Newsweek

TRAVEL GUIDE TO THE UNITED STATES

edited by Peter & Craig Norback

NEWSWEEK BOOKS, New York

Printed in the United States of America.

Third Printing 1980

Library of Congress Catalog in Publication Data

Norback, Peter G. ,
Newsweek Travel Guide to the United States

(Newsweek books)

1. United States — Description and Travel —
1960 — Guide - books. I. Norback, Craig T.,
joint author. II. Title.
E158.N79   917.3'04'926   78-65503
ISBN 0-88225-267-4

Book Design: Jerry Hood
Cover Design- Mary Gale Moyes

Contents

ix

Introduction

There are travel books that tell you what quaint little New England Inn to stay in. There are travel books that tell you how to fly or how to drive or where to sleep or how to bike. There is even a book on how to travel and attain your goals in life. And although the subject of travel has been dissected in nearly every way imaginable, there appears to be one common theme running through the lot of them; they all tell you what to do.

Unfortunately, what a travel author might do and what you might do in the same situation is often quite a different story. For instance, the author might find the bathroom charming in that quaint New England Inn, but you may find the charmer is located "out back." Or you may not appreciate flying at 3 a.m. just to save $10, or driving at exactly 55 mph for 6 straight hours with 4-minute pit stops at 2-pump gas stations that don't accept credit cards to make up 1 hour's driving time.

The NEWSWEEK TRAVEL GUIDE TO THE UNITED STATES doesn't tell you where to go, where to stay, how to fly or anything of that nature. It simply gives you as much information as possible on places to be and see, and lets you make the choice.

All of the information has been furnished by State Tourism Offices, the Federal Government, and reputable professional associations. This book does not contain "ratings" of the places listed; our own selection criteria, based on size, interest, location and other factors, have eliminated many places which seemed less acceptable; and obviously, the states and federal government want to encourage repeat tourist business by making reliable recommendations. As for those recommended by professional associations, few fly-by-night companies are willing to pay dues, and so they seldom join such organizations.

Following is a brief explanation of the categories and some of the terminology contained in the book, along with the rationale for qualifying and/or omitting certain material.

WEATHER - The general weather conditions of each state are synopsized in approximately 200 words and are followed by a chart illustrating the average monthly high and low temperatures. These averages are given for the two possible weather extremes in each state, usually the northern and southern regions.

STATE CHAMBER OF COMMERCE - This is simply a listing of the name, address and telephone number of the state's Chamber of Commerce. The Chamber may be contacted for specific data about the state, travel, business or other information.

STATE & CITY TOURISM OFFICES - These are the state and local government departments that promote tourism and/or business development in the state. All such information about a state is free for the asking and much of it is quite extensive and helpful. State offices are shown first, followed by major metropolitan areas that have promotion departments.

STATE HIGHWAY DEPARTMENT - This is a listing of each state's highway department (name, address and telephone number). The department can provide information on road conditions, alternate routes, state rules and regulations on load capacities, etc.

HIGHWAY WELCOMING CENTERS - Some of these centers are open year round while others operate only in the summer months. Also, they vary in size and services offered, but in general they are a good place to pick up directions, location of highway restaurants, roadside picnic areas and other state tourism information.

STATE POLICE - The headquarters address and telephone number is given for emergency assistance, for general information about traffic conditions on major arteries, and for other police-related business.

SPECIAL NOTE: To contact the State Police, call the Operator and you will be put through to the nearest station. (If you are in or near a metropolitan area, you will most likely be connected with the local or county police, because the jurisdiction of State Police is restricted to state thoroughfares and certain counties.) In addition to calling the Operator, you may get help from toll attendants. Normally, each toll area has a direct line to the State Police. CB Channel 9 (the emergency channel) is also monitored by the State Police. Patrol cars are not generally CB equipped, but each State Police station has a CB unit.

HUNTING & FISHING LICENSES - General requirements and fees are listed for resident and non-resident sportsmen. (Fees change from year to year, so ask for the most recent fee schedule when filing for a license.) In addition, the address and telephone number is given for each state's hunting and fishing commission to facilitate the filing of an application by mail.

CAMPGROUNDS - These include both private and state (public) campgrounds. Each facility's listing indicates the number of sites, water and bathroom facilities, picnic areas, swimming, boating, and so on. The criterion used to select campgrounds for each state was different (50 campsites minimum, 100 campsites minimum, etc.) depending on the actual number of campgrounds in the state and the average number of campsites at each. However, every effort was made to insure adequate coverage of those campgrounds located along heavily traveled routes.

In those states where no information was available on private and public campgrounds, a cross-reference is made to State Parks and to National Parks and Forests if they are also located in the state.

RESORTS & BEACHES - These are large recreation areas not operated by the state governments. For example, Atlantic City, New Jersey and Miami Beach, Florida are probably the most famous Resorts and Beaches.

During the early stages of research on this book, it was discovered that many states either do not define, or have not compiled information on, their Resort and Beach areas. Every effort was made to obtain this information from each state, but in addition to the scarcity of available data, certain other factors confuse the picture somewhat. Very few of the inland states have Resort and Beach areas at all; and states like Alaska and Arizona contain resort areas that are more properly characterized as, respectively, "Wilderness Lodges" and "Guest Ranches."

Other states, Nebraska and Ohio, for instance, consider their major lakes to be their resort areas. When this is the case, a cross-reference to Boating Areas and State Parks is made.

Another exception appears in New York, California and the like, where no specific resorts are listed, but rather entire areas that cater to the tourist, Niagara Falls, Los Angeles, etc., are described.

More comprehensive Resort and Beach information should be available to travelers in the near future: many of the state tourism offices contacted did say that their staffs were in the process of collecting just such data, at the present time.

Where Resorts and Beaches are listed for states in this book, the name and location of each area is given, along with a description of activities and services available.

BOATING AREAS - These are locations for pleasure boating in each state where power boats may be operated. Detailed information is given on the launching site, e.g., whether gas, food, fishing gear, boat rental, etc., are available.

Most inland states have compiled succinct listings on their pleasure boating areas; however, certain states like Michigan, which has more than 10,000 lakes, pose a problem. It would obviously be impractical to list all of that state's lakes in a volume of this size.

The solution — for Michigan and other states with too many boating areas to list, and for states where no information was available at all — has been to make a cross-reference to the State Parks and to the National Parks and Forests if they are also found within the state. These generally contain lakes and launching sites.

BICYCLE TRAILS - These are a selection of trails taken from "American Youth Hostels' North American Bicycle Atlas" by Warren Asa and the "Greater Washington Area Bicycle Atlas" by Alan Berkowitz and Dave Gilbert. Both books were published by American Youth Hostels, Inc.

Many of the trails are for avid cyclists who are able to travel great distances per day. However, family-type routes which do not require sophisticated bicycles or cycling skills are also included. Each trail is rated according to its degree of difficulty. The trails are listed alphabetically by name for the whole state, rather than by their starting point, since such routes are often chosen for their length and degree of difficulty rather than for their point of origin.

Accommodations for cyclists can be found at the Youth Hostels along the trails. For a listing of those hostels, see the HOSTELS section in each state.

TRAILS - In 1968, a National Trails System was established which set aside land to be used for foot, horse, and sometimes bicycle. The trails listed are foot or foot and/or horse trails; however, all have been designated foot trails in this book.

The trails listed are those which would appeal to families, more than to seasoned hiking enthusiasts.

SKI AREAS - Downhill ski areas in each snow state are listed along with pertinent details on the slopes, such as number, length, degree of difficulty, number of lifts, whether there are nearby restaurants and lodging, etc. When restaurants and lodging are shown, the establishments are within 15 or 20 miles of the slopes.

Cross-country ski areas were not listed because many of these can be found in National Parks and Forests and State Parks and Forests. In addition, the very nature of the sport simply calls for snow and wide open expanses of country.

AMUSEMENT PARKS & ATTRACTIONS - All major amusement parks (10 major rides or more) are listed in each state, along with interesting or unusual attractions. Single entries contain the number of rides, restaurants, games, dates the park is open, fee if any, and other factors. Exceptions to the above guideline are states such as South Dakota, where the population apparently does not warrant having a major amusement park. In this and similar states, smaller parks and attractions are listed, which represent the largest in the state.

STATE FAIR - The name, address, telephone number and date of each state's major fair is given.

NATIONAL PARKS - Campground areas within each National Park are listed with a description of facilities available, e.g., number of sites, length of stay permitted, boating, fishing, sanitary station, water and bathroom facilities, cabins, National Parks Service (NPS) guided tours, laundry, and others.

NATIONAL FORESTS - There are 154 in all, situated in 34 states, and most are assessible within a day's drive. In addition to nature trails, fishing, horse back riding, boating, hiking, and special attractions such as natural bridges and small game hunting, National Forests offer a limited number of camping sites and picnic areas.

STATE PARKS - These are replicas of the National Parks but in most cases are smaller in land area, which in turn, limits the scope of the facilities offered. (Whereas a National Park might have 15 campgrounds, a State Park may have only 5.) Otherwise, the State Parks will be quite similar in all other respects. When a state does not have a National Park within its boundaries, the State Parks will prove to be the state's major recreation areas.

All of the State Parks listed have a land area of 1000 acres or more except for those States with few but significant parks.

STATE FORESTS - A number of states only allow camping (generally primitive sites), hunting, fishing and hiking in their State Forests. The reason is that most of the forested land is undeveloped and the state wants to keep it that way, at least for the time being. On the other hand, there are State Forests which duplicate the services and facilities offered in the National Forests, only on a smaller scale.

All of the State Forests listed have a land area of over 1000 acres except for those states with few but significant forests.

HISTORIC SITES - These are the most interesting historical places in each state. In most instances, both the exact location and a brief description of the historical background are given.

Many states have created either driving or walking tours that make looking back in time an entertaining activity for the entire family.

Hours of operation are given only when they are unusual, i.e., weekends only, Monday through Friday, 6 - 8 p.m., etc. Otherwise, expect the sites to be open during normal business hours, 5 to 7 days a week.

HOSTELS - The word "hostel" comes from an archaic word meaning inn. Today's general definition of a hostel is a building that provides clean, simple, inexpensive overnight accommodations for people of all ages. It caters particularly to young people traveling independently or in groups on holiday or for educational purposes. In the United States and Canada, hostels include lodges, converted lifeguard stations (as on the Island of Nantucket), community centers, remodeled sorority houses — even an old city jail, as in the case of the hostel in Ottawa.

Most hostels have separate men's and women's dormitories with double-deck bunks. Each provides bathroom facilities, usually a fully equipped kitchen where travelers can prepare their own food, and a common room — a great deal like the main room at a mountain lodge — where hostelers meet at the end of the day to enjoy each other's company.

Some hostels have family quarters available, but for the most part, families may have to split up for the night, which provides an exciting, new adventure for most children. Hostels are supervised by resident houseparents who assure that International Youth Hostel Federation rules and regulations are followed.

Hosteling means traveling "under your own power," such as hiking, bicycling, canoeing, or skiing. But obviously it is impractical to expect hostelers to travel exclusively by such means in the United States because hostels are so far apart. If motorized transportation is used, as is allowed where time and distance make traveling "under your own power" unsafe or impractical, you are expected ing, canoeing, or skiing. But obviously it is impractical to expect hostelers to travel exclusively by such means in the United States because hostels are so far apart. If motorized transportation is used, as is allowed where time and distance make traveling "under your own power" unsafe or impractical, you are expected to become involved in a hosteling activity while staying there. This may include exploring caves or walking to historical or cultural places of interest.

Hostelers need a current youth hostel pass if they are members of AYH, their own sheets or "sheet-sleep sack" (where required), and eating utensils. Hostels are open between 4 p.m. and 7 p.m., and lights go out around 11 p.m. Wake-up time is around 7 a.m., and all hostelers are out by 9:30 a.m. (Hostels are closed from 9:30 a.m. until 4 or 4:30 p.m.)

Most hostelers buy and cook their own food and pitch in with the chores. It is the custom to leave every hostel in better and cleaner condition than it was when one arrived. Alcoholic beverages are taboo and smoking is allowed in designated areas only.

The customary limit of stay at a hostel is three days. However, special arrangement may be made with the houseparents for longer periods. Each hosteler is required to present at check-in a valid membership pass which he or she turns in to the houseparents and receives back when he or she departs. (Hostelers without passes are generally charged a higher room rate.)

Overnight charges at hostels range from $.90 to about $3.50 a night. In some areas where seasonal rates might apply, such as in ski areas during the winter, hostelers may have to pay as much as $4.25 a night.

For information on hosteling and a membership application, call or write the American Youth Hostels, Inc., Travel Department, National Campus, Delaplane, VA 22025, (703) 592-3271.

POINTS OF INTEREST - These are fascinating places to visit which do not fit easily into any other category in the book. Examples of Points of Interest would be caves, covered bridges, a world-famous zoo, a unique garden, or an entire village in miniature.

Whether stated in each listing or not, most places conduct tours or allow self-guided tours.

As noted under Historic Sites, unusual hours of operation are given if the place is open outside normal business hours.

Peter & Craig Norback

ALABAMA

In 1819, Alabama was admitted into the Union as the 22nd State. Then on January 11, 1861, Alabama seceded from the Union and became the Republic of Alabama. During the early days of the Civil War, Montgomery was selected as the site for the first capital of the Confederacy. (Later the capital was moved to Richmond, Virginia.)

Alabama is mostly an agricultural state with cotton, corn, peanuts, soybeans, broilers, cattle and eggs heading the list of products produced. Industry in the state consists of food, steel, textiles, paper, machinery and apparel products. Birmingham, often called the "Pittsburgh of the South," is the center for most of the state's steel and pig iron production.

State capital: Montgomery. State bird: Yellowhammer. State tree: Southern pine. State flower: Camellia.

WEATHER

The land slopes gradually upward from the low coastal plains around Mobile to the foothills in the central part of the State and then rises sharply in the northeastern counties. The Appalachians' average elevation in this area is about 800 feet, although Mount Chea reaches 2,047 feet while several other peaks top 2,000 feet.

The climate of Alabama is temperate, becoming largely subtropical near the coast. The summers are long, hot, and humid, with little day-to-day temperature change. The temperatures are lower in the northeastern counties due to the higher elevations. From late June through mid-August, approximately a third of the evenings are made comfortable by local afternoon thunderstorms which bring cool breezes over widely scattered areas. In the coldest months of December, January, and February, there are frequent shifts between mild air, which has been moistened and warmed by the Gulf, and dry, cool continental air. Severely cold weather seldom occurs.

Average daily temperature for each month.

	Northern	Southern
Jan.	51.4 to 29.1	62.6 to 36.9
Feb.	55.2 to 31.3	66.2 to 39.1
Mar.	62.8 to 37.5	72.6 to 44.4
Apr.	73.9 to 47.5	81.1 to 52.0
May	81.4 to 54.6	87.2 to 58.1
Jun.	87.7 to 62.3	91.8 to 64.8
Jul.	90.1 to 66.2	92.9 to 67.9
Aug.	90.2 to 65.0	92.5 to 67.4
Sept.	85.4 to 59.4	88.4 to 63.3
Oct.	75.1 to 46.3	80.3 to 50.8
Nov.	62.9 to 36.4	70.1 to 41.5
Dec.	54.5 to 31.7	64.3 to 38.5
Year	72.6 to 47.3	79.2 to 52.1

STATE CHAMBER OF COMMERCE

Alabama Chamber of Commerce
468 South Perry Street
Montgomery, AL 36101
(205) 834-6000

STATE & CITY TOURISM OFFICES

State

Alabama Development Office
3734 Atlanta Highway
Montgomery, AL 36130
(205) 832-6810

Bureau of Publicity and Information
State Highway Building
Montgomery, AL 36130
(800) 633-5761

Local

Birmingham Convention and Visitors Bureau
1909 7th Avenue, North
Birmingham, AL 35203
(205) 252-9825

Travel and Convention Department
Mobile Area Chambers of Commerce
P.O. Box 2187
Mobile, AL 36601
(205) 433-6951

STATE HIGHWAY DEPARTMENT

State of Alabama Highway Department
State Highway Building
11 South Union Street
Montgomery, AL 36104
(205) 832-5440

HIGHWAY WELCOMING CENTERS

Hodgesville

MADRID WELCOME CENTER - U. S. Highway 231, near Florida border.

Mobile

GRAND BAY WELCOME CENTER - Interstate 10, near Mobile.

ALABAMA

STATE POLICE

Department of Public Safety
Montgomery, AL 36130
(205) 832-6735

HUNTING & FISHING

Hunting

Resident

State, $5 plus 25 cents issuance fee.
County, $2.50 plus 25 cents issuance fee.
Over 65, 25 cents plus 15 cents issuance fee.

Non-resident

Annual (all game), $50 plus 25 cents issuance fee. Annual (small game), $15 plus 25 cents issuance fee. 7-day trip (small game), $10 plus 25 cents issuance fee. 7-day trip (all game), $25 plus 25 cents issuance fee. Non-residents under age 16 are exempt from having to purchase a license.

A $3 (plus 15 cents issuance fee) Management Area Deer and Turkey License in addition to a regular hunting license and Management Area permit is required for hunting deer and turkey on Management Areas.

Fishing

Resident

Annual rod and reel, $3 plus 25 cents issuance fee. (Residents who purchase $3 license may also fish with hook and line in salt and fresh waters without buying additional licenses.) Hook and line, $1 plus 25 cents issuance fee. (No license required when fishing in county of legal residence with hook and line only.) Over 65, lifetime license upon payment of 15 cents issuance fee to Judge of Probate or License Commissioner. Disabled, 25 cents plus 15 cents issuance fee.

Non-resident

Annual, $10 plus 25 cents issuance fee. 7-day trip, $4 plus 25 cents issuance fee. Children less than 16 years of age are not required to have hunting or fishing license. All military personnel are required to have license.

Annual non-resident for salt water, $10 for less than 1,200' depth. $20 for 1,200' - 1,800' depth. $40 for 1,800'-2,400' depth.

For more information contact:

Alabama Department of Conservation and
 Natural Resources
64 North Union Street
Montgomery, AL 36130
(205) 832-6300

CAMPGROUNDS

Private

Andalusia

OPEN POND
U.S.F.S. Box 310
Andalusia, AL 36420
(205) 222-3517
LOCATION: 15 mi. southwest of Andalusia via U.S. 29 and 137, then 1½ mi. southeast of 24 and 336.
FACILITIES: Open year round; 27 sites; campsite fee; sanitary stations; water and bathroom facilities; picnic area; swimming; hiking; fishing; boating; pets permitted.

Centre

BAY SPRINGS CAMPGROUND
Rt. 3, Box 83-A
Centre, AL 35960
(205) 927-8224
LOCATION: Off U.S. 411, 2 mi. west of Centre.
FACILITIES: Open Mar.-Oct.; 75 sites; campsite fee; electrical outlets; water and bathroom facilities; picnic area; swimming; fishing; boating; playground; pets permitted.

Centreville

PAYNE LAKE
U.S.F.S. Box 67
Centreville, AL 35042
(205) 926-9765
LOCATION: 16 mi. northwest of Greensboro on 25.
FACILITIES: Open May 1 - Dec. 1; 62 sites; campsite fee; sanitary stations; water and bathroom facilities; picnic area; swimming (May 1 - Oct. 1); hiking; fishing; boating (May 1 - Oct. 1); pets permitted.

Cullman

GOOD HOPE CAMPGROUND
Rt. 12, Box 330
Cullman, AL 35055
(205) 739-1319
LOCATION: On I-65 at Good Hope exit.
FACILITIES: Open year round; 50 sites; campsite fee; electrical outlets; sanitary stations; water and bathroom facilities; picnic area; hiking; playground; pets permitted.

Dadeville

BAMA PARK
R.F.D. No. 1, Box 601
Dadeville, AL 36853
(205) 825-7344
LOCATION: Hwy. 50, 5 mi. east of Martin Dam.
FACILITIES: Open Apr. 1 - Sept. 3; 65 sites; campsite fee; electrical outlets; sanitary stations; water and bathroom facilities; food service; picnic area; swimming; fishing; boating; playground; pets permitted.

Decatur

POINT MALLARD CAMPGROUND
3101 8th Street, SE
Decatur, AL 35601
(205) 355-9249

CAMPGROUNDS (continued)

LOCATION: Mallard Drive off I-65 in city of Decatur.
FACILITIES: Open year round; 175 sites; campsite fee; electrical outlets; sanitary stations; water and bathroom facilities; food service; picnic area; swimming; hiking; fishing; boating; tennis; golf; playground; pets permitted.

Double Springs

CORINTH RECREATIONAL AREA
U.S.F.S. Box 278
Double Springs, AL 35553
(205) 489-5317
LOCATION: 4 mi. east of Double Springs via U.S. 278, then 3 mi. south on 113.
FACILITIES: Open Apr. 1 - Oct. 31; 68 sites; campsite fee; sanitary stations; water and bathroom facilities; swimming; fishing; boating; pets permitted.

Eclectic

WHISPERING SPRINGS CAMPGROUND
R.R. 2, Box 88AA
Eclectic, AL 36024
(205) 857-3713
LOCATION: Hwy. 63 to Hwy. 229, first paved road to the left.
FACILITIES: Open year round; 60 sites; campsite fee; electrical outlets; sanitary stations; water and bathroom facilities; picnic area; swimming; hiking; fishing; boating; playground; pets permitted.

Eufaula

LAKE EUFAULA KOA KAMPGROUND
P.O. Box 47
Eufaula, AL 36027
(205) 687-9013
LOCATION: Junction Hwys. 431 and 82 on Chewalla Creek.
FACILITIES: Open year round; 100 sites; campsite fee; electrical outlets; sanitary stations; water and bathroom facilities; picnic area; swimming; fishing; boating; mini golf; playground; pets permitted.

Gulf Shores

LAGUNA PARK
P.O. Box 238
Gulf Shores, AL 36542
LOCATION: 3 mi. west on Hwy. 180 from intersection of Hwy. 59 and 180.
FACILITIES: Open May 1 - Oct. 15; 50 sites; campsite fee; electrical outlets; sanitary stations; water and bathroom facilities; picnic area; swimming; hiking; fishing; boating; playground; pets permitted.

SEASIDE TRAILER PARK
P.O. Box 513
Gulf Shores, AL 36542
(205) 981-4456
LOCATION: 4 mi. east of Gulf Shores via Hwy. 182.
FACILITIES: Open year round; 102 sites; campsite fee; electrical outlets; sanitary stations; water and bathroom facilities; food service; picnic area; swimming; fishing; pets permitted.

SOUTHPORT TRAVEL PARK
P.O. Box 453
Gulf Shores, AL 36542
(205) 968-7268
LOCATION: Hwy. 59 south, left or right at high rise bridge.
FACILITIES: Open year round; 78 sites; campsite fee; electrical outlets; sanitary stations; water and bathroom facilities; picnic area; swimming; hiking; fishing; boating; playground; pets permitted.

Helfin

COLEMAN LAKE
U.S.F.S. Box 548
Helfin, AL 36264
(205) 463-2273
LOCATION: 8 mi. north of Helfin via U.S. 78, then 3 mi. northwest via Hwy. 61, then 6 mi. north on Hwy. 553 and 500.
FACILITIES: Open May 1 - Sept. 30; 49 sites; campsite fee; sanitary stations; water and bathroom facilities; picnic area; swimming; hiking; fishing; boating; pets permitted.

Hope Hull

MONTGOMERY KOA KAMPGROUND
Route No. 1, Box 154
Hope Hull, AL 36043
(205) 288-0728
LOCATION: Junction of I-65 and U.S. 31, south of Montgomery at Hope Hull Interchange.
FACILITIES: Open year round; 140 sites; campsite fee; electrical outlets; sanitary stations; water and bathroom facilities; picnic area; swimming; hiking; fishing; boating; playground; pets permitted.

Jemison

JEMISON-PEACH QUEEN KOA
Route 2, Box 179A
Jemison, AL 35085
(205) 688-2573
LOCATION: 1,000 feet east at Jemison exit and I-65.
FACILITIES: Open year round; 110 sites; campsite fee; electrical outlets; sanitary stations; water and bathroom facilities; food service; picnic area; swimming; hiking; mini golf; playground; pets permitted.

Lanett

BURNT VILLAGE PARK
P.O. Box 205
Lanett, AL 36863
(205) 644-3959
LOCATION: Left off I-85 on U.S. 29 for 8 mi.
FACILITIES: Open year round; 120 sites; campsite fee; electrical outlets; sanitary stations; water and bathroom facilities; food service; picnic area; swimming; hiking; fishing; boating; playground; pets permitted.

Lillian

PERDIDO BAY KOA KAMPGROUND

ALABAMA

CAMPGROUNDS (continued)

Star Route, Box 875
Lillian, AL 36549
(205) 962-4373
LOCATION: 1 mi. south of U.S. 98 at west
of Lillian Alabama Bridge.
FACILITIES: Open year round; 85 sites;
campsite fee; electrical outlets; sanitary
stations; water and bathroom facilities; picnic
area; swimming; hiking; fishing; boating; playgrounds; pets permitted.

Mobile

DOG RIVER KOA KAMPGROUND
P.O. Box 6173
Mobile, AL 36606
(205) 661-5004
LOCATION: Exit I-10 at U.S. 90 west, 2 mi.
to 32, 2 mi. to Range Line Road.
FACILITIES: Open year round; 130 sites;
campsite fee; electrical outlets; sanitary
stations; water and bathroom facilities; picnic
area; swimming; fishing; boating; playground;
pets permitted.

Pell City

SHADY OAKS KOA KAMPGROUND
P.O. Box 545
Pell City, AL 35125
(205) 338-3316
LOCATION: I-20 exit at Riverside exit 162,
go 1 mi. west on Hwy. 78, turn at KOA Road.
FACILITIES: Open year round; 53 sites;
campsite fee; electrical outlets; sanitary
stations; water and bathroom facilities; food
service (Jun. - Aug.); picnic area; swimming;
hiking; mini golf; playground; pets permitted.

Robertsdale

MOBILE-PENSACOLA KOA
Route 1, Box 110-1
Robertsdale, AL 36567
(205) 964-5998
LOCATION: (Styx River-Mobile E); I-10 at
Wilcox Exit.
FACILITIES: Open year round; 114 sites;
campsite fee; electrical outlets; sanitary
stations; water and bathroom facilities; picnic
area; swimming; hiking; fishing; golf; playground; pets permitted.

Valley Head

SEQUOYAH CAVERNS KOA CAMP-
GROUND
Route 1
Valley Head, AL 35989
(205) 635-2311
LOCATION: Take Ider-Sulphur Springs exit
south or Valley Head exit north off I-59, then
off U.S. 11.
FACILITIES: Open year round; 85 sites;
campsite fee; electrical outlets; sanitary
stations; water and bathroom facilities; food
service; picnic area; swimming; hiking; playground; pets permitted.

Public

Demopolis

DEER LICK

P.O. Box 520
Demopolis, AL 36732
(205) 289-3540
LOCATION: 15 mi. north of Tuscaloosa on
Hwy. 69.
FACILITIES: Open year round; 39 sites;
campsite fee; picnic area; swimming; hiking;
fishing; boating; pets permitted.

RESORTS & BEACHES

Dadeville

STILL WATER ON LAKE MARTIN
Dadeville, AL 36853
(205) 825-4062
LOCATION: 1-hour drive from Montgomery
on I-85.
FACILITIES: Sand beach; launching ramps;
boating supplies; groceries; gas; sailing; tennis;
golf; swimming pool; hunting; fishing; villa,
on a daily or year round basis.

Dothan

OLYMPIA SPA
Highway 231 South
Dothan, AL 36301
(205) 677-3321
LOCATION: 80 mi. north of Panama City.
FACILITIES: 30 mi. of sand beaches; deep-
sea and fresh-water fishing; hunting; boating;
skiing; golf; tennis; historic tours.

BOATING AREAS

Abbeville

Walter F. George Dam (Chattahoochee River)

HIGHLAND PARK BOAT LANDING
LOCATION: Old River Road off Hwy. 10
east, 14 mi. east of Abbeville.
FACILITIES: Launching; tent camping; trailer camping; picnic area; restrooms; open 24
hrs.

Adger

Bankhead Lake (Warrior River System)

DUNN'S MARINA
LOCATION: Adger.
FACILITIES: Launching, $1; boat storage;
marine gas and oil; dockside pump; groceries;
snacks; tackle; open 7 days, 10 hrs.

KNIGHT'S CAMP
LOCATION: Adger.
FACILITIES: Launching, $1; boat storage;
marine gas and oil; dockside pump; boat and
motor rental; picnic area; restrooms; groceries; snacks; bait and tackle; open 7 days, 14
hrs.

LIGHTHOUSE
LOCATION: Gwin's Slough.
FACILITIES: Launching, $1.50; boat storage;
marine gas and oil; dockside pump; boat
rental; cabins; restrooms; snacks; bait and
tackle; cafe; open 7 days, 12 hrs.

SMITH FISHING CAMP
LOCATION: 27 mi. northwest of Bessemer.

BOATING AREAS (continued)

FACILITIES: Launching, $1; boat storage; marine gas and oil; dockside pump; boat rental; picnic area, $1; groceries; snacks; bait and tackle; open 24 hrs.

YACHT CLUB
LOCATION: 25 mi. northwest of Bessemer.
FACILITIES: Launching, $1; marine gas and oil; dockside pump; boat rental; restrooms; bait and tackle; cafe; open 7 days, 18 hrs.

YELLOW CREEK FISHING CAMP, INC.
LOCATION: 2 mi. above Bankhead Lock and Dam on right side of road.
FACILITIES: Launching, $1; boat storage; marine gas and oil; dockside pump; boat rental; open 7 days, 10 hrs.

Akron

Black Warrior Lake

OLD LOCK NO. 8
LOCATION: 3 mi. west of Akron.
FACILITIES: Launching; tent camping; trailer camping; tables; water; cookers; picnic area; open 24 hrs.

Alexander City

Martin Lake (Tallapoosa River)

ADCOX'S MARINA
LOCATION: Turn northeast in Equality on Hwy. 259, go to the second paved road to the right; go to the end of the road.
FACILITIES: Launching, $1; marine gas and oil; dockside pump; restrooms; groceries; snacks; bait and tackle; open 7 days, 17 hrs.

KOWALIGIA SPORT SHOP
LOCATION; 8 mi. east of Eclectic on Hwy. 63 at bridge.
FACILITIES: Launching; boat and motor sales and repairs; boat storage; marine gas and oil; dockside pump; cabins; $125 weekly; restrooms; groceries; bait and tackle; cafe; open 7 days, 10 hrs.

LAKE MARTIN MARINA
LOCATION: ¼ mi. north of River Bridge on Hwy. 280 between Alexander City and Dadeville.
FACILITIES: Launching; marine gas and oil; dockside pump; boat and motor rental; tent camping, $1.50 per night; picnic area, $1; restrooms; groceries; bait and tackle; ice; houseboat docking; cold beverages; open 7 days, 16 hrs.

MARINE SERVICE CENTER
LOCATION: ¼ mi. off Hwy. 128 between Alexander City and Wind Creek State Park at the mouth of Elkhatchee Creek.
FACILITIES: Launching; motor sales and repairs; boat storage; marine gas and oil; dockside pump; boat rental; restrooms; groceries; bait and tackle; ice; cold beverages; open 7 days, 15 hrs.

VEAZEY'S MARINA
LOCATION: Hwy. 63 turn at Ourtown, follow signs 2 mi.

FACILITIES: Launching, $1; boat storage; marine gas and oil; dockside pump; boat and motor rental; restrooms; groceries; bait and tackle; beverages; marine supplies; open 7 days, 14 hrs.

WIND CREEK STATE PARK
LOCATION: ¼ mi. off Hwy. 128 between Alexander City and Ourtown.
FACILITIES: Launching; boat storage; marine gas and oil; dockside pump; boat rental; cabins, $6 per night; tent camping, $3; picnic area; restrooms; groceries; bait and tackle; ice; beaches with lifeguards; open 7 days, 14 hrs.

Ashville

Neely Henry Lake (Coosa River)

CANOE CREEK MARINA
LOCATION: U.S. Hwy. 411, ½ mi. south of Etowah County Line.
FACILITIES: Launching, 50 cents; marine gas and oil; dockside pump; snacks; bait and tackle; open 24 hrs.

GREENSPORT MARINA
LOCATION: 4 mi. south of Etowah County Line on Greensport Road.
FACILITIES: Launching, $1; boat storage; marine gas and oil; dockside pump; boat rental; tent camping, $3; trailer camping, $3; picnic area, $2; restrooms; snacks; groceries; open Apr. to Sept., 24 hrs.

Athens

Wheeler Lake (Tennessee River)

BLUE SPRINGS FISH CAMP
LOCATION: 6 mi. upstream Lee High Bridge, 6 mi. east of Hwy. 72.
FACILITIES: Launching; marine gas and oil; dockside pump; boat and motor rental; cabins, $10; tent camping, $3; trailer camping, $3; picnic area; snacks; bait and tackle; open 7 days, 18 hrs.

ELK RIVER LODGE STATE PARK
LOCATION: Lee High Bridge on U.S. Hwy. 72 (on Elk River).
FACILITIES: Launching; marine gas and oil; dockside pump; boat rental; cabins, $3; restrooms; picnic area; snacks; bait and tackle; open 7 days, 16 hrs.

SPORTSMAN PARK or ELK RIVER MILLS
LOCATION: 11 mi. upstream from Lee High Bridge, 12 mi. northwest of Athens on Elk River Mills Road (on Elk River).
FACILITIES: Launching; marine gas and oil; boat rental; picnic area; restrooms; groceries; snacks; bait and tackle; open 7 days, 15 hrs.

Bay Minette

Tensaw River

CLIFF'S LANDING
LOCATION: On Tensaw River off Hwy. 225.
FACILITIES: Launching, $1.50; motor sales and repairs; boat storage; marine gas and oil; dockside pump; boat rental, $2.50; motor rental; tent camping, $1; trailer camping, $10

ALABAMA

per month; restrooms; groceries; snacks; bait and tackle; open 7 days, 12 hrs.

CLOVERLEAF LANDING
LOCATION: (with nearest access to Raft River), 1.9 mi. off Hwy. 225, 6 mi. from Spanish Fort.
FACILITIES: Launching, $1; boat storage; marine gas and oil; boat rental; groceries; bait and tackle; open 7 days, dawn to dusk.

PATRICK'S LANDING
LOCATION: North of Bay Minette off Hwy. 225.
FACILITIES: Launching, $1.50; boat storage; marine gas and oil; dockside pump; boat rental; trailer camping, $10 per month; picnic area; restrooms; groceries; snacks; bait and tackle; open 7 days, 17 hrs.

PERKIN'S LANDING
LOCATION: On Hurricane Bayou end of Hurricane Road.
FACILITIES: Launching, $1; boat storage; marine gas and oil; boat rental; tent camping; trailer camping, $1.50 daily; restrooms; groceries; snacks; bait and tackle; bar; open 7 days, 17 hrs.

Bessemer

Bankhead Lake (Warrior River System)

BILL'S LANDING
LOCATION: Warrior River Road.
FACILITIES: Launching, $1; marine gas and oil; dockside pump; boat rental; restrooms; groceries; snacks; bait and tackle; cafe; open 24 hrs.

CLEVENGER'S MARINA
LOCATION: Taylor's Ferry Road.
FACILITIES: Launching, $1; boat and motor repairs; boat storage; marine gas and oil; dockside pump; boat rental; tent camping, $2; trailer camping, $2; picnic area; restrooms; bait and tackle; cafe; open 7 days, 18 hrs.

Bladon Springs

Coffeeville Lake (Tom River)

BOBBY'S FISH CAMP
LOCATION: ½ mi. off Hwy. 84 on Tombigbee River.
FACILITIES: Launching, $1; marine gas and oil; dockside pump; boat rental; cabins, $5 per day; trailer camping, $2; tent camping, $1; restrooms; bait and tackle; cafe; ice; open 24 hrs.

Burkville

Jones Bluff Lake (Alabama River)

CAMP MANACK
LOCATION: 12 mi. west of Montgomery on Old Selma Road.
FACILITIES: Launching, 50 cents; boat storage; marine gas and oil; dockside pump; boat rental; tent and trailer camping, $1; picnic area, 50 cents; restrooms; groceries; bait and tackle; cafe; open 24 hrs.

JANE'S LANDING
LOCATION: Burkville.
FACILITIES: Launching, $1; boat storage; marine gas and oil; dockside pump; boat rental; restrooms; groceries; snacks; bait and tackle; cafe; open 6 days.

Camden

Millers Ferry (Alabama River)

CAMDEN STATE PARK
LOCATION: 6 mi. north of Camden.
FACILITIES: Launching; cabins (reservation necessary); golf course; camping for tents and campers; water and electricity; restrooms; open 7 days, 18 hrs.

SHELL CREEK LODGE
LOCATION: 14 mi. west of Camden on Hwy. 28.
FACILITIES: Launching; cabins; bait and tackle; groceries; restrooms; open 24 hrs.

Cedar Bluff

Weiss Lake (Coosa River)

CHEROKEE CAMPER SITE
LOCATION: 2 mi. east of Cedar Bluff, 1 mi. off Hwy. 9.
FACILITIES: Launching; marine gas and oil; dockside pump; boat and motor rental; cabins, $10; tent camping, $2; trailer camping, $4; picnic area, $1; restrooms; groceries; snacks; bait and tackle; open 24 hrs.

CHESTNUT RECREATION
LOCATION: 4 mi. northeast off Leesburg on Hwy. 44.
FACILITIES: Launching; boat storage; marine gas and oil; tent camping, $3; trailer camping, $3; dockside pump; cabins, $10; picnic area, 50 cents; restrooms; showers; groceries; bait and tackle; open 24 hrs.

LITTLE RIVER MARINA
LOCATION: 4 mi. west of Cedar Bluff on Little River.
FACILITIES: Launching; boat and motor sales and repairs; boat storage; marine gas and oil; dockside pump; boat and motor rental; tent camping, $2; trailer camping, $2; picnic area; restrooms; groceries; bait and tackle; cafe; open 7 days, 12 hrs.

SCOTT'S ARCO
LOCATION: Cedar Bluff.
FACILITIES: Launching; marine gas and oil; dockside pump; restrooms; snacks; bait and tackle; open 7 days, 14 hrs.

YELLOW CREEK FALLS FISH CAMP
LOCATION: 5 mi. north of Leesburg on Hwy. 273.
FACILITIES: Launching; marine gas and oil; dockside pump; boat rental; tent camping; trailer camping; restrooms; groceries; bait and tackle; open 24 hrs.

Centre

Weiss Lake (Coosa River)

BOATING AREAS (continued)

ANDERSON'S FISH CAMP
LOCATION: 5 mi. east of Centre on Hwy. 22, Spring Creek.
FACILITIES: Launching; tent camping, $2; marine gas and oil; dockside pump; boat rental; trailer camping, $2; picnic area, $1; restrooms; groceries; bait and tackle; open 7 days, 12 hrs.

BAY SPRINGS MARINA
LOCATION: 4 mi. west of Centre, 2 mi. north Hwy. 411.
FACILITIES: Launching; boat and motor sales and repairs; boat storage; marine gas and oil; dockside pump; boat and motor rental; motel, $15; tent camping, $3; trailer camping, $3; picnic area, $1; restrooms; snacks; bait and tackle; cafe; open 7 days, 12 hrs.

PRUETT'S FISH CAMP
LOCATION: 5 mi. east of Centre on Hwy. 16.
FACILITIES: Launching; boat and motor sales and repairs; boat storage; marine gas and oil; dockside pump; tent camping, $2; trailer camping, $2; picnic area; restrooms; groceries; bait and tackle; cafe; open 7 days, 17 hrs.

TAB'S FISH BOW VILLA
LOCATION: Centre.
FACILITIES: Launching; marine gas and oil; boat and motor rental; tent camping, $2; trailer camping, $2; picnic area; restrooms; groceries; bait and tackle; cafe; open 24 hrs.

Cherokee

Pickwick Lake (Tennessee River)

BEAR CREEK FISH CAMP
LOCATION: 8 mi. west of Cherokee on U.S. Hwy. 72.
FACILITIES: Launching; marine gas and oil; boat rental; cabins, $12.60; restrooms; groceries; bait and tackle; cafe; open 7 days, 15 hrs.

SPRING VALLEY FISH CAMP
LOCATION: Cherokee.
FACILITIES: Launching, 50 cents; boat storage; marine gas and oil; dockside pump; boat and motor rental; cabins, $12.60; tent camping; trailer camping, $1.50; bait and tackle; cafe; open 7 days, 15 hrs.

Chickasaw

Mobile River

CHICKASAW MARINA (Chickasaw Creek)
LOCATION: Hwy. 43, Chickasaw Bough Creek.
FACILITIES: Launching, $1.50; boat storage; dockside pump; restrooms; snacks; bait and tackle; open 24 hrs.

Clanton

Lay Lake (Coosa River)

PINEVIEW CAMP
LOCATION: ¾ mi. above Lay Dam off Lay Dam Road.

FACILITIES: Launching, $1; marine gas and oil; dockside pump; boat and motor rental; tent camping, $2; restrooms; groceries; bait and tackle; open 7 days, 16 hrs.

Mitchell Lake (Coosa River)

DIXIE'S CAMP
LOCATION: On Blue Creek Road off Hwy. 22 east.
FACILITIES: Launching, $1; marine gas and oil; dockside pump; boat rental; snacks; bait and tackle; open 7 days, 14 hrs.

LAVADA'S CAMP AND CAFE
LOCATION: Camp is located at the end of Ferry Road, ¾ mi. below Lay Dam.
FACILITIES: Launching, $1; motor repairs; boat storage; marine gas and oil; dockside pump; boat rental; tent camping; trailer camping, $25 per month; restrooms; bait and tackle; cafe; open 7 days, 16 hrs.

SEAB AND SAM CAMP
LOCATION: Camp is located on Yellow Leaf Creek off Ferry Road, ¾ mi. below Lay Dam.
FACILITIES: Launching, $1; marine gas and oil; dockside pump; boat rental; cabins by year; tent camping, $2; trailer camping; picnic area; restrooms; groceries; bait and tackle; open 7 days, 15 hrs.

WYATT'S CAMP
LOCATION: Camp is on Walnut Creek, turn off Higgins Ferry Road.
FACILITIES: Launching; boat storage; marine gas and oil; dockside pump; boat rental; cabins, $3; restrooms; groceries; bait and tackle; open 7 days, 16 hrs.

Coffeeville

Coffeeville Lake (Tom River)

COFFEEVILLE LAKE ACCESS AREA
LOCATION: ¼ mi. above Coffeeville Lock and Dam.
FACILITIES: Launching; tent camping; trailer camping; picnic area; restrooms; open 24 hrs.

Crane Hill

Lewis Smith Lake (Warrior River System)

BAILEY'S FISH CAMP
LOCATION: Mouth of Crooked Creek.
FACILITIES: Launching, $1; marine gas and oil; dockside pump; boat rental; cabins, $6; tent camping, $1; trailer camping, $1.50; picnic area; restrooms; groceries; snacks; bait and tackle; hunting and fishing license; open 24 hrs.

BIG BRIDGE FISH CAMP
LOCATION: Ryans Creek on Cullman County Road 15.
FACILITIES: Launching, $1; boat storage; marine gas and oil; dockside pump; boat rental; motel, $11; cabins, $11; tent camping, $1; picnic area; restrooms; groceries; bait and tackle; cafe; open 7 days, 16 hrs.

D. B. SPEEGLE FISH CAMP
LOCATION: 10 mi. west of Cullman, Cull-

ALABAMA

BOATING AREAS (continued)

man County Road 22, at Trimble.
FACILITIES:Launching, $1; marine gas and oil; dockside pump; boat rental; tent camping, $1.50; picnic area, $1; restrooms; groceries; bait and tackle; cafe; open 24 hrs.

GLENN'S FISH CAMP
LOCATION: 10 mi. northeast of I-65 on Cullman County 15 at Big Bridge.
FACILITIES: Launching, $1; motor repairs; boat storage; marine gas and oil; dockside pump; boat rental; cabins, $8; tent camping, $3; trailer camping, $3; picnic area; restrooms; bait and tackle; cafe; open 7 days, 17 hrs.

ROCKCREEK MARINA & CAMPING AREA INC.
LOCATION: Near Crane Hill on Rockcreek.
FACILITIES: Launching, $1; boat storage; marine gas and oil; dockside pump; tent camping, $2 per day; trailer camping, $2 per day; picnic area, $1 per day; restrooms; snacks; bait and tackle; hunting and fishing license; open 7 days, 12 hrs.

Creola

Mobile River

DEAD LAKE FISHING & HUNTING CAMP
LOCATION: End of Dead Lake Road.
FACILITIES: Launching, $1; boat storage; marine gas and oil; dockside pump; boat rental; cabins, $6 nightly; picnic area; restrooms; snacks; bait and tackle; open 24 hrs.

Cropwell

Logan Martin Lake (Coosa River)

BELL'S MARINA
LOCATION: 4 mi. south of Pell City off Hwy. 231.
FACILITIES: Launching, $1; boat and motor repairs; boat storage; marine gas and oil; dockside pump; boat rental; picnic area, $1; restrooms; snacks; bait and tackle; open 24 hrs.

COOSA ISLAND MARINA
LOCATION: 3 mi. west of Logan Martin Dam, 12 mi. south of Pell City.
FACILITIES: Launching, $1; boat and motor repairs; boat storage; marine gas and oil; dockside pump; boat and motor rental; cabins, $500 to $800 per year; picnic area, $1; restrooms; groceries; bait and tackle; cafe; open 24 hrs.

GENERAL LEE MARINA & CAMP-GROUND
LOCATION: 8½ mi. south of Pell City on U.S. Hwy. 231.
FACILITIES: Launching, $1; boat and motor sales; boat storage; marine gas and oil; dockside pump; boat rental; tent camping, $3; trailer camping, $3; picnic area, $1.50; groceries; snacks; bait and tackle; restrooms; open 24 hrs.

HOLIDAY MARINA & CAMPGROUND
LOCATION: Hwy. 34, 5 mi. southeast of Pell City.
FACILITIES: Launching, $1; boat storage;

marine gas and oil; dockside pump; boat rental; tent camping, $3; trailer camping, $3; picnic area, $1.50; restrooms; groceries; snacks; bait and tackle; open 24 hrs.

NICK'S FISH CAMP
LOCATION: 10 mi. southeast of Pell City on Hwy. 34, at Stemley Bridge.
FACILITIES: Launching, 50 cents; marine gas and oil; dockside pump; boat rental; tent camping, $3; picnic area, $1; restrooms; groceries; snacks; bait and tackle; open Apr. - Oct. 15.

PIER 59 ISLAND MARINA
LOCATION: 3 mi. west of Logan Martin Dam.
FACILITIES: Launching, $1; boat sales and repairs; boat storage; marine gas and oil; boat rental; dockside pump; restrooms; groceries; snacks; bait and tackle; cafe; open Apr. - Oct.; weekends in winter.

PINE HARBOR MARINA
LOCATION: 6 mi. southeast of Pell City on Hwy. 34.
FACILITIES: Launching, $1; boat and motor sales and repairs; boat storage; marine gas and oil; dockside pump; motel, $12; picnic area; restrooms; snacks; cafe; open 24 hrs.

POWELLS HIDEAWAY
LOCATION: 10 mi. southeast of Pell City on Hwy. 34.
FACILITIES: Launching, $1; marine gas and oil; dockside pump; tent camping, $3; trailer camping, $3; picnic area, $1; restrooms; snacks; bait; open Apr. - Oct. 15.

RABBIT BRANCH MARINA
LOCATION: 8 mi. south of Pell City on Hwy 231.
FACILITIES: Launching, $1; marine gas and oil; dockside pump; boat rental; picnic area, 50 cents; restrooms; groceries; snacks; bait and tackle; cafe; open 24 hrs.

ST. CLAIR SHORES MARINA
LOCATION: 8 mi. south of Pell City on U.S. Hwy. 231.
FACILITIES: Launching, 50 cents; boat storage; marine gas and oil; dockside pump; cabins, $79 per week; picnic area, $1; restrooms; groceries; snacks; bait and tackle; cafe; open 24 hrs.

TOWN & COUNTRY FOOD MART
LOCATION: 6 mi. south of Pell City on U.S. Hwy. 231.
FACILITIES: Launching, $1; marine gas and oil; dockside pump; boat and motor rentals; restrooms; groceries; snacks; bait and tackle; open 24 hrs.

Cullman

Lewis Smith Lake (Warrior River System)

B.B. CALVERT'S FISHING CAMP
LOCATION: 3 mi. off Hwy. 69 on Cullman County Road 15.
FACILITIES: Launching, 50 cents; marine gas and oil; dockside pump; tent camping, $1; restrooms; picnic area; snacks; bait and tackle; open 7 days, 15 hrs.

BOATING AREAS (continued)

BAGWELL'S SAVE A STOP & FISH CAMP
LOCATION: Cullman County Road 22 at Trimble, 10 mi. west of Cullman.
FACILITIES: Launching; marine oil; boat rental; restrooms; groceries; bait and tackle; open 7 days, 16 hrs.

HAMES FISH CAMP
LOCATION: Simpson Creek, 1 mi. north of Hwy. 69.
FACILITIES: Launching, $1; marine gas and oil; dockside pump; boat rental; picnic area; restrooms; snacks; bait and tackle; open 7 days, 15 hrs.

SCOTT'S FISH CAMP
LOCATION: Simpson Creek off of Cullman County Road 15.
FACILITIES: Launching, $1; boat storage; marine gas and oil; dockside pump; boat rental; tent camping, $2; picnic area, $1; restrooms; groceries; snacks; bait and tackle; open 24 hrs.

SMITH LAKE FISHING LODGE
LOCATION: Ryans Creek at Trimble off Cullman County Road 22.
FACILITIES: Launching, $1; boat storage; marine gas and oil; dockside pump; boat and motor rentals; cabins, $12.50; restrooms; snacks; bait and tackle; open 24 hrs.

SMITH LAKE PARK
LOCATION: 6 mi. southwest of I-65, 69, Cullman, Good Hope Interchange.
FACILITIES: Launching; trailer parking; boat storage and houses; marine gas and oil, (dockside); camping area; restrooms; bait and tackle; picnic facilities; playgrounds; open 24 hrs.

TURNER'S FISH CAMP
LOCATION: Simpson Creek.
FACILITIES: Launching, $1; marine gas and oil; dockside pump; boat rental; tent camping, $2; picnic area, $1; restrooms; bait and tackle; cafe; open 7 days, 12 hrs.

Dadeville

Martin Lake (Tallapoosa River)

BONE'S PLACE
LOCATION: 6 mi. south of Dadeville on Hwy. 49 at Blue Creek.
FACILITIES: Launching, 50 cents; boat storage; marine gas and oil; dockside pump; boat and motor rental; trailers, $35 weekly; picnic area; restrooms; groceries; bait and tackle; marine supplies; open 7 days, 15 hrs.

CHUCK'S MARINA
LOCATION: Turn west on Hwy. 50 at Rock Store and Hwy. 49, go 5 mi., turn right, go 1½ mi.
FACILITIES: Launching, 50 cents; boat and motor sales; boat storage; marine gas and oil; dockside pump; boat and motor rental; restrooms; groceries; bait and tackle; ice; marine supplies; cabins, $50 to $70; open 7 days, 14 hrs.

COKER'S MARINA
LOCATION: 5 mi. west of Dadeville on Coker's Landing Road on Big Sandy Creek.
FACILITIES: Launching; marine gas and oil; dockside pump; picnic area; restrooms; soft drinks; open 24 hrs.

PLEASURE POINT PARK
LOCATION: Pace Peninsula Lake Martin, 5 mi. south of Dadeville on Hwy. 49, turn west on black top, go 8 mi.
FACILITIES: Launching; boat storage; marine gas and oil; dockside pump; boat and motor rental; tent camping, $3; trailer camping, $4.50; restrooms; groceries; bait and tackle; boating; building and marine supplies; open 7 days, 14 hrs.

STILLWATERS
LOCATION: 4 mi. south of Dadeville on Hwy. 49 turn west on black top, go ½ mi. turn left.
FACILITIES: Launching; boat and motor sales and repairs; boat storage (wet and dry); marine gas and oil; dockside pump; boat rental (sail); restrooms; groceries; snacks; bait and tackle; fishing license; marine and beach supplies; open May - Nov., 14 hrs.

Daleville

Little Choctawhatchee River

CHOCTAWHATCHEE WELLS
LOCATION: 3 mi. southeast of Daleville on Hwy. 92.
FACILITIES: Launching; tent camping, $3.50 per night; trailer camping, $3.50 per night; picnic area; restrooms; snacks; bait; open 7 days, 8 hrs.

Daphne

Tensaw River

AUTREY'S FISH CAMP
LOCATION: Mobile Causeway, Mobile east.
FACILITIES: Launching; motor repairs; boat storage; marine gas and oil; dockside pump; boat and motor rental; restrooms; snacks; bait and tackle; open 24 hrs.

BERRY'S FISH CAMP
LOCATION: Mobile Causeway, Mobile.
FACILITIES: Launching, $1; boat storage; marine gas and oil; dockside pump; boat and motor rental; restrooms; snacks; bait and tackle; open 24 hrs.

HERD'S FISHING CAMP
LOCATION: Battleship Parkway on bank of Chacoloochee Bay.
FACILITIES: Launching, 50 cents; boat storage; marine gas and oil; dockside pump; boat rental; restrooms; snacks; bait and tackle; cold beverages; open 7 days, 15 hrs.

SHELL BANK FISH CAMP
LOCATION: East end of Battleship Parkway at foot of Spanish Fort Hill.
FACILITIES: Launching, 50 cents; marine gas and oil; dockside pump; boat rental; snacks; bait and tackle; open 7 days, dawn to dusk.

TENSAW FISHING CAMP
LOCATION: Battleship Parkway on east end

ALABAMA

BOATING AREAS (continued)

of Tensaw River Bridge.
FACILITIES: Launching, 50 cents; boat storage; marine gas and oil; dockside pump; boat rental; restrooms; snacks; bait and tackle; open 7 days, dawn to dusk.

RAY'S FISH CAMP
LOCATION: Mobile Causeway (east).
FACILITIES: Launching, 50 cents; boat storage; marine gas and oil; dockside pump; boat rental; restrooms; snacks; bait and tackle; open 24 hrs.

Small Tributaries (Blakely River)

BUZBEE FISHING CAMP
LOCATION: Hwy. 225 at Bay Minette Creek Bridge.
FACILITIES: Launching, $1; boat and motor rental; restrooms; bait and tackle; cold beverages; open 7 days, dawn to dusk.

Dauphin Island

Mobile Bay

DAUPHIN ISLAND MARINA
LOCATION: Dauphin Island south end of bridge.
FACILITIES: Launching, $1; boat and motor sales and repairs; boat storage (dry & wet); marine gas and oil; dockside pump; restrooms; groceries; snacks; bait and tackle; cafe; charter; open 7 days, 16 hrs.

Deatsville

Jordan Lake (Coosa River)

BLACKWELL FISHING LODGE
LOCATION: 12 mi. northwest of Wetumpka on Hwy. 111, 1 mi. north on 23.
FACILITIES: Launching, 50 cents; boat and motor repairs; boat storage; marine gas and oil; dockside pump; boat rental; tent camping, $3; picnic area, 50 cents; restrooms; groceries; snacks; bait and tackle; open 7 days, 15 hrs.

LAKE JORDAN MARINA
LOCATION: 11 mi. northwest on Hwy. 111, from Wetumpka to Slapout.
FACILITIES: Launching, 50 cents; boat and motor repairs; motor sales; boat storage; marine gas and oil; dockside pump; boat and motor rental; motel, $15; cabins, $50; tent camping, $2; trailer camping, $3; apartments; restrooms; groceries; snacks; bait and tackle; cafe; swimming pool; cold beverages; open 7 days, dawn to dusk.

Decatur

Wheeler Lake (Tennessee River)

DECATUR BOAT HARBOR
LOCATION: At Tennessee River Bridge.
FACILITIES: Launching; boat storage; marine gas and oil; dockside pump; boat rental; picnic area; restrooms; snacks; bait and tackle; open 24 hrs.

Demopolis

Dem Lake (Tom River)

CALDWELL'S BOAT AND BAIT
LOCATION: 990 West Jackson Street.
FACILITIES: Launching; boat and motor sales and repairs; boat storage; regular gas and oil; dockside pump; boat and motor rental; restrooms; snacks; bait and tackle; ice; open 7 days, 12 hrs.

DEMOPOLIS ACCESS AREA
LOCATION: 1 mi. above Demopolis Lock, Foscue Park.
FACILITIES: Launching; tent camping; trailer camping; picnic area; restrooms; open 24 hrs.

Double Springs

Lewis Smith Lake (Warrior River System)

CORINTH RECREATION AREA
LOCATION: 4 mi. east of Double Springs then 2½ mi. south.
FACILITIES: Launching, $1; tent camping, $1; picnic area, $1; restrooms; open 24 hrs.

ROCKHOUSE CREEK RESORT
LOCATION: 4 mi. east of Double Springs, then 2½ mi. south.
FACILITIES: Launching; marine gas and oil; dockside pump; boat rental; tent camping, $3; trailer camping, $3; picnic area, $1; restrooms; groceries; bait and tackle; cafe; hunting and fishing license; open 6 days, 15 hrs.

WINSTON MARINA
LOCATION: 5 mi. east of Double Springs off Hwy. 278.
FACILITIES: Launching; boat storage; marine gas and oil; dockside pump; restrooms; groceries; snacks; bait and tackle; hunting and fishing license; open 24 hrs.

Dunavant

Purdy Lake (Alabama River)

LAKE PURDY BOAT LANDING
LOCATION: 2½ mi. east of Hwy. 280 on Hwy. 119.
FACILITIES: Launching; marine gas and oil; boat rental; restrooms; snacks; bait and tackle; fishing and hunting license; open 24 hrs.

Eclectic

Martin Lake (Tallapoosa River)

CASTAWAY ISLAND
LOCATION: 6 mi. east of Eclectic, 5 mi. north of Kent.
FACILITIES: Launching; boat storage; marine gas and oil; dockside pump; boat and motor rental; cabins, $10; picnic area; restrooms; snacks; bait and tackle; cafe; open 7 days, 12 hrs.

Equality

Martin Lake (Tallapoosa River)

REAL ISLAND MARINA
LOCATION: 6 mi. east of Hwy. 9.
FACILITIES: Launching, $1; boat storage; marine gas and oil; dockside pump; picnic

BOATING AREAS (continued)

area, $1; restrooms; groceries; tackle; open 7 days, 14 hrs.

Eufaula

Walter F. George (Chattahoochee River)

CHEWACLA CREEK MARINA
LOCATION: City limits of Eufaula on Chewala Creek, Hwy. 431.
FACILITIES: Launching; boat and motor sales and repairs; boat storage; marine gas and oil; dockside pump; boat and motor rental; restrooms; groceries; bait and tackle; open 7 days, 14 hrs.

LAKE EUFAULA KAMPGROUND (KOA)
LOCATION: ¼ mi. west of intersection Hwy. 431 and 82.
FACILITIES: Launching; marine gas and oil; tent camping, $3.50 nightly; trailer camping, $3.50; restrooms; groceries; bait and tackle; open 24 hrs.

WHITE OAK CREEK LANDING
LOCATION: 12 mi. south of Eufaula on Hwy. 95.
FACILITIES: Launching; boat storage; marine gas and oil; dockside pump; boat rental; tent camping; trailer camping; picnic area; restrooms; groceries; bait and tackle; open 24 hrs.

Eutaw

Black Warrior Lake

JENNINGS FERRY LANDING
LOCATION: 1 mi. south of Hwy. 14 at Underwood Bridge near Eutaw.
FACILITIES: Launching; tent camping; trailer camping; tables; water; picnic area; open 24 hrs.

Fairhope

Fish River

DAMON'S MARINA
LOCATION: On Fish River near Marlow Road on west side of river.
FACILITIES: Launching; boat storage; marine gas and oil; dockside pump; boat rental; cabins, $8 single, $4 each additional; picnic area; restrooms; groceries; bait and tackle; open 7 days, 11 hrs.

Florence

Wilson Lake (Tennessee River)

BACHLOR VILLA
LOCATION: Shoals Creek, 8 mi. north of Florence on County Road 47.
FACILITIES: Launching, $1; marine gas and oil; dockside pump; boat and motor rental; restrooms; groceries; bait and tackle; trailer rentals, $15 per day; open 24 hrs.

Foley

Bon Secour River

CAMPBELL'S BON SECOUR RESORT

LOCATION: Bon Secour Bridge, Hwy. 10.
FACILITIES: Launching; marine gas and oil; dockside pump; boat rental; cabins, $10; restrooms; bait and tackle; open 24 hrs.

Magnolia River

NOLTE CREEK MARINA
LOCATION: 2 mi. south and 2 mi. west of Magnolia Springs.
FACILITIES: Launching, $1; marine gas and oil; dockside pump; boat rental; open 7 days, 14 hrs.

Forkland

Lake Demopolis (Black Warrior River)

KELLEY'S MARINA
LOCATION: ¼ mi. north of River Bridge on Hwy. 43 on Greene County Road 4.
FACILITIES: Launching; boat and motor repairs; boat storage; marine gas and oil; dockside pump; snacks; open 7 days, dawn to dusk.

Gadsden

Neely Henry Lake (Coosa River)

BUCK'S BOATS
LOCATION: 1 mi. below South Side Bridge, 15 mi. up from Henry Dam.
FACILITIES: Launching, $2; boat and motor sales and repairs; boat storage; marine oil; restrooms; open 7 days, 14 hrs.

CAPTAIN RILEY'S RAINBOW MARINA
LOCATION: At South Side Bridge.
FACILITIES: Launching; marine gas and oil; dockside pump; restrooms; groceries; bait and tackle; open 6 days, 8 hrs.

LEE'S FISH CAMP
LOCATION: 4 mi. west of Weiss Powerhouse.
FACILITIES: Launching, 50 cents; marine gas and oil; dockside pump; boat rental; tent camping, $2; trailer camping, $2; picnic area; restrooms; snacks; bait and tackle; open 7 days, 14 hrs.

PAYNE'S MARINA
LOCATION: Green Valley Lake Estates 6½ mi. up river from Henry Dam.
FACILITIES: Launching; boat storage; marine gas and oil; dockside pump; snacks; bait and tackle; open 7 days, 13 hrs.

TOMMY'S MARINA
LOCATION: 1 mi. north of South Side Bridge.
FACILITIES: Launching, 50 cents; boat storage; marine gas and oil; dockside pump; snacks; bait and tackle; open 7 days, 6 hrs.

Gallion

Lake Demopolis (Black Warrior River)

OLD LOCK NO. 5
LOCATION: 5 mi. west off Hwy. 69 between Gallion and Greensboro.
FACILITIES: Launching; tent camping; trailer camping; tables; water; picnic area; restrooms; open 24 hrs.

ALABAMA

BOATING AREAS (continued)

Gantt

Gantt Lake (Conecuh River)

LINDSEY'S WATERFRONT
LOCATION: 1 mi. east of Hwy. 29.
FACILITIES: Launching; marine gas and oil; dockside pump; picnic area; restrooms; snacks; bait and tackle; cafe; open 7 days, 15 hrs.

SLEEPY'S PLACE
LOCATION: 1 mi. east of Hwy. 29.
FACILITIES: Launching, 50 cents; marine gas and oil; dockside pump; tent camping; trailer camping; picnic area; restrooms; groceries; bait and tackle; open 7 days, 16 hrs.

Gilbertown

Coffeeville Lake (Tom River)

OKATUPPA CREEK LAUNCHING RAMP
LOCATION: 6 mi. east of Gilbertown.
FACILITIES: Launching; tent camping; trailer camping; picnic area; restrooms; open 24 hrs.

Grant

Guntersville Lake (Tennessee River)

HONEYCOMB BOAT DOCK
LOCATION: 7 mi. north of Guntersville.
FACILITIES: Launching; minor boat repairs; motor repairs; boat storage; marine gas and oil; dockside pump; boat rental; tent camping, $3; picnic area; restrooms; snacks; bait and tackle; cafe; open 7 days, 12 hrs.

MINK CREEK LODGE
LOCATION: 9 mi. south of Scottsboro on Hwy. 79.
FACILITIES: Launching, $1; boat storage; cabins; tent camping, $3; trailer camping, $3; picnic area, $2; restrooms; open 7 days, 8 hrs.

Greensboro

Black Warrior River

PAYNE LAKE
LOCATION: 16 mi. north of Greensboro off Hwy. 25.
FACILITIES: Launching; tent camping; trailer camping; picnic area; restrooms; open 24 hrs.

Guntersville

Guntersville Lake (Tennessee River)

ALRED MARINA
LOCATION: 3 mi. north of Guntersville west on Hwy. 431.
FACILITIES: Launching, $1; boat repairs; inboard motor repairs; boat storage; marine gas and oil; dockside pump; restrooms; open 7 days, 10 hrs.

BEECH CREEK FISHING CAMP
LOCATION: 3 mi. south of Hwy. 69 from Warrenton.

FACILITIES: Launching, 50 cents; boat storage; marine gas and oil; dockside pump; boat and motor rental; tent camping; trailer camping; picnic area; restrooms; groceries; bait and tackle; cafe; open 24 hrs.

CATFISH CAFE
LOCATION: South of Guntersville on Hwy. 431, just across Spring Creek on southside.
FACILITIES: Launching, $1; boat storage; marine gas and oil; dockside pump; boat and motor rental; picnic area, $1 per table; restrooms; snacks; bait and tackle; cafe; open 6 days, 12 hrs.

GUNTERSVILLE BOAT MART AND FISH CAMP
LOCATION: Located on Brown Creek, Hwy. 69 between Guntersville and Arab.
FACILITIES: Launching; boat and motor sales and repairs; boat storage; marine gas and oil; dockside pump; boat and motor rentals; restrooms; groceries; bait and tackle; open 7 days, dawn to dusk.

LAKEWOOD MOTEL
LOCATION: ¼ mi. north of Guntersville Bridge on Hwy. 431.
FACILITIES: Launching; marine gas and oil; boat rental; motel, $8; cabins, $8; restrooms; picnic area; groceries; bait and tackle; cafe; open 7 days, 14 hrs.

RIVERBEND MARINA
LOCATION: Scottsboro Hwy. 5 mi north of Guntersville.
FACILITIES: Launching, $1; boat storage; marine gas and oil; dockside pump; restrooms; snacks; marine supplies; open 7 days, 9 hrs.

STREET BLUFF FISH CAMP
LOCATION: 3 mi. west of Guntersville on Hwy. 69 to intersection of Cha-La-Kee Road, 1½ mi. north.
FACILITIES: Launching; boat storage; marine gas and oil; dockside pump; boat rental; tent camping, $1.50; trailer camping, $2; picnic area; restrooms; snacks; bait and tackle; cafe; open 7 days, 15 hrs.

TOWN CREEK LAUNCHING RAMPS
LOCATION: 9 mi. north of Guntersville on Hwy. 227.
FACILITIES: Launching; marine gas and oil; dockside pump; boat rental; tent camping, $3; trailer camping, $3; picnic area; restrooms; groceries; snacks; bait and tackle; open 24 hrs.

TURNER'S MARINA
LOCATION: 9 mi. north of Guntersville on Hwy. 79.
FACILITIES: Launching, $1; boat storage; marine gas and oil; dockside pump; picnic area; restrooms; snacks; bait and tackle; cafe; trailer rentals; open 7 days, 13 hrs.

Hillsboro

Wheeler Lake (Tennessee River)

MALLARD CREEK FISH CAMP
LOCATION: 15 mi. west of Decatur.
FACILITIES: Launching; marine gas and oil; dockside pump; picnic area; groceries; bait and tackle; open 7 days, 14 hrs.

BOATING AREAS (continued)

Hollywood

Guntersville Lake (Tennessee River)

MUD CREEK FISH CAMP
LOCATION: 9 mi. east of Scottsboro on U.S.
Hwy. 72.
FACILITIES: Launching; boat and motor
sales and repairs; boat storage; gas and oil;
dockside pump; motel, $8; picnic area; rest-
rooms; snacks; bait and tackle; cafe; open 7
days, 14 hrs.

Houston

Lewis Smith Lake (Warrior River System)

YELLOW CREEK DOCKS
LOCATION: 6 mi. south of Hwy. 278,
through Houston Hwy. 63.
FACILITIES: Launching; boat storage;
marine gas and oil; dockside pump; boat rental; tent camping, $2; trailer camping, $2; picnic area; restrooms; snacks; bait and tackle;
cafe; hunting and fishing licenses; open 24
hrs.

Huntsville

Wheeler Lake (Tennessee River)

MADISON COUNTY BOAT HARBOR
LOCATION: 2 mi. east of Hwy. 231 on
Hobb's Island Road.
FACILITIES: Launching; boat storage;
marine gas and oil; dockside pump; picnic
area; snacks; open 7 days, 14 hrs.

Jackson Gap

Martin Lake (Tallapoosa River)

WHITE'S MARINA
LOCATION: 3½ mi. off U.S. 280 turn at the
RC sign, follow it to the second RC sign on
east side of bridge, and turn and follow it until you come to the marina.
FACILITIES: Launching, 50 cents; boat storage; marine gas and oil; dockside pump; boat
rental; restrooms; groceries; bait and tackle;
marine supplies; beverages; open 7 days, 12
hrs.

Jasper

Lewis Smith Lake (Warrior River System)

CLEAR CREEK MARINA
LOCATION: 4 mi. east of Hwy. 195 on Clear
Creek.
FACILITIES: Launching, $1; boat storage;
marine gas and oil; dockside pump; boat rental; restrooms; snacks; bait and tackle; hunting
and fishing license; open 24 hrs.

DUSKIN POINT MARINA
LOCATION: 15 mi. from Jasper, approximately 6 mi. on County Road 43.
FACILITIES: Launching; boat and motor repairs; boat storage; marine gas and oil; dockside pump; boat rental; restrooms; groceries;
snacks; bait and tackle; cafe; open 7 days, 12
hrs.

HUEY'S MARINA
LOCATION: At Duncan Bridge on 257.
FACILITIES: Launching; boat sales; boat
and motor repairs; boat storage; marine gas
and oil; dockside pump; boat rental; tent
camping; trailer camping; restrooms; groceries; bait and tackle; cafe; hunting and fishing
license; open 24 hrs.

MAULDIN'S FISHING CAMP
LOCATION: 15 mi. from Jasper, County
Road 43.
FACILITIES: Launching, $1; marine gas and
oil; dockside pump; boat and motor rental;
motel, $15; tent camping, $3; trailer camping,
$20 per month; picnic area, $1; restrooms;
groceries; snacks; bait and tackle; swimming
area; hunting and fishing license; ice; open 7
days, 12 hrs.

Killen

Wilson Lake (Tennessee River)

EMERALD BEACH
LOCATION: 1 mi. north of Shoals Creek
Bridge on Hwy. 72.
FACILITIES: Launching, $1; boat storage;
marine gas and oil; dockside pump; boat
rental; motel, $15; tent camping, $2; trailer
camping, $2; restrooms; groceries; bait and
tackle; cafe; open 7 days, 19 hrs.

Langston

Guntersville Lake (Tennessee River)

CUNNINGHAM FISH CAMP
LOCATION: 17 mi. south of Scottsboro on
County Road 67 near South Sauty Creek.
FACILITIES: Launching; marine gas and oil;
restrooms; groceries; snacks; bait and tackle;
open 24 hrs.

SOUTH SAUTY CREEK CAMP
LOCATION: 13 mi. northeast of Guntersville
on Hwy. 227 to Five Points, turn left 7 mi.,
17 mi. southeast of Scottsboro on Hwy. 67.
FACILITIES: Launching; boat and motor
sales and repairs; boat storage; marine gas and
oil; dockside pump; boat and motor rental;
motel, $10; tent camping, $1; trailer camping,
$1; picnic area; restrooms; groceries; bait and
tackle; cafe; open 7 days, 14 hrs.

Leesburg

Weiss Lake (Coosa River)

CONNELL'S EXXON STATION
LOCATION: 3 mi. west of Leesburg on Hwy.
411.
FACILITIES: Launching; marine gas and oil;
tent camping, $2; trailer camping, $2; picnic
area; restrooms; groceries; bait; open 7 days,
12 hrs.

JONES FISH CAMP
LOCATION: 2 mi. west of Leesburg off Hwy.
411.
FACILITIES: Launching, 50 cents; marine
gas and oil; dockside pump; boat rental; tent
camping, $2; trailer camping, $2; picnic area,
$1; restrooms; groceries; snacks; bait and
tackle; open 7 days, 14 hrs.

ALABAMA

BOATING AREAS (continued)

E. C. LACK'S FISH CAMP
LOCATION: 3 mi. west of Leesburg, 1 mi. off Hwy. 411.
FACILITIES: Launching, 50 cents; marine gas and oil; dockside pump; boat rental; tent camping, $1.50; trailer camping, $15 per month; picnic area, $1; restrooms; groceries; snacks; bait and tackle; open 7 days, 12 hrs., Apr. to Oct.

Levaca

Coffeeville Lake (Tom River)

EZELL'S FISH CAMP
LOCATION: 15 mi. east of Butler on Hwy. 10.
FACILITIES: Launching; marine gas and oil; dockside pump; restrooms; cafe; open 24 hrs.

Lincoln

Logan Martin Lake (Coosa River)

CLEAR SPRINGS MARINA
LOCATION: On Hwy. 63 between I-20 and Hwy. 78.
FACILITIES: Launching, $1; boat storage; marine gas and oil; dockside pump; boat rental; tent camping, $3 per night; trailer camping, $3 per night; restrooms; groceries; snacks; bait and tackle; open 24 hrs.

HIGHWAY 78 BOAT DOCK
LOCATION: On Hwy. 78.
FACILITIES: Launching, $1; boat and motor sales and repairs; boat storage; marine gas and oil; dockside pump; tent camping, $1; trailer camping, $1; picnic area, $1; restrooms; bait and tackle; cafe; open 7 days, 14 hrs.

INGRAM'S BLUE EYE MARINA
LOCATION: On Hwy. 63 between I-20 and Hwy. 78.
FACILITIES: Launching; boat and motor sales and repairs; boat storage; marine gas and oil; dockside pump; boat and motor rental; tent camping, $1; trailer camping, $3.50; picnic area, $1; restrooms; snacks; bait and tackle; cafe; mobile homes for rent; swimming area; open 7 days, 14 hrs.

Little River

Alabama River

DIXIE LANDING
LOCATION: Near Monroe County Line at Little River.
FACILITIES: Launching, $2; marine gas and oil; dockside pump; boat rental; motel, $5; tent camping, $1; trailer camping, $1; groceries; snacks; bait and tackle; cafe; open 7 days, 16 hrs.

Magnolia Springs

Fish River

FISH RIVER FISHING CAMP
LOCATION: Fish River Bridge on Hwy. 98.
FACILITIES: Launching, 75 cents; boat storage; marine gas and oil; dockside pump; boat

and motor rental; picnic area; restrooms; groceries; bait and tackle; open 7 days, 14 hrs.

McIntosh

Bates Lake (Tom River)

DICK'S LANDING
LOCATION: 2 mi. east of Hwy. 43 at McIntosh.
FACILITIES: Launching; marine gas and oil; snacks; bait; open 24 hrs.

Millers Ferry

Millers Ferry (Alabama River)

WILCOX MARINA
LOCATION: 10 mi. west of Camden on Hwy. 28.
FACILITIES: Launching, $1; boat and motor sales and repairs; marine gas and oil; dockside pump; boat rental; tent camping, $3; restrooms; groceries; bait and tackle; open 7 days, 16 hrs.

Mobile

Dog River

BEACHCOMBER DOCKS
LOCATION: Dog River Bridge.
FACILITIES: Launching, $1; boat storage; marine gas and oil; dockside pump; snacks; bait and tackle; open 7 days, dawn to dusk.

DOG RIVER K.O.A. KAMPGROUND
LOCATION: Rangeline Road off Hamilton Blvd., 2 mi. west of Dog River Bridge Bywater.
FACILITIES: Launching; boat rental; tent camping, $4 for 2 people; trailer camping, $4 for 2 people; picnic area; restrooms; groceries; snacks; bait and tackle; campers for rent; open 24 hrs.

FROST MARINE
LOCATION: Dog River Bridge south side.
FACILITIES: Launching, $1; boat and motor repairs; boat sales; boat storage; marine gas and oil; dockside pump; restrooms; snacks; bait and tackle; cafe; open 7 days, 10 hrs.

HOPPE'S FISHING CAMP
LOCATION: ¼ mi. north of Dog River Bridge.
FACILITIES: Launching, 50 cents; marine gas and oil; boat and motor rental; restrooms; snacks; bait and tackle; open 7 days, dawn to dusk.

PARKWAY SEAFOOD
LOCATION: ¼ mi. north of Dog River Bridge.
FACILITIES: Launching, 50 cents; boat and motor rental; restrooms; groceries; bait and tackle; open 7 days, 19 hrs.

Montgomery

Black Warrior River

MOUNDVILLE PUBLIC USE AREA
LOCATION: 5 mi. southwest of Moundville on east side of river.

14

BOATING AREAS (continued)

FACILITIES: Launching; tent camping; trailer camping; picnic area; restrooms; open 24 hrs.

RIVERVIEW COOKOUT
LOCATION: 2¼ mi. from Hunters Station west on Washington Ferry.
FACILITIES: Launching, $1; boat storage; oil; dockside pump; boat and motor rental; cabins, $12; tent camping, $4; trailer camping, $4; picnic area, $1.50; restrooms; snacks; bait and tackle; open 24 hrs.

WASHINGTON FERRY MARINA
LOCATION: 2¼ mi. from Hunters Station west on Washington Ferry.
FACILITIES: Launching, $1; boat storage; marine gas and oil; dockside pump; boat rental; tent camping, $2; trailer camping, $3.50; picnic area; restrooms; groceries; bait and tackle; open 24 hrs.

Northport

North River

BUSTER'S PLACE
LOCATION: ½ mi. off Hwy. 69, 12 mi. from Northport.
FACILITIES: Launching, $1; boat storage; marine gas and oil; dockside pump; picnic area; restrooms; groceries; bait and tackle; tent and trailer camping areas; open 24 hrs.

SMITH BOAT LANDING
LOCATION: 10 mi. north of Tuscaloosa on Hwy. 43, ¼ mi. off Hwy. 43.
FACILITIES: Launching, $1; boat storage; marine gas and oil; dockside pump; tent camping; trailer camping; picnic area; restrooms; snacks; bait and tackle; open 5 days, 12 hrs.

Ohatchee

Logan Martin Lake (Coosa River)

CANE BREAK
LOCATION: Mouth of Ohatchee Creek and Coosa River on Hwy. 77.
FACILITIES: Launching; boat rental; tent camping; trailer camping; picnic area; restrooms; groceries; bait and tackle; cafe; open 7 days, 20 hrs.

RIO VISTA
LOCATION: Hwy. 77 in Ohatchee.
FACILITIES: Launching; tent camping, $1; picnic area, $1; restrooms; snacks; bait and tackle; open 7 days, 14 hrs.

Neely Henry Lake (Coosa River)

LAKESHORE FISH CAMP
LOCATION: 2 mi. north of Ohatchee on Hwy. 77.
FACILITIES: Launching, 50 cents; marine gas and oil; dockside pump; boat rental; tent camping, $1.50; trailer camping, $1.50; picnic area, $1; restrooms; groceries; snacks; bait and tackle; open 24 hrs.

Oneonta

Inland Lake (Black Warrior Lake)

BOAT LANDING
LOCATION: East end of lake, 7 mi. south of Oneonta.
FACILITIES: Launching, $2; boat storage; marine gas and oil; dockside pump; boat rental; groceries; bait and tackle; cafe; open 24 hrs.

Orrville

Millers Ferry (Alabama River)

RIVERS RETREAT
LOCATION: 8 mi. south of Orrville on Hwy. 33.
FACILITIES: Launching, $1; marine gas and oil; dockside pump; boat rental; tent camping; trailer camping; picnic area; restrooms; groceries; bait and tackle; swimming lake; guide service; catfish restaurant; open 24 hrs.

Parrish

Lewis Smith Lake (Warrior River System)

HOWARD CHAPPELL
LOCATION: 15 mi. south of Jasper on County Road 269.
FACILITIES: Launching, $1; marine gas and oil; boat and motor rental; restrooms; snacks; bait and tackle; open 7 days, 12 hrs.

Pell City

Logan Martin Lake (Coosa River)

HUB'S FOOD MART
LOCATION: Hwy. 63.
FACILITIES: Launching; marine gas and oil; dockside pump; boat rental; trailer camping, $1; restrooms; groceries; snacks; bait and tackle; open 7 days, 14 hrs.

Peterson

Holt Lake (Black Warrior River)

TOXEY MARINA
LOCATION: ½ mi. above Holt Lock and Dam on east side of river.
FACILITIES: Launching; boat storage; marine gas and oil; dockside pump; restrooms; open 6 days, 14 hrs.

Phenix City

Oliver Lake (Chattahoochee River)

LAKE OLIVER MARINA RAMP
LOCATION: 4½ mi. below Goat Rock Dam.
FACILITIES: Launching, 50 cents; marine oil; dockside pump; tent camping, $1.50; picnic area, 25 cents; restrooms; groceries; snacks; bait and tackle; open 24 hrs.

Ragland

Logan Martin Lake (Coosa River)

KIKER'S CAMP
LOCATION: 7 mi. northeast of Pell City on Emory's Bend.
FACILITIES: Launching, $1; marine gas and oil; dockside pump; tent camping, $2; trailer camping, $2.50; picnic area, $1; restrooms;

ALABAMA

BOATING AREAS (continued)

groceries; snacks; bait and tackle; open 24 hrs.

Neeley Henry Lake (Coosa River)

NEELEY HENRY PARK
LOCATION: ½ mi. west of Henry Dam.
FACILITIES: Launching; tent camping, $2;
trailer camping, $2; picnic area; restrooms;
groceries; snacks; bait and tackle; open 24 hrs.

Riverside

Logan Martin Lake (Coosa River)

BUCKNER'S MARINA
LOCATION: 1 mi. north of I-20.
FACILITIES: Launching, $1; boat and motor
sales and repairs; marine gas and oil; groceries;
snacks; bait and tackle; dockside pump; open
24 hrs.

RIVERSIDE MARINA
LOCATION: Intersection of I-20 and 78 at
Riverside.
FACILITIES: Launching, $1; boat and motor
sales and repairs; boat storage; marine gas and
oil; dockside pump; picnic area, 50 cents, $1;
restrooms; groceries; snacks; cafe; open 24
hrs.

Riverview

Hardins Lake (Chattahoochee River)

CAMP HALAWAKA RAMP
LOCATION: Hwy. 87 Long Bridge, Halawaka
Creek, 16 mi. east of Opelika.
FACILITIES: Launching, 50 cents; dockside
pump; restrooms; groceries; snacks; cafe; open
7 days, 12 hrs.

COOK'S LANDING RAMP
LOCATION: Blanton Road, 18 mi. east of
Opelika.
FACILITIES: Launching, 50 cents; boat rental; restrooms; groceries; snacks; bait and
tackle; Poor Boy Landing, near Camp Halawaka, free lunch; open 7 days, 14 hrs.

Rockford

Mitchell Lake (Coosa River)

BARRETT'S FISH CAMP
LOCATION: Turn north at Hulls store on
Hwy. 22, 3 mi. east of the Coosa River
Bridge, go to the end of the road.
FACILITIES: Launching, $1; marine gas and
oil; dockside pump; boat rental; cabins, $4;
tent camping, $1; trailer camping, $1; picnic
area; restrooms; snacks; bait and tackle; open
7 days, 12 hrs.

HOWELL'S FISH CAMP
LOCATION: Turn north at Kelly's crossroads
on Hwy. 22, 8 mi. west of Rockford.
FACILITIES: Launching, 50 cents; boat rental; tent camping, $1; trailer camping, $1; picnic area; open 24 hrs.

Rogersville

Wheeler Lake (Tennessee River)

DAVIS FISH CAMP
LOCATION: 2 mi. east of Elgin Crossroads.
FACILITIES: Launching; marine gas and oil;
tent camping, $2; trailer camping, $2; picnic
area; restrooms; groceries; bait and tackle;
open 7 days, 16 hrs.

Salem

Harding Lake (Chattachoochee River)

SONIA'S MARINA RAMP
LOCATION: Near Long Bridge Hwy. 87, 17
mi. east of Opelika.
FACILITIES: Launching, 50 cents; boat storage; marine gas and oil; dockside pump; motel, $7 per night; cabins, $7 per night; tent
camping; trailer camping; restrooms; snacks;
groceries; bait and tackle; cafe; open 7 days,
14 hrs.

Satsuma

Mobile River

MACK'S BOAT LANDING
LOCATION: (Gunnison Creek) east end
Orange Avenue.
FACILITIES: Launching, $1.50; boat storage;
boat rental; picnic area; restrooms; snacks;
open 24 hrs.

ROGER'S MARINA
LOCATION: (Steel Creek) ¾ mi. east of red
light on Hwy. 43, at east end of Bayou Street.
FACILITIES: Launching, $1.50; boat storage;
marine gas and oil; dockside pump; boat rental; restrooms; groceries; snacks; bait and
tackle; dry storage; open 24 hrs.

Sawyerville

Black Warrior Lake

BARFIELD BAIT SHOP
LOCATION: Hwy. 14, 3 mi. east of Eutaw,
near Jennings Ferry Landing.
FACILITIES: Launching; marine gas and oil;
dockside pump; boat rental; trailer camping;
restrooms; groceries; bait and tackle; open 24
hrs.

Lake Demopolis (Black Warrior River)

OLD LOCK NO. 6
LOCATION: 5 mi. west of Sawyerville off
Hwy. 14.
FACILITIES: Launching; tent camping;
trailer camping; tables; water; picnic area;
restrooms; open 24 hrs.

Scottsboro

Guntersville Lake (Tennessee River)

COMER BRIDGE MARINA
LOCATION: 5 mi. east of Scottsboro on
Hwy. 35.
FACILITIES: Launching; boat storage;
marine gas and oil; tent camping; picnic area;
restrooms; snacks; groceries; bait and tackle;
open 7 days, 12 hrs.

JACKSON COUNTY PARK
LOCATION: 3 mi. southeast of Scottsboro

BOATING AREAS (continued)

on Roseberry Creek.
FACILITIES: Launching; boat and motor sales and repairs; boat storage; marine gas and oil; dockside pump; boat rental; tent camping, $3; trailer camping, $3; picnic area; restrooms; groceries; snacks; bait and tackle; cafe; open 7 days, 14 hrs.

NORTH SAUTY CREEK MARINA

LOCATION: 8 mi. south of Scottsboro on Hwy. 79.
FACILITIES: Launching; boat and motor sales and repairs; marine gas and oil; dockside pump; boat and motor rental; tent camping; trailer camping, $3; picnic area; restrooms; groceries; snacks; bait and tackle; open 7 days, 14 hrs.

SALT PETRE FISH CAMP

LOCATION: 8 mi. west of Scottsboro on County Road 11 on North Sauty Creek.
FACILITIES: Launching, 50 cents; boat rental; tent camping; picnic area; restrooms; snacks and groceries; bait and tackle; open 7 days, dawn to dusk.

Screamer

Walter F. George Dam (Chattahoochee River)

HARDRIDGE CREEK LANDING

LOCATION: 15 mi. east of Abbeville on Old River Road.
FACILITIES: Launching; marine gas and oil; boat rental; tent camping; trailer camping; picnic area; restrooms; groceries; bait and tackle; cafe; open 24 hrs.

THOMAS MILL CREEK AREA

LOCATION: Old River Road, about 18 mi. east of Abbeville.
FACILITIES: Launching; marine gas and oil; boat rental; tent camping; trailer camping; picnic area; groceries; bait and tackle; open 24 hrs.

Selma

Millers Ferry (Alabama River)

BEACH CREEK MARINA

LOCATION: River Road behind Selma Stockyards.
FACILITIES: Launching; boat storage; marine gas and oil; dockside pump; snacks; bait and tackle; open 24 hrs.

OLD CAHABA PARK

LOCATION: 5 mi. south of Selma on Hwy. 22, turn left on County Road 33 for 5 mi.
FACILITIES: Launching; gas; groceries; dirt launching ramp; picnic area; restrooms; sightseeing; open 24 hrs.

RIVERSIDE CAMPING

LOCATION: 6 mi. northeast of Selma on River Road.
FACILITIES: Launching, $1; tent camping, $3; trailer camping, $3; picnic area; restrooms (hot showers); open 24 hrs.

SELMA CITY MARINA

LOCATION: Hwy. 22 west behind Block Park.
FACILITIES: Launching; marine gas and oil; dockside pump; picnic area; restrooms; snacks; open 24 hrs.

Seminole

Perdido River

BROWN'S LANDING

LOCATION: 1½ mi. south of Hwy. 90 Bridge at Florida Line.
FACILITIES: Launching, $1; boat storage; open 7 days, dawn to dusk.

Shelby

Lay Lake (Coosa River)

ARMSTRONG FISH CAMP

LOCATION: 3 mi. south of Shelby on County Road 47 to intersection 47 & 71, turn right 4 mi.
FACILITIES: Launching, $1; marine gas and oil; dockside pump; boat rental; cabins, $10 daily; restrooms; snacks; bait and tackle; cafe; mobile home space; fishing and hunting license; open 7 days, 12 hrs.

BOZO FISH CAMP

LOCATION: 3 mi. south of Shelby on County Road 47 to 71, then 5 mi. on 71, turn right.
FACILITIES: Launching, $1; marine gas and oil; dockside pump; boat and motor rental; restrooms; groceries; snacks; bait and tackle; fishing and hunting license; open 24 hrs.

CAMP OKOMO

LOCATION: From Columbiana south to Shelby on County Road 71, turn left on 47, about 3 mi. left to camp.
FACILITIES: Launching, $1; marine gas and oil; dockside pump; boat rental; restrooms; snacks; bait and tackle; cafe; fishing and hunting license; mobile home park; open 7 days, 12 hrs.

CAMP WAXHATCHIE

LOCATION: 3 mi. south of Shelby, on County Road 47 to intersection 47 and 71 turn right 4 mi.
FACILITIES: Launching, $1; marine gas and oil; dockside pump; boat rental; tent camping; trailer camping; restrooms; snacks; bait and tackle; open 7 days, 16 hrs.

LA COOSA MARINA

LOCATION: 3 mi. south of Shelby on County Road 47 to 71 then about 4 mi.
FACILITIES: Launching, $1; boat storage; marine gas and oil; dockside pump; boat and motor rental; tent camping, $1; trailer camping, $3; picnic area; restrooms; snacks; groceries; bait and tackle; fishing and hunting license; open 7 days, 18 hrs.

SPRING CREEK GROCERY & FISH CAMP

LOCATION: 1 mi. south of Shelby on County Road 47 to intersection 46, turn left 3 mi. at end of road.
FACILITIES: Launching, $1; marine gas and oil; boat and motor rental; tent camping, $2; trailer camping, $2; picnic area; restrooms; groceries; snacks; bait and tackle; fishing and

ALABAMA

BOATING AREAS (continued)

hunting license; open 24 hrs.

Stockton

Tensaw River

BRYANT'S LANDING
LOCATION: Hwy. 225.
FACILITIES: Launching, $1.50; boat storage
and rental; cabins; trailer camping; picnic
area; restrooms; groceries; snacks; bait and
tackle; cafe; open 7 days, 16 hrs.

HUBBARD LANDING
LOCATION: 3 mi. north of Stockton.
FACILITIES: Launching, $2; marine gas and
oil; boat and motor rental; cabins, $12.50;
tent camping and trailer camping, $3.50 daily;
picnic area; restrooms; groceries; snacks; bait
and tackle; ice; open 7 days, 17 hrs.

LIVEOAK LODGE
LOCATION: Stockton.
FACILITIES: Launching, $1.50; boat storage;
marine gas and oil; boat rental; trailer camping,
$1.50; trailer camping, $20 per month; picnic
area, $1 per table; restrooms; open 7 days, 18
hrs.

Sylacauga

Lay Lake (Coosa River)

CEDAR CREEK MARINA
LOCATION: 12 mi. southwest of Sylacauga
on Cedar Creek.
FACILITIES: Launching, $1; boat and motor
sales and repairs; boat storage (wet); marine
gas and oil; dockside pump; boat and motor
rental; tent camping, $2; trailer camping, $2;
picnic area; restrooms; groceries; snacks; bait
and tackle; swimming area; open 7 days, 16
hrs.

J & M MARINA AND RESTAURANT
LOCATION: 12 mi. southwest of Sylacauga
on Cedar Creek.
FACILITIES: Launching, $1; boat sales and
repairs; motor repairs; boat storage; marine
gas and oil; dockside pump; boat and motor
rental; trailer camping, $2; restrooms; snacks;
groceries; bait and tackle; cafe; open 7 days,
15 hrs.

LITTLE TOM'S FISH CAMP
LOCATION: Paint Creek, turn west in Weogufka on County Hwy. to Unity Crossroads,
turn left and keep straight and follow signs.
FACILITIES: Launching, $1; marine gas and
oil; dockside pump; boat rental; cabins, $8;
restrooms; groceries; snacks; bait and tackle;
open 7 days, 15 hrs.

Mitchell Lake (Coosa River)

RAYFIELDS MARINA
LOCATION: Turn north on Hwy. 22 at Hull's
Store, 3 mi. east of the Coosa River Bridge
take second left dirt road.
FACILITIES: Launching; marine gas and oil;
dockside pump; boat and motor rental; bait
and tackle; open 6 days, 16 hrs.

Talladega

Logan Martin Lake (Coosa River)

BAKER HARBOR
LOCATION: 1 mi. off Hwy. 42 at mouth of
Clear Creek.
FACILITIES: Launching, $1; boat storage;
marine gas and oil; dockside pump; boat rental; tent camping, $3.50; trailer camping,
$3.50; picnic area, $2; restrooms; groceries;
snacks; bait and tackle; dairy bar; swimming
area; open 7 days, 12 hrs.

FISHERMAN'S WHARF
LOCATION: 3/10 of a mi. off Hwy. 63 on
Howell's Branch.
FACILITIES: Launching, $1; boat storage;
marine gas and oil; dockside pump; tent
camping, $5 per week; trailer camping, $5 per
week; picnic area; restrooms; groceries;
snacks; bait and tackle; open 7 days, 12 hrs.

Theodore

Fowl River

BAILEY'S MARINA
LOCATION: ¼ mi. north of Fowl River
Bridge.
FACILITIES: Launching; boat storage;
marine gas and oil; dockside pump; restrooms;
snacks; bait and tackle; cafe; open 7 days, 15
hrs.

FOWL RIVER MARINA
LOCATION: Fowl River Bridge on Dauphin
Island Parkway.
FACILITIES: Launching, 75 cents; boat storage; marine gas and oil; dockside pump; restrooms; snacks; bait and tackle; cafe; open 7
days, 16 hrs.

Titus

Jordan Lake (Coosa River)

JOE'S LANDING
LOCATION: Weoka Creek.
FACILITIES: Launching; marine gas and oil;
dockside pump; boat rental; restrooms; groceries; snacks; bait and tackle; open 7 days,
dawn to dusk.

Toxey

Coffeeville Lake (Tom River)

LENOIR'S LANDING
LOCATION: 8 mi. east of Toxey at the
mouth of Tallawompa Creek.
FACILITIES: Launching; tent camping; trailer camping; picnic area; restrooms; open 24
hrs.

Tuscaloosa

Oliver Lake (Black Warrior River)

BENNETT'S MARINA
LOCATION: West side of river at Tuscaloosa
(Oliver Pool).
FACILITIES: Launching; free with sale or
service; boat and motor sales and repairs; oil;
gas and restrooms; open 6 days, 10 hrs.

BOATING AREAS (continued)

Holt Lake (Black Warrior River)

BLUE CREEK PUBLIC USE AREA
LOCATION: 16 mi. above Holt Lock and Dam on west side of river off Hwy. 69 north.
FACILITIES: Launching; tent camping; trailer camping; picnic area; restrooms; open 7 days, 16 hrs.

DEER LICK PUBLIC USE AREA
LOCATION: ½ mi. above Holt Lock and Dam on west side of river.
FACILITIES: Launching; tent camping; trailer camping; swimming area; picnic area; restrooms; open 24 hrs.

OLD LOCK 15 PUBLIC USE AREA
LOCATION: 10 mi. above Holt Lock Dam on west side of river.
FACILITIES: Launching; tent camping; trailer camping; picnic area; restrooms; open 24 hrs.

ROCK QUARRY PUBLIC USE AREA
LOCATION: ¾ mi. above Holt Lock Dam on east side of river.
FACILITIES: Launching; tent camping; trailer camping; picnic area; restrooms; open 24 hrs.

ROCKY BRANCH PUBLIC USE AREA
LOCATION: 3 mi. above Holt Lock Dam on east side of river.
FACILITIES: Launching; tent camping; trailer camping; swimming area; picnic area; restrooms; open 24 hrs.

Verbena

Jordan Lake (Coosa River)

COOSA FISHING LODGE
LOCATION: ¾ mi. below Mitchell Dam off Hwy. 22 east near Coosa River Bridge.
FACILITIES: Launching, $1; marine gas and oil; dockside pump; boat rental; cabins, $4, $6; restrooms; groceries; bait and tackle; open 7 days, 15 hrs.

LOG CABIN BEACH
LOCATION: ¾ mi. below Mitchell Dam off Hwy. 22 east, near Coosa River Bridge.
FACILITIES: Launching, $1; boat and motor rental; cabins, $5; tent camping, $1.50; trailer camping, $1.50; picnic area; restrooms; snacks; open 7 days, 16 hrs.

Mitchell Lake (Coosa River)

BLUE CREEK LODGE
LOCATION: On Blue Creek Road off Hwy. 22 east.
FACILITIES: Launching, $1; motor repairs; boat storage; marine gas and oil; dockside pump; boat and motor rental; tent camping, $3; picnic area; restrooms; bait and tackle; cafe; open 7 days, 16 hrs.

INMAN'S CAMP
LOCATION: Turn off Hwy. 22 east on Blue Creek Road, camp is located at end of road.
FACILITIES: Launching, $1; boat storage; marine gas and oil; dockside pump; boat rental; restrooms; groceries; bait and tackle; open 7 days, 15 hrs.

Vincent

Logan Martin Lake (Coosa River)

BURN'S MARINA
LOCATION: 1 mi. west of Logan Martin Dam.
FACILITIES: Launching, $1; boat storage; marine gas and oil; dockside pump; boat rental; picnic area, 75 cents; restrooms; snacks; bait and tackle; open 7 days, 16 hrs., Apr. - Oct.

Waterloo

Pickwick Lake (Tennessee River)

SPORTSMAN RESTAURANT & TACKLE SHOP
LOCATION: On Second Creek, Bumpus Creek Road off County Road 14.
FACILITIES: Restrooms; groceries; bait and tackle and ammunition; open 6 days, 14 hrs.

Wedgeworth

Black Warrior Lake

OLD LOCK NO. 7
LOCATION: 5 mi. off Hwy. 14 west of Wedgeworth.
FACILITIES: Launching; tent camping; trailer camping; tables; water; picnic area; open 24 hrs.

Weogufka

Mitchell Lake (Coosa River)

TOMMY WILL'S FISH CAMP
LOCATION: 1 mi. below Lay Dam turn west in Weogufka on County Hwy. to Unity Crossroads, turn left and keep straight.
FACILITIES: Launching, $1; marine gas and oil; boat rental; tent camping, $2; trailer camping, $2; picnic area, $2; restrooms; snacks; bait and tackle; river ferry; open 24 hrs.

Wetumpka

Jordan Lake (Coosa River)

BONNER'S FISHING LODGE
LOCATION: 8 mi. north of Wetumpka on Hwy. 111.
FACILITIES: Launching; boat storage; marine gas and oil; dockside pump; boat rental; trailer camping, $3; restrooms; groceries; bait and tackle; open 7 days, 14 hrs.

SEAR'S MARINA
LOCATION: 9 mi. north of Hwy. 231 from Wetumpka.
FACILITIES: Marine gas and oil; dockside pump; boat rental; restrooms; snacks; bait and tackle; open 7 days, dawn to dusk.

BICYCLE TRAILS

See FLORIDA - Gulf Coast Trail

See MISSISSIPPI - Natchez Trail

ALABAMA

TRAILS

Montgomery

BARTRAM TRAIL - 1 mi. foot trail. The trailhead in Tuskegee National Forest is located on Forest Road 900 approximately 1½ mi. southwest of Hwy. 80. The trail is named after William Bartram who traveled through this area in 1776. The trail terminates at Choctafaula Creek where a white sand beach invites wading in cool water before returning. A wide variety of plant species is encountered along the route with transitions from common pine species of the ridges to bottomland species with ferns, cane and dogwood.

SKI AREAS

CLOUDMONT RESORT
Mentone, AL 35984
(205) 634-3841
FACILITIES: Cloudmont is Alabama's only ski area. It features a 300 foot poly-slope for all-weather skiing and a 1000 foot run for the winter season. In addition, Cloudmont offers tennis, swimming, horseback riding, golf and hiking.

AMUSEMENT PARKS & ATTRACTIONS

Birmingham

CASCADE PLUNGE
6815 Second Avenue, South
Birmingham, AL 35212
(205) 591-6451
FACILITIES: Pool; ballrooms; athletic field; picnic area; Arnold Palmer putting course; miniature golf; picnic catering; restaurant; refreshment stands; pay gate; free parking; open May 30 - Sept. 1: Weekends, all year.

FAIR PARK KIDDIELAND
2331 Bessemer Road
Birmingham, AL 35208
(205) 787-2641
FACILITIES: Major rides; kiddie rides; fun house; walk-thru; refreshment stand; penny arcade; athletic field; race track; picnic area; free gate; free parking.

Gulf Shores

HOLLYWOOD PARK
P.O. Box 274
Gulf Shores, AL 36542
(205) 968-7370
FACILITIES: Major rides; kiddie rides; games; refreshment stands; restaurant; arcade; shooting gallery; minature golf; free gate and parking; open Mar. - Labor Day.

Huntsville

ALABAMA SPACE AND ROCKET CENTER
  (Space museum)
Tranquility Base
Huntsville, AL 35807
(205) 837-3400
FACILITIES: Refreshment stands; restaurant; museum; exhibits; picnic area; theatre; stage shows; pay gate; free parking; open all year, closed Christmas Day only.

Mobile

U.S.S. ALABAMA BATTLESHIP COMMIS-
  SION (Attraction)
P.O. Box 65
Battleship Parkway (U.S.90)
Mobile, AL 36601
(205) 433-2703
FACILITIES: Military exhibits; museum; walk-thrus (USS Alabama & Submarine USS Drum); picnic area; refreshment stand; pay gate; free parking; open all year.

Oxford

OXFORD PARK & RECREATION DEPART-
  MENT
McCullar Lane
P.O. Box 3383
Oxford, AL 36201
(205) 831-2660
FACILITIES: Refreshment stands; swimming pool; athletic field; picnic area; crafts; par 3 golf course; tennis; miniature golf; stage shows; orchestras; name bands; fireworks; free acts; free & pay gate; parking.

St. Bernard

AVE MARIA GROTTO (Attraction)
St. Bernard Abbey
St. Bernard, AL 35138
(205) 734-9890; 734-4110
FACILITIES: Exhibits (miniatures in 4 acre park); picnic area; snack bar; open daily 7:00 A.M. to sunset.

Theodore

BELLINGRATH   GARDENS   &   HOME
  (Attraction)
Rt. 1, Box 60
Theodore, AL 36582
(205) 973-2217
FACILITIES: 75 acres of gardens; home tour with rare furnishings; gift shop; snack bar; cafeteria; pay gate; free parking; open all year.

Tuscumbia

SPRING PARK
300 S. Main Street
Tuscumbia, AL 35674
(205) 383-5152
FACILITIES: Kiddie rides; refreshment stand; pool; picnic area; exhibits; books free acts; free gate; free parking; open all year.

Valley Head

SEQUOYAH CAVERNS & CAMPGROUNDS
  (Attraction)
Valley Head, AL 35989
(205) 635-2311
FACILITIES: Caverns; swimming pool; camping; exhibits; athletic field; picnic area; buffalo, white deer, llama, rainbow trout; zoo; free gate & parking; open all year.

Vinemont

HURRICANE CREEK PARK

AMUSEMENT PARKS (continued)

Rt. 4, Box 183
Vinemont, AL 35179
(205) 734-2125
FACILITIES: Souvenir shop; picnic area; natural trails; cable car lift; pay gate; free parking; open all year.

STATE FAIR

Alabama State Fair
P.O. Box 3800-B
Birmingham, AL 35208
(205) 787-2641
DATE: October

NATIONAL PARKS

There are no National Parks in Alabama.

NATIONAL FORESTS

National Forests
Montgomery, AL 36101
(205) 832-7630

Cullman

WILLIAM B. BANKHEAD NATIONAL FOREST
ATTRACTIONS: Limestone gorges;, Lewis Smith Reservoir, two natural bridges, wildlife refuge and management area. Deer, turkey, and squirrel hunting. Bass and bream fishing in Brushy Lake.
FACILITIES: 3 camp and picnic sites, 4 picnic only, 2 swimming sites.
NEARBY TOWNS: Decatur, Haleyville, Jasper, and Russellville.

Andalusia

CONECUH NATIONAL FOREST
ATTRACTIONS: Large, clear ponds. Bass and bream fishing. Deer, turkey, and small-game hunting.
FACILITIES: 1 camp and picnic site, 2 picnic only; 2 swimming sites.

Talladega

TALLADEGA NATIONAL FOREST
ATTRACTIONS: South Sandy Wildlife Management Area; Skyway Motorway; Mount Cheaha, 2,047 feet, highest point in Alabama; Lake Chinnabee. Deer, turkey, duck, and squirrel hunting, bass, bream, and perch fishing; swimming at Cheaha State Park.
FACILITIES: 5 camp and picnic sites, 11 picnic only; 3 swimming sites. Resort hotel, and cabins at Cheaha State Park.
NEARBY TOWNS: Anniston, Centerville, Heflin, Marion, Selma, Sylacauga, and Tuscaloosa.

Tuskegee

TUSKEGEE NATIONAL FOREST
ATTRACTIONS: Pine plantation of advanced size. Bream fishing in streams.
FACILITIES: 1 camp and picnic site, 1 picnic only.
NEARBY TOWN: Auburn.

STATE PARKS

Alexander City

WIND CREEK STATE PARK
Route 2
Alexander City, AL 35010
(205) 234-2101
LOCATION: 7 mi. southeast of Alexander City.
FACILITIES: Open year round; 378 sites; campsite fee; electrical outlets; water and bathroom facilities; food service; picnic area; swimming; hiking; fishing; golf; playground; pets permitted.

Atmore

LITTLE RIVER STATE PARK
Route 2, Box 47
Atmore, AL 36502
(205) 862-2511
LOCATION: 17 mi. north of Atmore.
FACILITIES: Open year round; primitive sites; campsite fee; picnic area; swimming; fishing; boating; pets permitted.

Auburn

CHEWACLA STATE PARK
Route 2, Box 350
Auburn, AL 36830
(205) 887-5621
LOCATION: 4 mi. south of Auburn.
FACILITIES: Open year round; primitive sites; family cottages: 6; food service; picnic area; swimming; hiking; fishing; boating; playground; pets permitted.

Bladon Springs

BLADON SPRINGS STATE PARK
Bladon Springs, AL 36902
(205) 754-9452
LOCATION: 1 mi. north of Bladon Springs.
FACILITIES: Open year round; primitive sites; campsite fee; picnic area; pets permitted.

Camden

ROLAND COOPER STATE PARK
P.O. Box 128
Camden, AL 36726
(205) 682-4838
LOCATION: 6 mi. northeast of Camden.
FACILITIES: Open year round; 41 sites; campsite fee; electrical outlets; sanitary stations; water and bathroom facilities; family cottages: 5; food service; picnic area; swimming; fishing; boating; golf; playground; pets permitted.

Clio

BLUE SPRINGS STATE PARK
Route 1
Clio, AL 36107
(205) 397-8703; 397-4875

ALABAMA

STATE PARKS (continued)

LOCATION: 6 mi. east of Clio.
FACILITIES: Open year round; 50 sites;
campsite fee; electrical outlets; sanitary stations; water and bathroom facilities; picnic
area; swimming; tennis; playground; pets permitted.

Coker

LAKE LURLEEN STATE PARK
Route 1, Box 146
Coker, AL 35452
(205) 339-1558
LOCATION: 12 mi. northwest of Tuscaloosa.
FACILITIES: Open year round; 86 sites;
campsite fee; electrical outlets; sanitary stations; water and bathroom facilities; food service; picnic area; swimming; hiking; fishing;
boating; playground; pets permitted.

Eufaula

LAKEPOINT RESORT STATE PARK
Route 2, Box 94
Eufaula, AL 36027
(205) 687-6676
LOCATION: 7 mi. north of Eufaula.
FACILITIES: Open year round; 190 sites;
campsite fee; electrical outlets; sanitary stations; water and bathroom facilities; family
cottages: 29; inns; food service; picnic area;
swimming; hiking; fishing; boating; tennis;
golf; playground; pets permitted.

Florala

FLORALA STATE PARK
Florala, AL 36442
(205) 858-6425
LOCATION: In Florala.
FACILITIES: Open year round; picnic area;
swimming; fishing; boating; playgrounds; pets
permitted.

Fort Payne

DE SOTO STATE PARK
Route 1, Box 210
Fort Payne, AL 35967
(205) 845-0051
LOCATION: 8 mi. northeast of Fort Payne.
FACILITIES: Open year round; 78 sites;
campsite fee; electrical outlets; sanitary stations; water and bathroom facilities; family
cottages: 22; inns: 25; food service; picnic
area; swimming; hiking; fishing; boating; tennis; playground; pets permitted.

Gallion

CHICKASAW STATE PARK
Route 1
Gallion, AL 36742
(205) 295-8230
LOCATION: 4 mi. north of Linden.
FACILITIES: Open year round; primitive
sites; campsite fee; water and bathroom facilities; picnic area; hiking; playground; pets permitted.

Gordon

CHATTAHOOCHEE STATE PARK
Gordon, AL 36343

(205) 522-3607
LOCATION: 11 mi. southeast of Gordon.
FACILITIES: Open year round; primitive
sites; campsite fee; picnic area; fishing; boating; playground; pets permitted.

Grove Oak

BUCK'S POCKET STATE PARK
Route 1, Box 24
Grove Oak, AL 35975
(205) 659-2000
LOCATION: 2 mi. north of Grove Oak.
FACILITIES: Open year round; 60 sites;
campsite fee; electrical outlets; sanitary stations; water and bathroom facilities; food service; picnic area; hiking; fishing; boating; playground; pets permitted.

Gulf Shores

GULF STATE PARK
Star Route, Box 9
Gulf Shore, AL 36542
(205) 698-7544
LOCATION: On Gulf of Mexico at Gulf
Shores.
FACILITIES: Open year round; 468 sites;
campsite fee; electrical outlets; sanitary stations; water and bathroom facilities; family
cottages: 20; inns: 144; food service; picnic
area; swimming; hiking; fishing; boating; tennis; golf; playground; pets permitted.

Guntersville

LAKE GUNTERSVILLE STATE PARK
Star Route, Box 52
Guntersville, AL 35976
(205) 582-3666
LOCATION: 6 mi. northeast of Guntersville.
FACILITIES: Open year round; 322 sites;
campsite fee; electrical outlets; sanitary stations; water and bathroom facilities; family
cottages: 36; inns: 100; food service; picnic
area; swimming; hiking; fishing; boating; tennis; golf; playgrounds; pets permitted.

Huntsville

MONTE SANO STATE PARK
Huntsville, AL 35801
(205) 534-3757
LOCATION: In Huntsville.
FACILITIES: Open year round; primitive
sites; campsite fee; family cottages: 14; food
service; picnic area; hiking; playground; pets
permitted.

Lineville

CHEAHA STATE PARK
Lineville, AL 36266
(205) 488-5111
LOCATION: 17 mi. north of Lineville.
FACILITIES: Open year round; 73 sites;
campsite fee; electrical outlets; sanitary stations; water and bathroom facilities; family
cottages: 13; inns: 31; food service; picnic
area; swimming; hiking; playground; pets permitted.

McCalla

TANNCHILL STATE PARK
Route 1, Box 124

STATE PARKS (continued)

McCalla, AL 35111
(205) 477-6571
LOCATION: 11 mi. west of Bessemer, ½ mi.
east of Bucksville exit on I-59.
FACILITIES: Open year round; 112 sites;
campsite fee; electrical outlets; sanitary stations; water and bathroom facilities; food service; picnic area; swimming; hiking; fishing;
pets permitted.

Moundville

MOUND STATE MONUMENT
Moundville, AL 35474
(205) 371-2572 (museum)
LOCATION: Take 69 south from Tuscaloosa
to Moundville.
FACILITIES: Open year round; 31 sites;
campsite fee; electrical outlets; sanitary stations; water and bathroom facilities; food service; picnic area; hiking; pets permitted.

Pelham

OAK MOUNTAIN STATE PARK
P.O. BOX 278
Pelham, AL 35124
(205) 663-6771
LOCATION: 15 mi. south of Birmingham.
FACILITIES: Open year round; 150 sites;
campsite fee; electrical outlets; sanitary stations; water and bathroom facilities; family
cottages: 10; food service; picnic area; swimming; hiking; fishing; boating; tennis; golf;
playground; pets permitted.

Selma

PAUL M. GRIST STATE PARK
Route 2
Selma, AL 36701
(205) 872-5846
LOCATION: 15 mi. north of Selma.
FACILITIES: Open year round; primitive
sites; campsite fee; food service; picnic area;
swimming; hiking; fishing; boating; playground; pets permitted.

Town Creek

JOE WHEELER STATE PARK
Route 2
Town Creek, AL 35672
(205) 685-3306
LOCATION: Near Town Creek.
FACILITIES: Open year round; primitive
sites; campsite fee; electrical outlets; sanitary
stations; water and bathroom facilities; family
cottages: 26; inns: 75; food service; picnic
area; swimming; hiking; fishing; boating;
tennis; golf; playgrounds; pets permitted.

Warrior

RICKWOOD CAVERNS STATE PARK
Route 3, Box 68-C
Warrior, AL 35180
(205) 647-9692
LOCATION: 20 mi. north of Birmingham,
near Warrior.
FACILITIES: Open year round; primitive
sites; campsite fee; electrical outlets; water
and bathroom facilities; picnic area; swimming; hiking; playground; pets permitted.

STATE FORESTS

There are no State Forests in Alabama.

HISTORIC SITES

Anniston

ANNISTON MUSEUM OF NATURAL HIS-
TORY - Seventh largest collection of natural
history specimens in the U.S. Nature trails on
187 acres surrounding the museum. Free (donations).
OPEN 10 a.m. - 5 p.m. Mon. - Fri.; 1 p.m. - 5
p.m. Sat. and Sun.

Birmingham

ARLINGTON ANTEBELLUM HOME AND
GARDENS - Gardens are right out of the
19th century; inside Victorian treasures. Ad-
mission charged, children under 6 free.
OPEN: 9 a.m. - 5 p.m. weekdays, closed
Mon. 1 p.m. - 6 p.m. on Sun.

Childersburg

DESOTO CAVERNS - Oldest recorded U.S.
Caverns; brimming with history and folklore.
Admission charged; group rates available;
children under 5 free. (By appointment,
school groups may go any day during closed
months).
OPEN: 9 a.m. - 6 p.m. daily. 12:30 - 6 p.m.,
weekends. Apr. - Sept., open every day. Oct.,
Nov., Feb. & Mar., weekends only. Dec. - Jan.
closed.

Cullman

AVE MARIE GROTTO - Benedictine monk
spent his lifetime creating these minature religious buildings, shrines, and settings from
scraps; over 150 of them are exhibited about
the hillside of this park. Admission charged.
OPEN: 7 a.m. - sunset.

Dauphin Island

DAUPHIN ISLAND - When the French landed here to colonize Louisiana, they called it
Massacre Island because the beaches were
covered with bleached human bones.

FORT GAINES - After English, Spanish and
French troops had occupied the site, the U.S.
built Fort Gaines in the early 1800's. Admission charged; group rates available.
OPEN 9 a.m. - 6 p.m. May - Sept.; 9 a.m. -
5:30 p.m. Oct. - Apr.

Demopolis

BLUFF HALL - Home built in 1832 on river
cliffs as man's gift to his daughter.
OPEN: 10 a.m. - 5 p.m. Tue. - Sat.; 2 p.m. -
5 p.m. Sun.

GAINESWOOD - Greek Revival Mansion, the
center of a large plantation when the Black
Belt was in its prime. Admission charged.
OPEN: 9 a.m. - 5 p.m. daily.

ALABAMA

HISTORIC SITES (continued)

Florence

W.C. HANDY HOME & MUSEUM - Right in this log cabin the "Father of the Blues" was born and raised. You can sit down at the piano where Handy himself wrote "St. Louis Blues." Admission charged.
OPEN: 9 a.m. - 12 noon, 1 p.m. - 4 p.m. Tue. - Sat. By appointment only on Sun. & Mon.

INDIAN MOUND MUSEUM - The largest mound on the Tennessee River, built for a temple foundation by Alabama's prehistoric residents, the Mound Builders. Admission charged.
OPEN: 9 a.m. - 12 p.m.; 1 p.m. - 4 p.m. Tue. - Sat. Closed Sun. & Mon.

POPE'S TAVERN - A century and a half of history in this old house, from stage stop and tavern to Confederate hospital. Admission charged.
OPEN: 9 a.m. - 12 p.m.; 1 p.m. - 4 p.m. Tue. - Sat. Closed Sun. & Mon.

Fort Rucker

ARMY AVIATION MUSEUM - Army aviation from its beginning.
OPEN: 10 a.m. - 5 p.m. weekdays; 1 p.m. - 5 p.m. weekends & holidays.

Gadsden

NOCCALULA FALLS - Breathtaking vegetation; rocks and falling water. It's also a legendary Indian lover's leap. Free.
OPEN: daily.

Greensboro

MAGNOLIA GROVE HOBSON MEMORIAL - 145 year old antebellum home of Rear Admiral Hobson, who sank the Merrimac during the Spanish-American War. Free (donation).
OPEN: 9 a.m. - 12 p.m.; 2 p.m. - 4 p.m. Tue. - Sat.; 2 p.m. - 4 p.m. Sun.

Gulf Shores

FORT MORGAN - Civil War history comes alive, especially when you see the bloodstains of the Confederate soldier that stayed on the fort's steps; last Confederate fort to fall.
OPEN: 8 a.m. - sunset year round.
Museum hours: 8 a.m. - 6 p.m. Jun. 1 - Labor Day.

Haleyville

NATURAL BRIDGE - The longest natural bridge east of the Rockies, with nothing to disturb the surrounding natural beauty except picnic tables and nature paths. Admission charged, children under 6 free; group rates available.
OPEN: Sunup to sunset.

Hillsboro

JOE WHEELER HOME - Confederate army hero, Gen. Joe Wheeler's home. Contains antiques of the period, including rare china that was buried during the Civil War to protect it. Admission charged.
OPEN: 9 a.m. - 7 p.m. Mon. - Sat.; 12:30 p.m. - 7 p.m. Sun.

Jacksonville

FRANCIS-DOCTOR'S OFFICE & APOTHECARY - Pharmaceutical and medical objects are on display in this century-and-a-quarter-old place.
OPEN: 9 a.m. - 12 noon weekdays; weekends and holidays by appointment.

Mobile

BERNSTEIN - BUSH HOUSE - A museum of the history of Mobile under 5 flags. Free.
OPEN: 10 a.m. - 5 p.m. Tue. - Sat.; 1 p.m. - 5 p.m. Sun.

CARLEN HOUSE MUSEUM - Charming house in the Creole Cottage style of architecture which originated in Mobile in 1842. Free.
OPEN: 10 a.m. - 5 p.m. Tue. - Sat.; 1 p.m. - 5 p.m. Sun.

CATHEDRAL OF THE IMMACULATE CONCEPTION - This beautifully massive cathedral of Roman design is built on old Spanish burial grounds. Free.
OPEN: daily; tours by appointment.

FORT CONDE - CHARLOTTE HOUSE - One-time Mobile jail; now furnished to depict period of Mobile's history. Admission charged.
OPEN: 10 a.m. - 4 p.m. Tue. - Sat.

OAKLEIGH - A mansion in the fullest sense.
OPEN: 10 a.m. - 4 p.m. weekdays; 2 p.m. - 4 p.m. Sun. Closed Christmas week and legal holidays.

PHOENIX MUSEUM - An old fire station, stocked with firefighting equipment of another era.
OPEN: 10 a.m. - 5 p.m. Tue. - Sat.; 1 p.m. - 5 p.m. Sun.

Mobile Bay

BATTLESHIP U.S.S. ALABAMA MEMORIAL PARK - You can walk the decks of this historic WWII battleship that floats in Mobile Bay.
OPEN: 8 a.m. - sunset daily.

U.S.S. DRUM SUBMARINE - See how submarine crews lived, fired torpedoes and operated their ship.
OPEN: 8 a.m. - sunset daily.

Montgomery

GOVERNOR'S MANSION - Dignified, stately and set amid lovely landscaped grounds. Free.
OPEN: 9 a.m. - 12 p.m.; 1 p.m. - 3 p.m. Mon. - Fri. Closed during Christmas.

ORDEMAN-SHAW COMPLEX ON OLD NORTH HULL - 11 buildings that house a museum portraying urban living in the Old South. Free.
OPEN: 9:30 a.m. - 4 p.m. Tue. - Sat.; 1:30

HISTORIC SITES (continued)

p.m. - 4 p.m. Sun. Closed Thanksgiving, Christmas; New Year's.

STATE CAPITOL OF ALABAMA - A bronze star marks the spot where Jefferson Davis stood to become President of the Confederacy. Free.
OPEN: 8 a.m. - 5 p.m. daily. Closed New Year's, July 4; Labor Day, Thanksgiving, and Christmas.

TUMBLING WATERS MUSEUM OF FLAGS - Features a wide variety of flags and other items of historical significance. Free.
OPEN: 10 a.m. - 4 p.m. daily. Special group tours on request.

WHITE HOUSE OF THE CONFEDERACY - When Montgomery was capital of the Confederacy, Davis and his family lived here. Now the old house is full of important relics of the Civil War and furniture and personal belongings of the Davis family. Free.
OPEN: 9 a.m. - 4:30 p.m. daily; Closed 11:30 - 12:30 Sat. & Sun.

Moundville

MOUND STATE MONUMENT - Indian mounds; village; burial grounds and museum. Admission charged.
OPEN: 9 a.m. - 5 p.m. except Christmas.

Oneonta

HORTON MILL COVERED BRIDGE - It's 220 feet over the water; the highest covered bridge in America. Free.
OPEN: daily.

Scottsboro

FIRST MONDAY - First Monday of every month; century-old observation of barter day on Courthouse Square. Quilts; homemade bread; axe handles, for swap; trade and barter; all going on to lively banjoing and fiddling.

Selma

STURDIVANT HALL - Once one of the most stunning homes in the Black Belt. Admission charged, children under 12 free.
OPEN: 9 a.m. - 4 p.m. Mon. - Sat.; 2 p.m. - 4 p.m. Sun.

Troy

PIKE PIONEER MUSEUM - Full of artifacts of the Alabama pioneers. Antique farm implements; looms; log house; and a country store.
OPEN: 10 a.m. - 5 p.m. weekdays; 1 p.m. - 5 p.m. Sun.

Tuscaloosa

GORGAS HOME - The only building at the University of Alabama to survive the Civil War. Built as a dining room for students in 1829, now a memorial full of old furniture and furnishings. Free (donations).

OLD TAVERN - In the 1820's, before the state capitol building was built in Montgomery, the legislature met here. Free.
OPEN: 9 a.m. - 5 p.m. Wednesday (closed 1 hr. for lunch); 2 p.m. - 5 p.m. weekends.

Tuscumbia

HELEN KELLER'S BIRTHPLACE IVY GREEN - This charming place contains the Keller family furniture and hundreds of additional mementos. Admission charged; children under 6 free.
OPEN: 8:30 a.m. - 4:30 p.m. weekdays; 1 p.m. - 4:30 p.m. Sun.
"The Miracle Worker" performed on the grounds Friday nights in Jul. & Aug.

Tuskegee

GEORGE WASHINGTON CARVER MUSEUM - The great variety of this collection tells something of the depth and greatness of Dr. Carver himself. Includes his laboratory, artwork, hundreds of things he developed from peanut by-products.
OPEN: 10 a.m. - 4 p.m. Mon. - Sat.; 1 p.m. - 4 p.m. Sun.

Wetumpka

FORT TOULOUSE - An 18th Century French fortress and 19th Century munitions depot. Free.
OPEN: 8 a.m. - 7 p.m. daily.

HOSTELS

There are no Hostels in Alabama.

POINTS OF INTEREST

Bayou LaBatre

BLESSING OF THE SHRIMP FLEET - Shrimp boats glide down the bayou through floating blossoms to receive the priest's blessings.

Birmingham

BIRMINGHAM BOTANICAL GARDENS - Continously changing flower show. 7 acres of Japanese Gardens. Free.
OPEN: every day from dawn to dusk.

BIRMINGHAM MUSEUM OF ART - Enjoy thousands of exhibits in the 25 galleries including the world's largest private collection of delicate Wedgewood. Free.
OPEN: 10 a.m. - 5 p.m. daily; till 9 p.m. Thurs.; 2 p.m. - 6 p.m. Sun.

BIRMINGHAM ZOO - One of the largest zoos in the southeast. Over 1,000 animals on exhibit. Admission charged.
OPEN: 9:30 a.m. - 5 p.m. daily.

FESTIVAL OF ARTS - Every year a different country is honored in the oldest continuous arts festival in America.
OPEN: Annually in Spring; dates available if desired.

ALABAMA

VULCAN - How many places can you speed right up 179 feet to an iron man's head? Besides the elevator ride, the view from the top is absolutely breathtaking. Admission charged for park and vehicles; children under 2 free.
OPEN: 9 a.m. - 10 p.m. (last ticket sold at 9 p.m.).

Bridgeport

RUSSELL CAVE MONUMENT - Three thousand years before the Great Pyramid, the first Indians in Russell Cave were building their fires. Free.
OPEN: 8 a.m. - 6 p.m. Memorial Day - Labor Day; 8 a.m. - 5 p.m. winter.

Eufaula

TOM MANN'S FISH WORLD - Alabama's most unique freshwater fish exhibit; 38,000 gallon aquarium and 10 smaller aquariums containing freshwater species of fish native to Alabama. Other attractions include Indian Museum. Admission charged.
OPEN: all year; 9 a.m. - 5 p.m. Mon. - Fri.; 9 a.m. - 9 p.m. Sat. - Sun. Closed Thanksgiving and Christmas.

Fort Payne

DESOTO FALLS - If it isn't enough to watch wild-flower-surrounded waters cascade down 110 feet into a rock basin, you can picnic, swim, boat and fish. Free.
OPEN: 8 a.m. to sunset.

LITTLE RIVER CANYON - One of the deepest gorges east of the Rockies. It's called the Little Grand Canyon by some. Free.
OPEN: daily, year-round.

MANITOU CAVE - More underground Alabama, featuring a guided tour through roomy passageways with ceilings from 9-90 feet high. Admission charged, children 5 and under free.
OPEN: 7 a.m. - 7 p.m. summer; 8 a.m. - 5 p.m. Oct. - May, weekends only.

Hodges

ROCK BRIDGE CANYON - Interesting rock formations, waterfall, massive natural bridge. Admission charged.
OPEN: 8 a.m. - 6:30 p.m. daily.

Huntsville

ALABAMA SPACE & ROCKET CENTER - Experience first-hand the sights and sounds of space. Admission charged, children 5 and under free; group rates available.
OPEN: 9 a.m. - 6 p.m. Jun. - Aug.; 9 a.m. - 5 p.m. Sept. - May.

Mobile

AZALEA TRAIL - Azaleas were brought to Mobile from France in 1754, and when you see this trail of the most beautiful specimens, you'll be grateful to the French for the idea.
OPEN: Feb. - Mar.

Montgomery

W.A. GAYLE PLANETARIUM - Lie back in one of the 236 reclining seats and watch a celestial panorama on the fifty foot dome overhead. Experience and learn with a variety of astronomical and astrological programs.
OPEN: 8 a.m. - 5 p.m. Mon. - Fri.

MONTGOMERY ZOO - Animals from Kinkajou to hairy Armadillos.
OPEN: 9:30 a.m. - 4:30 p.m. winter; 9:30 a.m. - 5:30 p.m. summer.

Munford

CHEAHA MOUNTAIN - Reach up just a little and touch the sky on the highest place in Alabama - 2,047 feet above sea level.

Phil Campbell

DISMAL WONDER GARDENS - Mysterious twinkle-in-the-dark worms (Dismalities) and exotic plants in this enormous gulch. Admission charged.
OPEN: 8 a.m. - sunset daily.

Theodore

BELLINGRATH GARDENS AND HOME - World famous gardens of every season and home filled with fine furnishings and rare art objects.
OPEN: 7 a.m., dusk gardens. 8:30 a.m. - 5 p.m., home; last tour begins at 4:15 p.m.

Valley Head

SEQUOYAH CAVE - The prettiest caverns you'll ever see anywhere. With looking glass lakes and elegant lighting, looks more like an underground palace. Admission charged, children 5 and under free.
OPEN: 8 a.m. - 7 p.m. Memorial Day - Labor Day; 8:30 a.m. - 5 p.m. Sept. - May.

Vance

BAMA SCENIC ROCK GARDENS - Impressive natural rock formations among wildflowers, ferns and wildlife.
OPEN: 9 a.m. - 6 p.m. daily.

Wetumpka

JASMINE HILL - Twelve acres of Greek sculpture, ruins and various art objects amid flowering trees and fragrant blossoms. A classic attraction.
OPEN: 9 a.m. - 5 p.m. Sat. - Sun. only during Dec. - Feb.; Tues. - Sun. during Mar. - Nov.

ALASKA

Acquired by purchase from Russia in 1867, Alaska entered the Union in 1959 as the fiftieth state. It has the largest land area and the smallest population, 300,000 people, according to late 1970's figures. Two major reasons account for people's unwillingness to settle in the state permanently, the weather and the difficult terrain.

Summers, below the arctic line, are brief, warm and pleasant, but the winters are quite long and severe and the mountains of Alaska, each higher than the next, make it difficult to traverse the state. Today much is being done to accommodate state travelers. Some areas formerly accessible only on foot, on horseback or by dogsled are now reachable by plane or boat. Roads, along with air facilities, are continually being improved.

Alaska's most important industries are fishing and forestry. However, tourism has become a significant growth industry because of the increased popularity of sportfishing and hunting in the state.

State capital: Juneau. State Bird: Willow ptarmigan. State tree: Sitka spruce. State flower: Forget-me-not.

WEATHER

Alaska contains 375 million acres of land and many thousands of lakes. The state's coastline is 33,000 miles in length. The highest peak (20,320 feet above sea level) in the North American Continent, Mt. McKinley, is located in south-central Alaska.

The geographical features have a significant effect on Alaska's climate, which falls into five major zones: (1) a maritime zone which includes southeastern Alaska, the south coast, and southwestern islands; (2) a maritime-continental zone which includes the western portions of Bristol Bay and west-central zones. In this zone the summer temperatures are moderated by the open waters of the Bering Sea, but winter temperatures are more continental in nature due to the presence of sea ice during the coldest months of the year; (3) a transition zone between the maritime and continental zones in the southern portion of the Copper River zone, the Cook Inlet zone, and the northern extremes of the south coast zone; (4) a continental zone made up of the remainders of the Copper River and west-central divisions, and the interior basin; and (5) an arctic zone.

The greatest contrast in seasonal temperature is found in the central and eastern portion of the continental interior. Elsewhere in the state, temperature contrasts are much more moderate. In the maritime zone the summer to winter range of average temperatures is from near 60 to the 20's. In the transition zone, temperatures range from the low 60's to near zero; in the maritime-continental zone the range is from the low 60's to 10 below zero. The arctic slope has a range extending from the upper 40's to 20 below zero.

Average daily temperature for each month.

	Northwestern	Southeastern
Jan.	3.2 to -10.6	34.6 to 23.0
Feb.	3.3 to -11.8	39.6 to 27.0
Mar.	8.1 to - 9.1	41.8 to 27.5
Apr.	22.3 to 3.7	47.3 to 31.7
May	37.8 to 23.7	53.2 to 37.3
Jun.	49.6 to 37.3	57.1 to 43.4
Jul.	58.7 to 47.1	60.5 to 47.9
Aug.	55.9 to 45.4	61.5 to 48.5
Sept.	46.5 to 35.7	58.2 to 44.0
Oct.	28.7 to 18.5	50.5 to 37.4
Nov.	13.4 to 2.0	42.6 to 31.4
Dec.	2.6 to -10.3	37.7 to 27.6
Year	27.5 to 14.3	48.7 to 35.6

STATE CHAMBER OF COMMERCE

Alaska State Chamber of Commerce
310 Second Street
Juneau, AK 99801
(907) 586-2323

STATE & CITY TOURISM OFFICES

State

Alaska Division of Tourism
Department of Economic Development
Pouch E
Juneau, AK 99811
(907) 465-2010

STATE HIGHWAY DEPARTMENT

Department of Transportation and
 Public Facilities
Pouch Z
Juneau, AK 99811
(907) 364-2121

HIGHWAY WELCOMING CENTERS

Haines

HAINES CENTER - Mile 1 and Haines Hwy.

ALASKA

Tok

TOK CENTER - Alaska Hwy., near Tok junction.

STATE POLICE

Alaska State Troopers
Juneau, AK 99811
(907) 465-4305

HUNTING & FISHING

Hunting

Resident

No license is required of an Alaskan resident under 16 years of age, for hunting or trapping. Licenses and big game tags are required of all nonresidents, regardless of age, for hunting and trapping. However, all residents, regardless of age, intending to hunt brown/grizzly bears, are required to possess a resident brown/grizzly bear tag.

Fees for resident licenses and tags are as follows: Trapping license, $3; hunting license, $12; hunting and trapping license, $15; hunting and sport fishing license, $22; hunting, trapping, & sport fishing license, $25; fur dealer license, $50; taxidermy license, $75; fish, fur or game farming license, $100.

Big game tags: Muskoxen, each $500; Bear, brown or grizzly, each $25; resident or nonresident permit application fee (all species for which a limited drawing is conducted, except muskoxen), $5; resident or nonresident permit application fee for muskoxen, each $10.

All non-residents, regardless of age, must have a valid hunting license and tag(s) in their possession while taking or attempting to take game.

Non-resident

Fees for non-resident licenses are as follows: Hunting license, $60; hunting & sport fishing license, $90; hunting & trapping license, $200; fur dealer license, $200; taxidermy license, $200.

Fees for non-resident big game locking tags are as follows: Bear, black, each $100; bear, brown or grizzly, each $250; bear, polar, each $250; bison, each $250; caribou, each $200; deer, each $35; elk, each $125; goat, each $125; moose, each $200; muskoxen, each $1,000; sheep, each $250; walrus, each $250; wolf, each $50; wolverine, each $50.

Alien persons not lawfully admitted to the United States are prohibited from taking game, including marine mammals, in the State of Alaska or its waters.

Metal locking tags are issued to an individual and are nonrefundable and nontransferable.

Metal locking tags must be affixed and locked to an animal immediately upon taking and must remain affixed and locked until the animal is prepared for storage, consumed, or exported.

Fishing

A sport fishing license is required and must be in the possession of all persons 16 years of age or older while taking or attempting to take any freshwater, marine, or anadronous fish for personal use and while sport digging razor clams or dip-netting for smelt (hooligan).

The license period is from January 1 through December 31, inclusive, of the current calendar year.

Resident

Sport fishing license, $10; (blind) sport fishing license, 25 cents; hunting and sport fishing license, $22; hunting, trapping, and sport fishing license, $25.

Non-resident

Visitor's special sport fishing license: Valid for one (1) day, $5; Valid for ten (10) days, $15; sport fishing license, $30; hunting and sport fishing license, $90; military sport fishing, $10; military sport fishing and small game hunting, $22.

For more information contact:

Alaska Department of Fish & Game
Subport Building
Juneau, AK 99801
(907) 465-4112

CAMPGROUNDS

Private

Anchorage

HILLSIDE MOTEL & CAMPER PARK
2150 Gambell Street
Anchorage, AK 99503
(907) 277-5124
FACILITIES: Open year round; water and bathroom facilities; sanitary station; electrical hookup; laundry; pets permitted.

JOHNSON CAMPER PARK & MOTEL
3543 Mt. View Drive
Anchorage, AK 99504
(907) 277-4332
FACILITIES: Open year round; 43 sites; water and bathroom facilities; sanitary station; electrical hookup; laundry; no pets.

Delta Junction

BERGSTAD'S TRAVEL & TRAILER PARK
Box 273
Delta Junction, AK 99737
(907) 895-4856
FACILITIES: Open year round; 105 sites; water and bathroom facilities; sanitary station; electrical hookup; guided tour.

Fairbanks

GOOD HILL CAMPGROUND
Box 81706
Fairbanks, AK 99708

CAMPGROUNDS (continued)

LOCATION: Mile 4 on George Parks Hwy.
(Alaska Route 3).
FACILITIES: Open year round; 200 sites;
water and bathroom facilities; sanitary station; electrical hookup; food service; hiking.

NORLITE CAMPGROUND, INC.
1660 Peger Road
Fairbanks, AK 99701
(907) 452-4206
FACILITIES: Open year round; 250 sites;
water and bathroom facilities; sanitary station; electrical hookup; laundry; food service;
guided tour.

TANANA VALLEY FAIRGROUNDS CAMP-
GROUND
Box 188
Fairbanks, AK 99707
(907) 452-3750
FACILITIES: Open May 15 - Sept. 15; 30
sites; campsite fee, $5 per day; water and
bathroom facilities; firewood; laundry.

Glennallen

TOLSONA WILDERNESS CAMPGROUND
Box 23
Glennallen, AK 99588
(907) 822-3865
LOCATION: Mile 173 Glenn Hwy., about 14
mi. west of Glennallen.
FACILITIES: Open year round; 40 sites;
water and bathroom facilities; sanitary station; fishing.

Kenai Peninsula

SUNRISE KOA CAMPGROUND
5117 Shorecrest Drive
Anchorage, AK 99502
(907) 243-4470
LOCATION: 80 mi. from Anchorage and 7½
mi. off the Seward Hwy. on Hope Road.
FACILITIES: Open year round; water and
bathroom facilities; electrical hookup; laundry; food service; fishing; gold panning.

Mantanuska Glacier

GLACIER PARK OF ALASKA
Box 4 - 2615
Anchorage, AK 99509
(907) 822-3748
LOCATION: 102 mi. north of Anchorage on
Glenn Hwy. between Palmer and Glennallen.
FACILITIES: Open year round; water and
bathroom facilities; sanitary station; electrical
hookup; laundry; playground; food service;
self-guided tour; lodging.

Mount McKinley National Park Area

BEARWALK TRADING POST & CAMP-
GROUNDS
Box 397
Nenana, AK 99760
(907) 683-2252
LOCATION: Mile 276 on George Parks Hwy.
(Alaska Route 3).
FACILITIES: Open year round; water and
bathroom facilities; cabins; laundry; food ser-
vice; hunting; fishing.

KOA KAMPGROUND
Box 34
Healy, AK 99243
(907) 683-2379
LOCATION: Mile 248 on George Parks Hwy.
(Alaska Route 3).
FACILITIES: Open May 15 - Sept. 15; water
and bathroom facilities; electrical hookup;
firewood; laundry; picnic area; food service.

SUMMER SHADES CAMPGROUND
Route 2
Mile 290 Parks Hwy.
Nenana, AK 99760
(907) 832-5418
LOCATION: Mile 290 on George Parks Hwy.
FACILITIES: Open year round; water and
bathroom facilities; sanitary station; cabins;
laundry; food service.

Palmer Region

BARRY'S RESORT
Box 745
Palmer, AK 99645
(907) 745-3939
FACILITIES: Open year round; 40 sites;
water and bathroom facilities; food service;
fishing; lodging.

HIDEAWAY
Star Route C
Box 257B
Palmer, AK 99645
LOCATION: Lake Louise, 17 miles on access
road from Mile 160, turn off on Glenn Hwy.
FACILITIES: Open year round; cabins; boat
rental; boat or fly-in only.

KEPLER PARK
Star Route Box S- 820
Palmer, AK 99645
(907) 745-4756
LOCATION: Mile 37 ¼ on Glenn Hwy.
FACILITIES: Open year round; boating; boat
rental; fishing.

MATANUSKA LAKE PARK
Star Route A
Box 70
Palmer, AK 99645
(907) 745-3693
LOCATION: Junction of Glenn and Park
Hwys., 7 mi. southwest of Palmer.
FACILITIES: Open year round; picnic area;
swimming; boating; hiking; horseback riding;
bicycle trail; lodging.

SHEEP MOUNTAIN LODGE
Star Route C
Box 130
Palmer, AK 99645
(907) 822-3777
LOCATION: Mile 133 on Glenn Hwy., 65 mi.
northeast of Palmer.
FACILITIES: Open year round; 8 sites;
water; sanitary station; cabins; food service;
lodging; air field.

Sterling

BING BROWN'S SPORTSMEN'S SERVICE
Box 256
Star Route 2
Sterling, AK 99672

ALASKA

CAMPGROUNDS (continued)

(907) 262-4780
LOCATION: Mile 81 on Sterling Hwy., Kenai Peninsula.
FACILITIES: Open year round; water and bathroom facilities; sanitary station; cabins; laundry; food service; fishing.

Tok

GOLDEN BEAR MOTEL
Box 276
Tok, AK 99780
(907) 883-2561
LOCATION: On Glenn Hwy. near junction of Glenn and Alaska Hwys.
FACILITIES: Open year round; water and bathroom facilities; electrical hookup; trailer village vehicle sites; laundry; picnic area; lodging; tent campers.

TUNDRA LODGE
Box 336
Tok, AK 99780
(907) 883-2291
LOCATION: On Alaska Hwy. near junction of Glenn and Alaska Hwys.
FACILITIES: Open year round; water and bathroom facilities; electrical hookup; trailer village vehicle sites; laundry; picnic area; tent campers.

Willow

NANCY LAKE MARINA
Box 114
Willow, AK 99688
(907) 495-6284
FACILITIES: Open year round; 26 sites; water and bathroom facilities; cabins; food service; boat rental.

Public

Anchorage

CENTENNIAL CAMPER PARK
Parks & Recreation Division
City of Anchorage
Pouch 6-650
Anchorage, AK 99502
(907) 264-4474
FACILITIES: Open year round; limit of stay, 7 days; 88 sites; water and bathroom facilities; sanitary station; electrical hookup; firewood; laundry; picnic area.

LION'S CAMPER PARK
Park's & Recreation Division
City of Anchorage
Anchorage, AK 99502
(907) 264-4474
LOCATION: Russian Jack Springs.
FACILITIES: Open year round; limit of stay, 7 days; 50 sites; water and bathroom facilities; sanitary station; electrical hookup; firewood; picnic area; hiking; tent campers.

Fairbanks

HARDING LAKE RECREATION AREA
Mile 42 Richardson Hwy.
Fairbanks, AK 99701
LOCATION: North shore of Harding Lake.

FACILITIES: Open year round; limit of stay, 7 days; 89 sites; water and bathroom facilities; sanitary station; electrical hookup; picnic area; swimming; boating; fishing.

SALCHA RIVER WAYSIDE
Harding Lake Recreation Area
Mile 42 Richardson Hwy.
Fairbanks, AK 99701
FACILITIES: Open year round; bathroom facilities; trailer village vehicle sites; boating; tent campers.

Skagway

HANOUFEK PARK
Parks Department
City of Skagway
Skagway, AK 99840
LOCATION: 14th and Broadway.
FACILITIES: Open May 15 - Oct. 1; 24 sites; water and bathroom facilities; sanitary station.

RESORTS

Wilderness Lodges

Anchorage

ALASKA PENINSULA LODGE
Providence Professional Building
3300 Providence Drive
Anchorage, AK 99504
(907) 279-3566
LOCATION: 50 mi. north of King Salmon.
FACILITIES: 8 rooms to accommodate 16; modern communal baths; dining and lounge; guided sportsfishing in summer; hunting in spring and fall; 1 to 3 day guided float trips.

ALEXANDER LAKE LODGE
Box 4-212
Anchorage, AK 99509
(907) 277-1443, ask for radio unit 0400
LOCATION: 50 air mi. northwest of Anchorage on Alexander Lake.
FACILITIES: Big game animals and sportfishing; heated cabins sleep 2-4; bar and dining room for family-style meals.

BATTLE RIVER WILDERNESS CAMP
1513 "F" Street
Anchorage, AK 99501
(907) 272-0903
LOCATION: Alaska Peninsula, southwest of Anchorage.
FACILITIES: Cabins; family-style meals; sportfishing.

BEAR TRACK LODGE
Box 3-385
Anchorage, AK 99504
(907) 277-7275
LOCATION: 25 mi. northwest of Cordova.
FACILITIES: Accommodations for 12 with bath and individual cabins; charter yacht with 3 staterooms and baths.

BROOK'S LODGE
Wien Air Alaska
4100 International Airport Road
Anchorage, AK 99502
(907) 243-4100

RESORTS (continued)

LOCATION: Mouth of Brooks River in Katmai National Monument.
FACILITIES: Fly-in via King Salmon Airport; reservations required; daily tours during season to Valley of Ten Thousand Smokes; open Jun. 10 - Sept. 30.

CHULITNA LODGE
Rust's Flying Service, Inc.
Box 1452Q
Star Route A
Anchorage, AK 99502
(907) 243-1595
LOCATION: Alaska Peninsula, west side of Cook Inlet.
FACILITIES: Wilderness sportfishing and sporthunting; rustic and remote log lodge and sleeping cabins; sauna; family-style meals.

FISHING UNLIMITED
Box 6301
Anchorage, AK 99502
(907) 243-5899
LOCATION: Iliamna, Lake Clark, Tikchik Lake areas.
FACILITIES: Main lodge; cabins with modern plumbing; sauna; daily fly-out sportfishing, only 8 fishermen per week.

GRACIOUS HOUSE LODGE
3233 Richmond Avenue
Anchorage, AK 99504
(907) 272-8686
LOCATION: Mile 82.2 Denali Highway (Alaska Route 8).
FACILITIES: Lodge; air taxi with floats; skiing; horseback riding; track vehicle; airboats; registered guide.

GOLDEN HORN LODGE
Box 546
Anchorage, AK 99510
(907) 276-1390
LOCATION: 55 mi. north of Dillingham in Wood River-Tikchik Lakes area.
FACILITIES: Sportfishing; bookings limited to 16 per week; meals; fly-outs.

GROSVENOR LAKE LODGE
Wein Air Alaska
4100 International Airport Road
Anchorage, AK 99502
(907) 243-4100
LOCATION: Channel connecting Lake Coville and Lake Grosvenor in Katmai National Monument.
FACILITIES: Fly-in lodge via Brooks Camp or direct from King Salmon Airport; sportfishing; accommodates 8 in rustic comfort; reservations.

HAYES RIVER LODGE
Box 6184
Anchorage, AK 99502
(907) 277-9403
LOCATION: Hayes River, south side of the Alaska Range, about 100 mi. northwest of Anchorage.
FACILITIES: Sportfishing; hunting; lodge; guide.

ILIAMNA LODGE
6361 Nielson Way
Anchorage, AK 99502
(907) 571-1267
LOCATION: On Iliamna Lake, 200 mi. southwest of Anchorage.
FACILITIES: Dining room; cocktail lounge; accommodations for 40; floatplanes; fishing boats; fly-in via Anchorage Airport; open May 1 - Nov. 1.

KULIK LODGE
Wien Air Alaska
4100 International Airport Road
Anchorage, AK 99502
(907) 243-2400
LOCATION: Between Kulik and Nonvianuk lakes, 60 mi. northeast of King Salmon.
FACILITIES: Fly-in; log cottages; lodge with fireplace; sportfishing; guides and charters; reservations; open Jul. 15 - Sept. 30.

LAKE CREEK LODGE
SKS Outfitters
Box 8-229
Anchorage, AK 99508
(907) 333-7692
LOCATION: Lake Creek and the Yentna River, 65 mi. northwest of Anchorage.
FACILITIES: Fly-in; sportfishing; lodge; lounge; dining area; bar; modern plumbing; licensed air taxi; float trips; jet boats; open Jun. - Sept.

MIDNIGHT SUN LODGE
1306 East 26th Avenue
Anchorage, AK 99504
(907) 277-8829
LOCATION: 90 mi. northwest of Kotzebue (northwest arctic coast), 30 mi. upstream from Kivalina.
FACILITIES: Riverboats; rafts and light aircraft; heated cabins with modern facilities; family-style meals in main lodge; guide service; sportfishing.

MOTHER GOOSE LAKE LODGE
4203 Minnesota Drive
Anchorage, AK 99503
(907) 277-7756
LOCATION: Mother Goose Lake.
FACILITIES: Guided sporthunting; sportfishing parties; accommodate 8 persons.

NEWHALEN LODGE
Box 799
Anchorage, AK 99510
(907) 279-4236
LOCATION: Village of Nondalton, 15 min. via air from Lake Iliamna.
FACILITIES: Home-cooked meals; sportfishing; open Jun. 1 - Aug. 10.

RAINY PASS LODGE
3090 Amber Bay Loop
Anchorage, AK 99502
(907) 349-4976
LOCATION: Puntilla Lake, 125 air mi. northwest of Anchorage.
FACILITIES: Fly-in; main lodge; modern log cabins; high-wall tents on wooden frames and wooden floors.

SILVERTIP LODGES
Box 6389
Anchorage, AK 99502
(907) 243-1416

ALASKA

RESORTS (continued)

LOCATION: Headwaters the Talachulitna River, 75 mi. west and northwest of Anchorage.
FACILITIES: Fly-in; lodge; meals; guiding service; fishing equipment and boats.

TALACHULITNA RIVER LODGE
Box 6595
Anchorage, AK 99502
(907) 278-2123
LOCATION: 65 air mi. west of Anchorage.
FACILITIES: Fly-in; sportfishing.

U.S. FOREST SERVICE CABINS
Forest Supervisor
Chugach National Forest
U.S. Forest Service
Pouch 6606
Anchorage, AK 99502
(907) 274-6061
LOCATION: 34 isolated locations throughout the Chugach National Forest in southcentral Alaska.
FACILITIES: Cabins equipped with wooden furniture (no bedding); electricity or plumbing; some lakesites have skiffs; cost of cabins $5 per night; reservations made up to 6 mos. in advance.

WILDERNESS LAKE ADVENTURES
Box 4-2048
Anchorage, AK 99509
(907) 349-5761
LOCATION: 60 mi. west of Nenana and north of Mount McKinley National Park.
FACILITIES: Cabins on lake.

WRANGELL MOUNTAIN LODGE
308 East Northern Lights Boulevard
Anchorage, AK 99503
(907) 279-7454
LOCATION: Camps at Pt. Hope, Copper River and Cinder River.
FACILITIES: Fly-in; sportfishing; sporthunting; modern plumbing, electricity and camp kitchen.

Angoon

KOOTZNAHOO LODGE
Box 134
Angoon, AK 99820
(907) 788-3501
LOCATION: Kootznahoo Inlet, Favorite Bay, Admiralty Island.
FACILITIES: Motel with private baths; 6 units with fully equipped kitchens; homestyle meals in dining room by reservations; laundry facilities; skiff and motor rentals; charter boat fishing; registered guides.

RAVEN-BEAVER LODGE
Angoon, AK 99820
(907) 788-3441
LOCATION: Admiralty Island, 70 air mi. from Juneau.
FACILITIES: Sportfishing; kitchen appliances plus cooking utensils and tableware.

Bell Island

BELL ISLAND HOT SPRINGS
Bell Island, AK 99950

(206) 242-0466
LOCATION: 42 mi. north of Ketchikan.
FACILITIES: Sportfishing; lodge with restaurant, cocktail lounge; olympic-sized swimming pool; cabins; fishing boats.

Bettles

BETTLES LODGE
General Delivery
Bettles, AK 99726
(907) 692-5111
LOCATION: South side of Brooks Range, 190 air mi. northwest of Fairbanks.
FACILITIES: Dining room; store; float dock; aviation gas.

Central

ARCTIC CIRCLE HOT SPRINGS RESORT
General Delivery
Central, AK 99730
(907) 452-6255
LOCATION: Short distance off the Steese Highway (Route 6), approximately 137 mi. from Fairbanks. Northern most resort in Alaska.
FACILITIES: Natural mineral hot springs; scenic tundra countryside; sportfishing; goldpanning; indoor swimming pool; restaurant; cocktail lounge; open year round.

Chitina

KENNICOTT GLACIER LODGE
Chitina, AK 99566
(907) 344-1798
LOCATION: Wrangall Mountains in McCarthy, 3 mi. south of historic mining settlement of Kennicott.
FACILITIES: Sky tours of surrounding mountains and mining settlements; lodge.

Cooper Landing

GWIN'S LODGE
Mile 52 Sterling Highway
Cooper Landing, AK 99572
Radio Phone KBU 3049
LOCATION: Mile 52 Sterling Highway on Kenai Peninsula, about 105 mi. south of Anchorage.
FACILITIES: Lodge; restaurant; sportfishing.

KENAI LAKE LODGE
Box 669
Cooper Landing, AK 99572
(907) 595-9293
LOCATION: Kenai Lake, Mile 47.5 Sterling Highway.
FACILITIES: Lodge with dining room; cafe; bar.

SPORTMAN'S LODGE
Mile 56 - Sterling Highway
Cooper Landing, AK 99572
(907) 595-9294
LOCATION: Kenai Peninsula at Cooper Landing, 30 mi. northwest of Steward, on the bank of the Russian River, where Russian and Kenai Rivers meet.
FACILITIES: Motel; cabins; campsites; trailer spaces; restaurants; grocery store; gas; tire service; garage.

RESORTS (continued)

Delta Junction

GEORGE LAKE LODGE
Mile 1385 Alaska Highway
Delta Junction, AK 99737
(907) 895-4885
LOCATION: Mile 1385 Alaska Highway, 40 mi. from Delta Junction.
FACILITIES: Riverboat trips for sportfishing and sporthunting.

SUMMIT LAKE LODGE
Mile 195 Richardson Highway
Delta Junction, AK 99737
LOCATION: Upper Gulkana Basin, Summit Lake, Mile 195 Richardson Highway.
FACILITIES: Unguided or guided sportfishing; boats.

Dillingham

ROYAL COACHMAN LODGE
Box 10068
Dillingham, AK 99576
(907) 344-7595
LOCATION: Nuyakuk River, at the outlet of the Tikchik Lakes, 375 mi. southwest of Anchorage and 60 mi. north of Dillingham.
FACILITIES: Lodge; sportfishing; lounge; dining area.

Dot Lake

DOT LAKE LODGE
Mile 1361 Alaska Highway
Dot Lake, AK 99737
(907) 883-2691
LOCATION: Mile 1361 Alaska Highway, 40 mi. northeast of Tok.
FACILITIES: Camping; cafe; grocery store; river boat tours.

Eagle River

BECHAROF LODGE AND CAMPS
Box 632
Eagle River, AK 99577
LOCATION: Alaska Peninsula, 45 mi. south of King Salmon at the head of Egegik River and Lake, southwest of Katmai National Monument.
FACILITIES: Sportfishing, Jun. - Sept.; unguided sporthunting, Sept. - Oct.; wildlife and scenic photographic safaris, Jun. - Nov.

IGIUGIG LODGE
Box 503
Eagle River, AK 99577
(907) 694-2625
LOCATION: About 250 mi. southwest of Anchorage.
FACILITIES: Lodge; sportfishing; boating; scenic tours.

Fairbanks

ALATNA LODGE
Box 80424
Fairbanks, AK 99708
(907) 479-6354
LOCATION: Alatna River headwaters, north of treeline in the arctic tundra.
FACILITIES: Float trips; hikes; canoes; rafts;

registered guides; sporthunting; sportfishing; open Jul. - mid-Sept.

THE CACHES
Box 60531
Fairbanks, AK 99706
(907) 479-6939
LOCATION: 34 mi. northwest of Fairbanks.
FACILITIES: Fly-in; cabin or platform tents; boats; gas; cooking facilities; bedding; simple fishing gear; sportfishing.

INIAKUK LAKE LODGE
Bernd Gaedeke
Box 80424
Fairbanks, AK 99708
(907) 479-6354
LOCATION: Remote lodge above the Arctic Circle in the Brooks Range.
FACILITIES: Fly-in; lodge accommodates 12; boats; float plane; sportfishing; float trips; scenic flights; guided hunts; family-style meals; limited bookings from Jun. - Sept.

MIDWAY LODGE
Star Route Box 90684
Fairbanks, AK 99701
(907) 488-2939
LOCATION: 49 Mile Richardson Highway, midway between Delta Junction and Fairbanks.
FACILITIES: Lodge accommodates 20; sportfishing; sporthunting; ice fishing; family-style meals; cocktail lounge.

WOOD RIVER LODGE
Box 1616
Fairbanks, AK 99707
LOCATION: Main camp 100 mi. south of Fairbanks in heart of Alaska Range.
FACILITIES: Fly-in or on horseback; summer pack trips; fall sporthunting.

Galena

MELOZI HOT SPRINGS LODGE
Box 226
Galena, AK 99741
LOCATION: 200 air mi. west of Fairbanks and 17 air mi. north of Kokrines Village.
FACILITIES: Main lodge for dining and recreation; one all-season guest cabin with bath; 4 summer cabins without bath (all bathing in hot springs); swimming pool; sportfishing; hiking; photography; tent camping spots with facilities; reservations.

Gustavus

GLACIER BAY LODGE
Box 108
Gustavus, AK 99826
(907) 697-3221

Suite 312 (Winter)
Park Place Building
Seattle, WA 98101
(206) 624-8551
LOCATION: Bartlett Cove, Glacier Bay National Monument, 90 mi. west of Juneau by air.
FACILITIES: Lodge; dining room; cocktail lounge; campgrounds; sightseeing cruises; sportfishing; air tours; marine fuel station; marina; hiking. Only hotel overnight accommodations within the monument. National

ALASKA

RESORTS (continued)

Park Service naturalist programs; open May - Sept.

GUSTAVUS INN
Box 31
Gustavus, AK 99526
(907) 697-3311
LOCATION: Gustavus adjacent to Glacier Bay National Monument.
FACILITIES: Glacier Bay tours; sportfishing; bicycling; family-style meals.

Healy

MERCER'S RANCH
Bert Mercer
Mercer Ranch
Healy, AK 99743
(907) 683-2359
LOCATION: Near Mt. McKinley National Park.
FACILITIES: Trail rides; pack trips into the western area of Mt. McKinley National Park.

PAUL'S HEALY ROADHOUSE
Healy, AK 99734
(907) 682-2244
LOCATION: Mile 245 George Parks Highway (Alaska Route 3).
FACILITIES: Motel rooms; dining room; cocktail lounge; gas station; open year round.

Homer

KACHEMAK BAY WILDERNESS LODGE
China Poot Bay
Homer, AK 99603
(907) 235-8910
LOCATION: Kenai Peninsula, across Kachemak Bay from Homer.
FACILITIES: Fly-in or boat; lodge accommodates 8; cabins; sauna; sportfishing; duck hunting; bird and wildlife photography; open year round.

WILLARD'S MOOSE CAMP
Caribou Lake
Homer, AK 99603
Radio Phone KSG 96, Caribou Lake
LOCATION: Caribou Lake on Kenai Peninsula.
FACILITIES: Meals; lodging; boats; horseback riding; sportsfishing.

Iliamna

ILIASKA LODGE
Box 28
Iliamna, AK 99606
(907) 571-1221
LOCATION: Lake Iliamna region, southwest of Anchorage.
FACILITIES: Lodge; fly-out sportfishing.

NORTH COUNTRY LODGE
Box 49
Iliamna, AK 99606
LOCATION: Near Lake Iliamna, southwest of Anchorage.
FACILITIES: Fly-out sportfishing; river float trips.

RAINBOW KING LODGE
Box 106

Iliamna, AK 99606
(907) 571-1277 (summer)
(509) 924-8077 (winter)
LOCATION: Bristol Bay Trophy sportfish area southwest of Anchorage.
FACILITIES: Daily fly-out seven-day sportfishing trips only.

Juneau

HOOD BAY WILDERNESS CAMP
Rural Route 5
Box 5610
Juneau, AK 99803
(907) 789-0776
LOCATION: Admiralty Island in Alaska's "Inside Passage."
FACILITIES: Fly-in or boat; sportfishing; wildlife observation; photography; hiking; meals; bedding.

U.S. FOREST SERVICE CABINS
Regional Forest Supervisor
U.S. Forest Service
Box 1628
Juneau, AK 99802
(907) 586-7484
LOCATION: 146 isolated locations throughout the Tongass National Forest in Southeast Alaska.
FACILITIES: Cabins equipped with wood furniture (no bedding); electricity; plumbing; some lakesites have skiffs; cabins $5 per night; reservations made up to 6 months in advance.

Karluk

KARLUK LODGE
General Delivery
Karluk, AK 99608
LOCATION: Karluk River, northern coast of Kodiak Island.
FACILITIES: Lodge; meals; sportfishing; float trips on Karluk River.

Kenai

BEAR LAKE LODGE
Box 152
Kenai, AK 99611
(907) 283-4761
LOCATION: Bear Lake, Port Moller, western Alaska coast.
FACILITIES: Lodge; cabins; family-style meals featuring locally caught fish and seafoods; lounge.

COPPER RIVER FLY FISHING LODGE
Pope Vanoy Landing (summer)
Iliamna, AK 99606

Box 260, Star Route 1 (winter)
Kenai, AK 99611
LOCATION: Copper River near Lake Iliamna, southwest of Anchorage.
FACILITIES: Jet boats; canoes; complete board and room in tent houses; sportfishing.

Ketchikan

CLOVER PASS RESORT
Box 7322
Ketchikan, AK 99901
(907) 247-2234

RESORTS (continued)

LOCATION: 15 mi. from Ketchikan.
FACILITIES: Lodge; cabins; restaurant; lounge; boat rentals; open Apr. 15 - Sept. 15.

THAYER LAKE LODGE
Box 5416
Ketchikan, AK 99901
(907) 225-3343
LOCATION: Wilderness lodge on Admiralty Island, 60 air mi. southwest of Juneau.
FACILITIES: Fly-in or trail (6 mi. of wilderness trails, connecting inland lakes); sportfishing; boating; hiking; boat and motors; open Jun. 1 - Sept. 30.

WATERFALL CANNERY RESORT
Box 8600
Ketchikan, AK 99901
(907) 225-2502
LOCATION: Historic cannery now operating as a wilderness resort located 62 mi. west of Ketchikan.
FACILITIES: Hotel; cabins; meeting rooms; moorings; fuel; store; wildlife; hiking; beachcombing; sightseeing by boat; clam beaches; sportfishing.

King Salmon

ENCHANTED LAKE LODGE
Box 97
King Salmon, AK 99613
LOCATION: Alaska Peninsula, 60 mi. east of King Salmon and north of Katmai National Monument.
FACILITIES: Sportfishing; open Jun. 1 - Oct. 10.

UGASHIK LAKE LODGE
Box 323 (Spring)
King Salmon, AK 99613
(907) 486-3276, ask for KIZ-25

Box 349 (Fall)
Vancouver, WA 98661
(206) 696-0283
LOCATION: Alaska Peninsula, 100 mi. below King Salmon, between Upper and Lower Ugashik Lakes.
FACILITIES: Lodge; restaurant; sportfishing; waterfowl and bird hunting.

Klawock

FIREWEED LODGE
Box 116
Klawock, AK 99925
(907) 755-2226
LOCATION: One-half mi. east of Klawock on Hollis Highway.
FACILITIES: Lodge; private baths; restaurant; lounge; bicycles; boats; canoes; fishing gear; sportfishing.

LOG CABIN TENTERS LODGE
Box 54
Klawock, AK 99925
(907) 755-2205
LOCATION: 56 mi. west of Ketchikan on Prince of Wales Island.
FACILITIES: Large heated tents on raised beds; sportfishing; canoe trips; fly-ins; restaurant; skiffs; outboards; bicycles.

PRINCE OF WALES LODGE
Box 72
Klawock, AK 99925
(907) 755-2227
LOCATION: In Klawock on Prince of Wales Island.
FACILITIES: Lodge; restaurant; native village; totems; sportfishing; photography; hiking; sporthunting in season; boat charters.

Kodiak

ARCTIC TERN LODGE
Box 402
Kodiak, AK 99615
LOCATION: On Wein Lake, 100 air mi. southwest of Fairbanks.
FACILITIES: Family sportfishing; home-cooked meals; cabins with fireplace and twin beds; recreational facilities; flightseeing tours of Mount McKinley National Park.

MUNSEY'S BEAR CAMP
Park-Munsey
Box 1186
Kodiak, AK 99615
(907) 486-3040 (Apr. - Nov.)
(808) 325-7640 (Dec. - Mar.)
LOCATION: 70 mi. southwest of Kodiak on Kodiak Island.
FACILITIES: Lodge; camera safaris for wildlife; sportfishing.

McGrath

FAREWELL LAKE LODGE
McGrath, AK 99627
LOCATION: 55 mi. southeast of McGrath, approximately 225 air mi. northwest of Anchorage.
FACILITIES: Lodge; meals served family-style; bath house; laundry.

MYSTIC LAKE LODGE
Box 111
McGrath, AK 99627
(907) 524-3123
LOCATION: Upper Tonzona River.
FACILITIES: Log lodge with sauna and plumbing; jet boat; sportfishing.

Mentasta

MENTASTA LODGE
Mile 78 Tok Cutoff
Mentasta, AK 99586
(907) 883-2634
LOCATION: Mile 78 Tok Cutoff (Glenn Highway).
FACILITIES: Lodge; cafe; bar; modern motel; garage; oil and gas; guide service.

Naknek

KVICHAK LODGE
Box 37
Naknek, AK 99633
(907) 246-3291
LOCATION: Kvichak River, Iliamna, southwest of Anchorage.
FACILITIES: Sportfishing; electricity; oil heat; inside plumbing; open Jun. 12 - Oct. 10.

ALASKA

RESORTS (continued)

Nome

CAMP BENDELEBEN
Box 941
Nome, AK 99762
(907) 443-2880
LOCATION: Council, approximately 75 mi.
northeast of Nome on Seward Peninsula.
FACILITIES: Sportfishing; sporthunting; ice
fishing in Nov. & Dec.; hunting in Mar. &
Apr.; family groups welcomed for fully
guided and outfitted trips; family-style meals;
private cabins sleep up to 4 people; canoes;
rafts for rent as well as other camping equipment; reservations; open year round.

Palmer

ALASKA WILDERNESS TRAILS
Box 142, Star Route C
Palmer, AK 99645
(907) 822-3311
LOCATION: Chugach and Talkeetna
mountains.
FACILITIES: Lodge; horseback riding; 2-4
day hiking and backpacking trips; photographic safaris.

BARRY'S RESORT
Box 745
Bogard Road
Palmer, AK 99645
(907) 745-3939
LOCATION: On Bogard Road, 7 mi. west of
Palmer on Finger Lake.
FACILITIES: Lodge; restaurant; lounge; 40
campsites with running water and modern
plumbing; sportfishing; boat rentals; golf
course.

EVERGREEN LODGE
Box 264, Star Route C
Palmer, AK 99643
(907) 344-9811
LOCATION: Mile 160 Glenn Highway (Alaska Route 1).
FACILITIES: Lounge; dining area; snack bar;
cabins; family-style dinners; restaurant; bait
and tackle; licenses; boat rentals; trailer park;
campgrounds; sportfishing.

GUNSIGHT MOUNTAIN LODGE
Star Route C, Box 145
Palmer, AK 99645
(907) 822-3272
LOCATION: Mile 123 Glenn Highway, 75 mi.
northeast of Palmer.
FACILITIES: Lodge; cafe; bar; sporthunting;
sportfishing; photography; backpacking.

HIDEAWAY
Box 257
Palmer, AK 99645
LOCATION: Lake Louise near Glennallen, 17
mi. from turn-off Mile 160 Glenn Highway.
FACILITIES: Fly-in or boat; housekeeping
cabins; boat rental.

LAKE LOUISE LODGE
Box 265B, Star Route C
Palmer, AK 99645
Radio Phone KEP 7728
LOCATION: Access road leading from turn-

off Mile 160 Glenn Highway.
FACILITIES: Lodge; cabins; bunkhouse; bar;
cafe; boat docking and mooring; tackle and
sundries; camping.

SHEEP MOUNTAIN LODGE
Star Route C, Box 130
Palmer, AK 99645
(907) 822-3777
LOCATION: Mile 113 Glenn Highway, 65 mi.
northeast of Palmer.
FACILITIES: Cabins; motel; air stream trailers; 8 camper and trailer sites with sanitary
disposal; restaurant; bar.

TAZLINA GLACIER LODGE
Ray Williams
Box 250, Star Route C
Palmer, AK 99645
(907) 822-3280
LOCATION: Located on Glenn Highway
(Alaska Route 1), 156 mi. from Anchorage.
FACILITIES: Roadside lodge; cafe; bar;
sleeping cabins; trading post.

Port Alsworth

KOKSETNA CAMP
Port Alsworth, AK 99653
LOCATION: Lake Clark, southwest of
Anchorage.
FACILITIES: Lodge; meals; sportfishing; bird
watching; float trips on the Chulitna River.

VAN VALIN'S ISLAND LODGE
Port Alsworth, AK 99653
(907) 344-7361
LOCATION: Lake Clark Area, southwest of
Anchorage.
FACILITIES: Fly-in; log lodge; cabins; sport-
fishing; river float trips; backpacking; scenic
flights.

Seal Bay

AFOGNAK WILDERNESS LODGE
Seal Bay, AK 99697
LOCATION: Seal Bay, northeast end of Afog-
nak Island of Kodiak Island, southwest of
Anchorage.
FACILITIES: Lodge; family-style meals; pho-
tography; bird watching; sportfishing; open
spring - fall.

Seldovia

CHESLOKNU CABINS
Box 197
Seldovia, AK 99663
(907) 234-7890
LOCATION: Seldovia Bay, Kenai Peninsula,
directly across from community of Seldovia.
FACILITIES: Cabins; tent campers.

SELDOVIA LODGE
Box 136
Seldovia, AK 99663
(907) 234-7654
LOCATION: Lower Kenai Peninsula seacoast,
facing on Cook Inlet.
FACILITIES: Lodge; restaurant; lounge;
scenic hiking; sportfishing; photography; boat
rentals; clam digging.

RESORTS (continued)

Seward

KAKHONAK FISHING CAMP
Box 1241
Seward, AK 99664
(907) 224-5486
LOCATION: 12 mi. southeast of Soldotna on
the Kenai Peninsula.
FACILITIES: Canoe trips; sportfishing; pho-
tography; backpacking.

LABOUNTY'S MONTAGUE ISLAND
RESORT
Montague Island Resort
Star Route
Seward, AK 99664
LOCATION: MacLeod Harbor, Montague
Island, in Prince William Sound, approximate-
ly 115 air mi. southeast of Anchorage.
FACILITIES: Fly-in or boat; cabins equipped
for light housekeeping; beachcombing; pho-
tography; sportfishing; berry picking; canning;
birding; open year round.

Sterling

PEDERSEN'S MOOSE RIVER RESORT
Box 223, Star Route 2
Sterling, AK 99672
(907) 262-4515
LOCATION: Mile 83 Sterling Highway, Kenai
Peninsula.
FACILITIES: Cabins; canoes; boats; camp-
grounds; tackle; miniature golf course; open
May - Sept.

SPORTSMEN'S SERVICE
Box 256, Star Route 2
Sterling, AK 99672
(907) 262-4780
LOCATION: Mile 81 Sterling Highway, Kenai
Peninsula.
FACILITIES: Light housekeeping cabins;
camper laundry; dumping facilities; retail
store; sporting goods; licenses; camping supplies; year round boat parking; guided fishing
tours.

Skwentna

A WILDERNESS PLACE
Skwentna, AK 99667
LOCATION: 65 air mi. northwest of Anchor-
age on Lake Creek.
FACILITIES: Log cabin; guided sportfishing;
reservations.

Unalakleet

UNALAKLEET LODGE
Box 27
Unalakleet, AK 99684
(907) 624-3333
LOCATION: Western arctic coast, 412 air mi.
west of Fairbanks.
FACILITIES: Lodge; meals; sportfishing;
sporthunting; boat and motors for rent; open
May - Oct.

Wasilla

CALL OF THE WILD
Star Route A, Box 2594

Wasilla, AK 99681
(907) 892-6274
LOCATION: West end, Big Lake.
FACILITIES: Fly-in (summer); ice road (winter); cabins; restaurant; bar; sportfishing;
boating; water-skiing; hiking; ice fishing.

INNOKO RIVER LODGE
Box 246
Wasilla, AK 99687
(907) 376-5725
LOCATION: Alaska's Innoko River District
between the Yukon and Kuskokwin deltas.
FACILITIES: Lodging; boat and motors;
portable suction gold dredges.

NO-SEE-UM LODGE
Box 311 (Jun. - Aug.)
King Salmon, AK 99613

Box 506 (Sept. - May)
Wasilla, AK 99687
LOCATION: Kvichak River, 50 mi. north of
King Salmon in Iliamna trophy trout area,
300 mi. southwest of Anchorage.
FACILITIES: Lodge; family-style meals;
sportfishing.

Wrangell

JUDITH ANN
Box 12
Wrangell, AK 99929
LOCATION: 65-foot riverboat moored in a
wilderness location near Wrangell.
FACILITIES: Quarters for up to 10 persons;
guide; sportfishing; open Jun. 1 - Oct. 31.

Yakutat

GLACIER BEAR LODGE
Box 303
Yakutat, AK 99689
(907) 784-3202
LOCATION: Yakutat on Gulf of Alaska.
FACILITIES: Lodge; lounge; dining facilities;
charter boat sightseeing; sportfishing.

Yes Bay

YES BAY LODGE
Yes Bay, AK 99950
Radio phone KOJ 89
LOCATION: 50 mi. northwest of Ketchikan.
FACILITIES: Lodge; family-style meals;
sportfishing with fish smoking and packaging
service; scenic photography tours; hiking;
beachcombing; open May 1 - Oct. 1.

BOATING AREAS

Anchor Point

ANCHOR RIVER WAYSIDE
LOCATION: Kenai-Kodiak district.
FACILITIES: Open year round; limit of stay,
15 days; 7 sites; bathroom facilities; fishing.

SILVER KING WAYSIDE
LOCATION: Kenai-Kodiak district.
FACILITIES: Open year round; limit of stay,
15 days; 38 sites; water and bathroom facilities; fishing; self-guided trail.

ALASKA

BOATING AREAS (continued)

STARISKI WAYSIDE
LOCATION: Kenai-Kodiak district.
FACILITIES: Open year round; limit of stay, 15 days; 12 sites; water and bathroom facilities.

Copper Center

LITTLE TONSINA WAYSIDE
LOCATION: Copper Basin district.
FACILITIES: Open year round; limit of stay, 15 days; 6 sites; water and bathroom facilities; fishing.

SQUIRREL CREEK WAYSIDE
LOCATION: Copper Basin district.
FACILITIES: Open year round; limit of stay, 15 days; 7 sites; water and bathroom facilities; fishing.

Delta Junction

CLEARWATER WAYSIDE
LOCATION: Interior district.
FACILITIES: Open year round; limit of stay, 15 days; 12 sites; water and bathroom facilities; boating; fishing.

DONNELLY CREEK WAYSIDE
LOCATION: Interior district.
FACILITIES: Open year round; limit of stay, 15 days; 12 sites; bathroom facilities.

QUARTZ LAKE WAYSIDE
LOCATION: Interior district.
FACILITIES: Open year round; bathroom facilities; swimming; boating; fishing.

Eagle River

MIRROR LAKE WAYSIDE
LOCATION: Chugach district.
FACILITIES: Open year round; water and bathroom facilities; picnic area; swimming; boating; fishing.

PETERS CREEK WAYSIDE
LOCATION: Chugach district.
FACILITIES: Open year round; limit of stay, 4 days; 32 sites; water and bathroom facilities; fishing.

Fairbanks

CHATANIKA RIVER WAYSIDE
LOCATION: Interior district.
FACILITIES: Open year round; limit of stay, 15 days; 25 sites; water and bathroom facilities; boating; fishing.

CHENA RIVER RECREATION AREA
LOCATION: Interior district.
FACILITIES: Open year round; picnic area; boating; fishing.

CHENA RIVER STATE RECREATION AREA
LOCATION: Interior district.
FACILITIES: Open year round; boating; fishing; area is undeveloped.

CHENA RIVER WAYSIDE
LOCATION: Interior district.

FACILITIES: Open year round; limit of stay, 5 days; 62 sites; water and bathroom facilities; picnic area; boating.

Glennallen

DRY CREEK WAYSIDE
LOCATION: Copper Basin district.
FACILITIES: Open year round; limit of stay, 15 days; 10 sites; bathroom facilities; fishing.

LAKE LOUISE WAYSIDE
LOCATION: Copper Basin district.
FACILITIES: Open year round; limit of stay, 15 days; 5 sites; bathroom facilities; boating; fishing.

LITTLE NELCHINA WAYSIDE
LOCATION: Copper Basin district.
FACILITIES: Open year round; limit of stay, 15 days; 6 sites.

TOLSONA CREEK WAYSIDE
LOCATION: Copper Basin district.
FACILITIES: Open year round; limit of stay, 15 days; 5 sites; bathroom facilities.

Haines

CHILKOOT LAKE WAYSIDE
LOCATION: Southeast district.
FACILITIES: Open year round; limit of stay, 15 days; 32 sites; water and bathroom facilities; swimming; boating; fishing.

MOSQUITO LAKE WAYSIDE
LOCATION: Southeast district.
FACILITIES: Open year round; limit of stay, 15 days; 13 sites; water and bathroom facilities; swimming; boating; fishing.

PORTAGE COVE WAYSIDE
LOCATION: Southeast district.
FACILITIES: Open year round; limit of stay, 15 days; 9 sites; bathroom facilities.

Juneau

JUNEAU TRAIL SYSTEM
LOCATION: Southeast district.
FACILITIES: Open year round; fishing; self-guided trail; historic site.

Kenai

BERNICE LAKE WAYSIDE
LOCATION: Kenai-Kodiak district.
FACILITIES: Open year round; limit of stay, 7 days; 11 sites; water and bathroom facilities; swimming; boating.

CAPTAIN COOK STATE RECREATION AREA
LOCATION: Kenai-Kodiak district.
FACILITIES: Open year round; limit of stay, 15 days; 20 sites; water and bathroom facilities; picnic area; swimming; boating.

BISHOP CREEK
LOCATION: Kenai-Kodiak district.
FACILITIES: Open year round; limit of stay, 15 days; 12 sites; water and bathroom facilities; fishing; self-guided trail.

ALASKA

BOATING AREAS (continued)

DISCOVERY CAMPGROUND
LOCATION: Kenai-Kodiak district.
FACILITIES: Open year round; limit of stay, 15 days; 57 sites; water and bathroom facilities.

DISCOVERY PICNIC AREA
LOCATION: Kenai-Kodiak district.
FACILITIES: Open year round; bathroom facilities; picnic area.

STORMY LAKE
LOCATION: Kenai-Kodiak district.
FACILITIES: Open year round; limit of stay, 15 days; 10 sites; water and bathroom facilities; cabins; picnic area; swimming; boating; fishing; self-guided trail.

SWANSON RIVER CANOE LANDING
LOCATION: Kenai-Kodiak district.
FACILITIES: Open year round; bathroom facilities; boating; fishing.

Ketchikan

REFUGE COVE PICNIC WAYSIDE
LOCATION: Southeast district.
FACILITIES: Open year round; bathroom facilities; picnic area; swimming.

TOTEM BRIGHT HISTORIC SITE
LOCATION: Southeast district.
FACILITIES: Open year round; bathroom facilities; historic site.

Kodiak

FORT ABERCROMBIE
LOCATION: Kenai-Kodiak district.
FACILITIES: Open year round; limit of stay, 7 days; 14 sites; water and bathroom facilities; swimming; fishing; historic site.

North Pole

HARDING LAKE STATE RECREATION AREA
LOCATION: Interior district.
FACILITIES: Open year round; limit of stay, 15 days; 95 sites; picnic area; swimming; boating; fishing.

SALCHA RIVER PICNIC AREA
LOCATION: Interior district.
FACILITIES: Open year round; water and bathroom facilities; picnic area; boating; fishing.

Ninilchik

DEEP CREEK WAYSIDE
LOCATION: Kenai-Kodiak district.
FACILITIES: Open year round; limit of stay, 15 days; 20 sites; bathroom facilities; picnic area; boating; fishing.

NINILCHIK WAYSIDE
LOCATION: Kenai-Kodiak district.
FACILITIES: Open year round; limit of stay, 15 days; 15 sites; bathroom facilities.

Palmer

BONNIE LAKE WAYSIDE
LOCATION: Mat-Su district.
FACILITIES: Open year round; limit of stay, 15 days; 8 sites; bathroom facilities; boating; fishing.

FINGER LAKE WAYSIDE
LOCATION: Mat-Su district.
FACILITIES: Open year round; limit of stay, 15 days; 41 sites; water and bathroom facilities; boating; fishing; self-guided trail.

KING MOUNTAIN WAYSIDE
LOCATION: Mat-Su district.
FACILITIES: Open year round; limit of stay, 15 days; 22 sites; water and bathroom facilities.

LONG LAKE WAYSIDE
LOCATION: Mat-Su district.
FACILITIES: Open year round; limit of stay, 15 days; 8 sites; water and bathroom facilities; boating; fishing.

MATANUSKA GLACIER WAYSIDE
LOCATION: Mat-Su district.
FACILITIES: Open year round; limit of stay, 15 days; 6 sites; bathroom facilities; fishing; self-guided trail.

MOOSE CREEK WAYSIDE
LOCATION: Mat-Su district.
FACILITIES: Open year round; limit of stay, 15 days; 8 sites; water and bathroom facilities.

Seldovia

KECHEMAK WILDERNESS PARK
LOCATION: Kenai Peninsula accessible by aircraft or boat only.
FACILITIES: Open year round; boating; fishing; area is undeveloped.

Sitka

HALIBUT POINT WAYSIDE
LOCATION: Southeast district.
FACILITIES: Open year round; bathroom facilities; picnic area; fishing; historic site.

OLD SITKA HISTORIC SITE
LOCATION: Southeast district.
FACILITIES: Open year round; fishing; historic site.

Skagway

CHILKOOT TRAIL
LOCATION: Southeast district.
FACILITIES: Open year round; bathroom facilities; fishing; self-guided trail; historic site.

LIARSVILLE WAYSIDE
LOCATION: Southeast district.
FACILITIES: Open year round; limit of stay, 15 days; 7 sites; bathroom facilities; fishing.

Soldotna

CLAM GULCH PICNIC

ALASKA

BOATING AREAS (continued)

LOCATION: Kenai-Kodiak district.
FACILITIES: Open year round; limit of stay,
15 days; 15 sites; water and bathroom facilities; picnic are; fishing.

IZAAK WALTON WAYSIDE
LOCATION: Kenai-Kodiak district.
FACILITIES: Open year round; limit of stay,
15 days; 32 sites; bathroom facilities; boating;
fishing.

JOHNSON LAKE WAYSIDE
LOCATION: Kenai-Kodiak district.
FACILITIES: Open year round; limit of stay,
15 days; 20 sites; bathroom facilities; swimming; boating; fishing.

KASILOF RIVER WAYSIDE
LOCATION: Kenai-Kodiak district.
FACILITIES: Open year round; limit of stay,
15 days; 10 sites; water and bathroom facilities; picnic area; fishing.

Tok

DEADMAN LAKE WAYSIDE
LOCATION: Interior district.
FACILITIES: Open year round; limit of stay,
15 days; 16 sites; bathroom facilities; swimming; boating; fishing.

EAGLE TRAIL WAYSIDE
LOCATION: Interior district.
FACILITIES: Open year round; limit of stay,
15 days; 40 sites; water and bathroom facilities; picnic area; fishing; self-guided trail.

GARDINER CREEK WAYSIDE
LOCATION: Interior district.
FACILITIES: Open year round; limit of stay,
15 days; 6 sites; bathroom facilities; fishing.

LAKEVIEW WAYSIDE
LOCATION: Interior district.
FACILITIES: Open year round; limit of stay,
15 days; 8 sites; bathroom facilities; swimming; boating; fishing.

MOON LAKE WAYSIDE
LOCATION: Interior district.
FACILITIES: Open year round; limit of stay,
15 days; 15 sites; bathroom facilities; swimming; boating.

PORCUPINE CREEK WAYSIDE
LOCATION: Copper Basin district.
FACILITIES: Open year round; limit of stay,
15 days; 12 sites; water and bathroom facilities; self-guided trail.

TOK RIVER WAYSIDE
LOCATION: Interior district.
FACILITIES: Open year round; limit of stay,
15 days; 10 sites; water and bathroom facilities; swimming; boating; fishing.

Valdez

BLUEBERRY LAKE WAYSIDE
LOCATION: Copper Basin district.
FACILITIES: Open year round; limit of stay,
15 days; 6 sites; bathroom facilities; fishing.

WORTHINGTON GLACIER WAYSIDE
LOCATION: Copper Basin district.
FACILITIES: Open year round; limit of stay,
15 days; 6 sites; bathroom facilities.

Wasilla

BIG LAKE (EAST) WAYSIDE
LOCATION: Mat-Su district.
FACILITIES: Open year round; limit of stay,
15 days; 14 sites; water and bathroom facilities; swimming; boating.

BIG LAKE (SOUTH) WAYSIDE
LOCATION: Mat-Su district.
FACILITIES: Open year round; limit of stay,
15 days; 13 sites; water and bathroom facilities; picnic area; boating; fishing.

NANCY LAKE STATE RECREATION AREA
LOCATION: Mat-Su district.
FACILITIES: Open year round; limit of stay,
15 days; 106 sites; picnic area; boating; fishing.

SOUTH ROLLY LAKE CAMPGROUND
LOCATION: Mat-Su district.
FACILITIES: Open year round; limit of stay,
15 days; 106 sites; water and bathroom facilities; picnic area; boating; fishing.

ROCK LAKE WAYSIDE
LOCATION: Mat-Su district.
FACILITIES: Open year round; limit of stay,
15 days; 10 sites; water and bathroom facilities; boating.

Willow

NANCY LAKE WAYSIDE
LOCATION: Mat-Su district.
FACILITIES: Open year round; limit of stay,
15 days; 30 sites; water and bathroom facilities; picnic area; boating; fishing.

WILLOW CREEK WAYSIDE
LOCATION: Mat-Su district.
FACILITIES: Open year round; limit of stay,
15 days; 17 sites; bathroom facilities; fishing.

BICYCLE TRAILS

YUKON TRAIL - 2,200 mi; rugged terrain,
gravel surfaces, long distances per day, adverse
climatic conditions, primitive campsites; 10-
speed bikes necessary.

This is a long (2,200 miles), arduous journey, only to be attempted by skilled bike
tourists after considerable planning. You will
have to carry food to last as long as a week,
and as dehydrated foods are not generally
available along the route, you may want to
mail food parcels to yourself in care of General Delivery at various spots along the way.
It was reported that 1,700 miles of the route
was gravel. In fact, a 4-mile section between
Telegraph Creek and Hazelton was uncompleted and a sea of mud. This section is now
open but much of this route will remain gravel for some years.

You will need tents, warm sleeping bags,
insect protection, and your own cooking gear.

BICYCLE TRAILS (continued)

Start with bikes in top shape and carry as much repair equipment and spare parts as possible. You might even consider having new tires waiting for you at Hazelton.
Trail: Anchorage to Mount McKinley National Park, to Dawson, to Whitehorse, to Telegraph Creek to Hazelton to Prince George to Jasper to Banff to Calgary.

TRAILS

Fairbanks

PINNELL MOUNTAIN TRAIL - 24 mi. foot trail. This is the northernmost maintained hiking trail in the United States and is located off the Steese Hwy. about 90 mi. North of Fairbanks. It traverses alpine ridge tops with outstanding vistas of the Alaska Range, Brook Range and Yukon River Valley. Beautiful wild flower displays, as well as views of the midnight sun, can be seen in the latter part of June. Unique plank construction permits hikers to cross marshy muskeg areas safely.

SKI AREAS

Girdwood

ALYESKA RESORT
Girdwood, AK 99587
(907) 783-6000
LOCATION: About 40 mi. from Anchorage.
FACILITIES: 7 double chairlifts; 2 tow ropes; 1 poma lift; slopes for expert, intermediate and beginning skiers; ski instruction; ski rental; restaurants; lodging.

Juneau

EAGLECREST
Parks & Recreation Dept.
City & Borough of Juneau
490 S. Franklin
Juneau, AK 99801
(907) 586-3300 Ext. 26
LOCATION: About 15 mi. from Juneau on Fish Creek Road.
FACILITIES: 2 chairlifts; slopes for expert, intermediate and beginning skiers; ski instruction; ski rental; longest run, 2½ mi.; restaurants; lodging.

AMUSEMENT PARKS & ATTRACTIONS

Anchorage

TOTEM TOWN AMUSEMENT PARK
100 Fireweed Lane
Anchorage, AK 99503
(907) 272-8334
FACILITIES: Seven major rides; 3 kiddie rides; ice rink, picnic area; zoo; museum; refreshments; entertainment; free gate and parking.

Juneau

MENDENHALL GLACIER VISITOR INFORMATION CENTER
Juneau, AK 99801
(907) 789-7235
FACILITIES: 13 mi. from downtown Juneau. The observatory affords a spectacular view of the glacier ½ mi. away. A naturalist is on duty during summer visitor season.

STATE FAIR

Alaska State Fair
Box 1128
Palmer, AK 99645
(907) 745-4827
DATE: Late August - Labor Day.

NATIONAL PARKS

McKinley Park

MOUNT MCKINLEY NATIONAL PARK
McKinley Park, AK 99755
(907) 683-2294

IGLOO
LOCATION: Mile 34.
FACILITIES: Open May 25 - Sept. 25; limit of stay: 14 days; 7 sites; bathroom facilities; tents; reservations; primitive site.

MORINO
LOCATION: Mile 2.
FACILITIES: Open May 25 - Oct. 1; limit of stay: 14 days; 10 sites; walk-in only; tents.

RILEY CREEK
LOCATION: Mile 1.
FACILITIES: Open year round; limit of stay: 14 days; 102 sites; NPS campsite fee: $4; water and bathroom facilities; picnic area; food service; hiking; museum; living history program; NPS guided tour; self-guiding tour.

SANCTUARY
LOCATION: Mile 22.
FACILITIES: Open May 25 - Sept. 25; limit of stay: 14 days; 7 sites; bathroom facilities; reservations; primitive site.

SAVAGE
LOCATION: Mile 12.
FACILITIES: Open May 25 - Oct. 1; limit of stay: 14 days; 24 sites; group camps; NPS campsite fee: $4; water and bathroom facilities; picnic area; food service; fishing; hiking; museum; living history program; NPS guided tour; self-guiding tour.

TEKLANIKA
LOCATION: Mile 29.
FACILITIES: Open May 25 - Sept. 25; limit of stay: 14 days; 35 sites; NPS campsite fee: $2; water and bathroom facilities; reserva-

ALASKA

tions; primitive site.

WONDER LAKE
LOCATION: Mile 85.
FACILITIES: Open Jun. 10 - Sept. 10; limit of stay: 14 days; 23 sites; group camps; NPS campsite fee: $4; water and bathroom facilities; picnic area; food service; fishing; hiking; museum; living history program; NPS guided tour; self-guiding tour; tents only; reservations.

NATIONAL FORESTS

National Forests
P.O. Box 1628
Juneau, AK 99802
(907) 586-7151

Anchorage

CHUGACH NATIONAL FOREST
ATTRACTIONS: Fiords and glaciers, lakes and rivers. Unexcelled scenery. Salmon spawning runs, salmon, crab, and clam canneries. Kenai Mountains with access by road system throughout the Kenai Peninsula. and saltwater fishing. Hunting for moose, sheep, mountain goats. Alaskan brown bear and elk, also for waterfowl and grouse.
FACILITIES: 39 camp and picnic sites, 9 picnic only; 2 winter sports areas.
NEARBY TOWNS: Cordova, Kodiak, Seward, Valdez, and Whittier.

Juneau

TONGASS NATIONAL FOREST
ATTRACTIONS: Rugged Alaska coast; hundreds of islands, fiords, snowcapped mountains above the sea; totems; territorial museum and Indian villages. Salmon canneries. Gateway to Canadian hinterland and Yukon, "Trail of '98" gold mines. Glaciers; "Ice Cap" back of Juneau; fiords of Tracy Arm. Admiralty Island. Trout fishing, also saltwater fishing for salmon and halibut. Hunting for Alaska brown and grizzly bear, mountain goat, and deer. Boating on lakes and inland waterways. Scenic wilderness trails; mountain climbing.
FACILITIES: 95 camp and picnic sites, 14 picnic only; 1 swimming site; 2 winter sports areas.
NEAREST TOWNS: Petersburg, Sitka, Skagway.

Ketchikan

TONGASS NATIONAL FOREST
ATTRACTIONS: Fiords of Walker Cove and Rudyerd Bay of the Behm Canal, and Portland Canal. Trout fishing; salt-water fishing for salmon and halibut. Alaskan brown, black, and grizzly bear, goat, and deer hunting. Totems. Indian villages. Salmon canneries; pulpmill. Boating on inland waterways.
FACILITIES: 10 camp and picnic sites, 1 picnic only; 3 swimming sites; 1 winter sports area.

NEAREST TOWN: Wrangell.

STATE PARKS

Headquarters

Department of Natural Resources
Division of Parks
619 Warehouse Avenue
Anchorage, AK 99501
(907) 274-4676

District Headquarters

Chugach District
Alaska Division of Parks
2601 Commercial Drive
Anchorage, AK 99501
(907) 279-3413

Interior District
Alaska Division of Parks
4420 Airport Way
Fairbanks, AK 99071
(907) 479-2243

Kenai-Kodiak District
Alaska Division of Parks
Box 1247
Soldonta, AK 99699
(907) 262-5581

Mat-Su & Copper Basin District
Alaska Division of Parks
P.O. Box 182
Palmer, AK 99645

Southeast District
Alaska Division of Parks
Pouch M
Juneau, AK 99801
(907) 465-2421

Anchorage

CHUGACH STATE PARK
LOCATION: Eastern edge of Anchorage metropolitan area and stretches from the Knik River to the Girdwood valley.
FACILITIES: Open year round; limit of stay: 15 days; 40 sites; water and bathroom facilities; picnic area; hunting; fishing; cross country skiing; hiking; self-guided trail.

BIRD CREEK STATE PARK
LOCATION: Chugach district.
FACILITIES: Open year round; limit of stay, 7 days; 25 sites; water and bathroom facilities; picnic area; fishing.

MCHUGH CREEK STATE PARK
LOCATION: Chugach district.
FACILITIES: Open year round; bathroom facilities; picnic area; self-guided trail.

Eagle River

EAGLE RIVER STATE PARK
LOCATION: Chugach district.
FACILITIES: Open year round; limit of stay, 4 days; 36 sites; water and bathroom facilities; picnic area; boating; fishing.

STATE PARKS (continued)

EKLUTNA BASIN STATE PARK
LOCATION: Chugach district.
FACILITIES: Open year round; limit of stay,
15 days; 30 sites; bathroom facilities; self-
guided trail.

THUNDERBIRD FALLS STATE PARK
LOCATION: Chugach district.
FACILITIES: Open year round; bathroom
facilities; picnic area; self-guided trail.

Seldovia

KACHEMAK BAY STATE PARK
LOCATION: Kenai Peninsula accessible by
aircraft or boat only.
FACILITIES: Open year round; limit of stay,
15 days; 5 sites; boating; fishing; area is undeveloped.

Haines

CHILKAT STATE PARK
LOCATION: Chilkat Peninsula, 1½ mi. south
of Haines.
FACILITIES: Open year round; limit of stay,
15 days; 30 sites; water and bathroom facilities; picnic area; boating; fishing; self-guided
trail.

Cantwell

DENALI STATE PARK
LOCATION: 130 mi. north of Anchorage.
FACILITIES: Open year round; limit of stay,
18 days; 50 sites; water and bathroom facilities; picnic area; swimming; boating; fishing;
self-guided trail.

BYERS LAKE STATE PARK
LOCATION: Mat-Su district.
FACILITIES: Open year round; limit of stay,
18 days; 61 sites; water and bathroom facilities; swimming; boating; fishing; self-guided
trail.

Wrangell

PATS CREEK WAYSIDE STATE PARK
LOCATION: Southeast district.
FACILITIES: Open year round; limit of stay,
15 days; 9 sites; bathroom facilities; fishing;
self-guided trail.

STATE FORESTS

There are no State Forests in Alaska.

HISTORIC SITES

Fairbanks

PLEASANT CAMP - Location of a Northwest
Mounted Police (now the Royal Canadian
Mounted Police) border station on Dalton
Trail during the Klondike Goldrush of the
1890's. When the final border surveys were
made, Pleasant Camp was determined to be in
the United States territory. Located near the
mouth of Jarvis Creek, Mile 40 on the Haines
Highway (Alaska Route 8).

**GEORGE C. THOMAS MEMORIAL
LIBRARY** - Built in 1909 and still in use; the
library is a tribute to American missionary
activity in Alaska; purchased from the Episcopal Church in 1942.

Juneau

HOUSE OF WICKERSHAM - Home once
owned by Judge James Wickersham, one of
Alaska's outstanding statesmen, historian and
pioneering federal judge. He established the
first government in Far North Alaska (1900),
named Fairbanks (1903); was elected delegate
to Congress (1907); secured Alaska Railroad
legislation (1914); University of Alaska bill
(1915); establishment of Mt. McKinley National Park (1917). The home contains impressive array of Alaskana; conducted tours
available. Located at 213 Seventh Avenue.

**SAINT NICHOLAS RUSSIAN ORTHODOX
CHURCH** - (Orthodox Church in America).
Built in 1894, the church is one of the oldest
log buildings in the Southeast Alaska and first
church built in Juneau. Contains numerous
church artifacts and several interesting ikons.
Guided tours available daily during summer.
Located at 326 Fifth Street.

Kenai

**CHURCH OF THE ASSUMPTION OF THE
VIRGIN MARY** - Built in 1894, the church is
considered the best preserved example of
nineteenth century Russian Orthodox Church
constructed on the quadrilateral ground plan;
the building still holds regularly scheduled
services; a number of original religious and art
objects imported from Russia in 1849 may be
seen. Special tours available by appointment.
Located on the east shore of Cook Inlet.

Ketchikan

CREEK STREET HISTORIC DISTRICT -
Ketchikan's famous "district" where Black
Mary, Dolly, Frenchie and others plied their
trade for over a half century; Creek Street is a
wooden street on pilings along Ketchikan
Creek; this area is being restored and the
houses renovated into shops and business offices and is within walking distance of downtown Ketchikan.

TOTEM BRIGHT - Features a community
house and totem park with 13 totems; situated on a point overlooking Tongass Narrows.
Located about 25 min. north of Ketchikan.

TOTEM HERITAGE CENTER - Old totems
of the Tlingit and Haida people of Southeast
Alaska. Located at 601 Deermount.

Kenai Peninsula

ALASKA NELLIES HOMESTEAD - The
roadhouse of Nellie Neal and her husband
Billie Lawing. For years the roadhouse was a
stop on the Alaska Railroad between Seward

ALASKA

HISTORIC SITES (continued)

and Anchorage. Located near Mile 23 on the Seward-Anchorage Highway (Route 9).

Kodiak

BARANOF MUSEUM - The oldest remaining Russian-built structure in Alaska. The foundation dates from the 1790's. Displays of 500 items such as a 3-hole kayak, samovars, vintage implements, ikons, Attu basketry. Located at 101 Marine Way.
OPEN: 11 a.m. - 3 p.m. Mon. - Fri. (summer); 1 p.m. - 3 p.m. Wed., Fri., Sat., Sun. (winter).

Metlakatla

DUNCAN COTTAGE MUSEUM - A missionary's house which consists of the room which was his office; his private bedroom; the room used as his clinic; a room formerly used as a school classroom; a guest sitting room and bedroom; many personal artifacts, including the Ediphone built by Thomas Edison; and many historic photographs.
OPEN: Daily 9 a.m. - 5 p.m.

Sitka

CASTLE HILL - Site of the 1st raising of the Stars and Stripes when the United States purchased Russian America from Czarist Russia in 1867. Free. Located off Lincoln Street.
OPEN: Year round.

OLD SITKA - Site of the first attempt of Russians to establish a trading post in southeast Alaska. The post established in 1799 was called St. Michael. The garrison was massacred by the warlike Tlingit Indians in June, 1802. There are no surface remains of the fort. Located 6 mi. from Sitka.

SAINT MICHAEL'S RUSSIAN ORTHODOX CATHEDRAL - Destroyed by fire in 1966 and now completely restored; the church built in 1840's is one of the best surviving examples of Russian Orthodox "country" cathedral architecture in the world. It contains the famed Sitka Madonna ikon and many other art treasures. The Cathedral is headquarters for the Russian Orthodox Church in Alaska. Located on Lincoln Street.
OPEN: Daily during summer; other times by appointment.

SHELDON JACKSON MUSEUM - The first museum and the first concrete building in the state was built by the Rev. Sheldon Jackson, the first ordained missionary to come to Alaska following the purchase from Russia in 1867. Admission $1. Located on Sheldon Jackson College Campus.
OPEN: Jun. - Sept.; Oct. - May by appointment only.

Skagway

GOLDEN NORTH HOTEL - A hotel/museum of Alaskana furnished in goldrush era appointments from the basic room furniture to details such as crocheted and embroidered dresser scarves and doilies, needlepoint chair covers, period photographs, flocked wallpaper and functioning old-style radiators which heat the rooms and hallways. Located at Third & Broadway.

SKAGWAY - Has the largest and finest collection of original buildings still standing that reflect the spirit of the greatest and most important mining stampede in Alaska. This was the most direct and heavily traveled route of the gold seekers to the Klondike gold fields of the Yukon Territory of Canada. The first route in the area was from the neighboring town of Dyea; now almost completely obliterated, over the Chilkoot Pass (3,739 feet) to the headwaters of the Yukon River. After a disastrous avalanche in the spring of 1898, the center of activity shifted to nearby Skagway and the White Pass (2,900 feet), where the railroad to Whitehorse was under construction.

Soldotna

FORT ABERCROMBIE HISTORIC SITE - The fort was a part of the coastal defenses of Kodiak Island during World War II; the site lies but a short driving distance from the town of Kodiak.

Teller

NORGE LANDING SITE - It was here that the "Norge," first dirigible to fly over the North Pole, landed May 13, 1926. The craft, damaged in landing after its 71-hour cruise from Spitsbergen, was dismantled and shipped to Italy. Later it was lost in another polar attempt.

Wrangell

BEAR TRIBAL HOUSE - Tlingit tribal house of the Bear Clan on Chief Shakes Island, it contains a collection of totems. Accessible from the mainland by a footbridge at the bottom of Front Street.
OPEN: Year round.

HOSTELS

Juneau

JUNEAU YOUTH HOSTEL, INC.
Box 186
11th and B Streets
Juneau, AK 99801
(907) 586-3131
FACILITIES: Open Jun. 1 - Sept.1; 20 beds, men; 10 beds, women; modern bathrooms; nearest hostels: Ketchikan, 200 mi. south (by air or ferry); overnight charges: $2 ($1 AYH members); houseparents: Theresa & Michael Reda.

Ketchikan

KETCHIKAN UNITED METHODIST CHURCH
Box 8515
Grant and Main Streets
Ketchikan, AK 99901
(907) 225-3780
FACILITIES: Open Jun. 1 - Sept. 1; 15 beds, men; 15 beds, women; modern bathrooms;

ALASKA

HOSTELS (continued)

nearest hostels: Juneau, 200 mi. north (by air or ferry); overnight charges: $2; houseparents: Daryl & Margaret Guthrie.

Nome

COMMUNITY UNITED METHODIST CHURCH
Box 907
Nome, AK 99762
(907) 443-2865
FACILITIES: Open year round; 10 beds, men; 10 beds, women; modern and semi-modern bathrooms; cooking; nearest hostels: Ketchikan, Juneau; overnight charges: $2.50; houseparents: John & Barbara Shaffer.

POINTS OF INTEREST

Anchorage

ANCHORAGE FUR RENDEZVOUS - Held in February. Alaska's largest winter celebration, includes the World Championship Sled Dog races; snowshoe baseball game; a fur auction; Native dances; blanket toss exhibitions.

ANCHORAGE HISTORICAL & FINE ARTS MUSEUM - City of Anchorage museum, with collections and exhibitions on native peoples, history and arts of Alaska, and varied temporary exhibitions, changed monthly; museum houses the collection of the Cook Inlet Historical Society. No charge for admission. 121 West Seventh Ave.
OPEN: 9-5 p.m. Mon., Wed., Fri., Sat.; 9-9 p.m. Tues. & Thur.; 1-5 p.m. Sun. (summer).

NATIONAL BANK OF ALASKA HERITAGE LIBRARY - A collection of early Alaskana; features original paintings by Sydney Laurence, Eustace Ziegler, Tom Lambert, Fred Machetanz and many others; collections of old publications; maps; artifacts, etc. No admission charge. Located on the corner of Northern Lights Boulevard and C Street.
OPEN: 1-4 p.m. Mon. - Fri.

OLD ST. NICHOLAS RUSSIAN ORTHODOX CHURCH - The vestments and ikons in the chapel were brought to Alaska from the Soviet Union sometime during the 1920's. In 1962, Old St. Nicholas was replaced as an active church by an adjacent frame structure. The Eklutna residents, however, have preserved the chapel as an historic building. Located in the Village of Eklutna, at Mile .5 of the Eklutna Village Road, about 25 road miles north of Anchorage.

WILDLIFE MUSEUM - Contains over 150 native Alaska species of wildlife. No admission charge. Located at Elmendorf Air Force Base.
OPEN: Mon. - Fri. 7:45 - 11:45 a.m.; 12:45 - 4:45 p.m..

Bethel

YUGTARVIK - Formerly Bethel Museum, offers a collection of Eskimo artifacts of Southwestern Alaska, Kuskokwim and Yukon deltas. Authentic Eskimo arts and crafts for sale. Free.
OPEN: Tue. - Sat. 9 a.m. - 6 p.m.; closed Sun. & Mon.

Fairbanks

ALASKALAND - City-operated outdoor "theme park"; featuring historical exhibits & artifacts from all over Alaska; interesting zoo with major Alaskan wildlife species. Located on Airport Way between Peger Road and Moore Street.

CRIPPLE CREEK RESORT - Company mining town with former buildings largely intact; features the Malamute Saloon, an old time theater; museum and hotel. In Ester, 7 mi. west of Fairbanks on the George Parks Highway (Alaska Route 3) on the way to Mount McKinley National Park.
OPEN: 12 p.m. - 5 a.m., May - Sept., 7 days a week.

EQUINOX MARATHON - Conducted annually on the Fairbanks campus of the University of Alaska on the Saturday closest to the autumnal equinox; the event has grown from its initial 67 finishers in 1963 to a present-day finishing number of around 600 people; participants are a combination of intensely competitive racers and many recreation-fitness non-competitive runners and hikers; event considered 2nd only to the Pike's Peak Marathon in the severity of its terrain which features a differential of approximately 2,000 feet from the lowest to the highest point; $1 entry fee.

GILMORE CREEK TRACKING STATION - NASA Satellite Tracking Station. Located at Mile 13.5 on the Steese Highway (Alaska Route 6) north of Fairbanks.
OPEN: Mon. - Fri. 9 a.m. - 3 p.m.

GOLDEN DAYS CELEBRATION - Held annually during the week that includes July 22nd; citywide pageant commemorating the finding of gold near Fairbanks in July 1902 by Felix Pedro.

RIVERBOAT DISCOVERY I AND II - Authentic reproductions of historic Yukon River sternwheelers which make 4 hr. cruises on the Chena River and Tananna River; departure from Discovery Landing, near Fairbanks International Airport.
OPEN: Daily, Jun. - Sept.

UNIVERSITY OF ALASKA MUSEUM - Features collection of Alaskan ethnographic and archaeological materials, wildlife and bird specimens; historical collections; interpretive displays. Free. On main campus of University of Alaska.
OPEN: Mid-May - Labor Day; 9 a.m. - 5 p.m.; winter hours 1 - 5 p.m. daily, except Christmas.

Homer

ALASKA WILD BERRY PRODUCTS - Jams, jellies, syrups and sauces cooked by hand. Prepared from wild berries of the Kenai Peninsula. Guided tours of the kitchen and processing plant available year round.

ALASKA

POINTS OF INTEREST (continued)

Juneau

ALASKA STATE MUSEUM - Located in Juneau Subport Area, contains wide-ranging collection of Aleut, Athapaskan, Tlingit, Haida and Eskimo artifacts and materials. Interpretative exhibits and dioramas, also. Guided tours provided Jun. 1 - Sept. 30. Free. OPEN: May 15 - Oct. 1, 9 a.m. - 9 p.m., Mon. - Fri. Weekends, 1 p.m. - 4:30 p.m. Winter hours, 9 a.m. - 5 p.m., Mon. - Fri. Weekends, 1 p.m. - 4:30 p.m.

Kotzebue

KOTZEBUE COMMUNITY MUSEUM - "Ootukakuktuvik," an Eskimo word meaning a "Place of old things"; features a collection of Eskimo artifacts and craft items from the Kotzebue region.
OPEN: Summers, 2:30 p.m. - 6:30 p.m.

LIVING MUSEUM OF THE ARCTIC - Features dioramas of arctic environment; animals and sea life as well as Eskimo cultural exhibits.
OPEN: Summer.

Nome

CARRIE MCLAIN MEMORIAL MUSEUM - The collections include native Eskimo art works and artifacts; exhibits of gold rush history of Nome; including photographs and historical objects. Located on Front Street in the Kegayah Public Library.
OPEN: Mon. - Wed. 10 a.m. - 7 p.m.; Tue., Thur., Fri. 10 a.m. - 5 p.m.; Sat. 10 a.m. - 4 p.m.; closed Sun. and legal holidays.

North Pole

NORTH POLE, ALASKA - Specializes in Christmas gifts available from Santa Claus House, this house annually receives thousands of letters addressed to "Santa Claus, North Pole, AK 99705" written by children the world round. Located on the Richardson Highway (Alaska Route 4) about 14 mi. east of Fairbanks.

Palmer

INDEPENDENCE MINE - Gold mining operations recorded as early as 1897; the mines became the 2nd largest in Alaska behind the Alaska-Juneau mine and the largest in south-central Alaska. Rising mining costs and government established price of $35 per gold ounce made operation unprofitable and the mine closed down in 1950. Located at Mile 23 Fishook Road, northwest of Palmer.

Pribilof Islands

FUR SEAL ROOKERIES - The Pribilof Islands in the Bering Sea are the breeding grounds of the largest herd of Pacific northern fur seals in the world. Over 1¼ million strong, as well as a sanctuary for more than 100 million birds, representing some 180 species. Closely regulated by international treaty among the United States, Canada, Russia and Japan, the annual harvest of fur seals is carried out by the Aleut inhabitants of the island. Air tours are available Jun. - Sept. Contact Alaska Tour & Marketing Service, Park Place Building, Seattle, WA 98101, (206) 624-8851.

Seward

RESURRECTION BAY HISTORICAL SOCIETY MUSEUM - Offers a collection of historical artifacts, early-day mining tools, furniture used by early settlers, Aleut baskets and other items. Small entry fee.

Skagway

DAYS OF '98 SHOW - Revue commemorating goldrush days of 1898 in Skagway; produced by an all-volunteer cast; the show is scheduled to coincide with ferryliner and cruiseship arrivals. Located Eagle Hall, located corner of 6th & Broadway. Admission $3.
OPEN: Jun. - Sept.

TRAIL OF '98 MUSEUM - Features outstanding collection of early Native and pioneer era artifacts; one of the best collections of the goldrush memorabilia in the state with particular emphasis on the goldrush to the Klondike in 1898. Located at Second and Spring Streets on second floor of the first granite building built in Alaska.
OPEN: 8 a.m. - 8 p.m. Oct. - May, by appointment only.

ARIZONA

Arizona, the last continental state to adopt statehood, joined the Union in 1918 as the forty-eighth state. Much of the state's land was annexed to the United States following the war with Mexico in 1848. Five years later, Mexico gave up the remainder through the Gadsden Purchase.

Arizona's early history is steeped in constant conflicts with the whites fighting the Mexicans and Indians for land, the Union soldiers fighting the Confederates, the sheepherders fighting the cattlemen for grazing land, and the Indians, cattlemen, sheepherders and bordering states all fighting for water rights.

The state is rich in Wild West folklore, too, with such notables as Wyatt Earp, Doc Holliday, Johnny Rings, Cochise and Geronimo heading the famous cowboys and Indians.

Also Arizona boasts numerous tourist attractions, among them, Tombstone, "the town too tough to die," Boothill, the most infamous old West cemetery, the Painted Desert, the reconstructed London Bridge, the mile-wide Grand Canyon and the Hoover Dam, the largest structure of its kind.

Other leading revenue earners for the

INTRODUCTION (continued)

state, in addition to tourism, are cattle and sheep production, and copper mining with Arizona providing more than half of the United States supply.

State capital: Phoenix. State bird: Cactus wren. State tree: Paloverde. State flower: Saguaro cactus.

WEATHER

Arizona covers 113,909 square miles, with about 350 square miles of water surface. The state has three main topographical areas: (1) a high plateau averaging between 5,000 and 7,000 feet in elevation in the northeast; (2) a mountainous region oriented southeast to northwest with maximum elevation between 9,000 and 12,000 feet above mean sea level; (3) low mountain ranges and desert valleys in the southwestern portion of the state.

Cold air masses from Canada sometimes penetrate into the state, bringing temperatures well below zero in the high plateau and mountainous regions of central and northern Arizona. The lowest readings can dip to 35 degrees F below zero. High temperatures are common throughout the summer months at the lower elevations. Temperatures over 125 degrees F have been observed in the desert area. Great extremes occur between day and night temperatures throughout Arizona. During winter months, daytime temperatures may average 70 degrees F, with night temperatures often falling to freezing or slightly below in lower desert valleys. In the summer the pine-clad forests in the central part of the state may have afternoon temperatures of 80 degrees F, while night temperatures drop to 35 degrees to 40 degrees F.

Average daily temperature for each month.

	Northern	Southern
Jan.	39.5 to 20.6	67.7 to 33.4
Feb.	42.7 to 22.6	72.0 to 36.2
Mar.	48.6 to 26.3	77.2 to 40.0
Apr.	59.1 to 32.9	86.0 to 45.7
May	70.5 to 42.2	95.5 to 54.0
Jun.	81.2 to 52.1	104.5 to 63.4
Jul.	86.9 to 58.5	107.3 to 74.5
Aug.	83.4 to 56.5	104.0 to 72.9
Sept.	76.2 to 50.2	100.9 to 64.7
Oct.	63.8 to 40.2	90.3 to 52.2
Nov.	48.6 to 28.7	76.6 to 40.8
Dec.	39.6 to 21.4	67.9 to 34.2
Year	61.7 to 37.7	87.5 to 51.0

STATE CHAMBER OF COMMERCE

Arizona State Chamber of Commerce
3216 North Third Street
Suite 103
Phoenix, AZ 85012
(602) 248-9172

STATE & CITY TOURISM OFFICES

State

Arizona Department of Economic Planning & Development
1645 West Jefferson Street
Phoenix, AZ 85007
(602) 271-5371

Local

Tourist Development Department
Phoenix Metropolitan Chamber of Commerce
805 N. Second Street
Phoenix, AZ 85004
(602) 254-5521

Visitor's Bureau
Tucson Chamber of Commerce
P.O. Box 991
Tucson, AZ 85702
(602) 792-1212

STATE HIGHWAY DEPARTMENT

Arizona Department of Transportation
206 South 17th Avenue
Phoenix, AZ 85007
(602) 261-7011

HIGHWAY WELCOMING CENTERS

Willcox

WILLCOX CENTER - Interstate 10, east of Willcox.

Yuma

YUMA CENTER - Interstate 8, west of Yuma.

STATE POLICE

Department of Public Safety
P.O. Box 6638
Phoenix, AZ 85005
(602) 262-8011

HUNTING & FISHING

Hunting

Anyone age 14 or over hunting animals or

47

ARIZONA

HUNTING & FISHING (continued)

birds in Arizona must have in his possession either a Class G General Hunting License or a Class F Combination Hunting and Fishing license.

A person under age 14 may hunt wildlife other than big game when accompanied by a person 18 years of age or older holding a valid Arizona hunting license. No more than two unlicensed children may accompany each license holder. No person under the age of 14 may take big game without having satisfactorily completed the Arizona Firearms Safety Training Course. Appropriate licenses, tags and permits are required of all persons taking big game. No person under age 10 may be certified to hunt big game under the firearms safety course, but an attendance verification will be issued.

Resident

Fees charged for hunting and fishing licenses, tags, stamps and permits are as follows: Class F Combination Hunting and Fishing, $12; Class G General Hunting Licenses, $7; Javelina tag, $3; Turkey tag, $3; Bear tag, $2; Mountain Lion tag, $1; Deer tag, $4; Antelope tag, $20; Elk tag, $20; Bighorn Sheep tag, $50; Buffalo permit (residents only): Adult bulls, $500; Yearling, $160; Kaibab North Special Deer Hunting Permit, $5; Trapping license, $30.

Non-resident

Fees charged for hunting and fishing licenses, tags, stamps and permits are as follows: Class F Combination Hunting and Fishing, $45; Class G General Hunting licenses, $30; Javelina tag, $20; Turkey tag, $10; Bear tag, $25; Mountain Lion tag, $10; Deer tag, $30; Antelope tag, $50; Elk tag, $75; Bighorn Sheep tag, $250; Kaibab North Special Deer Hunting Permit, $5; Trapping license, $150.

Fishing

Any person fishing shall possess a valid fishing license, except that:(1) A resident or non-resident of the state under the age of 14 years may fish during the open season without a license; (2) A blind resident of the state may fish during the open season without a license.

A valid Nevada-Colorado River special use stamp and a valid Arizona fishing license, or a valid Arizona-Colorado River special use stamp and a valid Nevada fishing license are required of any person fishing from a boat or other floating device on the waters of Lake Mead, Lake Mohave, and the Colorado River forming the mutual boundary between Arizona and Nevada.

A valid California-Colorado River special use permit (stamp) and a valid Arizona fishing license, or a valid Arizona-Colorado River special use permit (stamp) and a valid California fishing license are required of any person fishing from a boat or other floating device on the waters of the Colorado River south of the Nevada-California boundary to Morelos Dam.

A valid Arizona fishing license or a valid Utah resident fishing license with an Arizona

Lake Powell stamp shall be required of any person fishing in the Arizona portion of Lake Powell.

Resident

Licenses: General fishing, $4; 1-day fishing, all species, $3; combination general all fishing and hunting, $12.

Stamps: Trout stamp for Class A, $3; California Colorado River, $3; Nevada-Colorado River, $3; Lake Powell (Utah portion), $6.

Non-resident

Licenses: General fishing, $12; 9-day fishing, all species, $8; 5-day fishing, all species, $6; 1-day fishing, all species, $3; Colorado River fishing, all species, $12; Combination General all fishing and hunting, $45.

Stamps: Trout stamp for Class A, $8; California Colorado River, $3; Nevada-Colorado River, $3.

For more information contact:

Arizona Game & Fish Department
2222 W. Greenway Road
Phoenix, AZ 85023
(602) 942-3000

CAMPGROUNDS

See Boating Areas, National Parks and State Parks.

RESORTS

Guest Ranches

Alpine

SPRUCEDALE RANCH
Alpine, AZ 85925
(602) 333-2156
FACILITIES: Horseback riding every morning; ranch work in the afternoon or trout fishing in nearby lakes and streams; weekly round-up and calf-branding; weekly gymkhana-type rodeo with ribbons for the winners.

Amado

REX RANCH
P.O. Box 87
Amado, AZ 85640
(602) 398-2311
FACILITIES: Horseback riding; heated swimming pool; frequent sight-seeing and shopping trips to Tucson, or Nogales on the Mexican border.

Douglas

PRICE CANYON RANCH
P.O. Box 1065
Douglas, AZ 85607
(602) 558-2383
FACILITIES: A year round working ranch - not a resort - where guests can participate in general ranch life; 10 hookups for trailers, campers or mobile homes; family-style meals; horseback riding; trail rides; fishing; trips to Agua Prieta, Mexico; summer riding program for children.

RESORTS (continued)

Globe

ELLISON RANCH
P.O. Box 2443
Globe, AZ 85501
No telephone.
FACILITIES: Pack trips for big game hunting or fishing.

Mesa

SAHUARD LAKE GUEST RANCH
P.O. Box 4066
Mesa, AZ 85201
(602) 985-1330
FACILITIES: Horseback riding in the Tonto Forest with some 20 different trails; noon cookouts, breakfast rides and moonlight rides; Saturday night Sundown Steak Fry; heated swimming pool; a variety of sports and games; golf nearby; lake fishing; boating; water skiing; excellent rock-hounding; bird watching; photography and painting opportunities.

Patagonia

CIRCLE Z RANCH
Patagonia, AZ 85624
(602) 287-2091 (Nogales)
FACILITIES: A working cattle ranch; horseback riding; heated pool; tennis; Audubon Sanctuary.

Payson

KOHL'S RANCH
Payson, AZ 85541
(602) 478-4211
FACILITIES: Cocktail lounge; coffee shop; grocery store; swimming pool; sauna baths and exercise rooms; horseback riding.

Pearce

SUNGLOW MISSION RANCH, INC.
Star Route
Pearce, AZ 85625
(602) 824-3364
FACILITIES: Horseback riding; hike; birdwatch; rock hunt; fish (bass filled lakes on the premises.); all units have kitchens; dishes; linens and tableware; no public food service.

Sasabe

RANCHO DE LA OSA
Sasabe, AZ 85633
(602) 323-4321
FACILITIES: Desert and mountain horseback riding; heated, outdoor swimming pool; recreation room; side trips to Desert Museum, Kitt Peak, and Mexico arranged.

Springerville

SOUTH FORK GUEST RANCH
P.O. Box 627
Springerville, AZ 85938
(602) 333-4456
FACILITIES: Fishing; swimming in heated pool; games; outdoor picnics and barbeques; biking trails; horseback riding facilities; Indian ruins; hunting and ski area.

Tucson

BRAVE BULL RANCH RESORT
Box 335, Route 19
Tucson, AZ 85704
(602) 792-4990
FACILITIES: Horseback riding; overnight pack horse trips; barbeques and cookouts; hay rides; sing-alongs; deluxe heated pool; tennis courts; shuffleboard; horse shoes; pool table; movies; hiking trails; bird watching; pilots fly directly to 3,200-foot airstrip, and a ranch wagon will pick you up.

DOUBLE U RANCH, INC.
P.O. Box 6148
Tucson, AZ 85733
(602) 749-4334
FACILITIES: Large heated pool; counselors for children during Christmas and Spring Vacations; fully equipped play area; horseback riding; cookouts; tennis; birding; golf; whirlpool bath and exercise room; ping-pong; shuffleboard; square dancing; movies; television and card rooms.

EL CARNILA RANCH
9061 E. Woodland (Tanque Verde Road)
Tucson, AZ 85715
(602) 298-2347
FACILITIES: Horseback riding; heated swimming pool; tennis; square dancing; movies.

ELKHORN RANCH
Sasabe Star Route
Tucson, AZ 85736
(602) 822-1040
FACILITIES: Desert and mountain riding; working cattle; swimming; tennis; bird watching; meals served family-style.

HACIENDA del SOL
Hacienda del Sol Road
Tucson, AZ 85718
(602) 299-1501
FACILITIES: Large library; heated pool; enclosed hot therapeutic pool; exercise room; shuffleboard; putting green; tennis court.

JACK JACKSON'S "SUNDANCER" RANCH (formerly)
Saddle and Surrey Ranch Resort
4110 Sweetwater Drive
Tucson, AZ 85705
(602) 743-0411
FACILITIES: Horseback riding; breakfast; cookout; day and moonlight rides; heated pool; tennis court; hydrotheraphy spa; putting green; pool table; shuffleboard; private sunning tower; dancing; sightseeing; 5 golf courses; bird watching.

LAZY K BAR RANCH
Route 9, Box 560
Tucson, AZ 85704
(602) 297-0702
FACILITIES: Horseback riding; tennis on lighted courts; breakfast rides; hayrides; cookouts; poolside buffets; dances; movies.

SAHUARO VISTA RANCH
Route 14, Box 554
Tucson, AZ 85704
(602) 297-0502
FACILITIES: Horseback riding; tennis; swim-

ARIZONA

RESORTS (continued)

ming; cookouts.

TANGQUE VERDE RANCH
Route 8, Box 66
Tucson, AZ 85710
(602) 296-6275
FACILITIES: Steak fries; breakfast cookouts; all-day rides; marked hiking trails; heated indoor and outdoor pools; jacuzzi pool; saunas; exercise room; 3 tennis courts; shuffleboard; putting green, with golf nearby; separate dining room and counselor supervision for children.

WHITE STALLION RANCH
Route 9, Box 567
Tucson, AZ 85704
(602) 297-0252
FACILITIES: Horseback riding; bird-watching; rock hunting; hiking; heated pool; redwood hot tub; therapy pool; 2 tennis courts; library; hayrides; movies; shuffleboard; croquet; ping-pong; a pool table; putting green; bridge; chess; rodeos; pet Longhorn steers and 60 pens of exotic birds.

WILD HORSE RANCH CLUB
P.O. Box 5505
Tucson, AZ 85703
(602) 297-2266
FACILITIES: Horseback riding; 200 species of birds seen within a 2 mile radius of the ranch; nature walk with 100 varieties of labeled desert vegetation; riding; heated pool; tennis courts; golf.

Tumacacori

RANCHO SANTA CRUZ
P.O. Box 8
Tumacacori, AZ 85640
(602) 398-2261
FACILITIES: Horseback riding; swimming pool; badminton; ping-pong; shuffleboard; horsehoes; archery; golf; cookouts; luncheon rides.

Wickenburg

DIAMOND P RANCH
P.O. Box S2
Wickenburg, AZ 85358
(602) 684-2169
FACILITIES: A working cattle ranch; accommodations for 12; references required.

FLYING E RANCH
P.O. Box EEE
Wickenburg, AZ 85358
(602) 684-2690
FACILITIES: Horseback riding; swimming; sauna; desert dining; golfing; tennis; ping-pong and shuffleboard.

RANCHO CASITAS
P.O. Drawer A-3
Wickenburg, AZ 85358
(602) 684-2628
FACILITIES: Horseback riding; swimming pool.

RANCH de los CABALLEROS
P.O. Box 1148
Wickenburg, AZ 85358
(602) 684-5484
FACILITIES: Horseback riding; tennis; golf; swimming; skeet; activities for the kids.

THE WICKENBURG INN TENNIS & GUEST RANCH
P.O. Box P
Wickenburg, AZ 85358
(602) 684-7811
FACILITIES: Weekly tennis clinics; horseback riding; resident naturalist; 2 fully equipped arts and crafts studios; swimming pool; special programs and counseling during holidays for children.

BOATING AREAS

Blythe

Blythe to Yuma (Colorado River)

COCOPAH INDIAN RESERVATION
FACILITIES: Launch ramp.

FISHER'S LANDING
FACILITIES: Launch ramp; campground; lodging; food; water; bathroom facilities; boat supplies; fuel.

HUNTER'S HOLE
FACILITIES: Launch ramp.

IMPERIAL OASIS
FACILITIES: Launch ramp; campground; food; water; bathroom facilities; boat supplies; fuel; repairs; sanitary station.

LAGUNA DAM
FACILITIES: Launch ramp; campground; food; water; bathroom facilities; fuel.

MARTINEZ LAKE
FACILITIES: Launch ramp; campground; lodging; food; water; bathroom facilities; boat supplies; fuel; repairs.

MITTRY LAKE
FACILITIES: Launch ramp; campground.

Carefree

BARTLETT LAKE
FACILITIES: Launch ramp; campground.

Flagstaff

UPPER LAKE MARY
FACILITIES: Launch ramp; campground; bathroom facilities.

Globe

SAN CARLOS LAKE
FACILITIES: Launch ramp; campground; food; bathroom facilities; fuel.

Holbrook

CHOLLA LAKE
FACILITIES: Launch ramp; bathroom facilities.

BOATING AREAS (continued)

Meadview

Lake Mead (See also Boating Areas - Nevada)

TEMPLE BAR
FACILITIES: Launch ramp; campground; lodging; food; water; bathroom facilities; boat supplies; fuel; repairs.

SOUTH COVE
FACILITIES: Launch ramp.

New River

LAKE PLEASANT
FACILITIES: Launch ramp; campground; food; water; bathroom facilities.

Page

Lake Powell (See also Boating Areas - Utah)

BULLFROG
FACILITIES: Launch ramp; campground; lodging; food; water; bathroom facilities; boat supplies; fuel; repairs; sanitary station.

HALLS CROSSING
FACILITIES: Launch ramp; campground; food; water; bathroom facilities; fuel; repairs.

HITE
FACILITIES: Campground; food; water; bathroom facilities; fuel.

RAINBOW BRIDGE
FACILITIES: Food; water; bathroom facilities; fuel.

WAHWEAP
FACILITIES: Launch ramp; campground; lodging; food; water; bathroom facilities; boat supplies; fuel; repairs; sanitary station.

Parker

Parker Dam to Headrock Dam (Colorado River)

AH-VILLA PARK
FACILITIES: Launch ramp; campground; water; bathroom facilities; sanitary station.

AQUA HOLIDAY RESORT
FACILITIES: Launch ramp; lodging; food; water; fuel.

BADENOCK'S RIVER MARINA
FACILITIES: Launch ramp; food; water; bathroom facilities; boat supplies; fuel; repairs.

BLUE WATER MARINA
FACILITIES: Launch ramp; campground; food; water; bathroom facilities; boat supplies; fuel; repairs.

BRANSON'S RESORT
FACILITIES: Launch ramp; lodging; water; bathroom facilities; fuel.

PLEASURE ISLAND
FACILITIES: Launch ramp; campgrounds; food; water; bathroom facilities; fuel.

RED ROCK
FACILITIES: Launch ramp; campground; food; water; bathroom facilities; fuel.

Patagonia

PATAGONIA LAKE
FACILITIES: Launch ramp; campground; food; bathroom facilities; boat supplies; fuel.

Roosevelt

Salt River Lake

APACHE LAKE
FACILITIES: Launch ramp; campground; lodging; food; water; bathroom facilities; fuel.

CANYON LAKE
FACILITIES: Launch ramp; campground; lodging; water; bathroom facilities; fuel; repairs.

ROOSEVELT LAKE
FACILITIES: Launch ramp; lodging; food; water; bathroom facilities; boat supplies; fuel; repairs.

St. Johns

LYMAN LAKE
FACILITIES: Launch ramp; campground; food; water; bathroom facilities.

Wenden

Bill Williams River

ALAMO LAKE
FACILITIES: Launch ramp; campground; water; bathroom facilities; sanitary station.

Willow Beach

Lake Mohave (See also Boating Areas - Nevada)

KATHERINE LANDING
FACILITIES: Launch ramp; campground; lodging; food; water; bathroom facilities; fuel; repairs; sanitary station.

WILLOW BEACH
FACILITIES: Launch ramp; campground; lodging; food; water; bathroom facilities; boat supplies; fuel; repairs; sanitary station.

BICYCLE TRAILS

CANYONS AND MESAS TRAIL - 232 mi; mountainous terrain, canyons, steep grade, high elevation from 2,900 to 6,800 feet, possible heavy traffic; 10-speed bicycle necessary.

This is a great one-week trip for experienced cyclists during the spring or fall. The South Rim of the Grand Canyon offers campgrounds, lodge accommodations, stores; hiking and breath-taking scenery. The ride to Flagstaff is across a high plateau of forest and scrub.

Trail: South Rim of Grand Canyon, south to Flagstaff, Alternate 89 to Sedona to Clark-

ARIZONA

BICYCLE TRAILS (continued)

dale to Jerome to Prescott to Yarnell to Wickenburg.

FLAGSTAFF FOREST TRAIL - 100 mi; short distances, mountainous terrain, high elevations. 3-speed & 10-speed bicycles.

This is high country with elevations ranging from 5,500 to 7,000 feet. However, it is a relatively short trip, and many families could try this one during this summer or early fall.

Trail: Flagstaff to Mormon Lake to Happy Jack to Long Valley to Pine to Payson.

PETRIFIED FOREST TRAIL - 30 mi; any bicycle. Along the route you will view such unusual items as a bridge consisting of an agate log, Indian petroglyphs, and the painted desert. Spring and fall are the best seasons. The summer period is hot but not impossible; and the winters are very cold.

Trail: Visitors Center just off of I-S 40 (old US 66) to the Rainbow Forest entrance just off of US 180.

SAGUARO FOREST TRAIL - 20 mi.; poor road surfaces; 10-speed bicycle recommended. This is a rough ride of about 20 mi. with gravel and dirt a good part of the way and many dips in the road, but you pass through a wonderland of Saguaro cactus.

Trail: "The Outfit" youth Hostel near Cortaro, about 13 mi. north of Tucson, to the Desert Museum, then return to the hostel.

TORTILLA FLAT TRAIL - 34 mi.; hilly terrain; 10-speed bicycle recommended.

This ride starts fairly flat, then gets into a few hills and ends with some long climbs. A good late fall, winter, or early spring ride. If there has been some rain in the mountains you will have to ford Tortilla Creek. The creek has a solid bottom and markers to tell you the depth of the water.

Trail: Apache Junction, 30 mi. east of Phoenix, to Tortilla Flat.

TRAILS

Phoenix

NORTH MOUNTAIN TRAIL - .9 mi. foot trail. In North Mountain Park, 10 mi. north of the center of Phoenix, this trail begins at the 1,400-foot contour and terminates at an observation platform at the 2,138-foot level, providing a panoramic view of the area. The trail passes interesting formations of sandstone, schist and granite, and sparse amounts of cactus, mesquite, ironwood, and greasewood.

SOUTH MOUNTAIN PARK TRAIL - 14 mi. foot trail. The trail, located in the center of South Mountain Park, is on desert terrain, sparsely vegetated with brush and a wide variety of cactus and other plant life. Unusual geologic formations can be seen. This is the initial component of a proposed 110-mi. loop trail for hiking and riding, originally conceived by the Arizona State Horsemen's Association. There is an extensive network of connecting trails.

SQUAW PEAK TRAIL - 1.2 mi. foot trail. The trail, located in Squaw Peak Park, ascends Squaw Peak along a series of switch-backs through fissured ledges, to the bare rock summit. There is a pronounced grade with several moderate-to-near-level portions. The environment is sparsely vegetated desert in a gravelly, sand-like soil. Birds and small mammals are plentiful. An observation point below the summit provides a good trail terminus for those not wishing to climb the last steep segment.

Picacho Peak State Park

HUNTER TRAIL - 2.3 mi. foot trail. The trail starts near the park entrance, some 45 mi. west of Tucson, and ascends to the summit of Picacho Peak. The peak is a fairly well preserved volcanic cone. Vegetation is sparse and is comprised of cactus, typical of the Sonoran Desert, as well as some introduced species. The area supports small mammals and reptiles, wild burros, and coyotes. The peak provides a 360-degree panorama of surrounding lands, distant mountains, and sheer cliffs up to 1,000 feet high.

SKI AREAS

Flagstaff

ARIZONA SNOW BOWL
P.O. Box 158
Flagstaff, AZ 86002
(602) 774-0562
LOCATION: 7 mi. off U.S. 180 north of Flagstaff in the San Francisco Peaks.
FACILITIES: Riblet double chair lift; Poma lift, 3 handle tows; one tow rope; ski rentals; ski instructions; toboggan and whirlybird runs; 20 miles of trails for beginners through expert skiers; restaurants; inns; lodges; open 7 days a week, 9 a.m. - 4 p.m., Thanksgiving to Easter.

McNary

SUNRISE SKI AREA
Box 217
McNary, AZ 85930
(602) 334-2144
LOCATION: 6 mi. west of State Route 73, between McNary and Springerville.
FACILITIES: 3 double chair lifts; mighty mite lift; ski rentals; ski instructions; snowmobile rentals; 15 runs to accommodate beginners through experts; restaurants; inns; lodges; open 7 days a week, Nov. - Apr.

Mount Lemmon

MOUNT LEMMON SKI VALLEY
Box 612
Mount Lemmon, AZ 85619
(602) 791-9721
LOCATION: 33 mi. northeast from Tucson.
FACILITIES: Herron-Poma double chair lifts; pony lift; longest run, 3 mi.; ski rentals; ski instructions; whirlybird runs; beginners to expert slopes; restaurants; inns; lodges; open 7 days a week, year round, but usual season runs from Dec. - Apr.

SKI AREAS (continued)

Williams

BILL WILLIAMS SKI AREA
Kaibab National Forest
Williams Ranger District
Box 434
Williams, AZ 86046
(602) 635-2633
LOCATION: 4 mi. south of Williams on
Route 66.
FACILITIES: Poma lift; tow rope; ski rentals;
ski instruction; beginner's area but some expert runs; snack bar; lodge; inns; open: weekends and Christmas Holiday Season.

AMUSEMENT PARKS & ATTRACTIONS

Phoenix

ROYAL LONDON WAX MUSEUM (Attraction)
5555 E. Van Buren
Phoenix, AZ 85008
(602) 273-1368
FACILITIES: 150 wax figures; 45 scenes; exhibits; gift shop; open all year.

Scotsdale

RAWHIDE (Attraction)
23023 N. Scotsdale Road
Scotsdale, AZ 85252
(602) 992-6111
FACILITIES: 2 kiddie rides; walk thru; 2 refreshment stands; restaurants; museum; stage shows; free gate; free parking.

Tempe

BIG SURF
1500 N. Hayden Road
Tempe, AZ 85281
(602) 947-2478
FACILITIES: Ocean swimming; surfing in world's largest filtered swimming lagoon; arcade; swimming pool; bathing beach; 300' surf slide; ice rink; 5 refreshment stands; pay gate; free parking; open Mar. 15 - Sept. 30.

LEGEND CITY (Attraction)
1200 W. Washington Street
Tempe, AZ 85281
(602) 275-8551
FACILITIES: 25 major rides; 10 kiddie rides; 10 games; 12 refreshment stands; 4 restaurants; 12 shops; gold panning; 2 arcades; shooting gallery; picnic facilities; zoo; paddle boats; 18 hole miniature golf; theatre; name bands; orchestra; stage shows; vaudeville; fireworks; free acts; pay gate; free parking; open Mar. - Dec.

Tucson

OLD TUCSON (Attraction)
201 S. Kinney Road
Tucson, AZ 85705
(602) 883-0100

FACILITIES: Theme rides; walk thrus; 4 refreshment stands; 2 restaurants; ice cream parlor; old fashioned 1890 town; working movie lot; arcade; picnic facilities; old-fashioned movie theatre; live action gunfight & stunt shows; exhibits & museums of Old West & motion picture sound stage tours; stage shows; original ranch set of High Chaparral & countless T.V. & commercials; fireworks; pay gate; free parking; open all year.

STATE FAIR

Arizona State Fair
1826 West McDowell
Phoenix, AZ 85005
(602) 252-6771
DATE: October

NATIONAL PARKS

Grand Canyon

GRAND CANYON NATIONAL PARK
Grand Canyon, AZ 86023
(602) 638-2443

NORTH RIM
LOCATION: 13 mi. south of north entrance.
FACILITIES: Open May - Oct.; entrance fee; limit of stay: 7 days; 82 sites; group camps: 1; NPS campsite fee: $3; water and bathroom facilities; sanitary station; cabins; laundry; picnic area; food service; boating; hiking; horseback riding; bicycle trail; exhibit; museum; environmental study area; NPS guided tour; self-guiding tour; medical service.

DESERT VIEW
LOCATION: ½ mi. west of east entrance.
FACILITIES: Open May - Oct.; entrance fee; limit of stay: 7 days; 50 sites; NPS campsite fee: $2; water and bathroom facilities; cabins; picnic area; food service; boating; hiking; bicycle trail; exhibit; museum; environmental study area; NPS guided tour; self-guiding tour; medical service.

MATHER
LOCATION: Grand Canyon Village.
FACILITIES: Open year round; entrance fee; limit of stay: 7 days; 327 sites; group camps: 7; NPS campsite fee: $3; water and bathroom facilities; sanitary station; cabins; laundry; picnic area; food service; boating; hiking; bicycle trail; exhibit; museum; environmental study area; NPS guided tour; self-guiding tour; medical service; reservations by mail, Jun. 1 - Sept. 1.

MONUMENT
LOCATION: Toroweap Point.
FACILITIES: Open year round; limit of stay: 14 days; 10 sites.

TRAILER VILLAGE
LOCATION: Grand Canyon Village.
FACILITIES: Open year round; limit of stay: 7 days; water and bathroom facilities; sanitary

ARIZONA

NATIONAL PARKS (continued)

station; trailer village vehicle sites and fee: 192, $4; laundry; food service.

BRIGHT ANGEL CREEK
LOCATION: Phantom Ranch.
FACILITIES: Open year round; limit of stay: 2 days; 75 sites; water and bathroom facilities; hike in campgrounds; reservations; no wood or charcoal fires.

COTTONWOOD
LOCATION: North Kaibab Trail.
FACILITIES: Open Apr. - Oct.; limit of stay: 2 days; 40 sites; water and bathroom facilities; fishing; hike-in campground; reservations; no wood or charcoal fires.

INDIAN GARDENS
LOCATION: Bright Angel Trail.
FACILITIES: Open year round; limit of stay: 2 days; 75 sites; water and bathroom facilities; hike-in campground; reservations; no wood or charcoal fires.

NATIONAL FORESTS

National Forests
Southwestern Region
517 Gold Avenue, SW
Albuquerque, NM 87102
(505) 766-2444

Flagstaff

COCONINO NATIONAL FOREST
ATTRACTIONS: Graceful San Francisco Peaks, 12,611 feet, highest in Arizona. Numerous national monuments nearby plus Lowell Astronomical Observatory, Museum of Northern Arizona, Flagstaff; Meteor Crater near Painted Desert. Deer, antelope, turkey, elk, mountain lion hunting; lake and stream fishing; horseback riding; boating on Lake Mary.
FACILITIES: 16 camp and picnic sites, 15 picnic only; Arizona Snow Bowl Winter Sports Area. Resort hotels, dude ranches.
NEARBY TOWNS: Camp Verde, Clarkdale, Cottonwood, Sedona, and Winslow.

Holbrook

SITGREAVES NATIONAL FOREST
ATTRACTIONS: Pueblo ruins; deer, turkey, antelope, bear hunting. Saddle and pack trips.
FACILITIES: Public golf and swimming at White Mountain Country Club; 8 camp and picnic sites, 3 picnic only; numerous resorts, hotels, summer homes, guest ranches.
NEARBY TOWNS: Lakeside, Pinetop, Show Low, Snowflake, Winslow.

Phoenix

TONTO NATIONAL FOREST
ATTRACTIONS: Semidesert to pine-fir forests, lakes, boating, swimming, skindiving, water skiing, bass fishing, public boat ramps at most lakes. Boats and tackle also for rent. Limited trout fishing in high country; deer, elk, bear, javelina, turkey and mountain lion hunting. Saddle and pack trips. Scenic drive.

FACILITIES: 42 camp and picnic sites, 13 picnic only; no lifeguards. Resorts, dude ranches.
NEARBY TOWNS: Globe, Mesa, Miami, Payson, Pine, Superior, and Young.

Prescott

PRESCOTT NATIONAL FOREST
ATTRACTIONS: Rugged back country, many roads primitive. Limited trout fishing. Jerome, nation's largest ghost town. Deer, antelope, dove, quail hunting; horse trails; scenic drives.
FACILITIES: 18 camp and picnic sites, 1 picnic only. Resorts, motels, and dude ranches.
NEARBY TOWNS: Clarkdale, Cottonwood, Jerome, Mayer.

Springerville

APACHE NATIONAL FOREST
ATTRACTIONS: Scenic Coronado Trail and other drives through spruce and mountain-meadow country. Cliff dwellings; lake and stream trout fishing. Elk, deer, bear, antelope, turkey hunting. Horseback riding; pack trips; hiking.
FACILITIES: 30 camp and picnic sites, 4 picnic only; boats without motors for rent on Big and Luna Lakes. Resorts and motels.
NEARBY TOWNS: Alpine, Greer, Luna and Reserve, NM.

Tuscon

CORONADO NATIONAL FOREST
ATTRACTIONS: Rugged mountains rising abruptly from surrounding deserts; cactus to fir trees, swimming to skiing in an hour's time - 40 miles apart. Mount Lemmon Snow Bowl, southernmost winter sports area in the Continental U.S. Bass fishing 4 miles from the international boundary with Mexico. Nearby are Arizona-Sonora Desert Museum, Colossal Cave State Park, Tucson Mountain Park. Deer, javelina, mountain lion, quail, dove hunting. Scenic drives; pack-trip and hiking trails (caution: carry adequate water). Dude ranch and winter resort country.
FACILITIES: 22 camp and picnic sites, 27 picnic only.
NEARBY TOWNS: Benson, Bisbee, Mexican border towns of Douglas and Nogales, Fort Huachuca, Patagonia, Safford, San Simon, Tombstone and Wilcox.

Williams

KAIBAB NATIONAL FOREST
ATTRACTIONS: Grand Canyon National Game Preserve with the famous North Kaibab deer herd, a wild buffalo herd and the only habitat of the Kaibab squirrel. Indian village in Havasu Canyon. Deer, elk, antelope, bear, mountain lion, turkey and limited buffalo hunting. Scenic drives, fishing, riding, pack trips. Photographic opportunities; wildlife and vivid geologic formations.
FACILITIES: 8 camp and picnic sites, 1 picnic only. Motels, resorts, guest ranches. Hunting camps with groceries open in season.
NEARBY TOWNS: Ashfork, Cottonwood, Flagstaff, Fredonia, Grand Canyon, Kanab, Utah.

NATIONAL FORESTS (continued)

See GILA NATIONAL FOREST - New Mexico.

STATE PARKS

Arizona State Parks
1688 West Adams
Phoenix, AZ 85007
(602) 271-4174

Apache Junction

LOST DUTCHMAN STATE PARK
LOCATION: 6 mi. northeast of Apache Junction on AZ 88.
FACILITIES: Open year round; water and bathroom facilities; picnic area; hiking; self-guided trail.

Camp Verde

FORT VERDE STATE PARK
LOCATION: 3 mi. east of I-17.
FACILITIES: Open year round; water and bathroom facilities; sanitary station; picnic area; museum; living history program; medical service.

Cottonwood

DEAD HORSE STATE PARK
LOCATION: Across the river from Cottonwood, enter on N 5th Street.
FACILITIES: Open year round; 45 sites; water and bathroom facilities; sanitary station; electrical hookup; picnic area; fishing; hiking.

Florence

MCFARLAND STATE PARK
LOCATION: In town.
FACILITIES: Open year round; water and bathroom facilities; museum; living history program; medical service.

Gila Bend

PAINTED ROCK STATE PARK
LOCATION: 12 mi. west of Gila Bend.
FACILITIES: Open year round; 25 sites; water and bathroom facilities; picnic area; playground; hiking; living history program.

Jerome

JEROME STATE PARK
LOCATION: In town.
FACILITIES: Open year round; water and bathroom facilities; picnic area; museum; living history program.

Lake Havasu City

LAKE HAVASU STATE PARK

CATTAIL COVE
LOCATION: 15 mi. south of Lake Havasu City, 1 mi. west of Route 95.
FACILITIES: Open year round; 90 sites; water and bathroom facilities; sanitary station; electrical hookup; picnic area; food service; swimming; boating; boat rental; fishing; hiking.

PITTSBURG POINT
LOCATION: West of Lake Havasu City across London Bridge.
FACILITIES: Open year round; 718 sites; water and bathroom facilities; sanitary station; electrical hookup; picnic area; playground; food service; swimming; boating; fishing; medical service; motel.

WINDSOR BEACH
LOCATION: North of London Bridge at end of Crystal Ave.
FACILITIES: Open year round; water and bathroom facilities; picnic area; swimming; boating; fishing; hiking.

Nogales

PATAGONIA LAKE STATE PARK
LOCATION: 12 mi. east of Nogales on Route 82; 4 mi. north on gravel road.
FACILITIES: Open year round; 300 sites; water and bathroom facilities; sanitary station; electrical hookup; picnic area; food service; swimming; boating; fishing; hiking; self-guided trail.

Parker

BUCKSKIN STATE PARK
LOCATION: 11 mi. north of Parker on Route 95.
FACILITIES: Open year round; 48 sites; water and bathroom facilities; sanitary station; electrical hookup; picnic area; playground; food service; swimming; boating; fishing; hiking; self-guided trail.

Safford

ROPER LAKE STATE PARK
LOCATION: 6 mi. south of Safford, ½ mi. east of U.S. 666.
FACILITIES: Open year round; 24 sites; water and bathroom facilities; picnic area; playground; swimming; boating; fishing; hiking; self-guided trail.

St. Johns

LYMAN STATE PARK
LOCATION: 11 mi. south of St. Johns, 1 mi. east of U.S. 666.
FACILITIES: Open year round; 46 sites; water and bathroom facilities; sanitary station; electrical hookup; picnic area; food service; swimming; boating; boat rental; fishing; hiking; self-guided trail.

Superior

BOYCE THOMPSON STATE PARK
LOCATION: 3 mi. west of Superior.
FACILITIES: Open year round; water and bathroom facilities; picnic area; swimming; hiking; self-guided trail.

Tombstone

TOMBSTONE STATE PARK
LOCATION: In town.
FACILITIES: Open year round; water and bathroom facilities; museum; living history program; medical service.

ARIZONA

STATE PARKS (continued)

Tubac

TUBAC STATE PARK
LOCATION: In town.
FACILITIES: Open year round; water and bathroom facilities; picnic area; museum; living history program.

Tucson

PICACHO PEAK STATE PARK
LOCATION: 35 mi. north of Tucson on I-10.
FACILITIES: Open year round; 29 sites; water and bathroom facilities; electrical hookup; picnic area; swimming; boating; fishing; hiking; self-guided trail.

Wenden

ALAMO LAKE STATE PARK
LOCATION: 38 mi. north of U.S. 60-70 at Wenden.
FACILITIES: Open year round; 450 sites; water and bathroom facilities; sanitary station; electrical hookup; picnic area; food service; swimming; boating; boat rental; fishing; hiking; self-guided trail.

Yuma

YUMA STATE PARK
LOCATION: In town.
FACILITIES: Open year round; water and bathroom facilities; picnic area; museum; living history program.

STATE FORESTS

There are no State Forests in Arizona.

HISTORIC SITES

Camp Verde

MONTEZUMA CASTLE NATIONAL MONUMENT - Its history shrouded in the mist of centuries, located near Camp Verde.

Clarkdale

TUZIGOOT NATIONAL MONUMENT - A pre-Columbian ruin dating about 1300 A.D. Two mi. east of Clarkdale.

Clifton

CORONADO TRAIL - Scenic trail said to have been followed by the Spanish Explorer, Coronado, in his trek northward in search of the fabulous Seven Cities of Cibola; U.S. 666 from Clifton to Alpine.

Cochise

COCHISE STRONGHOLD - 10½ mi. from U.S. Highway 666, in the heart of the Dragoon Mountains. For many years the hiding place of the famous Apache chief.

Coolidge

CASA GRANDE RUINS NATIONAL MONUMENT - The well-preserved ruins of a four-storied prehistoric community dwelling near Coolidge, with remains of an extensive canal system.

Flagstaff

WALNUT CANYON NATIONAL MONUMENT - Many cliff-dwellings make this one of the most interesting points in the state.

WUPATKI NATIONAL MONUMENT - Between Flagstaff and Tuba City, prehistoric Indian ruins.

Grand Canyon

THE GRAND CANYON NATIONAL MONUMENT AND PARK - The world's greatest natural wonder. For 200 mi. the Colorado River flows through this great canyon, appearing a mere thread when viewed from the rim a mile above.

Jerome

JEROME - Historic mining town picturesquely located on a steep mountainside, liveliest ghost city in America. Jerome Mine Museum is a treasure-house of archaeological, mining and historical lore.

Kingman

HOOVER DAM - Located 72 mi. north of Kingman, the largest of all federal reclamation projects and one of the greatest feats of all time. Hoover Dam is the highest concrete dam in the U.S. 727 feet high, reservoir 115 mi. long, covering 227 square mi. with a storage capacity of 30,500,000 acre feet.

Lake Havasu City

LONDON BRIDGE - Lake Havasu City and Lake Havasu State Park. The transplanting of the famed London Bridge to the desert shores of Arizona has generated an unusual tourist interest to this area.

Lee's Ferry

NAVAJO BRIDGE - 7 mi. below the historic Lee's Ferry. The bridge floor is 467 feet above the water level of the Colorado River, the span across being 616 feet in length.

Moccasin

PIPE SPRINGS NATIONAL MONUMENT - One of Arizona's historical and picturesque spots, a landmark of pioneer history.

Phoenix

PUEBLO GRANDE - Ancient Indian ruin in Phoenix, extensively excavated, flourished about 1200 A.D.

HISTORIC SITES (continued)

Prescott

PRESCOTT TERRITORIAL CAPITOL - Site of the first capitol of Arizona Territory. Also Sharlot Hall Museum, The Plaza (Bucky O'Neil Rough Rider's Statue), Smoki Museum.

Second Mesa

HOPI INDIAN VILLAGES - Walpi, Oraibi, Hateville, Shongapovi, and so on, where the annual and world-famous snake dance is held late in Aug. These villages may be reached from Holbrook, Winslow and Flagstaff. Oraibi is believed to be the oldest continuously inhabited village in North America, dating back to 1200 A.D.

Sentinel

PAINTED DESERT - Here Nature has swung a reckless brush and painted the mountainside sands to gorgeous hues.

Tombstone

TOMBSTONE - An old mining town "too tough to die," features Boothill Graveyard, Wells Fargo Museum and the O.K. Corral.

Tucson

MISSION SAN XAVIER DEL BAC - Located 9 mi. south of Tucson, this mission is conceded to be the most beautiful mission structure in the Southwest. Established 1700. Original mission destroyed in Pima Revolt of 1751. Present mission built by Franciscans during 1783-1797.

OLD TUCSON - In Tucson Mt. Park, 13 mi. southwest of Tucson. Reconstructed village showing Tucson as it appeared in the middle 1880s. Over 60 motion pictures filmed here.

Tumacacori

TUMACACORI MISSION NATIONAL MONUMENT - Established in 1690 by the Jesuit priest, Father Kino, the ruins of this structure show the Spanish influence characteristic of all historic missions.

Willcox

CHIRICAHUA NATIONAL MONUMENT - Nature has fashioned a weird and silent community through the erosive agency of wind and water. Sometimes called Rhyolite Park or Wonderland of Rocks.

Window Rock

WINDOW ROCK - Capitol of the Navajo Indians. Museum located nearby.

Winslow

METEOR CRATER - Regarded as one of Arizona's strangest wonders, formed perhaps by the landing of some visitor from outer space.

HOSTELS

Flagstaff

1ST CONGREGATIONAL CHURCH
740 N. Turquoise Drive
Flagstaff, AZ 86001
(602) 774-0890
FACILITIES: Open year round; 15 beds, men; 15 beds, women (foam pads); modern bathrooms; nearest hostel: Holbrook, 97 mi. SE; overnight charge: $2.

Holbrook

ARIZONA RANCHO MOTOR LODGE
Corner of Apache Dr. & Tovar St.
Holbrook, AZ 86025
(602) 524-6770
FACILITIES: Open year round; 10 beds, men; 10 beds, women, also family rooms; modern bathroom; nearest hostel: Flagstaff, 97 mi. W; overnight charges: $3; houseparent: Mrs. Lloyd M. Taylor.

Phoenix

SOUTH MOUNTAIN YOUTH HOSTEL
1346 E. South Mountain Avenue
Phoenix, AZ 85040
(602) 268-3723
FACILITIES: Open year round; 12 beds, men; 12 beds, women; modern bathroom; nearest hostel: Flagstaff, 180 mi.; overnight charges: $2; houseparents: David and Phyllis Harkins.

POINTS OF INTEREST

Ajo

ORGAN PIPE CACTUS NATIONAL MONUMENT - South of Ajo and bordering on Mexico. This cactus is so named because its branches resemble the pipes of the pipe organ.

Apache Junction

APACHE TRAIL - Beginning at Apache Junction, 34 mi. east of Phoenix, this world-famous trail winds through gorgeous mountain scenery to Globe. Highlights of this trip are the dams and lakes on the Salt River.

Bisbee

LAVENDER PIT - Located at Bisbee, an important copper development of the Phelps-Dodge Corporation.

Flagstaff

SUNSET CRATER NATIONAL MONUMENT - A cone-shaped crater of volcanic cinder, near Flagstaff, gray at the base and tapering to a red tip, which reflects the rays of the sun with gorgeous effect.

Kingman

DAVIS DAM - This dam, built to harness the lower Colorado River, is 67 river miles below

ARIZONA

POINTS OF INTEREST (continued)

Hoover Dam and 32 mi. west of Kingman. Its reservoir, Lake Mohave, has a capacity of 1,890,000 acre feet.

Phoenix

DESERT BOTANICAL GARDEN - Only one of its kind in the U.S. Blooming season is from late February to May. Located on E. Van Buren Street.

Scottsdale

SCOTTSDALE - "The West's most western town" includes reconstructed storefronts and arts and crafts shops.

Tucson

ARIZONA-SONDORA DESERT MUSEUM - This museum, located in Tucson Mountains 16 mi. west of Tucson, features exhibits of desert botany, zoology, geology, and anthropology. Nature trails and live animal collections are outstanding.

COLOSSAL CAVE - One of the state's wonders, 28 mi. southwest of Tucson.

Yuma

TERRITORIAL PRISON - For 33 years in territorial days, this prison at Yuma housed some of the most dangerous and daring desperados of the wild and wooly West.

ARKANSAS

America's only diamond producing state, Arkansas entered the Union in 1836 as the twenty-fifth state. A quarter of a century later, the state, decidedly in favor of the Union at the onset of the Civil War, suddenly seceded when asked by President Lincoln to provide support troops.

Arkansas is among the states leading in the production of livestock, especially razorback hogs, rice, soybeans, bauxite ore, from which aluminum is derived, and lumber.

Tourism plays a major role in the state's economy, also, aided by the excellent hunting and fishing. Well over half of the state is thickly forested and the hundreds of unspoiled rivers, lakes and streams add to Arkansas's wild and picturesque terrain. In addition, world famous Hot Springs National Park with its 47 thermal springs draws thousands of people each year to immerse themselves in the soothing waters of the natural health spa.

State capital: Little Rock. State bird: Mockingbird. State tree: Pine. State flower: Apple blossom.

WEATHER

Arkansas is divided geographically into two principal divisions. The dividing line between these two sections cuts diagonally across the state from the northeast to the southwest. West and north of this line are the interior highlands; to the east and south are the lowlands. Climatic differences between the two areas are not as great as the local differences between mountain and valley stations in the highlands. Generally, the climate of western and northern Arkansas is a little cooler and there are greater temperature extremes; humidities are lower and there is less cloudiness.

Average temperatures show little variation over the state. Temperatures vary more from northwest to southeast in winter than in summer. Maximum temperatures exceed 100 degrees F at times during July and August, particularly at valley stations in the highlands. The winters are short, but cold periods of brief duration do occur. In the northern part of the state, zero temperatures occasionally occur in January and February and zero has been recorded along the southern border. The absolute temperature range for the state is from 120 degrees to minus 29 degrees F.

Average daily temperature for each month.

	Northern	Southern
Jan.	51.4 to 23.7	55.1 to 31.3
Feb.	55.2 to 27.1	59.6 to 34.2
Mar.	62.4 to 34.0	67.1 to 40.8
Apr.	74.0 to 45.4	76.8 to 51.3
May	80.7 to 52.8	83.6 to 59.1
Jun.	88.1 to 61.0	90.5 to 66.8
Jul.	92.2 to 64.7	93.6 to 70.2
Aug.	91.7 to 62.6	93.2 to 68.5
Sept.	85.3 to 56.0	87.9 to 62.0
Oct.	75.9 to 44.0	78.2 to 50.0
Nov.	62.6 to 33.8	66.1 to 39.4
Dec.	53.6 to 27.0	57.2 to 33.5
Year	72.8 to 44.3	75.7 to 50.6

STATE CHAMBER OF COMMERCE

Arkansas State Chamber of Commerce
911 Wallace Building
Little Rock, AR 72201
(501) 374-9225

STATE & CITY TOURISM OFFICES

State

Arkansas Department of Parks & Tourism
149 State Capitol Building
Little Rock, AR 72201
(501) 371-7777

Arkansas Industrial Development Commission
205 State Capitol Building
Little Rock, AR 72201
(501) 371-2052

Local

Hot Springs Convention Bureau
P.O. Box 1500
Hot Springs, AR 71901
(501) 321-1703

Little Rock Chamber of Commerce
1 Spring Building
Little Rock, AR 72201
(501) 374-4871

STATE HIGHWAY DEPARTMENT

Arkansas State Highway and Transportation Department
State Highway Department Building
9500 New Benton Highway
Little Rock, AR 72202
(501) 569-2000

HIGHWAY WELCOMING CENTERS

Ashdown

ASHDOWN TOURIST CENTER - Hwy. 71 north.

Bentonville

BENTONVILLE WELCOME CENTER - Hwy. 71 south, near Missouri border.

Blytheville

BLYTHEVILLE CENTER - Interstate 55 south, near Missouri and Tennessee border.

Corning

CORNING WELCOME CENTER - Interstate 67 south, near Missouri border.

Dora

DORA/VAN BUREN CENTER - Interstate 40 east, near Fort Smith.

El Dorado

EL DORADO CENTER - Interstate 167 north.

Texarkana

TEXARKANA TOURIST CENTER - Interstate 30 north.

West Memphis

WEST MEMPHIS CENTER - Interstate 40 west.

STATE POLICE

Department of Public Safety
P.O. Box 4005
Little Rock, AR 72214
(501) 371-2151

HUNTING & FISHING

Hunting

Resident

All persons who have established a bonafide or actual residence of at least sixty (60) days prior to applying for a license, and who declare their intentions of becoming a citizen of Arkansas are residents. Servicemen stationed in Arkansas, and servicemen from Arkansas stationed out of state, are considered residents. Also, any student enrolled in any college or university in Arkansas is considered as a resident. Possession of property in Arkansas does not itself constitute residency.

Non-resident

Seasons vary from year to year and non-resident license fees vary according to species hunted. For complete hunting and fishing information write: Arkansas Game & Fish Commission.

Fishing

License and trout permit not required on any person, resident or non-resident, under 16 years of age. No closed season on sport fishing in Arkansas.

Resident

Fishing license, $7.50; trout permit (required in addition to license) $3.

Non-resident

14 day trip license, $7.50; non-resident annual, $10.30; trout permit (required in addition to license), $3.

For more information contact:

Arkansas Game & Fish Commission
No. 2 Capitol Mall
Little Rock, AR 72201
(501) 371-1025

ARKANSAS

CAMPGROUNDS

Private

Alma

KOA - FORT SMITH/ALMA
Rt. 2, Box 203A
Alma, AR 72921
(501) 632-2704
FACILITIES: Open year round; 60 sites.

Arkadelphia

KOA - LAKE DEGRAY
P.O. Box 555
Arkadelphia, AR 71923
(501) 246-4922
FACILITIES: Open year round; 90 sites.

Bluff City

WHITE OAK LAKE
Bluff City, AR 71722
(501) 685-2748
FACILITIES: Open year round; 300 sites.

Bull Shoals

RIVERSIDE MOBILE & RIVER PARK
P.O. Box 167
Lakeview, AR 72642
(501) 431-8260
FACILITIES: Open year round; 60 sites.

Carlisle

PONDEROSA CAMPGROUND
Carlisle, AR 72024
(501) 552-3304
FACILITIES: Open year round; 50 sites.

Clinton

RAINBOW RANCH CAMPING PARK
Clinton, AR 72031
No telephone.
FACILITIES: Open year round; 50 sites.

Cotter

KOA - WHITE RIVER
Box 99
Cotter, AR 72626
(501) 453-2299
FACILITIES: Open year round; 105 sites.

Dogpatch

MILL CREEK CAMPGROUND
Dogpatch, AR 72648
(501) 446-5507
FACILITIES: Open year round; 50 sites.

Eureka Springs

KOA - EUREKA SPRINGS
RFD 2
Eureka Springs, AR 72632
(501) 253-9916
FACILITIES: Open year round; 110 sites.

PINE HAVEN CAMPGROUND
Eureka Springs, AR 72632
(501) 253-9930

FACILITIES: Open year round; 55 sites.

Hardy

KELLEY'S SPRING RIVER CAMPGROUND
Hardy, AR 72542
(501) 856-3753
FACILITIES: Open year round; 235 sites.

Harrison

KOA - HARRISON
RFD 2, Box 20
Harrison, AR 72601
(501) 743-2000
FACILITIES: Open year round; 83 sites.

OZARK SAFARI CAMP
Box 932
Harrison, AR 72601
(501) 743-2343
FACILITIES: Open year round; 75 sites.

ROCK CANDY MOUNTAIN CAMP-
GROUND
Hwy. 7 South
Harrison, AR 72601
(501) 743-1531
FACILITIES: Open year round; 100 sites.

Heber Springs

BILL LINDSEY'S RAINBOW RESORT AND
TROUT DOCK
Rt. 3, Box 89
Heber Springs, AR 72543
(501) 362-8857
FACILITIES: Open year round; 100 sites.

Hot Springs

KOA - HOT SPRINGS
P.O. Box 1218
Hot Springs, AR 71901
(501) 624-5912
FACILITIES: Open year round; 114 sites.

PHIL'S TRAILER CITY
938 Whittington
Hot Springs, AR 71901
(501) 623-3062
FACILITIES: Open year round; 50 sites.

Little Rock Area

KOA - BENTON
RFD 7, Box 1440
Benton, AR 72015
(501) 778-1244
FACILITIES: Open year round; 87 sites.

YOGI BEAR'S JELLYSTONE PARK CAMP-
GROUND
Rt. 1, Box 772
Benton, AR 72015
(501) 778-7222
FACILITIES: Open year round; 113 sites.

KOA - NORTH LITTLE ROCK
P.O. Box 917
North Little Rock, AR 72115
(501) 758-4598
FACILITIES: Open year round; 100 sites

CAMPGROUNDS (continued)

Mena

KOA -MENA
Rt. 4, Box 612AA
Mena, AR 71953
(501) 394-3021
FACILITIES: Open year round; 75 sites.

Morrilton

KOA - MORRILTON/CONWAY
Box 259
Morrilton, AR 72110
(501) 354-8262
FACILITIES: Open year round; 100 sites.

Mountain Home

WILDERNESS POINT CAMPGROUND
P.O. Box 307
Henderson, AR 72544
(501) 488-5340
FACILITIES: Open year round; 180 sites.

Mountain View

HOLIDAY INN TRAV-L PARK
Hwy. 14 NW
Mountain View, AR 72560
(501) 585-2231
FACILITIES: Open year round; 113 sites.

Rogers

BEAVER LAKE SAFARI CAMP
Rt. 6, Box 340
Rogers, AR 72756
(501) 636-2011
FACILITIES: Open year round; 140 sites.

KOA - ROGERS/PEA RIDGE
P.O. Box 456
Rogers, AR 72656
(501) 451-8566
FACILITIES: Open year round; 60 sites.

Texarkana

KOA - TEXARKANA
Rt. 8, Box 254
Texarkana, AR 75501
(501) 772-0751
FACILITIES: Open year round; 100 sites.

West Memphis Area

KOA - LAKESIDE
Rt. 1
Heth, AR 72346
(501) 657-2422
FACILITIES: Open year round; 57 sites.

SAFARI CAMPGROUND
Rt. 2, Box 397U
Marion, AR 72364
(501) 739-3864
FACILITIES: Open year round; 108 sites.

Winslow

SILVER LEAF CAMPARK
Rt. 1, Box 436
Winslow, AR 72959
(501) 634-9051

FACILITIES: Open year round; 71 sites.

"Y" City

DIAMOND "J" CAMPER PARK
Boles, AR 72926
(501) 577-2489
FACILITIES: Open year round; 71 sites.

RESORTS & BEACHES

Arkadelphia

DEGRAY LAKE AREA - One of Arkansas' newest lakes is DeGray, where a major new state park is under development. Nearby is the old Ouachita river port of Arkadelphia, Henderson State College, Ouachita Baptist University, and one of Arkansas' largest and most modern thoroughbred breeding farms. (See Boating Areas.)

Clarksville

LAKE DARDANELLE AREA - 43,000 acres of water offering all the fishing and cruising excitement you could want. Mount Nebo and Lake Dardanelle State Parks and surrounding areas offer approximately 650 private and public use campsites. Historical sites and modern locks and dams add to the fascination of this area.

Eureka Springs

EUREKA SPRINGS AREA - The "Little Switzerland of America," Eureka Springs is a Victorian showplace. Blue Springs, Onyx Cave, the Passion Play, the Christ of the Ozarks, and the Holiday Island Exotic Animal Parks are only a few of the many sights. In nearby Berryville, the Saunders Memorial Museum offers an outstanding display of firearms.

Fayetteville

BEAVER LAKE AREA - A place of many faces in the heart of the Ozarks, the Beaver Lake area features approximately 880 private and public use campsites, outstanding fishing in the 28,000 acres of the lake and the winding waters of the White River. (See Boating Areas.)

Fort Smith

FORT SMITH AREA - Once an outpost that guarded the frontier, Fort Smith is today a bustling modern center of industry. The past lives again at the Fort Smith National Historic Site where "Hanging Judge" Isaac Parker's courtroom has been restored along with the infamous gallows on which desperadoes ended their days. Fort Smith's main street, Garrison Avenue, once served as the parade grounds.

Hardy

HARDY AREA - Visit the Arkansas Traveller Folk Theater, marvel at the world's largest spring, Mammoth Spring, look in on resort developments like Horseshoe Bend and Cherokee Village. Approximately 397 private and

ARKANSAS

RESORTS (continued)

public use campsites.

Harrison

HARRISON AREA - Daisy Mae and Little Abner, and all the characters of Al Capp's famous comic strip welcome you to a unique theme park, Dogpatch, U.S.A. Explore Dogpatch Caverns, fish for trout or go ice skating year-round. Approximately 452 private and public use campsites in the area.

Helena

HELENA - WEST HELENA AREA - Antebellum homes, historical sites, Civil War relics and battlefield, the geologic oddity, Kudzu-covered Crowley's Ridge. Explore the St. Francis National Forest and try your luck at landing the big ones on Old Town Lake. (See National Forests.)

Heber Springs

GREERS FERRY AREA - Greers Ferry Lake is ideal for sailing, water skiing, scuba diving, swimming, and fishing. The Little Red River below the dam vies with the lake for fishing trophies. Tour the Federal Fish Hatchery, hike the Sugar Loaf Nature Trail. (See Boating Area.)

Little Rock

LITTLE ROCK - NORTH LITTLE ROCK AREA - Arkansas' capitol city blends tradition and contemporary action in a beautiful setting of rolling hills and dramatic river views. Three capitols - the Territorial Restoration, the First State House, and the present State Capitol - are open for your inspection. A brand new convention center, the Arkansas Arts Center, the Museum of Science and Natural History, War Memorial Stadium, a fine collection of city parks which includes a municipal zoo, in-city campgrounds, modern tennis complexes and challenging golf courses.

Mountain Home

TWIN LAKES AREA - Centered around mammoth Bull Shoals and Norfork Lakes. Try a float fishing trip in a "John" boat on the cold waters of the White or North Fork Rivers brimming with Rainbow trout. Bull Shoals State Park, Penrod's Museum, Mountain Village 1890, the Norfork Federal Fish Hatchery, Arkansas' oldest home, the Wolf House. Approximately 900 private and public use campsites and resorts. (See Boating Areas.)

Mountain View

MOUNTAIN VIEW AREA - Return to the era of the dulcimer, the fiddle, and the pickin' bow when the Rackensack Society musicians assemble for the evening performance at the new Ozark Folk Center. Watch mountain craftsmen explore folklore galore, eat your heart out on mountain specialities, and join in the jig dancing at the Folk Center. Tour under ground at Blanchard Springs Caverns.

Above ground, go fishing, hike the nature trails in the Sylamore District of the Ozark National Forest, or canoe on the fabled Buffalo National River. (See National Forests.)

Murfreesboro

CRATER OF DIAMONDS STATE PARK AREA - Crater of Diamonds State Park is the happy hunting grounds for the only diamonds found in their natural matrix in North America. Here, finders are keepers where hardly a week goes by without a find. Here, too, the Caddo Indian Burial Grounds.

Texarkana

TEXARKANA AREA - Texarkana is the gateway to Arkansas from the Great Southwest. Texarkana lies in both Texas and Arkansas, with a post office building that straddles the state line, a popular background for photographers. Not far away is Hope, home of the world's largest watermelons, and Old Washington State Historic Park, a restored town that figured prominently in the history of the Southwest. Here, Sam Houston, Davey Crockett and Jim Bowie once walked, the Bowie knife was forged, and the Arkansas Legislature fled during Union occupation of Little Rock from 1863 to 1865.

West Memphis

WEST MEMPHIS AREA - Summer months bring dog racing to Southland Greyhound Park. The mighty Mississippi laps at the edge of the city, and at its outskirts, the cotton, rice, and soybean fields stretch as far as the eye can see. Close by, the Great River Road leads north and south through this historic land where conquistadors once came in search of gold.

BOATING AREAS

Arkadelphia

DeGray Lake Areas

ARLIE MOORE
LOCATION: Halfway between DeGray Dam and Bismarck on State 7, turn left at Morrison's store, then 2 mi. to area.
FACILITIES: 87 campsites; heated showers; water; dump station; restrooms; electricity; boat ramp; shelter; day use area; swimming beaches. User's fee charged.

CADDO DRIVE
LOCATION: 15 mi. north of Arkadelphia, turn off State 7 at Orr's One Stop, 3 mi. into area.
FACILITIES: 72 campsites; heated showers; water; electricity; restrooms; boat ramp. User's fee charged.

EDGEWOOD
LOCATION: 15 mi. north of Arkadelphia, turn off State 7 at Orr's One Stop, 4 mi. into area.
FACILITIES: 51 campsites; heated showers; water; restrooms; electricity. User's fee charged.

BOATING AREAS (continued)

IRON MOUNTAIN
LOCATION: Off State 7, 2½ mi. west of De-Gray Dam to area.
FACILITIES: 69 campsites; heated showers; water; dump station; restrooms; boat ramp; day use area; electricity. User's fee charged.

SHOUSE FORD
LOCATION: 10½ mi. from Bismarck on State 84, turn left at Point Cedar, then 2 mi. to area.
FACILITIES: 100 campsites; heated showers; restrooms; water; dump station; boat ramp; electricity; day use area; swimming beaches. User's fee charged.

Arkansas Post

River Areas Between Arkansas Post and Pine Bluff

MERRISACH
LOCATION: ½ mi. west of Lock No. 2 on paved access road.
FACILITIES: 35 campsites; boat ramp; water; restrooms; group shelter; playground.

STE. MARIE
LOCATION: 4 mi. northeast of Pine Bluff city limits along paved access road.
FACILITIES: 22 campsites; boat ramp; restrooms; water.

Ashdown

Millwood Lake Areas

BEARD'S BLUFF
LOCATION: 13 mi. east of Ashdown.
FACILITIES: 33 campsites; boat ramp; water; swimming; recreation area is upstream of the east embankment of the dam.

COTTONSHED LANDING
LOCATION: 8 mi. southwest of Mineral Springs and Tollette.
FACILITIES: 50 campsites; boat ramp; dump station; water.

MILLWOOD PARK
LOCATION: 7 mi. east of Ashdown on State 32, then 3½ mi. north on State 317.
FACILITIES: 91 campsites; boat ramp; water.

PARALOMA LANDING
LOCATION: 1½ mi. south of Paraloma on access road.
FACILITIES: 68 campsites; boat ramp; water; dump station.

SARATOGA LANDING
LOCATION: 1 mi. south, then 1 mi. west of Saratoga.
FACILITIES: 35 campsites; boat ramp; water.

Heber Springs

Greers Ferry Lake Areas

CHEROKEE
LOCATION: 7½ mi. west of Drasco on State 92, then 4½ mi. on gravel access road.

FACILITIES: 33 campsites; boat ramp; water; restrooms; swimming.

CHOCTAW
LOCATION: 5 mi. south of Clinton on U.S. 65, then 3½ mi. on State 330.
FACILITIES: 115 campsites; boat dock; boat ramp; water; restrooms; swimming; amphitheater; dump station.

COVE CREEK
LOCATION: 6½ mi. northeast of Quitman on State 25, then 3 mi. northwest on State 16, then 1¼ mi. on access road.
FACILITIES: 55 campsites; boat ramp; water; restrooms; swimming.

DAM SITE
LOCATION: 3 mi. north of Heber Springs on State 25.
FACILITIES: 321 campsites; dump station; showers; boat dock; boat ramp; water; restrooms; swimming; amphitheater; marine dump station.

DEVILS FORK
LOCATION: ½ mi. north of Stark on State 16.
FACILITIES: 55 campsites; boat ramp; water; restrooms; swimming; dump station.

HEBER SPRINGS
LOCATION: 1 mi. west of Heber Springs on Eden Isle Road, then ½ mi. north on access road.
FACILITIES: 144 campsites; boat dock; boat ramp; water; restrooms; showers; dump station; marine dump; swimming.

HILL CREEK
LOCATION: 12 mi. west of Drasco on State 92, then 3 mi. northwest on county road, then 1½ mi. south on gravel access road.
FACILITIES: 31 campsites; boat dock; boat ramp; water; restrooms; swimming.

MILL CREEK
LOCATION: 6½ mi. northeast of Quitman on State 25, then 13½ mi. north on State 16, then 3 mi. on gravel access road.
FACILITIES: 27 campsites; boat ramp; water; restrooms; swimming.

NARROWS
LOCATION: 6½ mi. northeast of Quitman on State 25, then 16 mi. on State 16.
FACILITIES: 60 campsites; boat dock; boat ramp; water; restrooms; dump station; electricity.

OLD HIGHWAY
LOCATION: 6¼ mi. north of Heber Springs on State 25, then 3 mi. west on old State 25.
FACILITIES: 98 campsites; boat ramp; water; restrooms; swimming; dump station.

SHILOH
LOCATION: 14½ mi. southeast of Shirley on State 16, then 2½ mi. on access road.
FACILITIES: 104 campsites; boat dock; boat ramp; water; restrooms; dump stations; swimming.

SUGAR LOAF
LOCATION: 6½ mi. northeast of Quitman on

ARKANSAS

BOATING AREAS (continued)

State 25, then 13 mi. northwest on State 16, then 1 mi. west on State 92, then 1 mi. west on State 337.
FACILITIES: 80 campsites; boat dock; boat ramp; water; restrooms; swimming; dump station.

VAN BUREN
LOCATION: 2 mi. south of Shirley on State 16, then 5 mi. on State 330.
FACILITIES: 65 campsites; boat dock; boat ramp; water; restrooms; swimming; dump station.

Little Rock

River Areas Between Little Rock and Dardanelle

CHEROKEE
LOCATION: 3 mi. south of Morrilton off Cherokee Street.
FACILITIES: 38 campsites; showers; water; restrooms; dump station; boat ramp.

MAUMELLE
LOCATION: 3 mi. off State 10 on old Penal Farm Road.
FACILITIES: 24 campsites; restrooms; showers; dump station; boat ramp; water.

POINT REMOVE
LOCATION: 1.4 mi. south of Morrilton off Cherokee Street.
FACILITIES: 21 campsites; showers; restrooms; boat ramp.

SEQUOYA
LOCATION: 4 mi. south of Morrilton on State 9, then right 1.6 mi. on Lock and Dam 9 access road.
FACILITIES: 25 campsites; water; showers; restrooms; boat ramp.

SWEEDEN ISLAND
LOCATION: 8 mi. south of Atkins on State 105.
FACILITIES: 69 campsites; water; restrooms; boat ramp.

TOAD SUCK FERRY
LOCATION: 4½ mi. west of Conway on State 60.
FACILITIES: 34 campsites; showers; boat ramp; restrooms; water.

Mountain Home

Bull Shoals Lake Areas

BUCK CREEK
LOCATION: 5½ mi. south of Protem, MO, on State 125.
FACILITIES: 34 campsites; dump station; electricity; swimming beach; boat ramps; restrooms; water; playground.

DAM SITES
LOCATION: 1 mi. southwest of town of Bull Shoals.
FACILITIES: 35 campsites; water; restrooms; dump station.

HIGHWAY 125
LOCATION: 14 mi. northwest of Yellville on State 14, then north on State 125 for 13 mi.
FACILITIES: 32 campsites; dump station; electricity; swimming beach; water; restrooms; playgrounds; boat dock and ramp.

LAKEVIEW
LOCATION: 1 mi. north of Lakeview on State 178.
FACILITIES: 81 campsites; dump station; electricity; showers; swimming beach; group shelter; playground; boat dock and ramp; water.

LEAD HILL
LOCATION: 4 mi. north of Lead Hill on State 7.
FACILITIES: 78 campsites; dump station; electricity; water; restrooms; heated fishing dock; swimming beach; marine dump station; group shelter; playground; boat ramp.

OAKLAND
LOCATION: 8 mi. north of Midway on State 5, then 10 mi. west on State 202.
FACILITIES: 34 campsites; marine dump station; swimming beach; boat dock; dump station; water; restrooms; boat ramp.

OZARK ISLE
LOCATION: 5 mi. southwest of Oakland.
FACILITIES: 118 campsites; showers; boat dock; nearby swimming beach; boat ramps; restrooms; water; group shelter; playground; group camp area.

POINT RETURN
LOCATION: Northeast of town of Bull Shoals on access road.
FACILITIES: 28 campsites; dump station; swimming beach; water; restrooms; boat ramp.

TUCKER HOLLOW
LOCATION: 7 mi. northwest of Lead Hill on State 14, then 3 mi. north on State 281.
FACILITIES: 30 campsites; boat dock; water; restrooms; swimming beach; dump station; boat ramp.

Norfolk Lake Area

BIDWELL POINT
LOCATION: 10 mi. northeast of Mt. Home on State 101, cross lake on ferry and take first access road to the right.
FACILITIES: 48 campsites; dump station; electricity; swimming beach; change shelter; water; restrooms.

CRANFIELD
LOCATION: 5½ mi. northeast of Mt. Home on U.S. 62, then 2 mi. north on paved access road.
FACILITIES: 74 campsites; dump station; electricity; swimming beach; change shelter; water; restrooms; boats and motors.

GAMALIEL
LOCATION: 15 mi. northeast of Mt. Home, cross ferry at State 101, then 4½ mi. north on State 101, then 3 mi. southeast on paved access road.
FACILITIES: 29 campsites; dump station; boat ramp; water; restroom; swimming beach;

BOATING AREAS (continued)

boats and motors.

HENDERSON
LOCATION: 10 mi. east of Mt. Home on U.S. 62, across lake on ferry and turn left.
FACILITIES: 39 campsites; dump station; boats and motors; boat ramp; water; restrooms; swimming beach.

JORDAN
LOCATION: 3 mi. east of Norfork Dam on State 177, then 3 mi. north on gravelled access road.
FACILITIES: 33 campsites; dump station; electricity; swimming beach; change shelter; boat dock; water; restrooms.

PANTHER BAY
LOCATION: 10 mi. east of Mt. Home on U.S. 62.
FACILITIES: 28 campsites; marine dump station; swimming beach; water; restrooms; boat ramp and boat dock.

QUARRY COVE AND DAM SITE
LOCATION: 3 mi. northeast of Norfork on State 5, then 2 mi. east on State 177.
FACILITIES: 59 campsites; dump station; restrooms; water; boat dock; swimming; bathhouse.

ROBINSON POINT
LOCATION: 9 mi. east of Mt. Home on U.S. 62, then 2½ mi. south on paved access road.
FACILITIES: 102 campsites; dump station; electricity; swimming; beach; bathhouse; water; restrooms; showers.

Mountain Pine

Lake Ouachita Areas

BRADY MOUNTAIN
LOCATION: 10 mi. west of Hot Springs on U.S. 270, then 7 mi. north on access road.
FACILITIES: 71 campsites; boat ramp; water; showers; restrooms; dump station; beach; nature trail; restaurant; marina; store.

CRYSTAL SPRINGS
LOCATION: 15 mi. west of Hot Springs on U.S. 270, then 2 mi. north on access road.
FACILITIES: 60 campsites; boat ramp; water; showers; restrooms; dump station; beach; restaurant; marina; store.

DENBY POINT
LOCATION: 8 mi. east of Mt. Ida on U.S. 270, then 1 mi. north on access road.
FACILITIES: 40 campsites; boat ramp; water; restrooms; dump station; amphitheater; nature trail; restaurant; marina.

JOPLIN (MOUNTAIN HARBOR)
LOCATION: 11 mi. east of Mt. Ida on U.S. 270, then 2 mi. north on access road.
FACILITIES: 63 campsites; boat ramp; water; restrooms; showers; dump station; beach; restaurant; marina.

LITTLE FIR
LOCATION: 5 mi. southeast of Mt. Ida on State 27, then 9 mi. east on State 188.
FACILITIES: 25 campsites; boat ramp; wa-

ter; restrooms; marina.

SPILLWAY
LOCATION: 3 mi. west of Hot Springs on U.S. 270, then 8 mi. north on State 227, then 3 mi. west on access road.
FACILITIES: 21 campsites; boat ramp; water; restrooms; beach; restaurant; marina.

TOMPKINS BEND
LOCATION: 10 mi. east of Mt. Ida on U.S. 270, then 3 mi. north on access road.
FACILITIES: 63 campsites; boat ramp; water; restrooms; showers; dump station; amphitheater; restaurant; marina.

Murfreesboro

Lake Greeson Areas

ARROWHEAD POINT
LOCATION: 5½ mi. east of Newhope on U.S. 70, then 1/5 mi. south on access road.
FACILITIES: 21 campsites; boat ramp; water; restrooms.

BEAR CREEK
LOCATION: ½ mi. south of Kirby on State 27, then 1¾ mi. west on access road.
FACILITIES: 20 campsites; boat ramp; water; nature trail; restrooms.

COWHIDE COVE
LOCATION: 9 mi. north of Murfreesboro on State 27, then 2 mi. west on access road.
FACILITIES: 60 campsites; showers; water; restrooms; dump station.

KIRBY LANDING
LOCATION: 2½ mi. west of Kirby on U.S. 70, then 1¼ mi. south on access road.
FACILITIES: 78 campsites; boat dock; boat ramp; water; nature trail; showers; rental boats; restrooms; dump station.

LAUREL CREEK
LOCATION: 5¼ mi. south of Kirby on State 27, then 4 mi. west on gravel access road.
FACILITIES: 30 campsites; boat ramp; water; nature trails; restrooms.

NARROWS DAM SITE
LOCATION: 6 mi. north of Murfreesboro on State 19.
FACILITIES: 90 campsites; dump station; restrooms; water; boat dock; boat ramp; nature trails; showers; rental boats.

PARKER CREEK
LOCATION: 6 mi. north of Murfreesboro on State 19, then 6 mi. northwest of Dam on access road.
FACILITIES: 30 campsites; boat ramp; water; restrooms.

SELF CREEK
LOCATION: 1 mi. west of Daisy on U.S. 70.
FACILITIES: 53 campsites; showers; restrooms; water; boat dock; boat ramp; rental boats.

STAR OF THE WEST
LOCATION: 2¾ mi. east of Newhope on U.S. 70.
FACILITIES: 26 campsites; water; restrooms.

ARKANSAS

BOATING AREAS (continued)

Ozark

River Areas Between Ozark and Fort Smith

CITADEL BLUFF
LOCATION: 2 mi. southeast of Ozark. Day use area only.
FACILITIES: 36 campsites; picnic area; nature trail; playground.

CLEAR CREEK
LOCATION: 8 mi. southeast of Alma.
FACILITIES: 40 campsites; boat ramp; water; showers; dump station; restrooms.

DAM SITE 13 SOUTH
LOCATION: 2 mi. north of Barling.
FACILITIES: 64 campsites; boat ramp; water; showers; dump station; restrooms.

FORT SMITH PARK
LOCATION: Just northeast of Ft. Smith city limits. Near 6th Street and Clayton Expressway.
FACILITIES: 33 campsites; picnic; water; restrooms; boat ramp.

OZARK DAM SITE SOUTH
LOCATION: 1 mi. south of Ozark.
FACILITIES: 41 campsites; water; restrooms; boat ramp.

RIVER RIDGE
LOCATION: 11 mi. west of Cecil.
FACILITIES: 24 campsites; boat ramp; water; restrooms; group shelter.

VACHE GRASSE
LOCATION: 3.5 mi. northwest of Lavaca.
FACILITIES: 30 campsites; boat ramp; water; restrooms; group shelter.

Pine Bluff

River Areas Between Pine Bluff and Little Rock

TAR CAMP
LOCATION: 6 mi. east of Redfield.
FACILITIES: 20 campsites; boat ramp; restrooms; water; playground; group shelter.

WILLOW BEACH
LOCATION: 2 mi. southeast of Baucum, then ½ mi. southwest on paved access road.

Plainview

Nimrod Lake Areas

COUNTY LINE
LOCATION: 6 mi. east of Plainview on State 60, then ¼ mi. south on access road.
FACILITIES: 20 campsites; boat dock; water; swimming; restrooms; dump station.

QUARRY COVE
LOCATION: 7 mi. southeast of Ola on State 7, then ½ mi. west on State 60 to access road.
FACILITIES: 31 campsites; boat ramp; water; restrooms; swimming; dump station.

SUNLIGHT BAY
LOCATION: 1½ mi. east of Plainview on State 60, then 2 1/3 mi. southwest on gravelled access road.
FACILITIES: 24 campsites; boat ramp; water; restrooms; dump station.

Rogers

Beaver Lake Areas

DAM SITE
LOCATION: 9 mi. west of Eureka Springs on U.S. 62, then 2.5 mi. south on paved access road State 187 to dam.
FACILITIES: 78 campsites; dump station; electricity; water; restrooms; boat ramps; overlook; swimming.

HICKORY CREEK
LOCATION: 4 mi. north of Springdale on U.S. 71, then 7 mi. east on paved State 264.
FACILITIES: 38 campsites; boat dock; dump station; electricity; water; restrooms; boat ramp; swimming.

HORSESHOE BEND
LOCATION: 8 mi. east of Rogers on State 94.
FACILITIES: 103 campsites; boat dock; boat ramp; water; restrooms; swimming; showers; dump station.

INDIAN CREEK
LOCATION: 1½ mi. east of Gateway on 62, then south 5 mi. on gravel access road.
FACILITIES: 42 campsites; water; restrooms; boat ramps; swimming.

LOST BRIDGE
LOCATION: 5 mi. southeast of Garfield on State 127.
FACILITIES: 80 campsites; boat dock; dump station; water; restrooms; boat ramp; electricity; swimming; youth group camp area.

PRAIRIE CREEK
LOCATION: 3¼ mi. east of Rogers on State 12, then 1 mi. on access road.
FACILITIES: 119 campsites; boat dock; restrooms; water; boat ramp; electricity; trailer and marine dump station; swimming.

ROCKY BRANCH
LOCATION: 11 mi. east of Rogers on State 12, then 4½ mi. northeast on paved access road on State 303.
FACILITIES: 50 campsites; electricity; boat dock; water; restrooms; boat ramp; swimming.

STARKEY
LOCATION: 4 mi. west of Eureka Springs on U.S. 62, then 7 mi. southwest on paved access road.
FACILITIES: 32 campsites; electricity; boat dock; water; restrooms; boat ramp.

WAR EAGLE
LOCATION: 10 mi. east of Springdale on State 68, then 3 mi. north on paved access road.
FACILITIES: 22 campsites; electricity; boat dock; dump station; water; restrooms; boat ramp; swimming.

BOATING AREAS (continued)

Russellville

Dardanelle Lake Areas

DAM SITE WEST
LOCATION: ¾ mi. north of Dardanelle on paved road to Dam.
FACILITIES: 22 campsites; overlook; water; restrooms.

PINEY BAY
LOCATION: 2/3 mi. east of Piney on U.S. 64, then 4 mi. north on State 359.
FACILITIES: 39 campsites; dump station; water; restrooms; group shelters; boat ramps; electricity.

SHOAL BAY
LOCATION: 2 mi. north of New Blaine on access road.
FACILITIES: 60 campsites; dump station; marine dump station; electricity; boat dock; boat ramp; water; restrooms; group shelter; nature trail.

SPADRA
LOCATION: 2 mi. south of Clarksville on State 103 to Jamestown, then 1 mi. on access road.
FACILITIES: 31 campsites; dump station; boat dock; boat ramp; water; restrooms; showers; group shelter.

Waveland

Blue Mountain Lake Areas

OUTLET AREA
LOCATION: 3 mi. south of Waveland on paved road. Located below the dam on Petit Jean River.
FACILITIES: 21 campsites; dump station; water; restrooms.

WAVELAND PARK
LOCATION: 2 mi. southwest of Waveland on paved road.
FACILITIES: 47 campsites; dump station; boat ramp; restrooms; water.

For additional information on the Boating Areas in Arkansas, contact:

U.S. Corps of Engineers Office
P.O. Box 867
Little Rock, AR 72203
(501) 378-5551

BICYCLE TRAILS

No information was available on Bicycle Trails in Arkansas.

TRAILS

Crossett

LEVI WILCOXON DEMONSTRATION FOREST TRAIL - .75 mi. foot trail. Located with the Levi Wilcoxon Demonstration Forest, the trail is natural and rustic. Topography is of gently-rolling hills shrouded by old-growth stands of loblolly pine, winged elm, wild grape and dogwood shrubs; a second-growth stand; and a new stand of pines. Interpretive devices are located at points of interest to explain the types of vegetation, management technique, and supportive ecosystems of the forest.

Greer Ferry Lake

SUGAR LOAF MOUNTAIN NATURE TRAILS - 1 mi. foot trail. This nature trail is constructed on an island rising 560 feet above the man-made lake. There is a wide variety of vegetation ranging from lichens and mosses through many species of trees. The island houses a wildlife refuge. Interesting sandstone formations can be observed. Access is by concessioner-operated barge or via visitor's own boat. Built by the Corps of Engineers, this trail has been specially honored by the Chief of Engineers.

Petit Jean State Park

CEDAR CREEK SELF-GUIDING TRAIL - 1.5 mi. foot trail. Cedar Creek is the focal point of this nature trail, which was built in 1933 by the Civilian Conservation Corps. Steps were carved out of the rock, and bridges over Cedar Creek consist of single logs with handrails. Several pools in the creek provide habitat for warm-water fish species. An interpretive booklet is available to help identify the wide variety of flora and fauna along the trail.

SEVEN HOLLOWS TRAIL - 3.5 mi. foot trail. This nature trail passes through pine-hardwood forests and elongated sandstone canyons. Rock outcropping, geologic formations, caves, a natural bridge and Indian pictographs are among the special features of the trail. The natural bridge, 70 feet high, is the third highest in the United States. The trail is part of an extensive trail system in the State Park.

SKI AREAS

There are no organized Ski Areas in Arkansas.

AMUSEMENT PARKS & ATTRACTIONS

Dogpatch

DOGPATCH U.S.A., INC. (Attraction)
Dogpatch, AR 72648
(501) 743-1111
FACILITIES: 12 major rides; 8 kiddie rides; 15 walk thrus; 5 games; 11 refreshment stands; 3 restaurants; gravity house; arcade; shooting gallery; swimming pool; ice rink; marina; camping; picnic facilities; petting zoo; theater; crafts; stage shows; orchestras; vaudeville; name bands; free acts; pay gate; free parking; open Memorial Day - Labor Day.

ARKANSAS

AMUSEMENT PARKS (continued)

Hot Springs

ANIMAL WONDERLAND (Attraction)
4800 Albert Pike
Hot Springs, AR 71901
(501) 767-5056
FACILITIES: Petting zoo; animal exhibits; deer farm; aviary; gift shop; picnic facilities; dolphin show; macaw show; 2 refreshment stands; pay gate; free parking; open May - Oct. 31.

Little Rock

WAR MEMORIAL AMUSEMENT PARK
P.O. Box 5499
Little Rock, AR 72205
(501) 663-9817
FACILITIES: 4 refreshment stands; 9 games; arcade; shooting gallery; swimming pool; picnic facilities; golf driving range; zoo; fireworks; free gate; free parking; open Jun. 1 - Sept. 1, weekends, all year.

North Little Rock

BURNS PARK FUNLAND, INC.
P.O. Box 352
North Little Rock, AR 72115
(501) 753-7307
FACILITIES: 7 major rides; 8 kiddie rides; refreshment stand; free gate; free parking; open Mar. 1 - Labor Day.

STATE FAIR

Arkansas State Fair and Livestock Show
P.O. Box 907
Little Rock, AR 72202
(501) 372-8341
DATE: September.

NATIONAL PARKS

Hot Springs National Park

HOT SPRINGS NATIONAL PARK
Hot Springs National Park, AR 71901
(501) 321-5202

GULPHA GORGE
LOCATION: 2 mi. east of Hot Springs.
FACILITIES: Open year round; limit of stay: 30 days (14, Apr. 1 - Oct. 31); 47 sites; NPS campsite fee: $3; water and bathroom facilities; sanitary station; picnic area; hiking; bicycle trail; exhibit; environmental study area; living history program; NPS guided tour; self-guiding tour.

NATIONAL FORESTS

National Forests
Southern Region
1720 Peachtree Road, NW
Atlanta, GA 30309
(404) 881-4177

Hot Springs

OUACHITA NATIONAL FOREST
ATTRACTIONS: 8 major and numerous smaller artificial lakes in or near the National Forest. Caddo Gap, where DeSoto fought Indians. Bass fishing; deer, quail, squirrel hunting; scenic drives; hiking; swimming.
FACILITIES: 21 camp and picnic sites, 23 picnic only. Hotels, resorts, and cabin camps.
NEARBY TOWNS: Booneville, Heavener and Poteau, OK.

Russellville

OZARK NATIONAL FOREST
ATTRACTIONS: Scenic drives; three recreational lakes; lake fishing, deer, small-game hunting, 2 large reservoirs near the National Forest.
FACILITIES: 24 camp and picnic sites, 21 picnic only; 9 swimming sites. Mountain Magazine Lodge and cabins. White Rock Mountain cabins, others nearby.
NEARBY TOWNS: Clarksville, Fayetteville, Ft. Smith, Harrison, Ozark, Paris.

STATE PARKS

Headquarters

Department of Parks and Tourism
Tourism Division
Room 149
State Capitol
Little Rock, AR 72201
(501) 371-1511

Ashdown

MILLWOOD STATE PARK
LOCATION: From Texarkana, 16 mi. north on U.S. 71, then 8 mi. east on State 32.
FACILITIES: Open year round; 91 sites; water and bathroom facilities; electrical hookup; boating; boat rental; fishing.

Bismarck

DEGRAY STATE PARK
LOCATION: From Arkadelphia exit off I-30, 7 mi. north of State 7.
FACILITIES: Open year round; 113 sites; water and bathroom facilities; electrical hookup; laundry; boating; boat rental; fishing; bicycle trail.

Bluff City

WHITE OAK LAKE STATE PARK
LOCATION: From I-30, 30 mi. east of Prescott on State 24 to Bluff City, then 2 mi. south on State 387.
FACILITIES: Open year round; 48 sites; water and bathroom facilities; electrical hookup; food service; swimming; boating; boat rental.

Conway

WOOLLY HOLLOW STATE PARK
LOCATION: From I-30 at Conway, 12 mi. north on U.S. 65, then 6 mi. east on State 285.

STATE PARKS (continued)

FACILITIES: Open year round; 17 sites; water and bathroom facilities; swimming; boating; boat rental; fishing; hiking; living history program; electric motors only.

Daisy

DAISY STATE PARK
LOCATION: ¼ mi. south of Daisy off U.S. 70.
FACILITIES: Open year round; 108 sites; water and bathroom facilities; sanitary station; electrical hookup; cabins; food service; boating; only known diamond field in North America.

Dardanell

MT. NEBO STATE PARK
LOCATION: 7 mi. west of Dardanell on State 155.
FACILITIES: Open year round; 30 sites; water and bathroom facilities; electrical hookup; cabins; food service; swimming; hiking.

Harrisburg

LAKE POINSETT STATE PARK
LOCATION: 1 mi. east of Harrisburg on State 14, then 2 mi. south on State 163.
FACILITIES: Open year round; 25 sites; water and bathroom facilities; electrical hookup; food service; boating; boat rental; fishing.

Hot Springs

LAKE CATHERINE STATE PARK
LOCATION: 1 mi. north of Malvern on I-30, then 12 mi. west on State 171.
FACILITIES: Open year round; 70 sites; water and bathroom facilities; sanitary station; electrical hookup; cabins; laundry; food service; boating; fishing; water skiing; hiking.

Huntsville

WITHROW SPRINGS STATE PARK
LOCATION: 5 mi. north of Huntsville on State 23.
FACILITIES: Open year round; 25 sites; water and bathroom facilities; electrical hookup; food service; swimming pool; fishing.

Jersey

MORO BAY STATE PARK
LOCATION: 20 mi. northeast of El Dorado on State 15.
FACILITIES: Open year round; 21 sites; water and bathroom facilities; sanitary station; food service; swimming; boating; boat rental; fishing.

Lake Village

LAKE CHICOT STATE PARK
LOCATION: 8 mi. northeast of Lake Village on State 144.
FACILITIES: Open year round; 127 sites; water and bathroom facilities; sanitary station; electrical hookup; cabins; laundry; food service; boating; boat rental; fishing.

Mena

QUEEN WILHELMINA STATE PARK
LOCATION: 13 mi. northwest of Mena on State 88.
FACILITIES: Open year round; 42 sites; water and bathroom facilities; electrical hookup; cabins; laundry; food service.

Morrilton

PETIT JEAN STATE PARK
LOCATION: 6 mi. south of Morrilton on State 9, then 12 mi. west on State 154.
FACILITIES: Open year round; 127 sites; water and bathroom facilities; sanitary station; electrical hookup; cabins; laundry; food service; swimming pool; boating; boat rental; fishing; hiking; horseback riding.

Mountain Home

BULL SHOALS STATE PARK
LOCATION: 11 mi. west of Mountain Home on State 178.
FACILITIES: Open year round; 105 sites; water and bathroom facilities; sanitary station; electrical hookup; laundry; food service; boating; boat rental; fishing; hiking.

Mountain Pine

LAKE OUACHITA STATE PARK
LOCATION: 3 mi. west of Hot Springs on U.S. 270, then 15 mi. north on State 227.
FACILITIES: Open year round; 95 sites; water and bathroom facilities; cabins; laundry; food service; boating; boat rental.

Mountainburg

LAKE FORT SMITH STATE PARK
LOCATION: 1 mi. east off U.S. 71 north of Mountainburg.
FACILITIES: Open year round; 12 sites; water and bathroom facilities; electrical hookup; food service; swimming; boating; boat rental; fishing.

Pocahontas

OLD DAVIDSONVILLE STATE PARK
LOCATION: 2 mi. west of Pocahontas on U.S. 62, then 9 mi. southwest on State 166.
FACILITIES: Open year round; 12 sites; water and bathroom facilities; boating; fishing; site of first courthouse, post office and land office in Arkansas.

Powhatan

LAKE CHARLES STATE PARK
LOCATION: 8 mi. northwest of Hoxie on U.S. 63, then 6 mi. southwest on State 25.
FACILITIES: Open year round; 130 sites; water and bathroom facilities; food service; swimming; boating; fishing; 10hp motor units on lake.

Russellville

LAKE DARDANELLE STATE PARK
LOCATION: 2 mi. off U.S. 64, then west on State 326.

ARKANSAS

STATE PARKS (continued)

FACILITIES: Open year round; 97 sites; water and bathroom facilities; food service; boating; boat rental; fishing; water skiing.

Walcott

CROWLEY'S RIDGE STATE PARK
LOCATION: 15 mi. north of Jonesboro on State 141.
FACILITIES: Open year round; 18 sites; water and bathroom facilities; electrical hookup; cabins; food service; swimming; boat rental; fishing.

West Fork

DEVIL'S DEN STATE PARK
LOCATION: 8 mi. south of Fayetteville on U.S. 71, then 18 mi. west on State 170.
FACILITIES: Open year round; 96 sites; water and bathroom facilities; sanitary station; cabins; laundry; food service; boat rental; hiking; environmental study area.

Wynne

VILLAGE CREEK STATE PARK
LOCATION: 12 mi. north from I-40 at Forrest City on State 284.
FACILITIES: Open year round; 104 sites; water and bathroom facilities; laundry; food service; swimming; boating; boat rental; fishing; hiking.

STATE FORESTS

There are no State Forests in Arkansas.

HISTORIC SITES

Boxley

CAVERN - The Cavern which was known as Bat Cave and Salt Peter Cave is located at Boxley. The saltpeter found in the cave was used during the Civil War for making gun powder. A detachment of 25-30 men from Huntsville captured the cave and destroyed the iron pots and boiler. All of the nine pots were damaged, but are still in existence.

Bradley

WALNUT HILL - James Sevier Conway, the state's first govenor, obtained a large plantation of 3,200 acres in the 1820's. He did not live on his plantation until after he had served four years as governor - from 1836 to 1840. He died of pneumonia at the age of 58 and was buried in the family cemetery. In 1950 a marker was erected at the foot of Governor Conway's grave with this inscription: "James Sevier Conway, First Governor of the State of Arkansas - 1836-40, erected by the Caddo Chapter of the Daughters of the American Revolution."

Camden

CHIDESTER HOUSE or Stagecoach Inn - The Chidester House was built by Col. John Chidester about 1847, and was one of the stagecoach house centers of a long mail route. It was used by both General Sterling Price of the Confederate Army and General Frederick Steele of the Union forces. The house remained in continuous use by the Chidester family and the original furniture remains, with very few modern conveniences installed by the last occupants.

Chismville

CHISMVILLE - Chismville was the site of the residence-tavern of Dr. Stephen H. Chism, built around 1840. Roads from Fort Smith to Little Rock and from Ozark to Waldron crossed at Chismville. The old house harbored many notables as well as outlaws such as Belle Starr.

Clarendon

LOUISIANA PURCHASE LANDMARK - Survey markers on a gum tree contain marks which designated the tree as probably the most interesting and important geographic point west of the Mississippi River. The tree (landmark) is the starting point from which all township and section lines in Arkansas, Missouri, Iowa, and Minnesota are based.

Dardanelle

COUNCIL OAKS - Two great oaks grew on the riverbank behind the waterworks on North Front Street. They shaded an important meeting in 1820 between Robert Crittenden, Secretary of the Arkansas Territory, and leaders of the Cherokee. The purpose of the conference was to arrange an agreement whereby the Indians would yield, for white settlement, part of their treaty-granted land in Arkansas.

Gateway

BUTTERFIELD OVERLAND MAIL ROAD - (Elkhorn Tavern, to Fort Smith and Memphis west to Fort Smith). By Act of Congress in March, 1857, John Butterfield of New York, mail contractor, was authorized to carry mail from St. Louis, Missouri, and Memphis, Tennessee, to San Francisco. He organized the Overland Mail Company which later became the Butterfield Overland Mail Company. The government agreed to pay $600,000 a year for six years for this service. The first mail started from St. Louis and Memphis the same day, September 16, 1858. From St. Louis, the stage's first stop in Arkansas was at Callahan's Tavern the morning of September 18 and both stages met at Fort Smith on the same day, Sunday, September, 19.

Heber Springs

SUGAR LOAF MOUNTAIN - Sugar Loaf Mountain is about 2.5 miles east of Heber Springs, rises about 500 feet perpendicularly. It has a flat top, capped by a massive layer of limestone and pine trees. A legend holds that Sugar Loaf Mountain was shaped by Indians who sought to make the plateau impregnable in time of war.

HISTORIC SITES (continued)

Helena

DESOTO TRAIL - In June 1541, Hernando DeSoto reached Chickasaw Bluffs, below Memphis, coming from Yazoo territory. He crossed the Mississippi River into Arkansas and was the first white man on Arkansas soil. He traveled southwest to places later established as Arkansas Post, Little Rock, Hot Springs (the healing waters) and wintered near Champagnolle on the Quachita River. In 1542 his trail led south into Louisiana passing near El Dorado.

Junction City

BLANCHARD SPRINGS - At one time Blanchard Springs had four large hotels to accommodate visitors seeking the health restoring properties of the spring waters. Later when the big oak tree near the springs died, they ceased to flow. This brought about the end of the thriving resort.

Little Rock

ARKOPOLIS - In 1820, Dr. Matthew Cunningham "built this second house in Little Rock, a log cabin. a short distance away from the 'little rock' and in . . . a dense forest with deep shadows." Arkopolis was the name proposed for Little Rock on February 3, 1821. A large and respectable meeting was held to give a name to Little Rock. The combination of the first syllable of Arkansas and the Greek word "polis" (city) was suggested. The name was soon abandoned.

TEN-MILE HOUSE - The old brick stagecoach house in a yard fringed by cedars was designed in 1836 by Gideon Shryock. He designed the Old State House in Little Rock. A paneled door, with the original lock and brass key, open into a central hall, from which a walnut stairway leads to the second floor. Early-day chandeliers and furniture ornament the place. When General Frederick Steele's Federal Army occupied Little Rock, the house became a military headquarters and a few Confederate prisoners were kept there; one name and the autographer's profane opinion of "Damn Yankees" is still a legible scrawl on the wall. The woods nearby witnessed the capture of David O. Dodd, a 17 year-old Confederate dispatch bearer, who was hanged in Little Rock on the University Technology Campus in 1864.

Monticello

MONTICELLO - Monticello was the site of the last skirmish of the Civil War in Arkansas on May 24, 1865.

North Little Rock

ARGENTA or North Little Rock - Argenta was incorporated as a town in 1871. Nearby the town of Baring Cross grew up around the railroad shops and was later joined to Argenta. In 1890 Little Rock annexed that part of Argenta between Clendenin Hill, about 13th Street, and the river. In 1903 North Little Rock was voted back into Argenta. The name of the city was officially changed to North Little Rock in 1917 by the town council.

Pittman

HIX'S FERRY - Hix's Ferry was the first ferry established in Arkansas at what is now Pittman.

Rogers

CALLAHAN - Callahan's tavern, the first Butterfield Stagecoach station in Arkansas, was located in the northeast corner of what is now the city of Rogers. The first stage arrived at Callahan about 7 o'clock on the morning of September 18, 1858.

TRAIL OF TEARS - During the 1830's long miserable processions of Indians passed westward through Arkansas. The true "trail of tears" was the forced march by the United States Army following the Indian Removal Act of 1830 when the Indians had to give up their land in the Southern Appalachians. The portion through northern Arkansas was surveyed by the late Sam A. Leath, Eureka Springs, who claimed to be the only white man to follow the Trail of Tears.

Washington

WASHINGTON - Washington was a flourishing trading point early in the 19th century. Washington is said to be the birth place of Texas. It is the "Home of the Bowie Knife" made by James Black. There now stands a building that is a reproduction of the Blacksmith Shop. Washington was the Confederate Capitol from 1863 to 1865 and the original building remains. A gun museum of over 600 different guns is on display in an old bank building. The largest Magnolia tree in the state is located here.

West Helena

CLEBURNE MONUMENT - A monument has been erected to General Patrick Cleburne whose grave is in the Confederate Cemetery. General Cleburne was the most outstanding military figure of the Confederacy during the Civil War in Arkansas.

Western Grove

MARBLE FALLS - Marble Falls got its name from the marble for which it was noted. The first water mill at the water falls was built by Peter Bellar in 1829. In 1834 a slab of marble was sent to Washington, D.C., and was used in the Washington Monument. The Marble Falls property was sold by Bellar to Wilcoxon who established the first Post Office in 1880.

HOSTELS

There are no Hostels in Arkansas.

ARKANSAS
POINTS OF INTEREST

Booneville

GOLDEN CITY - This ghost town south of Booneville was laid out and named in the flush of a gold boom in 1886-87. Reports of a rich gold strike caused great excitement until the ores were found to be worthless.

Bull Shoals

MOUNTAIN VILLAGE - A modern attempt to recreate an annonymous village of an earlier era, for the benefit of tourists. Mountain Village is located one mile from Bull Shoals Dam.

Center Point

EBENEZER CAMP MEETING or Methodist Meeting - Ebenezer Camp Meeting began in 1837 and has been at the present site, a mile and a half north of Center Point, since 1857. Bushwhackers burned the buildings in 1865, and the camp was rebuilt five years later. Some of the camp houses erected then are still standing. Meetings are held in August of each year. It is one of the oldest camp meetings still operating in the South.

Central

MAGNET COVE - Magnet Cove is a valley surrounded by low hills, looks much like any other piece of pasture land in the Ouachita foothills, but its small area (5.1 square miles) comprises one of the most remarkable assortments of minerals in America. Geologists have counted 42 kinds of minerals here.

Deer

NATURAL BRIDGE - The Natural Bridge is a natural formation of rock and is located about three miles northeast of Deer. The Natural Bridge and vicinity has been developed for a tourist attraction by the Ozark Forest Service. The bridge has a 130 foot span natural bridge carved from solid rock by a small stream. It is about 12 feet wide and 25 feet high. It continues along the trail across Alum Cove to large rooms weathered out of the rocky cliff over thousands of years.

Eureka Springs

HATCHET HALL - Hatchet Hall on East Mountain in Eureka Springs was the last home of the late Carry Nation, temperance crusader of the early 1900's, and is now occupied by Louis and Elsie Freund, contemporary artists.

Ft. Smith

JUDGE PARKER COURT AND GALLOWS - This was an old fort and once was the scene of the spectacular trials at which Judge Isaac C. Parker sat in judgement. It was originally intended as a barracks. Later the stone building was remodeled into a courtroom and jail. Nearby is the site of the Old Gallows, where 83 men "stood on nothing, a-lookin' up a rope." The platform had a trap wide enough to accommodate 12 men, but half that number was the highest ever hanged at once, on two occasions.

Hot Springs

WILDWOOD - Wildwood was the home Prosper Harvey Ellsworth started in 1878. Mrs. Ellsworth came from Washington, DC, having been reared in a highly cultured society. The barns were built first and one was occupied as a home following the great fire in Hot Springs in 1913; Wildwood was built in 1884. It is of the Queen Anne style. There is not a square room in the thousands of square feet of floor space.

Huntsville

GOVERNOR'S HILL - Governor's Hill is located on the eastern edge of the city of Huntsville. It was the site of Governor Isaac Murphy's home, also that of Governor Orval E. Faubus. A very picturesque view of the surrounding countryside may be had from the top of the hill. A fallout shelter is located in the side of the hill and is used as a State Police Headquarters.

Lake Village

LINDBERGH MONUMENT - Colonel Charles A. Lindbergh's Monument is located two miles north of Lake Village on the J. L. Foster property on North Lakeshore Drive. It commemorates the first night flight of Lindbergh in April, 1923, when he flew over Lake Chicot.

Mammoth Spring

MAMMOTH SPRING - The source of Spring River, and the largest spring in the world. It flows 200,000,000 gallons of water each day.

Manila

HERMAN DAVIS MONUMENT - The Herman Davis Monument is located in Manila. He was named by General Pershing on his list of 100 outstanding World War I heroes.

Marianna

PATTERSON MONUMENT - The homestead and grave of John Patterson, 1790-1886, is southeast of Marianna on Crowley's Ridge. He is said to be the first native-born child of Anglo-Saxon parentage. This riddle describes part of his life: "I was born in a kingdom (Spain). Reared in an empire (France). At tained manhood in a territory (Louisiana). And, now a citizen of a state, I have never been 100 miles from where I was born."

Marshall

MYSTERY CAVE (Search County) - Mystery Cave is a short distance off Highway 27, 12 miles north of Marshall. Massive and beautiful rock formations will thrill lovers of subterranean beauty and mystery. Some rooms have ceilings 60 feet high with as much space between the walls.

ARKANSAS

POINTS OF INTEREST (continued)

Mc Genee

FIRST RAILROAD - The Mississippi, Ouachita and Red River railroad charted in 1852 was the first railroad chartered and built in Arkansas. A marker is placed at the northwest side of the junction of highways 65 and 35 in Chicot County. It was scheduled to run from Gaines Landing to Fulton on the Red River. The plans were to run four miles south of Monticello then to Warren and on to Camden. Estimated cost was $12,897 per mile. The estimated daily cost to operate over the 155 miles of track was $88.49. A severe drouth in 1855 stopped the work and the road was abandoned. The road bed was completed as far as Camden and the tracks laid to Monticello.

Murfreesboro

DIAMOND MINES - The Arkansas Diamond Mines are located two and one-half miles southeast of Murfreesboro. These are the only diamond mines in the United States, discovered by John Huddleston in 1906. Many valuable diamonds have been found in the past. Some have been uncovered recently.

Norristown

NORRISTOWN - Norristown on the Arkansas River was at one time the County Seat for ten years. It was settled in 1829. This was the last stop for the Butterfield Overland Mail before it crossed the Arkansas River. It was also the place where Edward Payson Washburn painted "The Arkansas Traveler" in 1858.

Zion

WILD HAWS (Izard County) - The old Wild Haws home was the first colonial house built in Izard County by Dr. Owen T. Watkins in 1853. The first post office in the county was established across the road and named "Wild Haws." It is a beautiful two-story house with a fireplace in every room.

CALIFORNIA

The only mainland state with an active volcano (Lassen Peak), California joined the Union in 1850 as the thirty-first state. Two years earlier, gold fever engulfed the state with the discovery of the precious yellow metal by James Marshall near Coloma. Within one year (1849) California's population increased nearly 20 fold.

The discovery of gold and the subsequent influx of Americans is probably the most significant event in the state's history. By sheer numbers alone, the territory was firmly established as American soil and the Mexican government had no recourse but to relinquish control.

Following the 49'ers were the wine makers, the oil men, the fishermen, the lumberjacks and the film makers, all lured to the sunny state by stories and dreams of striking it rich.

California leads all other states in commercial fishing and in the production of agricultural products such as lettuce, citrus fruits and tomatoes. Also, the state's lumber and oil industries are among the nation's top producers.

Other notable achievements for California include firsts in population and automobile ownership.

State capital: Sacramento. State bird: Valley quail. State tree: Redwood. State flower: Golden poppy.

WEATHER

The state of California extends along the shore of the Pacific Ocean. Its more than 1,340 miles of coastline constitutes nearly three-fourths of the Pacific coastline of the conterminous United States. With its major axis oriented in a northwest-southeast direction the state is 800 miles in length. Its greatest east-west dimension is about 360 miles though its average width is only 250 miles.

The topography is varied and includes Death Valley, the lowest point in the U.S., with an elevation of 276 feet below sea level and less than 85 miles away, Mt. Whitney, the highest peak in the conterminous states at 14,495 feet above sea level.

Within the state are to be found a variety of climates, ranging from one extreme to the other. Temperatures have been recorded from minus 45 degrees to 134 degrees F. Temperature tends toward uniformity from day to day and from season to season on the ocean side of the Coast Range and in coastal valleys. East of the Sierra Nevada temperature patterns are continental in character with wide excursions from high readings to low. Between the two mountain chains and over much of the desert area the temperature regime is intermediate between the maritime and the continental models. Hot summers are the rule while winters are moderate to cold.

Average daily temperature for each month.

	Northern	Southern
Jan.	44.2 to 22.6	65.2 to 38.5
Feb.	49.0 to 25.4	69.7 to 42.3
Mar.	52.1 to 26.8	74.1 to 45.6
Apr.	60.4 to 30.2	81.3 to 52.2
May	69.8 to 36.4	89.2 to 59.1
Jun.	78.5 to 42.6	98.4 to 66.8
Jul.	87.6 to 45.8	104.4 to 76.0

73

CALIFORNIA

WEATHER (continued)

Aug.	86.1 to 44.2	102.7 to 74.9
Sept.	80.5 to 39.0	98.4 to 67.0
Oct.	68.4 to 33.2	87.5 to 56.4
Nov.	53.8 to 28.6	74.3 to 46.1
Dec.	46.0 to 24.4	66.2 to 39.3
Year	64.7 to 33.3	84.3 to 55.4

STATE CHAMBER OF COMMERCE

California Chamber of Commerce
P.O. Box 1736
Sacramento, CA 95808
(916) 444-6670

STATE & CITY TOURISM OFFICES

State

Office of Visitor Services
1120 N. Street
Sacramento, CA 95814
(916) 322-1396

Department of Economic & Business Development
1120 N. Street
Sacramento, CA 95805
(916) 322-5665

Local

Anaheim Visitor and Convention Bureau
800 West Katella Avenue
Anaheim, CA 92802
(714) 533-5536

Long Beach Convention and News Bureau
555 E. Ocean Blvd.
Long Beach, CA 90802
(213) 436-1236

Los Angeles Convention and Visitors Bureau
505 South Flower St., Level B
Los Angeles, CA 90071
(213) 488-9100

Southern California Visitor's Council
705 West 7th Street
Los Angeles, CA 90017
(213) 628-3101

Convention and Tourist Bureau
Chamber of Commerce
1320 Webster Street
Oakland, CA 94612
(415) 451-7800

Palm Springs Convention and Visitor's Bureau
Suite 101, Municipal Airport Terminal
Palm Springs, CA 92262
(714) 327-8411

Sacramento Convention and Visitor's Bureau
1100 14th Street
Sacramento, CA 95814
(916) 449-5291

Convention and Visitor's Bureau
1200 3rd Avenue, Suite 824
San Diego, CA 92101
(714) 232-3101

The Redwood Empire Association
476 Post Street
San Francisco, CA 94102
(415) 421-6554

San Francisco Convention and Visitor's Bureau
1390 Market Street, Suite 260
San Francisco, CA 94102
(415) 626-5500

STATE HIGHWAY DEPARTMENT

Department of Transportation
1120 North Street
Sacramento, CA 95814
(916) 445-2201

HIGHWAY WELCOMING CENTERS

There are no Highway Welcoming Centers in California.

STATE POLICE

Department of Public Safety
Sacramento, CA 95804
(916) 445-1564

HUNTING & FISHING

Hunting

A state hunting license is required for the taking of any bird or mammal. Hunters must carry licenses and be prepared to show them on request. Guns and other equipment used in hunting must be shown on request.

In addition to a state hunting license, state and federal duck stamps are necessary for the taking of migratory waterfowl (except hunters under 16 years of age); deer tags are necessary for the taking of deer and bear tags are necessary for the taking of bear.

A trapping license is required to trap or sell furs of furbearing mammals or nongame mammals.

"Resident" means any person who has resided continuously in California for six months or more immediately prior to date of application for license, persons on active military duty with the Armed Forces of the United States or an auxiliary branch thereof, or Job Corps enrollees.

Resident

Hunting license: resident, under 16 years, $2; resident, $10; General deer tag, $3; Option deer tag, (option tag must be puchased in

HUNTING & FISHING (continued)

addition to a general tag), $5; Bear tag (deer tags and bear tags cannot be issued to anyone under 12 years of age), $1; Trapping (license required to sell furs of furbearing mammals and nongame mammals regardless of how taken); resident, $10; under 16 years of age, resident, $5.

Non-resident

Hunting license, $35; General tag, $25; Option tag (option tag must be purchased in addition to a general tag), $35; Trapping (license required to sell furs of furbearing mammals and nongame mammals regardless of how taken), $25.

Fishing

A fishing license is required of any person 16 years of age, or over, including members of the Armed Forces of the United States, for the taking of any kind of fish, mollusk, invertebrate, amphibian or crustacean in California, except of persons fishing from a public pier in waters of the Pacific Ocean (the public pier must be in the open sea adjacent to the coast and islands of California or in the waters of those open bays or enclosed bays contiguous to the ocean). No license is required for the taking of reptiles.

Fishing license stamps: No license stamp is required for taking frogs and other amphibians or for fishing in ocean waters. To fish in inland waters, an inland water license stamp is required in addition; when fishing in inland waters for trout, steelhead or salmon, a California Trout and Salmon Stamp is required. All stamps must be permanently affixed to licenses.

Sport fishing license year: January 1 to December 31.

"Resident" means any person who has resided continously in California for six months or more immediately before date of application for license, or persons on active military duty with the armed forces of the United States or auxiliary branch thereof.

Resident

Resident license, $4; Special 3-day waters of the Pacific Ocean, $2; Inland water license stamp, $2; Trout & salmon license stamp, $3; Colorado River special use stamp, $3.

Non-resident

Non-resident license, $15; Special 10-day non-resident license, $5.

For more information contact:

Department of Fish & Game
Resources Building
1416 Ninth Street
Sacramento, CA 95814
(916) 445-3531

CAMPGROUNDS

Public

Department of Parks & Recreation

P.O. Box 2390
Sacramento, CA 95811
(916) 445-6477

Bodega Bay

SONOMA COAST STATE BEACH
LOCATION: On Hwy. 1.
FACILITIES: Open year round; 128 sites; water and bathroom facilities; sanitary station; trailer village vehicle sites; picnic area; fishing; hiking; horseback riding.

Cardiff

SAN ELIJO STATE BEACH
LOCATION: On old Hwy. 101 in Cardiff.
FACILITIES: Open year round; 171 sites; water and bathroom facilities; trailer village vehicle sites; food service; swimming; fishing.

Carlsbad

SOUTH CARLSBAD STATE BEACH
LOCATION: 3 mi. south of Carlsbad on Carlsbad Blvd.
FACILITIES: Open year round; 226 sites; water and bathroom facilities; trailer village vehicle sites; swimming; fishing.

Colusa

COLUSA-SACRAMENTO RIVER STATE RECREATION AREA
LOCATION: In Colusa, 9 mi. east of I-5.
FACILITIES: Open year round; 24 primitive sites; trailer village vehicle sites; picnic area; fishing.

Corning

WOODSON BRIDGE STATE RECREATION AREA
LOCATION: 6 mi. east of Corning and I-5 on South Ave.
FACILITIES: Open year round; 46 sites; water and bathroom facilities; trailer village vehicle sites; swimming; fishing; self-guided trail.

Corona

LAKE ELSINORE STATE RECREATION AREA
LOCATION: 22 mi. southeast of Corona via Hwys. 71 and 74.
FACILITIES: Open year round; 176 sites; water and bathroom facilities; electrical hookup; trailer village vehicle sites; picnic area; food service; swimming; fishing.

Dana Point

DOHENY STATE BEACH
LOCATION: South end of Dana Point on Hwy. 1.
FACILITIES: Open year round; 119 sites; sanitary station; trailer village vehicle sites; picnic area; food service; swimming; fishing.

Delhi

MCCONNELL STATE RECREATION AREA
LOCATION: 5 mi. southeast of Delhi on Pepper Road.

CALIFORNIA

CAMPGROUNDS (continued)

FACILITIES: Open year round; 17 sites; water and bathroom facilities; trailer village vehicle sites; picnic area; swimming; fishing.

Essex

PROVIDENCE MOUNTAINS STATE RECREATION AREA
LOCATION: 17 mi. northwest of I-40 near Essex on Essex Road.
FACILITIES: Open year round; 6 primitive sites; water and bathroom facilities; trailer village vehicle sites; exhibit; self-guided trail.

Folsom

FOLSOM LAKE STATE RECREATION AREA
LOCATION: 7806 Folsom-Auburn Road.
FACILITIES: Open year round; 150 sites; water and bathroom facilities; sanitary station; electrical hookup; trailer village vehicle sites; picnic area; food service; swimming; fishing; hiking; horseback riding; exhibit; self-guided trail.

Fresno

MILLERTON LAKE STATE RECREATION AREA
LOCATION: 20 mi. northeast of Fresno on Hwy. 41 and Friant Road.
FACILITIES: Open year round; 71 sites; water and bathroom facilities; sanitary station; trailer village vehicle sites; picnic area; food service; swimming; fishing; horseback riding; exhibit; self-guided trail.

Garberville

BENBOW LAKE STATE RECREATION AREA
LOCATION: 2 mi. south of Garberville on U.S. 101.
FACILITIES: Open year round; 76 sites; water and bathroom facilities; trailer village vehicle sites; picnic area; swimming; fishing.

Guerneville

AUSTIN CREEK STATE RECREATION AREA
LOCATION: 2 mi. north of Guerneville on Armstrong Woods Road.
FACILITIES: Open year round; 25 primitive sites; water and bathroom facilities; picnic area; hiking; horseback riding.

Half Moon Bay

HALF MOON BAY STATE BEACH
LOCATION: ½ mi. west of Hwy. 1 on Kelly Ave.
FACILITIES: Open year round; 50 sites; trailer village vehicle sites; picnic area; fishing; horseback riding.

Hollister

HOLLISTER HILLS STATE VEHICULAR RECREATION AREA
LOCATION: 8 mi. south of Hollister via Cienega Road.

FACILITIES: Open year round; 100 primitive sites; water and bathroom facilities; trailer village vehicle sites; picnic area; food service; hiking; motorbike trail.

Indio

SALTON SEA STATE RECREATION AREA
LOCATION: 25 mi. southeast of Indio on Hwy. 111.
FACILITIES: Open year round; 190 sites; sanitary station; trailer village vehicle sites; picnic area; swimming; fishing; exhibit; self-guided trail.

Jackson

INDIAN GRINDING ROCK STATE HISTORIC PARK
LOCATION: 11 mi. northeast of Jackson, 1.4 mi. from Hwy. 88 on Pine Grove-Volcano Road.
FACILITIES: Open year round; 21 sites; water and bathroom facilities; trailer village vehicle sites; picnic area; exhibit; guided tour; self-guided trail.

Leggett

STANDISH-HICKEY STATE RECREATION AREA
LOCATION: 1 mi. north of Leggett on U.S. 101.
FACILITIES: Open year round; 162 sites; water and bathroom facilities; trailer village vehicle sites; picnic area; swimming; fishing; hiking.

Los Banos

SAN LUIS RESERVOIR STATE RECREATION AREA
LOCATION: 12 mi. west of Los Banos on Hwy. 152.
FACILITIES: Open year round; 79 sites; water and bathroom facilities; trailer village vehicle sites; picnic area; swimming; fishing; exhibit; motorbike trail.

Merced

GEORGE J. HATFIELD STATE RECREATION AREA
LOCATION: 28 mi. west of Merced on Kelly Road.
FACILITIES: Open year round; 7 primitive sites; water and bathroom facilities; trailer village vehicle sites; picnic area; swimming; fishing.

Modesto

TURLOCK LAKE STATE RECREATION AREA
LOCATION: 22 mi. east of Modesto off Hwy. 132.
FACILITIES: Open year round; 65 sites; water and bathroom facilities; trailer village vehicle sites; picnic area; food service; swimming; fishing; hiking.

Mojave

RED ROCK CANYON STATE RECREATION AREA

CAMPGROUNDS (continued)

LOCATION: 25 mi. northeast of Mojave on Hwy. 14.
FACILITIES: Open year round; 50 primitive sites; water and bathroom facilities; sanitary station; trailer village vehicle sites; hiking.

Morro Bay

ATASCADERO STATE BEACH
LOCATION: Hwy. 1 at Yerba Buena.
FACILITIES: Open year round; 92 sites; water and bathroom facilities; trailer village vehicle sites; swimming; fishing.

Navarro

PAUL M. DIMMICK WAYSIDE CAMPGROUND
LOCATION: 8 mi. east of Hwy. 1 on Hwy. 128.
FACILITIES: Open year round; 28 sites; trailer village vehicle sites; picnic area; swimming; fishing.

Nevada City

MALAKOFF DIGGINS STATE HISTORIC PARK
LOCATION: 16 mi. northeast of Nevada City on North Bloomfield Road.
FACILITIES: Open year round; 30 primitive sites; water and bathroom facilities; picnic area; swimming; fishing; hiking; horseback riding; exhibit; guided tour; self-guided trail.

Oroville

LAKE OROVILLE STATE RECREATION AREA
LOCATION: 7 mi. east of Oroville on Hwy. 162.
FACILITIES: Open year round; 137 sites; water and bathroom facilities; sanitary station; electrical hookup; trailer village vehicle sites; picnic area; food service; swimming; fishing; hiking; horseback riding; exhibit; self-guided trail.

Perris

LAKE PERRIS STATE RECREATION AREA
LOCATION: 4 mi. northeast of Perris on Hwy. 395, Ramona Exp.
FACILITIES: Open year round; 431 sites; water and bathroom facilities; sanitary station; electrical hookup; trailer village vehicle sites; picnic area; food service; swimming; fishing; horseback riding; bicycle trail; exhibit; self-guided trail; scuba diving.

Pismo Beach

PISMO STATE BEACH & PISMO DUNES STATE VEHICULAR RECREATION AREA
LOCATION: 2 mi. south of Pismo Beach on Hwy. 1.
FACILITIES: Open year round; 143 sites; water and bathroom facilities; sanitary station; electrical hookup; trailer village vehicle sites; fishing; hiking; self-guided trail.

Point Arena

MANCHESTER STATE BEACH
LOCATION: 7 mi. north of Point Arena on Hwy. 1.
FACILITIES: Open year round; 48 primitive sites; water and bathroom facilities; sanitary station; trailer village vehicle sites; picnic area; fishing.

Rio Vista

BRANNAN ISLAND STATE RECREATION AREA
LOCATION: 3 mi. south of Rio Vista on Hwy. 160.
FACILITIES: Open year round; 100 sites; water and bathroom facilities; sanitary station; trailer village vehicle sites; picnic area; swimming; fishing.

San Bernardino

SILVERWOOD LAKE STATE RECREATION AREA
LOCATION: 30 mi. north of San Bernardino on Hwy. 138.
FACILITIES: Open year round; 95 sites; water and bathroom facilities; sanitary station; trailer village vehicle sites; picnic area; food service; swimming; fishing; hiking; exhibit; self-guided trail.

San Clemente

SAN CLEMENTE STATE BEACH
LOCATION: South end of San Clemente on I-5.
FACILITIES: Open year round; 85 sites; water and bathroom facilities; sanitary station; electrical hookup; trailer village vehicle sites; picnic area; swimming; fishing; hiking.

SAN ONOFRE STATE BEACH
LOCATION: 3 mi. south of San Clemente on I-5 (Basilone Road).
FACILITIES: Open year round; 273 sites; water and bathroom facilities; sanitary station; trailer village vehicle sites; swimming; fishing; hiking.

San Simeon

SAN SIMEON STATE BEACH
LOCATION: 5 mi. south of San Simeon on Hwy. 1.
FACILITIES: Open year round; 134 sites; water and bathroom facilities; trailer village vehicle sites; picnic area; fishing.

Santa Barbara

CARPINTERIA STATE BEACH
LOCATION: 12 mi. south of Santa Barbara on U.S. 101.
FACILITIES: Open year round; 175 sites; water and bathroom facilities; sanitary station; electrical hookup; trailer village vehicle sites; picnic area; swimming; fishing.

EL CAPITAN STATE BEACH
LOCATION: 20 mi. northwest of Santa Barbara on U.S. 101.
FACILITIES: Open year round; 142 sites; wa-

CALIFORNIA

CAMPGROUNDS (continued)

hicle sites; picnic area; food service; swimming; fishing; exhibit.

REFUGIO STATE BEACH
LOCATION: 23 mi. northwest of Santa Barbara on U.S. 101.
FACILITIES: Open year round; 85 sites; water and bathroom facilities; trailer village vehicle sites; picnic area; food service; swimming; fishing.

Santa Cruz

NEW BRIGHTON STATE BEACH
LOCATION: 4 mi. south of Santa Cruz on Hwy. 1.
FACILITIES: Open year round; 115 sites; trailer village vehicle sites; picnic area; swimming; fishing.

SEACLIFF STATE BEACH
LOCATION: 5 mi. south of Santa Cruz on Hwy. 1.
FACILITIES: Open year round; 26 sites; water and bathroom facilities; sanitary station; electrical hookup; trailer village vehicle sites; picnic area; swimming; fishing; hiking.

SUNSET STATE BEACH
LOCATION: 16 mi. south of Santa Cruz on Hwy. 1, take San Andreas Road turnoff.
FACILITIES: Open year round; 90 sites; water and bathroom facilities; trailer village vehicle sites; picnic area; fishing.

Tahoe City

TAHOE STATE RECREATION AREA
LOCATION: ¼ mi. east of Tahoe City on Hwy. 28.
FACILITIES: Open year round; 39 sites; water and bathroom facilities; trailer village vehicle sites; picnic area; swimming; fishing.

Ventura

EMMA WOOD STATE BEACH
LOCATION: 4 mi. north of Ventura on U.S. 101.
FACILITIES: Open year round; 150 primitive sites; water and bathroom facilities; trailer village vehicle sites; swimming; fishing.

MCGARTH STATE BEACH
LOCATION: From U.S. 101, Ventura, take Seaward Ave., then south on Harbor.
FACILITIES: Open year round; 174 sites; water and bathroom facilities; sanitary station; trailer village vehicle sites; swimming; fishing.

Winterhaven

PICACHO STATE RECREATION AREA
LOCATION: 25 mi. south of Winterhaven.
FACILITIES: Open year round; 50 primitive sites; water and bathroom facilities; trailer village vehicle sites; picnic area; fishing; hiking; exhibit.

RESORTS & BEACHES

Los Angeles

LOS ANGELES AREA - The largest city in the country, Los Angeles is filled with literally thousands of sights from the Sunset Strip, alive with people and glitter to the gigantic letters of the word "Hollywood" lighting up Hollywood Hills. If it's sun, fun and surf you want, visit the sandy shores of Santa Monica, Manhattan Beach, Redondo Beach, Long Beach and Huntington Beach. Then, of course, Los Angeles has all those exciting movie studio tours where you can chat with the stars or stand back and watch them work. Just beyond the city limits you'll find Pasadena, the home of the Tournament of Roses, or Catalina Island with its glass-bottomed boats.

Monterey

MONTEREY PENINSULA - You'll find great sailing, deep-sea fishing, tennis at 19 court locations and golf courses for the player or spectator, including world-famous Pebble Beach. Among the sights to see are Monterey's Fisherman's Wharf, the historic Old Custom House and California's first capitol.

Newport Beach

NEWPORT BEACH AREA - Expansive Pacific beaches where you can enjoy superb sailing, tidepooling, golf, tennis, horseback riding along the water's edge, bicycle trails, challenging water sports, deep sea fishing and whale watching. Nearby is Disneyland with all its enchanted thrills, and chartered cruises past the homes of John Wayne and other famous movie stars.

Palm Springs

PALM SPRINGS AREA - In the "golf capital of the world," you can play on any one of the 36 courses, or you may swim, horseback ride, hike, get revitalized in a mineral bath or take a 2½ mile high adventure ride in the Aerial Tramway. Nearby enjoy a chuck-wagon breakfast ride, and fish or play in the Salton Sea. Palm Springs is also the winter headquarters for baseball's American League Angels. Their spring training games are always open to visitors.

Sacramento

SACRAMENTO AREA - In the city itself, Sacramento boasts the largest attraction of living monuments depicting California's Gold Rush. Walk down board sidewalks surrounded by gas lights, cobblestone streets and 100-year-old structures, relive the Pony Express or wait for a train in an authentic turn-of-the-century atmosphere. Only minutes from the metropolitan area you may journey into the foothills to historic Folsom and the vast gold country or head into wine country through hundreds of miles of delta area.

RESORTS (continued)

San Diego

SAN DIEGO AREA - County beaches stretch more than 70 miles from just below San Clemente southward to the Mexican border. Enjoy water sports in an area which boasts Mediterranean climate. East of the city in the pine-studded Laguna Mountains, hike and mountain climb in the summer, sled and toboggan in the winter. And since less than 40 percent of the land in the country is urbanized, there is plenty of room for horseback riding, hunting, picnicking and camping, as well as several fresh water lakes for fishing.

San Francisco

SAN FRANCISCO AREA - The Golden Gate City is surprisingly compact with most interesting sights within walking distance of one another. In less than an hour you can go from Union Square to Chinatown, cut through the financial district and end at the Embarcadero on the waterfront. And if you're tired of walking, there is always the fun and fascination of taking a cable car. Just outside the city, in almost any direction, you'll discover majestic 1200-year old redwoods, unspoiled beaches, and famous vineyards and wineries.

Santa Barbara

SANTA BARBARA AREA - Take the "Red Tile Tour," a walking tour of 12 blocks that encompasses more than 150 years of California history. Then see nearby vineyards and wineries or the charming Danish village. Also, there is a still-active stagecoach, a cave with walls colorfully painted by the Chumash Indians ages ago, and unspoiled natural beauty at every turn.

Ventura

VENTURA AREA - From Early Chumash Indian tribes through founding of Mission San Buenaventura and the California Pioneers, Ventura is a city rich in historical discoveries. In addition, you'll enjoy beaches, parks, golf courses, fishing, swimming, surfing, tennis, bike riding and more.

BOATING AREAS

Aguanga

VAIL LAKE
FACILITIES: Launching; supplies.

Alameda

ALAMEDA MARINA
FACILITIES: Launching; berths; fuel; supplies.

ALAMEDA MUNICIPAL RAMP
FACILITIES: Launching.

ALAMEDA PUBLIC RAMP
FACILITIES: Launching.

ALAMEDA YACHT HARBOR
FACILITIES: Launching; berths; fuel; supplies.

BALLENA BAY YACHT HARBOR
FACILITIES: Launching; berths; fuel; supplies.

PACIFIC MARINA
FACILITIES: Launching; berths.

Albion

Albion River

ALBION FLATS FISHING VILLAGE
FACILITIES: Launching; berths; fuel; supplies.

SCHOONER'S LANDING
FACILITIES: Launching; berths; fuel; supplies.

Almanor

Lake Almanor

ALMANOR INN AND MARINA
FACILITIES: Launching; berths; fuel; supplies.

LAKE ALMANOR LAUNCHING RAMP
FACILITIES: Launching.

PLUMAS PINES
FACILITIES: Launching; fuel; supplies.

Alpine

LAKE ALPINE
FACILITIES: Launching; fuel; supplies. .

Alturar

BIG SAGE RESERVOIR
FACILITIES: Launching.

Alviso

ALVISO BOAT WORKS & MARINA
FACILITIES: Launching; berths; supplies.

ALVISO MARINA
FACILITIES: Launching; berths.

Anaheim

ANAHEIM LAKE
FACILITIES: Launching; supplies.

Antioch

ANTIOCH PUBLIC RAMP
FACILITIES: Launching.

BIG BREAK RESORT
FACILITIES: Launching; berths; fuel; supplies.

LAURITZEN YACHT HARBOR
FACILITIES: Launching; berths; fuel.

Atascadero

ATASCADERO LAKE

CALIFORNIA

BOATING AREAS (continued)

FACILITIES: Launching; supplies.

Bartel

MEDICINE LAKE RAMP
FACILITIES: Launching.

Bayside

ARCATA LAUNCHING RAMP
FACILITIES: Launching.

Benicia

BENICIA PUBLIC BOAT RAMP
FACILITIES: Launching.

SAM'S HARBOR
FACILITIES: Launching.

Berkeley

ARCO FUEL DOCK
FACILITIES: Launching; berths; fuel; supplies.

BERKELEY AQUATIC
FACILITIES: Launching.

BERKELEY MARINA
FACILITIES: Launching; berths; fuel; supplies.

LARRY KOHLER YACHT SALES
FACILITIES: Launching; berths; fuel; supplies.

Big Bear Lake

BIG BEAR BOAT LANDING
FACILITIES: Launching; berths; fuel; supplies.

BIG BEAR MARINA
FACILITIES: Launching; berths; fuel; supplies.

BIG BEAR PUBLIC LAUNCHING RAMP
FACILITIES: Launching.

BOULDER BAY MARINA
FACILITIES: Launching; berths; fuel; supplies.

CLUSTER PINES RESORT
FACILITIES: Launching; berths; fuel; supplies.

HOLLOWAY'S LANDING AND MARINA
FACILITIES: Launching; berths; fuel; supplies.

JUNIPER BOAT LANDING
FACILITIES: Launching; berths; supplies.

LAKE SHORE LANDING
FACILITIES: Launching; berths; fuel; supplies.

PLEASURE POINT LANDING
FACILITIES: Launching; berths; fuel; supplies.

Big Pine

LAKE SABRINA BOAT LANDING
FACILITIES: Launching; berths; fuel; supplies.

Blythe

Colorado River

BLYTHE MARINA KOA
FACILITIES: Launching; supplies.

QUESHAN PARK
FACILITIES: Launching; berths; fuel; supplies.

Colorado River Road (Colorado River)

MAYFLOWER PARK
FACILITIES: Launching.

SPORTSMEN'S HIDE-A-WAY
FACILITIES: Launching; supplies.

Parker Star Route (Colorado River)

AHA QUIN TRAILER PARK
FACILITIES: Launching; berths; fuel; supplies.

HAAKER'S SKI CAMP
FACILITIES: Launching; berths; supplies.

PARADISE POINT CAMP
FACILITIES: Launching; fuel.

TWIN PALM TRAILER PARK
FACILITIES: Launching; fuel; supplies.

Boca

BOCA RESERVOIR
FACILITIES: Launching.

PROSSER LAKE
FACILITIES: Launching.

Bodega Bay

DORAN PARK
FACILITIES: Launching.

MASON'S BODEGA BAY MARINA
FACILITIES: Launching; berths; fuel.

PORTA BODEGA
FACILITIES: Launching; berths; supplies.

WESTSHORE PARK
FACILITIES: Launching.

Bombay Beach

BOB'S PLAYA RIVIERA
FACILITIES: Launching.

BOMBAY MARINA
FACILITIES: Launching; berths; fuel; supplies.

CORVINA MARINA
FACILITIES: Launching; berths; fuel; supplies.

BOATING AREAS (continued)

NILAND MARINA
FACILITIES: Launching; supplies.

Boulder Creek

LOCH LOMOND RESERVOIR
FACILITIES: Launching; supplies.

Bradley

SAN ANTONIO LAKE
FACILITIES: Launching; berths; fuel; supplies.

Brawley

WIEST LAKE
FACILITIES: Launching.

Bridgeport

Bridgeport Lake

BRIDGEPORT LAKE ACCESS FACILITIY
FACILITIES: Launching.

Twin Lakes

MONO VILLAGE
FACILITIES: Launching; berths; fuel; supplies.

TWIN LAKE STORE
FACILITIES: Launching; berths; fuel; supplies.

THE CRAGS RESORT
FACILITIES: Launching; berths; fuel; supplies.

Burney

Lake Britton

JAMO POINT FISHING ACCESS
FACILITIES: Launching.

MCARTHUR-BURNEY FALLS MEMORIAL STATE PARK
FACILITIES: Launching; berths; supplies.

NORTH SHORE
FACILITIES: Launching.

Calpella

Lake Mendocino

LAKE MENDOCINO FISHING ACCESS
FACILITIES: Launching.

LAKE MENDOCINO MARINA
FACILITIES: Launching; berths; fuel; supplies.

LAKE MENDOCINO PUBLIC RAMP
FACILITIES: Launching.

Campbell

VASONA LAKE
FACILITIES: Launching.

Canyon Dam

Butt Valley Reservoir

COOL SPRINGS
FACILITIES: Launching.

PONDEROSA FLAT
FACILITIES: Launching.

Lake Almanor (Canyon Dam)

LAKE ALMANOR COUNTY PUBLIC LAUNCHING RAMP
FACILITIES: Launching.

Lake Almanor (East Shore)

BIG COVE RESORT
FACILITIES: Launching; fuel; supplies.

BOSWORTHS LAKE ALMANOR RESORT
FACILITIES: Launching; berths; fuel; supplies.

CRAWFORDS LAKESIDE RESORT
FACILITIES: Launching; berths; fuel; supplies.

EASTSHORE MOTEL-RESORT
FACILITIES: Launching; berths.

LAKE HAVEN RESORT
FACILITIES: Launching; berths; fuel; supplies.

LASSEN VIEW RESORT
FACILITIES: Launching; berths; fuel; supplies.

Lake Almanor (Peninsula)

BRATTON'S RESORT
FACILITIES: Launching; berths; fuel; supplies.

CAMPOTEL ALMANOR
FACILITIES: Launching; berths; fuel; supplies.

COUNTRY CLUB RESORT
FACILITIES: Launching; berths; supplies.

HARBOR LITES RESORT
FACILITIES: Launching.

KNOTTY PINE RESORT
FACILITIES: Launching; berths; fuel; supplies.

LITTLE NORWAY RESORT
FACILITIES: Launching; fuel; supplies.

Carmel

Carmel Bay

STILLWATER COVE
FACILITIES: Launching; berths.

Castaic

Castaic Reservoir

CASTAIC OVERLOOK BOAT RAMP

CALIFORNIA

BOATING AREAS (continued)

FACILITIES: Launching.

CASTAIC RIDGE BOAT RAMP
FACILITIES: Launching.

Lake Piru

LAKE PIRU
FACILITIES: Launching.

Pyramid Reservoir

PYRAMID RESERVOIR
FACILITIES: Launching.

Chambers Lodge

HELL HOLE RESERVOIR
FACILITIES: Launching.

Chico

Sacramento River

PINE CREEK LANDING
FACILITIES: Launching; fuel; supplies.

SCOTTY'S BOAT LANDING
FACILITIES: Launching; berths; fuel; supplies.

Chilcoot

FRENCHMAN LAKE
FACILITIES: Launching.

Chowchilla

BERENDA RESERVOIR
FACILITIES: Launching.

Chula Vista

LOWER OTAY LAKE
FACILITIES: Launching; fuel; supplies.

Cisco

LAKE VALLEY RESERVOIR
FACILITIES: Launching.

Clarksburg

CLARKSBURG PUBLIC RAMP
FACILITIES: Launching.

Colusa

Sacramento River

COLUSA-SACRAMENTO RIVER STATE RECREATION AREA
FACILITIES: Launching; supplies.

CRUISE'N TARRY MARINA TRAILER PARK
FACILITIES: Launching; berths; fuel; supplies.

Comptonville

Bullards Bar Reservoir

COTTAGE CREEK PUBLIC LAUNCHING RAMP
FACILITIES: Launching.

DARK DAY PUBLIC LAUNCHING RAMP
FACILITIES: Launching.

Confidence

CHERRY LAKE
FACILITIES: Launching.

Copperopolin

SALT SPRINGS RESERVOIR
FACILITIES: Launching.

Cottonwood

Sacramento River (Shasta County)

BALL'S FERRY FISHING ACCESS
FACILITIES: Launching.

BALL'S FERRY FISHING RESORT
FACILITIES: Launching; berths; fuel; supplies.

REDDING ISLAND FISHING ACCESS
FACILITIES: Launching.

Coulterville

Lake McClure

BAGBY MARINA
FACILITIES: Launching; fuel; supplies.

HORSESHOE BEND MARINA
FACILITIES: Launching; berths; fuel; supplies.

HUNTERS VALLEY POINT MARINA
FACILITIES: Launching; fuel; supplies.

MCCLURE POINT
FACILITIES: Launching; berths; fuel; supplies.

SWICKARD'S MARINA
FACILITIES: Launching; berths; fuel; supplies.

Courtland

COURTLAND DOCK
FACILITIES: Launching; supplies.

TYE-A-LEE DOCKS
FACILITIES: Launching; berths.

Covington Mill

South Clair Engle Lake

CEDAR STOCK & MARINA
FACILITIES: Launching; berths; fuel; supplies.

ESTRELLITA MARINA
FACILITIES: Launching; berths; fuel; supplies.

BOATING AREAS (continued)

FAIRVIEW MARINA
FACILITIES: Launching; berths; fuel; supplies.

STUART FORK BOAT RAMP
FACILITIES: Launching.

Crescent City

CRESCENT CITY PUBLIC FISHING ACCESS
FACILITIES: Launching; berths.

Cuyamaca Lake

CUYAMACA LAKE FISHING RESORT
FACILITIES: Launching; fuel; supplies.

Dana Point

EMBARCADERO MARINA
FACILITIES: Launching; fuel.

Davis Dam

Bullhead City (Colorado River)

FISH & FUN RESORT
FACILITIES: Launching; fuel.

GRANDVIEW LANDING
FACILITIES: Launching.

HOLIDAY SHORES MARINA
FACILITIES: Launching; berths; fuel.

Delana

LAKE WOOLOMES
FACILITIES: Launching.

Desert Shores

Desert Shores-Thermal (Salton Sea)

DESERT SHORES TRAILER PARK & MARINA
FACILITIES: Launching; berths; fuel; supplies.

FISHERMAN'S WHARF
FACILITIES: Launching; fuel; supplies.

HELEN'S BEACH HOUSE & HARBOR
FACILITIES: Launching.

MARINA MOBILE ESTATES
FACILITIES: Launching; berths; fuel; supplies.

RANCHO MARINA
FACILITIES: Launching; fuel; supplies.

SALTON SEA BEACH MARINA
FACILITIES: Launching; fuel; supplies.

Dos Palos

LOS BANOS RESERVOIR
FACILITIES: Launching.

Eays

Parker Dam-California Shore (Colorado River)

BIG BEND RESORT
FACILITIES: Launching; berths; fuel; supplies.

CALIFORNIA
FACILITIES: Launching; fuel; supplies.

FISHING VILLAGE
FACILITIES: Launching; supplies.

RIVER LODGE RESORT
FACILITIES: Launching; fuel; supplies.

THE RITE SPOT
FACILITIES: Launching; fuel; supplies.

TOM'S LANDING
FACILITIES: Launching; supplies.

Parker Strip-California Shore (Colorado River)

BERMUDA PALMS
FACILITIES: Launching; berths.

ECHO TRAILER PARK
FACILITIES: Launching; fuel; supplies.

KINDER'S COLORADO RIVER CAMP
FACILITIES: Launching; fuel; supplies.

RIVERLAND RESORT
FACILITIES: Launching; fuel; supplies.

RIVER SHORE RESORT
FACILITIES: Launching; berths.

RIVER VIEW TRAILER PARK
FACILITIES: Launching.

SPORTSMANS TRAILER PARK
FACILITIES: Launching; fuel.

STIFFLER'S DESERT RIVIERA
FACILITIES: Launching.

WHEEL-ER IN FAMILY RESORT
FACILITIES: Launching; fuel; supplies.

WINDMILL TRAILER PARK
FACILITIES: Launching; berths.

Edison

LAKE MING
FACILITIES: Launching.

Edna

LOPEZ LAKE
FACILITIES: Launching; fuel; supplies.

El Cajon

LAKE MURRAY
FACILITIES: Launching; fuel; supplies.

El Centio

SUNBEAM LAKE
FACILITIES: Launching.

CALIFORNIA

BOATING AREAS (continued)

Elk Creek

STONY GORGE RESERVOIR
FACILITIES: Launching; fuel; supplies.

Escondida

LAKE WOHLFORD
FACILITIES: Launching; fuel; supplies.

Eureka

Humboldt Bay

EUREKA MOORING BASIN
FACILITIES: Launching; fuel.

FAIRHAVEN LAUNCHING RAMP
FACILITIES: Launching.

SAMOA PENINSULA COASTAL ACCESS
FACILITIES: Launching.

Fall River

Eastman Lake

CROGAN'S SPORTSMAN'S LODGE
FACILITIES: Launching; fuel; supplies.

Fields Landing

Humboldt Bay

E-Z BOAT LANDING & TRAILER PARK
FACILITIES: Launching; berths; fuel; supplies.

FIELDS LANDING BOAT RAMP
FACILITIES: Launching.

JOHNNY'S LANDING & TRAILER COURT
FACILITIES: Launching; berths; fuel; supplies.

PAT'S PLACE
FACILITIES: Launching; fuel; supplies.

Firebaugh

MENDOTA POOL RESERVOIR PUBLIC BOAT LAUNCHING FACILITY
FACILITIES: Launching.

Folsom

BEALE'S POINT
FACILITIES: Launching.

GRANITE BAY
FACILITIES: Launching.

PENINSULA CAMPGROUND
FACILITIES: Launching.

RATTLESNAKE BAR
FACILITIES: Launching.

South Shore

BROWNS RAVINE

FACILITIES: Launching; berths; fuel; supplies.

DYKE 8
FACILITIES: Launching.

Forest Glen

Ruth Lake

HUBERT'S LAKESIDE RESORT & MARINA
FACILITIES: Launching; berths; fuel; supplies.

RUTH LAKE COMMUNITY SERVICES DISTRICT RAMP
FACILITIES: Launching.

Fort Bidwell

FEE RESERVOIR
FACILITIES: Launching.

Fort Bragg

Noyo River

ANCHOR MARINE INC.
FACILITIES: Launching; berths; supplies.

DOLPHIN COVE MARINA
FACILITIES: Launching; berths; fuel.

MACKERRICHER STATE PARK
FACILITIES: Launching; fuel; supplies.

NOYO MOORING BASIN
FACILITIES: Launching; berths.

SPORTSMAN'S DOCK
FACILITIES: Launching; fuel; supplies.

Fort Dick

LAKE EARL
FACILITIES: Launching.

SMITH RIVER ANGLING ACCESS
FACILITIES: Launching; supplies.

Freeport

GARCIA BEND PUBLIC RAMP
FACILITIES: Launching.

Fremont

LAKE ELIZABETH
FACILITIES: Launching; supplies.

Georgetown

LAKE EDSON
FACILITIES: Launching.

Glenhaven

GLENHAVEN BEACH
FACILITIES: Launching; berths; fuel; supplies.

INDIAN BEACH RESORT
FACILITIES: Launching; berths.

BOATING AREAS (continued)

JOHNSON'S MARINA & LODGING RE-
SORT
FACILITIES: Launching; berths; fuel; sup-
plies.

MCALLISTER'S GLENHAVEN INN
FACILITIES: Launching; berths; fuel.

POWARS RESORT
FACILITIES: Launching.

PLAGG'S RESORT
FACILITIES: Launching; berths; fuel.

SCHOUX STRAIGHT RESORT
FACILITIES: Launching; berths; supplies.

SHAMROCK RESORT
FACILITIES: Launching; berths; supplies.

STARLITE RESORT
FACILITIES: Launching.

Gold Run

Rollins Lake

GREENHORN
FACILITIES: Launching.

LONG RAVINE
FACILITIES: Launching; fuel; supplies.

ORCHARD SPRINGS
FACILITIES: Launching; berths; fuel; supplies.

PENINSULA LAUNCHING
FACILITIES: Launching.

Goleta

GOLETA BEACH
FACILITIES: Launching.

Grimes

GRIMES BOAT LANDING
FACILITIES: Launching; berths; fuel; supplies.

Guerneville

Russian River

JOHNSON'S RESORT
FACILITIES: Launching; supplies.

Homewood

Lake Tahoe

HOMEWOOD HIGH & DRY MARINA
FACILITIES: Launching; fuel; supplies.

OBEXERS BOAT & MOTOR SALES
FACILITIES: Launching; berths; fuel; supplies.

Hornbrook

Copco Lake

COPCO LAKE STORE
FACILITIES: Launching; fuel; supplies.

MALLARD COVE
FACILITIES: Launching.

Humphrey's Station

Pine Flat Reservoir

DEER CREEK
FACILITIES: Launching.

DRIFTWOOD TRAILER PARK
FACILITIES: Launching.

ISLAND PARK
FACILITIES: Launching.

LAKERIDGE MARINA
FACILITIES: Launching; berths; fuel; supplies.

LAKEVIEW
FACILITIES: Launching.

LOMBARDO'S LAKEVIEW RESORT
FACILITIES: Launching; berths; fuel; supplies.

TRIMMER ENTERPRISES
FACILITIES: Launching; berths; fuel; supplies.

TRIMMER VIEW
FACILITIES: Launching.

Inglewood

Marina Del Rey

AMMARINE LTD.
FACILITIES: Launching; supplies.

CHRIS CRAFT PACIFIC
FACILITIES: Launching; berths; supplies.

FORTY-FOUR DEL REY MARINA
FACILITIES: Launching; fuel.

PUBLIC BEACH & HAND LAUNCHING
FACILITIES: Launching.

PUBLIC LAUNCHING RAMP
FACILITIES: Launching.

Ione

LAKE AMADOR
FACILITIES: Launching; berths; supplies.

PARDEE LAKE
FACILITIES: Launching; berths; fuel; supplies.

Isabella

Lake Isabella

ISABELLA PENINSULA PUBLIC LAUNCH-
ING FACILITY
FACILITIES: Launching.

KERN VALLEY MARINA
FACILITIES: Launching; fuel; supplies.

CALIFORNIA

BOATING AREAS (continued)

OLD ISABELLA ROAD PUBLIC LAUNCH-
ING FACILITY
FACILITIES: Launching.

Isleton

VIERRA'S RESORT
FACILITIES: Launching; berths; fuel; supplies.

Jenner

Russian River

BRIDGEHAVEN RESORT
FACILITIES: Launching; berths; supplies.

RIVER'S END RESORT
FACILITIES: Launching; supplies.

June Lake

GRANT LAKE
FACILITIES: Launching; supplies.

Gull Lake

GULL LAKE BOAT LANDING
FACILITIES: Launching; berths; fuel; supplies.

UPPER GULL LAKE PUBLIC RAMP
FACILITIES: Launching.

June Lake

BIG ROCK LANDING
FACILITIES: Launching; berths; fuel; supplies.

JUNE LAKE PUBLIC RAMP
FACILITIES: Launching.

JUNE LAKE MARINA
FACILITIES: Launching; berths; fuel; supplies.

Kane Spring

BENSON'S LANDING
FACILITIES: Launching; fuel; supplies.

Kingsburg

KINGS RIVER
FACILITIES: Launching; fuel.

Kirkwood

CAPLES LAKE
FACILITIES: Launching; berths; fuel; supplies.

Kit Carson

Silver Lake

KAY'S SILVER LAKE RESORT
FACILITIES: Launching; supplies.

Klamath

Klamath River

CHINOOK TRAILER RESORT
FACILITIES: Launching; berths; fuel.

CHUB'S CAMP
FACILITIES: Launching; fuel; supplies.

KING SALMON RESORT
FACILITIES: Launching; berths; fuel; supplies.

PANTHER CREEK RESORT
FACILITIES: Launching; berths; fuel.

REQUA BOAT DOCK & TRAILER PARK
FACILITIES: Launching; berths; fuel; supplies.

Klamath Glen

KLAMATH GLEN
FACILITIES: Launching; supplies.

Knights Landing

Sacramento River

KNIGHTS LANDING BOAT CLUB
FACILITIES: Launching; fuel.

KNIGHTS LANDING PUBLIC FISHING AC-
CESS
FACILITIES: Launching.

YOLO-SUTTER BOAT CLUB, INC.
FACILITIES: Launching.

La Grange

Don Pedro Reservoir

LAKE DON PEDRO MARINA
FACILITIES: Launching; fuel; supplies.

Lake Elsinore

LAKE ELSINORE STATE RECREATION
AREA
FACILITIES: Launching; berths; fuel; sup-
plies.

Lakehead

Lake Shasta

ANTLER'S RESORT
FACILITIES: Launching; fuel; supplies.

RIVERVIEW RESORT
FACILITIES: Launching; berths; supplies.

Lakeport

AQUA VILLAGE
FACILITIES: Launching; berths; fuel.

COUNTY PUBLIC LAUNCHING RAMP
FACILITIES: Launching.

EARLS HARBOR
FACILITIES: Launching.

EL DORADO BOTEL
FACILITIES: Launching.

BOATING AREAS (continued)

FIFTH STREET PUBLIC LAUNCHING FACILITY
FACILITIES: Launching.

HILLCREST PARK RESORT
FACILITIES: Launching.

LAKEPORT PUBLIC DOCK
FACILITIES: Launching.

MARV'S SKI BOAT
FACILITIES: Launching; berths; supplies.

NORTHPORT TRAILER RESORT
FACILITIES: Launching.

PARK VIEW RESORT
FACILITIES: Launching.

ROBIN HILL
FACILITIES: Launching.

ROCKY POINT
FACILITIES: Launching; fuel; supplies.

SANTA RITA
FACILITIES: Launching.

SHADY BEACH
FACILITIES: Launching.

SKYLARK MOTEL
FACILITIES: Launching.

SPORTSMENS PIT STOP
FACILITIES: Launching; berths; fuel; supplies.

STILLWOOD RESORT
FACILITIES: Launching.

SUNRISE RESORT
FACILITIES: Launching.

WALNUT BEACH MARINA
FACILITIES: Launching; fuel; supplies.

WESTERN HILL RESORT
FACILITIES: Launching.

WILL-O-POINT RESORT
FACILITIES: Launching; fuel; supplies.

Lakeside

EL CAPITAN LAKE
FACILITIES: Launching; fuel; supplies.

LAKE JENNINGS
FACILITIES: Launching; supplies.

SAN VICENTE LAKE
FACILITIES: Launching; fuel; supplies.

Lakeshore

FLORENCE LAKE BOATHOUSE
FACILITIES: Launching; fuel; supplies.

Huntington Lake

DEER CREEK PUBLIC RAMP
FACILITIES: Launching.

HUNTINGTON LAKE RESORT MARINA
FACILITIES: Launching; berths; fuel; supplies.

RANCHERIA PUBLIC RAMP
FACILITIES: Launching.

WAGNER'S MAMMOTH POOL RESORT
FACILITIES: Launching; fuel; supplies.

Las Crucer

REFUGIO STATE BEACH
FACILITIES: Launching; supplies.

Lee Vining

ELLERY LAKE
FACILITIES: Launching.

Tiogas Lake

SADDLEBAG LAKE RESORT
FACILITIES: Launching; supplies.

Lemoncove

Lake Kaweah

KAWEAH MARINA
FACILITIES: Launching; berths; fuel; supplies.

LEMON HILL
FACILITIES: Launching.

Likely

WEST VALLEY RESERVOIR
FACILITIES: Launching.

Livermore

DEL VALLE RESERVOIR
FACILITIES: Launching.

Long Beach

Anaheim Bay-Sunset Aquatic Park

HUNTINGTON HARBOR
FACILITIES: Launching; berths; supplies.

SUNSET AQUATIC MARINA
FACILITIES: Launching; berths.

Cabrillo Beach

CABRILLO BEACH PUBLIC LAUNCHING FACILITY
FACILITIES: Launching.

Cerritos Channel East Basin

CERRITOS YACHT ANCHORAGE
FACILITIES: Launching; berths.

Fish Harbor

AL LARSON MARINA
FACILITIES: Launching; berths; supplies.

GOLDEN AVENUE LAUNCHING RAMP
FACILITIES: Launching.

CALIFORNIA

BOATING AREAS (continued)

HARBOR PARK LAKE
FACILITIES: Launching.

Long Beach Marina, Alamitos Bay

CHANNEL BOAT YARD
FACILITIES: Launching; supplies.

LONG BEACH MARINA
FACILITIES: Launching; berths; fuel; supplies.

MARINA SHIPYARD
FACILITIES: Launching; supplies.

MARINE STADIUM EAST LAUNCHING RAMP
FACILITIES: Launching.

MARINE STADIUM WEST LAUNCHING RAMP
FACILITIES: Launching.

Los Angeles River

CLAIR YACHTS, INC.
FACILITIES: Launching.

Outer Los Angeles Harbor

CABRILLO BOAT SHOP & YACHT BASIN
FACILITIES: Launching; berths; supplies.

SHELTER POINT YACHT SERVICES, INC.
FACILITIES: Launching; berths; supplies.

SOUTHWIND MARINA
FACILITIES: Launching; berths; fuel.

Los Banos

San Luis Reservoir

O'NEILL FOREBAY
FACILITIES: Launching.

SAN LUIS STATE RECREATION AREA
FACILITIES: Launching.

Los Gator

LEXINGTON RESERVOIR
FACILITIES: Launching.

Los Malinos

Sacramento River

HIDDEN HARBOR
FACILITIES: Launching; berths; fuel.

MILL CREEK RECREATION AREA
FACILITIES: Launching; fuel; supplies.

PELHAMS BAY RESORT
FACILITIES: Launching; berths; fuel; supplies.

RIVER INN MOBILE PARK
FACILITIES: Launching; berths; fuel.

Lucerne

ARROW PARK & BAIT SHOP
FACILITIES: Launching; supplies.

BAMBOO HOLLOW
FACILITIES: Launching; fuel.

BEACHCOMBER RESORT
FACILITIES: Launching; fuel.

LAKE SANDS RESORT
FACILITIES: Launching.

LUCERNE PUBLIC LAUNCHING RAMP
FACILITIES: Launching.

RIVIERA BEACH CLUB
FACILITIES: Launching.

SNUFFY'S
FACILITIES: Launching.

WE FLOATERS
FACILITIES: Launching.

Malibu

PARADISE COVE PIER
FACILITIES: Launching; supplies.

Mammoth Lakes

Lake George

WOODS LODGE
FACILITIES: Launching; berths; fuel; supplies.

Lake Mamie

WILDYRIE
FACILITIES: Launching; berths; supplies.

Lake Mary

LAKE MARY STORE
FACILITIES: Launching; fuel; supplies.

Markleeville

LOWER BLUE LAKE
FACILITIES: Launching.

Marshall

Tomales Bay

GOLDEN HINDE BOATEL
FACILITIES: Launching; berths; fuel; supplies.

LAWSON'S LANDING
FACILITIES: Launching; fuel; supplies.

MARCONI COVE MARINA
FACILITIES: Launching; berths; fuel.

MARSHALL BOAT WORKS
FACILITIES: Launching; berths; fuel; supplies.

MILLER PARK BOAT LAUNCH
FACILITIES: Launching.

BOATING AREAS (continued)

MILLER PARK MARINA
FACILITIES: Launching; berths; fuel; supplies.

NORTH SHORE BOATS
FACILITIES: Launching; fuel; supplies.

Martinez

MARTINEZ MARINA
FACILITIES: Launching; berths; fuel; supplies.

Maxwell

EAST PARK RESERVOIR
FACILITIES: Launching; fuel; supplies.

McKinleyville

MAD RIVER BOAT RAMP
FACILITIES: Launching.

Mecca

North Shore

NORTH SHORE MARINA
FACILITIES: Launching; berths; fuel; supplies.

SALTON SEA STATE RECREATION AREA
FACILITIES: Launching.

Meeks Bay

Lake Tahoe

MEEKS BAY RESORT
FACILITIES: Launching; berths; fuel; supplies.

Meyers

Echo Lake

ECHO LAKE RESORT
FACILITIES: Launching; fuel; supplies.

Mird Monte

LAKE CASITAS RECREATION AREA
FACILITIES: Launching; berths; fuel; supplies.

Miramar

MIRAMAR LAKE
FACILITIES: Launching; fuel; supplies.

Milford

ANTELOPE LAKE
FACILITIES: Launching.

Monte

Russian River

CASINI RANCH CAMPGROUND
FACILITIES: Launching; supplies.

MONTE RIO ANGLING ACCESS
FACILITIES: Launching; supplies.

Monterey

Monterey Bay

HOVER EQUIPMENT CO.
FACILITIES: Launching; supplies.

JOE'S BOAT HOIST
FACILITIES: Launching; supplies.

MONTEREY HARBOR
FACILITIES: Launching; berths; fuel; supplies.

Morgan Hill

ANDERSON LAKE
FACILITIES: Launching.

CALERO RESERVOIR
FACILITIES: Launching.

CHESBRO RESERVOIR
FACILITIES: Launching.

Morro Bay

MIDWAY MARINA
FACILITIES: Launching; berths.

MORRO BAY COASTAL ANGLING
FACILITIES: Launching.

MORRO BAY MARINA
FACILITIES: Launching; berths; fuel; supplies.

R & M MARINE
FACILITIES: Launching; berths; supplies.

Moss Landing

WOODWARD BOAT BROKERAGE
FACILITIES: Launching; fuel.

Mount Shasta

LAKE SISKIYOU
FACILITIES: Launching; fuel; supplies.

Mountain Center

LAKE HEMET
FACILITIES: Launching; supplies.

Mountain Gate

Bailey Cove (Lake Shasta)

BAILEY COVE PUBLIC LAUNCHING RAMP
FACILITIES: Launching.

HOLIDAY HARBOR
FACILITIES: Launching; berths; supplies.

Jones Valley (Lake Shasta)

JONES VALLEY PUBLIC BOAT RAMP
FACILITIES: Launching; fuel.

CALIFORNIA

BOATING AREAS (continued)

JONES VALLEY RESORT & MARINA
FACILITIES: Launching; berths; fuel; supplies.

Lake Shasta

BRIDGE BAY RESORT & MARINA
FACILITIES: Launching; berths; fuel; supplies.

CENTIMUDI BAY PUBLIC BOAT RAMP
FACILITIES: Launching.

DIGGER BAY MARINA
FACILITIES: Launching; berths; fuel; supplies.

LAKEVIEW RESORT
FACILITIES: Launching; berths; fuel; supplies.

PACKERS BAY PUBLIC LAUNCHING
RAMP
FACILITIES: Launching.

POINT MCCLOUD RESORT
FACILITIES: Launching; fuel; supplies.

SILVERTHORN BAY RESORT
FACILITIES: Launching; fuel.

Lakeshore (Lake Shasta)

LAKESHORE VILLA TRAILER PARK &
CAMPGROUND
FACILITIES: Launching; berths.

O'Brien Creek Inlet (Lake Shasta)

SHASTA MARINA
FACILITIES: Launching; berths; fuel; supplies.

Salt Creek (Lake Shasta)

HOLIDAY FLOTELS
FACILITIES: Launching; berths; fuel; supplies.

SALT CREEK LODGE
FACILITIES: Launching; berths; fuel; supplies.

Sugarloaf (Lake Shasta)

SUGARLOAF BEACH & MARINA
FACILITIES: Launching; berths; fuel; supplies.

SUGARLOAF COTTAGES
FACILITIES: Launching.

Napa

Napa River

CITY OF NAPA MARINA
FACILITIES: Launching.

MOORE'S RESORT
FACILITIES: Launching; fuel; supplies.

NAPA VALLEY MARINA
FACILITIES: Launching; berths; fuel; supplies.

Needles

Colorado River

NEEDLES MARINA PARK
FACILITIES: Launching; berths; fuel; supplies.

RAINBO BEACH MARINA
FACILITIES: Launching; fuel.

WETMORE'S BEACH & TRAILER COURT
FACILITIES: Launching.

YOGI BEAR'S JELLYSTONE PARK
FACILITIES: Launching; berths; fuel; supplies.

Nevada City

Scotts Flat Lake

SCOTTS FLAT LAKE MARINA
FACILITIES: Launching; fuel; supplies.

Newport Beach

Balboa

DAVEY'S LOCKER, INC.
FACILITIES: Launching; fuel; supplies.

Bayshores

BAY SHORE PARK
FACILITIES: Launching; berths.

Lido Isle-Lido Peninsula

SCHOCK HARDWARE & REPAIR
FACILITIES: Launching; berths; supplies.

28TH STREET MARINA
FACILITIES: Launching; berths.

Upper Newport Bay

DEANZA BAYSIDE BOAT LAUNCH
FACILITIES: Launching; berths; fuel.

Newport Bay—Main Channel & Turning Basin

BOATSWAIN'S LOCKER, INC.
FACILITIES: Launching; supplies.

VIKINGS PORT
FACILITIES: Launching; berths.

**Upper Newport Bay-Newport Dunes Aquatic
Park**

NEWPORT DUNES
FACILITIES: Launching; berths; fuel.

Nice

AURORA RESORT
FACILITIES: Launching; supplies.

BAYWOOD BEACH RESORT
FACILITIES: Launching; fuel; supplies.

BOATING AREAS (continued)

CASTAWAY HOUSEBOAT RENTAL
FACILITIES: Launching; berths; fuel; supplies.

DRIFT INN TRAILER RESORT
FACILITIES: Launching.

HOLIDAY HARBOR
FACILITIES: Launching; berths; fuel; supplies.

LEN-LEE TRAILER RESORT
FACILITIES: Launching; berths.

SHADE & SHORE RESORT
FACILITIES: Launching; berths; supplies.

THE HARBOR
FACILITIES: Launching; fuel.

TIKI TIKI
FACILITIES: Launching; berths; supplies.

TONY'S CAMPGROUND
FACILITIES: Launching; fuel; supplies.

TREEHAVEN RESORT
FACILITIES: Launching.

WATEREDGE
FACILITIES: Launching.

WAYNE'S RESORT
FACILITIES: Launching.

Niland

RED HILL MARINA
FACILITIES: Launching; fuel; supplies.

North Shore

Lake Shasta

KINGS BEACH
FACILITIES: Launching.

Novato

BLACK POINT BOAT LAUNCH RAMP
FACILITIES: Launching.

Oakdale

WOODWARD RESERVOIR
FACILITIES: Launching; berths; fuel; supplies.

Oakhurst

Bass Lake

BASS LAKE RECREATIONAL AREA
FACILITIES: Launching; supplies.

MCDOUGALD'S
FACILITIES: Launching; berths; fuel; supplies.

PINES MARINA
FACILITIES: Launching; fuel; supplies.

THE FORKS RESORT
FACILITIES: Launching; fuel; supplies.

Oakland

BOAT MART
FACILITIES: Launching; berths; fuel; supplies.

JACK LONDON MARINA
FACILITIES: Launching; berths; fuel; supplies.

LAKE MERRITT RECREATION AREA
FACILITIES: Launching.

OAKLAND MARINA
FACILITIES: Launching; berths; fuel; supplies.

OAKLAND PUBLIC RAMP
FACILITIES: Launching.

Oceanside

OCEANSIDE HARBOR
FACILITIES: Launching; berths.

OCEANSIDE HARBOR LAUNCHING RAMP
FACILITIES: Launching.

Orland

Black Butte Reservoir

BUCKHORN
FACILITIES: Launching.

EAGLE PASS
FACILITIES: Launching.

ORLAND BUTTES
FACILITIES: Launching.

Oroville

ENTERPRISE
FACILITIES: Launching.

LIME SADDLE RECREATION AREA
FACILITIES: Launching; berths; fuel; supplies.

Southwest Shore

BIDWELL CANYON
FACILITIES: Launching; berths; fuel; supplies.

LOAFER CREEK
FACILITIES: Launching.

SPILLWAY
FACILITIES: Launching.

THERMALITO AFTERBAY
FACILITIES: Launching.

Pacific Grove

Monterey Bay

HOVER EQUIPMENT CO.
FACILITIES: Launching.

CALIFORNIA

BOATING AREAS (continued)

JOE'S BOAT HOIST
FACILITIES: Launching; supplies.

MONTEREY HARBOR
FACILITIES: Launching; berths; fuel; supplies.

Palo Alto

PALO ALTO YACHT HARBOR
FACILITIES: Launching; berths.

Palo Verde

Colorado River

ARPS TRAILER PARK
FACILITIES: Launching; berths; fuel.

BUREAU OF RECLAMATION BOAT RAMP
FACILITIES: Launching.

COCO PALMS MOBILE PARK
FACILITIES: Launching.

DAVY CROCKETT CAMP
FACILITIES: Launching; berths; supplies.

PALO VERDE COUNTY PARK
FACILITIES: Launching.

SANDBAR TRAILER PARK
FACILITIES: Launching.

Peddler Hill

Bear River Reservoir

LOWER BEAR RIVER RESORT
FACILITIES: Launching; supplies.

Petaluma

Petaluma River

GILARDI'S FISHING RESORT
FACILITIES: Launching; berths; fuel; supplies.

MIRA MONTE MARINA
FACILITIES: Launching; berths; fuel.

PETALUMA LAUNCHING RAMP
FACILITIES: Launching.

Picacho

Colorado River

IMPERIAL OASIS
FACILITIES: Launching; fuel; supplies.

Imperial Reservoir (Colorado River)

FISHER'S LANDING
FACILITIES: Launching; berths; fuel; supplies.

MARTINEZ LAKE MARINA
FACILITIES: Launching; berths; fuel; supplies.

PICACHO STATE RECREATION AREA
FACILITIES: Launching.

WALTER'S CAMP
FACILITIES: Launching; fuel.

Pinale

Rodeo

JOSEPH'S FISHING RESORT
FACILITIES: Launching; fuel; supplies.

RODEO MARINA
FACILITIES: Launching; berths; fuel; supplies.

Pinecrest

PINECREST LAKE
FACILITIES: Launching; fuel; supplies.

Pine Ridge

MILLERTON LAKE STATE RECREATION
AREA
FACILITIES: Launching; berths; fuel; supplies.

Wishon Reservoir

WISHON VILLAGE
FACILITIES: Launching; fuel; supplies.

Pittsburg

Honker Bay

MCAVOY YACHT HARBOR
FACILITIES: Launching; berths; fuel; supplies.

Pittsburg

HARRIS YACHT HARBOR
FACILITIES: Launching; berths; fuel; supplies.

PITTSBURG MARINA
FACILITIES: Launching; berths.

Point Arena

ARENA COVE SPORTS CENTER
FACILITIES: Launching; fuel; supplies.

Pollock Pines

Jenkinson Reservoir

SLY PARK RECREATION AREA
FACILITIES: Launching; berths.

Port Hueneme

Channel Islands Harbor

CHANNEL ISLANDS HARBOR PUBLIC
LAUNCHING RAMP
FACILITIES: Launching; berths.

CHANNEL ISLANDS LANDING
FACILITIES: Launching; berths; supplies.

BOATING AREAS (continued)

CHANNEL ISLANDS MARINA
FACILITIES: Launching; berths; fuel; supplies.

PENINSULA YACHT ANCHORAGE
FACILITIES: Launching; berths; fuel; supplies.

Port San Luis

Avila Beach

HARBOR ASSOCIATES
FACILITIES: Launching; supplies.

PORT SAN LUIS MARINA
FACILITIES: Launching.

Portola

LAKE DAVIS
FACILITIES: Launching.

Potter Valley

Lake Pillsbury

BOGNER'S LAKE PILLSBURY PINES
FACILITIES: Launching; berths; fuel; supplies.

LAKE PILLSBURY RESORT
FACILITIES: Launching; berths; fuel; supplies.

Red Bluff

Sacramento River

BEND MOBILE PARK
FACILITIES: Launching; fuel.

BOW RIVER MARINA & TRAILER PARK
FACILITIES: Launching; fuel.

LLOYD E. SMITH BOAT SHOP
FACILITIES: Launching; berths; fuel; supplies.

RED BLUFF CITY MARINA
FACILITIES: Launching; berths; fuel; supplies.

Redding

Lake Redding

CALDWELL PARK BOAT RAMP
FACILITIES: Launching.

POSSE GROUNDS BOAT RAMP
FACILITIES: Launching.

Redondo Beach

REDONDO BEACH MARINA
FACILITIES: Launching; berths; fuel.

Redwood City

DOCKTOWN MARINA
FACILITIES: Launching; berths; fuel; supplies.

HOWARD'S YACHT SALES
FACILITIES: Launching; fuel; supplies.

REDWOOD CITY MUNICIPAL MARINA
FACILITIES: Launching; berths.

Richmond

PACIFIC BOAT WORKS
FACILITIES: Launching; fuel; supplies.

RED ROCK MARINA
FACILITIES: Launching; berths; fuel; supplies.

RICHMOND PUBLIC RAMP
FACILITIES: Launching.

Rio Vista

DELTA MARINA YACHT HARBOR
FACILITIES: Launching; berths; fuel; supplies.

HAP'S BAIT & SPORTS STORE
FACILITIES: Launching; berths; fuel; supplies.

RIO VISTA PUBLIC RAMP
FACILITIES: Launching.

Ripley

Colorado River

PETER MCINTYRE COUNTY PARK
FACILITIES: Launching.

Rutherford

LAKE HENNESSEY
FACILITIES: Launching.

Sacramento

Andrus Island

B & W BOAT RESORT
FACILITIES: Launching; berths; fuel; supplies.

KORTH'S PIRATES LAIR MARINA
FACILITIES: Launching; berths; fuel; supplies.

LIGHTHOUSE RESORT
FACILITIES: Launching; berths; fuel; supplies.

BETHANY RESERVOIR
FACILITIES: Launching.

Bethel Island

BEACON HARBOR
FACILITIES: Launching; berths; fuel.

BETHEL HARBOR
FACILITIES: Launching; berths; fuel; supplies.

DELTA RESORT
FACILITIES: Launching; berths; fuel; supplies.

CALIFORNIA

BOATING AREAS (continued)

FARRAR PARK HARBOR & DRY DOCK
FACILITIES: Launching; berths; supplies.

FRANK'S MARINA
FACILITIES: Launching; berths; fuel; supplies.

RUSSO'S MARINA
FACILITIES: Launching; berths; fuel; supplies.

Brannan Island

BRANNAN ISLAND STATE RECREATION AREA
FACILITIES: Launching; berths.

Buckley's Cove

BUCKLEY'S COVE PUBLIC RAMP
FACILITIES: Launching.

FORE 'N AFT
FACILITIES: Launching; fuel; supplies.

HOFFMAN ANCHORAGE
FACILITIES: Launching; berths; supplies.

LADDS STOCKTON MARINA
FACILITIES: Launching; berths; supplies.

WINDMILL COVE MARINA
FACILITIES: Launching; berths; fuel; supplies.

Collinsville Resort

COLLINSVILLE FISHING RESORT
FACILITIES: Launching; berths; fuel; supplies.

Coney Island

DEL'S BOAT HARBOR
FACILITIES: Launching; fuel; supplies.

Dos Reis Access Area

DOS REIS PUBLIC FISHING ACCESS
FACILITIES: Launching.

HAVENS ACRES RIVER CLUB
FACILITIES: Launching; berths; fuel; supplies.

Dutch Slough

CAROL'S HARBOR & MARINA
FACILITIES: Launching; berths; fuel; supplies.

ED-DE'S MARINA
FACILITIES: Launching; berths.

Empire Tract

HERMAN & HELEN'S RESORT
FACILITIES: Launching; berths; fuel; supplies.

Schad Landing

EDDO'S BOAT HARBOR
FACILITIES: Launching; berths; fuel; supplies.

Steamboat Slough

GRAND ISLAND PUBLIC RAMP
FACILITIES: Launching.

SNUG HARBOR RESORT
FACILITIES: Launching; berths; fuel; supplies.

Terminous

TOWER PARK MARINA
FACILITIES: Launching; berths; fuel; supplies.

VILLAGE WEST MARINA
FACILITIES: Launching; berths; supplies.

Woodbridge

LOUIS PARK FORE 'N AFT
FACILITIES: Launching; fuel; supplies.

Salton City

LIDO PALMS MARINA
FACILITIES: Launching; berths; fuel; supplies.

SALTON BAY MARINA
FACILITIES: Launching; berths; fuel; supplies.

SALTON BAY YACHT CLUB
FACILITIES: Launching; berths.

SALTON CITY CAMPGROUND
FACILITIES: Launching; fuel; supplies.

San Andreas

NEW HOGAN RESERVOIR
FACILITIES: Launching; berths; fuel; supplies.

San Diego

Bahia Point-Ventura Point

BAHIA HOTEL
FACILITIES: Launching; berths; supplies.

Chula Vista

CHULA VISTA LAUNCHING FACILITY
FACILITIES: Launching.

Commercial Basin

KETTENBURG MARINA
FACILITIES: Launching; supplies.

Coronado

CORONADO MUNICIPAL RAMP
FACILITIES: Launching.

BOATING AREAS (continued)

Dana Basin-Perez Cove

DANA BASIN
FACILITIES: Launching; berths; fuel; supplies.

DANA MARINA INC.
FACILITIES: Launching; berths; supplies.

PEREZ COVE MARINA
FACILITIES: Launching.

De Anza Cove

DEANZA COVE RAMP
FACILITIES: Launching.

DEANZA TRAILER HARBOR
FACILITIES: Launching.

MISSION BAY CAMPLAND
FACILITIES: Launching; berths; fuel; supplies.

Grand Island

GREENING'S KO-KET RESORT
FACILITIES: Launching; fuel.

Grant Line Canal

TONY'S ALL YEAR FISHING & BOATING HARBOR
FACILITIES: Launching; fuel; supplies.

Indian Slough

NEW ORWOOD RESORT
FACILITIES: Launching; berths; fuel; supplies.

King Island (Disappointment Slough)

LODI LAKE PARK
FACILITIES: Launching.

UNCLE BOBBIE'S MARINA SALES
FACILITIES: Launching; berths; fuel; supplies.

Miller Park

MILLER PARK PUBLIC RAMP
FACILITIES: Launching.

SACRAMENTO BOAT HARBOR
FACILITIES: Launching; berths; fuel.

Mokelumne River - South Fork

NEW HOPE LANDING
FACILITIES: Launching; berths; fuel; supplies.

WIMPY'S NEW HOPE MARINA
FACILITIES: Launching; berths; fuel; supplies.

Oakwood Lake

OAKWOOD LAKE
FACILITIES: Launching.

Rindge Tract

PARADISE POINT MARINA
FACILITIES: Launching; berths; fuel; supplies.

Roberts Island

TIKI LAGUN RESORT MARINA
FACILITIES: Launching; berths; fuel; supplies.

Sacramento River

BRODERICK PUBLIC LAUNCHING RAMP
FACILITIES: Launching.

DISCOVERY PARK PUBLIC RAMP
FACILITIES: Launching.

TOWER BRIDGE MARINA
FACILITIES: Launching; berths; fuel; supplies.

VILLAGE MARINA
FACILITIES: Launching; berths; fuel; supplies.

Sacramento River - Garcia Bend

GARCIA BEND PUBLIC RAMP
FACILITIES: Launching.

Sacramento River - I-5 Bridge

ELKHORN BRIDGE PUBLIC LAUNCHING RAMP
FACILITIES: Launching.

Sacramento River - Miller Park

MILLER PARK PUBLIC RAMP
FACILITIES: Launching.

SACRAMENTO BOAT HARBOR
FACILITIES: Launching; berths; fuel.

San Joaquin River

ISLANDER MARINA & TRAILER PARK
FACILITIES: Launching; berths; fuel; supplies.

MOSSDALE TRAILER PARK
FACILITIES: Launching.

PERRY'S PLACE
FACILITIES: Launching.

WETHERBEE LAKE RESORT
FACILITIES: Launching; berths; fuel; supplies.

Fiesta Island

THE HILTON INN BOAT DOCK
FACILITIES: Launching; berths; fuel; supplies.

Mission Bay

EAST VACATION ISLE-SKI BEACH
FACILITIES: Launching.

CALIFORNIA

BOATING AREAS (continued)

SANTA CLARA POINT
FACILITIES: Launching.

National City

NATIONAL CITY LAUNCHING FACILITY
FACILITIES: Launching.

Quivira Basin

HANA KAI LANDING, INC.
FACILITIES: Launching; berths; supplies.

MISSION BAY AQUATIC PARK
FACILITIES: Launching.

Shelter Island

DRISCOLL CUSTOM BOATS, INC.
FACILITIES: Launching.

SHELTER ISLAND PUBLIC LAUNCHING
RAMP
FACILITIES: Launching.

SHELTER ISLAND YACHT CLUB
FACILITIES: Launching; berths; supplies.

San Dimar

PUDDINGSTONE RESERVOIR
FACILITIES: Launching; supplies.

San Francisco

China Basin

MISSION ROCK RESORT
FACILITIES: Launching; berths; supplies.

SAN FRANCISCO PUBLIC RAMPS
FACILITIES: Launching.

THE RAMP
FACILITIES: Launching; fuel; supplies.

Coyote Point

COYOTE POINT MARINA
FACILITIES: Launching; berths; fuel; supplies.

COYOTE POINT MARINA SERVICE
FACILITIES: Launching; fuel.

Lake Merced

LAKE MERCED BOAT HOUSE
FACILITIES: Launching; supplies.

San Francisco Bay

GAS HOUSE COVE MARINA, INC.
FACILITIES: Launching; berths; fuel; supplies.

MISSION ROCK RESORT
FACILITIES: Launching; berths; supplies.

SAN FRANCISCO MARINA
FACILITIES: Launching; berths; fuel; supplies.

South San Francisco

OYSTER POINT MARINA
FACILITIES: Launching; berths; fuel.

San Leandro

SAN LEANDRO MARINA
FACILITIES: Launching; berths; fuel.

San Martin

COYOTE LAKE
FACILITIES: Launching.

UVAS RESERVOIR
FACILITIES: Launching.

San Mateo

DARCY'S MARINA
FACILITIES: Launching; fuel; supplies.

MARINA SLOUGH
FACILITIES: Launching.

Smith Lake

WOODBRIDGE INN
FACILITIES: Launching; berths; supplies.

San Miguel

Nacimiento Reservoir

WORLD WATER RESORTS
FACILITIES: Launching; berths; fuel; supplies.

San Pablo

SAN PABLO RESERVOIR
FACILITIES: Launching.

San Rafael

THE BOATYARD
FACILITIES: Launching; supplies.

CHINA CAMP
FACILITIES: Launching.

HARBOR BOAT REPAIR
FACILITIES: Launching.

LOCH LOMOND MARINA
FACILITIES: Launching; berths; fuel; supplies.

PIER 15 RESTAURANT
FACILITIES: Launching.

Gallinas Creek

BUCKS BOAT LANDING
FACILITIES: Launching.

Santa Barbara

MARINE CENTER, INC.
FACILITIES: Launching; supplies.

PUBLIC LAUNCHING RAMP
FACILITIES: Launching.

BOATING AREAS (continued)

SANTA BARBARA HARBOR
FACILITIES: Launching; berths; fuel; supplies.

Santa Cruz

ALDO'S
FACILITIES: Launching.

CAPITOLA WHARF
FACILITIES: Launching; fuel; supplies.

SANTA CRUZ BOAT RENTAL
FACILITIES: Launching; berths; supplies.

SANTA CRUZ SMALL CRAFT HARBOR
FACILITIES: Launching; berths; fuel; supplies.

Santa Margarita

SANTA MARGARITA LAKE
FACILITIES: Launching; berths; fuel; supplies.

Santa Monica

Santa Monica Harbor

PETE PETERSON CO.
FACILITIES: Launching.

Santa Rosa

LAKE RALPHINE
FACILITIES: Launching.

Santa Yney

CACHUMA LAKE RECREATION AREA
FACILITIES: Launching; fuel; supplies.

Santa Ysabel

LAKE SUTHERLAND
FACILITIES: Launching; fuel; supplies.

Saratoga

STEVENS CREEK RESERVOIR
FACILITIES: Launching.

Sausalito

ANDERSON'S BOAT YARD
FACILITIES: Launching.

CLIPPER YACHT HARBOR
FACILITIES: Launching; berths; fuel; supplies.

EDGEWATER YACHT SALES
FACILITIES: Launching.

SAUSALITO PUBLIC RAMP
FACILITIES: Launching.

Shasta

KESWICK RESERVOIR FISHING ACCESS
FACILITIES: Launching.

Whiskeytown Lake

BRANDY CREEK MARINA
FACILITIES: Launching; berths.

OAK BOTTOM MARINA
FACILITIES: Launching; berths; fuel; supplies.

WHISKEY CREEK RAMP
FACILITIES: Launching.

Shaver Lake Heights

Shaver Lake

CAMP EDISON
FACILITIES: Launching.

DUANE TAYLOR'S MARINA
FACILITIES: Launching; fuel; supplies.

PUBLIC RAMP
FACILITIES: Launching.

Sierraville

Jackson Meadows Reservoir

PASS CREEK
FACILITIES: Launching.

WOOD CAMP
FACILITIES: Launching.

Stampede Reservoir

CAPTAIN ROBERTS BOAT RAMP
FACILITIES: Launching.

Smartville

Collins Lake

COLLINS LAKE RECREATION AREA
FACILITIES: Launching; berths; fuel; supplies.

Englebright Reservoir

ENGLEBRIGHT MAIN RECREATION AREA
FACILITIES: Launching; berths.

ENGLEBRIGHT MARINA - JOE MILLER RAVINE
FACILITIES: Launching; berths; fuel; supplies.

Smith River

SALMON HARBOR RESORT
FACILITIES: Launching; berths; fuel; supplies.

SHIP ASHORE RESORT
FACILITIES: Launching; fuel; supplies.

TRAILS END RESORT
FACILITIES: Launching; supplies.

Snelling

LAKE MCSWAIN MARINA

CALIFORNIA

BOATING AREAS (continued)

FACILITIES: Launching; berths; fuel; supplies.

Soda Bay

Buckingham Point

BUCKINGHAM MARINA
FACILITIES: Launching.

Clearlake Highlands

AUSTIN'S RESORT
FACILITIES: Launching; berths; fuel; supplies.

B & B LIGHTHOUSE
FACILITIES: Launching; fuel.

CLEAR LAKE BOAT
FACILITIES: Launching.

DON'S MARINA
FACILITIES: Launching; fuel; supplies.

GALAXY RESORT
FACILITIES: Launching.

GARNERS RESORT
FACILITIES: Launching; berths; fuel; supplies.

HAMILTON'S MOBILE HOME PARK
FACILITIES: Launching.

HARBOR LITE RESORT
FACILITIES: Launching; berths.

HOLIDAY ISLAND MOBILE PARK
FACILITIES: Launching.

JULES RESORT
FACILITIES: Launching; berths; fuel.

LAKELAND MOBILE PARK & RESORT
FACILITIES: Launching; berths; fuel; supplies.

LAKESIDE RESORT
FACILITIES: Launching.

LAMPLIGHTER RESORT
FACILITIES: Launching.

LOTOWAHA VILLAGE
FACILITIES: Launching.

RED BUD PARK PUBLIC LAUNCHING RAMP
FACILITIES: Launching.

SHIP 'N' SHORE RESORT
FACILITIES: Launching; berths; fuel; supplies.

TAMARACK LODGE
FACILITIES: Launching; berths.

TROMBETTA'S BEACH RESORT
FACILITIES: Launching; berths; fuel.

WILLOW TREE RESORT
FACILITIES: Launching; berths.

Clearlake Oaks

BOB'S MARINA RESORT
FACILITIES: Launching; berths; fuel; supplies.

EL MAR HOTEL
FACILITIES: Launching.

INDIAN BEACH RESORT
FACILITIES: Launching.

ISLAND PARK TRAILER COURT
FACILITIES: Launching.

KILGORES HARBOR MOTEL
FACILITIES: Launching.

LAKE MARINA MOTEL
FACILITIES: Launching.

LAKEHAVEN COTTAGE
FACILITIES: Launching.

SHORT ST. PUBLIC LAUNCHING RAMP
FACILITIES: Launching.

20 OAKS
FACILITIES: Launching.

Lower Lake

END OF THE RAINBOW
FACILITIES: Launching.

OAKES WATERFRONT PARK
FACILITIES: Launching; fuel; supplies.

SHAWS SHADY ACRES
FACILITIES: Launching.

WESTWIND MOBILE PARK
FACILITIES: Launching.

Soda Bay

CLEAR LAKE STATE PARK
FACILITIES: Launching; berths.

EDGEWATER RESORT
FACILITIES: Launching; berths; fuel; supplies.

FERNDALE RESORT
FACILITIES: Launching; fuel; supplies.

LAKESIDE COUNTY PARK
FACILITIES: Launching.

LAKEWOOD RESORT
FACILITIES: Launching.

ROYAL OAKS RESORT
FACILITIES: Launching; berths; fuel.

SKI HAVEN RESORT
FACILITIES: Launching; berths.

SODA BAY BOAT CLUB
FACILITIES: Launching.

Sonora

LYONS LAKE
FACILITIES: Launching; supplies.

BOATING AREAS (continued)

South Lake Tahoe

Fallen Leaf Lake

FALLEN LEAF LODGE
FACILITIES: Launching; berths; fuel; supplies.

Lake Tahoe

BENDER'S CAMP RICHARDSON MARINA
FACILITIES: Launching; fuel; supplies.

LAKE FOREST FISHING ACCESS
FACILITIES: Launching.

SIERRA BOAT COMPANY
FACILITIES: Launching; berths; fuel; supplies.

South Lake Tahoe

BEACH & HARBOR MARINA
FACILITIES: Launching; fuel; supplies.

BEACHCOMBER MOTEL & PORT
FACILITIES: Launching.

EL DORADO RECREATION AREA
FACILITIES: Launching.

LAKESIDE YACHT & HARBOR CLUB
FACILITIES: Launching; berths; fuel; supplies.

TAHOE KEYS MARINA
FACILITIES: Launching; berths; fuel; supplies.

SUNNYSIDE RESORT
FACILITIES: Launching; berths; fuel; supplies.

Spring Gardens

LITTLE GRASS VALLEY RESERVOIR
FACILITIES: Launching; supplies.

Springville

Lake Success

FAIRVIEW MARINA
FACILITIES: Launching; berths; fuel; supplies.

ROCKY HILL
FACILITIES: Launching

SUCCESS MARINA
FACILITIES: Launching; fuel; supplies.

TULE
FACILITIES: Launching; berths.

Stockton

STOCKTON PUBLIC RAMP
FACILITIES: Launching.

Storrie

Bucks Lake

BUCKS LAKE LODGE MARINA
FACILITIES: Launching; berths; fuel; supplies.

HASKINS VALLEY RESORT
FACILITIES: Launching; berths; fuel; supplies.

LAKESHORE
FACILITIES: Launching; berths; supplies.

Suisun City

PAUL'S BOAT HARBOR
FACILITIES: Launching; berths; fuel; supplies.

SUISUN CITY PUBLIC FISHING ACCESS
FACILITIES: Launching; berths.

SUISUN PACIFIC MARINA
FACILITIES: Launching; berths; fuel.

Surf

OCEAN BEACH COUNTY PARK
FACILITIES: Launching.

Susanville

EAGLE LAKE FISHING ACCESS
FACILITIES: Launching.

EAGLE LAKE MARINA-GALLATIN BEACH
FACILITIES: Launching; berths; fuel; supplies.

Tahoe City

Lake Tahoe

THE BOATWORKS
FACILITIES: Launching; berths; fuel; supplies.

Topaz Junction

Topaz Lake

PINE NUT LODGE
FACILITIES: Launching; fuel; supplies.

TOPAZ LAKE MARINA
FACILITIES: Launching.

TOPAZ LAKE RESORT
FACILITIES: Launching; supplies.

Topock

Lake Havasu (Colorado River)

BLACK MEADOW LANDING
FACILITIES: Launching; berths; fuel; supplies.

CRAZY HORSE CAMPGROUND
FACILITIES: Launching; berths; supplies.

CALIFORNIA

BOATING AREAS (continued)

HAVASU LANDING
FACILITIES: Launching; berths; fuel; supplies.

HAVASU PALMS
FACILITIES: Launching; berths; fuel; supplies.

LAKE HAVASU MARINA
FACILITIES: Launching; berths; fuel; supplies.

Colorado River

CATFISH PARADISE
FACILITIES: Launching; berths; fuel; supplies.

FIVE MILE LANDING
FACILITIES: Launching; fuel; supplies.

GOLDEN SHORE MARINA
FACILITIES: Launching; berths; fuel; supplies.

PARK MOABI MARINA
FACILITIES: Launching; berths; fuel.

Trinidad

Trinidad Bay

BOB'S BOAT BASIN
FACILITIES: Launching; berths; fuel; supplies.

Trinity Center

RECREATION PLUS
FACILITIES: Launching; berths; fuel; supplies.

TRINITY CENTER PUBLIC RAMP
FACILITIES: Launching.

WYNTOON PARK
FACILITIES: Launching; fuel; supplies.

Truckee

Donner Lake

DONNER SHORE RESORT
FACILITIES: Launching; fuel; supplies.

LAKESHORE MOTEL
FACILITIES: Launching; fuel; supplies.

TRUCKEE-DONNER RECREATION AND PARK DISTRICT
FACILITIES: Launching; fuel.

Tuttle

Lake Yosemite

LAKE YOSEMITE BOAT LAUNCHING RAMP
FACILITIES: Launching.

Ukiah

Blue Lakes

LAKEVIEW HAVEN RESORT
FACILITIES: Launching; berths; supplies.

NARROWS LODGE
FACILITIES: Launching; fuel; supplies.

PINE ACRES BLUE LAKE RESORT & MOTEL
FACILITIES: Launching.

Vallejo

Goodyear Slough

PIERCE HARBOR & REEL INN
FACILITIES: Launching; berths; fuel; supplies.

Hudeman Slough

HUDEMAN SLOUGH FISHING ACCESS
FACILITIES: Launching.

Napa River

BRINKMAN'S MARINE SERVICE
FACILITIES: Launching; supplies.

NAPA VALL FISHING RESORT
FACILITIES: Launching; berths; supplies.

VALLEJO BOAT CENTER
FACILITIES: Launching; berths; fuel; supplies.

VALLEJO LAUNCHING RAMP
FACILITIES: Launching.

VALLEJO MUNICIPAL MARINA
FACILITIES: Launching; berths; fuel; supplies.

Valley Acres

BUENA VISTA LAKE
FACILITIES: Launching.

Valley Springs

Lake Camanche

LAKE CAMANCHE NORTH SHORE
FACILITIES: Launching; berths; fuel; supplies.

SOUTH CAMANCHE
FACILITIES: Launching; berths; fuel; supplies.

Ventura

ANCHORS WAY MARINE
FACILITIES: Launching; supplies.

LAUNCHING RAMP
FACILITIES: Launching.

VENTURA MARINA
FACILITIES: Launching; berths; fuel; supplies.

Verona

RIO RAMAZA MARINA
FACILITIES: Launching; berths; fuel; supplies.

BOATING AREAS (continued)

Sacramento River

ELKHORN BRIDGE PUBLIC LAUNCHING RAMP
FACILITIES: Launching.

Vernatir

GARDNER'S COVE RESORT
FACILITIES: Launching; supplies.

Vidal

Colorado River

LOST LAKE RESORT
FACILITIES: Launching; fuel; supplies.

WATER WHEEL CAMP
FACILITIES: Launching.

Vina

Sacramento River - Woodson Bridge

RIVERSIDE SPORTSMAN'S MOBILE HOME RESORT
FACILITIES: Launching; berths; fuel; supplies.

Warmer Springs

LAKE HENSHAW
FACILITIES: Launching; supplies.

Waterford

Modesto Reservoir

MODESTO RESERVOIR RESORT
FACILITIES: Launching; berths; fuel; supplies.

Turlock Lake

TURLOCK LAKE STATE RECREATION AREA
FACILITIES: Launching; fuel; supplies.

Watsonville

PINTO LAKE
FACILITIES: Launching; supplies.

Weaverville

Lewiston Lake

PINE COVE MARINA
FACILITIES: Launching; berths; fuel; supplies.

Wheatland

CAMP FAR WEST
FACILITIES: Launching; fuel.

White Hall

Loon Lake Reservoir

CRYSTAL BASIN RECREATION AREA
FACILITIES: Launching.

Union Valley Reservoir

UNION VALLEY RAMP
FACILITIES: Launching.

YELLOW JACKET RAMP
FACILITIES: Launching.

White Hot Springs

Convict Lake

CONVICT LAKE RESORT
FACILITIES: Launching; fuel; supplies.

U.S. FOREST SERVICE RAMP
FACILITIES: Launching.

Lake Crowley

LAKE CROWLEY
FACILITIES: Launching; berths; fuel.

Winten

Lake Berryessa - Monticello Dam

MARKELY COVE RESORT
FACILITIES: Launching; berths; fuel; supplies.

Lake Berryessa - Northwest Shore

PUTAH CREEK PARK
FACILITIES: Launching; berths; fuel; supplies.

LAKE BERRYESSA - NORTH SHORE RESORT MARINA
FACILITIES: Launching; fuel; supplies.

Lake Berryessa - Southwest Shore

SPANISH FLAT RESORT
FACILITIES: Launching; berths; fuel; supplies.

STEELE PARK RESORT
FACILITIES: Launching; berths; fuel; supplies.

Lake Berryessa - West Shore

LAKE BERRYESSA MARINA RESORT
FACILITIES: Launching; berths; fuel; supplies.

RANCHO HERMOSA MARINA
FACILITIES: Launching; fuel; supplies.

RANCHO MONTICELLO RESORT
FACILITIES: Launching; berths; fuel; supplies.

Yosemite Junction

Tulloch Lake

COPPER COVE LODGE
FACILITIES: Launching; berths; fuel.

POKER FLAT LODGE
FACILITIES: Launching; berths; fuel; supplies.

CALIFORNIA

BOATING AREAS (continued)

Yuba City

Feather River

YUBA CITY PUBLIC RAMP
FACILITIES: Launching.

YUBA SUTTER BOAT DOCK
FACILITIES: Launching; berths; fuel; supplies.

Zephyr Cove

Lake Tahoe

LOGAN SHOALS HARBOR
FACILITIES: Launching; berths; fuel.

BICYCLE TRAILS

ANGEL ISLAND TRAIL - SAN FRANCISCO
BAY - 5.5 mi.; any bicycle.
This trip combines a ferry ride, sea breeze and great views of the San Francisco Bay area.
Trail: Ayala Cove to West Garrison to Mt. Linermore.

BIG BEAR LAKE TRAIL - 16 mi.; some hills; 10-speed bicycle recommended.
You will pass through stands of pine and cedar and through the towns of Big Bear and Fawnskin. Avoid weekends if you want more open road and fewer cars. Be prepared for a few hills. Although this is an ideal summer ride it can be done throughout the year whenever the road is free of snow.
Trail: 16 mi. trip around Big Bear Lake and in the San Bernadino Mountains.

BORDER AREA TRAIL - 370 mi.; steep hills, desert areas; 10-speed bicycle necessary.
This tour can be made in a week but you may profitably spend from 10 to 14 days along the route. On your first day you will encounter some stiff climbs and steep downhill runs.
When crossing into Mexico at Mexicali it is important to be neat and clean. The stretch inside Mexico is sparsely populated. It is advisable to carry food, water, and to be prepared to camp. In the U.S., stay off Interstate 5. At Camp Pendleton you will be asked to sign a waiver at the gate in order to pass.
Trail: Hemet to Radec to Warner Springs to Julian to Brawley to Calexico to Mexicali to Rumorosa to Tecate to Tijuana to San Diego to Oceanside to Camp Pendleton to Laguna Beach to Long Beach.

CALIFORNIA AQUEDUCT TRAIL - 60 mi.; gusty winds; some hills, hazards of aqueduct; 10-speed bicycle recommended.
This bicycle route offers the biker 60 mi. of traffic-free riding. The entire route roughly parallels Interstate 5 so you can start or stop your ride at several spots.
Strong winds are possible so keep your trip plan flexible; you may decide to go in the opposite direction to take advantage of the tail wind.
It is suggested that you stay away from the Aqueduct as the water moves rapidly and the sides are slippery.
Trail: Bethany Reservoir (Between San Jose and Stockton) to San Luis Reservoir on California Route 152.

DEATH VALLEY TRAILS - 110 & 120 mi.; harsh weather conditions; 10-speed bicycle recommended.
The harsh environment of Death Valley rules out summer cycling but from Nov. - Apr. the weather is more temperate. This is not to say that every day is sunny and mild, as you may encounter cold weather and stiff winds. The best way to appreciate the Valley is to get into the side canyon and other out-of-the-way areas.
Motel-type accommodations are available at Furnace Creek, Stove Pipe Wells, and Wildrose from Feb. - mid-May and reservations are advised. There are nine easily accessible campsites in the Valley.
Trails: (1) Shoehone to 178 west to Badwater to Furnace Creek to 190 north to Sand Dunes to Mesquite Springs to Ubehebe Crater-about 120 mi.; (2) Follow 190 to Emigrant Junction to Stovepipe Wells to Sand Dunes to Furnace Creek to Death Valley Junction - about 110 mi.

HEMET VALLEY TRAIL - Hills; 10-speed bicycle recommended.
One hundred miles southeast of Los Angeles in the shadow of 10,700 foot Mt. San Jacinto is the Hemet Valley.
Some of the hills in this area are very steep. Some portions of Route 71 around Temecula and in the Elsinore-Lake Mathews area are divided road. Bicyclists are permitted on these roads but caution is recommended.
The portions of this trip at lower elevations can be made any time of the year, but the summers are warm. The higher portions are best traveled after the snow melts.
Trails: (1) Valle Vista to Mountain Center to Anza to Aguaga to Radec to Temecula to Winchester to Valle Vista; (2) Valle Vista to San Jacinto to Lakeview to Nuevo to Sun City to Elsinore to 71 west right on Cajalco Road, left on Perris Blvd., right on Alessandro Blvd., right on Gilman Springs Road to Valle Vista.

JULIAN TRAILS - 30 mi.; some hills; some rugged terrain; 10-speed bicycle recommended.
The smallest loop to the south of Julian takes in Cuyamaca Reservoir and offers camping at Pasa Picacho Campground a few miles south of the Lake on Route 79.
On the other loop you have some major changes in elevation to contend with. You will have great downhill runs into the desert of Anza-Borrego State Park.
Trails: (1) Julian to Cuyamaca Reservoir to Pine Hills to Julian; (2) Julian to Camp Stevens Hostel, to 78 east, left on S3 to Tamarisk Grove Campground to Borrego Springs to Ranchita to S22 west, left on 79 to Santa Ysabel to Julian.

NEVADA CITY TRAILS - 14 mi., 30 mi. & 43 mi.; rugged terrain,; 10-speed bicycle necessary.
Interstate 80 between Sacramento and Reno. The biking in this area is rugged with

CALIFORNIA

BICYCLE TRAILS (continued)

thousand foot drops into the valleys being commonplace. In general, the country consists of steep hills, with a covering of pines and small oaks. Spring and fall are the best seasons, but if you don't mind the heat, summer is okay.

Trails: (1) Nevada City to Grass Valley to Rough & Ready, back to Nevada City - 14 mi; (2) Nevada City to N. San Juan to Camptonville to Downieville - 43 mi.; (3) Nevada City to Grass Valley to Cedar Ridge to Chicago Park to Dutch Flat - about 30 mi.

PLACERVILLE TRAILS - 20, 40 & 100 mi. some hills; 10-speed bicycle recommended.

Placerville is situated at 1,800 feet and enjoys fine cycling weather most of the year but especially in the spring and fall.

Trails: (1) Placerville to Coloma to Garden Valley to Kelsey to Placerville - about 40 mi.; (2) Placerville to Gold Hill to Coloma to Placerville - about 20 mi.; (3) Placerville to Diamond Springs to Gutenberger's Corners to Somerset to Pleasant Valley to Pollock Pines to Camino to Placerville - about 100 mi.

POINT REYES TRAILS - 27, 28, 46 & 64 mi; any bicycle.

There is a great combination of rides including beaches, farm land, lakes, and charming small towns. All mileages are figured from the Laguna Ranch Youth Hostel in Point Reyes National Seashore.

Trails: (1) Laguna Ranch Hostel to Inverness Park to Inverness to Tomales Bay State Park - 28 mi.; (2) Laguna Hostel to Olema to Samuel P. Taylor State Park - 27 mi.; (3) Laguna Hostel to Inverness Park to North Beach to South Beach to Drakes Beach - 46 mi.; (4) Hostel to Point Reyes Station to Marshall to cheese factory to Nicasio to San Geronimo to Olema to Laguna Hostel - about 64 mi.

REDWOOD TRAIL - 84 mi.; some hills, smooth roads and some gravel, traffic; 10-speed bicycle recommended.

From Redway to South Fork you will be riding the Avenue of the Giants, famous for its groves of arrow straight, coastal redwoods. The road is smooth with generally easy riding, but there are a few hills.

The ride can be made in either direction almost any time of the year.

Trail: Redway to Phillipsville to Miranda to Myers Flat to Weott to South Fork. Follow Mattole Road to Honeydew to Wilder Ridge Road to Ettersburg to Briceland to Redway.

SANTA BARBARA TRAIL - 45 mi.; hills, some irregular surfaces; 10-speed bicycle recommended.

This ride follows less traveled roads through wooded hills and through beautiful residential areas. You will also have some fine ocean views.

Trail: Stow Grove to Noguerra to Coneja to Salinas to Olive Mill to Cabrillo Beach to Loma Alta to Miramonte to Via Presada to Stow Grove.

WINE COUNTRY TRAIL - 120 mi.; rolling hills; any bicycle.

This trip into the California wine country north of San Francisco can take from three days to a week.

The months from Apr. - Nov. offer the best cycling. Most of the wineries offer tours.

Trail: Santa Rosa to East Windsor to Healsburg to Alexander Valley to Calistoga to St. Helena to Rutherford to Oakville to Napa to Sonoma to Glen Ellen to Santa Rosa.

TRAILS

California City

TWENTY MULE TEAM TRAIL - 12 mi. foot trail. This trail has historical significance as it is a segment of the original trail used to carry borax from Death Valley to Mojave, California. It traverses Galileo Park, which is dominated by the Queen Mountain, Castle Butte, and Mt. Whitney.

East Oakland

YORK TRAIL - 3.5 mi. foot trail. The trail takes an easterly course from Leona Park to Skyline Boulevard, passing through two canyons and along a spring-fed stream while climbing 900 feet. The lower canyon is densely vegetated with second-growth redwoods, ferns, and flowering shrubs. Brush and grass-covered hills are found at higher elevations. Old mine workings and evidence of early logging add historical interest. There are excellent views of the San Francisco Bay area.

Folsom

WESTERN STATES PIONEER EXPRESS TRAIL - 50 mi. foot trail. This trail is the site of the annual Tevis Cup 100-mile one-day ride, which attracts up to 200 horse riders. It extends from Folsom Lake State Recreation Area to the border of Tahoe National Forest and follows the main stem of the American River to Auburn, passing orchards, grazing lands and undeveloped hillsides. Above Auburn, the trail generally parallels the Middle Fork American River and passes through semi-wild, heavily forested countryside. This is a portion of the historical route of Adams Express Company and Wells Fargo & Company Express Riders.

Fresno

LOST LAKE NATURE TRAIL - 2 mi. foot trail. Located within Fresno County's Lost Lake Recreation Area, this nature trail is popular with school children on field trips. A special feature of the trail is the Indian grinding holes, in which corn and other grains were ground into meal. Another attraction is a 65-acre bird sanctuary lying between the trail and the nearby San Joaquin River. Side trails lead to the river and to Lost Lake, both of which are heavily used by fishermen.

Huntington Beach

SANTA ANA RIVER TRAIL - 15.7 mi. foot trail. The trail starts at Brookhurst Street in Huntington Beach and ends at Katella Avenue

CALIFORNIA

TRAILS (continued)

in Anaheim. Access to the trail is from four major highways and 17 roads which cross it. Along the west and east river levees, the trail lies on an asphalt-surfaced maintenance road for bicycles.

Lake Tahoe

LAKE TAHOE BICYCLE AND PEDESTRIAN WAY - 5 mi. foot trail. This is an 8-foot wide, surfaced path along the northwestern shore of Lake Tahoe. It lies inside the right-of-way for Star Route 28 north of Tahoe City and the right-of-way for State Route 89 south of Tahoe City. The trail passes through numerous recreation areas on the shore of Lake Tahoe, and access points are provided to the waterfront at several points along the way. For most of its length, the trail traverses scattered-to-heavily-forested countryside.

Monterey

TORO RIDING AND HIKING TRAILS - 6 mi. foot trail. This is a loop trail which starts along an oak-filled canyon and passes through dense chaparral, grassy hillsides, and scattered oaks and sycamores. On the 2,000-foot-high crest, the hiker or rider has an excellent view of Monterey Bay, the Coast Range Mountains, and the Salinas Valley. This undeveloped land supports a wide variety of upland bird life and a large deer population. Bobcats and coyotes are occasionally sighted.

Nevada City

SOUTH YUBA TRAIL - 6 mi. foot trail. Located along the north side of the South Yuba River Canyon, the initial 1½ miles of the trail is a self-guided nature trail. The trail traverses a rugged canyon with trees, flowers, and spectacular views of the river and surrounding country. Historical remnants of Gold Rush days can be found. There is good hiking and hunting with an abundance of small game.

Pasadena

GABRIELINO TRAIL - 28 mi. foot trail. This trail, entirely within the Angeles National Forest, forms a huge semi-circle from Chantry Flats, along several rivers, to the city of Pasadena. Hikers go through canyon bottoms and along ridge tops with the highest point being 4,100 feet. Both deciduous and coniferous trees are found along the chaparral country and the ruins of an old resort. A peaceful Indian tribe, which formerly lived along the coast in summer and on the mountains in winter, gave the trail its name.

Rubidoux

SANTA ANA RIVER TRAIL - 10 mi. foot trail. This trail, as the 100th national recreation trail, marks a major milestone in the National Trails System program. The 10-mile trail winds along the banks of the Santa Ana River in Riverside County, roughly connecting the cities of Rubidoux, Riverside, and Norco. The Santa Ana River Trail is planned

to extend from San Bernardino County to the Pacific Ocean via connections with the Riverside County and Orange County portions of the trail.

Sacramento

JEDEDIAH SMITH TRAIL - 26 mi. foot trail. From Discovery Park, at the confluence of the Sacramento and American Rivers, to Nimbus Dam at Lake Natoma, the entire trail lies within the American River Parkway of metropolitan Sacramento and other heavily populated areas.

San Francisco

EAST BAY SKYLINE TRAIL - 14 mi. foot trail. This trail lies between Redwood Regional Park and Anthony Cabot Park along the eastern skyline of San Francisco Bay. It passes near 315-acre Lake Chabot. Much of the area is chaparral, grass, and mixed woodlands. Higher elevations along the trail provide unusually fine vistas of the bay. Plans include an eventual extension, both north and south, up to a distance of 25 miles.

MUIR WOODS INTERPRETIVE TRAIL - .88 mi. foot trail. Located 17 miles north of San Francisco, at Muir Woods National Monument, the trail is set within a remnant redwood forest and parallels the banks of Redwood Creek. The trail offers a vast variety of vegetation for nature appreciation, and Redwood Creek allows hikers an opportunity to view spawning silver salmon and steelhead trout during the winter. Other features of the trail include: a self-guiding nature trail, and a Braille trail.

San Jose

PENITENCIA CREEK TRAIL - 5.5 mi. foot trail. Starting at Alum Rock Park's northwest entrance, this loop trail follows Penitencia Creek, climbs the Mt. Hamilton sub-range and returns to its beginning point along the creek. The trail features California's inner coast range terrain, flora, and fauna; and there are trail-side mineral water springs.

Stockton

CALIFORNIA AQUEDUCT BIKEWAY - 67 mi. foot trail. This trail is on the levee of the northernmost portion of the aqueduct from Bethany Reservoir through portions of three counties to O'Neil Forebay, at San Luis Creek State Recreation Area.

SKI AREAS

Bear Valley

MT. REBA AT BEAR VALLEY
P.O. Box 38
Bear Valley, CA 95223
(209) 753-2301
LOCATION: 104 mi. east of Stockton via Ebbetts Pass Hwy. 4.
FACILITIES: 7 chairlifts; slopes for expert, intermediate and beginning skier; ski instruc-

SKI AREAS (continued)

tion; ski rental; nursery; 2100 ft. vertical drop; longest run, 3 mi.; restaurants; lodging.

Big Bear Lake

GOLDMINE
Box 6812
Big Bear Lake, CA 92315
(714) 585-2517
LOCATION: Hwy. 330 from San Bernardino to Hwy. 18 at Running Springs.
FACILITIES: 3 chairlifts; 3 tow ropes; slopes for expert, intermediate and beginning skier; ski instruction; ski rental; 1500 ft. vertical drop; longest run, 2½ mi.; restaurants; lodging.

SNOW SUMMIT
Box 77
Big Bear Lake, CA 92315
(714) 866-4621
LOCATION: 100 mi. east of Los Angeles on I-15.
FACILITIES: 5 double and 1 quad chairlift; 3 tow ropes; slopes for expert, intermediate and beginning skier; ski instruction; ski rental; nursery; 1200 ft. vertical drop; longest run, 1¼ mi.; restaurants; lodging.

Eureka

LASSEN PARK
519 Sixth South
Eureka, CA 95501
(707) 422-5789
LOCATION: 10 mi. west of Willow Creek off Route 299.
FACILITIES: 3 tow ropes; slopes for expert, intermediate and beginning skier.

Green Valley

GREEN VALLEY
Box 202
Green Valley, CA 92341
(714) 867-2338
LOCATION: 100 mi. from Los Angeles via I-15E to Crosstown Hwy. to Route 330.
FACILITIES: 2 T-bars; 2 tow ropes; slopes for expert, intermediate, and beginning skier; ski instruction; ski rental; 300 ft. vertical drop; longest run, 2000 ft.

Homewood

HOMEWOOD
P.O. Box 165
Homewood, CA 95718
(916) 525-7256
LOCATION: 6 mi. south of Tahoe City on Hwy. 89.
FACILITIES: 3 chairlifts; 1 tram; 4 T-bars; 2 mitey mites; slopes for expert, intermediate and beginning skier; ski instruction; ski rental; 1670 ft. vertical drop; longest run, 2 mi.

TAHOE SKI BOWL
Box 305
Homewood, CA 95718
(916) 525-5224
LOCATION: 7 mi. south of Tahoe City on Hwy. 89.
FACILITIES: 2 chairlifts; 1 T-bar; 2 tow

ropes; slopes for expert, intermediate and beginning skier; ski instruction; ski rental; nursery; 1630 ft. vertical drop; longest run, 2 mi.; restaurants; lodging.

June Lake

JUNE MOUNTAIN
Box 146
June Lake, CA 93529
(714) 648-7733
LOCATION: Route 385, June Lake Loop exit.
FACILITIES: 5 chairlifts; 1 T-bar; slopes for expert, intermediate beginning skier; ski instruction; ski rental; 2400 ft. vertical drop; longest run, 2 mi.

Kirkwood

KIRKWOOD SKI AREA
P.O. Box 1
Kirkwood, CA 95646
(209) 258-6000
LOCATION: 30 mi. south of Lake Tahoe on Hwy. 88.
FACILITIES: 8 chairlifts; 1 T-bar; slopes for expert, intermediate and beginning skier; ski instruction; ski rental; nursery; 2000 ft. vertical drop; longest run, 2½ mi.; restaurants; lodging.

La Canada

KRATKA RIDGE
Box 186
La Canada, CA 91011
(213) 842-1051
LOCATION: From Los Angeles via Route 2, 36 mi. beyond I-210.
FACILITIES: 1 chairlift; 6 tow ropes; slopes for expert, intermediate and beginning skier; ski instruction; ski rental; 900 ft. vertical drop; longest run, ½ mi.

MT. WATERMAN
817 Lynnhaven
La Canada, CA 91011
(213) 790-2002
LOCATION: 43 mi. from Los Angeles via Route 2.
FACILITIES: 2 chairlifts; slopes for expert, intermediate and beginning skier; ski instruction; ski rental; 830 ft. vertical drop; longest run, 1 mi.

Lakeshore

CHINA PEAK
Box 236
Lakeshore, CA 93636
(209) 893-3316
LOCATION: 75 mi. from Fresno via Route 168.
FACILITIES: 3 chairlifts; 2 T-bar; 1 tow rope; slopes for expert, intermediate and beginning skier; ski instruction; ski rental; 1709 ft. vertical drop; longest run, 3 mi.; restaurants; lodging.

Mammoth Lakes

MAMMOTH
P.O. Box 24
Mammoth Lakes, CA 93546

CALIFORNIA

SKI AREAS (continued)

(714) 934-2571
LOCATION: 6 mi. north on Hwy. 203 from Hwy. 395 junction.
FACILITIES: 16 chairlifts; 2 trams; 4 T-bars; slopes for expert, intermediate and beginning skier; ski instruction; ski rental; 3100 ft. vertical drop; longest run, 2½ mi.; restaurants; lodging.

Mill Creek

HORSE MOUNTAIN
Mill Creek, CA 96061
(916) 595-3306
LOCATION: In Lassen National Park, 230 mi. from San Francisco via I-5.
FACILITIES: 1 T-bar; 2 tow ropes; slopes for expert, intermediate and beginning skier; ski instruction; ski rental; 600 ft. vertical drop; longest run, ½ mi.; restaurants; lodging.

Mount Shasta City

SKI SHASTA
Mount Shasta City, CA 96067

This ski area has been closed by an avalanche.

Mt. Baldy

MT. BALDY
Box 459
Mt. Baldy, CA 91759
(714) 982-4208
LOCATION: 5 mi. from Los Angeles via San Bernardino Hwy.
FACILITIES: 4 chairlifts; slopes for expert, intermediate and beginning skier; ski instruction; ski rental; 2100 ft. vertical drop; longest run, 2 mi.

Truckee

BOREAL RIDGE
Box 39
Truckee, CA 95734
(916) 426-3666
LOCATION: 10 mi. west of Truckee on I-80 at Castle Peak Interchange.
FACILITIES: 7 chairlifts; slopes for expert, intermediate and beginning skiers; ski instruction; ski rental; 600 ft. vertical drop; longest run, 7/8 mi.; restaurants; lodging.

NORTHSTAR
P.O. Box 129
Truckee, CA 95734
(916) 562-1010
LOCATION: 40 mi. from South Shore via Hwy. 50, Hwy. 28 and State Hwy. 267.
FACILITIES: 7 chairlifts; 1 tow rope; slopes for advanced, intermediate and beginning skier; ski instruction; ski rental; 2200 ft. vertical drop; longest run, 2½ mi.; restaurants; lodging.

TAHOE DONNER
Drawer G
Truckee, CA 95734
(916) 587-6046
LOCATION: Off I-80 at first Truckee exit, 1 mi. to Northwood, turn left 5 mi.

FACILITIES: 2 chairlifts; 1 tow rope; slopes for intermediate and beginning skier; ski instruction; ski rental; 600 ft. vertical drop; longest run, 1 mi.; restaurants; lodging.

Twin Bridges

SIERRA SKI RANCH
Twin Bridges, CA 95735
(916) 659-7453
LOCATION: 12 mi. west of South Lake Tahoe on Hwy. 50.
FACILITIES: 6 chairlifts; slopes for expert, intermediate and beginning skier; ski instruction; ski rental; 1585 ft. vertical drop; longest run, 2½ mi.; restaurants; lodging.

Wrightwood

HOLIDAY HILL
Box 327
Wrightwood, CA 92397
(714) 249-3256
LOCATION: I-14 or I-15 North to Hwy. 138. Take Hwy. 138 to Hwy. 2 to 2½ mi. west of Wrightwood.
FACILITIES: 4 chairlifts; 1 T-bar; 2 tow rope; slopes for expert, intermediate and beginning skier; ski rental; 1600 vertical drop; longest run, 1½ mi.; restaurants; lodging.

MOUNTAIN HIGH
Hwy. 2
Wrightwood, CA 92379
(714) 249-3226
LOCATION: I-15 from Los Angeles to the Wrightwood cutoff.
FACILITIES: 2 chairlifts; slopes for expert, intermediate and beginning skier; ski instruction; ski rental; 1400 ft. vertical drop; longest run, 4200 ft.

SKI SUNRISE
Box 645
Wrightwood, CA 92397
(714) 249-6150
LOCATION: 1½ hrs. northwest of Los Angeles off Hwys. 15 and 138.
FACILITIES: 3 T-bars and pomas; 3 tow ropes; slopes for advanced, intermediate and beginning skier; ski instruction; nursery; 800 ft. vertical drop; longest run, 1½ mi.

Yosemite National Park

BADGER PASS
Yosemite National Park, CA 95389
(209) 372-4691
LOCATION: 89 mi. north of Fresno on Hwy. 41.
FACILITIES: 3 chairlifts; 2 T-bars; 1 tow rope; slopes for expert, intermediate and beginning skiers; ski instruction; ski rental; nursery; 900 ft. vertical drop.

Norden

DONNER SKI RANCH
P.O. Box 66
Norden, CA 95724
(916) 426-3578
LOCATION: 90 mi. east of Sacramento via I-80.
FACILITIES: 6 chairlifts; 3 tow ropes; slopes

SKI AREAS (continued)

for expert , intermediate and beginning skier; ski instruction; ski rental; 826 ft. vertical drop; longest run, ¾ mi.; restaurants; lodging.

SUGAR BOWL
Norden, CA 95724
(916) 426-3651
LOCATION: 90 mi. east of Sacramento off I-80.
FACILITIES: 7 chairlifts; slopes for expert, intermediate and beginning skier; ski instruction; ski rental; 1500 ft. vertical drop; longest run, 2 mi.; restaurants; lodging.

Olympic Valley

SQUAW VALLEY
Box 2007
Olympic Valley, CA 95730
(916) 583-6966
LOCATION: 10 mi. south of I-80 at Truckee off ramp.
FACILITIES: 1 gondola; 24 chairlifts; 1 tram; 2 pomas; slopes for expert, intermediate and beginning skier; ski instruction; ski rental; nursery; 2700 ft. vertical drop; longest run, 3 mi.; restaurants; lodging.

Pinecrest

DODGE RIDGE
Box 1188
Pinecrest, CA 95364
(209) 965-3474
LOCATION: 30 mi. east of Sonora on Hwy. 108.
FACILITIES: 6 chairlifts; 3 tow ropes; slopes for expert, intermediate and beginning skier; ski instruction; ski rental; nursery; 1000 ft. vertical drop; longest run, 4200 ft.; restaurants; lodging.

Running Springs

SNOW VALLEY
Box 8
Running Springs, CA 92382
(714) 867-3677
LOCATION: 85 mi. from Los Angeles, east on I-10 to I-15E to Crosstown Hwy. to Hwy. 330.
FACILITIES: 7 chairlifts; 3 tow ropes; slopes for expert, intermediate and beginning skier; ski instruction; ski rental; 1000 ft. vertical drop; longest run, ½ mi.; restaurants; lodging.

South Lake Tahoe

HEAVENLY VALLEY
P.O. Box AT
South Lake Tahoe, CA 95705
LOCATION: Off Hwy. 50 at South Lake Tahoe.
FACILITIES: 1 triple and 14 double chairlifts; 1 tram; 3 T-bars; 6 mitey mites; slopes for expert, intermediate and beginning skier ; ski instruction; ski rental; nursery; 4000 ft. vertical drop; longest run, 7 mi.; restaurants; lodging.

Tahoe City

ALPINE MEADOWS

P.O. Box AM
Tahoe City, CA 95730
(916) 583-4232
LOCATION: Via I-80; 120 mi. from Sacramento.
FACILITIES: 9 chairlifts; 4 T-bars; slopes for expert, intermediate and beginning skiers; ski instruction; ski rental; nursery; 1730 ft. vertical drop; longest run, 1 mi.; restaurants; lodging.

POWDER BOWL
Box 1641
Tahoe City, CA 95730
(916) 583-4373
LOCATION: 185 mi. from San Francisco via I-80, south on Route 89, right on Alpine Meadows Road.
FACILITIES: 2 T-bars; slopes for expert, intermediate and beginning skiers; ski instruction; ski rental; 800 ft. vertical drop; longest run, 1 mi.

AMUSEMENT PARKS & ATTRACTIONS

Anaheim

DISNEYLAND (Attraction)
1313 Harbor Blvd.
Anaheim, CA 92803
(714) 533-4456
FACILITIES: 53 major attractions; adventures and rides; including 8 animated three-dimensional figures; 12 restaurants and 40 refreshment stands and carts; 63 merchandise stands and gift shops; top-name bands and orchestras; entertainment stars and acts; parades; house-talent performances; variety shows; holiday-theme celebrations; special events; pay gate; pay parking.

Buena Park

MOVIELAND WAX MUSEUM & PALACE OF LIVING ART
7711 Beach Blvd.
Buena Park, CA 90620
(714) 522-1154
FACILITIES: Hall of Fame; museum; arcade; exhibits; 2 refreshment stands; 2 restaurants; candy shop; name bands; pay gate; free parking; open all year.

El Cajon

MARSHAL SCOTTY'S PLAYLAND AND PARK
14011 Ridgehill Road
El Cajon, CA 92021
(714) 443-2377
FACILITIES: 9 major rides; 10 kiddie rides; 3 games; refreshment stand; arcade; swimming pool; miniature golf; picnic facilities; free and pay gate; free parking; open all year.

Escondido

SAN DIEGO WILD ANIMAL PARK
(Attraction)
Hwy. 78
Escondido, CA 92025

CALIFORNIA

AMUSEMENT PARKS (continued)

(714) 747-8704
FACILITIES: 5 mile 1880 steam railroad; 2 walk thrus (aviary and tropical America); 5 refreshment stands; 2 restaurants; exhibits; picnic facilities; zoo; horse show; elephant show; bird of prey show; pay gate; free parking; open all year.

Felton

ROARING CAMP AND BIG TREES NAR-
ROW GAUGE RAILROAD (Attraction)
Roaring Camp & Graham Hill Road
Felton, CA 95018
(408) 335-4484
FACILITIES: 5 mile 1880 steam railroad; refreshment stand; outdoor barbeque; picnic facilities; general store; 180 acre redwood grove; free gate; free parking; open all year.

Irvine

THE FUNDROME (Attraction)
4872 Kron Street
Irvine, CA 92714
(714) 559-5959
FACILITIES: 18 major rides; 5 kiddie rides; fun house; 2 walk thrus; 12 games; 10 refreshment stands; 12 restaurants; arcade; shooting gallery; exhibits; picnic facilities; theatre; stage shows; orchestras; name bands; vaudeville; free acts; pay gate; free parking; open all year.

Klamath

TREES OF MYSTERY (Attraction)
Hwy. 101
Klamath, CA 95548
FACILITIES: A trail of nature's oddities; restaurant; cocktail lounge; Indian museum; pay gate; free parking; open Feb. 10 - Jan. 10.

Long Beach

QUEEN MARY TOURS (Attraction)
Pier J
Long Beach, CA 90801
(213) 435-4747
FACILITIES: 3½ hour tour; swimming pool; museum; exhibits; picnic facilities; theatre; stage shows; orchestras; name bands; free acts; vaudeville; fireworks; pay gate; pay parking; open all year.

"THE PIKE"
LONG BEACH AMUSEMENT CO.
444 W. Ocean Blvd.
Long Beach, CA 90802
(213) 432-7404
FACILITIES: 18 major rides; 5 kiddie rides; fun house; walk thru; 5 refreshment stands; 3 restaurants; arcade; shooting gallery; picnic facilities; free gate; pay parking; open all year.

Morongo Valley

MORONGO WILDLIFE RESERVE
(Attraction)
P.O. Box 694
Morongo Valley, CA 92256
(714) 363-6114

FACILITIES: Wildlife reserve; nature trails; riding trails; picnic facilities; free gate.

Newhall

CALLAHAN'S OLD WEST (Attraction)
Rt. 1
13660 Sierra Highway
Newhall, CA 91321
(805) 252-1515
FACILITIES: Historical; educational Old West shows; Boot Hill; Indian museum; burro rides; 4 trails; barn dances; old time movies; western shoot-outs; ice rink; picnic facilities; miniature golf; theatre; orchestras; vaudeville; pay gate; free parking.

Obrien

LAKE SHASTA CAVERNS (Attraction)
P.O. Box 801
Obrien, CA 96070
(916) 238-2341
FACILITIES: Largest caverns on west coast; 3 refreshment stands; museum; camping; exhibits; picnic facilities; free parking; open all year.

Palos Verdes Peninsula

MARINELAND
Palos Verdes Peninsula, CA 90274
(213) 377-1571
FACILITIES: 2 major rides; world's largest collection of marine mammals & fish; sky tower; restaurant; snack bars; vending machines; cruise boats; picnic facilities; gift shops; camera shops; camping; pay gate; pay parking.

Redwood City

MARINE WORLD - AFRICA U.S.A. (Attraction)
Marine World Parkway
Redwood City, CA 94065
(415) 591-7676
FACILITIES: 3 major rides; 2 kiddie rides; 8 walk thrus; 9 games; 6 refreshment stands; 3 restaurants; 5 major animal shows; water ski and boat shows; "Whale-of-a-Time" Children's playground; arcade; shooting gallery; exhibits; zoo; petting zoo; gift shops; aquarium; dolphin petting pool; seal cove; safari raft ride; camel and elephant rides; stage shows; free acts; pay gate; pay parking; open Memorial Day - Labor Day; weekends: all year.

San Diego

SAN DIEGO ZOO (Attraction)
Park Blvd.
San Diego, CA 92112
(714) 231-1515
FACILITIES: Guided bus tours; sky ride; children's zoo; 5 refreshment stands; restaurant; 5 snack stands; exhibits; picnic facilities; zoo; seal lion show; pay gate; free parking; open all year.

SEA WORLD OF SAN DIEGO (Attraction)
1720 South Shores Road
San Diego, CA 92109
(714) 222-6363

AMUSEMENT PARKS (continued)

FACILITIES: 3 major rides; 2 kiddie rides; 4 refreshment stands; 2 restaurants; 5 major show attractions; all aquatic with trained performing animals; marine exhibits & displays; stage shows; pay gate; free parking.

San Francisco

WAX MUSEUM AT FISHERMAN'S WHARF (Attraction)
145 Jefferson Street
San Francisco, CA 94133
(415) 885-4834
FACILITIES: Arcade; museum; animated ride; open all year.

San Jose

FRONTIER VILLAGE AMUSEMENT PARK (Attraction)
4885 Monterey Road
San Jose, CA 95111
(408) 225-1500
FACILITIES: 15 major rides; 1 walk thru; 3 games; 9 refreshment stands; restaurant; arcade; shooting gallery; museum; picnic facilities; petting zoo; stage shows; name bands; free acts; pay gate; free parking; open all year.

WINCHESTER MYSTERY HOUSE (Attraction)
525 S. Winchester Blvd.
San Jose, CA 95128
(408) 247-2000
FACILITIES: 160 room, beautiful but bizarre mansion built by Sarah Winchester of rifle fame; arcade; refreshments; gift shop; museum; exhibits; guided tours; wax and artifacts; pay gate; free parking; open daily except Christmas Day.

Santa Clara

MARRIOTT'S GREAT AMERICA (Attraction)
One Great America Parkway
Santa Clara, CA 95052
(408) 988-1776
FACILITIES: 21 major rides; 7 kiddie rides; 21 games; 21 refreshment stands; 28 restaurants; 3 arcades; shooting gallery; 5 theaters; crafts; fireworks; pay gate; pay parking.

Santa Cruz

SANTA CRUZ SEASIDE COMPANY (Santa Cruz Beach Boardwalk)
Box 625
Santa Cruz, CA 95061
(408) 423-5590
FACILITIES: 18 major rides; 5 kiddie rides; 26 games; 15 refreshment stands; 6 restaurants; 3 arcades; 2 shooting galleries; beach; miniature golf (indoor); marionette theatre; banquet facilities; stage shows; orchestras; name bands; free acts; pay parking; open May 15 - Sept. 15; weekends: all year.

Universal City

UNIVERSAL CITY STUDIO TOURS
100 Universal City Plaza
Universal City, CA 91608
(213) 985-4321
FACILITIES: Movie lot tour.

Valencia

MAGIC MOUNTAIN
Magic Mountain Parkway
Valencia, CA 91355
(805) 259-7272
FACILITIES: 28 major rides; 9 kiddie rides; 5 restaurants; 18 major gift shops; 16 games of skill; 2 arcades; shooting gallery; petting farm; fun village; animal chatter show; showcase theatre (amphitheatre); stage shows; orchestras; name bands; free acts; fireworks; picnic facilities; kennel facilities; camping adjacent; pay gate; pay parking; open May - Sept., weekends all year, and designated holidays.

Van Nuys

BUSCH BIRD SANCTUARY (Attraction)
16000 Roscoe Blvd.
Van Nuys, CA 91406
(213) 997-1171
FACILITIES: Major ride; arcade; exhibits (animal); theatre (live and trained birds); free-flight aviary; theatre with live entertainment and trained birds; zoo; crafts; audio-visual show, "Day of the Balloons"; free gate; pay parking; open year round.

STATE FAIR

California State Fair
P.O. Box 15649
Sacramento, CA 95813
(916) 641-2311
DATE: August

NATIONAL PARKS

Crescent City

REDWOOD NATIONAL PARK
Crescent City, CA 95531
(707) 464-6101
LOCATION: Near Crescent City.
FACILITIES: Open year round; entrance fee; limit if stay: 7 days; 100 sites; NPS campsite fee: $2; water and bathroom facilities; cabins; picnic area; swimming; boating.

Mineral

LASSEN VOLCANIC NATIONAL PARK
Mineral, CA 96063
(916) 595-4444

BUTTE LAKE
LOCATION: Northeast corner of park.
FACILITIES: Open May 30 - Oct. 15; entrance fee; limit of stay: 7 days; 98 sites; NPS campsite fee: $2; water and bathroom facilities; cabins; picnic area; swimming; boating; fishing; hiking; horseback riding; exhibit; living history program; handicapped access restrooms; medical service; reservations; no motor boats; lodging.

CALIFORNIA

NATIONAL PARKS (continued)

CRAGS
LOCATION: 48 mi. east of Reading.
FACILITIES: Open May 30 - Oct. 10; limit of stay: 7 days; 45 sites; NPS campsite fee: $1; water and bathroom facilities.

JUNIPER LAKE
LOCATION: 13 mi. north of Chester.
FACILITIES: Open Jun. 30 - Oct. 1; limit of stay: 7 days; 18 sites; group camps: 1 (reservations); bathroom facilities; swimming; boating; fishing; no motor boats; primitive site.

LOST CREEK
LOCATION: 5 mi. east of Manzanita Lake.
FACILITIES: Open Jun. 15 - Oct. 1; limit of stay: 7 days; group camps: 9; water and bathroom facilities; reservations; primitive site.

MANZANITA LAKE
LOCATION: Northwest of entrance.
FACILITIES: Open May 30 - Oct. 15; entrance fee; limit of stay, 7 days; 183 sites; NPS campsite fee: $2; water and bathroom facilities; sanitary station; cabins; picnic area; food service; swimming; boating; fishing; hiking; exhibit; living history program; handicapped access/restroom; NPS guided tour; self-guiding tour; medical service; lodging.

SOUTHWEST
LOCATION: Southwest of entrance.
FACILITIES: Open Jun. 15 - Oct. 20; entrance fee; limit of stay: 21 days; NPS campsite fee: $1; water and bathroom facilities; cabins; picnic area; food service; hiking; horseback riding; exhibit; living history program; handicapped access/restroom; NPS guided tour; self-guiding tour; medical service; lodging; walk in.

SUMMIT LAKE
LOCATION: 12 mi. south of Manzita Lake.
FACILITIES: Open Jun. 15 - Sept. 10; entrance fee; limit of stay: 7 days; 94 sites; NPS campsite fee: $2; water and bathroom facilities; cabins; picnic area; swimming; boating; fishing; hiking; horseback trail; exhibit; living history program; handicapped access restroom; NPS guided tour; self-guiding tour; medical service; lodging.

WARNER VALLEY
LOCATION: 16 mi. northwest of Chester.
FACILITIES: Open Jun. 1 - Oct. 1; limit of stay: 7 days; 15 sites; NPS campsite fee: $1; bathroom facilities; fishing; horseback riding; no large trailers; primitive site.

Three Rivers

KINGS CANYON NATIONAL PARK
Three Rivers, CA 93271
(209) 565-3341

AZALEA
LOCATION: ½ mi. north of Grant Grove.
FACILITIES: Open year round; entrance fee; limit of stay: 14 days; 108 sites; NPS campsite fee: $2; water and bathroom facilities; sanitary station; cabins; picnic area; food service; fishing; guide for hire; hiking; horseback riding; bicycle trail; exhibit; museum; environmental study area; living history program; handicapped access/restroom; medical service; lodging; limited trailer space.

CANYON VIEW
LOCATION: 31 mi. northeast of Grant Grove (cedar Grove area).
FACILITIES: Open May 20 - Sept. 15; entrance fee; limit of stay: 14 days; 67 sites; NPS campsite fee: $2; water and bathroom facilities; sanitary station; cabins; picnic area; food service; fishing; guide for hire; hiking; horseback riding; bicycle trail; exhibit; museum; environmental study area; living history program; handicapped access/restroom; NPS guided tour; self-guiding tour; medical service; lodging.

CRYSTAL SPRINGS
LOCATION: ½ mi. north of Canyon Grove.
FACILITIES: Open Jun. 15 - Sept. 15; entrance fee; limit of stay: 14 days; 57 sites; NPS campsite fee: $2; water and bathroom facilities; cabins; picnic area; food service; fishing; guide for hire; hiking; horseback riding; bicycle trail; exhibit; museum; environmental study area; living history program; handicapped access/restroom; NPS guided tour; self-guiding tour; medical service; lodging.

MORAINE
LOCATION: 32 mi. northeast of Grant Grove (Cedar Grove area).
FACILITIES: Open May 20 - Sept. 15; entrance fee; limit of stay: 14 days; 124 sites; group camps: 7 (25 cents per person); NPS campsite fee: $2; water and bathroom facilities; cabins; picnic area; food service; fishing; guide for hire; hiking; horseback riding; bicycle trail; exhibit; museum; environmental study area; living history program; handicapped access/restroom; NPS guided tour; self-guiding tour; medical service; lodging.

SENTINEL
LOCATION: 30 mi. northeast of Grant Grove (Cedar Grove area).
FACILITIES: Open May 20 - Sept. 15; entrance fee; limit of stay: 14 days; 86 sites; NPS campsite fee: $2; water and bathroom facilities; cabins; picnic area; food service; fishing; guide for hire; hiking; horseback riding; bicycle trail; exhibit; museum; environmental study area; living history program; handicapped access/restroom; NPS guided tour; self-guiding tour; medical service; no trailers; lodging.

SHEEP CREEK
LOCATION: 29 mi. northeast of Grant Grove (Cedar Grove area).
FACILITIES: Open May 20 - Nov. 1; entrance fee; limit of stay: 14 days; 113 sites; NPS campsite fee: $2; water and bathroom facilities; sanitary station; cabins; picnic area; food service; fishing; guide for hire; hiking; horseback riding; bicycle trail; exhibit; museum; environmental study area; living history program; handicapped access/restroom; NPS guided tour; self-guiding tour; medical service; lodging.

SUNSET
LOCATION: ½ mi. south of Grant Grove.

NATIONAL PARKS (continued)

FACILITIES: Open May 20 - Oct. 15; entrance fee; limit of stay: 14 days; 213 sites; NPS campsite fee: $2; water and bathroom facilities; cabins; picnic area; food service; fishing; guide for hire; hiking; horseback riding; bicycle trail; exhibit; museum; environmental study area; living history program; handicapped access/restroom; NPS guided tour; self-guiding tour; medical service; lodging; limited trailer space.

SWALE
LOCATION: 1 mi. northwest of Grant Grove.
FACILITIES: Open Jun. 15 - Sept. 15; entrance fee; limit of stay: 14 days; 56 sites; NPS campsite fee: $2; water and bathroom facilities; cabins; picnic area; food service; fishing; guide for hire; hiking; bicycle trail; exhibit; museum; environmental study area; living history program; handicapped access/restroom; NPS guided tour; self-guiding tour; medical service; lodging.

SEQUOIA NATIONAL PARK
Three Rivers, CA 93271
(209) 565-3341

ATWELL
LOCATION: 20 mi. east of Hammond.
FACILITIES: Open May 25 - Sept. 25; limit of stay: 14 days; 23 sites; water and bathroom facilities; fishing; no trailers.

BUCKEYE FLAT
LOCATION: 5 mi. north of headquarters.
FACILITIES: Open Apr. 15 - Nov. 1; entrance fee; limit of stay: 14 days; 29 sites; NPS campsite fee: $2; water and bathroom facilities; cabins; picnic area; fishing; guide for hire; hiking; bicycle trail; exhibit; museum; environmental study area; living history program; handicapped access/restroom; medical service; no trailers; lodging.

DORST
LOCATION: 28 mi. north of headquarters.
FACILITIES: Open May 15 - Sept. 15; entrance fee; limit of stay: 14 days; 238 sites; group camps: 6; NPS campsite fee: $2; water and bathroom facilities; sanitary stations; cabins; picnic area; fishing; guide for hire; hiking; bicycle trail; exhibit; museum; environmental study area; living history program; handicapped access/restroom; NPS guided tour; self-guiding tour; medical service; lodging.

LODGEPOLE
LOCATION: 21 mi. north of headquarters.
FACILITIES: Open year round; entrance fee; limit of stay: 14 days; 261 sites; NPS campsite fee: $2; water and bathroom facilities; sanitary stations; cabins; picnic area; food service; fishing; guide for hire; hiking; horseback riding; bicycle trail; exhibit; museum; environmental study area; living history program; handicapped access/restroom; NPS guided tour; self-guiding tour; medical service; lodging.

POTWISHA
LOCATION: 3 mi. north of headquarters.
FACILITIES: Open year round; limit of stay:

14 days; 44 sites; NPS campsite fee: $2; water and bathroom facilities; sanitary station; cabins; picnic area; fishing; guide for hire; hiking; bicycle trail; exhibit; museum; environmental study area; living history program; handicapped access/restroom; NPS guide tour; self-guiding tour; medical service; lodging.

SOUCH FORK
LOCATION: 15 mi. south of Three Rivers.
FACILITIES: Open year round; limit of stay: 14 days; 12 sites; water and bathroom facilities; fishing; no water in winter.

Yosemite National Park

YOSEMITE NATIONAL PARK
Yosemite National Park, CA 95389
(209) 372-4461

BRIDALVEIL CREEK
LOCATION: 24 mi. from Yosemite Valley.
FACILITIES: Open May 30 - Oct. 1; entrance fee; limit of stay: 30 days (14, Jun. 1 - Sept. 15); 110 sites; NPS campsite fee: $3; water and bathroom facilities; cabins; picnic area; fishing; hiking; bicycle trail; exhibit; museum; environmental study area; living history program; handicapped access/restroom; NPS guided tour; self-guiding tour; medical service; lodging.

CRANE FLAT
LOCATION: 9 mi. south of Big Oak Flat entrance.
FACILITIES: Open May 30 - Oct. 15; entrance fee; limit of stay: 30 days (14, Jun. 1 - Sept. 15); 164 sites; NPS campsite fee: $3; water and bathroom facilities; cabins; picnic area; hiking; bicycle trail; exhibit; museum; environmental study area; living history program; handicapped access/restroom; NPS guided tour; self-guiding tour; medical service; lodging.

HODGDON MEADOW
LOCATION: ½ mi. south of Big Oak Flat.
FACILITIES: Open May 1 - Nov. 1; entrance fee; limit of stay: 30 days (14, Jun. 1 - Sept. 15); 110 sites; group camps: 7; NPS campsite fee: $3; cabins; picnic area; hiking; bicycle trail; exhibit; museum; environmental study area; living history program; handicapped access/restroom; NPS guided tour; self-guiding tour; medical service; lodging.

PORCUPINE FLAT
LOCATION: 6 mi. west of Tenaya Lake.
FACILITIES: Open May 30 - Oct. 30; limit of stay: 30 days (14, Jun. 1 - Sept. 15); 50 sites; NPS campsite fee: $1.

SMOKEY JACK
LOCATION: 10 mi. east of Crane Flat.
FACILITIES: Open May 30 - Oct. 30; limit of stay: 30 days (14, Jun. 1 - Sept. 15); 25 sites; NPS campsite fee: $1.

TAMARACK FLAT
LOCATION: 5 mi. southeast of Crane Flat.
FACILITIES: Open May 30 - Oct. 15; limit of stay: 30 days (14, Jun. 1 - Sept. 15); 80 sites; NPS campsite fee: $1; fishing.

CALIFORNIA

NATIONAL PARKS (continued)

TENAYA LAKE
LOCATION: 8 mi. west of Tioga Pass.
FACILITIES: Open May 30 - Oct. 30; entrance fee; limit of stay: 30 days (14, Jun. 1 - Sept. 15); NPS campsite fee: $2; water and bathroom facilities; cabins; picnic area; swimming; boating; fishing; hiking; bicycle trail; exhibit; museum; environmental study area; living history program; handicapped access/restroom; NPS guided tour; self-guiding tour; medical service; walk in; no pets; lodging.

TUOLUMNE BACKPACKERS
LOCATION: 4 mi. west of Tioga Pass.
FACILITIES: Open May 27 - Sept. 4; entrance fee; limit of stay: 30 days (14, Jun. 1 - Sept. 15); 30 sites; water and bathroom facilities; food service; fishing; walk in.

TUOLUMNE MEADOWS
LOCATION: 4 mi. west of Tioga Pass.
FACILITIES: Open May 30 - Oct. 30; entrance fee; limit of stay: 30 days (14, Jun. 1 - Sept. 15); 600 sites; group camps: 4 ($6 per group); NPS campsite fee: $2; water and bathroom facilities; sanitary station; cabins; picnic area; food service; fishing; hiking; horseback riding; bicycle trail; exhibit; museum; environmental study area; living history program; handicapped access/restroom; NPS guided tour; self-guiding tour; medical service; lodging.

WAWONA
LOCATION: 6 mi. north of south entrance.
FACILITIES: Open year round; entrance fee; limit of stay: 30 days (14, Jun. 1 - Sept. 15); 110 sites; group camps: 1 (25 cents per person); NPS campsite fee: $3; water and bathroom facilities; cabins; picnic area; food service; fishing; hiking; horseback riding; bicycle trail; exhibit; museum; environmental study area; living history program; handicapped access/restroom; NPS guided tour; self-guiding tour; medical service; lodging.

WHITE WOLF
LOCATION: 25 mi. west of Tioga Pass.
FACILITIES: Open May 30 - Sept. 15; entrance fee; limit of stay: 30 days (14, Jun. 1 - Sept. 15); 86 sites; NPS campsite fee: $3; water and bathroom facilities; cabins; food service; fishing; hiking; horseback riding; bicycle trail; exhibit; museum; environmental study area; living history program; handicapped access/restroom; NPS guided tour; self-guiding tour; medical service; lodging.

YOSEMITE CREEK
LOCATION: 17 mi. west of Tioga Pass.
FACILITIES: Open May 30 - Oct. 15; limit of stay: 30 days (14, Jun. 1 - Sept. 15); 100 sites; NPS campsite fee: $1; fishing.

YOSEMITE VALLEY: LOWER PINES
FACILITIES: Open year round; entrance fee; limit of stay: 30 days (7, Jun. 1 - Sept. 15); 183 sites; NPS campsite fee: $4; water and bathroom facilities; cabins; picnic area; food service; swimming; fishing; hiking; horseback riding; bicycle trail; exhibit; museum; environmental study area; living history program; handicapped access/restroom; NPS guided

tour; self-guiding tour; medical service; no pets; lodging.

YOSEMITE VALLEY: LOWER RIVER
FACILITIES: Open Apr. 1 - Oct. 15; entrance fee; limit of stay: 30 days (7, Jun. 1 - Sept. 15); 154 sites; NPS campsite fee: $4; water and bathroom facilities; sanitary station; cabins; picnic area; food service; swimming; fishing; hiking; horseback riding; bicycle trail; exhibit; museum; environmental study area; living history program; handicapped access/restroom; NPS guided tour; self-guiding tour; medical service; no pets; lodging.

YOSEMITE VALLEY: MUIR TREE
FACILITIES: Open May 27 - Oct. 15; entrance fee: 25 cents; limit of stay: 30 days (7, Jun. 1 - Sept. 15); 25 sites; water and bathroom facilities; swimming; fishing; walk in.

YOSEMITE VALLEY: NORTH PINES
FACILITIES: Open Apr. 1 - Oct. 31; entrance fee; limit of stay: 30 days; 101 sites; NPS campsite fee: $4; water and bathroom facilities; cabins; picnic area; food service; swimming; fishing; hiking; horseback riding; bicycle trail; exhibit; museum; environmental study area; living history program; handicapped access/restroom; NPS guided tour; self-guiding tour; medical service; no pets; lodging.

YOSEMITE VALLEY: SUNNYSIDE
FACILITIES: Open year round; entrance fee; limit of stay: 30 days (7, Jun. 1 - Sept. 15); NPS campsite fee: $2; water and bathroom facilities; cabins; picnic area; food service; swimming; fishing; hiking; bicycle trail; exhibit; museum; environmental study area; living history program; handicapped access/restroom; NPS guided tour; self-guiding tour; medical service; walk in; no pets; lodging.

YOSEMITE VALLEY: UPPER PINES
FACILITIES: Open Apr. 1 - Oct. 31; limit of stay: 30 days (7, Jun. 1 - Sept. 15); 240 sites; NPS campsite fee: $4; water and bathroom facilities; sanitary stations; cabins; picnic area; food service; swimming; fishing; hiking; horseback riding; bicycle trail; exhibit; museum; environmental study area; living history program; handicapped access/restrooms; NPS guided tour; self-guiding tour; medical service; lodging.

YOSEMITE VALLEY: UPPER RIVER
FACILITIES: Open May 1 - Sept. 30; entrance fee; limit of stay: 30 days (7, Jun. 1 - Sept. 15); 124 sites; NPS campsite fee: $4; water and bathroom facilities; cabins; picnic area; food service; swimming; fishing; hiking; horseback riding; bicycle trail; exhibit; museum; environmental study area; living history program; handicapped access/restroom; NPS guided tour; self-guiding tour; medical service; no pets; lodging.

YOSEMITE VALLEY: YOUTH GROUP
FACILITIES: Open Apr. 1 - Oct. 31; limit of stay: 30 days (7, Jun. 1 - Sept. 15); group camps: 14 ($6 per site); NPS campsite fee; water and bathroom facilities; food service; swimming; fishing; horseback riding; no pets; reservations.

NATIONAL FORESTS

National Forests
630 Sansome Street
San Francisco, CA 94111
(415) 556-0122

Alturas

MODOC NATIONAL FOREST
ATTRACTIONS: Remote northeast corner of California; scenic rides; wilderness trails; lava flows; scene of Modoc Indian wars. Winter range of interstate deer herd, Clear Lake Reservoir migratory bird refuge; stream and lake fishing; mule deer, waterfowl hunting.
FACILITIES: 20 camp and picnic sites, 4 picnic only. Swimming, winter sports, hotels, cabins; hunters' camp during deer season.
NEARBY TOWNS: Adin, Canby, Cedarville, Tulelake.

Bishop

INYO NATIONAL FOREST
ATTRACTIONS: Palisade Glacier, southernmost glacier in the United States. Ancient Bristlecone Pine Forest Botanical Area with many 4,000-year-old trees - the oldest living things on earth. Many wild granite peaks 12,000 to more than 14,000 feet in elevation. Mount Whitney, 14,495 feet, highest point in continental United States. Lake and stream fishing, deer hunting, wilderness trips.
FACILITIES: 17 camp and picnic sites; boating, swimming, winter sports; resorts; motels.
NEARBY TOWNS: Bigpine, Independence, Leevining, and Lone Pine.

Eureka

SIX RIVERS NATIONAL FOREST
ATTRACTIONS: Giant coast redwood and fir forests stretching 135 miles south from the Oregon line. Trout, steelhead, salmon fishing; deer and bear hunting; riding trails,; scenic drives.
FACILITIES: 28 camp and picnic sites; 2 picnic only; resorts, hotels, cabins.
NEARBY TOWNS: Arcata, Crescent City, Fortuna, Klamath, Orick, and Orleans.

Fresno

SIERRA NATIONAL FOREST
ATTRACTIONS: Giant sequoia trees. Lakes and stream fishing; deer, bear, quail hunting; boating; mountain climbing; pack and saddle trips; winter sports.
FACILITIES: 111 camp and picnic sites, 20 picnic only. Swimming, boating, winter sports. Hotels, resorts, dude ranches.
NEARBY TOWN: North Fork.

Nevada City

TAHOE NATIONAL FOREST
ATTRACTIONS: Squaw Valley. Outstanding conditions and facilities for winter sports. Lake and stream fishing; deer and bear hunting; riding and hiking trails; scenic drives through historic gold mining towns.
FACILITIES: 70 camp and picnic sites, 11 picnic only. Swimming, boating, winter sports. Summer resorts, cabins, hotels.
NEARBY TOWNS: Downieville, Grass Valley, Sierra City, Sierraville, Truckee, CA; Carson City and Reno, NV.

Pasadena

ANGELES NATIONAL FOREST
ATTRACTIONS: Old Baldy, chiefly a chaparral forest that serves as a watershed for the Los Angeles area; scenic drives; riding and hiking trails; skiing; fishing; hunting; swimming; boating.
FACILITIES: 98 camp and picnic sites, 33 picnic only. (No open campfires are permitted in this National Forest.) Resorts, cabins, hotels and motels in Los Angeles and foothill towns.
NEARBY TOWN: Los Angeles.

Placerville

ELDORADO NATIONAL FOREST
ATTRACTIONS: Rugged mountains in the Sierra Nevada; lakes including south shore of Lake Tahoe, 23 miles long, 13 miles wide; California Gold Rush Country; Mother Lode mining communities including site of Sutter's Mill. Lake and stream fishing, deer, bear hunting; scenic drives; riding trails; wilderness trips.
FACILITIES: 47 camp and picnic sites, 26 picnic only. Boating; swimming; winter sports. Resorts; motels; and dude ranches.
NEARBY TOWNS: Sacramento, CA; Carson City and Reno, NV.

Porterville

SEQUOIA NATIONAL FOREST
ATTRACTIONS: Giant sequoia big trees, high mountain lakes and stream fishing; home of the golden trout; mule deer, bear hunting; scenic drives; wilderness hiking; riding trails.
FACILITIES: 10 camp and picnic sites. Swimming; boating; winter sports. Motels, resorts, lodges.
NEARBY TOWNS: Bakersfield, Fresno, Visalia.

Quincy

PLUMAS NATIONAL FOREST
ATTRACTIONS: Feather Falls, one of the highest and most picturesque waterfalls in the United States. Historic gold mining areas of La Porte, Johnsville, and Rich Bar; extensive hydroelectric developments. Limestone caves; lake and stream fishing; mule and black-tailed deer, bear, duck, geese, quail, and dove hunting. Scenic drives.
FACILITIES: 9 camp and picnic sites, 2 picnic only. Boating, winter sports. Resorts, hotels, and cabins.
NEARBY TOWNS: Chico, Greenville, Marysville, Oroville, Sacramento, Sierraville.

Redding

SHASTA-TRINITY NATIONAL FOREST
ATTRACTIONS: Beautiful Mount Shasta with eternal snow, 5 living glaciers. Lake and stream fishing; home of Dolly Varden trout. Waterfowl, upland birds, deer, bear, small game hunting. Limestone caves, lava caves,

CALIFORNIA

and chimneys. Riding trails; skiing; scenic drives.
FACILITIES: 102 camp and picnic sites, 14 picnic only. Swimming, boating, winter sports. Resorts, hotels, motels, guest ranches.
NEARBY TOWNS: Callahan, Dunsmur, McCloud, Mount Shasta, Weaverville, Weed.

San Bernardino

SAN BERNARDINO NATIONAL FOREST
ATTRACTIONS: Highest mountains in southern California; historic landmarks. Lake and stream fishing, deer hunting. Life zones from desert to alpine within a few miles. Camping and pack trips, winter sports.
FACILITIES: 11 camp and picnic sites, 2 picnic only. Swimming and winter sports. (No open campfires are permitted in this National Forest.) Resorts, hotels, motels, cabins at Arrowhead, Big Bear Lakes, Idyllwild.
NEARBY TOWNS: Banning, Indio, Palm Springs, Riverside.

San Diego

STANISLAUS NATIONAL FOREST
ATTRACTIONS: Primarily a watershed forest with an unusually mild climate, between the desert and the sea. The world's largest telescope at Palomar Observatory on Mount Palomar. Camping; warm water fishing; duck, deer, pigeon, quail hunting. The Mexico-to-Oregon Trail starts here.
FACILITIES: 57 camp and picnic sites, 11 picnic only. (No open campfires are permitted in this National Forest.) Dude ranches; resorts; motels.
NEARBY TOWNS: El Centro, Los Angeles, Oceanside.

Santa Barbara

LOS PADRES NATIONAL FOREST
ATTRACTIONS: Undeveloped, rugged country, varying from lonely coast to semidesert, from brush to oak country to pine timber; home of the rare California condor. Quail, pigeon, deer, wild boar hunting; trout fishing; scenic drives; oceanside camping; wilderness trips.
FACILITIES: 325 camp and picnic sites, 22 picnic only. (No open campfires are permitted in this National Forest.) Swimming and winter sports areas including Kern County Ski Lodge. Hotels, cabins, a few dude ranches.
NEARBY TOWNS: Atascadero, Carmel, King City, Monterey, Ojai, Paso Robles, Taft, San Luis Obispo, Santa Maria, and Ventura.

Sonora

STANISLAUS NATIONAL FOREST (includes Calaveras Big Tree National Forest)
ATTRACTIONS: Deep canyons; fine timber stands; Gold Rush Country. Routes of pioneers; fishing in lakes and streams; deer and bear hunting; scenic drives; saddle and pack trips; winter sports.
FACILITIES: 67 camp and picnic sites, 10 picnic only. Swimming, boating; winter sports. Resorts, cabins, stores, boating, packer stations.

NEARBY TOWNS: Angels Camp, Columbia, Groveland, Jamestown, San Andrews.

Susanville

LASSEN NATIONAL FOREST
ATTRACTIONS: Lakes; volcanic lava flow tubes; hot springs; mud pots; Indian pictographs and hieroglyphics; old emigrant trails. Lake and stream fishing for rainbow, Lochleven, and steelhead trout; deer and bear hunting; riding and hiking trails.
FACILITIES: 44 camp and picnic sites, 9 picnic only. Boating; swimming; winter sports. Privately owned resorts, hotels, cabins.
NEARBY TOWNS: Chester, Chico, Mill Creek, Red Bluff, and Redding.

Willows

MENDOCINO NATIONAL FOREST
ATTRACTIONS: Hunting, fishing, saddle and pack trips.
FACILITIES: 325 camp and picnic sites, 22 picnic only. Dude ranches, motels.
NEARBY TOWNS: Corning, Laytonville, Sacramento, Ukiah, Willits.

Yreka

KLAMATH NATIONAL FOREST
ATTRACTIONS: Big timber forest. Klamath River and tributaries, famous for salmon and steelhead. High mountain lakes and streams; deer hunting; hiking; riding; pack trips.
FACILITIES: 28 camp and picnic sites, 4 picnic only. Motels, resorts, dude ranches.
NEARBY TOWNS: Eureka, Mount Shasta, CA; Medford, OR.

See TOIYAKE NATIONAL FOREST - Nevada.

See ROGUE RIVER NATIONAL FOREST - Oregon.

See SISKIYOU NATIONAL FOREST - Oregon.

STATE PARKS

Headquarters

Department of Parks & Recreation
P.O. Box 2390
Sacramento, CA 95812
(916) 445-4624

Aptos

THE FOREST OF NISENE MARKS STATE PARK
LOCATION: 4 mi. north of Aptos on Aptos Creek Road.
FACILITIES: Open year round; picnic area; hiking.

Arnold

CALAVERAS BIG TREES STATE PARK
LOCATION: 4 mi. northeast of Arnold on Hwy. 4.
FACILITIES: Open year round; 129 sites; wa-

STATE PARKS (continued)

ter and bathroom facilities; sanitary station; picnic area; swimming; fishing; hiking; exhibit; self-guiding trail.

Blairsden

PLUMAS - EUREKA STATE PARK
LOCATION: 5 mi. west of Blairsden on County Road A-14.
FACILITIES: Open year round; 67 sites; water and bathroom facilities; picnic area; fishing; hiking; horseback riding; exhibit; living history program; self-guiding trail.

Boonville

HENDY WOODS STATE PARK
LOCATION: 10 mi. northwest of Boonville, 1 mi. from Hwy. 128.
FACILITIES: Open year round; 92 sites; water and bathroom facilities; sanitary station; picnic area; swimming; fishing; hiking; horseback riding; self-guiding trail.

Burney

MCARTHUR-BURNEY FALLS MEMORIAL STATE PARK
LOCATION: 11 mi. northeast of Burney on Hwy. 89.
FACILITIES: Open year round; 118 sites; water and bathroom facilities; sanitary station; picnic area; food service; swimming; boating; fishing; hiking; exhibit; self-guiding trail.

Calabasas

MALIBU CREEK STATE PARK
LOCATION: 4 mi. south of U.S. 101 on Las Virgenes/Malibu Canyon Road.
FACILITIES: Open year round; fishing; hiking; horseback riding.

Carmel

ANDREW MOLERA STATE PARK
LOCATION: 21 mi. south of Carmel on Hwy. 1.
FACILITIES: Open year round; hiking; hike-in campground.

PFEIFFER BIG SUR STATE PARK
LOCATION: 26 mi. south of Carmel on Hwy. 1.
FACILITIES: Open year round; 218 sites; water and bathroom facilities; sanitary station; cabins; picnic area; food service; swimming; fishing; hiking; exhibit; self-guiding trail.

JULIA PFEIFFER BURNS STATE PARK
LOCATION: 37 mi. south of Carmel on Hwy. 1.
FACILITIES: Open year round; picnic area; hiking.

Crescent City

DEL NORTE COAST REDWOODS STATE PARK
LOCATION: 7 mi. south of Crescent City on U.S. 101.
FACILITIES: Open year round; 145 sites; water and bathroom facilities; sanitary station;

picnic area; fishing; hiking; exhibit; self-guiding trail.

JEDEDIAH SMITH REDWOODS STATE PARK
LOCATION: 9 mi. east of Crescent City on Hwy. 199.
FACILITIES: Open year round; 108 sites; water and bathroom facilities; sanitary station; picnic area; swimming; fishing; hiking; exhibit; self-guiding trail.

Danville

MOUNT DIABLO STATE PARK
LOCATION: 5 mi. east of I-680 on Diablo Road.
FACILITIES: Open year round; 60 sites; water and bathroom facilities; picnic area; hiking; horseback riding; exhibit.

Escondido

PALOMAR MOUNTAIN STATE PARK
LOCATION: From Escondido, north on Hwy. S6, east 5 mi. on Hwy. 76, north 9 mi. on Hwy. S6, west on Hwy. S7, 3 mi. to park.
FACILITIES: Open year round; 51 sites; water and bathroom facilities; picnic area; fishing; hiking; self-guiding trail.

Eureka

DRY LAGOON STATE PARK
LOCATION: 31 mi. north of Eureka on U.S. 101.
FACILITIES: Open year round; picnic area; fishing.

HUMBOLDT REDWOODS STATE PARK
LOCATION: 45 mi. south of Eureka via U.S. 101 and Hwy. 254 (Avenue of Giants).
FACILITIES: Open year round; 247 sites; water and bathroom facilities; sanitary station; picnic area; swimming; fishing; hiking; horseback riding; exhibit; self-guiding trail.

PATRICK'S POINT STATE PARK
LOCATION: 25 mi. north of Eureka on U.S. 101.
FACILITIES: Open year round; 123 sites; water and bathroom facilities; picnic area; fishing; hiking; exhibit; museum; self-guiding trail.

PRAIRIE CREEK REDWOODS STATE PARK
LOCATION: 50 mi. north of Eureka on U.S. 101.
FACILITIES: Open year round; 100 sites; water and bathroom facilities; picnic area; fishing; hiking; exhibit; self-guiding trail.

Ft. Bragg

MACKERRICHER STATE PARK
LOCATION: 3 mi. north of Ft. Bragg on Hwy. 1.
FACILITIES: Open year round; 143 sites; water and bathroom facilities; sanitary station; picnic area; fishing; hiking; horseback riding; self-guiding trail.

CALIFORNIA

STATE PARKS (continued)

Garberville

RICHARDSON GROVE STATE PARK
LOCATION: 8 mi. south of Garberville on U.S. 101.
FACILITIES: Open year round; 169 sites; water and bathroom facilities; sanitary station; picnic area; food service; swimming; fishing; hiking; self-guiding trail.

Hydesville

GRIZZLY CREEK REDWOODS STATE PARK
LOCATION: 18 mi. east of U.S. 101 on Hwy. 36.
FACILITIES: Open year round; 30 sites; water and bathroom facilities; picnic area; swimming; fishing; hiking; exhibit; self-guiding trail.

Idyllwild

MOUNT SAN JACINTO STATE PARK
LOCATION: On Hwy. 243 near Idyllwild.
FACILITIES: Open year round; 33 sites; water and bathroom facilities; picnic area; food service; hiking; horseback riding; exhibit; self-guiding trail.

Inverness

TOMALES BAY STATE PARK
LOCATION: 4 mi. north of Inverness on Sir Francis Drake Blvd.
FACILITIES: Open year round; water and bathroom facilities; picnic area; swimming; fishing; exhibit; self-guiding trail.

Jenner

SALT POINT STATE PARK
LOCATION: 20 mi. north of Jenner on Hwy. 1.
FACILITIES: Open year round; 31 sites; picnic area; fishing; hiking; horseback riding.

Julian

CUYAMACA RANCHO STATE PARK
LOCATION: 9 mi. north of I-8 on Hwy. 79.
FACILITIES: Open year round; 182 sites; water and bathroom facilities; sanitary station; picnic area; fishing; hiking; horseback riding; exhibit; living history program; self-guiding trail.

Kelseyville

CLEAR LAKE STATE PARK
LOCATION: 4 mi. northeast of Kelseyville on Soda Bay Road.
FACILITIES: Open year round; 82 sites; water and bathroom facilities; sanitary station; picnic area; swimming; boating; fishing; hiking; self-guiding trail.

Lancaster

SADDLEBACK BUTTE STATE PARK
LOCATION: 17 mi. east of Lancaster on Avenue J East.
FACILITIES: Open year round; 50 sites; water and bathroom facilities; picnic area; hiking.

Los Osos

MONTANA DE ORO STATE PARK
LOCATION: 7 mi. south of Los Osos on Pecho Road.
FACILITIES: Open year round; 46 sites; picnic area; swimming; fishing; hiking; self-guiding trail.

Markleeville

GROVER HOT SPRINGS STATE PARK
LOCATION: 3 mi. west of Markleeville on Hot Springs Road.
FACILITIES: Open year round; 76 sites; water and bathroom facilities; picnic area; swimming; fishing; hiking; self-guiding trail; hot springs pool.

Mendocino

MENDOCINO HEADLANDS STATE PARK
LOCATION: Surrounds town of Mendocino.
FACILITIES: Open year round; fishing; hiking.

RUSSIAN GULCH STATE PARK
LOCATION: 2 mi. north of Mendocino on Hwy. 1.
FACILITIES: Open year round; 30 sites; water and bathroom facilities; picnic area; fishing; hiking; bicycle trail; exhibit; self-guiding trail.

VAN DAMME STATE PARK
LOCATION: 3 mi. south of Mendocino on Hwy. 1.
FACILITIES: Open year round; 74 sites; water and bathroom facilities; picnic area; fishing; hiking; bicycle trail; exhibit; self-guiding trail.

Morgan Hill

HENRY W. COE STATE PARK
LOCATION: 14 mi. east of Morgan Hill on E. Dunne Ave.
FACILITIES: Open year round; 20 sites; water and bathroom facilities; hiking; horseback riding; exhibit; living history program.

Morro Bay

MORRO BAY STATE PARK
LOCATION: In the town.
FACILITIES: Open year round; 115 sites; bathroom facilities; sanitary station; electrical hookup; trailer village vehicle sites; picnic area; food service; swimming; boating; fishing; hiking; exhibit; museum; living history program; self-guiding trail.

Mill Valley

MOUNT TAMALPAIS STATE PARK
LOCATION: 6 mi. west of Mill Valley on Panoramic Hwy.
FACILITIES: Open year round; 18 sites; water and bathroom facilities; picnic area; fishing; hiking; horseback riding; exhibit; self-guiding trail.

STATE PARKS (continued)

Oxnard

POINT MUGU STATE PARK
LOCATION: 15 mi. south of Oxnard on Hwy. 1.
FACILITIES: Open year round; 150 sites; water and bathroom facilities; picnic area; swimming; fishing; hiking; exhibit.

Pescadero

BUTANO STATE PARK
LOCATION: 7 mi. south of Pescadero on Cloverdale Road.
FACILITIES: Open year round; 21 sites; picnic area; hiking.

PORTOLA STATE PARK
LOCATION: Portola State Park road, 3 mi. west of Hwy. 35 on Alpine Road.
FACILITIES: Open year round; 52 sites; water and bathroom facilities; picnic area; fishing; hiking; exhibit; self-guiding trail.

Ripon

CASWELL MEMORIAL STATE PARK
LOCATION: 6 mi. south of Ripon on Austin Road.
FACILITIES: Open year round; 65 sites; water and bathroom facilities; picnic area; swimming; fishing; hiking; exhibit; self-guiding trail.

St. Helena

BOTHE-NAPA VALLEY STATE PARK
LOCATION: 4 mi. north of St. Helena on Hwy. 29/128.
FACILITIES: Open year round; 35 sites; water and bathroom facilities; sanitary station; picnic area; swimming; hiking; horseback riding; exhibit; self-guiding trail.

San Diego

ANZA-BORREGO DESERT STATE PARK
LOCATION: 85 mi. northeast of San Diego.
FACILITIES: Open year round; 90 sites; water and bathroom facilities; electrical hookup; picnic area; hiking; horseback riding; exhibit; self-guiding trail.

BORDEN FIELD STATE PARK
LOCATION: 15 mi. south of San Diego via I-5 and Monument Road.
FACILITIES: Open year round; swimming; fishing; hiking; horseback riding; self-guiding trail.

San Francisco

ANGEL ISLAND STATE PARK
LOCATION: By ferry from Tiburon, San Francisco or Berkeley.
FACILITIES: Open year round; water and bathroom facilities; picnic area; food service; boating; fishing; hiking; exhibit; self-guiding trail.

San Juan Bautista

FREMONT PEAK STATE PARK
LOCATION: 11 mi. south of San Juan Bautista on San Juan Canyon Road.
FACILITIES: Open year round; 12 sites; water and bathroom facilities; picnic area.

San Rafael

SAMUEL P. TAYLOR STATE PARK
LOCATION: 15 mi. west of San Rafael on Sir Francis Drake Blvd.
FACILITIES: Open year round; 65 sites; water and bathroom facilities; picnic area; swimming; fishing; hiking; horseback riding; exhibit; self-guiding trail.

Santa Barbara

GAVIOTA STATE PARK
LOCATION: 33 mi. west of Santa Barbara on U.S. 101.
FACILITIES: Open year round; 59 sites; water and bathroom facilities; food service; swimming; boating; fishing; hiking; horseback riding.

Santa Cruz

BIG BASIN REDWOODS STATE PARK
LOCATION: 20 mi. north of Santa Cruz via Hwys. 9 and 236.
FACILITIES: Open year round; 143 sites; water and bathroom facilities; sanitary station; picnic area; food service; hiking; horseback riding; exhibit; self-guiding trail.

HENRY COWELL REDWOODS STATE PARK
LOCATION: 5 mi. north of Santa Cruz on Hwy. 9.
FACILITIES: Open year round; 113 sites; water and bathroom facilities; sanitary station; picnic area; food service; fishing; hiking; horseback riding; exhibit; self-guiding trail.

Santa Rosa

ANNADEL STATE PARK
LOCATION: Channel Drive east off Montgomery Drive.
FACILITIES: Open year round; fishing; hiking; horseback riding; bicycle trail.

SUGARLOAF RIDGE STATE PARK
LOCATION: 7 mi. east of Santa Rosa on Hwy. 12, 3 mi. north on Adobe Canyon Road.
FACILITIES: Open year round; 50 sites; picnic area; hiking; horseback riding.

Saratoga

CASTLE ROCK STATE PARK
LOCATION: 2 mi. south of intersection of Hwys. 9 and 35 on Skyline Blvd.
FACILITIES: Open year round; 25 sites; picnic area; hiking; self-guiding trail.

Tahoe City

D.L. BLISS STATE PARK
LOCATION: 17 mi. south of Tahoe City on Hwy. 89.
FACILITIES: Open year round; 168 sites; water and bathroom facilities; picnic area; swimming; hiking; self-guiding trail.

117

CALIFORNIA

STATE PARKS (continued)

EMERALD BAY STATE PARK
LOCATION: 22 mi. south of Tahoe City on Hwy. 89.
FACILITIES: Open year round; 100 sites; water and bathroom facilities; picnic area; swimming; boating; fishing; hiking; exhibit; guided tour.

SUGAR PINE POINT STATE PARK
LOCATION: 10 mi. south of Tahoe City on Hwy. 89.
FACILITIES: Open year round; 175 sites; water and bathroom facilities; sanitary station; picnic area; swimming; fishing; hiking; exhibit; museum; self-guiding trail.

Truckee

DONNER MEMORIAL STATE PARK
LOCATION: On Old Hwy. 40, 2 mi. west of Truckee.
FACILITIES: Open year round; 154 sites; water and bathroom facilities; picnic area; swimming; fishing; exhibit; living history program; self-guiding trail.

STATE FORESTS

Fort Bragg

JACKSON STATE FOREST
820 N. Main Street
Fort Bragg, CA 95437
(707) 964-5673
LOCATION: 5 mi. south of Fort Bragg.
FACILITIES: Open year round; camping; picnic area; water; horseback riding; hiking; hunting; fishing; jeep trails.

Lower Lake

BOGGS MOUNTAIN STATE FOREST
c/o Konocti Conservation Camp
Lower Lake, CA 95457
(707) 994-2441
LOCATION: Adjacent to Lower Lake.
FACILITIES: Open year round; camping by permit only; picnic area; water; horseback riding; hiking; hunting; fishing.

Shingletown

LATOUR STATE FOREST
1000 Cypress Street
Redding, CA 96001
(916) 243-0954
LOCATION: Adjacent to Shingletown, about 25 mi. south of Redding.
FACILITIES: Open year round; camping; picnic area; water; horseback riding; hiking; hunting; fishing; nature trails.

Springville

MOUNTAIN HOME STATE FOREST
Hwy. 190
Springville, CA 93265
(209) 539-2855
LOCATION: Adjacent to Springville.
FACILITIES: Open Jun. - Oct.; camping; picnic area; water; horseback riding; hiking; hunting; fishing; jeep trails.

HISTORIC SITES

Blairsden

PIONEER SKI AREA OF AMERICA - Plumas-Eureka State Park, from Hwy. 70 south to Mohawk and west on County Road A 14. The first sport ski area in the western hemisphere was in the Sierra Nevada, and by 1860 races were being held in the Plumas-Sierra region.

Blythe

GIANT DESERT FIGURES - Hwy. 95, 18 mi. north of Blythe. Times of origin and meaning of the giant figures, the largest of which is 167 feet long and the smallest 95 feet, remain a mystery. There are three figures, two of animals and one of a coiled serpent, and some interesting lines. (Sandstone pebbles glazed on one side with "desert varnish," strewn over the surface of the mesa, have been moved away, leaving the earth forming the figures; the pebbles were placed in windows about the edge as an outline.)

Chico

HOOKER OAK - Manzanita Ave. between Vallombrosa and Hooker Oak Ave, Bidwell Park. This enormous tree is estimated to be a thousand years old. It is 96 feet tall; at 8 feet from the ground its trunk is 29 feet in circumference and 9 feet in diameter. From the tip of the north branches to the tip of the south branches is 53 feet; circumference of outside branches is 481 feet. Allowing 2 square feet per person, 8,000 people could stand under this tree. The largest south branch measures 111 feet from the trunk to its tip. In 1887 Annie E.K. Bidwell named the tree in honor of English botanist Sir Joseph Hooker.

Coloma

MARSHALL MONUMENT - Marshall Gold Discovery State Historic Park. A monument to commemorate James Marshall, who in 1848 discovered gold near Coloma. Marshall's discovery started the "gold rush". The figure of Marshall atop the monument is pointing to the place of discovery on the South Fork of the American River.

Coronado

FIRST MILITARY FLYING SCHOOL IN AMERICA - Naval Air Station, North Island. Glenn Curtiss founded the first military flying school in America here on January 17, 1911. The Army operated Rockwell Field until January 31, 1939; the Navy commissioned the present air station on November 8, 1917.

Cucamonga

CUCAMONGA RANCHO WINERY - 0.5 mi. west of Cucamonga. Established by Tiburcio Tapia, to whom the Cucamonga Rancho was granted March 3, 1839, by Governor Juan Bautista Alvarado of Mexico.

HISTORIC SITES (continued)

Daly City

BRODERICK-TERRY DUELING PLACE - 1100 Lake Merced Blvd. In the early morning of September 13, 1859, US Senator David C. Broderick and Chief Justice David S. Terry of the California Supreme Court fought the famous duel that ended dueling in California in a ravine east of here, near the shore of Lake Merced. Senator Broderick was mortally wounded.

Fellows

WELL "2-6" - 0.25 mi. west of Fellows on Broadway. Near an area of small 40-and 50-barrel wells, it blew in over the derrick top November 27, 1909, with a production of 2,000 barrels a day and started one of the greatest oil booms California ever experienced.

Fremont

LELAND STANFORD WINERY - From I-680 take Mission Blvd. north 0.5 mi. to Stanford Ave., turn east to winery in Mission San Jose District. This winery was founded in 1869 by Leland Stanford - railroad builder, Governor of California, United States Senator, and founder of Stanford University. The vineyard, planted by his brother Josiah, helped to prove that wines equal to any in the world could be produced in California. The restored buildings and winery are now occupied and operated by Weibel Champagne Vineyards.

French Corral

THE WORLD'S FIRST LONG-DISTANCE TELEPHONE LINE - On Pleasant Valley Rd. The first long-distance telephone in the world, built in 1877 by the Ridge Telephone Company, connected French Corral with French Lake, 58 mi. away. It was operated by the Milton Mining Company from a building on this site that had been erected about 1853.

Hemet

HEMET MAZE STONE - 5 mi. west of Hemet. This pictograph, representing a maze, is an outstanding example of the work of prehistoric peoples.

Hollywood

CECILE B. DEMILLE STUDIO BARN - Paramount Studios. Cecil B. DeMille rented half of this structure, then used as a barn, as the studio in which was made the first feature-length motion picture in Hollywood - The Squaw Man - in 1913. Associated with Mr. DeMille in making The Squaw Man were Samuel Goldwyn and Jesse Lakey, Sr. Originally located at the corner of Selma and Vine Streets, in 1927 the barn was transferred to Paramount Studios.

OLDEST HOUSE IN HOLLYWOOD - 7377 Santa Monica Blvd. Known as the "Oldest House in Hollywood," this house was built in the 1870s by Eugene Raphael Plummer.

Livermore

CONCANNON VINEYARD - 2 mi. southeast of Livermore via Livermore Ave. and Tesla Rd. Here, in 1883, James Concannon founded the Concannon Vineyard. The quality it achieved in sacramental and commercial wines helped established Livermore Valley as one of America's select winegrowing districts.

CRESTA BLANCA WINERY - Arroyo Road south of Livermore. Here Charles A. Wetmore planted his vineyard in 1882. The Cresta Blanca wine he made from its fruit won for California the first International Award the highest honor at the 1889 Paris Exposition, thus assuring California winegrowers that they could grow wines comparable to the finest in the world.

Mojave

20-MULE-TEAM BORAX TERMINUS - Mojave. Just west of this point was the Southern Pacific terminus for the 20-mule-team borax wagons that operated between Death Valley and Mojave from 1884 to 1889. The route ran from the Harmony Borax Mining Company works, later acquired by the Pacific Coast Borax Company, to the railroad loading dock in Mojave over 165 miles of mountains and desert trail. A round trip required 20 days. The Oregon wagons, which hauled a payload of 24 tons, were designed by J.W.S. Perry, Borax Company superintendent in Death Valley, and built in Mojave at a cost of $900 each. New borax discoveries near Barstow ended the Mojave shipments in 1889.

Monterey

COLTON HALL - Pacific between Jefferson and Madison. In this building met the convention that drafted the Constitution under which California was admitted to statehood on September 9, 1850.

Placerville

STUDEBAKER'S SHOP (SITE OF) - 543 Main St. This shop was built in the early 1850s and John Mohler Studebaker rented a part of the rear where he repaired and worked on wagon wheels and the like. A little later he began to make wheelbarrows for the miners and ammunition wagons for the Union Army; from that grew his extensive wagon and carriage business and, eventually, the automobile business.

Plymouth

D'AGOSTINI WINERY - 8 mi. northeast of Plymouth. D'Agostini Winery was started in 1856 by Adam Uhlinger, a Swiss immigrant. The original wine cellar, with walls made from rock quarried from nearby hills, hand-hewn beams, and oak casks, is part of the present winery; some of its original vines are still in production.

Point Loma

OLD POINT LOMA LIGHTHOUSE - Gabrillo

CALIFORNIA

HISTORIC SITES (continued)

National Monument. Here at Point Loma Head on the afternoon of September 28, 1542, Juan Rodriguez Cabrillo made his first Alta California landfall and thus discovered what is now the State of California. The distinguished Portuguese navigator, in the service of Spain, was commanding the flagship San Salvador.

Red Bluff

RESIDENCE OF GENERAL WILLIAM B. IDE - 1.5 mi. north of Red Bluff. Built about 1846 by General Ide, who helped organize the revolt against the Mexican mandate requiring Americans to leave California, and was the first and only President of the California Republic, under Bear Flag Party proclamation.

Sacramento

CALIFORNIA'S FIRST PASSENGER RAILROAD - 3rd and R Streets. The Sacramento Valley Railroad, running from Sacramento to Folsom, was begun at this site on February 12, 1855.

SUTTER'S FORT - Fascinating fort dating from the California gold rush days. Located at 28th and L Sts.

St. Helena

BERINGER BROTHERS WINERY - In continuous operation since its construction by Chinese laborers in 1876. The tunnels dug into the limestone hills where the wine is aged, maintain an average temperature of 58 degrees, and never vary more than 2 degrees, summer or winter.

CHARLES KRUG WINERY - Krug Ranch. Founded in 1861 by Charles Krug (1825-1892), this is the oldest operating winery in Napa Valley.

San Diego

MISSION SAN DIEGO DE ALCALA - On San Diego Mission Rd., near Friars Rd. This is the "mother" mission of the chain of 21 founded in California by the Franciscan Order. It was established at what is now known as Presidio Hill on July 16, 1769, by Junipero Serra. In 1774 the mission was moved to its present site, which the Indians called Nipaguay, in search of a better water supply.

San Fernando

GRIFFITH RANCH - Northeast corner, Vaughan St. and Foothill Blvd. This ranch, purchased by David Ward Griffith, revered pioneer of silent motion pictures, provided the locale for many western thrillers, and was the inspiration for the immortal production, "Birth of a Nation."

San Francisco

EASTERN TERMINUS OF CLAY STREET HILL RAILROAD - Portsmouth Plaza, Clay and Kearny. First cable railroad system in the world was invented and installed by Andrew S. Hallidie. Started operation on August 1, 1873, and ceased on February 15, 1942.

MISSION SAN FRANCISCO DE ASIS - Unusual architectural design, a combination of Moorish, Mission and Corinthian styles, with rawhide used to lash the roof timbers together. Located on Dolores St.

PRESIDIO - One of the oldest army forts on the West Coast, built in 1776. The Spanish headquarters building still stands. Park roads offer spectacular views of San Francisco Bay and the Pacific Ocean shoreline. Entrance to the park is situated at the junction of Presidio Blvd. and Letterman Drive.

SITE OF FIRST U.S. BRANCH MINT IN CALIFORNIA — 608-610 Commercial St. First U.S. branch mint in San Francisco was authorized by Congress July 3, 1852, and opened for operation April 3, 1854.

San Juan Capistrano

MISSION SAN JUAN CAPISTRANO - Famous for its swallows. Festivities held on March 19th (arrival day), and Oct. 23 (departure day), whether the swallows stick to their legendary itinerary or not. Located off Route 74.

San Jose

ALMADEN VINEYARDS - Kooser Rd., south of San Jose. On this site in 1852, Charles LeFranc made the first commercial planting of fine European wine grapes in Santa Clara County to found Almaden Vineyards.

Saratoga

PAUL MASSON MOUNTAIN WINERY - Pierce Rd. Premium wines and champagne have flowed continously since 1852 from the winery that bears the name of Paul Masson, even during Prohibition under a special government license.

Stanford

EADWARD MUYBRIDGE AND THE DEVELOPMENT OF MOTION PICTURES - Extensive photographic experiment portrays the attitudes of men and animals in motion. Consecutive instantaneous exposures were provided for by a battery of 24 cameras fitted with electroshutters. Located at Stanford University.

Sonoma Plaza

BEAR FLAG MONUMENT - Spain and 1st St. East, Sonoma Plaza. On June 14, 1846, the Bear Flag Party raised the Bear Flag on this spot and declared California free from Mexican rule.

Tehachapi

TEHACHAPI LOOP - 7 mi. west of Tehacha-

HISTORIC SITES (continued)

pi. From this spot may be seen a portion of the world-renowned Loop completed in 1876 under the direction of William Hood, Southern Pacific railroad engineer. In gaining elevation around the central hill of the Loop, a 4,000-foot train will cross 77 feet above its rear cars in the tunnel below.

Tuttletown

MARK TWAIN CABIN - 1 mi. west of Tuttletown off Hwy. 49. This is a replica of Mark Twain's cabin, with original chimney and fireplace. Here on Jackass Hill, young Mark Twain, while guest of the Gillis Brothers in 1864-65, gathered material for "The Jumping Frog of Calaveras County," which first brought him fame, and for "Roughing It."

HOSTELS

Bear Valley

THE MOUNTAIN SCHOOL
P.O. Box 86
84 Monty Wolf Road
Bear Valley, CA 95223
(209) 753-2533
FACILITIES: Open all year; 16-18 beds, men; 16-18 beds, women; modern bathroom; nearest hostel: Sacramento, 100 mi. west; overnight charges: $5; houseparent: Joanne Burton.

Los Altos

HIDDEN VALLEY RANCH YOUTH HOSTEL
26870 Moody Road
Los Altos, CA 94022
(415) 948-4690 or 948-4814
FACILITIES: Open year round; limited in July and August; 12 beds, men; 12 beds, women; 12 bunks in cabins; modern bathroom; overnight charges: $2; houseparents: Eric & Beverly Jorgensen.

Los Angeles

WESTCHESTER YMCA
8015 S. Sepulveda Blvd.
Los Angeles, CA 90045
(213) 776-0922
FACILITIES: Open from Jun. 1 - Sept. 3; 15 beds, men; 10 beds, women; modern bathroom; overnight charges: $4; houseparent: Shawn Bennett.

Mount Shasta

MT. SHASTA KOA
P.O. Box 176
900 No. Mt. Shasta Blvd.
Mount Shasta, CA 96067
(916) 926-4029
FACILITIES: Open year round; 10 beds, men; 10 beds, women; modern bathroom; nearest hostel: Sacramento, 180 mi.; overnight charges: $3; houseparents: Gary & Kathleen Linden.

Norden

SKI INN
P.O. Box 7
Norden, CA 95724
(916) 426-3079
FACILITIES: Open year round; reservations required; 40 beds, men; 40 beds, women; modern bathroom; nearest hostel: Sacramento, 100 mi.; overnight charges: dorm., $3.50 (summer); $5.50 (winter); sleeping bag accommodation; private room rate: $14 double (summer); $16 double (winter); houseparents: Mayo & Melva Torgerson.

Point Reyes

LAQUANA RANCH HOLIDAY HOSTEL
P.O. Box 59
Point Reyes, CA 94956
FACILITIES: Open year round; 20 beds, men; 20 beds, women; modern bathroom; nearest hostel: San Francisco, 40 mi.; overnight charges: $3; houseparents: Roger and Sharon Sierra.

Sacramento

CAL-EXPO YOUTH HOSTEL
Cal-Expo Fair Grounds
Sacramento, CA 95813
(916) 927-3819
FACILITIES: Open year round; reservations required; 40 beds, men; 40 beds, women; modern bathroom; overnight charges: dorm $1.50; hostel $2.50; houseparents: Butch & Diane Haydel.

San Diego

ARMED SERVICES Y.M.C.A.
500 West Broadway
San Diego, CA 92101
(714) 232-1133
FACILITIES: Open year round; 100 men and women in private rooms; modern bathroom; nearest hostel: Julian, 75 mi.; overnight charges: private rooms $5.83; dorms, $3; houseparent: Mrs. Anna Mae Wright.

San Francisco

SAN FRANCISCO AT DUBOCE PARK
101 Steiner Street
San Francisco, CA 94117
(415) 626-8361
FACILITIES: Open year round; 15 beds, men; 15 beds, women; modern bathroom; nearest hostel: Point Reyes, 60 mi., north; overnight charges: $3.25; reservations by mail only, send deposit; houseparents: Holy Order of MANS Staff.

Santa Cruz

SANTA CRUZ HOSTEL PROJECT
717 Pacific Avenue
Santa Cruz, CA 95062
(408) 426-4161
FACILITIES: Open Jun. 14 - Sept. 5; 50 beds for men and women; modern bathroom; nearest hostel: San Francisco, north 75 mi.; overnight charges: $2.75.

CALIFORNIA
POINTS OF INTEREST

Allensworth

ALLENSWORTH - Site of only town founded (1908), financed and governed by Black Americans.

Badwater

DEATH VALLEY - At 282' below sea level, Badwater, south of Furnace Creek, is lowest spot in U.S.

Bishop

BRISTLECONE PINES - East of Bishop are world's oldest living things. One tree is 4,600 years old.

Buena Park (Los Angeles)

KNOTT'S BERRY FARM - Enjoy an "Old West" flavored attraction.

MOVIELAND WAX MUSEUM/MOVIELAND OF THE AIR - Movie stars, old planes.

Burney

McARTHUR - BURNEY FALLS - Breath-taking double waterfalls near Burney, off Hwy. 89.

Crescent City

TREES OF MYSTERY - An amazing stand of redwoods on the highway between Crescent City and Klamath.

Felton

ROARING CAMP & BIG TREES RAILROAD - Take a ride through the forest near Felton on an old steamer.

Fresno

UNDERGROUND GARDENS - Plants flourish in underground rooms. Tours.

Glendale

FOREST LAWN MEMORIAL PARK - Beautifully landscaped cemetery featuring a museum and a stained-glass reproduction of "The Last Supper" by Leonardo da Vinci.

Lassen

LASSEN VOLCANO - Only active volcano in contiguous U.S.; just north are the Subway Caves.

Los Angeles

LA BREA TAR PITS/LOS ANGELES ART MUSEUM/WATTS TOWERS - Prehistoric relics and spectacular art, in Los Angeles area.

CALIFORNIA MUSEUM OF SCIENCE AND INDUSTRY - Fascinating achievements on display.

MANN'S CHINESE THEATRE - Impressions of famous movie stars' hands and footprints imbedded in the pavement in front of this unique movie house. (Formerly Grauman's Chinese Theatre.) Located at 6925 Hollywood Blvd.

Long Beach

H. M. S. QUEEN MARY - Now a floating museum and "Living Sea" oceanographic display.

Malibu

GETTY MUSEUM - J. Paul Getty's treasures, displayed in a transplanted Roman palace near Malibu.

Marysville

BOK KAI TEMPLE - Oldest Buddist temples in the State; built during the Gold Rush.

Mesquite Spring

SCOTTY'S CASTLE - Now a museum in Death Valley's desert where temperatures can reach 150 degrees.

Sacramento

ALMOND PLAZA - Tour the world's largest "almond factory."

WINE COUNTRY CENTRAL - In Santa Cruz/Monterey; Lodi/Sacramento; Modesto/Ripon/Escalon; and Fresno/San Joaquin county districts. (See Historic Sites.)

San Diego

WINE COUNTRY SOUTH - Cucamonga/Etiwanda/Ontario/Guasti districts; and near San Diego and Escondido. (See Historic Sites.)

San Francisco

ANGEL AND ALCATRAZ ISLANDS - Go by boat to Angel from Tiburon, or from San Francisco to Alcatraz.

CHINATOWN / FISHERMAN'S WHARF/ GHIRADELLI SQUARE - Three unique areas for shops and cafes.

FORT POINT - Built during the Civil War, you can now tour this fort spanned by the Golden Gate Bridge.

MARITIME HISTORIC PARK - Tour old time sail and steam ships at foot of Hyde Street.

Santa Clara

WINE COUNTRY NORTH - In Santa Clara/ Livermore Valley; Napa and Sonoma regions. (See Historic Sites.)

Visalia

SEQUOIA FOREST - See the biggest trees on earth in groves east of Visalia.

COLORADO

Colorado, one of the wildest places in the Old Wild West, joined the Union in 1876 as the thirty-eighth state. In the early days, following the discovery of gold and the withdrawal of Union troops to fight in the Civil War, the territory broke wide open.

Indian attacks on white settlers were as common as shootouts in front of the local saloon. But with the return of the Federal troops after the Civil War and the advent of the transcontinental railroad, Colorado settled down in preparation for statehood.

Most of the world's supply of molybdenum, a metal used to strengthen the steel used in rocketry and other industries, is mined in Colorado. Agriculture, specifically livestock and its by-products, plays an important role in the state's economy, as does tourism.

Colorado is rich in natural attractions which annually lure thousands of hunters, fishermen, skiers, campers and sightseers to the magnificent mountains and valleys.

State capital: Denver. State bird: Lark bunting. State tree: Blue spruce. State flower: Rocky Mountain columbine.

WEATHER

Colorado lies astride the highest mountains of the Continental Divide. Although primarily a mountain state, nearly 40 percent of its area is taken up by the eastern high plains. The principal features of Colorado geography are its inland continental location in the middle latitudes, and the mountains and ranges extending north and south approximately through the middle of the state. Roughly three-quarters of the Nation's land above 10,000 foot altitude lies within its borders. The high plains of Colorado slope gently upward for a distance of some 200 miles from the eastern border to the base of the foothills of the Rocky Mountains.

Most of Colorado has a cool and invigorating climate that could be termed a highland or mountain climate of a continental location. During summer there are hot days in the plains, but these are often relieved by afternoon thundershowers. Mountain regions are nearly always cool. Humidity is generally quite low; this favors rapid evaporation and a relatively comfortable feeling even on hot days. The thin atmosphere allows greater penetration of solar radiation and results in pleasant daytime conditions even during the winter. This is why skiers at high elevations are often pictured in very light clothing, although surrounded by heavy snow.

Average daily temperature for each month.

	Northern	Southern
Jan.	30.3 to .7	46.7 to 21.2
Feb.	33.1 to 2.0	48.9 to 22.3
Mar.	38.0 to 7.3	53.4 to 25.1
Apr.	47.4 to 17.5	63.2 to 33.2
May	58.9 to 25.9	73.0 to 42.4
Jun.	68.7 to 31.2	83.0 to 50.7
Jul.	74.8 to 36.0	86.8 to 56.6
Aug.	73.0 to 35.6	84.6 to 55.3
Sept.	66.7 to 27.9	78.5 to 47.7
Oct.	56.4 to 20.6	68.3 to 38.1
Nov.	40.4 to 10.1	55.0 to 27.7
Dec.	31.5 to 2.3	47.9 to 22.3
Year	51.6 to 18.1	65.8 to 36.9

STATE CHAMBER OF COMMERCE

Colorado Association of Commerce & Industry
1390 Logan Street
Suite 308
Denver, CO 80203
(303) 831-7411

STATE & CITY TOURISM OFFICES

State

Division of Commerce and Development
500 State Centennial Building
Denver, CO 80203
(303) 839-2350

Travel Marketing Section
Colorado Division of Commerce & Development
602 State Capitol Annex
Denver, CO 80203
(303) 839-3045

Local

Denver and Colorado Convention and Visitor's Bureau
225 West Colfax Avenue
Denver, CO 80202
(303) 892-1112

STATE HIGHWAY DEPARTMENT

State Department of Highways
4201 East Arkansas Avenue
Denver, CO 80222
(303) 757-9011

HIGHWAY WELCOMING CENTERS

There are Welcoming Centers run by local

123

COLORADO

WELCOMING CENTERS (continued)

chambers of commerce. (Listing of exact locations not available.)

STATE POLICE

Department of Public Safety
4201 East Arkansas Avenue
Denver, CO 80222
(303) 757-9011

HUNTING & FISHING

Hunting

To purchase a hunting license, all persons born on or after January 1, 1949, must successfully complete a hunter safety training course. A certificate attesting to successful completion of an approved course must be presented at the time of purchase. Appropriate training certification from other states is honored in Colorado.

A small game license is required for the hunting of both game birds and animals (however, the hunting of turkey requires a separate turkey license) as well as waterfowl and varmints. A federal migratory bird stamp is an additional requirement to hunt waterfowl. A trapping license is required to trap furbearers. The hunting of all small game species and turkeys is open to both residents and non-residents.

A resident is any person who has been domiciled in Colorado for six months or more immediately preceding the date of application for a license or permit and who resides in this state with the genuine intent of making this state his place of permanent abode and who, when absent, intends to return to this state. Also included under this definition are members of the armed services of the United States or any nation allied with the United States, who are on active duty in this state under permanent orders, and students who are attending and have been enrolled at least six months in any school, college or university in Colorado.

Resident

Combination, $10; extra rod stamp, $3; small game, $5; deer, $13; elk, $16; bear, $10; mountain lion, $25; antelope, $13; turkey, $5; trapping, $5; bighorn sheep, $75; Rocky Mountain goat, $75.

Non-resident

Extra rod stamp, $3; small game, $25; deer, $90; elk, $135; bear, $50; mountain lion, $200; antelope, $100; turkey, $20; trapping, $50.

Fishing

See resident requirement paragraph above.

Resident

Fishing, $7.50.

Non-resident

Fishing, $25; 5-day fishing, $10.

For more information contact:

Department of Natural Resources
Division of Wildlife
6060 Broadway
Denver, CO 80216
(303) 825-1192

CAMPGROUNDS

Public

Colorado Campground Association, Inc.
5101 Pennsylvania Ave.
Boulder, CO 80303
(303) 499-9343

Aurora

SHADY MEADOWS TRAVEL TRAILER PARK
2075 Potomac Street
Aurora, CO 80011
(303) 364-9483
LOCATION: 9 mi. east of Denver. Exit from I-225 at East Colfax (U.S. 40 & 287).
FACILITIES: Open year round; 300 sites; water and bathroom facilities; electrical hookup; laundry; small indoor pets only; car and trailer wash.

Bailey

LAZY OUR'S
Box 175
Bailey, CO 80421
(303) 838-5576
LOCATION: On U.S. Hwy. 285.
FACILITIES: Open year round; 50 sites; water and bathroom facilities; electrical hookup; cabins; tent sites.

Basalt

ASPEN-BASALT KOA KAMPGROUNDS
Box 880
Basalt, CO 81621
(303) 927-3532
LOCATION: 2 mi. west of Basalt on Colorado Hwy. 82.
FACILITIES: Open year round; 125 sites; water and bathroom facilities; sanitary station; electrical hookup; laundry.

Bayfield

FIVE BRANCHES CAMPER PARK
4677 County Road, 501-A
Bayfield, CO 81122
(303) 884-2582
LOCATION: 28 mi. northeast of Durango.
FACILITIES: Open May 15 - Oct. 15; 100 sites; water and bathroom facilities; sanitary station; electrical hookup; laundry.

Boulder

BOULDER KOA CAMPGROUND
5868 Valmont Road

CAMPGROUNDS (continued)

Boulder, CO 80301
(303) 442-3513
LOCATION: In Boulder.
FACILITIES: Open Mar. 15 - Oct. 15; 144
sites; water and bathroom facilities; sanitary
station; electrical hookup; laundry.

Breckenridge

CUTTY'S OF TIGER RUN
Box 1418
Breckenridge, CO 80424
(303) 453-2231
LOCATION: Frisco (old exit No. 38) mile-
post exit 203 from I-70, then 6 mi. south on
Hwy. 9, turn at road sign.
FACILITIES: Open year round; 65 sites; wa-
ter and bathroom facilities; sanitary station;
electrical hookup; laundry.

Buena Vista

BUENA VISTA KOA
2770 County Road 303
Buena Vista, CO 81211
(303) 395-8318
LOCATION: On U.S. Hwy. 285 and 24, 3 mi.
southeast of Buena Vista, ¾ mi. east of Johnson Village and Arkansas River.
FACILITIES: Open May - Nov.; 100 sites; water and bathroom facilities; sanitary station;
electrical hookup; laundry.

CRAZY HORSE CAMPING RESORT
U.S. Hwy. 24
Buena Vista, CO 81211
(303) 395-2323
LOCATION: 5 mi. north of Buena Vista on
U.S. Hwy. 24.
FACILITIES: Open year round; 100 sites; wa-
ter and bathroom facilities; sanitary station;
electrical hookup; laundry; trailers for rent.

Burlington

CAMPLAND, INC.
475 Webster, Route 4
Box 78
Burlington, CO 80807
(303) 346-8763
LOCATION: North on U.S. Hwy. 385 within
city limits of Burlington.
FACILITIES: Open year round; 50 sites; water and bathroom facilities; electrical hookup;
no tent sites.

Canon City

WHISPERING PINE CAMPGROUND
P.O. Box 1025
Canon City, CO 81212
(303) 275-2128
LOCATION: 9 mi. west of U.S. Hwy. 50 at
junction of Colorado Hwy. 9.
FACILITIES: Open Apr. - Nov.; 75 sites; water and bathroom facilities; electrical hookup;
laundry.

Cascade

LONE DUCK CAMPGROUND
P.O. Box 25

Cascade, CO 80809
(303) 684-9907
LOCATION: 2½ mi. west of Pikes Peak Hwy.
FACILITIES: Open May 15 - Sept. 15; 75
sites; water and bathroom facilities; sanitary
station; electrical hookup.

Cedaredge

ASPEN TRAILS CAMPGROUND
Box 134-E
Cedaredge, CO 81413
(303) 856-6321
LOCATION: Grand Mesa, 3 mi. north of Cedaredge on Colorado Hwy. 65.
FACILITIES: Open year round; 50 sites; water and bathroom facilities; sanitary station;
electrical hookup.

Coaldale

CUTTY'S CAMPING RESORT
Coaldale, CO 81222
(303) 942-3455
LOCATION: 37 mi. west of Canon City on
U.S. Hwy. 50, and 3½ mi. south into San Isabel National Forest.
FACILITIES: Open May 15 - Sept. 15; 225
sites; water and bathroom facilities; sanitary
station; electrical hookup; laundry.

Colorado Springs

FORD'S MOUNTAINDALE RANCH RV
PARK
Box 164
Colorado Springs, CO 80906
(303) 576-0619
LOCATION: 18 mi. southwest of Colorado
Springs on Colorado Hwy. 115, 2 mi. in on
Good County Road.
FACILITIES: Open May 15 - Sept. 15; 50
sites; water and bathroom facilities; sanitary
station; electrical hookup; laundry.

GARDEN OF THE GODS CAMPGROUND
3700 West Colorado Avenue
Colorado Springs, CO 80904
(303) 475-9450
LOCATION: From I-25, exit at mile post No.
141, west on U.S. business route 24, north 1
block on Ridge Road, then west 2 blocks.
FACILITIES: Open year round; 250 sites;
water and bathroom facilities; sanitary station; electrical hookup; laundry.

GOLDEN EAGLE RANCH SAFARI CAMP-
GROUNDS
Box 101
Colorado Springs, CO 80906
(303) 576-0450
LOCATION: 9 mi. southwest of Colorado
Springs on Colorado Hwy. 115.
FACILITIES: Open Apr. 15 - Sept. 30; 509
sites; water and bathroom facilities; sanitary
station; electrical hookup; laundry.

GOLDEN LANE CAMPGROUND
3023 ½ West Colorado Avenue
Colorado Springs, CO 80904
(303) 633-2192
LOCATION: 3½ mi. west on U.S. Hwy. 24
by-pass, exit 31st Street, right at next light, ½
block.
FACILITIES: Open year round; 125 sites; wa-

COLORADO

CAMPGROUNDS (continued)

ter and bathroom facilities; sanitary station; electrical hookup; laundry.

PEAK VIEW
4954 West Nevada Avenue
Colorado Springs, CO 80907
(303) 598-1434
LOCATION: From I-25 take milepost exit No. 146 (old exit No. 65) to North Nevada Avenue.
FACILITIES: Open year round; 125 sites; water and bathroom facilities; sanitary station; electrical hookup; laundry.

Cotopaxi

LOMA LINDA KOA
Box 331
Cotopaxi, CO 81223
(303) 275-9972
LOCATION: On U.S. Hwy. 50 between Canon City and Salida.
FACILITIES: Open May 26 - Sept. 5; 96 sites; water and bathroom facilities; sanitary station; electrical hookup; cabins; laundry.

Del Norte

AQUA RAMON KOA
Del Norte, CO 81132
(303) 873-5500
LOCATION: 12 mi. west of Del Norte on U.S. Hwy. 160.
FACILITIES: Open May 15 - Oct. 15; 100 sites; water and bathroom facilities; sanitary station; electrical hookup; laundry.

Delta

SWITZERLAND OF AMERICA
Route 2, Box 321
Delta, CO 81416
(303) 325-4736
LOCATION: Junction of U.S. 550 and Colorado 23.
FACILITIES: Open Apr. 15 - Oct. 30; 150 sites; water and bathroom facilities; sanitary station; electrical hookup; laundry.

Durango

LIGHTNER CREEK SAFARI CAMP
P.O. Box 3038
Durango, CO 81301
(303) 247-5406
LOCATION: 2½ mi. west on U.S. Hwy. 160 to Lightner Creek Road, then 1½ mi. north.
FACILITIES: Open May - Oct.; 87 sites; water and bathroom facilities; sanitary station; electrical hookup; laundry.

UNITED CAMPGROUND OF DURANGO
1322 County Road 203
Durango, CO 81301
(303) 247-3853
LOCATION: 1¼ mi. north of Durango on U.S. Hwy. 550.
FACILITIES: Open year round; 152 sites; water and bathroom facilities; sanitary station; electrical hookup; laundry.

Estes Park

ESTES PARK CAMPGROUND
Box 3517
Estes Park, CO 80517
(303) 586-4188
LOCATION: 5 mi. southwest on Colorado spur Hwy. 66.
FACILITIES: Open Jun. 1 - Sept. 1; limit of stay, 14 days; 50 sites; water and bathroom facilities; firewood; tent sites.

MARY'S LAKE CAMPGROUND & TRAILER PARK
Box 1558
Estes Park, CO 80517
(303) 586-4411
LOCATION: 3½ mi. south of Estes Park on Hwy. 7, then 1 mi. west on Peak View Drive.
FACILITIES: Open May - Oct.; 100 sites; water and bathroom facilities; sanitary station; electrical hookup; laundry.

Ft. Collins

HOWARD'S PINE LAKE RESORT & CAMPGROUND
Rt. 4, Box 115
Ft. Collins, CO 80521
(303) 493-9956
LOCATION: In Ft. Collins.
FACILITIES: Open year round; 50 sites; water and bathroom facilities; sanitary station; electrical hookup; laundry.

Glenwood Springs

ROCK GARDENS
1308 County Road 129
Glenwood Springs, CO 81601
(303) 945-6737
LOCATION: 1½ mi. east of Glenwood Springs exit milepost 119 (old exit No. 25) off I-70.
FACILITIES: Open year round; 90 sites; water and bathroom facilities; sanitary station; electrical hookup.

Golden

CHIEF HOSA CAMPGROUND
Route 3, Box 282
Golden, CO 80401
(303) 277-0364
LOCATION: 20 mi. west of Denver at milepost exit 253 (old exit No. 56) off I-70.
FACILITIES: Open May 1 - Nov. 1; 240 sites; water and bathroom facilities; sanitary station; electrical hookup; laundry.

Grand Lake

WINDING RIVER RV CAMPGROUND
Box 629
Grand Lake, CO 80447
(303) 627-3215
LOCATION: 1½ mi. north of Grand Lake on U.S. Hwy 34, then turn left 1 mi.
FACILITIES: Open Jun. 3 - Sept. 4; 93 sites; water and bathroom facilities; sanitary station; electrical hookup; laundry.

Greeley

SCOTTY'S CAMP

CAMPGROUNDS (continued)

501 E. 27th
Greeley, CO 80631
(303) 353-6476
LOCATION: Open year round; 94 sites; water and bathroom facilities; sanitary station; electrical hookup; laundry; pets permitted on beach; tent sites.

Green Mountain Falls

HI-VU
Box 215
Green Mountain Falls, CO 80819
(303) 684-9044
LOCATION: 15 mi. west of Colorado Springs on U.S. 24.
FACILITIES: Open May - Oct.; 78 sites; water and bathroom facilities; sanitary station; electrical hookup; cabins; laundry.

Gunnison

GUNNISON KOA KAMPGROUND
Box 1144
Gunnison, CO 81230
(303) 641-1358
LOCATION: 1 mi. west of Gunnison on U.S. Hwy. 50, south at Long's Motel.
FACILITIES: Open May 12 - Oct. 15; 75 sites; water and bathroom facilities; sanitary station; electrical hookup; laundry; tent sites.

Lake George

TRAV-L-PORT CAMPGROUND
P.O. Box 108
Lake George, CO 80827
(303) 748-3794
LOCATION: 38 mi. west of Colorado Springs on U.S. Hwy. 24 in Lake George.
FACILITIES: Open May 1 - Oct. 31; 52 sites; water and bathroom facilities; sanitary station; electrical hookup; laundry.

Leadville

SUGER LOAFIN' CAMPGROUND
Lake County Hwy. 4
Leadville, CO 80461
(303) 486-1031
LOCATION: In Leadville turn off U.S. Hwy. 24 at 6th Street, go 3 mi. west on Lake County Hwy. 4.
FACILITIES: Open May 15 - Oct. 15; 95 sites; water and bathroom facilities; sanitary station; electrical hookup; laundry; tent sites.

Loveland

RIVERVIEW CAMPGROUND
Star Route 603A
Loveland, CO 80537
(303) 667-9910
LOCATION: 3 mi. east of Loveland on U.S. Hwy. 34, west of I-25.
FACILITIES: Open year round; 90 sites; water and bathroom facilities; sanitary station; electrical hookup; laundry.

UNITED CAMPGROUND OF LOVELAND
P.O. Box 786
Loveland, CO 80537

(303) 667-1204
LOCATION: 3 mi. east of Loveland on U.S. Hwy. 34 west of I-25.
FACILITIES: Open Apr. - Dec.; 150 sites; water and bathroom facilities; sanitary station; electrical hookup; laundry.

Mancos

LAZY G CAMPGROUND
Rt. 2, Box 171A
Mancos, CO 81328
(303) 565-8924
LOCATION: 7 mi. west of Mancos on U.S. Hwy. 160, take Mesa Verde exit, then north to Frontage Road and east 300 yards.
FACILITIES: Open Apr. - Nov. 15; 50 sites; water and bathroom facilities; electrical hookup.

Manitou Springs

CRYSTAL KANGAROO CAMPGROUND
810 Crystal Park Road
Manitou Springs, CO 80829
(303) 685-5010
LOCATION: Exit U.S. Hwy. 24 at Manitou Avenue (business 24), then 1 block to Crystal Park Road, turn left, follow signs 1½ mi.
FACILITIES: Open Mar. 1 - Nov. 30; 95 sites; water and bathroom facilities; electrical hookup; laundry.

PIKES PEAK CAMPGROUNDS
320 Manitou Avenue
Manitou Springs, CO 80829
(303) 685-9459
LOCATION: 6 mi. west of I-25 on U.S. Hwy. 24 to Manitou Avenue exit, then 2 blocks west in Manitou Springs.
FACILITIES: Open year round; 95 sites; water and bathroom facilities; sanitary station; electrical hookup; laundry.

Montrose

HIGHLANDER KOA, INC.
Rt. 4, Box 172
Montrose, CO 81401
(303) 249-9177
LOCATION: 10 blocks east of junction Hwy. 50 and 550 at Cedar Avenue.
FACILITIES: Open May - Nov.; 82 sites; water and bathroom facilities; sanitary station; electrical hookup; laundry.

Monument

THE PINES
Box 383
Monument, CO 80132
(303) 481-2336
LOCATION: 17 mi. north of Colorado Springs, east side of I-25 between milepost exits 161 and 163.
FACILITIES: Open May 1 - Oct. 15; 80 sites; water and bathroom facilities; sanitary station; electrical hookup; laundry.

New Castle

NEW CASTLE KOA
0581 County Road 241
New Castle, CO 81647

COLORADO

CAMPGROUNDS (continued)

(303) 984-2240
LOCATION: 2½ mi. north of New Castle, exit milepost 105 (old exit No. 20) off I-70.
FACILITIES: Open May - Nov.; 64 sites; water and bathroom facilities; sanitary station; electrical hookup; tent sites.

Pagosa Springs

ELK MEADOWS CAMPGROUND AND RECREATION AREA
P.O. Box 238
Pagosa Springs, CO 81147
(303) 968-5482
FACILITIES: Open Apr. 15 - Nov. 15; 50 sites; water and bathroom facilities; sanitary station; electrical hookup; laundry; reservation deposit required.

Pueblo

PUEBLO KOA
4131 I-25 North
Pueblo, CO 81004
(303) 542-2273
LOCATION: 5 mi. north of Pueblo on I-25 at milepost exit No. 108 (old exit No. 47).
FACILITIES: Open year round; 90 sites; water and bathroom facilities; sanitary station; cabins; laundry; tent sites.

Steamboat Springs

SKI TOWN KOA
P.O. Box 608
Steamboat Springs, CO 80477
(303) 879-0273
LOCATION: 2 mi. west of Steamboat on U.S. Hwy. 40.
FACILITIES: Open year round; 100 sites; water and bathroom facilities; sanitary station; electrical hookup; laundry.

Strasburg

STRASBURG KOA
Box 597
Strasburg, CO 80136
(303) 622-9274
LOCATION: 30 mi. east of Denver on I-70 at Strasburg exit.
FACILITIES: Open Apr. - Nov.; 60 sites; water and bathroom facilities; sanitary station; electrical hookup; laundry.

Walsenburg

DAKOTA CAMP
P.O. Box 8
Walsenburg, CO 81089
(303) 738-9912
LOCATION: On U.S. Hwy. 85-87, south from milepost exit No. 52 (old exit No. 19) off I-25.
FACILITIES: Open year round; 50 sites; water and bathroom facilities; sanitary station; electrical hookup; laundry; tent sites.

Woodland Park

DIAMOND CAMPGROUND
Star Route 1102

Woodland Park, CO 80863
(303) 687-9684
LOCATION: West of Colorado Springs on Hwy. 24, then ½ mi. north of Woodland Park on Colorado Hwy. 67.
FACILITIES: Open May 15 - Oct. 1; 80 sites; water and bathroom facilities; sanitary station; electrical hookup; tent sites.

SOLAR RV PARK
510 North Hwy. 10
Woodland Park, CO 80863
(303) 687-9518
LOCATION: 14 mi. west of Colorado Springs via lane U.S. Hwy. 24, then 5 blocks north on Colorado Hwy. 67.
FACILITIES: Open May - Oct.; 50 sites; water and bathroom facilities; sanitary station; electrical hookup; laundry.

RESORTS

Guest Ranches

Colorado Dude & Guest Ranch Association
P.O. Box 6440 Cherry Creek Station
Denver, CO 80206
(303) 674-4906

Allenspark

LAZY H GUEST RANCH
Allenspark, CO 80510
(303) 747-2532
FACILITIES: Horseback riding; heated pool; trap shooting; pack trips; fishing; hiking; children's counselors; teen activities.

Antonito

RAINBOW TROUT LODGES & DUDE RANCH
Antonito, CO 81120
(303) 376-5659
FACILITIES: Horseback riding; heated pool; tennis; fishing; river raft rides; overnight pack trips; hay-rides; dances.

Bayfield

WILDERNESS TRAILS RANCH
Box A
Bayfield, CO 81122
(303) 884-2581
FACILITIES: Horseback riding; trap shooting; rodeo; cookouts; sailing; fishing; overnight pack trips; square dancing; supper rides; children's and teen programs.

Bellevue

SKY CORRAL RANCH
Bellevue, CO 80512
(303) 484-1362
FACILITIES: Horseback riding; heated pool; volleyball; badminton; ping-pong; pack trips; tennis; fishing; hunting; children's program; no pets.

Crawford

BAR X BAR RANCH
P.O. Box 27X

RESORTS (continued)

Crawford, CO 81415
(303) 921-6321
FACILITIES: Horseback riding; fishing; pack trips.

Deckers

LOST VALLEY RANCH
Deckers, CO 80135
(303) 647-2311
FACILITIES: Horseback riding; cattle round-ups; rodeo; fishing; heated pool; tennis; children's counselors; teen program.

Durango

COLORADO TRAILS RANCH
Box 848G
Durango, CO 81301
(303) 247-5055
FACILITIES: Horseback riding; tennis; heated pool; riflery; archery; trap shooting; fishing; pack trips; hayrides; breakfast rides; square dancing; children's programs.

Estes Park

DOUBLE JK RANCH
Longs Peak Route, Box D
Estes Park, CO 80517
(303) 586-3537
FACILITIES: Horseback riding; hayrides; hiking; heated pool; volleyball; horseshoes; square dancing; jeeping; fishing; children's counselor; no pets.

INDIAN HEAD GUEST RANCH
P.O. Box 2260
Estes Park, CO 80517
(303) 586-5291
FACILITIES: Horseback riding; fishing; hiking; heated pool; breakfast rides; steak fries; golf; tennis.

LONGS PEAK INN & GUEST RANCH
Longs Peak Route, Box 10
Estes Park, CO 80517
(303) 586-2110
FACILITIES: Horseback riding; breakfast rides; cookouts; hiking trails; heated pool; children's counselor.

WIND RIVER RANCH
Estes Park, CO 80517
(303) 586-4212
FACILITIES: Horseback riding; heated pool; fishing; square dances; picnics; children's counselor.

Fraser

DEVIL'S THUMB RANCH
Box 125
Fraser, CO 80442
(303) 726-8155
FACILITIES: Horseback riding; hiking; fishing; jogging trails; playground.

Glendevey

RAWAH RANCH
Glendevey, CO 82063
(303) 484-5585
FACILITIES: Horseback riding; hiking; cookouts; hunting.

Granby

ARAPAHO VALLEY RANCH
Box 142D
Granby, CO 80446
(303) 887-3495
FACILITIES: Horseback riding; pack trips; breakfast rides; fishing; boating; canoeing; heated pool; playground; square dancing; hayrides; children's counselor.

C LAZY RANCH
Box 378
Granby, CO 80446
(303) 887-3344
FACILITIES: Horseback riding; heated pool; square dancing; fishing; tennis; volleyball; children's counselor.

DROWSY WATER RANCH
Box 147A
Granby, CO 80446
(303) 725-3456
FACILITIES: Horseback riding; heated pool; breakfast rides; pack trips; rodeos; hayrides; cookouts; steak fries; fishing; golf; tennis; children's counselor.

Grand Lake

SUN VALLEY GUEST RANCH
Box 470-A
Grand Lake, CO 80447
(303) 627-3670
FACILITIES: Horseback riding; heated pool; fishing; hunting; breakfast rides; pack trips; hiking.

Grant

TUMBLING RIVER RANCH
Grant, CO 80448
(303) 838-5981
FACILITIES: Horseback riding; rodeos; heated pool; jeep trails; fishing; square dancing; hiking; children's counselors.

Gunnison

HARMEL'S RANCH RESORT
P.O. Box 944D
Gunnison, CO 81230
(303) 641-1740
FACILITIES: Horseback riding; pack trips; heated pool; golf; river rafting; hayrides.

WAUNITA HOT SPRINGS RANCH
Route 2, Box 56D
Gunnison, CO 81230
(303) 641-1266
FACILITIES: Horseback riding; hot springs pool; cookouts; breakfast rides; hayrides; jeep trips; hiking; fishing; no alcoholic beverages.

Gypsum

SEVEN W GUEST RANCH
Sweetwater Creek
Gypsum, CO 81637
(303) 524-9328
FACILITIES: Horseback riding; fishing; hunt-

COLORADO

ing; pack trips; cookouts; square dancing; hiking.

Hideway Park

SITZMARK GUEST RANCH
Box 1239
Hideway Park, CO 80450
(303) 726-5453
FACILITIES: Horseback riding; sauna; square dancing; cookouts; golf; tennis; fishing; jeep trips; children's counselor.

IDLEWILD GUEST RANCH
P.O. Box 1
Hideaway Park, CO 80450
(303) 726-5562
FACILITIES: Horseback riding; tennis; heated pool; fishing; hiking; river rafting; breakfast and lunch rides; square dancing; hayrides; children's counselor.

Kremmling

SNOWSHOE RANCH
Box 2370
Kremmling, CO 80459
(303) 724-3596
FACILITIES: Horseback riding; cookouts; archery; shuffleboard; ping-pong; volleyball; fishing; hunting.

Lake George

TARRYALL RIVER RANCH
Box A8
Lake George, CO 80827
(303) 748-3255
FACILITIES: Horseback riding; heated pool; supper rides; pack trips.

Loveland

SYLVAN DALE RANCH
2939 N. County Road 31D
Loveland, CO 80537
(303) 667-3915
FACILITIES: Horseback riding; pack trips; breakfast rides; round ups; fishing; tennis; heated pool; volleyball; ping-pong; horseshoes; shuffleboard; square dancing; hayrides; children's counselor.

Lyons

PEACEFUL VALLEY LODGE & GUEST RANCH
Dept. C8, Star Route
Lyons, CO 80540
(303) 747-2582
FACILITIES: Horseback riding; square dancing; chuckwagon meals; jeep trips; luncheon rides; pack trips; heated pool; fishing; children's & teen programs.

Mancos

CHERRY CREEK GUEST RANCH
P.O. Box 236
Mancos, CO 81328
(303) 533-7581
FACILITIES: Horseback riding; pack trips; hunting.

LAKE MANCOS RANCH
P.O. Box 218A
Mancos, CO 81328
(303) 533-7900
FACILITIES: Horseback riding; jeep trips; heated pool; fishing; children's counselor.

McCoy

BLACK MOUNTAIN RANCH
Box 607A
McCoy, CO 80463
(303) 926-3400
FACILITIES: Horseback riding; cookouts; pack trips; fishing; breakfast rides; hiking; volleyball; ping-pong; horseshoes; square dancing; swimming; hayrides; children's counselor.

Meredith

HORSESHOE BEND GUEST RANCH
Meredith, CO 81642
(303) 927-3570
FACILITIES: Horseback riding; fishing; hunting; cookouts; jeep trails; packing; hiking; rafting; sports; hayrides.

Nathrop

DEER VALLEY RANCH
Box R
Nathrop, CO 81236
(303) 395-2353
FACILITIES: Horseback riding; 2 natural hot springs; ranch activities; jeep trails; fishing; pack trips; no alcoholic beverages.

FUTURITY LODGE GUEST RANCH
Box 11
Nathrop, CO 81236
(303) 395-2353
FACILITIES: Horseback riding; hiking; cookouts.

Parshall

BAR LAZY GUEST RANCH
Box ND
Parshall, CO 80468
(303) 725-3437
FACILITIES: Horseback riding; heated pool; ping-pong; volleyball; shuffleboard; horseshoes; square dancing; tennis; golf; children's counselor.

Pueblo

THE DON K RANCH
2677 S. Siloam Road
Pueblo, CO 81005
(303) 784-6600
FACILITIES: Horseback riding; heated pool; trap shooting; ranch activities; children's counselor; no pets.

Rifle

COULTER LAKE GUEST RANCH
Box 906A
Rifle, CO 81650
(303) 625-1473
FACILITIES: Horseback riding; fishing; hunting; cookouts; square dancing; horseshoes; trap shooting; hiking.

RESORTS (continued)

Slater

FOCUS RANCH
P.O. Box 22
Slater, CO 81653
(303) 583-2410
FACILITIES: Horseback riding; swimming; picnics; hiking; jeep rides; steak fries; square dancing; volleyball; baseball; steer roping; hunting; fishing; children's programs.

Steamboat Springs

VISTA VERDE GUEST RANCH
Box 465
Steamboat Springs, CO 80477
(303) 879-3858
FACILITIES: Horseback riding; pack trips; fishing; hiking; hayrides.

Virginia Dale

TWO BARS SEVEN RANCH
Box 39
Virginia Dale, CO 80548
(303) 568-3844
FACILITIES: Horseback riding; cattle drives; hayrides; pack trips; rodeos; fishing; hunting.

Winter Park

BEAVER VILLAGE GUEST RANCH
Box 43
Winter Park, CO 80482
(303) 726-5741
FACILITIES: Horseback riding; lunch rides; fishing; heated pool; hayrides; hiking; cookouts; square dancing; children's counselor.

TALLY HO RANCH
Box 51
Winter Park, CO 80482
(303) 726-5958
FACILITIES: Horseback riding; cookouts; heated pool; rodeo; fishing; hayrides; children's counselor.

Woodland Park

TRIPLE "B" GUEST RANCH
Woodland Park, CO 80863
(303) 687-9082
FACILITIES: Horseback riding; heated pool; cookouts; dancing;.

BOATING AREAS

Department of Natural Resources
Colorado Division of Parks & Outdoor Recreation
1313 Sherman
Denver, CO 80203
(303) 839-3311

Antero Junction

ANTERO STATE RECREATION AREA
(303) 748-3401
LOCATION: 4 mi. northeast of Antero Junction.

FACILITIES: Launching; bathroom facilities; picnic area; boat rental; water skiing.

Arboles

NAVAJO STATE RECREATION AREA
(303) 883-2208
LOCATION: 1 mi. south of Arboles.
FACILITIES: Launching; bathroom facilities; picnic area; boat rental; water skiing.

Burlington

BONNY STATE RECREATION AREA
(303) 354-7306
LOCATION: 22 mi. north of Burlington.
FACILITIES: Launching; bathroom facilities; picnic area; boat rental; water skiing.

Collbran

VEGA STATE RECREATION AREA
(303) 487-3201
LOCATION: 12 mi. east of Collbran.
FACILITIES: Launching; bathroom facilities; picnic area; water skiing.

Crawford

CRAWFORD STATE RECREATION AREA
(303) 921-5721
LOCATION: 1 mi. south of Crawford.
FACILITIES: Launching; bathroom facilities; picnic area; boat rental; water skiing.

Delta

SWITZER LAKE STATE RECREATION AREA
(303) 874-4258
LOCATION: 2 mi. south of Delta.
FACILITIES: Launching; bathroom facilities; picnic area; water skiing.

Denver

CHATFIELD STATE RECREATION AREA
(303) 979-5449
LOCATION: 8 mi. southwest of Denver.
FACILITIES: Launching; bathroom facilities; picnic area; boat rental; water skiing.

CHERRY CREEK STATE RECREATION AREA
(303) 755-0766
LOCATION: Adjacent to Denver city limits, southeast.
FACILITIES: Launching; bathroom facilities; picnic area; boat rental; water skiing.

Flagler

FLAGLER STATE RECREATION AREA
(303) 354-7366
LOCATION: In Flagler.
FACILITIES: Launching; bathroom facilities; picnic area; water skiing.

Ft. Collins

BOYD STATE RECREATION AREA
(303) 669-1739
LOCATION: 7 mi. south of Ft. Collins via 287.

COLORADO

BOATING AREAS (continued)

FACILITIES: Launching; bathroom facilities; boat rental; water skiing.

Fort Morgan

JACKSON STATE RECREATION AREA
(303) 645-2405
LOCATION: 22 mi. northeast of Fort Morgan.
FACILITIES: Launching; bathroom facilities; boat rental; water skiing.

Grand Junction

ISLAND ACRES STATE RECREATION AREA
(303) 464-7297
LOCATION: 15 mi. east of Grand Junction.
FACILITIES: Launching; bathroom facilities; picnic area; hand propelled craft only.

Jefferson

TARRYALL STATE RECREATION AREA
(303) 836-2521
LOCATION: 15 mi. southeast of Jefferson.
FACILITIES: Launching; bathroom facilities; picnic area; water skiing.

Lake George

ELEVEN MILE STATE RECREATION AREA
(303) 748-3401
LOCATION: 8 mi. west of Lake George.
FACILITIES: Launching; bathroom facilities; boat rental.

Loma

HIGHLINE STATE RECREATION AREA
(303) 858-7208
LOCATION: 6 mi. north of Loma.
FACILITIES: Launching; bathroom facilities; picnic area; water skiing; hand propelled boats only on Mack Mesa Lake.

Longmont

BARBOUR PONDS STATE RECREATION AREA
(303) 482-2602
LOCATION: 7 mi. east of Longmont.
FACILITIES: Launching; bathroom facilities; picnic area; hand propelled craft only.

Norwood

MIRAMONTE STATE RECREATION AREA
(303) 837-4664
LOCATION: 17 mi. south of Norwood.
FACILITIES: Launching; bathroom facilities; picnic area; water skiing.

Paonia

PAONIA STATE RECREATION AREA
(303) 921-5721
LOCATION: 16 mi. northeast of Paonia.
FACILITIES: Launching; bathroom facilities; water skiing.

Pueblo

PUEBLO STATE RECREATION AREA
(303) 561-9320
LOCATION: 6 mi. west of Pueblo.
FACILITIES: Launching; bathroom facilities; water skiing.

Ramah

RAMAH STATE RECREATION AREA
(303) 745-2500
LOCATION: 3 mi. west of Ramah.
FACILITIES: Launching; bathroom facilities; picnic area; water skiing.

Rifle

RIFLE GAP-FALLS STATE RECREATION AREA
(303) 625-1607
LOCATION: 10 mi. north of Rifle.
FACILITIES: Launching; bathroom facilities; picnic area; water skiing.

BICYCLE TRAILS

No information was available on bicycle trails in Colorado.

TRAILS

Aurora

HIGHLINE CANAL TRAIL - 13 mi. foot trail. This lies along another segment of the 80-mile Highline Canal which winds through metropolitan Denver. Constructed along the tree-lined maintenance road on the bank of the Canal.

Denver

HIGHLINE CANAL TRAIL - 18 mi. foot trail. This is a segment of the 80-mile Highline Canal winding through metropolitan Denver. Constructed along the tree-lined maintenance road on the bank of the Canal, the trail provides visual relief and physical separation of the human communities within the urban area.

SKI AREAS

Aspen

ASPEN HIGHLANDS
P.O. Box T
Aspen, CO 81611
(303) 925-5300
LOCATION: 255 mi. from Denver via I-70 to Glenwood Springs, Hwy. 82 to Aspen.
FACILITIES: 8 double chairlifts; 4 pomas; slopes for expert, intermediate and beginning skiers; ski instruction; ski rental; nursery; 3800 ft. vertical drop; longest run, 3 mi.; restaurants; lodging.

SKI AREAS (continued)

ASPEN MOUNTAIN
P.O. Box 1248
Aspen, CO 81611
(303) 925-1220
LOCATION: 205 mi. from Denver via I-70 and Hwy. 82.
FACILITIES: 7 double chairlifts; slopes for expert, intermediate and beginning skiers; ski instruction; ski rental; nursery; 3282 ft. vertical drop; longest run, 3 mi.; restaurants; lodging.

BUTTERMILK
P.O. Box 1248
Aspen, CO 81611
(303) 925-1220
LOCATION: 205 mi. from Denver via I-70 and Hwy. 82.
FACILITIES: 5 double chairlifts; 1 T-bar; 1 pony lift; slopes for intermediate and beginning skiers; ski instruction; ski rental; nursery; 1972 ft. vertical drop; longest run, 2 mi.; restaurants; lodging.

SNOWMASS
P.O. Box 1248
Aspen, CO 81611
(303) 923-2085
LOCATION: 205 mi. from Denver via I-70 and Hwy. 82.
FACILITIES: 1 triple chairlift; 11 double chairlifts; slopes for expert, intermediate and beginning skiers; ski instruction; ski rental; nursery; 3563 ft. vertical drop; longest run, 3½ mi.; restaurants; lodging.

Breckenridge

BRECKENRIDGE
P.O. Box 1058
Breckenridge, CO 80424
(303) 453-2368
LOCATION: 70 mi. from Denver via I-70, exit 38 to Hwy. 9.
FACILITIES: 1 triple chairlift; 9 double chairlifts; 2 T-bars; 2 pomas; slopes for expert, intermediate and beginning skiers; ski instruction; ski rental; nursery; 2213 ft. vertical drop; longest run, 2.6 mi.; restaurants; lodging.

Canon City

CONQUISTADOR
601 Yale Place
Canon City, CO 81212
(303) 275-2049
LOCATION: 55 mi. from Pueblo via Hwy. 96.
FACILITIES: 2 pony lifts; slopes for expert, intermediate and beginning skiers; ski instruction; ski rental; nursery; 250 ft. vertical drop; longest run, ¼ mi.; restaurants; lodging.

Colorado Springs

PIKES PEAK
96 Raven Hills Ct.
Colorado Springs, CO 80918
(303) 684-9868
LOCATION: 20 mi. from Colorado Springs via U.S. 24.
FACILITIES: 1 tow rope; 2 pomas; slopes for expert, intermediate and beginning skiers; ski instruction; ski rental; 1000 ft. vertical drop; longest run, 1 mi.; restaurants; lodging.

SKI BROADMOOR
Broadmoor Hotel, Inc.
P.O. Box 1439
Colorado Springs, CO 80901
(303) 634-7711
LOCATION: 4 mi. from Colorado Springs via U.S. 85-87 and Hwy. 122.
FACILITIES: 1 double chairlift; slopes for expert, intermediate and beginning skiers; ski instruction; ski rental; nursery; 600 ft. vertical drop; longest run, 2/3 mi.; restaurants; lodging.

Copper Mountain

COPPER MOUNTAIN
P.O. Box 1
Copper Mountain, CO 80443
(303) 668-2882
LOCATION: 75 mi. from Denver via I-70.
FACILITIES: 8 double chairlifts (1 covered); 1 poma; 1 mitey mite; slopes for expert, intermediate and beginning skiers; ski instruction; ski rental; nursery; 2450 ft. vertical drop; longest run, 2½ mi.; restaurants; lodging.

Crested Butte

CRESTED BUTTE
P.O. Box 528
Crested Butte, CO 81244
(303) 349-6611
LOCATION: 30 mi. from Gunnison via Hwy. 135.
FACILITIES: 5 double chairlifts; 1 double enclosed cabin chair; 1 T-bar; slopes for expert, intermediate and beginning skiers; ski instruction; ski rental; nursery; 2150 ft. vertical drop; longest run, 1½ mi.; restaurants; lodging.

Dillon

A-BASIN
P.O. Box 267
Dillon, CO 80435
(303) 468-2608
LOCATION: 67 mi. from Denver via I-70 to Loveland Pass west side.
FACILITIES: 5 double chairlifts; 1 poma; slopes for expert, intermediate and beginning skiers; ski instruction; ski rental; nursery; 1700 ft. vertical drop; longest run, 2.5 mi.; restaurants; lodging.

Durango

PURGATORY
P.O. Box 666
Durango, CO 81301
(303) 247-9000
LOCATION: 25 mi. from Durango via U.S. 550.

COLORADO

SKI AREAS (continued)

FACILITIES: 4 double chairlifts; 1 tow rope; slopes for expert, intermediate and beginning skiers; ski instruction; ski rental; nursery; 1600 ft. vertical drop; longest run, 2 mi.; restaurants; lodging.

Estes Park

HIDDEN VALLEY
P.O. Box 98
Estes Park, CO 80517
(303) 576-4165
LOCATION: 75 mi. from Denver via I-25, Hwy. 66 west, Hwy. 36 to Estes Park, 10 mi. west in Rocky Mountain National Park on U.S. 34 or 36.
FACILITIES: 2 T-bars; 2 pomas; slopes for expert, intermediate and beginning skiers; ski instruction; ski rental; nursery; 2000 ft. vertical drop; longest run, 1¼ mi.; restaurants; lodging.

Garfield

MONARCH
Garfield, CO 81277
(303) 539-4060
LOCATION: 45 mi. from Gunnison via U.S. 50.
FACILITIES: 2 double chairlifts; 1 poma; slopes for expert, intermediate and beginning skiers; ski instruction; ski rental; nursery; 1000 ft. vertical drop; longest run, 1½ mi.; restaurants; lodging.

Georgetown

LOVELAND BASIN & VALLEY
P.O. Box 455
Georgetown, CO 80444
(303) 569-2288
LOCATION: 56 mi. from Denver via I-70, exit 40.
FACILITIES: 6 double chairlifts; 2 tow ropes; 2 pomas; slopes for expert, intermediate and beginning skiers; ski instruction; ski rental; nursery; 1430 ft. vertical drop; longest run, 1.5 mi.; restaurants; lodging.

Glenwood Springs

SUNLIGHT
P.O. Box 1061
Glenwood Springs, CO 81601
(303) 945-7481
LOCATION: 40 mi. from Aspen via Hwy. 82.
FACILITIES: 2 double chairlifts; 1 poma; slopes for expert, intermediate and beginning skiers; ski instruction; ski rental; nursery; 1850 ft. vertical drop; longest run, 4 mi.; restaurants; lodging.

Grand Junction

POWDERHORN
P.O. Box 1826
Grand Junction, CO 81501
(303) 268-5482
LOCATION: 42 mi. from Grand Junction via I-70 and Hwy. 65.

FACILITIES: 2 double chairlifts; 1 poma; slopes for expert, intermediate and beginning skiers; ski instruction; ski rental; 1600 ft. vertical drop; longest run, 2 mi.; restaurants; lodging.

Grant

GENEVA BASIN
P.O. Box 65
Grant, CO 80448
(303) 569-9872
LOCATION: 65 mi. from Denver via U.S. 285, 10 mi. off 285 at Grant on Guanella Pass Road.
FACILITIES: 2 double chairlifts; 2 pomas; slopes for expert, intermediate and beginning skiers; ski instruction; ski rental; nursery; 1250 ft. vertical drop; longest run, 1 mi.; restaurants; lodging.

Greeley

SHARKTOOTH SKI AREA
1721 13th Avenue
Greeley, CO 80631
(303) 353-2565
LOCATION: 5 mi. from Greeley via U.S. 34 west.
FACILITIES: 1 pony lift; slopes for intermediate and beginning skiers; ski instruction (handicapped); ski rental; 150 ft. vertical drop; longest run, 1000 ft.; restaurants; lodging.

Idaho Springs

BERTHOUD PASS
P.O. Box 520
Idaho Springs, CO 80435
(303) 569-9885
LOCATION: 57 mi. from Denver via I-70 and U.S. 40.
FACILITIES: 1 T-bar; slopes for expert, intermediate and beginning skiers; ski instruction; ski rental; 978 ft. vertical drop; longest run, ¾ mi.; restaurants; lodging.

Keystone

ARAPAHOE BASIN
P.O. Box 38
Keystone, CO 80435
(303) 468-2608
LOCATION: 66 mi. from Denver via I-70.
FACILITIES: 1 triple chairlift; 3 double chairlifts; 1 T-bar; slopes for expert, intermediate and beginning skiers; ski instruction; ski rental; 1640 ft. vertical drop; longest run, 1½ mi.; restaurants; lodging.

KEYSTONE
P.O. Box 38
Keystone, CO 80435
(303) 468-2316
LOCATION: 72 mi. from Denver via I-70 to Dillon, 5 mi. east on U.S. 6.
FACILITIES: 8 double chairlifts; 1 poma; slopes for expert, intermediate and beginning skiers; ski instruction; ski rental; nursery; 2340 ft. vertical drop; longest run, 3 mi.; restaurants; lodging.

SKI AREAS (continued)

Leadville

SKI COOPER
P.O. Box 973
Leadville, CO 80461
(303) 486-2277
LOCATION: 30 mi. from Vail via U.S. 24.
FACILITIES: 1 double chairlift; 1 T-bar; 1 poma; slopes for intermediate and beginning skiers; ski instruction; ski rental; 1200 ft. vertical drop; longest run, 1¼ mi.; restaurants; lodging.

Nederland

ELDORA
P.O. Box 430
Nederland, CO 80466
(303) 258-3211
LOCATION: 21 mi. from Boulder via Hwy. 119.
FACILITIES: 4 double chairlifts; 1 T-bar; slopes for expert, intermediate and beginning skiers; ski instruction; ski rental; nursery; 1400 ft. vertical drop; longest run, 2 mi.; restaurants; lodging.

Pagosa Springs

WOLF CREEK
P.O. Box 1036
Pagosa Springs, CO 81147
(303) 968-2533
LOCATION: 249 mi. from Denver via I-25 or U.S. 285 and U.S. 160.
FACILITIES: 1 double chairlift; 2 pomas; slopes for expert, intermediate and beginning skiers; ski instruction; ski rental; nursery; 1125 ft. vertical drop; longest run, 1½ mi.; restaurants; lodging.

Steamboat Springs

STEAMBOAT
P.O. Box 1178
Steamboat Springs, CO 80477
(303) 879-2220
LOCATION: 157 mi. from Denver via I-70 to Silverthorne (exit 205), Hwy. 9 to Kremmling and U.S. 40 to Steamboat.
FACILITIES: 11 double chairlifts; 2 pomas; 1 pony lift; 1 gondola; slopes for expert, intermediate and beginning skiers; ski instruction; ski rental; nursery; 3600 ft. vertical drop; longest run, 2½ mi.; restaurants; lodging.

Stoner

STONER SKI AREA
P.O. Box 218
Cortez, CO 81321
(303) 882-4437
LOCATION: Northeast of Cortez on Hwy. 145.
FACILITIES: 1 T-bar; 1 tow rope; slopes for expert, intermediate and beginning skiers; ski instruction; ski rental; 1250 ft. vertical drop; longest run, 4000 ft.; restaurants; lodging.

Telluride

TELLURIDE
P.O. Box 307
Telluride, CO 81435
(303) 728-3856
LOCATION: 62 mi. from Montrose via U.S. 550, Hwy. 62 and Hwy. 145.
FACILITIES: 6 double chairlifts; slopes for expert, intermediate and beginning skiers; ski instruction; ski rental; nursery; 3200 ft. vertical drop; longest run, 4 mi.; restaurants; lodging.

Vail

VAIL
P.O. Box 7
Vail, CO 81657
(303) 476-5601
LOCATION: 100 mi. from Denver via I-70 and U.S. 6.
FACILITIES: 2 triple chairlifts; 14 double chairlifts; 1 children's poma; 1 gondola; slopes for expert, intermediate and beginning skiers; ski instruction; ski rental; nursery; 3050 ft. vertical drop; longest run, 4.5 mi.; restaurants; lodging.

Winter Park

SKI IDLEWILD
P.O. Box 3
Winter Park, CO 80482
(303) 726-5564
LOCATION: 70 mi. from Denver via I-70 and U.S. 40.
FACILITIES: 12 double chairlifts; 1 T-bar; slopes for expert, intermediate and beginning skiers; ski instruction; ski rental; nursery; 2125 ft. vertical drop; longest run, 2 mi.; restaurants; lodging.

WINTER PARK
P.O. Box 36
Winter Park, CO 80482
(303) 726-5514
LOCATION: 67 mi. from Denver via I-70 and U.S. 40.
FACILITIES: 12 double chairlifts; 1 T-bar; slopes for expert, intermediate and beginning skiers; ski instruction; ski rental; nursery; 2125 ft. vertical drop; longest run, 2 mi.; restaurant; lodging.

AMUSEMENT PARKS & ATTRACTIONS

Canon City

"BUCKSKIN JOE" & "FUN COUNTRY"
(Attractions)
Royal Gorge Park
P.O. Box 8
Canon City, CO 81212
(303) 275-5149
FACILITIES: Authentic 1860 Boom Town; movie & TV location and park; 8 major rides; 8 kiddie rides; 3 fun houses; 28 walk thrus; 12 games; 3 refreshment stands; 2 restaurants; ar-

COLORADO

AMUSEMENT PARKS (continued)

cade; shooting gallery; swimming pool; 20 museums; camping; 20 exhibits; picnic facilities; miniature golf; zoo; theater; crafts; old antique photos; silversmith; stage shows; orchestras; name bands; vaudeville; free acts (gun fights); pay gate; free parking; open mid-Apr. - mid-Nov.

Denver

CELEBRITY SPORTS CENTER
888 South Colorado Blvd.
Denver, CO 80222
(303) 757-3321
FACILITIES: Olympic swimming pool; shooting gallery; 80 bowling lanes; 2 arcades; Po-Jo Billiard Golf; skeeball; pro-shop; coffee shop; soda bar; hofbrau; free gate; free parking; free nursery; open all year.

THE ELITCH GARDENS COMPANY, INC.
4620 W. 38th Avenue
Denver, CO 80212
(303) 455-4771
FACILITIES: 17 major rides; 12 kiddie rides; 2 fun houses; shooting gallery; 5 games; 12 refreshment stands; restaurant; arcade; picnic facilities; miniature golf; theatre; stage shows; free acts; pay gate; free parking; open May 1 - Sept. 14.

LAKESIDE AMUSEMENT PARK
4601 Sheridan Blvd.
Denver, CO 80212
(303) 477-1621
FACILITIES: 26 major rides; 16 kiddie rides; fun house; 7 games; 9 refreshment stands; 2 restaurants; arcade; race track; picnic facilities; fireworks; pay gate; free parking.

Grand Junction

FUN JUNCTION AMUSEMENT PARK
2878 North Avenue
Grand Junction, CO 81501
(303) 243-1522
FACILITIES: 10 major rides; 8 kiddie rides; 3 games; refreshment stand; arcade; space pillow; go-karts; picnic facilities; miniature golf; free gate; free parking; open Apr. - Sept.

North Pole

SANTA'S WORKSHOP (Attraction)
Pikes Peak Hwy.
North Pole, CO 80809
(303) 684-9432
FACILITIES: 6 major rides; 13 kiddie rides; fun house; walk thru; 2 refreshment stands; restaurant; petting zoo; ice cream parlor; candy kitchen; 8 shops; Santa's House; picnic facilities; crafts; magic shows; pay gate; free parking; open Mid-May - Dec. 24; closed Thurs. in May and Fall.

STATE FAIR

Colorado State Fair
Fairgrounds
Pueblo, CO 81004
(303) 561-8484
DATE: August

NATIONAL PARKS

Estes Park

ROCKY MOUNTAIN NATIONAL PARK
Estes Park, CO 80517
(303) 586-2371

ASPENGLEN
LOCATION: Fall River entrance.
FACILITIES: Open year round; entrance fee; limit of stay: 7 days; 82 sites; NPS campsite fee: $4; water and bathroom facilities; picnic area; food service; boating; fishing; hiking; snowmobile route; exhibit; museum; environmental study area; living history program; handicapped access/restroom.

GLACIER BASIN
LOCATION: 5 mi. on Bear Lake Road.
FACILITIES: Open Jun. - Sept.; limit of stay: 7 days; 202 sites; group camps: 25; NPS campsite fee: $4; water and bathroom facilities; sanitary station; picnic area; food service; boating; fishing; hiking; horseback riding; snowmobile route; exhibit; museum; environmental study area; living history program; handicapped access/restroom; NPS guided tour; self-guiding tour.

LONGS PEAK
LOCATION: 11 mi. south of Estes Park.
FACILITIES: Open Jun. - Sept.; limit of stay: 3 days; 30 sites; NPS campsite fee: $4; water and bathroom facilities; picnic area; food service; boating; hiking; snowmobile route; exhibit; museum; environmental study area; living history program; handicapped access/restroom; NPS guided tour; self-guiding tour.

MORAINE PARK
LOCATION: 2 mi. on Bear Lake Road.
FACILITIES: Open Jun. - Sept.; limit of stay: 7 days; 260 sites; NPS campsite fee: $4; water and bathroom facilities; sanitary station; picnic area; food service; boating; fishing; hiking; horseback riding; snowmobile route; exhibit; museum; environmental study area; living history program; handicapped access/restroom; NPS guided tour; self-guiding tour.

TIMBER CREEK
LOCATION: 11 mi. north of Grand Lake.
FACILITIES: Open Jun. - Sept.; limit of stay: 7 days; 100 sites; NPS campsite fee: $4; water and bathroom facilities; sanitary station; picnic area; food service; boating; fishing; hiking; snowmobile route; exhibit; museum; environmental study area; living history program; handicapped access/restroom; NPS guided tour; self-guiding tour.

Mesa Verde National Park

MESA VERDE NATIONAL PARK
Mesa Verde National Park, CO 81330
(303) 529-4465

MORFIELD CANYON
LOCATION: 5 mi. south of entrance.
FACILITIES: Open May 1 - Oct. 31; limit of stay: 14 days; 494 sites; group camps: 17; NPS campsite fee: $2; water and bathroom facilities; sanitary station; picnic area; hiking.

NATIONAL FORESTS

National Forests
Rocky Mountain Region
11177 West 8th Avenue
Lakewood, CO 80225
(303) 234-3914

Colorado Springs

PIKE NATIONAL FOREST
ATTRACTIONS: Pikes Peak with highway to summit, historic Cripple Creek and Alma gold camps. Hunting and fishing; scenic drives. Mountain sheep and other wildlife.
FACILITIES: 46 camp and picnic sites, 46 picnic only; 3 winter sports areas. Commercial hotels, resorts, motels in and near the National Forest.
NEARBY TOWNS: Cripple Creek, Denver.

Delta

GRAND MESA-UNCOMPAHGRE NATIONAL FORESTS (Two National Forests).
ATTRACTIONS: Cliffs; canyons; waterfalls; wildflowers; lake and stream fishing. Deer, elk, bear, duck hunting; scenic drives; saddle trips.
FACILITIES: 30 camp and picnic sites, 8 picnic only; winter sports areas. Motels, resorts in and near the National Forest.
NEARBY TOWNS: Grand Junction, Montrose, Norwood, Ouray, and Telluride.

Durango

SAN JUAN NATIONAL FOREST
ATTRACTIONS: Canyons, waterfalls, cataracts, peculiar geologic formations; archeological ruins; historic mines. Fishing; deer, elk, bear, mountain lion, grouse, duck hunting; scenic drives; saddle and pack trips.
FACILITIES: 38 camp and picnic sites, 10 picnic only; 2 winter sports areas. Motels and dude ranches in and near the National Forest.
NEARBY TOWNS: Cortez, Pagosa Springs, Silverton, CO; Farmington, NM.

Fort Collins

ROOSEVELT NATIONAL FOREST
ATTRACTIONS: Boating; fishing; deer, elk, mountain sheep, bear, mountain lion, grouse, duck hunting; saddle and pack trips; scenic drives.
FACILITIES: 27 camp and picnic sites, 32 picnic only; winter sports area. Motels and dude ranches in and near National Forest.
NEARBY TOWNS: Boulder, Denver, Estes Park, Longmont, Loveland.

Glenwood Springs

WHITE RIVER NATIONAL FOREST
ATTRACTIONS: Spectacular Glenwood mineral hot springs; caves; canyon; hanging lake; Bridal Veil Falls. Source of marble for Lincoln Memorial and Tomb of the Unknown Soldier. Fishing; elk, deer, bear hunting; saddle and pack trails; scenic drives.
FACILITIES: 45 camp and picnic sites, 4 picnic only; 6 winter sports areas. Motels and dude ranches in and near the National Forest.

NEARBY TOWNS: Aspen, Craig, Eagle, Gypsum, Leadville, Meeker, Rifle.

Golden

ARAPAHO NATIONAL FOREST
ATTRACTIONS: Highest auto road in U.S. to the crest of Mount Evans, 14,260 ft. Gold, silver mining; ghost towns. Moffat Tunnel, 6.2 miles long under Continental Divide. Lake and stream fishing; elk, deer, bear, small-game hunting; riding trails; wilderness trips.
FACILITIES: 38 camp and picnic sites, 29 picnic only; 7 winter sports areas. Resorts, hotels, cabins, dude ranches.
NEARBY TOWNS: Denver, Dillon, Granby, Grand Lake, Hot Sulphur Springs, Idaho Springs, Kremming.

Gunnison

GUNNISON NATIONAL FOREST
ATTRACTIONS: Many high lakes; ghost towns; trout fishing; elk, deer, mountain sheep, bear hunting; saddle trips; wilderness trips.
FACILITIES: 45 camp and picnic sites; winter sports areas. Commercial hotels, resorts, motels in and near National Forest.
NEARBY TOWNS: Lake City, Montrose, Salida.

Monte Vista

RIO GRANDE NATIONAL FOREST
ATTRACTIONS: Mountain lakes and trout streams; fishing; deer, elk, duck hunting; saddle and pack trips; scenic drives.
FACILITIES: 40 camp and picnic sites, 15 picnic only; winter sports area. Motels in and near the National Forest.
NEARBY TOWNS: Alamosa, Antonito, Creede, Saguache.

Pueblo

SAN ISABEL NATIONAL FOREST
ATTRACTIONS: Highest average elevation of any National Forest; Sangre de Cristo Range: 12 peaks more than 14,000 feet; molybdenum mines. Fishing; deer, elk, bear, mountain goat, grouse, duck hunting; scenic drives; saddle and pack trips.
FACILITIES: 19 camp and picnic sites, 14 picnic only; 2 winter sports areas. Motels and dude ranches in and near the National Forest.
NEARBY TOWNS: Canon City, Leadville, Salida, Walsenburg.

Steamboat Springs

ROUTT NATIONAL FOREST
ATTRACTIONS: Continental Divide with perpetual ice and snow, trout streams and alpine lakes; fishing; deer, elk, grouse, duck hunting; saddle and pack trips; scenic drives.
FACILITIES: 26 camp and picnic sites, 8 picnic only; winter sports area. Commercial cabins, motels in and near the National Forest.
NEARBY TOWNS: Craig, Kremmling, Walden, Yampa.

See CARSON NATIONAL FOREST - New Mexico.

COLORADO

NATIONAL FORESTS (continued)

See MANTI-LA SAL NATIONAL FOREST - Utah.

STATE PARKS

Headquarters

Department of Natural Resources
Colorado Division of Parks & Outdoor Recreation
1313 Sherman
Denver, CO 80203
(303) 839-3311

Blackhawk

GOLDEN GATE CANYON STATE PARK
(303) 642-3171
LOCATION: 7 mi. north of Blackhawk on Colorado Hwy. 119.
FACILITIES: Open year round; 135 sites; water and bathroom facilities; laundry; picnic area; hiking; horseback riding; self-guided trail.

Denver

BARR LAKE STATE PARK
(303) 654-6005
LOCATION: 18 mi. northeast of Denver via I-76.
FACILITIES: Open year round; water and bathroom facilities; hiking; horseback riding; self-guided trail.

Ft. Collins

LORY STATE PARK (Horsetooth)
(303) 493-1623
LOCATION: 5 mi. west of Ft. Collins.
FACILITIES: Open year round; water and bathroom facilities; picnic area; hiking; horseback riding; self-guided trail.

Franktown

CASTLEWOOD STATE PARK
(303) 755-0766
LOCATION: 3 mi. southwest of Franktown.
FACILITIES: Open year round; water and bathroom facilities; hiking; self-guided trail.

Steamboat Springs

STEAMBOAT LAKE STATE PARK
(303) 873-3922
LOCATION: 25 mi. north of Steamboat Springs.
FACILITIES: Open year round; 210 sites; water and bathroom facilities; food service; boating; boat rental; skiing; hiking; horseback riding.

Walsenburg

LATHROP STATE PARK
(303) 738-2376
LOCATION: 3 mi. west of Walsenburg.
FACILITIES: Open year round; 99 sites; water and bathroom facilities; sanitary station; electrical hookup; laundry; picnic area; boating; boat rental; hiking; horseback riding.

STATE FORESTS

Department of Natural Resources
Colorado Division of Parks & Outdoor Recreation
1313 Sherman
Denver, CO 80203
(303) 839-3311

Ft. Collins

STATE FOREST
(303) 723-8366
LOCATION: 21 mi. southeast of Walden.
FACILITIES: Open year round; 165 sites; water and bathroom facilities; boating; skiing; horseback riding; self-guided trail.

HISTORIC SITES

Central City

CENTRAL CITY - BLACKHAWK - Once known as the "richest square mile on earth," this gold-veined area 35 mi. west of Denver abounds in remnants of the past including ghost towns such as Nevadaville and Apex. Home of the Teller House and 1878 Opera House.

Fort Garland

OLD FORT GARLAND - Restored U.S. Army post, 1858-1883. Colonel Kit Carson commanded here 1866-1867. Adobe barracks, soldiers' theater, dioramas and historical objects.

Georgetown

GEORGETOWN LOOP - In Clear Creek County, 45 mi. west of Denver, in the scenic valley between Georgetown and Silver Plum. A working and living full-scale frontier mining complex.

La Jara

PIKE'S STOCKADE - Replica of moated log stockade built by Capt. Zebulon Pike in 1807 in what was then Spanish territory. East of the town of La Jara, 232 mi. from Denver on U.S. 285 south of Alamosa.

Leadville

H.A.W. TABOR HOME - Residence of Horace Tabor, whose love for Baby Doe was the subject of one of America's great operas.

HEALY HOUSE & DEXTER CABIN - Museums depicting household life in the silver mining days in the Rockies in the 1880s.

Platteville

FORT VASQUEZ - Life-size reproduction of Fort Vasquez, fur trading post built in the 1830s.

Trinidad

OLD BACA HOUSE & BLOOM HOUSE - Op-

HISTORIC SITES (continued)

posite the Post Office on Main Street. Felipe Baca home, two-story adobe, built in 1869, with museum in separate building, depicts time of the Santa Fe Trail, Kit Carson, and open-range cattle days. Adjoining is the Bloom House, restored Victorian home of a mining and cattle baron in the 1880s.

HOSTELS

Boulder

BOULDER INTERNATIONAL HOSTEL
1107 12th Street
Boulder, CO 80306
(303) 442-0522
FACILITIES: Open year round; 50 beds, men; 50 beds, women; modern bathroom; nearest hostel: Nederland, 120 mi. west; overnight charges: $2.50; houseparent: Ronald A. Mitchell.

Breckenridge

GALBREATH'S FIRESIDE INN
Box 2252
Breckenridge, CO 80424
(303) 453-6456
FACILITIES: Open Jun. 15 - Oct. 15; 33 beds, men and women; modern bathroom; nearest hostel: Georgetown, 35 mi. northeast; overnight charges: $8.50 summer rate (includes breakfast and dinner); $9 winter rate (only bed); houseparents: Joan & Gale Galbreath.

Colorado Springs

COLORADO SPRINGS HOSTEL
17 N. Farragut Avenue
Colorado Springs, CO 80909
(303) 471-2938
FACILITIES: Open year round; 20 beds, men; 20 beds, women; modern bathroom; nearest hostel: Denver, 70 mi.; overnight charges: $3.25; houseparent: Mrs. Connie Halley.

Denver

DENVER UNITED YOUTH HOSTEL
1432 Lafayette
Denver, CO 80218
(303) 832-9996
FACILITIES: Open year round; 16 beds, men; 9 beds, women; modern bathroom; nearest hostel: Boulder, 30 mi.; overnight charges: $3; houseparent: Holy Order of MANS.

Estes Park

H BAR G RANCH HOSTEL
P.O. Box 1260
Estes Park, CO 80517
(303) 586-3688
FACILITIES: Open May 27 - Sept. 10; reservation required; 65 beds, men; 65 beds, women; modern bathroom; nearest hostels: Grand Lake, 50 mi. west; Nederland, 47 mi. south; Boulder, 36 miles southeast; overnight charges: $2.75; houseparent: Lou Livingston.

Grand Lake

SHADOWCLIFF WORLD FRIENDSHIP CENTER YOUTH HOSTEL
Tunnel Road
Grand Lake, CO 80447
(303) 627-9966
FACILITIES: Open Jun. 1 - Sept. 1; 20 beds, men; 12 beds, women; modern facilities; nearest hostel: Estes Park, 48 mi. east; overnight charges: $2.50; houseparent: Warren Rempel.

Nederland

NEDERLAND
1005 Jackson Street
Nederland, CO 80466
(303) 258-9925
FACILITIES: Open year round; 10 beds, women; 10 beds, men; modern bathroom; nearest hostel: Boulder, 20 mi. east; overnight charges: $2; houseparent: Gregg Fletcher.

Steamboat Springs

HAYSTACK LODGE YOUTH HOSTEL
P.O. Box 1356
Steamboat Springs, CO 80477
(303) 879-0587
FACILITIES: Open year round; 100 beds, men; 100 beds, women; modern bathroom; nearest hostel: Winter Park, 95 mi. southeast; overnight charges: $3 summer, $4.25 winter; houseparents: J.R. & Maudie Johnson.

Winter Park

WINTER PARK YOUTH HOSTEL
P.O. Box 255
Winter Park, CO 80450
(303) 726-5356
FACILITIES: Open year round; 72 beds, men; 72 beds, women; modern bathroom; nearest hostels: Grand Lake, 29 mi. north; Boulder, 80 mi. east; Georgetown, 30 mi. south; Denver, 72 mi. east; overnight charges: Summer: $2.75; winter: $4; houseparents: Mr. & Mrs. Stuart Crook.

POINTS OF INTEREST

Aspen

ASPEN - In 1893 was considered the richest silver mining town in the world. See ghost towns of Ashcroft, Independence, and Marble.

Carbondale

POTATO DAY - In mid-October on the Saturday before the opening of hunting season, this picturesque community at the base of Mt. Sopris holds a typical western style celebration.

Colorado Springs

CHUCK WAGON DINNERS & SUPPERS - Ranch-style dinners and suppers are served Jun. - Sept. in the picturesque setting of the Garden of the Gods and in the shadow of Pikes Peak. Also chuck wagon suppers are served near Durango, CO.

COLORADO

POINTS OF INTEREST (continued)

U.S. AIR FORCE ACADEMY - Military institution for the training of U.S. Air Force officers. Tours available. Located north of Colorado Springs.

Cripple Creek

CRIPPLE CREEK - VICTOR - Called the "World's greatest gold camp," Cripple Creek is located 115 mi. south of Denver. Many excellent ghost towns are in the area, such as Altman, Elkton, and Goldfield. Mine tours, narrow-gauge train rides and melodrama.

Creede

CREEDE - "There's no night in Creede," one of Colorado's liveliest mining camps, great for reliving history. Located on State Hwy. 149 about 30 mi. northwest of South Fork on U.S. 160.

Denver

U.S. Mint - Tour the famous mint and watch money being made. No free samples. Located on W. Colfax Ave.

Durango

"TRIP INTO YESTERDAY" VIA NARROW GAUGE R.R. - A thrilling trip through the Rio de Las Animas Canyon via America's last passenger narrow-gauge railroad. This is one of Colorado's most rugged and historic areas. OPEN: Daily from Jun. - Sept.

La Junta

KOSHARE INTERPRETATIVE INDIAN DANCERS - A troop of world-famous Boy Scouts interpret ancient Indian dances and rituals in authentic Kiva. Museum containing many priceless Indian artifacts is open all year. Winter ceremonials are a late Dec. event.

Littleton

LITTLE BRITCHES RODEO - A mid-August event, this is world's largest junior rodeo.

Silverton

SILVERTON - Located on the spectacular Million Dollar Highway (U.S.550). Famed mining and movie location town is also accessible via Durango-Silverton Narrow Gauge. Ghost towns of Eureka, Animas Forks, and Ironton are nearby.

CONNECTICUT

Connecticut, a densely populated, highly industrial state, joined the Union in 1788 as the fifth state. Early settlers were not bothered by the fact that over one half of the state's land was forested. They farmed what open land there was and made by hand most of their own wares. But in the late 1800s, Connecticut's population swelled with the advent of better roads and transportation.

With more people and limited farm lands, the state turned to industry to support itself. In the manufacturing of electronic products, nuclear submarines, ball and roller bearings, airplane engines and helicopters, Connecticut ranks first in the nation.

Farming still provides a significant income for the state with tobacco, eggs and dairy products heading the list. In recent years, a new dimension has been added to the state's economy. Because of its proximity and easy access to New York City, numerous major corporations have set up headquarters offices in the state, among them Pepsico, Union Carbide and IBM.

State capital: Hartford. State bird: Robin. State tree: White oak. State flower: Mountain laurel.

WEATHER

Connecticut occupies the southwester portion of the region known as New England. The state extends for 90 miles in an east-west direction and 75 miles from north to south. The topography of Connecticut is predominantly hilly. The highest terrain is found in the northwest portion of the state, with elevations of 1,000 to 2,000 feet.

The chief characteristics of Connecticut's climate may be summarized as follows: equable distribution of precipitation among the four seasons; large ranges of temperature both daily and annual; great differences in the same season or month of different years; and considerable diversity of the weather over short periods of time.

Despite the small size of Connecticut there is a difference of about 6 degrees F in mean annual temperature from north to south. The greatest contrast of temperature occurs during the winter season, while summer temperatures are comparatively uniform over the state.

During the warmest month of the summer, the average minimum temperature ranges from about 56 degrees F in the cool northwest corner of the state to about 63 degrees F in the warmer coastal sections. Over most of the state, the average July minimum temperature is within a degree or two of 60 degrees F.

Average daily temperature for each month.

WEATHER (continued)

	Northern	Southern
Jan.	28.1 to 11.7	36.2 to 18.4
Feb.	30.0 to 12.5	38.6 to 20.3
Mar.	38.0 to 21.1	45.9 to 27.7
Apr.	52.5 to 32.5	58.6 to 36.7
May	64.5 to 42.6	68.6 to 45.6
Jun.	73.1 to 52.4	77.8 to 55.5
Jul.	77.6 to 57.3	82.7 to 61.0
Aug.	75.6 to 55.4	81.2 to 59.6
Sept.	68.3 to 48.7	74.5 to 52.5
Oct.	57.2 to 38.1	64.7 to 42.0
Nov.	44.1 to 29.0	52.0 to 33.3
Dec.	32.0 to 17.3	40.1 to 22.6
Year	53.4 to 34.9	60.1 to 39.6

STATE CHAMBER OF COMMERCE

Connecticut Business & Industry Association
Suite 1202
60 Washington Street
Hartford, CT 06106
(203) 547-1661

STATE & CITY TOURISM OFFICES

State

Connecticut Department of Commerce
210 Washington Street
Hartford, CT 06106
(203) 566-5546

Tourism Promotion Service
Connecticut Department of Commerce
210 Washington Street
Hartford, CT 06106
(203) 566-3977

Local

Hartford Convention and Visitor's Bureau
1 Civic Center Plaza
Hartford, CT 06103
(203) 728-6789

STATE HIGHWAY DEPARTMENT

Department of Transportation
20 Wolcott Hill Road
Weathersfield, CT 06109
(203) 566-3477

HIGHWAY WELCOMING CENTERS

Danbury

DANBURY WELCOME CENTER - Interstate 84.

Darien

DARIEN WELCOME CENTER - Interstate 95, between Stamford and Norwalk-New York Border, Greenwich Merritt Parkway.

Southington

SOUTHINGTON WELCOME CENTER - Interstate 84.

Stonington

STONINGTON CENTER - Interstate 95.

Wallingford

WALLINGFORD CENTER - Interstate 91.

Westbrook

WESTBROOK CENTER - Interstate 95, near Clinton.

STATE POLICE

Department of Public Safety
Hartford, CT 06101
(203) 566-3200

HUNTING & FISHING

Hunting

Licenses required of persons 16 years of age or over. Minors under 16 may trap without being accompanied by a licensed trapper.

Licenses must be displayed on outer clothing at all times while hunting, trapping or fishing (including the taking of bait fish and bait species). In order to be issued a free fishing license for mentally retarded, proof in the form of a certificate issued by any person licensed to practice medicine and surgery in this state must be presented.

No license to trap will be issued to a non-resident.

Any active, full-time member of the armed forces who, at time of his induction, enlistment or re-enlistment was a legal resident of this state and any non-resident active full-time member of the armed forces may purchase a combination license to hunt, trap and fish for the fees listed below. When using this license, credentials indicating active, full-time membership in the armed forces or discharge or separation from the service subsequent to the issuance of the license prior to its expiration date must be carried.

No license to hunt will be issued to any person unless he has held a license to hunt with firearms in any state or country within 10 years from the date of application, or unless he possesses a certificate of competency issued by a Connecticut certified Hunter Safety Instructor. Names of instructors are available at any town clerk's office. This does not apply to the use of bow and arrow only in hunting, or to trapping only.

Resident

Hunting and trapping, $4.35; hunting,

CONNECTICUT

HUNTING & FISHING (continued)

trapping and fishing, $6.35.

Non-resident

Hunting, $13.35; armed forces member, $1.35; 65 years of age or over, free; hunting and fishing, $17.35.

Fishing

See Hunting above.

Resident

Fishing, $4.35; hunting, trapping and fishing, $6.35.

Non-resident

Fishing season, $8.35; 3-day fishing license, $3.85 (available for any 3 consecutive days between Jul. 1 - Dec. 31.)

Special Licenses (Resident or non-resident)

Fishing for blind or mentally retarded, free.

For more information contact:

Department of Environmental Protection
State Office Building
Hartford, CT 06115
(203) 566-5599

CAMPGROUNDS

Private

Abington

BEAUPRES'
(203) 974-1373
LOCATION: Route 44, 2½ mi. west of Abington.
FACILITIES: Open year round; 125 sites; water and bathroom facilities; sanitary station; electrical hookup; trailer village vehicle sites; swimming; boating; fishing; tent camping.

Baltic

SALT ROCK
(203) 822-8728
LOCATION: Route 97, 2 mi. north of Baltic.
FACILITIES: Open year round; 109 sites; water and bathroom facilities; sanitary station; electrical hookup; trailer village vehicle sites; tent camping.

Bantam

COZY HILLS
(203) 567-0042
LOCATION: Route 202, Bantam.
FACILITIES: Open year round; 175 sites; water and bathroom facilities; sanitary station; electrical hookup; trailer village vehicle sites; tent camping.

Brooklyn

BIG VALLEY
(203) 774-5810
LOCATION: Brickyard Road, off Route 6, 2 mi. east of Brooklyn.
FACILITIES: Open Apr. 15 - Oct. 1; 250 sites; water and bathroom facilities; sanitary station; electrical hookup; trailer village vehicle sites; tent camping.

FOX TAIL
(203) 774-6334
LOCATION: Route 205, halfway between Wauregan and Brooklyn.
FACILITIES: Open Apr. 15 - Oct. 15; 150 sites; water and bathroom facilities; sanitary station; electrical hookup; trailer village vehicle sites; laundry; boating; tent camping.

Canaan

LONE OAK
(203) 824-7051
LOCATION: Route 44, 4 mi. east of Canaan.
FACILITIES: Open Apr. 15 - Oct. 15; 450 sites; water and bathroom facilities; sanitary station; electrical hookup; trailer village vehicle sites; laundry; tent camping.

Chaplin

NATCHAUG MEADOWS
(203) 455-9511
LOCATION: Route 198, 2 mi. south of Route 44.
FACILITIES: Open Apr. 15 - Sept. 30; 100 sites; water and bathroom facilities; sanitary station; electrical hookup; trailer village vehicle sites; boating; bicycle trail; tent camping.

NICKERSON PARK
(203) 455-0007
LOCATION: Route 198 between Routes 6 & 44.
FACILITIES: Open Apr. 15 - Nov. 1; 100 sites; water and bathroom facilities; sanitary station; electrical hookup; trailer village vehicle sites; laundry; boating; tent camping.

Clinton

RIVERDALE FARM
(203) 669-5388
LOCATION: River Road, northwest of Clinton.
FACILITIES: Open Apr. 15 - Nov. 1; 250 sites; water and bathroom facilities; sanitary station; electrical hookup; trailer village vehicle sites; laundry; boating; tent camping.

Colchester

ACORN ACRES
(203) 859-1020
LOCATION: Route 2 exit, 22 mi. east of Colchester.
FACILITIES: Open May 1 - Oct. 15; 160 sites; water and bathroom facilities; sanitary station; electrical hookup; trailer village vehicle sites; swimming; tent camping.

LAUREL LOCK
(203) 859-1424

CAMPGROUNDS (continued)

LOCATION: Gardner Lake, west of Route 52 exit 80.
FACILITIES: Open Apr. 15 - Oct. 15; 125 sites; water and bathroom facilities; sanitary station; electrical hookup; trailer village vehicle sites; boating; tent camping.

Danielson

ROSS HILL PARK
(203) 376-9606
LOCATION: Ross Hill Road, off Route 52 exit 84.
FACILITIES: Open year round; 200 sites; water and bathroom facilities; sanitary station; electrical hookup; trailer village vehicle sites; laundry; food service; swimming; boating; boat rental; tent camping.

East Haddam

WOLF'S DEN
(203) 873-9681
LOCATION: Route 82, 2½ mi. south of East Haddam.
FACILITIES: Open May 1 - Oct. 15; 200 sites; water and bathroom facilities; sanitary station; electrical hookup; trailer village vehicle sites; laundry; swimming; bicycle trail; tent camping.

East Hampton

NELSON'S
(203) 267-4561
LOCATION: Mott Hill Road, 2 mi. north of Route 66 via N. Main St.
FACILITIES: Open Apr. 15 - Oct. 15; 100 sites; water and bathroom facilities; sanitary station; electrical hookup; trailer village vehicle sites; boating; tent camping.

East Killingly

HIDE-A-WAY COVE
(203) 774-1128
LOCATION: North Road, ¼ mi. north of East Killingly off Route 101.
FACILITIES: Open May 1 - Oct. 1; 340 sites; water and bathroom facilities; sanitary station; electrical hookup; trailer village vehicle sites; laundry; swimming; boating; tent camping.

STATE LINE
(203) 774-3016
LOCATION: Route 101, 5 mi. east of Route 52 exit 93.
FACILITIES: Open May 15 - Oct. 15; 200 sites; water and bathroom facilities; sanitary station; electrical hookup; trailer village vehicle sites; laundry; swimming; boating; tent camping.

East Lyme

PONDEROSA
(203) 739-2629
LOCATION: Route 161, north of I-95 exit 74.
FACILITIES: Open year round; 146 sites; water and bathroom facilities; sanitary station; electrical hookup; trailer village vehicle sites;

laundry; tent camping.

Kent

SMILING FOREST
(203) 927-3555
LOCATION: Kenico Road, 5½ mi. east of junction of Routes 7 & 341.
FACILITIES: Open May 15 - Nov. 15; 262 sites; water and bathroom facilities; sanitary station; electrical hookup; trailer village vehicle sites; laundry; swimming; bicycle trail; tent camping.

Niantic

CAMP NIANTIC
(203) 739-9321
LOCATION: Route 156, west of I-95 exit 72, near Rocky Neck State Park.
FACILITIES: Open May 1 - Nov. 1; 130 sites; water and bathroom facilities; sanitary station; electrical hookup; trailer village vehicle sites; tent camping.

North Stonington

HIGHLAND ORCHARDS
(203) 599-5101
LOCATION: Route 49, north of I-95.
FACILITIES: Open year round; 160 sites; water and bathroom facilities; sanitary station; electrical hookup; trailer village vehicle sites; laundry; food service; swimming; tent camping.

Old Mystic

SEAPORT KOA
(203) 536-4044
LOCATION: North on Route 27 from I-95, ½ mi. right on Route 184.
FACILITIES: Open Apr. - Nov.; 130 sites; water and bathroom facilities; sanitary station; electrical hookup; trailer village vehicle sites; laundry; swimming; boating; bicycle trail; tent camping.

Oneco

RIVER BEND
(203) 564-3440
LOCATION: Route 14A, Oneco, 5 mi. east of Route 52 exit 88.
FACILITIES: Open May - Oct.; 100 sites; water and bathroom facilities; sanitary station; electrical hookup; trailer village vehicle sites; laundry; boating; boat rental; bicycle trail; tent camping.

Plymouth

GENTILE'S CAMPSITES
(203) 283-8437
LOCATION: Route 262 (Mt. Tobe Road), off Route 6 south of Terryville.
FACILITIES: Open Apr. - Oct.; 150 sites; water and bathroom facilities; sanitary station; electrical hookup; trailer village vehicle sites; bicycle trail; tent camping.

Preston

HIDDEN ACRES
(203) 887-9633

CONNECTICUT

CAMPGROUNDS (continued)

LOCATION: River Road (Route 52 exit 85, right 1 mi. to Palmer Road, 3 mi. to River Road).
FACILITIES: Open Apr. - Nov.; 130 sites; water and bathroom facilities; sanitary station; electrical hookup; trailer village vehicle sites; laundry; boating; boat rental; tent camping.

STRAWBERRY PARK KOA
(203) 886-1944
LOCATION: Pierce Road, off Route 165.
FACILITIES: Open Apr. - Nov.; 100 sites; water and bathroom facilities; sanitary station; electrical hookup; trailer village vehicle sites; horseback riding; tent camping.

Salem

WITCH MEADOW LAKE
(203) 859-1542
LOCATION: Witch Meadow Road.
FACILITIES: Open May 1 - Oct. 31; 150 sites; water and bathroom facilities; sanitary station; electrical hookup; trailer village vehicle sites; boating; bicycle trail; tent camping.

Scotland

HIGHLAND
(203) 423-5684
LOCATION: Route 97, ½ mi. south of Scotland.
FACILITIES: Open year round; 170 sites; water and bathroom facilities; sanitary station; electrical hookup; trailer village vehicle sites; laundry; tent camping.

Stafford Springs

ROARING BROOK
(203) 684-3131
LOCATION: Route 190, 3 mi. east of Stafford Springs.
FACILITIES: Open Apr. 15 - Oct. 15; 200 sites; water and bathroom facilities; sanitary station; electrical hookup; trailer village vehicle sites; swimming; fishing; tent camping.

Voluntown

NATURE'S
(203) 376-4203
LOCATION: Route 49, ½ mi. north of Voluntown.
FACILITIES: Open May - Nov.; 200 sites; water and bathroom facilities; sanitary station; electrical hookup; trailer village vehicle sites; laundry; swimming; boating; tent camping.

West Willington

MOOSE MEADOW KOA
(203) 429-7451
LOCATION: Moose Meadow Road, off Route 44, east of I-86 exit 100.
FACILITIES: Open May - Nov.; 200 sites; water and bathroom facilities; sanitary station; electrical hookup; trailer village vehicle sites; laundry; tent camping.

Winchester

WHITE PINES
(203) 379-0124
LOCATION: Old North Road, off Route 44, 1 mi. east of Winsted.
FACILITIES: Open May 1 - Oct. 15; 152 sites; water and bathroom facilities; sanitary station; electrical hookup; trailer village vehicle sites; tent camping.

RESORTS & BEACHES

New London

OCEAN BEACH PARK - A mile-long boardwalk adjoins scenic sandy beach. Enjoy salt water or pool bathing, amusement park rides, miniature golf and a score of other activities. Dine at many fine restaurants and stay at nearby resort hotels.

BOATING AREAS

Barkhamsted

COMPENSATING RESERVOIR
LOCATION: 4 mi. northeast of New Hartford.
FACILITIES: Launching.

Bridgewater

LAKE LILLINONAH
LOCATION: 9 mi. south of New Milford.
FACILITIES: Launching; fishing.

East Haddam

BASHAN LAKE
LOCATION: On Ballahack Road.
FACILITIES: Launching; fishing.

Ellington

CRYSTAL LAKE
LOCATION: Off Route 30.
FACILITIES: Launching; fishing.

Lakeville

WONONSCOPOMUC LAKE
LOCATION: In Lakeville.
FACILITIES: Launching; fishing.

Old Lyme

ROGERS LAKE
LOCATION: On Grassy Hill Road.
FACILITIES: Launching; fishing.

Salem-Montville

GARDNER LAKE
LOCATION: Off Route 82.
FACILITIES: Launching; fishing.

Shelton

LAKE HOUSATONIC
LOCATION: 2½ mi. northwest of Shelton, off Route 110.
FACILITIES: Launching.

BOATING AREAS (continued)

Southbury

LAKE ZOAR
LOCATION: 2½ mi. south of Route 6.
FACILITIES: Launching; fishing.

Thompson

QUADDICK RESERVOIR
LOCATION: 4 mi. north of East Putnam and
U.S. 44.
FACILITIES: Launching; fishing.

Union

MASHAPAUG LAKE
LOCATION: 2½ mi. north of Route 197.
FACILITIES: Launching.

Voluntown

BEACH POND
LOCATION: Off Route 165.
FACILITIES: Launching.

Winchester

HIGHLAND LAKE
LOCATION: 100 yards west of the dam at
the north end of the lake.
FACILITIES: Launching.

WINCHESTER LAKE
LOCATION: 2 mi. northeast of Winchester.
FACILITIES: Launching.

Windsor

RAINBOW RESERVOIR
LOCATION: Access area located approxi-
mately 2 mi. west of Rainbow.
FACILITIES: Launching.

BICYCLE TRAILS

HOUSATONIC RIVER TRAIL - 70 mi.; any
bicycle.
   Here is a ride along the Housatonic River
for the entire family, even the young ones
who can only pedal ten or fifteen miles per
day. There are a few hills along this route but
generally it is flat to rolling countryside. Favorable conditions exist from May - Oct.
   Trail: Cornwall Bridge to Lime Rock to
Ashley Falls, MA to Sheffield to Konkapot
to Falls Village, CT to Cornwall Bridge.

See MASSACHUSETTS - Springfield Trail.

See NEW YORK - Westchester-Fairfield Trail.

TRAILS

There are no National Trails System Foot
Trails in Connecticut.

SKI AREAS

Burrville

LAKERIDGE SKI AREA
Burr Mountain Road
Burrville, CT 06790
(203) 482-9303
LOCATION: In Burrville.
FACILITIES: 1 chairlift; slopes for expert, intermediate and beginning skiers; ski instruction; ski rental; 180 ft. vertical drop; longest
run, 1800 ft.; restaurants; lodging.

Cornwall

MOHAWK MOUNTAIN SKI AREA
Cornwall, CT 06796
(203) 672-6100
LOCATION: Off Route 4.
FACILITIES: 4 chairlifts; 9 tow ropes; 1
poma; slopes for expert, intermediate and beginning skiers; ski instruction; ski rental; 460
ft. vertical drop; longest run, 1 mi.; restaurants; lodging.

Middlefield

POWDER RIDGE SKI AREA
Middlefield, CT 06455
(203) 349-3454
LOCATION: Off Route 147.
FACILITIES: 1 quad chairlift; 3 double chairlifts; 2 tow ropes; 2 T-bars; slopes for expert,
intermediate and beginning skiers; ski instruction; ski rental; nursery; 500 ft. vertical drop;
longest run, 1¼ mi.; restaurants; lodging.

New Hartford

SKI SUNDOWN
Ratlum Road
New Hartford, CT 06057
(203) 379-0610
LOCATION: 2 mi. north of New Hartford.
FACILITIES: 1 triple chairlift; 1 double
chairlift; 1 poma; slopes for expert, intermediate and beginning skiers; ski instruction; ski
rental; 550 ft. vertical drop; longest run, 1
mi.; restaurants; lodging.

Southington

MT. SOUTHINGTON SKI AREA
P.O. Box 347
Southington, CT 06489
(203) 628-0954
LOCATION: Off I-84.
FACILITIES: 1 double chairlift; 1 triple
chairlift; 3 T-bars; 1 J-bar; slopes for expert,
intermediate and beginning skiers; ski instruction; ski rental; 460 ft. vertical drop; longest
run, 1 mi.; restaurants; lodging.

Woodbury

WOODBURY SKI AND RACQUET
Route 47
Woodbury, CT 06798
(203) 263-2203
LOCATION: 4 mi. north of Woodbury.
FACILITIES: 1 double chairlift; 1 tow rope;
1 T-bar; slopes for expert, intermediate and
beginning skiers; ski instruction; ski rental;

CONNECTICUT

SKI AREAS (continued)

290 ft. vertical drop; longest run, ½ mi.; restaurants; lodging.

Woodstock

OHOHO SKI AREA
Bungay Hill Road
Woodstock, CT 06281
(203) 974-1040
LOCATION: ½ mi. northwest of West Woodstock.
FACILITIES: 3 tow ropes; 1 T-bar; slopes for expert, intermediate and beginning skiers; ski instruction; ski rental; 300 ft. vertical drop; longest run, 3000 ft.; restaurants; lodging.

AMUSEMENT PARKS & ATTRACTIONS

Bristol

LAKE COMPOUNCE
Lake Avenue
Bristol, CT 06010
(203) 582-6333
FACILITIES: 9 major rides; 5 kiddie rides; 7 games; 6 refreshment stands; restaurant; penny arcade; beach; picnic facilities; miniature golf; orchestras; name bands; free acts; fireworks; free gate; free parking; pay parking, Sun. & Holidays.

Middlebury

LAKE QUASSAPAUG AMUSEMENT PARK, INC.
Route 64
Middlebury, CT 06762
(203) 758-2913
FACILITIES: 10 major rides; 6 kiddie rides; 6 games; 3 refreshment stands; restaurant; arcade; beach; miniature golf; catering; picnic facilities; orchestras; free acts; fireworks; free gate; free parking; pay parking, Sun. & holidays; open Apr. 1 - Sept. 30. Weekends, Apr., May & Sept.

New London

OCEAN BEACH PARK
New London, CT 06320
(203) 447-3031
FACILITIES: 13 major rides; 6 kiddie rides; 4 refreshment stands; restaurant; cafeteria; 2 cocktail lounges; arcade; shooting gallery; salt water pool; beach; picnic facilities; 18 hole miniature golf course; free acts; fireworks; pay gate; open Memorial Day - Labor Day.

STATE FAIR

Connecticut State Fair
Durham, CT 06422
(203) 349-9495
DATE: July

NATIONAL PARKS

There are no National Parks in Connecticut.

NATIONAL FORESTS

There are no National Forests in Connecticut.

STATE PARKS

Headquarters

Department of Environmental Protection
Parks and Recreation Unit
Hartford, CT 06115
(203) 566-2304

Bloomfield

PENWOOD STATE PARK
LOCATION: 4 mi. west of Bloomfield on Route 185.
FACILITIES: Open year round; picnic area; hiking; environmental study area.

Bolton

GAY CITY STATE PARK
LOCATION: 3 mi. south of Bolton on Route 85.
FACILITIES: Open year round; picnic area; swimming; fishing; hiking.

East Haddam

DEVIL'S HOPYARD STATE PARK
LOCATION: 3 mi. north of intersection of Routes 82 & 156.
FACILITIES: Open Apr. 15 - Sept. 30; 27 sites; water and bathroom facilities; picnic area; fishing; hiking; tent camping.

Groton

BLUFF POINT COASTAL RESERVE STATE PARK
LOCATION: Route 117 exit from Connecticut Turnpike, right on Route 1, left on Depot Road, continue under R.R. overpass.
FACILITIES: Open year round; picnic area; fishing; hiking; environmental study area.

Hamden

SLEEPING GIANT STATE PARK
LOCATION: 2 mi. north of Hamden off Route 10.
FACILITIES: Open Apr. 15 - Sept. 30; 6 sites; water and bathroom facilities; picnic area; fishing; hiking; tent camping.

Jewett City

HOPEVILLE POND STATE PARK
LOCATION: 3 mi. east of Jewett City on Route 201.
FACILITIES: Open Apr. 15 - Sept. 30; 81 sites; water and bathroom facilities; trailer village vehicle sites; picnic area; food service; swimming; boating; fishing; hiking; tent camping.

STATE PARKS (continued)

Kent

MACEDONIA BROOK STATE PARK
LOCATION: 4 mi. northwest of Kent off Route 341.
FACILITIES: Open Apr. 15 - Sept. 30; 84 sites; water and bathroom facilities; trailer village vehicle sites; picnic area; fishing; tent camping.

Madison

HAMMONASSET BEACH STATE PARK
LOCATION: 1 mi. south of Exit 62 from Route I-95.
FACILITIES: Open Apr. 15 - Sept. 30; 541 sites; water and bathroom facilities; trailer village vehicle sites; picnic area; food service; fishing; tent camping.

Mansfield

MANSFIELD HOLLOW STATE PARK
LOCATION: 1 mi. east of Mansfield Center off Route 89.
FACILITIES: Open year round; picnic area; boating; fishing; hiking.

Middle Haddam

HURD STATE PARK
LOCATION: 2 mi. south of Middle Haddam on Route 151.
FACILITIES: Open year round; picnic area; hiking.

Niantic

ROCKY NECK STATE PARK
LOCATION: 3 mi. west of Niantic.
FACILITIES: Open Apr. 15 - Sept. 30; 169 sites; water and bathroom facilities; trailer village vehicle sites; picnic area; swimming; fishing; hiking; tent camping.

Putnam

MASHAMOQUET BROOK STATE PARK
LOCATION: 5 mi. southwest of Putnam on Route 44.
FACILITIES: Open Apr. 15 - Sept. 30; 80 sites; water and bathroom facilities; trailer village vehicle sites; picnic area; swimming; fishing; tent camping.

Sharon

HOUSATONIC MEADOWS STATE PARK
LOCATION: 1 mi. north of Cornwall Bridge on Route 7.
FACILITIES: Open Apr. 15 - Sept. 30; 100 sites; water and bathroom facilities; trailer village vehicle sites; picnic area; fishing; tent camping.

Simsbury

TALCOTT MOUNTAIN STATE PARK
LOCATION: 3 mi. south of Simsbury on Route 185.
FACILITIES: Open year round; picnic area; hiking.

Southbury

KETTLETOWN STATE PARK
LOCATION: 5 mi. south of Southbury.
FACILITIES: Open Apr. 15 - Sept. 30; 80 sites; water and bathroom facilities; trailer village vehicle sites; swimming; hiking; self-guided trail; tent camping.

Torrington

BURR POND STATE PARK
LOCATION: 5 mi. north of Torrington on Route 8.
FACILITIES: Open Apr. 15 - Sept. 30; 40 sites; water and bathroom facilities; picnic area; food service; swimming; boating; fishing; hiking; camping nearby.

JOHN A. MINETTO STATE PARK
LOCATION: 6 mi. north of Torrington on Route 272.
FACILITIES: Open year round; picnic area; swimming; fishing; hiking.

SUNNYBROOK STATE PARK
LOCATION: 2 mi. north of Torrington on Newfield Road.
FACILITIES: Open year round; picnic area; swimming; fishing; hiking.

Union

BIGELOW HOLLOW STATE PARK
LOCATION: 2 mi. east of Union on Route 197.
FACILITIES: Open year round; picnic area; boating; fishing; hiking.

Watertown

BLACK ROCK STATE PARK
LOCATION: 2 mi. west of Thomaston on Route 6.
FACILITIES: Open Apr. 15 - Sept. 30; 90 sites; water and bathroom facilities; picnic area; food service; swimming; fishing; hiking; tent camping.

STATE FORESTS

Department of Environmental Protection
Parks and Recreation Unit
Hartford, CT 06115
(203) 566-2304

Beacon Falls

NAUGATUCK STATE FOREST
LOCATION: 1 mi. north of Beacon Falls.
FACILITIES: Open year round; picnic area; hunting; hiking.

Chester

COCKAPONSET STATE FOREST
LOCATION: 3 mi. west of Chester on Route 148.
FACILITIES: Open Apr. 15 - Sept. 30; 12 sites; water and bathroom facilities; picnic area; hunting; fishing; hiking; tent camping.

CONNECTICUT

STATE FORESTS (continued)

Goshen

MOHAWK STATE FOREST
LOCATION: 4 mi. west of Goshen on Route 4.
FACILITIES: Open year round; picnic area; fishing; hiking.

Phoenixville

NATCHAUG STATE FOREST
LOCATION: 4 mi. south of Phoenixville on Route 198.
FACILITIES: Open year round; picnic area; hunting; fishing; hiking; horseback riding.

Pleasant Valley

AMERICAN LEGION STATE FOREST
LOCATION: 1 mi. north of Pleasant Valley on West River Road.
FACILITIES: Open Apr. 15 - Sept. 30; 30 sites; water and bathroom facilities; picnic area; hunting; fishing; hiking; tent camping.

PEOPLES STATE FOREST
LOCATION: 1 mi. north of Pleasant Valley on East River Road.
FACILITIES: Open year round; picnic area; hunting; fishing; hiking.

South Chaplin

JAMES L. GOODWIN STATE FOREST
LOCATION: 3 mi. east of South Chaplin on Route 6.
FACILITIES: Open year round; fishing; hiking; environmental study area.

Voluntown

PACHAUG STATE FOREST
LOCATION: 1 mi. south of Voluntown.
FACILITIES: Open Apr. 15 - Sept. 30; 18 sites; water and bathroom facilities; swimming; hunting; fishing; hiking; horseback riding; tent camping.

HISTORIC SITES

Canterbury

PRUDENCE CRANDALL HOUSE - Georgian-style home where Miss Crandall, in 1832, established state's first all-Black school for girls. Located at junction of Routes 169 & 14.

Coventry

NATHAN HALE HOMESTEAD - Deacon Richard Hale, father of the patriot, built the house in 1776 and held court there as a justice of the peace. Located on South Street.

East Granby

OLD NEW-GATE PRISON & COPPER MINE America's first chartered copper mine (1707), Revolutionary War prison (1775-1782), and Connecticut's first state prison (1776-1827). Visitors may tour copper mine where prisoners were chained at night. Located on Newgate Road.

Farmington

FARMINGTON MUSEUM (Stanley - Whitman House) - This 1660 homestead, beautifully restored, has lovely period furnishings, artifacts, beautiful herb and flower gardens. Located at 37 High Street.

Guilford

WHITFIELD HOUSE MUSEUM - New England's oldest stone house (1639-40), originally a parsonage, fort and community hall. Located on Whitfield Street.

Hartford

MUSEUM OF CONNECTICUT HISTORY - Priceless historic displays: original Royal Charter, Colt Collection of Firearms, Connecticut-made clocks. Located on Capitol Avenue (opposite State Capitol).

Lebanon

JONATHAN TRUMBULL HOUSE (1735) - Home of the only colonial governor to support independence. During the Revolutionary War the house was connected by tunnel with the War Office nearby. Located on Lebanon Green.

Litchfield

TAPPING REEVE HOUSE & LAW SCHOOL - America's first law school (1784); graduates included Aaron Burr and 2 other U.S. Vice Presidents, 130 members of Congress. Located on South Street.

Norwalk

LOCKWOOD-MATHEWS MANSION (1864) - America's first chateau. A 40-room Victorian palace with stenciled walls, inlaid woodwork, great skylight rotunda. Located at 295 West Street.

South Woodstock

QUASSET SCHOOL - Nation's oldest one-room school in continuous service (1748 - 1945). Located off Route 169.

Stonington

OLD LIGHTHOUSE MUSEUM - Said to be the first government lighthouse in Connecticut (1823). Located on The Point.

Wethersfield

JOSEPH WEBB HOUSE (1752) - Outstanding example of colonial architecture. Site of historic strategy conference (1781) between Washington and Rochambeau that led to British defeat at Yorktown. Located on Main Street.

HISTORIC SITES (continued)

SILAS DEANE HOUSE (1766) - Built by member of First Continental Congress and Commissioner to France. Located on Main Street.

Woodbury

GLEBE HOUSE (1740) - Birthplace of American Episcopacy. Site of Samuel Seabury's election as first bishop of Episcopal Church in America. Located on Hollow Road.

HOSTELS

Lakeside

BANTAM LAKE YOUTH HOSTEL
E. Shore Road
Lakeside, CT 06758
(203) 567-9258 Litchfield
FACILITIES: Open year round; 20 beds for men & women; modern bathroom; overnight charges: $2.50 May 1 - Sept. 30; $3.25 Oct. 1 - Apr. 30; houseparent: Alex Sobolewski.

New London

MITCHELL COLLEGE YOUTH HOSTEL
361 Pequot Avenue
New London, CT 06320
(203) 443-2811
FACILITIES: Open year round; 50 beds for men and women; modern bathroom; overnight charges: $3 summer; $4.25 winter; houseparents: Mitchell College staff.

POINTS OF INTEREST

Bridgeport

BRIDGEPORT JAI ALAI - Pari-mutuel betting, lounges, snack bars. Located at 255 Kossuth Street.

Glastonbury

FERRY BOAT RIDE - Across the Connecticut River to Rocky Hill (Route 160). The oldest ferry in continuous operation in the country (since 1655).

Greenwich

MUSEUM OF CARTOON ART & HALL OF FAME - Unique collection of original cartoons, from Thomas Nast and Charles Dana Gibson to Peanuts. Located at 384 Field Point Road.

U.S. TOBACCO COMPANY MUSEUM - History of tobacco on five continents traced in a collection of pipes, snuff boxes, and other tobacco-related artifacts. Located at 100 W. Putnam Avenue.

Hartford

MARK TWAIN MEMORIAL AND HARRIET BEECHER STOWE HOUSE - Adjacent houses consist of the extravagant Victorian mansion of Mark Twain and home of the author of "Uncle Tom's Cabin." Both are located on Farmington Avenue at Forest Street.

WADSWORTH ATHENEUM - The nation's first free public art museum. Collections illustrate the arts of all ages. Located on 600 Main Street.

Litchfield

LITCHFIELD NATURE CENTER & MUSEUM - State's largest nature center. Located on Route 202.

Manchester

LUTZ JUNIOR MUSEUM - A "do touch" museum to encourage self-discovery through handling displays and participating in special projects. Located at 126 Cedar Street.

Mystic

MYSTIC SEAPORT - Nationally acclaimed "living" museum, 19th century maritime village with authentic ships, shops, homes, crafts, planetarium, and the last of the wooden whalers: the Charles W. Morgan. Located on Route 27.

New Haven

YALE UNIVERSITY ART GALLERY - Nation's oldest college art museum. Located at 111 Chapel Street.

Old Lyme

NUT MUSEUM - Unusual and charming collection of nuts and nutwood products from all parts of the world. Located at 303 Ferry Road.

Plainfield

PLAINFIELD GREYHOUND PARK - Greyhound racing, pari-mutuel betting. Located on Lathrop Road.

Terryville

LOCK MUSEUM OF AMERICA - Unique historic collection of 18,000 locks and keys (largest in U.S.) from 19th century. Located at 114 Main Street.

Washington

AMERICAN INDIAN ARCHAEOLOGICAL INSTITUTE AND MUSEUM - Exhibits include the state's only mastodon skeleton, artifacts from local Paleo-Indian campsite 12,000 years old, nature/habitat trail and longhouse. Located off Route 199.

West Hartford

NOAH WEBSTER HOUSE & MUSEUM - Eighteenth century farmhouse, birthplace of author of "Blue-Backed Speller" (1783) and "American Dictionary" (1828). Located at 227 S. Main Street.

DELAWARE

Delaware, geographically situated within 300 miles of the East Coast's important industrial centers, was admitted to the Union in 1787 as the first state. This proximity to New York, Philadelphia, Baltimore, Washington, D.C., and Richmond set the stage for the state's stand during the Civil War.

Although the people of Delaware tended to favor slavery, their feelings for remaining with the Union were far stronger.

The state is heavily industrial. Its largest city, Wilmington, boasts the world's largest braided rubber hose manufacturer and cotton dyeing and finishing works in addition to being "the chemical capital of the world."

Even with Delaware's economic emphasis on major industry, the state also manages to produce an impressive amount of peaches and broilers. The state's peaches are nationally renowned and its broiler production leads all other states.

State capital: Dover. State bird: Blue hen chicken. State tree: American holly. State flower: Peach blossom.

WEATHER

Delaware lies in a north-south position, spanning a distance of 96 miles. The width increases from 9 miles in the northern portion to 35 miles in the extreme southern portion. The total area of the state is 2,057 square miles. Although Delaware ranks as one of the smallest states with minor physiographic features, the southern portion, which lies closest to the bays and ocean, experiences somewhat milder weather than the northern portion.

The climate of Delaware is "humid, temperate" with hot summers and mild winters. The winter climate is intermediate between the cold of the northeast and the mild weather of the south. Summer is characterized by considerable warm weather, including at least several hot, humid periods. However, nights are usually quite comfortable.

Average daily temperature for each month.

	Northern	Southern
Jan.	39.0 to 23.5	43.6 to 25.5
Feb.	41.3 to 24.9	46.2 to 26.7
Mar.	49.3 to 32.0	53.8 to 32.9
Apr.	61.9 to 41.8	66.0 to 42.2
May	71.5 to 51.0	75.2 to 51.5
Jun.	80.5 to 60.6	83.5 to 60.8
Jul.	84.6 to 65.6	87.1 to 65.4
Aug.	82.6 to 64.2	85.3 to 63.5
Sept.	76.5 to 57.5	79.5 to 56.9
Oct.	65.9 to 46.5	69.0 to 46.0
Nov.	53.3 to 36.6	57.7 to 36.5
Dec.	42.7 to 27.7	47.1 to 28.9
Year	62.4 to 44.3	66.2 to 44.7

STATE CHAMBER OF COMMERCE

Delaware State Chamber of Commerce, Inc.
1102 West Street
Wilmington, DE 19801
(302) 655-7221

STATE & CITY TOURISM OFFICES

State

Delaware Department of Community Affairs and Economic Development
630 State College Road
Dover, DE 19901
(302) 678-4254

STATE HIGHWAY DEPARTMENT

Department of Transportation
Highway Department Administration Bldg.
Dover, DE 19901
(302) 678-4301

HIGHWAY WELCOMING CENTERS

Delaware

DELAWARE MEMORIAL BRIDGE CENTER - Interstate 295.

STATE POLICE

Department of Public Safety
P.O. Box 430
Dover, DE 19901
(302) 734-5973

HUNTING & FISHING

Hunting

Licenses required for persons 15 years or over.

Residents and members of the immediate family who live on farms in the state containing 20 acres or more are not required to purchase a license to hunt, fish or trap on their land.

HUNTING & FISHING (continued)

Residents under 15 years of age may hunt without a license in this state when accompanied by a person who is the lawful holder of a hunting license or has a lawful right to hunt.

All persons under the age of 18 must successfully complete a 6-hour hunter safety instruction course before obtaining a resident hunting license.

Residents over 65 years do not need to obtain a license.

Non-residents to hunt only on regulated shooting preserves when it is lawful to do so, but nowhere else.

Non-residents other than aliens who are under 15 years of age may hunt without a license in this State when accompanied by a person who is the lawful holder of a hunting license or has a lawful right to hunt.

A Federal Migratory Bird Hunting Stamp is required for any person 16 years or older to hunt waterfowl.

Resident

Hunting and trapping fee, $5.20.

Non-resident

Hunting, $3; hunting & trapping, $40.25.

Fishing

A license is required for anyone 16 years of age and older to fish ponds and non-tidal streams.

A trout stamp is required for all licensed anglers to fish designated trout streams.

No fishing license is required to fish waters where the tide is regularly ebbs and flows including the C&D Canal.

Residents over 65 years of age do not need to obtain a license or a trout stamp.

Anglers legally fishing without a license should have proof of their age (drivers license, student I.D., etc.) in their possession.

No trout stamp is required to fish for trout from July 1 until the first Saturday of April each year. All other trout fishing regulations are in effect year round.

Resident

Fish ponds & non-tidal stream, $4.20; trout stream, $2.10.

Non-resident

Fish pond & non-tidal stream, $9.50; trout stream, $5.25; 7-day fishing license, $3.20.

For more information contact:

Department of National Resources and Environmental Control
Division of Fish & Wildlife
Dover, DE 19901
(302) 678-4431

CAMPGROUNDS

Private

Dagsboro

JIM'S HIDE-A-WAY
R.D. 2, Box 157A
Dagsboro, DE 19939
(302) 539-6095
LOCATION: 1 mi. north of Route 26 on Route 347.
FACILITIES: Open year round; 140 sites; water and bathroom facilities; sanitary station; electrical hookup; trailer village vehicle sites; picnic area; tent camping.

TUCKAHOE ACRES CAMPING RESORT
Dagsboro, DE 19939
(302) 539-9841 or 732-6457
LOCATION: On Indian River Bay.
FACILITIES: Open year round; 480 sites; water and bathroom facilities; sanitary station; electrical hookup; trailer village vehicle sites; food service; boating; fishing; tent camping.

Georgetown

HOMESTEAD CAMPSITES
R.F.D. 4, Box 205
Georgetown, DE 19947
(302) 684-4278
LOCATION: On Road 254, 6 mi. east of Georgetown.
FACILITIES: Open year round; 86 sites; water and bathroom facilities; sanitary station; electrical hookup; trailer village vehicle sites; food service; boating; fishing.

Glasgow

NORTH DEL A-OK CAMPGROUND
Box 275
Bear, DE 19701
(302) 834-7100
LOCATION: 2½ mi. east of Del 896 at Glasgow on U.S. 40 & U.S. 301 north.
FACILITIES: Open year round; 300 sites; water and bathroom facilities; electrical hookup; trailer village vehicle sites; food service; swimming pool; boating; fishing; hiking; horseback riding; tent camping.

Greenwood

WOODENHAWK CAMPGROUND
R.D. 2, Box 189C
Greenwood, DE 19950
(302) 349-4967
LOCATION: Rt. 404 west 7 mi. from Bridgeville, then north on Rt. 571 for 2 mi.
FACILITIES: Open year round; 200 sites; water and bathroom facilities; sanitary station; electrical hookup; trailer village vehicle sites; fishing; tent camping.

Harrington

CALLOWAY'S HITCHING RAIL CAMPGROUND
R.D. 1, Box 167
Harrington, DE 19952
(302) 422-4094
LOCATION: 5 mi. east of Harrington on Rt.

DELAWARE

CAMPGROUNDS (continued)

14 to Route 398; turn left 1½ mi., or turn west on Route 14 at Milford 3 mi. to Route 398, then turn right 1½ mi.
FACILITIES: Open year round; 165 sites; water and bathroom facilities; sanitary station; electrical hookup; trailer village vehicle sites; picnic area; boating; fishing; tent camping.

Laurel

LOWE'S LAKE VIEW RECREATION AREA
R.D. 1, Box 266
Laurel, DE 19956
(302) 875-3067
LOCATION: Off U.S. 13 at Laurel, east on Rt. 24, 1 mi. to sign.
FACILITIES: Open year round; 150 sites; water and bathroom facilities; sanitary station; electrical hookup; trailer village vehicle sites; picnic area; swimming; boating; tent camping.

Lewes

LOG CABIN HILL CAMPING AREA
R.D. 1, Box 221
Lewes, DE 19958
(302) 684-8934
LOCATION: 3 mi. west of Rt. 1.
FACILITIES: Open year round; 250 sites; water and bathroom facilities; sanitary station; electrical hookup; trailer village vehicle sites; food service; tent camping.

STEAMBOAT LANDING
P.O. Box 300
Lewes, DE 19958
(302) 645-6500
LOCATION: 1 mi. east of Lewes on Rt. 258 off Rts. 1 & 14.
FACILITIES: Open year round; 300 sites; water and bathroom facilities; sanitary station; electrical hookup; trailer village vehicle sites; fishing; tent camping.

Milford

PINE HAVEN CAMP SITE
R.D. 1, Box 122A
Milford, DE 19963
(302) 422-7117
LOCATION: 5 mi. south of Milford on Rts. 1 & 14 just west of Argo's Corner.
FACILITIES: Open year round; 110 sites; water and bathroom facilities; electrical hookup; trailer village vehicle sites; picnic area; food service; fishing.

Millsboro

HOLLY LAKE CAMPSITE
R.D. 1, Box 326A
Millsboro, DE 19966
(302) 945-3410
LOCATION: 4 mi. south of Route 1 on north side of Route 24.
FACILITIES: Open year round; 900 sites; water and bathroom facilities; sanitary station; electrical hookup; trailer village vehicle sites; picnic area; food service; boating; tent camping.

LEISURE POINT CAMPGROUND
R.D. 1, Box 306B

Millsboro, DE 19966
(302) 945-2000
LOCATION: Between Millsboro and Rehoboth Beach, just 1½ mi. off Rt. 24 on Rt. 22.
FACILITIES: Open year round; 400 sites; water and bathroom facilities; sanitary station; electrical hookup; trailer village vehicle sites; boating; fishing.

Ocean View

BAY SHORES CAMP SITES
Ocean View, DE 19970
(302) 539-7200
LOCATION: 2 mi. north of Rt. 26 on Central Avenue.
FACILITIES: Open year round; 300 sites; water and bathroom facilities; sanitary station; electrical hookup; trailer village vehicle sites; food service; boating; fishing.

PINE TREE CAMPSITES
Ocean View, DE 19970
(302) 539-7006
LOCATION: Rt. 14 south, turn right on Cedar Neck (Rd. 360) 1½ mi. north of Rt. 26 on Central Avenue.
FACILITIES: Open year round; 115 sites; water and bathroom facilities; sanitary station; electrical hookup; trailer village vehicle sites; picnic area; food service; swimming; tent camping.

SANDY COVE
Rt. 1, Box 118
Ocean View, DE 19970
(302) 539-6245
LOCATION: 2 mi. north of Rt. 26 on Central Avenue.
FACILITIES: Open year round; 160 sites; water and bathroom facilities; sanitary station; electrical hookup; trailer village vehicle sites; picnic area; food service; boating; fishing; tent camping.

Rehoboth Beach

BIG OAKS FAMILY CAMPGROUNDS
P.O. Box 342
Rehoboth Beach, DE 19971
(302) 645-6838
LOCATION: ¼ mi. east of the intersection of Rt. 1.
FACILITIES: Open year round; 400 sites; water and bathroom facilities; sanitary station; electrical hookup; trailer village vehicle sites; picnic area; food service; swimming; boating.

SHAWN'S HIDEAWAY
P.O. Box 302
Rehoboth Beach, DE 19971
(302) 945-3133
LOCATION: From Rt. 14 west on Rt. 24 7½ mi. to 298.
FACILITIES: Open year round; 93 sites; water and bathroom facilities; sanitary station; electrical hookup; trailer village vehicle sites; picnic area; food service; swimming; boating; tent camping.

THREE SEASON CAMPING RESORT
P.O. Box 156
Rehoboth Beach, DE 19971
(302) 227-2564
LOCATION: 1½ mi. west on County Road

CAMPGROUNDS (continued)

273, off Routes 1 & 14.
FACILITIES: Open year round; 150 sites; water and bathroom facilities; sanitary station; electrical hookup; trailer village vehicle sites; swimming; boating; fishing; tent camping.

Selbyville

TREASURE BEACH CAMPGROUND & TRAVEL TRAILER PARK
Selbyville, DE 19975
(302) 436-8001
LOCATION: Fenwick Island on Route 54.
FACILITIES: Open year round; 613 sites; water and bathroom facilities; sanitary station; electrical hookup; trailer village vehicle sites; food service; swimming; boating; fishing.

RESORTS & BEACHES

Rehoboth Beach

REHOBOTH BEACH - Stroll the boardwalk or the miles of uncrowded beaches. Swim in the sunny surf or lounge around the pool. Then sample the distinctive fare at the dozens of fine restaurants and nightclubs. There's bicycling, horseback riding along the shore, sailing, saltwater fishing and clam digging.

BOATING AREAS

See State Parks.

BICYCLE TRAILS

FLATLANDS TRAIL - 47.4 mi.; any bicycle.
   A tour to suit almost any cyclist, between the Chesapeake Bay and the Delaware River, using only low-use country roads.
   Trail: Bohemia Manor School, Chesapeake City, to Route 286 east, left on Route 433 to Summit Bridge, right on Route 412, right on Route 414, left on Route 15, becomes 420, left on Route 2, right on Route 417, right on Route 9, right on Route 423, left on Route 9 (County 424), to Odessa, to Armstrong, left on Route 435, right on Route 437, right on St. Augustine Road, left on Route 310, to St. Augustine, right on Route 342, to Chesapeake City Bridge to Route 213 south to Bohemia Manor School.

TRAILS

There are no National Trails System Foot Trails in Delaware.

SKI AREAS

There are no organized Ski Areas in Delaware.

AMUSEMENT PARKS & ATTRACTIONS

Rehoboth Beach

SEASIDE AMUSEMENTS (FUNLAND)
Delaware Ave. & Boardwalk
Rehoboth Beach, DE 19971
(302) 227-2785
FACILITIES: 4 major rides; 8 kiddie rides; shooting gallery; refreshment stand; 4 games; arcade; free gate; open May 6 - Sept. 10.

Winterthur

THE HENRY FRANCIS du PONT WINTERTHUR MUSEUM (Attraction)
Winterthur, DE 19735
(302) 656-8591
FACILITIES: 2 walk-thrus; restaurant; museum; free parking.

STATE FAIR

Delaware State Fair
P.O. Box 28
Harrington, DE 19952
(302) 398-3269
DATE: July

NATIONAL PARKS

There are no National Parks in Delaware.

NATIONAL FORESTS

There are no National Forests in Delaware.

STATE PARKS

Headquarters

Department of Natural Resources & Environmental Control
Edward Tatnall Bldg.
Dover, DE 19901
(302) 687-4506

Delaware City

FORT DELAWARE STATE PARK
Pea Patch Island
Delaware City, DE 19706
LOCATION: On Pea Patch Island.
FACILITIES: Open Apr. 15 - Oct. 15; water and bathroom facilities; picnic area; museum; environmental study area.

Felton

KILLENS POND STATE PARK
Rt. 1
Box 198A
Felton, DE 19943
LOCATION: South of Felton.
FACILITIES: Open year round; water and bathroom facilities; swimming; boating; fish-

DELAWARE

STATE PARKS (continued)

ing; environmental study area; primitive tent camping.

Kirkwood

LUMS POND STATE PARK
Route 71
Kirkwood, DE 19708
LOCATION: Route 896 along Route 71 near Kirkwood.
FACILITIES: Open year round; 72 sites; water and bathroom facilities; sanitary station; electrical hookup; trailer village vehicle sites; picnic area; swimming; boating; boat rental; fishing; hiking; tent camping.

Laurel

TRAP POND STATE PARK
Box 331
Route 2
Laurel, DE 19956
LOCATION: East of Laurel on Route 24.
FACILITIES: Open Apr. - Oct.; 140 sites; water and bathroom facilities; sanitary station; electrical hookup; trailer village vehicle sites; picnic area; swimming; boating; boat rental; fishing; tent camping.

Lewes

CAPE HENLOPEN STATE PARK
Lewes, DE 19958
LOCATION: North of Lewes off Route 1 on Atlantic Ocean.
FACILITIES: Open Apr. 1 - Oct. 31; 162 sites; water and bathroom facilities; sanitary station; electrical hookup; trailer village vehicle sites; picnic area; swimming; boating; fishing; bicycle trail; tent camping.

Millville

HOLTS LANDING STATE PARK
P.O. Box 76
Millville, DE 19967
LOCATION: North of Millville, off Route 26.
FACILITIES: Open year round; water and bathroom facilities; picnic area; swimming; boating.

Newark

WALTER S. CARPENTER, JR. STATE PARK
Route 896
Newark, DE 19711
LOCATION: North of Newark on Route 896.
FACILITIES: Open year round; picnic area; hiking; environmental study area; primitive tent camping.

Rehoboth Beach

DELAWARE SEASHORE STATE PARK
P.O. Box 850
Route 2
Rehoboth Beach, DE 19971
LOCATION: North of Fenwick Island.
FACILITIES: Open year round; 299 sites; water and bathroom facilities; sanitary station; electrical hookup; trailer village vehicle sites;

picnic area; food service; boating; boat rental; fishing; tent camping.

Wilmington

BRANDYWINE CREEK STATE PARK
P.O. Box 3782
Wilmington, DE 19702
LOCATION: Off Concord Pike at junction of Routes 100 & 92.
FACILITIES: Open year round; water and bathroom facilities; picnic area; fishing; environmental study area.

STATE FORESTS

Headquarters

Department of Agriculture
Forestry Section
Drawer D
Dover, DE 19901
(302) 678-4820

Redden

REDDEN STATE FOREST
LOCATION: Near Georgetown.
FACILITIES: Open year round; picnic area; hunting.

Smyrna

BLACKBIRD STATE FOREST
LOCATION: North of Smyrna.
FACILITIES: Open year round; hunting; primitive tent camping.

HISTORIC SITES

Dover

THE JOHN DICKINSON MANSION - The boyhood home of one of Delaware's foremost Revolutionary patriots. John Dickinson is often called "the Penman of the Revolution." Located on Kills Hummock Road.

THE OLD STATE HOUSE - Figured in many episodes from Delaware history. Built in 1772 as the Kent County Court House. Located on Court Street.

Frederica

BARRATT'S CHAPEL - The Methodist Church in America was organized here in 1784. Located on Route 113 near Frederica.

Lewes

THE DOCTOR'S OFFICE - Museum showing a doctor's office at the turn of the century. Located on Market and Front Street.

THE ZWAANENDAEL MUSEUM - A replica of the ancient Town Hall in Hoorn, Holland, was erected by the State of Delaware in 1931 to commemorate the 300th anniversary of the founding of the first Dutch settlement on Delaware soil. Located on Kings Highway and Savannah Road.

HISTORIC SITES (continued)

New Castle

OLD DUTCH HOUSE MUSEUM - The only complete house dating to the Dutch colonial period built before 1700. Located on Third Street.

THE OLD COURT HOUSE - Delaware's colonial capitol and meeting place of the State Assembly until 1777. Located on "The Green" in New Castle.

WELSH TRACT BAPTIST CHURCH - It is the oldest Baptist Church still in use in the United States. Located on Welsh Tract Road.

South Bowers

ISLAND FIELD MUSEUM - Man has lived on Milford Neck for ten thousand years. An archaeological study collection and a library on regional prehistory are housed at the museum. Located on Route 19.

Wilmington

OLD SWEDES CHURCH - The oldest Protestant church in the United States standing as originally built. Located at 606 Church Street.

HOSTELS

There are no Hostels in Delaware.

POINTS OF INTEREST

Dover

DELAWARE STATE MUSEUM - An extensive collection of exhibits and memorabilia tracing the history of Delaware from the landing of the Dutch in 1631 to the moon walk of Neil Armstrong is on display here. A little known fact is that the space suits were made right here in Dover. Located on Governors Avenue & North Street.

DOVER AIR FORCE BASE - Dover is the home of the world's largest cargo-transport plane, the C-5 Galaxy. Located 5 mi. south of Dover.

Seaford

WOODLAND FERRY - Has been in existence for about 200 years. One of the last cable-drawn ferries still running in the country. Located at Nanticoke River about 4 mi. southwest of Seaford.

Wilmington

THE HAGLEY MUSEUM - A 19th-century historic indoor-outdoor complex on the site of the original Du Pont black powder works. Located 3 mi. north of Wilmington via Routes 52 and 141.

ROCKWOOD MANOR - A country estate in the true 19th-century sense; is Delaware's finest surviving example of Rural Gothic architecture and the Gardenesque school of landscape design. Located on Shipley Road off Route 95.

Winterthur

THE HENRY FRANCIS DU PONT WINTERTHUR MUSEUM AND GARDENS - The Winterthur contains an incomparable collection of decorative arts made or used in America from 1640 to 1840. Located off Route 52.

DISTRICT OF COLUMBIA

The location of the nation's capital was a compromise. New Englanders wanted the city situated in New England; Southerners demanded a Dixie capital. George Washington came up with the solution: build the capital half-way between New England and Georgia. He selected the exact site and asked Maryland and Virginia to give up a portion of their land.

In 1791, Pierre Charles L'Enfant was assigned the job of designing the city and became America's first city planner.

Washington was not considered a pleasant place to live prior to the Civil War. Depending on the season, the capital was either muddy or dusty. Ambassadors who resided there drew hardship pay from their governments.

The Federal government is the city's major industry, augumented by tourism and most recently, research and development companies.

⮞ SPECIAL NOTE ⮜

Most of the activities in the city of Washington, a District approximately 69 square miles in area, are centered around sightseeing. The following categories will not be found in the District of Columbia: Highway Welcoming Centers, State Police, Hunting & Fishing, Campgrounds, Resorts & Beaches, Boating Areas, Ski Areas, State Fair, National Parks, National Forests, State Parks, and State Forests.

DISTRICT OF COLUMBIA

WEATHER

See Maryland Weather.

DISTRICT CHAMBER OF COMMERCE

The Metropolitan Washington Board of Trade
1129-20th Street, NW
Washington, DC 20036
(202) 857-5900

DISTRICT TOURISM OFFICES

Public Citizen Visitors Center
1200 15th Street, NW
Washington, DC 20005
(202) 659-9053

Washington Area Convention & Visitor's
Bureau
1129 20th Street, SW
Washington, DC 20036
(202) 857-5500

DISTRICT HIGHWAY DEPARTMENT

Department of Transportation
Presidential Building
415 12th Street, NW
Washington, DC 20004
(202) 628-6000

BICYCLE TRAILS

COLLEGE PARK TRAIL - 8 mi.; any bicycle.
A good suburban cycling route connecting the University of Maryland with downtown Washington.
Trail: Rock Creek Park, north on West Beach Drive, right, then left onto East Beach Drive, right onto North Portal, to Colesville Road, right onto Ellsworth, right on Dixon, left on Wayne, right on Sligo Creek Parkway, left on New Hampshire Avenue, right on Erskine, right on Riggs, left on Chapman, left on Stanford, left onto Adelphi, right onto Campus Drive and bicycle trail into University of Maryland.

CROSS- ALEXANDRIA TRAIL - 6.3 mi.; any bicycle.
This trail crosses Alexandria east to west from the waterfront at Pendleton and Union Streets to the William Ramsey School on Holmes Run Parkway.
Trail: Pendleton Street, right on West Street for one-half block, left on Braddock Road for about four mi., straight along the bicycle path past the Tyler School, left onto Dawes Avenue, left on N. Stevens Street, right on Fillmore Avenue, left on N. Chambliss Street, and left on Holmes Run Parkway to the William Ramsey School.

FORT CIRCLE AND EAST CAPITOL STREET TRAIL - 10 mi.; steep hills, hairpin turns, gravel surfaces; 10-speed bicycle recommended.
The Fort Circle Trail is an interesting tour of old fort sites.
Trail: Fort Stanton to Fort Davis to Fort Chaplin, left on Benning Road to Dix Street to Benning Road to Oklahoma Avenue, right on A Street, left on 19th Street, right on East Capitol Street to Lincoln Square to Capitol Hill.

FOUR MILE RUN TRAIL - 7.2 mi.; irregular surfaces; any bicycle.
This trail travels through attractive woods for most of its length, but is not well marked. The trail is identified at road and parking lot crossings by green gates.
Water crossings in Glen Carlyn, provided with concrete fords, limit the effective use of the trail to periods of low flow and make for continuously wet crossings. There are also confusing spur trails, particularly in this area.
Trail: I-95 and Gunston Road, right on Gunston, right on South Quincy, left on Arlington Mill to Falls Church.

ROCK CREEK TRAIL - 11 mi.; one creek ford, some traffic; any bicycle.
A major corridor through the Washington Metropolitan Area.
Trail: Lincoln Memorial to Rock Creek Parkway North, cross Rock Creek, Pennsylvania Avenue, Rock Creek twice, Calvert Street to National Zoo, and Rock Creek below Klingle Road Bridge, bear left off bike path to Beach Drive. Arrive at East-West Highway.

WHEATON REGIONAL PARK TRAIL - 15 mi.; any bicycle.
A good cycling corridor from DC to Wheaton Regional Park.
Trail: Lincoln Memorial, north to Rock Creek Bike Path, left on Beach Drive, right on West Beach Drive, left on Primrose which becomes Grubb Road, right on Washington Avenue, cross East-West Highway, road becomes Sundale Drive, right onto 4th Avenue, left on Grace Church Road, follow Dale Drive to right, left on Crosby Road to end, left on Sligo Creek Bike Path north, left on Francewell Avenue, right on Nairn Road to Wheaton Regional Park.

TRAILS

FORT CIRCLE PARKS TRAIL - 19.5 mi. foot trail. The trail now consists of several segments in and around a number of units of the National Capital Parks system. Portions have been constructed in Rock Creek Park, Fort Dupont Park and Anacostia Park. Some 23 miles of designated National Recreation Trail, in non-continuous segments, loosely join fourteen forts and batteries which protected the Capital during the Civil War. In addition to

TRAILS (continued)

those historic sites, from which it takes its name, the trail traverses stream valleys, flood plains, pine woods, and upland forests as well as landscaped areas. Connections to other trails, walks, and roads to Mount Vernon, Arlington National Cemetery, Haines Point, the C & O Canal, and other sites of great beauty and historic significance in and near the Capital City.

AMUSEMENT PARKS & ATTRACTIONS

NATIONAL HISTORICAL WAX MUSEUM (Attraction)
333 E. Street, SW
Washington, DC 20024
(202) 488-5588
FACILITIES: Wax museum of historical figures.

HISTORIC SITES

ARLINGTON HOUSE - Home of Robert E. Lee. Open daily, Oct. - Mar., 9:30 a.m. - 4:30 p.m.; Apr. - Sept., 9:30 a.m. - 6 p.m. (703) 557-3153. Located at Arlington National Cemetery, Arlington, VA.

ARLINGTON NATIONAL CEMETERY - The Tomb of the Unknown Soldier, Amphitheater, Arlington House, graves of John F. Kennedy and William Howard Taft. Changing of the guard at the Tomb of the Unknown Soldier every hour; during summer every ½ hour. Open daily, Oct. - Mar., 8 a.m. - 5 p.m.; Apr. - Sept., 8 a.m. - 7 p.m. (202) 692-0931. Located in Arlington, VA.

DECATUR HOUSE - Commodore Stephen Decatur's town house, erected in 1818, has played a colorful role in Washington history for more than 150 years. Open weekdays, 10 a.m. - 2 p.m.; Sat. & Sun., 12 noon - 4 p.m. (202) 638-1204. Located at 748 Jackson Place, NW.

FREDERICK DOUGLAS HOME - Restored home of educator-diplomat. Open Mon. - Sat., 9 a.m. - 4 p.m.; Sun., 10 a.m. - 5 p.m. (202) 889-1736. Located at 1411 W Street, SE.

FORD'S THEATRE & LINCOLN MUSEUM - Site of Abraham Lincoln's assassination in 1865 by John Wilkes Booth. Open daily, 9 a.m. - 5 p.m. Free except for theatre performances. (202) 347-6360. Located at 511 10th Street, NW.

JEFFERSON MEMORIAL - Reflects the classic style the third President, Thomas Jefferson, used in designing the rotunda of the University of Virginia and his home, Monticello. In the center of the circular memorial rooms stands the 19-foot Rudolph Evans statue of

DISTRICT OF COLUMBIA

the man who drafted the Declaration of Independence. Open daily, 24 hours a day. (202) 426-6821. Located on South Bank of Tidal Basin.

LINCOLN MEMORIAL - Dedicated on Memorial Day in 1922, the 21-foot statue of the seated Lincoln, the 16th President, is surrounded by 36 marble columns, one for each state in the Union when he died. Fifty-six steps, one for every year of his life, lead up to the inner chamber where his imposing statue stands. Open daily, 8 a.m. to midnight. (202) 426-6895. Located in West Potomac Park, foot of 23rd Street, NW.

MARINE CORPS MEMORIAL (IWO JIMA) - Statue depicts famed flag-raising on Iwo Jima. Located on Route 50 across Arlington Memorial Bridge.

MOUNT VERNON - Home and burial site of George Washington. Open Mar. - Oct., 9 a.m. - 5 p.m.; Nov. - Feb., 9 a.m. - 4 p.m. (703) 780-2000. Located in Mount Vernon, VA.

NATIONAL ARCHIVES - Repository of the Declaration of Independence, Constitution, and many other historic documents. Open Mar. - Sept., Mon. - Sat., 9 a.m. - 10 p.m., Sun., 1 - 6 p.m.; Oct. - Mar., daily till 6 p.m. (202) 523-3216. Located at 7th Street & Constitution Avenue, NW.

PETERSEN HOUSE - House where Lincoln died after being shot by John Wilkes Booth. Open daily, 9 a.m. - 5 p.m. (202) 426-6830. Located at 516 10th Street, NW, across from Ford's Theatre.

WASHINGTON MONUMENT - Tallest masonry structure in the world, 555 feet, and visible from most sections of the city. Open daily, Mar. 20 - Labor Day, 8 a.m. - midnight; Labor Day - Mar. 19, 9 a.m. - 5 p.m. (202) 426-6839. Located on the Mall at 15th Street, NW.

HOSTELS

WASHINGTON INTERNATIONAL YOUTH HOSTEL
1332 I Street, NW
Washington, DC 20005
(202) 347-3125; 387-3169
FACILITIES: Open year round; 200 beds, men; 200 beds, women; modern bathroom; overnight charges: $4.50; houseparents: Herman & Joan Voogel.

POINTS OF INTEREST

ALEXANDRIA - Christ's Church, George Washington Masonic National Memorial, Gadsby's Tavern, Carlyle House. Metrobus coaches leave 12th & Pennsylvania Avenue, NW every 10 minutes. Located 8 mi. south of Washington over the beautiful George Washington Memorial Parkway.

BOTANIC GARDENS - Exotic tropical gar-

DISTRICT OF COLUMBIA

POINTS OF INTEREST (continued)

den, waterfall. Open May - Sept., 9 a.m. - 6 p.m.; mid-Sept. - Apr., 9 a.m. - 5 p.m. (202) 225-8333. Located at 1st Street & Maryland Avenue, SW.

BUREAU OF ENGRAVING AND PRINTING - See money and stamps made. Open Mon. - Fri., 8 - 11:30 a.m. and 12:30 - 2 p.m. (202) 447-9709. Located at 14th & C Streets, SW.

THE CAPITOL - Classic Roman design building contains the Senate and House of Representatives. Open daily, 9 a.m. - 4:30 p.m. Tours, 9 a.m. - 3:45 p.m. (202) 224-3121. Located on Capitol Hill.

CHERRY BLOSSOM TIME - Mar. - Apr. The blossoming of the cherry trees marks the beginning of the tourist season in the nation's capital.

CONSTITUTION GARDENS - New 42-acre park features 6-acre lake, food facilities, gardens, amphitheatres and information center. Located near Constitution Avenue & 17th Street, NW.

CORCORAN GALLERY OF ART - Privately-owned museum. Open Tues. - Sun., 11 a.m. - 5 p.m. (202) 638-3211. Located at 17th Street and New York Avenue, NW.

DUMBARTON OAKS - Formal gardens open daily, 2 - 4:45 p.m.; museum open daily, except Mon. & holidays, 2 - 4:45 p.m. Both closed July 1 - Labor Day. (202) 232-3101. Located at 1703 32nd Street, NW.

EXPLORERS HALL, NATIONAL GEOGRAPHIC SOCIETY - Displays depict archaeology, astronomy, adventure and discovery. Open weekdays, 9 a.m. - 6 p.m.; Sat., 9 a.m. - 5 p.m.; Sun., 10 a.m. - 5 p.m. (202) 857-7588. Located at 17th and M Streets, NW.

FEDERAL BUREAU OF INVESTIGATION - An inside look at the nation's leading crime fighting organization. You will see the famous FBI laboratory and demonstrations of the latest crime detection techniques. Open Mon.- Fri., 9 a.m. - 4 p.m. Hour tours every 15 minutes. (202) 324-3447. Located on E Street between 9th and 10th Streets, NW.

FESTIVAL OF AMERICAN FOLKLIFE - Sponsored by Smithsonian Institution usually in the early fall, this outdoor festival spotlights culture from around the country and around the world. (202) 737-8811.

FOLGER (SHAKESPEARE) LIBRARY - An extensive collection of works and research on William Shakespeare. Open daily, 10 a.m. - 4:30 p.m. (202) 546-5370. Located at 201 East Capitol Street, SE.

FOURTH OF JULY CELEBRATION - More fireworks than you've ever seen before. Located at the base of the Washington Monument, July 4.

GEORGETOWN - Old Stone House, oldest standing house in Washington. Also shopping boutiques, restaurants and night clubs located in this old colonial section of Washington. Site of spring Home and Garden tours. Georgetown University, C & O Canal. Located West of Rock Creek Park.

ISLAMIC CENTER - One of the few mosques in the country. Open daily, 9 a.m. - 4 p.m. Friday Congregation Prayers at noon. (202) 332-3451. Located at 2551 Massachusetts Avenue, NW.

JOHN F. KENNEDY CENTER FOR THE PERFORMING ARTS - Contains opera house, concert hall, and Eisenhower Theatre. Latter is home of the American Film Institute which presents classic movies. Free concerts. Open Mon. - Sat., 10 a.m. - 5 p.m. for tours. (202) 254-3600. Located on Rock Creek Parkway at end of New Hampshire Avenue, NW.

THE MARTIN LUTHER KING, JR. MEMORIAL LIBRARY - Main branch of Washington's public library system. Of special interest are the Black Studies Division and the Washingtoniana Collection, a huge compilation of material on the history of the nation's capital. Open Mon. - Thurs., 9 a.m. - 9 p.m.; Fri. - Sat., 9 a.m. - 5:30 p.m. (202) 727-1111. Located at 901 G Street, NW.

LIBRARY OF CONGRESS - The world's largest library. Open Mon. - Fri., 8:30 a.m. - 9:30 p.m.; Sat., Sun. & holidays, 8:30 a.m. - 6 p.m. Tours available Mon. - Fri., 9 a.m. - 4 p.m. on the hour. (202) 426-5000. Located at 10 First Street, SE.

MUSEUM OF AFRICAN ART - Open Mon. - Fri., 11 a.m. - 5 p.m.; weekends, 12 noon - 5 p.m. (202) 547-7424. Located at 316 A Street, NE.

NATIONAL AQUARIUM - Over 2000 specimens of freshwater and marine animals, representing almost 3000 species. Displayed in 68 aquariums: sharks, octopus, exotic tropical fish and rare endangered species. Open daily, 9 a.m. - 5 p.m. (202) 377-2825. Located in basement of Dept. of Commerce, 14th and Constitution Avenue, NW.

NATIONAL ARBORETUM - 415 acres of flowering trees and shrubs. Open Apr. - Oct., Mon. - Fri., 8 a.m. - 7 p.m., Sat. & Sun., 10 a.m. - 7 p.m.; Nov. - Mar., Mon. - Fri., 8 a.m. - 5 p.m., Sat. & Sun., 10 a.m. - 5 p.m. (202) 399-5400. Located at 24th & R Streets, NE.

NATIONAL GALLERY OF ART - Only American gallery to own a Leonardo da Vinci. Open daily, 10 a.m. - 5:30 p.m.; Sun., 12 noon - 9 p.m.; Apr. 1 - Sept. 6, until 9 p.m.; Sept. - June, Sun. concerts, 7 p.m., in the East Garden Court. (202) 737-4215. Located at 6th Street & Constitution Avenue, NW.

NATIONAL PAGEANT OF PEACE - The President lights the National Christmas Tree, usually about Dec. 15. Carols and music nightly until the New Year.

NATIONAL SHRINE OF THE IMMACU-

POINTS OF INTEREST (continued)

LATE CONCEPTION - Largest Catholic church in the United States. Call for Mass times. Open daily, 7 a.m. - 8 p.m. (202) 526-8300. Located at 4th & Michigan Avenue, NE.

NATIONAL ZOOLOGICAL PARK - More than 2,000 animals: many rare and unusual. Panda bears from China are perhaps the most renowned. Grounds open daily, 6 a.m. - 8 p.m.; buildings open daily, 9 a.m. - 6:30 p.m. (202) 232-7703. Located at 3001 Connecticut Avenue, NW.

THE OCTAGON - Historical, architectural exhibits. Open Tue. - Sat., 10 a.m. - 4 p.m.; Sun., 1 - 4 p.m. (202) 638-3105. Located at 18th & New York Avenue, NW.

ORGANIZATION OF AMERICAN STATES - Formerly Pan American Union, features tropical courtyard gardens, Hall of Americas, Gallery of Heroes. Open Mon. - Fri., 9 a.m. - 4 p.m. (202) 331-1010. Located at 17th & Constitution Avenue, NW.

PHILLIPS COLLECTION - Modern art collection. Open Tue. - Sat., 10 a.m. - 5 p.m.; Sun., 2 - 7 p.m. (202) 387-2151. Located at 1600-1612 21st Street, NW.

PRESIDENTIAL INAUGURATION - January 20th every four years. See the inauguration of the President at noon at the Capitol building and Washington's greatest parade immediately following. This is the nation's most important quadrennial celebration.

PRESIDENT'S CUP REGATTA - World-famed unlimited hydroplane powerboats compete for Presidential awards usually in early June on the Potomac River.

SMITHSONIAN INSTITUTION GROUP - The Smithsonian was founded in 1846, at the bequest of James Smithson who left his entire fortune of $550,000 to the people of the United States to build in Washington "an establishment for the increase and diffusion of knowledge among men." Today there are ten separate branches to the Smithsonian. All listed here are open daily, 10 a.m. - 5:30 p.m.; summer months, 10 a.m. - 9 p.m. (202) 737-8811.

   AIR AND SPACE MUSEUM - 7th Street & Independence Avenue, SW.

   ART AND INDUSTRIES BUILDING - 9th Street & Jefferson Drive, SW.

   FREER GALLERY OF ART - 12th Street & Jefferson Drive, SW.

   HIRSHHORN MUSEUM AND SCULPTURE GARDEN - 7th Street & Independence Avenue, SW.

   MUSEUM OF HISTORY AND TECHNOLOGY - 14th Street & Constitution Avenue, NW.

   MUSEUM OF NATURAL HISTORY - 10th Street & Constitution Avenue, NW.

DISTRICT OF COLUMBIA

NATIONAL COLLECTION OF FINE ARTS - 8th & G Streets, NW.

NATIONAL PORTRAIT GALLERY - 8th & F Streets, NW.

RENWICK GALLERY - 7th Street & Pennsylvania Avenue, NW.

SMITHSONIAN BUILDING - Administration. 10th Street & Jefferson Drive, SW.

SUPREME COURT - Building that houses the highest court in the land is constructed of white marble in classic Corinthian design. Courtroom presentations (tour and examination) can be seen when the Court is not in session (usually Jul. - Sept.), from 9:30 a.m. - 4 p.m. Building open Mon. - Fri., 9 a.m. - 4:30 p.m. (202) 252-3000. Located at 1st Street & Maryland Avenue, NE.

TREASURY DEPARTMENT - Displays of money, both real and counterfeit; also sales of uncirculated coins. Open Tue. - Sat., 9:30 a.m. - 3:30 p.m. (202) 566-5221. Located at 15th Street & Pennsylvania Avenue, NW.

TRUXTON-DECATUR NAVAL MUSEUM - The history of the U.S. Navy from its inception in 1775 to present day. Open daily, 10:30 a.m. - 4 p.m. (202) 783-2573. Located at 1610 H Street, NW.

U.S. NAVAL MEMORIAL MUSEUM - Depicts history of U.S. Navy. Open Mon. - Fri., 9 a.m. - 4 p.m.; Sat., Sun. & holidays, 10 a.m. - 5 p.m. (202) 433-2651. Located at 9th & M Streets, SE.

U.S. NAVAL OBSERVATORY - The nation's official timekeeper. Open Mon. - Fri., 10 a.m. - 3 p.m. (202) 254-4533. Located at 34th Street & Massachusetts Avenue, NW.

VOICE OF AMERICA - Division which spreads American ideas and ideals around the world. Tours Mon. - Fri., 9 a.m. - 4 p.m. except 12 noon. (202) 755-4744. Located at 330 Independence Avenue, SW.

WASHINGTON CATHEDRAL - Probably the last great Gothic cathedral to be built (still under construction). Conducted tours Mon. - Sat., 10 a.m. - 3:15 p.m.; Sun., 12:15 p.m., 1:30 p.m. and 2:30 p.m. (202) 966-3500. Located on Wisconsin & Massachusetts Avenues, NW.

WHITE HOUSE - The mansion which took 8 years to build was completed in 1800, one year after the death of George Washington. Every President but Washington, for whom the city was named, has lived and worked there. Open Tue. - Sat., 10 a.m. - 12 noon, closed some holidays. (202) 456-1414. Located at 1600 Pennsylvania Avenue, NW.

WOLF TRAP FARM PARK FOR THE PERFORMING ARTS - First National Park for the performing arts: Opera, symphonic music, pop concerts and ballet. Open during warm weather only. (703) 938-3800. Located on Route 7 near Vienna, VA. Accessible (for program performances only) via Dulles Airport access highway.

FLORIDA

The Sunshine State was admitted to the Union as the twenty-seventh state in 1845, seceded in 1861 and was readmitted seven years later. Prior to Florida's Civil War involvement, the white settlers were engaged in a bitter struggle with the Seminole Indians.

In the early 1840s, following many years of fighting, the Indians were forced to surrender or retreat into the Everglades. Many chose the latter rather than be relocated on reservations in the state or in Oklahoma.

Today, the fishing industry and agriculture, specifically oranges, provide a sizeable portion of the state's revenues. However, dollars earned from tourism far outstrip both industries combined. Nearly constant sunshine, pleasant sea breezes and abundant fresh and saltwater fishing and sports activities make the state an irresistable vacationland.

Now, interestingly enough, there is a balance of tourist trade throughout the year. Just a few years ago, Florida was still thought of strictly as a "Winter Vacation" resort for the wealthy. The development of major attractions such as Disney World in Orlando, and Busch Gardens in Tampa, helped to extend and broaden the tourism market in the state.

State capital: Tallahassee. State bird: Mockingbird. State tree: Sabal palm. State flower: Orange blossom.

WEATHER

Florida is largely a lowland peninsula comprising about 54,100 square miles of land area, and is surrounded on three sides by the waters of the Atlantic Ocean and the Gulf of Mexico. No point in the state is more than 70 miles from salt water, and the highest natural land in the Northwest Division is only 345 feet above sea level.

General climatic conditions range from a zone of transition between temperate and subtropical conditions in the northern interior portion of the state to the tropical conditions found on the Florida Keys.

Summers throughout the state are long, warm, and relatively humid; winters, although punctuated with periodic invasions of cool to occasionally cold air from the north, are mild because of the southern latitude and relatively warm adjacent ocean waters. Summertime mean temperatures are about the same throughout the state, 81 degrees to 82 degrees; during the coolest months, temperatures average about 13 degrees lower in northern than in southern Florida. July and August temperature averages are the warmest in all areas, and December and January temperature averages are the coolest in the northern and central portions of the state. January and February, on the average, are the coolest months in the extreme south and on the Keys.

Average daily temperature for each month.

	Northern	Southern
Jan.	63.7 to 42.0	76.9 to 53.7
Feb.	67.2 to 44.2	77.6 to 54.1
Mar.	73.1 to 49.3	81.2 to 57.3
Apr.	81.4 to 56.7	84.3 to 61.6
May	87.9 to 63.1	87.1 to 65.6
Jun.	91.2 to 68.8	88.7 to 69.7
Jul.	91.9 to 70.8	90.2 to 71.0
Aug.	91.8 to 70.6	90.9 to 71.4
Sept.	88.2 to 67.7	89.3 to 71.4
Oct.	80.8 to 58.0	85.6 to 67.3
Nov.	71.4 to 48.2	81.2 to 59.9
Dec.	65.5 to 43.4	77.6 to 54.6
Year	79.5 to 56.9	84.2 to 63.1

STATE CHAMBER OF COMMERCE

Florida Chamber of Commerce
P.O. Box 5497
Tallahassee, FL 32301
(907) 222-2831

STATE & CITY TOURISM OFFICES

State

Division of Economic Development
Florida Department of Commerce
107 West Gaines Street
Tallahassee, FL 32304
(904) 488-6300

Division of Tourism
Florida Department of Commerce
107 West Gaines Street
Tallahassee, FL 32304
(904) 487-1462

Local

Convention and Tourism Bureau
Daytona Beach Area Chamber of Commerce
City Island, P.O. Box 2775
Daytona Beach, FL 32015
(904) 255-0981

Jacksonville Convention and Visitor's Bureau
133 W. Monroe Street
Jacksonville, FL 32202
(904) 353-9736

Miami Metro Development of Publicity & Tourism
499 Biscayne Blvd.
Miami, FL 33132
(305) 579-6327

Miami Beach Tourist Development Authority
555 17th Street
Miami Beach, FL 33139
(305) 673-7070

TOURISM OFFICES (continued)

Convention and Visitor's Bureau
Orlando Area Chamber of Commerce
P.O. Box 1913
Orlando, FL 32802
(305) 425-5563 or 423-5527

Tourist Department
Greater Tampa Chamber of Commerce
P.O. Box 420
Tampa, FL 33601
(813) 228-7777

STATE HIGHWAY DEPARTMENT

Florida Department of Transportation
Haydon Burns Building
605 Swannee Street
Tallahassee, FL 32304
(904) 488-8772

HIGHWAY WELCOMING CENTERS

Campbellton

CAMPBELLTON CENTER - U.S. 231, near Alabama border.

Fernandina

FERNANDINA MARINA - Coastal Waterway.

Hilliard

HILLIARD CENTER - Hwy. 301.

Jennings

JENNINGS CENTER - Interstate 75 near Georgia border, north of Lake City.

Pensacola

PENSACOLA CENTER - Interstate 10.

Tallahassee

TALLAHASSEE CENTER - Hwy. 27.

Yulee

YULEE CENTER - Interstate 95.

STATE POLICE

Department of Public Safety
Tallahassee, FL 32301
(904) 488-8676

HUNTING & FISHING

Hunting

All hunters must possess a hunting license, except children under 15 and Florida residents age 65 and older. Residents are those citizens who have resided continuously in the state for 1 year and in a particular county for at least 6 months. Servicemen stationed in Florida are considered residents when purchasing licenses.

Duck stamps are required of anyone 16 years of age and older when taking ducks.

Wildlife Management Area Permits are required for residents under age 65 and all non-residents for hunting on such areas. Underage permits are required of hunters under 15 years of age.

Archery permits are required, in addition to a hunting license, by anyone hunting with a bow and arrow during the general archery season. Exceptions are hunters under 15 and residents age 65 and over.

Resident

Statewide hunting-fishing combination (series AK), $10.50; statewide hunting (series K), $7.50; home county (series I), $2; other than home county (series J), $4.50; Wildlife Management Area Permit (series RS regular), $10; underage (series AB), $2.50; archery season permit, $5; hunting on licensed private hunting preserves: resident or non-resident (series H), $5.50; alien hunting, $50.

Non-resident

Statewide annual (series L), $50.50; statewide, 10-day continuous (series M), $15.50; hunting on licensed private hunting preserves, resident or non-resident (series H), $5.50.

Fishing

All Florida fishermen, except residents 65 years of age and over and children under 15, must possess a fishing license when freshwater fishing. No license shall be required of any resident when fishing in his county of residence with not more than three (3) poles or lines for noncommercial purposes, except in Fish Management Areas.

No fishing license shall be required of military personnel who are Florida residents while they are home on leave for a period of 30 days or less, provided that they shall exhibit a copy of their military leave orders upon request of a wildlife officer.

No license is required for saltwater fishing.

Resident

Statewide annual fishing (series A), $3; fishing-hunting combination (series AK), $10.50.

Non-resident

Annual (series B), $10.50; 14-day continuous (series C), $7.50; 5-day continuous (series D), $5.50.

For more information contact:

Game and Fresh Water Fish Commission
Tallahassee, FL 32403
(904) 488-1960

FLORIDA

CAMPGROUNDS

Private

Apopka

APOPKA-CLARCONA CAMPGROUND
LOCATION: 3½ mi. south of Apopka on Hwy. 435.
FACILITIES: Open year round; 300 sites; water and bathroom facilities; sanitary station; electrical hookup; trailer village vehicle sites; laundry; food service; swimming; fishing.

Bradenton

ARBOR TERRACE PARK
LOCATION: 3 mi. southeast of Bradenton off U.S. 41.
FACILITIES: Open year round; 428 sites; water and bathroom facilities; trailer village vehicle sites; laundry; swimming.

Clearwater

TRAVEL TOWNE RESORT
LOCATION: 5 mi. north of Clearwater on U.S. 19.
FACILITIES: Open year round; 360 sites; water and bathroom facilities; sanitary station; electrical hookup; trailer village vehicle sites; laundry; food service; swimming.

TRAVEL WORLD CAMPGROUND
LOCATION: 8 mi. south of Clearwater on U.S. 19.
FACILITIES: Open year round; 340 sites; laundry; swimming.

Daytona Beach

ORANGE ISLES CAMPGROUND
LOCATION: On Hwy. 5A-S.
FACILITIES: Open year round; 350 sites; water and bathroom facilities; sanitary station; electrical hookup; trailer village vehicle sites; laundry; food service; swimming.

Destin

HOLIDAY INN TRAV-L-PARK
LOCATION: 9 mi. east of Destin.
FACILITIES: Open year round; 300 sites; water and bathroom facilities; sanitary station; electrical hookup; trailer village vehicle sites; laundry; food service; swimming; boating; fishing.

Eustis

EUSTIS RV PARK
LOCATION: 1½ mi. northwest of Eustis on Hwy. 452.
FACILITIES: Open year round; 488 sites; water and bathroom facilities; sanitary station; electrical hookup; trailer village vehicle sites.

Fiesta Key

FIESTA KEY RESORT
LOCATION: In Fiesta Key.
FACILITIES: Open year round; 400 sites; water and bathroom facilities; sanitary station; electrical hookup; trailer village vehicle sites; laundry; food service; swimming; boating; boat rental; fishing.

Ft. Lauderdale

HOLIDAY INN TRAV-L-PARK
LOCATION: Exit 12 off Florida Turnpike.
FACILITIES: Open year round; 372 sites; water and bathroom facilities; sanitary station; electrical hookup; trailer village vehicle sites; laundry; food service; swimming; boating; boat rental; fishing.

Ft. Myers

KOA - FT. MYERS BEACH
LOCATION: 2 mi. north of Ft. Myers on Hwy. 865.
FACILITIES: Open year round; 300 sites; water and bathroom facilities; sanitary station; electrical hookup; trailer village vehicle sites; laundry; food service.

Ft. Pierce

BRYN MAWR CAMP RESORT
LOCATION: 5 mi. north of Ft. Pierce on Hwy. A1A.
FACILITIES: Open year round; 319 sites; water and bathroom facilities; sanitary station; electrical hookup; trailer village vehicle sites; laundry; food service; swimming; boating; boat rental; fishing.

Hollywood

HOLIDAY TOWERS
LOCATION: 3300 Pembrooke Road.
FACILITIES: Open year round; 350 sites; water and bathroom facilities; sanitary station; electrical hookup; trailer village vehicle sites; laundry; swimming.

Homestead

DESOTO TRAVEL PARK
LOCATION: 100 NE 6th Avenue.
FACILITIES: Open year round; 400 sites; water and bathroom facilities; sanitary station; electrical hookup; trailer village vehicle sites; laundry; swimming.

FLORIDA CITY CAMPGROUND
LOCATION: ½ mi. south of Homestead at City Park.
FACILITIES: Open year round; 300 sites; water and bathroom facilities; sanitary station; electrical hookup; trailer village vehicle sites.

GOLDCOASTER PARK
LOCATION: 31 mi. south of Homestead on U.S. 1, then 1 mi. west on Hwy. 27.
FACILITIES: Open year round; 300 sites; water and bathroom facilities; sanitary station; electrical hookup; trailer village vehicle sites; laundry; swimming.

Homosassa Springs

NATURE'S CAMPGROUND
LOCATION: 1½ mi. west of Homosassa Springs.
FACILITIES: Open year round; 400 sites; water and bathroom facilities; sanitary station;

CAMPGROUNDS (continued)

electrical hookup; trailer village vehicle sites; laundry; food service; swimming; boating; boat rental; fishing.

Jacksonville

HANNA PARK CAMPGROUND
LOCATION: Wonderwood Drive.
FACILITIES: Open year round; 300 sites; water and bathroom facilities; sanitary station; electrical hookup; trailer village vehicle sites; laundry; food service; swimming; boating; boat rental; fishing.

Jensen Beach

HOLIDAY OUT AT ST. LUCIE
LOCATION: 2½ mi. east of Jensen Beach on Hwy. A1A.
FACILITIES: Open year round; 536 sites; water and bathroom facilities; sanitary station; electrical hookup; trailer village vehicle sites; food service; swimming; boating; boat rental; fishing.

OUTDOOR RESORTS OF AMERICA AT NETTLES ISLAND
LOCATION: 3½ mi. north of Jensen Beach on Hwy. A1A.
FACILITIES: Open year round; 1585 sites; water and bathroom facilities; sanitary station; electrical hookup; trailer village vehicle sites; laundry; food service; swimming; boating; boat rental; fishing.

Key West

VENTURE OUT AT CUDJOE CAY
LOCATION: 23 mi. east of Key West on U.S. 1.
FACILITIES: Open year round; 655 sites; water and bathroom facilities; sanitary station; electrical hookup; trailer village vehicle sites; laundry; swimming; boating; fishing.

Kissimmee

HOLIDAY INN TRAV-L-PARK
LOCATION: 7 mi. west of Kissimmee on U.S. 192.
FACILITIES: Open year round; 438 sites; water and bathroom facilities; sanitary station; electrical hookup; trailer village vehicle sites; laundry; food service; swimming; fishing.

KOA-SUN INNS CAMPGROUND
LOCATION: 4 mi. west of Kissimmee on U.S. 192.
FACILITIES: Open year round; 645 sites; water and bathroom facilities; sanitary station; electrical hookup; trailer village vehicle sites; laundry; food service; swimming; boating; boat rental; fishing.

Lake Wales

SADDLEBAG LAKE CAMPGROUND
LOCATION: 7 mi. east of Lake Wales on Hwy. 60.
FACILITIES: Open year round; 318 sites; water and bathroom facilities; sanitary station; electrical hookup; trailer village vehicle sites;

laundry; food service; swimming; boating; boat rental; fishing.

Lakeland

SANLAN RANCH CAMPGROUND
LOCATION: 3 mi. south of Lakeland on U.S. 98.
FACILITIES: Open year round; 300 sites; water and bathroom facilities; sanitary station; electrical hookup; trailer village vehicle sites; laundry; food service; swimming; boating; boat rental; fishing.

Leesburg

HOLIDAY INN TRAV-L-PARK
LOCATION: 3 mi. south of Leesburg on U.S. 27, then ½ mi. west on Hwy. 33.
FACILITIES: Open year round; 371 sites; water and bathroom facilities; sanitary station; electrical hookup; trailer village vehicle sites; laundry; food service; swimming; boating; boat rental; fishing.

Long Key

OUTDOOR RESORTS OF AMERICA
LOCATION: In town on U.S. 1.
FACILITIES: Open year round; 418 sites; water and bathroom facilities; sanitary station; electrical hookup; trailer village vehicle sites; laundry; food service; swimming; boating; boat rental; fishing.

Marathon

SUNSHINE KEY TRAV-L-PARK
LOCATION: 8 mi. south of Marathon on U.S. 1.
FACILITIES: Open year round; 400 sites; water and bathroom facilities; sanitary station; electrical hookup; trailer village vehicle sites; laundry; food service; swimming; boating; boat rental; fishing.

Melbourne Beach

OCEAN HOLIDAY RESORT
LOCATION: 4½ mi. south of Melbourne Beach off U.S. 192 on Hwy. A1A.
FACILITIES: Open year round; 576 sites; water and bathroom facilities; sanitary station; electrical hookup; trailer village vehicle sites; laundry; food service; swimming; boating; fishing.

Miami

KOA-MIAMI
LOCATION: 20675 SW 162nd Ave.
FACILITIES: Open year round; water and bathroom facilities; sanitary station; electrical hookup; trailer village vehicle sites; laundry; food service; swimming.

Ocala

LAKE BRYANT CAMP
LOCATION: 17 mi. east of Ocala.
FACILITIES: Open year round; 500 sites; water and bathroom facilities; sanitary station; electrical hookup; trailer village vehicle sites; laundry; swimming; boating; fishing.

FLORIDA

CAMPGROUNDS (continued)

Okeechobee

OKEE-TANTIE CAMPGROUND
LOCATION: 6 mi. south of Okeechobee on Hwy. 78 at Kissimmee River.
FACILITIES: Open year round; 300 sites; water and bathroom facilities; trailer village vehicle sites; food service; swimming; boating; fishing.

Orlando

CAMPTOWN CAMPGROUND
LOCATION: 15 mi. southeast of Orlando at junction of Hwys. 530 & 15.
FACILITIES: Open year round; 350 sites; water and bathroom facilities; sanitary station; electrical hookup; trailer village vehicle sites; laundry; food service; swimming; boating; boat rental; fishing.

GREEN ACRES TRAILER CAMP
LOCATION: 9701 Forest City Road.
FACILITIES: Open year round; 652 sites; water and bathroom facilities; sanitary station; electrical hookup; trailer village vehicle sites; laundry; food service; swimming.

KOA-ORLANDO 27
LOCATION: 20 mi. southwest of Orlando on I-4 to U.S. 192, 9 mi. west to U.S. 27, then north.
FACILITIES: Open year round; 319 sites; water and bathroom facilities; sanitary station; electrical hookup; trailer village vehicle sites; laundry; food service; swimming.

LAKEWOOD EAST CAMPGROUND
LOCATION: Southwest of Orlando on I-4, exit U.S. 192, then 3 mi. east.
FACILITIES: Open year round; 500 sites; water and bathroom facilities; sanitary station; electrical hookup; trailer village vehicle sites; laundry; food service; swimming; boating; boat rental; fishing.

LAKEWOOD SOUTH CAMPGROUND
LOCATION: Southwest of Orlando on I-4 to U.S. 192, west to Hwy. 545, then south 5 mi.
FACILITIES: Open year round; 300 sites; water and bathroom facilities; sanitary station; electrical hookup; trailer village vehicle sites; laundry; food service; swimming.

OUTDOOR RESORTS OF AMERICA AT ORLANDO
LOCATION: 5 mi. west of Disney World on U.S. 192.
FACILITIES: Open year round; 900 sites; water and bathroom facilities; sanitary station; electrical hookup; trailer village vehicle sites; laundry; food service; swimming; boating; boat rental; fishing.

TRAV-TRA PARK CAMPGROUND
LOCATION: 1600 West 33rd Street.
FACILITIES: Open year round; 477 sites; water and bathroom facilities; sanitary station; electrical hookup; trailer village vehicle sites; laundry; food service; swimming; boating; boat rental; fishing.

YOGI BEAR'S JELLYSTONE PARK
LOCATION: 9202 E. Sand Lake Road.
FACILITIES: Open year round; 400 sites; water and bathroom facilities; sanitary station; electrical hookup; trailer village vehicle sites; laundry; food service; swimming; boating; boat rental; fishing.

YOGI BEAR'S JELLYSTONE PARK
LOCATION: 5½ mi. west of I-4 on U.S. 192.
FACILITIES: Open year round; 510 sites; water and bathroom facilities; sanitary station; electrical hookup; trailer village vehicle sites; laundry; food service; swimming; boating; boat rental; fishing.

Palm Harbor

RAMADA CAMP INN
LOCATION: 400 U.S. 19 north.
FACILITIES: Open year round; 400 sites; water and bathroom facilities; sanitary station; electrical hookup; trailer village vehicle sites; laundry; food service; swimming; boating; boat rental; fishing.

Panama City Beach

VENTURE OUT AT PANAMA CITY BEACH
LOCATION: 3 mi. east of Panama City Beach on Hwy. 392.
FACILITIES: Open year round; 504 sites; water and bathroom facilities; sanitary station; electrical hookup; trailer village vehicle sites; food service; swimming; boating; fishing.

Pinellas Park

SUNSET PARK
LOCATION: 1 mi. east of Pinellas Park on Hwy. 694.
FACILITIES: Open year round; 300 sites; water and bathroom facilities; swimming.

Pompano Beach

BREEZY HILL PARK
LOCATION: 800 NE 48th Street.
FACILITIES: Open year round; 600 sites; water and bathroom facilities; sanitary station; electrical hookup; trailer village vehicle sites; laundry; swimming.

Punta Gorda

POLYNESIAN PALMS CAMPGROUND
LOCATION: 10½ mi. east of Punta Gorda on Hwy. 764.
FACILITIES: Open year round; 400 sites; water and bathroom facilities; sanitary station; electrical hookup; trailer village vehicle sites; laundry; food service; swimming; boating; boat rental; fishing.

St. Petersburg

HOLIDAY CAMPGROUND
LOCATION: 10 mi. northwest of St. Petersburg on Hwy. 694.
FACILITIES: Open year round; 354 sites; water and bathroom facilities; sanitary station; electrical hookup; trailer village vehicle sites; laundry; food service; swimming; boating; boat rental; fishing.

CAMPGROUNDS (continued)

KOA-ST. PETERSBURG CAMPGROUND
LOCATION: 5400 - 95th Street N.
FACILITIES: Open year round; 421 sites; water and bathroom facilities; sanitary station; electrical hookup; trailer village vehicle sites; laundry; food service; swimming; boating; fishing.

TRAVEL TOWNE RESORT
LOCATION: 5 mi. north of St. Petersburg on U.S. 19.
FACILITIES: Open year round; 385 sites; electrical hookup; laundry; food service; swimming.

Sarasota

SUN "N" FUN TRAVEL TRAILER CAMP-GROUND
LOCATION: 6 mi. east of Sarasota.
FACILITIES: Open year round; 550 sites; water and bathroom facilities; sanitary station; electrical hookup; trailer village vehicle sites; swimming; boating; boat rental; fishing.

Silver Springs

SALT SPRINGS CAMPGROUND
LOCATION: 22 mi. northeast of Silver Springs via Hwys. 40 & 314.
FACILITIES: Open year round; 360 sites; water and bathroom facilities; sanitary station; electrical hookup; trailer village vehicle sites; laundry; food service; swimming; boating; boat rental; fishing.

Tarpon Springs

HOLIDAY TRAVEL PARK
LOCATION: 10 mi. north of Tarpon Springs on Alt. U.S. 19.
FACILITIES: Open year round; 470 sites; water and bathroom facilities; sanitary station; electrical hookup; trailer village vehicle sites; laundry; swimming; boating; boat rental; fishing.

Venice

KING'S GATE CAMPGROUND
LOCATION: 1500 Kings Way.
FACILITIES: Open year round; 300 sites; water and bathroom facilities; sanitary station; electrical hookup; trailer village vehicle sites; laundry; swimming; boating; boat rental; fishing.

Weeki Wachee

SON-MAR TRAVEL PARK
LOCATION: 10 mi. south of Weeki Wachee on U.S. 19.
FACILITIES: Open year round; 300 sites; water and bathroom facilities; sanitary station; electrical hookup; trailer village vehicle sites; laundry; food service.

Wildwood

CONTINENTAL CAMPER
LOCATION: 4 mi. east of Wildwood on Hwy. 44.
FACILITIES: Open year round; 534 sites; water and bathroom facilities; sanitary station; electrical hookup; trailer village vehicle sites; food service; swimming; boating; fishing.

HEARTY HOST CAMPGROUND
LOCATION: 1½ mi. east of Wildwood on Hwy. 44.
FACILITIES: Open year round; 305 sites; water and bathroom facilities; sanitary station; electrical hookup; trailer village vehicle sites; laundry; food service; swimming; boating; boat rental; fishing.

Winter Garden

KOA-WINTER GARDEN-ORLANDO CAMP-GROUND
LOCATION: 2 mi. west of Winter Garden on Hwy. 50.
FACILITIES: Open year round; 320 sites; water and bathroom facilities; sanitary station; electrical hookup; trailer village vehicle sites; laundry; food service; swimming.

RESORTS & BEACHES

Daytona Beach

DAYTONA BEACH AREA - With 23 mi. of white sandy beaches, you can swim, fish, surf or simply bathe in the warm sunshine. Accommodations abound as do restaurants, golf courses, tennis courts and sightseeing attractions. For the spectator-sportsman, Daytona Beach offers the world famous Daytona International Speedway, greyhound racing and jai-alai.

Ft. Lauderdale

FT. LAUDERDALE AREA - Easter Week college vacation made Ft. Lauderdale famous, or maybe it was the other way around. Whichever came first really doesn't matter, because you can enjoy the fun of sunning, surfing and beach strolling anytime of the year on Ft. Lauderdale's white sandy beach. For the adventurous, there is sailing and deep-sea fishing; for the curious, sightseeing tours.

Miami Beach

MIAMI BEACH AREA - The world's most famous playground, Miami Beach offers relaxation in the sun or high-pitched excitement at the race tracks. Or perhaps you'd rather spend the time in the water, swimming, skin diving, scuba diving, and water skiing. But if you wish less down-to-earth activities, you can take a blimp or helicopter ride. Of course, there is plenty of tennis and golf, too.

Palm Beach

PALM BEACH AREA - Just to the north of Miami Beach is Palm Beach with its towering royal palms which edge the roadways and shelter the beaches' land sides. Golf courses and tennis courts are readily available when you wish a break from swimming and sunning. Evening hours can be spent dining and being entertained in any one of the score of fabulous night spots.

FLORIDA

BOATING AREAS

Avon Park

EAST TWIN LAKE
LOCATION: East of Route 700.
FACILITIES: Launching.

LAKE LOTELA
LOCATION: Off Route 17.
FACILITIES: Launching.

Bonifay

LAKE VICTOR
LOCATION: 24 mi. northwest of Bonifay off Route 2.
FACILITIES: Launching.

SMITH LAKE
LOCATION: 2 mi. south of Bonifay.
FACILITIES: Launching.

Brooksville

MOUNTAIN LAKE
LOCATION: 7 mi. southeast of Brooksville.
FACILITIES: Launching.

Carrabelle

HITCHCOCK LAKE
LOCATION: 15 mi. north of Carrabelle.
FACILITIES: Launching.

WHITEHEAD LAKE
LOCATION: 18 mi. north of Carrabelle.
FACILITIES: Launching.

Catherine

SILVER LAKE
LOCATION: Near Catherine.
FACILITIES: Launching.

Century

LAKE STONE
LOCATION: 3 mi. south of Century.
FACILITIES: Launching.

Clermont

JOHNS LAKE
LOCATION: 6 mi. east of Clermont.
FACILITIES: Launching.

Coleman

LAKE PANASOFFKEE
LOCATION: 2 mi. west of Coleman.
FACILITIES: Launching.

Compass Lake

COMPASS LAKE
LOCATION: Off U.S. 231.
FACILITIES: Launching.

Crawfordville

LAKE ELLEN
LOCATION: 4 mi. southwest of Crawford-ville.

FACILITIES: Launching.

Crescent City

CRESCENT LAKE
LOCATION: Off U.S. 17.
FACILITIES: Launching.

LAKE STELLA
LOCATION: Off Route 308.
FACILITIES: Launching.

Crestview

LAKE KARICK
LOCATION: 18 mi. north of Crestview.
FACILITIES: Launching.

SILVER LAKE
LOCATION: 4 mi. north of Crestview.
FACILITIES: Launching.

Cross City

GOVERNOR HILL LAKE
LOCATION: 8 mi. northeast of Cross City.
FACILITIES: Launching.

DeFuniak Springs

JUNIPER LAKE
LOCATION: 4 mi. north of DeFuniak Springs.
FACILITIES: Launching.

DeLand

INDIAN LAKE
LOCATION: 8 mi. northeast of DeLand.
FACILITIES: Launching.

LAKE DIAS
LOCATION: 10 mi. north of DeLand.
FACILITIES: Launching.

Eustis

DOE LAKE
LOCATION: 16 mi. northwest of Eustis.
FACILITIES: Launching.

FARLES LAKE
LOCATION: 18 mi. north of Eustis.
FACILITIES: Launching.

LAKE EUSTIS
LOCATION: Off Route 19.
FACILITIES: Launching.

SELLAR'S LAKE
LOCATION: 30 mi. north of Eustis.
FACILITIES: Launching.

Hawthorne

COWPEN LAKE
LOCATION: 6 mi. east of Hawthorne.
FACILITIES: Launching.

Keystone Heights

LOWERY LAKE
LOCATION: Near Keystone Heights.
FACILITIES: Launching.

BOATING AREAS (continued)

MAGNOLIA LAKE
LOCATION: Near Keystone Heights.
FACILITIES: Launching.

Kissimmee

LAKE TOHOPEKALIGA
LOCATION: Near Kissimmee.
FACILITIES: Launching.

Lake Alfred

LAKE SWOOPE
LOCATION: Near city limits.
FACILITIES: Launching.

Lake City

ALLIGATOR LAKE
LOCATION: Near Lake City.
FACILITIES: Launching.

WATERTOWN LAKE
LOCATION: 1 mi. east of Lake City.
FACILITIES: Launching.

Lake Mary

LAKE MARY
LOCATION: Near Lake Mary.
FACILITIES: Launching.

Lake Placid

LAKE CLAY
LOCATION: 1 mi. north of Lake Placid.
FACILITIES: Launching.

LAKE FRANCIS
LOCATION: 4 mi. northwest of Lake Placid.
FACILITIES: Launching.

LAKE JOSEPHINE
LOCATION: 6 mi. south of Lake Placid.
FACILITIES: Launching.

LAKE PLACID
LOCATION: 3 mi. south of Lake Placid.
FACILITIES: Launching.

Lake Wales

CROOKED LAKE
LOCATION: 13 mi. south of Lake Wales.
FACILITIES: Launching.

Lakeland

LAKE BONNY
LOCATION: South of Route 600.
FACILITIES: Launching.

LAKE HUNTER
LOCATION: North of Route 600.
FACILITIES: Launching.

LAKE PARKER
LOCATION: North of Route 600-A.
FACILITIES: Launching.

Madison

MYSTIC LAKE

LOCATION: 1 mi. west of Madison.
FACILITIES: Launching.

Mt. Dora

LAKE DORA
LOCATION: Near city limits.
FACILITIES: Launching.

Ocala

MILL DAM LAKE
LOCATION: 30 mi. east of Ocala on Hwy. 40.
FACILITIES: Launching.

Oklawaha

LAKE WEIR
LOCATION: 3 mi. southwest of Oklawaha.
FACILITIES: Launching.

Orlando

CLEAR LAKE
LOCATION: In southwest Orlando.
FACILITIES: Launching.

LAKE LAWNE
LOCATION: 3 mi. west of Orlando.
FACILITIES: Launching.

Port Richey

MOON LAKE
LOCATION: 8 mi. east of Port Richey.
FACILITIES: Launching.

Punta Gorda

DEEP CREEK LAKE
LOCATION: 8 mi. north of Punta Gorda.
FACILITIES: Launching.

Sebring

LAKE JACKSON
LOCATION: Near city limits.
FACILITIES: Launching.

LAKE LETTA
LOCATION: 3 mi. northwest of Sebring.
FACILITIES: Launching.

LITTLE RED WATER LAKE
LOCATION: 5 mi. northwest of Sebring.
FACILITIES: Launching.

LAKE SEBRING
LOCATION: 4 mi. northwest of Sebring.
FACILITIES: Launching.

Seffner

LAKE WEEKS
LOCATION: Near city limits.
FACILITIES: Launching.

Seville

LAKE GEORGE
LOCATION: Navy dock near Seville.
FACILITIES: Launching.

FLORIDA

BOATING AREAS (continued)

Starke

LAKE SAMPSON
LOCATION: 4 mi. west of Starke.
FACILITIES: Launching.

Tallahassee

LAKE MUNSON
LOCATION: 5 mi. south of Tallahassee on Crawfordville Road.
FACILITIES: Launching.

Titusville

LAKE FOX
LOCATION: 3 mi. southwest of Titusville.
FACILITIES: Launching.

Umatilla

LAKE DALHOUSIE
LOCATION: 4 mi. southeast of Umatilla.
FACILITIES: Launching.

LAKE HOLLY
LOCATION: 4 mi. west of Umatilla.
FACILITIES: Launching.

LAKE UMATILLA
LOCATION: Near city limits.
FACILITIES: Launching.

Vero Beach

BLUE CYPRESS LAKE
LOCATION: 30 mi. west of Vero Beach on Blue Cypress Road.
FACILITIES: Launching.

Wewahitchka

CYPRESS LAKE
LOCATION: 7 mi. northwest of Wewahitchka.
FACILITIES: Launching.

DEAD LAKES (WEST ARM)
LOCATION: 1 mi. north of Wewahitchka.
FACILITIES: Launching.

Wildwood

LAKE MIONA
LOCATION: North of Wildwood on Route 472.
FACILITIES: Launching.

BICYCLE TRAILS

EVERGLADES TRAIL - 106 mi.; winds and rain; 10-speed bicycle recommended.
Most of the ride is over flat country with sawgrass, palmettos, and pines. You may find stiff breezes in this area. Be prepared for rain, carry some food and a filled water bottle.
Trail: Musselwhite Park to Everglades National Park to Royal Palm Center to Long Pine Key campground to Flamingo, back through Everglades to Musselwhite Park.

GULF COAST TRAIL - 700 mi.; long dis-
tances per day; 10-speed bicycle necessary.
An ambitious trip through four southeastern states, starting in New Orleans, LA and ending in Orlando. Traffic varies from light to heavy along the route.
Trail: New Orleans to Mobile, AL to Pensacola, FL to Panama City to Apalachicola to Perry to High Springs to Williston to Inverness to Wildwood to Leesburg to Orlando.

INLAND FLORIDA TRAIL - 180 mi.; narrow roads, traffic hazard, much rain; 10-speed bicycle recommended.
The major cities of southern Florida are mainly along the coast leaving a vast interior of small towns and lightly traveled roads for the bicycle tourist. The ride starts and ends at Hillsborough River State Park which is east of the city of Tampa.
Back roads in Florida are reasonably safe, but most are narrow, and the few cars that travel them do so rather fast. Extreme caution should be exercised. Be ready for rain and insects.
Trail: Hillsborough River State Park to Keysville to Wauchula to Zolfo Springs to Highlands Hammock State Park.

OLD DIXIE HIGHWAY TRAIL - 28 mi.; any bicycle.
This flat ride starts and ends in Bulow State Park. Good cycling all year, but be prepared for rain, especially on summer afternoons.
Trail: Bulow State Park, 5A South to Old Dixie Highway South, left on 40, left on Halifax Avenue to Anderson Drive to Bulow State Park.

PANHANDLE TRAIL - 100 mi. loop; some hills; 10-speed bicycle recommended.
This is basically flat country except for the hills that you will encounter along Route 29.
Trail: Pensacola to Gonzales to Barth to Century to Jay to Munson to Milton to Pensacola.

PENSACOLA TRAILS - 21, 33 & 38 mi.; strong winds; any bicycle.
Pensacola has summer temperatures of 80 to 90 degrees F.; winter nights may go as low as 30 degrees F.
Trails: (1) Pensacola Bay Bridge to Gulf Breeze to Ft. Pickens - 38 mi.; (2) Pensacola to Route 90 north to University of Florida to Route 291 south to Pensacola - 21 mi.; (3) Pensacola to Route 292 west to Gulf Beach and Ona Island and back - 33 mi.

TRAILS

Bristol

APALACHICOLA BLUFFS TRAIL - .8 mi. foot trail. The setting for the trail is the Torreya State Park. Beginning at the historic Gregory House, which is situated on a high bluff overlooking the Apalachicola River, the trail winds its way down the steep bluff past several Civil War-period cannon emplacements, travels along the river, and eventually circles back up to the Gregory House.

TRAILS (continued)

Milton

JACKSON TRAIL - 21 mi. foot trail. This hiking trail is located entirely within the Blackwater River State Forest, 20 miles northeast of Milton. Primitive in nature, the trail retraces the earliest trade route of Indians and settlers. The trail traverses a variety of vegetational types including pine, mixed hardwoods and bottomland species. The area offers an excellent opportunity for wildlife and nature study. The Jackson Trail is a part of the Florida Trails System.

Palatka

RICE CREEK TRAIL - 3 mi. foot trail. This trail, composed of three hiking paths with other names, is located in the 2000-acre Rice Creek Wildlife Sanctuary approximately 6 miles west of Palatka, just off Route 100. It begins at a developed picnic area and is not a difficult trail, thereby appealing to hikers of varying interests. Abundant wildlife, a richly varied flora including wild flowers and wild azaleas, and the historic rice fields provide the center of interest for hikers. The sanctuary is open year round to the public without charge.

SKI AREAS

There are no organized Ski Areas in Florida.

AMUSEMENT PARKS & ATTRACTIONS

Clermont

WOMETCO'S FLORIDA CITRUS TOWER (Attraction)
U.S. 27
Clermont, FL 32711
(904) 395-2145
FACILITIES: Citrus packing plant; glass blowing artist's workshop; candy factory; restaurant; ice cream parlor; gift shop; pay gate; free parking.

Cypress Gardens

FLORIDA CYPRESS GARDENS
Cypress Gardens Blvd.
Cypress Gardens, FL 33880
(813) 324-2111
FACILITIES: 2 major rides; 2 walk thrus; 2 restaurants; 3 refreshment stands; picnic facilities; crafts; free acts; pay gate; free parking; open all year.

Dunnelon

RAINBOW SPRINGS (Attraction)
P.O. Box 98
Dunnelon, FL 32630
(904) 489-2256
FACILITIES: Snack bar; restaurant; underwater cruise; Rainbow Queen double deck paddleboat cruise; Rainbow Raft adventure; rodeo shows; Forest Flite monorail; animal park; swamp garden; bird park; gardens; pay gate; free parking.

Ft. Lauderdale

OCEAN WORLD, INC. (Attraction)
1701 S. E. 17th Street
Ft. Lauderdale, FL 33316
(305) 525-6612
FACILITIES: 2 major rides; refreshment stand; gift shop; marina; picnic facilities; porpoise show; oceanarium; pay gate; free parking; open all year.

Ft. Myers

THOMAS EDISON WINTER HOME AND BOTANICAL GARDENS (Attraction)
2350 McGregor Blvd.
Ft. Myers, FL 33901
(813) 334-3614
FACILITIES: Conducted tours; refreshment stand; museum; exhibits; picnic facilities; botanical gardens; chemical laboratory; pay gate; free parking; open all year.

Haines City

RINGLING BROS. & BARNUM & BAILEY CIRCUS WORLD (Attraction)
I-4 & U.S. 27 South
Haines City, FL 33844
(813) 424-2421
FACILITIES: 1 major ride; 6 games; 7 refreshment stands; 2 restaurants; 5 major shows; shooting gallery; exhibits; theater; carousel; 6-story movie-circus house; stage shows; free parking.

Jacksonville

JACKSONVILLE ZOOLOGICAL PARK & SOCIETY
8605 Zoo Road
Jacksonville, FL 32218
(904) 765-4431
FACILITIES: 3 major rides; 2 refreshment stands; zoo; safari train ride; gift shop; pay gate; free parking; open all year.

Jacksonville Beach

GRIFFIN AMUSEMENT PARK
P.O. Box 43
Jacksonville Beach, FL 32050
(904) 249-4741
FACILITIES: 9 major rides; 4 kiddie rides; beach; 2 games; picnic facilities; fireworks; beach beauty contest; water show concerts; Spring band festival; free gate; free & pay parking.

Kennedy Space Center

KENNEDY SPACE CENTER TOURS (Attraction)
P.O. Box 21222
Kennedy Space Center, FL 32815
(305) 269-3000
FACILITIES: Museum; theatre; restaurant; movies; space exhibits; space demonstrations; 50-mile bus tour of Kennedy Space Center and Cape Canaveral Air Force Station; free parking; open all year, except Christmas.

FLORIDA

AMUSEMENT PARKS (continued)

Key West

KEY WEST CONCH TOUR TRAIN
303 Front Street
Key West, FL 33040
(305) 294-5161
FACILITIES: 14-mile, 1½ hour narrated
tram-train tour; refreshment stand; gift shop;
pay gate; free parking.

Lake Buena Vista

WALT DISNEY WORLD
P.O. Box 40
Lake Buena Vista, FL 32830
(305) 824-2222
FACILITIES: 45 major rides; 25 refreshment
stands; 72 restaurants; arcade; shooting gallery; swimming pool; bathing beach; marina;
camping; exhibits; picnic facilities; golf driving range; River Country (world's largest man-
made swimming facility); theatre; crafts; stage
shows; orchestras; name bands; vaudeville;
free acts; fireworks; pay gate; pay parking.

Loxahatchee

LION COUNTRY SAFARI (Attraction)
State Route 80
Loxahatchee, FL 33470
(305) 793-1084
FACILITIES: 3 major rides; 2 kiddie rides;
refreshment stand; restaurant; picnic facilities;
zoo; 2 walk thrus; free parking; open all year.

Miami

THE MIAMI SERPENTARIUM (Attraction)
12655 S. Dixie Hwy.
Miami, FL 33156
(305) 235-5722
FACILITIES: Spectacular venom attractions;
stage shows; pay gate; free parking; open all
year.

MONKEY JUNGLE (Attraction)
14805 SW 216 Street
Miami, FL 33170
(305) 235-1611
FACILITIES: Picnic facilities; private zoo;
pay gate; free parking; open all year.

PARROT JUNGLE (Attraction)
11000 SW 57th Avenue
Miami, FL 33156
(305) 666-7834
FACILITIES: Parrot exhibit and shows; landscaped natural jungle and garden; flamingo parade; refreshment stand; restaurant; cafeteria;
pay gate; free parking; open all year.

PLANET OCEAN (Attraction)
3979 Rickenbacker Causeway
Miami, FL 33149
(305) 361-5786
FACILITIES: Marine exposition; 7 theaters;
100 exhibits; museum; pay gate; free parking;
open all year.

WOMETCO MIAMI SEAQUARIUM (Attraction)
4400 Rickenbacker Causeway
Miami, FL 33149

(305) 361-5705
FACILITIES: 4 walk thrus; 3 refreshment
stands; restaurant; 5 marine mammal shows;
shark show; exhibits; picnic facilities; stage
shows; pay gate; free parking; open all year.

Orlando

SEA WORLD OF FLORIDA (Attraction)
7007 Sea World Drive
Orlando, FL 32809
(305) 351-3600
FACILITIES: 6 restaurants; 8 gift shops; exhibits; picnic facilities; beach; 9 refreshment
stands; zoo; theatre; skytower; marine-life
shows and feeding pools; stage shows; orchestras; name bands; free acts; pay gate; free
parking; open all year.

STARS HALL OF FAME (Attraction)
6825 Starway Drive
Orlando, FL 32809
(305) 351-1120
FACILITIES: World's largest movie-TV wax
museum; 4 games; 2 refreshment stands; restaurant; arcade; shooting gallery; museum;
theatre; pay gate; free parking; open all year.

Panama City

MIRACLE STRIP AMUSEMENT PARK
12001 West Hwy. 98
Panama City, FL 32401
(904) 234-3333
FACILITIES: 16 major rides; 10 kiddie
rides; 3 fun houses; 3 walk thrus; 7 refreshment stands; restaurant; arcade; 2 shooting
galleries; bathing beach; miniature golf; scenic
tower; 4 gift shops; giant water slide; jungle-
land; pay gate; pay parking; open mid-May -
Labor Day; weekends, Mar. - May 30.

PETTICOAT JUNCTION
P.O. Box 9110
Panama City, FL 32401
(904) 234-2563
FACILITIES: 13 major rides; 8 kiddie rides; 3
fun houses; 12 walk thrus; 4 refreshment
stands; 9 games; shooting gallery; arcade;
pool; bathing beach; museum; miniature golf;
zoo; nature trail; hourly gunfights; hourly
stage performances; antique steam locomotives operating every 30 minutes; name bands;
free acts; fireworks; free gate; free parking.

St. Augustine

MARINELAND OF FLORIDA (Attraction)
Route 1
St. Augustine, FL 32084
(904) 829-5607
FACILITIES: 11 marine exhibits and 6 daily
shows; restaurant; swimming pool; exhibits;
picnic facilities; bathing beach; marina; complete oceanfront resort; pay gate; free parking; open all year.

ST. AUGUSTINE ALLIGATOR FARM (Attraction)
Hwy. A1A South
St. Augustine, FL 32084
(904) 824-3337
FACILITIES: Alligator shows; wildlife birds;
museum; exhibits; zoo; stage show (alligator

AMUSEMENT PARKS (continued)

wrestling); refreshment stand; free parking; open all year.

St. Petersburg

FLORIDA'S SUNKEN GARDENS (Attraction)
1825 4th Street North
St. Petersburg, FL 33704
(813) 896-3186
FACILITIES: Exotic plants; birds and animals; 2 walk-thru aviaries; 2 refreshment stands; restaurant; museum; crafts; orchid house; exhibits; fudge kitchen; zoo; pay gate; free parking; open all year.

MGM'S BOUNTY EXHIBIT (Attraction)
345 Second Avenue, Northeast
St. Petersburg, FL 33701
(813) 896-3117
FACILITIES: Replica of ship made famous in "Mutiny on the Bounty"; pay gate; free parking; open all year.

Sarasota

CIRCUS HALL OF FAME
6255 N. Tamiami Trail
Sarasota, FL 33580
(813) 355-5095
FACILITIES: Refreshment stand; arena; museum; exhibits; theatre puppets; circus acts, winter - summer season; open all year; pay gate; free parking.

RINGLING MUSEUMS (Attraction)
5401 Bayshore Road
Sarasota, FL 33578
(813) 355-5101
FACILITIES: Refreshment stand; museum; exhibits; theater; pay gate; free parking; free gate for grounds only; children under 12 admitted free; open all year.

Silver Springs

SIX GUN TERRITORY (Attraction)
4901 Silver Springs Blvd.
Silver Springs, FL 32688
(904) 236-2211
FACILITIES: 10 major rides; 9 kiddie rides; 3 restaurants; 7 refreshment stands; 2 games; arcade; shooting gallery; picnic facilities; museum; exhibits; gun fights; Palace Saloon shows; theatre; petting zoo; Indian dances; stage show; pay gate; pay parking; open all year.

Tampa

BUSCH GARDENS (Attraction)
3000 Busch Blvd.
Tampa, FL 33612
(813) 988-8360
FACILITIES: 6 major rides; 1 kiddie ride; 3 restaurants; nocturnal mountain-cave with birds and animals; free-flight cage; small animal zoo and contact area; bird gardens; animal shows; crafts; exhibits; camping; live entertainment; theater; stage shows; trained animal acts; name bands; pay gate; pay parking; open all year.

FUNLAND AMUSEMENT PARK
4406 W. Hillsborough Avenue
Tampa, FL 33614
(813) 876-7244
FACILITIES: 7 major rides; 3 kiddie rides; 2 games; refreshment stand; go-karts; arcade; roller rink; picnic facilities; miniature golf; free gate; free parking; open all year.

FAIRYLAND LOWRY PARK
Tampa, FL 33601
(813) 935-5503
FACILITIES: 6 major rides; 11 kiddie rides; arcade; gift shop; birthday house; 1¼ mi. train ride; picnic facilities; miniature golf; zoo; free gate; free parking; open all year.

West Panama City Beach

MAGIC WORLD
U.S. 98
West Panama City Beach, FL 32401
(813) 234-3441
FACILITIES: 5 major rides; kiddie ride; walk-thru; bathing beach; jungle boat ride; animal show; refreshment stand; picnic facilities; miniature golf; free gate; free parking.

White Springs

STEPHEN FOSTER MEMORIAL (Attraction)
White Springs, FL 32096
(904) 397-2192
FACILITIES: Major ride; museum; exhibits; restaurant; refreshment stand; crafts; picnic facilities; free acts; pay gate; free parking; open all year, closed Thanksgiving and Christmas Days.

STATE FAIR

Florida State Fair
P.O. Box 11766
Tampa, FL 33680
(813) 621-7821
DATE: March

NATIONAL PARKS

Homestead

EVERGLADES NATIONAL PARK
Homestead, FL 33030
(305) 247-6211

FLAMINGO
LOCATION: 38 mi. south of entrance.
FACILITIES: Open year round; entrance fee; limit of stay: 14 days (30, Apr. 30 - Nov. 1); 297 sites; group camps: 4; NPS campsite fee: $3; water and bathroom facilities; sanitary station; cabins; picnic area; food service; boating; boat rental; fishing; exhibit; museum; environmental study area; handicapped access/restroom; NPS guided tour; self-guiding tour; medical service; no trailer hook-ups; lodging.

LONG PINE KEY
LOCATION: 6 mi. west of entrance.
FACILITIES: Open year round; entrance fee;

FLORIDA

NATIONAL PARKS (continued)

limit of stay: 14 days (30, Apr. 30 - Nov. 1); 106 sites; NPS campsite fee: $3; water and bathroom facilities; picnic area; exhibit; museum; environmental study area; NPS guided tour; self-guiding tour; medical service; lodging.

NATIONAL FORESTS

National Forests
Southern Region
1720 Peachtree Road, NW
Atlanta, GA 30309
(404) 881-4177

Tallahassee

APALACHICOLA NATIONAL FOREST
ATTRACTIONS: Pine-hardwood forests. Natural sinks, bottomland and hardwood swamps along large rivers with trees typically found far to the north. Bass, bream, perch fishing; quail, deer, bear hunting; boating; swimming.
FACILITIES: 27 camp and picnic sites, 33 picnic only; 16 swimming sites. Hotels not far away.
NEARBY TOWNS: Apalachicola, Blountstown, Bristol.

OCALA NATIONAL FOREST
ATTRACTIONS: Large clear-flowing streams through subtropical wilderness; botanical lore, palms, hardwoods, and pine. The Big Scrub, characterized by vast stands of sand pine, is unique. Annual deer and bear hunts; fishing; camping sites.
FACILITIES: 7 camp and picnic sites, 16 picnic sites; 4 swimming sites; hunting camps; commercial accommodations near the forest.
NEARBY TOWNS: Deland, Eustis, Leesburg, Mount Dora, Ocala, Palatka.

OSCEOLA NATIONAL FOREST
ATTRACTIONS: Flat country, dotted with numerous ponds, sinks, and cypress swamps. State game breeding ground. Bass, perch, bream fishing; deer, turkey, quail, dove hunting; swimming; boating at Ocean Pond.
FACILITIES: 2 camp and picnic sites, 5 picnic only; 2 swimming sites.
NEARBY TOWNS: Jacksonville, Lake City.

STATE PARKS

Headquarters

Department of Natural Resources
Division of Recreation and Parks
Crown Bldg.
Tallahassee, FL 32304
(904) 488-7326

Bristol

TORREYA STATE PARK
LOCATION: Between Bristol and Greensboro.
FACILITIES: Open year round; 35 sites; water and bathroom facilities; electrical hookup; trailer village vehicle sites; picnic area; museum; living history program; guided tour; self-guided trail; tent camping.

Chiefland

MANATEE SPRINGS STATE PARK
LOCATION: 6 mi. west of Chiefland.
FACILITIES: Open year round; 100 sites; water and bathroom facilities; sanitary station; electrical hookup; trailer village vehicle sites; picnic area; food service; swimming; boating; boat rental; fishing; self-guided trail; tent camping.

DeLand

HONTOON ISLAND STATE PARK
LOCATION: 6 mi. west of DeLand.
FACILITIES: Open year round; 24 sites; water and bathroom facilities; electrical hookup; trailer village vehicle sites; cabins; laundry; picnic area; food service; boating; boat rental; fishing.

Dunedin

CALADESI ISLAND STATE PARK
LOCATION: Offshore Dunedin.
FACILITIES: Open year round; picnic area; swimming; boating; fishing; self-guided trail.

Fernandina Beach

FORT CLINCH STATE PARK
LOCATION: In Fernandina Beach.
FACILITIES: Open year round; 67 sites; water and bathroom facilities; sanitary station; electrical hookup; trailer village vehicle sites; laundry; picnic area; food service; swimming; boating; fishing; museum; guided tour; self-guided trail; tent camping.

Ft. White

ICHETUCKNEE SPRINGS STATE PARK
LOCATION: 4 mi. northwest of Ft. White.
FACILITIES: Open year round; picnic area; swimming.

Jacksonville

LITTLE TALBOT ISLAND STATE PARK
LOCATION: 17 mi. northeast of Jacksonville.
FACILITIES: Open year round; 59 sites; water and bathroom facilities; sanitary station; electrical hookup; trailer village vehicle sites; picnic area; food service; swimming; boating; fishing; tent camping.

Key Largo

JOHN PENNEKAMP CORAL REEF STATE PARK
LOCATION: In Key Largo.
FACILITIES: Open year round; 60 sites; water and bathroom facilities; sanitary station; electrical hookup; trailer village vehicle sites; picnic area; food service; swimming; boating; fishing; guided tour; self-guided trail.

Keystone Heights

MIKE ROESS GOLD HEAD BRANCH

STATE PARKS (continued)

STATE PARK
LOCATION: 6 mi. northeast of Keystone Heights.
FACILITIES: Open year round; 107 sites; water and bathroom facilities; sanitary station; electrical hookup; trailer village vehicle sites; cabins; laundry; picnic area; food service; swimming; boating; fishing; tent camping.

Lake City

O'LENO STATE PARK
LOCATION: 20 mi. south of Lake City.
FACILITIES: Open year round; 65 sites; water and bathroom facilities; sanitary station; electrical hookup; trailer village vehicle sites; picnic area; swimming; boating; fishing; tent camping.

Live Oak

SUWANNEE RIVER STATE PARK
LOCATION: 13 mi. west of Live Oak.
FACILITIES: Open year round; 32 sites; water and bathroom facilities; electrical hookup; trailer village vehicle sites; picnic area; food service; swimming; boating; fishing; self-guided trail; tent camping.

Marianna

FLORIDA CAVERNS STATE PARK
LOCATION: 3 mi. north of Marianna.
FACILITIES: Open year round; 43 sites; water and bathroom facilities; electrical hookup; trailer village vehicle sites; picnic area; food service; swimming; boating; fishing; museum; guided tour; self-guided trail; tent camping.

Milton

BLACKWATER RIVER STATE PARK
LOCATION: 15 mi. northeast of Milton.
FACILITIES: Open year round; 18 sites; water and bathroom facilities; sanitary station; electrical hookup; trailer village vehicle sites; picnic area; swimming; fishing; self-guided trail.

Naples

COLLIER-SEMINOLE STATE PARK
LOCATION: 17 mi. south of Naples.
FACILITIES: Open year round; 130 sites; water and bathroom facilities; sanitary station; electrical hookup; trailer village vehicle sites; picnic area; boating; fishing; museum; self-guided trail.

Orlando

WEKIWA SPRINGS STATE PARK
LOCATION: In North Orlando.
FACILITIES: Open year round; water and bathroom facilities; picnic area; swimming; boating; fishing; self-guided trail.

Ormond Beach

TOMOKA STATE PARK
LOCATION: 2 mi. north of Ormond Beach.
FACILITIES: Open year round; 100 sites; water and bathroom facilities; sanitary station; electrical hookup; trailer village vehicle sites; laundry; picnic area; food service; boating; boat rental; fishing; museum; guided tour; self-guided trail; tent camping.

Port St. Joe

T.H. STONE MEMORIAL STATE PARK
LOCATION: Near Port St. Joe.
FACILITIES: Open year round; 115 sites; water and bathroom facilities; sanitary station; electrical hookup; trailer village vehicle sites; cabins; picnic area; food service; swimming; boating; fishing; bicycle trail; self-guided trail.

St. Augustine

FAVER-DYKES STATE PARK
LOCATION: 15 mi. south of St. Augustine.
FACILITIES: Open year round; 24 sites; water and bathroom facilities; electrical hookup; trailer village vehicle sites; picnic area; boating; fishing; self-guided trail.

Sarasota

MYAKKA RIVER STATE PARK
LOCATION: 17 mi. east of Sarasota.
FACILITIES: Open year round; 76 sites; water and bathroom facilities; electrical hookup; trailer village vehicle sites; cabins; picnic area; food service; boating; boat rental; fishing; bicycle trail; guided tour; self-guided trail; tent camping.

Sebring

HIGHLANDS HAMMOCK STATE PARK
LOCATION: 6 mi. west of Sebring.
FACILITIES: Open year round; 140 sites; water and bathroom facilities; sanitary station; electrical hookup; trailer village vehicle sites; picnic area; food service; fishing; guided tour; self-guided trail; tent camping.

Sopchoppy

OCHLOCKONEE RIVER STATE PARK
LOCATION: 4 mi. south of Sopchoppy.
FACILITIES: Open year round; 30 sites; water and bathroom facilities; electrical hookup; trailer village vehicle sites; picnic area; food service; swimming; boating; self-guided trail; tent camping.

Stuart

JONATHAN DICKINSON STATE PARK
LOCATION: 13 mi. south of Stuart.
FACILITIES: Open year round; 135 sites; water and bathroom facilities; sanitary station; electrical hookup; trailer village vehicle sites; cabins; laundry; food service; swimming; boating; fishing; self-guided trail; tent camping.

Zephyrhills

HILLSBOROUGH RIVER STATE PARK
LOCATION: 6 mi. southwest of Zephyrhills.
FACILITIES: Open year round; 118 sites; water and bathroom facilities; sanitary station; electrical hookup; trailer village vehicle sites; cabins; picnic area; food service; swimming; boating; boat rental; fishing; self-guided trail; tent camping.

FLORIDA

STATE FORESTS

Headquarters

Division of Forestry
Larson Bldg.
Tallahassee, FL 32301
(904) 488-4274

Crestview

BLACKWATER RIVER STATE FOREST
LOCATION: 15 mi. west of Crestview.
FACILITIES: Open year round; water and
bathroom facilities; electrical hookup; trailer
village vehicle sites; picnic area; swimming;
fishing; tent camping.

Dade City

WITHLACHOOCHEE STATE FOREST
LOCATION: 10 mi. north of Dade City.
FACILITIES: Open year round; water and
bathroom facilities; electrical hookup; trailer
village vehicle sites; picnic area; swimming;
boating; fishing; tent camping.

HISTORIC SITES

Apalachicola

TRINITY EPISCOPAL CHURCH - This
original structure of white pine had previously
been cut into sections in New York and trans-
ported by sailing vessel down the Atlantic
Coast and around the Florida Keys before it
was erected on this site. Located across from
Gorrie Museum.

Garden Key

FT. JEFFERSON - Largest 19th century
coastal fort built in the country and was at
one time considered "Key to the Gulf of Mexico." Located at Tortugas Harbor on Garden
Key.

Jacksonville

FT. CAROLINE NATIONAL MEMORIAL -
French Huguenots chose this spot overlooking the St. Johns River to establish the first
Protestant colony in America in 1564. Located at 12713 Ft. Caroline Road.

KINGSLEY PLANTATION - The oldest plantation home still standing in Florida is preserved at the Zephaniah Kingsley Plantation
on Ft. George Island. Located about 35 min.
north of Jacksonville; I-95 to Hwy. 105
(Heckscher Dr.).

Key Biscayne

CAPE FLORIDA LIGHTHOUSE - Cape Florida, the southern tip of Key Biscayne, was discovered by John Cabot in 1497, less than five
years after Columbus first landed in the West
Indies. The lighthouse was raised to its present height of 95 feet in 1855.

Madison

THE FOUR FREEDOMS MONUMENT - The
Four Freedoms were stated by President
Franklin D. Roosevelt in his Annual Message
to Congress, January 6, 1941. Freedom of
speech and expression, freedom of worship,
freedom from want, and freedom from fear
everywhere in the world became the ideals of
American policy. Located in City Park off
U.S. 90.

Pensacola

CHRIST CHURCH - Erected in 1832, this is
the oldest church building in Florida still
standing on its original site. Tradition ascribes
the church's design to Sir Christopher Wren.
Located at the corner of East Zarragossa &
Adams South.

St. Augustine

FOUNTAIN OF YOUTH - Memorial to Ponce
de Leon, who discovered Florida in 1513.

ST. AUGUSTINE - Don Pedro Menendez de
Aviles founded St. Augustine in 1565, making
this city the oldest continuously occupied
European settlement in the United States. Im-
portant sites in the restoration area include
the "Oldest Wooden Schoolhouse" in the
United States, the Ortega House, the Ribera
House, Maria Triay House and many more.
Located in downtown St. Augustine.

Tampa Bay

DE SOTO MEMORIAL - A large stone monument commemorating De Soto's landing on
the Florida West Coast and his leading of the
first major exploration of the southern United
States. Located 5 mi. west of Bradenton.

HOSTELS

Orlando

THE EPICENTER HOSTEL
5135 Sand Lake Road
Orlando, FL 32809
(305) 351-2391
FACILITIES: Open year round; 50 beds men
and women; modern bathroom; nearest hostel: Plymouth, 18 mi.; overnight charges: $3
plus $1.25 linen charge; houseparent: Nancy
Baunhover.

Plymouth

CAMP WEWA YMCA
Highway U.S. 441
Plymouth, FL 32768
(305) 886-1240
FACILITIES: Open year round (except Jun.
10 - Aug. 15, camp season); 20 beds, men; 20
beds, women; modern bathroom; overnight
charges: $2.50; houseparent: Chester Gullick-
son.

POINTS OF INTEREST

Bradenton

GAMBLE MANSION AND PLANTATION - The Gamble Mansion, built principally of native materials, 1845-1850, is an outstanding example of antebellum construction and stands today as a monument to pioneer ingenuity and craftsmanship. Located near Parrish.

Clermont

CITRUS TOWER - Observation tower at Central Florida's highest point; view more than 17 million citrus trees.

Daytona Beach

DAYTONA INTERNATIONAL SPEEDWAY- High speed auto and motorcycle raceway; site of Daytona 500, Firecracker 400.

Ellenton

BOUNTY EXHIBIT - Florida's first marine historical exhibit located at the Municipal Pier in St. Petersburg. The Bounty, reminiscent of Capt. Bligh and Fletcher Christian, was seen by millions in "Mutiny on the Bounty."

Hollywood

HOLLYWOOD DOG TRACK - Greyhound racing track.

Kissimmee

GATORLAND ZOO - Thousands of alligators and crocodiles; reptiles and birds from throughout the world.

Lake Wales

SPOOK HILL - Optical illusion site where cars appear to roll uphill.

Miami

JAPANESE GARDENS - Gardens and tearoom in Watson Park; gift to the city from Japan.

Riviera Beach

OCEANOGRAPHY USA-WORLD OCEAN SCIENCE CENTER - First complete entertainment and education center devoted entirely to ocean science and oceanography.

Silver Springs

FLORIDA'S SILVER SPRINGS - Natural spring attraction featuring glass-bottom boat tours over springs, jungle cruise on Silver River; reptile institute with snake and alligator shows.

Tallahassee

WAKULLA SPRINGS - Deepest natural spring in the world featuring glass-bottom boat tours, recreation area, and alligator pool.

GEORGIA

Georgia, the first Deep South state to send a President to the White House since the Civil War, joined the Union in 1788 as the fourth state. Settled by James Oglethorpe and a band of English social outcasts, the state grew in a few short years to become a major cotton producer.

The Civil War devastated much of the state's land and the spirit of the people. It wasn't until many years after the war that Georgia became a productive state again.

Today, the state leads all others in the production of peanut and poultry products and its textile, tobacco and cotton industries are listed among the nation's major producers.

Tourism is another growing state industry fostered by agreeable weather, splendid natural surroundings and extraordinary attractions such as Stone Mountain Monument (figures of Jefferson Davis, Robert E. Lee and Stonewall Jackson), the world's largest work of sculptural art.

State capital: Atlanta. State bird: Brown thrasher. State tree: Live oak. State flower: Cherokee rose.

WEATHER

Georgia, with an area of over 58,000 square miles, is the largest state east of the Mississippi River. Its land area is made up of four principal physiographic provinces: the Blue Ridge or Mountain Province, located in the northeastern part of the state; the Valley and Ridge Province, located in northwest Georgia; the Piedmont Plateau Province, a wide area extending from the foothills of the Appalachian Mountains to the Coastal Plain and comprising nearly one-third of the area of the state; the Coastal Plain Province, which includes all of Georgia south of the Fall Line and comprises about three-fifths of the total area of the state.

Due to its latitude and its proximity to the warm waters of the Gulf of Mexico and the Atlantic Ocean, most of Georgia has warm, humid summers and short, mild winters. However, in the northern part of the state, altitude becomes the more predominant influence with resulting cool summers and colder, but not severe, winters.

All four seasons are apparent, but spring is usually short and blustery. In autumn long periods of mild, sunny weather are the rule for all Georgia.

GEORGIA

WEATHER (continued)

Average daily temperature for each month.

	Northern	Southern
Jan.	50.5 to 31.6	63.1 to 39.9
Feb.	53.5 to 32.6	65.6 to 41.5
Mar.	60.9 to 38.7	72.0 to 47.3
Apr.	71.2 to 47.7	79.7 to 54.4
May	78.4 to 55.1	86.1 to 61.3
Jun.	84.1 to 61.6	90.1 to 66.9
Jul.	86.7 to 65.0	91.5 to 69.3
Aug.	86.2 to 64.5	91.6 to 69.1
Sept.	81.0 to 59.4	87.6 to 65.6
Oct.	71.9 to 48.4	80.3 to 55.4
Nov.	60.7 to 39.0	71.2 to 45.1
Dec.	52.0 to 33.3	64.7 to 40.1
Year	69.8 to 48.1	78.6 to 54.7

STATE CHAMBER OF COMMERCE

Georgia State Chamber of Commerce
1200 Commerce Building
Atlanta, GA 30303
(404) 524-8481

STATE & CITY TOURISM OFFICES

State

Georgia Department of Community Development
1400 North Omni International
Atlanta, GA 30301
(404) 656-3556

Tourist Division
Bureau of Industry and Trade
P.O. Box 38097
Atlanta, GA 30334
(404) 656-3590

Local

Department of Public Information
Atlanta Chamber of Commerce
P.O. Box 1740
Atlanta, GA 30301
(404) 521-0845

Savannah Chamber of Commerce
P.O. Box 530
Savannah, GA 31402
(912) 233-3067

STATE HIGHWAY DEPARTMENT

Department of Transportation
No. 2 Capitol Square
Atlanta, GA 30334
(404) 656-5200

HIGHWAY WELCOMING CENTERS

Augusta

AUGUSTA CENTER - Interstate 20, east.

Columbus

COLUMBUS CENTER - Hwy. 27.

Florida

FLORIDA BORDER - Interstate 95.

Savannah

SAVANNAH CENTER - Hwy. 17.

South Carolina

SOUTH CAROLINA BORDER - Hwy. 301.

SOUTH CAROLINA BORDER - Interstate 85.

Tennessee

TENNESSEE BORDER - Interstate 75, south of Chattanooga, TN.

Valdosta

VALDOSTA CENTER - Interstate 75, south, just below Valdosta.

STATE POLICE

Department of Public Safety
Atlanta, GA 30301
(404) 656-5890

HUNTING & FISHING

Hunting

Hunters 16 years of age or over are required to have a valid hunting license for all hunting, except when hunting on lands owned by them or their immediate family residing in the same household.

Residents 65 or over must obtain an honorary license. Non-residents must have the appropriate non-resident license.

Bow hunters must have a valid bow and arrow hunting license.

Anyone hunting deer or turkey in Georgia must have a valid big game license in addition to the regular hunting license or bow and arrow license.

Residents under 16 and over 65 and landowners hunting on their property must have complimentary deer tags issued by the License Division to take deer. Non-residents must purchase all appropriate licenses, regardless of age.

Resident

Hunting license, $4.25; hunting and fish-

HUNTING & FISHING (continued)

ing combination, $7.25; bow and arrow hunting license, $3.25; big game license, $3.25; trapping license, $25.

Non-resident

Hunting license (10-day trip), $15.25; season hunting license, $25.25; archery license (10-day trip), $12.50; season archery license, $25.25; big game (season), $25; public shooting preserve permit, $5.25; private shooting preserve permit, $12.50; trapping license, $250.

Fishing

All fishermen age 16 or older must have a current Georgia fishing license in possession while fishing in fresh water, with the exception of landowners and their immediate family who may fish without a license on their own property. Any violation of the fishing laws or regulations can cause your fishing license to be revoked.

Residents who are 65 or over, blind or totally disabled may obtain an honorary license free of charge by applying to the Atlanta Game and Fish office.

All non-resident fishermen and all resident fishermen between 16 and 65 must have a trout stamp to fish for and possess trout. Residents with honorary licenses and residents under 16 are not required to have a trout stamp.

Resident

Fishing license, $3.25; combination hunting and fishing, $7.25; trout stamp, $2.25.

Non-resident

Fishing (5-day trip), $3.25; season fishing license, $10.25; trout stamp (5-day), $3.25; season trout stamp, $10.25.

For more information contact:

Department of Natural Resources
270 Washington Street, SW
Atlanta, GA 30334
(404) 393-7263

CAMPGROUNDS

Private

Acworth

PONDEROSA PARK CAMPING AREA
LOCATION: U.S. 41.
FACILITIES: Open year round; water and bathroom facilities; electrical hookup; trailer village vehicle sites; swimming; boating; tent camping.

Atlanta

ARROWHEAD CAMPGROUND SIX FLAGS
LOCATION: 10 mi. west of Atlanta on I-20 at Six Flags Road.

FACILITIES: Open year round; water and bathroom facilities; electrical hookup; trailer village vehicle sites; swimming; tent camping.

Bainbridge

BASS ISLAND CAMPGROUND
LOCATION: 15 mi. southwest of Bainbridge on Route 97, then 3 mi. north on Route 310.
FACILITIES: Open year round; water and bathroom facilities; electrical hookup; trailer village vehicle sites; swimming; boating; tent camping.

Barnesville

PONDEROSA PARK CAMPGROUND
LOCATION: 12 mi. east of Barnesville.
FACILITIES: Open year round; water and bathroom facilities; electrical hookup; trailer village vehicle sites; swimming.

Buford

LAKE LANIER ISLANDS CAMPGROUND
LOCATION: Exit 2 off Route 365.
FACILITIES: Open year round; water and bathroom facilities; electrical hookup; trailer village vehicle sites; swimming; boating; tent camping.

Clarkesville

TALLULAH FALLS KOA KAMPGROUND
LOCATION: 12 mi. north of Clarkesville on U.S. 441.
FACILITIES: Open year round; water and bathroom facilities; electrical hookup; trailer village vehicle sites; swimming; boating.

Columbus

HILLS OF HARRIS CAMPGROUND
LOCATION: River Road.
FACILITIES: Open year round; water and bathroom facilities; electrical hookup; trailer village vehicle sites; swimming; tent camping.

LAKE PINES CAMPGROUND
LOCATION: 12 mi. east of Columbus on U.S. 80, then 1 block south on Garrett Road.
FACILITIES: Open year round; water and bathroom facilities; electrical hookup; trailer village vehicle sites; swimming; tent camping.

Cordele

ARABI CAMPER VILLAGE
LOCATION: 10 mi. south of Cordele on I-75.
FACILITIES: Open year round; water and bathroom facilities; electrical hookup; trailer village vehicle sites; swimming; tent camping.

Douglas

HOLIDAY BEACH CAMPGROUND
LOCATION: 3 mi. west of Douglas on Route 158.
FACILITIES: Open year round; water and bathroom facilities; electrical hookup; trailer village vehicle sites; swimming; boating; tent camping.

GEORGIA

CAMPGROUNDS (continued)

Eastman

JAY BIRD SPRINGS CAMPGROUND
LOCATION: 13 mi. south of Eastman on
U.S. 341, then 2 mi. east on county road.
FACILITIES: Open year round; water and
bathroom facilities; electrical hookup; trailer
village vehicle sites; swimming; tent camping.

McDonough

HOLIDAY INN TRAV-L-PARK
LOCATION: I-75 and Route 351.
FACILITIES: Open year round; water and
bathroom facilities; electrical hookup; trailer
village vehicle sites; swimming; boating; tent
camping.

KAMPGROUNDS OF AMERICA
LOCATION: I-75 and Route 351.
FACILITIES: Open year round; water and
bathroom facilities; electrical hookup; trailer
village vehicle sites; swimming; tent camping.

Pembroke

RAMBLING CREEK CAMPORAMA
LOCATION: 9 mi. east of Pembroke off U.S.
280.
FACILITIES: Open year round; water and
bathroom facilities; electrical hookup; trailer
village vehicle sites; swimming; boating; tent
camping.

Perry

CROSSROADS CAMPGROUND
LOCATION: I-75 and Route 341.
FACILITIES: Open year round; water and
bathroom facilities; electrical hookup; trailer
village vehicle sites; swimming; tent camping.

Savannah

BELLAIRE WOODS CAMPGROUNDS
LOCATION: 12 mi. south of Savannah on
U.S. 17, then 3½ mi. west on Route 204.
FACILITIES: Open year round; water and
bathroom facilities; electrical hookup; trailer
village vehicle sites; swimming; boating; tent
camping.

SAVANNAH SOUTH KOA KAMPGROUND
LOCATION: U.S. 17 at I-95.
FACILITIES: Open year round; water and
bathroom facilities; electrical hookup; trailer
village vehicle sites; swimming; tent camping.

Savannah Beach

RIVERS END FAMILY CAMPGROUND
LOCATION: North end of island on the Savannah riverfront.
FACILITIES: Open year round; water and
bathroom facilities; electrical hookup; trailer
village vehicle sites; swimming; boating; tent
camping.

Sparks

ARROWHEAD CAMPSITE
LOCATION: Barneyville exit off I-75.

FACILITIES: Open year round; water and
bathroom facilities; electrical hookup; trailer
village vehicle sites; swimming; tent camping.

Stone Mountain

STONE MOUNTAIN CAMPGROUND
LOCATION: East of Atlanta on Stone Mountain Freeway.
FACILITIES: Open year round; water and
bathroom facilities; electrical hookup; trailer
village vehicle sites; swimming; boating; tent
camping.

Valdosta

BAILEY'S MANOR CAMPING AREA
LOCATION: 3 mi. north of Valdosta on U.S.
41.
FACILITIES: Open year round; water and
bathroom facilities; electrical hookup; trailer
village vehicle sites; swimming; tent camping.

GEORGIA-FLORIDA KOA CAMPING
AREA
LOCATION: 12 mi. southeast on I-75 at
Clyattville Twin Lakes exit.
FACILITIES: Open year round; water and
bathroom facilities; electrical hookup; trailer
village vehicle sites; swimming; tent camping.

PONDEROSA PARK
LOCATION: North Valdosta Road.
FACILITIES: Open year round; water and
bathroom facilities; electrical hookup; trailer
village vehicle sites; swimming; tent camping.

RIVER PARK CAMPING AREA
LOCATION: 3 mi. west of Valdosta at junction of I-75 and Route 94.
FACILITIES: Open year round; water and
bathroom facilities; electrical hookup; trailer
village vehicle sites; swimming; tent camping.

RESORTS & BEACHES

Brunswick

SEA ISLAND - Three semitropical islands a
short distance off the Georgia coast near
Brunswick. On St. Simons Island, visit Fort
Frederica where the English defeated the
Spanish in this country's first major confrontation. On Jekyll Island, lounge on the
miles of white sandy beaches or stroll along
the 2-mile boardwalk. Sea Island has miles of
delightfully sunny beaches, too, plus tennis,
golf, horseback riding, and surf fishing. The
islands are accessible by automobile via
bridges from Brunswick.

Pine Mountain

CALLAWAY GARDENS - A 2500-acre family resort famous for its wildflowers of the
Southern Appalachians. This is a nature
lover's paradise with miles of scenic drives and
walking trails. You can also enjoy golf, fishing, horseback riding, hunting, and sport
shooting. Or you may spend all your time
strolling through the lush greenhouses.

BOATING AREAS

Acworth

ALLATOONA LAKE
LOCATION: Route 92 to U.S. 41.
FACILITIES: Launching; fishing; swimming; camping.

Bainbridge

LAKE SEMINOLE
LOCATION: Southwest of Bainbridge via Route 97.
FACILITIES: Launching; fishing; swimming; camping.

Blairsville

LAKE NOTTELY
LOCATION: 10 mi. northwest of Blairsville.
FACILITIES: Launching; fishing; swimming; camping.

Blue Ridge

BLUE RIDGE LAKE
LOCATION: 4 mi. east of Blue Ridge via U.S. 76.
FACILITIES: Launching; fishing; swimming; camping.

Covington

LAKE JACKSON
LOCATION: Off Route 212.
FACILITIES: Launching; fishing; swimming; camping.

Fort Gaines

LAKE WALTER F. GEORGE
LOCATION: 2 mi. north of Fort Gaines.
FACILITIES: Launching; fishing; swimming; camping.

Gainesville

LAKE LANIER
LOCATION: Off Route 369.
FACILITIES: Launching; fishing; swimming; camping.

Hiawassee

LAKE CHATAGE
LOCATION: Off U.S. 76.
FACILITIES: Launching; fishing; swimming; camping.

Lakeland

BANKS LAKE
LOCATION: Off U.S. 221 and Route 122.
FACILITIES: Launching; fishing; swimming; camping.

Ray City

RAY'S MILL POND
LOCATION: Off U.S. 129 and Route 37.
FACILITIES: Launching; fishing; swimming; camping.

BICYCLE TRAILS

LAKE ALLATOONA TRAIL - 56 mi.; some hills; 10-speed bicycle recommended.

From Sandy Springs to Allatoona Lake is a ride of only 28 mi. with a few hills. This ride would be suitable for most families that have been bicycling together for a few seasons.

Old Route 92 is the more scenic route but it also has the most hills. Route 92 has fewer hills and is the faster road. Try going out one way and coming back the other.

Trail: Sandy Springs, north to Johnson Ferry, left on Shallow Ford Road, right on Trimble to Route 92 west to Allatoona Lake to Old Route 92, right on Route 205, left on Route 92, retrace to Sandy Springs.

HENRY COUNTY TRAIL - 22 mi.; any bicycle.

Make the ride in a counter-clockwise direction. Be careful not to miss the Thurman turnoff when going southeast on Atlanta Highway. Also be alert for the confusing intersection of Fairview and Panola.

Trail: Boulder Crest Road south, left on Stage Coach Road, left on Rex, right on Atlanta Hwy, left on Thurman, left on Fairview, cross Panola to Flakes Mill, left on River Road, to Boulder Crest.

TRAILS

Atlanta

STONE MOUNTAIN TRAIL - 6.5 mi. foot trail. This trail network within the Stone Mountain Memorial Park (a Confederate Memorial) is noted for its unusual monolithic granite outcropping. The trail is mostly level, winding around the base of the mountain, in an area of oak-hickory climax forest with lovely wild flowers.

SKI AREAS

Dillard

SKY VALLEY SKI AREA
Dillard, GA 30537
(404) 746-5301
LOCATION: Northeast from Dillard on Route 246.
FACILITIES: 1 double chairlift; 1 tow rope; slopes for expert, intermediate and beginning skiers; ski instruction; ski rental; 250 ft. vertical drop; longest run, ½ mi.; restaurants; lodging.

AMUSEMENT PARKS & ATTRACTIONS

Atlanta

SIX FLAGS OVER GEORGIA
P.O. Box 43187
Atlanta, GA 30336
(404) 948-9290

GEORGIA

AMUSEMENT PARKS (continued)

FACILITIES: 35 major rides; 9 kiddie rides; fun house; 3 walk thrus; 9 games; 27 refreshment stands; 8 restaurants; 2 arcades; 2 shooting galleries; exhibits; picnic facilities; petting zoo; 5 theaters; crafts; stage shows; name bands; free acts; fireworks; pay gate; pay parking; open mid-Mar. - mid-Nov.

Douglas

HOLIDAY BEACH
Hwy. 158 West
Douglas, GA 31533
(912) 384-6090
FACILITIES: 12 major rides; 4 kiddie rides; 8 games; 3 refreshment stands; paddle boats; ski shows; live entertainment and special events; arcade; bathing beach; roller rink; marina; camping; picnic facilities; crafts; miniature golf; stage shows; name bands; free acts; fireworks; pay gate; free parking; open all year.

Stockbridge

KINGDOMS 3 (Theme Attraction)
Stockbridge, GA 30281
(404) 474-1461
FACILITIES: 15 major rides; 6 kiddie rides; fun house; 3 walk-thrus; 2 games; 6 refreshment stands; restaurant; large drive-thru animal safari; 565-acre park; arcade; shooting gallery; marina; exhibits; picnic facilities; zoo; theatre; crafts; stage shows; orchestras; name bands; vaudeville; free acts; fireworks; pay gate; free parking; open all year.

Stone Mountain

GEORGIA'S STONE MOUNTAIN
P.O. Box 778
Stone Mountain, GA 30086
(404) 469-9831
FACILITIES: A 3200-acre park surrounds world's largest granite monolith: huge sculpture of Civil War heroes carved on face of mountain, viewable from skylift; 5-mile steam train ride around mountain; riverboat; attractions; 3 major rides; 2 restaurants; 7 snack bars; bathing beach; marina; museum; camping; exhibits; picnic facilities; game ranch; antique auto and music museum; Civil War museum; carillon concerts; antebellum plantation; nature trails; boating; 18-hole championship golf course; orchestras; fireworks; pay parking.

Warm Springs

THE LITTLE WHITE HOUSE - F.D.R. MEMORIAL
85 West
Warm Springs, GA 31830
(404) 655-6511
FACILITIES: Museum in house where President Franklin D. Roosevelt lived; snack bar; exhibits; picnic facilities; free parking; open all year.

STATE FAIR

Georgia State Fair
P.O. Box 5260
Macon, GA 31208
(912) 746-7184
DATE: October

NATIONAL PARKS

There are no National Parks in Georgia.

NATIONAL FORESTS

National Forests
Southern Region
1720 Peachtree Road, NW
Atlanta, GA 30309
(404) 881-4177

Gainesville

CHATTAHOOCHEE NATIONAL FOREST
ATTRACTIONS: Visitor Center at Brasstown Bald, 4,784 feet, highest point in Georgia; waterfalls; southern end of Appalachian Trail. Deer, small-game hunting; archery hunting for deer; trout, bass fishing; swimming; boating; hiking.
FACILITIES: 25 camp and picnic sites, 23 picnic only; 6 swimming sites.
NEARBY TOWNS: Atlanta, Blue Ridge, Clarkesville, Clayton, Dahlonega, Dalton, and Toccoa; Chattanooga, TN.

OCONEE NATIONAL FOREST
ATTRACTIONS: Archaeological remains, effigy of eagle; large 4-H center; deer, small-game hunting; bass, bream fishing.
FACILITIES: 2 camp and picnic sites, 4 picnic only; 1 swimming site.
NEARBY TOWNS: Eatonton, Greensboro, and Madison.

STATE PARKS

Headquarters

Department of Natural Resources
Parks & Historic Sites Division
270 Washington, SW
Atlanta, GA 30334
(404) 656-3530

Appling

MISTLETOE STATE PARK
LOCATION: 5 mi. north of Appling.
FACILITIES: Open year round; 107 sites; water and bathroom facilities; sanitary station; electrical hookup; trailer village vehicle sites; cabins; laundry; picnic area; food service; swimming; boating; fishing; hiking; tent camping.

Bell

BOBBY BROWN STATE PARK
LOCATION: 6 mi. east of Bell.
FACILITIES: Open year round; 59 sites; water and bathroom facilities; sanitary station; electrical hookup; trailer village vehicle sites; laundry; picnic area; food service; swimming; boating; fishing; tent camping.

STATE PARKS (continued)

Blairsville

VOGEL STATE PARK
LOCATION: South of Blairsville on U.S. 19.
FACILITIES: Open year round; 80 sites; water and bathroom facilities; sanitary station; electrical hookup; trailer village vehicle sites; cabins; laundry; picnic area; food service; boating; boat rental; fishing; hiking.

Blakely

KOLOMOKI MOUNDS STATE PARK
LOCATION: 8 mi. north of Blakely.
FACILITIES: Open year round; 35 sites; water and bathroom facilities; electrical hookup; trailer village vehicle sites; laundry; picnic area; food service; boating; boat rental; fishing; hiking; museum; tent camping.

Canton

RED TOP MOUNTAIN STATE PARK
LOCATION: 6 mi. southwest of Canton.
FACILITIES: Open year round; 282 sites; water and bathroom facilities; sanitary station; electrical hookup; trailer village vehicle sites; picnic area; food service; swimming; boating; fishing; tent camping.

Carlton

WATSON MILL BRIDGE STATE PARK
LOCATION: 5 mi. south of Carlton.
FACILITIES: Open year round; 25 sites; water and bathroom facilities; electrical hookup; trailer village vehicle sites; picnic area; fishing; tent camping.

Carrollton

JOHN TANNER STATE PARK
LOCATION: 2 mi. west of Carrollton.
FACILITIES: Open year round; 80 sites; water and bathroom facilities; sanitary station; electrical hookup; trailer village vehicle sites; cabins; laundry; picnic area; food service; boating; boat rental; fishing; tent camping.

Chappel

HIGH FALLS STATE PARK
LOCATION: 3 mi. east of Chappel.
FACILITIES: Open year round; 142 sites; water and bathroom facilities; sanitary station; electrical hookup; trailer village vehicle sites; laundry; picnic area; food service; swimming; boating; boat rental; fishing; tent camping.

Chatsworth

FORT MOUNTAIN STATE PARK
LOCATION: 5 mi. east of Chatsworth.
FACILITIES: Open year round; 125 sites; water and bathroom facilities; electrical hookup; trailer village vehicle sites; cabins; laundry; picnic area; food service; swimming; boating; boat rental; fishing; hiking.

Clayton

MOCCASIN CREEK STATE PARK
LOCATION: 10 mi. southwest of Clayton.

FACILITIES: Open year round; 33 sites; water and bathroom facilities; sanitary station; electrical hookup; trailer village vehicle sites; food service; boating; fishing.

Cordele

GEORGIA VETERANS MEMORIAL STATE PARK
LOCATION: 7 mi. west of Cordele.
FACILITIES: Open year round; 50 sites; water and bathroom facilities; sanitary station; electrical hookup; trailer village vehicle sites; cabins; laundry; food service; swimming; boating; boat rental; fishing; hiking; museum; tent camping.

Dillard

BLACK ROCK MOUNTAIN STATE PARK
LOCATION: 5 mi. south of Dillard.
FACILITIES: Open year round; 50 sites; water and bathroom facilities; electrical hookup; trailer village vehicle sites; cabins; laundry; picnic area; food service; hiking; tent camping.

Douglas

GENERAL COFFEE STATE PARK
LOCATION: 5 mi. east of Douglas.
FACILITIES: Open year round; 50 sites; water and bathroom facilities; sanitary station; electrical hookup; trailer village vehicle sites; picnic area; fishing; museum; tent camping.

Ellenton

REED BINGHAM STATE PARK
LOCATION: 3 mi. east of Ellenton.
FACILITIES: Open year round; 85 sites; water and bathroom facilities; sanitary station; electrical hookup; trailer village vehicle sites; laundry; picnic area; food service; swimming; boating; fishing.

Ellijay

AMICALOLA FALLS STATE PARK
LOCATION: Near Ellijay.
FACILITIES: Open year round; 25 sites; water and bathroom facilities; electrical hookup; trailer village vehicle sites; cabins; laundry; picnic area; food service; swimming; boating; boat rental; fishing; hiking; tent camping.

Fargo

STEPHEN C. FOSTER STATE PARK
LOCATION: 15 mi. northeast of Fargo in Okefenokee Swamp Park.
FACILITIES: Open year round; 68 sites; water and bathroom facilities; sanitary station; electrical hookup; trailer village vehicle sites; cabins; laundry; picnic area; food service; boating; boat rental; fishing; museum; tent camping.

Franklin Springs

VICTORIA BRYANT STATE PARK
LOCATION: Near Franklin Springs.
FACILITIES: Open year round; 25 sites; water and bathroom facilities; sanitary station; electrical hookup; trailer village vehicle sites;

GEORGIA

STATE PARKS (continued)

laundry; picnic area; food service; swimming; fishing; tent camping.

Georgetown

GEORGE BAGBY STATE PARK
LOCATION: 10 mi. south of Georgetown.
FACILITIES: Open year round; 50 sites; water and bathroom facilities; sanitary station; electrical hookup; trailer village vehicle sites; cabins; picnic area; boating; fishing.

Hartwell

HART STATE PARK
LOCATION: 7 mi. east of Hartwell.
FACILITIES: Open year round; 50 sites; water and bathroom facilities; sanitary station; electrical hookup; cabins; picnic area; food service; swimming; boating; fishing; tent camping.

Helen

UNICOI STATE PARK
LOCATION: 3 mi. northeast of Helen.
FACILITIES: Open year round; 103 sites; water and bathroom facilities; sanitary station; electrical hookup; trailer village vehicle sites; cabins; picnic area; food service; boating; boat rental; fishing; hiking; tent camping.

Indian Springs

INDIAN SPRINGS STATE PARK
LOCATION: Near Indian Springs.
FACILITIES: Open year round; 125 sites; water and bathroom facilities; sanitary station; electrical hookup; trailer village vehicle sites; cabins; laundry; picnic area; food service; boating; boat rental; fishing; museum; environmental study area; tent camping.

Keller

RICHMOND HILL STATE PARK
LOCATION: 3 mi. east of Keller.
FACILITIES: Open year round; 30 sites; water and bathroom facilities; sanitary station; electrical hookup; trailer village vehicle sites; picnic area; boating; boat rental; fishing.

Kingsland

CROOKED RIVER STATE PARK
LOCATION: 10 mi. northeast of Kingsland.
FACILITIES: Open year round; 100 sites; water and bathroom facilities; sanitary station; electrical hookup; trailer village vehicle sites; cabins; laundry; picnic area; food service; swimming; boating; fishing; tent camping.

LaFayette

CLOUDLAND CANYON STATE PARK
LOCATION: 3 mi. north of LaFayette.
FACILITIES: Open year round; 48 sites; water and bathroom facilities; electrical hookup; trailer village vehicle sites; cabins; laundry; food service; hiking; tent camping.

Lincolnton

ELIJAH CREEK STATE PARK
LOCATION: 4 mi. north of Lincolnton.
FACILITIES: Open year round; 141 sites; water and bathroom facilities; sanitary station; electrical hookup; trailer village vehicle sites; cabins; laundry; picnic area; food service; swimming; boating; boat rental; fishing.

Madison

HARD LABOR CREEK STATE PARK
LOCATION: 4 mi. north of Madison.
FACILITIES: Open year round; 105 sites; water and bathroom facilities; sanitary station; electrical hookup; trailer village vehicle sites; cabins; laundry; picnic area; food service; swimming; boating; boat rental; fishing; tent camping.

Martin

TUGALOO STATE PARK
LOCATION: 4 mi. east of Martin.
FACILITIES: Open year round; 130 sites; water and bathroom facilities; sanitary station; electrical hookup; trailer village vehicle sites; laundry; picnic area; food service; swimming; boating; boat rental; fishing; tent camping.

McRae

LITTLE OCMULGEE STATE PARK
LOCATION: Near McRae.
FACILITIES: Open year round; 60 sites; water and bathroom facilities; sanitary station; electrical hookup; trailer village vehicle sites; cabins; laundry; picnic area; food service; swimming; boating; fishing; hiking; tent camping.

Millen

MAGNOLIA SPRINGS STATE PARK
LOCATION: 5 mi. north of Millen.
FACILITIES: Open year round; 100 sites; water and bathroom facilities; sanitary station; electrical hookup; trailer village vehicle sites; picnic area; food service; swimming; boating; fishing; hiking; tent camping.

Mitchell

HAMBURG STATE PARK
LOCATION: 5 mi. west of Mitchell.
FACILITIES: Open year round; 30 sites; water and bathroom facilities; sanitary station; electrical hookup; trailer village vehicle sites; cabins; picnic area; food service; swimming; boating; boat rental; fishing; museum.

Reynoldsville

SEMINOLE STATE PARK
LOCATION: 7 mi. south of Reynoldsville.
FACILITIES: Open year round; 50 sites; water and bathroom facilities; sanitary station; electrical hookup; trailer village vehicle sites; cabins; laundry; picnic area; food service; swimming; boating; fishing; tent camping.

Savannah Beach

SKIDAWAY ISLAND STATE PARK

STATE PARKS (continued)

LOCATION: On Skidaway Island.
FACILITIES: Open year round; 100 sites; water and bathroom facilities; sanitary station; electrical hookup; trailer village vehicle sites; picnic area; swimming.

Warm Springs

FRANKLIN D. ROOSEVELT STATE PARK
LOCATION: 5 mi. south of Warm Springs.
FACILITIES: Open year round; 140 sites; water and bathroom facilities; sanitary station; electrical hookup; trailer village vehicle sites; cabins; picnic area; food service; boating; fishing; hiking; bicycle trail; museum; tent camping.

Waycross

LAURA S. WALKER STATE PARK
LOCATION: 7 mi. southeast of Waycross.
FACILITIES: Open year round; 100 sites; water and bathroom facilities; sanitary station; electrical hookup; trailer village vehicle sites; laundry; picnic area; food service; tent camping.

Winder

FORT YARGO STATE PARK
LOCATION: Near Winder.
FACILITIES: Open year round; 34 sites; water and bathroom facilities; electrical hookup; trailer village vehicle sites; picnic area; food service; swimming; boating; boat rental; fishing; handicapped access/restroom; tent camping.

STATE FORESTS

There are no State Forests in Georgia.

HISTORIC SITES

Andersonville

ANDERSONVILLE - Actively being restored as a Civil War village to appear much as it was when Northern prisoners were unloaded from trains and taken to the Andersonville Prison across the road. Located on Route 49.

Appling

OLD KIOKEE BAPTIST CHURCH - The oldest Baptist church in Georgia. Established in 1771. Located 3 mi. north on Old Augusta-Washington Highway.

Atlanta

DR. MARTIN LUTHER KING, JR.'s TOMB - Tomb beside the Ebenezer Baptist Church which he co-pastored with his father. Located at 413 Auburn Avenue, NE.

Augusta

COTTON EXCHANGE BUILDING - The center of cotton trading in the area when Augusta streets were lined with bales being bought and sold. Located at 775 Reynolds Street.

SIGNERS' MONUMENT - A 50-foot high obelisk of Stone Mountain granite, honoring Georgia's signers of the Declaration of Independence. Located on Greene Street at Monument Street.

ZERO MILE POST - Erected in 1850, it marks the Southwestern terminus of the Western & Atlantic Railroad. This is the birthplace of the City of Atlanta. Located under Central Avenue Bridge near Decatur Street.

Blakely

CONFEDERATE FLAG POLE - Erected in 1861, it is the last remaining Confederate flag pole. Located on Court House Square in Blakely.

Cartersville

ETOWAH INDIAN MOUNDS - The largest and most important Indian settlement in the Etowah Valley. Occupied between 1000 A.D. and 1500 A.D. Located 3 mi. south of Cartersville.

Chickamauga

GORDON-LEE HOME - Served the Union Army first as headquarters and then as a hospital during the two bloodiest days of the Civil War. Located in the Chickamauga Battlefield area on Route 27.

Dahlonega

COURTHOUSE GOLD MUSEUM - Commemorates the exciting era when the nation's first major gold rush took place in 1828, and scores of prospectors converged on the area. Sites of a branch of the United States Mint in 1838. Located on the town square.

Jefferson

CRAWFORD W. LONG MUSEUM - Site of Dr. Long's office where he performed the first operation with ether. Located in downtown Jefferson.

Sandersville

OLD WOODEN JAIL - This historic structure, built around 1783, was the site of Aaron Burr's incarceration in 1807 while en route to Virginia to stand trial for treason. Located north of Sandersville on Route 15.

Savannah

CHRIST EPISCOPAL CHURCH - The first church established in the colony. Present structure replaced two others and was erected in 1840. John Wesley preached here, founding what is thought to be the world's first Sunday School. Located at 28 Bull Street.

JULIETTE GORDON LOW BIRTHPLACE - Home of the founder of the Girl Scouts of

GEORGIA

HISTORIC SITES (continued)

America. Located at 142 Bull Street.

OGLETHORPE BEACH - Commemorates the landing of James Edward Oglethorpe at this spot on February 12, 1733. Oglethorpe, along with his band of colonists, founded Georgia and Savannah. Located on Bay Street, ½ block east of City Hall.

Thompson

OLD ROCK HOUSE - The only known stone residence from the Revolutionary period in Georgia when brick and wood were the predominant building materials in the area. Located 3 mi. northwest of Thompson on Stephens Hunter Road.

HOSTELS

Atlanta

HOSTEL GEORGIAN TERRACE
Peachtree at Ponce de Leon
Atlanta, GA 30308
(404) 872-6671
FACILITIES: Open year round; 50 beds, men; 60 beds, women; modern bathroom; nearest hostel: Bryson City, NC; overnight charges: $5 in quad, $6 in triple, $7 in double, $12 in single, reservations preferred; houseparent: Joanna Claire Leifer.

Brunswick

HOSTEL IN THE FOREST
P.O. Box 1496
Brunswick, GA 31522
(912) 264-9676
FACILITIES: Open year round; 31 beds, men; 18 beds, women; nearest hostel: Orlando, FL; overnight charges: $3, $1 extra for linens; houseparents: Thomas E. Jr., & Marie B. Dennard.

POINTS OF INTEREST

Athens

DOUBLE-BARRELED CANNON - Only one of its kind in the world. Invented in 1863 for use in the War Between the States, it was to have simultaneously fired two balls connected by a chain. It failed to fire accurately, however, and was relegated to its present location as an object of curiosity. Located on City Hall lawn.

FOUNDER'S MEMORIAL GARDEN - A memorial to the founders of the first garden club in the United States (organized in 1891 by 12 ladies). Located on Babcock Drive and Lumpkin Street.

Atlanta

STONE MOUNTAIN MEMORIAL CARVING - Figures of Jefferson Davis, General Robert E. Lee and Stonewall Jackson carved from the granite mountain make this the world's largest work of sculptural art.

Augusta

OLD SLAVE MARKET COLUMN - Legend says a traveling minister, once refused permission to preach in the Lower Market, went into a rage and declared the Market Place would be destroyed and every stone would fall to the ground except one. He swore that whoever touched the remaining stone would be killed. In 1878 a cyclone destroyed the building, save this one stone pillar. Some say the preacher's curse persists. Located on Broad at 5th Street.

Baxley

EDWIN I. HATCH NUCLEAR VISITORS CENTER - A showcase of nuclear power. Located 10 mi. north of Baxley on U.S. 1.

Blakely

PEANUT MONUMENT - A constant reminder that Early County is one of the nation's largest producers of peanuts. Located on the Court House Square.

Brunswick

LOVER'S OAK - The tree is over 900 years old. Located on Albany Street near Prince Street.

Columbus

THE PEMBERTON HOUSE - This cottage, occupied by Dr. John Styth Pemberton from 1855-1860, is of international importance because Dr. Pemberton originated the Coca-Cola formula. Located at 11 Seventh Street.

Eatonton

UNCLE REMUS MUSEUM - Represents the slave cabin setting of Joel Chandler Harris' stories about Uncle Remus and his famous "critters." Located mid-town.

Fayetteville

FIFE HOUSE - The only unaltered antebellum home in the county. Housed the faculty and students of the Fayetteville Academy (1855-1857), which was attended by the fictional Scarlett O'Hara in Margaret Mitchell's "Gone with the Wind." Located at 140 W. Lanier.

Fort Benning

FORT BENNING INFANTRY MUSEUM - Traces the evolution of the infantry from French and Indian Wars to the present. Located on Ingersoll Street, Building 1234.

Helen

TOWN OF HELEN - Bavarian Alps architecture is used throughout Helen, and the buildings feature gingerbread trim and face paintings. Enjoy stone streets, unique shops

POINTS OF INTEREST (continued)

and a picture-book setting. Located at junction of Route 75 and Route 348.

Macon

AVENUE OF THE FLAGS - Features the flag of each state, as well as the territorial flags of the United States. Located on Poplar Street.

GRAND OPERA HOUSE - Has the largest stage in the United States. Built in 1906 and recently restored, the structure is the center for performing arts in middle Georgia. Located at 651 Mulberry Street.

Plains

PLAINS - The small town of Plains has received national exposure as a result of Jimmy Carter. Points of interest include the home of the President, Carter's birthplace, downtown, old Railroad Depot (Campaign Headquarters),

and peanut warehouses.

Tallulah Falls

TALLULAH GORGE - Believed to be the oldest natural gorge in North America. It is 1½ mi. long and reaches a depth of 2000 feet. Located on U.S. 441.

Tate

GEORGIA MARBLE - Has been used throughout the world for buildings and monuments, and an almost unlimited supply is found here in the Long Swamp valley region. Located at intersection of Route 5 and Route 53.

Tifton

AGRIRAMA - Experience the flavor of rural Georgia prior to 1900. Over 25 authentic structures faithfully restored. Located at intersection of I-75 and 8th Street.

HAWAII

Hawaii, a group of eight islands some 2,400 miles west of the mainland, joined the Union in 1959 as the fiftieth state. Around the turn of the century, with the growth of pineapple and sugar plantations on the islands, the United States annexed the territory and established major trade routes.

Hawaii also proved to be strategic militarily, especially in light of the world's hostilities prevalent in the 1930s; but although experts warned of imminent attack by Japanese forces, no special precautions were taken un-

til Pearl Harbor was bombed on December 7, 1941. Today, all branches of the Armed Forces are stationed in Hawaii.

The pineapple and sugar industries are no longer the state's leading revenue earners. With the advent of lower air fares and shorter flying time from the West Coast, vacationers have flocked to the sunny shores in record-breaking numbers, creating a tourism boom.

State capital: Honolulu. State bird: Hawaiian goose. State tree: Kukui. State flower: Hibiscus.

►— SPECIAL NOTE —◄

Hawaii is composed of 8 islands; the most important are the 6 major islands: Hawaii (4,038 sq. mi.), Kauai (555 sq. mi.), Lanai (140 sq. mi.), Maui (729 sq. mi.), Molokai

(261 sq. mi.), and Oahu (608 sq. mi.). The information in this state pertains to the 6 major islands only and is arranged in alphabetical order.

WEATHER

There are six major islands in the state of Hawaii which occupy a narrow zone 430 miles long. From west to east these are Kauai, Oahu, Molokai, Lanai, Maui, and Hawaii. The islands are terrestrial, summit portions of the long range of volcanic mountains that comprise the Hawaiian Chain. Kauai, in the west, is geologically the oldest of the six major islands and is, therefore, most strongly eroded. Hawaii, in the east, is geologically the youngest. Its dominant physiographic features are the large mountain masses of Mauna Loa and Mauna Kea, both of which rise to over 13,000

feet above the mean sea level, and both of which have suffered only slight erosion. All the islands are bordered by coral reefs, and all have coasts that consist, in part, of cliffs.

In general, the Hawaiian climate is characterized by a two-season year, by mild and fairly uniform temperature conditions everywhere except at high elevations, by strikingly marked geographic differences in rainfall, by generally humid conditions and high cloudiness, except on the driest coasts and high elevations, and by a general dominance of trade-wind flow, especially at elevations below a few thousand feet.

HAWAII

WEATHER (continued)

Average daily temperature for each month.

	Mountainous	Coastal
Jan.	74.3 to 56.8	79.6 to 62.8
Feb.	73.5 to 56.4	79.4 to 62.6
Mar.	73.4 to 57.2	78.8 to 63.3
Apr.	73.7 to 58.5	79.8 to 64.6
May	74.8 to 59.4	81.3 to 65.6
Jun.	76.4 to 60.4	82.7 to 66.5
Jul.	77.0 to 61.4	83.0 to 67.5
Aug.	77.6 to 62.0	83.5 to 68.2
Sept.	78.3 to 61.1	83.6 to 67.6
Oct.	77.9 to 60.8	83.2 to 66.7
Nov.	75.6 to 59.9	81.3 to 65.6
Dec.	74.1 to 58.1	79.4 to 63.7
Year	75.6 to 59.3	81.3 to 65.4

STATE CHAMBER OF COMMERCE

Chamber of Commerce of Hawaii
Dillingham Building
Honolulu, HI 96813
(808) 531-4111

STATE & CITY TOURISM OFFICES

State

Hawaii Visitors Bureau
P.O. Box 2274
Honolulu, HI 96804
(808) 923-1811

Planning and Economic Development
P.O. Box 2359
Honolulu, HI 96804
(808) 548-4025

STATE HIGHWAY DEPARTMENT

Department of Transportation
869 Punchbowl Street
Honolulu, HI 96813
(808) 548-3205

HIGHWAY WELCOMING CENTERS

There are no Highway Welcoming Centers in Hawaii.

STATE POLICE

Honolulu Police Department *
1455 South Beretania St.
Honolulu, HI 96814
(808) 955-8111

*Hawaii does not have a State Police department. Each of the six islands maintains a local police department which reports to the mayor of the island. Listed above is the state's largest police force.

HUNTING & FISHING

Hunting

Hunting is open to persons of all ages who are permitted to hunt in any of the other forty-nine states.

Each island has its own game mammal regulations, which include maps of Game Management Areas, calendars listing specific seasons for hunting within these areas, bag limits and permissable hunting methods, plus other pertinent information available from the respective Island office of the Division of Fish and Game.

Resident

Hunting, $7.50.

Non-resident

Hunting, $15.

Fishing

Fishing the waters of the Islands is a 12-months-a-year challenge; and for saltwater fishing there are no seasons, no limits and no licenses.

Freshwater fishing consists exclusively of introduced species with the exception of one group of fish called gobies. Due to the nature of the mountainous, volcanic terrain, there are few natural freshwater bodies of water. The state maintains five public fishing areas.

Resident

Freshwater fishing, $3.75.

Non-resident

Freshwater fishing, $3.75.

For more information contact:

Department of Land and Natural Resources
Division of Fish and Game
Honolulu, HI 96813
(808) 548-4002

CAMPGROUNDS

See National Parks and State Parks.

RESORTS & BEACHES

Hawaii

KAILUA - Once the capital of the Hawaiian kingdom, Kailua is a mixture of the old and new Hawaii. Modern hotels and low Polyne-

RESORTS (continued)

sian-type buildings surround the bay where deep-sea charter fishing boats troll for marlin. For the inquisitive, glass-bottomed excursion boats and a Chinese junk (also glass-bottomed) are available for exploring the underwater reefs.

Maui

KAANAPALI - The vistas here are stunning, a collaboration of nature in a benevolent mood and man with an appreciative eye. There are gardens to stroll through, boats to sail, fish to catch, sports to play and sun-soaked beaches to relax on.

Oahu

WAIKIKI - Perhaps the most famous beach of all, Waikiki has a miracle mile of hotels, international shops, restaurants and clubs that appeal to natives and visitors alike. All your time can be taken up with playing games in the sun. You may choose tennis or golf, then suit up for surfing or sailing. Or for a change of pace, interesting and historic sites, such as Pearl Harbor, are nearby.

BOATING AREAS

There are no inland Boating Areas in Hawaii.

BICYCLE TRAILS

TRAILS AROUND KAUAI AND MAUI - Any bicycle.

Although there are a limited number of roads in Hawaii, the cycling is unique, featuring tropical plants, waterfalls, great beaches, and unusual fruits and vegetables.

Be sure to go to a police station to get a license for each bicycle. While at the police station or at a county office, make reservations for the county parks in which you plan to camp. These parks are patrolled and a reservation permit is required.

Trails: KAUAI - Haena to Hanalei to Kapaa to Lihue to Kekaha.
MAUI - (1) Honokahua to Lahaina to Makena; (2) Waihee to Kahuli to Paia to Hana to Kipahulu; (3) Honokahua to Lahaina to Waihee.

TRAILS

There are no National Trails System Foot Trails in Hawaii.

SKI AREAS

There are no organized Ski Areas in Hawaii.

AMUSEMENT PARKS & ATTRACTIONS

Ewa Beach

E. K. FERNANDEZ SHOWS
91-246 Oihana Street
Ewa Beach, HI 96707
(808) 682-5767
FACILITIES: 16 major rides; 9 kiddie rides; walk thru; 40 games; 2 confectionery wagons; arcade; shooting gallery; exhibits; jewelry and novelty sales; free acts; fireworks; free and pay gate; free and pay parking.

STATE FAIR

50th State Fair
Aloha Stadium
Honolulu, HI 96820
(808) 531-4333
DATE: May

NATIONAL PARKS

Hawaii National Park

HAWAII VOLCANOES NATIONAL PARK
Hawaii Volcanoes National Park, HI 96718
(808) 967-7311

KAMOAMOA
LOCATION: 52 mi. southeast of Park headquarters.
FACILITIES: Open year round; limit of stay: 7 days; 10 sites; bathroom facilities; no water.

KIPUKA NENE
LOCATION: 12 mi. south of Park headquarters.
FACILITIES: Open year round; limit of stay: 7 days; 6 sites; water and bathroom facilities; cabins; picnic area; food service; fishing; hiking; exhibit; museum; living history program; NPS guided tour; self-guiding tour; lodging.

NAMAKANI PAIO
LOCATION: 3 mi. west of Park headquarters.
FACILITIES: Open year round; limit of stay: 7 days; 6 sites; group camps: 2; water and bathroom facilities; cabins; picnic area; food service; fishing; hiking; exhibit; museum; living history program; NPS guided tour; self-guiding tour; lodging.

Makawao

HALEAKALA NATIONAL PARK
Maui, HI 96768
(808) 572-7749

HOLUA
LOCATION: Near Holua Cabin.
FACILITIES: Open year round; limit of stay: 2 days; 5 sites; water and bathroom facilities; cabins; picnic area; hiking; horseback riding; exhibit; NPS guided tour; self-guiding tour; no pets; no open fires; reservations 60 days in advance.

HAWAII

NATIONAL PARKS (continued)

HOSMER GROVE
LOCATION: ½ mi. east of north entrance.
FACILITIES: Open year round; limit of stay:
3 days; 5 sites; water and bathroom facilities;
cabins; picnic area; hiking; horseback riding;
exhibit; NPS guided tour; self-guiding tour;
reservations 60 days in advance.

KIPAHULA
LOCATION: Near Oheo Gulch.
FACILITIES: Open year round; limit of stay:
3 days; 10 sites; bathroom facilities; cabins;
picnic area; swimming; fishing; hiking; horseback riding; exhibit; NPS guided tour; self-
guiding tour; no water; reservations 60 days in
advance.

PALIKU
LOCATION: Near Paliku Cabin.
FACILITIES: Open year round; limit of stay:
2 days; 5 sites; water and bathroom facilities;
cabins; picnic area; hiking; horseback riding;
exhibit; NPS guided tour; self-guiding tour; no
pets; no open fires; reservations 60 days in
advance.

NATIONAL FORESTS

There are no National Forests in Hawaii.

STATE PARKS

Headquarters

Department of Land & Natural Resources
Division of Parks, Outdoor Recreation and
   Historical Sites
1151 Punchbowl Street
Honolulu, HI 96813
(808) 548-7455

Island of Hawaii
P.O. Box 936
Hilo, HI 96720
(808) 961-7200

Hilo

MAUNA KEA STATE PARK
LOCATION: 10 mi. east of Pahoa off Hwy.
137.
FACILITIES: Open year round; water and
bathroom facilities; cabins; picnic area; hiking.

WAILUKU RIVER STATE PARK
LOCATION: In Hilo.
FACILITIES: Open year round; water and
bathroom facilities.

Honomu

AKAKA FALLS STATE PARK
LOCATION: 2 mi. from Honomu.
FACILITIES: Open year round; water and
bathroom facilities; picnic area.

Pahoa

MACKENZIE STATE PARK

LOCATION: 10 mi. east of Pahoa off Hwy.
137.
FACILITIES: Open year round; water and
bathroom facilities; trailer village vehicle sites;
picnic area; fishing; tent camping.

Island of Kauai
P.O. Box 1671
Kauai, HI 96766
(808) 245-4444

Bonham Air Force Base

POLIHALE STATE PARK
LOCATION: 5 mi. north of Bonham Air
Force Base.
FACILITIES: Open year round; water and
bathroom facilities; picnic area; swimming;
tent camping.

Kauai (western coast)

NA PALI COAST STATE PARK
LOCATION: 5 mi. from Polihale landing.
FACILITIES: Open year round; water and
bathroom facilities; electrical hookup; trailer
village vehicle sites; picnic area; boating; fishing; tent camping.

Kekaha

KOKEE STATE PARK
LOCATION: 15 mi. north of Kekaha on
Hwy. 55.
FACILITIES: Open year round; water and
bathroom facilities; electrical hookup; trailer
village vehicle sites; picnic area; food service;
hunting; fishing; hiking; horseback riding; tent
camping.

WAIMEA CANYON STATE PARK
LOCATION: 12 mi. north of Kekaha on
Hwy. 55.
FACILITIES: Open year round; water and
bathroom facilities; picnic area; hiking.

Lihue

WAILUA RIVER STATE PARK
LOCATION: 6 mi. north of Lihue on Hwy.
56.
FACILITIES: Open year round; water and
bathroom facilities; picnic area; swimming;
fishing; tent camping.

Island of Maui
P.O. Box 1049
Maui, HI 96793
(808) 244-4352

Hana

WAIANAPANAPA STATE PARK
LOCATION: 4 mi. north of Hana.
FACILITIES: Open year round; water and
bathroom facilities; fishing; hiking; tent camping.

Island of Molokai
P.O. Box 627
Molokai, HI 96748
(808) 553-5415

STATE PARKS (continued)

Kualapuu

PALAAU STATE PARK
LOCATION: 3 mi. north of Kualapuu off
Hwy. 47.
FACILITIES: Open year round; water and
bathroom facilities; picnic area; tent camping.

Island of Oahu
1151 Punchbowl Street
Honolulu, HI 96813
(808) 548-7455

Honolulu

AINA MOANA STATE PARK
LOCATION: Aina Moana, Honolulu.
FACILITIES: Open year round; water and
bathroom facilities; picnic area; swimming.

KAHANA VALLEY STATE PARK
LOCATION: 26 mi. from Honolulu on Route
83.
FACILITIES: Open year round; water and
bathroom facilities; picnic area; swimming.

STATE FORESTS

There are no State Forests in Hawaii.

HISTORIC SITES

Hawaii

FIRST CHRISTIAN CHURCH - Was erected
by American missionaries who first landed on
this coast in 1820. Located at Kailua-Kona.

HULIHEE PALACE - Was once the summer
palace of Hawaiian royalty, and now houses a
rare collection of Hawaiiana. Located in the
village of Kailua-Kona.

KAMEHAMEHA STATUE - Was lost at sea
and later recovered after a replica had been
made and erected in Honolulu. Located in
Kohala.

LYMAN MISSION HOUSE AND MUSEUM -
Contains a collection of ancient Hawaiian historic relics. Located in Hilo.

Kauai

CAPTAIN COOK'S LANDING, WAIMEA
BAY - First place in which the intrepid British
explorer set foot in Hawaii, this bay was for
many years a favorite provisioning port with
Pacific traders and whalers. Located on southwest shore.

Lanai

LUAHIWA PETROGLYPHS - En route to
Palawai Basin, site of an old Mormon Colony,
these petroglyphs are among the best preserved in Hawaii. Located on east shore.

Maui

JODO MISSION - A Buddhist cultural park
built between 1968 and 1970. It includes a
Buddhist Temple and Japanese cultural garden with the largest Buddha outside of Japan.
Located on northwest shore.

KAAHUMANU CHURCH - Oldest Congregational Hawaiian church on central Maui. Original section was built in 1837. Located on
north shore.

LAHAINALUNA SCHOOL - Oldest school
west of the Rocky Mountains, established in
1831. Its first building of poles and grass was
replaced by a stone building which still stands
on the modern school grounds. Located on
northwest shore.

LAHAINA - First capital of the Islands and
historic heart of Maui. This colorful town is
steeped in the memories and evidences of
whaling days, missionaries, ancient Hawaiian
rulers and the plantation workers of various
ethnic orgins who migrated to this island. Located on northwest shore.

Molokai

FATHER DAMIEN'S STATUE - Built in
memory of Father Damien de Veuster whose
missionary work among the victims of Han-
sen's disease was renowned throughout the
world. This statue stands in a grassy glade on
the isolated Kalaupapa Peninsula on Molokai's
north shore.

Oahu

IOLANI PALACE - Only throne room under
the American flag, where Hawaii's kings and
queens lived and ruled. Located in Honolulu.

MISSION HOUSES - The oldest existing
building erected by the first missionary con-
tingent to Honolulu are in the civic center
area, which is also the locale of many other
historic sites.

NUUANU PALI - Oahu's scenic masterpiece,
at the head of Nuuanu Valley. Here Kamehameha the Great defeated the Oahuans in a
bloody battle in 1795, thus adding Oahu to
his realm.

PEARL HARBOR - The attack on this naval
base by the Japanese on December 7, 1941,
precipitated the United States' entry into
World War II. Located on south shore.

HOSTELS

Captain Cook

DR. B.J. KEITH INSTITUTE FOR GIFTED
    STUDENTS
R.R. 1, Box 64
Captain Cook, HI 96704
(808) 328-2323
FACILITIES: Open year round; paid reservations only; 12 beds, men; 12 beds, women; 10
extra bunks with mattresses and trailer; mod-

HAWAII

HOSTELS (continued)

ern bathroom; nearest hostel: Honolulu; overnight charges: $3; inquiries and reservations require stamped, self-addressed envelope; houseparent: Dr. Bruno J. Keith.

Honolulu

HALE ALOHA YOUTH HOSTEL
2323 Sea View Avenue
Honolulu, HI 96822
(808) 946-0591
FACILITIES: Open year round (send stamped return envelope, one night deposit for reservation); 16 beds, men; 6 beds, women; modern bathroom; nearest hostel: Captain Cook; overnight charges: $2; houseparents: John K. Akau, Jr. & Thelma I. Akau.

Wailuku

KEANAE YMCA YOUTH HOSTEL
Maui, P.O. Box 820
Wailuku, HI 96793
(808) 248-8355
FACILITIES: Open year round; 30 beds, men; 30 beds, women; modern bathroom; nearest hostels: Honolulu, Captain Cook; overnight charges: $3; houseparents: David & Bud Aronson.

POINTS OF INTEREST

Hawaii

CAPTAIN COOK MONUMENT - A tribute to the British navigator and discoverer of the Hawaiian islands who was killed here in 1779. Located at Kealakekua Bay, west shore.

PARKER RANCH - The largest single-owner ranch under the American flag. Located at foot of Mauna Kea.

Kauai

FERN GROTTO - Hauntingly beautiful cave, luxuriantly festooned with growing ferns. Located on east shore.

KALALAU LOOKOUT - One of the most breathtaking views in all the islands, where the valley drops 4,000 feet to the shores of the Pacific. The valley is bounded by razor-sharp cliffs sprinkled by many waterfalls. Located just off Route 55 above Kokee Park.

LUMAHAI BEACH - Chosen for Nurses' Beach in "South Pacific," this lovely spot is undoubtedly the most photographed on Kauai. Located on north shore.

PARADISE PACIFICA - An expansive 23-acre field with gardens, lagoons, exotic birds and unique narrated train rides which meander through replicas of a rain forest, a Polynesian village, a Japanese island, a Filipino village, and other interesting and colorful exhibits. Located on east shore.

SLEEPING GIANT - Outline of mountain ridge shows striking resemblance to reclining giant. Located on east shore.

Lanai

GARDEN OF THE GODS - Weird rock formations near Kanepuu change color with the setting sun. Located on west shore.

LANAIHALE - From this 3370-foot vantage point, all of Hawaii's islands, except Kauai and Niihau, can be seen on a clear day. Located on northeast shore.

LANAI CITY - Often likened to a New England village, this picturesque town is backed by towering Norfolk pine trees and surrounded by silvery fields of pineapples. Dole Company's offices are here.

Maui

BANYAN TREE - Planted in 1873, this magnificent tree is said to be the largest banyan tree in all Hawaii. Located on northwest shore.

WAIANPANAPA CAVES - By diving into a pool and swimming underwater, the boldly curious can reach a big inner cave, a legendary trysting place for lovers of old. Located on southeast shore.

Molokai

MOAULA FALLS - Legend has it that the pool at the bottom of these falls is safe for swimming only if a ti leaf floats when thrown on the water. Located on northeast shore of island.

Oahu

BLOW HOLE - Playful Mother Nature forces the mighty sea through a tiny hole in a lava ledge and blows miniature geysers high into the air. Located near Koko Head.

DIAMOND HEAD - This world renowned landmark bounds Waikiki Beach on the south. An extinct volcano, it is said to have once been the home of Pele, the Fire Goddess. Located on Waikiki Beach.

POLYNESIAN CULTURAL CENTER AT LAIE - Made up of six native villages representative of those in Fiji, Tonga, New Zealand, Tahiti-Marquesas, Samoa and Hawaii. Located on the north shore of Oahu.

QUEEN EMMA SUMMER PALACE - A charming home, this former summer palace has been restored to its original appearance and houses a fine collection of Hawaiiana. Located in Nuuanu Valley.

IDAHO

Idaho, the nation's largest silver-producing state, was admitted to the Union in 1890 as the forty-third state. Since the 1860s, mining has played a significant role in shaping the state's history and economy.

There were years of violent conflicts and bloodshed between unions and mineowners culminating in 1899, when martial law had to be declared and federal troops called in to restore order.

Besides leading in silver production, Idaho today also mines more lead and cobalt than any other state. But even with all this activity deep in the ground, agricultural products, such as corn, wheat, barley, hops, apples and the famous potato, produce more revenues for the state.

Tourism is beginning to develop into a strong revenue earner, too. Thousands of vacationers are taking advantage of Idaho's rugged wilderness, natural hot springs and abundant lakes and reservoirs.

State capital: Boise. State bird: Mountain bluebird. State tree: Western pine. State flower: Syringa.

WEATHER

Idaho lies entirely west of the Continental Divide, which forms its boundary for some distance westward from Yellowstone National Park. The northern part of the state averages lower in elevation than the much larger central and southern portions, where numerous mountain ranges form barriers to the free flow of air from all points of the compass. Comprising rugged mountain ranges, canyons, high grassy valleys, arid plains, and fertile lowlands, the state reflects, in its topography and vegetation, a wide range of climates. Located some 300 miles from the Pacific Ocean, Idaho is, nevertheless, influenced by maritime air. Particularly in winter, the maritime influence is noticeable in the greater average cloudiness, greater frequency of precipitation, and mean temperatures which are above those at the same latitude and altitude in midcontinent. Eastern Idaho's climate has a more continental character than the west and north, a fact quite evident not only in the somewhat greater range between winter and summer temperatures, but also in the reversal of the wet winter-dry summer pattern.

In summer, periods of extreme heat extending beyond a week are quite rare, and the same can be said of periods of extremely low temperatures in winter. In both cases the normal progress of weather systems across the state generally results in rather frequent changes.

Average daily temperature for each month.

	Eastern	Western
Jan.	28.1 to 11.1	38.6 to 22.8
Feb.	34.3 to 15.9	45.7 to 26.7
Mar.	42.9 to 21.8	54.3 to 30.5
Apr.	55.8 to 30.5	63.4 to 36.9
May	67.8 to 39.1	72.2 to 45.0
Jun.	75.5 to 45.7	79.3 to 51.8
Jul.	86.5 to 51.3	88.4 to 57.3
Aug.	84.6 to 49.7	86.3 to 55.2
Sept.	73.2 to 40.7	77.2 to 46.4
Oct.	60.5 to 31.3	65.0 to 37.1
Nov.	43.2 to 22.6	50.1 to 29.9
Dec.	30.5 to 13.4	39.9 to 24.6
Year	56.9 to 31.1	63.4 to 38.7

STATE CHAMBER OF COMMERCE

Idaho Association of Commerce & Industry
P.O. Box 389
Boise, ID 83701
(208) 343-6666

STATE & CITY TOURISM OFFICES

State

Commerce and Development
State Capitol Building
Boise, ID 83720
(208) 384-2470

Division of Tourism and Industrial Development
State Capitol Building
Boise, ID 83720
(208) 384-2470

STATE HIGHWAY DEPARTMENT

State of Idaho Transportation Department
3311 West State Street
Boise, ID 83707
(208) 384-3699

HIGHWAY WELCOMING CENTERS

Boise

BOISE CENTER - Interstate 80, exit 54, near Boise.

Coeur D'Alene

COEUR D'ALENE CENTER - Interstate 90.

Wallace

WALLACE CENTER - Interstate 90 east of Coeur D'Alene.

IDAHO

STATE POLICE

Department of Public Safety
Box 34
Boise, ID 83731
(208) 384-2900

HUNTING & FISHING

Hunting

Any persons hunting or fishing in Idaho must have a valid license or permit, except no license is required for children under 14 years of age. Non-resident children under 14 years of age must be accompanied by a valid fishing license holder, and their fish must be included in his limit in order to fish without a license.

A person must be a resident of the State for six months in order to qualify for a resident license.

Persons 14 years of age and older who do not qualify as residents must purchase a non-resident license.

Resident

Game, $5; juvenile (12-17 years) game, $3; elk, $8; deer, $4; moose, $45; sheep, $45; goat, $15; antelope, $10; mountain lion, $5; bear, $4; turkey, $4; archery hunting, $3.

Non-resident

Game, $50; gun (non-game, Jan. - Aug. only), $5; elk (limited number to be sold), $100; deer (limited number to be sold), $35; sheep, $100; mountain lion, $35; antelope, $25; goat, $35; bear, $15; turkey, $7; archery hunting, $3.

Fishing

See above regulations.

Resident

Fish, $6; juvenile (14-17 years) fish, $4; fish and game, $10; juvenile (14-17 years) fish and game, $6; steelhead fishing, $2; salmon fishing, $2.

Non-resident

Season fishing, $20; 7-day fishing, $7; 1-day fishing, $3; steelhead fishing, $2; salmon fishing, $2.

For more information contact:

Idaho Department of Fish and Game
600 South Walnut
Box 25
Boise, ID 83707
(208) 384-3700

CAMPGROUNDS

See National Forests and State Parks.

RESORTS

Hot Springs

Idaho's natural hot springs, with their soothing mineral waters, are among the state's major attractions. Following are those hot springs which are situated in or near a city with a local Chamber of Commerce. Contact the Chamber for information on facilities offered.

American Falls

INDIAN SPRINGS
LOCATION: 1 mi. west of American Falls.

AMERICAN FALLS CHAMBER OF COMMERCE
Box 207
American Falls, ID 83211
(208) 226-5084

Boise

TWIN SPRINGS
LOCATION: East of Atlanta on Middle Fork of Boise.

BOISE CHAMBER OF COMMERCE
Box 2368
Boise, ID 83701
(208) 344-5515

Buhl

BANBURY HOT SPRINGS
LOCATION: Between Buhl and Hagerman on U.S. 30.

BUHL CHAMBER OF COMMERCE
Box 28
Buhl, ID 83316
(208) 543-6682

Council

STARKEY HOT SPRINGS
LOCATION: 8 mi. north of Council.

COUNCIL CHAMBER OF COMMERCE
General Delivery
Council, ID 83612
(208) 253-3489

Hailey

CLARENDON HOT SPRINGS
LOCATION: 7 mi. northwest of Hailey.

HAILEY CHAMBER OF COMMERCE
Box 1340
Hailey, ID 83333
(208) 788-4505

Marsing

GIVENS HOT SPRINGS
LOCATION: 12 mi. south of Marsing.

MARSING CHAMBER OF COMMERCE
Marsing, ID 83639
(208) 896-4122

RESORTS (continued)

McCall

BURGDORF HOT SPRINGS
LOCATION: 30 mi. north of McCall.

MCCALL CHAMBER OF COMMERCE
Box D
McCall, ID 83638
(208) 634-5400

Preston

VINCENT HOT SPRINGS
LOCATION: Near Hwy. 36, midway between
Mink Creek and Preston, at southern end of
Oneida Narrows.

PRESTON CHAMBER OF COMMERCE
27½ W. Oneida
Preston, ID 83263
(208) 852-2703

Riggins

RIGGINS HOT SPRINGS
LOCATION: 9 mi. east of Riggins.

RIGGINS CHAMBER OF COMMERCE
Box 289
Riggins, ID 83549
(208) 628-3414

Salmon

BEARDSLEY HOT SPRINGS
LOCATION: South of Salmon on U.S. 93.

SALMON HOT SPRINGS
LOCATION: South of Salmon on U.S. 93.

SHARKEY HOT SPRINGS
LOCATION: 20 mi. southeast of Salmon near
Hwy. 28.

SALMON CHAMBER OF COMMERCE
Box 657
Salmon, ID 83467
(208) 756-2714

Soda Springs

HOOPER SPRING
LOCATION: 1 mi. north of Soda Springs.

MAMMOTH SODA SPRING
LOCATION: 3 mi. north of Soda Springs.

SULPHUR SPRINGS
LOCATION: 8 mi. southeast of Soda Springs
on U.S. 30N.

SODA SPRINGS CHAMBER OF COM-
MERCE
Box 697
Soda Springs, ID 83276
(208) 547-3238

Stanley

MINERAL SPRINGS
LOCATION: 2 mi. south of Stanley on U.S.
93.

STANLEY HOT SPRINGS
LOCATION: Junction of Valley Creek and
U.S. 93.

SUNBEAM HOT SPRINGS
LOCATION: 13 mi. east of Stanley on U.S.
93.

STANLEY CHAMBER OF COMMERCE
Box 45
Stanley, ID 83278
(208) 774-3380

Other Idaho Hot Springs

For specific information on facilities offered,
contact the state tourism office.

Bruneau

BRUNEAU HOT SPRINGS
LOCATION: 8 mi. southeast of Bruneau.

Challis

CHALLIS HOT SPRINGS
LOCATION: On Warm Springs Creek, east of
Challis off U.S. 93.

Downey

DOWNATA HOT SPRINGS
LOCATION: 5 mi. south of Downey.

Dubois

LIDY HOT SPRINGS
LOCATION: 16 mi. west of Dubois on Hwy.
22.

Elk City

RED RIVER HOT SPRINGS
LOCATION: 27 mi. east of Elk City.

Garden City

SILVER CREEK PLUNGE
LOCATION: North of Hwy. 23 in Garden
City.

Lava Hot Springs

LAVA HOT SPRINGS
LOCATION: In Lava Hot Springs.

Malad City

PLEASANTVIEW WARM SPRINGS
LOCATION: 5 mi. west of Malad City.

New Meadows

MEADOWS VALLEY HOT SPRINGS
LOCATION: 5 mi. north on U.S. 95.

SULPHUR HOT SPRINGS
LOCATION: 14 mi. north of New Meadows
off Hwy. 95.

Newdale

GREEN CANYON HOT SPRINGS
LOCATION: Off Hwy. 33, southeast of New-
dale.

IDAHO

RESORTS (continued)

ZIM'S PLUNGE
LOCATION: 7 mi. north of New Meadows
off Hwy. 95.

Pollock

BOULDER CREEK RESORT
LOCATION: 8 mi. south of Pollock.

Ririe

HEISE HOT SPRINGS
LOCATION: About 5 mi. east of Ririe.

BOATING AREAS

See State Parks.

BICYCLE TRAILS

LAKE COEUR D'ALENE TRAIL - 36 mi.;
hilly terrain; 10-speed bicycle recommended.
Expect some thousand foothills along with
scenic vistas of the lake. The road has little or
no shoulder so select a time of light traffic for
your ride.
Trail: Interstate 90 to State Route 3.

LEWIS AND CLARK TRAIL - 320 mi.;
mountainous terrain, long distances per day,
poor roads; 10-speed bicycle necessary.
This trip starts in Missoula, Montana, and
follows closely the route taken by the Lewis
& Clark Expedition in 1805 to Kooskia. On
this leg of the triangle you climb 5,200 foot
Lolo Pass and have a down-hill run on the
west side.
At Elk City, Montana, the pavement ends
and you have 90 mi. of passable but rough
road to reach Conner, Montana.
The last leg of the triangle takes you along
the Bitterroot River back to Missoula. The
trip is best tackled in Jul., Aug., or Sept.
Trail: Missoula, MT to Lolo, MT to Lowell, ID to Kooskia to Harpster to Golden to
Elk City to Conner, MT to Hamilton to Lolo
to Missoula.

RED FISH LAKE TRAIL - 400 mi.; long distances per day, rugged terrain, cold climate;
10-speed bicycle necessary.
Many campsites, operated by both the
Forest Service and commercial groups, dot
the hay fields along the Salmon River.
Trail: Stanley to Clayton to Challis to Salmon to Leadore to Arco to Carey to Ketchum
to Stanley.

TRAILS

There are no National Trails System Foot
Trails in Idaho.

SKI AREAS

Albion

MAGIC MOUNTAIN

P.O. Box 158
Albion, ID 83311
(208) 638-5555
LOCATION: 35 mi. southeast of Twin Falls.
FACILITIES: 1 double chairlift; 1 tow rope;
1 poma; ski instruction; ski rental; 800 ft. vertical drop; restaurants.

POMERELLE
P.O. Box 158
Albion, ID 83311
(208) 638-5555
LOCATION: 28 mi. southeast of Burley off
I-80.
FACILITIES: 2 double chairlifts; 1 tow
rope; ski instruction; ski rental; 1000 ft. ver-
tical drop; restaurants; lodging.

Ashton

BEAR GULCH
P.O. Box 937
Idaho Falls, ID 83401
(208) 522-1865
LOCATION: 10 mi. northeast of Ashton on
Route 47.
FACILITIES: 1 double chairlift; 1 T-bar; ski
instruction; ski rental; 1240 ft. vertical drop;
restaurants; lodging.

Boise

BOGUS BASIN
731 North 15th
Boise, ID 83702
(208) 336-4500
LOCATION: 16 mi. north of Boise.
FACILITIES: 6 double chairlifts; 4 tow
ropes; 1 poma; ski instruction; ski rental;
nursery; 1800 ft. vertical drop; restaurants;
lodging.

Cottonwood

COTTONWOOD BUTTE
P.O. Box 335
Cottonwood, ID 83522
(208) 962-3166
LOCATION: 5 mi. west of Cottonwood off
U.S. 95.
FACILITIES: 1 T-bar; 1 tow rope; ski instruc-
tion; ski rental; 845 ft. vertical drop; restau-
rants; lodging.

Driggs

TARGHEE
Driggs, ID 83422
(307) 353-2304
LOCATION: 12 mi. north of Driggs.
FACILITIES: 3 double chairlifts; 1 tow
rope; ski instruction; ski rental; nursery;
2200 ft. vertical drop; restaurants; lodging.

Fairfield

SOLDIER MOUNTAIN
P.O. Box 337
Fairfield, ID 83327
(208) 764-2260
LOCATION: 12 mi. north of Fairfield off
Route 68.
FACILITIES: 2 double chairlifts; 1 J-bar; 2
tow ropes. ski instruction; ski rental; 1400 ft.
vertical drop; restaurants; lodging.

SKI AREAS (continued)

Grangeville

SNOWHAVEN
305 North Mill
Grangeville, ID 83530
(208) 983-0740
LOCATION: 7 mi. south of Grangeville.
FACILITIES: 1 T-bar; 1 tow rope; ski instruction; ski rental; 400 ft. vertical drop; restaurants; lodging.

Idaho Falls

KELLY CANYON
2034 Virginia
Idaho Falls, ID 83401
(208) 523-3709
LOCATION: 8 mi. east of Ririe off U.S. 26.
FACILITIES: 3 double chairlifts; 3 tow ropes; ski instruction; ski rental; 870 ft. vertical drop; restaurants; lodging.

TAYLOR MOUNTAIN
1975 North Yellowstone Highway
Idaho Falls, ID 83401
(208) 523-3383
LOCATION: 13 mi. southeast of Idaho Falls.
FACILITIES: 1 double chairlift; 1 poma; ski instruction; ski rental; 750 ft. vertical drop; restaurants; lodging.

Kellogg

SILVERHORN
P.O. Box 417
Kellogg, ID 83838
(208) 786-9521
LOCATION: 7 mi. south of Kellogg off I-90.
FACILITIES: 1 double chairlift; 1 tow rope; ski instruction; ski rental; nursery; 1900 ft. vertical drop; restaurants; lodging.

McCall

BRUNDAGE MOUNTAIN
P.O. Box 1072
McCall, ID 83638
(208) 634-2244
LOCATION: 7 mi. north of McCall on Route 55.
FACILITIES: 2 double chairlifts; 1 poma; ski instruction; ski rental; 1600 ft. vertical drop; restaurants; lodging.

Montpelier

MONTPELIER
909 Washington
Montpelier, ID 83254
(208) 847-1133
LOCATION: Near Montpelier.
FACILITIES: 1 tow rope; 300 ft. vertical drop; restaurants; lodging.

Orofino

BALD MOUNTAIN
Route 3
Orofino, ID 83544
(208) 476-2311
LOCATION: 6 mi. north of Pierce on Route 11.
FACILITIES: 1 T-bar; 1 tow rope; ski instruction; ski rental; 975 ft. vertical drop; restaurants; lodging.

Pocatello

CARIBOU
Buckskin Road
Pocatello, ID 83201
(208) 233-6134
LOCATION: 6 mi. east of Pocatello.
FACILITIES: 1 double chairlift; ski instruction; ski rental; 670 ft. vertical drop; restaurants; lodging.

SKYLINE
398 Hyde Avenue
Pocatello, ID 83201
(208) 775-3744
LOCATION: 17 mi. southeast of Pocatello off I-15.
FACILITIES: 1 double chairlift; 3 pomas; ski instruction; ski rental; 1650 ft. vertical drop; restaurants; lodging.

Sandpoint

SCHWEITZER BASIN
P.O. Box 815
Sandpoint, ID 83864
(208) 263-3331
LOCATION: 11 mi. northwest of Sandpoint off U.S. 95.
FACILITIES: 7 double chairlifts; 1 T-bar; ski instruction; ski rental; nursery; 2000 ft. vertical drop; restaurants; lodging.

Sun Valley

SUN VALLEY
Sun Valley, ID 83353
(208) 726-4471
LOCATION: 1 mi. off U.S. 75 at Ketchum.
FACILITIES: 8 triple chairlifts; 8 double chairlifts; 1 T-bar; ski instruction; ski rental; nursery; 3400 ft. vertical drop; restaurants; lodging.

Troy

TAMARACK
Route 1, Box 169
Troy, ID 83871
(208) 835-4714
LOCATION: 6 mi. north of Troy.
FACILITIES: 1 T-bar; 1 tow rope; ski instruction; ski rental; 600 ft. vertical drop; restaurants; lodging.

Wallace

LOOKOUT PASS
Idaho Ski Club
P.O. Box 983
Wallace, ID 83983
(208) 752-1188
LOCATION: 12½ mi. east of Wallace on I-90.
FACILITIES: 2 tow ropes; 2 pomas; ski instruction; ski rental; 850 ft. vertical drop; restaurant; lodging.

IDAHO

AMUSEMENT PARKS & ATTRACTIONS

Idaho Falls

TAUTPHAUS PARK
P.O. Box 276
Idaho Falls, ID 83401
(208) 522-9814
FACILITIES: 4 major rides; 3 kiddie rides; 12 games; 2 refreshment stands; restaurant; penny arcade; picnic facilities; food catering; miniature golf; zoo; orchestras; free acts; fireworks; free gate; free parking.

Lava Hot Springs

FUNTASIA AMUSEMENT PARK
P.O. Box 657
Lava Hot Springs, ID 83246
(208) 776-5646
FACILITIES: 6 major rides; 4 kiddie rides; 10 games; 2 refreshment stands; arcade; shooting gallery; swimming pool; camping; picnic facilities; miniature golf; free gate; free parking.

Pocatello

ROSS PARK PLEASURELAND
Ross Park
Pocatello, ID 83201
(208) 232-9680
FACILITIES: 6 major rides; 2 kiddie rides; 2 games; 1 refreshment stand; arcade; shooting gallery; swimming pool; miniature golf; zoo; picnic facilities; free gate; free parking.

STATE FAIR

East Idaho State Fair
P.O. Box 228
Blackfoot, ID 83221
(208) 785-2480
DATE: September

NATIONAL PARKS

There are no National Parks in Idaho.

NATIONAL FORESTS

National Forests
Northern Region
Federal Building
Missoula, MT 59807
(406) 329-3316

Boise

BOISE NATIONAL FOREST
ATTRACTIONS: Scenes of early Indian camps and massacres. Virgin stands of ponderosa pine; trout, salmon fishing; bear, elk, deer hunting; scenic drives.
FACILITIES: 116 camp sites, 5 picnic sites; swimming site; resorts, motels, dude ranches.
NEARBY TOWNS: Cascade, Emmett, Horseshoe Bend, Idaho City, Mountain Home.

Challis

CHALLIS NATIONAL FOREST
ATTRACTIONS: Mount Borah, 12,655 feet, highest peak in Idaho; headwaters of the Salmon River. Stream and lake trout, salmon fishing. Deer, elk, mountain goat, mountain sheep, antelope, bear hunting; scenic drive; riding and hiking trails; wilderness boating and pack trips.
FACILITIES: 52 camp sites, 7 picnic sites; resorts, hotels, cabins, and dude ranches; commercial packers and guides.
NEARBY TOWNS: Mackay, Salmon, Stanley.

Coeur d'Alene

COEUR D'ALENE NATIONAL FOREST
ATTRACTIONS: Fishing; hunting elk, deer. Rich Coeur d'Alene mining district (zinc, lead, silver); several large sawmills.
FACILITIES: 9 camp and picnic sites, 5 picnic only; Lookout Pass Winter Sports Area; resort hotels and cabins.
NEARBY TOWNS: Kellogg, Spirit Lake, Wallace, ID; Spokane, WA.

Grangeville

NEZ PERCE NATIONAL FOREST
ATTRACTIONS: Elk, deer, bear hunting; lake and stream fishing; hiking and horse trails; wilderness pack trips; scenic drives.
FACILITIES: 36 camp and picnic sites, 6 picnic only; resorts, hotels, cabins, pack trip outfitters.
NEARBY TOWNS: Kamiah, Kooskia, Riggins.

McCall

PAYETTE NATIONAL FOREST
ATTRACTIONS: Deepest gorge in the U.S.; trout, salmon fishing; deer, elk, mountain goat, bighorn sheep, bear hunting; scenic drives; wilderness trips.
FACILITIES: 26 camp sites; Payette Lake Winter Sports Area; dude ranches.
NEARBY TOWNS: Cascade, Council, New Meadows, Weiser.

Orofino

CLEARWATER NATIONAL FOREST
ATTRACTIONS: Spring log drive on the Middle Fork and North Fork, Clearwater River; large stands of virgin white pine. Trout, salmon fishing; elk, deer, bear hunting; scenic drives.
FACILITIES: 23 camp and picnic sites, 4 picnic only; motels, cabins; pack trip outfitters available.
NEARBY TOWNS: Kooskia, Lewistown, Pierce, ID; Hot Springs, and Missoula, MT.

Pocatello

CARIBOU NATIONAL FOREST
ATTRACTIONS: High country; towering mountain ranges divided by beautiful valleys. Historic markers and trails, natural soda springs; stream fishing; game bird, deer, bear hunting; scenic drives; numerous riding trails into wilderness country.

NATIONAL FORESTS (continued)

FACILITIES: 21 camp sites, 6 picnic sites; winter sports area; resorts and motels.
NEARBY TOWNS: Idaho Falls, Malad City, Montpelier, Soda Springs, Swan Valley, ID; Afton, WY.

St. Anthony

TARGHEE NATIONAL FOREST
ATTRACTIONS: Lake and stream fishing; bear, deer, elk, moose hunting; riding and hiking trails; scenic drives.
FACILITIES: 26 campsites, 3 picnic only; Bear Gulch, Moose Creek, and Pine Basin Winter Sports Areas; resorts; motels; dude ranches; boating facilities; pack outfits for hunting parties; fishing camps.
NEARBY TOWNS: Ashton, Driggs, Dubois, Idaho Falls, Rexburg, Rigby, Victor, ID; Afton and Jackson, WY.

St. Maries

ST. JOE NATIONAL FOREST
ATTRACTIONS: Virgin stands of white pine; large timber operations; elk, deer, bear, mountain goat hunting; fishing; scenic drives.
FACILITIES: 22 camp and picnic sites, 3 picnic only; swimming site; North-South Winter Sports Area; dude ranches nearby, cabins on St. Joe River.
NEARBY TOWNS: Avery, Clarkia, Moscow, Potlatch.

Salmon

SALMON NATIONAL FOREST
ATTRACTIONS: Historic Lewis and Clark Trail; fishing; deer, elk, bighorn sheep, mountain goat, bear, cougar, antelope hunting; boat trips.
FACILITIES: 20 camp sites, 2 picnic only; dude ranches.
NEARBY TOWN: Leadore.

Sandpoint

KANIKSU NATIONAL FOREST
ATTRACTIONS: Rugged back country; lake and stream fishing; big game hunting; scenic drives; boating.
FACILITIES: 26 camp and picnic sites, 11 picnic only; 3 swimming sites; Schweitzer Basin Winter Ski Area; resorts, hotels, lodges, cabins.
NEARBY TOWNS: Bonners Ferry, Clark Fork, Priest River.

Twin Falls

SAWTOOTH NATIONAL FOREST
ATTRACTIONS: Lakes, hot springs; Sun Valley with its four-season opportunities for outdoor sports. "Silent City of Rocks," fantastic formations worn by wind and water. Fishing; swimming; big-game grouse hunting; saddle and pack trips; scenic drives.
FACILITIES: 64 camp sites, 14 picnic only; swimming site; 8 winter sports areas; numerous dude ranches; camps, and motels.
NEARBY TOWNS: Burley, Gooding, Sun Valley.

See BITTERROOT NATIONAL FOREST and KOOTENAI NATIONAL FOREST - Montana.

See CACHE NATIONAL FOREST - Utah.

STATE PARKS

Headquarters

Parks and Recreation Department
Statehouse
Boise, ID 83707
(208) 384-2154

American Falls

MASSACRE ROCKS STATE PARK
LOCATION: On U.S. 30N, 20 mi. southwest of American Falls.
FACILITIES: Open year round; 52 sites; water and bathroom facilities; sanitary station; electrical hookup; trailer village vehicle sites; picnic area.

Athol

FARRAGUT STATE PARK
LOCATION: 4 mi. east of U.S. 95 and Athol.
FACILITIES: Open May - Oct.; 100 sites; water and bathroom facilities; picnic area; swimming; boating; fishing; hiking.

Boise

LUCKY PEAK STATE PARK
LOCATION: 8 mi. east of Boise on Route 21.
FACILITIES: Open May - Sept.; water and bathroom facilities; picnic area; swimming; boating; fishing.

Bruneau

BRUNEAU DUNES STATE PARK
LOCATION: 5 mi. north and 2 mi. east of Bruneau on Hwy. 51.
FACILITIES: Open Mar. - Sept.; 48 sites; water and bathroom facilities; sanitary station; electrical hookup; trailer village vehicle sites; picnic area; fishing.

Emmett

BLACK CANYON STATE PARK
LOCATION: 2 mi. east of Black Canyon Dam.
FACILITIES: Open Mar. - Oct.; water and bathroom facilities; picnic area; swimming; boating; fishing.

Glenns Ferry

THREE ISLAND STATE PARK
LOCATION: At Glenns Ferry off U S. 30.
FACILITIES: Open year round; 5 sites; water and bathroom facilities; sanitary station; electrical hookup; trailer village vehicle sites; picnic area; boating; fishing.

Lava Hot Springs

LAVA HOT SPRINGS STATE PARK

IDAHO

STATE PARKS (continued)

LOCATION: At Lava Hot Springs on U.S. 30.
FACILITIES: Open year round; water and bathroom facilities; picnic area; swimming; fishing.

Macks Inn

HENRY'S LAKE STATE PARK
LOCATION: 10 mi. north of Macks Inn.
FACILITIES: Open May - Oct.; 32 sites; water and bathroom facilities; swimming; boating.

McCall

PONDEROSA STATE PARK
LOCATION: In McCall.
FACILITIES: Open Jun. - Oct.; 170 sites; water and bathroom facilities; sanitary station; electrical hookup; trailer village vehicle sites; picnic area; swimming; boating; fishing.

McCammon

INDIAN ROCKS STATE PARK
LOCATION: McCammon Interchange on I-15.
FACILITIES: Open May - Oct.; 51 sites; water and bathroom facilities; living history program.

New Meadows

PACKER JOHN'S CABIN STATE PARK
LOCATION: On Hwy. 15.
FACILITIES: Open year round; 40 sites; water and bathroom facilities; picnic area.

Plummer

HEYBURN STATE PARK
LOCATION: On Hwy. 5, off U.S. 95 between Plummer and St. Maries.
FACILITIES: Open May - Oct.; 136 sites; water and bathroom facilities; trailer village vehicle sites; picnic area; swimming; boating; fishing.

Priest River

INDIAN CREEK STATE PARK
LOCATION: 35 mi. north of Priest River at road end.
FACILITIES: Open May - Nov.; limit of stay, 15 days; 73 sites; water and bathroom facilities; electrical hookup; firewood; trailer village vehicle sites; picnic area; swimming; fishing.

St. Charles

BEAR LAKE STATE PARK
LOCATION: 2 mi. east of Hwy. 89 at Bear Lake.
FACILITIES: Open Jun. - Sept.; water and bathroom facilities; swimming; boating; fishing.

Sandpoint

ROUND LAKE STATE PARK
LOCATION: 8 mi. south of Sandpoint and 2 mi. west on U.S. 95.

FACILITIES: Open May - Nov.; 53 sites; water and bathroom facilities; picnic area; swimming; boating; fishing.

Weiser

MANN CREEK STATE PARK
LOCATION: 13 mi. north of Weiser on U.S. 95.
FACILITIES: Open year round; water and bathroom facilities; picnic area; swimming; boating; fishing; tent camping.

STATE FORESTS

There are no State Forests in Idaho.

HISTORIC SITES

Hailey

EMMANUEL EPISCOPAL CHURCH - Oldest Episcopalian church in Idaho.

Hope

KULLYSPELL HOUSE MONUMENT - Marks the first trading post in Idaho. It was built in Sept. 1809. Located on Route 200.

Kellogg

OLD MISSION - An historic mission that is over 120 years old. Located 10 mi. west of Kellogg.

SUNSHINE MEMORIAL MONUMENT - A 12½ foot statue of a miner using jackleg drill as memorial to Sunshine Mine disaster of May 2, 1972. Located 4 mi. east of Kellogg.

HOSTELS

There are no Hostels in Idaho.

POINTS OF INTEREST

Arco

CRATERS OF THE MOON - Weird volcanic basalt shapes of black lava tubes, trees, and cones. Located off U.S. 20.

Buhl

BALANCED ROCK - One of nature's oddities. Located 16 mi. west of Buhl.

FERRY ON THE SNAKE RIVER - Large wall mural. Located in Buhl Post Office.

Hagerman

FOSSIL BEDS - Prehistoric remains. Located west of Hagerman across river.

Hope

INDIAN HIEROGLYPHICS - Carved in rock

POINTS OF INTEREST (continued)

on Hope Peninsula's eastern shoreline and on the peninsula's Memaloose point.

Mackay

OLD EMPIRE MINE - In shadow of Mt. Borah, Idaho's highest peak.

Soda Springs

GEYSER - Tapped in the 1930s while the townspeople were looking for a water source for a swimming pool. Located behind the Enders Hotel on Main Street.

Weiser

PYTHIAN CASTLE - Built in 1904 for $9,000. Located at 30 East Idaho Street.

ILLINOIS

A state steeped in paradoxes, Illinois entered the Union in 1818 as the twenty-first state. Abraham Lincoln, perhaps the state's most famous citizen, ultimately lost the 1858 Senate race in which he debated the question of slavery with Stephen A. Douglas; but his stand on the subject won him fame and the Presidency 3 years later.

States with excellent surface transport networks do not necessarily have equally good air connections; Illinois has both. Waterways abound there, as do railroad lines and interstate highways, making the transporta-

tion of manufactured products a major industry. The state also has O'Hare International Airport, the largest and busiest airport in the country.

And although Illinois is basically an agrarian state, producing sizeable crops of corn, soybeans, and hogs and other farm animals, it also contains Chicago, the second largest metropolitan area in the U.S. (after New York).

State capital: Springfield. State bird: Cardinal. State tree: Oak. State flower: Native violet.

WEATHER

Illinois lies midway between the Continental Divide and the Atlantic Ocean and some 500 miles north of the Gulf of Mexico. The irregularly-shaped area of the state has a width of less than 200 miles at most points, but extends for 385 miles in the north-south direction. Except for a few low hills in the extreme south and a small unglaciated area in the extreme northwest, the terrain is flat. Differences in elevation have no significant influence on the climate.

Its climate is typically continental with cold winters, warm summers, and frequent short-period fluctuations in temperature, humidity, cloudiness, and wind direction. Because Illinois extends so far in a north-south direction, the contrasts in winter temperature conditions are rather large. The north has frequent snows and temperatures drop to below zero several times each winter. During the summer the sun heats the entire state quite strongly and uniformly. The north-south range of mean temperatures in July is only about 6 degrees F.

Average daily temperature for each month.

	Northern	Southern
Jan.	29.7 to 12.3	43.8 to 24.3
Feb.	34.5 to 16.8	48.2 to 27.5
Mar.	44.6 to 25.8	57.4 to 35.2
Apr.	60.0 to 37.8	70.9 to 46.5
May	71.2 to 47.4	80.0 to 54.6
Jun.	81.1 to 57.6	88.6 to 63.3
Jul.	84.1 to 61.5	91.4 to 66.8
Aug.	82.7 to 60.0	90.4 to 64.4
Sept.	76.2 to 52.4	84.5 to 57.3
Oct.	65.1 to 41.6	73.3 to 45.6
Nov.	48.0 to 29.2	57.9 to 35.8
Dec.	34.8 to 18.4	46.8 to 28.4
Year	59.3 to 38.4	69.4 to 45.8

STATE CHAMBER OF COMMERCE

Illinois State Chamber of Commerce
20 North Wacker Drive
Chicago, IL 60606
(312) 372-7373

STATE & CITY TOURISM OFFICES

State

Office of Tourism
Illinois Department of Business and Economic Development
205 W. Wacker Drive, Room 1100
Chicago, IL 60606
(312) 793-4732

Illinois Department of Business and Economic Development
222 South College
Springfield, IL 62706
(217) 782-7500

ILLINOIS

TOURISM OFFICES (continued)

Local

Convention and Tourism Bureau
332 S. Michigan Avenue
Room 2050
Chicago, IL 60604
(312) 922-3530

STATE HIGHWAY DEPARTMENT

Illinois Department of Transportation
2300 South Dirksen Parkway
Springfield, IL 62764
(217) 782-2632

HIGHWAY WELCOMING CENTERS

Effingham

EFFINGHAM CENTER - Interstate 70, southwest, just outside of Effingham.

Minooka

MINOOKA CENTER - Interstate 80, west.

Monee

MONEE CENTER - Interstate 57, south.

Union County

UNION COUNTY/LICK CREEK - Interstate 57, north.

STATE POLICE

Department of Public Safety
103 Armory Building
Springfield, IL 62706
(217) 782-7762

HUNTING & FISHING

Hunting

Hunters must have a valid license in their possession at all times when afield, and are required to purchase a Federal and State Migratory Bird Hunting Stamp before taking migratory waterfowl. Illinois residents exempt from the purchase of a hunting license or a State Migratory Waterfowl stamp include: (1) Persons 65 years or older, physically disabled, or on leave from the U.S. Armed forces; (2) an owner or tenant and his immediate family who reside and hunt on the land.

A person under 16 needs the written consent of a parent or guardian, plus a hunter safety certificate or proof of a previous hunting license to purchase a current license.

All hunters who have a firearm in their possession, whether they own it or not, must have a valid Firearm Owner's Identification Card from the Illinois Department of Law Enforcement. Exemptions include: (1) Non-resident hunters if their state has no such requirement; (2) a minor accompanied by a parent, guardian or any adult who has a valid card in his possession.

Resident

Hunting license, $3.25; trapping license, $3.25; state migratory stamp, $5; federal migratory stamp, $5.

Non-resident

Hunting license, reciprocal (minimum is $15).

Fishing

A sport fishing license entitles an angler to take all species of fish, turtles or bullfrogs within established limits, except for endangered species. Thirty days residency is required for a resident's license; persons on active duty in the Armed Forces are considered residents.

No license is required of those under 16 years of age, senior citizens, handicapped and blind, of those fishing at licensed daily fee fishing areas, of landowners fishing on their property, or of Illinois residents in the Armed Forces while on leave.

Resident

Sport fishing annual, $2.25; salmon stamp, $2.25.

Non-resident

Sport fishing (10 days), $4.25; annual, reciprocal (minimum is $6); salmon stamp, $2.25.

For more information contact:

Department of Conservation
Division of Wildlife Resources
100½ East Washington Street
Springfield, IL 62706
(217) 782-6384

CAMPGROUNDS

Private

Aledo

LITTLE PONDEROSA
(309) 582-2460
LOCATION: Off Route 94.
FACILITIES: Open Apr. 15 - Oct. 15; 450 sites; water and bathroom facilities; sanitary station; electrical hookup; trailer village vehicle sites; food service; swimming; boating; boat rental; fishing; tent camping.

Amboy

CRYSTAL LAKE CAMPGROUND
(815) 857-3860

CAMPGROUNDS (continued)

LOCATION: Near Amboy.
FACILITIES: Open year round; 400 sites; water and bathroom facilities; sanitary station; electrical hookup; trailer village vehicle sites; food service; swimming; boating; boat rental; fishing; tent camping.

GREEN RIVER OAKS CAMPING RESORT
(815) 857-2815
LOCATION: Near Amboy.
FACILITIES: Open Apr. - Nov.; 450 sites; water and bathroom facilities; sanitary station; electrical hookup; trailer village vehicle sites; food service; swimming; fishing; tent camping.

Antioch

DEER LAKE CAMPING OUTDOOR RECREATION CLUB
(312) 395-7414
LOCATION: Near Antioch
FACILITIES: Open year round; 500 sites; water and bathroom facilities; sanitary station; electrical hookup; trailer village vehicle sites; swimming; boating; boat rental; fishing; tent camping.

TIMBER LAKE PARK
(312) 395-4281
LOCATION: Near Antioch.
FACILITIES: Open year round; 430 sites; water and bathroom facilities; sanitary station; electrical hookup; trailer village vehicle sites; food service; swimming; boating; boat rental; fishing; tent camping.

Belvedere

BIG TROUT CAMPGROUND
(815) 543-0555
LOCATION: 5710 Shattuck Road.
FACILITIES: Open May 1 - Oct. 15; 350 sites; water and bathroom facilities; sanitary station; electrical hookup; trailer village vehicle sites; food service; swimming; fishing; tent camping.

Bushnell

LAKE WILDWOOD HAVEN
(309) 772-3454
LOCATION: 325 N. Sperry Street.
FACILITIES: Open year round; 1000 sites; water and bathroom facilities; sanitary station; electrical hookup; trailer village vehicle sites; food service; swimming; boating; boat rental; fishing; tent camping.

TIMBERVIEW LAKES
(309) 772-3609
LOCATION: Near Bushnell.
FACILITIES: Open Apr. - Nov.; 350 sites; water and bathroom facilities; sanitary station; electrical hookup; trailer village vehicle sites; food service; swimming; fishing; tent camping.

Carbondale

CRAB ORCHARD RECREATION AREA
(618) 985-6913
LOCATION: Near Carbondale.

FACILITIES: Open Apr. 15 - Sept. 15; 300 sites; water and bathroom facilities; sanitary station; electrical hookup; trailer village vehicle sites; swimming; boating; fishing; tent camping.

Carlyle

THE PAMPERED CAMPER
(618) 594-4111
LOCATION: Off Route 1.
FACILITIES: Open May 1 - Sept. 15; 200 sites; water and bathroom facilities; sanitary station; electrical hookup; trailer village vehicle sites; food service; swimming; fishing; tent camping.

DuQuoin

HAYES FAIR ACRES
(618) 542-4705
LOCATION: Off U.S. 51 south.
FACILITIES: Open Apr. - Nov.; 200 sites; water and bathroom facilities; sanitary station; electrical hookup; trailer village vehicle sites; swimming; fishing; tent camping.

Galesburg

LAKE STOREY CAMPGROUND
(309) 343-4181
LOCATION: Near Galesburg.
FACILITIES: Open Apr. 15 - Oct. 15; 400 sites; water and bathroom facilities; sanitary station; electrical hookup; trailer village vehicle sites; swimming; boating; boat rental; fishing; tent camping.

Goodfield

TIMBERLINE RECREATION PARK
(309) 965-2275
LOCATION: ½ mi. east of I-74.
FACILITIES: Open year round; 600 sites; water and bathroom facilities; sanitary station; electrical hookup; trailer village vehicle sites; food service; swimming; fishing; tent camping.

Hillsdale

WRIGHT'S LANDUIT'S LAKE
(309) 755-2268
LOCATION: 2700 290th Street, N.
FACILITIES: Open Apr. 15 - Oct. 15; 1350 sites; water and bathroom facilities; sanitary station; electrical hookup; trailer village vehicle sites; food service; swimming; boating; boat rental; fishing; tent camping.

Jacksonville

LAKE JACKSONVILLE
(217) 245-6903
LOCATION: Near Jacksonville.
FACILITIES: Open Apr. 15 - Oct. 15; 300 sites; water and bathroom facilities; sanitary station; electrical hookup; trailer village vehicle sites; food service; swimming; boating; fishing; tent camping.

Marion

PYRAMID ACRES
(618) 993-2784

ILLINOIS

CAMPGROUNDS (continued)

LOCATION: Off Route 4.
FACILITIES: Open Mar. 15 - Nov. 1; 330 sites; water and bathroom facilities; sanitary station; electrical hookup; trailer village vehicle sites; food service; swimming; boating; boat rental; fishing; tent camping.

Marseilles

GLENWOOD FARMS
(815) 795-2195
LOCATION: Off Route 3.
FACILITIES: Open Apr. 15 - Nov. 1; 500 sites; water and bathroom facilities; sanitary station; electrical hookup; trailer village vehicle sites; food service; swimming; tent camping.

WILDERNESS CAMPGROUND
(815) 496-2618
LOCATION: Off Route 2.
FACILITIES: Open year round; 600 sites; water and bathroom facilities; sanitary station; electrical hookup; trailer village vehicle sites; food service; swimming; fishing; tent camping.

Mt. Carroll

TIMBERLAKE RESORT LTD.
(815) 244-8744
LOCATION: Black Oak Road.
FACILITIES: Open Apr. - Nov.; 350 sites; water and bathroom facilities; sanitary station; electrical hookup; trailer village vehicle sites; food service; swimming; boating; boat rental; fishing; tent camping.

Palestine

LEAVERTON PARK
(618) 586-2147
LOCATION: Near Palestine.
FACILITIES: Open year round; 300 sites; water and bathroom facilities; electrical hookup; trailer village vehicle sites; tent camping.

Round Lake

FISH LAKE BEACH
(312) 546-2228
LOCATION: Near Round Lake.
FACILITIES: Open May 15 - Oct. 15; 450 sites; water and bathroom facilities; sanitary station; electrical hookup; trailer village vehicle sites; food service; swimming; boating; boat rental; fishing; tent camping.

Sheridan

NELSON'S VIKING VILLAGE CAMPING RESORT
(815) 496-2405
LOCATION: Off Route 71.
FACILITIES: Open year round; 650 sites; water and bathroom facilities; sanitary station; electrical hookup; trailer village vehicle sites; swimming; boating; boat rental; fishing; tent camping.

Smithboro

BONANZA CAMPING
(618) 326-7261

LOCATION: Hwy. 140 and I-70.
FACILITIES: Open Apr. - Dec.; 210 sites; water and bathroom facilities; sanitary station; electrical hookup; trailer village vehicle sites; food service; swimming; boating; boat rental; fishing; tent camping.

Yorkville

HIDE-A-WAY LAKES
(312) 553-6323
LOCATION: Van Emmon Road.
FACILITIES: Open year round; 1000 sites; water and bathroom facilities; sanitary station; electrical hookup; trailer village vehicle sites; food service; swimming; boating; boat rental; fishing; tent camping.

RESORTS & BEACHES

Most of the state's resort activities center around the major lakes and include fishing, swimming, boating, water skiing and camping. Also, there are five resort-type State Parks: Giant City State Park, Illinois Beach State Park, Pere Marquette State Park, Starved Rock State Park and White Pines State Park. (See Boating Areas and State Parks.)

BOATING AREAS

Baldwin

BALDWIN LAKE
LOCATION: 3 mi. north of Baldwin.
FACILITIES: Launching.

Carbondale

CEDAR LAKE
LOCATION: 4 mi. southwest of Carbondale.
FACILITIES: Launching.

CRAB ORCHARD LAKE
LOCATION: 4 mi. east of Carbondale.
FACILITIES: Launching.

Carlyle

CARLYLE LAKE
LOCATION: ½ mi. northeast of Carlyle.
FACILITIES: Launching.

Fox Lake

FOX LAKE (CHAIN O'LAKES)
LOCATION: Near Fox Lake.
FACILITIES: Launching.

PISTAKEE LAKE (FOX CHAIN O'LAKES)
LOCATION: Near Fox Lake.
FACILITIES: Launching.

Murphysboro

KINKAID LAKE
LOCATION: 3 mi. northwest of Murphysboro.
FACILITIES: Launching.

Olive Branch

HORSESHOE LAKE

BOATING AREAS (continued)

LOCATION: Near Olive Branch.
FACILITIES: Launching.

Sesser

REND LAKE
LOCATION: 3 mi. east of Sesser.
FACILITIES: Launching.

Spring Grove

GRASS LAKE (FOX CHAIN O'LAKES)
LOCATION: 2 mi. east of Spring Grove.
FACILITIES: Launching.

Springfield

LAKE SPRINGFIELD
LOCATION: South edge of Springfield.
FACILITIES: Launching.

SANGCHRIS LAKE
LOCATION: 14 mi. southeast of Springfield.
FACILITIES: Launching.

BICYCLE TRAILS

FARMLAND TRAIL - 350 mi.; long distances
per day; 10-speed bicycle recommended.

On this tour you will travel almost the
length of Illinois on paved roads with light
traffic. These roads are generally flat and pass
through some of the most fertile fields in the
world, periodically interrupted by small
towns. Fall is the ideal time for this ride.

Trail: Palos Park Hostel to Wilmington to
Chatsworth to Elliot to Champaign to Urbana
to Camargo to Charleston to Toledo to Diet-
erich to Kinmundy to Salem to Mt. Vernon to
Benton to Carbondale to Little Grassy Hostel.

LAKE TRAIL - 26 mi.; any bicycle.

Three lakes offering a wide variety of water sports are along this route.

Trail: Little Grassy Lake Youth Hostel
(Carbondale), right on County Road, left on
Old Highway 13, left on Giant City Road to
Youth Hostel.

SHAWNEE FOREST TRAIL - 190 mi.; steep
hills; 10-speed bicycle necessary.

Cycle through the beautiful hardwood
forest of southern Illinois. This area usually
has temperatures just above freezing from
mid-Mar. until mid-Nov. The summers tend to
be hot and humid but rideable.

Watch for Tunnel Hill Road after leaving
Goreville. Turn east through a railroad under-
pass. You will climb seven tough hills on this
30 mi. run.

Trails: Carbondale to Pulleys Mill to Goreville to Tunnel Hill to Simpson to Glendale to
Dixon Springs to Paducah to Metropolis to
Mermet to Karnak to West Vienna to Goreville to Pulleys Mill to Carbondale.

SOUTHERN ILLINOIS TRAILS - 20 mi.;
some hills, some rough terrain; 10-speed bicycle recommended.

Nestled between the Mississippi and Ohio
Rivers, this is a collection of rides in Southern

Illinois centering on the Carbondale area. The
area you will be bicycling through is hilly
with woodlands, farms, and lakes.

Trails: (1) Little Grassy Lake Hostel to
Glendale to Dixon Springs State Park to Cave-
in-Rock State Park; (2) Carbondale to Mur-
physboro to Campbell Hill to Bremen to Fort
Kaskaskia State Park; (3) Carbondale to Little
Grassy Youth Hostel to U.S. 51 south to
Mounds to Horseshoe Lake.

TRAILS

Chicago

THE ILLINOIS PRAIRIE PATH - 22.7 mi.
foot trail. This trail, located on a portion of
an abandoned railroad right-of-way, is used as
a hiking trail, as well as by urban residents
whose homes often abut the trail. There are
several street and rail crossings, as well as a
variety of second-growth vegetation, including
many shrub and tree species. This was the
first trail formally submitted to the Secretary
of the Interior for inclusion in the National
Trails System.

SKI AREAS

Bartlett

VILLA OLIVIA SKI AREA
Bartlett, IL 60103
(312) 695-7669
LOCATION: Near Bartlett.
FACILITIES: 1 quad chairlift; 12 tow ropes;
ski instruction; ski rental; 180 ft. vertical
drop; longest run, ¼ mi.; restaurants; lodging.

Galena

CHESTNUT MOUNTAIN
Galena, IL 61036
(815) 777-1320
LOCATION: On Blackjack Road.
FACILITIES: 2 triple chairlifts; 1 double
chairlift; 7 tow ropes; ski instruction; ski rental; 465 ft. vertical drop; longest run, 3200 ft.;
restaurants; lodging.

Ingleside

HOLIDAY PARK
P.O. Box 156
Ingleside, IL 60041
(312) 546-8222
LOCATION: 3 mi. south of Fox Lake.
FACILITIES: 1 double chairlift; 5 tow ropes;
ski instruction; ski rental; 200 ft. vertical
drop; longest run, 1400 ft.; restaurants; lodging.

Lincolnshire

MARRIOTT'S LINCOLNSHIRE RESORT
Lincolnshire, IL 60015
(312) 634-0100
LOCATION: 14901 Half Day Road.
FACILITIES: 1 T-bar; ski instruction; ski
rental; 50 ft. vertical drop; longest run, 600
ft.; restaurants; lodging.

ILLINOIS

SKI AREAS (continued)

Lisle

FOUR LAKES SKI AREA
P.O. Box 430
Lisle, IL 60532
(312) 964-2550
LOCATION: In Lisle.
FACILITIES: 6 tow ropes; ski instruction; ski rental; 250 ft. vertical drop; longest run, 1100 ft.; restaurants; lodging.

Shannon

PLUMTREE SKI AREA
P.O. Box 200
Shannon, IL 61078
(815) 493-2881
LOCATION: In Shannon.
FACILITIES: 1 double chairlift; 1 T-bar; ski instruction; ski rental; 185 ft. vertical drop; restaurants; lodging.

Spring Grove

LOST VALLEY
Spring Grove, IL 60081
(815) 675-2302
LOCATION: 1609 North Route 12.
FACILITIES: 2 double chairlifts; 2 tow ropes; ski instruction; ski rental; 200 ft. vertical drop; longest run, ¼ mi.; restaurants; lodging.

AMUSEMENT PARKS & ATTRACTIONS

Addison

ADVENTURE LAND
Route 20
Addison, IL 60101
(312) 529-8880
FACILITIES: 25 major rides; 12 kiddie rides; fun house; walk thru; 15 games; 10 refreshment stands; arcade; picnic facilities; outdoor disco; stage shows; name bands; pay gate; free parking; open Mother's Day - Labor Day; weekends, through Sept.

Bolingbrook

OLD CHICAGO
555 S. Bolingbrook Drive
Bolingbrook, IL 60439
(312) 759-1895
FACILITIES: 23 major rides; 5 kiddie rides; 21 games; 23 refreshment stands; 9 restaurants; 200 stores; arcade; shooting gallery; miniature golf; stage shows; exhibits; theatre; orchestras; free acts; pay gate; free parking; open all year.

Chicago

FUNTOWN AMUSEMENT PARK
1711 East 95th Street
Chicago, IL 60617
(312) 221-2311
FACILITIES: 13 major rides; 8 kiddie rides; 10 refreshment stands; penny arcades; 21 games; golf driving range; arcade; skee-ball palace; shooting gallery; miniature golf; picnic facilities; stage shows; free acts; fireworks; free gate; free parking; pay gate; open Apr. 27 - Sept. 5.

Gurnee

MARRIOTT'S GREAT AMERICA
One Great America Parkway
Gurnee, IL 60031
(312) 249-2000
FACILITIES: 31 major rides; 20 games; 28 restaurants; buffets and snack shops; 35 shops; parade/cartoon characters (Warner Bros.); arcade; shooting gallery; exhibits; theaters; crafts; stage shows; pay gate; open late Apr. - mid-Oct.; weekends, spring and fall.

Lyons

FAIRYLAND PARK, INC.
3938 South Harlem Avenue
Lyons, IL 60534
(312) 447-3279
FACILITIES: 8 major rides; 12 kiddie rides; 2 refreshment stands; penny arcade; shooting gallery; zoo; picnic facilities; free gate; free parking.

Melrose Park

KIDDIELAND
8400 W. North Avenue
Melrose Park, IL 60160
(312) 343-1050
FACILITIES: 8 major rides; 13 kiddie rides; 2 games; arcade; shooting gallery; 2 refreshment stands; novelty stand; shooting waters game; 2 fire engines; free gate; free parking; open Apr. - Oct.; weekends, Apr. and May.

Willow Springs

PLAYLAND AMUSEMENT PARK
79th LaGrange Road
Willow Springs, IL 60480
FACILITIES: 18 major rides; 15 kiddie rides; 10 games; 4 refreshment stands; fun house; arcade; shooting gallery; picnic facilities; 12 stores; free gate; free parking; open last Sun. in Apr. - Labor Day.

STATE FAIR

DuQuoin State Fair
P.O. Box 182
DuQuoin, IL 62832
(618) 542-4705
DATE: September

NATIONAL PARKS

There are no National Parks in Illinois.

NATIONAL FORESTS

National Forests
Eastern Region

NATIONAL FORESTS (continued)

633 West Wisconsin Avenue
Milwaukee, WI 53203
(414) 291-3693

Harrisburg

SHAWNEE NATIONAL FOREST
ATTRACTIONS: Prehistoric stone forts and
Indian mounds; stream and river fishing;
quail, migratory waterfowl, squirrel, rabbit,
fox, raccoon hunting; boating and swimming.
FACILITIES: 14 camp and picnic sites, 32
picnic only; 2 swimming sites; hotels and
cabins.
NEARBY TOWNS: Anna, Cairo, Carbondale,
Marion, Metropolis, and Murphysboro, IL;
Paducah, KY; St. Louis, MO.

STATE PARKS

Department of Conservation
Division of Land & Historic Sites
405 E. Washington
Springfield, IL 62706
(217) 782-3340

Benton

WAYNE FITZGERRELL STATE PARK
Benton, IL 62812
(618) 438-6781
LOCATION: Near Benton.
FACILITIES: Open year round; limit of stay:
14 days; water and bathroom facilities; electrical hookup; trailer village vehicle sites; picnic area; boating; hunting; fishing; hiking;
horseback riding.

Bourbonnais

KANKAKEE RIVER STATE PARK
Bourbonnais, IL 60914
(815) 933-1383
LOCATION: Near Bourbonnais.
FACILITIES: Open year round; limit of stay,
14 days; water and bathroom facilities; sanitary station; electrical hookup; trailer village
vehicle sites; food service; boating, 10 h.p.;
hunting; fishing; hiking; horseback riding;
museum.

Caledonia

ROCK CUT STATE PARK
Caledonia, IL 61011
(815) 885-3311
LOCATION: Near Caledonia.
FACILITIES: Open year round; limit of stay,
14 days; water and bathroom facilities; sanitary station; electrical hookup; trailer village
vehicle sites; picnic area; food service; boating, 10 h.p.; fishing; hiking; environmental
study area.

Carlyle

ELDON HAZLET STATE PARK
Carlyle, IL 62231
(618) 594-3015
LOCATION: Near Carlyle.
FACILITIES: Open year round; limit of stay,

14 days; water and bathroom facilities; sanitary station; electrical hookup; trailer village
vehicle sites; boating; hunting; fishing; hiking;
environmental study area.

Clayton

SILOAM SPRINGS STATE PARK
Clayton, IL 62324
(217) 894-6205
LOCATION: Near Clayton.
FACILITIES: Open year round; limit of stay,
14 days; water and bathroom facilities; sanitary station; electrical hookup; trailer village
vehicle sites; picnic area; boating, electric;
hunting; fishing; horseback riding; environmental study area.

Colchester

ARGYLE LAKE STATE PARK
Colchester, IL 62326
(309) 776-3422
LOCATION: Near Colchester.
FACILITIES: Open year round; limit of stay,
14 days; water and bathroom facilities; sanitary station; electrical hookup; trailer village
vehicle sites; picnic area; food service; boating, 10 h.p.; hunting; fishing; hiking; environmental study area.

E. St. Louis

FRANK HOLTEN STATE PARK
E. St. Louis, IL 62205
(618) 874-7920
LOCATION: Near E. St. Louis.
FACILITIES: Open year round; water and
bathroom facilities; electrical hookup; trailer
village vehicle sites; picnic area; food service;
boating, 10 h.p.; fishing; environmental study
area.

Goreville

FERNE CLYFFE STATE PARK
Goreville, IL 62939
(618) 995-2411
LOCATION: Near Goreville.
FACILITIES: Open year round; limit of stay,
14 days; sanitary station; electrical hookup;
trailer village vehicle sites; picnic area; hunting; fishing; hiking; horseback riding; environmental study area.

Grafton

PERE MARQUETTE STATE PARK (Resort)
R. R. 1
Grafton, IL 62037
(618) 786-3785
LOCATION: Near Grafton.
FACILITIES: Open year round; limit of stay,
14 days; water and bathroom facilities; sanitary station; electrical hookup; trailer village
vehicle sites; picnic area; food service; boating; hunting; fishing; hiking; horseback riding;
environmental study area.

Kewanee

JOHNSON SAUK TRAIL STATE PARK
Kewanee, IL 61443
(309) 853-5589
LOCATION: Near Kewanee.

ILLINOIS

STATE PARKS (continued)

FACILITIES: Open year round; limit of stay, 14 days; water and bathroom facilities; sanitary station; electrical hookup; trailer village vehicle sites; picnic area; boating, electric; hunting; fishing.

Kinmundy

STEPHEN A. FORBES STATE PARK
Kinmundy, IL 62854
(618) 547-3381
LOCATION: Near Kinmundy.
FACILITIES: Open year round; limit of stay, 14 days; water and bathroom facilities; sanitary station; electrical hookup; trailer village vehicle sites; picnic area; food service; boating; hunting; fishing; hiking; horseback riding; environmental study area.

LeRoy

MORAINE VIEW STATE PARK
LeRoy, IL 61752
(309) 724-8032
LOCATION: Near LeRoy.
FACILITIES: Open year round; limit of stay, 14 days; water and bathroom facilities; sanitary station; electrical hookup; trailer village vehicle sites; picnic area; boating, 10 h.p.; hunting; fishing; hiking; horseback riding; environmental study area.

Makanda

GIANT CITY STATE PARK (Resort)
Makanda, IL 62958
(618) 457-4836
LOCATION: Near Makanda.
FACILITIES: Open year round; limit of stay, 14 days; water and bathroom facilities; sanitary station; electrical hookup; trailer village vehicle sites; picnic area; boating, 10 h.p.; hunting; fishing; hiking; horseback riding; environmental study area.

McHenry

MORAINE HILLS STATE PARK
McHenry, IL 60050
(815) 385-1624
LOCATION: Near McHenry.
FACILITIES: Open year round; limit of stay, 14 days; water and bathroom facilities; picnic area; food service; boating, 15 h.p.; fishing; hiking; museum.

Morris

I & M CANAL STATE PARK
Morris, IL 60450
(815) 942-0796
LOCATION: Near Morris.
FACILITIES: Open year round; limit of stay, 14 days; water and bathroom facilities; trailer village vehicle sites; picnic area; boating, no motor; fishing; hiking.

Morrison

MORRISON - ROCKWOOD STATE PARK
Morrison, IL 61720
(815) 772-4708
LOCATION: Near Morrison.

FACILITIES: Open year round; water and bathroom facilities; sanitary station; trailer village vehicle sites; boating, 10 h.p.; fishing; horseback riding.

Newton

SAM PARR STATE PARK
Newton, IL 62448
(618) 783-2661
LOCATION: Near Newton.
FACILITIES: Open year round; limit of stay, 14 days; water and bathroom facilities; picnic area; boating, 10 h.p.; hunting; fishing; hiking.

Oakwood

KICKAPOO STATE PARK
Oakwood, IL 61858
(217) 442-4915
LOCATION: Near Oakwood.
FACILITIES: Open year round; limit of stay, 14 days; water and bathroom facilities; sanitary station; electrical hookup; trailer village vehicle sites; picnic area; boating, electric; hunting; fishing; hiking; environmental study area.

Pickneyville

PYRAMID STATE PARK
Pickneyville, IL 62274
(618) 357-2574
LOCATION: Near Pickneyville.
FACILITIES: Open year round; water and bathroom facilities; sanitary station; trailer village vehicle sites; picnic area; boating, 10 h.p.; hunting; fishing; hiking; horseback riding.

Ramsey

RAMSEY LAKE STATE PARK
Ramsey, IL 62080
(618) 423-2215
LOCATION: Near Ramsey.
FACILITIES: Open year round; limit of stay, 14 days; water and bathroom facilities; sanitary station; electrical hookup; trailer village vehicle sites; food service; boating, electric; hunting; fishing; hiking; environmental study area.

Rochester

SANGCHRIS LAKE STATE PARK
Rochester, IL 62563
(217) 637-9208
LOCATION: Near Rochester.
FACILITIES: Open year round; limit of stay, 14 days; water and bathroom facilities; sanitary station; electrical hookup; trailer village vehicle sites; picnic area; boating, 10 h.p.; hunting; fishing; hiking.

Savanna

MISSISSIPPI PALISADES STATE PARK
Savanna, IL 61074
(815) 273-2731
LOCATION: Near Savanna.
FACILITIES: Open year round; limit of stay, 14 days; water and bathroom facilities; sanitary station; electrical hookup; trailer village vehicle sites; picnic area; boating; fishing; hik-

STATE PARKS (continued)

ing; horseback riding; environmental study area.

Spring Grove

CHAIN O'LAKES
Spring Grove, IL 60081
(312) 587-5512
LOCATION: Near Spring Grove.
FACILITIES: Open year round; limit of stay, 14 days; water and bathroom facilities; sanitary station; electrical hookup; trailer village vehicle sites; picnic area; boating, 10 h.p.; hunting; fishing; hiking; environmental study area.

Utica

STARVED ROCK STATE PARK (Resort)
Utica, IL 61373
(815) 667-4726
LOCATION: Near Utica.
FACILITIES: Open year round; limit of stay, 14 days; water and bathroom facilities; sanitary station; electrical hookup; trailer village vehicle sites; food service; boating; fishing; hiking; environmental study area.

Windsor

EAGLE CREEK STATE PARK
Windsor, IL 61957
(217) 756-8260
LOCATION: Near Windsor.
FACILITIES: Open year round; limit of stay, 14 days; water and bathroom facilities; sanitary station; electrical hookup; trailer village vehicle sites; boating; hunting; fishing; hiking.

WOLF CREEK STATE PARK
Windsor, IL 61957
(217) 459-2831
LOCATION: Near Windsor.
FACILITIES: Open year round; limit of stay, 14 days; water and bathroom facilities; sanitary station; electrical hookup; trailer village vehicle sites; picnic area; boating; fishing; hiking; horseback riding; environmental study area.

Yorkville

SILVER SPRINGS STATE PARK
Yorkville, IL 60560
(312) 553-6297
LOCATION: Near Yorkville.
FACILITIES: Open year round; limit of stay, 14 days; water and bathroom facilities; picnic area; food service; boating; hunting; fishing; hiking.

Zion

ILLINOIS BEACH STATE PARK (Resort)
Zion, IL 60099
(312) 662-4811
LOCATION: Near Zion.
FACILITIES: Open year round; limit of stay, 14 days; water and bathroom facilities; sanitary station; electrical hookup; trailer village vehicle sites; picnic area; boating, no motors; hunting; fishing; hiking; museum.

STATE FORESTS

Department of Conservation
Division of Forestry
100 E. Washington
Springfield, IL 62706
(217) 782-2361

Forest City

SAND RIDGE STATE FOREST
P.O. Box 82
Forest City, IL 61532
(309) 597-2212
FACILITIES: Open year round; limit of stay, 14 days; water and bathroom facilities; trailer village vehicle sites; picnic area; hunting; hiking; horseback riding.

Jonesboro

TRAIL OF TEARS STATE FOREST
R.R. 2
Jonesboro, IL 62952
(618) 833-6125
FACILITIES: Open year round; limit of stay, 14 days; water and bathroom facilities; sanitary station; trailer village vehicle sites; picnic area; hunting; museum.

Keithsburg

BIG RIVER STATE FOREST
Keithsburg, IL 61442
(309) 374-2496
FACILITIES: Open year round; limit of stay, 14 days; water and bathroom facilities; sanitary station; trailer village vehicle sites; picnic area; boating; hunting; fishing.

Strasburg

HIDDEN SPRINGS STATE FOREST
Box 110
Strasburg, IL 62465
(217) 644-3091
FACILITIES: Open year round; limit of stay, 14 days; water and bathroom facilities; sanitary station; trailer village vehicle sites; picnic area; hunting; hiking; museum.

HISTORIC SITES

Bement

BRYANT COTTAGE - Where Lincoln and Douglas met to make arrangements for their historic confrontations.

Cahokia

CAHOKIA COURTHOUSE - Oldest building west of the Alleghenies, and one of but a few remaining examples of French pioneer log architecture.

Galena

ULYSSES S. GRANT HOME - Gift to General Grant, 18th President, from the people of Galena when he returned home after the Civil War.

ILLINOIS

HISTORIC SITES (continued)

Grand Detour

JOHN DEERE BLACKSMITH SHOP - Site where Deere perfected and forged his first steel plow.

Nauvoo

BRIGHAM YOUNG HOME - House of famous leader who led the Mormons west to the Valley of the Great Salt Lake.

Petersburg

NEW SALEM VILLAGE - Lincoln lived here for six years. More than twelve timber houses, the Rutledge Tavern, plus stores and a country school have been restored to mirror life of the prairie in the 1830s.

Springfield

LINCOLN DEPOT - Lincoln delivered famous Farewell Address from this original depot when he departed for Washington on February 11, 1861. Located on Monroe between 9th and 10th Streets.

LINCOLN HOME - Modest clapboard house built in 1839, purchased in 1844 and occupied until the family's move to Washington. It is the only home Abraham Lincoln, 16th President, owned. Located on 8th and Jackson.

LINCOLN HOME MALL - Gas lights and brick sidewalks remind visitors of more quiet days. Four square blocks restored to their appearance in Lincoln's time. Located on 8th and Jackson.

NINIAN EDWARDS HOME - Also called the Lincoln Marriage Home and Lincoln Life Museum. Here Lincoln courted and wed Mary Todd. Wedding parlor restored, excellent dioramas portray Lincoln's life. Located at 406 South 8th Street.

OAK RIDGE CEMETERY - Lincoln Tomb, with its towering obelisk, marks the President's final resting place.

HOSTELS

There are no Hostels in Illinois.

POINTS OF INTEREST

Bishop Hill

BISHOP HILL - Old colonial settlement in western Illinois remains much the same as when Swedish Utopists arrived in 1846.

Cahokia

JARROT MANSION - Probably the oldest brick structure in the Upper Mississippi Valley.

MONK'S MOUND - Largest built by industrious Mound Dwellers, and greater in bulk and area than the famous Egyptian pyramids. Located near E. St. Louis.

Chester

KASKASKIA - Settled by French missionaries in 1675 and became the state's first seat of government in 1818. Today, following a flood in 1888, the tiny island is isolated from the Illinois mainland and, ironically, can only be reached by traveling through Missouri. Located on Route 3.

Chicago

CHICAGO - Midtown, renowned for its outdoor gallery, offers startling works of art: Chagall's 3000-square-foot mosaic, Picasso's 50-foot steel sculpture, and Calder's 50-ton "Flamingo."

SEARS TOWER - World's tallest building with 110 floors reaching 1454 feet into the heavens.

Nauvoo

JOHN BROWNING HOUSE (Blacksmith, Gunsmith and Locksmith) - Home of world-famous inventor of Browning firearms.

Springfield

OLIVER P. PARKS MUSEUM - Nation's largest collection of antique telephone equipment.

INDIANA

Indiana, the name meaning home of the Indian, entered the Union in 1816 as the nineteenth state. Late in the 1700s, trouble erupted between the settlers and the Indians, but was soon quelled. However, William Henry Harrison, then territorial governor, purchased several million acres of Indian land which infuriated Tecumseh, a Shawnee chief, who went on the warpath.

After several years of fighting, Harrison finally defeated Tecumseh in 1811 at the Battle of Tippecanoe. The deed and the name stuck with Harrison, and he won the Presidency with the famous slogan, "Tippecanoe and Tyler, too." (John Tyler was his running mate.)

Today Indiana, the state with the most famous auto race in the country, the "Indianapolis 500," is also a major automobile manufacturing center.

INTRODUCTION (continued)

Another important revenue earner is agriculture, especially the wheat, corn and soybean crops.

State capital: Indianapolis. State bird: Cardinal. State tree: Tulip. State flower: Peony.

WEATHER

The three principal land regions in Indiana are: the Great Lakes Plain in the north, the Central Till Plains and, in the south, the Interior Low Plateau that is characterized by hills, ridges, knolls, caves and waterfalls.

Indiana, because of its location in the middle latitudes in the interior of the continent, has an invigorating climate with warm summers and cool winters. Imposed on the well-known daily and seasonal temperature fluctuations are changes occurring every few days as surges of polar air move southward or tropical air moves northward. These changes are more frequent and pronounced in the winter than in the summer. A winter may be unusually cold or a summer cool if the influence of polar air is persistent. Similarly, a summer may be unusually warm or a winter mild if air of tropical origin predominates. These systems are least active in midsummer and during this season frequently pass north of Indiana. Climatological variations within the state are caused by differences of latitude, elevation, terrain, soil, and lakes. Temperatures can range from around minus 35 degrees to plus 115 degrees F, although prolonged severe hot or cold spells are uncommon.

Average daily temperature for each month.

	Northern	Southern
Jan.	32.9 to 15.8	40.0 to 20.1
Feb.	37.1 to 19.2	43.8 to 22.3
Mar.	47.1 to 27.3	52.7 to 30.0
Apr.	62.3 to 38.4	66.9 to 41.8
May	73.5 to 48.0	76.4 to 50.1
Jun.	83.4 to 57.2	84.6 to 59.4
Jul.	86.1 to 60.9	87.8 to 63.1
Aug.	84.6 to 58.8	87.0 to 60.7
Sept.	78.4 to 51.8	81.1 to 53.7
Oct.	66.4 to 41.7	70.2 to 41.6
Nov.	49.5 to 31.1	54.5 to 32.1
Dec.	37.1 to 21.7	43.5 to 24.4
Year	61.5 to 39.3	65.7 to 41.6

STATE CHAMBER OF COMMERCE

Indiana State Chamber of Commerce, Inc.
201-212 Board of Trade Building
Indianapolis, IN 46204
(317) 634-6407

STATE & CITY TOURISM OFFICES

State

Indiana Department of Commerce
State House
Indianapolis, IN 46204
(317) 633-5300

Tourism Development Division
Indiana Department of Commerce
State House, Room 336
Indianapolis, IN 46204
(317) 633-5423

Local

Community Information
Indianapolis Chamber of Commerce
320 N. Meridan Avenue
Indianapolis, IN 46204
(317) 635-4747

STATE HIGHWAY DEPARTMENT

State Highway Commission
State Office Building
100 North Senate Avenue
Indianapolis, IN 46204
(317) 633-5816

HIGHWAY WELCOMING CENTERS

Auburn

AUBURN CENTER - Interstate 69, south.

Batesville

BATESVILLE CENTER - Interstate 74, east.

Centerville

CENTERVILLE CENTER - Interstate 70, west.

Henryville

HENRYVILLE CENTER - Interstate 65, north.

Kankakee

KANKAKEE CENTER - Interstate 65, south.

Plainfield

PLAINFIELD CENTER - Interstate 70, east.

Taylorsville

TAYLORSVILLE CENTER - Interstate 65, south.

INDIANA
STATE POLICE

Department of Public Safety
100 North Senate Avenue
Indianapolis, IN 46204
(317) 633-5271

HUNTING & FISHING
Hunting

Any individual person must have and carry a license to hunt or chase, with or without dogs, any wild animal, except;

Resident or non-resident participating in a field trial sanctioned by the Director.

Owner of farmland and a resident of Indiana, his spouse and children living with him while hunting, fishing or trapping on the land he owns.

Tenant of farmland who is a resident of Indiana and his spouse and children living with him while hunting, fishing or trapping on the farm upon which they reside.

Military personnel on active duty and stationed within Indiana may lawfully hunt or fish upon obtaining a resident license.

A resident is a person who has lived in Indiana continuously for a full period of 90 days preceding the date of application for a license or permit. All other persons are non-residents.

Resident

Hunting, fishing & trapping, $5.25; hunting & trapping, $3.25; fishing, $3.50; trout-salmon stamp, $2.25; deer hunting—archery, $5.75; deer hunting—shotgun, $5.75; deer hunting—muzzle-loading rifle, $5.75; turkey hunting, $5.25; waterfowl stamp, $5.

Non-resident

Hunting & fishing, $25.25; annual fishing, $7.50; annual hunting, $20.25; annual trapping, $25.25; 14-day fishing, $3.25; trout-salmon stamp, $2.25; 5-day hunting, $5.25; deer hunting—archery, $30.75; deer hunting—shotgun, $30.75; deer hunting—muzzle—loading rifle, $30.75; waterfowl stamp, $5.

Fishing

A resident is a person who has lived in Indiana continuously for a full period of 90 days preceding the date of license purchase.

Every person must carry his license or permit when engaged in any activity allowed by that license or permit, and produce that license or permit on the request of any Conservation Enforcement Officer (or any other authorized Peace Officer).

Residents between the ages of 16 and 65 are required to possess a fishing license. This same age group is required to possess a trout-salmon stamp to fish for trout and salmon. Non-residents of all ages are required to have a fishing license, except:

The owner of farmland who is a resident of Indiana, his wife and children living with him, may fish, hunt and trap on said land without a license.

A tenant of farmland, his wife and children living with him, may fish, hunt and trap without a license only upon the farm upon which he lives.

No fishing license is required to fish on private ponds. A license would be required, however, to possess fish off private property.

Resident

Hunting, fishing & trapping, $5.25; fishing only, $3.50; trout-salmon stamp, $2.25.

Non-resident

Hunting & fishing only, $25.25; annual fishing only, $7.50; 14-day fishing only, $3.25; trout-salmon stamp, $2.25.

For more information contact:

Department of Natural Resources
Division of Fish & Wildlife
607 State Office Bldg.
Indianapolis, IN 46204
(317) 633-7696

CAMPGROUNDS
Private

Akron

OAKRIDGE CAMPGROUND
(219) 893-4503
LOCATION: 1 mi. south of Akron on Route 19, then ½ mi. west on County Road 250S.
FACILITIES: Open Apr. 1 - Oct. 30; water and bathroom facilities; sanitary station; electrical hookup; trailer village vehicle sites; swimming; boating; fishing; horseback riding; tent camping.

Angola

CIRCLE PARK CAMPGROUND
(219) 488-2185
LOCATION: 13½ mi. southeast of Angola on Circle Park Road.
FACILITIES: Open May - Nov.; water and bathroom facilities; sanitary station; electrical hookup; trailer village vehicle sites; laundry; food service; swimming; boating; boat rental; fishing; horseback riding; tent camping.

Cannelton

ROCKY POINT MARINA
(812) 547-7416
LOCATION: 4 mi. east of Cannelton at junction Routes 66 and 166.
FACILITIES: Open year round; water and bathroom facilities; sanitary station; electrical hookup; trailer village vehicle sites; food service; boating; boat rental; fishing; horseback riding; tent camping.

Clinton

HORSESHOE LAKES
(317) 832-6717
LOCATION: 7 mi. south of Newport on Route 63, 5 mi. west on U.S. 36, then 8 mi.

CAMPGROUNDS (continued)

south on Route 71.
FACILITIES: Open year round; water and bathroom facilities; sanitary station; electrical hookup; trailer village vehicle sites; swimming; boating; boat rental; fishing; horseback riding; tent camping.

Covington

SYCAMORE VALLEY CAMPGROUND
(317) 397-3864
LOCATION: 8 mi. south of Covington on I-74, then ½ mi. west on Yeddo Road.
FACILITIES: Open year round; water and bathroom facilities; sanitary station; electrical hookup; trailer village vehicle sites; swimming; boating; boat rental; fishing; horseback riding; tent camping.

Crawfordsville

LAKE WAVELAND
(317) 435-2073
LOCATION: 15 mi. southwest of Crawfordsville on Route 47.
FACILITIES: Open Mar. 26 - Oct. 1; water and bathroom facilities; sanitary station; electrical hookup; trailer village vehicle sites; food service; swimming; boating; boat rental; fishing; horseback riding; tent camping.

Fort Wayne

INDIAN SPRINGS CAMPGROUND
(219) 489-5680
LOCATION: 12 mi. north of Fort Wayne on Coldwater Road, then west on County Road 64.
FACILITIES: Open year round; water and bathroom facilities; sanitary station; electrical hookup; trailer village vehicle sites; laundry; swimming; boating; fishing; horseback riding; tent camping.

Fremont

1000 ACRE CAMPING
(219) 495-9115
LOCATION: 2 mi. northeast of Fremont on Ray Clear Lake Road.
FACILITIES: Open May 15 - Sept. 7; water and bathroom facilities; sanitary station; electrical hookup; trailer village vehicle sites; food service; swimming; boating; fishing; horseback riding; tent camping.

Goshen

TU-CO CAMPGROUND
(219) 848-4487
LOCATION: 14 mi. north of Goshen on Route 15, then east 1 mi. on Route 120.
FACILITIES: Open year round; water and bathroom facilities; sanitary station; electrical hookup; trailer village vehicle sites; food service; swimming; boating; fishing; horseback riding; tent camping.

Greenfield

RAMADA CAMP INN
(317) 326-3171
LOCATION: 2 mi. north of Greenfield, then

3½ mi. west on County Road 300N.
FACILITIES: Open year round; water and bathroom facilities; sanitary station; electrical hookup; trailer village vehicle sites; laundry; picnic area; food service; swimming; fishing; tent camping.

S & H CAMPGROUND
(317) 545-4081
LOCATION: 4 mi. west of Greenfield on County Road 100N.
FACILITIES: Open May - Nov.; water and bathroom facilities; sanitary station; electrical hookup; trailer village vehicle sites; food service; swimming; boating; horseback riding; tent camping.

LaGrange

ATWOOD SHORES CAMPGROUND
(219) 854-2214
LOCATION: 9 mi. south of LaGrange on Route 9, then 3 mi. west on County Line Road.
FACILITIES: Open year round; water and bathroom facilities; sanitary station; electrical hookup; trailer village vehicle sites; boating; boat rental; hunting; fishing; tent camping.

GORDON'S CAMPING
(219) 351-3383
LOCATION: 15½ mi. southeast of LaGrange on County Road 600S.
FACILITIES: Open year round; sanitary station; electrical hookup; trailer village vehicle sites; swimming; boating; boat rental; fishing; horseback riding; tent camping.

TWIN MILLS RESORT
(219) 562-3212
LOCATION: 6 mi. north of LaGrange on Route 9, then 2 mi. west on Route 120.
FACILITIES: Open year round; water and bathroom facilities; sanitary station; electrical hookup; trailer village vehicle sites; food service; swimming; boating; boat rental; fishing; horseback riding; tent camping.

Logansport

FRANCE PARK
(219) 753-2928
LOCATION: 4 mi. west of Logansport on U.S. 24.
FACILITIES: Open year round; water and bathroom facilities; sanitary station; electrical hookup; trailer village vehicle sites; food service; swimming; boating; fishing; horseback riding; tent camping.

Palmyra

BUFFALO TRACE
(812) 738-4865
LOCATION: East edge of Palmyra on U.S. 50.
FACILITIES: Open Apr. - Nov.; water and bathroom facilities; sanitary station; electrical hookup; trailer village vehicle sites; food service; swimming; fishing; tent camping.

Roselawn

LAKE HOLIDAY CAMPGROUND
(219) 987-3132

INDIANA

CAMPGROUNDS (continued)

LOCATION: ½ mi. east of Roselawn on Route 10.
FACILITIES: Open year round; water and bathroom facilities; sanitary station; electrical hookup; trailer village vehicle sites; laundry; food service; swimming; boating; fishing; horseback riding; tent camping.

Richmond

POW WOW RIDGE KAMPGROUND
(317) 962-1487
LOCATION: 5 mi. northeast of Richmond on Smyrna Road.
FACILITIES: Open year round; water and bathroom facilities; sanitary station; electrical hookup; trailer village vehicle sites; laundry; food service; swimming; boating; boat rental; fishing; horseback riding; tent camping.

Washington

YOUNG'S DOGWOOD LAKE LODGE
(812) 644-3534
LOCATION: 10 mi. south of Washington on Route 257.
FACILITIES: Open Mar. 1 - Dec. 7; water and bathroom facilities; sanitary station; electrical hookup; trailer village vehicle sites; food service; boating; boat rental; fishing; tent camping.

Winamac

WILDERNESS PARK CAMPGROUNDS
(219) 946-4370
LOCATION: 2½ mi. north of Winamac on Route 35, then 2 mi. east off County Road 215.
FACILITIES: Open Apr. 15 - Nov. 15; water and bathroom facilities; sanitary station; electrical hookup; trailer village vehicle sites; laundry; picnic area; swimming; boating; fishing; horseback riding; tent camping.

RESORTS & BEACHES

Bloomington

BLOOMINGTON (LAKE MONROE) - This is the place for those who want to get back to nature and hanker to horseback ride, swim, fish, canoe or stroll in the woods.

French Lick

FRENCH LICK - Sixteen hundred acres of natural, wooded land in the rolling hills of southern Indiana. If you're the energetic type, you may want to try your hand at tennis, trap and skeet, Putt-Putt golf, badminton, volleyball, croquet or softball. Or perhaps you'd rather sun yourself on the patio or next to the shimmering swimming pool.

Monticello (Lake Shafer)

INDIANA BEACH - Over 100 miles of shoreline offering fishing, swimming and boating plus all the water sports. You can walk the boardwalk, play golf, watch a ski show or spend the afternoon sampling the 23 amusement rides.

BOATING AREAS

Bloomington

MONROE RESERVOIR
LOCATION: 1 mi. east on Route 46, then 7 mi. south on Route 446.
FACILITIES: Launching.

Brookville

BROOKVILLE RESERVOIR
LOCATION: 1 mi. north on Route 101.
FACILITIES: Launching.

Huntington

HUNTINGTON RESERVOIR
LOCATION: 2 mi. south on Route 5 at junction of Routes 224 and 5.
FACILITIES: Launching.

SALAMONIE RESERVOIR
LOCATION: Huntington, 12 mi. south on Routes 9 and 37.
FACILITIES: Launching.

Peru

MISSISSINEWA RESERVOIR
LOCATION: Peru, 7 mi. south on Route 21, then 3 mi. east on County Road 500 S.
FACILITIES: Launching.

Scottsburg

HARDY LAKE RESERVOIR
LOCATION: 5 mi. east on Route 56, then 8 mi. north on Route 203.
FACILITIES: Launching.

BICYCLE TRAILS

COUNTRY ROADS TRAIL - 70 mi.; any bicycle.
Farm lined country roads, shaded forest lanes, and three large reservoirs await the cyclist who travels this route.
Trail: Marion to Jalapa to Somerset to Peoria to Wabash to Andrews to Huntington to Van Buren to Landess to Marion.

COVERED BRIDGE TRAILS - 38, 40 & 44 mi.; some gravel surfaces; 10-speed bicycle recommended.
Parke County in western Indiana, beside the Wabash River, calls itself Covered Bridge County. The county boasts 39 of these picturesque structures. The town of Rockville, where U.S. 36 and 41 cross, is the center of Indiana Covered Bridge Country.
Trails: (1) Rockville to Raccoon State Park to Mansfield to Fallen Rock to Rockville - 38 mi.; (2) Rockville to Mecca to Rosedale to Rockville - 38 mi.; (3) Rockville to Coloma to Sylvania to Bloomingdale to Rockville - 40 mi.; (4) Rockville to Turkey Run State Park to Judson to Rockville - 44 mi.

BICYCLE TRAILS (continued)

THE RESERVOIR TRAIL - 70 mi.; any bicycle.

    Start from Marion on paved roads. On the return ride you can retrace your steps or travel on the north side of Mississinewa Reservoir.

    Trail: Marion to Jalapa to Vernon, turn south on Route 13, then west to Peonia, to Peru.

TRAILS

Portage

CALUMET TRAIL - 9.2 mi. foot trail. The trail is located on an electric powerline corridor adjacent to the Indiana Dunes National Lakeshore. To the south of the trail, the urban character is clearly evident with many views of railroads, highways, commercial development and the powerline towers. To the north, the trail is bordered for nearly its entire length by forested land.

SKI AREAS

La Porte

SKI VALLEY
550 N. Forrester Road
La Porte, IN 46350
(219) 362-1212
LOCATION: 5 mi. west of La Porte.
FACILITIES: 1 T-bar; 5 tow ropes; ski instruction; ski rental; restaurants; lodging.

New Paris

MT. WAWASEE SKI AREA
New Paris, IN 46553
(219) 831-4112
LOCATION: Near New Paris.
FACILITIES: 1 T-bar; 8 tow ropes; ski instruction; ski rental; nursery; 150 ft. vertical drop; restaurants; lodging.

Paoli

PAOLI PEAKS SKI AREA
P.O. Box 67
Paoli, IN 47454
(812) 723-4698
LOCATION: Near Paoli.
FACILITIES: 1 quad chairlift; 2 tow ropes; ski instruction; ski rental; restaurants; lodging.

Valparaiso

SKI PINES
674 N. Meridan
Valparaiso, IN 46383
(219) 462-4179
LOCATION: Near Valparaiso.
FACILITIES: 4 T-bars; 5 tow ropes; ski instruction; ski rental; 135 ft. vertical drop; restaurants; lodging.

AMUSEMENT PARKS & ATTRACTIONS

Chesterton

ENCHANTED FOREST AMUSEMENT PARK, INC.
U.S. 20 & Indiana 49
Chesterton, IN 46304
(219) 926-2161
FACILITIES: 16 major rides; 12 kiddie rides; fun house; 20 games; 2 refreshment stands; 2 restaurants; 2 snack stands; 2 arcades; shooting gallery; picnic facilities; zoo; gift shop; free acts; pay gate; free parking; open May 1 - Labor Day.

Geneva

AMISHVILLE USA (Attraction)
Rt. 2
Geneva, IN 46740
(219) 589-3536
FACILITIES: Amish House tours; buggy rides; pedal boats; canoe; livery; farm animals; restaurant; snack bar; bathing beach; camping; picnic facilities; free gate; free parking; open all year.

Lafayette

COLUMBIAN PARK
1915 Scott Street
Lafayette, IN 47904
(317) 447-6984
FACILITIES: 5 major rides; 7 kiddie rides; live ponies; 2 refreshment stands; pool; beach; picnic facilities; miniature golf; zoo; outdoor theater; fireworks; free gate; free & pay parking.

Marengo

CAVE PARK (Attraction)
Hwy. 64
Marengo, IN 47140
(812) 365-2705
FACILITIES: Commercial cave; 2 refreshment stands; swimming pool; exhibits; picnic facilities; nature trails; free gate; free parking; open all year.

Monticello

INDIANA BEACH
306 Indiana Beach Road
Monticello, IN 47960
(219) 583-4141
FACILITIES: 18 major rides; 8 kiddie rides; 8 games; 10 refreshment stands; 3 restaurants; penny arcade; shooting gallery; bathing beach; sightseeing boats; miniature golf; marina; hotel; camp grounds; cottages; picnic facilities; orchestras; name bands; free acts; fireworks; pay gate; free parking.

Muncie

JAKE'S JUNCTION-SHROYER'S VILLAGE-
R.R. 13
Muncie, IN 47302
(317) 288-4191
FACILITIES: Major ride; 2 refreshment

INDIANA

AMUSEMENT PARKS (continued)

stands; toy train museum; camping; picnic facilities; petting zoo; books free acts; free parking.

North Webster

ADVENTURELAND
Hwy. 13 North
North Webster, IN 46555
(219) 834-2554
FACILITIES: 10 major rides; 4 kiddie rides; 3 games; 2 refreshment stands; restaurant; 3 arcades; picnic facilities; petting zoo; 2 miniature golf courses; pay gate; free parking.

Santa Claus

SANTA CLAUS LAND
Highways 162 & 245
Santa Claus, IN 47579
(812) 937-4401
FACILITIES: 6 major rides; 11 kiddie rides; 5 walk thrus; 9 games; 4 refreshment stands; 3 restaurants; petting zoo; bathing beach; museum; exhibits; picnic facilities; arcade; camping; miniature golf; crafts; stage shows; pay gate; free parking; open May - Sept. 6; weekends: Sept. - Oct., Nov. & Dec. til Christmas.

STATE FAIR

Indiana State Fair
State Fairgrounds
Indianapolis, IN 46205
(317) 923-3431
DATE: August

NATIONAL PARKS

There are no National Parks in Indiana.

NATIONAL FORESTS

National Forests
Eastern Region
633 West Wisconsin Avenue
Milwaukee, WI 53203
(414) 291-3693

Bedford

HOOSIER NATIONAL FOREST
ATTRACTIONS: Outstanding specimen of black walnut; final outlet of Lost River; Old trail of migrating buffalo between Western Plains and French Lick. Squirrel, fox, quail hunting; catfish, bass, bluegill fishing; scenic drives.
FACILITIES: 13 camp and picnic sites, 24 picnic only; swimming site; hotels and motels.
NEARBY TOWNS: Bloomington, Evansville, Jasper, Paoli, Tell City.

STATE PARKS

Department of Natural Resources
Division of State Parks

616 State Office Bldg.
Indianapolis, IN 46204
(317) 633-4164

Albion

CHAIN O'LAKES STATE PARK
(219) 636-2654
LOCATION: 5 mi. southeast of Albion.
FACILITIES: Open year round; water and bathroom facilities; sanitary station; electrical hookup; trailer village vehicle sites; food service; swimming; boating; fishing; hiking; tent camping.

Anderson

MOUNDS STATE PARK
(317) 642-6627
LOCATION: 2 mi. west of Anderson on I-69.
FACILITIES: Open year round; water and bathroom facilities; electrical hookup; trailer village vehicle sites; picnic area; food service; boating; fishing; hiking; horseback riding.

Angola

POKAGON STATE PARK
(219) 665-9613
LOCATION: On U.S. 27 & I-69 near Angola.
FACILITIES: Open year round; water and bathroom facilities; sanitary station; electrical hookup; trailer village vehicle sites; food service; swimming; boating; hiking; horseback riding; bicycle trail; environmental study area; tent camping.

Chesterton

INDIANA DUNES STATE PARK
(219) 926-1215
LOCATION: On U.S. 12 & Indiana 49 north of Chesterton.
FACILITIES: Open year round; water and bathroom facilities; sanitary station; electrical hookup; trailer village vehicle sites; picnic area; food service; swimming; hiking; environmental study area; tent camping.

Cloverdale

RICHARD LIEBER STATE PARK
(317) 795-4576
LOCATION: On Indiana 42 & 243, southwest of Cloverdale.
FACILITIES: Open year round; water and bathroom facilities; sanitary station; electrical hookup; trailer village vehicle sites; swimming; boating; fishing; hiking; tent camping.

Jasonville

SHAKAMAK STATE PARK
(812) 665-2158
LOCATION: On Indiana 48 & 159, near Jasonville.
FACILITIES: Open year round; water and bathroom facilities; sanitary station; electrical hookup; trailer village vehicle sites; food service; swimming; boating; fishing; hiking; horseback riding; bicycle trail.

Liberty

WHITEWATER STATE PARK

STATE PARKS (continued)

(317) 458-5565
LOCATION: On Route 101, south of Liberty.
FACILITIES: Open year round; water and bathroom facilities; sanitary station; electrical hookup; trailer village vehicle sites; picnic area; swimming; boating; fishing; horseback riding; bicycle trail; environmental study area; tent camping.

Lincoln City

LINCOLN STATE PARK
(812) 937-4710
LOCATION: On Route 162 near Lincoln City.
FACILITIES: Open year round; water and bathroom facilities; sanitary station; electrical hookup; trailer village vehicle sites; swimming; boating; fishing; hiking; tent camping.

Madison

CLIFTY FALLS STATE PARK
(812) 273-5495
LOCATION: On Routes 107 & 56 near Madison.
FACILITIES: Open year round; water and bathroom facilities; sanitary station; electrical hookup; trailer village vehicle sites; swimming; hiking; bicycle trail; environmental study area; tent camping.

Marshall

TURKEY RUN STATE PARK
(317) 597-2635
LOCATION: On Route 47 near Marshall.
FACILITIES: Open year round; water and bathroom facilities; sanitary station; electrical hookup; cabins; food service; swimming; hiking; horseback riding; bicycle trail; environmental study area; tent camping.

Mitchell

SPRING MILL STATE PARK
(812) 849-4129
LOCATION: On Route 69 near Mitchell.
FACILITIES: Open year round; water and bathroom facilities; sanitary station; electrical hookup; trailer village vehicle sites; cabins; food service; swimming; boating; fishing; hiking; horseback riding; environmental study area; tent camping.

Nashville

BROWN COUNTY STATE PARK
(812) 988-2825
LOCATION: On Routes 46 & 135 near Nashville.
FACILITIES: Open year round; water and bathroom facilities; sanitary station; electrical hookup; trailer village vehicle sites; swimming; fishing; hiking; horseback riding; bicycle trail; tent camping.

Spencer

MCCORMICK'S CREEK STATE PARK
(812) 829-2235
LOCATION: On Route 46 near Spencer.

FACILITIES: Open year round; water and bathroom facilities; sanitary station; electrical hookup; food service; swimming; hiking; horseback riding; bicycle trail; environmental study area; tent camping.

Versailles

VERSAILLES STATE PARK
(812) 689-6424
LOCATION: 1 mi. east of Versailles on U.S. 50.
FACILITIES: Open Apr. - Nov.; water and bathroom facilities; sanitary station; electrical hookup; trailer village vehicle sites; food service; swimming; boating; fishing; hiking; horseback riding; environmental study area.

Waveland

SHADES STATE PARK
(317) 435-2810
LOCATION: Off Route 234 near Waveland.
FACILITIES: Open year round; boating; fishing; hiking; environmental study area; tent camping.

Winamac

TIPPECANOE RIVER STATE PARK
(219) 946-3213
LOCATION: Just north of Winamac on U.S. 35.
FACILITIES: Open year round; water and bathroom facilities; sanitary station; electrical hookup; trailer village vehicle sites; boating; fishing; hiking; horseback riding; environmental study area; tent camping.

STATE FORESTS

Department of Natural Resources
Division of State Parks
616 State Office Bldg.
Indianapolis, IN 46204
(317) 633-4164

Brownstown

JACKSON-WASHINGTON STATE FOREST
(812) 358-2160
LOCATION: 3 mi. southeast of Brownstone on Route 250.
FACILITIES: Open year round; boating; hunting; fishing; hiking; horseback riding; environmental study area; tent camping.

Jasper

FERDINAND STATE FOREST
(812) 367-1524
LOCATION: 9 mi. south of Jasper on Route 162, then 7 mi. east on Route 264.
FACILITIES: Open year round; water and bathroom facilities; swimming; boating; hunting; fishing; hiking; tent camping.

Largo

SALAMONIE RIVER STATE FOREST
(219) 782-2349
LOCATION: South of Largo on Route 524.
FACILITIES: Open year round; boating;

INDIANA

STATE FORESTS (continued)

hunting; fishing; hiking; horseback riding; bicycle trail; tent camping.

Leavenworth

HARRISON-CRAWFORD STATE FOREST
(812) 738-2722
LOCATION: 6 mi. east of Leavenworth on U.S. 460, then 3 mi. south on Route 462.
FACILITIES: Open year round; hunting; fishing; hiking; horseback riding; environmental study area; tent camping.

Martinsville

MORGAN-MONROE STATE FOREST
(317) 342-4026
LOCATION: 3 mi. south of Martinsville on Route 37, then 3 mi. east on "old" 37.
FACILITIES: Open year round; cabins; boating; hunting; fishing; hiking; environmental study area; tent camping.

Nashville

YELLOWWOOD STATE FOREST
(812) 988-7945
LOCATION: 7 mi. west of Nashville on Yellowwood Lake Road.
FACILITIES: Open year round; boating; hunting; fishing; hiking; horseback riding; tent camping.

Petersburg

PIKE STATE FOREST
(812) 789-5251
LOCATION: 11 mi. south of Petersburg on Route 61, then east on Route 364.
FACILITIES: Open year round; hunting; fishing; hiking; horseback riding; tent camping.

Scottsburg

CLARK STATE FOREST
(812) 294-4306
LOCATION: 11 mi. south of Scottsburg on U.S. 31.
FACILITIES: Open year round; water and bathroom facilities; sanitary station; electrical hookup; trailer village vehicle sites; boating; hunting; fishing; hiking; environmental study area; tent camping.

Shoals

MARTIN STATE FOREST
(812) 247-3496
LOCATION: 3 mi. east of Shoals on U.S. 50.
FACILITIES: Open year round; picnic area; hunting; fishing; hiking; environmental study area; tent camping.

Spencer

OWEN-PUTNAM STATE FOREST
(317) 795-4821
LOCATION: 5 mi. north of Spencer on U.S. 231.
FACILITIES: Open year round; hunting; fishing; hiking; horseback riding; tent camping.

HISTORIC SITES

Berne

FIRST MENNONITE CHURCH - Berne was founded in 1852, and its first settlers were Mennonite immigrants from Berne, Switzerland. With a seating capacity of 2,000, the First Mennonite Church is the largest of its kind in the United States. Located at corner of U.S. 27 and Route 218.

Crawfordsville

OLD JAIL MUSEUM - The Old Jail was built in 1882 and contains the only operating rotary cell block unit known in existence. Located at 225 North Washington Street.

Fountain City

LEVI COFFIN HOUSE STATE MEMORIAL - Referred to as the Grand Central Station of the Underground Railroad. Located on U.S. 27.

Gentryville

LINCOLN BOYHOOD NATIONAL MEMORIAL - The pioneer life of Abraham Lincoln's early years (1816-1830) is brought vividly to life at this Living Historical Farm, located on a portion of the original family tract. Located 2 mi. east off Route 162.

Indianapolis

PRESIDENT BENJAMIN HARRISON MEMORIAL HOME - The home of the nation's 23rd President and only President elected from Indiana. Located at 1230 North Delaware Street.

JAMES WHITCOMB RILEY HOME - Residence of famous Hoosier poet. Located at 528 Lockerbie Street.

Marion

SHUGART HOUSE - Secret passages between the walls hid runaway slaves in this historic Quaker pioneer house, once an underground slave station. Located south on Route 37.

Millville

WILBUR WRIGHT STATE MEMORIAL - "Magnificent Men in Flying Machines" can trace their heritage to the birthplace of Wilbur Wright. Located off Route 38.

Salem

JOHN HAY CENTER - Birthplace of John Milton Hay, the statesman, author and diplomat who served as private secretary to President Lincoln and Secretary of State under Presidents McKinley and Teddy Roosevelt Located at 307 East Market.

South Bend

SAINT MARY'S COLLEGE - Founded in 1844 by the Sisters of the Holy Cross; na-

HISTORIC SITES (continued)

tion's first chartered Catholic college for women. Located on U.S. 231 north of South Bend.

Vincennes

GROUSELAND - The spacious home of William Henry Harrison, built in 1803-04 and set in a grove of walnut trees near the Wabash River, is said to be the first brick building in Vincennes. Before becoming the 9th President of the United States, Harrison served as first Governor of the Indiana Territory. Located at 3 West Scott Street.

SONOTABAC PREHISTORIC INDIAN MOUND - Largest Indian mound in Indiana, built some 2,300 years ago by the mound-builder cult that archaeologists now call the Hopewellen People who used the mound to worship their god, the sun. Located at 2401 Wabash Avenue.

Wabash

WABASH COUNTY COURT HOUSE - On March 31, 1880, Wabash became the first electrically lighted city in the world. Reminiscent of this great day when "in the evening's darkness, burst forth such a flood of light as to shock spectators into a rigid silence," a huge electric lamp, one of the first, is displayed inside the court house. Located on Hill and Main Streets.

HOSTELS

Porter

CORONADO LODGE YOUTH HOSTEL
R.R. 3, Box 218
Chesterton, IN 46304
(219) 926-1528
FACILITIES: Open year round; 35 beds, men; 35 beds, women; modern bathroom; overnight charges: $2.50 (May 2 - Oct. 31); $3.25 (Nov.1 - May 1).

San Pierre

RIVER BEND CAMPGROUND
R.R. 1, Box 128
San Pierre, IN 46374
(219) 896-3339
FACILITIES: Open Apr. 1 - Nov. 1; 18 beds, men; 18 beds, women; modern bathroom; overnight charges: $2; houseparent: Edward Miller.

POINTS OF INTEREST

Cloverdale

CATARACT FALLS - Indiana's largest natural waterfall tumbles and gushes into the southern end of the 1,500-acre Cataract Lake. Located on Route 42 at south end of Cataract Lake.

Crawfordsville

GENERAL LEW WALLACE STUDY AND MUSEUM - It was here that the author created the widely read historical novel, "Ben Hur." Many furnishings and mementos have been preserved. Located on Wallace Avenue and East Pike Streets.

Crown Point

OLD LAKE COUNTY JAIL - This 94-year-old jail, which retains its original interior, gained national notoriety when John Dillinger made his daring escape using a gun carved from soap on March 3, 1934. Located at 212-228 South Main Street.'

Indianapolis

CIVIC THEATRE OF INDIANAPOLIS - The Booth Tarkington Civic Theatre is the oldest continually operated community theatre in the country. Located at 1200 West 38th Street.

INDIANAPOLIS MOTOR SPEEDWAY AND MUSEUM - Take a ride around the famous "Indy 500" track or leisurely browse through the museum and Auto Racing Hall of Fame. The 2½-mile oval is site of the world's largest one-day sporting event. Located at 4790 West 16th Street.

Kokomo

ELWOOD HAYNES MUSEUM - This was the home of Elwood Haynes, who built America's first automobile with a clutch and electric ignition. He was also the inventor of stainless steel and stellito. Located at 1915 South Webster Street.

Lebanon

BOONE COUNTY COURT HOUSE - Built of granite and Indiana limestone in 1857, the court house's eight huge limestone pillars are said to be the largest one-piece limestone columns in the world. Each column is over 35 feet high and weighs 30 tons. Located on Washington and Lebanon Streets.

Matthews

CUMBERLAND COVERED BRIDGE - Built in 1877, this Howe-design covered bridge is considered one of the longest single-span truss-type covered bridges ever constructed. It was first built as an open bridge and covered later. Located on the northeast corner of town on County Road 1000E.

Michigan City

MICHIGAN CITY PIER AND LIGHTHOUSE - Indiana's only operating lighthouse beckons ships cruising Lake Michigan's temperamental waters to a snug Michigan City harbor. Located at entrance of harbor on Lake Michigan shoreline.

Nappanee

AMISH ACRES - Visit a living historical farm

INDIANA

POINTS OF INTEREST (continued)

where Amish folk, "Plain People," religiously adhere to the lifestyle and beliefs of their forefathers who settled here in 1850. Located at 1600 West Market Street.

Pleasant Lake

LITTLE RIVER RAILROAD - The railroad preserves the sights, sounds and smells of steam railroading in the early 1900s. The engine is the smallest standard-gauge 4-6-2 locomotive ever built. Located in downtown Pleasant Lake.

Vevay

MARTHA A. GRAHAM SIDEWHEEL FERRYBOAT - The last Indiana sidewheel ferryboat on the Ohio River invites motorists to drive aboard and chug across the river on a remnant of an earlier time. Located at riverfront.

SWISS VALLEY WINERY - Vevay is believed to be the birthplace, in 1803, of commercial wine in the nation. Located at 101 South Ferry Street.

West Baden

NORTHWOOD INSTITUTE - Once known as the "Eighth Wonder of the World," the West Baden Springs Hotel prospered as a grandiose resort during the early part of the century. The highly reputed "Pompeiian Court" was the central feature of the hotel. Visitors today, as in the past, can marvel at the ornate imported marble flooring of the court, as well as its ceiling, said to be the largest unsupported dome in the world at the time it was built. Located adjacent to French Lick.

Wyandotte

WYANDOTTE CAVE - One of the largest underground caverns in the world.

Zionsville

COLONIAL VILLAGE OF ZIONSVILLE - The reconstruction of this 125-year-old village has developed into a community-wide project. Colonial and early American architectural styles prevail among the antique shops and residential sections. Located 3 mi. north of I-465 on Route 421, then 1 mi. east on County Road 334.

IOWA

Iowa, the land of the farmer, joined the Union in 1846 as the twenty-ninth state. Its first permanent inhabitants, the Mound Builders, were essentially farmers who planted crops and domesticated animals.

Much trouble broke out between the white settlers and the Indians when the white settlers began setting up homesteads in Iowa around the turn of the 19th century. The struggle persisted for nearly fifty years and was considered over when the Sioux gave up their claim to the land in 1851.

Today, Iowa's rich farmlands produce 10 percent of the country's food supply, with corn, soybeans and oats heading the list of bountiful crops. The state's livestock industry is a winner, too, simply because of the readily available feed supply.

But surprisingly enough, manufacturing, which is centered in Cedar Rapids, Des Moines, Dubuque and Waterloo, is Iowa's major source of revenue.

State capital: Des Moines. State bird: Eastern goldfinch. State tree: Oak. State flower: Wild rose.

WEATHER

The state of Iowa comprises 56,290 square miles, primarily of rolling prairie. Changes in elevation are small across the state, varying from 1,675 feet on Ocheyedan Mound in the northwest to 477 feet at the mouth of the Des Moines River in the southeast. There is some rugged terrain, mainly of forest soils, in the northeast. Most of the state's lakes are located in the northwest.

Iowa's climate, because of latitude and interior continental location, is characterized by marked seasonal variations. During the six warm months of the year the prevailing moist, southerly flow from the Gulf of Mexico produces a summer rainfall maximum. The prevailing northwesterly flow of dry Canadian air in the winter causes this season to be cold and relatively dry. At intervals throughout the year, air masses from the Pacific Ocean moving across the western United States reach Iowa, producing comparatively mild and dry weather. The autumnal "Indian Summers" are a result of the dominance of these modified Pacific air masses. Hot, dry winds, originating in the desert southwestern U.S. occasionally sweep into Iowa during the summer, producing unusually high temperatures.

Average daily temperature for each month.

	Northern	Southern
Jan.	21.9 to 4.0	31.0 to 12.9
Feb.	27.7 to 9.6	37.3 to 18.6
Mar.	37.4 to 20.1	47.0 to 27.2
Apr.	56.2 to 35.0	62.8 to 40.8
May	69.3 to 46.4	74.2 to 51.6
Jun.	79.1 to 56.7	83.0 to 61.1
Jul.	82.2 to 60.7	87.1 to 65.2
Aug.	81.1 to 58.7	85.4 to 63.3

WEATHER (continued)

Sept.	71.8 to 48.9	77.6 to 54.8
Oct.	61.7 to 38.9	67.5 to 44.6
Nov.	43.1 to 24.6	50.1 to 30.8
Dec.	28.0 to 11.7	36.4 to 19.6
Year	55.0 to 34.6	61.6 to 40.9

STATE CHAMBER OF COMMERCE

Iowa Development Commission
250 Jewett Building
Des Moines, IA 50309
(515) 281-3251

STATE & CITY TOURISM OFFICES

State

Iowa Development Commission
250 Jewett Building
Des Moines, IA 50309
(515) 281-3619

Travel Development Division
Iowa Development Commission
250 Jewett Building
Des Moines, IA 50309
(515) 281-3401

Local

Convention Bureau
800 High Street
Des Moines, IA 50307
(515) 283-1777

STATE HIGHWAY DEPARTMENT

Iowa Department of Transportation
State Capitol
Des Moines, IA 50319
(515) 296-1101

HIGHWAY WELCOMING CENTERS

Davis City

DAVIS CITY CENTER - Interstate 35, north.

Des Moines

DES MOINES CENTER - Interstate 80, west.

Mason City

MASON CITY CENTER - Interstate 35 south, then north on Mason City Road.

Sioux City

SIOUX CITY CENTER - Interstate 29, south, just south of Sioux City.

Underwood

UNDERWOOD CENTER - Interstate 80, east, west edge of state.

Victor

VICTOR CENTER - Interstate 80, east, west of Iowa City.

Wilton

WILTON CENTER - Interstate 80, west, near Illinois border.

STATE POLICE

Department of Public Safety
Wallace State Office Building
Des Moines, IA 50319
(515) 281-5114

HUNTING & FISHING

Hunting

Hunting license not required for: Owners or tenants of land and their children who hunt on their own land, with the exception of deer and wild turkey where special licenses are required.

Residents under sixteen (16) years of age if accompanied by a licensed parent or guardian or in the company with any other competent licensed adult with the consent of the parent or guardian, providing, however, that one licensed adult accompanies each person under age 16.

Minor inmates of state institutions under the Department of Social Services. This does not apply to inmates of state penal institutions.

Inmates of county homes.

Military personnel on active duty and who are legal residents of Iowa when on authorized leave.

Resident

Hunting, $5; combination hunting & fishing, $8; combination hunting & fishing (annual), $2.50; lifetime hunting, $6; lifetime combination hunting & fishing, $8.

Residency of 30 days in Iowa entitles an individual to resident small game hunting and trapping license privileges.

Non-resident

Hunting, $25.

Deer: Legal residents only. Required in addition to regular hunting license. Shotgun, $10; bow, $10.

State Duck Stamp: No person shall hunt duck or geese in Iowa without possessing an Iowa Migratory Waterfowl Stamp. The face of the stamp must be signed, $1.

Federal Duck Stamp: All persons of age

219

IOWA

HUNTING & FISHING (continued)

16 or older hunting migratory waterfowl must have with them an unexpired Migratory Bird Hunting Stamp validated by their signature on the face of the stamp. These stamps can be bought at post office, $5.

Landowner-Tenant Deer License: Special licenses to hunt deer are required of landowners and tenants. These licenses are free and valid only on land upon which the licenses resides. Applications must be submitted by early November to assure applicants of a license before the opening day of gun season. Only one free deer license will be issued to a farm unit.

Fishing

A fishing license not required for the following: Owners or tenants of land and their children may fish on their own land without a license.

Residents under sixteen (16) years of age.

Non-residents under fourteen (14) years of age.

Minor pupils of the state school for the blind, state school for the deaf, or minor inmates of other state institutions under the Department of Social Services. This does not apply to inmates in state penal institutions.

Military personnel on active duty and who are legal residents of Iowa when on authorized leave.

Resident

Fishing license, $4; combination hunting & fishing, $8; resident 65 or older (annual), $1.25; combination hunting & fishing (annual), $2.50; lifetime fishing, $6; lifetime combination hunting & fishing, $8.

Non-resident

Fishing license (required of either sex 14 years of age and older), $10; 6-day license, $6; 1-day for resident or non-resident, $1.

Trout Stamp: No person, resident or non-resident, required to have a fishing license, shall have in his possession trout unless at the time of such possession he has on his person an unexpired special trout license stamp validated by his signature written across the face of the stamp in ink or a receipt or other evidence showing that such trout was acquired lawfully. A person who has not reached his sixteenth birthday is not required to have a trout license stamp. Special trout license stamp, $5.

For more information contact:

Iowa Conservation Commission
Wallace State Office Bldg.
Des Moines, IA 50319
(515) 281-5918

CAMPGROUNDS

Private

Adel

DES MOINES WEST KOA
Route 2
Adel, IA 50003
(515) 834-2729
LOCATION: 1½ mi. north of I-80 at Exit 106.
FACILITIES: Open year round; 150 sites; water and bathroom facilities; sanitary station; electrical hookup; trailer village vehicle sites; food service.

Burlington

LAKE WILDERNESS
Box 9
Burlington, IA 52601
(319) 837-6516
LOCATION: West of Denmark on Route 16.
FACILITIES: Open Apr. - Nov.; 200 sites; water and bathroom facilities; sanitary station; electrical hookup; trailer village vehicle sites; food service; boating; fishing.

Colo

TWIN ANCHORS CAMPGROUND
Colo, IA 50056
(515) 377-2243
LOCATION: 11 mi. east of I-35 at Ames on U.S. 30.
FACILITIES: Open year round; 164 sites; water and bathroom facilities; electrical hookup; trailer village vehicle sites; laundry; food service; boating; fishing.

Council Bluffs

OMAHA-COUNCIL BLUFFS KOA
Box 41
Crescent, IA 51526
(712) 545-3202
LOCATION: 12 mi. north of Omaha.
FACILITIES: Open Mar. - Dec.; 100 sites; water and bathroom facilities; sanitary station; electrical hookup; trailer village vehicle sites; food service.

Davenport

LAKESIDE MANOR PARK
Route 2
Davenport, IA 52804
(319) 381-3413
LOCATION: Exit 6 at I-280, then ¼ mi. west on U.S. 61 south.
FACILITIES: Open year round; 200 sites; water and bathroom facilities; sanitary station; electrical hookup; trailer village vehicle sites; laundry; food service; swimming; hiking.

Garnavillo

PARADISE VALLEY
Route 2
Garnavillo, IA 52049
(319) 873-2079
LOCATION: 4 mi. east of Garnavillo, 2 mi. north X56, the Great River Road.

CAMPGROUNDS (continued)

FACILITIES: Open Apr. 15 - Oct. 15; 165 sites; water and bathroom facilities; sanitary station; electrical hookup; trailer village vehicle sites; food service.

J.W. PARK CAMPGROUND
Route 2
Garnavillo, IA 52049
(319) 964-2113
LOCATION: 4 mi. east of Garnavillo on C17 at junction of Great River Road.
FACILITIES: Open Apr. - Nov.; 175 sites; water and bathroom facilities; sanitary station; electrical hookup; firewood; trailer village vehicle sites; laundry; food service; swimming.

Iowa Falls

GEHRKE'S LAKE
Route 1
Iowa Falls, IA 50126
(515) 855-4348
LOCATION: 9 mi. south of Iowa Falls on U.S. 65, 2½ mi. west on D41.
FACILITIES: Open May - Nov.; 100 sites; water and bathroom facilities; sanitary station; electrical hookup; trailer village vehicle sites; swimming; hiking.

Knoxville

HICKORY RIDGE
Knoxville, IA 50138
(515) 842-5963
LOCATION: 3 mi. north, & 1 mi. east of Knoxville.
FACILITIES: Open Apr. - Nov.; 200 sites; water and bathroom facilities; sanitary station; electrical hookup; trailer village vehicle sites; laundry; food service; boating; hiking.

North Liberty

JOLLY ROGER RECREATION AREA
Box 190
North Liberty, IA 52317
(319) 626-2171
LOCATION: I-380 to Exit 4, North Liberty, north ½ mi., then east 3 mi. to Coralville Lake.
FACILITIES: Open Apr. - Nov.; 100 sites; water and bathroom facilities; sanitary station; electrical hookup; trailer village vehicle sites; food service; boating.

Onawa

ONAWA KOA
R.R. 2
Onawa, IA 51040
(712) 423-1633
LOCATION: ½ mi. west of Onawa I-29 exit, then north 1½ mi.
FACILITIES: Open May - Oct.; 100 sites; water and bathroom facilities; sanitary station; electrical hookup; trailer village vehicle sites; laundry; food service.

Story City

WHISPERING OAKS
Box 66
Story City, IA 50248
(515) 733-2521
LOCATION: 10 mi. north of Ames on I-35, Story City Exit 124. Take access road north between Mobile and Skelly stations at Happy Chief.
FACILITIES: Open Apr. 15 - Nov. 15; 100 sites; water and bathroom facilities; electrical hookup; trailer village vehicle sites; food service; fishing.

Tama

BOLEN'S ARROWHEAD
R.R. 2
Tama, IA 52339
(515) 484-3018
LOCATION: 2 mi. west of Tama on E-49 (old Hwy. 30.)
FACILITIES: Open year round; 100 sites; water and bathroom facilities; electrical hookup; trailer village vehicle sites; boating; fishing.

SHADY HILLS
R.R. 2
Tama, IA 52339
(515) 484-4717
LOCATION: 2 mi. west of Toledo on U.S. 30, then 1 mi. south of Tama.
FACILITIES: Open Apr. 15 - Oct. 15; 225 sites; water and bathroom facilities; sanitary station; electrical hookup; trailer village vehicle sites; food service; boating; fishing.

Tipton

KOCH'S MEADOW LAKE
R.R. 1
Tipton, IA 52772
(319) 886-6273
LOCATION: From I-80, exit 267, Tipton, then 2 mi. north, 2 mi. east and 3 mi. north.
FACILITIES: Open Apr. - Oct.; 100 sites; sanitary station; electrical hookup; trailer village vehicle sites; laundry; swimming; boating; fishing.

Vinton

HIDDEN VALLEY CAMPGROUND
Box 130
Vinton, IA 52349
(319) 472-2002
LOCATION: 1½ mi. east of Vinton.
FACILITIES: Open May - Oct.; 200 sites; water and bathroom facilities; sanitary station; electrical hookup; trailer village vehicle sites; food service; boating; fishing.

RESORTS & BEACHES

Most of the state's resort activities center around the major lakes and include fishing, swimming, boating, water skiing and camping. (See Boating Areas.)

IOWA

BOATING AREAS

Centerville

RATHBUN LAKE
LOCATION: Near Centerville.
FACILITIES: Launching.

Clear Lake

CLEAR LAKE
LOCATION: Near Clear Lake.
FACILITIES: Launching.

Knoxville

RED ROCK LAKE
LOCATION: Near Knoxville.
FACILITIES: Launching.

North Liberty

CORALVILLE LAKE
LOCATION: Near North Liberty.
FACILITIES: Launching.

Saylorville

SAYLORVILLE LAKE
LOCATION: Near Saylorville.
FACILITIES: Launching.

Spirit Lake

IOWA GREAT LAKES
LOCATION: Near Spirit Lake.
FACILITIES: Launching.

BICYCLE TRAILS

No information was available on Bicycle
Trails in Iowa.

TRAILS

Cedar Rapids

SAC AND FOX TRAIL - 5 mi. foot trail. This
trail follows the Cedar River and Indian Creek
within an 800-acre linear greenbelt. It bisects
the 130-acre Indian Creek Nature Center.
Special features include scenic views of the
bluffs and limestone palisades. The riverbanks
are lined with willow, birch, cottonwood and
sycamore trees.

SKI AREAS

Boone

SKI VALLEY
Boone, IA 50036
(515) 432-2413
LOCATION: 3 mi. west on U.S. 30.
FACILITIES: 3 tow ropes; slopes for expert,
intermediate and beginning skiers; ski instruction; ski rental; 180 ft. vertical drop; restaurants; lodging.

Crescent

CRESCENT SKI HILLS
Crescent, IA 51526
(712) 328-9547
LOCATION: 7 mi. north of Council Bluffs on
Hwy. 183.
FACILITIES: 1 T-bar; 1 poma; slopes for expert, intermediate and beginning skiers; ski instruction; ski rental; 200 ft. vertical drop; restaurants; lodging.

Decorah

NOR-SKI RUNS
Decorah, IA 52101
(319) 382-9962
LOCATION: 1½ mi. north of U.S. 52 and
Route 9 junction.
FACILITIES: 4 tow ropes; slopes for expert,
intermediate and beginning skiers; ski instruction; ski rental; 250 ft. vertical drop; restaurants; lodging.

Dexter

DEER RUN SPORTS AREA
Dexter, IA 50070
(515) 789-4575
LOCATION: 2½ mi. north of Dexter on Road
P48.
FACILITIES: 3 tow ropes; slopes for expert,
intermediate and beginning skiers; ski instruction; ski rental; 200 ft. vertical drop; restaurants; lodging.

Dubuque

SUNDOWN
Dubuque, IA 52001
(319) 556-6676
LOCATION: 5½ mi. west of Dubuque on
Asbury Road.
FACILITIES: 1 triple chairlift; 2 double
chairlifts; 3 tow ropes; slopes for expert, intermediate and beginning skiers; ski instruction; ski rental; 475 ft. vertical drop; restaurants; lodging.

VETERANS' MEMORIAL PARK SKI AREA
Dubuque, IA 52001
(319) 588-1478
LOCATION: On 32nd Street, off U.S. 52.
FACILITIES: 2 tow ropes; slopes for expert,
intermediate and beginning skiers; 200 ft. vertical drop; restaurants; lodging.

Estherville

HOLIDAY MOUNTAIN SKI AREA
Estherville, IA 51334
(712) 362-9028
LOCATION: 1 mi. south of Estherville.
FACILITIES: 2 T-bars; 2 tow ropes; slopes
for expert, intermediate and beginning skiers;
ski instruction; ski rental; 190 ft. vertical
drop; restaurants; lodging.

Hardy

WINTER WORLD
Hardy, IA 50545
(515) 332-3329
LOCATION: ½ mi. north of Humboldt on
Hwy. 3.

SKI AREAS (continued)

FACILITIES: 3 tow ropes; slopes for expert, intermediate and beginning skiers; ski instruction; ski rental; restaurants; lodging.

Milford

HORSESHOE BEND
Milford, IA 51351
(712) 338-4007
LOCATION: 2 mi. south of Milford, then 3 mi. west.
FACILITIES: 2 tow ropes; slopes for expert, intermediate and beginning skiers; ski instruction; ski rental; 100 ft. vertical drop; restaurants; lodging.

Montezuma

FUN VALLEY
Montezuma, IA 50171
(515) 623-3456
LOCATION: 8 mi. south of I-80, then 2½ mi. west of International Store on Hwy. 63.
FACILITIES: 5 tow ropes; 2 cable hand tows; slopes for expert, intermediate and beginning skiers; ski instruction; ski rental; 200 ft. vertical drop; restaurants; lodging.

Pella

SUNSET SKI SLOPE
Pella, IA 50219
(515) 626-3291
LOCATION: South of Pella on Elevator Road.
FACILITIES: 3 tow ropes; slopes for expert, intermediate and beginning skiers; ski instruction; ski rental; 100 ft. vertical drop; restaurants; lodging.

Waverly

SKI VILLA
Waverly, IA 50677
(319) 352-9922
LOCATION: In Waverly.
FACILITIES: 6 tow ropes; slopes for expert, intermediate and beginning skiers; ski instruction; ski rental; restaurants; lodging.

AMUSEMENT PARKS & ATTRACTIONS

Arnolds Park

LAKE OKOBOJI AMUSEMENTS
Box 438
Arnolds Park, IA 51331
(712) 332-5658
FACILITIES: 12 major rides; 10 kiddie rides; 1 fun house; 2 walk thrus; 5 games; 9 refreshment stands; restaurant; excursion-boat; paddle boats; 2 arcades; shooting gallery; bathing beach; roller rink; exhibits; picnic facilities; miniature golf; crafts; stage shows; orchestras; name bands; free acts; fireworks; free gate; free parking.

Des Moines

ADVENTURELAND

I-80 at Hwy. 65
Des Moines, IA 50316
(515) 266-2121
FACILITIES: 16 major rides; 3 kiddie rides; 8 games; 4 refreshment stands; picnic facilities; stage shows; shooting gallery; 5 restaurants; arcade; pool; camping; orchestras; name bands; fireworks; pay gate; pay parking; open Memorial Day - Labor Day.

NEW RIVERVIEW AMUSEMENT CO., DIV. OF MORLES INC.
8th & Corning
Des Moines, IA 50313
(515) 288-3621
FACILITIES: 13 major rides; 5 kiddie rides; walk thru; 7 games; 4 refreshment stands; restaurant; arcade; miniature train; shooting gallery; picnic facilities; miniature golf; zoo; orchestras; free acts; fireworks; pay gate; free parking; open early May - Labor Day.

STATE FAIR

Iowa State Fair
State House
Des Moines, IA 50319
(515) 262-3111
DATE: August

NATIONAL PARKS

There are no National Parks in Iowa.

NATIONAL FORESTS

There are no National Forests in Iowa.

STATE PARKS

Headquarters

Department of Conservation
Wallace State Office Bldg.
Des Moines, IA 50319
(515) 281-5886

Anita

LAKE ANITA STATE PARK
Lake Anita, IA 50020
(712) 762-3564
LOCATION: 3 mi. south of Anita Interchange.
FACILITIES: Open year round; 144 sites; water and bathroom facilities; sanitary station; electrical hookup; trailer village vehicle sites; picnic area; food service; swimming; boating, 6 h.p.; fishing.

Bedford

LAKE OF THREE FIRES STATE PARK
Bedford, IA 50833
(712) 523-2700
LOCATION: 3 mi. northeast of Bedford.
FACILITIES: Open year round; 160 sites; water and bathroom facilities; sanitary station;

IOWA

STATE PARKS (continued)

electrical hookup; trailer village vehicle sites; cabins; picnic area; food service; swimming; boating, 6 h.p.; fishing; hiking.

Clear Lake

CLEAR LAKE STATE PARK
Clear Lake, IA 50428
(515) 357-4212
LOCATION: 2 mi. south of Clear Lake.
FACILITIES: Open year round; 222 sites; water and bathroom facilities; sanitary station; electrical hookup; picnic area; swimming; boating; fishing.

Danville

GEODE STATE PARK
Danville, IA 52623
(319) 392-4601
LOCATION: 4 mi. southwest of Danville.
FACILITIES: Open year round; 216 sites; water and bathroom facilities; sanitary station; electrical hookup; picnic area; food service; swimming; boating, 6 h.p.; fishing; hiking.

Davis City

NINE EAGLES STATE PARK
Davis City, IA 50065
(515) 442-3333
LOCATION: 6 mi. southeast of Davis City.
FACILITIES: Open year round; 128 sites; water and bathroom facilities; sanitary station; electrical hookup; picnic area; food service; swimming; boating, electric; fishing; hiking.

Drakesville

LAKE WAPELLO STATE PARK
Drakesville, IA 52552
(515) 722-3371
LOCATION: 6 mi. west of Drakesville.
FACILITIES: Open year round; 128 sites; water and bathroom facilities; sanitary station; electrical hookup; trailer village vehicle sites; cabins; picnic area; food service; swimming; boating, 6 h.p.; fishing; hiking.

Dundee

BACKBONE STATE PARK
Dundee, IA 52038
(319) 924-2527
LOCATION: 4 mi. southwest of Strawberry Point.
FACILITIES: Open year round; 232 sites; water and bathroom facilities; sanitary station; electrical hookup; trailer village vehicle sites; cabins; picnic area; food service; swimming; boating, 6 h.p.; fishing; hiking.

Eldora

PINE LAKE STATE PARK
Eldora, IA 50627
(515) 858-5832
LOCATION: ½ mi. northeast of Eldora.
FACILITIES: Open year round; 128 sites; water and bathroom facilities; sanitary station; electrical hookup; trailer village vehicle sites; cabins; picnic area; food service; swimming; boating, 6 h.p. & electric; fishing; hiking.

Guthrie Center

SPRINGBROOK STATE PARK
Route 1
Guthrie Center, IA 50015
(515) 747-3591
LOCATION: 8 mi. northeast of Guthrie Center.
FACILITIES: Open year round; 200 sites; water and bathroom facilities; sanitary station; electrical hookup; cabins; picnic area; food service; swimming; boating, electric; fishing; hiking.

Hampton

BEEDS LAKE STATE PARK
Hampton, IA 50441
(515) 456-2047
LOCATION: 3 mi. northwest of Hampton.
FACILITIES: Open year round; 144 sites; water and bathroom facilities; sanitary station; electrical hookup; picnic area; food service; swimming; boating, 6 h.p.; fishing; hiking.

Indianola

LAKE AHQUABI
Indianola, IA 50125
(515) 961-7101
LOCATION: 5½ mi. southwest of Indianola.
FACILITIES: Open year round; 176 sites; sanitary station; electrical hookup; trailer village vehicle sites; picnic area; food service; swimming; boating, 6 h.p.; fishing; hiking.

Kellogg

ROCK CREEK STATE PARK
Kellogg, IA 50135
(515) 236-3722
LOCATION: 6 mi. northeast of Kellogg.
FACILITIES: Open year round; 280 sites; water and bathroom facilities; sanitary station; electrical hookup; trailer village vehicle sites; picnic area; food service; swimming; boating, 6 h.p.; fishing; hiking.

Keosauqua

LACEY-KEOSAUQUA STATE PARK
Keosauqua, IA 52565
(319) 293-3502
LOCATION: Adjoins Keosauqua.
FACILITIES: Open year round; 176 sites; electrical hookup; trailer village vehicle sites; cabins; picnic area; food service; swimming; boating, electric; fishing; hiking.

Lake View

BLACK HAWK LAKE STATE PARK
Lake View, IA 51450
(712) 657-8712
LOCATION: In Lake View.
FACILITIES: Open year round; 176 sites; sanitary station; electrical hookup; trailer village vehicle sites; picnic area; swimming; boating; fishing.

Milford

EMERSON BAY STATE PARK
Route 2
Milford, IA 51351

STATE PARKS (continued)

(712) 337-3634
LOCATION: 2½ mi. north of Milford.
FACILITIES: Open year round; 144 sites; picnic area; swimming; boating; fishing.

Missouri Valley

WILSON ISLAND STATE PARK
Missouri Valley, IA 51555
(712) 642-2069
LOCATION: 5 mi. west of Loveland.
FACILITIES: Open year round; 238 sites; water and bathroom facilities; sanitary station; electrical hookup; trailer village vehicle sites; picnic area; swimming; boating; hunting; hiking.

Moravia

HONEY CREEK STATE PARK
Moravia, IA 52571
(515) 724-3739
LOCATION: Near Moravia.
FACILITIES: Open year round; 134 sites; water and bathroom facilities; electrical hookup; sanitary station; trailer village vehicle sites; picnic area; swimming; boating; fishing.

Sidney

WAUBONSIE STATE PARK
Hamburg, IA 51640
(712) 382-2786
LOCATION: 7 mi. southwest of Sidney.
FACILITIES: Open year round; 128 sites; water and bathroom facilities; sanitary station; electrical hookup; trailer village vehicle sites; picnic area; hiking.

Solon

LAKE MACBRIDE STATE PARK
Solon, IA 52333
(319) 644-2200
LOCATION: 4 mi. west of Solon.
FACILITIES: Open year round; 160 sites; water and bathroom facilities; sanitary station; electrical hookup; trailer village vehicle sites; picnic area; food service; swimming; boating, 6 h.p.; fishing; hiking.

STATE FORESTS

Chariton

STEPHENS FOREST
Chariton, IA 50049
(515) 774-4554
LOCATION: East of Chariton.
FACILITIES: Open year round; picnic area; boating, electric; hunting; hiking; tent camping.

Farmington

SHIMEK FOREST
Farmington, IA 52626
(319) 878-3811
LOCATION: 1 mi. east of Farmington.
FACILITIES: Open year round; picnic area; boating, electric; hunting; hiking; tent camping.

Waukon

YELLOW RIVER FOREST
McGregor, IA 52157
(319) 586-2254
LOCATION: 14 mi. southeast of Waukon.
FACILITIES: Open year round; picnic area; hunting; hiking; tent camping.

HISTORIC SITES

Clarion

4-H HISTORICAL BUILDING - One-room rural schoolhouse from Lake Township, District No. 6, credited as the birthplace of the 4-H emblem. Located on Central Avenue West.

Council Bluffs

GENERAL DODGE HOUSE - Home of General Granville Mellen Dodge, who, while president of 16 railroad companies, surveyed and built more railroad mileage than any other American. Located at 605 3rd Street.

Croton

CROTON CIVIL WAR MEMORIAL PARK - Iowa's only Civil War battle scars are at Croton. Cannonballs that fell here afford the only instance in which hostile cannonfire landed on Iowa soil.

Dubuque

GRAVE OF JULIEN DUBUQUE - Circular Galena limestone tower erected in 1897 on the Mississippi River bluffs, at the mouth of Catfish Creek, contains the grave of Julien DuBuque, founder of the city of Dubuque, and reportedly the first white man to settle permanently in Iowa. Located beyond the end of Rowan Street, south of Dubuque.

WILLIAM NEWMAN HOUSE - Log cabin, built prior to 1827, is reputedly the oldest building in Iowa. Occupied originally by French hunters and miners. Located at 2241 Lincoln Avenue.

Mount Pleasant

IOWA WESLEYAN COLLEGE - First college west of the Mississippi River. Sponsored by Methodist Church, the college was first named Mount Pleasant Collegiate Institute, renamed Iowa Wesleyan University in 1849 and Iowa Wesleyan College in 1911. Located in Mount Pleasant.

West Bend

GROTTO OF THE REDEMPTION - Largest grotto (small cavern) and collection of minerals and petrification in the world. Started by Father Paul Dobberstein, who labored 42 years setting ornamental rocks and gems in concrete, the Grotto, actually a composite of

IOWA

HISTORIC SITES (continued)

nine separate grottos, portrays nine scenes in the life of Christ.

West Branch

HERBERT HOOVER NATIONAL HISTORIC SITE - Herbert Hoover Presidential Library and Museum includes public papers, personal correspondence, books, manuscripts, audiovisual materials, and memorabilia of Herbert Clark Hoover, 31st President. Two-room birthplace cottage restored in 1938 to its original appearance contains many possessions of the Hoover family. Located in West Branch.

HOSTELS

Sioux City

YMCA OF SIOUXLAND
722 Nebraska Street
Sioux City, IA 51101
(712) 252-3276
FACILITIES: Open year round; 20 beds men only; beds up to 70 with advance reservations required; modern bathroom; overnight charges: $2.50; houseparent: John Wais.

POINTS OF INTEREST

Adair

SITE OF JESSE JAMES TRAIN ROBBERY - Locomotive wheel marks the site of the first robbery of a moving train in the West. On July 21, 1873, Jesse James and his gang derailed the Chicago, Rock Island and Pacific train, killing engineer, John Rafferty. Located west of Adair on U.S. 6.

Burlington

SNAKE ALLEY - Curving, narrow street built on a limestone bluff consisting of 5 half curves and 2 quarter curves, descending over a distance of 275 feet. Featured in "Believe It or Not" as the "crookedest street in the world." The curves were designed to permit horses to descend the hill at safe speeds. Located on North 6th Street between Washington and Columbia Streets.

Charles City

GIRLHOOD HOME OF CARRIE LANE CHAPMAN CATT - Two-story frame farmhouse, the girlhood home of Carrie Lane Chapman Catt, international leader of women's suffrage and peace movements. In 1890, she succeeded Susan B. Anthony as president of the National American Woman Suffrage Association. Located southeast of Charles City.

Dyersville

BASILICA OF ST. FRANCIS XAVIER - One of the 18 Minor Basilicas in the United States. The name "Basilica," bestowed by the Pope, denotes a church of unusual architectural design, native nobility, and antiquity.

Exira

PLOW IN OAK PARK - Roadside park containing an ancient oak tree with an old iron plow embedded in its heart. The plow was leaned against the young oak by the son of a pioneer farmer and left undisturbed. As the tree grows, less and less of the plow is visible and it no longer rests on the ground. Located 1 mi. south of Exira on U.S. 71.

Fayette

BUFFALO RANCH MUSEUM - Herd of live buffalo, in addition to old-time general store and saloon with items dating back to pioneer days. Located at 310 Lovers Lane.

Festina

ST. ANTHONY OF PADUA CHAPEL - "Smallest cathedral in the world." This little chapel seats 8 people. Built in 1885 on the south bank of the Turkey River by Johann Gaertner who served as a soldier under Napoleon.

Little Amana

THE AMANAS - Seven little villages filled with old world charm and hospitality. Settled in 1854 by members of the Community of True Inspiration, originally an offshoot of Lutheranism, the 26,000 acre area contains general stores, meat shops, a woolen mill, furniture shop, bakery, winery, and other craft-type businesses. Located off I-80.

Manning

HOLSTEIN-FRIESIAN MUSEUM - Only Holstein museum in America, features antiques and memorabilia donated by breeders of the black and white cows, the most popular dairy animal in the world. Items include milk stool and neck chain of the late College Ormsby Burke (Mama), holder of the lifetime record for milk production, 334,219 pounds. Loccated at 507 Main.

Nashua

GLACIAL ROCK - Largest glacial rock in the Midwest. Deposited by the Wisconsin Glacier, the last of the glaciers to invade Iowa, more than 50,000 years ago. Rock is in the middle of a field, on the east side of road. Located 3 mi. west of Nashua on Route 54, then ¾ mi. south on gravel road.

Peru

ORIGINAL DELICIOUS APPLE TREE - In 1870 a chance seedling apple tree was found in an orchard planted in the 1860s by Jesse Hiatt, a Quaker who came to Madison County in 1856. From this original tree, Stark Nurseries developed the Delicious Apple. Some 10,000,000 trees have since come from its branches. Located near Peru.

POINTS OF INTEREST (continued)

Winterset

JOHN WAYNE BIRTHPLACE - Marion

Michael Morrison (John Wayne), son of a druggist, was born on May 26, 1907 in Winterset. The family lived in several different homes in the town.

KANSAS

Kansas, the "Nation's Breadbasket," entered the Union in 1861 as the thirty-fourth state. Early explorers, Lewis and Clark and Zebulon Pike, inhibited the settlement of the state because they thought the area desertlike. Consequently, many of the displaced Indians were resettled in the Kansas territory, and it wasn't until the 1820s that permanent white settlements were established. Ironically, these were forts built as protection against Indian attacks.

Today, more wheat is grown and flour milled in Kansas than any other state; hence the title "Nation's Breadbasket," but agriculture takes second place to the rapidly expanding manufacturing industry.

Airplane, tire and railroad car manufacturing accounts for a large share of Kansas' industrial revenues. And because the state is nearly equidistant between the two coasts, making it an ideal distribution point, major companies are looking to Kansas when expanding their operations.

State capital: Topeka. State bird: Western meadowlark. State tree: Cottonwood. State flower: Sunflower.

WEATHER

Kansas has a distinctly continental climate with characteristically changeable temperatures and wide variation in precipitation. Its day-to-day weather is affected largely by two physical features, both some distance from the state: the Rock Mountains to the west and the Gulf of Mexico to the south. The mountains on the west prevent the importation of moisture from the Pacific Ocean, while the Gulf is the source of much of the state's precipitation.

Differences in elevation also have influence on the climate. Elevation changes are quite gradual, rising from 800 or 1,000 feet above sea level in a number of extreme eastern and southeastern counties to approximately 1,500 feet in the center of the state, (north to south), and to 3,500 feet at the Colorado line.

During much of the year there is a progressive increase in mean temperature from the higher northwestern counties to the southeastern area. The exception is during the warm summer months when the higher mean temperatures are found in the central and south-central counties.

Average daily temperature for the month.

	Northern	Southern
Jan.	40.2 to 14.9	45.0 to 21.7
Feb.	46.7 to 20.4	50.9 to 26.1
Mar.	54.0 to 26.8	58.9 to 32.9
Apr.	67.9 to 39.4	71.3 to 44.9
May	77.6 to 50.6	80.4 to 54.8
Jun.	88.0 to 61.1	90.3 to 64.5
Jul.	93.3 to 66.2	94.9 to 69.0
Aug.	92.2 to 64.5	94.2 to 67.3
Sept.	82.6 to 54.2	84.9 to 59.2
Oct.	71.9 to 42.0	74.1 to 47.5
Nov.	54.8 to 28.2	58.0 to 34.0
Dec.	43.1 to 18.9	46.9 to 25.0
Year	67.7 to 40.6	70.8 to 45.6

STATE CHAMBER OF COMMERCE

Kansas Association of Commerce & Industry
500 First National Tower
One Townsite Plaza
Topeka, KS 66603
(913) 357-6321

STATE & CITY TOURISM OFFICES

State

Kansas Department of Economic Development
503 Kansas Avenue
Topeka, KS 66603
(913) 296-3841

Tourist Division
Kansas Department of Economic Development
122 South State Office Building
Topeka, KS 66612
(913) 296-3483

Local

Wichita Area Chamber of Commerce
350 W. Douglas
Wichita, KS 67202
(316) 265-7771

STATE HIGHWAY DEPARTMENT

Kansas Department of Transportation
State Office Building
Topeka, KS 66612
(913) 296-3461

KANSAS

HIGHWAY WELCOMING CENTERS

There are no Highway Welcoming Centers in Kansas.

STATE POLICE

Department of Public Safety
200 E. 6th Street
Topeka, KS 66603
(913) 296-3102

HUNTING & FISHING

Hunting

Unless otherwise exempt, all persons hunting or taking wildlife in Kansas are required to possess a valid hunting license. In addition, all persons born on or after July 1, 1957 are required to have passed an approved hunter safety course before taking to the field to hunt. (Approved hunter safety courses are now offered in nearly every state in the nation.)

Owners or tenants of land leased for agricultural purposes and their immediate families living with them may hunt on such land without a hunting license. Kansas residents who have not reached their 16th birthday or have passed their 65th birthday do not need a license to hunt. Also, certain Kansas resident American Indians are exempt from the license requirements.

All non-residents, regardless of age, are required to possess an appropriate license to hunt unless they are hunting on land owned or leased by them for agricultural purposes. Kansas residents may take coyotes without a license.

Resident

Hunting, $5.

Non-resident

Hunting, $25.

Fishing

Any person age 16 to 65 who has been a bona fide resident of the state for 60 days then last past (immediately prior to buying a license) must have a resident license in possession when fishing in Kansas, except for exemptions listed below. All non-residents of the state, except those under 16 years, must have a non-resident fishing license in possession while fishing in Kansas. Licenses expire December 31 each year, except the 10-day fishing licenses.

EXEMPTIONS: A landowner and his immediate family living with him, and tenants renting land for agricultural purposes, and members of their immediate family living with them, may fish by legal methods on such lands without licenses. Any Kansas resident who is enrolled as an American Indian on tribal membership roll maintained by the Bureau of Indian Affairs of the U.S. Department of the Interior, may fish without a license, providing all other laws and regulations are observed. A Kansas resident on active duty in the Armed Forces and who entered the service while a resident of this state is not required to have a fishing license, provided he can produce proof of residency and has leave or furlough papers on his person while fishing. A non-resident on active military duty and stationed in Kansas is entitled to a resident fishing license, which he must have on his person along with evidence of current active military duty.

Resident

Fishing license, $5; combination fishing & hunting license, $10.

Non-resident

Fishing license, $10; trip fishing, 10 days, $5.

For more information contact:

Kansas Fish and Game Commission
Box 54A, Route 2
Pratt, KS 67124
(316) 672-5411

CAMPGROUNDS

Private

Abilene

SAFARI INN
Abilene, KS 67410
(913) 598-2212
LOCATION: 6 mi. east of Abilene to Enterprise exit (I-70 exit 281).
FACILITIES: Open year round; 100 sites; water and bathroom facilities; sanitary station; electrical hookup; trailer village vehicle sites; laundry; food service; swimming pool; fishing; hiking.

VIOLA LAKE CAMPGROUND
Route 4
Abilene, KS 67410
(913) 263-1868
LOCATION: 2 mi. west of Abilene to Talmage exit (I-70 exit 272), 1½ mi. north.
FACILITIES: Open year round; 100 sites; water and bathroom facilities; sanitary station; electrical hookup; trailer village vehicle sites; food service; boating; boat rental; fishing; bicycle trail.

Dodge City

WATER SPORTS CAMPGROUND
Box 430
Dodge City, KS 67801
(316) 227-9325
LOCATION: 2 blocks south of River Bridge in Dodge City, then 4 blocks east on Cherry Street.
FACILITIES: Open year round; 60 sites; water and bathroom facilities; sanitary station; electrical hookup; laundry; food service;

CAMPGROUNDS (continued)

swimming; boating; boat rental; fishing; hiking.

Fort Scott

FORT SCOTT KOA
Route 6
Fort Scott, KS 66701
(316) 233-3440
LOCATION: North on Hwy. 69 to junction 69 & 54, then ½ mi. north on Hwy. 69.
FACILITIES: Open year round; 75 sites; water and bathroom facilities; sanitary station; electrical hookup; trailer village vehicle sites; laundry; food service; swimming pool.

Goodland

GOODLAND KOA
Hwy. 24
Goodland, KS 67735
(913) 899-2352
LOCATION: East Goodland junction I-70 & Hwy. 24.
FACILITIES: Open year round; 116 sites; water and bathroom facilities; sanitary station; electrical hookup; trailer village vehicle sites; laundry; food service; horseback riding; bicycle trail.

MID-AMERICA CAMP IN
Route 1
Goodland, KS 67735
(913) 899-5431
LOCATION: Junction Hwy. 27 & I-70 West Interchange at Goodland, south to Park.
FACILITIES: Open year round; 109 sites; water and bathroom facilities; sanitary station; electrical hookup; trailer village vehicle sites; laundry; swimming pool.

Kinsley

ROADRUNNER'S ROOST
Box 38
Kinsley, KS 67547
(316) 659-3548
LOCATION: 3 blocks west of Hwys. 50 & 183 junction at Kinsley.
FACILITIES: Open year round; 50 sites; water and bathroom facilities; sanitary station; laundry; food service; swimming; boating.

Lawrence

LAWRENCE KOA
Route 3
Lawrence, KS 66044
(913) 824-3877
LOCATION: Near Lawrence.
FACILITIES: Open year round; 85 sites; water and bathroom facilities; sanitary station; electrical hookup; trailer village vehicle sites.

Oakley

CAMP INNS TRAILER PARK
Oakley, KS 67748
(913) 672-3538
LOCATION: At junction of Hwy. 83 & I-70 at Oakley.
FACILITIES: Open Apr. 15 - Oct. 15; 100 sites; water and bathroom facilities; sanitary

station; electrical hookup; trailer village vehicle sites; laundry; food service; swimming pool.

Paxico

CLIFF 'N CREEK
Box 54
Paxico, KS 66526
(913) 636-8142
LOCATION: 1 mi. off I-70 at Paxico.
FACILITIES: Open Apr. - Nov.; 100 sites; water and bathroom facilities; sanitary station; electrical hookup; trailer village vehicle sites; boating; hiking.

Sabetha

SYCAMORE SPRINGS
Sabetha, KS 66534
(913) 284-2436
LOCATION: 6 mi. north of Sabetha on U.S. 75, 2 mi. east & 1½ mi. south.
FACILITIES: Open Apr. - Dec.; 150 sites; water and bathroom facilities; sanitary station; electrical hookup; trailer village vehicle sites; laundry; food service; fishing.

Salina

SALINA KOA
Box 903
Salina, KS 67401
(913) 827-3182
LOCATION: 1 block north of alternate Route 81 & I-70 (Exit 252), ½ mi. west on Diamond Drive.
FACILITIES: Open year round; 150 sites; water and bathroom facilities; sanitary station; electrical hookup; trailer village vehicle sites; laundry; food service; swimming pool; fishing; bicycle trail.

SUNDOWNER WEST
Route 2
Salina, KS 67401
(913) 823-8335
LOCATION: 7 mi. west of Salina on I-70 (exit 244), ½ mi. north.
FACILITIES: Open year round; 80 sites; water and bathroom facilities; sanitary station; electrical hookup; trailer village vehicle sites; laundry; food service; swimming pool; boating; boat rental; fishing; hiking; horseback riding; bicycle trail.

Topeka

CROCKER'S MOBILE HOME PARK
2834 Topeka Blvd.
Topeka, KS 66611
(913) 267-1000
LOCATION: U.S. 75 & 29th Street south.
FACILITIES: Open year round; 75 sites; water and bathroom facilities; sanitary station; electrical hookup; trailer village vehicle sites; food service.

WaKeeney

WAKEENEY KOA
Box 843
WaKeeney, KS 67672
(913) 743-5612
LOCATION: Exit 127, junction I-70 & U.S. 283.

KANSAS

CAMPGROUNDS (continued)

FACILITIES: Open year round; 74 sites; water and bathroom facilities; sanitary station; electrical hookup; trailer village vehicle sites; laundry; playground; food service.

Wellington

WHEATLAND KOA
Route 1
Wellington, KS 67152
(316) 326-7930
LOCATION: 1 mi. east of Wellington on U.S. 160.
FACILITIES: Open year round; 54 sites; water and bathroom facilities; sanitary station; electrical hookup; trailer village vehicle sites; laundry; food service.

RESORTS & BEACHES

Most of the state's resort activities center around the major lakes and reservoirs and include fishing, swimming, boating, water skiing and camping. (See Boating Areas).

BOATING AREAS

Atchison

ATCHISON COUNTY LAKE
LOCATION: Near Atchison:
FACILITIES: Launching.

STATE LAKE
LOCATION: Near Atchison.
FACILITIES: Launching.

WARNOCK LAKE
LOCATION: Near Atchison.
FACILITIES: Launching.

Augusta

SANTA FE LAKE
LOCATION: 3½ mi. west of Augusta on U.S. 54.
FACILITIES: Launching.

Burlington

JOHN REDMOND RESERVOIR
LOCATION: Near Burlington.
FACILITIES: Launching.

Council Grove

COUNCIL GROVE RESERVOIR
LOCATION: North of Council Grove.
FACILITIES: Launching.

El Dorado

MUNICIPAL TWIN LAKES
LOCATION: Northeast of El Dorado.
FACILITIES: Launching.

Horton

MISSION LAKE
LOCATION: Near Horton.

FACILITIES: Launching.

Junction City

MILFORD LAKE
LOCATION: Near Junction City.
FACILITIES: Launching.

Kingsdown

CLARK COUNTY LAKE
LOCATION: 11 mi. southwest of Kingsdown.
FACILITIES: Launching.

Kirwin

KIRWIN RESERVOIR
LOCATION: Near Kirwin.
FACILITIES: Launching.

Lawrence

PERRY RESERVOIR
LOCATION: Near Lawrence.
FACILITIES: Launching.

Manhattan

TUTTLE CREEK LAKE
LOCATION: 5 mi. north of Manhattan.
FACILITIES: Launching.

Mankato

LOVEWELL RESERVOIR
LOCATION: Near Mankato.
FACILITIES: Launching.

Marion

MARION RESERVOIR
LOCATION: Near Marion.
FACILITIES: Launching.

Winfield

WINFIELD CITY LAKE
LOCATION: Near Winfield.
FACILITIES: Launching.

BICYCLE TRAILS

No information was available on Bicycle Trails in Kansas.

TRAILS

Atchison

INTERNATIONAL FOREST OF FRIENDSHIP TRAIL - .56 mi. foot trail. The trail is located within the 40-acre International Forest of Friendship, adjacent to the Warnock Lake Recreation Center. The trail winds through the man-made forest which contains trees from all 50 states and 30 foreign countries.

SKI AREAS

There are no organized Ski Areas in Kansas.

AMUSEMENT PARKS & ATTRACTIONS

Dodge City

BOOT HILL MUSEUM
500 West Wyatt Earp
Dodge City, KS 67801
(316) 227-8188
FACILITIES: 2 historical museums; 2 refreshment stands; restaurants; exhibits; stagecoach ride; theater; stage shows; free gate (donation basis); free parking; open all year.

Seneca

FORT MARKLEY & INDIAN VILLAGE (Theme)
Seneca, KS 67401
(913) 336-2285
FACILITIES: Old Western town; cowboy jail; livery stable; log cabin; fire station; old fort; live buffalo; covered wagons; museum; general store; land office; souvenir shop; swimming pool; restaurant; picnic facilities; golf range; theatre; camping; fishing; boating; rifle range; name bands; free acts; pay gate; free parking.

Topeka

JOYLAND PARK
27th & California Avenue
Topeka, KS 67205
(913) 266-6400
FACILITIES: 10 major rides; 10 kiddie rides; 1 refreshment stand; game; arcade; shooting gallery; race track; miniature golf; free gate; free parking.

Wichita

HISTORIC WICHITA, COW TOWN
1717 Sim Park Drive
Wichita, KS 67203
(316) 264-8452
FACILITIES: 28 walk thrus; 3 refreshment stands; restaurants; exhibits; museum; crafts; theatre; vaudeville; melodramas; pay gate; free parking; open Mar. 1 - Nov. 30.

JOYLAND AMUSEMENT PARK
2801 So. Hillside
Wichita, KS 67216
(316) 684-0179
FACILITIES: 12 major rides; 9 kiddie rides; 7 games; 2 refreshment stands; arcade; shooting gallery; roller rink; miniature golf; picnic facilities; puppet theatre; go-karts; stage shows; fireworks; free parking; pay gate; open Mar. 15 - Oct. 15.

STATE FAIR

Kansas State Fair
State Fairgrounds
Hutchinson, KS 67501
(316) 662-6611
DATE: September

NATIONAL PARKS

There are no National Parks in Kansas.

NATIONAL FORESTS

There are no National Forests in Kansas.

STATE PARKS

State Park and Resources Authority
503 Kansas
P.O. Box 977
Topeka, KS 66601
(913) 296-2281

Beloit

GLEN ELDER STATE PARK
LOCATION: 10 mi. west of Beloit on U.S. 24.
FACILITIES: Open year round; sanitary station; boating; boat rental; fishing.

El Dorado

EL DORADO STATE PARK
LOCATION: 5 mi. east of El Dorado on Route 177.
FACILITIES: Under construction.

Ellsworth

KANOPOLIS STATE PARK
LOCATION: 21 mi. southeast of Ellsworth on Route 41.
FACILITIES: Open year round; 15 sites; sanitary station; electrical hookup; trailer village vehicle sites; picnic area; food service; boating; boat rental; fishing.

Fredonia

FALL RIVER STATE PARK
LOCATION: 17 mi. northwest of Fredonia on Route 96.
FACILITIES: Open year round; 30 sites; water and bathroom facilities; sanitary station; electrical hookup; trailer village vehicle sites; picnic area; boating; fishing.

Girard

CRAWFORD STATE PARK
LOCATION: North of Girard on Route 7.
FACILITIES: Open year round; 30 sites; water and bathroom facilities; sanitary station; electrical hookup; trailer village vehicle sites; picnic area; food service; boating; boat rental; fishing.

Hutchinson

SAND HILLS STATE PARK
LOCATION: 3 mi. northeast of Hutchinson.
FACILITIES: Open year round; hiking.

Independence

ELK CITY STATE PARK
LOCATION: 7 mi. northwest of Independence on U.S. 160.
FACILITIES: Open year round; 30 sites; water and bathroom facilities; sanitary station; electrical hookup; trailer village vehicle sites; picnic area; boating; fishing.

KANSAS

STATE PARKS (continued)

Junction City

MILFORD STATE PARK
LOCATION: 2 mi. northwest of Junction City on Route 57.
FACILITIES: Open year round; 60 sites; water and bathroom facilities; sanitary station; electrical hookup; trailer village vehicle sites; picnic area; food service; boating; boat rental; fishing.

Lawrence

CLINTON STATE PARK
LOCATION: 4 mi. west of Lawrence off U.S. 40.
FACILITIES: Open year round; 45 sites; water and bathroom facilities; sanitary station; electrical hookup; trailer village vehicle sites; picnic area; food service; boating; fishing.

Lyndon

MELVERN STATE PARK
LOCATION: 8 mi. southwest of Lyndon on K 278.
FACILITIES: Open year round; water and bathroom facilities; picnic area; boating; fishing.

Manhattan

TUTTLE CREEK STATE PARK
LOCATION: 5 mi. north of Manhattan on U.S. 24.
FACILITIES: Open year round; 102 sites; water and bathroom facilities; sanitary station; electrical hookup; trailer village vehicle sites; picnic area; food service; boating; boat rental; fishing.

Mankato

LOVEWELL STATE PARK
LOCATION: 15 mi. northeast of Mankato on K 14.
FACILITIES: Open year round; 30 sites; water and bathroom facilities; sanitary station; electrical hookup; trailer village vehicle sites; food service; boating; boat rental; fishing.

Meade

MEADE STATE PARK
LOCATION: 13 mi. southwest of Meade on Route 23.
FACILITIES: Open year round; 15 sites; water and bathroom facilities; sanitary station; electrical hookup; picnic area; fishing.

Norton

PRAIRIE DOG STATE PARK
LOCATION: 3 mi. west of Norton on U.S. 36.
FACILITIES: Open year round; water and bathroom facilities; picnic area; boating; fishing.

Ottawa

POMONA STATE PARK
LOCATION: 16 mi. west of Ottawa on Route 368.
FACILITIES: Open year round; 101 sites; water and bathroom facilities; sanitary station; electrical hookup; trailer village vehicle sites; picnic area; food service; boating; boat rental; fishing.

Scott City

SCOTT STATE PARK
LOCATION: 12 mi. north of Scott City on Route 95.
FACILITIES: Open year round; 30 sites; water and bathroom facilities; electrical hookup; trailer village vehicle sites; food service; boating; boat rental; fishing.

Stockton

WEBSTER STATE PARK
LOCATION: 8 mi. west of Stockton on U.S. 24.
FACILITIES: Open year round; 20 sites; water and bathroom facilities; sanitary station; electrical hookup; trailer village vehicle sites; picnic area; boating; fishing.

Topeka

PERRY STATE PARK
LOCATION: 16 mi. northeast of Topeka on Route 237.
FACILITIES: Open year round; 60 sites; water and bathroom facilities; sanitary station; electrical hookup; trailer village vehicle sites; picnic area; boating; fishing.

WaKeeney

CEDAR BLUFF STATE PARK
LOCATION: 23 mi southeast of WaKeeney on Route 47.
FACILITIES: Open year round; 45 sites; water and bathroom facilities; sanitary station; electrical hookup; trailer village vehicle sites; picnic area; food service; boating; fishing; self-guided trail.

Wichita

CHENEY STATE PARK
LOCATION: 20 mi. northwest of Wichita on Route 251.
FACILITIES: Open year round; 90 sites; water and bathroom facilities; sanitary station; electrical hookup; trailer village vehicle sites; picnic area; food service; boating; boat rental; fishing.

Wilson

WILSON STATE PARK
LOCATION: North of Wilson on Route 232.
FACILITIES: Open year round; 51 sites; sanitary station; electrical hookup; trailer village vehicle sites; picnic area; food service; boating; boat rental; fishing.

Yates Center

TORONTO STATE PARK
LOCATION: 17 mi southwest of Yates Center on Route 105.
FACILITIES: Open year round; 15 sites; wa-

KANSAS

STATE PARKS (continued)

ter and bathroom facilities; sanitary station; electrical hookup; trailer village vehicle sites; picnic area; food service; boating; boat rental; fishing.

STATE FORESTS

There are no State Forests in Kansas.

HISTORIC SITES

Argonia

SLATER HOME - World's first woman mayor, Susanna Medora Slater, was elected by the city of Argonia April 4, 1887. Home of Mrs. Slater and a museum open Jun. - Sept.

Caldwell

CALDWELL - Seven lodge Indian village dating back to the 1300s.

Hanover

THE HOLLENBERG STATION - Only original unaltered Pony Express Station left standing today. Located 2 mi. northeast of Hanover.

Kiowa

KIOWA - Carry Nation began crusade against demon rum by smashing her first saloon here in July, 1900.

Leavenworth

FORT LEAVENWORTH - Oldest army post in continuous use west of the Mississippi River. Fort is also site of the world-famous U.S. Command and General Staff College.

Rock City

ROCK CITY - National historic landmark, 200 or more unusually large, well-formed, sandstone masses of geological significance.

Wallace

MONUMENT ROCKS — Unique windcarved, water-eroded chalk formations designated first natural national landmark in Kansas. Chalk outcroppings, rising abruptly to heights of 60 feet from the valley of the Smokey Hill River, are sedimented remains of ancient marine life. Located near Wallace.

HOSTELS

Marion

STONE PRAIRIE LIFE CENTER
Route 1
Marion, KS 66861
(316) 382-2057
FACILITIES: Open Mar. - Nov.; 15 beds, men; 15 beds, women; modern bathroom; overnight charges: $3.50, May - Oct.; $2.50, Nov., Mar. & Apr.; houseparents: Wendell & Nancy Hendricks.

POINTS OF INTEREST

Abilene

EISENHOWER CENTER - Contains Eisenhower family home, Presidential Library building with exhibit areas, and "A Place of Meditation," the final resting place of Dwight D. Eisenhower, 34th President.

Bonner Springs

AGRICULTURAL HALL OF FAME AND NATIONAL CENTER - Living monument to agriculture, once this nation's largest industry. Three buildings with exhibits on "the evolution of agriculture."

Independence

"LITTLE HOUSE ON THE PRAIRIE" - Childhood home of Laura Ingalls Wilder, author of numerous stories on growing up in the West. Located 10 mi. southwest of Independence.

Meade

DALTON GANG HIDEOUT - Visitors go through secret escape tunnel from the house to the barn which contains a western museum with one of the nation's finest gun collections. Located on Main Street.

Salina

PREHISTORIC BURIAL PIT - Contains more than 140 skeletal remains of Indians six feet tall and taller. Located 4 mi. east of Salina off I-70.

Sedan

KELLY MUSEUM - Emmett Kelly Museum commemorates world-famous circus clown's birthplace. Located in Sedan.

KENTUCKY

Kentucky, where opposing ideas flourished and often clashed, joined the Union in 1792 as the fifteenth state. Daniel Boone's early attempt to settle the territory was thwarted by the resident Indians, but two years later he returned to establish Boonesboro.

Thirty-four years following Boone's town-building episode, Jefferson Davis, the man who became the President of the Confederacy, was born in Kentucky. Abraham Lincoln,

233

KENTUCKY

INTRODUCTION (continued)

also a Kentuckian, was born in 1809, the very next year.

Perhaps the most famous Kentucky confrontation was between the Hatfields and McCoys, a family feud that lasted 14 years with no decisive winner.

Tourism is now beginning to develop in Kentucky, aided by a growing national interest in thoroughbred racing and the Kentucky Derby, the building of better roadways and the enhancing of state resort parks. However, the state's big moneymakers are still tobacco farming, coal mining and manufacturing.

State capital: Frankfort. State bird: Cardinal. State tree: Tulip poplar. State flower: Goldenrod.

WEATHER

Kentucky has a land surface of 40,109 square miles. It is essentially an eroded plateau that slopes downward gradually to the southwest, with elevations ranging from about 400 feet above sea level at the western edge to 1,000 feet in the central districts to above 4,000 feet near the southeastern border.

The climate of Kentucky is essentially continental in character, with rather wide extremes of temperature and precipitation. The state lies within the path of storms and in the belt of westerly winds. The temperature generally varies as the storms move across the state. Thus in winter and summer there are occasional cold and hot spells of short duration. In the spring and fall, the storm systems have a lower frequency, temperatures are more consistent, and fewer extremes are experienced.

Average daily temperature for the month.

	Eastern	Western
Jan.	45.1 to 23.6	45.1 to 25.5
Feb.	48.5 to 25.2	49.4 to 28.1
Mar.	57.4 to 33.0	58.1 to 35.8
Apr.	69.8 to 42.3	70.8 to 46.9
May	77.9 to 50.4	78.8 to 54.6
Jun.	84.7 to 58.4	86.2 to 62.6
Jul.	87.3 to 62.6	89.3 to 66.2
Aug.	86.4 to 61.1	88.6 to 64.1
Sept.	81.4 to 54.5	83.0 to 57.4
Oct.	71.2 to 42.5	72.6 to 45.8
Nov.	57.6 to 33.0	58.4 to 36.0
Dec.	48.0 to 27.0	48.2 to 29.2
Year	67.9 to 42.8	69.0 to 46.0

STATE CHAMBER OF COMMERCE

Kentucky Chamber of Commerce
Versailles Road
P.O. Box 817
Frankfort, KY 40601
(502) 223-8261

STATE & CITY TOURISM OFFICES

State

Division of Advertising and Travel Promotion

Capitol Annex
Frankfort, KY 40601
(502) 564-4930

Kentucky Department of Commerce
Capital Plaza Towers
Frankfort, KY 40601
(502) 564-4270

Local

Louisville Visitors Bureau
300 West Liberty
Louisville, KY 40202
(502) 582-2421

STATE HIGHWAY DEPARTMENT

Department of Transportation
State Office Building
High and Clinton Streets
Frankfort, KY 40601
(502) 564-4890

HIGHWAY WELCOMING CENTERS

Beaver Dam

BEAVER DAM CENTER - West Kentucky Parkway.

Florence

FLORENCE CENTER - Interstate 75.

Franklin

FRANKLIN CENTER - Interstate 65.

Fulton

FULTON CENTER - Interstate 24, Purchase Parkway.

Georgetown

GEORGETOWN CENTER - Interstate 75.

Pineville

PINEVILLE CENTER - U.S. 25, east. West of junction with U.S. 119.

Richmond

RICHMOND CENTER - Interstate 75, south.

WELCOMING CENTERS (continued)

Shepherdsville

SHEPHERDSVILLE CENTER - Interstate 65.

STATE POLICE

Department of Public Safety
Frankfort, KY 40601
(502) 227-2221

HUNTING & FISHING
Hunting

All hunters must have in possession a valid Kentucky hunting license and, if hunting deer, a deer permit, except:

A resident owner of farmlands, his wife or dependent children hunting upon farmland of which they are bona fide owners. Also tenants or their dependent children, residing upon said farmlands.

Residents 65 years of age or older who instead must carry an affidavit stating the year of birth and place of residence.

Resident servicemen on furlough of more than 3 days may hunt in the county of legal residence at the time of entrance into the service but must carry proper identification and papers showing furlough status.

All above exempted persons shall notify the Department of Fish and Wildlife in writing as to deer killed and those exempted must have written permission from a conservation officer or deer check station before removing a deer from their land.

Deer hunting permit required for both residents and non-residents in addition to an annual hunting license.

Resident

Statewide hunting (annual), $5; juvenile hunting (under 16 years), $3.50; combined hunting & fishing, $9; trapping, $5; furbuyers, $7.50; deer permits, $10.50.

Non-resident

Statewide hunting (annual), $27.50; statewide hunting (small game only) 3-days, $10; juvenile hunting (under 16 years), $27.50; trapping, $27.50; furbuyers, $100; deer permits, $10.50.

Fishing

All persons are required to procure the proper license to fish ponds, lakes and streams except:

No license required of persons under 16 years of age.

Residents 65 years of age or older may fish without license by carrying on person affidavit of year of birth and place of residence.

The resident owner of farmlands, his wife, or dependent children, or tenants and their dependent children, residing upon said farmland shall, without procuring a license have the right to take fish or hunt during the open season (except trapping) on said farmlands of which they are bona fide owners, or wife or dependent children of such owners, or tenants or dependent children of such tenants.

Resident

Statewide fishing, $5; combined hunting and fishing, $9; trout stamp, $2.25.

Non-resident

Statewide fishing, $10; 15-day fishing, $4; 3-day fishing, $2.50; trout stamp, $2.25; Ohio River fishing license for residents of Ohio, Indiana, Illinois, $5.

For more information contact:

Department of Fish & Wildlife Resources
Capital Plaza
Frankfort, KY 40601
(502) 564-4336

CAMPGROUNDS
Private

Benton

MOORS RESORT
(502) 362-4356
LOCATION: Off U.S. 68 on Route 963.
FACILITIES: Open Mar. 15 - Nov. 1; 150 sites; water and bathroom facilities; sanitary station; electrical hookup; trailer village vehicle sites; food service; swimming; boating; boat rental; fishing; tent camping.

WILL VERA VILLAGE
(502) 354-6422
LOCATION: U.S. 68E at Fairdealing, turn north on Route 962 and go 3 mi.
FACILITIES: Open Mar. 15 - Nov. 1; 200 sites; water and bathroom facilities; sanitary station; electrical hookup; trailer village vehicle sites; food service; swimming; boating; boat rental; tent camping.

Burkesville

DALE HOLLOW KOA CAMPGROUND
(502) 433-7200
LOCATION: 6½ mi. south of Burkesville on Route 61, then 2½ mi. south on Route 485.
FACILITIES: Open Apr. 1 - Oct. 1; 100 sites; sanitary station; electrical hookup; trailer village vehicle sites; laundry; food service; swimming; boating; boat rental; fishing; tent camping.

Campbellsville

GREEN RIVER LAKE KOA CAMPGROUND
(502) 465-3916
LOCATION: 7 mi. south of Campbellsville on Route 55.
FACILITIES: Open Mar. 1 - Nov. 30; 100 sites; water and bathroom facilities; sanitary

KENTUCKY

CAMPGROUNDS (continued)

station; electrical hookup; trailer village vehicle sites; laundry; food service; swimming; tent camping.

HOLMES BEND CAMPGROUND
(502) 384-4623
LOCATION: 12 mi. south of Campbellsville on Route 55, then 6 mi. north on Holmes Bend Road.
FACILITIES: Open year round; 125 sites; water and bathroom facilities; sanitary station; electrical hookup; trailer village vehicle sites; swimming; boating; boat rental; fishing; tent camping.

Cave City

YOGI BEAR'S JELLYSTONE PARK CAMP-RESORT
(502) 773-3840
LOCATION: ½ mi. west of I-65 Cave City Exit (No. 53), on Route 70.
FACILITIES: Open year round; 148 sites; water and bathroom facilities; sanitary station; electrical hookup; trailer village vehicle sites; laundry; food service; swimming; fishing; tent camping.

Crittenden

KOA RESORT CAMPGROUND
(606) 428-2000
LOCATION: From I-75 Crittenden exit (No. 166) go south 2 mi. on U.S. 25.
FACILITIES: Open year round; 100 sites; water and bathroom facilities; sanitary station; electrical hookup; trailer village vehicle sites; laundry; food service; swimming; fishing; tent camping.

Danville

PIONEER PLAYHOUSE CAMPGROUND
(606) 236-2747
LOCATION: Take Old U.S. 150 south at city limits.
FACILITIES: Open Apr. - Oct.; 100 sites; water and bathroom facilities; sanitary station; electrical hookup; trailer village vehicle sites; food service; swimming; recreation vehicles only.

Eddyville

DAYTONA SHORES CAMPGROUND
(502) 388-7709
LOCATION: 5 mi. south of Eddyville on KY 293E.
FACILITIES: Open Apr. 10 - Nov. 1; 200 sites; water and bathroom facilities; sanitary station; electrical hookup; trailer village vehicle sites; laundry; swimming; boating; recreation vehicles only.

HOLIDAY HILLS CAMPING RESORT
(502) 388-2419
LOCATION: 5 mi. south of Eddyville on KY 93.
FACILITIES: Open Mar. 21 - Nov. 1; 116 sites; water and bathroom facilities; sanitary station; electrical hookup; trailer village vehicle sites; laundry; swimming; boating; boat rental; tent camping.

Frankfort

ELKHORN CAMPGROUND
(502) 695-9117
LOCATION: 2 mi. east of Frankfort on U.S. 460.
FACILITIES: Open Mar. 1 - Nov. 1; 120 sites; water and bathroom facilities; sanitary station; electrical hookup; trailer village vehicle sites; food service; swimming; fishing; tent camping.

Grand River

HILLMAN FERRY CAMPGROUND
(502) 924-5602
LOCATION: 3 mi. south of Barkley Canal on the Kentucky Lake shoreline in the northern portion of Land Between the Lakes.
FACILITIES: Open year round; 800 sites; water and bathroom facilities; sanitary station; electrical hookup; trailer village vehicle sites; swimming; boating; fishing; tent camping.

Horse Cave

HORSE CAVE KOA KAMPGROUND
(502) 786-2819
LOCATION: I-65 and Route 218 Interchange, Horse Cave Interchange (Exit 58).
FACILITIES: Open year round; 110 sites; water and bathroom facilities; sanitary station; electrical hookup; trailer village vehicle sites; laundry; food service; swimming; fishing; horseback riding; tent camping.

Jamestown

FOLEY'S CAMPER COURT
(502) 343-4616
LOCATION: 9 mi. south of Jamestown on U.S. 127, on Lake Cumberland.
FACILITIES: Open year round; 100 sites; water and bathroom facilities; electrical hookup; trailer village vehicle sites; food service; tent camping.

Monticello

CONLEY BOTTOM CAMPGROUND
(606) 348-6351
LOCATION: 9 mi. north of Monticello on KY 1275.
FACILITIES: Open Mar. 1 - Nov. 1; 125 sites; water and bathroom facilities; sanitary station; electrical hookup; trailer village vehicle sites; food service; swimming; boating; boat rental; tent camping.

Muldraugh

ROBIN WOODS CAMPGROUND
(502) 583-3577
LOCATION: 2½ mi. west of Muldraugh on Route 1638.
FACILITIES: Open Mar. 15 - Oct. 15; 151 sites; water and bathroom facilities; sanitary station; electrical hookup; trailer village vehicle sites; laundry; food service; swimming; boating; horseback riding; tent camping.

CAMPGROUNDS (continued)

Park City

CEDAR HILL CAMPGROUND
(502) 749-8941
LOCATION: 2½ mi. west of Park City.
FACILITIES: Open Apr. 1 - Oct. 31; 100 sites; water and bathroom facilities; sanitary station; electrical hookup; trailer village vehicle sites; laundry; food service; swimming; fishing; tent camping.

DIAMOND CAVERNS KOA CAMPGROUND
(502) 749-4400
LOCATION: From Park City exit from I-65, go 1½ mi. north on Route 255.
FACILITIES: Open year round; 200 sites; water and bathroom facilities; sanitary station; electrical hookup; trailer village vehicle sites; laundry; food service; swimming; fishing; tent camping.

Russell Springs

INDIAN HILLS KOA CAMPGROUND
(502) 866-5616
LOCATION: 3 mi. east of Russell Springs on Route 80, then 8 mi. southeast on Routes 910, 76 & 1383.
FACILITIES: Open Apr. 1 - Oct. 31; 179 sites; water and bathroom facilities; sanitary station; electrical hookup; laundry; food service; swimming; boating; boat rental; fishing; horseback riding; tent camping.

Scottsville

WALNUT CREEK CAMPGROUND
(502) 622-5858
LOCATION: 8 mi. north of Scottsville on U.S. 31E, then 2 mi. east on Route 1855.
FACILITIES: Open year round; 150 sites; water and bathroom facilities; electrical hookup; trailer village vehicle sites; boating; boat rental; tent camping.

Public

Bowling Green

BEECH BEND PARK CAMPGROUND
(502) 842-8101
LOCATION: Take exit I-65 to U.S. 31W bypass, turn right 3 mi. to park.
FACILITIES: Open May 15 - Labor Day; 6500 sites; water and bathroom facilities; sanitary station; electrical hookup; laundry; food service; swimming; fishing; horseback riding; tent camping.

Burlington

RIVER EDGE PARK CAMPGROUND
(606) 586-7282
LOCATION: I-75 south to Route 18 to Burlington, continue on Route 18 to large sign on barn, turn on River Road.
FACILITIES: Open Apr. 1 - Oct. 31; 102 sites; water and bathroom facilities; sanitary station; electrical hookup; trailer village vehicle sites; food service; swimming; boating; fishing; recreation vehicles only.

Grand Rivers

CAMP ENERGY CAMPGROUND
(502) 924-5602
LOCATION: Energy Lake in the northern portion of the project, east of The Trace.
FACILITIES: Open year round; 200 sites; water and bathroom facilities; sanitary station; electrical hookup; trailer village vehicle sites; swimming; boating; fishing; tent camping.

Hardinsburg

AXTEL CAMPGROUND
(502) 257-2061
LOCATION: Near junction of Route 79 & Route 259.
FACILITIES: Open year round; 160 sites; water and bathroom facilities; sanitary station; laundry; food service; swimming; boating; boat rental; fishing; tent camping.

NORTH FORK CAMPGROUND
(502) 257-2061
LOCATION: Near Junction of Route 79 & Route 259 on Rough River Lake.
FACILITIES: Open year round; 107 sites; water and bathroom facilities; sanitary station; trailer village vehicle sites; laundry; food service; swimming; boating; tent camping.

Leitchfield

CAVE CREEK CAMPGROUND
(502) 257-2061
LOCATION: South of Route 79, 5 mi. from Rough River Dam.
FACILITIES: Open year round; 150 sites; water and bathroom facilities; trailer village vehicle sites; swimming; boating; fishing; tent camping.

MOUTARDIER CAMPGROUND
(502) 286-4813
LOCATION: 10 mi. south on Route 259, then turn left.
FACILITIES: Open year round; 167 sites; water and bathroom facilities; sanitary station; trailer village vehicle sites; laundry; food service; swimming; boating; boat rental; fishing; tent camping.

Owensboro

WINDY HOLLOW RECREATION AREA
(502) 785-4150
LOCATION: 10 mi. southwest of Owensboro, 2 mi. off Route 81.
FACILITIES: Open Apr. - Oct.; 140 sites; water and bathroom facilities; sanitary station; electrical hookup; trailer village vehicle sites; food service; swimming; fishing; tent camping.

RESORTS & BEACHES

See State Parks.

BOATING AREAS

See State Parks.

KENTUCKY

BICYCLE TRAILS

LEXINGTON TRAIL - 104 mi.; some hills; 10-speed bicycle recommended.

This six-county tour is in the heart of the Blue Grass Country.

Trail: Keene to Troy-Keene Road, north, right on Clays Mill Road, left on Ash Grove Park, left on Tates Creek Road, right on Bryan Avenue to Muir, right on Muir Pike, left on Todd Road, left on Van Meter Road, left on Hutchinson Road, left on Harp Innis Road, left on Russell Cave Park, right on Ironworks Pike, left on Yarnallton Road, left on Shannons Run Road to Pinckard to Keene.

RED RIVER TRAIL - 170 mi.; steep hills, narrow roads; 10-speed bicycle necessary.

This hilly tour of the scenic Red River Gorge features forest, sheer bluffs, and natural bridges.

The Nada Tunnel is dangerous. It is a one-lane, dark, wet tunnel and the safest way to get through is to wait for a line of cars going your way. If tunnel riding is not your thing, plan on having a wagon take you through. After the tunnel, the descent into the Red River Gorge is very steep on a curving, narrow road which, as an added inducement for caution, sometimes has loose gravel on its surface.

Trail: Lexington to Winchester to Goffs Corner to Powell Valley to Nada to Route 77 to Route 715 to Pine Ridge to Slade to Nada to Lexington.

See ILLINOIS - Shawnee Forest Trail.

TRAILS

Golden Pond

LONG CREEK TRAIL - .25 mi. foot trail. The ¼-mile demonstration trail, within the Land Between the Lakes Conservation Education Center (a large woodland area near Lake Barkley), is designed to enable physically handicapped people to become acquainted with the outdoors. The wide flat trail along a creek is paved and can easily be used by the blind with the aid of a companion, or by people on crutches or in wheelchairs. There are nine interpretive stations and a shelter for quiet appreciation of the songbirds and wildlife in the area.

Land Between the Lakes

HILLMAN HERITAGE TRAIL - 10 mi. foot trail. The trail system which starts from Hillman Ferry Campground consists of two loops and ten connector trails which wind along ridgetops and bottomlands treating the hiker to a variety of forest habitats, scenic vistas and historical sites. The longest loop of the trail system is five miles and approximately half of the system follows abandoned roads which show little evidence of the former use. Trail width varies from three to ten feet and the loops and connectors are well marked with trail blazing symbols.

SKI AREAS

There are no organized Ski Areas in Kentucky.

AMUSEMENT PARKS & ATTRACTIONS

Bowling Green

BEECH BEND PARK
Rt. 16
Bowling Green, KY 42101
(502) 842-8101
FACILITIES: 25 major rides; 7 kiddie rides; walk thrus; 24 games; fun house; 22 refreshment stands; 2 restaurants; cafeteria; arcade; shooting gallery; pool; roller rink; zoo; race track; miniature golf; go karts; trampolines; picnic facilities; crafts; camping; fishing; stock car and drag races; horseback riding; orchestras; name bands; free acts; fireworks; pay gate; free parking; open Easter - mid Oct.

Paducah

NOBLE PARK FUNLAND, INC.
2600 North 10th Street
Paducah, KY 42001
(502) 442-3713
FACILITIES: 11 major rides; 7 kiddie rides; fun house; games; 2 refreshment stands; swimming pool; pool-a-round; picnic facilities; free acts; fireworks; free gate; free parking.

Slade

NATURAL BRIDGE SKY LIFT (Attraction)
341 S. Lake Drive
Slade, KY 40376
(606) 886-2364
FACILITIES: Aerial ride; picnic facilities; restaurant; snack bars; souvenirs & novelties.

STATE FAIR

Kentucky State Fair
P.O. Box 21179
Louisville, KY 40221
(502) 366-9592
DATE: September

NATIONAL PARKS

Mammoth Cave

MAMMOTH CAVE NATIONAL PARK
Mammoth Cave, KY 42259
(502) 758-2328

HEADQUARTERS
FACILITIES: Open year round; limit of stay: 14 days; 145 sites; group camping; NPS campsite fee: $3; water and bathroom facilities; sanitary station; cabins; laundry; picnic area; food service; boating; fishing; hiking; horseback riding; handicapped access/restroom; ferry available; lodging.

NATIONAL PARKS (continued)

HOUCHIN'S FERRY
LOCATION: 2 mi. northeast of Brownsville.
FACILITIES: Open year round; limit of stay:
14 days; 12 sites; water and bathroom facilities; boating; fishing; no drinking water Nov. - Mar.

NATIONAL FORESTS

National Forests
Southern Region
1720 Peachtree Road, NW
Atlanta, GA 30309
(404) 881-4177

Winchester

DANIEL BOONE NATIONAL FOREST
ATTRACTIONS: Sandstone cliffs 100 feet high; natural arches; numerous limestone caves and mineral springs; bass and pike fishing; squirrel, deer, cottontails, upland game bird hunting.
FACILITIES: 27 camp and picnic sites, 30 picnic only; swimming; also hotels and cabins; motels; cottages.
NEARBY TOWNS: Boonesboro, Corbin, Lexington.

See SHAWNEE NATIONAL FOREST - Missouri.

See JEFFERSON NATIONAL FOREST - Virginia.

STATE PARKS

Headquarters

Department of Parks
Capital Plaza Office Tower
Frankfort, KY 40601
(502) 564-5410

Bardstown

MY OLD KENTUCKY HOME STATE PARK
(502) 348-3502
LOCATION: On Route 49, 2 mi. east of U.S. 150,
FACILITIES: Open Apr. 1 - Oct. 31; 40 sites; water and bathroom facilities; sanitary station; electrical hookup; trailer village vehicle sites; laundry; food service; tent camping.

Boonesboro

FORT BOONESBOROUGH STATE PARK
(606) 527-3328
LOCATION: Route 627 exit from I-75, then 5 mi. to park.
FACILITIES: Open year round; 187 sites; water and bathroom facilities; sanitary station; electrical hookup; trailer village vehicle sites; laundry; swimming; tent camping.

Burkesville

DALE HOLLOW LAKE STATE PARK
(502) 433-7431

LOCATION: 5 mi. east of Burkesville, 9 mi west from U.S. 127 to Route 449, 5 mi. south to Route 206, then 3 mi.
FACILITIES: Open Apr. 1 - Oct. 31; 144 sites; water and bathroom facilities; sanitary station; electrical hookup; trailer village vehicle sites; swimming; boating; boat rental; fishing; tent camping.

Burnside

GENERAL BURNSIDE STATE PARK
(606) 561-4104
LOCATION: 1 mi. south of Burnside on U.S. 27 on Lake Cumberland.
FACILITIES: Open Apr. 1 - Oct. 31; 129 sites; water and bathroom facilities; sanitary station; electrical hookup; trailer village vehicle sites; tent camping.

Campbellsville

GREEN RIVER LAKE STATE PARK
(502) 465-8255
LOCATION: 7 mi. south of Campbellsville on Route 65.
FACILITIES: Open Apr. 1 - Oct. 31; 90 sites; water and bathroom facilities; sanitary station; electrical hookup; trailer village vehicle sites; laundry; swimming; fishing; tent camping.

Columbus

COLUMBUS - BELMONT BATTLEFIELD STATE PARK
(502) 677-2327
LOCATION: Near Columbus.
FACILITIES: Open Apr. 1 - Oct. 31; 38 sites; water and bathroom facilities; sanitary station; electrical hookup; trailer village vehicle sites; food service; tent camping.

Dunmor

LAKE MALONE STATE PARK
(502) 657-2111
LOCATION: 2 mi. west of Dunmor on Route 973.
FACILITIES: Open Apr. 1 - Oct. 31; 20 sites; water and bathroom facilities; sanitary station; electrical hookup; trailer village vehicle sites; laundry; food service; swimming; boating; boat rental; fishing; tent camping.

Elkhorn City

BREAKS INTERSTATE PARK
(703) 865-4413
LOCATION: 7 mi. east of Elkhorn City on Route 80.
FACILITIES: Open Apr. 1 - Oct. 31; 122 sites; water and bathroom facilities; sanitary station; electrical hookup; trailer village vehicle sites; laundry; swimming; horseback riding; tent camping.

Falmouth

KINCAID LAKE STATE PARK
(606) 654-3531
LOCATION: 4 mi. north of Falmouth on Route 159.
FACILITIES: Open Apr. 1 - Oct. 31; 84 sites; water and bathroom facilities; sanitary sta-

KENTUCKY

STATE PARKS (continued)

tion; electrical hookup; trailer village vehicle sites; laundry; food service; swimming; boating; boat rental; tent camping.

Grayson

GRAYSON LAKE STATE PARK
(606) 474-9727
LOCATION: 10 mi. south of Grayson on Route 7.
FACILITIES: Open Apr. 1 - Oct. 31; 71 sites; water and bathroom facilities; electrical hookup; trailer village vehicle sites; laundry; swimming; boating; tent camping.

Henderson

JOHN JAMES AUDUBON STATE PARK
(502) 826-2247
LOCATION: 3 mi. north of Henderson on U.S. 41.
FACILITIES: Open year round; 64 sites; water and bathroom facilities; sanitary station; electrical hookup; trailer village vehicle sites; food service; swimming; tent camping.

Lexington

KENTUCKY STATE HORSE PARK
(606) 233-4304
LOCATION: I-75 Interchange, Iron Works Pike, then 1 mi. east.
FACILITIES: Open year round; 263 sites; water and bathroom facilities; sanitary station; electrical hookup; trailer village vehicle sites; laundry; food service; swimming; horseback riding; tent camping.

London

LEVI JACKSON WILDERNESS ROAD STATE PARK
(606) 864-5108
LOCATION: 3 mi. south of London on U.S. 25.
FACILITIES: Open year round; 200 sites; water and bathroom facilities; sanitary station; electrical hookup; trailer village vehicle sites; laundry; food service; swimming; horseback riding; tent camping.

Walton

BIG BONE LICK STATE PARK
(606) 384-3522
LOCATION: 4½ mi. west of Walton on Route 1292 to Route 338, then 3 mi.
FACILITIES: Open Apr. 1 - Oct. 31; 62 sites; water and bathroom facilities; sanitary station; electrical hookup; trailer village vehicle sites; laundry; food service; swimming; fishing; tent camping.

STATE FORESTS

Department of Natural Resources and Evironmental Protection
Division of Forestry
618 Teton Trail
Frankfort, KY 40601
(502) 564-4496

Bardstown

KNOB STATE FOREST
LOCATION: 5 mi. west of Bardstown.
FACILITIES: Open year round; trailer village vehicle sites; picnic area; hunting; fishing; hiking; tent camping.

Harlan

KENTENIA STATE FOREST
LOCATION: U.S. 421 to Little Shepherd Trail.
FACILITIES: Open year round; trailer village vehicle sites; picnic area; hunting; fishing; hiking; tent camping.

Middlesboro

KENTUCKY RIDGE STATE FOREST
LOCATION: 6 mi. northwest of Middlesboro.
FACILITIES: Open year round; trailer village vehicle sites; picnic area; hunting; fishing; hiking; tent camping.

Owingsville

OLYMPIC STATE FOREST
LOCATION: On I-64.
FACILITIES: Open year round; trailer village vehicle sites; picnic area; hunting; fishing; hiking; tent camping.

HISTORIC SITES

Bardstown

OLD TALBOTT TAVERN - Oldest American hotel west of Alleghenies in continuous operation. Located at 107 W. Stephen Foster Avenue.

Ft. Knox

THE PATTON MUSEUM OF CAVALRY AND ARMOR - Cavalry, armor displays, Revolutionary War to Vietnam. Personal effects of WW II General George S. Patton, Jr., plus much armor captured by his troops; tanks on grounds. Located off U.S. 31W near Chaffee Avenue.

Frankfort

DANIEL BOONE MONUMENT - Graves of Daniel Boone and wife Rebecca. Located at Frankfort Cemetery, E. Main Street.

Hodgenville

ABRAHAM LINCOLN BIRTHPLACE - Granite memorial shrine encloses log cabin birthplace of Abraham Lincoln, 16th President. Fifty-six steps lead to shrine, one for each of Lincoln's life. Located 3 mi. south of Hodgenville.

Lexington

ASHLAND - Estate of Kentucky statesman Henry Clay, U.S. Senator and Secretary of State. Located on Richmond Road.

HOSTELS

Pippa Passes

OLD KNOTT COUNTY HIGH SCHOOL
Box 15
Pippa Passes, KY 41844
(606) 368-2756 or 2753
FACILITIES: Open year round; 30 beds for men and women; modern bathroom; overnight charges: $2.50 summer; $3 winter; houseparents: Ed & Charlotte Madden.

POINTS OF INTEREST

Bardstown

BERNHEIM FOREST - A 10,000-acre gem of natural scenery and landscaping with four lakes, arboretums and nature trails. Located on Route 245.

MY OLD KENTUCKY HOME - Stately Georgian colonial mansion, home of Judge John Rowan visited by Pittsburgh cousin Stephen Foster in 1852. Soon after, Foster wrote the famous song, now the name of the Foster mansion and official Kentucky state song. Located 1 mi. east of U.S. 150, in state park.

Corbin

CUMBERLAND FALLS - Called "Niagara of the South," the 150 ft. wide falls drop 68 feet, largest east of the Rockies and south of Niagara. By night at full moon, the falls show only known "moonbow" on earth. Located within state park.

Covington

CATHEDRAL BASILICA OF THE ASSUMPTION - Largest stained glass window in the country. Located at Madison and 12th Street.

Ft. Knox

U.S. GOLD DEPOSITORY - Two-story granite, steel and concrete, bullion depository containing great part of U.S. gold reserve. Gold is in standard mint bars of almost pure gold or melted coin gold and worth approximately $20 billion. Located on Gold Vault Road.

Ft. Mitchell

MONTE CASSINO CHAPEL (Thomas More College) - Smallest chapel in the world. Built in 1879 by Benedictine monk. Interior about 6 feet by 9 feet. Located on the main campus.

Lexington

BURLEY TOBACCO MARKET - Largest Burley tobacco market in the world. Located off I-64, I-75, Blue Grass Parkway.

HORSE FARMS IN THE BLUEGRASS - Several hundred private horse farms are concentrated within a 35-mi. radius of Lexington. Farms range in size from a few acres to about 6,000 acres. Some of the world's foremost thoroughbred, standardbred and saddlebred horses are bred and trained in this area. Good views of the farms can be seen from Iron Works Pike, Paris Pike, Newton Pike and U.S. 60, 72, 68. There are miles of traditional fences (now mostly black or brown instead of white), lush bluegrass and glimpses of stately mansions.

Louisville

BELLE OF LOUISVILLE - Last authentic excursion sternwheeler in America. Located on 4th Street and River Road.

CHURCHILL DOWNS - America's most historic and famous thoroughbred racing track. Built in 1874, first Kentucky Derby held May 1875. Track is a one-mile oval. Also see Kentucky Derby Museum, fascinating records of all Derby winners, with flags modeled after winning silks. Located at 700 Central Avenue at South Fourth Street.

J.B. SPEED ART MUSEUM - Oldest and largest art museum. Outstanding medieval, Renaissance collections. Located at 2035 S. 3rd Street.

OLD FITZGERALD DISTILLERY - Since 1849, famous for production of Old Fitzgerald Kentucky, straight bourbon whiskey, 86 and 100 proof, one of bourbon connoisseurs' top choices the world over. Located on Fitzgerald Road.

Park City

JESSE JAMES CAVE - Legendary hideout of famous outlaw. Located at Park Mammoth Resort, 1 mi. west of U.S. 31W.

Somerset

SHORT CREEK - World's shortest creek, flows only 200 ft. between cliffs and powers grist mill. Located 12 mi. east on Route 80.

LOUISIANA

Acquired as part of the Louisiana Purchase from Napoleon Bonaparte in 1803, Louisiana entered the Union in 1812 as the eighteenth state. The French influence in the state has been a very strong factor beginning with La Salle's laying claim to the territory in the late 1600s. Nearly 100 years later, Acadians, French Canadians known locally as Cajuns,

LOUISIANA

INTRODUCTION (continued)

immigrated in great numbers to Baton Rouge, New Orleans and other cities in the southern portion of the state.

The French Quarter in New Orleans, one of the state's most famous and historic sections, now attracts thousands of tourists each year, especially during the pre-Lenten festivities of the Mardi Gras.

Louisiana is rich in oil and natural gas deposits, two vital commodities in this era of shortened energy supplies.

Agriculture plays a major role in the state's economy, too, with rice and sugar cane production among the highest in the country.

State capital: Baton Rouge. State bird: Brown pelican. State tree: Bald cypress. State flower: Magnolia.

WEATHER

The topography of Louisiana is characterized by low rolling hills in the north and coastal marshes and bayous in the south. In the east many bluffs dot the river plains. The Mississippi Delta, a fertile sedimentary deposit, comprises a third of the state's total area.

The principal influences that determine the climate of Louisiana are its subtropical latitude and its proximity to the Gulf of Mexico. The marine tropical influence is evident from the fact that the average water temperatures of the Gulf along the Louisiana shore range from 64 degrees F in February to 84 degrees in August.

In summer the prevailing southerly winds provide moist, semitropical weather, often favorable for afternoon thunderstorms. When westerly to northerly winds occur, periods of hotter and drier weather interrupt the prevailing moist condition. In the colder season the state is subjected alternately to tropical air and cold continental air, in periods of varying length. Although warmed by its southward journey, the cold air occasionally brings large and rather sudden drops in temperature, but conditions are usually not severe.

Average daily temperature for each month.

	Northern	Southern
Jan.	57.1 to 35.0	64.3 to 43.6
Feb.	61.1 to 37.4	66.6 to 45.5
Mar.	67.9 to 43.5	72.2 to 51.4
Apr.	77.2 to 53.4	80.0 to 59.5
May	84.0 to 60.5	85.7 to 65.3
Jun.	90.6 to 68.0	90.6 to 70.9
Jul.	93.3 to 71.0	91.8 to 72.9
Aug.	93.4 to 69.6	91.6 to 72.5
Sept.	88.3 to 64.1	88.9 to 69.4
Oct.	79.5 to 52.0	82.0 to 59.3
Nov.	67.8 to 42.5	72.6 to 50.2
Dec.	59.5 to 37.2	66.7 to 45.5
Year	76.6 to 52.9	79.4 to 58.8

STATE CHAMBER OF COMMERCE

Louisiana Association of Business & Industry
P.O. Box 3988
Baton Rouge, LA 70821
(504) 387-5372

STATE & CITY TOURISM OFFICES

State

Louisiana Department of Commerce and Industry
P.O. Box 44185, Capitol Station
Baton Rouge, LA 70804
(504) 389-5371

Louisiana Tourist Development Commission
P.O. Box 44291, Capitol Station
Baton Rouge, LA 70804
(504) 342-4889

Local

Greater New Orleans Tourist and Convention Commission
334 Royal Street
New Orleans, LA 70130
(504) 522-8772

Shreveport-Bossier Convention and Tourist Commission
P.O. Box 1761
Shreveport, LA 71166
(318) 222-9391

STATE HIGHWAY DEPARTMENT

Department of Transportation and Development
P.O. Box 44245
Capitol Station
Baton Rouge, LA 70804
(504) 389-2931

HIGHWAY WELCOMING CENTERS

Baton Rouge

BATON ROUGE - Front Street.

Greenwood

GREENWOOD CENTER - Interstate 20.

Kentwood

KENTWOOD CENTER - U.S. 55.

WELCOMING CENTERS (continued)

Logansport

LOGANSPORT CENTER - U.S. 84.

New Orleans

NEW ORLEANS - Royal Street.

Pearl River

PEARL RIVER - Interstate 59.

Vidalia

VIDALIA CENTER - U.S. 84.

Vinton

VINTON CENTER - Interstate 10.

STATE POLICE

Department of Public Safety
Baton Rouge, LA 70821
(504) 925-6425

HUNTING & FISHING

Hunting

Any non-resident from a state that has entered into reciprocal hunting or fishing license agreements with the state of Louisiana may hunt or fish within the state according to the agreement terms.

Persons in the Armed Forces of the United States, on active duty, shall for license purposes be allowed to purchase and use resident licenses.

Persons under 16 years of age, whether residents or non-residents, shall not be required to obtain basic licenses or pay fees to fish or hunt, but must be the holder of a big game permit issued free of charge to hunt deer, bear or wild turkey.

No fishing license is required of a resident using a rod (or fishing pole) or hook and line, without a reel or artificial bait.

Any person who has resided in Louisiana for two or more years just prior to application, and 60 years of age or older, shall be issued free hunting and fishing permits.

Resident

Basic season (excluding big game), $5; big game (required of all bear, deer and turkey hunters in addition to basic license), $5.

Non-resident

Basic season (excluding big game), $25; basic 3-day trip (excluding big game), $10; big game (required of all bear, deer and turkey hunters in addition to basic license), $20.

Fishing

See hunting regulations above.

Resident

Resident (expires June 30), $2.

Non-resident

Non-resident (expires June 30), $6; 7 consecutive days, $3.

For more information contact:

Department of Wildlife and Fisheries
400 Royal Street
New Orleans, LA 70130
(504) 568-5612

CAMPGROUNDS

Private

Abita Springs

SHADY LAKES CAMPGROUND
(504) 892-8402
LOCATION: 2 mi. from Abita Springs on Hwy. 435.
FACILITIES: Open year round; water and bathroom facilities; sanitary station; electrical hookup; trailer village vehicle sites; laundry; swimming; boating; boat rental; fishing; horseback riding; tent camping.

Denham Springs

BATON ROUGE EAST KOA KAMPGROUND
(504) 664-7281
LOCATION: 7 mi. east on I-12 at Denham Springs exit.
FACILITIES: Open year round; water and bathroom facilities; sanitary station; electrical hookup; trailer village vehicle sites; laundry; food service; swimming; tent camping.

New Orleans

PARC D'ORLEANS
(504) 241-3167
LOCATION: 7676 Chef Menteur Hwy.
FACILITIES: Open year round; water and bathroom facilities; sanitary station; electrical hookup; trailer village vehicle sites; laundry; food service; swimming; tent camping.

River Ridge

NEW ORLEANS EAST KOA KAMPGROUND
(504) 643-3850
LOCATION: 219 S. Starrett Road.
FACILITIES: Open year round; water and bathroom facilities; sanitary station; electrical hookup; trailer village vehicle sites; laundry; food service; swimming; tent camping.

Robert

YOGI BEAR JELLYSTONE CAMPGROUND
(504) 542-1507
LOCATION: From I-12, 2 mi. north on Route 445.
FACILITIES: Open year round; water and bathroom facilities; sanitary station; electrical

LOUISIANA

CAMPGROUNDS (continued)

hookup; trailer village vehicle sites; laundry; food service; swimming; boating; boat rental; fishing; tent camping.

St. Francisville

AUDUBON LAKE CAMPING RESORT
(504) 635-6118
LOCATION: 1½ mi. south of St. Francisville.
FACILITIES: Open year round; water and bathroom facilities; sanitary station; electrical hookup; trailer village vehicle sites; boating; boat rental; fishing; tent camping.

St. Joseph

LAKE BRUIN KOA KAMPGROUND
(318) 766-3334
LOCATION: 5 mi. north of St. Joseph.
FACILITIES: Open year round; water and bathroom facilities; sanitary station; electrical hookup; trailer village vehicle sites; laundry; food service; swimming; boating; boat rental; fishing; tent camping.

Scott

KOA OF LAFAYETTE
(504) 235-2739
LOCATION: 5 mi. west of I-10 at Hwy. 93 exit.
FACILITIES: Open year round; water and bathroom facilities; sanitary station; electrical hookup; trailer village vehicle sites; laundry; food service; swimming; boating; boat rental; fishing; tent camping.

Shreveport

KOA OF SHREVEPORT
(318) 687-4567
LOCATION: I-20 west, Flournoy Lucas exit to Hwy. 511.
FACILITIES: Open year round; water and bathroom facilities; sanitary station; electrical hookup; trailer village vehicle sites; laundry; food service; swimming; fishing; tent camping.

Vinton

VINTON-LAKE CHARLES KOA KAMP-GROUND
(318) 589-2300
LOCATION: 1514 Azema St.
FACILITIES: Open year round; water and bathroom facilities; sanitary station; electrical hookup; trailer village vehicle sites; laundry; food service; swimming; tent camping.

RESORTS & BEACHES

Most of the state's resort activities center around the major lakes and the State Parks, and include fishing, swimming, boating, water skiing and camping. (See Boating Areas and State Parks.)

BOATING AREAS

Campti

BLACK LAKE
LOCATION: 6 mi. from Campti.
FACILITIES: Launching.

Doyline

KEPLER LAKE
LOCATION: 10 mi. east of Lake Bistineau.
FACILITIES: Launching.

Farmerville

D'ARBONNE LAKE
LOCATION: 10 mi. southeast of Farmerville.
FACILITIES: Launching.

Florien

TOLEDO BEND
LOCATION: Near Florien.
FACILITIES: Launching.

Shreveport

CADDO LAKE
LOCATION: 18 mi. northwest of Shreveport.
FACILITIES: Launching.

CROSS LAKE
LOCATION: Near Shreveport.
FACILITIES: Launching.

LAKE O' THE PINES
LOCATION: 60 mi. northwest of Shreveport.
FACILITIES: Launching.

BICYCLE TRAILS

BREAUX BRIDGE TRAIL - 63 mi.; any bicycle.
An easy ride through flat but interesting country.
Trail: Breaux Bridge to St. Martinville to Loreauville to New Iberia to Delcambre to Abbeville.

GREAT RIVER ROAD TRAIL - 125 mi.; poor road surface; 10-speed bicycle recommended.
In the early days, the only way to go from New Orleans to Baton Rouge was by hugging the banks of the Mississippi along the winding River Road. There are "River Roads" on both east and west banks of the river today, following the levees, and without much traffic except in the New Orleans area.
In New Orleans, River Road traffic on the east bank is so dangerous that it is recommended you ride on top of the levee until you get out of the metropolitan area.
Free ferries at a half-dozen points connect the east and west bank river roads. Take the west bank close to New Orleans and again between Donaldsonville and Plaquemine, and in fact you might take it the whole way if not cycling from Plaquemine to Baton Rouge.
Trail: New Orleans to Baton Rouge along River Road.

See FLORIDA - Gulf Coast Trail.

BICYCLE TRAILS (continued)

ROLLER COASTER TRAIL - 55 mi.; low hills; 10-speed bicycle recommended.

Much of the Louisiana Panhandle is flat but the 55-mile section on Route 10 from St. Francisville to Fluker is a series of low hills. The local riders call it the "Roller Coaster Road" and consider it a fun ride.

Trail: St. Francisville to Fluker.

TRAILS

Shreveport

RED RIVER TRAIL - 5.25 mi. foot trail. The trail meanders along the banks of the Red River and is located almost entirely within the Clyde Fant Parkway. The trail runs north and south through the city and leads travelers to small shops, theaters, art centers, reflecting pools, historic sites, and park and playground areas. Along one section of the trail, there are numerous boulders and a large petrified tree stump believed to be between 50 and 60 million years old.

SKI AREAS

There are no organized Ski Areas in Louisiana.

AMUSEMENT PARKS & ATTRACTIONS

Alexandria

CITY PARK OF FUNLAND
1711 W. MacArthur
Alexandria, LA 71301
(318) 442-0206
FACILITIES: 5 major rides; 6 kiddie rides; refreshment stand; pool; miniature golf; zoo; 18 skee ball machines; picnic facilities; free acts; free gate; free parking; open Feb. - Nov.

Baton Rouge

FUN FAIR PARK
8475 Florida Blvd.
Baton Rouge, LA 70806
(504) 924-6266
FACILITIES: 6 major rides; 7 kiddie rides; 2 games; 2 refreshment stands; picnic facilities; arcade; souvenir shop; theater; free gate; free parking.

Denham Springs

THUNDERBIRD PARK & BEACH
Hwy. 1019
Denham Springs, LA 70726
(504) 665-2511
FACILITIES: 8 major rides; 4 kiddie rides; 3 refreshment stands; restaurant; arcade; swimming pool; bathing beach; camping; picnic facilities; miniature golf; crafts; pay gate; free parking.

New Orleans

PONTALBA HISTORICAL PUPPETORIUM
(Attraction)
514 St. Peter Street
Jackson Square
New Orleans, LA 70116
(504) 522-0344
Facilities: Fully animated museum; scenes from U.S. and Louisiana history; souvenirs; puppets and doll shops; pay gate; open all year.

PONTCHARTRAIN BEACH
Elysian Fields Avenue & Lakeshore Drive
New Orleans, LA 70122
(504) 288-7511
FACILITIES: 18 major rides; 7 kiddie rides; 16 games; 5 refreshment stands; restaurant; arcade; shooting gallery; magic show; high diving show; catering service; gift store; live bands; stage shows; fireworks; pay gate; free parking; open May 27 - Labor Day; weekends: Mar. 26 - May 22.

Tallulah

DELTA VILLAGE
Rt. 2
Tallulah, LA 71282
(318) 574-4131
FACILITIES: 7 major rides; 5 kiddie rides; 3 walk thrus; 8 games; 4 refreshment stands; picnic facilities; petting farm; stage shows; pay gate; free parking; open 1st weekend in May - Labor Day.

STATE FAIR

Louisiana State Fair
P.O. Box 9100
Shreveport, LA 71109
(318) 635-1361
DATE: May

NATIONAL PARKS

There are no National Parks in Louisiana.

NATIONAL FORESTS

National Forests
Southern Region
1720 Peachtree Road, NW
Atlanta, GA 30309
(404) 881-4177

Alexandria

KISATCHIE NATIONAL FOREST
ATTRACTIONS: Colonial homes; Natchitoches, oldest town in Louisiana on Old San Antonio Trail; Stuart Forest Service Nursery, one of the largest pine nurseries in the world; fishing; deer, quail, migratory bird hunting; boating; camping; scenic drives.
FACILITIES: 9 camp and picnic sites, 12 picnic only; 4 swimming sites; hotels.
NEARBY TOWNS: Leesville, Minden, Winnfield.

LOUISIANA

STATE PARKS

Headquarters

Louisiana State Parks & Recreation Commission
P.O. Drawer 1111
Baton Rouge, LA 70821
(504) 389-5761

Bastrop

CHEMIN-A-HAUT STATE PARK
LOCATION: 10 mi. north of Bastrop.
FACILITIES: Open year round; water and bathroom facilities; trailer village vehicle sites; cabins; picnic area; swimming; boating; boat rental; fishing; tent camping.

Covington

BOGUE FALAYA STATE PARK
LOCATION: In Covington.
FACILITIES: Open year round; water and bathroom facilities; picnic area; swimming; boating; fishing.

Doyline

LAKE BISTINEAU STATE PARK
LOCATION: Near Doyline.
FACILITIES: Open year round; water and bathroom facilities; trailer village vehicle sites; cabins; picnic area; swimming; boating; boat rental; fishing; tent camping.

Farmerville

LAKE D'ARBONNE STATE PARK
LOCATION: Near Farmerville.
FACILITIES: Open year round; water and bathroom facilities; picnic area; boating; boat rental; fishing.

Grand Isle

GRAND ISLE STATE PARK
LOCATION: On Route 1.
FACILITIES: Open year round; water and bathroom facilities; trailer village vehicle sites; picnic area; swimming; boating; fishing; tent camping.

Homer

LAKE CLAIBORNE STATE PARK
LOCATION: 7 mi. southwest of Homer.
FACILITIES: Open year round; water and bathroom facilities; trailer village vehicle sites; picnic area; swimming; boating; boat rental; fishing; tent camping.

Lake Charles

SAM HOUSTON STATE PARK
LOCATION: 12 mi. north of Lake Charles.
FACILITIES: Open year round; water and bathroom facilities; trailer village vehicle sites; cabins; picnic area; boating; boat rental; fishing; tent camping.

Madisonville

FAIRVIEW RIVERSIDE STATE PARK
LOCATION: 2 mi. east of Madisonville.
FACILITIES: Open year round; water and bathroom facilities; trailer village vehicle sites; picnic area; boating; fishing; tent camping.

Mandeville

FONTAINEBLEAU STATE PARK
LOCATION: Southeast of Mandeville on U.S. 190.
FACILITIES: Open year round; water and bathroom facilities; trailer village vehicle sites; picnic area; swimming; boating; fishing; tent camping.

St. Joseph

LAKE BRUIN STATE PARK
LOCATION: Near St. Joseph.
FACILITIES: Open year round; water and bathroom facilities; trailer village vehicle sites; picnic area; swimming; boating; boat rental; fishing; tent camping.

Ville Platte

CHICOT STATE PARK
LOCATION: 6 mi. north of Ville Platte.
FACILITIES: Open year round; water and bathroom facilities; trailer village vehicle sites; cabins; picnic area; swimming; boating; boat rental; tent camping.

STATE FORESTS

Louisiana State Parks & Recreation Commission
Forestry Commission
P.O. Drawer 1111
Baton Rouge, LA 70821
(504) 925-4500

Alexander

ALEXANDER STATE FOREST
LOCATION: 15 mi. south of Alexander.
FACILITIES: Open year round; water and bathroom facilities; sanitary station; electrical hookup; trailer village vehicle sites; picnic area; swimming; boating; fishing; tent camping.

HISTORIC SITES

Epps

POVERTY POINT INDIAN MOUNDS - Largest complex of ceremonial mounds yet discovered in North America. Artifacts discovered there prove this was the site of a trade system extending from Canada to Mexico and from coast to coast. Located northeast of Epps on Route 134.

New Orleans

THE CABILDO - Seat of Louisiana territorial government for France, Spain, the Confederacy and the United States. France and the U.S. concluded the Louisiana Purchase transaction in 1803 in a second floor room of this

HISTORIC SITES (continued)

building. Located in 700 block of Charles Street.

CATHEDRAL OF ST. LOUIS KING OF FRANCE - Oldest active cathedral in the United States. Located on Charles Street facing Jackson Square.

LAFITTE'S BLACKSMITH SHOP - Served as a front for smuggling operations of the pirate Jean Lafitte and his brother Pierre. Located at 941 Bourbon Street.

ST. CHARLES AVENUE STREETCAR LINE- Last functional streetcar line in the U.S.

URSULINE CONVENT - Oldest building on record in the Mississippi Valley. Located on corner of Chartres and Ursuline Streets.

Newellton

WINTER QUARTERS PLANTATION - Used as headquarters by General Grant, for a time, during the siege of Vicksburg. One of the few homes of the area spared the torch. Located 3 mi. southeast of Newellton on Route 608.

Shreveport

BIRTHPLACE OF SECESSION - Site of Rocky Mount town meeting, Nov. 26, 1860, first in the South to adopt a resolution favoring secession. Located on Route 160 at Route 157.

SYMPHONY HOUSE - Built in 1872 by Col. Robert H. Lindsay, unusually fine example of the transitional style of Southern residence between the Greek Revival and Late Victorian periods. One of the city's oldest structures, possibly the only existing immediate post-Civil War architecture of its type in Shreveport.

HOSTELS

There are no Hostels in Louisiana.

POINTS OF INTEREST

Bossier City

LOUISIANA DOWNS - Finest new racing facility, its multi-level, glass-enclosed, air conditioned stadium offers an unobstructed view from each of the 15,000 seats. Thoroughbred racing and parimutuel wagering. Located at 8,000 U.S. 80 east.

Franklin

OAKLAWN MANOR - Massive columned mansion set in the midst of formal gardens in the largest grove of live oaks in the world. Located on Sterling Road.

Lafayette

ACADIAN VILLAGE AND TROPICAL GARDENS - Number of Acadian dwellings brought together to represent an early "Cajun" bayou village. Located on Moulton Road, just south of Route 342.

Mandeville

LAKE PONTCHARTRAIN CAUSEWAY - Longest bridge in U.S., 24 mi., crosses America's largest inland saltwater lake. Connects U.S. 190 with U.S. 90.

Many

HODGES GARDENS - Nation's largest privately operated horticultural parkland and wildlife refuge. It contains multi-level formal gardens, natural scenic walks and drives, picnic areas, conservatory, greenhouses and a dramatic monument illustrating the Louisiana Purchase. Located south of Many on U.S.171.

New Orleans

THE FRENCH QUARTER - The famous French Quarter, or Vieux Carre (Old Square), was laid out on a grid plan in 1721 and remains one of the nation's greatest clusters of colonial and antebellum structures. Bounded by Canal Street, Esplanade, Ramparts and the Mississippi.

MARDI GRAS - A city-wide, pre-Lenten celebration with parades and festivities on the eve of Ash Wednesday.

VOODOO MUSEUM - Contains many artifacts of voodoo, the occult and the supernatural. Displays rituals and powers of voodoo from the earliest times to the present. Located at 739 Bourbon Street.

Opelousas

JIM BOWIE MUSEUM - Houses a fine collection of Bowie possessions and memorabilia. Located at 153 West Landry Street.

St. Francisville

AUDUBON ART GALLERY - While living in the St. Francisville area, John James Audubon painted at least 75 of his world-famous "Birds of America." Gallery houses complete collection of the artist's 435 life-sized bird portraits.

Shreveport

THE AMERICAN ROSE CENTER - 118 acres of water, trees and breathtaking roses in various garden settings. The final goal of this project is the largest garden in the world devoted primarily to roses.

Vacherie

OAK ALLEY PLANTATION - Most famous antebellum home in Louisiana. Built 1830-39 by Jacques Roman III, surrounded by upper and lower galleries and by 28 fluted Doric columns. Located on Route 18 between St. James and Vacherie.

MAINE

Maine, which is nearly 80 percent forested, entered the Union in 1820 as the twenty-third state. Unlike many western and midwestern states, early settlers had no trouble with resident Indians. In fact, white settlers often joined forces with the local Indians to fight off attacks by invading Iroquois.

In the mid-1800s, even with the number of lumberjacks, woodsmen, trappers and rugged individualists living in the territory, Maine went dry, abolishing all alcoholic beverages, and was the first state to do so. The law remained in force until the passage of the 21st Amendment in 1933.

Although winters are severe and summer nights cool, the low concentration of people in the state and the vastness of the natural surroundings prove to be irresistible to many a hunter, skier, camper and outdoor enthusiast. However, the state's major revenue source is and will remain its giant lumber and lumber byproducts industry.

State capital: Augusta. State bird: Chickadee. State tree: White pine. State flower: White pine cone and tassel.

WEATHER

Maine occupies 33,215 square miles, almost exactly one-half of New England's total area. The terrain is hilly. Elevations are generally less than 500 feet above sea level over the southeastern one-half of the state. The northwestern one-half is a plateau ranging in elevation from 1,000 to 1,500 feet, but sloping downward to 500 feet in the northeast from 1,000 feet in the north (Aroostook County). The coastal portion of the state has many inlets, bays, channels, fine harbors, rocky islands, and promontories which provide a treasure of scenic beauty. More than five-sixths of the state is forest land.

Maine's chief climatic characteristics include: changeableness of the weather; large ranges of temperature, both daily and annual; great differences between the same seasons in different years; equable distributions of precipitation; and considerable diversity from place to place. The regional climatic influences are modified in Maine by varying distances from the ocean, by elevations, and by types of terrain. Summer temperatures are usually cool and are reasonably uniform over the state. Average temperatures vary from place to place much more in winter than in summer.

Average daily temperature for each month.

	Northern	Southern
Jan.	21.8 to 3.2	32.4 to 15.2
Feb.	25.0 to 4.4	33.4 to 15.7
Mar.	34.2 to 15.4	40.5 to 24.6
Apr.	47.2 to 28.4	51.9 to 33.7
May	62.4 to 39.0	63.3 to 42.4
Jun.	72.8 to 49.6	71.8 to 50.8
Jul.	77.3 to 54.5	76.8 to 58.4
Aug.	74.4 to 51.8	75.4 to 56.0
Sept.	66.2 to 44.5	68.0 to 49.9
Oct.	54.0 to 35.5	58.5 to 41.9
Nov.	39.0 to 25.0	47.2 to 32.6
Dec.	25.4 to 8.7	36.1 to 20.2
Year	50.0 to 30.0	54.6 to 36.6

STATE CHAMBER OF COMMERCE

Maine State Chamber of Commerce
477 Congress Street
Portland, ME 04111
(207) 774-9871

STATE & CITY TOURISM OFFICES

State

State Development Office
State House
Augusta, ME 04333
(207) 289-2656

Maine Publicity Bureau
3 St. John Street
Portland, ME 04102
(207) 773-7266

Local

Tourism and Convention Bureau
Greater Portland Chamber of Commerce
142 Free Street
Portland, ME 04101
(207) 772-2811

STATE HIGHWAY DEPARTMENT

Department of Transportation
Transportation Building
Augusta, ME 04330
(207) 289-2551

HIGHWAY WELCOMING CENTERS

Bass Park

BASS PARK - In city of Bangor.

Calais

CALAIS INTERNATIONAL BRIDGE CENTER - Near Canadian border.

WELCOMING CENTERS (continued)

Fryeburg

FRYEBURG CENTER - Route 302, near New Hampshire border.

Kittery

KITTERY/YORK CENTER - Maine Turnpike, border of New Hampshire.

STATE POLICE

Department of Public Safety
Augusta, ME 04330
(207) 289-2155

HUNTING & FISHING

Hunting

A license is required for all persons, ages 10 through 69, who hunt or fish in the state. To qualify as a resident, a person must reside in the state 3 months prior to application.

Resident

Junior hunting (10-15 years inc.), $1.50; hunting (16 years and over), $7.50; combination hunting and fishing (over age 70), free; combination hunting and fishing (16 years and over), $12.50; serviceman combination, $3.50; archery hunting (10 years and over), $7.50; trapping (statewide), $13; guide (18 years and over), $32; deer transportation license, $40.50.

Non-resident

Citizen big game hunting (10 years and over), $60.50; alien big game hunting, $100; small game hunting (16 years and over), $30.50; junior small game hunting (10-15 years inc.), $15.50; archery deer hunting (12 years and over), $60.50; trapping, $250; guide (18 years and over), $125; alien guide, $150.

Fishing

See hunting regulations above.

Resident

Fishing (16 years and older), $7.50; combination hunting and fishing, $12.50; 70 years of age and older, free; 3-day, $7.50.

Non-resident

Season (age 16 and older), $25.50; 12-15 years inclusive, $4; 15-day, $15.50; 7-day, $12.50; 3-day, $7.50.

For more information contact:

Department of Inland Fisheries and Wildlife
284 State Street
Augusta, ME 04333
(207) 289-3651

CAMPGROUNDS

Private

Bangor

HAMMOND CAMPGROUND
(207) 848-3455
LOCATION: 4 mi. west of Bangor on U.S. 2.
FACILITIES: Open May 15 - Oct. 15; 200 sites; water and bathroom facilities; sanitary station; electrical hookup; trailer village vehicle sites; laundry; swimming; boating; tent camping.

Bar Harbor

BARCADIA T&T GROUNDS
(207) 288-3520
LOCATION: In Bar Harbor.
FACILITIES: Open May 25 - Oct. 1; 200 sites; water and bathroom facilities; sanitary station; electrical hookup; trailer village vehicle sites; laundry; food service; swimming; boating; fishing; tent camping.

Casco

POINT SEBAGO CAMPGROUND
(207) 655-3821
LOCATION: Off Maine Turnpike at Exit 8.
FACILITIES: Open year round; 435 sites; water and bathroom facilities; sanitary station; electrical hookup; trailer village vehicle sites; laundry; food service; swimming; boating; fishing; tent camping.

Damariscotta

LAKE PEMAQUID CAMPING
(207) 563-5202
LOCATION: In Damariscotta.
FACILITIES: Open May 1 - Oct. 15; 200 sites; water and bathroom facilities; sanitary station; electrical hookup; trailer village vehicle sites; laundry; food service; swimming; boating; fishing; tent camping.

North Waterford

PAPOSSE POND CAMPGROUND
(207) 583-4470
LOCATION: In North Waterford.
FACILITIES: Open May 30 - Oct. 1; 225 sites; water and bathroom facilities; sanitary station; electrical hookup; trailer village vehicle sites; laundry; food service; swimming; boating; fishing; tent camping.

Old Orchard Beach

OLD ORCHARD BEACH CAMPING
(207) 934-4477
LOCATION: Ocean Park Road.
FACILITIES: Open Apr. - Nov.; 600 sites; water and bathroom facilities; sanitary station; electrical hookup; trailer village vehicle sites; laundry; swimming; tent camping.

POWDER HORN TENT & TRAILER PARK
(207) 934-4733
LOCATION: On Hwy. 98.
FACILITIES: Open May 30 - Sept. 4; 350 sites; water and bathroom facilities; sanitary

MAINE

CAMPGROUNDS (continued)

station; electrical hookup; trailer village vehicle sites; food service; swimming; tent camping.

WILD ACRES CAMPGROUND
(207) 934-2535
LOCATION: Saco Ave.
FACILITIES: Open May 27 - Sept. 15; 300 sites; water and bathroom facilities; sanitary station; electrical hookup; trailer village vehicle sites; laundry; food service; swimming; boating; tent camping.

Small Point

HERMIT ISLAND
(207) 389-1747
LOCATION: 14 mi. south of Bath.
FACILITIES: Open May 30 - Oct. 15; 250 sites; water and bathroom facilities; trailer village vehicle sites; food service; swimming; boating; fishing; tent camping.

South Lebanon

THE KING'S/THE QUEEN'S COURTS
(207) 339-9465
LOCATION: Flat Rock Bridge Road.
FACILITIES: Open May 15 - Oct. 15; 450 sites; water and bathroom facilities; sanitary station; electrical hookup; trailer village vehicle sites; laundry; food service; swimming; fishing; tent camping.

Wells

WELLS BEACH RESORT CAMPGROUND
(207) 646-7570
LOCATION: On U.S. 1.
FACILITIES: Open May 30 - Oct. 12; 150 sites; water and bathroom facilities; sanitary station; electrical hookup; trailer village vehicle sites; food service; tent camping.

RESORTS & BEACHES

Boothbay

MID-COAST AREA - Seagoing peninsulas, quiet, peaceful inlets, colorful islands and busy coastal villages abound in the 70 or so miles from Boothbay to Stockton Springs. The heart of the region, Boothbay Harbor, offers fishing, bathing, yachting, boat trips, every imaginable fun under the sun.

Kittery

SOUTHERN COAST AREA - Long, white sand beaches, surf drenched cliffs and thriving cities make up this 60 mile stretch of Maine's coastline from Kittery to Popham Beach. In between is Portland and such famous resort areas as Wells Beach, Old Orchard Beach, York Beach, Ogunquit Beach, Freeport Beach and Small Point Beach where you can enjoy the warm summer sunshine.

Stonington

PENOBSCOT-ACADIA AREA - Seacoast beauty and island charm, extending from Stonington to Prospect Harbor, blend to create 50 miles of splendid natural surroundings. Bar Harbor, home of Acadia National Park, is the center of attention. But elsewhere on Mount Desert Island or Winter Harbor or a dozen other such places, you can sail, golf, hike, climb, swim, or simply relax in the sun.

BOATING AREAS

Acton

GREAT EAST LAKE
LOCATION: Near Acton.
FACILITIES: Launching.

Belgrade

MESSALONSKEE LAKE
LOCATION: Near Belgrade.
FACILITIES: Launching.

Bridgton

LONG LAKE
LOCATION: Near Bridgton.
FACILITIES: Launching.

Danforth

GRAND LAKE
LOCATION: Near Danforth.
FACILITIES: Launching.

Dover-Foxcroft

SEBEC LAKE
LOCATION: Near Dover-Foxcroft.
FACILITIES: Launching.

Eagle Lake

EAGLE LAKE
LOCATION: Near Eagle Lake.
FACILITIES: Launching.

Fort Kent

BLACK LAKE
LOCATION: Near Fort Kent.
FACILITIES: Launching.

Hartland

GREAT MOOSE LAKE
LOCATION: Near Hartland.
FACILITIES: Launching.

Hope

ALFORD LAKE
LOCATION: Near Hope.
FACILITIES: Launching.

Lincoln

MATTANAWCOOK LAKE
LOCATION: Near Lincoln.
FACILITIES: Launching.

Linneus

NICKERSON LAKE

BOATING AREAS (continued)

LOCATION: Near Linneus.
FACILITIES: Launching.

Madison

WASSERUNSETT LAKE
LOCATION: Near Madison.
FACILITIES: Launching.

Monmouth

COBBOSSEECONTEE LAKE
LOCATION: Near Monmouth.
FACILITIES: Launching.

Mt. Vernon

ECHO LAKE
LOCATION: Near Mt. Vernon.
FACILITIES: Launching.

New Limerick

DEWS LAKE
LOCATION: Near New Limerick.
FACILITIES: Launching.

Newport

SEBASTICOOK LAKE
LOCATION: Near Newport.
FACILITIES: Launching.

Norway

PENNESSEEWASSEE LAKE
LOCATION: Near Norway.
FACILITIES: Launching.

Orono

PUSHAW LAKE
LOCATION: Near Orono.
FACILITIES: Launching.

Portage

PORTAGE LAKE
LOCATION: Near Portage.
FACILITIES: Launching.

Readfield

MARANACOOK LAKE
LOCATION: Near Readfield.
FACILITIES: Launching.

St. Agatha

LONG LAKE
LOCATION: Near St. Agatha.
FACILITIES: Launching.

Vanceboro

SPEDNIK LAKE
LOCATION: Near Vanceboro.
FACILITIES: Launching.

BICYCLE TRAILS

ACADIA NATIONAL PARK TRAIL - 20

mi.; hilly terrain; 10-speed bicycle recommended.

All the roads on the island are good for bicycling. Particularly noteworthy is Ocean Drive, where a cyclist can experience the rare luxury of riding on a one way road for twenty miles. There is also a major network of roads from which automobiles are prohibited. They were built for carriages. Most are suitable for bicycling and some have been resurfaced for that purpose.

Trail: Mt. Desert Island.

TRAILS

There are no National Trails System Foot Trails in Maine.

SKI AREAS

Auburn

LOST VALLEY
Auburn, ME 04210
(207) 784-1561
LOCATION: Off Route 11.
FACILITIES: 2 double chairlifts; 1 tow rope; 1 poma; ski instruction; ski rental; 254 ft. vertical drop; restaurants; lodging.

Bangor

BANGOR RECREATION SKI AREA
Bangor, ME 04401
(207) 942-6602
LOCATION: Off Essex Street.
FACILITIES: 1 poma; ski instruction; 300 ft. vertical drop; restaurants; lodging.

Bethel

SUNDAY RIVER
Bethel, ME 04217
(207) 824-2187
LOCATION: Off Route 26.
FACILITIES: 1 double chairlift; 3 pomas; ski instruction; ski rental; 1500 ft. vertical drop; restaurants; lodging.

Bridgton

PLEASANT MOUNTAIN
Bridgton, ME 04009
(207) 647-2022
LOCATION: Off U.S. 302.
FACILITIES: 3 double chairlifts; 3 pomas; ski instruction; ski rental; 1256 ft. vertical drop; restaurants; lodging.

Camden

CAMDEN SNOW BOWL
Camden, ME 04843
(207) 236-4418
LOCATION: Off U.S. 1.
FACILITIES: 1 double chairlift; 2 pomas; ski instruction; ski rental; 900 ft. vertical drop; restaurants; lodging.

Caribou

CARIBOU SKI SLOPE

MAINE

SKI AREAS (continued)

Caribou, ME 04736
(207) 492-0891
LOCATION: Off Route 1.
FACILITIES: 1 poma; 360 ft. vertical drop;
restaurants; lodging.

Carrabasset Valley

SUGARLOAF USA
Carrabasset Valley, ME 04947
(207) 237-2000
LOCATION: Off Route 27.
FACILITIES: 5 double chairlifts; 5 pomas; 1
gondola; ski instruction; ski rental; 2600 ft.
vertical drop; restaurants; lodging.

E. Stoneham

EVERGREEN VALLEY
E. Stoneham, ME 04231
(207) 928-3300
LOCATION: Off Route 5.
FACILITIES: 3 pomas; ski instruction; ski
rental; 1050 ft. vertical drop; restaurants;
lodging.

Falmouth

HURRICANE SLOPE
Falmouth, ME 04105
(207) 797-4418
LOCATION: Off Route 26.
FACILITIES: 1 tow rope; ski instruction; 180
ft. vertical drop; restaurants; lodging.

Farmington

TITCOMB SLOPE
Farmington, ME 04938
(207) 778-9384
LOCATION: Off Route 4.
FACILITIES: 2 pomas; ski instruction; 500
ft. vertical drop; restaurants; lodging.

Ft. Fairfield

WHITE BUNNY
Ft. Fairfield, ME 04742
(207) 473-7190
LOCATION: Off Route 1.
FACILITIES: 1 poma; 250 ft. vertical drop;
restaurants; lodging.

Greenville

SQUAW MOUNTAIN
Greenville, ME 04441
(207) 695-2272
LOCATION: Off Routes 6 and 15.
FACILITIES: 1 double chairlift; 2 pomas; ski
instruction; ski rental; 1750 ft. vertical drop;
restaurants; lodging.

Hermon

HERMON MOUNTAIN
Hermon, ME 04401
(207) 848-5192
LOCATION: Off U.S. 2.
FACILITIES: 1 tow rope; 2 pomas; ski instruction; ski rental; 400 ft. vertical drop; restaurants; lodging.

Island Falls

MAY MOUNTAIN
Island Falls, ME 04747
(207) 463-2101
LOCATION: Off Route 2.
FACILITIES: 1 poma; ski instruction; ski
rental; 427 ft. vertical drop; restaurants; lodging.

Lee

MOUNT JEFFERSON
Lee, ME 04455
(207) 738-2377
LOCATION: Off Route 6.
FACILITIES: 1 tow rope; 1 poma; ski instruction; ski rental; 430 ft. vertical drop; restaurants; lodging.

Livermore Falls

SPRUCE MOUNTAIN
Livermore Falls, ME 04254
(207) 897-2796
LOCATION: Off Route 4.
FACILITIES: 4 tow ropes; ski instruction;
400 ft. vertical drop; restaurants; lodging.

Locke Mills

MOUNT ABRAM
Locke Mills, ME 04255
(207) 875-2601
LOCATION: Off Route 26.
FACILITIES: 1 double chairlift; 3 pomas; ski
instruction; ski rental; 1030 ft. vertical drop;
restaurants; lodging.

Mars Hill

BIG ROCK
Mars Hill, ME 04758
(207) 425-6711
LOCATION: Off U.S. 1.
FACILITIES: 1 tow rope; 2 pomas; ski instruction; ski rental; 900 ft. vertical drop; restaurants; lodging.

Millinocket

MUNICIPAL SLOPE
Millinocket, ME 04462
(207) 723-4097
LOCATION: Athletic Field.
FACILITIES: 1 tow rope; 100 ft. vertical
drop; restaurants; lodging.

Moscow

BAKER MOUNTAIN
Moscow, ME 04920
(207) 672-9369
LOCATION: Off U.S. 201.
FACILITIES: 1 tow rope; ski instruction; 329
ft. vertical drop; restaurants; lodging.

Rangeley

SADDLEBACK
Rangeley, ME 04970
(207) 864-3380
LOCATION: Off Route 4.
FACILITIES: 2 double chairlifts; 2 pomas;

SKI AREAS (continued)

ski instruction; ski rental; 1700 ft. vertical drop; restaurants; lodging.

Rumford

CHISHOLM WINTER PARK
Rumford, ME 04276
(207) 364-8977
LOCATION: Near Rumford.
FACILITIES: 1 poma; ski instruction; 500 ft. vertical drop; restaurants; lodging.

Temple

TATER MOUNTAIN
Temple, ME 04984
(207) 778-6283
LOCATION: Off Route 43.
FACILITIES: 1 poma; ski instruction; 320 ft. vertical drop; restaurants; lodging.

Waterville

COLBY SKI AREA
Waterville, ME 04901
(207) 872-9890
LOCATION: Off Route 104.
FACILITIES: 1 poma; 250 ft. vertical drop; restaurants; lodging.

Winterport

SNOW MOUNTAIN
Winterport, ME 04496
(207) 223-4455
LOCATION: Off Route 139.
FACILITIES: 1 poma; ski instruction; ski rental; 580 ft. vertical drop; restaurants; lodging.

AMUSEMENT PARKS & ATTRACTIONS

Caribou

FUNLAND
Presque Isle Road
Caribou, ME 04736
(207) 493-3157
FACILITIES: 5 major rides; 5 kiddie rides; refreshment stand; 3 games; baseball pitching machine; arcade; miniature golf; golf driving range; free gate; free parking; open May 1 - Sept. 30.

Old Orchard Beach

PALACE AMUSEMENT
1 Old Orchard Street
Old Orchard Beach, ME 04064
(207) 934-2001
FACILITIES: 12 major rides; 8 kiddie rides; 7 games; fun house; 5 refreshment stands; arcade; shooting gallery; free gate; pay parking; open Memorial Day - Labor Day.

Saco

FUNTOWN, U.S.A.
Portland Road
Saco, ME 04072

(207) 284-5139
FACILITIES: 8 major rides; 7 kiddie rides; 6 games; 3 refreshment stands; restaurant; arcade; shooting gallery; picnic facilities; crafts; miniature golf; free acts; free gate; free parking; open mid-Apr. - Labor Day.

York Beach

ANIMAL FOREST AMUSEMENT PARK
P.O. Box 404
York Beach, ME 03910
(207) 363-4911
FACILITIES: 8 major rides; 6 kiddie rides; zoo; arcade; refreshment stand; free gate; free parking.

STATE FAIR

Bangor State Fair
100 Dutton Street
Bangor, ME 04401
(207) 947-3542
DATE: July

NATIONAL PARKS

Bar Harbor

ACADIA NATIONAL PARK
Route 1
Bar Harbor, ME 04609
(207) 288-3338

BLACKWOODS
LOCATION: 5 mi. south of Bar Harbor.
FACILITIES: Open year round; limit of stay: 14 days; 325 sites; group camps: 5; NPS campsite fee: $4; water and bathroom facilities; sanitary station; picnic area; food service; swimming; boating; fishing; hiking; horseback riding; snowmobile route; exhibit; museum; environmental study area; NPS guided tour; self-guiding tour; no water Nov. 15 - May 15; reservations.

SEAWALL
LOCATION: 5 mi. south of Southwest Harbor.
FACILITIES: Open May 15 - Oct. 15; limit of stay: 14 days; 218 sites; group camps: 5; NPS campsite fee: $4; water and bathroom facilities; sanitary station; picnic area; food service; swimming; boating; fishing; hiking; horseback riding; snowmobile route; exhibit; museum; environmental study area; NPS guided tour; self-guiding tour; 104 walk-in sites ($2); reservations.

NATIONAL FORESTS

National Forests
Eastern Region
633 West Wisconsin Avenue
Milwaukee, WI 53203
(414) 291-3693

See WHITE MOUNTAIN NATIONAL FOREST - New Hampshire.

MAINE

STATE PARKS

Headquarters

Maine Department of Conservation
Bureau of Parks & Recreation
State Office Bldg.
Augusta, ME 04333
(207) 289-3821

Camden

CAMDEN HILLS STATE PARK
LOCATION: 2 mi. north of Camden.
FACILITIES: Open May 15 - Nov. 1; water
and bathroom facilities; sanitary station; trailer village vehicle sites; picnic area; hiking; tent
camping.

Dennysville

COBSCOOK BAY STATE PARK
LOCATION: South of Dennysville.
FACILITIES: Open May 15 - Oct. 15; water
and bathroom facilities; sanitary station; trailer village vehicle sites; picnic area; boating;
fishing; hiking; tent camping.

Ellsworth

LAMOINE STATE PARK
LOCATION: Route 184 near Ellsworth.
FACILITIES: Open May 30 - Oct. 15; trailer
village vehicle sites; picnic area; swimming;
boating; fishing; tent camping.

Freeport

BRADBURY MOUNTAIN STATE PARK
LOCATION: 6 mi. from Freeport.
FACILITIES: Open May 15 - Nov.1; water
and bathroom facilities; trailer village vehicle sites; picnic area; swimming; hiking; tent
camping.

Greenville

LILY BAY STATE PARK
LOCATION: North of Greenville.
FACILITIES: Open Apr. 1 - Oct. 15; water
and bathroom facilities; sanitary station; trailer village vehicle sites; picnic area; boating;
boat rental; fishing; tent camping.

Liberty

LAKE ST. GEORGE STATE PARK
LOCATION: On Route 3 near Liberty.
FACILITIES: Open May - Nov.; water and
bathroom facilities; sanitary station; trailer
village vehicle sites; picnic area; swimming;
boating; boat rental; fishing; tent camping.

Millinocket

BAXTER STATE PARK
LOCATION: 16 mi. from Millinocket.
FACILITIES: Open May 16 - Oct. 19; water
and bathroom facilities; trailer village vehicle
sites; cabins; picnic area; swimming; boating;
fishing; hiking; tent camping.

Naples

SEBAGO LAKE STATE PARK
LOCATION: Off U.S. 302 between Naples &
S. Casco.
FACILITIES: Open May 1 - Oct. 15; water
and bathroom facilities; sanitary station; trailer village vehicle sites; picnic area; food service; swimming; boating; fishing; hiking; tent
camping.

Presque Isle

AROOSTOCK STATE PARK
LOCATION: South of Presque Isle, off U.S.
1.
FACILITIES: Open May 15 - Oct. 15; water
and bathroom facilities; trailer village vehicle
sites; picnic area; swimming; boating; boat
rental; fishing; tent camping.

Rumford

RANGELY LAKE STATE PARK
LOCATION: Route 17 from Rumford.
FACILITIES: Open Apr. 1 - Oct. 15; water
and bathroom facilities; sanitary station; trailer village vehicle sites; picnic area; swimming;
boating; fishing; tent camping.

Warren Island

WARREN ISLAND STATE PARK
LOCATION: On Warren Island.
FACILITIES: Open May 30 - Sept. 30; trailer
village vehicle sites; picnic area; boating; fishing; hiking; tent camping.

Weld

MT. BLUE STATE PARK
LOCATION: Near Weld.
FACILITIES: Open May 30 - Oct. 15; water
and bathroom facilities; sanitary station; trailer village vehicle sites; picnic area; swimming;
boating; boat rental; fishing; hiking; tent
camping.

STATE FORESTS

There are no State Forests in Maine.

HISTORIC SITES

Augusta

FORT HALIFAX - Oldest blockhouse in the
U.S.; part of a larger fortification used as way-
station for Col. Benedict Arnold's expedition
through Maine wilderness to Quebec in 1775.
Located on U.S. 201, 1 mi. south of Winslow-
Waterville Bridge.

Lubec

CAMPOBELLO ISLAND - Summer home of
Franklin Delano Rosevelt, 32nd President;
now an international shrine.

Machias

FORT O'BRIEN OR FORT MACHIAS - Site

HISTORIC SITES (continued)

of the first naval engagement of the American Revolution, five days before Battle of Bunker Hill. During the fracus, an English warship was captured. Located 5 mi. from Machias on Route 92.

New Gloucester

NEW GLOUCESTER - Town where famous Shaker Society was organized in 1794. Shaker Village and Church located on road to Poland Spring.

Portsmouth

JOHN PAUL JONES MEMORIAL - As Captain of the U.S.S. Ranger, Jones received first salute by a foreign power given a man-of-war flying the Stars and Stripes. Ship was built and launched near this site in 1777. Located on U.S. 1.

HOSTELS

There are no Hostels in Maine.

POINTS OF INTEREST

Andover

EARTH STATION - Center for communications satellites. Located off Route 120.

Bristol

COLONIAL PEMAQUID RESTORATION - Site of extensive archaeological dig. Some 14 foundations, believed to be those of 16th and 17th century settlements, have been uncovered. Also hundreds of artifacts unearthed which show evidence of much earlier Indian habitation. Located on a point of land near the mouth of the Pemaquid River.

Georgetown

PHIPPS POINT - Birthplace of Sir William Phipps. First American knighted at the English court, in recognition for having donated to the Crown treasure taken from old Spanish galleons sunk in the Caribbean Sea.

Harpswell

EAGLE ISLAND - Home of Admiral Robert E. Peary. Equipped with pier to allow boaters access to the property.

MARYLAND

Maryland, the center of much conflict and controversy, joined the Union in 1788 as the seventh state. The son of the first Lord Baltimore established a Catholic colony in the mid-1600s only to have it forcefully taken from him by the more powerful Puritans. Then 21 years before statehood, the Mason-Dixon line was drawn separating Pennsylvania and Maryland and ending years of haggling between the two states.

Recently two major scandals surfaced. Governor Mendel was found guilty of criminal charges, and Vice President Agnew was forced to resign his office, the first such resignation in the history of the country. Interestingly enough, the charges brought against Vice President Agnew stemmed from activities while he, too, was governor of Maryland.

Near Baltimore, heavy industry generates a major portion of the state's income, while in the southern section, dairy and poultry farms are the important revenue producers.

State capital: Annapolis. State bird: Baltimore oriole. State tree: White oak. State flower: Blackeyed Susan.

WEATHER

The total area of Maryland is 12,303 square miles. The land rises more or less gradually from the Atlantic Ocean across the Coastal Plain (which virtually includes the Eastern Shore and Southern Maryland) and then more rapidly across the Piedmont Plateau (northern-central Maryland) and the ridges of the Appalachian Mountains and finally reaches its highest point at 3,340 feet above mean sea level on Backbone Mountain in the Allegheny Plateau of Garrett County.

Although Maryland ranks as one of the smaller states with respect to size, it encompasses an extremely wide range of physiographic features which contribute to a comparatively wide range of climatic conditions. The winter climate on the Piedmont and Coastal Plain sections of Maryland is intermediate between the cold of the Northeast and the mild weather of the South. Extremely cold air masses from the interior of the continent are moderated somewhat by passage over the Appalachian Mountains and, in some instances, by a short trajectory over the nearby ocean and bays. Weather on the Allegheny Plateau is frequently 10 degrees to 15 degrees F colder than it is in eastern portions of the state, and, at times, extremely low temperatures occur in winter. Summer is characterized by considerable warm weather, including several hot, humid periods; however, nights are usually quite comfortable.

Average daily temperature for each month.

MARYLAND

WEATHER (continued)

	Northern	Southern
Jan.	38.8 to 22.7	43.3 to 26.9
Feb.	41.3 to 23.8	46.0 to 28.8
Mar.	50.2 to 30.7	53.5 to 35.1
Apr.	63.4 to 41.0	65.5 to 45.3
May	72.5 to 49.8	74.9 to 54.5
Jun.	81.0 to 58.9	82.7 to 63.5
Jul.	84.9 to 63.5	86.7 to 68.2
Aug.	83.2 to 62.1	85.3 to 66.7
Sept.	76.8 to 55.4	79.7 to 60.0
Oct.	65.6 to 44.6	69.9 to 49.5
Nov.	52.8 to 35.0	57.9 to 39.3
Dec.	41.6 to 26.3	46.8 to 30.5
Year	62.7 to 42.8	66.0 to 47.4

STATE CHAMBER OF COMMERCE

Maryland State Chamber of Commerce
60 West Street
Annapolis, MD 21401
(301) 269-0642

STATE & CITY TOURISM OFFICES

State

Division of Tourist Development
Department of Economic & Community
  Development
1748 Forest Drive
Annapolis, MD 21401
(301) 269-2686

Maryland Department of Economic and Community Development
2525 Riva Road
Annapolis, MD 21401
(301) 269-3265

Local

Baltimore Promotion Council, Inc.
22 Light Street
Baltimore, MD 21202
(301) 727-5688

STATE HIGHWAY DEPARTMENT

Maryland Department of Transportation
Baltimore-Washington International
Airport, MD 21240
(301) 787-7397

HIGHWAY WELCOMING CENTERS

Allegany

ALLEGANY COUNTY CENTER - Baltimore and Green Streets, Cumberland.

Ann Arundel

ANN ARUNDEL COUNTY - City dock, Annapolis.

Frederick

FREDERICK CENTER - U.S. 15. exit 7.

Garrett

GARRETT COUNTY CENTER - Route 219 at Deep Creek Lake.

Ocean City

OCEAN CITY CENTER - U.S. Hwy. 50.

Talbot

TALBOT COUNTY CENTER - Route 50 at Easton.

Washington

WASHINGTON COUNTY - Summit and Washington Ave., Hagerstown.

Wicomico

WICOMICO COUNTY - Route 13, near Salisbury.

STATE POLICE

Department of Public Safety
Pikesville, MD 21208
(301) 391-0700

HUNTING & FISHING

Hunting

A license is required for all persons who hunt and fish in the state. To qualify as a resident, a person must reside in the state 90 days prior to application. No license is required for tidewater fishing.

Resident

Statewide license, $8; plus $1.25 statewide license fee (age 16 years - 64), $2.50 license fee (age 65 or older); $35.50 license fee (under age 16); deer-turkey stamp, $5.50; deer-turkey stamp (age 65 or older), $1; state waterfowl stamp, $1.10; migratory bird hunting stamp, $5; shooting preserve hunting license, $3.50.

Non-resident

Hunting, $30.50; hunting (under 16 years of age), $5; trapping, $25.50.

Fishing

See hunting regulations above.

HUNTING & FISHING (continued)

Resident

License, $4.50; license (65 years or older), $1; fee fishing lakes, $25; fish breeders license, $5; trout stamp, $3.50; trout stamp (age 65 years and older), $1.

Non-resident

License, $10.50; 7-day tourist license, $4.50; special license for residents of Virginia, West Virginia and District of Columbia for Potomac River, $4.50; fee fishing lakes, $25; fish breeders license, $5; trout stamp, $3.50.

For more information contact:

Department of Natural Resources
Wildlife Administration
Tawes State Office Bldg.
Annapolis, MD 21401
(301) 269-3195

CAMPGROUNDS

Private

Abingdon

BAR HARBOR CAMPGROUND
4228 Birch Ave.
Abingdon, MD 21009
(301) 679-0880
LOCATION: In Abingdon.
FACILITIES: Open year round; 175 sites; water and bathroom facilities; sanitary station; electrical hookup; trailer village vehicle sites; laundry; swimming; fishing; tent camping.

Big Pool

HOLIDAY PINES CAMPGROUNDS
Pectonville Road
Big Pool, MD 21711
(301) 842-2159
LOCATION: In Big Pool.
FACILITIES: Open year round; 100 sites; water and bathroom facilities; sanitary station; electrical hookup; trailer village vehicle sites; laundry; food service; swimming; fishing; hiking; bicycle trail; tent camping.

College Park

CHERRY HILL CAMP CITY
9530 Rose Hill Ave.
College Park, MD 20740
(301) 474-5069
LOCATION: At I-95 (Capital Beltway and U.S. 1, take exit 27N, on left behind Holiday Inn).
FACILITIES: Open year round; 100 sites; water and bathroom facilities; sanitary station; electrical hookup; trailer village vehicle sites; laundry; tent camping.

Greensboro

HOLIDAY PARK CAMPGROUND
P.O. Box 81
Greensboro, MD 21639

(301) 482-6797
LOCATION: At intersection of Hwys. 313 & 314, go east on Boyce Mill 1 mi., then north 2 mi. on Diapers Mill Road.
FACILITIES: Open year round; 150 sites; water and bathroom facilities; sanitary station; electrical hookup; trailer village vehicle sites; swimming; boating; tent camping.

Lothian

DUNCAN'S FAMILY KOA KAMPGROUNDS
P.O. Box 7
Lothian, MD 20820
(301) 627-3909
LOCATION: On Sands Road, off Route 408 from Maryland 4.
FACILITIES: Open year round; 25 sites; water and bathroom facilities; sanitary station; electrical hookup; trailer village vehicle sites; laundry; swimming; tent camping.

Ocean City

BALI-HI TRAVEL TRAILER PARK
8902 Coastal Hwy.
Ocean City, MD 21842
(301) 354-5477
LOCATION: West of Ocean City on Route 90 to Isle of Wright Road.
FACILITIES: Open May - Nov.; 115 sites; sanitary station; electrical hookup; trailer village vehicle sites; swimming; boating; boat rental; fishing; hiking.

CAMP WISHING WELL
105 70th Street
Ocean City, MD 21842
(301) 289-7601
LOCATION: On Coastal Hwy., 6 blocks north of Route 90 terminus.
FACILITIES: Open year round; 158 sites; water and bathroom facilities; sanitary station; electrical hookup; trailer village vehicle sites; laundry; food service; swimming; boating; boat rental; fishing; bicycle trail.

EAGLES NEST PARK
Box 488
Berlin, MD 21811
(301) 289-9097
LOCATION: 1 mi. south of Ocean City on Route 611.
FACILITIES: Open year round; 186 sites; water and bathroom facilities; sanitary station; electrical hookup; trailer village vehicle sites; food service; swimming; boating; boat rental; fishing; bicycle trail; tent camping.

WHITE HORSE CAMPGROUND
P.O. Box 691
Ocean City, MD 21842
(301) 641-1102
LOCATION: Left on Route 586 from U.S. 50, then left on Beauchamp Road.
FACILITIES: Open May 15 - Sept. 30; 175 sites; water and bathroom facilities; sanitary station; electrical hookup; trailer village vehicle sites; swimming; boating; fishing; hiking; tent camping.

Rock Hall

ELLENDALE CAMPSITES

MARYLAND

CAMPGROUNDS (continued)

Rock Hall, MD 21661
(301) 639-7485
LOCATION: In Rock Hall.
FACILITIES: Open May 8 - Oct. 31; 130
sites; water and bathroom facilities; electrical
hookup; trailer village vehicle sites; laundry;
food service; boating; boat rental; hiking.

RESORTS & BEACHES

Ocean City

OCEAN CITY - Miles and miles of white
sandy beaches and boardwalks for sunning
and surfing. There's golfing, boating, amusement parks, and since it's the "White Marlin
Capital of the World," plenty of fishing, too.

BOATING AREAS

See State Parks.

BICYCLE TRAILS

ANTIETAM BATTLEFIELD TRAIL - 32.3
mi.; very hilly; 10-speed bicycle necessary.
    This loop encounters the abrupt ridges on
the Potomac's north bank, the rustic farm
country in and around Sharpsburg, the his-
toric Antietam Battlefield, and the C & O
Canal below Antietam Creek.
    Trail: Sandy Hook, left on Sandy Hook
Road, becomes Harpers Ferry Road, right on
Mills Road, left on Burnside Bridge Road to
Sharpsburg, straight on Route 65 to Antietam
Battlefield, left on Harpers Ferry Road to C &
O Canal, left on C & O Canal, cross Antietam
Creek Aqueduct, left to leave towpath at
Lock No. 34, right on Harpers Ferry-Sandy
Hook Road to Sandy Hook.

C & O CANAL TRAIL - 184 mi.; rough surfaces, temporary washouts from river flood-
ing; any bicycle.
    Because of the rugged nature of this trail
heavy-duty tires are recommended, as well as
a more sturdy bicycle.
    Trail: Cumberland to North Branch to
Oldtown to Paw Paw to Little Orleans to Hancock to Big Pool to Williamsport to Sandy
Hook to Brunswick to Point of Rocks to
Monocacy to Seneca to Great Falls to Georgetown.

D.C.-SENECA TRAIL - 22.5 mi.; hilly terrain;
10-speed bicycle recommended.
    This route comprises the shortest route to
Seneca.
    Trail: Washington Circle at K and 23rd
Street, northwest on Pennsylvania Avenue,
becomes M Street, cross Wisconsin Avenue,
bear right on Foxall Road, left on MacArthur
Blvd., right on Persimmon Tree Road, left on
River Road to Potomac Village, left on Route
112 to Old Stonehouse Youth Hostel.

EASTERN SHORE TRAIL - 29 mi.; any bicycle.

    A level and attractive tour, much of it
along marked bicycle lanes, through an
area of quaint little towns and fishing areas.
    Trail: Start in Easton, Maryland (south of
the Chesapeake Bay Bridge on U.S. 50), go
south on Route 333 along bicycle route located on marked shoulders of the highway to
Oxford. Take ferry to Bellevue, from Bellevue, take road straight toward Royal Oak, go
left on road to Newcomb, left on Route 33,
along bicycle route to St. Michaels, go back
to Newcomb along Route 33, at Newcomb,
stay left along Route 33, return to Easton.

See DELAWARE - Flatlands Trail.

FREDERICK'S COVERED BRIDGE TRAIL-
47.5 mi.; hilly terrain; 10-speed bicycle recommended.
    This loop takes the cyclist through two
covered bridges and the quiet back roads of
Frederick County.
    Trail: Staley Park, Frederick, North on
Oppossumtown Pike, right on Bethel Road to
Lewistown to Thurmont, east on Route 77 to
covered bridge to Route 77 to second covered
bridge to Route 77 to Woodboro to Walkers-
ville to Frederick.

See PENNSYLVANIA - Gettysburg-Catochtin
Park Trail.

LOCH RAVEN RESERVOIR TRAIL - 17 mi;
rolling hills; 10-speed bicycle recommended.
    The Loch River Dam.
    Trail: Loch River Road, to Dulaney Valley
Road (Peerce's Plantation), turn right to
Manor Road (turning left), right turns to Car-
rol Manor Road, to Sweet Air Road, to Patterson Road, to Long Green Pike, to Glenarm,
right on Glenarm Road, right on Cromwell
Bridge Road right on Loch Raven Road.

SENECA TO GETTYSBURG TRAIL - 136.6
mi.; any bicycle.
    An excellent loop for an extended tour
with the family, combining refreshing countryside and rich history.
    Trail: Seneca, left on River Road, left on
Montevideo Road, right on Sugarland Road,
right on Route 107, left on Route 118 to
Neelsville to Damascus to Mt. Airy to New
Windsor to Keymar to Thurmont to Emmitsburg to Gettysburg to Emmitsburg to Lewistown to Frederick to Dickerson to Beallsville
to Poolesville to Seneca.

SENECA HORSE COUNTRY TRAIL - 42 mi;
hilly terrain; 10-speed bicycle recommended.
    Connecting Rock Creek Park with rural
Montgomery County, this loop offers a pleas-
ant one-day tour or a connecting route from
Washington, DC to Seneca.
    Trail: Start at Rock Creek Recreation Cen-
ter on Beach Drive just north of the Washing-
ton, DC border in Maryland. North on Beach
Drive, cross East-West Highway, straight on
Jones Mill Road, left on Beach Drive, Stoney-
brook Drive goes straight here just after pass-
ing under Beltway, left on connecting spur,
Beach Drive continues north, cross Rockville
Pike, follow Grosvenor Lane, right Old
Georgetown Road, left Tukerman Lane, left
Falls Road, right Glen Road, right South Glen

BICYCLE TRAILS (continued)

Road, cross bridge, left continue on Glen Road, left Query Mill Road, right Esworthy Road, left Seneca Road which becomes River Road, continue on River Road for Old Stonehouse Youth Hostel just up hill. Retrace route on River Road, right continue on River Road (190) to Potomac Village, continue on River Road, right Persimmon Tree Road, left MacArthur Road, left Goldsbor Road, straight on Goldsboro Road, cross River Road, right Bradley Blvd., continue Wisconsin & Conn. Avenues; Bradley Blvd. become Bradley Lane, left on Brookville Road, right Shepherd Street, become Pomander Lane after crossing Turner Lane, right Leland Street, left Beach Drive, return to Recreation Center.

SHAWAN TRAIL - 20 mi.; hilly terrain; 10-speed bicycle recommended.

A loop tour of Baltimore County.

Trail: Begins at school parking lot on Church Lane, just off York Road, west on Church Lane to Texas, right on Beaver Dam Road which becomes Cuba Road, left on Western Run Road to Falls Road, a jog right, then left, on Butler Road, left on Mantua Mill Road, left on Tufton Avenue to Falls Road, to Shawan Road and retrace the outgoing route back to the start.

URBANA TRAIL - 60 mi.; hills, unpaved roads; 10-speed bicycle recommended.

Urbana situated adjacent to Interstate 70, is the jumping point for a fine day or weekend of cycling. This is hilly country dotted with homes, farms, and towns. You may run into a few short stretches of unpaved road. Your return route is somewhat longer.

Trail: Urbana to New Market to Woodville to Unionville to Oak Orchard to Weldon to Sam's Creek to McKinstry's Mill to Union Bridge to Centerville to Mt. Pleasant to McKaig to Urbana.

WORCESTER COUNTY TRAIL - 100 mi.; any bicycle.

A background tour of Worcester County, where the flat semi-aquatic topography lend a rare beauty to the land. The trail is marked and rides predominantly on paved secondary roads, with a few stretches of gravel and dirt.

Trail: Berlin, west on Berlin-Libertytown Road to Whiton to Pokomoke State Forest to Route 364 South to Pokomoke City, south on Our Swamp Road, left on Tull Corner Road, right on Payne Road, right on Brantley Road, right on Sheephouse Road, left on Steel Pond Road, right on Little Mill Road, left on Route 366, right on Birdhill Road, right on Taylor Lodge Road, left on Hudson Road, right on Paw Paw Creek Road to Basket Switch to Newark to Berlin.

TRAILS

Baltimore

TOUCH OF NATURE TRAIL - .32 mi. foot & Braille trail. This trail loops through an oak-hickory forest just a few miles west of Baltimore in Patapsco State Park. Honeysuckle

provides groundcover over the hilly terrain. A donation by the American Legion Auxiliary funded construction of the trail on state land, and the Maryland State School for the Blind assisted in route layout and design, which includes Braille signs and a pavilion for listening to taped interpretive lectures.

SKI AREAS

Braddock Heights

BRADDOCK HEIGHTS SKI WAY
Braddock Heights, MD 21714
(301) 371-7131
LOCATION: Near Braddock Heights.
FACILITIES: 1 T-bar; 2 tow ropes; ski instruction; ski rental; 250 ft. vertical drop; longest run, 1200 ft.; restaurants; lodging.

Oakland

WISP
U.S. 19
Oakland, MD 21550
(301) 387-5503
LOCATION: 8 mi. north of Oakland.
FACILITIES: 2 double chairlifts; 1 T-bar; 1 tow rope; ski instruction; ski rental; 610 ft. vertical drop; longest run, 2 mi.; restaurants; lodging.

AMUSEMENT PARKS & ATTRACTIONS

Bryans Road

SPECTACULAR RIDES
Route 1
Bryans Road, MD 20616
(301) 375-7676
FACILITIES: 14 major rides; 4 kiddie rides; 8 games; 3 refreshment stands; arcade; picnic facilities; fireworks; pay gate; free parking; open May 3 - Labor Day.

Ellicott City

ENCHANTED FOREST
10040 Baltimore National Pike
Ellicott City, MD 21043
(301) 465-0707
FACILITIES: 8 major rides; 2 kiddie rides; 10 walk thrus; 3 refreshment stands; picnic facilities; exhibits; free acts; pay gate; free parking.

Ocean City

JOLLY ROGER PARK
30th Street
Ocean City, MD 21842
(301) 289-6505
FACILITIES: 7 major rides; 8 kiddie rides; refreshment stands; kart tracks; miniature golf; golf driving range; free gate; free parking.

OCEAN CITY AMUSEMENTS
607 Boardwalk
Ocean City, MD 21842
(301) 289-3108
FACILITIES: 6 major rides; 3 kiddie rides; 15

MARYLAND

AMUSEMENT PARKS (continued)

games; 4 refreshment stands; haunted house; laser light concert; free gate; free parking; open Easter - Labor Day.

PLAYLAND AMUSEMENT PARK
65th Street
Ocean City, MD 21842
(301) 289-8353
FACILITIES: 12 major rides; 8 kiddie rides; 12 games; 5 refreshment stands; restaurant; arcade; shooting gallery; picnic facilities; miniature golf; pay gate; free parking; open Apr. 30 - Weekend after Labor Day.

TRIMPER RIDES AND AMUSEMENTS
Boardwalk at Division Street
Ocean City, MD 21842
(301) 289-9391
FACILITIES: 14 major rides; 13 kiddie rides; 2 fun houses; walk thru; 30 games; 3 refreshment stands; restaurant; shooting gallery; bathing beach; free gate; free parking.

STATE FAIR

Maryland State Fair
P.O. Box 188
Timonium, MD 21093
(301) 252-0200
DATE: August

NATIONAL PARKS

There are no National Parks in Maryland.

NATIONAL FORESTS

There are no National Forests in Maryland.

STATE PARKS

Headquarters

Department of Natural Resources
Maryland Park Service
Tawes State Office Bldg.
Annapolis, MD 21401
(301) 269-3761

Baltimore

PATAPSCO VALLEY STATE PARK
(301) 747-6602
LOCATION: 6 mi. west of Baltimore.
FACILITIES: Open year round; 150 sites; water and bathroom facilities; picnic area; fishing; hiking; environmental study area.

Bel Air

ROCKS STATE PARK
(301) 557-7994
LOCATION: 8 mi. northeast of Bel Air.
FACILITIES: Open year round; picnic area; boating; fishing.

Boonsboro

WASHINGTON MONUMENT STATE PARK
(301) 432-8065
LOCATION: 2 mi. east of Boonsboro.
FACILITIES: Open Apr. - Nov.; 13 sites; water and bathroom facilities; picnic area; hiking; environmental study area.

Crisfield

JANES ISLAND STATE PARK
(301) 968-1565
LOCATION: 1½ mi. west of Crisfield.
FACILITIES: Open year round; 50 sites; water and bathroom facilities; picnic area; swimming; boating; fishing; hiking.

Cumberland

ROCKY GAP STATE PARK
(301) 777-2138
LOCATION: 7 mi. east of Cumberland along U.S. 40.
FACILITIES: Open Apr. 1 - Oct. 15; 280 sites; sanitary station; electrical hookup; trailer village vehicle sites; picnic area; food service; swimming; boating; boat rental; fishing; tent camping.

Denton

MARTINAK STATE PARK
(301) 479-1619
LOCATION: 2 mi. south of Denton.
FACILITIES: Open year round; 60 sites; water and bathroom facilities; picnic area; boating; fishing; hiking.

Fork

GUNPOWDER   FALLS   STATE   PARK
(301) 592-2897
LOCATION: 2 mi. north of Gunpowder Falls.
FACILITIES: Open Apr. 1 - Oct. 30; picnic area; food service; swimming; boating; boat rental; fishing.

Frederick

CUNNINGHAM FALLS STATE PARK
(301) 271-7574
LOCATION: 12 mi. north of Frederick off U.S. 15.
FACILITIES: Open Apr. - Nov.; 31 sites; water and bathroom facilities; sanitary station; trailer village vehicle sites; picnic area; food service; swimming; boating; boat rental; hunting; fishing; hiking; tent camping.

GAMBRILL STATE PARK
(301) 473-8360
LOCATION: 6 mi. northwest of Frederick.
FACILITIES: Open year round; 45 sites; water and bathroom facilities; picnic area; fishing; hiking; environmental study area; self-guided trail.

Frostburg

DAN'S MOUNTAIN STATE PARK
(301) 463-5564
LOCATION: 9 mi. south of Frostburg.
FACILITIES: Open year round; picnic area; fishing.

STATE PARKS (continued)

Grantsville

NEW GERMANY STATE PARK
(301) 895-5453
LOCATION: 5 mi. south of Grantsville off
U.S. 40.
FACILITIES: Open May 1 - Oct. 15; 38 sites;
water and bathroom facilities; picnic area;
swimming; boating; boat rental; fishing; hiking; guided tour.

Hagerstown

GREENBRIER STATE PARK
(301) 739-7877
LOCATION: 10 mi. east of Hagerstown on
U.S. 40.
FACILITIES: Open year round; 200 sites;
sanitary station; trailer village vehicle sites;
swimming; boating; boat rental; fishing; hiking; environmental study area; tent camping.

Havre de Grace

SUSQUEHANNA STATE PARK
(301) 939-0643
LOCATION: 3 mi. north of Havre de Grace.
FACILITIES: Open Apr. 1 - Oct. 31; 70 sites;
water and bathroom facilities; picnic area;
food service; boating; boat rental; fishing; hiking.

Indian Springs

FORT FREDERICK STATE PARK
(301) 842-2504
LOCATION: Near Indian Springs, off I-70 via
Route 56.
FACILITIES: Open year round; 28 sites; picnic area; food service; boating; boat rental;
fishing; living history program; guided tour.

North East

ELK NECK STATE PARK
(301) 287-5333
LOCATION: 9 mi. south of North East.
FACILITIES: Open year round; 330 sites; water and bathroom facilities; picnic area; food
service; swimming; boating; boat rental; fishing; hiking; environmental study area.

Oakland

HERRINGTON MANOR STATE PARK
(301) 334-9180
LOCATION: 5 mi. northwest of Oakland on
County Route 20.
FACILITIES: Open year round; cabins; picnic
area; food service; swimming; boating; boat
rental; fishing.

SWALLOW FALLS STATE PARK
(301) 334-9180
LOCATION: 10 mi. northwest of Oakland
on County Route 20.
FACILITIES: Open year round; 125 sites; water and bathroom facilities; picnic area; fishing; hiking; environmental study area; guided
tour.

Ocean City

ASSATEAGUE STATE PARK
(301) 641-2120
LOCATION: 6 mi. south of Ocean City.
FACILITIES: Open year round; 311 sites; water and bathroom facilities; picnic area; food
service; swimming; fishing; hiking; guided
tour; self-guided trail.

Pisgah

SMALLWOOD STATE PARK
(301) 743-7613
LOCATION: 4 mi. west of Pisgah.
FACILITIES: Open year round; picnic area;
hiking.

Point Lookout

POINT LOOKOUT STATE PARK
(301) 872-5688
LOCATION: In Point Lookout.
FACILITIES: Open year round; 146 sites; water and bathroom facilities; picnic area; swimming; boating; fishing; hiking; environmental
study area.

Prince Frederick

CALVERT CLIFFS STATE PARK
(301) 326-4728
LOCATION: 14 mi. south of Prince Frederick.
FACILITIES: Open year round; picnic area;
fishing; hiking.

Queen Anne

TUCKAHOE STATE PARK
(301) 634-2810
LOCATION: 6 mi. north of Queen Anne.
FACILITIES: Open Apr. 1 - Dec. 5; 71 sites;
water and bathroom facilities; picnic area;
boating; fishing; hiking.

Skidmore

SANDY POINT STATE PARK
(301) 974-1249
LOCATION: Near Skidmore.
FACILITIES: Open year round; picnic area;
food service; swimming; boating; boat rental;
fishing.

Thayerville

DEEP CREEK LAKE STATE PARK
(301) 387-5563
LOCATION: 1 mi. north of Thayerville off
U.S. 219.
FACILITIES: Open year round; 113 sites; water and bathroom facilities; picnic area; food
service; swimming; boating; fishing; hiking.

STATE FORESTS

Department of Natural Resources
Maryland Forest Service
Tawes State Office Bldg.
Annapolis, MD 21401
(301) 269-3776

MARYLAND

STATE FORESTS (continued)

Cumberland

GREEN RIDGE STATE FOREST
LOCATION: 20 mi. east of Cumberland.
FACILITIES: Open year round; hunting; fishing; hiking; primitive camp sites.

Doncaster

DONCASTER STATE FOREST
LOCATION: 2 mi. east of Doncaster.
FACILITIES: Open year round; hunting; fishing; hiking.

Easton

SETH STATE FOREST
LOCATION: Southeast of Easton off U.S. 50.
FACILITIES: Open year round; picnic area; hunting; fishing; hiking.

Grantsville

SAVAGE RIVER STATE FOREST
LOCATION: 1 mi. south of Grantsville.
FACILITIES: Open year round; hunting; fishing; primitive camp sites.

North East

ELK LAKE STATE FOREST
LOCATION: Between North East and Elkton.
FACILITIES: Open year round; picnic area; hunting; fishing; hiking; primitive camp sites.

Oakland

SWALLOW FALLS STATE FOREST
LOCATION: 5 mi. northwest of Oakland.
FACILITIES: Open year round; hunting; hiking; primitive camp sites.

Pittsville

WICOMICO STATE FOREST
LOCATION: 2 mi. south of Pittsville.
FACILITIES: Open year round; picnic area; hunting; fishing; hiking; primitive camp sites.

Snow Hill

POCOMOKE STATE FOREST
LOCATION: Between Snow Hill and Pocomoke City.
FACILITIES: Open year round; picnic area; hunting; fishing; hiking; primitive camp sites.

Tasker Corners

POTOMAC STATE FOREST
LOCATION: 2 mi. east of Tasker Corners.
FACILITIES: Open year round; hunting; fishing; hiking; primitive camp sites.

HISTORIC SITES

Baltimore

BASILICA OF THE ASSUMPTION (1863) - First Roman Catholic cathedral built in the U.S. Located on Cathedral and Mulberry Streets.

BATTLE MONUMENT AND PARK - First war monument in the U.S., erected to those slain in War of 1812. Located on Calvert and Fayette Streets.

FORT MCHENRY - Scene of the writing of the Star-Spangled Banner during the War of 1812. Located on Fort Avenue.

STAR-SPANGLED BANNER FLAG HOUSE - Home of Mary Pickersgill, who made the flag which inspired the writing of the National Anthem. Located at 844 E. Pratt Street.

U.S. FRIGATE CONSTELLATION - First ship of the U.S. Navy. Located on Constellation Dock, Pier 1, Pratt and Light Streets.

Frederick

BARBARA FRITCHIE MUSEUM - Reconstruction of the home of an ardent Unionist immortalized in John Greenleaf Whittier's poem. Located at 154 W. Patrick Street.

ROGER BROOKE TANEY HOUSE - Residence of U.S. Chief Justice Roger Brooke Taney who wrote the majority opinion in the Dred Scott Decision, which held slavery was legal under the Constitution. Located at 123 Bentz Street.

Glen Echo

CLARA BARTON HOUSE - Home of the founder of the American Red Cross and her headquarters until 1904. Located at 5801 Oxford Road.

St. Clement's Island

ST. CLEMENT'S ISLAND - Impressive 40 ft. cross marks the site where the "Ark" and the "Dove" landed with the state's original settlers on March 25, 1634, and where Father Andrew White celebrated first Roman Catholic mass in Maryland.

HOSTELS

Baltimore

MT. VERNON YOUTH HOSTEL
222 W. Monument Street
Baltimore, MD 21201
(301) 383-1180
FACILITIES: Open year round; 30 beds for men and women; modern bathroom; nearest hostel: Washington, DC, 30 mi. southeast; overnight charges: $3; houseparent: John Weston.

Grantsville

NATIONAL HOTEL
Box 224
Grantsville, MD 21536
(301) 895-5052
FACILITIES: Open year round; 20 beds for men and women; modern bathroom; nearest

HOSTELS (continued)

hostel: Morgantown, WV; overnight charges: $3; houseparents: Judith Miller & Mark Silberstein.

Knoxville (Sandy Hook)

KIWANIS YOUTH HOSTEL
Rt. 2, Box 304
Knoxville, MD 21758
(301) 834-9252
FACILITIES: Open Apr. 1 - Nov. 1; 10 beds, men; 10 beds, women; modern bathroom; nearest hostel: Williamsport, 25 mi. west; overnight charges: $ 2.50 summer; $3 winter; houseparent: David Gilbert.

Williamsport

FALLING WATERS YOUTH HOSTEL
Rural Route 1
Box 238-B
Williamsport, MD 21795
(301) 223-9208
FACILITIES: Open year round; 16 beds, men; 10 beds, women; modern bathroom; nearest hostel: Cumberland, 40 mi. west; Knoxville, 25 mi. southeast; overnight charges: $2; houseparent: Pamela Parrot.

POINTS OF INTERESTS

Annapolis

U.S. NAVAL ACADEMY - Academy's chapel contains the crypt of Adm. John Paul Jones. Museum has portraits of American navel heroes, battle flags, weapons, ship models, and other naval relics. Full-dress parades held each Wednesday during school term. Located on Severn River.

Baltimore

BABE RUTH BIRTHPLACE AND MUSEUM- Slide presentation, wax figures, and memorabilia from life of baseball hero. Located at 216 Emory Street.

B & O RAILROAD MUSEUM - World's finest collection of historic railroad equipment. Located on Pratt and Poppleton Streets.

SAINT ELIZABETH ANN SETON HOUSE - Home of the first American-born saint. Located at 600 N. Paca Street.

Barnesville

AL-MARAH - World's largest Arabian horse breeding farm, where more than 300 purebred Arabian horses roam 2,800 acres of rolling pasture land.

College Park

COLLEGE PARK AIRPORT - Oldest airport operating continuously in U.S. In 1909, Wilbur and Orville Wright trained the world's first military aviators here.

Glyndon

WOOD GAIT FARM - Home of famous thoroughbreds, show horses and historic hunts.

Greenbelt

GODDARD SPACE FLIGHT CENTER - Hub of all NASA tracking activities. Also responsible for development of unmanned sounding rockets in basic and applied science. Two weeks advance reservation required. Located on Greenbelt Road.

MASSACHUSETTS

Massachusetts, rich in the history of early America, joined the Union in 1788 as the sixth state. The original "Mayflower," blown off course in a storm, landed at Plymouth in 1620 with its cargo of outcast Puritans who set up this country's first colony. Banished to American shores because of religious intolerance in England, the Puritans practiced their own kind of fanaticism culminating with witch burning at Salem.

As early as 1770, trouble erupted in the colonies, but dampened for a time when British troops fired on a defenseless crowd. Three years following the Boston Massacre, the famous "Boston Tea Party" was held. Then the "shot heard around the world" was fired at Lexington and Concord in 1775, signaling the start of the American Revolution.

With the abundance of historic sites in Massachusetts, tourism is now a significant contributor to the state's economy. Other industries include commercial fishing and manufacturing of electronic equipment.

State capital: Boston. State bird: Chicadee. State tree: American elm. State flower: Mayflower.

WEATHER

Massachusetts occupies 8,266 square miles, nearly one-eighth of New England's total area. The land surface is mountainous along the western border and generally hilly elsewhere. However, the Cape and some other sections of the coastal area consist of flat land with numerous marshes and some small lakes and ponds.

Climatic characteristics of Massachusetts

MASSACHUSETTS

WEATHER (continued)

include: changeableness in the weather, large ranges of temperature, both daily and annual, great differences between the same seasons in different years, equable distribution of precipitation, and considerable diversity from place to place. The regional New England climatic influences are modified in Massachusetts by varying distances from the ocean, elevations, and types of terrain. These modifying factors divide the state into three climatological divisions: western, central, and coastal.

Summer temperatures are delightfully comfortable for the most part. Average temperatures vary from place to place more in winter than in summer.

Average daily temperature for each month.

	Northwestern	Southwestern
Jan.	29.7 to 11.7	36.8 to 17.3
Feb.	31.9 to 12.9	38.9 to 19.2
Mar.	40.1 to 23.1	45.7 to 26.8
Apr.	54.5 to 33.9	57.8 to 35.1
May	66.4 to 42.3	68.3 to 44.1
Jun.	76.2 to 52.2	77.2 to 54.3
Jul.	80.7 to 56.6	82.0 to 60.2
Aug.	78.5 to 54.1	80.3 to 58.2
Sept.	71.0 to 47.5	73.1 to 50.8
Oct.	60.6 to 37.0	63.8 to 40.0
Nov.	46.2 to 29.3	51.7 to 31.9
Dec.	33.7 to 18.1	40.6 to 21.7
Year	55.8 to 34.9	59.7 to 38.3

STATE CHAMBER OF COMMERCE

Massachusetts Department of Commerce & Development
Leverett Saltonstall Building
Government Center
100 Cambridge Street
Boston, MA 02202
(617) 727-3221

STATE & CITY TOURISM OFFICES

State

Division of Tourism
Massachusetts Department of Commerce and Development
100 Cambridge Street
Boston, MA 02202
(617) 727-3201

Massachusetts Department of Commerce and Development
100 Cambridge Street
Boston, MA 02202
(617) 727-3321

STATE HIGHWAY DEPARTMENT

Executive Office of Transportation and Construction
One Ashburne Place
Boston, MA 02108
(617) 727-7680

HIGHWAY WELCOMING CENTERS

Charlton

CHARLTON CENTER - MA Turnpike, Interstate 290 east, south of Auburn..

West Burn

WESTBURN - MA Turnpike, Interstate 495 west, exit 11.

STATE POLICE

Department of Public Safety
Boston, MA 02215
(617) 566-4500

HUNTING & FISHING

Hunting

Licenses required by all persons, male or female, over 15 years of age for: Fishing (in all inland waters) and hunting (any bird or mammal). Trapping license, 12 years and over.

Minors between the ages of 15 and 17 inclusive must have written consent of parent or guardian to obtain a sporting or hunting license.

No license required by any legal resident of the Commonwealth or member of his immediate family for hunting, fishing or trapping on land owned or leased by him which is used principally for agriculture.

To qualify as a resident, a person must reside in the state 6 months prior to application.

All license stamps valid from Jan. 1 - Dec. 31.

Resident

Hunting, $8.25; paraplegic blind and mentally retarded hunting, free; sporting, $13.50; sporting and trapping - persons over the age of 70, free; trapping - adult, $11.50; trapping, minors 12-17 years of age, $6.25; alien hunting, $16.25.

Non-resident

Big game (including deer and bear), $35.25; small game (except deer and bear), $20.25; 3-day hunting commercial shooting preserve only, $16.25.

HUNTING & FISHING (continued)

Fishing

See hunting regulations above.

Resident

Fishing, $8.25; minor fishing (ages 15-17), $6.25; the blind, paraplegics and mentally retarded, free.

Non-resident

Fishing, $14.25; 7-day fishing, $8.25.

For more information contact:

Division of Fisheries and Wildlife
100 Cambridge Street
Boston, MA 02202
(617) 727-3151

CAMPGROUNDS

Private

Bolton

CRYSTAL SPRINGS CAMPGROUND
(617) 779-2711
LOCATION: Route 117.
FACILITIES: Open Apr. 1 - Oct. 15; 200 sites; water and bathroom facilities; sanitary station; electrical hookup; trailer village vehicle sites; laundry; picnic area; food service; swimming; hiking; tent camping.

Bourne

BAY VIEW CAMPGROUNDS
(617) 759-7610
LOCATION: Route 28.
FACILITIES: Open Apr. 15 - Oct. 15; 280 sites; water and bathroom facilities; sanitary station; electrical hookup; trailer village vehicle sites; picnic area; food service; hiking; tent camping.

Brewster

SPRAWLING HILLS PARK
(617) 896-3939
LOCATION: Off Routes 6A & 124.
FACILITIES: Open May 15 - Sept. 15; 300 sites; water and bathroom facilities; electrical hookup; trailer village vehicle sites; laundry; swimming; boating; fishing; tent camping.

SWEETWATER FOREST CAMPGROUND
(617) 896-3773
LOCATION: Off Route 124.
FACILITIES: Open year round; 164 sites; water and bathroom facilities; electrical hookup; trailer village vehicle sites; picnic area; swimming; boating; fishing; hiking; tent camping.

East Brimfield

QUINEBAUG COVE CAMPSITES
(413) 245-9525
LOCATION: Off Route 20.

FACILITIES: Open Apr. 15 - Nov. 1; 160 sites; water and bathroom facilities; sanitary station; electrical hookup; trailer village vehicle sites; laundry; picnic area; food service; swimming; fishing; hiking; tent camping.

East Wareham

MAPLE PARK FAMILY CAMPGROUND
(617) 295-4945
LOCATION: Glen Charlie Road.
FACILITIES: Open May 1 - Oct. 15; 400 sites; water and bathroom facilities; sanitary station; electrical hookup; trailer village vehicle sites; laundry; food service; swimming; boating; fishing; tent camping.

Gloucester

CAPE ANN CAMP SITE
(617) 283-8683
LOCATION: Atlantic Street.
FACILITIES: Open May - Nov.; 200 sites; water and bathroom facilities; sanitary station; electrical hookup; trailer village vehicle sites; food service; tent camping.

Middleboro

PLYMOUTH ROCK KOA KAMPGROUND
(617) 947-6435
LOCATION: Route 44.
FACILITIES: Open year round; 200 sites; water and bathroom facilities; sanitary station; electrical hookup; trailer village vehicle sites; laundry; food service; swimming; hiking; tent camping.

North Egremont

CAMP THUNDERBIRD
(413) 528-1810
LOCATION: Off Route 51.
FACILITIES: Open May - Nov.; 150 sites; water and bathroom facilities; sanitary station; electrical hookup; laundry; food service; swimming; boating; fishing; hiking; horseback riding; bicycle trail; tent camping.

North Truro

HORTON'S PARK
(617) 487-1220
LOCATION: S. Highland Road off Route 6.
FACILITIES: Open Apr. 15 - Oct. 15; 210 sites; water and bathroom facilities; sanitary station; electrical hookup; trailer village vehicle sites; laundry; picnic area; food service; tent camping.

NORTH OF HIGHLAND CAMPING AREA
(617) 487-1191
LOCATION: Head of Meadow Road off Route 6.
FACILITIES: Open May 30 - Jun. 15; 218 sites; water and bathroom facilities; trailer village vehicle sites; laundry; water skiing; tent camping.

NORTH TRURO CAMPING AREA
(617) 487-1847
LOCATION: Highland Road.
FACILITIES: Open year round; 200 sites; water and bathroom facilities; sanitary station;

MASSACHUSETTS

CAMPGROUNDS (continued)

electrical hookup; trailer village vehicle sites; laundry; food service; tent camping.

Oakham

PINE ACRES FAMILY CAMPING AREA
(617) 882-9509
LOCATION: Bechan Road.
FACILITIES: Open year round; 250 sites; water and bathroom facilities; sanitary station; electrical hookup; trailer village vehicle sites; food service; swimming; fishing; skiing; hiking; tent camping.

Plainfield

BERKSHIRE GREEN ACRES
(413) 634-5385
LOCATION: Grant Street off Route 116.
FACILITIES: Open year round; 175 sites; water and bathroom facilities; sanitary station; electrical hookup; trailer village vehicle sites; laundry; swimming; hiking; tent camping.

Plymouth

ELLIS HAVEN CAMPGROUND
(617) 746-0803
LOCATION: Federal Furnace Road.
FACILITIES: Open May - Oct.; 400 sites; water and bathroom facilities; sanitary station; electrical hookup; trailer village vehicle sites; laundry; food service; swimming; boating; fishing; hiking; tent camping.

INDIANHEAD RESORT
(617) 888-3688
LOCATION: In Plymouth.
FACILITIES: Open Apr. 12 - Oct. 29; 180 sites; water and bathroom facilities; sanitary station; electrical hookup; trailer village vehicle sites; food service; swimming; boating; fishing; water skiing; tent camping.

Rochester

CAPE COD KOA KAMPGROUND
(617) 763-5911
LOCATION: High Street, Route 58 on Leonards Pond.
FACILITIES: Open Apr. - Nov.; 200 sites; water and bathroom facilities; sanitary station; electrical hookup; trailer village vehicle sites; laundry; picnic area; food service; swimming; boating; fishing; hiking; bicycle trail; tent camping.

Savoy

SHADY PINES CAMPGROUND
(413) 743-2694
LOCATION: Loop Road, Route 116.
FACILITIES: Open year round; 150 sites; water and bathroom facilities; sanitary station; electrical hookup; trailer village vehicle sites; laundry; picnic area; food service; swimming; fishing; hiking; tent camping.

South Dennis

AIRLINE MOBILE HOME PARK
(617) 385-3616

LOCATION: Old Chatham Road.
FACILITIES: Open Apr. 15 - Oct. 15; 200 sites; water and bathroom facilities; sanitary station; electrical hookup; trailer village vehicle sites; food service; swimming; tent camping.

South Sandwich

PETERS POND PARK
(617) 477-1775
LOCATION: Cotuit Road.
FACILITIES: Open year round; 350 sites; water and bathroom facilities; sanitary station; electrical hookup; trailer village vehicle sites; food service; swimming; boating; fishing; hiking; tent camping.

South Wellfleet

MAURICE'S TENT AND TRAILER PARK FAMILY CAMPGROUND
(617) 349-2029
LOCATION: Route 6.
FACILITIES: Open May 26 - Oct. 15; 220 sites; water and bathroom facilities; sanitary station; electrical hookup; trailer village vehicle sites; food service; water skiing; tent camping.

Sterling

STERLING SPRINGS
(617) 422-7992
LOCATION: Ford's Road.
FACILITIES: Open Apr. 15 - Oct. 15; 150 sites; water and bathroom facilities; sanitary station; electrical hookup; trailer village vehicle sites; food service; swimming; fishing; hiking; tent camping.

Sturbridge

MASHAPAUG PARK CAMPGROUND
(617) 347-7156
LOCATION: Mashapaug Road, Route I-86.
FACILITIES: Open Apr. 15 - Nov. 1; 150 sites; water and bathroom facilities; sanitary station; electrical hookup; trailer village vehicle sites; swimming; boating; fishing; water skiing; tent camping.

STURBRIDGE PINELAKE FAMILY CAMPING AREA
(617) 347-9570
LOCATION: River Road.
FACILITIES: Open year round; 150 sites; water and bathroom facilities; sanitary station; electrical hookup; trailer village vehicle sites; picnic area; food service; swimming; boating; fishing; hiking; tent camping.

Vineyard Haven

MARTHA'S VINEYARD FAMILY CAMPGROUND
(617) 693-3772
LOCATION: Edgartown Road.
FACILITIES: Open May 30 - Oct. 15; 180 sites; water and bathroom facilities; sanitary station; electrical hookup; trailer village vehicle sites; laundry; fishing; water skiing; horseback riding; tent camping; lodging.

CAMPGROUNDS (continued)

West Brookfield

HIGH VIEW CAMPGROUND
(617) 867-7800
LOCATION: John Gilbert Road.
FACILITIES: Open May 1 - Oct. 15; 150 sites; water and bathroom facilities; sanitary station; electrical hookup; trailer village vehicle sites; food service; swimming; hiking; tent camping.

Westford

WYMAN'S BEACH CAMPGROUND
(617) 692-6287
LOCATION: Dunstable Road.
FACILITIES: Open May 15 - Oct. 15; 160 sites; water and bathroom facilities; sanitary station; electrical hookup; firewood; trailer village vehicle sites; picnic area; food service; swimming pool; tent camping.

RESORTS & BEACHES

Falmouth - Provincetown

CAPE COD AREA - A 75-mile stretch of Atlantic Ocean seacoast where you can go on a clambake any day of the year. Under the summer sun, ride the dunes, bask on the white sandy beaches, or cast a line into the salty surf.

Martha's Vineyard

MARTHA'S VINEYARD - An island world of beaches, moors, lighthouses, grey-shingled homes, flower-covered cottages and fishing villages. A 45 minute ferry ride from Woods Hole on Cape Cod.

Nantucket

NANTUCKET - An island haven that still retains much of its 19th-century whaling port heritage. Walk the cobblestoned streets lined with the mansions of sea captains and stop at shops filled with relics from the age of sailing ships. Then head for the shore where you can swim, fish or simply relax in the pleasant summer sunshine. Ferry service from Woods Hole and Hyannis.

BOATING AREAS

Blandford

COBBLE MOUNTAIN RESERVOIR
LOCATION: South of Blandford.
FACILITIES: Launching.

Eastham

HERRING POND
LOCATION: In Eastham.
FACILITIES: Launching.

Erving

LAUREL LAKE
LOCATION: Near Erving.
FACILITIES: Launching.

Hardwick

QUABBIN RESERVOIR
LOCATION: Near Hardwick.
FACILITIES: Launching.

Lakeville

ASSAWOMPSETT POND
LOCATION: Near Lakeville.
FACILITIES: Launching.

GREAT QUITTACAS POND
LOCATION: Near Lakeville.
FACILITIES: Launching.

LONG POND
LOCATION: Near Lakeville.
FACILITIES: Launching.

Lawrence

PONTOOSUC LAKE
LOCATION: Off Route 7.
FACILITIES: Launching.

Otis

OTIS RESERVOIR
LOCATION: Near Otis.
FACILITIES: Launching.

Pittsfield

ONOTA LAKE
LOCATION: West of Pittsfield.
FACILITIES: Launching.

Shrewsbury

QUINSIGAMOND LAKE
LOCATION: In Shrewsbury.
FACILITIES: Launching.

Webster

WEBSTER LAKE
LOCATION: In Webster.
FACILITIES: Launching.

BICYCLE TRAILS

See VERMONT - All State Tour.

See CONNECTICUT - Housatonic River Trail.

LEXINGTON-CONCORD TRAIL - 12 mi.; any bicycle.
    This historic trail is well marked and it leads right to Concord.
    Trail: Start at Lexington to Massachusetts Road to Hwy. 128 to Battle Road to Concord.

MASSACHUSETTS BAY TRAIL - 300 mi.; long distances per day; 10-speed bicycle recommended.
    Here is a chance to mix salt air and colonial history on a bicycle tour. Allow from 10 days to 3 weeks for this ride. Ferries operate during the summer only, so this is the time to

MASSACHUSETTS

BICYCLE TRAILS (continued)

make the trip.

Trail: Provincetown to Truro to Orleans to Hyannis to Plymouth to Brockton to Sherborn to Marlborough to Concord to Ipswich to Gloucester to Salem to Marblehead to Boston.

THE SPRINGFIELD TRAIL - 240 mi.; steep hills; 10-speed bicycle necessary.

The hills in New England can be very steep. A low gear is suggested, especially if you are heavily loaded. Best trips are in summer and fall.

Trail: Springfield to Granville to Canton, CT to Harwinton to Litchfield to South Canaan to Sheffield, MA to Stockbridge to Washington to Hinsdale to Williamsburg to Sunderland to Springfield.

TRAILS

Boston

DR. PAUL DUDLEY WHITE BICYCLE PATHS - 6.5 mi. foot trail. Located in the heart of the metropolitan Boston area, the trail is named for the late Dr. Paul Dudley White of Boston, who was a leading physician to President Eisenhower in the 1950's. The trail parallels the course of the Charles River from the dam on the river to Watertown Square on the Cambridge side and includes bridges across the Charles River as connectors. A five-minute walk off the trail would lead to urban Boston or Cambridge. Sites on or along the trail include Beacon Hill, Harvard University, Boston University, Massachusetts Institute of Technology, and a bird sanctuary.

FREEDOM TRAIL - 2.5 mi. foot trail. This trail is America's 76th National Recreation Trail. In the shape of a figure eight, the 2.5 mile-route links 19 historic buildings, sites, and burying grounds within downtown Boston. All of the buildings played an important role in the American Revolution and colonial life. The trail is marked by signs and a red line which is painted on the sidewalks. Approximate walking time, including visits to the sites, is 2½ to 4 hours.

Northfield

NORTHFIELD MOUNTAIN TRAIL SYSTEM - 5 mi. foot trail. Located at the Northfield Mountain Pumped Storage Station, the trail has gradual ascents and descents of the nearly 800-foot vertical rise. A variety of views and distant vista offer numerous panoramas of the Connecticut River Valley, the Berkshire Mountain foothills and the Green Mountains of Vermont.

SKI AREAS

Amesbury

AMESBURY SKI TOWS
Amesbury, MA 01002

(617) 388-9205
LOCATION: On Route 107A.
FACILITIES: 2 tow ropes; 2 pomas; ski instruction; ski rental; restaurants; lodging.

Ashby

MT. WATATIC
Ashby, MA 01431
(617) 386-7921
LOCATION: On Route 119.
FACILITIES: 2 T-bars; 2 tow ropes; ski instruction; ski rental; 550 ft. vertical drop; restaurants; lodging.

Boxborough

FLAGG HILL RECREATION CLUB
Boxborough, MA 01921
(617) 263-3711
LOCATION: On Flagg Hill Road.
FACILITIES: 2 double chairlifts; ski instruction; ski rental; restaurants; lodging.

Canton

BLUE HILL SKI AREA
Canton, MA 02021
(617) 828-5070
LOCATION: North of Route 128 on Route 138.
FACILITIES: 1 double chairlift; 2 J-bars; 2 tow ropes; ski instruction; ski rental; restaurants; lodging.

Charlemont

BERKSHIRE EAST SKI AREA
Charlemont, MA 01339
(413) 339-6617
LOCATION: Off Route 2.
FACILITIES: 4 double chairlifts; 1 T-bar; 1 J-bar; ski instruction; ski rental; nursery; 1180 ft. vertical drop; restaurants; lodging.

CHICKLEY ALPS
Charlemont, MA 01339
(413) 339-4802
LOCATION: Route 8A off Route 2.
FACILITIES: 1 T-bar; 4 tow ropes; ski instruction; ski rental; restaurants; lodging.

Dunstable

BLANCHARD HILL SKI AREA
Dunstable, MA 01827
(617) 649-6137
LOCATION: On Main Street.
FACILITIES: 1 T-bar; 3 tow ropes; ski instruction; ski rental; restaurants; lodging.

East Northfield

THE NORTHFIELD INN
East Northfield, MA 01360
(413) 498-5341
LOCATION: Off Routes 10 and 63.
The Inn is no longer in operation; however, it may be possible to use the slopes, which are geared for beginning skiers. No facilities are available.

East Pepperell

INDIAN HEAD SKI AREA
East Pepperell, MA 01437

SKI AREAS (continued)

(617) 433-2249
LOCATION: Off Route 111.
FACILITIES: 2 T-bars; 1 tow rope; ski instruction; ski rental; restaurants; lodging.

Franklin

KLEIN INNSBRUCK SKI AREA
Franklin, MA 02038
(617) 528-5660
LOCATION: Off Route 495.
FACILITIES: 3 double chairlifts; 1 tow rope; ski instruction; ski rental; restaurants; lodging.

Great Barrington

BUTTERNUT BASIN
Great Barrington, MA 01230
(413) 528-2000
LOCATION: Near Great Barrington.
FACILITIES: 3 double chairlifts; 1 T-bar; 3 tow ropes ; ski instruction; ski rental; nursery; restaurants; lodging.

Groton

GROTON HILLS SKI AREA
Groton, MA 01450
(617) 448-5951
LOCATION: Route 3 to Route 40.
FACILITIES: 6 tow ropes; 2 pomas; ski instruction; ski rental; restaurants; lodging.

Hamilton

HAMILTON SKI SLOPES
Hamilton, MA 01936
(617) 468-4804
LOCATION: On Moulton Street.
FACILITIES: 1 J-bar; 5 tow ropes; ski instruction; ski rental; restaurants; lodging.

Hancock

JIMINY PEAK
Hancock, MA 01237
(413) 738-5431
LOCATION: 14 mi. northwest of Pittsfield off Routes 43 and 7.
FACILITIES: 2 double chairlifts; 2 T-bars; 1 tow rope; ski instruction; ski rental; nursery; restaurants; lodging.

Haverhill

BRADFORD SKI AREA
Haverhill, MA 01830
(617) 373-0071
LOCATION: On S. Cross Road.
FACILITIES: 1 T-bar; 3 tow ropes; ski instruction; ski rental; restaurants; lodging.

Holyoke

MT. TOM
Holyoke, MA 01040
(413) 536-0416
LOCATION: Off Route 5 between Holyoke and Northampton.
FACILITIES: 2 double chairlifts; 2 T-bars; 1 J-bar; 1 tow rope; ski instruction; ski rental; nursery; restaurants; lodging.

Lenox

EASTOVER
Lenox, MA 01240
(413) 637-0625
LOCATION: Off Route 7.
FACILITIES: 1 double chairlift; 1 tow rope; ski instruction; ski rental; restaurants; lodging.

Leominster

PHEASANT RUN SKI AREA
Leominster, MA 01453
(617) 537-9293
LOCATION: On Exchange Street.
FACILITIES: 2 T-bars; 4 tow ropes; ski instruction; ski rental; nursery; 225 ft. vertical drop; restaurants; lodging.

Littleton

HARTWELL HILL SKI AREA
Littleton, MA 01460
(617) 486-4546
LOCATION: On Route 495.
FACILITIES: 4 tow ropes; ski instruction; ski rental; restaurants; lodging.

Marlborough

JERICHO HILL
Marlborough, MA 01752
(617) 485-9730
LOCATION: Off Routes 20 and 85.
FACILITIES: 2 tow ropes; restaurants; lodging.

Methuen

MERRIMAC VALLEY SKI AREA
Methuen, MA 01844
(617) 686-2021
LOCATION: On Hampshire Road.
FACILITIES: 1 T-bar; 2 tow ropes; ski instruction; ski rental; restaurants; lodging.

New Ashford

BRODIE MOUNTAIN SKI AREA
New Ashford, MA 02137
(413) 443-4752
LOCATION: On U.S. 7.
FACILITIES: 3 double chairlifts; 1 T-bar; 3 tow ropes; ski instruction; ski rental; nursery; 1200 ft. vertical drop; restaurants; lodging.

North Andover

BOSTON HILL SKI AREA
North Andover, MA 01845
(617) 683-2733
LOCATION: On Route 114.
FACILITIES: 1 double chairlift; 3 tow ropes; ski instruction; ski rental; restaurants; lodging.

Otis

OTIS RIDGE
Otis, MA 01253
(413) 269-4444
LOCATION: ¼ mi. west off Route 8 on Route 23.
FACILITIES: 1 T-bar; 1 J-bar; 2 tow ropes; 1 poma; ski instruction; ski rental; nursery; res-

MASSACHUSETTS

SKI AREAS (continued)

taurants; lodging.

Palmer

HEMLOCK HILL SKI AREA
Palmer, MA 01609
(413) 283-6308
LOCATION: On Springfield Street.
FACILITIES: 4 tow ropes; ski instruction; ski rental; 300 ft. vertical drop; restaurants; lodging.

Phillipston

SNOW HILL SKI AREA
Phillipston, MA 01331
(617) 249-9255
LOCATION: On Route 2.
FACILITIES: 1 T-bar; 2 tow ropes; ski instruction; ski rental; 200 ft. vertical drop; restaurants; lodging.

Pittsfield

BOUSQUET SKI AREA
Pittsfield, MA 01201
(413) 442-2436
LOCATION: Off Routes 7 and 20.
FACILITIES: 1 double chairlift; 1 T-bar; 5 tow ropes; 2 pomas; ski instruction; ski rental; nursery; 750 ft. vertical drop; restaurants; lodging.

Princeton

WACHUSETT MOUNTAIN SKI AREA
Princeton, MA 01541
(617) 464-2355
LOCATION: Off Routes 2 and 140 south.
FACILITIES: 2 T-bars; 1 tow rope; ski instruction; ski rental; nursery; restaurants; lodging.

Shelburne

MT. MOHAWK
Shelburne, MA 01370
(413) 625-2643
LOCATION: Near Shelburne.
FACILITIES: 2 T-bars; 1 tow rope; ski instruction; ski rental; restaurants; lodging.

Shrewsbury

WARD HILL SKI AREA
Shrewsbury, MA 01545
(617) 842-6346
LOCATION: Old Post Road between Route 20 and Shrewsbury Center.
FACILITIES: 2 T-bars; 2 tow ropes; ski instruction; ski rental; restaurants; lodging.

South Egremont

CATAMOUNT SKI AREA
South Egremont, MA 01258
(518) 325-3200
LOCATION: On Route 23.
FACILITIES: 3 double chairlifts; 2 T-bars; 1 J-bar; ski instruction; ski rental; nursery; restaurants; lodging.

JUG END
South Egremont, MA 01258 ¯

(413) 528-0434
LOCATION: Near South Egremont.
FACILITIES: 1 T-bar; 2 tow ropes; ski instruction; ski rental; restaurants; lodging.

South Lee

OAK 'N SPRUCE
South Lee, MA 01260
(413) 243-3500
LOCATION: Off Route 102.
FACILITIES: 1 tow rope; ski instruction; ski rental; restaurants; lodging.

Waltham

PROSPECT HILL SKI AREA
Waltham, MA 02154
(617) 893-4040
LOCATION: Off Route 128 from Winter Street Exit.
FACILITIES: 1 T-bar; slopes for beginning skiers; ski instruction; ski rental; restaurants; lodging.

West Cummington

BERKSHIRE SNOW BASIN
West Cummington, MA 01265
(413) 634-8808
LOCATION: On Route 9.
FACILITIES: 3 T-bars; ski instruction; ski rental; restaurants; lodging.

Westford

NASHOBA VALLEY SKI AREA
Westford, MA 01886
(617) 692-7025
LOCATION: On Power Road.
FACILITIES: 1 T-bar; 7 tow ropes; ski instruction; ski rental; restaurants; lodging.

AMUSEMENT PARKS & ATTRACTIONS

Agawam

RIVERSIDE PARK
Main Street
Agawam, MA 01001
(413) 786-9300
FACILITIES: 50 rides & shows; 7 kiddie rides; 3 walk thrus; 30 games; 30 food stands; restaurant; arcade; shooting gallery; roller rink; race track; picnic facilities; miniature golf; bowling alley; stadium; auto racing; orchestras; vaudeville; free acts; fireworks; pay gate; free parking.

Boston

REVERE BEACH
151-161 Boulevard
Boston, MA 02151
(617) 284-7300
FACILITIES: 14 major rides; 4 kiddie rides; fun house; 15 games; 5 refreshment stands; restaurant; penny arcade; shooting gallery; beach; racetrack; picnic facilities; miniature golf; free acts; fireworks; free gate; free parking.

AMUSEMENT PARKS (continued)

Bourne

BOURNE'S SPORTSWORLD
320 McArthur Blvd.
Bourne, MA 02534
FACILITIES: Arcade; golf driving range;
miniature golf; bumper cars; refreshment
stand; restaurant; souvenirs & novelties; free
gate; free parking.

Brewster

SEALAND OF CAPE COD (Attraction)
Brewster, MA 02631
(617) 389-9252
FACILITIES: Aquarium; dolphin show; refreshment counter; souvenirs & novelties;
free parking; pay gate.

Hancock

HANCOCK SHAKER VILLAGE (Attraction)
P.O. Box 898
Hancock, MA 01237
(413) 447-7284
FACILITIES: Authentic Shaker Village;
guided tours; pay gate.

Holyoke

MOUNTAIN PARK
Rt. 5
Holyoke, MA 01040
(413) 532-4418
FACILITIES: 15 major rides; 12 kiddie rides;
2 fun houses; 2 walk thrus; 3 arcades; 16
games; 5 refreshment stands; picnic facilities;
miniature golf; books orchestras; name bands;
vaudeville; free acts; fireworks; free gate; free
parking.

Hull

PARAGON PARK
175 Nantasket Avenue
Hull, MA 02045
(617) 925-0115
FACILITIES: 27 major rides; 17 kiddie rides;
walk thru; 9 games; 6 refreshment stands;
restaurant; penny arcade; shooting gallery;
beach; picnic facilities; miniature golf; free
acts; fireworks; free gate; free parking.

Lunenburg

WHALOM PARK AMUSEMENT COMPANY
Route 13
Lunenburg, MA 01462
(617) 342-3707
FACILITIES: 18 major rides; 12 kiddie rides;
fun house; 20 games; 5 refreshment stands;
restaurant; arcade; beach; roller rink; picnic
facilities; miniature golf; motor launch; free
acts; fireworks; free gate; free parking; open
Easter Sunday - Oct. 1.

North Dartmouth

LINCOLN PARK AMUSEMENT CO.
State Road
North Dartmouth, MA 02747
(617) 999-6984

FACILITIES: 24 major rides; 25 kiddie rides;
2 fun houses; 22 games; 8 refreshment stands;
restaurant; walk thru; penny arcade; shooting
gallery; roller rink; bowling alley; miniature
golf; golf driving range; picnic facilities; giant
slide; zoo; orchestras; name bands; free acts;
fireworks; free gate; free parking.

Salisbury Beach

DEAN & FLYNN AMUSEMENTS, INC.
Ocean Front
Salisbury Beach, MA 01950
(617) 465-7261
FACILITIES: 11 major rides; 11 kiddie rides;
2 fun houses; 2 walk thrus; 5 refreshment stands; 4 restaurants; arcade; shooting gallery; exhibits; orchestras; free acts; fireworks; free gate; free parking.

SHAHEEN'S FUN PARK
26 Ocean Front
Salisbury Beach, MA 01950
(617) 462-6631
FACILITIES: 15 major rides; 18 games; fun
house; 4 refreshment stands; restaurants; arcade; electric shooting gallery; miniature golf;
beach; fireworks; free gate; pay parking.

STATE FAIR

Massachusetts State Fair
Wilson Street
Spencer, MA 01562
(617) 885-2635
DATE: September

NATIONAL PARKS

There are no National Parks in Massachusetts.

NATIONAL FORESTS

There are no National Forests in Massachusetts.

STATE PARKS

Headquarters

Department of Environmental Management
Division of Forests & Parks
100 Cambridge Street
Boston, MA 02202
(617) 727-3180

Abington

AMES NOWELL STATE PARK
LOCATION: Routes 18 & 123.
FACILITIES: Open year round; picnic area;
boating; fishing; skiing; hiking; horseback riding.

Agawam

ROBINSON STATE PARK
LOCATION: North Street, Feeding Hills.
FACILITIES: Open year round; picnic area;

MASSACHUSETTS

STATE PARKS (continued)

swimming; hunting; fishing; hiking; horseback riding.

Ashland

ASHLAND STATE PARK
LOCATION: Route 135.
FACILITIES: Open year round; picnic area; swimming; fishing; skiing; hiking; horseback riding.

Boston Harbor

BOSTON HARBOR ISLANDS STATE PARK
LOCATION: Boston Harbor.
FACILITIES: Open year round; picnic area; swimming; boating; fishing; hiking; bicycle trail; primitive camp sites.

Chicopee

CHICOPEE STATE PARK
LOCATION: Exit 6, Massachusetts Turnpike.
FACILITIES: Open year round; picnic area; swimming; hunting; fishing; skiing; hiking; horseback riding; bicycle trail.

Clarksburg

CLARKSBURG STATE PARK
LOCATION: Routes 2 & 8.
FACILITIES: Open year round; 47 sites; water and bathroom facilities; picnic area; swimming; boating; hunting; fishing; skiing; hiking; horseback riding.

Dalton

WAHCONAH FALLS STATE PARK
LOCATION: Routes 8A & 9.
FACILITIES: Open year round; picnic area; fishing; skiing; hiking; horseback riding.

Holland

HOLLAND STATE PARK
LOCATION: Route 20.
FACILITIES: Open year round; picnic area; swimming; hunting; fishing.

Hopkinton

HOPKINTON STATE PARK
LOCATION: Route 85.
FACILITIES: Open year round; picnic area; swimming; fishing; skiing; hiking; horseback riding; handicapped access/restroom.

WHITEHALL STATE PARK
LOCATION: Route 135.
FACILITIES: Open year round; boating; fishing; skiing; hiking; horseback riding.

Huntington

CHARLES M. GARDNER STATE PARK
LOCATION: Route 112.
FACILITIES: Open year round; picnic area; swimming; fishing; skiing; hiking; horseback riding.

Ludlow

LUDLOW STATE PARK
LOCATION: Via Plumbley Street & Tower Road.
FACILITIES: Open year round; picnic area; skiing; hiking; horseback riding.

Oxford

BUFFUMVILLE STATE PARK
LOCATION: Route 12.
FACILITIES: Open year round; picnic area; swimming; boating; hunting; fishing; skiing; hiking; horseback riding.

Paxton

MOORE STATE PARK
LOCATION: Route 31.
FACILITIES: Open year round; hunting; fishing; skiing; hiking; horseback riding.

Plum Island

PLUM ISLAND STATE PARK
LOCATION: Route 1A.
FACILITIES: Open year round; hunting; fishing; skiing; horseback riding.

Ruthland

RUTHLAND STATE PARK
LOCATION: Route 122.
FACILITIES: Open year round; picnic area; swimming; boating; fishing.

Sharon

BORDERLAND STATE PARK
LOCATION: Massapoag Ave.
FACILITIES: Open year round; fishing; skiing; hiking; horseback riding.

South Dartmouth

DEMAREST LLOYD STATE PARK
LOCATION: Route 6.
FACILITIES: Open year round; picnic area; swimming; boating; fishing; skiing; hiking; horseback riding.

South Hadley

SKINNER STATE PARK
LOCATION: Route 47.
FACILITIES: Open year round; picnic area; skiing; hiking; horseback riding.

Sturbridge

WELLS STATE PARK
LOCATION: Routes 20 & 49.
FACILITIES: Open year round; 50 sites; water and bathroom facilities; sanitary station; trailer village vehicle sites; swimming; boating; fishing; skiing; hiking; horseback riding; tent camping.

Taunton

MASSASOIT STATE PARK
LOCATION: Off Route 18.
FACILITIES: Open year round; 130 sites; wa-

STATE PARKS (continued)

ter and bathroom facilities; electrical hookup; trailer village vehicle sites; swimming; hunting; fishing; handicapped access/restroom; tent camping.

Topsfield

BRADLEY PALMER STATE PARK
LOCATION: Route 1.
FACILITIES: Open year round; picnic area; fishing; skiing; hiking; horseback riding; handicapped access/restroom.

Townsend

PEARL HILL STATE PARK
LOCATION: Route 119.
FACILITIES: Open year round; 50 sites; water and bathroom facilities; trailer village vehicle sites; picnic area; swimming; hunting; fishing; skiing; hiking; horseback riding; tent camping.

Winchendon

LAKE DENNISON STATE PARK
LOCATION: Route 202.
FACILITIES: Open year round; 150 sites; water and bathroom facilities; trailer village vehicle sites; picnic area; swimming; boating; hunting; fishing; skiing; hiking; horseback riding; tent camping.

STATE FORESTS

Department of Environmental Management
Division of Forests & Parks
100 Cambridge Street
Boston, MA 02202
(617) 727-3180

Ashby

WILLIARD BROOK STATE FOREST
LOCATION: Route 119.
FACILITIES: Open year round; 21 sites; water and bathroom facilities; trailer village vehicle sites; cabins; picnic area; swimming; hunting; fishing; skiing; hiking; horseback riding; tent camping.

Assonet

FREETOWN STATE FOREST
LOCATION: Routes 24 & 79.
FACILITIES: Open year round; picnic area; swimming; hunting; skiing; hiking; horseback riding.

Brewster

R.C. NICKERSON STATE FOREST
LOCATION: Route 6A.
FACILITIES: Open year round; 435 sites; water and bathroom facilities; sanitary station; trailer village vehicle sites; picnic area; swimming; boating; fishing; skiing; hiking; horseback riding; bicycle trail; tent camping.

Brimfield

BRIMFIELD STATE FOREST

LOCATION: Route 20.
FACILITIES: Open year round; picnic area; swimming; boating; hunting; fishing; skiing; hiking; horseback riding.

Charlemont

MOHAWK TRAIL STATE FOREST
LOCATION: Route 2.
FACILITIES: Open year round; 58 sites; water and bathroom facilities; trailer village vehicle sites; cabins; picnic area; swimming; hunting; fishing; skiing; hiking; horseback riding; handicapped access/restroom; tent camping.

Chester

CHESTER STATE FOREST
LOCATION: Route 20.
FACILITIES: Open year round; picnic area; swimming; hunting; fishing; skiing; hiking; horseback riding.

Colrain

CATAMOUNT STATE FOREST
LOCATION: Routes 2 & 112.
FACILITIES: Open year round; hunting; fishing; skiing; hiking; horseback riding.

H. O. COOK STATE FOREST
LOCATION: Route 8A.
FACILITIES: Open year round; picnic area; hunting; skiing; hiking; horseback riding.

Conway

CONWAY STATE FOREST
LOCATION: Route 116.
FACILITIES: Open year round; hunting; fishing; skiing; hiking; horseback riding.

Douglas

DOUGLAS STATE FOREST
LOCATION: Route 6.
FACILITIES: Open year round; picnic area; swimming; boating; hunting; fishing; skiing; hiking; horseback riding.

Erving

ERVING STATE FOREST
LOCATION: Route 2.
FACILITIES: Open year round; 32 sites; water and bathroom facilities; trailer village vehicle sites; picnic area; swimming; boating; hunting; fishing; skiing; hiking; horseback riding; tent camping.

Fitchburg

LEOMINSTER STATE FOREST
LOCATION: Routes 2 & 31.
FACILITIES: Open year round; picnic area; swimming; hunting; fishing; skiing; hiking; horseback riding.

Florida

SAVOY MOUNTAIN-FLORIDA STATE FOREST
LOCATION: Route 2.
FACILITIES: Open year round; 45 sites; wa-

MASSACHUSETTS

STATE FORESTS (continued)

ter and bathroom facilities; trailer village vehicle sites; cabins; picnic area; swimming; boating; hunting; fishing; skiing; hiking; horseback riding; tent camping.

Foxboro

GILBERT F. HILLS STATE FOREST
LOCATION: Routes 1 & 140.
FACILITIES: Open year round; hunting; skiing; hiking; horseback riding.

Georgetown

GEORGETOWN ROWLEY STATE FOREST
LOCATION: Route 133.
FACILITIES: Open year round; hunting; fishing; skiing; hiking; horseback riding.

Goshen

D.A.R. STATE FOREST
LOCATION: Route 9.
FACILITIES: Open year round; 50 sites; water and bathroom facilities; picnic area; swimming; boating; hunting; fishing; skiing; hiking; horseback riding.

Granville

GRANVILLE STATE FOREST
LOCATION: Route 57.
FACILITIES: Open year round; 39 sites; water and bathroom facilities; trailer village vehicle sites; picnic area; swimming; hunting; fishing; skiing; hiking; horseback riding.

Hawley

HAWLEY STATE FOREST
LOCATION: Route 8A.
FACILITIES: Open year round; picnic area; hunting; skiing; hiking; horseback riding.

Ipswich

WILLOWDALE STATE FOREST
LOCATION: Linebrook Road.
FACILITIES: Open year round; boating; hunting; fishing; skiing; hiking; horseback riding.

Lee

OCTOBER MOUNTAIN STATE FOREST
LOCATION: Route 7.
FACILITIES: Open year round; 50 sites; water and bathroom facilities; boating; hunting; skiing; hiking; horseback riding; handicapped access/restroom; tent camping.

Lowell

LOWELL DRACUT STATE FOREST
LOCATION: Mammoth Road.
FACILITIES: Open year round; picnic area; hunting; skiing; hiking; horseback riding.

Martha's Vineyard Island

MARTHA'S VINEYARD STATE FOREST
LOCATION: On Martha's Vineyard.

FACILITIES: Open year round; hunting; skiing; hiking; horseback riding; bicycle trail.

Monroe

MONROE STATE PARK
LOCATION: Route 2.
FACILITIES: Open year round; hunting; fishing; skiing; hiking; horseback riding.

Monterey

BEARTOWN STATE FOREST
LOCATION: Route 23.
FACILITIES: Open year round; 12 sites; water and bathroom facilities; trailer village vehicle sites; picnic area; swimming; boating; hunting; fishing; skiing; hiking; horseback riding; tent camping.

Mt. Washington

BASH BISH FALLS STATE PARK
LOCATION: Routes 23 & 41.
FACILITIES: Open year round; hunting; fishing; skiing; hiking; horseback riding.

Nantucket Island

NANTUCKET STATE FOREST
LOCATION: On Nantucket Island.
FACILITIES: Open year round; hunting; skiing; hiking; horseback riding.

Northfield

NORTHFIELD STATE FOREST
LOCATION: Route 2A.
FACILITIES: Open year round; hunting; fishing; skiing; hiking; horseback riding.

North Reading

HAROLD PARKER STATE FOREST
LOCATION: Route 125.
FACILITIES: Open year round; 134 sites; water and bathroom facilities; trailer village vehicle sites; picnic area; swimming; boating; hunting; fishing; skiing; hiking; horseback riding; tent camping.

Otis

OTIS STATE FOREST
LOCATION: Route 23.
FACILITIES: Open year round; boating; hunting; fishing; skiing; hiking; horseback riding.

TOLLAND OTIS STATE FOREST
LOCATION: Routes 8 & 23.
FACILITIES: Open year round; 70 sites; water and bathroom facilities; trailer village vehicle sites; picnic area; swimming; boating; hunting; fishing; skiing; hiking; horseback riding; handicapped access/restroom; tent camping.

Peru

PERU STATE FOREST
LOCATION: Route 143.
FACILITIES: Open year round; hunting; fishing; skiing; hiking; horseback riding.

STATE FORESTS (continued)

Petersham

FEDERAL WOMEN'S CLUB STATE FOREST
LOCATION: Route 122.
FACILITIES: Open year round; picnic area; hunting; fishing; skiing; hiking; horseback riding.

PETERSHAM STATE FOREST
LOCATION: Route 32.
FACILITIES: Open year round; hunting; fishing; skiing; hiking; horseback riding.

Pittsfield

PITTSFIELD STATE FOREST
LOCATION: Via West St.
FACILITIES: Open year round; 25 sites; water and bathroom facilities; trailer village vehicle sites; picnic area; swimming; boating; hunting; fishing; skiing; hiking; horseback riding; tent camping.

Sandisfield

SANDISFIELD STATE FOREST
LOCATION: Route 57.
FACILITIES: Open year round; picnic area; swimming; boating; hunting; fishing; skiing; hiking; horseback riding; handicapped access/ restroom.

Sandwich

SHAWNE CROWELL STATE FOREST
LOCATION: Routes 3, 6A & 130.
FACILITIES: Open year round; 230 sites; water and bathroom facilities; sanitary station; trailer village vehicle sites; picnic area; hunting; hiking; tent camping.

South Carver

MYLES STANDISH STATE FOREST
LOCATION: Route 3.
FACILITIES: Open year round; 492 sites; water and bathroom facilities; sanitary station; trailer village vehicle sites; picnic area; swimming; boating; hunting; fishing; skiing; hiking; horseback riding; handicapped access/ restroom; tent camping.

Southfield

CAMPBELLS FALLS STATE FOREST
LOCATION: Route 272.
FACILITIES: Open year round; picnic area; hunting; fishing; skiing; hiking; horseback riding.

Spencer

SPENCER STATE FOREST
LOCATION: Route 31.
FACILITIES: Open year round; picnic area; swimming; hunting; fishing; skiing; hiking; horseback riding.

Upton

UPTON STATE FOREST
LOCATION: Westborough Road.
FACILITIES: Open year round; hunting; fishing; skiing; hiking; horseback riding.

Warwick

MT. GRACE STATE FOREST
LOCATION: Route 78.
FACILITIES: Open year round; picnic area; hunting; fishing; skiing; hiking; horseback riding.

WARWICK STATE FOREST
LOCATION: Athol Road.
FACILITIES: Open year round; hunting; fishing; skiing; hiking; horseback riding.

Wendell

WENDELL STATE FOREST
LOCATION: Wendell Road.
FACILITIES: Open year round; picnic area; swimming; boating; hunting; fishing; skiing; hiking; horseback riding.

West Cummington

WINDSOR STATE FOREST
LOCATION: Route 9.
FACILITIES: Open year round; 24 sites; water and bathroom facilities; trailer village vehicle sites; picnic area; swimming; hunting; fishing; skiing; hiking; horseback riding; tent camping.

Winchendon

OTTER RIVER STATE FOREST
LOCATION: Route 202.
FACILITIES: Open year round; 102 sites; water and bathroom facilities; trailer village vehicle sites; picnic area; swimming; hunting; fishing; skiing; hiking; horseback riding; tent camping.

HISTORIC SITES

Boston

BOSTON TEA PARTY SHIP - Full-scale working replica of one of the original Tea Party ships. Visitors may throw tea overboard. Located at Congress Street Bridge.

THE COMMON - Oldest public park in the country, founded in 1634.

PAUL REVERE HOUSE - Famous Silversmith and Patriot lived here 1770-1800. Located at 19 North Square.

Brookline

JOHN FITZGERALD KENNEDY HOME - Here on May 29, 1917, John Kennedy, 35th President, was born. Located at 83 Beals Street.

Cambridge

HARVARD UNIVERSITY - A 45-minute walking tour of the nation's oldest university.

MASSACHUSETTS

HISTORIC SITES (continued)

LONGFELLOW HOME - Poet Henry Wadsworth Longfellow's home for 45 years, 1837-1882. Located at 105 Brattle Street.

Charlestown

BUNKER HILL MONUMENT - Memorial to Battle of Bunker Hill, June 17, 1775; completed 1843. Located on Monument Square.

Concord

NORTH BRIDGE - Here, on April 19, 1775, the embattled farmers stood and "fired the shot heard 'round the world," beginning the American Revolutionary War.

RALPH WALDO EMERSON HOUSE - Famous poet's home. Located at 28 Cambridge Turnpike.

SLEEPY HOLLOW CEMETERY - The Alcotts, Ralph Waldo Emerson, Nathaniel Hawthorne, Daniel Chester French, Henry David Thoreau are among the noted citizens buried here. Located on Bedford Street.

WALDEN POND - Site of Henry Thoreau's cabin, where he wrote his famous book.

Dedham

FAIRBANKS HOUSE - Built in 1636, oldest known frame house in the country. Located on East Street.

Hingham

OLD SHIP CHURCH - Oldest surviving church in the original 13 colonies, and the only 17th century church in New England.

Lexington

LEXINGTON GREEN - Site of first battle of the Revolutionary War between Minutemen (see the statue), and British troops.

Lynn

MARY BAKER EDDY HOUSE - Home of the founder of Christian Science church where she wrote a major part of "Science and Health." Located at 12 Broad Street.

North Oxford

CLARA BARTON BIRTHPLACE - Founder of the American Red Cross was born here in 1821. Located on Clara Barton Road.

Plymouth

MAYFLOWER II - Replica of Pilgrims' ship. Exhibits aboard ship show what life was like on the Pilgrims' 66-day voyage in 1620. "Mayflower II" sailed from England to Plymouth in 1957. Located on Water Street.

PLYMOUTH ROCK - Landing place of the Pilgrims in December 1620, on Water Street.

Quincy

ADAMS NATIONAL HISTORIC SITE - Home of the Adams family for four generations, including John Adams, 2nd President, and John Quincy Adams, 6th President. Located at 135 Adams Street.

West Barnstable

WEST PARISH CONGREGATIONAL CHURCH - Built in 1717, oldest Congregational Church in the world. Located at Exit 5 on Mid-Cape Route 6.

HOSTELS

Brookline

STRATHMORE LODGING
45 Strathmore Road
Brookline, MA 02146
(617) 566-8936
FACILITIES: Open year round; 20 beds, men; 20 beds, women; modern bathroom; nearest hostel: Littleton, 30 mi.; overnight charges: $3.50; houseparents: Kevin & Carol Ferguson.

Cedarville

CAMP MASSASOIT
Sandy Pond Road
R.F.D. 5, Box 636
Plymouth, MA 02360
(617) 888-2624
FACILITIES: Open May 15 - Sept. 15; 30 beds, men; 20 beds, women; modern bathroom; nearest hostel: Hyannis, south; East Bridgewater, north; overnight charges: $2.50; houseparents: Michael & Marion Collins.

East Bridgewater

STANDISH MUSEUMS YOUTH HOSTEL
234 Central Street
East Bridgewater, MA 02333
(617) 378-2467
FACILITIES: Open year round; 50 beds, women; 50 beds, women; modern bathroom; overnight charges: $2.50 summer; $3 winter; houseparents: Ruth C. Thayer and Rev. Paul Rich.

East Brookfield

CAMP FRANK A. DAY
East Brookfield, MA 01515
(617) 867-3780
FACILITIES: Open Jun. 1 - Aug. 31; 10 beds, men; 10 beds, women; modern bathroom; nearest hostel: Littleton, 50 mi. northeast; Springfield, 30 mi. west; Sunderland, 45 mi. west; overnight charges: $2.50; houseparent: John Donovan.

Hyannis

MASSACHUSETTS, HY LAND YOUTH HOSTEL

HOSTELS (continued)

465 Falmouth Road
Hyannis, MA 02601
(617) 771-1585
FACILITIES: Open year round; 20 beds, men; 20 beds, women; modern bathroom; nearest hostel: Martha's Vineyard by ferry from Hyannis and Wood's Hole; overnight charges: $2.50 summer (Jun. 1 - Sept. 30); $3.25 winter (Oct. 1 - May 31); houseparent: Linda Bird.

Littleton

FRIENDLY CROSSWAYS YOUTH HOSTEL
Littleton, MA 01460
(617) 456-3649
FACILITIES: Open year round; 30 beds, men; 40 beds, women; modern bathroom; overnight charges: $2.50 summer; $3.50 winter; houseparent: Martin Vesenka.

Martha's Vineyard

LILLIAN MANTER MEMORIAL YOUTH HOSTEL
Holiday Hotel
West Tisbury, MA 02575
(617) 693-2665
FACILITIES: Open Apr. 1 - Nov. 30; reservation required; send self-addressed stamped envelope; phone reservations accepted when followed by deposit; 42 beds, men; 43 beds, women; modern bathroom; overnight charges: $3.75; houseparent: Richard Cohen.

Nantucket

STAR OF THE SEA YOUTH HOSTEL
Surfside
Nantucket, MA 02554
(617) 228-0433
FACILITIES: Open May 26 - Sept. 10; 22 beds, men; 38 beds, women; modern bathroom; nearest hostel: Hyannis, Martha's Vineyard; overnight charges: $2.50.

Newburyport

CIVIC CENTER YMCA
96 State Street
Newburyport, MA 01950
(617) 462-6711 or 462-8811
FACILITIES: Open Jun. 15 - Labor Day; 20 beds, men; 20 beds, women; modern bathroom; overnight charges: $2.50; houseparent: David A. Brown.

Pittsfield

CAMP KARU
73 North Street
Pittsfield, MA 01201
(413) 623-9764
FACILITIES: Open year round; 35 beds, men; 28 beds, women; modern bathroom; nearest hostel: Sheffield, 35 mi. south; overnight charges: $3 summer; $3.50 winter; houseparent: Rudolph A. Sacco.

Sheffield

MOUNT EVERETT YOUTH HOSTEL
Under Mount Road

Sheffield, MA 01257
(413) 229-2043
FACILITIES: Open May 14 - Oct. 15; 20 beds, men; 20 beds, women; modern bathroom; nearest hostel: Pittsfield, 35 mi. north; overnight charges: $2.50; houseparent: Mildred Roys.

Springfield

SPRINGFIELD COLLEGE CAMP
701 Wilbraham Road
Springfield, MA 01109
(413) 782-0461
FACILITIES: Open Jul. 1 - Aug. 31; 20 beds, men; 20 beds, women; modern bathroom; nearest hostels: Granville, 25 mi. west; Sunderland, 32 mi. north; overnight charges: $1.50; houseparent: Charles T. Wilson.

Sunderland

LITTLE MEADOW YOUTH HOSTEL
Falls Road
Sunderland, MA 01375
(413) 665-4609
FACILITIES: Open Apr. 15 - Oct. 15; reservation required; 15 beds, men; 15 beds, women; modern bathroom; nearest hostel: Springfield, 32 mi. north; overnight charges: $2; bikers and hikers only; houseparent: Mrs. Carol Baldwin.

Truro

LITTLE AMERICA YOUTH HOSTEL
P.O. Box 402
Truro, MA 02666
(617) 349-3889
FACILITIES: Open Jun. 18 - Sept. 15; 23 beds, men; 23 beds, women; modern bathroom; overnight charges: $2.50.

POINTS OF INTEREST

Concord

ORCHARD HOUSE - Diorama of scenes from Little Women, written here by Louisa May Alcott. Also location of Bronson Alcott's School of Philosophy. Located at 399 Lexington Road.

Lowell

WHISTLER HOUSE AND PARKER GALLERY - Birthplace of James Abbott McNeil Whistler. Etchings by Whistler displayed. Located at 243 Worthern Street.

Marblehead

ABBOTT HALL - Houses A.M. Willard's famous painting, "Spirit of '76." Located on Washington Street.

New Bedford

WHALING MUSEUM - Half-scale replica of whaling ship (big enough to board). Also world's largest collection of whaling gear, marine paintings, scrimshaw and other intriguing exhibits. Located at 18 Johnny Cake Hill.

MASSACHUSETTS

POINTS OF INTEREST (continued)

North Adams

NATURAL BRIDGE - Natural water-eroded bridge of rock formations formed before plant life lived above the sea in North America. Located on Route 8 north.

North Salem

SALEM WITCH MUSEUM - Experience re-creation of 1692 through historically accurate audio/visual presentation. Located at 19½ Washington Square.

Plymouth

PILGRIM HALL - Oldest historical museum in the country. Contains finest known authentic collections of Pilgrim artifacts. Located at 75 Court Street.

PLIMOUTH PLANTATION - Full-scale re-creation of the Pilgrims' village as it appeared in 1627. Located on Warren Avenue.

Salem

HOUSE OF THE SEVEN GABLES - Made famous by Nathaniel Hawthorne's novel. Built in 1668 by Captain John Turner. Six rooms and the secret staircase are shown to guests. Located at 54 Turner Street.

Sandwich

SANDWICH GLASS MUSEUM - Charming white clapboard building housing extensive exhibits of famous glass manufactured at Sandwich from 1825 to 1888. Located on Route 130 at Town Hall Square.

South Hadley

DINOSAUR LAND - Natural history museum with the world's largest dinosaur footprint quarry.

Springfield

NATIONAL BASKETBALL HALL OF FAME - Shrine of basketball, game invented by Dr. James Naismith in Springfield in 1891. Located at 460 Alden Street.

Sturbridge

OLD STURBRIDGE VILLAGE - A re-created New England country town of homes, shops, mills, schools, meetinghouses, general stores, illustrating American rural life before the Industrial Revolution.

MICHIGAN

Michigan, involved in trade and manufacturing from the beginning, joined the Union in 1837 as the twenty-sixth state. Early French settlers, interested in developing a fur trading industry, allowed the British to move into the territory and take possession by establishing permanent settlements.

Following statehood, Michigan quickly built roads, railroads and Great Lakes waterways to accommodate growing trade and industry. Politics entered the picture in 1854 when the pro-business Republican Party was created in Jackson as a result of internal strife within the Whig Party.

Today, Michigan is the world's leading producer of automobiles, and the home of the United Auto Workers, the second largest union in the country.

Tourism, aided by the recreation facilities offered at the four Great Lakes surrounding the state and the more than 10,000 inland lakes, is another major source of state revenues.

State capital: Lansing. State bird: Robin. State tree: White pine. State flower: Apple blossom.

WEATHER

Michigan is located in the heart of the Great Lakes region and is composed of two large peninsulas. Many smaller peninsulas jut from these two peninsulas into the world's largest bodies of fresh water to give most of Michigan a quasi-marine-type climate in spite of its midcontinent location.

The Upper Peninsula is long and narrow. The terrain of the eastern half varies from level to gently rolling hills. The western table lands rise to elevations generally between 1,400 and 1,600 feet. The Lower Peninsula, occupying about 70 percent of Michigan's total land area, ranges from quite level terrain in the southeast to gently rolling hills in the southwest with elevations generally between 800 and 1,000 feet.

While latitude, by determining the amount of solar insolation, is the major climatic control, the Great Lakes and variations in elevation play an important role in the amelioration of Michigan's climate.

The lake effect imparts many interesting departures to Michigan's climate which one would not ordinarily expect to find at a midcontinental location. Because of the lake water's slow response to temperature changes and the dominating westerly winds, the arrival of both summer and winter are retarded. Temperature extremes are modified by the lakes. In general, there is a decrease in average temperature from the southern section of Michigan to the upper northeastern border.

WEATHER (continued)

Average daily temperature for each month.

	Northeastern	Southern
Jan.	23.1 to 8.4	31.1 to 17.4
Feb.	24.0 to 7.4	31.9 to 16.5
Mar.	31.7 to 15.8	40.7 to 24.1
Apr.	46.4 to 29.6	55.9 to 35.5
May	59.9 to 39.3	68.1 to 46.0
Jun.	69.9 to 48.0	78.4 to 56.3
Jul.	75.6 to 53.5	83.4 to 59.9
Aug.	74.0 to 54.0	81.6 to 58.8
Sept.	64.4 to 47.1	73.0 to 51.0
Oct.	54.5 to 38.1	61.4 to 41.1
Nov.	39.6 to 26.9	45.3 to 30.5
Dec.	27.3 to 14.4	34.0 to 21.0
Year	49.2 to 31.9	57.1 to 38.2

STATE CHAMBER OF COMMERCE

Michigan State Chamber of Commerce
501 South Capitol Avenue
Lansing, MI 48933
(517) 371-2100

STATE & CITY TOURISM OFFICES

State

Michigan Travel Commission
300 S. Capitol Avenue, Suite 102
Lansing, MI 48926
(517) 373-2090

Office of Economic Expansion
Michigan Department of Commerce
Law Building
Lansing, MI 48913
(517) 373-3530

Local

Metropolitan Detroit Convention and Visitors Bureau
1400 Book Building
Detroit, MI 48226
(313) 961-9010

STATE HIGHWAY DEPARTMENT

Michigan Department of State Highways and Transportation
425 West Ottawa
Lansing, MI 48904
(517) 373-2090

HIGHWAY WELCOMING CENTERS

Claire

CLAIRE CENTER - U.S. 27.

Cold Water

COLD WATER CENTER - Interstate 69.

Crystal Falls

CRYSTAL FALLS CENTER - In city of Crystal Falls.

Detroit

DETROIT CENTER - 2260 Walter Street.

Easterday

EASTERDAY CENTER - Interstate 75, at Sault Sainte Marie.

Ironwood

IRONWOOD CENTER - U.S. 2.

Mackinaw

MACKINAW CENTER - Interstate 75.

Menominee

MENOMINEE CENTER - In city of Menominee.

Monroe

MONROE CENTER - Interstate 75.

New Buffalo

NEW BUFFALO CENTER - In city of New Buffalo.

STATE POLICE

Department of Public Safety
East Lansing, MI 48823
(517) 332-2521

HUNTING & FISHING

Hunting

Any person who has resided in the state for 6 months prior to date of application and is at least 17 years old is qualified to apply for a resident license. Members of the Armed Forces on active duty and officially stationed in Michigan may buy a resident hunting license regardless of how long they have been stationed in this state. This also applies to Armed Forces personnel officially stationed outside the state who were residents of Michigan when they entered the service.

Resident

Sportsman's license, $22.50; senior sportsman's license, $5.50; firearm deer, $7.50; senior firearm deer, $1; muzzle loading deer, $7.50; senior muzzle loading deer, $1; archery deer, $7.50; senior archery deer, $1; small game, $5; senior small game, $1; bear, $5; bear-dog permit, $2; camp deer permit, $10; put-take pheasant permit, $10; waterfowl

MICHIGAN

HUNTING & FISHING (continued)

stamp, $2.10; Zone 3 public access stamp, $1.

Non-resident

Firearm deer, $40; muzzle loading deer, $40; archery deer, $20; small game, $25; bear, $25; bear-dog permit, $10; camp deer permit, $10; put-take pheasant permit, $10; waterfowl stamp, $2.10; Zone 3 public access stamp, $1.

Fishing

See hunting regulations above.

Resident

Sportsman's license (also covers spouse; good for all species), $22.50; senior sportsman's license (also covers spouse; good for all species), $5.50; annual (also covers spouse; good for all species except trout, salmon), $5.25; senior annual (also covers spouse and the blind; good for all species), $.75; daily (covers resident and non-residents and spouses; good for all species and waters), 1st day, $1.25, each successive day, $1; trout stamp (covers both residents and non-residents and also spouses; needed to fish for trout and salmon under resident and non-resident annual licenses), $5.25.

Non-resident

Annual (also covers spouse; good for all species except trout, salmon), $10.25; daily (covers residents and non-residents and spouses; good for all species and waters), 1st day, $1.25, each successive day, $1; trout stamp (covers both residents and non-residents and also spouses; needed to fish for trout and salmon under resident and non-resident annual licenses), $5.25.

For more information contact:

Department of Natural Resources
P.O. Box 30028
Lansing, MI 48909
(517) 373-1220

CAMPGROUNDS

Private

Almont

WOODLAND WATERS CAMPGROUND
(313) 798-9907
LOCATION: 2½ mi. south of Almont on Route 53.
FACILITIES: Open year round; 224 sites; water and bathroom facilities; sanitary station; electrical hookup; trailer village vehicle sites; picnic area; swimming; boating; boat rental; fishing; tent camping.

Buchanan

THREE BRAVES CAMPGROUND
(616) 695-9895

LOCATION: 5 mi. northwest of Buchanan.
FACILITIES: Open May 1 - Oct. 31; 150 sites; water and bathroom facilities; sanitary station; electrical hookup; trailer village vehicle sites; laundry; food service; swimming; fishing; tent camping.

Cedar

LEELANAU PINES
(616) 228-5742
LOCATION: 4 mi. north of Cedar on County Road.
FACILITIES: Open May - Nov.; 150 sites; water and bathroom facilities; sanitary station; electrical hookup; trailer village vehicle sites; laundry; picnic area; food service; swimming; boating; boat rental; fishing; tent camping.

Coldwater

WAFFLE FARM CAMPGROUND
(517) 278-4315
LOCATION: 3½ mi. north of Coldwater via Union County Road.
FACILITIES: Open Apr. 15 - Oct. 31; 273 sites; water and bathroom facilities; sanitary station; electrical hookup; trailer village vehicle sites; picnic area; food service; swimming; boating; boat rental; fishing; tent camping.

Dowagiac

RODGERS LAKE RECREATIONAL AREA
(616) 782-3207
LOCATION: 3 mi. north on Indian Lake Rd.
FACILITIES: Open Apr. 15 - Oct. 31; 216 sites; water and bathroom facilities; sanitary station; electrical hookup; trailer village vehicle sites; laundry; picnic area; food service; swimming; boating; boat rental; fishing; tent camping.

Edwardsburg

CAMP WILDWOOD
(616) 699-5331
LOCATION: 4½ mi. east of Edwardsburg.
FACILITIES: Open May - Nov.; 154 sites; water and bathroom facilities; sanitary station; electrical hookup; trailer village vehicle sites; food service; swimming; fishing; tent camping.

Evart

STRAWBERRY LAKE RESORT, INC.
(616) 734-5313
LOCATION: 1 mi. north on Main St. from traffic light in Evart.
FACILITIES: Open May 1 - Oct. 15; 170 sites; sanitary station; electrical hookup; trailer village vehicle sites; laundry; food service; swimming; boating; boat rental; tent camping.

Gowen

LINCOLN PINES RESORT
(616) 984-2100
LOCATION: 13033 19 Mi. Rd.
FACILITIES: Open year round; 314 sites; water and bathroom facilities; sanitary station; electrical hookup; trailer village vehicle sites; laundry; picnic area; food service; swimming; boating; boat rental; fishing; tent camping.

CAMPGROUNDS (continued)

Grayling

PINE KNOLL CAMPGROUND
(517) 348-7194
LOCATION: 2½ mi. southwest of Grayling.
FACILITIES: Open Apr. - Nov.; 275 sites; water and bathroom facilities; sanitary station; electrical hookup; trailer village vehicle sites; laundry; picnic area; food service; tent camping.

Howell

TAYLOR'S BEACH CAMPGROUNDS
(517) 546-2679
LOCATION: 6197 N. Burkhart Road.
FACILITIES: Open Apr. - Nov.; 189 sites; water and bathroom facilities; sanitary station; electrical hookup; trailer village vehicle sites; picnic area; food service; swimming; fishing; tent camping.

Iron Mountain

RIVERS BEND CAMPGROUNDS
(906) 774-4007
LOCATION: ½ mi. south on Pine Mountain Road.
FACILITIES: Open May 25 - Oct. 1; 130 sites; water and bathroom facilities; sanitary station; electrical hookup; trailer village vehicle sites; laundry; swimming; boating; boat rental; fishing; tent camping.

Lupton

LOST VALLEY CAMPGROUND
(517) 473-2201
LOCATION: 3700 E. Sage Lake Road.
FACILITIES: Open year round; 216 sites; water and bathroom facilities; sanitary station; electrical hookup; trailer village vehicle sites; laundry; picnic area; food service; swimming; boating; boat rental; fishing; tent camping.

Mackinaw City

MACKINAW CAMPGROUND
(616) 436-5584
LOCATION: 3 mi. south of the Mackinaw Bridge on U.S. 23 & Lake Huron.
FACILITIES: Open Apr. 1 - Oct. 31; 600 sites; sanitary station; electrical hookup; trailer village vehicle sites; food service; swimming; boating; fishing; tent camping.

Montague

WHITE RIVER CAMPGROUND
(616) 894-4708
LOCATION: U.S. 31 north of Muskegon to Fruitville Road.
FACILITIES: Open year round; 150 sites; water and bathroom facilities; sanitary station; electrical hookup; trailer village vehicle sites; laundry; picnic area; food service; swimming; boating; boat rental; fishing; tent camping.

Newberry

KOA KAMPGROUND
(906) 293-5762
LOCATION: In Newberry.

FACILITIES: Open year round; 120 sites; water and bathroom facilities; sanitary station; electrical hookup; trailer village vehicle sites; laundry; tent camping.

New Hudson

HAAS LAKE PARK
(313) 437-8485
LOCATION: 2 mi. east of New Hudson on Grand River Ave., 1½ mi. south on Haas Road at end of road.
FACILITIES: Open year round; 192 sites; water and bathroom facilities; sanitary station; electrical hookup; trailer village vehicle sites; food service; swimming; boating; fishing; tent camping.

Otter Lake

OTTER LAKE KOA KAMPGROUND
(313) 793-2725
LOCATION: 2½ mi. east of Route 15 on Farrand Road.
FACILITIES: Open May - Nov.; 180 sites; water and bathroom facilities; sanitary station; electrical hookup; trailer village vehicle sites; laundry; picnic area; food service; swimming; boating; boat rental; tent camping.

Petersburg

MONROE COUNTY KOA KAMPGROUND
(313) 856-4972
LOCATION: U.S. 23 at Summerfield Road.
FACILITIES: Open Apr. 15 - Oct. 31; 199 sites; water and bathroom facilities; sanitary station; electrical hookup; trailer village vehicle sites; laundry; food service; swimming; boating; boat rental; fishing; tent camping.

Rodney

HORSEHEAD LAKE CAMPGROUND INC.
(616) 972-8770
LOCATION: 3 mi. northeast of Rodney off Route 20.
FACILITIES: Open May 1 - Oct. 1; 280 sites; water and bathroom facilities; sanitary station; electrical hookup; trailer village vehicle sites; laundry; picnic area; swimming; boating; boat rental; fishing; tent camping.

St. Clair

ST. CLAIR WILDERNESS CAMPGROUND
(313) 329-2742
LOCATION: 1299 Wadhams Road.
FACILITIES: Open year round; 412 sites; water and bathroom facilities; sanitary station; electrical hookup; trailer village vehicle sites; laundry; picnic area; food service; fishing; tent camping.

Traverse City

HOLIDAY PARK CAMPGROUND
(616) 947-5001
LOCATION: 6 mi. south and 1 mi. west on U.S. 31 at Silver.
FACILITIES: Open year round; 149 sites; water and bathroom facilities; sanitary station; electrical hookup; trailer village vehicle sites; laundry; picnic area; food service; boating; boat rental; fishing; tent camping.

MICHIGAN

CAMPGROUNDS (continued)

YOGI BEAR'S JELLYSTONE PARK
(616) 947-2770
LOCATION: U.S. 31 & Hwy. 72 to Four Mile Road, 2 mi. south to Hammond Road, 2 mi. east on Hammond Road.
FACILITIES: Open year round; 190 sites; water and bathroom facilities; sanitary station; electrical hookup; trailer village vehicle sites; laundry; picnic area; food service; tent camping.

RESORTS & BEACHES

Most of the state's resort activities center around the major lakes and include fishing, swimming, boating, water skiing and camping. (See National Parks, National Forests, State Parks and State Forests.)

BOATING AREAS

Michigan is surrounded by the Great Lakes: Lake Huron and Lake Erie on the east, Lake Michigan on the west, and Lake Superior to the north. In addition, there are more than 11,000 inland lakes. For Boating Areas in major recreational areas throughout the state, see National Parks, National Forests, State Parks and State Forests.

BICYCLE TRAILS

GARDEN PENINSULA TRAIL - 50 mi.; any bicycle.
At the northern end of Lake Michigan, one hundred miles west of the Straits of Mackinac, a peninsula extends into the lake from Upper Peninsula. This is called the Garden Peninsula, and here a cyclist can find miles of nearly flat roads.
Trail: Start in Thompson on U.S. 2, to Garden to Fayette State Park to Fairport and return to Thompson.

LOWER PENINSULA TRAIL - 170 mi.; any bicycle.
This route (Hwy. 72) stays away from the larger cities, is in a scenic area, and uses paved but less traveled farm roads.
Trail: Glen Arbor (on Lake Michigan) to Empire to Traverse City to Kalkaska to Grayling to Red Oak to Curran to Harrisville (on Lake Huron).

TRAILS

There are no National Trails System Foot Trails in Michigan.

SKI AREAS

Alamo

TIMBER RIDGE
(616) 694-9449

LOCATION: 3½ mi. west of Alamo.
FACILITIES: 1 triple chairlift; 1 double chairlift 9 tow ropes; 1 poma; 11 ski runs; ski instruction; ski rental.

Bellaire

SHANTY CREEK LODGE
(616) 533-8621
LOCATION: 2 mi. south of Bellaire off Route 88.
FACILITIES: 2 double chairlifts; 1 T-bar; 1 tow rope; 15 ski runs; ski rental; nursery; restaurants; lodging.

Bessemer

BLACKJACK
(906) 229-5115
LOCATION: 2 mi. northeast of Bessemer and 1 mi. north of Ramsay.
FACILITIES: 3 double chairlifts; 2 tow ropes; 12 ski runs; ski instruction; ski rental; restaurants.

Boyne Falls

BOYNE MOUNTAIN
(616) 549-2441
LOCATION: At Boyne Falls.
FACILITIES: 1 quad chairlift; 5 double chairlifts; 1 tow rope; ski instruction; ski rental; restaurants; lodging.

THUNDER MOUNTAIN
(616) 549-2441
LOCATION: 5 mi. northeast of Boyne Falls.
FACILITIES: 1 quad chairlift; 1 double chairlift; 1 tow rope; 1 poma; 12 slopes; beginner's area; ski instruction; ski rental; restaurants.

Branch

WARD HILLS
(616) 266-5202
LOCATION: 6½ mi. north of Branch, between Ludington and Baldwin.
FACILITIES: 6 tow ropes; 8 slopes; 2 trails; ski instruction; ski rental; restaurants.

Brighton

MT. BRIGHTON SKI AREA
(313) 227-1451
LOCATION: 1 mi. west of Brighton off I-96.
FACILITIES: 2 chairlifts; 7 tow ropes; ski instruction; ski rental; 220 ft. vertical drop; longest run, 1500 ft.; restaurants; lodging.

Buchanan

ROYAL VALLEY
(616) 695-3847
LOCATION: 2 mi. north of Buchanan.
FACILITIES: 2 chairlifts; 7 tow ropes; 1 T-bar; 1 J-bar; beginner's area; 14 runs; ski instruction; ski rental; 210 ft. vertical drop; restaurants; lodging.

Cadillac

CABERFAE
(616) 862-3300

SKI AREAS (continued)

LOCATION: 15 mi. west of Cadillac on Route 55.
FACILITIES: 2 chairlifts; 6 T-bars; 16 tow ropes; ski instruction; ski rental; restaurants; lodging.

Cannonsburg

CANNONSBURG SKI AREA
(616) 874-6711
LOCATION: At Cannonsburg.
FACILITIES: 1 quad chairlift; 1 triple chairlift; 1 double chairlift; 2 T-bars; 14 tow ropes; 34 ski runs; ski instruction; ski rental; restaurants; lodging.

Clare

SNOWSNAKE MOUNTAIN
(517) 539-6583
LOCATION: 9 mi. north of Clare on U.S. 27, left at Lake George exit.
FACILITIES: 1 T-bar; 5 tow ropes; 15 slopes; slopes for expert, intermediate and beginning skiers; ski instruction; ski rental; 200 ft. vertical drop; restaurants; lodging.

Clarkston

PINE KNOB
(313) 394-0000
LOCATION: 3 mi. east of Clarkston.
FACILITIES: 3 triple chairlifts; 2 double chairlifts; 7 tow ropes; 8 slopes; beginner's area; ski instruction; ski rental; restaurants; lodging.

Farwell

MOTT MOUNTAIN
(517) 588-2945
LOCATION: 1½ mi. south of Farwell off U.S. 10.
FACILITIES: 1 chairlift; 4 tow ropes; 5 slopes; slopes for expert, intermediate and beginning skiers; ski instruction; ski rental; 200 ft. vertical drop; restaurants; lodging.

Gaylord

MICHAYWE SLOPES
(517) 939-8719
LOCATION: 7 mi. south of Gaylord off old U.S. 27.
FACILITIES: 1 chairlift; 2 tow ropes; 2 pomas; 9 slopes; slopes for expert, intermediate and beginning skiers; ski instruction; ski rental; 215 ft. vertical drop; longest run, 1200 ft.; restaurants; lodging.

SYLVAN KNOB
(517) 732-4733
LOCATION: 5 mi. east of Gaylord on Route 44.
FACILITIES: 4 tow ropes; 6 pomas; 17 slopes; ski instruction; ski rental; 225 ft. vertical drop; longest run, 1500 ft.; restaurants; lodging.

Gladstone

GLADSTONE SKI PARK

(906) 428-9130
LOCATION: In Gladstone.
FACILITIES: 1 T-bar; 4 tow ropes; 5 slopes.

Grand Rapids

PANDO SKI AREA
(616) 874-8343
LOCATION: 12 mi. northeast of Grand Rapids on Route 44.
FACILITIES: 6 tow ropes; 7 ski runs; slopes for beginners; ski instruction; ski rental; restaurants; lodging.

Grayling

RASMUS-HANSON RECREATION AREA
(517) 348-9266
LOCATION: 1½ mi. west of Grayling off Route 72 and Route 93.
FACILITIES: 1 T-bar; 4 tow ropes; 9 slopes; ski instruction; ski rental; restaurants; lodging.

SKYLINE
(517) 275-5445
LOCATION: 4 Mile Road, Exit 251 on I-75 south of Grayling.
FACILITIES: 1 chairlift; 10 tow ropes; 12 slopes; slopes for expert, intermediate and beginning skiers; ski instruction; ski rental; 215 ft. vertical drop; longest run, 1800 ft.; restaurants; lodging.

Harbor Springs

BOYNE HIGHLANDS
(616) 526-2171
LOCATION: 4 mi. northeast of Harbor Springs.
FACILITIES: 2 quad chairlifts; 4 triple chairlifts; 1 T-bar; 17 runs; ski instruction; ski rental; restaurants; lodging.

NUB'S NOB
(616) 526-2131
LOCATION: 5 mi. northeast of Harbor Springs on Pleasant View Road.
FACILITIES: 4 double chairlifts; 2 tow ropes; 1 poma; 13 slopes; beginner's area; ski rental; restaurants; lodging.

Houghton

MOUNT RIPLEY
(906) 487-2340
LOCATION: ½ mi. east of bridge on Route 26.
FACILITIES: 1 double chairlift; 1 T-bar; 1 tow rope; ski instruction; ski rental; 420 ft. vertical drop; restaurants; lodging.

Iron Mountain

PINE MOUNTAIN
(906) 774-2747
LOCATION: At Iron Mountain.
FACILITIES: 3 double chairlifts; 3 tow ropes; 12 slopes; ski instruction; restaurants; lodging.

Iron River

BRULE MOUNTAIN
(906) 265-4957
LOCATION: 7 mi. southwest of Iron River.

MICHIGAN

SKI AREAS (continued)

FACILITIES: 1 chairlift; 1 T-bar; 4 tow ropes; ski instruction; ski rental; restaurants.

Ironwood

BIG POWDERHORN
(906) 932-3100
LOCATION: 3 mi. northwest of Bessemer and 4 mi. northeast of Ironwood on U.S. 2.
FACILITIES: 5 double chairlifts; 2 tow ropes; 18 runs; ski instruction; ski rental; longest run, 1 mi.; restaurants; lodging.

Ishpeming

AL QUAAL RECREATION AREA
(906) 486-4841
LOCATION: At Ishpeming.
FACILITIES: 3 tow ropes; 3 slopes; restaurants; lodging.

Kewadin

MAPLEHURST SKI AREA
(616) 264-9675
LOCATION: At Kewadin.
FACILITIES: 1 tow rope; 1 poma; 8 slopes; ski instruction; ski rental; restaurants; lodging.

Lakeview

WINTERSKOL
(517) 352-7920
LOCATION: West of Lakeview off Route 46.
FACILITIES: 6 tow ropes; 1 poma; 12 ski runs; ski rental; restaurants; lodging.

Lewiston

SHERIDAN VALLEY
(517) 785-4822
LOCATION: 7 mi. northeast of Lewiston.
FACILITIES: 1 tow rope; 2 pomas; 5 slopes; slopes for expert, intermediate and beginning skiers; ski instruction; ski rental; restaurants; lodging.

Mancelona

MT. MANCELONA
(616) 587-8631
LOCATION: ½ mi. northeast of Mancelona on U.S. 131.
FACILITIES: 1 T-bar; 5 tow ropes; 2 pomas; 18 slopes; slopes for expert, intermediate and beginning skiers; ski instruction; ski rental; 380 ft. vertical drop; restaurants; lodging.

SCHUSS MOUNTAIN
(616) 587-9162
LOCATION: 6 mi. west of Mancelona on Route 88.
FACILITIES: 1 triple chairlift; 2 double chairlifts; 1 T-bar; 1 tow rope; ski instruction; ski rental; restaurants; lodging.

Marquette

CLIFFS RIDGE SKI AREA
(906) 225-0486
LOCATION: In Marquette.
FACILITIES: 1 double chairlift; 2 T-bars; 2 tow ropes; 13 slopes; ski instruction; ski rental; 600 ft. vertical drop; restaurants; lodging.

Mio

MIO MOUNTAIN
(517) 826-5569
LOCATION: 1 mi. west of Mio off Route 72.
FACILITIES: 4 tow ropes; 4 slopes; beginner's area; ski instruction; ski rental; 250 ft. vertical drop; longest run, 1500 ft.; restaurants; lodging.

Ontonagon

PORCUPINE MOUNTAIN
(906) 885-5170
LOCATION: 17 mi. west of Ontonagon.
FACILITIES: 1 double chairlift; 2 T-bars; 2 tow ropes; 10 slopes; ski rental; 600 ft. vertical drop; longest run, 6200 ft.

Oxford

MT. GRAMPIAN
(313) 628-2450
LOCATION: 2 mi. east of Oxford on Lakeville Road, off Route 24.
FACILITIES: 1 double chairlift; 1 J-bar; 8 tow ropes; ski instruction; ski rental; restaurants; lodging.

Pontiac

ALPINE VALLEY
(313) 887-2180
LOCATION: On Route 59, 10 mi. west of Pontiac.
FACILITIES: 9 double chairlifts; 11 tow ropes; 18 slopes; ski instruction; ski rental; longest run, 1500 ft.; restaurants; lodging.

MT. HOLLY
(313) 634-8260
LOCATION: 15 mi. north of Pontiac.
FACILITIES: 1 triple chairlift; 5 double chairlifts; 10 tow ropes; beginner's area; ski instruction; ski rental; restaurants; lodging.

Saginaw

APPLE MOUNTAIN
(517) 781-0170
LOCATION: 5 mi. northwest of Saginaw off Route 47.
FACILITIES: 10 tow ropes; 10 slopes; ski instruction; ski rental; 200 ft. vertical drop; longest run, 1000 ft.; restaurants; lodging.

Spruce

MT. MARIA
(517) 736-8377
LOCATION: In Spruce, at south end of Hubbard Lake.
FACILITIES: 1 double chairlift; 3 tow ropes; 1 poma; 7 slopes; ski instruction; ski rental; 285 ft. vertical drop; longest run, 4500 ft.; restaurants; lodging.

Thompsonville

CRYSTAL MOUNTAIN

SKI AREAS (continued)

(616) 378-2911
LOCATION: 2 mi. west of Thompsonville on Route 115.
FACILITIES: 1 quad chairlift; 2 double chairlifts; 2 tow ropes; 18 ski runs; slopes for expert, intermediate and beginning skiers; ski instruction; ski rental; nursery; restaurants; lodging.

Three Rivers

SWISS VALLEY
(616) 244-5635
LOCATION: 10 mi. west of Three Rivers off Route 60.
FACILITIES: 1 T-bar; 3 tow ropes; 1 poma; 14 slopes; slopes for expert, intermediate and beginning skiers; ski instruction; ski rental; restaurants; lodging.

Traverse City

SUGAR LOAF MOUNTAIN
(616) 228-5461
LOCATION: 18 mi. northwest of Traverse City.
FACILITIES: 5 double chairlifts; 1 J-bar; 23 ski runs; slopes for expert, intermediate and beginning skiers; ski instruction; ski rental; restaurants; lodging.

TRAVERSE CITY HOLIDAY
(616) 938-1360
LOCATION: 5 mi. east of Traverse City on U.S. 31 north.
FACILITIES: 2 T-bars; 5 tow ropes; 12 slopes; slopes for expert, intermediate and beginning skiers; ski instruction; ski rental; restaurants; lodging.

Vulcan

VULCAN, U.S.A.
(906) 563-9222
LOCATION: At Vulcan.
FACILITIES: 2 double chairlifts; 1 tow rope; 9 slopes; slopes for expert, intermediate and beginning skiers; ski instruction; ski rental; restaurants; lodging.

Wakefield

INDIANHEAD MOUNTAIN
(906) 229-5181
LOCATION: 9 mi. east of Ironwood, north of U.S. 2 between Bessemer and Wakefield.
FACILITIES: 1 quad chairlift; 1 triple chairlift; 2 double chairlifts; 2 T-bars; 10 runs; 5 slopes; slopes for expert, intermediate and beginning skiers; ski instruction; ski rental; 638 ft. vertical drop; longest run, 1 mi.; restaurants; lodging.

Walloon Lake

WALLOON HILLS
(616) 549-2441
LOCATION: 4½ mi. east of Walloon Lake junction of U.S. 131 and Route 75.
FACILITIES: Open weekends; quad chairlift; poma; 2 tow ropes; 10 slopes; ski instruction; restaurants; lodging.

AMUSEMENT PARKS & ATTRACTIONS

Detroit

BOB-LO ISLAND AMUSEMENT PARK
Michigan Ave. & Hwy. 18
Detroit, MI 48226
(313) 736-2194
FACILITIES: 30 major rides; 10 kiddie rides; 2 fun houses; 15 refreshment stands; restaurant; arcade; shooting gallery; roller rink; marina; miniature golf; ponies; excursion boats; picnic facilities; exhibits; stage shows; zoo; free acts; pay gate; pay parking.

EDGEWATER PARK
23500 W. 7 Mile Road
Detroit, MI 48219
(313) 731-2660
FACILITIES: 23 major rides; 5 kiddie rides; 2 fun houses; 15 games; 7 refreshment stands; penny arcade; shooting gallery; miniature golf; picnic facilities; free acts; name bands; vaudeville; pay gate; pay parking.

Muskegon

DEER PARK FUNLAND (Attraction)
4750 Whitehall Road
Muskegon, MI 49445
(616) 766-3377
FACILITIES: 8 major rides; 2 kiddie rides; 2 refreshment stands; 6 games; exhibits; arcade; souvenir shop; picnic facilities; zoo; pay gate; free parking; open May 22 - Sept. 6.

Ossineke

DINOSAUR GARDENS (Attraction)
11168 U.S. 23 S.
Ossineke, MI 49766
(517) 471-2181
FACILITIES: Prehistoric zoo; museum; exhibits; pay gate; open May 15 - Oct. 15.

Richmond

KING ANIMALAND PARK
62000 Gratiot Avenue
Richmond, MI 48062
(313) 749-5572
FACILITIES: 6 major rides; 9 kiddie rides; fun house; 9 games; refreshment stand; restaurant; souvenir shop; picnic facilities; free circus shows daily; magic show; children's zoo; free acts; pay gate; free parking; open May 28 - Sept. 5.

STATE FAIR

Michigan State Fair
State Fairgrounds
Detroit, MI 48203
(313) 368-1000
DATE: August

MICHIGAN

NATIONAL PARKS

Houghton

ISLE ROYALE NATIONAL PARK (Island)
Houghton, MI 49931
(906) 482-3310

BEAVER ISLAND
LOCATION: Washington Harbor.
FACILITIES: Open May - Oct.; limit of stay:
3 days; 3 sites; cabins; picnic area; food service; boating; boat rental; fishing; hiking; exhibit; NPS guided tour; self-guiding tour; boat access; lodging.

BELLE ISLE
LOCATION: North side.
FACILITIES: Open May - Oct.; limit of stay:
7 days; 12 sites; cabins; picnic area; boating; boat rental; fishing; hiking; exhibit; NPS guided tour; self-guiding tour; boat access; lodging.

BIRCH ISLAND
LOCATION: North side.
FACILITIES: Open May - Oct.; limit of stay:
3 days; 1 site; cabins; picnic area; boating; boat rental; fishing; hiking; exhibit; NPS guided tour; self-guiding tour; boat access; lodging.

CARIBOU ISLAND
LOCATION: Rock Harbor.
FACILITIES: Open May - Oct.; limit of stay:
3 days; 4 sites; cabins; picnic area; boating; boat rental; fishing; hiking; exhibit; NPS guided tour; self-guiding tour; boat access; lodging.

CHICKENBONE LAKE
LOCATION: Inland.
FACILITIES: Open May - Oct.; limit of stay:
2 days; 5 sites; group camps: 3; cabins; picnic area; fishing; hiking; exhibit; NPS guided tour; self-guiding tour; trail access; lodging.

CHIPPEWA HARBOR
LOCATION: South side.
FACILITIES: Open May - Oct.; limit of stay:
7 days; 4 sites; group camps: 2; cabins; picnic area; boating; boat rental; fishing; hiking; exhibit; NPS guided tour; self-guiding tour; boat and trail access; lodging.

DAISY FARM
LOCATION: Rock Harbor.
FACILITIES: Open May - Oct.; limit of stay:
3 days; 23 sites; group camps: 3; cabins; picnic area; boating; boat rental; fishing; hiking; exhibits; NPS guided tour; self-guiding tour; boat and trail access; lodging.

DUNCAN BAY
LOCATION: North side.
FACILITIES: Open May - Oct.; limit of stay:
7 days; 3 sites; cabins; picnic area; boating; boat rental; fishing; hiking; exhibit; NPS guided tour; self-guiding tour; boat access; lodging.

DUNCAN NARROWS
LOCATION: North side.
FACILITIES: Open May - Oct.; limit of stay:

7 days; 2 sites; cabins; picnic area; boating; boat rental; fishing; hiking; exhibit; NPS guided tour; self-guiding tour; boat access; lodging.

EAST CHICKENBONE LAKE
LOCATION: Inland.
FACILITIES: Open May - Oct.; limit of stay:
2 days; 6 sites; group camps: 3; cabins; picnic area; fishing; hiking; exhibit; NPS guided tour; self-guiding tour; trail access; lodging.

FELTMAN ISLAND
LOCATION: Inland.
FACILITIES: Open May - Oct.; limit of stay:
3 days; 3 sites; group camps: 3; cabins; picnic area; fishing; hiking; exhibit; NPS guided tour; self-guiding tour; trail access; lodging.

GRACE ISLAND
LOCATION: Grace Harbor.
FACILITIES: Open May - Oct.; limit of stay:
3 days; 2 sites; cabins; picnic area; boating; boat rental; fishing; hiking; exhibit; NPS guided tour; self-guiding tour; boat access; lodging.

HATCHET LAKE
LOCATION: Inland.
FACILITIES: Open May - Oct.; limit of stay:
2 days; 4 sites; group camps: 3; cabins; picnic area; fishing; hiking; exhibit; NPS guided tour; self-guiding tour; trail access; lodging.

HAY BAY
LOCATION: South side.
FACILITIES: Open May - Oct.; limit of stay:
3 days; 2 sites; cabins; picnic area; boating; fishing; hiking; exhibit; NPS guided tour; self-guiding tour; boat access; lodging.

HUGGININ CORE
LOCATION: Northwest end.
FACILITIES: Open May - Oct.; limit of stay:
2 days; 5 sites; cabins; picnic area; boating; boat rental; fishing; hiking; exhibit; NPS guided tour; self-guiding tour; boat and trail access; lodging.

ISLAND MINE
LOCATION: Inland.
FACILITIES: Open May - Oct.; limit of stay:
2 days; 6 sites; group camps: 3; cabins; picnic area; fishing; hiking; exhibit; NPS guided tour; self-guiding tour; trail access; lodging.

LAKE RICHIE
LOCATION: Inland.
FACILITIES: Open May - Oct.; limit of stay:
2 days; 3 sites; group camps: 2; cabins; picnic area; fishing; hiking; exhibit; NPS guided tour; self-guiding tour; trail access.

LANE COVE
LOCATION: Inland.
FACILITIES: Open May - Oct.; limit of stay:
2 days; 3 sites; cabins; picnic area; fishing; hiking; exhibits; NPS guided tour; self-guiding tour; trail access; lodging.

LITTLE TODD HARBOR
LOCATION: Inland.
FACILITIES: Open May - Oct.; limit of stay:
2 days; 3 sites; cabins; picnic area; fishing;

NATIONAL PARKS (continued)

...king; exhibit; NPS guided tour; self-guiding ...ur; trail access; lodging.

...CCARGO COVE
LOCATION: North side.
FACILITIES: Open May - Oct.; limit of stay: ...days; 8 sites; group camps: 2; cabins; picnic ...rea; boating; boat rental; fishing; hiking; ex...ibit; NPS guided tour; self-guiding tour; boat ...nd trail access; lodging.

...ALONE BAY
LOCATION: South side.
...ACILITIES: Open May - Oct.; limit of stay: ...days; 8 sites; group camps: 3; cabins; picnic ...rea; boating; boat rental; fishing; hiking; ex...ibit; NPS guided tour; self-guiding tour; boat ...nd trail access; lodging.

...ERRITT LANE
LOCATION: Northeast end.
...ACILITIES: Open May - Oct.; limit of stay: ...days; 2 sites; cabins; picnic area; boating; ...shing; hiking; exhibit; NPS guided tour; self-...uiding tour; boat access; lodging.

...OSKEY BASIN
LOCATION: Rock Harbor.
...ACILITIES: Open May - Oct.; limit of stay: ...days; 10 sites; group camps: 2; cabins; pic...ic area; boating; fishing; hiking; exhibit; NPS ...uided tour; self-guiding tour; boat and trail ...ccess; lodging.

...ORTH LAKE DESOR
LOCATION: Inland.
...ACILITIES: Open May - Oct.; limit of stay: ...days; 4 sites; group camps: 3; cabins; picnic ...rea; fishing; hiking; exhibit; NPS guided tour; ...elf-guiding tour; trail access; lodging.

...OCK HARBOR
...ACILITIES: Open May - Oct.; limit of stay: ...day; 20 sites; group camps: 3; cabins; laun...ry; picnic area; food service; boating; boat ...ental; fishing; hiking; exhibit; NPS guided ...our; self-guiding tour; boat and trail access; ...odging.

...ISKIWIT CAMP
LOCATION: South side.
...ACILITIES: Open May - Oct.; limit of stay: ...days; 4 sites; group camps: 2; cabins; picnic ...rea; boating; boat rental; fishing; hiking; ex...ibit; NPS guided tour; self-guiding tour; ...oat and trail access; lodging.

...OUTH LAKE DESOR
LOCATION: Inland.
...ACILITIES: Open May - Oct.; limit of stay: ...days; 4 sites; group camps: 3; cabins; picnic ...rea; fishing; hiking; exhibits; NPS guided ...our; self-guiding tour; trail access; lodging.

...HREE-MILE
LOCATION: Rock Harbor.
...ACILITIES: Open May - Oct.; limit of stay: ...day; 12 sites; group camps: 3; cabins; pic...ic area; boating; boat rental; fishing; hiking; ...xhibit; NPS guided tour; self-guiding tour; ...oat and trail access; lodging.

TODD HARBOR
LOCATION: North side.
FACILITIES: Open May - Oct.; limit of stay: 3 days; 7 sites; group camps: 3; cabins; picnic area; boating; boat rental; fishing; hiking; exhibit; NPS guided tour; self-guiding tour; boat and trail access; lodging.

TOOKERS ISLAND
LOCATION: Rock Harbor.
FACILITIES: Open May - Oct.; limit of stay: 3 days; 2 sites; cabins; picnic area; boating; boat rental; fishing; hiking; exhibit; NPS guided tour; self-guiding tour; boat access; lodging.

WASHINGTON CREEK
LOCATION: Washington Harbor.
FACILITIES: Open May - Oct.; limit of stay: 2 days; 16 sites; group camps: 3; cabins; picnic area; food service; boating; boat rental; fishing; hiking; exhibit; NPS guided tour; self-guiding tour; boat and trail access; lodging.

NATIONAL FORESTS

National Forests
Eastern Region
633 West Wisconsin Avenue
Milwaukee, WI 53203
(414) 291-3693

Cadillac

HURON NATIONAL FOREST
ATTRACTIONS: Trout fishing; deer, small-game, bird hunting.
FACILITIES: 13 camp and picnic sites, 6 picnic only; 2 swimming sites; Au Sable and Silver Valley Winter Sports Areas; many resorts, hotels, and cabins.
NEARBY TOWNS: Grayling, Harrisville, Mio, Oscoda, and Tawas City.

MANISTEE NATIONAL FOREST
ATTRACTIONS: Trout, bass, northern wall-eyed pike, perch fishing; deer, small-game hunting. Good skiing on northern part of the National Forest; canoeing.
FACILITIES: 17 camp and picnic sites, 17 picnic only; swimming site; Caberfae and Manistee Winter Sports Areas; many resorts, hotels, and cabins.
NEARBY TOWNS: Big Rapids, Ludington, Manistee, Muskegon, Reed City.

Escanaba

HIAWATHA NATIONAL FOREST
ATTRACTIONS: Small lake among mixed evergreen and hardwood forests; waterfalls. Trout, bass, northern and walleyed pike, perch fishing; smelt dipping; deer, black bear, ruffed sharptailed grouse hunting. Canoeing; scenic drives.
FACILITIES: 24 camp and picnic sites, 15 picnic only; 3 swimming sites; Gladstone Winter Sports Area; resorts, hotels, many cabins.
NEARBY TOWNS: Gladstone, Manistique, Munising, Rapid River, Saint Ignace, Sault Sainte Marie, and Trout Lake.

Ironwood

OTTAWA NATIONAL FOREST

MICHIGAN

NATIONAL FORESTS (continued)

ATTRACTIONS: Lake and stream fishing; deep-water trolling in Lake Superior; deer, bear hunting; scenic drives.
FACILITIES: 25 camp and picnic sites, 19 picnic only; 7 swimming sites; numerous hotels and cabins.
NEARBY TOWNS: Bessemer, Iron River, Ontonagon, Trout Creek, Wakefield, Watersmeet; Duluth, MN.

STATE PARKS

Headquarters

Department of Natural Resources
Parks Division
P.O. Box 30028
Lansing, MI 48909
(517) 373-1270

Algonac

ALGONAC STATE PARK
LOCATION: Off Route 29.
FACILITIES: Open year round; 300 sites; water and bathroom facilities; sanitary station; electrical hookup; trailer village vehicle sites; picnic area; hunting; fishing; hiking; tent camping.

Brighton

ISLAND LAKE STATE PARK
LOCATION: Off I-96.
FACILITIES: Open year round; 25 sites; water and bathroom facilities; trailer village vehicle sites; picnic area; swimming; hunting; fishing; tent camping.

Carp Lake

WILDERNESS STATE PARK
LOCATION: Off U.S. 31.
FACILITIES: Open year round; 210 sites; water and bathroom facilities; sanitary station; electrical hookup; trailer village vehicle sites; picnic area; swimming; boating; hunting; fishing; hiking; tent camping.

Champion

VAN RIPER STATE PARK
LOCATION: Off U.S. 41.
FACILITIES: Open year round; 226 sites; water and bathroom facilities; sanitary station; electrical hookup; trailer village vehicle sites; picnic area; food service; swimming; boating; fishing; hiking; tent camping.

Chelsea

WATERLOO STATE PARK
LOCATION: Off I-94.
FACILITIES: Open year round; 434 sites; water and bathroom facilities; sanitary station; electrical hookup; trailer village vehicle sites; picnic area; food service; swimming; boating; hunting; fishing; hiking; horseback riding; tent camping.

Fenton

SEVEN LAKES STATE PARK
LOCATION: Off U.S. 23.
FACILITIES: Open year round; water and bathroom facilities; picnic area; food service; swimming; boating; hunting; fishing; hiking.

Grayling

HARTWICK PINES STATE PARK
LOCATION: Off Route 93.
FACILITIES: Open year round; 46 sites; water and bathroom facilities; sanitary station; electrical hookup; trailer village vehicle sites; picnic area; food service; hunting; fishing; hiking; tent camping.

Holly

HOLLY STATE PARK
LOCATION: Off I-75.
FACILITIES: Open year round; 79 sites; water and bathroom facilities; trailer village vehicle sites; picnic area; food service; swimming; boating; hunting; fishing; hiking; tent camping.

Howell

BRIGHTON STATE PARK
LOCATION: Off I-96.
FACILITIES: Open year round; 222 sites; water and bathroom facilities; sanitary station; electrical hookup; trailer village vehicle sites; picnic area; food service; swimming; boating; hunting; fishing; hiking; horseback riding; tent camping.

Lake Orion

BALD MOUNTAIN STATE PARK
LOCATION: Off Route 24.
FACILITIES: Open year round; 25 sites; water and bathroom facilities; trailer village vehicle sites; picnic area; food service; swimming; boating; hunting; fishing; hiking; horseback riding; tent camping.

Ludington

LUDINGTON STATE PARK
LOCATION: Off Route 116.
FACILITIES: Open year round; 398 sites; water and bathroom facilities; sanitary station; electrical hookup; trailer village vehicle sites; picnic area; swimming; boating; hunting; fishing; hiking; tent camping.

Lupton

RIFLE RIVER STATE PARK
LOCATION: Off Route 33.
FACILITIES: Open year round; 159 sites; water and bathroom facilities; sanitary station; electrical hookup; trailer village vehicle sites; picnic area; swimming; boating; hunting; fishing; hiking; tent camping.

Mears

SILVER LAKE STATE PARK
LOCATION: Off U.S. 31.
FACILITIES: Open year round; 249 sites; wa-

STATE PARKS (continued)

ter and bathroom facilities; sanitary station; electrical hookup; trailer village vehicle sites; picnic area; food service; swimming; boating; fishing; hiking; tent camping.

Middleville

YANKEE SPRINGS STATE PARK
LOCATION: Off Route 37.
FACILITIES: Open year round; 345 sites; water and bathroom facilities; sanitary station; electrical hookup; trailer village vehicle sites; picnic area; food service; swimming; boating; hunting; fishing; hiking; horseback riding; tent camping.

Milford

HIGHLAND STATE PARK
LOCATION: Off Route 59.
FACILITIES: Open year round; 25 sites; water and bathroom facilities; electrical hookup; trailer village vehicle sites; picnic area; swimming; boating; hunting; fishing; hiking; horseback riding; tent camping.

PROUD LAKE STATE PARK
LOCATION: Off I-96.
FACILITIES: Open year round; 150 sites; water and bathroom facilities; sanitary station; electrical hookup; trailer village vehicle sites; picnic area; swimming; boating; hunting; fishing; hiking; tent camping.

Muskegon

HOFFMASTER STATE PARK
LOCATION: Off U.S. 31.
FACILITIES: Open year round; 333 sites; water and bathroom facilities; sanitary station; electrical hookup; trailer village vehicle sites; picnic area; food service; swimming; fishing; horseback riding; tent camping.

North Muskegon

MUSKEGON STATE PARK
LOCATION: Off Route 213.
FACILITIES: Open year round; 357 sites; water and bathroom facilities; electrical hookup; trailer village vehicle sites; picnic area; swimming; boating; fishing; hiking; tent camping.

Ontonagon

PORCUPINE MTS. STATE PARK
LOCATION: Off Route 107.
FACILITIES: Open year round; 199 sites; water and bathroom facilities; sanitary station; electrical hookup; trailer village vehicle sites; picnic area; boating; hunting; fishing; hiking; tent camping.

Ortonville

ORTONVILLE STATE PARK
LOCATION: Off Route 15.
FACILITIES: Open year round; 70 sites; water and bathroom facilities; trailer village vehicle sites; picnic area; food service; swimming; boating; hunting; fishing; hiking; horseback riding; tent camping.

Paradise

TAHQUAMENON FALLS STATE PARK
LOCATION: Off Route 123.
FACILITIES: Open year round; 319 sites; water and bathroom facilities; sanitary station; electrical hookup; trailer village vehicle sites; picnic area; food service; swimming; boating; hunting; fishing; hiking; tent camping.

Pinckney

PINCKNEY STATE PARK
LOCATION: Off Route 36.
FACILITIES: Open year round; 270 sites; water and bathroom facilities; sanitary station; electrical hookup; trailer village vehicle sites; picnic area; swimming; boating; hunting; fishing; hiking; horseback riding; tent camping.

Pontiac

PONTIAC LAKE STATE PARK
LOCATION: Off Route 59.
FACILITIES: Open year round; 25 sites; water and bathroom facilities; picnic area; boating; hunting; fishing; hiking; horseback riding; primitive camping sites.

Sawyer

WARREN DUNES STATE PARK
LOCATION: Off I-94.
FACILITIES: Open year round; 249 sites; water and bathroom facilities; sanitary station; electrical hookup; trailer village vehicle sites; picnic area; swimming; hunting; hiking; tent camping.

STATE FORESTS

Department of Natural Resources
Division of Forestry
Lansing, MI 48909
(517) 373-1275

Atlanta

AVERY LAKE STATE FOREST
LOCATION: 9 mi. southwest of Atlanta.
FACILITIES: Open year round; 29 sites; water and bathroom facilities; trailer village vehicle sites; picnic area; boating; fishing; hiking; tent camping.

JACKSON LAKE STATE FOREST
LOCATION: 6 mi. north of Atlanta on Route 33.
FACILITIES: Open year round; 22 sites; water and bathroom facilities; trailer village vehicle sites; picnic area; swimming; boating; fishing; hiking; tent camping.

Brutus

MAPLE BAY STATE FOREST
LOCATION: 4 mi. east of Brutus.
FACILITIES: Open year round; 36 sites; water and bathroom facilities; trailer village vehicle sites; picnic area; swimming; boating; fishing; hiking; tent camping.

MICHIGAN

STATE FORESTS (continued)

Curran

MCCULLUM LAKE STATE FOREST
LOCATION: 9 mi. northwest of Curran.
FACILITIES: Open year round; 24 sites; water and bathroom facilities; trailer village vehicle sites; picnic area; swimming; boating; fishing; tent camping.

Farwell

PIKE LAKE STATE FOREST
LOCATION: 10 mi. west of Farwell on U.S. 10.
FACILITIES: Open year round; 22 sites; water and bathroom facilities; trailer village vehicle sites; picnic area; swimming; boating; fishing; hiking; tent camping.

Frederic

JONES LAKE STATE FOREST
LOCATION: 9 mi. east of Frederic.
FACILITIES: Open year round; 42 sites; water and bathroom facilities; trailer village vehicle sites; picnic area; swimming; boating; fishing; hiking; tent camping.

Grayling

CANOE HARBOR STATE FOREST
LOCATION: 14 mi. southeast of Grayling.
FACILITIES: Open year round; 40 sites; water and bathroom facilities; trailer village vehicle sites; boating; fishing; tent camping.

LAKE MARGRETHE STATE FOREST
LOCATION: 5 mi. west of Grayling on Route 72.
FACILITIES: Open year round; 45 sites; water and bathroom facilities; trailer village vehicle sites; picnic area; swimming; boating; fishing; hiking; tent camping.

MANISTEE BRIDGE STATE FOREST
LOCATION: 8 mi. west of Grayling on Route 72.
FACILITIES: Open year round; 24 sites; water and bathroom facilities; trailer village vehicle sites; picnic area; boating; fishing; hiking; tent camping.

WHITE PINE STATE FOREST
LOCATION: 12 mi. east of Grayling.
FACILITIES: Open year round; 24 sites; water and bathroom facilities; trailer village vehicle sites; fishing; hiking; tent camping.

Hillman

ESS LAKE STATE FOREST
LOCATION: 8 mi. northwest of Hillman.
FACILITIES: Open year round; 30 sites; water and bathroom facilities; trailer village vehicle sites; picnic area; swimming; boating; fishing; hiking; tent camping.

Houghton Lake

HOUGHTON LAKE STATE FOREST
LOCATION: 7 mi. northeast of Houghton Lake on U.S. 27.

FACILITIES: Open year round; 50 sites; water and bathroom facilities; trailer village vehicle sites; picnic area; swimming; boating; fishing; hiking; tent camping.

REEDSBURG DAM STATE FOREST
LOCATION: 5 mi. northwest of Houghton Lake on Route 55.
FACILITIES: Open year round; 42 sites; water and bathroom facilities; trailer village vehicle sites; picnic area; fishing; hiking; tent camping.

Johannesburg

BIG BEAR LAKE STATE FOREST
LOCATION: 7 mi. southeast of Johannesburg.
FACILITIES: Open year round; 65 sites; water and bathroom facilities; trailer village vehicle sites; picnic area; swimming; boating; fishing; hiking; tent camping.

Lewiston

LITTLE WOLF LAKE STATE FOREST
LOCATION: 3 mi. southeast of Lewiston.
FACILITIES: Open year round; 35 sites; water and bathroom facilities; trailer village vehicle sites; picnic area; swimming; boating; fishing; hiking; tent camping.

Lovells

SHUPAC LAKE STATE FOREST
LOCATION: 1 mi. northeast of Lovells.
FACILITIES: Open year round; 24 sites; water and bathroom facilities; trailer village vehicle sites; picnic area; swimming; boating; fishing; hiking; tent camping.

Mio

MIO POND STATE FOREST
LOCATION: 3 mi. northwest of Mio.
FACILITIES: Open year round; 24 sites; water and bathroom facilities; trailer village vehicle sites; picnic area; swimming; boating; fishing; hiking; tent camping.

Onaway

BLACK LAKE STATE FOREST
LOCATION: 11 mi. north of Onaway.
FACILITIES: Open year round; 50 sites; water and bathroom facilities; trailer village vehicle sites; picnic area; swimming; boating; fishing; hiking; tent camping.

SHOEPAC LAKE STATE FOREST
LOCATION: 11 mi. southeast of Onaway.
FACILITIES: Open year round; 50 sites; water and bathroom facilities; trailer village vehicle sites; picnic area; boating; fishing; hiking; tent camping.

TOMAHAWK LAKE STATE FOREST
LOCATION: 11 mi. southeast of Onaway.
FACILITIES: Open year round; 39 sites; water and bathroom facilities; trailer village vehicle sites; picnic area; swimming; boating; fishing; tent camping.

Oscoda

VAN ETTEN LAKE STATE FOREST

STATE FORESTS (continued)

LOCATION: 5 mi. northwest of Oscoda.
FACILITIES: Open year round; 53 sites; water and bathroom facilities; trailer village vehicle sites; picnic area; swimming; boating; fishing; hiking; tent camping.

Ossineke

OSSINEKE STATE FOREST
LOCATION: 1 mi. east of Ossineke on U.S. 23.
FACILITIES: Open year round; 43 sites; water and bathroom facilities; trailer village vehicle sites; swimming; fishing; hiking; tent camping.

Rose City

RIFLE RIVER STATE FOREST
LOCATION: 12 mi. southeast of Rose City on Route 33.
FACILITIES: Open year round; 20 sites; water and bathroom facilities; trailer village vehicle sites; picnic area; fishing; hiking; tent camping.

Sanford

BLACK CREEK STATE FOREST
LOCATION: 3 mi. northwest of Sanford on U.S. 10.
FACILITIES: Open year round; 20 sites; water and bathroom facilities; trailer village vehicle sites; picnic area; fishing; hiking; tent camping.

Skeels

HOUSE LAKE STATE FOREST
LOCATION: 4 mi. northeast of Skeels on Route 18.
FACILITIES: Open year round; 42 sites; water and bathroom facilities; trailer village vehicle sites; picnic area; swimming; boating; fishing; hiking; tent camping.

TROUT LAKE STATE FOREST
LOCATION: 4 mi. northeast of Skeels on Route 18.
FACILITIES: Open year round; 35 sites; water and bathroom facilities; trailer village vehicle sites; picnic area; boating; fishing; hiking; tent camping.

Vanderbilt

PICKEREL LAKE STATE FOREST
LOCATION: 11 mi. northeast of Vanderbilt.
FACILITIES: Open year round; 45 sites; water and bathroom facilities; trailer village vehicle sites; picnic area; swimming; boating; fishing; hiking; tent camping.

PIGEON RIVER STATE FOREST
LOCATION: 14 mi. east of Vanderbilt.
FACILITIES: Open year round; 22 sites; water and bathroom facilities; trailer village vehicle sites; picnic area; fishing; hiking; tent camping.

West Branch

AMBROSE LAKE STATE FOREST
LOCATION: 11 mi. northwest of West Branch.
FACILITIES: Open year round; 30 sites; water and bathroom facilities; trailer village vehicle sites; picnic area; swimming; boating; fishing; hiking; tent camping.

HISTORIC SITES

Dearborn

GREENFIELD VILLAGE AND HENRY FORD MUSEUM - Original homes and workshops of Thomas Edison, Henry Ford, also Abe Lincoln. More than 200 antique autos.

Grand Rapids

NORTON MOUND GROUP - Among the best preserved burial mounds in the Great Lakes region. Eleven remain from the seventeen originally located here.

Mackinac Island

OLD FORT MACKINAC - One of the few sites in U.S. that has been under 3 flags - British, French and American.

Manistee

OUR SAVIOUR'S EVANGELICAL LUTHERAN CHURCH - Oldest Danish Lutheran Church in America, built in 1869.

Menominee

THE ALVIN CLARK (Mystery Ship) - Preserved deep in the fresh cold waters of Lake Michigan for over a hundred years, the "Alvin Clark" is a Great Lake schooner built in 1846, sunk in 1864, and raised in 1969. Oldest floating sailing ship on the Great Lakes.

HOSTELS

Bessemer

BESSEMER INDIANHEAD YOUTH HOSTEL
Eli Avenue
Bessemer, MI 49911
(906) 667-0915
FACILITIES: Open Nov. - Apr.; 64 beds, men; 64 beds, women; modern bathroom; overnight charges: $4.50; houseparent: Eugene Cocco.

Cassopolis

CAMP FRIENDENSWALD LODGE
Route 3
Cassopolis, MI 49031
(616) 476-2426
FACILITIES: Open year round; reservation required; 20 beds, men; 20 beds, women; modern bathroom; overnight charges: $3; houseparents: Orv & Mary Bontrager.

MICHIGAN

HOSTELS (continued)

East Lansing

MSU STUDENT HOUSING CO-OPS
311 B Student Service Building
East Lansing, MI 48823
(517) 355-8313
FACILITIES: Open year round; 10 beds,
men; 10 beds, women; modern bathroom;
nearest hostel: Milford, 50 mi. east; overnight charges: $2 summer; $3 winter; houseparent: Jacob Wind.

Kalkaska

BLUE LAKE
Route 1
Box 157
Kalkaska, MI 49646
(616) 587-8298
FACILITIES: Open year round; reservation
required; 20 beds, men; 20 beds, women;
modern bathroom; overnight charges: May 1 -
Sept. 30, $2.50; Oct. 1 - Apr. 30, $4; house-
parent: Lucille Heavner.

Milford

FOOTE YOUTH HOSTEL
1845 Dawson Road
Milford, MI 48042
(313) 378-8560
FACILITIES: Open year round; reservations
required; 25 beds, men; 25 beds, women;
modern bathroom; nearest hostel: E. Lansing;
overnight charges: $2.50 summer; $3.25 winter; houseparents: Glenn & Caroline Kruger.

Saginaw

SAGINAW VALLEY
Dept. of Residence Halls
Saginaw Valley College
2250 Pierce Road
Saginaw, MI 48710
(517) 793-9800
FACILITIES: Open year round; 10 beds,
men; 10 beds, women; reservations required;
modern bathroom; nearest hostels: Kalkaska,
125 mi. northwest; Milford, 90 mi. southeast;
overnight charges: $3 summer; $4 winter;
houseparents: Brian & Rhonda Gano.

POINTS OF INTEREST

Battle Creek

"CEREAL BOWL OF AMERICA" - Home of
Kellogg Company, located on Porter Street.

Dearborn

RIVER ROUGE PLANT - Largest integrated
industrial city in the world. Represents every
step of Ford manufacturing from production
of steel and other raw materials to assembly
of cars. Located at 3001 Miller Road.

Detroit

FAIRLANE SHOPPING MALL - Second largest in U.S., complete with "people mover."

Frankemuth

BRONNER'S CHRISTMAS WONDERLAND-
America's largest year-round display of Christmas decorations from around the world.

Grayling

FRED BEAR MUSEUM - World's largest private collection of archery artifacts and history.

Hancock

QUINCY MINE HOIST (the Nordberg Hoist)-
Largest steam-powered mine hoist ever manufactured.

Holland

WINDMILL ISLAND - Only authentic Dutch
windmill in U.S. "De Zwaan," 200-year-old,
60-ton mill with 80-foot wings was brought
from the Netherlands in 1964.

Ironwood

COPPER PEAK - Only ski-flying hill in America, and largest artificial slide in the world.
Designed to permit leaps of 500 feet and
more.

Ishpeming

UNITED STATES SKI ASSOCIATION
HALL OF FAME - Birthplace of organized
skiing in America. Displays of early skiing
equipment and memorabilia of skiers elected
to the Hall of Fame. Located on Mather Ave.

Kalamazoo

KALAMAZOO MALL - First pedestrian mall
in the nation. Four blocks of shopping, dining, and entertainment.

Little Traverse Bay

SKIN DIVERS SHRINE - Underwater in the
bay, life-size marble and black walnut cruci-
fix. Only one of its kind in U.S.

Mackinac Island

GRAND HOTEL - Largest summer hotel in
the world with longest front porch.

Manistique

SIPHON BRIDGE - Supported by water
which is atmospherically forced under it.
Roadway is approximately 4 feet below the
water level.

MINNESOTA

Minnesota, home of tall trees and tall stories, joined the Union in 1858 as the thirty-second state. About 10 years following statehood, its lumber industry entered a period of rapid growth that peaked just short of the Twentieth Century. In those few short years, the state experienced significant economic development and population expansion.

Besides lumber, a gigantic legend came out of the state's forests at that time, the famous lumberjack Paul Bunyan and his blue ox, Babe. Babe's monstrous footprints, it is said, created thousands of lakes in Minnesota.

Another giant name associated with the state, but this time in the medical profession, is Mayo, a father and two sons who established the world-renowned clinic in Rochester.

The importance of Minnesota's lumber industry has diminished, being replaced instead by agriculture, especially corn and wheat crops and livestock. Tourism also plays a major role in its economy.

State capital: St. Paul. State bird: Common loon. State tree: Norway pine. State flower: Pink and white lady's-slipper.

WEATHER

The state of Minnesota covers 84,068 square miles, of which 4,059 square miles are water (15,291 lakes greater than 10 acres). The highest point above sea level, Eagle Mountain in the extreme northeast, is at 2,301 feet, and the lowest is 602 feet along the shores of Lake Superior.

Minnesota has a continental-type climate and is subject to frequent gusts of continental polar air throughout the year, with occasional Artic weather during the cold season. Occasional periods of prolonged heat occur during the summer, particularly in the southern portion when warm air pushes northward from the Gulf of Mexico and the southwestern United States. Pacific Ocean air masses that move across the western United States produce comparatively mild and dry weather at all seasons.

Average daily temperature for each month.

	Northern	Southern
Jan.	15.4 to -9.4	22.9 to 2.5
Feb.	24.2 to -4.2	29.1 to 8.2
Mar.	37.0 to 9.9	39.5 to 20.1
Apr.	52.7 to 26.8	58.5 to 35.3
May	66.6 to 37.8	71.8 to 46.7
Jun.	76.0 to 48.3	81.3 to 56.8
Jul.	80.3 to 52.9	85.0 to 61.1
Aug.	78.3 to 51.1	83.3 to 58.9
Sept.	67.0 to 41.8	74.0 to 49.1
Oct.	56.6 to 33.4	63.8 to 39.3
Nov.	35.9 to 18.3	43.5 to 25.1
Dec.	21.9 to 1.1	29.0 to 11.4
Year	51.0 to 25.7	56.8 to 34.5

STATE CHAMBER OF COMMERCE

Minnesota Association of Commerce & Industry
200 Hanover Building
480 Cedar Street
St. Paul, MN 55101
(612) 227-9591

STATE & CITY TOURISM OFFICES

State

Department of Economic Development
480 Cedar Street
St. Paul, MN 55101
(612) 296-2755

Tourism Division
Minnesota Department of Economic Development
480 Cedar St., Hanover Bldg.
St. Paul, MN 55101
(612) 296-5027

Local

Minneapolis Convention and Tourism Commission
15 South 5th Street
Minneapolis, MN 55402
(612) 348-4330

Convention and Visitor's Bureau
St. Paul Area Chamber of Commerce
Suite 300, Osborn Bldg.
St. Paul, MN 55102
(612) 222-5561

STATE HIGHWAY DEPARTMENT

Department of Transportation
State Transportation Building
St. Paul, MN 55155
(612) 296-3000

HIGHWAY WELCOMING CENTERS

Albert Lea

ALBERT LEA CENTER - Interstate 90 & 35.

Beaver Creek

BEAVER CREEK CENTER - Interstate 90.

MINNESOTA

WELCOMING CENTERS (continued)

east, west of Beaver Creek.

Dresbach

DRESBACH CENTER - Interstate 90, north of Crescent.

Duluth-Thompson

DULUTH-THOMPSON CENTER - Hwy. 2 & Interstate 35.

Moorehead

MOOREHEAD CENTER - Interstate 95, east.

STATE POLICE

Department of Public Safety
St. Paul, MN 55155
(612) 482-5900

HUNTING & FISHING

Hunting

Resident license may be issued only to U.S. citizens who have maintained a legal residence in Minnesota for a period of 60 days immediately preceding the date of application for a license.

Residents serving the U.S. military or naval forces, or the reserve components thereof, who are stationed outside the state, may obtain a free deer license and seal from county auditors when in Minnesota on regularly granted leave or furlough provided that they have proper leave or furlough papers on their person.

A license is required to hunt big game regardless of the hunter's age. Anyone under the age of 16 must have a firearm or hunter safety certificate on his person to purchase a big game hunting license. A person under age 12 may not hunt big game.

Residents under age 14 must be accompanied by a parent or guardian when using firearms for any purpose. Residents over 14 but under 16 may hunt or possess firearms by themselves only if they have a firearm safety certificate in their possession.

A bow and arrow deer hunting license permits the licensee to hunt with bow and arrow during the entire deer season, including during the firearms season.

All non-residents, regardless of age, are required to procure an appropriate hunting license before attempting to hunt in Minnesota.

Non-residents attending schools in Minnesota are required to purchase a non-resident license for hunting deer or bear in Minnesota.

Big Game

Resident

Bow & arrow deer license, $10; firearms deer license, $10; bear license, $7.50.

Non-resident

Bow & arrow deer license, $25; firearms deer license, $60; bear license, $25.25.

Agent's Fee: An additional charge of $.75 will be made for issuing deer license and $.50 for all other licenses.

Small Game

Listed amounts are for restricted licenses. The fee for an unrestricted license is $1 extra. For those persons who purchased a restricted license and later desire to hunt on the Leech Lake Indian Reservation a $2 stamp may be purchased.

Resident

Small game, $7; state migratory waterfowl stamp, $3; beaver trapping, $2.50.

Non-resident

Small game, $27.

Agent's Fee: An additional charge of $.50 will be made for issuing the above licenses, including each state migratory waterfowl stamp if issued separately from the small game license.

Fishing

Resident licenses may be issued only to U.S. citizens who have maintained a legal residence in Minnesota for a period of 60 days immediately preceding the date of application for a license, except as provided below.

Residents under the age of 16 are not required to have an angling, spearing, or netting license.

A license to take fish shall be issued without charge to any citizen of Minnesota who is a recipient of supplemental security income for the aged, blind, or disabled.

Residents serving in the U.S. military or naval forces, or the reserve components thereof, who are stationed outside the state, may fish without a license when in Minnesota on regularly granted leave or furlough, provided they have proper leave or furlough papers on their person.

A non-resident under the age of 16 years is not required to have an angling license if his parent or legal guardian has obtained a non-resident angling license, and provided the child's fish are included in the daily possession limit of the parent or legal guardian. However, a non-resident under 16 may purchase a license and thereby be entitled to his own limit of fish.

Non-residents in the military or naval forces of the U.S., or in any reserve component of the military or naval service, who have officially transferred to and are stationed in Minnesota, are eligible for resident fishing licenses.

Non-resident full-time students at public or private educational institutions who reside in Minnesota during the full term of the school year may purchase a resident fishing license from the county auditor upon presenting proof of their status as students.

HUNTING & FISHING (continued)

Resident

Issuing fees, $.50; individual angling, $5; combination angling (husband and wife), $8; dark house spearing (additional to angling), $5; fish house or dark house (each must be licensed), $3; fish house or dark house used for rental (each must be licensed), $10; whitefish netting (additional to angling license) per 100-ft. net (2 nets permitted), each net, $3.

Non-resident

Individual angling (season), $10; individual angling (3 days), $5; combination angling (husband and wife), $15.

For more information contact:

Department of Natural Resources
Division of Fish & Wildlife
390 Centennial Bldg.
St. Paul, MN 55155
(612) 296-3325

CAMPGROUNDS
Private

Anoka

RAMBLIN' RUM CAMPGROUND
(612) 434-9490
LOCATION: 12 mi. north of Anoka on County Road 9.
FACILITIES: Open year round; 162 sites; water and bathroom facilities; sanitary station; electrical hookup; trailer village vehicle sites; laundry; picnic area; food service; swimming; boating; tent camping.

Battle Lake

OTTERTAIL LAKE CAMPGROUND
(218) 864-5848
LOCATION: 4½ mi. north of Battle Lake on Hwy. 78, then ½ mi. north on access road.
FACILITIES: Open May - Oct.; 100 sites; water and bathroom facilities; sanitary station; trailer village vehicle sites; laundry; picnic area; swimming; boating; boat rental; fishing; tent camping.

Baudette

BAUDETTE KOA KAMPGROUND
(218) 634-1694
LOCATION: 10 mi. northwest of Baudette on Route 172.
FACILITIES: Open year round; 125 sites; water and bathroom facilities; trailer village vehicle sites; swimming; boating; boat rental; hunting; tent camping.

Becker

SHERBURNE OAKS CAMPGROUND
(612) 261-9431
LOCATION: 9 mi. north of Becker on County Road 11.

FACILITIES: Open year round; 250 sites; water and bathroom facilities; sanitary station; electrical hookup; trailer village vehicle sites; food service; swimming; hiking; bicycle trail; tent camping.

Bemidji

GULL LAKE CAMPGROUND
(218) 586-2842
LOCATION: 10 mi. north of Bemidji on U.S. 71, then left on County Road 23, 5 mi.
FACILITIES: Open year round; 150 sites; water and bathroom facilities; sanitary station; electrical hookup; trailer village vehicle sites; laundry; food service; swimming; boating; fishing; tent camping.

Cannon Falls

CANNON FALLS KOA KAMPGROUND
(507) 263-3145
LOCATION: 2 mi. east of Cannon Falls on Route 19, then turn on Oak Lane.
FACILITIES: Open year round; 150 sites; water and bathroom facilities; sanitary station; electrical hookup; trailer village vehicle sites; swimming; boating; boat rental; tent camping.

Cass Lake

STONY POINT RESORT, TRAILER PARK & CAMPGROUND
(218) 335-6311
LOCATION: 2 mi. east of Cass Lake on U.S. 2.
FACILITIES: Open year round; 100 sites; water and bathroom facilities; sanitary station; electrical hookup; trailer village vehicle sites; cabins; picnic area; food service; swimming; boating; fishing; tent camping.

Cold Spring

EL RANCHO MANANA
(612) 597-2740
LOCATION: 5 mi. north of Cold Spring on County Road 9.
FACILITIES: Open Jun. - Sept.; 120 sites; water and bathroom facilities; sanitary station; electrical hookup; trailer village vehicle sites; picnic area; food service; swimming; boating; fishing; horseback riding; tent camping.

Elk River

CAMP ON THE MISSISSIPPI
(612) 441-1047
LOCATION: 3 mi. northwest of Elk River.
FACILITIES: Open Apr. 15 - Oct. 15; 150 sites; water and bathroom facilities; trailer village vehicle sites; food service; swimming; boating; boat rental; fishing; tent camping.

WAPITI PARK
(612) 441-1396
LOCATION: 3 mi. west of Elk River on U.S. 10.
FACILITIES: Open year round; 109 sites; water and bathroom facilities; sanitary station; electrical hookup; trailer village vehicle sites; picnic area; food service; swimming; boating; boat rental; fishing; bicycle trail; tent camping.

MINNESOTA

CAMPGROUNDS (continued)

Minneapolis

MINNEAPOLIS NORTHWEST I-94 KOA KAMPGROUND
(612) 425-5811
LOCATION: I-94 to Exit 213, 95th Avenue North (City Road 30), then 2 mi. west to Route 101, 1 mi. north on Route 101.
FACILITIES: Open May - Oct.; 130 sites; water and bathroom facilities; sanitary station; electrical hookup; trailer village vehicle sites; laundry; picnic area; food service; swimming; bicycle trail; tent camping.

MISSISSIPPI RIVERWOOD KOA KAMPERS RESORT
(612) 441-3530
LOCATION: 5 mi. north of I-94 at Rogers.
FACILITIES: Open year round; 207 sites; water and bathroom facilities; sanitary station; trailer village vehicle sites; laundry; food service; swimming; boating; fishing; bicycle trail; tent camping.

Mora

CAMPERVILLE
(612) 679-2326
LOCATION: 11 mi. north of Mora, then 2½ mi. east on Camperville Road.
FACILITIES: Open year round; 150 sites; water and bathroom facilities; sanitary station; electrical hookup; trailer village vehicle sites; picnic area; food service; swimming; boating; boat rental; fishing; tent camping.

Onamia

RUM RIVER VILLAGE
(612) 523-3166
LOCATION: 12 mi. north of Milaca on Hwy. 169.
FACILITIES: Open year round; 250 sites; water and bathroom facilities; sanitary station; electrical hookup; trailer village vehicle sites; picnic area; food service; swimming; boating; boat rental; fishing; bicycle trail; tent camping.

Park Rapids

BREEZE CAMPGROUND
(218) 732-5888
LOCATION: 9 mi. north of Park Rapids on U.S. 71.
FACILITIES: Open May - Oct.; 110 sites; water and bathroom facilities; sanitary station; electrical hookup; trailer village vehicle sites; laundry; picnic area; food service; swimming; boating; boat rental; fishing; horseback riding; tent camping.

Shakopee

VALLEYFAIR ENTERTAINMENT CENTER
(612) 445-6500
LOCATION: 3 mi. east of Shakopee on Hwy. 101.
FACILITIES: Open year round; 100 sites; water and bathroom facilities; trailer village vehicle sites; tent camping.

Stanchfield

SPRINGVALE CAMPGROUND
(612) 689-3208
LOCATION: 1 mi. west of Stanchfield on Hwy. 95, then north 6 mi. on County Road 14.
FACILITIES: Open Apr. 15 - Oct. 15; 105 sites; water and bathroom facilities; sanitary station; electrical hookup; trailer village vehicle sites; food service; swimming; boating; boat rental; hiking; bicycle trail; tent camping.

Thielman

WHIPPOORWILL SAFARI CAMPGROUND
(507) 534-3569
LOCATION: 1 mi. northeast of Plainview on Hwy. 42, then 8 mi. north on County Road 4.
FACILITIES: Open May - Nov.; 200 sites; water and bathroom facilities; electrical hookup; trailer village vehicle sites; laundry; food service; swimming; fishing; hiking; tent camping.

Walker

THE WEDGEWOOD
(218) 547-1443
LOCATION: 5 mi. north of Walker on Hwy. 371.
FACILITIES: Open May - Oct.; 100 sites; water and bathroom facilities; sanitary station; electrical hookup; trailer village vehicle sites; cabins; laundry; picnic area; food service; swimming; boating; boat rental; fishing; hiking; tent camping.

Waseca

KIESLER'S CLEAR LAKE CAMPGROUND
(507) 835-3179
LOCATION: 1 mi. east of Waseca on Hwy. 14.
FACILITIES: Open May - Oct.; 200 sites; water and bathroom facilities; sanitary station; trailer village vehicle sites; laundry; picnic area; food service; swimming; boating; boat rental; fishing; hiking; tent camping.

Waterville

KAMP DELS
(507) 362-8616
LOCATION: 1 mi. north of Routes 13 & 60 junction, then 4 blocks east on County Road 131.
FACILITIES: Open Apr. 15 - Oct. 15; 200 sites; water and bathroom facilities; sanitary station; electrical hookup; trailer village vehicle sites; laundry; picnic area; swimming; boating; boat rental; fishing; tent camping.

Zimmerman

CAMP IN THE WOODS
(612) 389-2516
LOCATION: 4 mi. north of Zimmerman on Hwy. 169, then 3 mi. west on County Road 9, then ¼ mi. south on County Road 1.
FACILITIES: Open May 15 - Oct. 1; 150 sites; water and bathroom facilities; sanitary station; electrical hookup; trailer village vehicle sites; picnic area; food service; swimming; bicycle trail; tent camping.

RESORTS & BEACHES

Beaver Creek

PIONEERLAND AREA - Many of the state's historic sites can be seen in this region, including Pipestone National Monument, the legendary pipestone quarries of Minnesota. Indians often traveled a thousand miles to obtain the red stone from which their pipes were made. The stone was sacred in Indian tradition and was never used to make anything else. Seventeen state parks and numerous county parks can be found in Pioneerland, offering opportunities for many recreational activities. Hardwood trees of every type, from sugar maples to the fire red oak, explode in fall colors that are unmatched anywhere in the world. The Beaver Creek Center, a 22-acre center, is located on the eastbound lane of Interstate 90 and serves as a gateway to the Pioneerland tourist region of southwestern Minnesota.

Brainerd

HEARTLAND AREA - Pine forests, birch groves, blue skies, clean, crisp air and lakes, 2,500 in all, abound in Minnesota's Heartland region. There are thousands of sunny beaches fronting more than 1,500 fine resorts, ranging from the most luxurious to the most rustic housekeeping cottages. Grownups and youngsters alike appreciate the boyhood home of Charles A. Lindbergh in Little Falls, where a new Interpretive Center displays mementos of the renowned "Lone Eagle." Also visit Brainerd International Raceway for big league sports car and speedway events. For vacationers who enjoy slower paced activities, the town of Nisswa has turtle races every summer Wednesday at 2 p.m., more or less.

For more information contact:

Heartland
411 Laurel
Brainerd, MN 56401
(218) 829-1615

Duluth

ARROWHEAD AREA - This area offers travelers the virtually untouched wilderness of the Boundary Waters Canoe Area, the cascading waters of Gooseberry Falls on the north shore of Lake Superior and the history of Grand Marais. Camping, fishing, and hiking can be enjoyed in complete privacy along three major wilderness trails in the northeastern tip of Minnesota. Travelers can view the oldest shaft mine on the Vermilion Range and can examine early mining equipment. Historic sites, state parks and excellent ski areas make the Arrowhead a year-round vacation region. The Thompson Hill Center, a 22-acre center located on Interstate 35 and Highway 2 on the western edge of Duluth, serves as a gateway to the Arrowhead tourist region of northeastern Minnesota.

LaCrescent

HIAWATHALAND AREA - This area is known for its spectacular river scenery; high, wooded, limestone bluffs; Indian summer scenery and more than 2,500 lakes. Apple orchards, historic homes, old railroad depots and museums provide a pleasant interlude in a bygone era. Area activities range from summer golfing, swimming, boating and waterskiing to hunting and cross-country skiing during the winter. Fishing and birdwatching can be enjoyed year round. The Dresbach Center, a 22-acre center on the Mississippi River, is located off the westbound lane of Interstate 90, about 1.5 mi. north of LaCrescent and serves as a gateway to the Hiawathaland tourist region of southeastern Minnesota.

Minneapolis

METROLAND - This eight county region offers city sophistication, with the Twin Cities of Minneapolis-St. Paul as its hub, and country serenity, with primitive camping no more than twenty minutes away. You can fish a wild river in the morning, take in a Minnesota Twins baseball game in the afternoon, spend the evening at the new Valleyfair Entertainment Center, then head back to your campground. Metroland offers sports fans a steady supply of major league action at Bloomington's Metropolitan Sports Area. You can root for baseball's Twins, football's Vikings, hockey's North Stars or the new Minnesota Kicks soccer team. Metroland presents lots of attractive distractions: swinging night life, Como Zoo, championship golf courses, the classic State Capitol, historic Fort Snelling, and Minnehaha Falls.

For more information contact:

Metroland
c/o Northern Dakota
County Chamber of Commerce
33 E. Wentworth, Suite 101
West St. Paul, MN 55118
(612) 222-5889

Moorhead

VIKINGLAND AREA - Artifacts such as firesteels, battle axes and swords that appear to be of 14th-century Scandinavian design, have been found in the area, indicating the possibility of a Viking exploration of this region. Hiking trails wander through virgin prairie land where marsh and prairie flowers abound. Sunfish and other game fish flourish in the many area lakes, which also provide good swimming, boating and waterskiing. Here, too, is the birthplace of the Mississippi River, Itasca State Park. And pioneer museums and Indian mounds provide glimpses of Vikingland's past. The Moorhead Center, a 22-acre center located off the eastbound lane of Interstate 94 about 2 mi. east of the Minnesota-North Dakota line, serves as a gateway to the Vikingland tourist region of northwestern Minnesota.

BOATING AREAS

See National Parks, National Forests, State Parks and State Forests.

MINNESOTA

BICYCLE TRAILS

CITY OF LAKES TRAIL - 15 mi.; any bicycle.

Five lakes and the Mississippi River surround this short tour through south Minneapolis and the downtown area. Sunday morning is the best time for this ride.

Trail: Nicollet Mall, right on Washington, right on Cedar, left on Riverside, left on Franklin, right on West River Road, right on Minnehaha Parkway, right on Harriet Blvd., right on Berry Drive, right on East Calhoun Blvd., continue to Lake of the Isles Blvd., right on Franklin, left on Hennepin, right on Harmon, right on Route 10 to Mall.

MISSISSIPPI RIVER TRAIL - 100 mi.; some hills; 10-speed bicycle recommended.

This is one of the most popular century rides in the Gopher State. You will pass through several towns near two lakes, and cross the Mississippi River twice.

The suggested direction of travel is clockwise. All on paved roads with light traffic.

Trail: Calhoun Beach to Route 16 west, right on Route 101, left on Route 6, right on Route 19 to Hanover to St. Michael, left on Route 130, right on Route 12, to Route 63, right on Route 22, left on Route 47, right on Route 24, right on Route 9, right on Route 58 to Route 7, right on Route 103 to West Broadway, right on Glenwood Parkway to Calhoun Beach.

TRAILS

Duluth

CONGDON CREEK PARK TRAIL - .75 mi. foot trail. A self-guided nature trail in a steep, wooded gorge. A brochure is available to help the user identify the bird and plant species and animal tracks seen along the route. It also describes the geology of the gorge and the process by which Tischers Creek cut through the lava flow, which is a billion years old.

LESTER PARK NATURE TRAIL - .8 mi. foot trail. A self-guided loop trail within Lester Park. A main attraction is the Lester River, which is a trout stream. The trail path follows first along the east branch, then cuts across to the west branch. Several rustic stone bridges constructed by the Works Progress Administration (WPA) contribute to the natural appeal of the trail environment. There are old-growth white and red pines, hardwoods, and other flora along the trail.

SKI AREAS

Ashby

VIKING VALLEY SKI AREA
Ashby, MN 56309
(218) 747-2542
LOCATION: Near Ashby.
FACILITIES: 6 tow ropes; ski instruction; ski rental; 180 ft. vertical drop; longest run, 1400 ft.; restaurants; lodging.

Bemidji

BUENA VISTA SKI AREA
Bemidji, MN 56601
(218) 243-2231
LOCATION: Near Bemidji.
FACILITIES: 2 double chairlifts; 6 tow ropes; ski instruction; ski rental; 200 ft. vertical drop; longest run, 1600 ft.; restaurants; lodging.

Biwabik

GIANT'S RIDGE SKI AREA
Biwabik, MN 55708
(218) 865-6315
LOCATION: Near Biwabik.
FACILITIES: 2 tow ropes; 1 poma; ski instruction; ski rental; 440 ft. vertical drop; longest run, 3700 ft.; restaurants; lodging.

Bloomington

HYLAND HILLS SKI AREA
8800 Chalet Road
Bloomington, MN 55437
(612) 835-4604
LOCATION: In Bloomington.
FACILITIES: 1 triple chairlift; 1 T-bar; 5 tow ropes; ski instruction; ski rental; 175 ft. vertical drop; restaurants; lodging.

Brainerd

SKI GULL
Brainerd, MN 56401
(218) 963-4353
LOCATION: Near Brainerd.
FACILITIES: 3 tow ropes; 1 T-bar; ski instruction; ski rental; 285 ft. vertical drop; longest run, 1700 ft.; restaurants; lodging.

Burnsville

BUCK HILL SKI AREA
15400 Buck Hill Road
Burnsville, MN 55337
(612) 435-7187
LOCATION: On Buck Hill Road.
FACILITIES: 4 double chairlifts; 1 J-bar; 4 tow ropes; ski instruction; ski rental; 304 ft. vertical drop; longest run, 2000 ft.; restaurants; lodging.

Coleraine

MT. ITASCA SKI AREA
Coleraine, MN 55722
(218) 245-1463
LOCATION: Near Coleraine.
FACILITIES: 2 tow ropes; ski instruction; ski rental; 200 ft. vertical drop; longest run, 1800 ft.; restaurants; lodging.

Detroit Lakes

DETROIT MOUNTAIN SKI AREA
Detroit Lakes, MN 56501
(218) 847-4703
LOCATION: Near Detroit Lakes.
FACILITIES: 1 double chairlift; 2 T-bars; 6 tow ropes; ski instruction; ski rental; 235 ft. vertical drop; longest run, 2400 ft.; restaurants; lodging.

SKI AREAS (continued)

Duluth

SPIRIT MOUNTAIN RECREATION AREA
Duluth, MN 55810
(218) 628-2891
LOCATION: Near Duluth.
FACILITIES: 2 triple chairlifts; 3 double
chairlifts; ski instruction; ski rental; 610 ft.
vertical drop; longest run, 3800 ft.; restaurants; lodging.

Ely

HIDDEN VALLEY SKI AREA
Ely, MN 55731
(218) 365-3097
LOCATION: Near Ely.
FACILITIES: 1 T-bar; 2 tow ropes; ski instruction; ski rental; 165 ft. vertical drop;
longest run, 1800 ft.; restaurants; lodging.

Fergus Falls

OLD SMOKEY SKI AREA
Fergus Falls, MN 56537
(218) 739-2251
LOCATION: Near Fergus Falls.
FACILITIES: 2 tow ropes; ski instruction; ski
rental; 115 ft. vertical drop; longest run, 1000
ft.; restaurants; lodging.

Frontenac

MT. FRONTENAC SKI AREA
Frontenac, MN 55026
(612) 388-5826
LOCATION: 9 mi. south of Red Wing.
FACILITIES: 1 double chairlift; 2 T-bars; 4
tow ropes; ski instruction; ski rental; 420 ft.
vertical drop; longest run, 1 mi.; restaurants;
lodging.

Glenwood

GLENHAVEN SKI AREA
Glenwood, MN 56334
(612) 634-9912
LOCATION: Near Glenwood.
FACILITIES: 2 tow ropes; ski instruction; ski
rental; 150 ft. vertical drop; longest run, 950
ft.; restaurants; lodging.

Grand Rapids

SUGAR HILLS SKI AREA
Grand Rapids, MN 55744
(218) 326-3473
LOCATION: Near Grand Rapids.
FACILITIES: 2 double chairlifts; 3 T-bars; 3
tow ropes; ski instruction; ski rental; 400 ft.
vertical drop; longest run, 4000 ft.; restaurants; lodging.

Grey Eagle

EAGLE MOUNTAIN SKI AREA
Grey Eagle, MN 56336
(612) 285-4567
LOCATION: Near Grey Eagle.
FACILITIES: 4 tow ropes; 1 poma; ski instruction; ski rental; 200 ft. vertical drop;
longest run, 2000 ft.; restaurants; lodging.

Hastings

AFTON ALPS SKI AREA
Hastings, MN 55033
(612) 436-5245
LOCATION: Near Hastings.
FACILITIES: 3 triple chairlifts; 14 double
chairlifts; ski instruction; ski rental; 330 ft.
vertical drop; longest run, 3000 ft.; restaurants; lodging.

Hill City

QUADNA SKI AREA
Hill City, MN 55748
(218) 697-2324
LOCATION: Near Hill City.
FACILITIES: 3 T-bars; 2 tow ropes; ski instruction; ski rental; 325 ft. vertical drop;
longest run, 3800 ft.; restaurants; lodging.

Kimball

POWDER RIDGE SKI AREA
Kimball, MN 55353
(612) 398-7200
LOCATION: Near Kimball.
FACILITIES: 1 double chairlift; 1 T-bar; 1 J-
bar; 3 tow ropes; ski instruction; ski rental;
310 ft. vertical drop; longest run, 2600 ft.;
restaurants; lodging.

Lake Benton

HOLE-IN-THE-MOUNTAIN COUNTY PARK
Lake Benton, MN 56149
(507) 368-9350
LOCATION: Near Lake Benton.
FACILITIES: 3 tow ropes; ski instruction; ski
rental; 175 ft. vertical drop; longest run, 1000
ft.; restaurants; lodging.

Lutsen

LUTSEN SKI AREA
Lutsen, MN 55612
(218) 663-7212
LOCATION: Near Lutsen.
FACILITIES: 3 double chairlifts; 1 T-bar; 2
tow ropes; ski instruction; ski rental; 600 ft.
vertical drop; longest run, 7000 ft.; restaurants; lodging.

Mankato

MT. KATO
Mankato, MN 56001
(507) 625-3363
LOCATION: On Hwy. 66.
FACILITIES: 4 quad chairlifts; 3 double
chairlifts; 2 tow ropes; ski instruction; ski
rental; 240 ft. vertical drop; longest run, 2000
ft.; restaurants; lodging.

Minneapolis

MT. WIRTH SKI AREA
Minneapolis, MN 55422
(612) 522-4584
LOCATION: Near Plymouth and Greenwood
Avenues.
FACILITIES: 3 tow ropes; ski instruction; ski
rental; 200 ft. vertical drop; longest run, 300
ft.; restaurants; lodging.

MINNESOTA

SKI AREAS (continued)

Orono

SKI TONKA
Orono, MN 55960
(612) 472-2827
LOCATION: Near Orono.
FACILITIES: 19 tow ropes; ski instruction; ski rental; 250 ft. vertical drop; longest run, 1000 ft.; restaurants; lodging.

Park Rapids

VAL CHATEL SKI AREA
Park Rapids, MN 56470
(218) 266-3306
LOCATION: Near Park Rapids.
FACILITIES: 6 tow ropes; ski instruction; ski rental; 270 ft. vertical drop; longest run, 1475 ft.; restaurants; lodging.

Red Lake Falls

TIMBERLAND SKI AREA
Red Lake Falls, MN 56750
(218) 253-2437
LOCATION: Near Red Lake Falls.
FACILITIES: 4 tow ropes; ski instruction; ski rental; 110 ft. vertical drop; longest run, 1200 ft.; restaurants; lodging.

Rochester

ROCHESTER SKI HILL
Rochester, MN 55901
(507) 288-6767
LOCATION: Near Rochester.
FACILITIES: 1 tow rope; 1 poma; ski instruction; ski rental; 140 ft. vertical drop; longest run, 800 ft.; restaurants; lodging.

St. Paul

BATTLE CREEK SKI AREA
St. Paul, MN 55119
(612) 770-1361
LOCATION: Off Winthrop St., 1 block south of Upper Afton Road.
FACILITIES: 3 tow ropes; ski instruction; ski rental; 90 ft. vertical drop; longest run, 1100 ft.; restaurants; lodging.

COMO PARK SKI AREA
St. Paul, MN 55101
(612) 489-1804
LOCATION: Near St. Paul.
FACILITIES: 2 tow ropes; ski instruction; ski rental; restaurants; lodging.

Sleepy Eye

GOLDEN GATE CAMPGROUND SKI AREA
Sleepy Eye, MN 56085
(507) 794-7459
LOCATION: Near Sleepy Eye.
FACILITIES: 2 tow ropes; ski instruction; ski rental; 150 ft. vertical drop; longest run, 1000 ft.; restaurants; lodging.

Taylor Falls

WILD MOUNTAIN SKI AREA
Taylor Falls, MN 55084

(612) 465-6365
LOCATION: Near Taylor Falls.
FACILITIES: 3 quad chairlifts; 2 tow ropes; ski instruction; ski rental; 300 ft. vertical drop; longest run, 4500 ft.; restaurants; lodging.

Wabasha

COFFEE MILL SKI AREA
Wabasha, MN 55981
(612) 565-4561
LOCATION: Near Wabasha.
FACILITIES: 2 double chairlifts; 1 poma; ski instruction; ski rental; 500 ft. vertical drop; longest run, 4000 ft.; restaurants; lodging.

Welch

WELCH VILLAGE SKI AREA
Welch, MN 55089
(612) 258-4567
LOCATION: Near Welch.
FACILITIES: 4 double chairlifts; 2 T-bars; 1 tow rope; 1 mitey mite; ski instruction; ski rental; 350 ft. vertical drop; longest run, 4000 ft.; restaurants; lodging.

West St. Paul

MARTHALER SKI AREA
1625 Humboldt Avenue
West St. Paul, MN 55118
(612) 455-9937
LOCATION: In West St. Paul.
FACILITIES: 1 tow rope; ski instruction; ski rental; 300 ft. vertical drop; longest run, 1000 ft.; restaurants; lodging.

AMUSEMENT PARKS & ATTRACTIONS

Apple Valley

MINNESOTA ZOOLOGICAL GARDEN
12101 Johnny Cake Ridge Road
Apple Valley, MN 55124
(612) 432-9000
FACILITIES: Zoo; 3 refreshment stands; restaurant; exhibits; pay gate.

Brainerd

PAUL BUNYAN CENTER
Hwys. 210 & 371
Brainerd, MN 56401
(218) 829-6342
FACILITIES: 7 major rides; 2 kiddie rides; 2 refreshment stands; restaurant; curio, souvenir & gift shops; arcade; helicopter rides; animated logging camp; free acts; pay gate; free parking; open Memorial Day - Labor Day.

LUMBERTOWN, U.S.A. (Attraction)
Route 6
Brainerd, MN 56401
(218) 829-8100
FACILITIES: 2 major rides; refreshment stand; restaurant; ice cream parlor; arcade; museum; exhibits; crafts; 30 authentic historical buildings; steamboat; saw mill; special railroad; free acts; orchestras; pay gate; free parking; open May 27 - Sept. 15.

AMUSEMENT PARKS (continued)

Marble

FAIRYLAND PARK (Attraction)
Hwy. 169
Marble, MN 55764
(218) 326-8160
FACILITIES: 35 life-sized, handmade scenes of fairy tales and folk tales; free parking; open May 30 - Labor Day.

St. Paul

O'NEIL AMUSEMENTS
Lexington Parkway
St. Paul, MN 55113
(612) 489-2323
FACILITIES: 8 major rides; 6 kiddie rides; 4 refreshment stands; swimming pool; picnic facilities; novelties; miniature golf; golf course; zoo; conservatory; fire engine & train exhibit; free gate; free parking; open Apr. - Oct.

Shakopee

VALLEY PARK, INC.
One Valleyfair Drive
Shakopee, MN 55379
(612) 445-7600
FACILITIES: 12 major rides; 3 kiddie rides; fun house; 12 games; 5 refreshment stands; 3 restaurants; arcade; shooting gallery; camping; zoo; crafts; stage shows; dolphin show; puppet show; free acts; pay gate; pay parking; open May 17 - Sept. 26.

STATE FAIR

Minnesota State Fair
St. Paul, MN 55108
(612) 645-2781
DATE: August

NATIONAL PARKS

International Falls

VOYAGEURS NATIONAL PARK
International Falls, MN 56649
(218) 283-9821

INDIVIDUAL SITES
FACILITIES: Open year round; limit of stay: 14 days; 65 sites; group camps; water and bathroom facilities; cabins; picnic area; food service; swimming; boating; boat rental; fishing; guide for hire; hiking; medical service; boat access; primitive site; untreated water; lodging.

KING WILLIAM
FACILITIES: Open year round; limit of stay: 14 days; 5 sites; group camps; water and bathroom facilities; cabins; picnic area; food service; swimming; boating; boat rental; fishing; guide for hire; hiking; medical service; boat access; primitive site; untreated water; lodging.

MUKOODA
FACILITIES: Open year round; limit of stay:

14 days; 5 sites; group camps; water and bathroom facilities; cabins; picnic area; food service; swimming; boating; boat rental; fishing; guide for hire; hiking; medical service; boat access; primitive site; untreated water; lodging.

NATIONAL FORESTS

National Forests
Eastern Region
633 West Wisconsin Avenue
Milwaukee, WI 53203
(414) 291-3693

Cass Lake

CHIPPEWA NATIONAL FOREST
ATTRACTIONS: Stands of virgin red pine; home and present headquarters of the Chippewa Indians. Walleyes, northern pike, and pan fish fishing; waterfowl, upland game bird, deer, black bear hunting; swimming; boating; water sports; winter sports including skiing, tobogganing, snowshoeing, and ice fishing.
FACILITIES: 25 camp and picnic sites; 21 picnic only; 4 swimming sites; Shingobee Winter Sports Area; 300 resorts in and adjacent to the National Forest; hotels; cabins.
NEARBY TOWNS: Bemidji, Blackduck, Deer River, Grand Rapids, Remer, Walker.

Duluth

SUPERIOR NATIONAL FOREST
ATTRACTIONS: 5,000 lakes; finest canoe country in the United States here in the land of the French voyageurs, along their historic water route to the Northwest. Lake and stream fishing; deer hunting; two ski areas nearby; scenic drives.
FACILITIES: 185 canoe camp sites, 63 camp and picnic sites, 24 picnic only; resorts; hotels; cabins outside the wilderness area.
NEARBY TOWNS: Ely, Grand Marais, International Falls, Two Harbors, Virginia.

See OTTAWA NATIONAL FOREST - Michigan.

STATE PARKS

Headquarters

Department of Natural Resources
Parks Division
658 Cedar
St. Paul, MN 55101
(612) 296-4776

Albert Lea

HELMER MYRE STATE PARK
LOCATION: 5 mi. east of Albert Lea.
FACILITIES: Open year round; 142 sites; water and bathroom facilities; sanitary station; trailer village vehicle sites; picnic area; fishing; hiking; tent camping.

Alexandria

LAKE CARLOS STATE PARK

MINNESOTA

STATE PARKS (continued)

LOCATION: 10 mi. north of Alexandria.
FACILITIES: Open year round; 146 sites; water and bathroom facilities; sanitary station; trailer village vehicle sites; picnic area; swimming; boating; fishing; hiking; horseback riding; tent camping.

Bemidji

LAKE BEMIDJI STATE PARK
LOCATION: 6 mi. northeast of Bemidji.
FACILITIES: Open year round; 113 sites; water and bathroom facilities; sanitary station; trailer village vehicle sites; picnic area; swimming; boating; fishing; hiking; handicapped access/restroom; tent camping.

Big Fork

SCENIC STATE PARK
LOCATION: 7 mi. southeast of Big Fork.
FACILITIES: Open year round; 74 sites; water and bathroom facilities; trailer village vehicle sites; picnic area; swimming; boating; fishing; hiking; tent camping.

Brainerd

CROW WING STATE PARK
LOCATION: 9 mi. southwest of Brainerd.
FACILITIES: Open year round; 101 sites; water and bathroom facilities; sanitary station; trailer village vehicle sites; picnic area; fishing; hiking; handicapped access/restroom; tent camping.

Duluth

JAY COOKE STATE PARK
LOCATION: 2 mi. west of Duluth.
FACILITIES: Open year round; 96 sites; water and bathroom facilities; sanitary station; trailer village vehicle sites; picnic area; fishing; hiking; handicapped access/restroom; tent camping.

Hinckley

ST. CROIX STATE PARK
LOCATION: 16 mi. east of Hinckley.
FACILITIES: Open year round; 224 sites; water and bathroom facilities; sanitary station; trailer village vehicle sites; picnic area; swimming; boating; fishing; hiking; horseback riding; bicycle trail; handicapped access/restroom; tent camping.

Isle

FATHER HENNEPIN STATE PARK
LOCATION: 1 mi. northwest of Isle.
FACILITIES: Open year round; 62 sites; water and bathroom facilities; sanitary station; trailer village vehicle sites; picnic area; swimming; fishing; hiking; tent camping.

Little Falls

CHARLES A. LINDBERGH STATE PARK
LOCATION: 2 mi. south of Little Falls.
FACILITIES: Open year round; 52 sites; water and bathroom facilities; sanitary station;

trailer village vehicle sites; picnic area; hiking; tent camping.

Luverne

BLUE MOUNDS STATE PARK
LOCATION: 7 mi. north of Luverne.
FACILITIES: Open year round; 76 sites; water and bathroom facilities; sanitary station; trailer village vehicle sites; picnic area; swimming; fishing; hiking; tent camping.

Mankato

MINNEOPA STATE PARK
LOCATION: 6 mi. west of Mankato.
FACILITIES: Open year round; 50 sites; water and bathroom facilities; trailer village vehicle sites; picnic area; fishing; hiking; tent camping.

McGregor

SAVANNA PORTAGE STATE PARK
LOCATION: 16 mi. northeast of McGregor.
FACILITIES: Open year round; 63 sites; water and bathroom facilities; trailer village vehicle sites; picnic area; swimming; boating; fishing; hiking; tent camping.

Montevideo

LAC QUI PARLE STATE PARK
LOCATION: 10 mi. northwest of Montevideo.
FACILITIES: Open year round; 50 sites; water and bathroom facilities; trailer village vehicle sites; picnic area; swimming; fishing; hiking; horseback riding; tent camping.

New London

SIBLEY STATE PARK
LOCATION: 5 mi. west of New London.
FACILITIES: Open year round; 85 sites; water and bathroom facilities; sanitary station; trailer village vehicle sites; picnic area; swimming; boating; fishing; hiking; horseback riding; tent camping.

Northfield

NERSTRAND WOODS STATE PARK
LOCATION: 16 mi. southeast of Northfield.
FACILITIES: Open year round; 62 sites; water and bathroom facilities; sanitary station; trailer village vehicle sites; picnic area; hiking; tent camping.

Onamia

MILLE LACS KATHIO STATE PARK
LOCATION: 5 mi. northwest of Onamia.
FACILITIES: Open year round; 71 sites; water and bathroom facilities; trailer village vehicle sites; picnic area; swimming; boating; fishing; hiking; horseback riding; tent camping.

Park Rapids

ITASCA STATE PARK
LOCATION: 28 mi. north of Park Rapids.
FACILITIES: Open year round; 237 sites; water and bathroom facilities; sanitary station;

STATE PARKS (continued)

trailer village vehicle sites; picnic area; swimming; boating; fishing; hiking; tent camping.

Pelican Rapids

MAPLEWOOD STATE PARK
LOCATION: 7 mi. southeast of Pelican Rapids.
FACILITIES: Open year round; 51 sites; water and bathroom facilities; trailer village vehicle sites; picnic area; swimming; fishing; hiking; horseback riding; tent camping.

Stillwater

WILLIAM O'BRIEN STATE PARK
LOCATION: 16 mi. north of Stillwater.
FACILITIES: Open year round; 125 sites; water and bathroom facilities; trailer village vehicle sites; picnic area; swimming; boating; fishing; hiking; handicapped access/restroom; tent camping.

Tower

BEAR HEAD LAKE STATE PARK
LOCATION: 16 mi. east of Tower.
FACILITIES: Open year round; 65 sites; water and bathroom facilities; trailer village vehicle sites; picnic area; swimming; boating; fishing; hiking; tent camping.

Two Harbors

GOOSEBERRY FALLS STATE PARK
LOCATION: 13 mi. northeast of Two Harbors.
FACILITIES: Open year round; 125 sites; water and bathroom facilities; sanitary station; trailer village vehicle sites; picnic area; fishing; hiking; tent camping.

Williams

ZIPPEL BAY STATE PARK
LOCATION: 9 mi. northeast of Williams.
FACILITIES: Open year round; 50 sites; water and bathroom facilities; trailer village vehicle sites; picnic area; swimming; fishing; hiking; tent camping.

Wykoff

FORESTVILLE STATE PARK
LOCATION: 7 mi. southeast of Wykoff.
FACILITIES: Open year round; 68 sites; water and bathroom facilities; trailer village vehicle sites; picnic area; fishing; hiking; horseback riding; tent camping.

STATE FORESTS

Department of Natural Resources
Forestry Division
444 Lafayette Road
St. Paul, MN 55101
(612) 296-5963

Brainerd

BIRCH LAKE STATE FOREST
Brainerd, MN 56401
(612) 693-8983
LOCATION: On Forest Road.
FACILITIES: Open year round; 20 sites; trailer village vehicle sites; picnic area; swimming; boating; fishing; hiking; tent camping.

CROW WING STATE FOREST
Brainerd, MN 56401
(218) 829-1411
LOCATION: Off County Road 14.
FACILITIES: Open year round; 33 sites; trailer village vehicle sites; picnic area; swimming; boating; fishing; tent camping.

Cambridge

SAND DUNES STATE FOREST
Cambridge, MN 55008
(612) 689-2832
LOCATION: Off County Road 4.
FACILITIES: Open year round; 27 sites; trailer village vehicle sites; swimming; tent camping.

Duluth

CLOQUET VALLEY STATE FOREST
Duluth, MN 55811
(218) 723-4669
LOCATION: On County Road 8.
FACILITIES: Open year round; 43 sites; trailer village vehicle sites; picnic area; swimming; boating; fishing; hiking; tent camping.

FINLAND STATE FOREST
Duluth, MN 55811
(218) 724-7606
LOCATION: On Hwy. 1 south.
FACILITIES: Open year round; 72 sites; trailer village vehicle sites; picnic area; boating; fishing; hiking; tent camping.

Hibbing

GEORGE WASHINGTON STATE FOREST
Hibbing, MN 55746
(218) 263-6405
LOCATION: Off Venning Road.
FACILITIES: Open year round; 137 sites; trailer village vehicle sites; picnic area; swimming; boating; fishing; hiking; tent camping.

Hill City

LAND O'LAKES STATE FOREST
Hill City, MN 55748
(218) 697-2476
LOCATION: On County Road 48.
FACILITIES: Open year round; 30 sites; trailer village vehicle sites; picnic area; swimming; boating; hiking; tent camping.

SAVANNA STATE FOREST
Hill City, MN 55748
(218) 697-2476
LOCATION: Off Hwy. 65.
FACILITIES: Open year round; 20 sites; trailer village vehicle sites; swimming; boating; fishing; hiking; tent camping.

Moose Lake

GENERAL C.C. ANDREWS STATE FOREST

MINNESOTA

STATE FORESTS (continued)

Moose Lake, MN 55767
(218) 485-4688
LOCATION: On Willow Road flowage.
FACILITIES: Open year round; 28 sites; trailer village vehicle sites; boating; fishing; tent camping.

NAMADJI STATE FOREST
Moose Lake, MN 55767
(218) 732-3309
LOCATION: Off County Road 104.
FACILITIES: Open year round; 42 sites; trailer village vehicle sites; picnic area; swimming; boating; tent camping.

Orr

KABETOGAMA STATE FOREST
Orr, MN 55771
(218) 757-3200
LOCATION: On Kabetogama Lake.
FACILITIES: Open year round; 100 sites; trailer village vehicle sites; picnic area; food service; swimming; boating; fishing; tent camping.

Park Rapids

HUNTERSVILLE STATE FOREST
Park Rapids, MN 56470
(218) 732-3309
LOCATION: On Crow Wing Saddle Trail on Crow Wing River.
FACILITIES: Open year round; 31 sites; trailer village vehicle sites; boating; fishing; tent camping.

HISTORIC SITES

Jeffers

JEFFERS PETROGLYPHS - Work of native Americans from as long ago as 3,000 B.C., these carvings comprise nearly two thousand reproductions of human figures, weapons and animals. Located on County Road 2.

Little Falls

CHARLES A. LINDBERGH HOUSE & INTERPRETIVE CENTER - Boyhood home of the first aviator to fly the Atlantic alone was built in 1906 by "Lucky Lindy's" father, a distinguished lawyer and congressman. Located on Lindbergh Drive.

Pine City

COMPANY FUR POST - In 1804, traders landed on the banks of the Snake River and set up a wintering post. Today an authentically reconstructed fur post is stocked with goods of those early times and guides dressed as voyageurs are engaged in activities typical of the post in the 1800s. Located off Interstate 35, 1½ mi. west on County Road 7.

St. Paul

ALEXANDER RAMSEY HOUSE - An 1872 French Renaissance mansion, it was the home of Alexander Ramsey who served as Governor, U.S. Senator and Secretary of War. It features walnut woodwork, marble fireplaces and Brussels carpeting. Located at 265 South Exchange Street.

FORT SNELLING - Built between 1820 and 1824 by U.S. soldiers under Col. Josiah Snelling, the fort was the indisputable guardian of American interests in the upper Northwest. Today, the fort is a living museum with costumed soldiers acting out aspects of the traditional military life of the 1820s. Located near Hwys. 5 & 55.

HOSTELS

Duluth

YWCA CAMP WANAKIWIN
202 W. 2nd Street
Duluth, MN 55802
(218) 722-7425
FACILITIES: Open Aug. 26 - Jun. 14; 40 beds, men; 40 beds, women; modern bathroom; overnight charges: $4; houseparent: Fern Anderson.

Grey Eagle

EAGLE MOUNTAIN SKI HOSTELS
P.O. Box 98
Grey Eagle, MN 56336
(612) 285-4567
FACILITIES: Open year round; 11 beds, men; 11 beds, women; modern bathroom; nearest hostel: Nimrod, 75 mi. north; overnight charges: $3.50; houseparent: Robert Lanners.

Nimrod

CROW WING TRAILS YOUTH HOSTEL
County Highway 27
Nimrod, MN 56477
(218) 472-3250
FACILITIES: Open Jun. 1 - Sept. 15; 10 beds, men; 10 beds, women; modern bathroom; nearest hostel: Grey Eagle, 75 mi. south; overnight charges: $2; houseparent: George Gloege.

St. Paul

CAPITOL CENTER YMCA
475 Cedar Street
St. Paul, MN 55101
(612) 222-0771
FACILITIES: Open year round; 10 beds, men; 10 beds, women; modern bathroom; overnight charges: $2; houseparent: Douglas G. Finch.

POINTS OF INTEREST

International Falls

GRAND MOUND INTERPRETIVE CENTER - Grand Mound, 136 feet long, 98 feet wide and 40 feet high, is the largest prehistoric Indian burial mound in Minnesota and

POINTS OF INTEREST (continued)

one of the largest in the Upper Midwest. Interpretive Center explains the culture of the people buried here. Located on Hwy. 11.

Le Sueur

W.W. MAYO HOUSE - An English immigrant, Dr. William W. Mayo, built this small Gothic house in 1859. Later he and his two sons es-tablished the world-renowned Mayo Clinic. Located at 118 North Main Street.

St. Paul

BURBANK-LIVINGSTON-GRIGGS HOUSE - Bordering Summit Avenue, street of F. Scott Fitzgerald, this lavish mansion was built in 1863 by shipping magnate James C. Burbank. It includes 10 European period rooms with 17th- and 18th-century appointments. Located at 432 Summit Avenue.

MISSISSIPPI

Mississippi, named after the great river which forms its western boundary, entered the Union in 1817 as the twentieth state. The French first tried to settle the state, but were hampered by persistant Indian attacks, and eventually relinquished their claim to Spain in the 1760s. Spain signed over the state's northern territorial rights to the United States, which then annexed the southern portion of the state based on its Louisiana Purchase.

The Civil War ravaged Mississippi's huge cotton plantations, and it took nearly a quarter of a century after Lee's surrender for the state to regain its economic stability.

Mississippi still relies on "King Cotton" and the related garment and textile industries. However, with the growth of the energy industry, the state now emphasises its natural gas and oil production.

Tourism is also a major contributor to the state's economy, aided by attractive state parks, sunny weather and the picturesque Gulf Coast.

State capital: Jackson. State bird: Mockingbird. State tree: Magnolia. State flower: Magnolia.

WEATHER

The topography of Mississippi consists of level lands in the "Delta" region in the northwest, the upland prairie in the northeast, and a series of ridges and valleys in between. A triangular area, comprising nearly one-third of the state, is composed of rolling hills 200 to 500 feet above sea level. The coastal strip has developed into a popular summer resort, since the waters of the Mississippi Sound provide a natural air-conditioning to ameliorate the summer heat.

Mississippi has a climate characterized by extreme heat in summer and absence of severe cold in winter. The prevailing southerly winds provide a moist, semitropical climate, with conditions often favorable for afternoon thunderstorms. In the colder season, the state is alternately subjected to warm tropical air and cold continental air, in periods of varying length. However, cold spells seldom last over 3 or 4 days.

Average daily temperature for each month.

	Northern	Southern
Jan.	50.9 to 30.2	61.5 to 37.8
Feb.	55.0 to 32.8	65.1 to 40.3
Mar.	62.3 to 39.8	71.8 to 46.0
Apr.	73.7 to 50.6	79.9 to 54.9
May	80.8 to 57.5	85.6 to 61.2
Jun.	87.9 to 65.4	91.6 to 67.6
Jul.	90.9 to 68.5	92.7 to 70.6
Aug.	90.6 to 66.9	92.3 to 69.7
Sept.	85.4 to 61.6	88.2 to 65.3
Oct.	75.3 to 49.0	80.2 to 53.2
Nov.	62.9 to 39.1	70.0 to 44.0
Dec.	54.0 to 33.0	63.7 to 39.9
Year	72.5 to 49.5	78.6 to 54.2

STATE CHAMBER OF COMMERCE

Mississippi Economic Council
The State Chamber of Commerce
P.O. Box 1849
Standard Life Building
Jackson, MS 39205
(601) 969-0022

STATE & CITY TOURISM OFFICES

State

Mississippi Agricultural and Industrial Board
1504 Walter Sillers Building
Jackson, MS 39205
(601) 354-6711

Travel and Tourism Department
Mississippi Agricultural and Industrial Board
1504 Walter Sillers Building
Jackson, MS 39205
(601) 354-6715

MISSISSIPPI

TOURISM OFFICES (continued)

Local

Natchez-Adams County Chamber of Commerce
P.O. Box 725
Natchez, MS 39120
(601) 445-4611

STATE HIGHWAY DEPARTMENT

State Highway Department
Woolfolk State Office Building
Northwest Street
Jackson, MS 39205
(601) 354-6594

HIGHWAY WELCOMING CENTERS

Lauderdale

LAUDERDALE COUNTY CENTER - Interstate 20, east, near Meridian.

Pike

PIKE COUNTY CENTER - Interstate 55, south, near Macomb.

STATE POLICE

Department of Public Safety
Jackson, MS 39205
(601) 982-1212

HUNTING & FISHING

Hunting

All persons except those exempt under state law are required to purchase an annual hunting and fishing license. Residents exempt from hunting licenses are those under 16 or over 65 years of age, those adjudged totally disabled by the Social Security Administration or those adjudged 100 percent service connected disabled by the Veteran's Administration.

Resident

Sportsman's, $25; combination hunting & fishing, $13; combination small game hunting & fishing, $9; small game hunting, $6; archery/primitive weapon permit, $7; state waterfowl stamp, $2. The archery/primitive weapon permit is included with the sportsman's license but must be bought in addition to the combination hunting & fishing license if hunting during special seasons.

Non-resident

Combination hunting & fishing, $65; all game hunting, $55; 7-day all game hunting, $25; 3-day all game hunting, $20; small game hunting, $25; 7-day small game hunting, $15; archery/primitive weapon permit, $20; state waterfowl stamp, $2. The archery/primitive weapon permit must be bought in addition to either a combination or annual all-game hunting license in order to hunt during the special archery/primitive weapons season.

Fishing

All persons not exempt under state law are required to have a valid fishing license in possession when fishing on public fresh waters of Mississippi. The following people are exempt from the license requirements: residents under the age of 16, non-residents under the age of 14, residents age 65 or over and residents who are blind, paraplegic, a multiple amputee or considered totally disabled by the Veterans or Social Security Administrations. All exempt residents except those under the age of 16 are required to have with them at all times when fishing an exempt license certificate available at no charge from their local clerk. No license is required for any person to fish, hunt or trap on lands in which the record title is vested in that person. In the case of a privately owned landlocked lake, no license is required of any person holding a written permit from the landowner to fish on that lake.

Resident

Sportsman's, $25; combination hunting & fishing, $13; combination small game hunting & fishing, $9; annual, $4; 7-day permit, $3.

Non-resident

7-day tourist permit, $7; annual fishing (cost equivalent to state of residency, but not less than $15); or combination hunting & fishing, $65.

For more information contact:

Mississippi Game & Fish Commission
P.O. Box 451
Jackson, MS 39205
(601) 354-7333

CAMPGROUNDS

Private

Gulfport

GAYWOOD CAMPGROUND
(601) 896-9831
LOCATION: 1100 Cowan Road.
FACILITIES: Open year round; 65 sites; water and bathroom facilities; sanitary station; electrical hookup; trailer village vehicle sites; swimming.

Jackson

CANE CREEK CAMPGROUND
(601) 825-5980

306

CAMPGROUNDS (continued)

LOCATION: On Hwy. 43, east.
FACILITIES: Open year round; 66 sites; water and bathroom facilities; sanitary station; electrical hookup; trailer village vehicle sites; laundry; tent camping.

JOHNNIE CLEVELAND'S TRAILER-TOWN
(601) 939-4873
LOCATION: 2 mi. southeast on old Hwy. 49, south.
FACILITIES: Open year round; 66 sites; water and bathroom facilities; sanitary station; electrical hookup; trailer village vehicle sites; swimming; tent camping.

LAKESHORE CAMPGROUND
(601) 939-3826
LOCATION: On Ross Barnett Reservoir.
FACILITIES: Open year round; 116 sites; water and bathroom facilities; sanitary station; electrical hookup; trailer village vehicle sites; laundry; food service; swimming; boating; fishing; tent camping.

Lucedale

KOA KAMPGROUND
(601) 947-8193
LOCATION: 1 mi. south via Hwy. 613 (on Mill Street exit).
FACILITIES: Open year round; 76 sites; water and bathroom facilities; electrical hookup; trailer village vehicle sites; laundry; food service; swimming; tent camping.

Meridian

CAMPGROUND TRAILER PARK
(601) 485-4549
LOCATION: 2 mi. from I-20 & I-59, DeKalb exit.
FACILITIES: Open year round; 50 sites; water and bathroom facilities; electrical hookup; trailer village vehicle sites; laundry; tent camping.

Morton

COOPER LAKE
(601) 537-3184
LOCATION: 5 mi. south of I-20 on Hwy. 13, Exit 25 (Morton-Puckett).
FACILITIES: Open Apr. - Sept.; 80 sites; water and bathroom facilities; electrical hookup; trailer village vehicle sites; laundry; food service; swimming; boating; fishing; tent camping.

Ocean Springs

KOA KAMPGROUND
(601) 875-2100
LOCATION: On Hwy. 57.
FACILITIES: Open year round; 118 sites; water and bathroom facilities; sanitary station; electrical hookup; trailer village vehicle sites; laundry; food service; swimming; fishing; horseback riding; tent camping.

Vaiden

KOA CARROLL COUNTY
(601) 464-9336

LOCATION: In Vaiden.
FACILITIES: Open year round; 90 sites; water and bathroom facilities; sanitary station; electrical hookup; trailer village vehicle sites; laundry; food service; swimming; tent camping.

RESORTS & BEACHES

Biloxi

MISSISSIPPI GULF COAST AREA - Twenty-six miles of white sand beaches edged by gracious homes and modern hotels. Swim, fish, sail, water ski, golf, play tennis or just sit back and relax in sunny, salty breezes that are frost-free nearly 300 days of the year.

BOATING AREAS

See National Forests and State Parks.

BICYCLE TRAILS

See FLORIDA - Gulf Coast Trail

NATCHEZ TRAIL - 450 mi.; long distances per day, few services; 10-speed bicycle recommended.
The Natchez Trail Parkway has one lane each way winding through scenic country with forests of oak, hickory and pine. Commercial traffic is prohibited and you meet few cars. The only drawback in cycling the Parkway is the fact that there are long stretches with no services.
Trail: Natchez to Natchez Trace Parkway to Nashville, TN.

TRAILS

Morton

SHOCKALOE TRAIL - 23 mi. foot trail. This loop trail, within 50 miles of Jackson and Meridian in the Bienville National Forest, is divided by all-weather gravel roads into nine sections of various lengths. Nature areas and examples of land-use management practices are included for visitor information and enjoyment.

SKI AREAS

There are no organized Ski Areas in Mississippi.

AMUSEMENT PARKS & ATTRACTIONS

Biloxi

BILOXI-GULFPORT AMUSEMENT PARK
3315 West Beach
Biloxi, MS 39531

MISSISSIPPI

AMUSEMENT PARKS (continued)

(601) 432-8946
FACILITIES: 7 major rides; 7 kiddie rides;
10 games; refreshment stand; shooting gallery;
picnic facilities; beach; free acts; fireworks;
free gate; free parking.

STATE FAIR

Mississippi State Fair
P.O. Box 892
Jackson, MS 39212
(601) 353-1187
DATE: October

NATIONAL PARKS

There are no National Parks in Mississippi.

NATIONAL FORESTS

National Forests
Southern Region
1720 Peachtree Road, NW
Atlanta, GA 30309
(404) 881-4177

BIENVILLE NATIONAL FOREST
ATTRACTIONS: Numerous forest management demonstration areas; quail hunting; fishing.
FACILITIES: 3 camp and picnic sites, 3 picnic only; swimming site.
NEARBY TOWN: Meridian.

DELTA NATIONAL FOREST
ATTRACTIONS: Fishing; waterfowl hunting.
FACILITIES: 2 picnic sites.
NEARBY TOWNS: Rolling Fork, Vicksburg.

DESOTO NATIONAL FOREST
ATTRACTIONS: Quail hunting; fishing; boating.
FACILITIES: 3 camp and picnic sites, 11 picnic only; swimming site.
NEARBY TOWNS: Biloxi, Gulfport, Hattiesburg, Laurel, Wiggins.

HOLLY SPRINGS NATIONAL FOREST
ATTRACTIONS: Intensive erosion control
projects; quail, small-game hunting.
FACILITIES: 2 camp and picnic sites, 3 picnic only; swimming site.
NEARBY TOWNS: Holly Springs, New Albany, Oxford.

HOMOCHITTO NATIONAL FOREST
ATTRACTIONS: One of the finest natural
timber-growing sites in the United States;
numerous forest management demonstration
areas; picturesque eroded loess country near
Natchez.
FACILITIES: 3 picnic sites and swimming
site.
NEARBY TOWNS: Brookhaven, Gloster,
Meadville, and Natchez.

TOMBIGBEE NATIONAL FOREST
ATTRACTIONS: Indian mounds; Natchez
Trace Parkway; deer, quail hunting; fishing;
boating.
FACILITIES: 3 camp and picnic sites, 3 pic-
nic only; swimming site.
NEARBY TOWNS: Ackerman, Houston, Kos-
ciusko, and Tupelo.

STATE PARKS

Headquarters

Mississippi Park Commission
717 Robert E. Lee Bldg.
Jackson, MS 39201
(601) 354-6638

Bay St. Louis

BUCCANEER STATE PARK
(601) 467-3822
LOCATION: 10 mi. west of Bay St. Louis off
U.S. 90.
FACILITIES: Open year round; water and
bathroom facilities; electrical hookup; trailer
village vehicle sites; laundry; picnic area; food
service; swimming; fishing; self-guided trail;
tent camping.

Columbus

LAKE LOWNDES STATE PARK
(601) 328-2110
LOCATION: 6 mi. southeast of Columbus off
Hwy. 69.
FACILITIES: Open year round; water and
bathroom facilities; sanitary station; electrical
hookup; trailer village vehicle sites; laundry;
picnic area; food service; boating; fishing; self-
guided trail; tent camping.

Dennis

TISHOMINGO STATE PARK
(601) 438-6914
LOCATION: 3 mi. north of Dennis off Hwy.
25.
FACILITIES: Open year round; water and
bathroom facilities; electrical hookup; trailer
village vehicle sites; cabins; laundry; picnic
area; food service; swimming; boating; fishing;
self-guided trail; tent camping.

Durant

HOLMES COUNTY STATE PARK
(601) 653-3351
LOCATION: 4 mi. south of Durant off I-55.
FACILITIES: Open year round; water and
bathroom facilities; electrical hookup; trailer
village vehicle sites; cabins; laundry; picnic
area; food service; swimming; boating; fishing;
self-guided trail; tent camping.

Grenada

HUGH WHITE STATE PARK
(601) 226-4934
LOCATION: 5 mi. east of Grenada.
FACILITIES: Open year round; water and
bathroom facilities; sanitary station; electrical
hookup; trailer village vehicle sites; cabins;

STATE PARKS (continued)

laundry; picnic area; food service; swimming; boating; fishing; self-guided trail; lodging; tent camping; reservation required.

Hattiesburg

PAUL B. JOHNSON STATE PARK
(601) 582-7721
LOCATION: 15 mi. south of Hattiesburg off U.S. 49.
FACILITIES: Open year round; water and bathroom facilities; electrical hookup; trailer village vehicle sites; cabins; laundry; picnic area; food service; swimming; boating; fishing; tent camping.

Hernando

ARKABUTLA STATE PARK
(601) 562-4385
LOCATION: 15 mi. west of Hernando off Hwy. 304.
FACILITIES: Open year round; water and bathroom facilities; sanitary station; electrical hookup; trailer village vehicle sites; laundry; picnic area; swimming; boating; fishing; tent camping; reservation required.

Hollandale

LEROY PERCY STATE PARK
(601) 827-5436
LOCATION: 6 mi. west of Hollandale off Hwy. 12.
FACILITIES: Open year round; water and bathroom facilities; electrical hookup; trailer village vehicle sites; cabins; laundry; picnic area; food service; swimming; boating; fishing; tent camping.

Holly Springs

WALL DOXEY STATE PARK
(601) 252-4231
LOCATION: 7 mi. south of Holly Springs off Hwy. 7.
FACILITIES: Open year round; water and bathroom facilities; electrical hookup; trailer village vehicle sites; cabins; laundry; picnic area; food service; swimming; boating; fishing.

Iuka

J.P. COLEMAN STATE PARK
(601) 423-6515
LOCATION: 13 mi. north of Iuka off Hwy. 25.
FACILITIES: Open year round; water and bathroom facilities; electrical hookup; trailer village vehicle sites; cabins; laundry; picnic area; food service; swimming; boating; fishing; self-guided trail; lodging; tent camping.

McComb

PERCY QUIN STATE PARK
(601) 684-3938
LOCATION: 6 mi. south of McComb off I-55.
FACILITIES: Open year round; water and bathroom facilities; electrical hookup; trailer village vehicle sites; cabins; laundry; picnic area; food service; swimming; boating; fishing; tent camping.

Meridian

CLARKCO STATE PARK
(601) 776-6651
LOCATION: 20 mi. south of Meridian off U.S. 45.
FACILITIES: Open year round; water and bathroom facilities; electrical hookup; trailer village vehicle sites; cabins; laundry; picnic area; food service; swimming; boating; fishing; self-guided trail; tent camping.

Morton

ROOSEVELT STATE PARK
(601) 732-6316
LOCATION: 2 mi. south of Morton off Hwy. 13.
FACILITIES: Open year round; water and bathroom facilities; electrical hookup; trailer village vehicle sites; cabins; laundry; picnic area; food service; swimming; boating; fishing; tent camping.

Oakland

YOCONA RIDGE STATE PARK
(601) 623-7356
LOCATION: 3 mi. east of Oakland off Hwy. 32.
FACILITIES: Open year round; water and bathroom facilities; electrical hookup; trailer village vehicle sites; cabins; laundry; picnic area; food service; swimming; boating; fishing; lodging; tent camping; reservation required.

Sardis

JOHN W. KYLE STATE PARK
(601) 487-1345
LOCATION: 9 mi. east of Sardis off Hwy. 315.
FACILITIES: Open year round; water and bathroom facilities; sanitary station; electrical hookup; trailer village vehicle sites; cabins; laundry; picnic area; food service; swimming; boating; fishing; self-guided trail; lodging; tent camping; reservation required.

Tupelo

TOMBIGBEE STATE PARK
(601) 842-7669
LOCATION: 6 mi. southeast of Tupelo off Hwy. 6.
FACILITIES: Open year round; water and bathroom facilities; electrical hookup; trailer village vehicle sites; laundry; picnic area; food service; swimming; boating; fishing; lodging; tent camping.

STATE FORESTS

There are no State Forests in Mississippi.

HISTORIC SITES

Alcorn

ALCORN STATE UNIVERSITY - First land-grant college for Blacks in the nation.

MISSISSIPPI

HISTORIC SITES (continued)

Biloxi

BEAUVOIR - Last home of Jefferson Davis, President of the Confederate States of America. Here he wrote "The Rise and Fall of the Confederate Government."

Jackson

OLD CAPITOL - Mississippi's legislature first met in unfinished building in 1839 and passed first law in America giving property rights to women.

Vicksburg

OLD WARREN COUNTY COURTHOUSE - Site of surrender of Vicksburg to General Grant on July 4, 1863, and symbol of Confederate resistance during the 47-day siege. Also houses one of the South's largest collections of Civil War Americana.

STEAMER SPRAGUE - Largest sternwheeler ever built. Relic now docked at the Vicksburg waterfront.

HOSTELS

There are no Hostels in Mississippi.

POINTS OF INTEREST

Biloxi

BLESSING OF THE SHRIMP FLEET - Carried over from old European customs; several hundred gaily decorated boats parade the Biloxi channel, each being blessed as it passes the priest from St. Michael's Catholic Church. Held the first weekend in June.

Flora

MISSISSIPPI PETRIFIED FOREST - Only petrified forest in eastern U.S. Giant stone trees dating back 30 million years: extinct species of maple, birch, fir, sequoia and spurge.

Natchez

CONNELLY'S TAVERN - A two-story structure with double galleries and canted roof built during the Spanish rule. Since many of the ceilings are arched, it is thought that the building was constructed from timbers of ships. A moat and drawbridges are other unique features.

LONGWOOD - Largest and most elaborate octagonal house in the country. Located near Natchez.

NATCHEZ-UNDER-THE-HILL - Old time den of iniquity at base of Natchez' high bluffs where river travelers stopped to gamble, carouse and fight, often ending up penniless. Called by an evangelist of the day the "worst hell-hole on earth."

Oxford

ROWAN OAK - Home of Nobel Prize and Pulitzer Prize winning author William Faulkner from 1930 until his death in 1962. Faulkner, considered by many scholars to be the "Shakespeare of the 20th century," wrote most of his internationally famous novels and short stories here. He was married and buried nearby.

Tupelo

ELVIS PRESLEY HOUSE - Boyhood town and home of the "King of Rock 'n Roll."

MISSOURI

Missouri, the Gateway to the West, joined the Union in 1821 as the twenty-fourth state. The French established their first settlement at Sainte Genevieve. St. Louis, the second site to be settled, eventually became the major supply and starting point for explorers, adventurers and wagon trains heading west.

The question of slavery arose early in Missouri, and hindered its entry into the Union. The issue was resolved in the famous "Missouri Compromise," which determined that all states above the 36th parallel, except Missouri, must be "free" states. Also, one

state opposed to slavery, Maine, in Missouri's case, had to enter the Union at the same time to strike a balance.

Today, most of the state's revenues come from manufacturing. Agriculture, and especially corn, is a second major income producer.

The state's tourism business, which features scenic lake resorts in the Ozark Mountains, also generates a substantial income.

State capital: Jefferson City. State bird: Bluebird. State tree: Flowering dogwood. State flower: Hawthorn.

WEATHER

Missouri's three main terrain features are the rolling prairies of the area north of the

Missouri River and of the west-central counties, the Ozarks, and the southeast lowlands, commonly called the "Bootheel."

Missouri is an inland state, thus its climate

WEATHER (continued)

is essentially continental. There are frequent changes in the weather, both from day to day and from season to season.

Missouri is in the path of cold air moving down out of Canada, warm moist air coming up from the Gulf of Mexico, and dry air from the west.

While winters are cold and summers are hot, prolonged periods of very cold or very hot weather are unusual. Occasional periods of mild, above freezing temperatures are noted almost every winter. Conversely, during the peak of the summer season, occasional periods of dry, cool weather break up stretches of hot, humid weather.

Average daily temperature for each month.

	Northern	Southern
Jan.	32.4 to 13.8	44.8 to 21.0
Feb.	38.2 to 19.2	49.3 to 25.0
Mar.	48.2 to 27.5	57.3 to 32.0
Apr.	63.3 to 41.1	69.6 to 43.0
May	73.8 to 51.6	77.5 to 51.6
Jun.	82.5 to 60.8	85.0 to 60.1
Jul.	87.3 to 65.0	89.4 to 64.3
Aug.	85.3 to 62.9	88.7 to 62.2
Sept.	77.4 to 54.8	81.4 to 55.3
Oct.	66.9 to 44.8	71.7 to 43.5
Nov.	50.6 to 31.2	57.3 to 32.2
Dec.	37.0 to 20.6	46.9 to 24.9
Year	61.9 to 41.1	68.2 to 42.9

STATE CHAMBER OF COMMERCE

Missouri Chamber of Commerce
P.O. Box 149
Jefferson City, MO 65101
(314) 634-3511

STATE & CITY TOURISM OFFICES

State

Missouri Division of Commerce and Industrial Development
Jefferson Building
Jefferson City, MO 65101
(314) 751-4241

Missouri Division of Tourism
P.O. Box 1055
Jefferson City, MO 65101
(314) 751-4133

Local

Convention and Tourist Board of Greater St. Louis
500 North Broadway
St. Louis, MO 63102
(314) 421-1023

Convention and Visitor's Bureau
1221 Baltimore Avenue
Kansas City, MO 64105
(816) 221-5242

STATE HIGHWAY DEPARTMENT

Missouri State Highway Department
State Highway Building
119 W. Capitol Avenue
Jefferson City, MO 65101
(314) 751-2551

HIGHWAY WELCOMING CENTERS

Joplin

JOPLIN CENTER - Interstate 44.

St. Louis

ST. LOUIS CENTER - Interstate 270.

STATE POLICE

Department of Public Safety
Jefferson City, MO 65101
(314) 755-3313

HUNTING & FISHING

Hunting

A license is required for all persons, ages 12 through 65, who hunt and fish in the state. To qualify as a resident, a person must reside in the state 30 days prior to application.

Resident

Hunting and fishing, $10; hunting, $5.50; deer hunting, $7.50; turkey hunting, $7.50; shooting area, $6; trapping, $5.50.

Non-resident

Deer hunting, $50; turkey hunting, $30; small game, $25.

Fishing

See hunting regulations above.

Resident

Fishing, $5.50; trout stamp, $4; 14-day fishing, $5; 3-day fishing, $3.

Non-resident

Fishing, $7.50; 14-day fishing, $5; 3-day fishing, $3.

For more information contact:

MISSOURI

HUNTING & FISHING (continued)

Department of Conservation
2901 N. Ten Mile Drive
Jefferson City, MO 65101
(314) 751-4115

CAMPGROUNDS

Private

Branson

YOGI BEAR'S JELLYSTONE PARK CAMP -
RESORT
(417) 334-4131
LOCATION: On Indian Point Road.
FACILITIES: Open year round; 360 sites; water and bathroom facilities; electrical hookup; trailer village vehicle sites; laundry; food service; swimming; boating; tent camping.

Cuba

YOGI BEAR'S JELLYSTONE PARK CAMP
(314) 885-2541
LOCATION: 3 mi. east of Cuba.
FACILITIES: Open year round; 215 sites; water an l bathroom facilities; sanitary station; electrical hookup; trailer village vehicle sites; laundry; food service; swimming; fishing; hiking.

Eureka

TOP NOTCH CAMP RESORT
(314) 587-3100
LOCATION: ¾ mi. on N service road.
FACILITIES: Open Mar. - Nov.; 294 sites; water and bathroom facilities; sanitary station; electrical hookup; trailer village vehicle sites; laundry; food service; swimming; fishing; hiking; tent camping.

Leasburg

DANIEL BOONE CAMPGROUND
(314) 245-6870
LOCATION: 6 mi. south of I-44 on Hwy. H.
FACILITIES: Open Apr. - Oct.; 590 sites; water and bathroom facilities; sanitary station; electrical hookup; trailer village vehicle sites; swimming; hunting; fishing; hiking.

Marquand

TRAILS END RANCH
(314) 783-2948
LOCATION: Road DD.
FACILITIES: Open year round; 450 sites; water and bathroom facilities; sanitary station; electrical hookup; trailer village vehicle sites; swimming; boating; hunting; fishing; hiking; tent camping.

Noel

WAYSIDE CAMPGROUND
(417) 475-3230

LOCATION: Hwys. 59 & 90 junction.
FACILITIES: Open Apr. - Oct.; 280 sites; water and bathroom facilities; electrical hookup; trailer village vehicle sites; swimming; boating; fishing; hiking; tent camping.

Wentzville

PINEWOODS PARK
(314) 327-8248
LOCATION: On Wilmer Road.
FACILITIES: Open year round; 260 sites; water and bathroom facilities; sanitary station; electrical hookup; trailer village vehicle sites; swimming; boating; hiking; tent camping.

TWIN ISLAND LAKE
(314) 623-3408
LOCATION: 8 mi. southeast of Wentzville.
FACILITIES: Open year round; 201 sites; water and bathroom facilities; sanitary station; electrical hookup; trailer village vehicle sites; food service; swimming; boating; fishing; hiking; tent camping.

RESORTS & BEACHES

Most of the state's resort activities center around the major lakes situated in State Parks and include fishing, swimming, boating, water skiing and camping. (See State Parks.)

BOATING AREAS

See National Forests and State Parks.

BICYCLE TRAILS

DEFIANCE TRAIL - 40 mi.; hilly terrain; 10-speed bicycle recommended.
This ride follows the Missouri River on Route 94. You will pass through beautiful farm country, but it is a rugged ride with many hills.
Trail: Defiance to Route 94 west to Hermann.

TRAILS

Graniteville

ELEPHANT ROCKS BRAILLE TRAIL - 1 mi. foot & Braille trail. This 5-foot-wide macadam path is located within Elephant Rocks State Park, which features massive granite outcroppings weathered and eroded to the color and configuration of carved elephants. Interpretive signs, both printed and in Braille, explain the natural and historic features of the park. A system of knotted ropes at trailside assists blind visitors in enjoying the trail.

SKI AREAS

There are no organized Ski Areas in Missouri.

AMUSEMENT PARKS & ATTRACTIONS

Blue Spring

HOMESTEAD FARM
Route 2
Blue Springs, MO 64015
(816) 229-3667
FACILITIES: 5 major rides; 10 kiddie rides;
games; refreshment stand; picnic facilities;
free gate; free parking.

Clarksville

CLARKSVILLE SKYLIFT (Attraction)
Hwy. 79
Clarksville, MO 63336
(314) 242-3454
FACILITIES: Major ride; walk thrus; 2 refreshment stands; picnic facilities; western
town; Indian burial grounds; Indian museum;
historical museum; country store; deer park;
observation tower; mystery house; free parking; open Easter - Sept. 30.

Eureka

SIX FLAGGS OVER MID-AMERICA
P.O. Box 666
Eureka, MO 63025
(314) 938-5300
FACILITIES: 28 major rides; 4 kiddie rides; 2
fun houses; walk thru; 15 games; 44 refreshment stands; 14 restaurants; 4 snack stands; 2
ice cream parlors; 4 live shows; arcade; shooting gallery; picnic facilities; zoo; theatre;
stage shows; orchestras; free acts; name bands;
fireworks; pay gate; pay parking; open Apr. -
Oct. 26.

Hannibal

MARK TWAIN CAVE (Attraction)
Hwy. 79 S.
Hannibal, MO 63401
(314) 221-1656
FACILITIES: Cameron Cave; refreshment
stand; exhibits; camping; picnic facilities;
free gate; free parking; open all year.

Kansas City

FAIRYLAND PARK
7501 Prospect Avenue
Kansas City, MO 63132
(816) 333-2040
FACILITIES: 26 major rides; 9 kiddie rides;
fun house; walk thru; 21 games; 6 refreshment stands; restaurant; penny arcade; shooting gallery; swimming pool; theatre; picnic
facilities; orchestras; name bands; pay gate;
free parking.

WORLDS OF FUN (Theme)
4545 Worlds of Fun Avenue
Kansas City, MO 64161
(816) 454-4545
FACILITIES: Sternwheel riverboat; pirate
ship; 105 major rides; 4 kiddie rides; 2 arcades; 2 shooting galleries; 48-alley skeeball
hall; 1 walk thru; crafts and trades; 2 theater
shows; 2 puppet shows; Dixieland show;
dolphin pool & show; on-grounds entertainment; costumed characters; petting zoo; name
entertainment; gauge steam train; sky lift; 9
restaurants; 13 refreshment stands; picnic
facilities; 15 shops; kennels; fireworks; pay
gate; pay parking; open Apr. - Oct. 30.

Lake Ozark

FUN CITY
P.O. Box 17
Lake Ozark, MO 65049
(314) 365-5607
FACILITIES: 10 major rides; 4 kiddie rides;
10 games; 2 refreshment stands; restaurant;
arcade; shooting gallery; stage shows; free
acts; free gate; free parking; open May 1 -
Labor Day.

Osage Beach

FORT OF THE OSAGE FAMILY FUN
  PARK
Hwy. 54
Osage Beach, MO 65065
(314) 348-3175
FACILITIES: 6 major rides; 2 kiddie rides; 2
games; 3 refreshment stands; 3 restaurants;
arcade; shooting gallery; museum; exhibits;
crafts; paddle boats; observation tower;
name bands; vaudeville; pay gate; free parking; open mid-Apr. - Oct. 15.

St. Louis

GRANT'S FARM
10501 Gravois Road
St. Louis, MO 63102
(314) 843-1700
FACILITIES: Trackless train ride; animal
contact area; bird show; elephant show;
stables; horse-drawn carriage collection; deer
park and game preserve; snack bar; Clydesdale
stallion stables; free gate; free parking; reservations required; open mid-Apr. - mid-Oct.

STATE FAIR

Missouri State Fair
P.O. Box 111
Sedalia, MO 65301
(816) 826-3430
DATE: August

NATIONAL PARKS

There are no National Parks in Missouri.

NATIONAL FORESTS

National Forests
Eastern Region
633 West Wisconsin Avenue
Milwaukee, WI 53203
(414) 291-3693

Rolla

CLARK NATIONAL FOREST
ATTRACTIONS: Smallmouth bass and other
fishing; squirrel, coon, fox hunting; float
trips; riverbank campsites in places.

MISSOURI

NATIONAL FORESTS (continued)

FACILITIES: 14 camp and picnic sites, 21 picnic only.
NEARBY TOWNS: Frederickstown, Ironton, Piedmont, Poplar Bluff, Potosi, St. Louis, and Salem.

Springfield

MARK TWAIN NATIONAL FOREST
ATTRACTIONS: Numerous caves; rock cairns; float trips; pan fish, bass, walleye fishing; deer, quail, small-game hunting.
FACILITIES: 19 picnic and 15 camp sites; 6 swimming sites; resorts and hotels.
NEARBY TOWNS: Branson, Doniphan, Van Buren, West Plains, Willow Springs.

STATE PARKS

Headquarters

Division of Parks & Recreation
P.O. Box 176
Jefferson City, MO 65101
(314) 751-3443

Branson

TABLE ROCK STATE PARK
LOCATION: 5 mi. west of Branson.
FACILITIES: Open year round; 388 sites; water and bathroom facilities; sanitary station; electrical hookup; trailer village vehicle sites; food service; swimming; boating; fishing; tent camping.

Cassville

ROARING RIVER STATE PARK
LOCATION: 7 mi. south of Cassville on Hwy. 112.
FACILITIES: Open year round; 550 sites; water and bathroom facilities; sanitary station; electrical hookup; trailer village vehicle sites; cabins; food service; swimming; fishing; horseback riding; lodging; tent camping.

Columbia

FINGER LAKES STATE PARK
LOCATION: 10 mi. north of Columbia on U.S. 63.
FACILITIES: Open year round; swimming; fishing.

ROCK BRIDGE MEMORIAL STATE PARK
LOCATION: 7 mi. south of Columbia.
FACILITIES: Open year round; picnic area; fishing; self-guided trail.

East Prairie

BIG OAK TREE STATE PARK
LOCATION: 10 mi. south of East Prairie.
FACILITIES: Open year round; fishing; self-guided trail.

Excelsior Springs

WATKINS MILL STATE PARK
LOCATION: 6½ mi. north of Excelsior Springs on U.S. 69.
FACILITIES: Open year round; 200 sites; water and bathroom facilities; sanitary station; electrical hookup; trailer village vehicle sites; swimming; boating; fishing; tent camping.

Florida

MARK TWAIN STATE PARK
LOCATION: Near Florida on Hwy. 107.
FACILITIES: Open year round; 118 sites; sanitary station; electrical hookup; trailer village vehicle sites; cabins; picnic area; swimming; fishing; tent camping.

French Village

ST. FRANCOIS STATE PARK
LOCATION: Near French Village on U.S. 67.
FACILITIES: Open year round; 260 sites; water and bathroom facilities; electrical hookup; trailer village vehicle sites; picnic area; swimming; boating; fishing; tent camping.

Fruitland

TRAIL OF TEARS STATE PARK
LOCATION: 10 mi. east of Fruitland.
FACILITIES: Open year round; 88 sites; water and bathroom facilities; electrical hookup; trailer village vehicle sites; boating; fishing; tent camping.

Kirksville

THOUSAND HILLS STATE PARK
LOCATION: 4 mi. west of Kirksville on Hwy. 6.
FACILITIES: Open year round; 280 sites; water and bathroom facilities; sanitary station; electrical hookup; trailer village vehicle sites; cabins; food service; swimming; boating; fishing; tent camping.

Knob Noster

KNOB NOSTER STATE PARK
LOCATION: At Knob Noster on U.S. 50.
FACILITIES: Open year round; 244 sites; water and bathroom facilities; sanitary station; electrical hookup; trailer village vehicle sites; swimming; fishing; tent camping.

Laclede

PERSHING STATE PARK
LOCATION: 2 mi. west of Laclede on U.S. 36.
FACILITIES: Open year round; 78 sites; water and bathroom facilities; sanitary station; electrical hookup; trailer village vehicle sites; swimming; fishing; tent camping.

Lebanon

BENNETT SPRINGS STATE PARK
LOCATION: 12 mi. west of Lebanon on Hwy. 64.
FACILITIES: Open year round; 470 sites; water and bathroom facilities; sanitary station; electrical hookup; trailer village vehicle sites; cabins; food service; swimming; boating; fishing; tent camping.

STATE PARKS (continued)

Lesterville

JOHNSON'S SHUT-INS STATE PARK
LOCATION: 8 mi. north of Lesterville on County Road M.
FACILITIES: Open year round; 280 sites; water and bathroom facilities; sanitary station; electrical hookup; trailer village vehicle sites; swimming; fishing; self-guided trail; tent camping.

Osage Beach

LAKE OF THE OZARKS STATE PARK
LOCATION: Near Osage Beach.
FACILITIES: Open year round; 440 sites; water and bathroom facilities; sanitary station; electrical hookup; trailer village vehicle sites; food service; swimming; boating; fishing; horseback riding; tent camping.

Patterson

SAM A. BAKER STATE PARK
LOCATION: 3 mi. north of Patterson on Hwy. 143.
FACILITIES: Open year round; 460 sites; water and bathroom facilities; sanitary station; electrical hookup; trailer village vehicle sites; cabins; food service; swimming; boating; fishing; tent camping.

Pittsburg

POMME DE TERRE STATE PARK
LOCATION: Two areas at Pittsburg and Hermitage, south of U.S. 54.
FACILITIES: Open year round; 638 sites; water and bathroom facilities; sanitary station; electrical hookup; trailer village vehicle sites; picnic area; food service; swimming; boating; boat rental; fishing; tent camping.

Poplar Bluff

LAKE WAPPAPELLO STATE PARK
LOCATION: 12 mi. north of Poplar Bluff on U.S. 67 and 9 mi. east on Hwy. 172.
FACILITIES: Open year round; 248 sites; water and bathroom facilities; sanitary station; electrical hookup; trailer village vehicle sites; cabins; swimming; boating; fishing; tent camping.

Potosi

WASHINGTON STATE PARK
LOCATION: 14 mi. northeast of Potosi on Hwy. 21.
FACILITIES: Open year round; 232 sites; water and bathroom facilities; electrical hookup; trailer village vehicle sites; cabins; picnic area; swimming; boating; fishing; tent camping.

St. Louis

DR. EDMUND A. BABLER MEMORIAL STATE PARK
LOCATION: 20 mi. west of St. Louis on Hwy. 109, off County Road CC.
FACILITIES: Open year round; 168 sites; water and bathroom facilities; sanitary station; trailer village vehicle sites; picnic area; swimming; horseback riding; handicapped access/restroom; tent camping.

Ste. Genevieve

HAWN STATE PARK
LOCATION: Between Ste. Genevieve and Farmington.
FACILITIES: Open year round; water and bathroom facilities; sanitary station; electrical hookup; trailer village vehicle sites; tent camping.

Salem

MONTAUK STATE PARK
LOCATION: 21 mi. southeast of Salem on Hwy. 119.
FACILITIES: Open year round; 400 sites; water and bathroom facilities; sanitary station; electrical hookup; trailer village vehicle sites; cabins; food service; fishing; tent camping.

Stockton

STOCKTON STATE PARK
LOCATION: South of Stockton along Hwy. 215.
FACILITIES: Open year round; 166 sites; water and bathroom facilities; sanitary station; electrical hookup; trailer village vehicle sites; picnic area; swimming; boating; fishing; tent camping.

Sullivan

MERAMEC STATE PARK
LOCATION: 4 mi. east of Sullivan on Hwy. 185.
FACILITIES: Open year round; 500 sites; water and bathroom facilities; sanitary station; electrical hookup; trailer village vehicle sites; cabins; food service; swimming; boating; fishing; tent camping.

Troy

CUIVRE RIVER STATE PARK
LOCATION: 5 mi. east of Troy on Hwy. 47.
FACILITIES: Open year round; 140 sites; water and bathroom facilities; sanitary station; electrical hookup; trailer village vehicle sites; picnic area; swimming; fishing; hiking; horseback riding; tent camping.

STATE FORESTS

Department of Conservation
P.O. Box 150
Jefferson City, MO 65101
(314) 751- 4115

Akers

CEDAR GROVE STATE FOREST
LOCATION: Near Akers.
FACILITIES: Open year round; water and bathroom facilities; trailer village vehicle sites; hunting; hiking; tent camping.

Alley Spring

ALLEY SPRING STATE FOREST

MISSOURI

STATE FORESTS (continued)

LOCATION: Near Alley Spring.
FACILITIES: Open year round; water and bathroom facilities; trailer village vehicle sites; hunting; fishing; hiking; tent camping.

Coldwater

COLDWATER STATE FOREST
LOCATION: Near Coldwater.
FACILITIES: Open year round; water and bathroom facilities; trailer village vehicle sites; hunting; fishing; hiking; tent camping.

Doniphan

FOURCHE CREEK STATE FOREST
LOCATION: Near Doniphan.
FACILITIES: Open year round; water and bathroom facilities; trailer village vehicle sites; hunting; fishing; hiking; tent camping.

LITTLE BLACK STATE FOREST
LOCATION: Near Doniphan.
FACILITIES: Open year round; water and bathroom facilities; trailer village vehicle sites; hunting; hiking; tent camping.

Ellington

CARDAREVA STATE FOREST
LOCATION: Near Ellington.
FACILITIES: Open year round; water and bathroom facilities; trailer village vehicle sites; hunting; hiking; tent camping.

CLEARWATER STATE FOREST
LOCATION: Near Ellington.
FACILITIES: Open year round; water and bathroom facilities; trailer village vehicle sites; hunting; fishing; hiking; tent camping.

DEER RUN STATE FOREST
LOCATION: Near Ellington.
FACILITIES: Open year round; water and bathroom facilities; trailer village vehicle sites; hunting; hiking; tent camping.

DICKENS VALLEY STATE FOREST
LOCATION: Near Ellington.
FACILITIES: Open year round; water and bathroom facilities; trailer village vehicle sites; hunting; hiking; tent camping.

LOGAN CREEK STATE FOREST
LOCATION: Near Ellington.
FACILITIES: Open year round; water and bathroom facilities; trailer village vehicle sites; hunting; fishing; hiking; tent camping.

PAINT ROCK STATE FOREST
LOCATION: Near Ellington.
FACILITIES: Open year round; water and bathroom facilities; trailer village vehicle sites; hunting; hiking; tent camping.

POWDER MILL STATE FOREST
LOCATION: Near Ellington.
FACILITIES: Open year round; water and bathroom facilities; trailer village vehicle sites; hunting; hiking; tent camping.

Eminence

BEAL STATE FOREST
LOCATION: Near Eminence.
FACILITIES: Open year round; water and bathroom facilities; trailer village vehicle sites; hunting; hiking; tent camping.

BLAIR CREEK STATE FOREST
LOCATION: Near Eminence.
FACILITIES: Open year round; water and bathroom facilities; trailer village vehicle sites; hunting; fishing; hiking; tent camping.

CLOW TRACT STATE FOREST
LOCATION: Near Eminence.
FACILITIES: Open year round; water and bathroom facilities; trailer village vehicle sites; hunting; hiking; tent camping.

MULE MOUNTAIN STATE FOREST
LOCATION: Near Eminence.
FACILITIES: Open year round; water and bathroom facilities; trailer village vehicle sites; hunting; hiking; tent camping.

ROCKY CREEK STATE FOREST
LOCATION: Near Eminence.
FACILITIES: Open year round; water and bathroom facilities; trailer village vehicle sites; hunting; fishing; hiking; tent camping.

SHANNONDALE STATE FOREST
LOCATION: Near Eminence.
FACILITIES: Open year round; water and bathroom facilities; trailer village vehicle sites; hunting; hiking; tent camping.

Hartshorn

HARTSHORN STATE FOREST
LOCATION: Near Hartshorn.
FACILITIES: Open year round; water and bathroom facilities; trailer village vehicle sites; hunting; hiking; tent camping.

Jonesburg

DANIEL BOONE STATE FOREST
LOCATION: Near Jonesburg.
FACILITIES: Open year round; water and bathroom facilities; trailer village vehicle sites; hunting; hiking; tent camping.

Leasburg

HUZZAH STATE FOREST
LOCATION: Near Leasburg.
FACILITIES: Open year round; water and bathroom facilities; trailer village vehicle sites; hunting; hiking; tent camping.

Piedmont

RIVERSIDE STATE FOREST
LOCATION: Near Piedmont.
FACILITIES: Open year round; water and bathroom facilities; trailer village vehicle sites; hunting; fishing; hiking; tent camping.

Pineville

HUCKLEBERRY RIDGE STATE FOREST
LOCATION: Near Pineville.

STATE FORESTS (continued)

FACILITIES: Open year round; water and bathroom facilities; trailer village vehicle sites; hunting; hiking; tent camping.

Salem

INDIAN TRAIL STATE FOREST
LOCATION: Near Salem.
FACILITIES: Open year round; water and bathroom facilities; trailer village vehicle sites; hunting; hiking; tent camping.

Warrenton

REIFSNIDER STATE FOREST
LOCATION: Near Warrenton.
FACILITIES: Open year round; water and bathroom facilities; trailer village vehicle sites; hunting; tent camping.

HISTORIC SITES

Jefferson City

JEFFERSON LANDING - The three historic buildings which comprise the landing date back to the mid-1800s when they were the center of river trade in the capital city. Located between the Governor's Mansion and State Capitol.

Laclede

JOHN J. PERSHING BOYHOOD HOME - The home of Gen. John J. Pershing who lived here from age 6 (1866) until 1882, when he left for West Point Military Academy. Located on Route 5.

Lamar

HARRY S. TRUMAN BIRTHPLACE - Harry S. Truman, the only Missourian ever elected President, was born here on May 8, 1884. He was the 32nd President, serving from 1945 - 1953. Located on U.S. 71.

Perry

MARK TWAIN BIRTHPLACE SHRINE - The shrine encloses the two-room cabin in which Mark Twain (Samuel Clemens) was born in 1835. Many of his personal items and a library of his books are displayed. Located in Mark Twain State Park near Perry.

Pilot Knob

FORT DAVIDSON - The scene of the Battle of Pilot Knob on Sept. 27, 1864, between the Union troops of Brig. Gen. Thomas Ewing, Jr., and the Confederate troops of Maj. Gen. Sterling Price. Price's troops attacked the Union-held fort and more than 1,000 men were killed or wounded in 20 minutes in a fierce engagement which ended in defeat for the Confederates. Located on Route 21.

St. Charles

FIRST STATE CAPITOL - The building housed Missouri's government from 1821 to 1826. It was here that Missouri's first governor, Alexander McNair, received official word that Missouri had been admitted to the Union. Located at 208 S. Main.

HOSTELS

Kansas City

LEWIS & CLARK YOUTH HOSTEL
12201 Blue River Road
Kansas City, MO 64146
(816) 942-0697
FACILITIES: Open year round; 7 beds, men; 7 beds, women; modern bathroom; nearest hostel: Marion, Kansas; overnight charges: $1.50; houseparents: David & Linda Robins.

POINTS OF INTEREST

Hannibal

NATIONAL TOM SAWYER FENCE PAINTING CONTEST - This contest, at Mark Twain's boyhood home, is the culmination of "Tom Sawyer Days." Other events include frog jumping, raft racing, and a fireworks display launched from a barge moored in the river. Held in early July.

Hermann

MAIFEST - This May Festival is perhaps Missouri's best-known authentic German celebration. Held in late May.

St. Louis

ANHEUSER-BUSCH BREWERY TOURS - One-hour tour of the brewery with a stop at the hospitality room. Home of the world-famous Budweiser Clydesdale 8-horse hitch. Six-story brew house dating from 1891-92. Free admission. Located at Broadway & Pestalozzi.
OPEN: Year round, 9:30 a.m. - 3:30 p.m. Mon. - Fri. Saturday tours May - Sept. No tours on holidays.

FOREST PARK BALLOON RALLY - The annual rally features giant hot-air balloons from around the country. Held in mid-September in huge Forest Park, one of America's largest municipal parks.

MISSOURI BOTANICAL GARDEN - One of the most beautiful and unusual botanical gardens in the United States. More than 79 acres of gardens, horticulture displays and historic buildings. Located at 2101 Tower Grove Ave. OPEN: Year round, May - Oct., 9 a.m. - 6 p.m.; Nov. - Apr., 9 a.m. - 5 p.m.

NATIONAL MUSEUM OF TRANSPORT - Visitors may see locomotives, railway cars, automobiles, streetcars, buses, trucks, horse-drawn vehicles, aircraft, as well as pipeline and communication devices. Located at 3015 Barret Station Road.
OPEN: Year round, 10 a.m. - 5 p.m.

MISSOURI

POINTS OF INTEREST (continued)

Ste. Genevieve

JOUR DE FETE - The oldest permanent town in Missouri, Ste. Genevieve, celebrates its founding in 1735 with this festival. There are tours of several homes dating back to 1770. Other popular features include folk dancing, a pageant, parades, arts and crafts, international cuisine, French costumes, and a King's Ball. Held in mid-August.

MONTANA

Montana, the site of the Pony Soldiers' most spectacular defeat at the hands of the Indians, entered the Union in 1889 as the forty-first state. On June 25, 1876, Crazy Horse and a small war party led General George A. Custer into a trap set by Chief Sitting Bull at Little Big Horn. Custer, aspiring to be a Presidential candidate, was annihilated with his company of over 200 men on that day.

Copper, coal and oil, in addition to a dozen other metals and minerals, were discovered in the late 1800s and played a major part in the development of Montana's economy. Today, mining is still one of the leading revenue earners. Cattle and sheep ranching, begun in the 1860s, is another.

Montana's abundant supply of small and big game, fish and scenic wilderness attracts a growing number of hunters, campers, and sightseers each year, making tourism a significant contributor to the state's revenues.

State capital: Helena. State bird: Western meadowlark. State tree: Ponderosa pine. State flower: Bitterroot.

WEATHER

Montana, with an area of 146,316 square miles, is the fourth largest state of the Union. Climatic variations are large. The Continental Divide, traversing the western half of the state in roughly a north-south direction, exerts a marked influence on the climate of adjacent areas. West of the Divide the climate might be termed a modified north Pacific coast type, while to the east, climatic characteristics are decidedly continental. On the west of the mountain barrier, winters are milder, precipitation is more evenly distributed throughout the year, summers are cooler, in general, and winds are lighter than on the eastern side. There is more cloudiness in the west in all seasons, and humidity runs a bit higher.

During the summer months hot weather occurs fairly often in the eastern parts of the state. Temperatures of over 100 degrees sometimes occur in the lower elevation areas west of the Divide, but hot spells are less frequent and of shorter duration than in the plains sections. Hot spells nowhere become oppressive, however, because summer nights almost invariably are cool and pleasant. In the areas with elevations above 4,000 feet, extremely hot weather is almost unknown. Summer days, however, are usually warm enough for light summer clothing.

Winters, while usually cold, have few extended cold spells. Between cold waves there are periods, sometime longer than 10 days, of mild but often windy weather. These warm, windy winter periods occur almost entirely along the eastern slopes of the Divide and are popularly known as "chinook" weather.

Average daily temperature for each month.

	Eastern		Western
Jan.	22.5 to	.1	33.3 to 18.5
Feb.	30.7 to	7.5	41.9 to 23.2
Mar.	40.4 to 16.5		48.8 to 25.3
Apr.	56.7 to 29.9		58.9 to 31.5
May	68.9 to 41.5		69.2 to 38.5
Jun.	77.7 to 51.0		76.3 to 45.4
Jul.	85.7 to 55.6		86.6 to 48.1
Aug.	85.6 to 53.5		85.2 to 46.8
Sept.	72.6 to 42.6		74.9 to 40.0
Oct.	61.0 to 32.9		59.6 to 33.0
Nov.	41.9 to 19.8		43.1 to 26.9
Dec.	29.6 to 8.3		34.8 to 32.1
Year	56.1 to 29.9		59.4 to 33.3

STATE CHAMBER OF COMMERCE

Montana Chamber of Commerce
P.O. Box 1730
Helena, MT 59601
(406) 442-2405

STATE & CITY TOURISM OFFICES

State

Office of Commerce and Small Business Development
State Capitol Building
Helena, MT 59601
(406) 449-3923

Travel Promotion Unit
Montana Department of Highways
Helena, MT 59601
(406) 449-2654

OURISM OFFICES (continued)

Local

hamber of Commerce
O. Box 2127
reat Falls, MT 59403
06) 453-1441

TATE HIGHWAY DEPARTMENT

partment of Highways
st Sixth Avenue & Roberts St.
elena, MT 59601
06) 449-2482

IGHWAY WELCOMING CENTERS

ardner

ARDNER CENTER - U.S. 89, entrance of ellowstone Park.

asgow

LASGOW CENTER - U.S. 2.

ardin

ARDIN CENTER - Interstate 90, just out of llings.

ungry Horse

UNGRY HORSE CENTER - U.S. 2 at acier Park.

ompson Falls

HOMPSON FALLS CENTER - U.S. 10 at perior.

est Yellowstone Park

EST YELLOWSTONE PARK CENTER - S. 287 & 191.

baux

IBAUX CENTER - North Dakota border, S. 10.

TATE POLICE

epartment of Public Safety
elena, MT 59601
06) 449-3000

UNTING & FISHING

Hunting

A license is required for all persons who unt (ages 15 through 62) and fish (ages 12

through 62) in the state. To qualify as a resident, a person must reside in the state 6 months prior to application. No license is required to hunt rabbit, ground squirrel, woodchuck, coyote, porcupine and other non-game and non-furbearing animals.

A Wildlife Conservation license is required before any fishing or hunting license may be purchased. You may apply for other licenses at the same time that you apply for a conservation license.

Resident

Conservation (prerequisite to hunting and fishing license except the sportsman's license), $1 (Montana residents 62 and older need only a conservation license to fish and hunt upland game birds other than turkey); sportsman's (contains a deer "A" tag, elk tag, a black bear tag, authorizes hunting of game birds and fishing), $35; bird (does not include turkey), $4; turkey tag (bird license or sportsman's license prerequisite), $2; deer "A" tag, $7; deer "B" tag (valid only in specified districts), $12; elk, $8 (residents under 15 years of age may buy bird, deer "A" and elk tags at $2 each); bow and arrow (required for special archery seasons only), $6; black bear, $6; grizzly bear, $25 (any person who has killed a grizzly bear in Montana shall not be eligible to apply for a grizzly bear hunting license for the next succeeding 7 years); grizzly bear trophy, $25 mountain lion, $5; mountain lion trophy (each hunter who kills a mountain lion must apply for a trophy license within 4 days after date of kill), no charge.

Non-resident

Conservation, $1; combination bird and fish (does not include turkey), $50; combination game, bird, fish (17,000 quota-first come, first served), contains deer "A" tag, an elk tag, black bear, authorizes hunting for game birds and fishing, $225; deer "B5" (valid in specified districts only, $1. For conservation license, $50 or $225, combination license prerequisite; upland bird (conservation license prerequisite does not include turkey), $30; turkey tag (any license authorizing upland bird hunting prerequisite), $2; black bear spring (conservation license prerequisite), $35; black bear, season ($50 combination license), prerequisite), $50; bow and arrow (required for special archery seasons only), $6; grizzly bear ($50 or $225 combination prerequisite) see grizzly bear restriction above, $125; grizzly trophy, $25; mountain lion ($50 or $225 combination prerequisite), $25; mountain lion trophy (see mountain lion restrictions above), no charge.

Fishing

See hunting regulations above.

Resident

Conservation license (62 years or older), $1; fishing license (stamp), $5; sportsman's license (includes Wildlife Conservation license), $35.

MONTANA

HUNTING & FISHING (continued)

Non-resident

Conservation license, $1; season fishing license (stamp), $20; temporary fishing license (6-day stamp), $10; temporary fishing license (1-day stamp), $2; combination bird and fish (serves as prerequisite to application for several Montana big game licenses), $50; fish, bird, and big game license (includes an elk tag, deer "A" tag, black bear tag, authorizes hunting of game birds and fishing) (quota of 17,000), $225.

For more information contact:

Department of Fish and Game
Helena, MT 59601
(406) 449-3089

CAMPGROUNDS

Private

Billings

SEVEN ZZZZZZ'S KAMPGROUND
(406) 245-0973
LOCATION: 3087 Graden Avenue.
FACILITIES: Open year round; 110 sites; water and bathroom facilities; sanitary station; electrical hookup; trailer village vehicle sites; food service; tent camping.

Bozeman

UNITED CAMPGROUND U.S.A.
(406) 587-1575
LOCATION: In Bozeman.
FACILITIES: Open year round; 100 sites; water and bathroom facilities; sanitary station; trailer village vehicle sites; laundry; food service; tent camping.

Clinton

THE ELKHORN GUEST RANCH
(406) 825-3220
LOCATION: In Clinton.
FACILITIES: Open year round; 150 sites; water and bathroom facilities; electrical hookup; trailer village vehicle sites; cabins; laundry; food service; swimming; horseback riding; tent camping.

Glendive·

GREEN VALLEY CAMPGROUND
(406) 365-4156
LOCATION: In Glendive.
FACILITIES: Open year round; 100 sites; water and bathroom facilities; sanitary station; electrical hookup; trailer village vehicle sites; laundry; food service; tent camping.

Helena

HELENA KOA KAMPGROUND
(406) 458-5110
LOCATION: 5820 North Montana Avenue.
FACILITIES: Open year round; 100 sites; water and bathroom facilities; sanitary station; trailer village vehicle sites; laundry; food service; tent camping.

VAGABOND CAMPGROUND
(406) 442-1821
LOCATION: 1803 Cedar.

FACILITIES: Open year round; 90 sites; water and bathroom facilities; electrical hookup; trailer village vehicle sites; laundry; food service; swimming; tent camping.

Hungry Horse

FLATHEAD RIVER RANCH RV PARK
(406) 387-5241
LOCATION: In Hungry Horse.
FACILITIES: Open year round; 152 sites; water and bathroom facilities; electrical hookup; trailer village vehicle sites; laundry; boating; tent camping.

Missoula

EL-MAR KOA KAMPGROUNDS
(406) 549-0881
LOCATION: 3695 Tina Avenue.
FACILITIES: Open year round; 200 sites; water and bathroom facilities; sanitary station; electrical hookup; trailer village vehicle sites; laundry; food service; swimming; tent camping.

Polson

KOA KAMPGROUND
(406) 883-2151
LOCATION: 4 mi. north of Polson.
FACILITIES: Open year round; 120 sites; water and bathroom facilities; sanitary station; electrical hookup; trailer village vehicle sites; laundry; food service; swimming; boating; tent camping.

St. Mary

ST. MARY KOA KAMPGROUND
(406) 732-5311
LOCATION: In St. Mary.
FACILITIES: Open year round; 225 sites; water and bathroom facilities; sanitary station; electrical hookup; trailer village vehicle sites; laundry; food service; tent camping.

Somers

SOMERS LANDING
(406) 857-3488
LOCATION: In Somers.
FACILITIES: Open year round; 100 sites; water and bathroom facilities; electrical hookup; trailer village vehicle sites; food service; swimming; boating; fishing; tent camping.

West Glacier

WEST GLACIER KOA KAMPGROUND
(406) 387-5341
LOCATION: In West Glacier.
FACILITIES: Open year round; 112 sites; water and bathroom facilities; sanitary station; electrical hookup; trailer village vehicle sites; laundry; food service; tent camping.

CAMPGROUNDS (continued)

West Yellowstone

WEST YELLOWSTONE UNITED CAMP-GROUND
(406) 646-7894
LOCATION: 2 mi. west on Routes 191 & 20.
FACILITIES: Open year round; 244 sites; water and bathroom facilities; sanitary station; electrical hookup; trailer village vehicle sites; laundry; food service; tent camping.

RESORTS & BEACHES

Most of the state's resort activities center around the major lakes and include fishing, swimming, boating, water skiing, and camping. (See Boating Areas, National Parks, National Forests, State Parks and State Forests.)

BOATING AREAS

Chester

TIBER RESERVOIR
LOCATION: 19 mi. southeast of Chester.
FACILITIES: Launching; campsites; fishing.

Choteau

PISHKUM RESERVOIR
LOCATION: 24 mi. southwest of Choteau.
FACILITIES: Launching; fishing.

Conrad

LAKE FRANCIS
LOCATION: 24 mi. northwest of Conrad.
FACILITIES: Launching; boat rental; campsites; fishing.

Dillon

CLARK CANYON RESERVOIR
LOCATION: 16 mi. south of Dillon.
FACILITIES: Launching; fuel; campsites; fishing.

HAP HAWKINS LAKE
LOCATION: 20 mi. south of Dillon.
FACILITIES: Launching; fuel; campsites; fishing.

Ennis

ENNIS LAKE
LOCATION: 7 mi. north of Ennis.
FACILITIES: Launching; boat rental; campsites; lodging; fishing.

Fort Peck

FORT PECK RESERVOIR
LOCATION: 35 mi. south of Fort Peck.
FACILITIES: Launching; campsites; fishing.

Harlowton

DEADMAN BASIN
LOCATION: 17 mi. east of Harlowton.
FACILITIES: Launching; campsites; fishing.

Haugen

CABINET RESERVOIR
LOCATION: Route 10 near Idaho line.
FACILITIES: Launching; campsites; fishing.

Helena

CANYON FERRY RESERVOIR
LOCATION: 23 mi. east of Helena.
FACILITIES: Launching; boat rental; fuel; campsites; lodging; fishing.

HAUSER RESERVOIR
LOCATION: 15 mi. northeast of Helena.
FACILITIES: Launching; boat rental; fuel; campsites; lodging; fishing.

Hungry Horse

HUNGRY HORSE RESERVOIR
LOCATION: Near Hungry Horse.
FACILITIES: Launching; campsites; lodging; fishing.

Libby

KOOCANUSA RESERVOIR
LOCATION: 13 mi. north of Libby.
FACILITIES: Launching; campsites; fishing.

Lima

LIMA RESERVOIR
LOCATION: 15 mi. east of Lima.
FACILITIES: Launching; fishing.

Polson

FLATHEAD LAKE
LOCATION: Near Polson.
FACILITIES: Launching; boat rental; fuel; campsites; lodging; fishing.

West Yellowstone

HEBGEN LAKE
LOCATION: 15 mi. northwest of West Yellowstone.
FACILITIES: Launching; boat rental; fuel; campsites; lodging; fishing.

Wolf Point

MISSOURI RIVER
LOCATION: Near Wolf Point.
FACILITIES: Launching; campsites; lodging; fishing.

BICYCLE TRAILS

CENTRAL MONTANA TRAIL - 114 mi.; mountainous terrain; 10-speed bicycle recommended.

During most of this ride you will be encircled by mountains. Although you will have some hard climbs there are no really high passes.

Trail: Lewistown to Brooks to Denton to Coffee Creek to Arrow Creek to Stanford to Windham to Moccasin to Hobson to Moore to Lewistown.

MONTANA

BICYCLE TRAILS (continued)

GLACIER NATIONAL PARK TRAIL - Mountainous terrain, high elevation; 10-speed bicycle necessary.

Start just over the Canadian border at Carway. Continue to Glacier National Park, where you will find along your route a visitor's center, five campgrounds, and a lodge. This is high country with cold rains and lofty places such as Logan Pass at 6600 feet, which is part of the Continental Divide. So be ready for mountain weather. There are compensations, however, in the form of clear air, alpine scenery, and abundant wildlife.

Trail: Carway Canada through Glacier National Park to West Glacier to U.S. 2 south to Kalispell.

See IDAHO - Lewis and Clark Trail

SWAN RIVER VALLEY TRAIL - 231 mi.; mountainous terrain; 10-speed bicycle recommended.

This is big country with open range, lakes, and mountains interspersed with small lumbering towns every 20 or 30 miles. So carry extra food, rain and cold-weather protection, and a good bicycle repair kit.

Trail: Missoula to Milltown to Greenough to Seeley Lake to Swan Lake to Kalispell to Polson to Ravalli to Missoula.

TRAIL AROUND CONTINENTAL DIVIDE - 370 mi.; mountains, unpaved roads; 10-speed bicycle necessary.

You will cross the Continental Divide three times during the trip. These crossings mean rugged climbs where a low alpine gear will be your fondest possession. Since the road is not paved part of the way from Clinton to Philipsburg, it is best to start this ride with new tires and tubes and to carry a spare tube.

Trail: Butte to Divide to Wisdom to Conner to Hamilton to Lolo to Missoula to Milltown to Clinton to Philipsburg to Anaconda to Divide to Butte.

TRAILS

There are no National Trails System Foot Trails in Montana.

SKI AREAS

Anaconda

DISCOVERY BASIN
Anaconda, MT 59711
(406) 653-2184
LOCATION: 20 mi. west of Anaconda.
FACILITIES: 1 double chairlift; 1 pony lift; ski instruction; ski rental; restaurants; lodging.

WRAITH HILL
Anaconda, MT 59711
(406) 563-2357
LOCATION: 12 mi. west of Anaconda.
FACILITIES: 1 T-bar; 1 tow rope; ski instruction; ski rental; restaurants; lodging.

Big Sky

BIG SKY OF MONTANA
Big Sky, MT 59716
(800) 548-4486
LOCATION: 43 mi. south of Bozeman o Hwy. 191.
FACILITIES: 1 triple chairlift; 2 doubl chairlifts; 1 gondola; ski instruction; ski ren al; restaurants; lodging.

Box Elder

BEAR PAW
Box Elder, MT 59521
No telephone
LOCATION: 30 mi. south of Havre.
FACILITIES: 1 double chairlift; 1 tow rope ski instruction; ski rental; restaurants; lodging

Bozeman

BRIDGER BOWL
Bozeman, MT 59715
(406) 587-2111
LOCATION: 16 mi. northeast of Bozeman.
FACILITIES: 3 double chairlifts; 1 T-bar; pony lift; ski instruction; ski rental; restau rants; lodging.

Butte

BEEF TRAIL
Butte, MT 59701
(406) 792-2242
LOCATION: 8 mi. southwest of Butte.
FACILITIES: 1 T-bar; 1 tow rope; ski instruc tion; ski rental; restaurants; lodging.

Choteau

TETON PASS
Choteau, MT 59422
(406) 466-5749
LOCATION: 32 mi. northwest of Choteau.
FACILITIES: 1 double chairlift; 1 tow rope 1 poma; 1 mitey mite; ski instruction; sk rental; restaurants; lodging.

Darby

LOST TRAIL
Darby, MT 59829
(406) 821-3574
LOCATION: 50 mi. south of Hamilton.
FACILITIES: 1 double chairlift; 2 tow ropes ski instruction; ski rental; restaurants; lodging.

Great Falls

SHOWDOWN
Great Falls, MT 59403
(406) 727-5511
LOCATION: 8 mi. south of Neihart.
FACILITIES: 1 double chairlift; 1 T-bar; 1 tow rope; 2 pomas; ski instruction; ski rental; restaurants; lodging.

Helena

BELMONT
Helena, MT 59602
No telephone
LOCATION: 25 mi. northwest of Helena.

SKI AREAS (continued)

FACILITIES: 1 T-bar; 2 tow ropes; 1 poma; ski instruction; ski rental; restaurants; lodging.

Libby

TURNER MOUNTAIN
Libby, MT 59923
No telephone
LOCATION: 22 mi. northwest of Libby.
FACILITIES: 1 T-bar; 1 tow rope; ski instruction; ski rental; restaurants; lodging.

Missoula

MARSHALL MOUNTAIN
Missoula, MT 59801
(406) 258-6619
LOCATION: 4 mi. east of Missoula.
FACILITIES: 1 triple chairlift; 1 T-bar; 4 tow ropes; 1 poma; ski instruction; ski rental; restaurants; lodging.

MONTANA SNOW BOWL
Missoula, MT 59801
(406) 549-9777
LOCATION: 13 mi. northwest of Missoula.
FACILITIES: 1 double chairlift; 1 T-bar; 1 tow rope; 1 poma; ski instruction; ski rental; restaurants; lodging.

Polaris

MAVERICK MOUNTAIN
Polaris, MT 59746
(406) 834-2412
LOCATION: 38 mi. northwest of Dillon on Hwy. 278.
FACILITIES: 1 double chairlift; 1 T-bar; 1 tow rope; ski instruction; ski rental; restaurants; lodging.

Red Lodge

RED LODGE MOUNTAIN
Red Lodge, MT 59068
(406) 466-2288
LOCATION: 6 mi. west of Red Lodge.
FACILITIES: 4 double chairlifts; 1 mitey mite; ski instruction; ski rental; restaurants; lodging.

Whitefish

THE BIG MOUNTAIN
Whitefish, MT 59937
(406) 862-3511
LOCATION: 8 mi. north of Whitefish.
FACILITIES: 1 triple chairlift; 2 double chairlifts; 1 T-bar; 1 tow rope; ski instruction; ski rental; restaurants; lodging.

Wise River

DEEP CREEK
Wise River, MT 59762
(406) 839-2129
LOCATION: Near Wise River.
FACILITIES: 1 T-bar; ski instruction; ski rental; restaurants; lodging.

AMUSEMENT PARKS & ATTRACTIONS

Helena

FRONTIER TOWN
U.S. 12
Helena, MT 59601
(406) 442-4560
FACILITIES: Western town; gift shop; chapel; museum; pay gate; free parking.

STATE FAIR

State Fair
P.O. Box 1524
Great Falls, MT 59403
(406) 452-6401
DATE: August

NATIONAL PARKS

West Glacier

GLACIER NATIONAL PARK
West Glacier, MT 59936
(406) 888-5441

APGAR
LOCATION: 2 mi. north of west entrance.
FACILITIES: Open May - Oct.; entrance fee; limit of stay: 14 days (7, Jul. & Aug.); 196 sites; group camps: 10; NPS campsite fee: $3; water and bathroom facilities; sanitary station; cabins; picnic area; food service; swimming; boating; boat rental; hunting; fishing; hiking; horseback riding; bicycle trail; exhibit; museum; living history program; handicapped access/restroom; lodging.

AVALANCHE
LOCATION: 16 mi. northeast of west entrance.
FACILITIES: Open Jun. - Labor Day; limit of stay: 14 days (7, Jul. & Aug.); 87 sites; NPS campsite fee: $3; water and bathroom facilities; sanitary station; cabins; picnic area; hunting; fishing; hiking; bicycle trail; exhibit; museum; environmental study area; living history program; handicapped access/restroom; NPS guided tour; self-guiding tour; lodging.

BOWMAN CREEK
LOCATION: ¼ mi. north of Poleridge entrance.
FACILITIES: Open Jun. - Sept.; limit of stay: 14 days (7, Jul. & Aug.); 6 sites; NPS campsite fee: $2; fishing.

BOWMAN LAKE
LOCATION: 6 mi. east of Poleridge entrance.
FACILITIES: Open Jun. - Sept.; limit of stay: 14 days (7, Jul. & Aug.); 48 sites; NPS campsite fee: $2; swimming; boating; fishing.

CUT BANK
LOCATION: 4 mi. west of U.S. 89.
FACILITIES: Open Jun. - Sept.; limit of stay: 14 days (7, Jul. & Aug.); 19 sites; NPS campsite fee: $2; fishing.

MONTANA

NATIONAL PARKS (continued)

FISH CREEK
LOCATION: 4 mi. northwest of west entrance.
FACILITIES: Open Jun. - Aug.; limit of stay: 14 days (7, Jul. & Aug.); 180 sites; NPS campsite fee: $3; water and bathroom facilities; sanitary stations; cabins; picnic area; food service; swimming; boating; boat rental; hunting; fishing; hiking; bicycle trail; exhibit; museum; environmental study area; living history program; handicapped access/restroom; NPS guided tour; self-guiding tour; lodging.

KINTLA LAKE
LOCATION: 15 mi. north of Poleridge entrance.
FACILITIES: Open Jun. - Sept.; limit of stay: 14 days (7, Jul. & Aug.); 19 sites; NPS campsite fee: $2; swimming; boating; fishing.

LOGGING CREEK
LOCATION: 14 mi. south of Poleridge entrance.
FACILITIES: Open Jun. - Sept.; limit of stay: 14 days (7, Jul. & Aug.); 8 sites; fishing.

MANY GLACIER
LOCATION: 13 mi. west of Babb.
FACILITIES: Open Jun. - Sept.; limit of stay: 14 days (7, Jul. & Aug.); 117 sites; group camps: 2; water and bathroom facilities; sanitary station; cabins; picnic area; food service; boating; boat rental; hunting; fishing; hiking; horseback riding; bicycle trail; exhibit; museum; environmental study area; living history program; handicapped access/restroom; NPS guided tour; self-guiding tour; lodging.

QUARTZ CREEK
LOCATION: 8 mi. south of Poleridge entrance.
FACILITIES: Open Jun. - Sept.; limit of stay: 14 days (7, Jul. & Aug.); 7 sites; NPS campsite fee: $2; fishing.

RISING SUN
LOCATION: 6 mi. west of St. Mary entrance.
FACILITIES: Open Jun. - Sept.; limit of stay: 14 days (7, Jul. & Aug); 82 sites; NPS campsite fee: $3; water and bathroom facilities; sanitary station; cabins; picnic area; food service; swimming; boating; boat rental; hunting; fishing; hiking; bicycle trail; exhibit; museum; environmental study area; living history program; handicapped access/restroom; NPS guided tour; self-guiding tour; lodging.

RIVER
LOCATION: North Fork, 2 mi. north of Poleridge entrance.
FACILITIES: Open Jun. - Sept.; limit of stay: 14 days (7, Jul. & Aug.); 7 sites; NPS campsite fee: $2; fishing.

ST. MARY LAKE
LOCATION: 1 mi. northwest of St. Mary entrance.
FACILITIES: Open Jun. - Sept.; limit of stay: 14 days (7, Jul. & Aug.); 156 sites; group camps: 4; NPS campsite fee: $3; water and bathroom facilities; cabins; picnic area; food service; swimming; boating; boat rental; hunt-ing; fishing; hiking; bicycle trail; exhibit; museum; environmental study area; living history program; handicapped access/restroom; NPS guided tour; self-guiding tour; lodging.

TWO MEDICINE
LOCATION: 7 mi. west of Hwy. 49.
FACILITIES: Open Jun. - Sept.; limit of stay: 14 days (7, Jul. & Aug.); 99 sites; group camps: 2; NPS campsite fee: $3; water and bathroom facilities; cabins; picnic area; food service; swimming; boating; boat rental; hunt-ing; fishing; hiking; bicycle trail; exhibit; museum; environmental study area; living history program; handicapped access/restroom; NPS guided tour; self-guiding tour; lodging.

SPRAGUE CREEK
LOCATION: 9 mi. north of west entrance.
FACILITIES: Open Jun. - Labor Day; limit of stay: 14 days (7, Jul. & Aug.); 25 sites; NPS campsite fee: $3; water and bathroom facilities; cabins; picnic area; food service; swimming; hunting; fishing; hiking; horseback riding; bicycle trail; exhibit; museum; environmental study area; living history program; handicapped access/restroom; NPS guided tour; self-guiding tour; tent and pickup campers only; lodging.

NATIONAL FORESTS

National Forests
Northern Region
Federal Building
Missoula, MT 59807
(406) 329-3316

Billings

CUSTER NATIONAL FOREST
ATTRACTIONS: Granite Peak (12,799 feet), highest point in Montana; Woodbine Falls, 900 feet high; glaciers and ice caverns; rich fossil beds, Indian hieroglyphics and burial grounds. Trout fishing; big game hunting; saddle and pack trips.
FACILITIES: 32 camp and picnic sites, 11 picnic only; Red Lodge Winter Sports Area; resorts, hotels, cabins, and dude ranches.
NEARBY TOWNS: Absarokee, Ashland, Columbus, Hardin, Laurel, Red Lodge.

Bozeman

GALLATIN NATIONAL FOREST
ATTRACTIONS: Snow-clad peaks; 11 outstanding waterfalls; lake and stream fishing; bear, moose, elkdeer hunting; scenic drives; trail riding; wilderness trips.
FACILITIES: 41 camp and picnic sites, 19 picnic only; Bridger Bowl and Lionhead Winter Sports Areas; resorts, hotels, cabins, and dude ranches.
NEARBY TOWNS: Big Timber, Gardiner, Livingston, West Yellowstone.

Butte

DEER LODGE NATIONAL FOREST
ATTRACTIONS: Lake and stream fishing; bear, moose, elk, deer hunting; scenic drives; trail riding; wilderness trips.

NATIONAL FORESTS (continued)

FACILITIES: 25 camp and picnic sites, 12 picnic only; Wraith Hill Winter Sports Area; resorts, hotels, cabins, and dude ranches.
NEARBY TOWNS: Anaconda, Boulder, Deer Lodge, Philipsburg, Whitehall.

Dillon

BEAVERHEAD NATIONAL FOREST
ATTRACTIONS: Bannack, the first capital of Montana; self-guided auto tours; fishing; deer, elk, moose, antelope, bear hunting; hot springs; wilderness trips; scenic drives.
FACILITIES: 36 camp and picnic sites, 5 picnic only; Rainy Mountain Winter Sports Area; resorts, hotels, cabins, and dude ranches in and near the National Forest.
NEARBY TOWNS: Ennis, Jackson, Lima, Sheridan, Virginia City, Wisdom.

Great Falls

LEWIS AND CLARK NATIONAL FOREST
ATTRACTIONS: Continental Divide, scenic limestone canyons; stream and lake fishing; deer, elk, antelope, grizzly, black bear hunting; wilderness trips; riding trails; scenic drives.
FACILITIES: 21 camp and picnic sites, 3 picnic sites; King's Hill Winter Sports Area; many resorts, cabins, and dude ranches.
NEARBY TOWNS: Augusta, Choteau, Harlowtown, Lewistown, and White Sulphur Springs.

Hamilton

BITTERROOT NATIONAL FOREST
ATTRACTIONS: Hot springs; ancient Indian hieroglyphics; lake and stream fishing; elk, deer, and mountain goat hunting; scenic drives; riding trails; wilderness trips.
FACILITIES: 30 camp and picnic sites; Lost Trail Winter Sports Area; resorts, hotels, cabins, and dude ranches.
NEARBY TOWNS: Corvallis, Missoula, Stevensville.

Helena

HELENA NATIONAL FOREST
ATTRACTIONS: Continental Divide; boat trip; old Fort Logan original blockhouse; ghost towns; lake and stream fishing; deer, elk hunting; scenic drives; hiking and horse trails; wilderness trips.
FACILITIES: 11 camp and picnic sites, 7 picnic only; Grass Mountain Winter Sports Area; resorts, hotels, cabins, and dude ranches.
NEARBY TOWNS: Lincoln, Townsend, Boulder, White Sulphur Springs.

Kalispell

FLATHEAD NATIONAL FOREST
ATTRACTIONS: Spectacular geological formations; hanging valleys; glaciers and scores of glacial lakes. Fishing; elk, deer, moose, bear, mountain sheep, goat hunting. Boating; canoeing; riding; scenic drives; wilderness trips.
FACILITIES: 35 camp and picnic sites, 13 picnic only; 2 swimming sites; Big Mountain Winter Sports Area; resorts, hotels, cabins, and dude ranches.
NEARBY TOWNS: Belton, Bigfork, Columbia Falls, Coram, Whitefish.

Libby

KOOTENAI NATIONAL FOREST
ATTRACTIONS: Lake and stream fishing; black bear, deer hunting; scenic drives; riding trails.
FACILITIES: 20 camp and picnic sites, 6 picnic only; Turner Mountain Winter Sports Area; hotels, cabins, and dude ranches.
NEARBY TOWNS: Eureka, Troy.

Missoula

LOLO NATIONAL FOREST
ATTRACTIONS: Stream and lake fishing; native grouse, elk, deer, bear hunting; wilderness pack trips; scenic drives; saddle trails; foot trails.
FACILITIES: 27 camp and picnic sites, 9 picnic only; swimming site; Snow Bowl Winter Sports Area; resorts, dude ranches.
NEARBY TOWNS: Alberton, Drummond, Ovando, Plains, St. Regis, Superior, Thompson Falls.

See CLEARWATER NATIONAL FOREST and KANIKSU NATIONAL FOREST - Idaho.

See SHOSHONE NATIONAL FOREST - Wyoming.

STATE PARKS

Headquarters

Department of Fish and Game
Division of Parks
1420 East Sixth Avenue
Helena, MT 59601
(406) 449-3750

Anaconda

LOST CREEK STATE PARK
LOCATION: Off U.S. 10A.
FACILITIES: Open year round; water and bathroom facilities; picnic area; tent camping.

Dillon

BANNACK STATE PARK
LOCATION: 21 mi. west of Dillon.
FACILITIES: Open year round; water and bathroom facilities; trailer village vehicle sites; picnic area; environmental study area; tent camping.

Ekalaka

MEDICINE ROCKS STATE PARK
LOCATION: 11 mi. north of Ekalaka.
FACILITIES: Open year round; water and bathroom facilities; trailer village vehicle sites; picnic area; tent camping.

Glendive

MAKOSHIKA STATE PARK

MONTANA

STATE PARKS (continued)

LOCATION: Near Glendive.
FACILITIES: Open year round; water and bathroom facilities; trailer village vehicle sites; picnic area; environmental study area; tent camping.

Great Falls

GIANT SPRINGS STATE PARK
LOCATION: Northeast of Great Falls.
FACILITIES: Open year round; water and bathroom facilities; trailer village vehicle sites; picnic area; environmental study area; tent camping.

Kalispell

LONE PINE STATE PARK
LOCATION: 3 mi. southwest of Kalispell.
FACILITIES: Open year round; water and bathroom facilities; picnic area.

WEST SHORE STATE PARK
LOCATION: 20 mi. south of Kalispell.
FACILITIES: Open year round; water and bathroom facilities; trailer village vehicle sites; picnic area; swimming; boating; environmental study area; tent camping.

Three Forks

LEWIS & CLARK CAVERNS STATE PARK
LOCATION: On U.S. 10, west of Three Forks.
FACILITIES: Open year round; water and bathroom facilities; sanitary station; trailer village vehicle sites; picnic area; environmental study area.

MISSOURI HEADWATERS STATE PARK
LOCATION: 3 mi. northeast of Three Forks.
FACILITIES: Open year round; water and bathroom facilities; sanitary station; trailer village vehicle sites; picnic area; boating; environmental study area; tent camping.

STATE FORESTS

Department of Fish and Game
Forestry Division
1420 East 6th Avenue
Helena, MT 59601
(406) 449-2535

Hamilton

STILLWATER STATE FOREST
LOCATION: Along U.S. 93.
FACILITIES: Open year round; trailer village vehicle sites; hunting; fishing; hiking; tent camping.

Happys Inn

THOMPSON RIVER STATE FOREST
LOCATION: Along U.S. 2.
FACILITIES: Open year round; trailer village vehicle sites; hunting; fishing; hiking; tent camping.

Lincoln

LINCOLN STATE FOREST
LOCATION: Along Routes 200 and 279.
FACILITIES: Open year round; trailer village vehicle sites; hunting; fishing; hiking; tent camping.

Swan Lake

SULA STATE FOREST
LOCATION: Along Route 209.
FACILITIES: Open year round; trailer village vehicle sites; hunting; fishing; hiking; tent camping.

SWAN RIVER STATE FOREST
LOCATION: On Hwy. 20 and Route 35.
FACILITIES: Open year round; trailer village vehicle sites; hunting; fishing; hiking; tent camping.

Tuscor

CLEARWATER STATE FOREST
LOCATION: Along Route 200 and U.S. 2.
FACILITIES: Open year round; trailer village vehicle sites; hunting; fishing; hiking; tent camping.

HISTORIC SITES

Cable

CABLE MINE - World's largest gold nugget ($19,000) discovered here. Located 26 mi. west of Anaconda on gravel road.

Hardin

CUSTER'S LAST STAND - In Battle of the Little Big Horn, June 25, 1876, General George A. Custer and entire Seventh Cavalry were slain by combined Sioux and Cheyenne Indian forces. Located 15 mi. south of Hardin.

Pompeys Pillar

POMPEYS PILLAR - Only remaining physical evidence of Lewis and Clark Expedition. Capt. Clark carved his name and date, July 25, 1806, on this 150 foot high sandstone block. Located northwest of Billings.

Virginia City

VIRGINIA CITY - Site of richest placer gold discovery ever made.

HOSTELS

Missoula

THE BIRCHWOOD
600 South Orange Street
Missoula, MT 59801
(406) 549-7124
FACILITIES: Open year round; 22 beds, men and women; 1 dormitory; modern bathroom; overnight charges: $3 summer; $3.25 winter; houseparent: Italo E. L. Franceschi.

POINTS OF INTEREST

Anaconda

ANACONDA SMELTER - World's largest brick smokestack.

Butte

RICHEST HILL ON EARTH - Gold, silver, copper, and zinc mines and open pits. Also, World Museum of Mining.

Darby

ALTA RANGER STATION - First Forest Service ranger station in U.S. Located in Bitterroot National Forest.

Great Falls

CHARLES M. RUSSELL HOUSE AND STUDIO - 1900 home and studio of famous western artist and sculptor. Located at 1217-1219 4th Avenue.

GIANT SPRINGS - One of the largest fresh-water springs in the world. Flows at a measured rate of 338 million gallons of water per day. Discovered by Lewis and Clark Expedition in 1805.

La Hood

LEWIS AND CLARK CAVERNS - Largest limestone cave system in the Northwest, and third largest in the nation. Summer tours.

Logan

MADISON BUFFALO JUMP - Prehistoric hunters stampeded buffalo and drove them over this sandstone cliff. Located 7 mi. south of Logan.

St. Ignatius

ST. IGNATIUS MISSION - Unique Catholic church contains 58 original murals on its walls and ceilings painted by Brother Joseph Carignano.

Wild Horse Island

WILD HORSE ISLAND - Largest single herd of mountain sheep in the U.S.

NEBRASKA

Nebraska, engaged in a classic range war for over half a century, entered the Union in 1867, as the thirty-seventh state.

Although the homesteaders owned the land, the cattlemen based their claim on primacy, that is being first in the territory. Congress ended the dispute in the early 1900s by turning over the last parcel of land to the farmers.

Ironically, today Nebraska farmlands produce more forage for domestic animals than any other state, in addition to huge corn, soybean, wheat, oat and bean crops.

The livestock industry fares well in Nebraska, too, with the Omaha area meat-packing business ranked number one in the country. On a world-wide scale, the state cattle industry is the second largest.

Recently, the state's tourism trade has been making a strong showing, particularly in the areas of big game hunting, fishing and camping.

State capital: Lincoln. State bird: Western meadowlark. State tree: American elm. State flower: Goldenrod.

WEATHER

Nebraska comprises 77,227 square miles, 705 of which are water. The landscape changes from gently rolling prairie in the east, to rounded sand hills in the north central part, to the high plains of the western section.

Nebraska's climate is typical of the interior of large continents in middle latitudes. Summers are hot and winters cool, with large seasonal and year-to-year variations in temperature and precipitation. The state lies in the path of alternating and interacting masses of air with different characteristics and sources. Consequently, the weather is subject to frequent and often sharp changes.

Although winters in Nebraska are classed as cold, there are usually several periods of mild pleasant weather when thawing occurs. The number and duration of mild intervals in midwinter increases southwestward across the state. From April through September, the Panhandle has the coolest mean monthly temperatures.

Average daily temperature for each month.

	Western	Eastern
Jan.	41.4 to 11.7	29.3 to 9.7
Feb.	46.6 to 16.4	36.0 to 15.8
Mar.	51.3 to 21.6	44.9 to 25.2
Apr.	63.7 to 31.7	61.8 to 38.9
May	73.7 to 43.0	72.7 to 50.4
Jun.	83.4 to 52.6	81.7 to 60.7
Jul.	90.7 to 58.2	85.8 to 64.9
Aug.	89.7 to 56.0	84.3 to 62.7
Sept.	79.8 to 45.0	75.0 to 53.1
Oct.	68.9 to 33.2	66.0 to 42.1
Nov.	52.4 to 21.5	49.1 to 28.2

NEBRASKA

WEATHER (continued)

Dec.   42.2 to 14.1   35.9 to 16.7

Year 65.3 to 33.8   60.2 to 39.0

STATE CHAMBER OF COMMERCE

Nebraska Association of Commerce & Industry
P.O. Box 81556
Lincoln, NE 68501
(402) 432-4273

STATE & CITY TOURISM OFFICES

State

Division of Travel & Tourism
Nebraska Department of Economic Development
P.O. Box 94666, State Capitol
Lincoln, NE 68509
(402) 471-3111

Nebraska Department of Economic Development
301 Centennial Mall South
Lincoln, NE 68509
(402) 471-3111

Local

Greater Omaha Chamber of Commerce
1620 Dodge Street, Suite 2100
Omaha, NE 68102
(402) 341-1234

STATE HIGHWAY DEPARTMENT

State Highway Department
Central Office Building
South Junction U.S. 77 and Hwy. 2
Lincoln, NE 68509
(402) 477-6012

HIGHWAY WELCOMING CENTERS

Alda

ALDA CENTER - Interstate 80, west.

Cozad

COZAD CENTER - Interstate 80, west.

Gibbon

GIBBON CENTER - Interstate 80, east.

Grand Island

GRAND ISLAND CENTER - Interstate 80, west.

GRAND ISLAND CENTER - Interstate 80, east.

Kearney

KEARNEY CENTER - Interstate 80, east.

KEARNEY CENTER - Interstate 80, west.

Lexington

LEXINGTON CENTER - Interstate 80, west.

Lincoln

LINCOLN CENTER - In city, State Capitol Building.

Maxwell

MAXWELL CENTER - Interstate 80, east.

MAXWELL CENTER - Interstate 80, west.

Ogallala

OGALLALA CENTER - Interstate 80, east.

OGALLALA CENTER - Interstate 80, west.

Omaha

OMAHA CENTER - Henry Doorly Zoo.

Seward

SEWARD CENTER - Interstate 80, east.

SEWARD CENTER - Interstate 80, west.

Sutherland

SUTHERLAND CENTER - Interstate 80, east.

SUTHERLAND CENTER - Interstate 80, west.

York

YORK CENTER - Interstate 80, east.

YORK CENTER - Interstate 80, west.

STATE POLICE

Department of Public Safety
Lincoln, NE 68509
(402) 477-3951

HUNTING & FISHING

Hunting

A license is required for all non-residents, regardless of age, who hunt for or possess either game or non-game animals or birds.

All non-residents, regardless of age, who hunt for or possess either game or non-game animals or birds.

Servicemen officially stationed in Nebras-

HUNTING & FISHING (continued)

ka may obtain a resident permit after being on active duty in the state for 30 consecutive days.

Non-resident students may purchase a resident permit on proof they have attended classes full-time for at least 30 days at any Nebraska university, college, junior college, or vocational school.

Any person duly enrolled and attending a civilian conservation center or similar government work or training facility for 30 consecutive days may obtain a resident hunting permit.

A small-game permit is not required in addition to the special permit for deer, antelope, or wild turkey.

A habitat stamp is required for every resident 16 years of age and older who hunts game species. Stamp must be signed in ink across the face. Every non-resident who hunts game species must have a stamp.

A waterfowl stamp is required for every person 16 years of age and older who hunts migratory waterfowl. Signature must be written in ink across the face of the stamp, and stamp attached to the regular hunting permit.

Resident

Combination hunting and fishing permit, $13.50; annual small-game hunting permit, $6.50; deer permit, $15; antelope permit, $15; wild turkey permit, $15; habitat stamp, $7.50; trapping, $7.

Non-resident

Annual small-game hunting permit, $30; deer permit, $50; antelope permit, $50; wild turkey permit, $35; habitat stamp, $7.50; trapping, $200.

Fishing

A resident is a person who has resided in Nebraska continuously for at least 90 days and who has a bona fide intention of becoming a legal resident of this state. Members of the armed forces on active duty and officially stationed in Nebraska may purchase a resident fishing permit after residing 30 consecutive days in the state.

Non-resident fishing permit required of all persons who are not residents of Nebraska, except those under 16 years of age accompanied by a person possessing a valid permit.

Resident fishing permit required of all residents 16 years of age or older.

Resident

Annual fishing, $7.50; combination hunting and fishing, $13.50.

Non-resident

Statewide annual, $30; statewide 5-day, $15; statewide 3-day, $10; Missouri River annual, $15; Missouri River 5-day, $5.

For more information contact:

Game and Parks Commission

P.O. Box 30370
Lincoln, NE 68503
(402) 464-0641

CAMPGROUNDS

Private

Big Springs

MCGREER CAMPER PARK
(308) 889-3489
LOCATION: Southeast corner of I-80 interchange.
FACILITIES: Open year round; 36 sites; water and bathroom facilities; sanitary station; electrical hookup; trailer village vehicle sites; laundry; food service; tent camping.

Brady

BUFFALO BILL CAMPGROUND
(308) 584-9407
LOCATION: 20 mi. east of North Platte on I-80, Brady interchange.
FACILITIES: Open year round; 60 sites; water and bathroom facilities; sanitary station; electrical hookup; trailer village vehicle sites; laundry; food service; fishing; tent camping.

Cozad

KAMPERVILLE
(308) 784-3700
LOCATION: 3 blocks north of I-80 at the Cozad exit.
FACILITIES: Open year round; 52 sites; water and bathroom facilities; sanitary station; electrical hookup; trailer village vehicle sites; laundry; food service; tent camping.

Grand Island

WEST HAMILTON CAMPGROUND
(402) 886-2249
LOCATION: 600 feet south of I-80 at Grand Island East exit & Hwy. 2.
FACILITIES: Open year round; 60 sites; water and bathroom facilities; sanitary station; electrical hookup; trailer village vehicle sites; laundry; food service; tent camping.

Kearney

SAFARI CAMP
(308) 234-1532
LOCATION: 3 blocks north of I-80 at the Kearney interchange.
FACILITIES: Open year round; 105 sites; water and bathroom facilities; sanitary station; electrical hookup; trailer village vehicle sites; laundry; food service; tent camping.

Linwood

CAMP MOSES MERRILL
(402) 666-5639
LOCATION: 6 mi. west from Hwy. 79 at Morse Bluff (road to Linwood), then ¼ mi. south.
FACILITIES: Open year round; 100 sites; water and bathroom facilities; sanitary station; electrical hookup; trailer village vehicle sites; laundry; food service; swimming; hiking.

NEBRASKA

CAMPGROUNDS (continued)

Norfolk

CIRCUS RIVER CAMPGROUND
(402) 379-0859
LOCATION: 1 mi. north of Norfolk on Hwy.
81.
FACILITIES: Open Apr. 30 - Oct. 30; 100
sites; water and bathroom facilities; sanitary
station; electrical hookup; trailer village vehicle sites; picnic area; tent camping.

North Platte

CUTTY'S CAMPING OF NORTH PLATTE
(308) 534-2265
LOCATION: In North Platte on Route 4.
FACILITIES: Open year round; 105 sites; water and bathroom facilities; sanitary station;
electrical hookup; trailer village vehicle sites;
laundry; swimming; tent camping.

Ogallala

OPEN CORRAL CAMPER COURT
(308) 284-4327
LOCATION: I-80, Ogallala exit.
FACILITIES: Open year round; 48 sites; water and bathroom facilities; sanitary station;
electrical hookup; trailer village vehicle sites;
laundry; swimming.

Potter

BUFFALO BEND CAMP-MOTEL
(308) 879-4431
LOCATION: 3 mi. east of Potter on Hwy. 30.
FACILITIES: Open year round; 104 sites; water and bathroom facilities; electrical hookup;
trailer village vehicle sites; laundry; food service; fishing; tent camping.

Seward

CAMP MIDWAY
(402) 643-2362
LOCATION: ¼ mi. south of I-80 at Seward
interchange.
FACILITIES: Open May - Nov.; 100 sites;
sanitary station; electrical hookup; trailer village vehicle sites; food service; tent camping.

York

RED ARROW CAMPGROUND
(402) 362-9939
LOCATION: ½ mi. north off I-80 at York &
U.S. 81 exit.
FACILITIES: Open year round; 60 sites; water and bathroom facilities; sanitary station;
electrical hookup; laundry; tent camping.

RESORTS & BEACHES

Most of the state's resort activities center
around the major lakes and include fishing,
swimming, boating, water skiing, and camping. (See Boating Areas and State Parks.)

BOATING AREAS

Beatrice

ROCKFORD LAKE
LOCATION: From Beatrice, 7 mi. east, then
2 mi. south.
FACILITIES: Launching; water and bathroom facilities.

Brownville

BROWNVILLE
LOCATION: In Brownville.
FACILITIES: Launching; water and bath-
room facilities.

Cambridge

MEDICINE CREEK RESERVOIR
LOCATION: From Cambridge, 2 mi. west,
then 7 mi. north.
FACILITIES: Launching.

Cozad

GALLAGHER CANYON
LOCATION: 8 mi. south of Cozad.
FACILITIES: Launching; water and bath-
room facilities.

Crofton

LEWIS AND CLARK LAKE
LOCATION: 15 mi. north of Crofton.
FACILITIES: Launching; water and bath-
room facilities.

Denton

CONESTOGA LAKE
LOCATION: 2 mi. north of Denton.
FACILITIES: Launching; water and bath-
room facilities.

Emerald

PAWNEE LAKE
LOCATION: From Emerald, 2 mi. west, then
3 mi. north.
FACILITIES: Launching; water and bathroom facilities.

Fremont

FREMONT LAKES
LOCATION: 3 mi. west of Fremont.
FACILITIES: Launching; water and bath-
room facilities; food service.

Hemingford

BOX BUTTE RESERVOIR
LOCATION: 9½ mi. north of Hemingford.
FACILITIES: Launching; water and bath-
room facilities.

Imperial

ENDERS RESERVOIR
LOCATION: From Imperial, 5 mi. east, then
4½ mi. south.
FACILITIES: Launching; water and bathroom facilities.

BOATING AREAS (continued)

Lexington

JOHNSON LAKE
LOCATION: 7 mi. south of Lexington.
FACILITIES: Launching; water and bathroom facilities.

Loup City

SHERMAN RESERVOIR
LOCATION: From Loup City, 4 mi. east,
then 1 mi. north.
FACILITIES: Launching; water and bathroom facilities; food service.

Malcolm

BRANCHED OAK LAKE
LOCATION: 3½ mi. north of Malcolm.
FACILITIES: Launching; water and bathroom facilities; food service.

McCook

RED WILLOW RESERVOIR
LOCATION: 11 mi. north of McCook.
FACILITIES: Launching; water and bathroom facilities; food service.

Nebraska City

RIVERVIEW MARINA
LOCATION: In Nebraska City.
FACILITIES: Launching; water and bathroom facilities.

North Platte

LAKE MAHONEY
LOCATION: 6 mi. south of North Platte.
FACILITIES: Launching; water and bathroom facilities.

Ogallala

LAKE MCCONAUGHY
LOCATION: 12 mi. north of Ogallala.
FACILITIES: Launching; water and bathroom facilities.

LAKE OGALLALA
LOCATION: 9 mi. northeast of Ogallala.
FACILITIES: Launching; water and bathroom facilities.

Scottsbluff

MINATARE LAKE
LOCATION: From Scottsbluff, 4 mi. east, 4
mi. north, then 4 mi. east.
FACILITIES: Launching; water and bathroom facilities; food service.

Sprague

BLUESTEM LAKE
LOCATION: 2½ mi. west of Sprague.
FACILITIES: Launching; water and bathroom facilities.

Trenton

SWANSON LAKE
LOCATION: 2 mi. west of Trenton.
FACILITIES: Launching; water and bathroom facilities; food service.

Valentine

MERRITT RESERVOIR
LOCATION: 25 mi. southwest of Valentine.
FACILITIES: Launching; water and bathroom facilities; food service.

BICYCLE TRAILS

PRAIRIE TRAIL - 435 mi.; long distances per
day; 10-speed bicycle necessary.
    The dividends of this trip are wide open
spaces, prairie, hay fields, and lots of blue
sky. It can be made in the summer but the
heat can be terrific. In late September or
early October you will normally find ideal
cycling. Only the larger towns have motels.
    Trail: Thedford to Mullen to Hyannis to
Ellsworth to Alliance to Chadron to Hay
Springs to Merriman to Martin, SD, to Rosebud to Mission to Valentine, NE, to Thedford.

TRAILS

Omaha

FONTENELLE FOREST TRAIL - 3.9 mi.
foot trail. The trail begins at Fontenelle Forest Nature Center and traverses an attractive
forested area affording a wide vista of the
Missouri River and surrounding country. The
first ¾ mile is a self-guided nature trail. An
extensive network of connecting foot trails
provides access to the entire 1,200-acre natural area of the Fontenelle Forest. Though privately owned, the trail is open to the general
public.

SKI AREAS

There are no organized Ski Areas in Nebraska.

AMUSEMENT PARKS & ATTRACTIONS

Minden

THE HAROLD WARP PIONEER VILLAGE
Hwy. 6 & 34
Minden, NE 68959
(308) 832-1181
FACILITIES: 24-building village illustrating
"The Story of America and How it Grew";
restaurant; snack bar; camping; picnic facilities; free parking.

Omaha

PEONY PARK
81st & Cass Streets
Omaha, NE 68114
(402) 391-6253
FACILITIES: 12 major rides; 8 kiddie rides; 6

NEBRASKA

AMUSEMENT PARKS (continued)

refreshment stands; beach; arcade; 8 games; shooting gallery; picnic facilities; miniature golf; orchestras; name bands; free acts; pay gate; free parking; open Memorial Day - Labor Day; weekends: May - Sept.

STATE FAIR

Nebraska State Fair
P.O. Box 81223
Lincoln, NE 68501
(402) 474-5371
DATE: August

NATIONAL PARKS

There are no National Parks in Nebraska.

NATIONAL FORESTS

National Forests
Rocky Mountain Region
11177 West 8th Avenue
Lakewood, CO 80225
(303) 234-3914

Lincoln

NEBRASKA NATIONAL FOREST
ATTRACTIONS: Extensive forest plantations on sand hills; entire forests in game refuge; mule deer; nesting ground of great blue heron, grouse, prairie chicken; fishing.
FACILITIES: 3 camp and picnic sites, 3 picnic only; swimming site; hotel accommodations.
NEARBY TOWNS: Broken Bow, Valentine, and Halsey.

STATE PARKS

Headquarters

Nebraska Game & Parks Commission
2200 North 33rd Street
Lincoln, NE 68503
(402) 464-0641

Chadron

CHADRON STATE PARK
LOCATION: 9 mi. south of Chadron.
FACILITIES: Open year round; water and bathroom facilities; sanitary station; electrical hookup; trailer village vehicle sites; cabins; picnic area; food service; swimming; boating; boat rental; fishing; tent camping.

Crawford

FORT ROBINSON STATE PARK
LOCATION: 3 mi. west of Crawford.
FACILITIES: Open year round; water and bathroom facilities; sanitary station; electrical hookup; trailer village vehicle sites; cabins; picnic area; food service; boating; hunting; fishing.

Niobrara

NIOBRARA STATE PARK
LOCATION: 1 mi. west of Niobrara on Route 12.
FACILITIES: Open year round; water and bathroom facilities; sanitary station; electrical hookup; trailer village vehicle sites; cabins; food service; swimming; boating; boat rental; fishing.

Ponca

PONCA STATE PARK
LOCATION: 2 mi. north of Ponca.
FACILITIES: Open year round; water and bathroom facilities; sanitary station; electrical hookup; cabins; picnic area; swimming; boating; fishing; tent camping.

STATE FORESTS

There are no State Forests in Nebraska.

HISTORIC SITES

Crawford

BEAVER WALL ESCARPMENT - Ceremonial gathering place for the Sioux led by Crazy Horse. Legend has it that he is buried at its base.

FORT ROBINSON - Log guardhouse and adjacent Adjutant's office, site of death of Sioux Chief Crazy Horse, September 5, 1877.

Fairview

WILLIAM JENNINGS BRYAN HOUSE - Home of the "Great Commoner," statesman and three-time Presidential candidate. Located at Sumner and 50th Street.

Fort Calhoun

FORT ATKINSON - Largest post in the west, with a garrison of over 1000 soldiers during its active period. Also, only permanent outpost built by the Yellowstone Expedition, group sent out to protect U.S. fur trade and exert American influence in area acquired in Louisiana Purchase.

North Platt

SCOTTS REST RANCH - Once winter quarters for "Buffalo Bill" Cody's world famous Wild West Show. Now a showcase to the famed scout who is also credited with starting the wild sport of rodeo when he staged the first "Old Glory Blowout" on July 4, 1882.

HOSTELS

Lincoln

CENTRAL YMCA
139 N. 11th Street
Lincoln, NE 68508
(402) 432-1251

HOSTELS (continued)

FACILITIES: Open year round; reservations required; 50 beds, men; 50 beds, women; modern bathroom; overnight charges $5 to $8.50; houseparent: Gladys Crist.

POINTS OF INTEREST

Bellevue

STRATEGIC AIR COMMAND MUSEUM - Display of aircraft, missiles, engines, uniforms and equipment. Also historical films of early flights.

Hastings

HASTINGS MUSEUM - Features over 35 habitat groups of mammals and birds, including world's largest collection of whooping cranes.

Keystone

KEYSTONE CHURCH - A tiny pioneer sanctuary with swiveling pews to serve both Catholic and Protestant congregations.

Lincoln

NEBRASKA'S UNICAMERAL - Home of only one-house legislature in the nation.

UNIVERSITY OF NEBRASKA - World's largest elephant displayed at Morrill Hall.

Ogallala

GOMORRAH OF THE PLAINS - Gamblers, gunfighters, and dance hall acts recreate rip-roaring end-of-trail cow town.

Omaha

BOYS TOWN - Institution for homeless boys founded by Father Flanagan. Tours available. Located 10 miles west on U.S. 6.

Southern Black Hills

CUSTER STATE PARK - Contains world's largest buffalo herd.

NEVADA

Never hampered by convention, Nevada joined the Union in 1804 as the thirty-sixth state. The famous Comstock Lode, containing both gold and silver, two metals seldom found together, was discovered near Virginia City in 1859. Then five years later, despite its failure to meet the population requirements, Nevada was allowed into the Union because of its great wealth and anti-slavery stand.

Nearly 90 percent of the land in Nevada is currently owned by the U.S. Government, yet the state boasts two of the most lavish and important resort areas in the country, Reno and Las Vegas. It's also the driest state, with less than 4 inches average annual rainfall, but visitors can engage in all types of water sports or downhill skiing at some of the country's finest skiing areas.

The Comstock Lode has played out, but mining, mostly copper and minerals, is the state's leading revenue earner followed closely by the expanding tourism industry.

State capital: Carson City. State bird: Mountain bluebird. State tree: Single-leaf pinon. State flower: Sagebrush.

WEATHER

Nevada is predominantly a plateau. The eastern part has an average elevation of between 5,000 and 6,000 feet. The western part is between 3,800 and 5,000 feet, the lower limit being in the vicinity of Pyramid Lake and Carson Sink. The southern part is generally between 2,000 and 3,000 feet. The Nevada plateau has several mountain ranges, most of them 50 to 100 miles long, running generally north-south. The only east-west range is in the northwest, where it forms the southern limit of the Columbia River Basin.

Nevada has great climatic diversity, ranging from scorching lowland desert in the south to cool mountain forests in the north. In the northeast, summers are short and hot; winters are long and cold. In the west, the summers are also short and hot, but the winters are only moderately cold. In the south the summers are long and hot, and winters short and mild. Long periods of extremely cold weather are rare, primarily because the mountains east and north of the state act as a barrier to the intensely cold continental arctic air masses. However, on occasion, a cold air mass spills over these barriers and produces prolonged cold waves. There is strong surface heating during the day and rapid nighttime cooling because of dry air, resulting in wide daily ranges in temperature.

Average daily temperature for each month.

	Northern	Southern
Jan.	37.7 to 17.9	57.1 to 28.7
Feb.	41.7 to 21.6	62.6 to 32.5
Mar.	45.0 to 23.0	68.2 to 36.5
Apr.	54.0 to 30.0	76.5 to 43.5
May	64.2 to 37.7	85.8 to 51.4
Jun.	73.2 to 44.0	95.6 to 59.5
Jul.	85.4 to 51.3	102.1 to 67.2
Aug.	83.3 to 49.8	99.7 to 65.8
Sept.	74.1 to 40.3	92.9 to 57.1

NEVADA

Oct.	63.0 to 31.8	80.7 to 46.9
Nov.	48.0 to 25.2	66.0 to 36.3
Dec.	39.2 to 18.8	57.6 to 29.4
Year	59.1 to 32.6	78.7 to 46.2

STATE CHAMBER OF COMMERCE

Nevada Chamber of Commerce Association
P.O. Box 3499
Reno, NV 89505
(702) 323-1877

STATE & CITY TOURISM OFFICES

State

Nevada Department of Economic Development
Blasdel Building
Carson City, NV 89701
(702) 882-7478

Tourism Division
Nevada Department of Economic Development
Capitol Complex
Carson City, NV 89701
(702) 885-4322

Local

Las Vegas Chamber of Commerce
2301 E. Sahara Avenue
Las Vegas, NV 89105
(702) 457-4664

STATE HIGHWAY DEPARTMENT

Nevada Department of Highways
Administration Building
1263 South Stewart Street
Carson City, NV 89712
(702) 885-5440

HIGHWAY WELCOMING CENTER

Las Vegas

LAS VEGAS - Interstate 15.

STATE POLICE

Department of Public Safety
Carson City, NV 89711
(702) 885-5302

HUNTING & FISHING

Hunting

No license to hunt or fish shall be required of residents of this state who have not yet attained their 12th birthday.

It is unlawful for any child who has not yet attained his 14th birthday to hunt any of the wild birds or animals with any firearm, unless such child is accompanied at all times by an adult person licensed to hunt.

No child under 12 years of age, whether accompanied by a qualified person or not, shall hunt big game in the state of Nevada. This section does not prohibit any child from accompanying an adult licensed to hunt.

Resident means any person who is a citizen of the United States and who has been actually present in the state of Nevada for 6 months immediately preceding his application for a license, tag or permit and who intends to make Nevada his permanent home.

Resident

General hunting license (for persons 16 years of age or older), $7; junior hunting license (for persons 12 through 15 years of age), $2; senior hunting license (for persons 65 years of age or older with 10 or more years of Nevada residence), $1.25; serviceman's hunting license (for Nevada residents who are servicemen on active duty outside Nevada), $2; Indian's hunting and fishing license (for resident Indians with certificate of eligibility), free; disabled veteran's hunting and fishing license (for veterans having permanent and total disabilities, upon certification by the Veterans' Administration pursuant to 38 U.S.C. 801), free; deer tags for special seasons, $9.

Non-resident

Regular hunting license (for persons of any age), $40; controlled general hunt (alien tags), $50; controlled archery hunt (alien tags), $10.

Fishing

See hunting regulations above.

Resident

General fishing license (for persons 16 years of age or older), $10; junior fishing license (for persons 12 through 15 years of age), $2; senior fishing license (for persons 65 years of age or older with 10 or more years of Nevada residence), $1.25; serviceman's fishing license (for Nevada residents who are servicemen on active duty outside Nevada), $2; Indian's hunting and fishing license (for resident Indians with certificate of eligibility), free; 10-day fishing permit, $7.50; 3-day fishing permit, $5.

Non-resident

Regular fishing license (for persons 16 years of age or older), $20; junior fishing license (for persons 12 through 15 years of age), $5; special Colorado River fishing li-

HUNTING & FISHING (continued)

cense (valid only on the reciprocal waters of the Colorado River, Lake Mead and Lake Mohave, for persons 14 years of age or older), $10; 10-day fishing permit, $10; 3-day fishing permit, $7.50.

For more information contact:

Department of Fish and Game
1100 Valley Road
Reno, NV 89520
(702) 784-6214

CAMPGROUNDS

See National Forests and State Parks.

RESORTS & BEACHES

Carson City

LAKE TAHOE AREA - Resorts with rustic charm surround the second largest lake in the world. You can water ski, swim, fish, sail, stretch out on sunny beaches or simply marvel at the magnificent view.

Las Vegas

LAS VEGAS AREA - The hotels are cities in themselves, with palm-tree lined golf courses, glamorous theatre restaurants, swimming pools, glittering casinos and plenty of sunshine.

Reno

RENO AREA - The "Biggest Little City in the World" lies at the foot of the purple Sierra Mountains, and through its downtown flows the Truckee River. Amid all this natural beauty are sparkling high-rise resort hotels where you can play tennis, golf, sun, swim or place a bet or two.

BOATING AREAS

Carson City

LAKE TAHOE
LOCATION: West of Carson City.
FACILITIES: Launching.

Hobson

RUBY LAKE
LOCATION: Near Hobson.
FACILITIES: Launching.

Las Vegas

LAKE MEAD
LOCATION: 30 mi. east of Las Vegas.
FACILITIES: Launching.

Lovelock

RYE PATCH RESERVOIR
LOCATION: 25 mi. north of Lovelock.
FACILITIES: Launching.

Pyramid

PYRAMID LAKE
LOCATION: 30 mi. north of Reno on Hwy. 33.
FACILITIES: Launching.

Ruby Valley

FRANKLIN LAKE
LOCATION: Near Ruby Valley.
FACILITIES: Launching.

Yerington

WALKER LAKE
LOCATION: 25 mi. southeast of Yerington.
FACILITIES: Launching.

BICYCLE TRAILS

See CALIFORNIA - Death Valley Trails.

TRAILS

There are no National Trails System Foot Trails in Nevada.

SKI AREAS

Incline Village

SKI INCLINE
Drawer AL
Incline Village, NV 89450
(702) 831-1821
LOCATION: Lake Tahoe's north shore, 28 mi. from Reno.
FACILITIES: 6 chairlifts; slopes for expert, intermediate and beginning skiers; ski instruction; ski rental; 900 ft. vertical drop; longest run, 1 mi.; restaurants; lodging.

Las Vegas

LEES CANYON
576 S. Decatur Blvd.
Las Vegas, NV 89107
(702) 870-4778
LOCATION: 35 mi. west of Las Vegas.
FACILITIES: 1 chairlift; 1 T-bar; 1 tow rope; slopes for expert, intermediate and beginning skiers; ski instruction; ski rental; 8500 ft. vertical drop; restaurants; lodging.

Reno

MT. ROSE - SLIDE MOUNTAIN
P.O. Box 2406
Reno, NV 89505
(702) 849-0704
LOCATION: 22 mi. southeast of Reno on Hwy. 27.
FACILITIES: 4 chairlifts; 3 T-bars; slopes for expert, intermediate and beginning skiers; ski instruction; ski rental; 1450 ft. vertical drop; longest run, 1 mi.; restaurants.

NEVADA

SKI AREAS (continued)

TANNENBAUM
550 Margrave Drive
Reno, NV 89502
(702) 849-9925
LOCATION: 18 mi. southwest of Reno on
Route 27.
FACILITIES: 2 T-bars; 1 tow rope; slopes
for intermediate and beginning skiers; ski instruction; ski rental; 450 ft. vertical drop;
longest run, 1 mi.; restaurants.

AMUSEMENT PARKS & ATTRACTIONS

Bonnie Springs

OLD NEVADA ENTERPRISES
P.O. Box 130
Bonnie Springs, NV 89004
(702) 875-4191
FACILITIES: 45 walk thrus; 3 refreshment
stands; 3 restaurants; arcade; theatre; stage
shows; pay gate; free parking; open all year.

Incline Village

PONDEROSA RANCH
Ponderosa Ranch Road
Incline Village, NV 89450
(702) 831-0691
FACILITIES: 6 walk thrus; 3 refreshment
stands; 5 restaurants; 2 museums; exhibits;
Frontier Town; Silver Dollar Saloon; picnic
facilities; petting farm; anti-gravity house;
riding stable; pay gate; free parking; open
May 1 - Oct. 26.

STATE FAIR

Nevada State Fair
P.O. Box 273
Reno, NV 89504
(702) 785-4280
DATE: September

NATIONAL PARKS

There are no National Parks in Nevada.

NATIONAL FORESTS

National Forests
Intermountain Region
324 25th Street
Ogden, UT 84401
(801) 399-6484

Elko

HUMBOLDT NATIONAL FOREST
ATTRACTIONS: Jarbridge; spectacular canyons, colorful cliffs, old historic mining
camps. Fishing; deer hunting; saddle and pack
trips.
FACILITIES: 20 camp sites, 6 picnic only;
Ward Mountain Winter Sports Area; resort

and dude ranch at Wildhorse Reservoir; ho-
tels.
NEARBY TOWNS: Ely, Mountain City,
Wells, Winnemucca.

Reno

TOIYABE NATIONAL FOREST
ATTRACTIONS: Lake Tahoe; historic ghost
towns; rugged High Sierra country. Trout fishing; hunting; saddle and pack trips; scenic
drives.
FACILITIES: 40 camp sites, 5 picnic only;
swimming sites; Lee Canyon and Reno Ski
Bowl Winter Sports Areas; motels, resorts,
dude ranches.
NEARBY TOWNS: Austin, Carson City, Minden, Tonopah.

See ELDORADO NATIONAL FOREST,
INYO NATIONAL FOREST and TAHOE
NATIONAL FOREST - California.

See DIXIE NATIONAL PARK - Utah.

STATE PARKS

Headquarters

Department of Conservation and Natural Resources
State Park System
201 South Fall Street
Carson City, NV 89701
(702) 885-4384

Caliente

KERSHAW-RYAN STATE PARK
LOCATION: 3 mi. south of Caliente.
FACILITIES: Open Apr. 15 - Oct. 31; 12
sites; water and bathroom facilities; trailer village vehicle sites; picnic area; hiking; tent
camping.

Gabbs

BERLIN-ICHTHYOSAUR STATE PARK
LOCATION: 23 mi. east of Gabbs.
FACILITIES: Open year round; 14 sites; water and bathroom facilities; sanitary station;
trailer village vehicle sites; picnic area; hiking;
tent camping.

Incline Village

LAKE TAHOE - NEVADA STATE PARK
LOCATION: On Hwy. 28.
FACILITIES: Open year round; picnic area;
swimming; boating; fishing; hiking; horseback
riding.

Overton

VALLEY OF FIRE STATE PARK
LOCATION: 5 mi. southwest of Overton.
FACILITIES: Open year round; 38 sites; water and bathroom facilities; sanitary station;
trailer village vehicle sites; picnic area; hiking;
tent camping.

Panaca

BEAVER DAM STATE PARK

STATE PARKS (continued)

LOCATION: Off U.S. 93, 6 mi. north of Caliente, then east 32 mi. on gravel road.
FACILITIES: Open Apr. 15 - Oct. 15; 52 sites; picnic area; swimming; boating; hunting; fishing; hiking; tent camping.

CATHEDRAL GORGE STATE PARK
LOCATION: North of Panaca.
FACILITIES: Open year round; 16 sites; water and bathroom facilities; trailer village vehicle sites; picnic area; hiking; tent camping.

Pioche

SPRING VALLEY STATE PARK
LOCATION: 18 mi. east of Pioche.
FACILITIES: Open year round; 37 sites; water and bathroom facilities; trailer village vehicle sites; picnic area; swimming; boating; fishing; hiking; tent camping.

STATE FORESTS

There are no State Forests in Nevada.

HISTORIC SITES

Carson City

FORT GENOA - Oldest town in state, created by gold rush. Located 1 mi. south of Carson City.

NEVADA STATE MUSEUM - Once the "U.S. Branch Mint at Carson City," features minting equipment and authentic reproduction of a silver mine with narrow tunnel and full-scale mining scenes. Located at Capitol Complex.

Virginia City

VIRGINIA CITY - "Queen of the Comstock Lode," best and largest existing authentic example of western mining metropolis.

HOSTELS

There are no Hostels in Nevada.

POINTS OF INTEREST

Boulder City

HOOVER DAM - One of the country's seven modern civil engineering wonders, the dam, rising 726 feet above bedrock, is the western hemisphere's highest concrete dam.

Elko

COMMERCIAL HOTEL - Home of one of world's largest stuffed polar bears.

Goldfield

GOLDFIELD - A fascinating gold camp of the early 1900s with many original buildings still standing. Also was scene of the Gans-Nelson world championship fist fight. Located 25 mi. east of Tonopah.

Reno

FLEISCHMANN ATMOSPHERIUM - Only one of its kind, features constantly changing shows depicting astronomical and meteorological phenomena. Located on Virginia Avenue.

HAROLD'S CLUB GUN COLLECTION - Houses more than 1000 historic firearms, one of the largest collections in the world. Located on Virginia Street.

HARRAH'S AUTOMOBILE COLLECTION - One of the largest of its type in world. More than 1100 antique, vintage, classic and special-interest cars, restored to their original factory specifications. Located off Glendale Ave.

WASHOE COUNTY COURTHOUSE - Possibly the nation's busiest divorce court; however, 10 times busier with marriages. Located at Virginia and Court Streets.

South Lake Tahoe

EMERALD BAY - Often called the most photographed scenic vista in the U.S.

Virginia City

VIRGINIA CITY CAMEL RACES - A race with a slow pace; unique event also includes ostrich races. Usually held in late summer.

NEW HAMPSHIRE

New Hampshire, decidely independent although bordered by three states and one country, entered the Union in 1788 as the ninth state. With so many neighbors, it is not surprising that border disputes comprise much of the state's history.

As early as 1841, the Massachusetts boundary was established, followed by Canada's nearly 100 years later. The Supreme Court had to settle the haggling between New Hampshire and Vermont and Maine in 1934.

New Hampshire was also a key element in the founding of the country. Upon ratifying the U.S. Constitution in 1788, the state completed the two-thirds majority necessary to make the document legal.

Most of New Hampshire's revenues are derived from manufacturing industries such as

NEW HAMPSHIRE

INTRODUCTION (continued)

electronics and heavy machinery. Also, in the past few years, tourism has grown in leaps and bounds because more and more skiers, hikers, campers and hunters are taking advantage of the state's highly developed outdoor facilities.

State capital: Concord. State bird: Purple finch. State tree: White birch. State flower: Purple lilac.

WEATHER

New Hampshire occupies 9,304 square miles, nearly one-seventh of New England's total area. The terrain is hilly to mountainous. Numerous hills and mountains extend to heights of 2,000 to 4,000 feet above sea level over most of the state, except in the southeast. Approximately 85 percent of New Hampshire is forested. Considerable areas, especially in the north, are sparsely settled.

Characteristics of New Hampshire climate are: changeability of the weather; large range of temperature, both daily and annual; great differences between the same seasons in different years; equable distribution of precipitation; and considerable diversity from place to place. The regional climatic influences are modified in New Hampshire by varying distances from the ocean, elevations, and types of terrain.

Summer temperatures are delightfully comfortable for the most part. They are reasonably uniform over the state, excepting topographical extremes. Average temperatures vary from place to place more in the winter than in the summer. Days with subzero readings are relatively few along the immediate coast but are common inland.

Average daily temperature for each month.

	Northern	Southern
Jan.	25.5 to 5.5	32.6 to 10.7
Feb.	28.9 to 7.3	36.0 to 13.2
Mar.	37.3 to 17.8	43.6 to 22.7
Apr.	50.8 to 29.8	58.3 to 32.7
May	64.3 to 40.2	70.2 to 42.1
Jun.	73.5 to 50.0	79.1 to 52.3
Jul.	77.3 to 54.4	83.5 to 56.5
Aug.	74.8 to 52.4	81.5 to 54.7
Sept.	67.6 to 45.3	73.9 to 47.6
Oct.	57.0 to 35.7	63.4 to 36.8
Nov.	41.9 to 25.7	48.1 to 28.9
Dec.	29.1 to 11.4	35.4 to 16.9
Year	52.3 to 31.3	58.8 to 34.6

STATE CHAMBER OF COMMERCE

Business & Industry Association of New Hampshire
23 School Street
Concord, NH 03301
(603) 224-5388

STATE TOURISM OFFICE

Office of Vacation Travel
Division of Economic Development
P.O. Box 856
Concord, NH 03301
(603) 271-2343

STATE HIGHWAY DEPARTMENT

Department of Public Works and Highways
John O. Morton Building
85 Loudon Road
Concord, NH 03301
(603) 271-3734

HIGHWAY WELCOMING CENTERS

Antrim

ANTRIM CENTER - Route 9.

Canterbury

CANTERBURY - NORTHFIELD CENTER - Route 93.

Colebrook

COLEBROOK CENTER - Route 3.

Salem

SALEM CENTER - Route 93.

STATE POLICE

Department of Public Safety
Concord, NH 03301
(603) 271-3636

HUNTING & FISHING

Hunting

A resident is a citizen of the United States who has lived and made his home within the state not less than 6 months just prior to his application for a license and who has not during that period claimed a residence in any other state for any purpose.

HUNTING & FISHING (continued)

All first-time hunters in New Hampshire must show a valid hunter safety training certificate or a hunting license for a prior year from any state before being issued a hunting license.

Resident

Hunting, $8.25; combination hunting and fishing, $14; archery license, $8; muzzle loaders license, $7; pheasant stamp, $4.

Non-resident

Minor's hunting, $36; hunting, $56; small game (season), $31; small game (3-day), $13; archery, $21; muzzle loaders, $19; pheasant stamp, $4.

Fishing

See hunting regulations above.

Resident

Fishing, $9.25.

Non-resident

Fishing (season), $21; 3-day fishing, $7.75; 7-day fishing, $11; 15-day fishing, $16.

For more information contact:

Fish and Game Department
34 Bridge Street
Concord, NH 03301
(603) 271-3512

CAMPGROUNDS

Private

Albany

PINE KNOLL CAMPING
(603) 447-8982
LOCATION: 5 mi. south of Conway on Lake Iona.
FACILITIES: Open May 15 - Oct. 15; 131 sites; water and bathroom facilities; electrical hookup; trailer village vehicle sites; cabins; swimming; tent camping.

Ashland

RIVERBEND CAMPING CLUB
(603) 536-3311
LOCATION: On Calley Road.
FACILITIES: Open year round; 140 sites; water and bathroom facilities; sanitary station; electrical hookup; trailer village vehicle sites; swimming; boating; hiking; tent camping.

SHADY LANE CAMPGROUND
(603) 968-3654
LOCATION: On Route 3B.
FACILITIES: Open May - Oct.; 200 sites; water and bathroom facilities; sanitary station; electrical hookup; trailer village vehicle sites;

swimming; boating; fishing; tent camping.

Barrington

LEN-KAY CAMPING AREA
(603) 664-9333
LOCATION: On Hall Road.
FACILITIES: Open May 15 - Sept. 15; 173 sites; water and bathroom facilities; sanitary station; electrical hookup; trailer village vehicle sites; swimming; boating; fishing; tent camping.

Brentwood

BRENTWOOD CAMPING AREA
(603) 679-8638
LOCATION: On Route 101.
FACILITIES: Open year round; 150 sites; water and bathroom facilities; electrical hookup; trailer village vehicle sites; swimming; tent camping.

Chester

SILVER SANDS CAMPING AREA
(603) 887-3638
LOCATION: On Route 102.
FACILITIES: Open year round; 100 sites; water and bathroom facilities; sanitary station; electrical hookup; trailer village vehicle sites; swimming; boating; fishing; horseback riding.

Center Ossipee

TERRACE PINES
(603) 539-6210
LOCATION: On Dan Hole Pond.
FACILITIES: Open May 15 - Oct.12; 125 sites; water and bathroom facilities; sanitary station; electrical hookup; trailer village vehicle sites; swimming; boating; fishing; tent camping.

Compton

GOOSE HOLLOW TRAVEL TRAILER PARK
(603) 726-4444
LOCATION: On Waterville Valley Road.
FACILITIES: Open year round; 110 sites; water and bathroom facilities; sanitary station; electrical hookup; trailer village vehicle sites; swimming; tent camping.

Conway

EASTERN SLOPE CAMPING AREA
(603) 447-5092
LOCATION: On Route 16.
FACILITIES: Open May - Nov.; 260 sites; water and bathroom facilities; electrical hookup; trailer village vehicle sites; tent camping.

Goffstown

COLD SPRING CAMPGROUND
(603) 529-2528
LOCATION: 5 mi. north of Goffstown.
FACILITIES: Open Apr. 15 - Oct. 15; 125 sites; water and bathroom facilities; sanitary station; electrical hookup; trailer village vehicle sites; tent camping.

NEW HAMPSHIRE

CAMPGROUNDS (continued)

Goshen

RAND POND CAMPGROUND
(603) 863-3350
LOCATION: On Route 49A.
FACILITIES: Open year round; 121 sites; water and bathroom facilities; sanitary station; electrical hookup; trailer village vehicle sites; boating; boat rental; fishing; tent camping.

Hampstead

EMERSON'S CAMPING AREA
(603) 329-6982
LOCATION: Emerson Avenue.
FACILITIES: Open May 30 - Sept. 15; 137 sites; water and bathroom facilities; electrical hookup; trailer village vehicle sites; swimming; fishing; tent camping.

Hampton Falls

WAKEDA CAMPGROUND
(603) 772-5274
LOCATION: On Route 88.
FACILITIES: Open May 1 - Oct. 15; 200 sites; water and bathroom facilities; sanitary station; electrical hookup; trailer village vehicle sites; tent camping.

Hancock

SEVEN MAPLES CAMPING AREA
(603) 525-3321
LOCATION: On Longview Road.
FACILITIES: Open Apr. - Nov.; 125 sites; water and bathroom facilities; sanitary station; electrical hookup; trailer village vehicle sites; swimming.

Laconia

GUNSTOCK
(603) 293-4341
LOCATION: On Route 11A.
FACILITIES: Open May 15 - Oct. 1; 300 sites; water and bathroom facilities; sanitary station; electrical hookup; trailer village vehicle sites; fishing; hiking.

Lancaster

ROGER'S CAMPGROUND
(603) 788-4885
LOCATION: On U.S. 2.
FACILITIES: Open May 1 - Oct. 1; 153 sites; water and bathroom facilities; sanitary station; electrical hookup; trailer village vehicle sites; cabins; swimming; tent camping.

Lochmere

WINNISQUAM BEACH CAMPGROUND
(603) 524-0021
LOCATION: On Union Road.
FACILITIES: Open May 1 - Oct. 15; 130 sites; water and bathroom facilities; sanitary station; electrical hookup; trailer village vehicle sites; swimming; boating; fishing; tent camping.

Raymond

PINE ACRES FAMILY CAMPGROUND
(603) 895-2519
LOCATION: Prescott Road.
FACILITIES: Open May 1 - Oct. 15; 350 sites; water and bathroom facilities; electrical hookup; trailer village vehicle sites; swimming; boating; boat rental; fishing; tent camping.

Richmond

SHIR-ROY CAMPING AREA
(603) 239-4768
LOCATION: 7 mi. from Route 12.
FACILITIES: Open May 15 - Oct. 12; 100 sites; water and bathroom facilities; sanitary station; electrical hookup; trailer village vehicle sites; swimming; boating; fishing; tent camping.

Rochester

GRAND VIEW CAMPING AREA
(603) 332-1263
LOCATION: 51 Four Rod Road.
FACILITIES: Open May 15 - Oct. 15; 100 sites; water and bathroom facilities; sanitary station; electrical hookup; trailer village vehicle sites; swimming; boating; fishing; tent camping.

South Hampton

TUXBURY POND CAMPING AREA
(603) 394-7660
LOCATION: W. Whitehall Road.
FACILITIES: Open year round; 130 sites; water and bathroom facilities; electrical hookup; trailer village vehicle sites; food service; swimming; boating; fishing.

Weare

ALL SEASONS
(603) 529-9907
LOCATION: On Buckley Road.
FACILITIES: Open year round; 120 sites; water and bathroom facilities; sanitary station; electrical hookup; trailer village vehicle sites; swimming; tent camping.

West Ossipee

SHAWTOWN
(603) 539-6611
LOCATION: On Ossipee Lake Road.
FACILITIES: Open May 15 - Oct. 12; 200 sites; water and bathroom facilities; sanitary station; electrical hookup; trailer village vehicle sites; hiking; bicycle trail; tent camping.

TOTEM POLE PARK
(603) 539-4420
LOCATION: On Ossipee Lake.
FACILITIES: Open May 15 - Sept. 15; 645 sites; water and bathroom facilities; sanitary station; electrical hookup; trailer village vehicle sites; swimming; fishing; tent camping.

WESTWARD SHORES CAMPING AREA
(603) 539-6445
LOCATION: On Ossipee Lake.
FACILITIES: Open May 1 - Oct. 15; 200

CAMPGROUNDS (continued)

sites; water and bathroom facilities; sanitary station; electrical hookup; trailer village vehicle sites; swimming; boating; boat rental; tent camping.

Winchester

FOREST LAKE CAMPING GROUND, INC.
(603) 239-4267
LOCATION: On Route 10.
FACILITIES: Open May - Oct.; 105 sites; water and bathroom facilities; sanitary station; electrical hookup; trailer village vehicle sites; swimming; boating; fishing; tent camping.

RESORTS & BEACHES

Most of the state's resort activities center around the major lakes and include fishing, swimming, boating, water skiing, and camping. (See Boating Areas.)

BOATING AREAS

Bristol

NEWFOUND LAKE
LOCATION: Near Bristol.
FACILITIES: Launching.

Clarksville

LAKE FRANCIS
LOCATION: Near Clarksville.
FACILITIES: Launching.

Conway

CONWAY LAKE
LOCATION: Near Conway.
FACILITIES: Launching.

Effingham

PROVINCE LAKE
LOCATION: Near Effingham.
FACILITIES: Launching.

Enfield

MASCOMA LAKE
LOCATION: Near Enfield.
FACILITIES: Launching.

Holderness

SQUAM LAKE
LOCATION: Near Holderness.
FACILITIES: Launching.

Laconia

PAUGUS BAY
LOCATION: Near Laconia.
FACILITIES: Launching.

Moultonboro

LAKE WINNIPESAUKEE
LOCATION: Near Moultonboro.
FACILITIES: Launching.

Newbury

LAKE SUNAPEE
LOCATION: Near Newbury.
FACILITIES: Launching.

Ossipee

OSSIPEE LAKE
LOCATION: Near Ossipee.
FACILITIES: Launching.

Pittsburg

FIRST CONNECTICUT LAKE
LOCATION: Near Pittsburg.
FACILITIES: Launching.

SECOND CONNECTICUT LAKE
Location: Near Pittsburg.
FACILITIES: Launching.

Strafford

BOW LAKE
LOCATION: Near Strafford.
FACILITIES: Launching.

Wolfeboro

WENTWORTH LAKE
LOCATION: Near Wolfeboro.
FACILITIES: Launching.

BICYCLE TRAILS

See VERMONT - Vermont - New Hampshire Trail.

See VERMONT - New England Trail.

SOUTHWEST NEW HAMPSHIRE TRAIL - 135 mi.; mountainous terrain; 10-speed bicycle necessary.

You will bicycle through a mountainous area of southwest New Hampshire dotted with ski lifts. Many of these lifts operate during the summer. They are an easy way to reach the high country. Use motels and campgrounds for your overnights.

Trail: Keene to Newport to Bradford to Henniker to Milford to South Weare to New Borton to Milford to Keene.

WHITE MOUNTAIN TRAILS - 42, 50, 57, and 105 mi.; mountainous terrain; 10-speed bicycle necessary.

The White Mountains of New Hampshire have long been famed for their rugged beauty. This tour is a selection of rides starting from North Woodstock or the nearby Loon Mountain Resort or one of the other resorts in the area. It is tough mountain cycling with passes over 1800 feet being quite common.

Trails: (1) North Woodstock to Route 112 west, right on Route 116 to Franconia, right on Route 18 to North Woodstock - 42 mi.; (2) North Woodstock to Route 175 south to Campton to Plymouth to Rumney Depot to Warren to North Woodstock - 57 mi.; (3)

NEW HAMPSHIRE

BICYCLE TRAILS (continued)

North Woodstock to Campton to Plymouth to North Sandwich, east on Route 113, left on Route 116, left on Route 112 to North Woodstock - 105 mi.

TRAILS

There are no National Trails System Foot Trails in New Hampshire.

SKI AREAS

Bartlett

ATTITASH
(603) 374-2386
LOCATION: Off Route 302.
FACILITIES: 4 double chairlifts; 1 beginner lift; slopes for expert, intermediate and beginning skiers; ski instruction; ski rental; nursery; 1550 ft. vertical drop; restaurants; lodging.

Bennington

BOBCAT SKI AREA
(603) 588-6330
LOCATION: Off Route 47.
FACILITIES: 1 bubble-double chairlift; 1 open double chairlift; 1 T-bar; slopes for expert, intermediate and beginning skiers; ski instruction; ski rental; nursery; 600 ft. vertical drop; restaurants; lodging.

Bretton Woods

BRETTON WOODS
(603) 278-5000
LOCATION: Off Route 302.
FACILITIES: 2 double chairlifts; 1 T-bar; slopes for expert, intermediate and beginning skiers; ski instruction; 100 ft. vertical drop; restaurants; lodging.

Brookfield

MOOSE MOUNTAIN SKI AREA
(603) 522-3639
LOCATION: Mountain Road.
FACILITIES: 1 chairlift; 2 T-bars; 1 tow rope; slopes for expert, intermediate and beginning skiers; ski instruction; ski rental; nursery; 1200 ft. vertical drop; restaurants.

Brookline

BIG BEAR
(603) 673-4600
LOCATION: Off Route 13.
FACILITIES: 1 T-bar; 1 tow rope; 1 pony lift; slopes for expert, intermediate and beginning skiers; ski instruction; ski rental; restaurants; lodging.

Danbury

RAGGED MOUNTAIN
(603) 768-3971
LOCATION: Off Route 104.
FACILITIES: 1 double chairlift; 1 T-bar; slopes for expert, intermediate and beginning skiers; ski instruction; ski rental; 1400 ft. vertical drop; restaurants; lodging.

Dixville Notch

WILDERNESS
(603) 255-3400
LOCATION: On Route 26.
FACILITIES: 1 double chairlift; 2 T-bars; slopes for expert, intermediate and beginning skiers; ski instruction; ski rental; nursery; 1000 ft. vertical drop; restaurants; lodging.

East Madison

KING PINE SKI AREA
(603) 367-4648
LOCATION: Off Route 153.
FACILITIES: 2 double chairlifts; 1 J-bar; slopes for expert, intermediate and beginning skiers; ski instruction; ski rental; nursery; 350 ft. vertical drop; restaurants; lodging.

Francestown

CROTCHED MOUNTAIN
(603) 588-6345
LOCATION: In Francestown.
FACILITIES: 1 double chairlift; 2 T-bars; 1 pony lift; slopes for expert, intermediate and beginning skiers; ski instruction; ski rental; nursery; 750 ft. vertical drop; restaurants; lodging.

Franconia

CANNON MOUNTAIN
(603) 823-7771
LOCATION: 3 mi. south of Franconia.
FACILITIES: 3 double chairlifts; 3 T-bars; 1 pony lift; 1 tram; slopes for expert, intermediate and beginning skiers; ski instruction; ski rental; nursery; 2146 ft. vertical drop; restaurants; lodging.

MITTERSILL
(603) 823-5511
LOCATION: Off Route 18.
FACILITIES: 1 double chairlift; 2 T-bars; slopes for expert, intermediate and beginning skiers; ski instruction; ski rental; 1600 ft. vertical drop; restaurants; lodging.

Hanover

DARTMOUTH SKIWAY
(603) 795-2143
LOCATION: Route 10 to Lyme Center.
FACILITIES: 2 chairlifts; 1 T-bar; slopes for expert, intermediate and beginning skiers; ski instruction; 900 ft. vertical drop; restaurants; lodging.

Henniker

PAT'S PEAK
(603) 428-8245
LOCATION: Flanders Road.
FACILITIES: 1 triple chairlift; 2 double chairlifts; 2 T-bars; 1 J-bar; slopes for expert, intermediate and beginning skiers; ski instruction; ski rental; nursery; 700 ft. vertical drop; restaurants; lodging.

SKI AREAS (continued)

Jackson

BLACK MOUNTAIN TRAMWAYS
(603) 383-4291
LOCATION: In Jackson.
FACILITIES: 1 double chairlift; 2 T-bars; 1 J-bar; slopes for expert, intermediate and beginning skiers; ski instruction; ski rental; nursery; 1100 ft. vertical drop; restaurants; lodging.

TYROL SKI AREA
(603) 383-4315
LOCATION: Off Route 16.
FACILITIES: 1 double chairlift; 1 T-bar; 1 poma; slopes for expert, intermediate and beginning skiers; ski instruction; ski rental; 960 ft. vertical drop; restaurants; lodging.

WILDCAT
(603) 466-3326
LOCATION: Off Route 16.
FACILITIES: 1 triple chairlift; 2 double chairlifts; 1 T-bar; 1 gondola; slopes for expert, intermediate and beginning skiers; ski instruction; ski rental; nursery; 2100 ft. vertical drop; restaurants; lodging.

Laconia

BRICKYARD MOUNTAIN
(603) 366-4316
LOCATION: Off Route 3.
FACILITIES: 1 double chairlift; 1 tow rope; slopes for expert, intermediate and beginning skiers; ski instruction; ski rental; 495 ft. vertical drop; restaurants; lodging.

GUNSTOCK AREA
(603) 293-4341
LOCATION: I-93 to Exit 20 on Route 11A Gilford.
FACILITIES: 3 double chairlifts; 1 single chairlift; 3 T-bars; 1 tow rope; slopes for expert, intermediate and beginning skiers; ski instruction; ski rental; nursery; 1400 ft. vertical drop; restaurants; lodging.

Lebanon

WHALEBACK
(603) 448-2607
LOCATION: In Lebanon.
FACILITIES: 1 double chairlift; 1 T-bar; 1 poma; slopes for expert, intermediate and beginning skiers; ski instruction; ski rental; nursery; 700 ft. vertical drop; restaurants; lodging.

Lincoln

LOON MOUNTAIN
(603) 745-8111
LOCATION: On Kancamagus Highway.
FACILITIES: 3 double chairlifts; 1 gondola; slopes for expert, intermediate and beginning skiers; ski instruction; ski rental; nursery; 1850 ft. vertical drop; restaurants; lodging.

Manchester

MCINTYRE SKI AREA
(603) 669-7931
LOCATION: Kennard Road.
FACILITIES: 2 double chairlifts; 1 pony lift; slopes for expert, intermediate and beginning skiers; ski instruction; ski rental; 169 ft. vertical drop; restaurants; lodging.

Moultonboro

OSSIPEE MOUNTAIN SKI AREA
(603) 253-4420
LOCATION: 1½ mi. south of Moultonboro.
FACILITIES: 1 T-bar; slopes for expert, intermediate and beginning skiers; ski instruction; 370 ft. vertical drop; restaurants; lodging.

Mt. Sunapee

MT. SUNAPEE
(603) 763-4020
LOCATION: Off I-89.
FACILITIES: 5 double chairlifts; 1 T-bar; 1 J-bar; 1 tow rope; slopes for expert, intermediate and beginning skiers; ski instruction; ski rental; nursery; 1500 ft. vertical drop; restaurants; lodging.

New London

KING RIDGE
(603) 526-4040
LOCATION: On I-89.
FACILITIES: 1 triple chairlift; 1 double chairlift; 2 T-bars; 3 J-bars; slopes for expert, intermediate and beginning skiers; ski instruction; ski rental; nursery; 800 ft. vertical drop; restaurants; lodging.

North Conway

MT. CRANMORE
(603) 356-5545
LOCATION: In Mt. Washington Valley.
FACILITIES: 3 double chairlifts; 1 poma; 2 trams; slopes for expert, intermediate and beginning skiers; ski instruction; ski rental; 1500 ft. vertical drop; restaurants; lodging.

Northfield

HIGHLAND SKI AREA
(603) 286-4055
LOCATION: Bear Hill Road.
FACILITIES: 2 T-bars; 1 poma; slopes for expert, intermediate and beginning skiers; ski instruction; ski rental; 700 ft. vertical drop; restaurants; lodging.

Peterborough

TEMPLE MOUNTAIN
(603) 924-6949
LOCATION: Off Route 101.
FACILITIES: 2 T-bars; 3 tow ropes; slopes for expert, intermediate and beginning skiers; ski instruction; ski rental; nursery; 550 ft. vertical drop; restaurants; lodging.

Plymouth

TENNEY MOUNTAIN
(603) 536-1717
LOCATION: Off Route 3A.
FACILITIES: 2 double chairlifts; 1 pony lift; slopes for expert, intermediate and beginning skiers; ski instruction; ski rental; 1600 ft. vertical drop; restaurants; lodging.

NEW HAMPSHIRE

SKI AREAS (continued)

Waterville Valley

WATERVILLE VALLEY SKI AREA - MT.
TECUMSEH
(603) 236-8311
LOCATION: Off Route 49.
FACILITIES: 5 double chairlifts; 1 T-bar; 1 J-bar; slopes for expert, intermediate and beginning skiers; ski instruction; ski rental; nursery; 2020 ft. vertical drop; restaurants; lodging.

WATERVILLE VALLEY - SNOW'S MOUNTAIN
(603) 236-8311
LOCATION: Off Route 49.
FACILITIES: 1 double chairlift; slopes for expert, intermediate and beginning skiers; nursery; 583 ft. vertical drop; restaurants; lodging; limited ticket ski area, only 600 skiers at one time.

West Ossipee

WHITTIER
(603) 539-2268
LOCATION: Off Route 25.
FACILITIES: 3 T-bars; 1 gondola; slopes for expert, intermediate and beginning skiers; ski instruction; ski rental; nursery; 1300 ft. vertical drop; restaurants; lodging.

AMUSEMENT PARKS & ATTRACTIONS

Gilford

ALPINE RIDGE
Gilford, NH 03246
(603) 293-4304
FACILITIES: Alpine toboggan slide; winter skiing; lodge; restaurant; snack bars; arcade; free parking.

Jefferson

SANTA'S VILLAGE
U.S. 2
Jefferson, NH 03583
(603) 586-4445
FACILITIES: Major ride; 2 kiddie rides; 3 fun houses; refreshment stand; theatre; picnic facilities; Gingerbread Forest; Santa Claus and Elves; 30 rooms of Christmas scenes; free acts; pay gate; free parking.

Laconia

THE ENCHANTED FOREST
Route 3
Laconia, NH 03241
(603) 366-4808
FACILITIES: 5 major rides; 2 kiddie rides; fun house; refreshment stand; arcade; exhibits; miniature golf; picnic facilities; zoo; free gate; free parking; open Jun. 15 - Labor Day.

Lincoln

NATURELAND'S FANTASY FARM (Attraction)

U.S. Route 3
Lincoln, NH 03251
(603) 745-8130
FACILITIES: 8 major rides; 3 refreshment stands; display of wild and tame animals; birds and fish including pet and feed areas; arcade; museum; picnic facilities; stage shows; free acts; open May 1 - Nov. 1.

Woodstock

LOST RIVER RESERVATION (Attraction)
P.O. Box 87
North Woodstock, NH 03262
(603) 745-8031
FACILITIES: Nature garden; museum; restaurant; picnic facilities; caves; pay gate; free parking; open May 14 - Oct. 13.

Salem

CANOBIE LAKE PARK
N. Policy Street
Salem, NH 03079
(603) 893-3506
FACILITIES: 17 major rides; 10 kiddie rides; fun house; walk thru; 8 games; 6 refreshment stands; restaurant; penny arcade; swimming pool; beach; roller rink; miniature golf; lake cruises; speed boats; races; orchestras; name bands; vaudeville; free acts; pay gate; free parking.

STATE FAIR

Plymouth State Fair
Plymouth, NH 03264
(603) 536-2654
DATE: August

NATIONAL PARKS

There are no National Parks in New Hampshire.

NATIONAL FORESTS

National Forests
Eastern Region
633 West Wisconsin Avenue
Milwaukee, WI 53203
(414) 291-3693

Laconia

WHITE MOUNTAIN NATIONAL FOREST
ATTRACTIONS: Mount Washington, 6288 feet, highest point in New England; brook trout fishing; deer, bear, small-game hunting; outstanding skiing with spring skiing often lasting into June; rock climbing; 1,000 miles of foot trails; swimming; scenic drives.
FACILITIES: 72 camp and picnic sites, 17 picnic only; 26 shelters and high-country cabins for hikers; swimming area; Wildcat, Tuckermans Ravine, Waterville Valley Winter Sports Area; cabins, motels, hotels.
NEARBY TOWNS: Berlin, Conway, Gorham, Lancaster, Littleton, Pinkham Notch.

STATE PARKS

Headquarters

Division of Parks
Concord, NH 03301
(603) 271-3556

Bartlett

CRAWFORD NOTCH STATE PARK
(603) 374-2272
LOCATION: 12 mi. north of Bartlett.
FACILITIES: Open May 24 - Oct. 12; 24 sites; water and bathroom facilities; picnic area; fishing; hiking; tent camping.

Colebrook

COLEMAN STATE PARK
(603) 237-4520
LOCATION: 12 mi. east of Colebrook.
FACILITIES: Open May 26 - Oct. 12; 30 sites; water and bathroom facilities; fishing; tent camping.

Gorham

MOOSE BROOK STATE PARK
(603) 466-3860
LOCATION: 2 mi. west of Gorham.
FACILITIES: Open May 26 - Sept. 7; 42 sites; water and bathroom facilities; picnic area; swimming; fishing.

Greenfield

GREENFIELD STATE PARK
(603) 547-3497
LOCATION: 1 mi. west of Greenfield.
FACILITIES: Open May 17 - Oct. 12; 252 sites; water and bathroom facilities; picnic area; food service; swimming; fishing; tent camping.

Hampton

HAMPTON BEACH STATE PARK
(603) 926-3784
LOCATION: Near Hampton.
FACILITIES: Open May - Oct.; 20 sites; picnic area; food service; swimming; boating.

Jaffrey

MONADNOCK STATE PARK
(603) 532-8862
LOCATION: 4 mi. west of Jaffrey.
FACILITIES: Open May 5 - Nov. 11; 21 sites; picnic area; hiking; tent camping.

North Woodstock

FRANCONIA NOTCH STATE PARK
(603) 823-5563
LOCATION: 8 mi. north of North Woodstock.
FACILITIES: Open year round; 98 sites; water and bathroom facilities; food service; swimming; boating; fishing; skiing; cross country skiing; hiking; tent camping.

Nottingham

PAWTUCKAWAY STATE PARK
(603) 895-3031
LOCATION: 4 mi. west of Nottingham.
FACILITIES: Open May 17 - Oct. 12; 170 sites; water and bathroom facilities; picnic area; food service; swimming; boating; fishing; hiking; tent camping.

Peterborough

MILLER STATE PARK
(603) 449-3444
LOCATION: 3 mi. east of Peterborough.
FACILITIES: Open Jun. 16 - Sept. 7; 12 sites; water and bathroom facilities; picnic area; fishing; hiking; tent camping.

Pittsburg

LAKE FRANCIS STATE PARK
No telephone.
LOCATION: 7 mi. north of Pittsburg on River Road.
FACILITIES: Open May 15 - Nov. 15; 36 sites; water and bathroom facilities; boating; fishing; tent camping.

Suncook

BEAR BROOK STATE PARK
(603) 485-9869
LOCATION: 8 mi. northeast of Suncook.
FACILITIES: Open Jun. - Sept.; 81 sites; water and bathroom facilities; vehicle sites; swimming; boating; boat rental; fishing; hiking; tent camping.

Washington

PILLSBURY STATE PARK
(603) 863-2860
LOCATION: 3 mi. north of Washington.
FACILITIES: Open May 26 - Sept. 7; 20 sites; picnic area; fishing; hiking; primitive campsites.

West Ossipee

WHITE LAKE STATE PARK
(603) 323-7350
LOCATION: North of West Ossipee.
FACILITIES: Open year round; 173 sites; water and bathroom facilities; swimming; boating; boat rental; fishing; hiking.

STATE FORESTS

Fish and Game Department
Division of Forestry
34 Bridge Street
Concord, NH 03301
(603) 271-3421

Hillsborough

FOX STATE FOREST
LOCATION: Near Hillsborough.
FACILITIES: Open year round; picnic area; hiking.

NEW HAMPSHIRE

HISTORIC SITES

Concord

STATE CAPITOL - Nation's oldest State Capitol in which the legislature meets in its original chambers. Located at Park and Main Streets.

Deerfield

SIMPSON HOUSE - Birthplace of Major John Simpson, who gained fame by the unauthorized firing of the first shot at Bunker Hill while serving as a private in Captain Dearborn's Company of Colonel Stark's Regiment. Although reprimanded for his disobedience, he afterward served his country with honor. Located on northwest corner of Route 107 and Old Center Road junction.

East Derry

SCOTCH-IRISH SETTLEMENT - In 1719, sixteen Presbyterian families settled here and planted America's first potato crop.

Exeter

EXETER TOWN HOUSE - Here on January 5, 1776, the Provincial Congress adopted and signed the first state constitution establishing an independent state government, the first of the thirteen colonies. Located at junction of Court and Front Streets.

Hillsborough

FRANKLIN PIERCE HOUSE - Home of the 14th President, only person from the state to attain the nation's highest office. Located on North State Street.

Mason

UNCLE SAM'S HOUSE - Boyhood home of Samuel Wilson, who was generally known as "Uncle Sam." He supplied the Army in 1812 with beef in barrels marked with "U.S." Transition from U.S. to Uncle Sam followed, and he became the popular symbol for the United States. Located on Route 123.

North Salem

MYSTERY HILL - "America's Stonehenge." Largest site of its kind in the country, built and used by ancient culture more than 2000 years ago.

Portsmouth

GOVERNOR LANGDON MANSION MEMORIAL - Home of John Langdon, five times Governor of the state, first President of the U.S. Senate, and Acting President of the country until the election of Washington, to whom he administered the oath of office.

Rye

ATLANTIC CABLE STATION AND SUNKEN FOREST - Receiving station for first Atlantic Cable, laid in 1874. Also, remains of Sunken Forests (remnants of the Ice Age) may be seen at low tide. Intermingled with these gnarled stumps are the remains of the original Cable.

Salisbury

BIRTHPLACE OF DANIEL WEBSTER - Born here January 18, 1732, statesman and lawyer, he served as U.S. Congressman from New Hampshire and Massachusetts, Senator from Massachusetts and Secretary of State under Presidents Harrison, Tyler and Fillmore. A noted orator, he achieved national recognition in the landmark Dartmouth College case. Also, one of the first men elected to U.S. Senate Hall of Fame. Located on Route 127 between Salisbury and Franklin.

HOSTELS

Alton

GREEN TOPS HOLIDAY HOSTEL
Roberts Cove Road
Alton, NH 03809
(603) 569-9878
FACILITIES: Open Jun. 25 - Sept. 8; 20 beds, men; 21 beds, women; modern bathroom; overnight charges: $3; houseparent: Willard Kempton.

Durham

UNIVERSITY OF NEW HAMPSHIRE
Randall Hostel
Randall Hall
College Road
Durham, NH 03824
(603) 862-2120
FACILITIES: Open Jun. 1 - Aug. 15; 15 beds, men; 15 beds, women; modern bathroom; nearest hostel: Alton, 50 mi.; overnight charges: $2.50; houseparents: resident graduate students.

Grantham

GRAY LEDGES
Route 10
Grantham, NH 03753
(603) 863-9880
FACILITIES: Open year round; 10 beds, men; 10 beds, women; modern bathroom; overnight charges: $2.50 summer; $3.75 winter; houseparents: Buck & Betty Martin.

Keene

DEAN'S HALL
Keene State College
Keene, NH 03431
(603) 352-1909, Ext. 230
FACILITIES: Open Jun. 15 - Aug. 20; 23 beds, men; 23 beds, women; modern bathroom; nearest hostel: Peterborough, 25 mi. southeast; overnight charges: $2.50; houseparents: resident graduate students.

North Haverhill

THE LIME KILNS YOUTH HOSTEL
Route 10

HOSTELS (continued)

North Haverhill, NH 03774
(603) 989-5656
FACILITIES: Open Jun. 15 - Oct. 15; 15
beds, men; 15 beds, women; modern bathroom; nearest hostel: Warren, VT, 45 mi.
west; overnight charges: $2; houseparents:
John J. & Keith O'Shaughnessy.

Peterborough

SHARION STUDIO BARN
c/o Shapley
RFD 2, Box 310
Peterborough, NH 03458
(603) 924-6928
FACILITIES: Mid-May - mid-Sept.; reservation required; 10 beds, men; 10 beds, women;
modern bathroom; nearest hostel: Littleton,
MA, southeast; Keene, NH; overnight charges:
$2.50 (sleeping bags; $1 for linens); houseparent: Carl Shapley.

Waterville Valley

WATERVILLE VALLEY BUNKHOUSE
Route 49
Waterville Valley, NH 03223
(603) 236-8326
FACILITIES: Open Thanksgiving - Apr. 30,
May 29 - Oct. 16; reservations required; 102
beds, men; 102 beds, women; modern bath-
room; overnight charges: $7; houseparents:
John & Patricia Sava.

POINTS OF INTEREST

Bean's Grant

MOUNT WASHINGTON COG RAILWAY -
Completed in 1869, this unique railway is
over 3 miles long. Average grade to 6293-foot
summit is 1 foot in 4. Made safe by toothed
wheel and ratchet. Second steepest in the
world and first of its type.

Franconia Notch

GREAT STONE FACE ("Old Man of the
Mountains") - Profile of granite head, 40
feet long, is situated 1200 feet above Profile Lake, south of town off U.S. 3.

Littleton

STEREOSCOPIC VIEW FACTORY - Here
from 1867 to 1909, world-famous Kilburn
brothers produced thousands of stereoscopic
views. Their collection, largest in the world
and collector's items today, provided popular
entertainment for generations. Located on
U.S. 302.

Newport

SARAH JOSEPHA BUELL HALE HOME -
Home of widowed mother of five who edited
"Godey's Ladies' Book" and composed poem
now called "Mary Had A Little Lamb." Located on Route 103.

Plymouth

STRAWBERY BANKE - Ten-acre outdoor
museum and historic preservation project featuring 30 homes from the 18th and 19th centuries. Located on Court Street.

Sugar Hill

FIRST SKI SCHOOL IN AMERICA - In 1929,
on the slopes of the hill to the east, Austrian-
born Sig Buchmayr established the first organized ski school in the U.S. Located at junction of Route 117 and Lover's Lane Road.

NEW JERSEY

New Jersey, a combination of manufacturing operations and seaside resorts, joined the
Union in 1787 as the third state. Four years
after statehood, Alexander Hamilton, who
was later killed in the famous duel with Aaron
Burr, established the first factory town in
America near present-day Patterson.

When the Civil War erupted, feelings in
New Jersey about the conflict were mixed.
Nearly all favored the anti-slavery stand but
were reluctant to go to war and disrupt trade
with the South.

Today, New Jersey is highly industrialized
and the most densely populated state in the
country. And since it is situated between two
major metropolitan areas, New York and
Philadelphia, its transportation systems, especially railroads and roadways, are among
the nation's most advanced.

Tourism is also big business in New Jersey.
Recently, its most famous resort area, Atlantic City, inaugurated casino gambling.

State capital: Trenton. State bird: Eastern
goldfinch. State tree: Red oak. State flower:
Purple violet.

WEATHER

New Jersey, though one of the smaller
states, has a varied topography. In the northwest, a section known as the Highlands and
Kittatinny Valley is traversed by several low
mountain ridges extending northeasterly a-
cross the state with valleys and rolling hills between. South and east of the Highlands is the
Red Sandstone Plain. It is generally hilly in its
northwestern part, becoming rolling and then
flat toward the south and southeast. The sea-

NEW JERSEY

WEATHER (continued)

coast section extends from Sandy Hook to
Cape May, a distance of about 125 miles. In
the southern interior, a region known as the
Pine Barrens is covered with scrubby forests
of pine and some oak. The land is low, and
some of it is swampy.

The extreme length of state is 166
miles, and its greatest width only about 65.
The difference in climate is quite marked between the southern tip at Cape May and the
northern extremity in the Kittatinny Mountains. Temperature differences between the
northern and southern parts of the state are
greatest in winter and least in summer. Nearly
every station has registered readings of 100
degrees F or higher at some time, and all have
records of zero or below.

Average daily temperature for each month.

	Northern	Southern
Jan.	34.2 to 15.3	40.4 to 21.4
Feb.	36.7 to 17.2	43.2 to 23.3
Mar.	45.6 to 26.2	50.5 to 29.8
Apr.	59.7 to 36.3	63.4 to 38.6
May	70.2 to 44.7	73.4 to 47.6
Jun.	79.7 to 54.2	82.4 to 57.1
Jul.	84.4 to 58.7	86.2 to 62.0
Aug.	82.2 to 56.5	84.3 to 60.6
Sept.	75.3 to 49.1	78.2 to 53.6
Oct.	64.2 to 38.0	67.7 to 42.5
Nov.	50.4 to 30.5	55.4 to 33.6
Dec.	38.2 to 20.6	44.0 to 25.2
Year	60.1 to 37.3	64.1 to 41.3

STATE CHAMBER OF COMMERCE

New Jersey State Chamber of Commerce
5 Commerce Street
Newark, NJ 07102
(201) 624-6888

STATE & CITY TOURISM OFFICES

State

Division of Economic Development
P.O. Box 2766
Trenton, NJ 08625
(609) 292-7757

Office of Tourism and Promotion
Department of Labor and Industry
P.O. Box 400
Trenton, NJ 08625
(609) 292-2470

Local

Greater Atlantic City Chamber of Commerce
10 Central Pier
Atlantic City, NJ 08401
(609) 345-2251

STATE HIGHWAY DEPARTMENT

Department of Transportation
1035 Parkway Avenue
Trenton, NJ 08625
(609) 292-3346

HIGHWAY WELCOMING CENTERS

Deepwater

DEEPWATER CENTER - Interstate 295.

Mondale

MONDALE CENTER - Garden State Parkway, near New York.

N.J. TURNPIKE - Several booths operated by
Exxon.

Phillipsburg

PHILLIPSBURG CENTER (mobile) - Route
22.

STATE POLICE

Department of Public Safety
West Trenton, NJ 08625
(609) 882-2000

HUNTING & FISHING

Hunting

It is unlawful for any person to obtain a
resident license in this state unless he is a
citizen of the United States and has had an
actual bona fide domicile in the state for six
months immediately prior to application.

It is unlawful for any non-resident or alien
upon reaching the age of 14 to hunt or trap
unless the proper license has been first pro-
cured; a non-resident's and alien's hunting license or a non-resident's and alien's trapping
license.

The division may, in its discretion, issue to
a citizen of the United States, 14 years of age
or older, a license authorizing such person to
hunt for 1 day only in areas licensed as semi-
wild or commercial shooting preserves. These
licenses are obtainable only in person at the
shooting preserve and are valid only on the
day of issue on the preserve for the species
covered by the preserve's license.

The division may issue a license to hunt
with a firearm or bow to citizens between the
ages of 10 and 14, when applied for by the
parent or legal guardian. Such persons must
first complete the appropriate hunter education course, and hunt only when accompanied
by a properly licensed adult above the age of
21.

HUNTING & FISHING (continued)

Resident

Resident firearm hunting, $10.25; bow & arrow hunting, $10.25; trapping, $10.25; citizen's 1-day hunting, $4.25; juvenile hunting, $2; special deer season (permit), $5; pheasant & quail stamp, $5.

Non-resident

Non-resident & alien firearm hunting, Reciprocal-Min., $25.25; bow & arrow hunting, Reciprocal-Min., $25.25; trapping, $100.25.

Fishing

It is unlawful for any person to obtain a resident license unless he is a citizen of the United States and has an actual bona fide domicile in the state for six months immediately prior to time of application.

Any non-resident or unnaturalized foreignborn person, 14 years of age or older, who intends to angle in any of the fresh waters of the state, including the Delaware River throughout its entire length, or in any inland tidal waters, must have a non-resident's and alien's fishing license.

There is available to non-residents and aliens a 3-day vacation fishing license, valid for a period of 3 consecutive days designated on license. Obtainable only after June 1 of each year.

No license is required of non-residents to fish in the Delaware Bay, or bays or waters of the Atlantic Ocean, but a license is required in all tidal rivers except Shark River and Manasquan River below Allenwood Bridge.

Resident

Family fishing (parents), $12.25; supplementary (each child 14-18), $1.25; fishing, $7.25; trout stamp, $4.

Non-resident

Non-resident & alien fishing, $12.25; trout stamp, $8; 3-day vacation fishing, $5.25.

For more information contact:

Division of Fish, Game & Shellfisheries
P.O. Box 1809
Trenton, NJ 08625
(609) 292-2965

CAMPGROUNDS

Private

Allentown

TIMBERLAND LAKE CAMPGROUND
(609) 758-2235
LOCATION: 6 mi. south of Allentown on Route 539.
FACILITIES: Open Apr. 1 - Oct. 31; 200 sites; water and bathroom facilities; sanitary station; electrical hookup; trailer village vehicle sites; picnic area; food service; swimming; boating; fishing; tent camping.

Beemerville

KYMER CAMPGROUND & GAME FARM
(201) 875-3167
LOCATION: Route 519 north 5 mi. to Beemerville.
FACILITIES: Open Apr. - Nov.; 230 sites; water and bathroom facilities; sanitary station; electrical hookup; trailer village vehicle sites; laundry; picnic area; food service; swimming; fishing; tent camping.

Cape May

CAPE ISLAND CAMPGROUND
(609) 884-5777
LOCATION: 3½ mi. south of Rio Grande and Route 47 on Route 9.
FACILITIES: Open May 1 - Sept. 30; 320 sites; water and bathroom facilities; sanitary station; electrical hookup; trailer village vehicle sites; picnic area; food service; swimming; tent camping.

HOLLY SHORES CAMPGROUND
(609) 886-1234
LOCATION: On Route 9.
FACILITIES: Open Apr. 1 - Sept. 30; 300 sites; water and bathroom facilities; sanitary station; electrical hookup; trailer village vehicle sites; laundry; picnic area; food service; swimming; tent camping.

LAKE LAURIE CAMPGROUND
(609) 884-3567
LOCATION: 2 mi. north of Garden State Parkway on Route 9.
FACILITIES: Open Apr. 1 - Oct. 15; 700 sites; water and bathroom facilities; sanitary station; electrical hookup; trailer village vehicle sites; picnic area; swimming; boating; fishing; tent camping.

SEASHORE CAMPSITES, INC.
(609) 884-4010
LOCATION: 1½ mi. north from O Exit, Garden State Parkway, on Route 9.
FACILITIES: Open May - Oct.; 500 sites; water and bathroom facilities; sanitary station; electrical hookup; trailer village vehicle sites; picnic area; food service; swimming; tent camping.

Cape May Court House

BIG TIMBER LAKE CAMPGROUND
(609) 465-4456
LOCATION: On Goshen-Swainton Road.
FACILITIES: Open May 15 - Oct. 1; 200 sites; water and bathroom facilities; sanitary station; electrical hookup; trailer village vehicle sites; laundry; picnic area; food service; swimming; tent camping.

BLUE DOLPHIN CAMPGROUND
(609) 465-4518
LOCATION: South on Route 9.
FACILITIES: Open May 15 - Sept. 10; 325 sites; water and bathroom facilities; sanitary station; electrical hookup; trailer village vehi-

NEW JERSEY

CAMPGROUNDS (continued)

cle sites; picnic area; food service; swimming; tent camping.

DRIFTWOOD CAMPGROUND, INC.
(609) 263-2677
LOCATION: 478 Shore Road.
FACILITIES: Open Apr. 15 - Oct. 15; 500 sites; water and bathroom facilities; sanitary station; electrical hookup; trailer village vehicle sites; laundry; picnic area; swimming; tent camping.

HACIENDA CAMPGROUND
(609) 465-7688
LOCATION: On Dennisville Road to Route 47, left on Route 47.
FACILITIES: Open Apr. 15 - Oct. 15; 200 sites; water and bathroom facilities; sanitary station; electrical hookup; trailer village vehicle sites; laundry; picnic area; swimming; boating; fishing; tent camping.

HIDEAWAY BEACH RESORT CAMP-GROUND
(609) 465-7097
LOCATION: On Route 47 next to Reeds Beach Road.
FACILITIES: Open May 15 - Sept. 15; 300 sites; water and bathroom facilities; sanitary station; electrical hookup; trailer village vehicle sites; laundry; picnic area; swimming; boating; fishing; horseback riding; tent camping.

KING NUMMY TRAIL CAMPGROUNDS
(609) 465-4242
LOCATION: 3 mi. west of Exit 6.
FACILITIES: Open May 1 - Sept. 15; 225 sites; water and bathroom facilities; sanitary station; electrical hookup; trailer village vehicle sites; swimming; boating; tent camping.

NORTH WILDWOOD CAMPGROUNDS
(609) 465-4440
LOCATION: 527L-J Shellbay Road.
FACILITIES: Open May 15 - Sept. 15; 200 sites; water and bathroom facilities; sanitary station; electrical hookup; trailer village vehicle sites; laundry; picnic area; food service; swimming; tent camping.

OLD STAGECOACH CAMPGROUND
(609) 465-4953
LOCATION: On Stagecoach Road.
FACILITIES: Open May 15 - Oct. 1; 235 sites; water and bathroom facilities; sanitary station; electrical hookup; trailer village vehicle sites; laundry; picnic area; food service; swimming; tent camping.

SHELLBAY CAMPGROUND
(609) 465-4770
LOCATION: 1 mi. south of Cape May Court House on Route 9.
FACILITIES: Open May 15 - Oct. 1; 296 sites; water and bathroom facilities; sanitary station; electrical hookup; trailer village vehicle sites; laundry; swimming; tent camping.

Chatsworth

KAMP OLYMPIK KAMPGROUNDS

(609) 965-4225
LOCATION: In Chatsworth.
FACILITIES: Open May 15 - Oct. 1; 250 sites; water and bathroom facilities; sanitary station; electrical hookup; trailer village vehicle sites; picnic area; food service; swimming; boating; fishing; tent camping.

Clermont

AVALON CAMPGROUND
(609) 263-3837
LOCATION: 492 Shore Road.
FACILITIES: Open Apr. 1 - Sept. 15; 250 sites; water and bathroom facilities; sanitary station; electrical hookup; trailer village vehicle sites; laundry; food service; swimming; boating; fishing; tent camping.

Egg Harbor

ATLANTIC CITY WEST KOA
(609) 965-1944
LOCATION: Heidelberg Ave.
FACILITIES: Open Apr. - Oct.; 165 sites; water and bathroom facilities; sanitary station; electrical hookup; trailer village vehicle sites; laundry; picnic area; swimming; tent camping.

Elmer

TALL PINES CAMPGROUND
(609) 451-7479
LOCATION: Beal Road.
FACILITIES: Open year round; 225 sites; water and bathroom facilities; sanitary station; electrical hookup; trailer village vehicle sites; laundry; picnic area; fishing; tent camping.

Farmingdale

DEEP HOLLOW PARK
(201) 938-2233
LOCATION: 1 mi. from Collingswood Circle, Routes 33 & 34.
FACILITIES: Open year round; 250 sites; water and bathroom facilities; sanitary station; electrical hookup; trailer village vehicle sites; food service; swimming; tent camping.

Green Bank

BEL HAVEN LAKE CAMPGROUND
(609) 965-2031
LOCATION: On Route 542.
FACILITIES: Open Apr. - Nov.; 285 sites; water and bathroom facilities; sanitary station; electrical hookup; trailer village vehicle sites; laundry; food service; swimming; boating; fishing; tent camping.

Green Creek

GREEN CREEK CAMPGROUNDS
(609) 886-7119
LOCATION: On Route 47.
FACILITIES: Open May - Oct.; 330 sites; water and bathroom facilities; sanitary station; electrical hookup; trailer village vehicle sites; laundry; picnic area; swimming; boating; fishing; tent camping.

CAMPGROUNDS (continued)

Hammonton

INDIAN BRANCH PARK CAMPGROUND
(609) 561-4719
LOCATION: From Hammonton, south 3½
mi. on Route 54 to U.S. 322, east 3½ mi.
FACILITIES: Open May - Oct.; 175 sites; water and bathroom facilities; sanitary station; electrical hookup; trailer village vehicle sites; picnic area; swimming; boating; fishing; tent camping.

Lakewood

TIP TAM CAMPING PARK, INC.
(201) 363-4036
LOCATION: 2½ mi. west of Lakewood.
FACILITIES: Open May 1 - Sept. 30; 200 sites; water and bathroom facilities; sanitary station; electrical hookup; trailer village vehicle sites; laundry; picnic area; food service; swimming; boating; fishing; tent camping.

Marmora

OAK RIDGE CAMPGROUND
(609) 399-0807
LOCATION: 518 South Shore Road.
FACILITIES: Open May - Oct.; 260 sites; water and bathroom facilities; sanitary station; electrical hookup; trailer village vehicle sites; laundry; picnic area; food service; tent camping.

WHIPPOORWILL CAMPGROUND
(609) 399-0547
LOCATION: 810 South Shore Road.
FACILITIES: Open Apr. 1 - Oct. 30; 288 sites; water and bathroom facilities; sanitary station; electrical hookup; trailer village vehicle sites; laundry; picnic area; tent camping.

New Gretna

CHIP'S FOLLY CAMPGROUND & TRAILER PARK
(609) 296-4434
LOCATION: On County Road 542.
FACILITIES: Open year round; 300 sites; water and bathroom facilities; sanitary station; electrical hookup; trailer village vehicle sites; laundry; picnic area; food service; swimming; boating; fishing; tent camping.

Newton

GREEN VALLEY BEACH, INC., CAMPGROUND
(201) 383-4026
LOCATION: 2 mi. south of Newton.
FACILITIES: Open year round; 250 sites; water and bathroom facilities; sanitary station; electrical hookup; trailer village vehicle sites; laundry; picnic area; food service; swimming; fishing; tent camping.

Ocean View

ECHO FARM CAMPGROUND
(609) 263-3465
LOCATION: South of Routes 9 & 50 intersection on Route 9.

FACILITIES: Open May - Oct.; 350 sites; water and bathroom facilities; sanitary station; electrical hookup; trailer village vehicle sites; laundry; picnic area; food service; swimming; tent camping.

LAKE AND SHORE CAMPGROUND
(609) 263-3775
LOCATION: On Route 550.
FACILITIES: Open Jun. - Oct.; 200 sites; water and bathroom facilities; sanitary station; electrical hookup; trailer village vehicle sites; laundry; food service; swimming; boating; tent camping.

OCEAN VIEW CAMPGROUND
(609) 263-8382
LOCATION: ½ mi. north of Sea Isle Blvd. on Route 9.
FACILITIES: Open Apr. 15 - Oct. 1; 700 sites; water and bathroom facilities; sanitary station; electrical hookup; trailer village vehicle sites; laundry; picnic area; food service; swimming; tent camping.

PINE HAVEN CAMPGROUND
(609) 263-8304
LOCATION: On Route 9.
FACILITIES: Open Mar. 15 - Sept. 30; 500 sites; water and bathroom facilities; sanitary station; electrical hookup; trailer village vehicle sites; picnic area; food service; swimming; boating; fishing; tent camping.

PLANTATION CAMPGROUND
(609) 263-3217
LOCATION: On Route 9.
FACILITIES: Open May 1 - Sept. 30; 225 sites; water and bathroom facilities; sanitary station; electrical hookup; trailer village vehicle sites; laundry; food service; tent camping.

TAMERLANE CAMPGROUND
(609) 263-3676
LOCATION: 1 mi. south of Exit 17 of Garden State Parkway on Route 9.
FACILITIES: Open May - Oct.; 250 sites; water and bathroom facilities; sanitary station; electrical hookup; trailer village vehicle sites; laundry; picnic area; swimming; tent camping.

YOGI BEAR'S JELLYSTONE PARK
(609) 263-3925
LOCATION: 1 mi. north of Sea Isle Blvd. on Route 9.
FACILITIES: Open Apr. 15 - Oct. 1; 500 sites; water and bathroom facilities; sanitary station; electrical hookup; trailer village vehicle sites; laundry; picnic area; food service; swimming; boating; fishing; tent camping.

Parsippany

BROOKWOOD LAKES CLUB
(201) 334-9907
LOCATION: On Route 46, ½ mi. east of Routes 287 & 202.
FACILITIES: Open year round; 200 sites; water and bathroom facilities; sanitary station; electrical hookup; trailer village vehicle sites; laundry; food service; swimming; boating; fishing; tent camping.

NEW JERSEY

CAMPGROUNDS (continued)

Pleasantville

DEER RUN CAMPGROUNDS
(609) 641-3085
LOCATION: 1997 Black Horse Pike.
FACILITIES: Open Mar. - Oct.; 180 sites; water and bathroom facilities; sanitary station; electrical hookup; trailer village vehicle sites; laundry; tent camping.

Port Republic

CHESTNUT LAKE CAMPGROUND
(609) 652-7251
LOCATION: Old New York Road.
FACILITIES: Open Mar. - Nov.; 200 sites; water and bathroom facilities; sanitary station; electrical hookup; trailer village vehicle sites; laundry; picnic area; food service; swimming; boating; fishing; tent camping.

RED WING LAKES CAMPGROUNDS
(609) 652-1939
LOCATION: In Port Republic.
FACILITIES: Open Apr. 15 - Sept. 15; 200 sites; water and bathroom facilities; sanitary station; electrical hookup; trailer village vehicle sites; swimming; boating; fishing; tent camping.

Rio Grande

FORT APACHE CAMPGROUNDS
(609) 886-1076
LOCATION: 1228 Delsea Drive.
FACILITIES: Open Mar. 15 - Sept. 15; 200 sites; water and bathroom facilities; sanitary station; electrical hookup; trailer village vehicle sites; laundry; picnic area; swimming; fishing; tent camping.

Stillwater

ACORN LAKE CAMPGROUND
(201) 383-8000
LOCATION: Route 80 Exit 15 north, to Route 206 north, to Route 521 south.
FACILITIES: Open Apr. 15 - Oct. 31; 250 sites; water and bathroom facilities; sanitary station; electrical hookup; trailer village vehicle sites; food service; boating; fishing; tent camping.

Sussex

PLEASANT ACRES FARM CAMPGROUND
(201) 875-4166
LOCATION: On DeWitt Road.
FACILITIES: Open May 15 - Oct. 15; 300 sites; water and bathroom facilities; sanitary station; electrical hookup; trailer village vehicle sites; laundry; picnic area; swimming; fishing; tent camping.

TALL TIMBER CAMPGROUND
(201) 875-7131
LOCATION: Between Hamburg & Sussex on Route 565.
FACILITIES: Open year round; 100 sites; water and bathroom facilities; sanitary station; electrical hookup; trailer village vehicle sites; laundry; swimming; boating; fishing; tent camping.

Tuckerton

ATLANTIC CITY NORTH KOA
(609) 296-9163
LOCATION: Exit 58 on Garden State Parkway, 2 mi. east of Bass River State Park.
FACILITIES: Open year round; 165 sites; water and bathroom facilities; sanitary station; electrical hookup; trailer village vehicle sites; laundry; picnic area; food service; swimming; tent camping.

Williamstown

HOSPITALITY CREEK CAMPGROUND
(609) 629-5140
LOCATION: 5 mi. east of Williamstown on U.S. Route 322.
FACILITIES: Open Apr. 15 - Oct. 15; 215 sites; water and bathroom facilities; sanitary station; electrical hookup; trailer village vehicle sites; laundry; food service; swimming; boating; fishing; tent camping.

Woodstown

FOUR SEASONS CAMPGROUND
(609) 769-0983
LOCATION: 4 mi. from Woodstown.
FACILITIES: Open year round; 422 sites; water and bathroom facilities; sanitary station; electrical hookup; trailer village vehicle sites; laundry; picnic area; food service; swimming; fishing; tent camping.

RESORTS & BEACHES

Asbury Park

ASBURY PARK
LOCATION: On Route 71.
FACILITIES: About 175 hotels, motels and guest houses; ocean and pool swimming, white sandy public beaches, surf and deep sea fishing; charter and sightseeing boats; water skiing; championship golf courses; wide boardwalk with pavilions and unique shops; amusement areas with sky-high rides; quaint parks; picturesque lakes; indoor and outdoor tennis courts; bicycling; movie theaters; nightclubs; horse racing at nearby Monmouth Park and harness racing at nearby Freehold Raceway.

Atlantic City

ATLANTIC CITY
LOCATION: Accessible via U.S. Routes 9, 30, 40, 322 and connecting highways, including Garden State Parkway Exits 36, 38 and Atlantic City Expressway from Philadelphia.
FACILITIES: 450 hotels and motels; 1500 guest homes and cottages; swimming; fishing (party boats, ½ day and full day charter fishing boats, pleasure excursion boats); 5 ocean piers (Steel Pier - newly remodeled with latest rides and top name entertainment; Garden Pier - concerts and Arts Center; Central Pier - exhibits, Sky Tower, rides, aquarium and miniature golf; Steeplechase Pier - games, rides; Million Dollar Pier - rides, games, miniature golf); tennis (24 courts, 12 indoor, year round); theaters; country club golf; 4½ mi.

RESORTS (continued)

beach and boardwalk; casino gambling.

Atlantic Highlands

ATLANTIC HIGHLANDS
LOCATION: Accessible via Route 36.
FACILITIES: Country club golf; fishing (party boats, charter boats, rowboats).

Avalon

AVALON
LOCATION: On Ocean Drive.
FACILITIES: 6 motels; 3 hotels; guest houses; protected beaches; sailing; boating; fishing in back bays as well as ocean; tennis.

Avon-by-the-Sea

AVON-BY-THE-SEA
LOCATION: On Route 71 near junction of Route 35.
FACILITIES: 3 hotels; 2 motels; 38 guest houses; 10 apartment units; many summer cottages; fishing (party boats, rowboats); swimming; ½ mi. beach and ½ mi. boardwalk.

Barnegat

BARNEGAT
LOCATION: On U.S. Route 9.
FACILITIES: Motel; guest house; 20 cottages; fishing (party boats, charter boats, rowboats); country club golf; horseback riding nearby; boat basins; municipal bathing beach; boat launching ramp and municipal dock.

Belmar

BELMAR
LOCATION: On Routes 71 & 35.
FACILITIES: Motels; 8 hotels; 164 guest houses; 600 cottages for rental; ocean swimming; pools; fishing (party boat); tennis courts; band concerts; golf courses; bathing beach 1½ mi. long; surfing beach; pier and jetty fishing.

Boro of Beachwood

BORO OF BEACHWOOD
LOCATION: On U.S. Route 9.
FACILITIES: Rental cottages; 1 private tennis court; public tennis courts; swimming; yacht club activities; ¾ mi. beach and ¾ mi. boardwalk.

Bradley Beach

BRADLEY BEACH
LOCATION: On Route 71.
FACILITIES: 6 hotels; 150 guest houses; 200 cottages; 2 motels; tennis; 2 nearby summer playhouses; theater; outdoor swimming pool; fishing (party boat, charter boat, rowboats); golf; horseback riding; 1 mi. of beach and boardwalk; games; ride; restaurants; surf fishing; dancing; band concerts.

Brielle

BRIELLE
LOCATION: On Routes 70, 71 & 35.

FACILITIES: 2 motels; 8 guest houses; 15 cottages; fishing (charter boats, party boats, rowboats); tennis (private & public courts); golf; horseback riding nearby; 11 boat basins (400 berths); restaurants.

Brigantine

BRIGANTINE
LOCATION: Accessible via U.S. 30, 9.
FACILITIES: Hotel; 23 motels; 200 apartment units; 400 cottages; beaches on both bay and ocean; boat rental; ocean fishing; pier; stores.

Budd Lake

BUDD LAKE
LOCATION: On Route 46.
FACILITIES: 4 hotels; 7 motels; 6 guest houses; cottages and bungalow colonies; public and private outdoor swimming pools; rowboats; golf; horseback riding; 7 mi. of shore; 2 swimming beaches.

Cape May

CAPE MAY CITY
LOCATION: "America's oldest seashore resort" at the southern tip of New Jersey, accessible by U.S. 9 and Garden State Parkway.
FACILITIES: 59 motels and hotels; 90 guest houses; 450 apartment units; 200 cottages; tennis courts; 2 movie theaters; fishing (party boats, charter boats); yacht club; marinas; golf; horseback riding.

Deal

DEAL
LOCATION: On Route 71.
FACILITIES: 80 cottages; 72 apartment units (on yearly or seasonal basis); 6 tennis courts; private outdoor swimming pool; golf; horseback riding.

Highlands

HIGHLANDS BOROUGH
LOCATION: Just off Route 36.
FACILITIES: 4 hotels; 3 guest houses; 3 colonies of cottages; fishing (party boats, charter boats, rowboats with or without outboards); marina; outdoor swimming pools; beaches; restaurants; river or ocean swimming.

Keansburg

KEANSBURG
LOCATION: South Shore of Raritan Bay just off Route 36.
FACILITIES: Hotels; cottages; guest houses; motels; theaters; outdoor swimming pool; fishing (party boats, rowboats); ½ mi. boardwalk; 3 mi. beach; restaurants; beach games.

Lakewood

LAKEWOOD
LOCATION: On U.S. Route 9.
FACILITIES: 20 hotels; 6 motels; theatres; indoor and outdoor swimming pools; fishing and boating on Lake Carasaljo; golf; indoor & outdoor tennis courts; driving range; horse-

NEW JERSEY

RESORTS (continued)

back riding; sport parachuting school; indoor ice skating; indoor swimming; carriage rides; primarily a winter resort.

Landing

LAKE HOPATCONG
LOCATION: Off U.S. 80.
FACILITIES: Hotel; 10 guest houses; 300 cottages; 4 motels; fishing & pleasure boats; golf; horseback riding; 45 mi. of lake front.

Lavallette

LAVALLETTE
LOCATION: On Route 35.
FACILITIES: Hotel; 13 motels and efficiency apartments; guest house; 1400 cottages; 4 tennis courts; basketball; baseball; rowboats; theater; 1½ mi. of sandy beaches; surf fishing.

Long Beach

BARNEGAT LIGHT
LOCATION: End of Route 72.
FACILITIES: 5 motels; 5 guest houses; cottages; restaurants; ocean & bay bathing; fishing; boating; charter boats; 2 mi. of beach.

HARVEY CEDARS
LOCATION: End of Route 72.
FACILITIES: Guest house; apartment unit; 800 cottages; boating; swimming; surf fishing.

SHIP BOTTOM
LOCATION: End of Route 72.
FACILITIES: 10 motels; hotel; 32 apartment houses; 1394 cottages; swimming; surfing; water skiing; boating; clamming; crabbing; bay & surf fishing; golf courses; horseback riding; 1 mi. of bay and 1 mi. of ocean beaches.

SURF CITY
LOCATION: End of Route 72.
FACILITIES: Hotel; 10 guest houses; 1000 cottages; fishing; swimming in bay and ocean; miniature golf courses; tennis courts; 1¼ mi. beach.

Long Branch

LONG BRANCH
LOCATION: On Route 36.
FACILITIES: Hotel; 11 motels; many guest houses; 3500 apartment units; tennis courts; outdoor pools; public fishing pier; golf; horseback riding nearby; boat basin; boardwalk and pier amusements; 2 mi. of boardwalk with 6 public beaches and a city-owned beach club with salt-water pool, bath houses and cabanas.

Manasquan

MANASQUAN
LOCATION: On Route 71.
FACILITIES: 2 hotels; 50 guest houses; cottages; 25 apartment units; 1¼ mi. of boardwalk and beach.

Margate City

MARGATE CITY

LOCATION: Accessible via Atlantic City Expressway, U.S. Routes 9, 30, 40 & 322.
FACILITIES: 30 motels; 50 guest houses; 500 apartment units; 50 cottages; golf; tennis; fishing (party boat, charter boat, rowboats); 1½ mi. of beach.

Middletown

MIDDLETOWN TOWNSHIP
LOCATION: On Route 35 between Raritan Bay and the Navesink River.
FACILITIES: Hotels; motels; restaurants; fishing (charter and rowboats); horseback riding; golf; beach.

Neptune

NEPTUNE
LOCATION: On Routes 18, 33, 35, 66, & 71, and Garden State Parkway.
FACILITIES: Motels; hotels; cottages; guest houses and apartments; ocean and pool swimming; surf fishing; public beaches; bicycling; fishing (charter boat, party boat); crabbing; skin diving; water skiing.

Ocean City

OCEAN CITY
LOCATION: Via the Atlantic City Expressway and Garden State Parkway.
FACILITIES: Hotels; guest houses; motels; apartment units, and rental homes; ocean and pool swimming; surf, ocean, and bay fishing; surf casting and fishing contest; charter and party boat rentals; sail and hobie cat regattas; golf; tennis courts; basketball; shuffleboard courts; 2½ mi. of boardwalk; 8 mi. of sandy beach; free concerts Mon. - Thurs. evening during the season, the oldest continuing series of concerts in the U.S. (Alcoholic beverages are forbidden.)

Ocean Gate

OCEAN GATE
LOCATION: On Barnegat Bay, 1 mi. off Route 9.
FACILITIES: Guest houses; cottages; apartment units; 1 mi. sandy beach; boating; sailing; tennis; fishing.

Ocean Grove

OCEAN GROVE
LOCATION: On Route 71.
FACILITIES: 100 hotels; motel; 200 cottages; 200 guest houses; 500 apartment units; ocean and pool swimming; surf fishing; bicycling; horseback riding; fishing (charter boats, party boats); 1 mi. beach; 1 mi. boardwalk.

Point Pleasant Beach

POINT PLEASANT BEACH
LOCATION: On Route 35.
FACILITIES: Hotels; motels; cabins; cottages; guest houses; outdoor swimming pool; sport fishing (charter and party boat fleets); small craft rentals; sailing; tennis; golf; bowling; horseback riding nearby; 1 mi. of boardwalk; 2 mi. of beach; restaurants; surf fishing.

RESORTS (continued)

Sea Bright

SEA BRIGHT
LOCATION: On Route 36.
FACILITIES: Hotel; 5 motels; 4 guest houses; 130 apartment units; cottages; fishing (charter boats, rowboats, party boats); golf; outdoor swimming pools; tennis courts; 3½ mi. of beach; salt water fishing; bicycling; swimming; private & public beach clubs.

Sea Girt

SEA GIRT
LOCATION: On Route 71.
FACILITIES: Hotel; 7 guest houses; tennis courts; golf; swimming; 1 mi. boardwalk and beach.

Sea Isle City

SEA ISLE CITY
LOCATION: On Route 585.
FACILITIES: 5 motels; 30 guest houses; 1000 apartment units; 1200 cottages and duplexes; tennis courts; shuffleboard; basketball court; fishing (party boats, charter boats, small craft); golfing; horseback riding nearby; Memorial Day parade and concert; beauty pageant in July; baby parade; Christmas parade; sailing and boating regattas; 1 mi. boardwalk; 5 mi. of beach.

Seaside Heights

SEASIDE HEIGHTS
LOCATION: On Route 35.
FACILITIES: 70 motels; 400 guest houses; 500 apartment units; 500 cottages; swimming; fishing; crabbing; boating (rowboat and motor boat rentals, party boats); bicycle riding; skateboard park; Olympic swimming pool; water skiing; tennis courts; golf; ice skating; roller skating rink; horseback riding; 2 mi. of boardwalk.

Seaside Park

SEASIDE PARK
LOCATION: On Route 35.
FACILITIES: 15 hotels and motels; 100 guest houses; 350 apartment units; 850 cottages; tennis courts; fishing; crabbing; horseback riding; golf; boardwalk amusement area; swimming pool; 2 mi. of beach and boardwalk.

Somers Point

SOMERS POINT
LOCATION: On U.S. Route 9.
FACILITIES: Hotel; 9 motels; 10 guest houses; boating; golf; horseback riding; water skiing.

Spring Lake

SPRING LAKE
LOCATION: Off Route 71.
FACILITIES: 7 hotels; 38 guest houses; tennis courts; swimming pools; horseback riding; 2 mi. of beach and boardwalk.

Stone Harbor

STONE HARBOR
LOCATION: On Route 585.
FACILITIES: 11 motels; 1000 apartment units; 800 cottages; many guest houses; tennis courts; fishing (party boats, charter boats, rowboats); horseback riding; golf; swimming off a 3 mi. beach.

Toms River

TOMS RIVER
LOCATION: On historic Toms River and Route 166, south of Route 37 juntion.
FACILITIES: 25 motels; tennis courts; swimming pools; golf.

Tuckerton

LITTLE EGG HARBOR
LOCATION: On U.S. Route 9.
FACILITIES: Motel; fishing (party boats, charter boats, rowboats, pleasure boats); golf; horseback riding; hunting area.

TUCKERTON
LOCATION: On U.S. Route 9.
FACILITIES: Motel; guest houses; cottages; fishing (party boats, charter boats, rowboats, U-drive boats); horseback riding; golf; tennis; swimming.

Ventnor City

VENTNOR CITY
LOCATION: On Route 585.
FACILITIES: 4 motels; 241 apartment units; 51 guest houses; 4 high rise apartments; 3 condominiums; ice skating; roller skating rink; tennis courts; shuffleboard; bocci courts; 2 mi. of protected beaches; surfing; sailing; fishing pier; golf courses; regatta; Miss Ventnor Beauty Contest.

Wildwood

THE WILDWOODS BY-THE-SEA
LOCATION: On Route 585.
FACILITIES: 12000 motel units; 80 hotels; 250 guest houses; 4000 apartment units; 500 cottages; tennis courts; shuffleboard courts; swimming pool; sailing; water skiing; fishing (pleasure boats, party boats, charter boats, rowboats); golf; horseback riding; amusement piers; 4½ mi. of boardwalk; 7 mi. of sandy beaches.

BOATING AREAS

Alpine

ALPINE BOAT BASIN
FACILITIES: Launching; fuel; water and bathroom facilities; food service.

ENGLEWOOD BOAT BASIN
FACILITIES: Launching; fuel; water and bathroom facilities; food service.

Amboy

PERTH AMBOY BOAT BASIN
FACILITIES: Launching; food service; water.

NEW JERSEY

BOATING AREAS (continued)

Atlantic Highlands

HARBOR COMMISSION
FACILITIES: Launching; fuel; water and bathroom facilities; food service.

Avalon

DARLING YACHT SALES (Ocean Drive)
FACILITIES: Launching; fuel; water and bathroom facilities.

DARLING YACHT SALES SERVICE CENTER (Old Avalon Blvd.)
FACILITIES: Launching; fuel; water and bathroom facilities.

Barnegat

EAST BAY MARINA
FACILITIES: Launching; fuel; water and bathroom facilities.

Barnegat Bay

BAYWOOD MARINA
FACILITIES: Launching; fuel; water and bathroom facilities.

Bayville

CEDAR CREEK MARINA
FACILITIES: Launching; fuel; water and bathroom facilities.

HARBOR LIGHT MARINA
FACILITIES: Launching; fuel; water and bathroom facilities; food service.

Beach Haven

SNUFFERY DOCK, INC.
FACILITIES: Launching; fuel; water and bathroom facilities; food service.

Brant Beach

SICKINGER'S MARINA
FACILITIES: Launching; fuel; water and bathroom facilities.

Bricktown

GREEN COVE MARINA
FACILITIES: Launching; fuel; water and bathroom facilities.

JOHNSON BOAT BASIN
FACILITIES: Launching; fuel; water and bathroom facilities.

MEADOWS MARINA, INC.
FACILITIES: Launching; fuel; water and bathroom facilities.

PARADISE CRAFTMEN'S MARINA
FACILITIES: Launching; fuel; water and bathroom facilities.

SPORTSMANS ISLAND MARINA
FACILITIES: Launching; fuel; water and bathroom facilities; food service.

Bridgeport

BRIDGEPORT BOAT YARD
FACILITIES: Launching; fuel; water and bathroom facilities.

Bridgeton

HUSTEDS LANDING, INC.
FACILITIES: Launching; fuel; water and bathroom facilities.

Brielle

ZUBERS SEACOAST BASIN, INC.
FACILITIES: Launching; water and bathroom facilities.

Brigantine

BAYSHORE MARINA
FACILITIES: Launching; fuel; water and bathroom facilities.

CIRCLE MARINA
FACILITIES: Launching; fuel.

COMMODORE MARINA
FACILITIES: Launching; fuel; water and bathroom facilities.

PETERSON'S MARINA
FACILITIES: Launching; fuel; water and bathroom facilities.

Burlington

CURTIN MARINA
FACILITIES: Launching; fuel; water and bathroom facilities.

Cape May

BREE ZEE YACHT BASIN
FACILITIES: Launching; fuel; water and bathroom facilities.

HINCH MARINA, INC.
FACILITIES: Launching; fuel; water and bathroom facilities.

MCNEILL MARINA
FACILITIES: Launching; fuel; water and bathroom facilities; food service.

PHARO'S MARINA
FACILITIES: Launching; fuel; water and bathroom facilities; food service.

Delanco

DAN'S BOAT YARD
FACILITIES: Launching; fuel; water and bathroom facilities; food service.

East Rutherford

FAVORITE MARINA
FACILITIES: Launching; fuel; water and bathroom facilities.

Forked River

BARA MARINA
FACILITIES: Launching; fuel; water and

BOATING AREAS (continued)

bathroom facilities; food service.

Fortescue

FORTESCUE PIER MARINA & TRAILER PARK
FACILITIES: Launching; fuel; water and bathroom facilities; food service.

FORTESCUE STATE MARINA
FACILITIES: Launching; fuel; water and bathroom facilities.

HIGBEE'S MARINA
FACILITIES: Launching; fuel; water and bathroom facilities; food service.

Greenwich

HITCH'S MARINA INC.
FACILITIES: Launching; fuel; water and bathroom facilities; food service.

Harvey Cedars

THE BOAT YARD
FACILITIES: Launching; fuel; water and bathroom facilities.

Heislerville

ANCHOR MARINA
FACILITIES: Launching; fuel; water and bathroom facilities; food service.

Hewitt

SPORTSMAN'S BOATS AND MOTORS
FACILITIES: Launching; fuel; water and bathroom facilities; food service.

Island Heights

COZY COVE MARINA
FACILITIES: Launching; fuel; water and bathroom facilities.

Jersey City

ROOSEVELT MARINA
FACILITIES: Launching; fuel; water and bathroom facilities; food service.

Lake Hopatcong

WOODPORT BOAT BASIN, INC.
FACILITIES: Launching; fuel; water and bathroom facilities.

Lavallette

OCEAN BEACH MARINA, INC.
FACILITIES: Launching; fuel; water and bathroom facilities; food service.

Long Beach

PATTEN AVE. MARINA
FACILITIES: Launching; fuel; water and bathroom facilities.

Manahawkin

DUCK INN MARINA & MOTEL
FACILITIES: Launching; fuel; water and bathroom facilities.

Manasquan

BURLEW'S ANCHORAGE
FACILITIES: Launching; fuel; water and bathroom facilities; food service.

CHRISTIANO'S MARINA
FACILITIES: Launching; fuel; water and bathroom facilities.

Mantoloking

WINTER YACHT BASIN, INC.
FACILITIES: Launching; fuel; water and bathroom facilities.

Margate

M.W. MARGATE MARINA, INC.
FACILITIES: Launching; fuel.

Marmora

ALL SEASONS MARINA
FACILITIES: Launching; fuel; water and bathroom facilities.

CLAYTON'S MARINA
FACILITIES: Launching; fuel; water and bathroom facilities.

Mays Landing

SMALL CRAFT MARINA
FACILITIES: Launching; fuel; water and bathroom facilities.

THOMPSON MARINE & ENGINE, INC.
FACILITIES: Launching; fuel.

Middle Township

JOHN F. GRANT MARINA, INC.
FACILITIES: Launching; fuel; water and bathroom facilities.

Millville

SPRING GARDEN BOAT WORKS
FACILITIES: Launching; fuel; water and bathroom facilities.

Monmouth Beach

CHANNEL CLUB MARINA
FACILITIES: Launching; fuel; water and bathroom facilities; food service.

Mt. Arlington

LEE'S PARK
FACILITIES: Launching; fuel; water and bathroom facilities; food service.

Neptune

SHARK RIVER HILLS MARINA
FACILITIES: Launching; fuel; water and bathroom facilities; food service.

NEW JERSEY

BOATING AREAS (continued)

Newport

GANDY'S BEACH MARINA
FACILITIES: Launching; fuel; water and
bathroom facilities.

MONEY ISLAND MARINA
FACILITIES: Launching; fuel; water and
bathroom facilities.

NEWPORT LANDING MARINA
FACILITIES: Launching; fuel; water and
bathroom facilities; food service.

North Wildwood

NORTH WILDWOOD MARINA
FACILITIES: Launching; fuel; water and
bathroom facilities.

Northfield

HACKNEY'S BOAT YARD, INC.
FACILITIES: Launching; fuel; water and
bathroom facilities; food service.

Ocean City

LEMONT'S MARINA, INC.
FACILITIES: Launching; fuel; water and
bathroom facilities; food service.

Ocean Gate

GOOD LUCK POINT MARINA
FACILITIES: Launching; fuel; water and
bathroom facilities.

OCEAN GATE YACHT BASIN, INC.
FACILITIES: Launching; fuel; water and
bathroom facilities; food service.

Point Pleasant

SHORE HAVEN MARINA, INC.
FACILITIES: Launching; fuel; water and
bathroom facilities.

Port Monmouth

GATEWAY MARINA
FACILITIES: Launching; fuel; water and
bathroom facilities.

PORT MONMOUTH MARINA
FACILITIES: Launching; fuel; water and
bathroom facilities.

Port Republic

CHESTNUT NECK BOAT YARD
FACILITIES: Launching; fuel; water and
bathroom facilities.

Riverside

RIVERSIDE MARINA, INC.
FACILITIES: Launching; fuel; water and
bathroom facilities; food service.

Salem

MARBORO MARINA, INC.

FACILITIES: Launching; fuel; water and
bathroom facilities.

Sea Bright

CHRIS'S LANDING
FACILITIES: Launching; water and bathroom facilities.

NAUVOO MARINA
FACILITIES: Launching; fuel; water and
bathroom facilities.

SURFSIDE MARINA, INC.
FACILITIES: Launching; fuel; water and
bathroom facilities.

Sea Isle City

ANCHORAGE MARINA
FACILITIES: Launching; fuel; water and
bathroom facilities; food service.

Sewaren

SEWAREN MARINE BASIN
FACILITIES: Launching; fuel; water and
bathroom facilities.

Somers Point

TIDEWATER MARINE COMPANY
FACILITIES: Launching.

South Amboy

BROWN'S MARINA
FACILITIES: Launching; fuel; water and
bathroom facilities.

Stone Harbor

DESCHAMPS BOAT YARD
FACILITIES: Launching; fuel; food service.

STONE HARBOR MARINA
FACILITIES: Launching; fuel; water and
bathroom facilities.

Strathmere

WHALE CREEK MARINA
FACILITIES: Launching; fuel; water and
bathroom facilities.

Trenton

ROSS MARINE SERVICE
FACILITIES: Launching; fuel; water and
bathroom facilities.

Toms River

CEDAR MAR MARINA, INC.
FACILITIES: Launching; fuel; water and
bathroom facilities; food service.

EAST DOVER MARINA
FACILITIES: Launching; fuel; water and
bathroom facilities.

SHELTER COVE MARINA
FACILITIES: Launching; fuel; water and
bathroom facilities.

BOATING AREAS (continued)

Tuckerton

CEDAR HARBOR MARINA
FACILITIES: Launching; fuel; water and bathroom facilities.

TUCKERTON MARINA
FACILITIES: Launching; fuel; water and bathroom facilities.

Villas

BAYVIEW MARINA & LUNCHEONETTE
FACILITIES: Launching; fuel; water and bathroom facilities; food service.

Waretown

HOLIDAY HARBOR MARINA, INC.
FACILITIES: Launching; fuel; water and bathroom facilities.

Wildwood

ANGLESEA MARINA, INC.
FACILITIES: Launching; fuel; water and bathroom facilities; food service.

BICYCLE TRAILS

See PENNSYLVANIA - Delaware River Trail.

JERSEY SHORE TRAIL - 200 mi.; long distances per day; 10-speed bicycle recommended.

This trip offers the cyclist scenic roads beside woodlands, streams, and shorelines. The trip is designed to use roads with light auto traffic.

Trails: Medford to Medford Lakes to Tabernacle to Wharton State Forest to Egg Harbor to Mays Landing to Ocean City to Cape May.

MORRISTOWN TRAIL - 34 mi.; any bicycle.

Morristown was the winter headquarters of General Washington in 1779 and 1780. The trail is located at Morris Avenue and Washington Place, approximately ½ mi. from the train station.

Trail: Morristown over Mt. Kimble Ave/Route 202 to Morristown National Historic Park to Bernardsville to Bedminister to Chester to Mendham to Morristown.

TRAILS

Fort Lee

PALISADES LONG PATH - 11 mi. foot trail. The path extends from the New Jersey side of the George Washington Bridge to the New York-New Jersey state line atop the Palisades cliffs, offering panoramic views of nearby New York City and the Hudson River Valley. Hikers can observe bridges and river traffic, as well as dense vegetation and huge rock formations, and can look down on trees growing on the riverbank and slopes.

PALISADES SHORE TRAIL - 11.25 mi. foot trail. Along the New Jersey shore of the Hudson River, the trail lies on extraordinary terrain at the foot of the Palisades, mostly at river's edge, affording hikers many views of the Palisades and New York City's skyline. It passes under the George Washington Bridge and among huge boulders and outcrops. Fall coloration is splendid along both Palisades trails.

SKI AREAS

Gladstone

PEAPACK SKI AREA
P.O. Box 15
Gladstone, NJ 07934
(201) 234-1344
LOCATION: 2 mi. north of Route 202 on Route 206.
FACILITIES: 1 tow rope; slopes for expert, intermediate and beginning skiers; ski instruction; ski rental; 200 ft. vertical drop; longest run, 1200 ft.; restaurants; lodging.

Hopewell

BELLE MOUNTAIN SKI AREA
Valley Road
Hopewell, NJ 08525
(609) 397-0043
LOCATION: On Valley Road off Route 29.
FACILITIES: 1 chairlift; 3 tow ropes; slopes for expert, intermediate and beginning skiers; ski instruction; 190 ft. vertical drop; longest run, 1100 ft.; restaurants; lodging.

Kenilworth

GALLOPING HILL SKI CENTER
Kenilworth Blvd.
Kenilworth, NJ 07033
(201) 352-8431
LOCATION: Galloping Hill Golf Course.
FACILITIES: 1 tow rope; slopes for intermediate and beginning skiers; ski instruction; ski rental; 150 ft. vertical drop; longest run, 800 ft.; restaurants; lodging.

Mahwah

CAMPGAW MOUNTAIN SKI CENTER
Campgaw Road
Mahwah, NJ 07430
(201) 327-7800
LOCATION: East face of Campgaw Mountain.
FACILITIES: 3 double chairlifts; slopes for expert, intermediate and beginning skiers; ski instruction; 255 ft. vertical drop; longest run, 1650 ft.; restaurants; lodging.

Marlboro

ARROWHEAD SKI AREA
YMCA
Marlboro, NJ 07746
(201) 946-4598
LOCATION: Opposite State Hospital on Route 520.
FACILITIES: 3 tow ropes; slopes for expert, intermediate and beginning skiers; ski instruction; ski rental; 100 ft. vertical drop; restaurants; lodging.

NEW JERSEY

SKI AREAS (continued)

McAfee

GREAT GORGE/VERNON VALLEY SKI AREA
Route 94
McAfee, NJ 07428
(201) 827-2000
LOCATION: On Route 94.
FACILITIES: 13 double chairlifts; 3 tow ropes; slopes for expert, intermediate and beginning skiers; ski instruction; ski rental; nursery; 1033 ft. vertical drop; longest run, 6023 ft.; restaurants; lodging.

Newfoundland

CRAIGMEUR SKI AREA
Green Pond Road
Newfoundland, NJ 07435
(201) 697-4501
LOCATION: 2¼ mi. off Route 23 between Routes 23 & 80.
FACILITIES: 1 chairlift; 1 T-bar; slopes for intermediate and beginning skiers; ski instruction; ski rental; nursery; longest run, 1200 ft.; restaurants; lodging.

Pine Hill

SKI MOUNTAIN SKI AREA
DeCou Road & Branch Avenue.
Pine Hill, NJ 08021
(609) 783-8484
LOCATION: DeCou Road & Branch Avenue.
FACILITIES: 1 T-bar; 2 tow ropes; 1 pony lift; slopes for expert, intermediate and beginning skiers; ski instruction; ski rental; nursery; longest run, 1800 ft.; restaurants; lodging.

Salem

HOLLY MOUNTAIN SKI AREA
Lower Alloways Creek
Salem County, NJ 08069
(609) 935-9888
LOCATION: On Jericho Road.
FACILITIES: 1 chairlift; 1 pony lift; slopes for expert, intermediate and beginning skiers; ski instruction; ski rental; 150 ft. vertical drop; longest run, 1000 ft.; restaurants; lodging.

Stillwater

FAIRVIEW LAKE SKI TOURING CENTER
R.D. 5, Box 210
Newton, NJ 07860
(201) 383-9282
LOCATION: Fairview Lake YMCA Camps in Stillwater.
FACILITIES: Slopes for expert, intermediate and beginning skiers; ski instruction; ski rental; restaurants; lodging.

Sussex

SLEEPY HOLLOW PARK KAMP GROUNDS
Route 565
Sussex, NJ 07461
(201) 875-6211
LOCATION: Route 565.
FACILITIES: School rates; lodging; ski touring and Nordic racing programs.

Vernon

HIDDEN VALLEY SKI AREA
Breakneck Road
Vernon, NJ 07462
(201) 764-4200
LOCATION: Breakneck Road.
FACILITIES: 1 triple chairlift; 1 double chairlift; slopes for expert, intermediate and beginning skiers; ski instruction; ski rental; nursery; 650 ft. vertical drop; longest run, 2700 ft.; restaurants; lodging.

AMUSEMENT PARKS & ATTRACTIONS

Asbury Park

PALACE AMUSEMENTS
207 Lake Avenue
Asbury Park, NJ 07712
(201) 775-7345
FACILITIES: 8 major rides; fun house; 6 games; refreshment stand; arcade; 2 shooting galleries; miniature golf; free gate; pay parking; open May 23 - Sept. 16; weekends rest of year.

Atlantic City

CENTRAL PIER
Boardwalk & Tennessee Avenue
Atlantic City, NJ 08401
(609) 344-1840
FACILITIES: 6 major rides; 3 fun houses; 200 games; 2 refreshment stands; 2 restaurants; 325 ft. space tower; miniature golf course; omnivision 180-degree hemospheric screen in 70 MM color; aquarium; penny arcade; mirror maze; free gate to pier, pay gate to space tower; rides and golf courses; open May 28 - Sept. 15; weekends, Sept. & Oct.

MILLION DOLLAR PIER
Boardwalk & Arkansas Avenue
Atlantic City, NJ 08401
(609) 345-7585
FACILITIES: 12 major rides; 12 kiddie rides; 21 games; 2 fun houses; walk thru; 11 refreshment stands; arcade; shooting gallery; beach; bowling alley; free gate; pay parking; open Jun. 18 - Sept. 11; weekends, Apr.

THE NEW STEEL PIER
Boardwalk & Virginia Avenue
Atlantic City, NJ 08401
(609) 344-2161
FACILITIES: 4 kiddie rides; fun house; 17 games; 9 refreshment stands; arcade; shooting gallery; exhibits; picnic facilities; theatre; crafts; petting zoo; stage shows; water shows; circus; Thrilsphere; Guinness World Record Show & Exhibit; pay gate; pay parking; open Jun. - Sept. 5.

STEEPLECHASE PIER
1106 Boardwalk
Atlantic City, NJ 08401
(609) 344-1085
FACILITIES: 13 major rides; 4 kiddie rides;

AMUSEMENT PARKS (continued)

fun house; walk thru; 17 games; 2 refreshment stands; shooting gallery; free gate.

Clementon

CLEMENTON LAKE AMUSEMENT PARK
144 Berlin Road
Clementon, NJ 08021
(609) 783-0263
FACILITIES: 15 major rides; 6 kiddie rides; fun house; walk thru; 9 games; 5 refreshment stands; restaurant; arcade; shooting gallery; picnic facilities; miniature golf; pay gate; free parking.

Jackson

GREAT ADVENTURE
Jackson, NJ 08527
(201) 928-2000
FACILITIES: 27 major rides; 7 kiddie rides; 2 walk thrus; 22 games; 12 refreshment stands; 3 restaurants; 18 specialty food outlets; arcade; shooting gallery; exhibits; picnic facilities; crafts; stage shows (diving, dolphin, tiger, magic, wild west); orchestras; name bands; free acts; pay gate; free parking; open Apr. 2 - Oct. 23; weekends, Apr. & Oct.

Long Branch

LONG BRANCH AMUSEMENT PIER
Ocean Avenue
Long Branch, NJ 07740
(201) 222-2624
FACILITIES: 6 major rides; 7 kiddie rides; 8 games; refreshment stands; 2 restaurants; arcades; free acts; free gate; pay parking.

Mt. Arlington

BERTRAND ISLAND PARK
Mt. Arlington, NJ 08060
(609) 398-0136
FACILITIES: 17 major rides; 7 kiddie rides; 20 games; fun house; 6 refreshment stands; restaurant; penny arcade; shooting gallery; beach; miniature golf; picnic facilities; free gate; free and pay parking.

Netcong

WILD WEST CITY
Route 206
Netcong, NJ 07857
(201) 347-8900
FACILITIES: 3 kiddie rides; 4 refreshment stands; restaurant; arcade; museum; exhibits; picnic facilities; zoo; stage shows; orchestras; pay gate; free parking; open May 1 - Oct. 31.

Ocean City

WONDERLAND PIER
6th & Boardwalk
Ocean City, NJ 08226
(609) 399-7082
FACILITIES: 13 major rides; 5 kiddie rides; 4 refreshment stands; arcade; pay parking.

Point Pleasant

POINT PLEASANT PAVILION

Arnold Avenue
Point Pleasant, NJ 08742
(201) 295-4334
FACILITIES: 10 major rides; 10 kiddie rides; fun house; arcade; beach; miniature golf; free and pay parking.

Scotch Plains

BOWCRAFT PLAYLAND
Route 22
Scotch Plains, NJ 07076
(201) 233-0675
FACILITIES: 9 major rides; 3 kiddie rides; 60 games; 2 refreshment stands; restaurant; arcade; picnic facilities; miniature golf; golf driving range; go karts; baseball batting machines; free gate; free parking; open all year.

Sea Isle City

FUN CITY AMUSEMENT PARK
32nd & Boardwalk
Sea Isle City, NJ 08243
(609) 263-3862
FACILITIES: 7 major rides; 8 kiddie rides; refreshment stand; 2 games; arcade; free gate; free parking.

Seaside Heights

CASINO PIER & POOL
Grant & Boardwalk
Seaside Heights, NJ 08751
(201) 793-6488
FACILITIES: 25 major rides; 22 kiddie rides; walk thru; 1 fun house; 52 games; 10 refreshment stands; 3 restaurants; 2 hotels; 3 night clubs; fishing pier; arcade; shooting gallery; pool; beach; exhibits; miniature golf; orchestras; name bands; free acts; free gate; pay parking; open May 1 - Sept. 15.

Wildwood

CASINO ARCADE PARK
Oak Avenue & Boardwalk
Wildwood, NJ 08260
(609) 522-5599
FACILITIES: 8 major rides; 6 kiddie rides; fun house; walk thru; 18 games; 9 refreshment stands; 2 restaurants; arcade; shooting gallery; tram trains; free gate.

FUN PIER
4001 Boardwalk
Wildwood, NJ 08260
(609) 522-5656
FACILITIES: 19 major rides; 8 kiddie rides; walk thru; 3 fun houses; 18 games; 4 refreshment stands; arcade; free gate; open May 28 - Sept. 6.

HUNT'S PIER
3511 Atlantic Avenue
Wildwood, NJ 08260
(609) 522-2429
FACILITIES: 15 major rides; 5 kiddie rides; 3 refreshment stands; walk thru; theaters; 18-hole miniature golf course; orchestras; name bands; free gate; pay parking.

MOREY'S PIER
25th & Boardwalk

NEW JERSEY

AMUSEMENT PARKS (continued)

Wildwood, NJ 08260
(609) 522-3050
FACILITIES: 15 major rides; 5 kiddie rides;
24 games; 2 refreshment stands; beach; arcade; shooting gallery; open Palm Sunday -
Sept. 21.

SPORTLAND PIER
23rd & Boardwalk
Wildwood, NJ 08260
(609) 522-2408
FACILITIES: 16 major rides; 5 kiddie rides;
10 games; 4 refreshment stands; restaurant;
swimming pool; trampolines; bicycles; aqua
circus; slides; motordome; beach; free gate.

STATE FAIR

New Jersey State Fair
1648 Nottingham Way
Trenton, NJ 08619
(609) 587-6300
DATE: September

NATIONAL PARKS

There are no National Parks in New Jersey.

NATIONAL FORESTS

There are no National Forests in New Jersey.

STATE PARKS

Headquarters

Environmental Protection Department
Division of Parks
John Fitch Plaza
Trenton, NJ 08625
(609) 292-2772

Centerton

PARVIN STATE PARK
LOCATION: Near Centerton.
FACILITIES: Open year round; water and
bathroom facilities; trailer village vehicle sites;
picnic area; food service; swimming; boating;
fishing; hiking; tent camping.

Clinton

SPRUCE RUN STATE PARK
LOCATION: 2 mi. north of Clinton.
FACILITIES: Open year round; picnic area;
food service; swimming; boating; hunting;
fishing; cross country skiing; hiking.

Farmingdale

ALLAIRE STATE PARK
LOCATION: 2 mi. south of Farmingdale.
FACILITIES: Open year round; water and
bathroom facilities; trailer village vehicle sites;
picnic area; food service; cross country skiing;
hiking; horseback riding; tent camping.

Glen Gardner

VOORHEES STATE PARK
LOCATION: 2 mi. east of Glen Gardner.
FACILITIES: Open year round; water and
bathroom facilities; trailer village vehicle sites;
picnic area; hunting; cross country skiing; hiking; tent camping.

Hackettstown

ALLAMUCHY MT. STATE PARK
LOCATION: 2 mi. north of Hackettstown.
FACILITIES: Open year round;.hunting; fishing; cross country skiing; hiking.

Hainesville

HIGH POINT STATE PARK
LOCATION: 4 mi. east of Hainesville.
FACILITIES: Open year round; water and
bathroom facilities; trailer village vehicle sites;
picnic area; swimming; boating; fishing; cross
country skiing; hiking; tent camping.

Island Beach

ISLAND BEACH STATE PARK
LOCATION: 1 mi. south of Island Beach.
FACILITIES: Open year round; picnic area;
food service; swimming; fishing; self-guided
trail.

Lebanon

ROUND VALLEY STATE PARK
LOCATION: Round Valley Road.
FACILITIES: Open year round; water and
bathroom facilities; trailer village vehicle sites;
picnic area; food service; swimming; boating;
hunting; fishing; cross country skiing; hiking;
tent camping.

Matawan

CHEESEQUAKE STATE PARK
LOCATION: In Matawan.
FACILITIES: Open year round; water and
bathroom facilities; trailer village vehicle sites;
picnic area; food service; swimming; fishing;
cross country skiing; hiking; horseback riding;
tent camping.

Newton

SWARTSWOOD STATE PARK
LOCATION: 4 mi. west of Newton.
FACILITIES: Open year round; water and
bathroom facilities; trailer village vehicle sites;
picnic area; food service; swimming; boating;
hunting; fishing; cross country skiing; tent
camping.

Raven Rock

DELAWARE & RARITAN CANAL STATE
PARK
LOCATION: Near Raven Rock.
FACILITIES: Open year round; water and
bathroom facilities; trailer village vehicle sites;
picnic area; boating; fishing; cross country skiing; tent camping.

STATE PARKS (continued)

Ringwood

RINGWOOD STATE PARK
LOCATION: Near Ringwood.
FACILITIES: Open year round; water and bathroom facilities; trailer village vehicle sites; swimming; boating; hunting; fishing; cross country skiing; hiking; tent camping.

STATE FORESTS

Environmental Protection Department
Division of Forestry
John Fitch Plaza
Trenton, NJ 08625
(609) 292-2520

Atsion

WHARTON STATE FOREST
LOCATION: In Atsion.
FACILITIES: Open year round; water and bathroom facilities; trailer village vehicle sites; picnic area; food service; swimming; boating; hunting; fishing; hiking; tent camping.

Belleplain

BELLEPLAIN STATE FOREST
LOCATION: 2 mi. south of Belleplain.
FACILITIES: Open year round; water and bathroom facilities; trailer village vehicle sites; picnic area; food service; swimming; boating; hunting; fishing; hiking; horseback riding; tent camping.

Branchville

STOKES STATE FOREST
LOCATION: 5 mi. northwest of Branchville.
FACILITIES: Open year round; water and bathroom facilities; trailer village vehicle sites; picnic area; food service; swimming; boating; hunting; fishing; hiking; tent camping.

Chatsworth

LEBANON STATE FOREST
LOCATION: 5 mi. north of Chatsworth.
FACILITIES: Open year round; water and bathroom facilities; trailer village vehicle sites; swimming; hunting; hiking; tent camping.

Hope

JENNY JUMP STATE FOREST
LOCATION: 3 mi. east of Hope.
FACILITIES: Open year round; water and bathroom facilities; trailer village vehicle sites; picnic area; hunting; hiking; self-guided trail; tent camping.

Jenkins

PENN STATE FOREST
LOCATION: 5 mi. north of Jenkins.
FACILITIES: Open year round; picnic area; boating; hunting; fishing; hiking; horseback riding.

New Gretna

BASS RIVER STATE FOREST
LOCATION: 4 mi. north of New Gretna.
FACILITIES: Open year round; water and bathroom facilities; trailer village vehicle sites; picnic area; food service; swimming; boating; hunting; fishing; hiking; horseback riding; self-guided trail; tent camping.

Ringwood

ABRAM S. HEWITT STATE FOREST
LOCATION: 5 mi. northwest of Ringwood.
FACILITIES: Open year round; hunting; cross country skiing; hiking.

RAMAPO MT. STATE FOREST
LOCATION: 4 mi. east of Ringwood.
FACILITIES: Open year round; fishing; cross country skiing; hiking.

Walnut Valley

WORTHINGTON STATE FOREST
LOCATION: 4 mi. north of Walnut Valley.
FACILITIES: Open year round; water and bathroom facilities; trailer village vehicle sites; picnic area; swimming; boating; hunting; fishing; hiking; tent camping.

Wanaque

NORVIN GREEN STATE FOREST
LOCATION: 3 mi. west of Wanaque.
FACILITIES: Open year round; hunting; cross country skiing; hiking; self-guided trail.

HISTORIC SITES

Caldwell

GROVER CLEVELAND BIRTHPLACE - In Caldwell. The birthplace of Grover Cleveland, 22nd & 24th President of the United States.

Elizabeth

BOXWOOD HALL - 1073 E. Jersey St. The home of Elias Boudinot, 1st President of the United States Continental Congress.

Haddonfield

INDIAN KING TAVERN - In Haddonfield. The meeting place of the New Jersey Assembly during the Revolution.

Hammonton

BATSTO VILLAGE - In Hammonton. The site of the William Richards Mansion and Ironworks, which produced cannon balls during the American Revolution.

Hancock's Bridge

HANCOCK HOUSE - In Hancock's Bridge. The site of a massacre of Quaker patriots at the hands of the British.

River Edge

VON STEUBEN HOUSE - In River Edge. Was

NEW JERSEY

HISTORIC SITES (continued)

presented to Baron Von Steuben in gratitude
for his services during the Revolutionary War.

Rocky Hill

ROCKINGHAM - In Rocky Hill. The last
headquarters of Washington during the Revolutionary War.

Somerville

OLD DUTCH PARSONAGE - In Somerville.
The house of Jacob Hardenbergh, the "Fighting Parson" of the Revolutionary War.

WALLACE HOUSE - The Headquarters of
Washington from December 11, 1778 to June
3, 1779. Located at 38 Washington Place.

WALLACE HOUSE - 38 Washington Place.
The headquarters of Washington from Decem-
ber 11, 1778, to June 3, 1779 during the
Revolutionary War.

West Orange

THOMAS EDISON HOME AND LABORA-
TORY - Thomas Edison lived here from 1886
until his death in 1931. His laboratory contains
the first phonograph, an early electric lamp,
and many of his other inventions.

HOSTELS

Layton

OLD MINE ROAD YOUTH HOSTEL
Box 81
Layton, NJ 07851
(201) 948-6750
FACILITIES: Open year round; reservation
required; 10 beds, men; 10 beds, women; modern bathroom; nearest hostel: Madison, 55
mi. southeast; overnight charges: $2.50, May -
May 1 - Sept. 30; $3.25 Oct. 1 - Apr. 30;
houseparents: Martin & Anne Hughes.

Madison

DICKINSON YOUTH HOSTEL
285 Madison Avenue

Fairleigh Dickinson University
Madison, NJ 07940
(201) 377-6541
FACILITIES: Open Jun. 1 - Aug. 24; 12 beds,
men; 12 beds, women; modern bathroom;
nearest hostels: Layton, 55 mi. northwest;
New York, 25 mi. east; overnight charges:
$4.50; houseparent: Joseph Akronowitz.

POINTS OF INTEREST

Camden

WALT WHITMAN HOUSE - 330 Mickle St.
The only home owned by the famed poet
Walt Whitman.

Farmington

HOWELL IRON WORKS - In Allaire State
Park. A silent reminder of the bog industry of
bygone days.

Hammonton

ABSECON LIGHTHOUSE - In Wharton State
Forest. Commissioned in 1857 and served sea-
farers for three-quarters of a century until
1933.

Matawan

TWIN LIGHTS - In Cheesequake State Park.
A maritime museum.

Ringwood

RINGWOOD MANOR HOUSE - In Ringwood
State Park. A spacious, rambling, old mansion
which represents the living conditions of Iron
Masters of the 19th century. It contains a valuable collection of Americana.

Seaside Park

BARNEGAT LIGHTHOUSE - In Island Beach
Park. Commissioned in 1834 and operated
without fail for over three-quarters of a century.

NEW MEXICO

New Mexico, home of one of the West's
wildest and most notorious outlaws, joined
the Union in 1912 as the forty-seventh state.
From the outset, it was apparent that the arid
grasslands in the state were not suitable for
farming. However, they were perfect for grazing animals, and by the late 1800s, New Mexico's cattle ranching industry was booming.

During this period, violent conflicts occurred between the cattlemen themselves,
over the rights to the limited water supply
and open range. Perhaps the most famous
confrontation was the Lincoln County War in

which William Bonner ("Billy the Kid")
fought and gained his gunslinging reputation.

Cattle ranching, still a major industry in
New Mexico, now shares the spotlight with
the energy industry, which provides much of
the nation's uranium and potash. Interestingly enough, the Atomic Age began in the state
in 1945 with the manufacture and explosion
of the world's first A-bomb.

State capital: Santa Fe. State bird: Road
runner. State tree: Nut pine. State flower:
Yucca.

NEW MEXICO

WEATHER

New Mexico is the fifth largest state in the Union, with a total area of 121,412 square miles. The state's topography consists mainly of high plateaus or mesas, with numerous mountain ranges, canyons, valleys, and normally dry arroyos.

New Mexico has a mild, arid or semi-arid, continental climate characterized by light precipitation totals, abundant sunshine, low relative humidities, and a relatively large annual and diurnal temperature range. The highest mountains have climate characteristics common to the Rocky Mountains. During the summer months, individual daytime temperatures quite often exceed 100 degrees F at elevations below 5,000 feet; but the average monthly maximum temperatures during July, the warmest month, range from slightly above 90 degrees F at lower elevations to the upper 70's at high elevations. In January, the coldest month, average daytime temperatures range from the middle 50's in the southern and central valleys, to the middle 30's in the higher elevations to the north.

Average daily temperature for each month.

	Northern	Southern
Jan.	46.5 to 18.7	57.1 to 27.5
Feb.	49.3 to 20.7	61.1 to 30.4
Mar.	54.6 to 25.0	67.6 to 36.3
Apr.	63.2 to 32.6	77.8 to 43.8
May	72.2 to 41.6	87.0 to 52.0
Jun.	81.0 to 49.6	95.7 to 61.7
Jul.	83.1 to 54.7	95.3 to 65.4
Aug.	80.8 to 53.0	92.7 to 63.7
Sept.	76.0 to 46.1	88.1 to 57.5
Oct.	67.4 to 36.4	77.9 to 46.1
Nov.	54.5 to 25.2	65.7 to 34.0
Dec.	47.4 to 19.4	57.1 to 27.7
Year	64.7 to 35.3	76.9 to 45.5

STATE CHAMBER OF COMMERCE

Association of Commerce & Industry of New Mexico
117 Quincy, NE
Albuquerque, NM 87108
(505) 265-5847

STATE & CITY TOURISM OFFICES

State

New Mexico Department of Development
113 Washington Avenue
Sante Fe, NM 87503
(505) 827-3101

Tourist Division
Department of Tourism
113 Washington Avenue
Santa Fe, NM 87503
(505) 827-3101 or (800) 545-9876

Local

Office of Tourism
Greater Albuquerque Chamber of Commerce
401 Second Street, NW
Albuquerque, NM 87101
(505) 842-0220

STATE HIGHWAY DEPARTMENT

New Mexico State Highway Department
State Highway Department Building
1120 Cerrillos Road
Santa Fe, NM 87503
(505) 983-0100

HIGHWAY WELCOMING CENTERS

Anthony

ANTHONY CENTER - Interstate 10 on Texas border, near El Paso.

Tucumcari

TUCUMCARI CENTER - Interstate 40, east.

STATE POLICE

Department of Public Safety
P.O. Box 1628
Santa Fe, NM 87501
(505) 827-2551

HUNTING & FISHING

Hunting

Anyone who hunts for protected game must have a license, regardless of age. All non-residents must be licensed, even for hunting unprotected (non-game) species such as rabbits, coyotes and bobcats.

To qualify for resident license privileges, you must be either a citizen of the United States and a bona fide resident of New Mexico, or have lived in New Mexico for 90 days immediately preceding the date you apply for the license.

Temporary residents who maintain their homes outside New Mexico do not qualify for resident license privileges.

With certain certification, some students in New Mexico educational institutions and members of U.S. Armed Forces stationed in New Mexico may qualify for resident license privileges.

Resident

Big game (deer, bear, fall turkey), $12.50; general hunting (deer, bear, fall turkey, squirrel, game birds), $15.50; general hunting and fishing (deer, bear, fall turkey, squirrel, game birds, game fish), $21; small game (squirrel, game birds other than turkey), $8.50; deer

NEW MEXICO

HUNTING & FISHING (continued)

(bow hunting only), any deer license legal; special season deer tag, $2.25; additional deer, $3.25; turkey (special season spring), $5.25; cougar, $15.50; antelope, $15.50; elk, $21; javelina, $15.50; bighorn sheep, $26; barbary sheep, $26; oryx (gemsbok), $26; ibex, $26; gazelle, $26; senior general hunting for persons 65 years and older (deer, bear, fall turkey, squirrel, game birds), $10.50.

Non-resident

Big game (deer, bear, fall turkey), $91; small game (squirrel, game birds other than turkey), $26; deer (bow hunting only), $31; special season deer tag, $2.25; additional deer, $6.50; bear only (non-deer season only), $51; turkey (special season spring), $51; cougar, $76; antelope, $101; elk, $136; javelina, $51; bighorn sheep, $301; barbary sheep, $301; oryx (gemsbok), $301; ibex, $301; gazelle, $301; non-game, $15.50 or a non-resident hunting license.

Fishing

A fishing license is not required until the 12th birthday.

A resident entitled to purchase a resident fishing license is any person:

Who is a citizen of the United States, and who has been a bona fide resident of New Mexico, or has actually lived in New Mexico, for 90 days immediately preceding the date of his license application.

Who is not a citizen of the United States but who is legally within the United States and has actually lived in New Mexico for 90 days immediately preceding his license application.

Certain students and military personnel stationed in New Mexico may qualify for resident privileges. A temporary resident who maintains a home outside of New Mexico is not eligible for resident license privileges.

Resident

Fishing, $7.50; 1-day fishing (good for 1-day only), $3.25; 5-day fishing, $8; junior-senior fishing (for residents from 12-14 years old, and those 65 years and over), $1.25; general hunting and fishing, $21; philmont (Boy Scouts), $1.10.

Non-resident

Fishing, $15.50; 1-day fishing (good for 1-day only), $3.25; 5-day fishing, $8; philmont (Boy Scouts), $1.10.

Trout-water

A trout-water validation (or trout stamp) is required for any fisherman 12 years of age and over who fishes in designated trout waters.

Resident

Fishing trout-water, $4 and $5; 1-day fishing (good for 1-day only), $2; 5-day fishing,

$3; junior-senior fishing (for residents from 12-14 years old, and those 65 years and over), $2; general hunting and fishing, $4.

Non-resident

Fishing trout-water, $4.25 and $5.25; 1-day fishing (good for 1 day only), $2.25; 5-day fishing, $3.25; junior-senior fishing (for residents from 12-14 years old, and those 65 years and over), $2.25; general hunting and fishing, $4.25.

For more information contact:

Department of Game and Fish
State Capital
Villagra Bldg.
Sante Fe, NM 87503
(505) 827-2143

CAMPGROUNDS

See National Parks, National Forests, and State Parks.

RESORTS & BEACHES

Most of the state's resort activities center around the major lakes in the State Parks and include fishing, swimming, boating, water skiing, and camping. (See State Parks.)

BOATING AREAS

See State Parks.

BICYCLE TRAILS

No information was available on Bicycle Trails in New Mexico.

TRAILS

Las Cruces

ORGAN MOUNTAIN TRAILS - 8.7 mi. foot trail. There are two segments which lead from the Acquirre Spring Recreation Area into the desert-mountain environment of Organ Mountain in southern New Mexico. The trails are designed to protect and interpret the natural environment which ranges from pinion-juniper through ponderosa pine, then spruce, and finally barren rock at the higher elevations.

SKI AREAS

Albuquerque

SANDIA PEAK SKI AREA
10 Tramway Loop, NE
Albuquerque, NM 87122
(505) 296-9585

SKI AREAS (continued)

LOCATION: 20 mi. northeast of Albuquerque.
FACILITIES: 2 double chairlifts; 3 pomas; 1 tram; ski instruction; ski rental; 1660 ft. vertical drop; restaurants; lodging.

Cloudcroft

SKI CLOUD COUNTRY
P.O. Box 14
Cloudcroft, NM 88317
(505) 682-2587
LOCATION: 2½ mi. east of Cloudcroft.
FACILITIES: 2 T-bars; 1 tow rope; ski instruction; ski rental; 500 ft. vertical drop; restaurants; lodging.

Eagle Nest

ANGEL FIRS SKI BASIN
Eagle Nest, NM 87718
(505) 377-2301
LOCATION: 12 mi. south of Eagle Nest.
FACILITIES: 3 double chairlifts; ski instruction; ski rental; 2180 ft. vertical drop; restaurants; lodging.

VAL VERDE SKI AREA
Eagle Nest, NM 87718
(505) 377-6011
LOCATION: 11 mi. south of Eagle Nest.
FACILITIES: 1 tow rope; 1 poma; ski instruction; ski rental; 350 ft. vertical drop; restaurants; lodging.

Raton

RATON SKI BASIN
P.O. Box 1043
Raton, NM 87740
(505) 445-5000
LOCATION: 4 mi. northeast of Raton.
FACILITIES: 1 double chairlift; 1 T-bar; ski instruction; ski rental; 1000 ft. vertical drop; restaurants; lodging.

Red River

POWDER PUFF MOUNTAIN
P.O. Box 786
Red River, NM 87558
(505) 754-2223
LOCATION: ¼ mi. west of Red River.
FACILITIES: 2 double chairlifts; 3 tow ropes; ski instruction; ski rental; 150 ft. vertical drop; restaurants; lodging.

RED RIVER SKI AREA
P.O. Box 303
Red River, NM 87558
(505) 754-2223
LOCATION: In Red River.
FACILITIES: 4 double chairlifts; 2 tow ropes; ski instruction; ski rental; 1530 ft. vertical drop; restaurants; lodging.

Ruidoso

SIERRA BLANCA SKI RESORT
P.O. Box 220
Ruidoso, NM 88345
(800) 545-4313
LOCATION: 16 mi. northwest of Ruidoso.

FACILITIES: 2 double chairlifts; 4 T-bars; 2 tow ropes; 1 gondola; ski instruction; ski rental; 1700 ft. vertical drop; restaurants; lodging.

Santa Fe

SANTA FE SKI BASIN
P.O. Box 2287
Santa Fe, NM 87501
(505) 882-4429
LOCATION: 16 mi. northeast of Santa Fe.
FACILITIES: 2 double chairlifts; ski instruction; ski rental; 1600 ft. vertical drop; restaurants; lodging.

Taos

TAOS SKI VALLEY
Taos, NM 87571
(505) 776-2291
LOCATION: 19 mi. northeast of Taos.
FACILITIES: 6 double chairlifts; 2 T-bars; ski instruction; ski rental; 2612 ft. vertical drop; restaurants; lodging.

Vadito

SIPAPU SKI AREA
Vadito, NM 87579
(505) 587-2240
LOCATION: 25 mi. south of Taos.
FACILITIES: 3 pomas; ski instruction; ski rental; 800 ft. vertical drop; restaurants; lodging.

AMUSEMENT PARKS & ATTRACTIONS

Albuquerque

UNCLE CLIFF'S FAMILYLAND
5301 San Mateo, NE
Albuquerque, NM 87109
FACILITIES: 11 major rides; 9 kiddie rides; 50 games; 18-hole miniature golf; arcade; picnic facilities; 2 refreshment stands; Dark Ride (Haunted House); free gate; pay gate; free & pay parking; open Apr. 1 - Oct. 15.

Carlsbad

PRESIDENT'S PARK
Lake Carlsbad
Carlsbad, NM 88220
(505) 885-5848
FACILITIES: 5 major rides; 40 games; 4 refreshment stands; arcade; beach; camping; picnic facilities; restaurant; paddle boats; golf driving range; Par 3 golf course; free gate; free parking; open Easter Day - Labor Day; weekends year round.

STATE FAIR

New Mexico State Fair
P.O. Box 8546
Albuquerque, NM 87108
(505) 265-1791
DATE: September

NEW MEXICO

NATIONAL PARKS

Carlsbad

CARLSBAD CAVERNS NATIONAL PARK
Carlsbad, NM 88220
(505) 758-2233
FACILITIES: Open year round; entrance fee;
picnic area; food service; hiking; bicycle trail;
exhibit; museum; handicapped access/rest-
room; NPS guided tour; self-guiding tour.

Dell City, TX

**GUADALUPE MOUNTAINS NATIONAL
PARK**
Dell City, TX 79837
(915) 828-3385

See TEXAS, National Parks, Guadalupe
Mountain National Park in Dell City.

NATIONAL FORESTS

National Forests
Southwestern Region
517 Gold Avenue, SW
Albuquerque, NM 87102
(505) 766-2444

Alamogordo

LINCOLN NATIONAL FOREST
ATTRACTIONS: Hiking trails; fishing; big-
game hunting; limited winter sports; scenic
drives; saddle and pack trips.
FACILITIES: 12 camp and picnic sites, 5 picnic only; winter sports area; resorts; hotels;
dude ranches; organization camps.
NEARBY TOWNS: Artesia, Capitan ("Birthplace of Smokey Bear"), Carlsbad, and Ros-
wells, NM; El Paso, TX.

Albuquerque

CIBOLA NATIONAL FOREST
ATTRACTIONS: Deer, antelope hunting; bighorn sheep often visible at Sandia Crest in
summer; Pueblo Indian villages; prehistoric
ruins; ancient "sky city" of Acoma; fishing;
scenic drives.
FACILITIES: 16 camp and picnic sites, 15
picnic only; Sandia Peak Ski Area in Sandia
Mountains; motels; hotels; dude ranches.
NEARBY TOWNS: Belen, Bernalillo, Gallup,
Grants, Magdalena, Mountainair, Socorro.

Santa Fe

SANTA FE NATIONAL FOREST
ATTRACTIONS: Wilderness pack trips; saddle trails; a dozen active Indian Pueblos nearby; great vistas; ancient ruins; Spanish missions; cliff dwellings; turkey, elk, deer, bear
hunting.
FACILITIES: 29 camp and picnic sites, 13
picnic only; winter sports at Santa Fe Basin;
scenic double chairlift to 11,600 feet oper-
ates summer by appointment; resorts; hotels;
guest ranches on Pecos River up as far as Cow-
les, and Jemez River near Jemez Springs.
NEARBY TOWNS: Albuquerque, Bernalillo,

Cuba, Espanola, Las Vegas, Pecos.

Silver City

GILA NATIONAL FOREST
ATTRACTIONS: Semi-desert to alpine country, most of it very remote and undeveloped;
pack trips; many historic ruins; fishing; black
bear, mule deer, white-tailed deer, antelope,
elk, mountain lion, turkey hunting; scenic
drives; riding and hiking trails.
FACILITIES: 13 camp and picnic sites, 3 picnic only; some motels; resorts; dude ranches.
NEARBY TOWNS: Deming, Las Cruces,
Lordsburg, Reserve, Truth or Consequences,
NM; Springerville, AZ.

Taos

CARSON NATIONAL FOREST
ATTRACTIONS: Wheeler Peak, 13,151 feet,
highest in New Mexico; Spanish-speaking villages. Taos: home and burial place of Kit Carson, and well-known art colony; Taos Indian
Pueblo; Ghost Ranch Museum near Abiquiu.
scenic drives.
FACILITIES: 40 camp and picnic sites, 4 picnic only; fine skiing at Red River, Taos Ski
Valley (Hondo Canyon), and Sipapu.
NEARBY TOWNS: Chama, Cimarron, Espanola, Farmington, Tierra Amarilla, NM; Alamosa and Pagosa Springs, CO.

See APACHE NATIONAL FOREST - Arizona.

See SAN JUAN NATIONAL FOREST - Colorado.

STATE PARKS
Headquarters

State Park and Recreation Commission
141 East De Vargas
Sante Fe, NM 87503
(505) 827-2726

Bernalillo

CORONADO STATE PARK
LOCATION: Near Bernalillo.
FACILITIES: Open year round; water and
bathroom facilities; sanitary station; trailer
village vehicle sites; picnic area; hiking; tent
camping.

Bloomfield

NAVAJO LAKE STATE PARK
LOCATION: 25 mi. east of Bloomfield via
U.S. 84 and Route 511.
FACILITIES: Open year round; water and
bathroom facilities; sanitary station; electrical
hookup; trailer village vehicle sites; picnic
area; boating; boat rental; fishing; hiking; tent
camping.

Carrizozo

VALLEY OF FIRES STATE PARK
LOCATION: 1 mi. west of Carrizozo via U.S.
380.
FACILITIES: Open year round; water and

STATE PARKS (continued)

bathroom facilities; trailer village vehicle sites; picnic area; hiking; tent camping.

Clayton

CLAYTON LAKE STATE PARK
LOCATION: 15 mi. north of Clayton via Route 370.
FACILITIES: Open year round; water and bathroom facilities; trailer village vehicle sites; picnic area; boating; fishing; hiking; tent camping.

Clovis

OASIS STATE PARK
LOCATION: 18 mi. southwest of Clovis via U.S. 60 and Route 467.
FACILITIES: Open year round; water and bathroom facilities; sanitary station; electrical hookup; trailer village vehicle sites; picnic area; fishing; hiking; tent camping.

Deming

CITY OF ROCKS STATE PARK
LOCATION: 28 mi. northeast of Deming via U.S. 180 and Route 61.
FACILITIES: Open year round; water and bathroom facilities; trailer village vehicle sites; picnic area; hiking; tent camping.

PANCHO VILLA STATE PARK
LOCATION: 35 mi. south of Deming via Route 11.
FACILITIES: Open year round; water and bathroom facilities; trailer village vehicle sites; picnic area; hiking; tent camping.

ROCK HOUND STATE PARK
LOCATION: 14 mi. southeast of Deming via Route 11.
FACILITIES: Open year round; water and bathroom facilities; electrical hookup; trailer village vehicle sites; picnic area; hiking; tent camping.

Fort Sumner

SUMNER LAKE STATE PARK
LOCATION: 16 mi. northwest of Fort Sumner on U.S. 84 and Route 203.
FACILITIES: Open year round; water and bathroom facilities; sanitary station; electrical hookup; trailer village vehicle sites; picnic area; swimming; boating; fishing; tent camping.

Gallup

RED ROCKS STATE PARK
LOCATION: 10 mi. east of Gallup via I-40 and Route 566.
FACILITIES: Open year round; water and bathroom facilities; sanitary station; electrical hookup; trailer village vehicle sites; picnic area; food service; hiking; tent camping.

Grants

BLUEWATER LAKE STATE PARK
LOCATION: 28 mi. west of Grants via I-40 and Route 12.
FACILITIES: Open year round; water and bathroom facilities; trailer village vehicle sites; picnic area; swimming; boating; boat rental; fishing; hiking; tent camping.

Hatch

CABALLO LAKE STATE PARK
LOCATION: 18 mi. north of Hatch via I-25.
FACILITIES: Open year round; water and bathroom facilities; electrical hookup; trailer village vehicle sites; picnic area; swimming; boating; boat rental; fishing; hiking; tent camping.

Las Cruces

LEASBURG DAM STATE PARK
LOCATION: 15 mi. north of Las Cruces via U.S. 85.
FACILITIES: Open year round; water and bathroom facilities; trailer village vehicle sites; picnic area; boating; fishing; hiking; tent camping.

Las Vegas

STORRIE LAKE STATE PARK
LOCATION: 6 mi. north of Las Vegas via Route 3.
FACILITIES: Open year round; water and bathroom facilities; trailer village vehicle sites; picnic area; swimming; boating; fishing; hiking; tent camping.

VILLA NUEVA STATE PARK
LOCATION: 13 mi. southwest of Las Vegas via I-25 and Route 3.
FACILITIES: Open year round; water and bathroom facilities; trailer village vehicle sites; fishing; hiking; tent camping.

Ledoux

MORPHY LAKE STATE PARK
LOCATION: 7 mi. west of Ledoux.
FACILITIES: Open year round; water and bathroom facilities; trailer village vehicle sites; picnic area; boating; fishing; hiking; tent camping.

Logan

UTE LAKE STATE PARK
LOCATION: 3 mi. west of Logan via Route 540.
FACILITIES: Open year round; water and bathroom facilities; sanitary station; electrical hookup; trailer village vehicle sites; picnic area; food service; swimming; boating; boat rental; fishing; lodging; tent camping.

Mora

COYOTE CREEK STATE PARK
LOCATION: 14 mi. north of Mora via Route 38.
FACILITIES: Open year round; water and bathroom facilities; sanitary station; electrical hookup; trailer village vehicle sites; picnic area; fishing; hiking; tent camping.

NEW MEXICO

STATE PARKS (continued)

Mountainair

MANZANA STATE PARK
LOCATION: 13 mi. northwest of Mountainair via Route 14.
FACILITIES: Open year round; water and bathroom facilities; sanitary station; trailer village vehicle sites; picnic area; hiking; tent camping.

Roswell

BOTTOMLESS LAKE STATE PARK
LOCATION: 16 mi. southeast of Roswell via U.S. 380 and Route 409.
FACILITIES: Open year round; water and bathroom facilities; electrical hookup; trailer village vehicle sites; picnic area; boating; boat rental; fishing; hiking; tent camping.

Roy

CHICOSA LAKE STATE PARK
LOCATION: 9 mi. northeast of Roy via Route 120.
FACILITIES: Open year round; water and bathroom facilities; trailer village vehicle sites; picnic area; hiking; tent camping.

Santa Fe

HYDE MEMORIAL STATE PARK
LOCATION: 12 mi. northeast of Santa Fe via Route 475.
FACILITIES: Open year round; water and bathroom facilities; sanitary station; trailer village vehicle sites; picnic area; food service; tent camping.

Taos

RIO GRANDE GORGE STATE PARK
LOCATION: 16 mi. southwest of Taos via Route 68.
FACILITIES: Open year round; water and bathroom facilities; trailer village vehicle sites; picnic area; fishing; hiking; tent camping.

Tierra Amarilla

EL VADO LAKE STATE PARK
LOCATION: 14 mi. southwest of Tierra Amarilla via Route 112.
FACILITIES: Open year round; water and bathroom facilities; trailer village vehicle sites; picnic area; food service; swimming; boating; boat rental; fishing; lodging; tent camping.

HERON LAKE STATE PARK
LOCATION: 11 mi. west of Tierra Amarilla via U.S. 84 and Route 95.
FACILITIES: Open year round; water and bathroom facilities; sanitary station; trailer village vehicle sites; picnic area; boating; fishing; hiking; tent camping.

Truth or Consequences

ELEPHANT BUTTE LAKE
LOCATION: 7 mi. north of Truth or Consequences via I-25.
FACILITIES: Open year round; water and bathroom facilities; sanitary station; electrical hookup; trailer village vehicle sites; picnic area; food service; swimming; boating; boat rental; fishing; hiking; lodging; tent camping.

PERCHA DAM STATE PARK
LOCATION: 21 mi. south of Truth or Consequences via I-25.
FACILITIES: Open year round; water and bathroom facilities; trailer village vehicle sites; picnic area; fishing; tent camping.

Tucumcari

CONCHAS LAKE STATE PARK
LOCATION: 34 mi. northwest of Tucumcari via Route 104.
FACILITIES: Open year round; water and bathroom facilities; sanitary station; electrical hookup; trailer village vehicle sites; picnic area; food service; swimming; boating; boat rental; fishing; lodging; tent camping.

STATE FORESTS

There are no State Forests in New Mexico.

HISTORIC SITES

Albuquerque

NATIONAL ATOMIC MUSEUM - Unique historical collection of nuclear weapons, including examples of the world's first two atomic bombs, "Little Boy" and "Fat Man."

Fort Sumner

FORT SUMNER - Abandoned by the Army in 1869, it became ranch headquarters of Lucien Maxwell, legendary holder of the largest land grant in the western hemisphere. Also, Billy the Kid was slain and buried here in 1881. Located 3 mi. east of Fort Sumner on Route 60.

Lincoln

LINCOLN COUNTY COURTHOUSE - Once housed a jail; Billy the Kid made his last jailbreak here in 1881.

Santa Fe

CHURCH OF CRISTO REY - Largest adobe structure in the nation, with walls from two to seven feet thick.

PALACE OF THE GOVERNORS - Oldest government building still in use in U.S.

ST. FRANCIS CATHEDRAL - North chapel contains the oldest representation of the Madonna in the U.S., "La Conquistadora," brought by the Spanish in the 15th century.

HOSTELS

Albuquerque

CANTERBURY YOUTH HOSTEL
1705 Mesa Vista, NE
Albuquerque, NM 87106
(505) 242-0996
FACILITIES: Open year round; 4 beds, men;
4 beds, women; modern bathroom; nearest
hostel: Flagstaff, AZ, west; overnight charges:
$3 summer; $3.25 winter; houseparents:
Diane DiGiacomo & the Rev. W.E. Crews.

POINTS OF INTEREST

Albuquerque

SANDIA PEAK TRAMWAY - Longest tramway in the U.S. (2.7 mi.), and second largest
in the world.

Carlsbad

CARLSBAD CAVERNS - Over 60 internationally famous limestone caverns 750 feet
underground. Located 27 mi. southwest of
Carlsbad on Route 7.

Chama

THE CUMBRES AND TOLTEC SCENIC
RAILROAD - One of the last remaining authentic coal-fired, steam-powered, narrow-
gauge railroads in the world.

Farmington

FOUR CORNERS - At northwest corner of

New Mexico, four states come together: New
Mexico, Arizona, Utah, and Colorado; the
only such spot in the U.S.

Isleta

SAN AUGUSTIN - Little mission church is
thought to be one of the oldest in America.
Fray Juan de Padilla, first Christian martyr on
American soil said to be buried here. Legend
has it that his cottonwood coffin rises to the
surface every 20 years, portending a year of
good crops and well-being for the people.

Jemez

REDONDO PEAK (VALLE GRANDE) - This
176 square mile area is world's largest extinct
volcanic crater.

Los Alamos

LOS ALAMOS SCIENTIFIC LABORATO-
RY - Museum with displays including nuclear
propulsion exhibit, working models of modern reactors, and ballistic cases of several nuclear weapons.

Raton

CAPULIN MOUNTAIN - Volcanic cone,
about 1000 feet high from its base, is considered to be one of the most symmetrical cones
in the world.

Santa Fe

FIESTA DE SANTA FE (Labor Day weekend) - Oldest community celebration in the
U.S.

NEW YORK

The nation's publishing, printing, financial, fashion, and communications capital,
New York entered the Union in 1788 as the
eleventh state. Its early history involved
power struggles among the Dutch, English and
French, with the English eventually winning.
However, before relinquishing their holdings,
the Dutch acquired Manhattan from the Indians for a paltry $24, an astonishing sum
considering the worth of the island today.

During the Civil War, New York's support
of the Union war effort was greater than any
other state's and included troops, supplies and

money. Another large venture which paid off
handsomely involved the influx of thousands
and thousands of immigrants in the early
1900s, who in turn were employed in its expanding manufacturing industries. Presently,
New York is the country's leading industrialized state.

With the Catskill and Adirondack Mountains and spectacular Niagara Falls, tourism is
also a major source of New York's revenues.

State capital: Albany. State bird: Bluebird. State tree: Sugar maple. State flower:
Rose.

WEATHER

New York State contains 49,576 square
miles, inclusive of 1,637 square miles of inland water. The principal highland regions of
the state are the Adirondacks in the northeast
and the Appalachian Plateau (Southern
Plateau) in the south. A long, narrow lowland
region lies along much of the eastern border

of New York, as well as along the northern
and western boundaries of the state.

The climate of New York State is broadly
representative of the humid continental type
which prevails in the northeastern United
States, but its diversity is not usually encountered within an area of comparable size. Many
atmospheric and physiographic controls on
the climate result in a considerable variation

WEATHER (continued)

of temperature over New York State.

The winters are long and cold in the Plateau Division; however, temperatures are moderated considerably in the Great Lakes Plain of western New York. Long Island and New York City experience below zero minimums in 2 or 3 winters out of 10, with low temperature generally near -5 degrees F.

The summer climate is cool in the Adirondacks, Catskills, and higher elevations of the Southern Plateau. The New York City area and lower portions of the Hudson Valley have rather warm summers by comparison, with some periods of high, uncomfortable humidity. The remainder of New York State enjoys pleasantly warm summers, marred by only occasional, brief intervals of sultry conditions.

Average daily temperature for each month.

	Eastern	Western
Jan.	28.9 to 11.7	31.4 to 15.2
Feb.	31.8 to 13.7	33.5 to 16.2
Mar.	40.1 to 23.2	41.5 to 23.9
Apr.	55.9 to 34.2	56.3 to 35.2
May	67.5 to 44.0	67.6 to 45.0
Jun.	76.6 to 53.6	77.6 to 54.8
Jul.	80.8 to 57.9	81.3 to 58.8
Aug.	78.6 to 56.0	79.3 to 57.1
Sept.	71.2 to 49.3	73.1 to 50.8
Oct.	60.6 to 39.3	62.5 to 41.2
Nov.	45.4 to 30.4	47.6 to 32.0
Dec.	33.0 to 18.4	35.6 to 21.1
Year	55.9 to 36.0	57.3 to 37.6

STATE CHAMBER OF COMMERCE

Empire State Chamber of Commerce, Inc.
150 State Street
Albany, NY 12207
(518) 472-9166

STATE & CITY TOURISM OFFICES

State

New York State Department of Commerce
99 Washington Avenue
Albany, NY 12245
(518) 474-2121

Travel Bureau
New York State Department of Commerce
99 Washington Avenue
Albany, NY 12245
(518) 474-4116

Local

New York Convention and Visitor's Bureau
90 East 42nd Street
New York, NY 10017
(212) 687-1300

Niagara Tourism
P.O. Box 1067, Falls Station
Niagara Falls, NY 14303
(716) 285-3191

Convention and Visitor's Bureau
Mony Plaza, 17th Floor
Syracuse, NY 13202
(315) 422-1343

STATE HIGHWAY DEPARTMENT

Department of Transportation
State Campus
1220 Washington Avenue
Albany, NY 12232
(518) 457-4422

HIGHWAY WELCOMING CENTERS

There are no Highway Welcoming Centers in New York.

STATE POLICE

Department of Public Safety
Albany, NY 12226
(518) 457-6811

HUNTING & FISHING

Hunting

All persons who hunt must have a hunting license, except:

Resident owners and lessees and members of their immediate families, and Indians resident owners and resident members of their immediate families when hunting on farm lands that they occupy and cultivate.

Active members of the U.S. Armed Forces who are residents of the state, but who are stationed elsewhere and are in the state no longer than 30 days.

Persons 16 years of age or over hunting waterfowl must obtain the special $5 federal duck stamp in addition to the regular small-game license. A federal duck stamp is not required to hunt woodcock, snipe or rails.

Persons hunting turkeys must possess a special $2 turkey permit.

Minors under the age of 14 may not obtain a hunting license or hunt wild birds or animals.

Minors 14 or 15 years of age may obtain a hunting license only upon: (1) Completing hunter training course; (2) being accompanied by a parent, guardian, or person over 18 designated in writing by parent or guardian; (3) obtaining the signature in ink of a parent, guardian, or person designated by a parent or guardian, across the face of the minor's license at the time of issuance.

When applying for a new license, persons previously licensed to hunt must show a previous license to hunt, or submit an affidavit from a license issuing agent showing that the

HUNTING & FISHING (continued)

applicant held such a license.

A resident is a person who is domiciled in New York State for 3 months or more immediately preceding the date of application. Active members of the U.S. Armed Forces stationed in the state are considered residents, as are full-time college students residing in the state during the school year.

Free hunting licenses are available to residents who are 70 years of age or over, members of the Shinnecock and Poospatuck tribes or the Six Nations residing on reservations in New York State, or honorably discharged veterans.

License year is Oct. 1 - Sept. 30.

Resident

Big game hunting, $5.25; small game hunting, $6.25; archery stamp, $4.25; junior archery stamp, $7.50; combination hunting and fishing, $11.25.

Non-resident

Big game hunting, $52.50; small game hunting, $32.50; archery stamp, $4.25.

Fishing

Any person who fishes must have a fishing license, except:

Persons under 16 years of age.

Citizen-resident owners, lessees and citizen members of their immediate families occupying and cultivating farm lands, when fishing on their own lands.

Active members of the U.S. Armed Forces who are New York State residents but are stationed elsewhere and are in the state for a maximum of 30 days.

Persons holding farm fish-pond licenses and members of their immediate families, when fishing on waters covered by their licenses.

Persons holding fishing preserve licenses and persons to whom permission has been given to fish preserve waters.

A fishing license is not required in the Marine District, or to take fish by angling or with tip-ups, spears, and longbows in the Hudson River south of the barrier dam at Troy.

Free fishing licenses are available for citizen-residents 70 years of age, the blind, members of the Shinnecock and Poospatuck tribes or the Six Nations residing on reservations in New York State, and honorably discharged disabled veterans.

To qualify for a resident license, one must be domiciled in New York State for 3 months or more immediately preceding date of application.

Active members of the U.S. Armed Forces stationed in the state, and full-time college students (citizens) in residence in the state during the school year also qualify for resident licenses.

License year is Oct. 1 - Sept. 30.

Resident

Fishing, $6.25; combination hunting and fishing, $11.25; small game hunting, $6.25.

Non-resident

Fishing, $17.25; 7-day fishing, $10.25; 3-day fishing, $5.50.

For more information contact:

Department of Environmental Conservation
50 Wolf Road
Albany, NY 12233
(518) 457-5861

CAMPGROUNDS

Private

Akron

CREEKSIDE CAMPGROUND
(716) 542-9595
LOCATION: 5 mi. north of Route 5 on Route 93.
FACILITIES: Open May - Oct.; 200 sites; water and bathroom facilities; sanitary station; electrical hookup; trailer village vehicle sites; food service; swimming; boating; boat rental; fishing; tent camping.

Corfu

SNYDER'S DARIEN LAKE CAMPGROUND
(716) 599-4501
LOCATION: 9993 Allegheny Road.
FACILITIES: Open May - Oct.; 200 sites; water and bathroom facilities; sanitary station; electrical hookup; trailer village vehicle sites; laundry; picnic area; food service; swimming; boating; boat rental; fishing; tent camping.

Corinth

ALPINE LAKE CAMPGROUND
(518) 654-6260
LOCATION: 2 mi. south of Corinth on Route 9N.
FACILITIES: Open May - Oct.; 235 sites; sanitary station; electrical hookup; trailer village vehicle sites; laundry; food service; swimming; boating; boat rental; fishing; tent camping.

Dansville

SKYBROOK CAMPGROUND
(716) 335-3904
LOCATION: 5 mi. southwest of Dansville on McCurdy Road.
FACILITIES: Open May - Oct.; 275 sites; water and bathroom facilities; sanitary station; electrical hookup; trailer village vehicle sites; picnic area; food service; swimming; fishing; tent camping.

East Nassau

TIMBER-VALE CAMPGROUND
(518) 794-8234
LOCATION: 1 mi. north of Route 20 on Route 66.
FACILITIES: Open May - Oct.; 25 sites; water and bathroom facilities; sanitary station;

NEW YORK

CAMPGROUNDS (continued)

electrical hookup; trailer village vehicle sites; laundry; swimming; fishing; tent camping.

Ellenville

BIRCHWOOD ACRES CAMPGROUND
(914) 434-4743
LOCATION: 9 mi. west of Ellenville.
FACILITIES: Open May - Oct.; 200 sites; water and bathroom facilities; sanitary station; electrical hookup; trailer village vehicle sites; laundry; picnic area; food service; swimming; boating; boat rental; fishing; tent camping.

RONDOUT VALLEY CAMPGROUND
(914) 626-5521
LOCATION: 9 mi. north of Ellenville.
FACILITIES: Open May - Oct.; 225 sites; water and bathroom facilities; sanitary station; electrical hookup; trailer village vehicle sites; laundry; picnic area; food service; swimming; tent camping.

Ellicottville

RAINBOW LAKE CAMPGROUND
(716) 699-2618
LOCATION: Northwest of Ellicottville.
FACILITIES: Open May - Oct.; 659 sites; water and bathroom facilities; sanitary station; electrical hookup; trailer village vehicle sites; laundry; picnic area; food service; swimming; boating; boat rental; fishing; tent camping.

TIMBER LAKE CAMPGROUND
(716) 699-4429
LOCATION: 7 mi. north of Ellicottville.
FACILITIES: Open May - Oct.; 302 sites; water and bathroom facilities; sanitary station; trailer village vehicle sites; laundry; picnic area; food service; boating; boat rental; fishing; tent camping.

Gainesville

WOODSTREAM CAMPGROUND
(716) 493-5643
LOCATION: 5440 School Road.
FACILITIES: Open May - Oct.; 200 sites; water and bathroom facilities; sanitary station; electrical hookup; trailer village vehicle sites; laundry; swimming; fishing; tent camping.

Gilboa

NICKERSON CAMPGROUND
(607) 588-7327
LOCATION: 1 mi. east of Gilboa.
FACILITIES: Open May - Oct.; 300 sites; water and bathroom facilities; sanitary station; electrical hookup; trailer village vehicle sites; laundry; food service; swimming; fishing; tent camping.

Glens Falls

LAKE GEORGE CAMPGROUND
(518) 792-9807
LOCATION: 6 mi. south of Lake George Village.
FACILITIES: Open May - Oct.; 200 sites; sanitary station; electrical hookup; trailer village vehicle sites; laundry; picnic area; food service; swimming; tent camping.

Gowanda

CAN-AM CAMPGROUND
(716) 532-9742
LOCATION: West Becker Road.
FACILITIES: Open May - Oct.; 200 sites; water and bathroom facilities; sanitary station; electrical hookup; trailer village vehicle sites; picnic area; food service; swimming; fishing; tent camping.

Kingston

HIDDEN VALLEY LAKE CAMPGROUND
(914) 338-4616
LOCATION: 5 mi. south of Kingston.
FACILITIES: Open May - Oct.; 240 sites; water and bathroom facilities; sanitary station; electrical hookup; trailer village vehicle sites; laundry; picnic area; food service; swimming; boating; boat rental; fishing; tent camping.

Mexico

DOWIE DALE BEACH CAMPGROUND
(315) 963-7899
LOCATION: 4 mi. northwest of Mexico.
FACILITIES: Open May - Oct.; 210 sites; water and bathroom facilities; sanitary station; electrical hookup; trailer village vehicle sites; food service; swimming; boating; fishing; tent camping.

Pulaski

BRENNAN BEACH CAMPGROUND
(315) 298-2242
LOCATION: 4 mi. west of Pulaski.
FACILITIES: Open May - Oct.; 400 sites; water and bathroom facilities; sanitary station; electrical hookup; trailer village vehicle sites; food service; swimming; fishing; tent camping.

WHITE SANDS BEACH CAMPGROUND
(315) 298-4050
LOCATION: 3 mi. north of Route 13 on Route 3.
FACILITIES: Open May - Oct.; 250 sites; water and bathroom facilities; sanitary station; electrical hookup; trailer village vehicle sites; picnic area; food service; swimming; boating; boat rental; fishing; tent camping.

Saratoga Springs

INTERLAKEN CAMPGROUND
(518) 587-1444
LOCATION: On Union Ave.
FACILITIES: Open May - Oct.; 200 sites; water and bathroom facilities; electrical hookup; trailer village vehicle sites; laundry; picnic area; food service; swimming; boating; boat rental; fishing; tent camping.

Schuyler Falls

MACOMB RESERVATION CAMPGROUND
(518) 634-9952
LOCATION: Off Route 22B.
FACILITIES: Open May - Oct.; 200 sites; water and bathroom facilities; sanitary station; trailer village vehicle sites; food service; swimming; fishing; tent camping.

CAMPGROUNDS (continued)

Stow

CHAUTAUQUA CAMPGROUND
(716) 789-3435
LOCATION: Off Route 394.
FACILITIES: Open May - Oct.; 450 sites; water and bathroom facilities; sanitary station; electrical hookup; trailer village vehicle sites; picnic area; food service; swimming; boating; boat rental; fishing; tent camping.

Summitville

WANDERWOOD CAMPGROUND
(914) 888-2161
LOCATION: Mt. Vernon Road.
FACILITIES: Open May - Oct.; 200 sites; water and bathroom facilities; sanitary station; electrical hookup; trailer village vehicle sites; laundry; food service; swimming; boating; fishing; tent camping.

Weedsport

RIVER FOREST CAMPGROUND
(315) 834-9458
LOCATION: Off Route 34.
FACILITIES: Open May - Oct.; 200 sites; water and bathroom facilities; sanitary station; electrical hookup; laundry; picnic area; food service; swimming; boating; boat rental; fishing; tent camping.

Westfield

BLUEWATER BEACH CAMPGROUND
(716) 326-3540
LOCATION: East Lake Road.
FACILITIES: Open May - Oct.; 200 sites; water and bathroom facilities; sanitary station; electrical hookup; trailer village vehicle sites; picnic area; food service; swimming; fishing; tent camping.

Public

Hague

ROGERS ROCK CAMPGROUND
(518) 585-6746
LOCATION: 3 mi. north of Hague.
FACILITIES: Open May - Oct.; 301 sites; water and bathroom facilities; sanitary station; trailer village vehicle sites; picnic area; swimming; boating; fishing; tent camping.

Haines Falls

NORTH LAKE CAMPGROUND
(518) 589-5058
LOCATION: 3 mi. northeast of Haines Falls.
FACILITIES: Open May - Oct.; 218 sites; water and bathroom facilities; sanitary station; trailer village vehicle sites; picnic area; swimming; boating; boat rental; tent camping.

Inlet

LIMEKILN LAKE CAMPGROUND
(315) 357-4401
LOCATION: 1 mi. east of Inlet.
FACILITIES: Open May - Oct.; 273 sites; water and bathroom facilities; sanitary station; trailer village vehicle sites; picnic area; swimming; boating; boat rental; fishing; tent camping.

Lake George Village

HEARTHSTONE POINT CAMPGROUND
(518) 668-5193
LOCATION: 2 mi. north of Lake George.
FACILITIES: Open May - Oct.; 254 sites; water and bathroom facilities; sanitary station.

LAKE GEORGE: GLEN ISLAND CAMPGROUND
(518) 644-9696
LOCATION: Bolton Landing (access by boat only).
FACILITIES: Open May - Oct.; 217 sites.

Paul Smiths

MEACHAM LAKE CAMPGROUND
(518) 483-5116
LOCATION: 19 mi. north of Lake Clear.
FACILITIES: Open May - Oct.; 222 sites; sanitary station; trailer village vehicle sites; laundry; picnic area; swimming; boating; boat rental; fishing; tent camping.

Plattsburgh

CUMBERLAND BAY CAMPGROUND
(518) 563-5240
LOCATION: 1 mi. north of Plattsburgh.
FACILITIES: Open May - Oct.; 210 sites; water and bathroom facilities; sanitary station; trailer village vehicle sites; picnic area; swimming; fishing; tent camping.

Raquette Lake

GOLDEN BEACH CAMPGROUND
(315) 354-4230
LOCATION: 3 mi. north of Raquette Lake.
FACILITIES: Open May - Oct.; 207 sites; water and bathroom facilities; sanitary station; trailer village vehicle sites; picnic area; swimming; boating; boat rental; fishing; tent camping.

Sabael

LEWEY LAKE CAMPGROUND
(518) 648-5266
LOCATION: 8 mi. south of Sabael on Route 30.
FACILITIES: Open May - Oct.; 215 sites; water and bathroom facilities; sanitary station; trailer village vehicle sites; picnic area; swimming; boating; boat rental; fishing; tent camping.

Saranac Lake

FISH CREEK POND CAMPGROUND
(518) 891-4560
LOCATION: 12 mi. east of Tupper Lake.
FACILITIES: Open May - Oct.; 351 sites; water and bathroom facilities; sanitary station; trailer village vehicle sites; picnic area; swimming; boating; fishing; tent camping.

ROLLINS POND CAMPGROUND
(518) 891-3239
LOCATION: 12 mi. east of Tupper Lake.

NEW YORK

CAMPGROUNDS (continued)

FACILITIES: Open May - Oct.; 288 sites; water and bathroom facilities; trailer village vehicle sites; boating; boat rental; fishing; tent camping.

Speculator

MOFFITT BEACH CAMPGROUND
(518) 548-7102
LOCATION: 2 mi. west of Speculator on Route 8.
FACILITIES: Open May - Oct.; 257 sites; water and bathroom facilities; trailer village vehicle sites; picnic area; swimming; fishing; tent camping.

Youngstown

FOUR MILE CREEK ANNEX CAMP-GROUND
(716) 745-3802
LOCATION: 3 mi. east of Youngstown.
FACILITIES: Open May - Oct.; 50 sites; water and bathroom facilities; sanitary station; electrical hookup; trailer village vehicle sites; fishing; tent camping.

RESORTS & BEACHES

Albany

CAPITAL - SARATOGA AREA - Albany, home of the fabulous Empire State Plaza and State Capitol, is a center of cultural, political and historical importance. Nearby, at Saratoga Springs, watch some of the world's finest thoroughbred horse racing, or take an invigorating mineral bath.

Alexandria Bay

1000 ISLANDS - SEAWAY AREA - More than 1800 green-thatched islets are scattered like stepping stones in the waters of the St. Lawrence River. Alexandria Bay, with Heart Island, home of gothic Boldt Castle, is the perfect place to begin taking in the sights. Clayton and Cape Vincent are picturesque spots, and at Messena visit the Moses-Saunders Power Dam and watch ocean vessels transit the St. Lawrence Seaway.

Catskill

CATSKILLS AREA - Some of the best trout fishing in the state can be found in the Catskills, as well as a full range of summer and winter outdoor activities. Swim, sail, ski, sunbathe or head indoors and enjoy Broadway entertainment and deluxe cuisine at some of the country's most plush resorts.

Geneva

FINGER LAKES AREA - Canandaigua, Cayuga, Keuka, Owasco, Seneca, Skaneatele, are Indian names for the deep blue lakes that are the fingers of the Finger Lakes. In addition to swimming, boating, skiing and fishing, you can marvel at Genesee Gorge, "The Grand Canyon of the East," or sample the fine wines at Hammondsport, the heart of New York's wine country. In Rochester visit Corning Glass Center, and Kodak's Museum of Photography. The Canal Museum and Erie Canal boat trips from Syracuse, and world-famous waterfall-dotted Watkins Glen, are other essential stops.

Lake Placid

ADIRONDACKS AREA - Hundreds of miles of hiking trails wind around and through the Adirondacks' crystal lakes and rugged mountains. And when it comes to summertime, sunshine fun, it's hard to beat the likes of Lake Placid, Lake George, Lake Champlain, the Saranacs, Great Sacandaga Lake and the Fulton Chain of Lakes.

New York City

NEW YORK CITY AREA - Shopping, culture, sports, sightseeing, New York has it all and in more abundance than anywhere else in the world. You can see the 110-story World Trade Center Towers, the 102-story Empire State Building, the Statue of Liberty, Radio City Music Hall, Rockefeller Center, United Nations, Lincoln Center for the Performing Arts, or perhaps a Broadway show.

Niagara Falls

NIAGARA FRONTIER AREA - Home of one of the greatest natural wonders of the world, Niagara Falls. South of the Falls is the city of Buffalo with its cultural attractions, top-flight entertainment and major professional sports center. Other "must-sees" include the Niagara Power Project, Iroquois arts and crafts at the Tuscarora Indian Reservation in Lewiston, and Old Fort Niagara at Youngstown.

Salamanac

CHAUTAUQUA-ALLEGANY AREA - Vineyards and fruit orchards stretch across the Lake Erie Plain, the state's most picturesque region. Adding to the natural beauty are blue lakes and hardwood forests. Chautauqua Lake is a fisherman's paradise, and on its shore, the world-famous Chautauqua Institute offers opera, drama, and symphony concerts as well as lectures and classes.

South Hampton

LONG ISLAND AREA - New York State's ocean oasis extends a sandy 120 miles east from New York City into the Atlantic. You can spend your time sunbathing, saltwater fishing, surfing or beachcombing. There's plenty of golf and tennis, too. Head for East Hampton if you're looking for elegance, Fire Island if Bohemian atmosphere appeals to you, and Jones Beach if you can't decide.

BOATING AREAS

Argyle

COSSAYUNA LAKE
LOCATION: Off Route 40 at Argyle.

BOATING AREAS (continued)

FACILITIES: Launching.

Blue Mountain Lake

LAKE DURANT
LOCATION: 2 mi. east of Blue Mountain Lake on Route 28.
FACILITIES: Launching.

Bridgeport

ONEIDA LAKE
LOCATION: 1 mi. east of Bridgeport off Route 31.
FACILITIES: Launching.

Chautauqua

CHAUTAUQUA LAKE
LOCATION: On Route 17J in Chautauqua.
FACILITIES: Launching.

Conesus

CONESUS LAKE
LOCATION: 3 mi. west of Conesus off Route 15.
FACILITIES: Launching.

Deerland

FORKED LAKE
LOCATION: 5 mi. west of Deerland off Route 30.
FACILITIES: Launching.

Dunkirk

LAKE ERIE
LOCATION: Off Route 5 in Dunkirk.
FACILITIES: Launching.

Gloversville

CAROGA LAKE
LOCATION: 9 mi. northwest of Gloversville on Route 29A.
FACILITIES: Launching.

Hague

LAKE GEORGE
LOCATION: 3 mi. north of Hague on Route 9N.
FACILITIES: Launching.

Honeoye

HONEOYE LAKE
LOCATION: 4 mi. south of Honeoye off Route 20A.
FACILITIES: Launching.

Inlet

FOURTH LAKE
LOCATION: 28 mi. north of Inlet on Route 28.
FACILITIES: Launching.

LIMEKILN LAKE
LOCATION: 3 mi. southeast of Inlet off

Route 28.
FACILITIES: Launching.

Lake Clear

MEACHAM LAKE
LOCATION: 19 mi. north of Lake Clear on Route 30.
FACILITIES: Launching.

Lake Placid

LAKE PLACID
LOCATION: Off Route 86 in Lake Placid.
FACILITIES: Launching.

Long Lake

LAKE EATON
LOCATION: 2 mi. west of Long Lake on Route 30.
FACILITIES: Launching.

LONG LAKE
LOCATION: Off Route 30.
FACILITIES: Launching.

Lowville

STILLWATER RESERVOIR
LOCATION: 28 mi. east of Lowville on Stillwater Road.
FACILITIES: Launching.

Merrill

UPPER CHATEAUGAY LAKE
LOCATION: ½ mi. north of Merrill off Route 374.
FACILITIES: Launching.

Morristown

BLACK LAKE
LOCATION: 2 mi. west of Edwardsville in Morristown.
FACILITIES: Launching.

Newcomb

LAKE HARRIS
LOCATION: 3 mi. north of Newcomb off Route 28N.
FACILITIES: Launching.

Northville

GREAT SACANDAGA LAKE
LOCATION: In Northville.
FACILITIES: Launching.

Oxbow

PAYNE LAKE
LOCATION: 1 mi. west of Oxbow.
FACILITIES: Launching.

Raquette

RAQUETTE LAKE
LOCATION: 3 mi. east of Raquette on Route 28.
FACILITIES: Launching.

NEW YORK

BOATING AREAS (continued)

Richfield Springs

CANADARAGO LAKE
LOCATION: 3 mi. south of Richfield Springs.
FACILITIES: Launching.

Saranac Lake

SARANAC LAKE, LOWER
LOCATION: 5 mi. west of Saranac Lake on Route 3.
FACILITIES: Launching.

SARANAC LAKE, UPPER
LOCATION: Off Route 30.
FACILITIES: Launching.

Saratoga

SARATOGA LAKE
LOCATION: Off Route 9P.
FACILITIES: Launching.

Speculator

LEWEY LAKE
LOCATION: 14 mi. north of Speculator off Route 30.
FACILITIES: Launching.

SACANDAGA LAKE
LOCATION: 4 mi. west of Speculator.
FACILITIES: Launching.

Tupper Lake

TUPPER LAKE
LOCATION: 2 mi. south of Tupper Lake on Route 30.
FACILITIES: Launching.

Wolcott

LAKE ONTARIO
LOCATION: 3½ mi. north of Wolcott on West Port Bay Road.
FACILITIES: Launching.

Westport

LAKE CHAMPLAIN
LOCATION: Adjacent to Route 22 in Westport.
FACILITIES: Launching.

BICYCLE TRAILS

ALCOVE RESERVOIR TRAIL - 29 mi.; any bicycle.
Starting from Clarksville, a cyclist can take a ride around Alcove Reservoir. It is advisable to carry snacks and water on your ride.
Trail: Clarksville to Route 43 west, left on Route 301, right on Route 109, right onto Route 32 south, left on Route 411, left on Route 111, left on Route 143, left on Route 32 south, right on Route 411, right on Route 312, right on Route 43 east to Clarksville.

ALLEGANY STATE PARK TRAIL - 80 mi.; mountainous terrain; 10-speed bicycle recommended.

This trip from Buffalo to Allegany State Park is through mountainous and wooded country; Hwy. 240 has light traffic.
Trail: Buffalo to Route 240 south to Webster Corners to Ellicott Heights to Glenwood to Riceville to Ellicottville to Salamanca to Allegany State Park.

See VERMONT - All State Trail.

COOPERSTOWN TRAIL - 15 mi.; any bicycle.
Cooperstown in central New York State is best known as the home of the Baseball Hall of Fame.
Trail: Glimmerglass State Park on the east side of Otsego Lake (County Route 31) to Glimmerglass State Park.

See PENNSYLVANIA - Delaware River Trail.

DOWNSVILLE TRAIL - 110 mi.; hilly terrain; 10-speed bicycle recommended.
This ride is in the valleys below the Catskills but you skirt the northwest boundary of the Catskill Forest Preserve.
Trail: Deposit to Walton to Delhi to Stamford to Grand Gorge to Roxbury to Arkville to Downsville.

FINGER LAKES TRAIL - 200 mi.; hilly terrain, heavy traffic; 10-speed bicycle necessary.
This area is not for the novice biker, because the hills are steep and the traffic tends to be heavy.
Trail: Auburn to Geneva to Potter to Naples to Wayland to Hammondsport to Corning to Watkins Glen to Elmira.

OLD ERIE CANAL TRAIL - 47 mi.; any bicycle.
Bicycle along a portion of the Erie Canal while traveling from Syracuse to Rome. This is basically flat pedaling using lightly traveled roads.
Trail: Start at Syracuse on Towpath Road to Green Lake State Park to Canastata to Durhamville to Rome to Pinti Field.

OSWEGO TRAIL - 8 mi.; any bicycle.
The historic town of Oswego is noted for its 19th-century architecture in the downtown area and Greek Revival architecture in the residential area. It is an easy ride for all riders but especially novices during the winter months.
Trail: Intersection of Route 170 and IBM Parkway, north on IBM Parkway, left on Taylor Road, right on Davis Road, left on Main Street, right on Erie Street, left on McMasters Street, right on Elm Street, left on Marvin Park, right on Main Street, left on Canal Street, left on River Street, right on Front Street, right on Route 170 to Intersection.

SARATOGA TRAIL - 220 mi.; traffic, some hills; 10-speed bicycle recommended.
Your route roughly parallels Interstate 90 and will bring you to the Saratoga Historic Park.
Trail: Rome to Utica to Little Falls to St. Johnsville to Stone Arabia to Johnstown to Amsterdam to Ballston Springs to Saratoga Historic Park to Saratoga Springs to

BICYCLE TRAILS (continued)

Gloversville to Caroga Lake to Salisbury Center to Poland to Westernville to Rome.

SCHENECTADY TO CARINTH TRAIL - 36 mi.; any bicycle.

Here is a fine weekend ride in the eastern New York State for the average cyclist. The route is mainly on local and country roads.

Trails: Schenectady, north on Bradth to Ashdown to Lake, left on Outlet, right on Middle Line, left on Devils Lane, right on Route 48, right on Lewis, and Route 43, left on Route 59, and Route 29, right on Sodemar, right on Route 21, left on Hy Spot, left on Route 36, left on Locust Grover, right on Route 25, left on Angel, and Wall to Corinth.

SUSQUEHANNA CRESCENT TRAILS - 27, 40, 56, 110 mi.; hilly terrain; 10-speed bicycle recommended.

Tucked away in the extreme northeast corner of Pennsylvania and extending into New York State is a region of hills, farms, and small towns bounded by the Susquehanna River.

Trails: (1) Vestal to Lawton to Rushville on Route 106, to Apalachin on Route 858, to Vestal on Route 434 - 56 mi.; (2) Little Meadows to Warren Center, southeast to Route 467 to Le Raysville, to Route 467 south, to Route 106 east to Rushville, to Route 858 north to Little Meadows - 40 mi.; (3) Vestal to Apalachin, south on Route 757 to Rushville, west on Route 106 to Camptown to Wyalusing to Wysox to Towanda to North Towanda, cross the Susquehanna River at Smithboro, Route 17C to Owego to Vestal-110 mi.

WESTCHESTER-FAIRFIELD TRAIL - 35 mi.; any bicycle.

This is a ride over lightly traveled roads through beautiful portions of Westchester County, NY, and Fairfield County, CT.

Trail: Westchester County Airport, left on Kings Street, right on Cliffdale Avenue, right on Riversville Road, left on Porchuck Road, right on Old Mill Road, left on Lake Avenue, right on Upper Cross, left on North Street to Banksville Road, right on Hickory Road to Bedford Village, left on Pound Ridge Road, right on Mianus River Road, left on E. Middle Patent Road to Taconic Road, right on S. Stanwich Road, right on North Street, left on Lower Cross, left on Lake Avenue, left on Burying Hill Road, left on Highland Farm Road to Cherry Valley Road, right on Old Mill Road, left on Riversville Road, left on John Street, left on Bedford Road, left on King Street to airport.

TRAILS

Glens Falls

CRANDALL PARK INTERNATIONAL SKI TRAILS - 2.2 mi. foot trail. The cross country ski trails are a continuous interlocking loop system in 49 acres of pine and hardwood forest, crossing historic Halfway Brook at four points. The trails are lighted for evening skiing and are open to the public without charge. When the skiing season is over, the trails are used for nature walks, environmental study, and limited bicycling. A ½-mile interpretive nature trail with 25 stations is contained within the trail system.

Haverstraw

HARRIMAN LONG PATH - 16 mi. foot trail. The path is located near the Hudson River in Harriman State Park, about 20 miles northwest of New York City. The trail winds along wooded ridge tops in 45,000 acres of uplands, drops occasionally into valleys, and crosses a portion of the Appalachian National Scenic Trail.

SKI AREAS

Addison

ADDISON PINNACLE SKI CENTER
Addison, NY 14801
(607) 359-2767
LOCATION: Near Addison.
FACILITIES: 2 chairlifts; 1 tow rope; ski instruction; ski rental; 725 ft. vertical drop; restaurants; lodging.

Alfred

HAPPY VALLEY SKI CENTER
Alfred, NY 14802
(607) 587-3442
LOCATION: West of Alfred.
FACILITIES: 1 chairlift; 1 tow rope; ski instruction; ski rental; 300 ft. vertical drop; restaurants; lodging.

Allegany

WING HOLLOW SKI CENTER
Allegany, NY 14706
(716) 372-2288
LOCATION: Near Allegany.
FACILITIES: 2 chairlifts; ski instruction; ski rental; 813 ft. vertical drop; restaurants; lodging.

Andes

CATSKILL SKI CENTER
Andes, NY 13731
(914) 676-3143
LOCATION: North of Andes.
FACILITIES: 2 chairlifts; ski instruction; ski rental; 1050 ft. vertical drop; restaurants; lodging.

Canandaigua

BRISTOL MOUNTAIN SKI CENTER
Canandaigua, NY 14424
(716) 374-6422
LOCATION: Southwest of Canandaigua.
FACILITIES: 5 chairlifts; ski instruction; ski rental; nursery; 1050 ft. vertical drop; restaurants; lodging.

Cazenovia

IRONWOOD RIDGE SKI CENTER

NEW YORK

SKI AREAS (continued)

Cazenovia, NY 13035
(315) 652-7753
LOCATION: West of Cazenovia.
FACILITIES: 1 chairlift; 3 tow ropes; ski instruction; ski rental; 500 ft. vertical drop; restaurants; lodging.

Cortland

GREEK PEAK SKI CENTER
Cortland, NY 13045
(607) 835-6111
LOCATION: South of Cortland.
FACILITIES: 7 chairlifts; ski instruction; ski rental; nursery; 780 ft. vertical drop; restaurants; lodging.

Easton

WILLARD MOUNTAIN SKI CENTER
Easton, NY 12834
(518) 642-7337
LOCATION: North of Easton.
FACILITIES: 2 chairlifts; 2 tow ropes; ski instruction; ski rental; nursery; 505 ft. vertical drop; restaurants; lodging.

Elizabethtown

OTIS MOUNTAIN SKI CENTER
Elizabethtown, NY 12932
(518) 873-6448
LOCATION: Near Elizabethtown.
FACILITIES: 1 chairlift; 1 tow rope; ski instruction; ski rental; 375 ft. vertical drop; restaurants; lodging.

Ellenville

MOUNT CATHALIA SKI CENTER
Ellenville, NY 12428
(914) 647-7171
LOCATION: Southeast of Ellenville.
FACILITIES: 2 chairlifts; ski instruction; ski rental; 525 ft. vertical drop; restaurants; lodging.

Ellicottville

HOLIDAY VALLEY SKI CENTER
Ellicottville, NY 14731
(716) 699-2345
LOCATION: South of Ellicottville.
FACILITIES: 5 chairlifts; 1 tow rope; ski instruction; ski rental; nursery; 750 ft. vertical drop; restaurants; lodging.

Fabius

TOGGENBURG SKI CENTER
Fabius, NY 13063
(315) 683-5382
LOCATION: East of Fabius.
FACILITIES: 4 chairlifts; 1 tow rope; ski instruction; ski rental; nursery; 600 ft. vertical drop; restaurants; lodging.

Farmingville

BALD HILL SKI CENTER
Farmingville, NY 11727
(516) 732-5610

LOCATION: Near Farmingville.
FACILITIES: 1 chairlift; 2 tow ropes; ski instruction; ski rental; 120 ft. vertical drop; restaurants; lodging.

Fayetteville

ACRES SKI CENTER
Fayetteville, NY 13066
(315) 637-9023
LOCATION: East of Fayetteville.
FACILITIES: 2 tow ropes; ski instruction; ski rental; 100 ft. vertical drop; restaurants; lodging.

Findley Lake

PEEK 'N PEAK SKI CENTER
Findley Lake, NY 14724
(716) 355-4141
LOCATION: Near Findley Lake.
FACILITIES: 7 chairlifts; ski instruction; ski rental; 400 ft. vertical drop; restaurants; lodging.

Glens Falls

WEST MOUNTAIN SKI CENTER
Glens Falls, NY 12801
(518) 793-6606
LOCATION: Near Glens Falls.
FACILITIES: 4 chairlifts; 1 tow rope; ski instruction; ski rental; 1010 ft. vertical drop; restaurants; lodging.

Glenwood

KISSING BRIDGE SKI CENTER
Glenwood, NY 14069
(716) 592-4963
LOCATION: Near Glenwood.
FACILITIES: 8 chairlifts; 3 tow ropes; ski instruction; ski rental; nursery; 500 ft. vertical drop; restaurants; lodging.

Greenwood Lake

MOUNT PETER SKI CENTER
Greenwood Lake, NY 10925
(914) 986-4992
LOCATION: Near Greenwood Lake.
FACILITIES: 2 chairlifts; ski instruction; ski rental; 400 ft. vertical drop; restaurants; lodging.

Haines Falls

CORTINA VALLEY SKI CENTER
Haines Falls, NY 12436
(518) 589-6500
LOCATION: Near Haines Falls.
FACILITIES: 2 chairlifts; 1 tow rope; ski instruction; ski rental; 625 ft. vertical drop; restaurants; lodging.

Harrisville

JUNIPER HILLS SKI CENTER
Harrisville, NY 13648
(315) 543-2737
LOCATION: East of Harrisville.
FACILITIES: 2 chairlifts; ski instruction; ski rental; 200 ft. vertical drop; restaurants; lodging.

SKI AREAS (continued)

Highmount

BELLEAYRE SKI CENTER
Highmount, NY 12465
(914) 254-5601
LOCATION: Near Highmount.
FACILITIES: 7 chairlifts; ski instruction; ski rental; nursery; 1265 ft. vertical drop; restaurants; lodging.

HIGHMOUNT SKI CENTER
Highmount, NY 12441
(914) 254-5265
LOCATION: Near Highmount.
FACILITIES: 4 chairlifts; 1 tow rope; ski instruction; ski rental; 1050 ft. vertical drop; restaurants; lodging.

Hillsdale

CATAMOUNT SKI CENTER
Hillsdale, NY 12529
(518) 325-3200
LOCATION: East of Hillsdale.
FACILITIES: 6 chairlifts; ski instruction; ski rental; nursery; 1000 ft. vertical drop; restaurants; lodging.

Hunter

HUNTER MOUNTAIN SKI CENTER
Hunter, NY 12442
(518) 263-4223
LOCATION: Near Hunter.
FACILITIES: 12 chairlifts; 3 tow ropes; ski instruction; ski rental; nursery; 1600 ft. vertical drop; restaurants; lodging.

Jay

PALEFACE SKI CENTER
Jay, NY 12941
(518) 946-2272
LOCATION: Near Jay.
FACILITIES: 2 chairlifts; ski instruction; ski rental; nursery; 730 ft. vertical drop; restaurants; lodging.

Johnstown

ROYAL MOUNTAIN SKI CENTER
Johnstown, NY 12095
(518) 835-6445
LOCATION: Northwest of Johnstown.
FACILITIES: 2 chairlifts; ski instruction; ski rental; 550 ft. vertical drop; restaurants; lodging.

Lake Placid

MOUNT WHITNEY
Lake Placid, NY 12946
(518) 523-2031
LOCATION: Near Lake Placid.
FACILITIES: 2 chairlifts; ski instruction; ski rental; 408 ft. vertical drop; restaurants; lodging.

LeRoy

FROST RIDGE SKI CENTER
LeRoy, NY 14482
(716) 768-9730
LOCATION: Near LeRoy.
FACILITIES: 1 chairlift; 3 tow ropes; ski instruction; ski rental; 150 ft. vertical drop; restaurants; lodging.

Little Falls

SHU-MAKER MOUNTAIN SKI CENTER
Little Falls, NY 13365
(315) 823-1110
LOCATION: South of Little Falls.
FACILITIES: 3 chairlifts; 1 tow rope; ski instruction; ski rental; 750 ft. vertical drop; restaurants; lodging.

Malone

MOON VALLEY SKI CENTER
Malone, NY 12953
(518) 483-7320
LOCATION: 6 mi. south of Malone.
FACILITIES: 2 chairlifts; ski instruction; ski rental; 600 ft. vertical drop; restaurants; lodging.

Monticello

HOLIDAY MOUNTAIN SKI CENTER
Monticello, NY 12701
(914) 796-3161
LOCATION: East of Monticello.
FACILITIES: 6 chairlifts; 3 tow ropes; ski instruction; ski rental; 400 ft. vertical drop; restaurants; lodging.

Newark

BRANTLING SKI CENTER
Newark, NY 14551
(315) 331-2365
LOCATION: Between Newark and Sodus.
FACILITIES: 2 chairlifts; 3 tow ropes; ski instruction; ski rental; 240 ft. vertical drop; restaurants; lodging.

New Paltz

MOHONK SKI CENTER
New Paltz, NY 12561
(914) 255-6655
LOCATION: Near New Paltz.
FACILITIES: 1 chairlift; 3 tow ropes; ski instruction; ski rental; 475 ft. vertical drop; restaurants; lodging.

SKI MINNEWASKA SKI CENTER
New Paltz, NY 12561
(914) 255-6000
LOCATION: West of New Paltz.
FACILITIES: 3 chairlifts; 1 tow rope; ski instruction; ski rental; nursery; 385 ft. vertical drop; restaurants; lodging.

New Woodstock

MYSTIC MOUNTAIN SKI CENTER
New Woodstock, NY 13122
(315) 662-3322
LOCATION: Near New Woodstock.
FACILITIES: 3 chairlifts; ski instruction; ski rental; 590 ft. vertical drop; restaurants; lodging.

NEW YORK

SKI AREAS (continued)

North Creek

GORE MOUNTAIN SKI CENTER
North Creek, NY 12853
(518) 251-2411
LOCATION: Near North Creek.
FACILITIES: 7 chairlifts; ski instruction; ski rental; nursery; 2100 ft. vertical drop; restaurants; lodging.

NORTH CREEK SKI BOWL SKI CENTER
North Creek, NY 12853
(518) 251-2021
LOCATION: Near North Creek.
FACILITIES: 2 chairlifts; ski instruction; ski rental; 960 ft. vertical drop; restaurants; lodging.

Old Forge

MCCAULEY MOUNTAIN SKI CENTER
Old Forge, NY 13420
(315) 369-3225
LOCATION: Near Old Forge.
FACILITIES: 3 chairlifts; 2 tow ropes; ski instruction; ski rental; 633 ft. vertical drop; restaurants; lodging.

Patterson

BIR BURCH SKI CENTER
Patterson, NY 12563
(914) 878-3181
LOCATION: Near Patterson.
FACILITIES: 3 chairlifts; 2 tow ropes; ski instruction; ski rental; 450 ft. vertical drop; restaurants; lodging.

Petersburg

MOUNT RAIMER SKI CENTER
Petersburg, NY 12138
(518) 658-3399
LOCATION: East of Petersburg.
FACILITIES: 2 chairlifts; 1 tow rope; ski instruction; ski rental; 850 ft. vertical drop; restaurants; lodging.

Phoenicia

PHOENICIA SKI CENTER
Phoenicia, NY 12464
(914) 688-5637
LOCATION: Near Phoenicia.
FACILITIES: 4 tow ropes; ski instruction; ski rental; 440 ft. vertical drop; restaurants; lodging.

Richfield Springs

GUNSET SKI CENTER
Richfield Springs, NY 13439
(315) 858-1140
LOCATION: West of Richfield Springs.
FACILITIES: 2 chairlifts; 1 tow rope; ski instruction; ski rental; 330 ft. vertical drop; restaurants; lodging.

Roxbury

PLATTEKILL MOUNTAIN SKI CENTER
Roxbury, NY 12474

(607) 326-7547
LOCATION: West of Roxbury.
FACILITIES: 3 chairlifts; ski instruction; ski rental; 970 ft. vertical drop; restaurants; lodging.

Salamanca

BOVA SKI CENTER
Salamanca, NY 14779
(716) 354-2535
LOCATION: Near Salamanca.
FACILITIES: 2 tow ropes; ski instruction; ski rental; 220 ft. vertical drop; restaurants; lodging.

Saranac Lake

MOUNT PISGAH SKI CENTER
Saranac Lake, NY 12983
(518) 891-1990
LOCATION: On Trudeau Road.
FACILITIES: 1 chairlift; 300 ft. vertical drop; restaurants; lodging.

Saratoga Springs

ADIRONDACK SKI CENTER
Saratoga Springs, NY 12822
(518) 654-6245
LOCATION: North of Saratoga Springs.
FACILITIES: 3 chairlifts; ski instruction; ski rental; 1000 ft. vertical drop; restaurants; lodging.

Schenectady

MAPLE SKI RIDGE SKI CENTER
Schenectady, NY 12306
(518) 377-5172
LOCATION: West of Schenectady.
FACILITIES: 1 chairlift; 4 tow ropes; ski instruction; ski rental; 225 ft. vertical drop; restaurants; lodging.

Sinclairville

COCKAIGNE SKI CENTER
Sinclairville, NY 14723
(716) 287-3223
LOCATION: East of Sinclairville.
FACILITIES: 3 chairlifts; ski instruction; ski rental; 430 ft. vertical drop; restaurants; lodging.

South Fallsburg

PINE SKI CENTER
South Fallsburg, NY 12779
(914) 434-6000
LOCATION: Near South Fallsburg.
FACILITIES: 2 chairlifts; 2 tow ropes; ski instruction; ski rental; 200 ft. vertical drop; restaurants; lodging.

Speculator

OAK MOUNTAIN SKI CENTER
Speculator, NY 12164
(518) 548-7311
LOCATION: Near Speculator.
FACILITIES: 3 chairlifts; 1 tow rope; ski instruction; ski rental; 650 ft. vertical drop; restaurants; lodging.

SKI AREAS (continued)

Stamford

SCOTCH VALLEY SKI CENTER
Stamford, NY 12167
(607) 652-7332
LOCATION: North of Stamford.
FACILITIES: 4 chairlifts; 1 tow rope; ski instruction; ski rental; 750 ft. vertical drop; restaurants; lodging.

Stormville

MOUNT STORM SKI CENTER
Stormville, NY 12582
(914) 226-4288
LOCATION: Near Stormville.
FACILITIES: 1 chairlift; 1 tow rope; ski instruction; ski rental; 600 ft. vertical drop;
restaurants; lodging.

Swain

SWAIN SKI CENTER
Swain, NY 14884
(607) 545-8886
LOCATION: Near Swain.
FACILITIES: 5 chairlifts; ski instruction; ski
rental; 607 ft. vertical drop; restaurants; lodging.

Truxton

LABRADOR SKI CENTER
Truxton, NY 13158
(607) 842-6221
LOCATION: North of Truxton.
FACILITIES: 5 chairlifts; ski instruction; ski
rental; nursery; 680 ft. vertical drop; restaurants; lodging.

Tully

SONG MOUNTAIN SKI CENTER
Tully, NY 13159
(315) 696-5711
LOCATION: Near Tully.
FACILITIES: 5 chairlifts; ski instruction; ski
rental; nursery; 700 ft. vertical drop; restaurants; lodging.

Tupper Lake

BIG TUPPER SKI CENTER
Tupper Lake, NY 12986
(518) 359-3651
LOCATION: South of Tupper Lake.
FACILITIES: 3 chairlifts; 1 tow rope; ski instruction; ski rental; 800 ft. vertical drop; restaurants; lodging.

Turin

SNOW RIDGE SKI CENTER
Turin, NY 13473
(315) 348-8456
LOCATION: Near Turin.
FACILITIES: 6 chairlifts; 1 tow rope; ski instruction; ski rental; nursery; 500 ft. vertical
drop; restaurants; lodging.

Tuxedo

STERLING FOREST SKI CENTER :
Tuxedo, NY 10987
(914) 351-5707
LOCATION: Near Tuxedo.
FACILITIES: 4 chairlifts; ski instruction; ski
rental; 450 ft. vertical drop; restaurants; lodging.

Utica

VAL BIALIS SKI CENTER
Utica, NY 13502
(315) 798-3294
LOCATION: Near Utica.
FACILITIES: 2 chairlifts; 1 tow rope; 400 ft.
vertical drop; restaurants; lodging.

Warrensburg

HICKORY SKI CENTER
Warrensburg, NY 12885
(518) 623-9866
LOCATION: West of Warrensburg.
FACILITIES: 3 chairlifts; 1 tow rope; 1200
ft. vertical drop; restaurants; lodging.

Warsaw

HONEY HILL SKI CENTER
Warsaw, NY 14569
(716) 786-9896
LOCATION: South of Warsaw.
FACILITIES: 1 chairlift; 3 tow ropes; ski instruction; ski rental; 200 ft. vertical drop; restaurants; lodging.

Wells

SILVER BELLS SKI CENTER
Wells, NY 12190
(518) 725-2198
LOCATION: Near Wells.
FACILITIES: 1 chairlift; 1 tow rope; ski instruction; ski rental; 450 ft. vertical drop;
restaurants; lodging.

West Chazy

BEARTOWN SKI CENTER
West Chazy, NY 12901
(518) 563-2975
LOCATION: Near West Chazy.
FACILITIES: 1 chairlift; 3 tow ropes; ski instruction; ski rental; 125 ft. vertical drop;
restaurants; lodging.

Westernville

WOODS VALLEY SKI CENTER
Westernville, NY 13486
(315) 827-4721
LOCATION: Near Westernville.
FACILITIES: 3 chairlifts; ski instruction; ski
rental; 500 ft. vertical drop; restaurants; lodging.

Wilmington

WHITEFACE SKI CENTER
Wilmington, NY 12997
(518) 946-2223
LOCATION: Near Wilmington.
FACILITIES: 7 chairlifts; 2 tow ropes; ski instruction; ski rental; 3216 ft. vertical drop;
restaurants; lodging.

NEW YORK

SKI AREAS (continued)

Windham

WINDHAM MOUNTAIN CLUB SKI CEN-
TER
Windham, NY 12496
(518) 734-4300
LOCATION: Near Windham.
FACILITIES: 4 chairlifts; ski instruction; ski
rental; nursery; 1500 ft. vertical drop; restau-
rants; lodging.

Woodridge

BIG VANILLA SKI CENTER
Woodridge, NY 12789
(914) 434-5321
LOCATION: Near Woodridge.
FACILITIES: 7 chairlifts; 2 tow ropes; ski
instruction; ski rental; nursery; 500 ft. vertical
drop; restaurants; lodging.

Yorkshire

BLUEMONT SKI CENTER
Yorkshire, NY 14173
(716) 496-6041
LOCATION: West of Yorkshire.
FACILITIES: 2 chairlifts; 2 tow ropes; ski instruction; ski rental; 800 ft. vertical drop; restaurants; lodging.

AMUSEMENT PARKS & ATTRACTIONS

Brooklyn

ASTROLAND AMUSEMENT PARK
1000 Surf Avenue
Brooklyn, NY 11224
(212) 372-0275
FACILITIES: 11 major rides; 15 kiddie rides;
6 games; 2 refreshment stands; restaurant; 2
walk thrus; shooting gallery; arcade; free gate;
open Apr. 1 - Sept. 1; weekends: Sept. - Nov.

THE NEW YORK AQUARIUM
Boardwalk at West 8th Street
Brooklyn, NY 11224
(212) 266-8500
FACILITIES: Marine life exhibits; education
hall; refreshment stand; restaurant; picnic
facilities; museum; whale and dolphin training; pay gate; pay parking.

STEEPLECHASE AMUSEMENT PARK
600 Surf Avenue
Brooklyn, NY 11224
(212) 372-7099
FACILITIES: 13 major rides; 14 kiddie rides;
restaurant; batting range; beach; picnic facilities; free acts; pay parking.

Buffalo

CRYSTAL BEACH AMUSEMENT PARK
P.O. Box 640
Crystal Beach, Ontario LOS IBO
(416) 894-2240
FACILITIES: 26 major rides; 12 kiddie rides;
18 games; 18 refreshment stands; tavern;
shooting gallery; restaurant; arcade; beach;
miniature golf; picnic facilities; pay gate; pay
parking; open mid-May - Labor Day.

Canandaigua

ROSELAND PARK
Lake Shore Drive
Canandaigua, NY 14424
(716) 394-1140
FACILITIES: 13 major rides; 7 kiddie rides;
fun house; 7 games; 3 refreshment stands;
restaurant; arcade; shooting gallery; picnic
facilities; slot car; race track; pay gate; free
parking; open May 1 - Labor Day; weekends:
Apr., May - Jun. 15.

Catskill

CATSKILL GAME FARM
R.D. 1
Catskill, NY 12414
(518) 678-3350
FACILITIES: 9 kiddie rides; 5 refreshment
stands; cafeteria; 4 animal food stands; zoo;
exhibits; pay gate; free parking; open mid-
Apr. - mid-Nov.

Corfu

SNYDER'S DARIEN LAKE
Corfu, NY 14306
(716) 266-8500
FACILITIES: Beach; kiddie rides; camping; 3
restaurants; swimming pool; zoo; bike rental.

E. Farmingdale

ADVENTURELAND
2245 Broadhollow Road
E. Farmingdale, NY 11735
(516) 694-6868
FACILITIES: 13 major rides; 6 kiddie rides;
75 games; refreshment stand; restaurant; arcade; shooting gallery; pay gate; pay parking;
open all year.

Elmira

ELDRIDGE PARK
Park
Elmira, NY 14901
(607) 733-5118
FACILITIES: 10 major rides; 6 kiddie rides; 4
games; 2 refreshment stands; 2 restaurants;
penny arcade; shooting gallery; picnic facilities; miniature golf; bands; free acts; free gate;
free parking.

Grand Island

FANTASY ISLAND (Theme)
2400 Grand Island Blvd.
Grand Island, NY 14072
(716) 773-7591
FACILITIES: 14 major rides; 8 kiddie rides;
2 walk thrus; 8 refreshment stands; 3 restaurants; arcade; electric shooting gallery; picnic
facilities; miniature golf; theatre; petting zoo;
puppets; shoot-outs; circus show; books free
acts; fireworks; pay gate; free parking; open
Jun. 25 - Sept. 5.

AMUSEMENT PARKS (continued)

Lake George

GASLIGHT VILLAGE
Route 9
Lake George, NY 12845
(518) 668-5459
FACILITIES: 10 major rides; 4 kiddie rides;
fun house; 2 refreshment stands; restaurant;
arcade; shooting gallery; ice rink for performers (Ice Revue); museum (Cavalcade of Cars);
exhibits; skee ball; theater; books stage shows;
vaudeville; free acts; pay gate; free parking;
open mid-Jun. - mid-Sept.

STORYTOWN U.S.A.
P.O. Box 511
Lake George, NY 12845
(518) 792-6568
FACILITIES: 17 major rides; 2 kiddie rides; 2
walk thrus; 4 games; 5 refreshment stands; 2
restaurants; arcade; shooting gallery; exhibits;
marionette show; picnic facilities; zoo animals
to fit stories; theater; circus; water thrill
show; western shows and shoot-outs; vaudeville; free acts; pay gate; free parking; open
Memorial Day - mid-Oct.

Maple Springs

MIDWAY PARK
Route 17
Maple Springs, NY 14756
(716) 386-3165
FACILITIES: 6 major rides; 8 kiddie rides;
3 refreshment stands; restaurant; penny arcade; shooting gallery; roller rink; miniature
golf; picnic facilities; free gate; free parking.

Niagara Falls

**MAID OF THE MIST CORPORATION (At-
traction)**
151 Buffalo Avenue
Niagara Falls, NY 14303
(716) 284-8897
FACILITIES: Scenic boat ride; open mid-
May - mid-Oct.

NIAGARA POWER PROJECT (Attraction)
5777 Lewiston Road
Niagara Falls, NY 14302
(716) 285-3211
FACILITIES: Power plant; exhibits; free gate;
free parking; open all year.

Old Forge

**THE ENCHANTED FOREST OF THE AD-
IRONDACKS (Theme)**
P.O. Box 181
Old Forge, NY 13420
(315) 369-6145
FACILITIES: 5 major rides; 9 kiddie rides; 2
refreshment stands; arcade; exhibits; picnic
facilities; stage shows; storybook displays; pay
gate; free parking; open May 28 - Sept. 5.

Pottersville

**NATURAL STONE BRIDGE & CAVES
(Attraction)**
Shore Bridge Road

Pottersville, NY 12860
(518) 494-2283
FACILITIES: Mineral exhibits; refreshment
stand; mermaid shows; self guided tours in
lighted caves; pay gate; free parking; open
May 1 - Oct. 31.

Rochester

OLYMPIC PARK
1300 Scottsville Road
Rochester, NY 14624
(716) 436-9180
FACILITIES: 14 major rides; 14 kiddie rides;
8 games; 2 refreshment stands; 2 restaurants;
arcade; picnic facilities; golf driving range;
miniature golf; roller rink; free acts; pay
gate; free parking.

SEA BREEZE PARK
4600 Culver Road
Rochester, NY 14622
(716) 467-3422
FACILITIES: 15 major rides; 4 kiddie rides;
7 games; 2 refreshment stands; restaurant;
arcade; miniature golf; picnic facilities; free
gate; free parking; open Apr. 20 - Labor Day.

Rockaway Beach

ROCKAWAY'S PLAYLAND
185 Beach 97th Street
Rockaway Beach, NY 11693
(212) 945-7000
FACILITIES: 13 major rides; 11 kiddie rides;
fun house; 25 games; 8 refreshment stands;
arcade; 3 shooting galleries; beach; picnic facilities; excursion boats; miniature golf; penny
falls and splashdown games; pay gate; free
gate; pay parking; free parking; open Mar. 5 -
Sept. 30; weekends: Mar., May, Sept.

Rye

**WESTCHESTER COUNTY PLAYLAND
COMMISSION**
Playland Park
Rye, NY 10580
(914) 967-2040
FACILITIES: 28 major rides; 17 kiddie rides;
walk thru; 25 games; 20 refreshment stands;
restaurant; shooting gallery; beach; fishing
boats; picnic facilities; miniature golf; fishing
pier; wildlife reservation; pay parking; open
May 22 - Sept. 6; weekends: May 1.

Tioga Center

SKYLINE AMUSEMENT PARK
Tioga Center, NY 13845
(607) 687-9807
FACILITIES: 8 major rides; 6 kiddie rides;
fun house; 5 games; 2 refreshment stands;
books free acts; free gate; free parking.

STATE FAIR

New York State Fair
State Fairgrounds
Syracuse, New York 13209
(315) 487-7711
DATE: August

NEW YORK

NATIONAL PARKS

There are no National Parks in New York.

NATIONAL FORESTS

There are no National Forests in New York.

STATE PARKS

Headquarters

Parks and Recreation
Empire State Plaza
Albany, NY 12238
(518) 474-0456

Albion

LAKESIDE BEACH STATE PARK
(716) 682-5246
LOCATION: 10 mi. north of Albion.
FACILITIES: Open May - Oct.; 274 sites; water and bathroom facilities; sanitary station; electrical hookup; trailer village vehicle sites; picnic area; fishing; tent camping.

Alexandria

KEEWAYDIN STATE PARK
(315) 482-2625
LOCATION: Off Route 12.
FACILITIES: Open May - Oct.; 46 sites; water and bathroom facilities; sanitary station; trailer village vehicle sites; picnic area; swimming; boating; boat rental; fishing; tent camping.

Alexandria Bay

CANOE-PICNIC POINT STATE PARK
(315) 482-9929
LOCATION: In the bay (access by boat only).
FACILITIES: Open May - Oct.; 35 sites; water and bathroom facilities; picnic area; fishing; tent camping.

CEDAR ISLAND STATE PARK
(315) 482-9929
LOCATION: In the bay (access by boat only).
FACILITIES: Open May - Oct.; 12 sites; water and bathroom facilities; picnic area; tent camping.

GRASS POINT STATE PARK
(315) 482-9929
LOCATION: Off Route 81.
FACILITIES: Open May - Oct.; 88 sites; water and bathroom facilities; sanitary station; trailer village vehicle sites; picnic area; swimming; boating; boat rental; fishing; tent camping.

MARY ISLAND STATE PARK
(315) 482-9929
LOCATION: In the bay (access by boat only).
FACILITIES: Open May - Oct.; 12 sites; water and bathroom facilities; picnic area; fishing; tent camping.

Binghamton

CHENANGO VALLEY STATE PARK
(607) 648-5251
LOCATION: 12 mi. north of Binghamton.
FACILITIES: Open May - Oct.; 220 sites; water and bathroom facilities; sanitary station; electrical hookup; trailer village vehicle sites; laundry; picnic area; swimming; boating; boat rental; fishing; tent camping.

Boonville

PIXLEY FALLS STATE PARK
(315) 942-4713
LOCATION: 6 mi. south of Boonville on Route 46.
FACILITIES: Open May - Oct.; 18 sites; water and bathroom facilities; trailer village vehicle sites; fishing; tent camping.

Brocton

LAKE ERIE STATE PARK
(716) 792-9214
LOCATION: North of Brocton.
FACILITIES: Open May - Oct.; 95 sites; water and bathroom facilities; sanitary station; electrical hookup; trailer village vehicle sites; laundry; swimming; fishing; tent camping.

Carmel

FAHNESTOCK STATE PARK
(914) 225-7207
LOCATION: Off Route 301.
FACILITIES: Open May - Oct.; 83 sites; water and bathroom facilities; trailer village vehicle sites; picnic area; swimming; boating; boat rental; tent camping.

Cazenovia

CHITTENANGO FALLS STATE PARK
(315) 655-9620
LOCATION: 5 mi. north of Cazenovia.
FACILITIES: Open May - Oct.; 30 sites; water and bathroom facilities; trailer village vehicle sites; picnic area; fishing; tent camping.

Clayton

BURNHAM POINT STATE PARK
(315) 654-2324
LOCATION: Off Route 12E.
FACILITIES: Open May - Oct.; 52 sites; water and bathroom facilities; electrical hookup; trailer village vehicle sites; boating; boat rental; fishing; tent camping.

CEDAR POINT STATE PARK
(315) 654-2522
LOCATION: Off Route 12E.
FACILITIES: Open May - Oct.; 186 sites; water and bathroom facilities; sanitary station; electrical hookup; trailer village vehicle sites; swimming; boating; boat rental; fishing; tent camping.

Colton

HIGLEY FLOW STATE PARK
(315) 262-2010

STATE PARKS (continued)

LOCATION: Coldbrook Drive.
FACILITIES: Open May - Oct.; 143 sites; water and bathroom facilities; sanitary station; electrical hookup; trailer village vehicle sites; swimming; boating; boat rental; fishing; tent camping.

Copake Falls

TACONIC STATE PARK
(518) 329-3993
LOCATION: East of Route 22.
FACILITIES: Open May - Oct.; 171 sites; water and bathroom facilities; sanitary station; trailer village vehicle sites; picnic area; swimming; fishing; tent camping.

Dansville

STONY BROOK STATE PARK
(716) 987-8111
LOCATION: 3 mi. south of Dansville.
FACILITIES: Open May - Oct.; 100 sites; water and bathroom facilities; sanitary station; trailer village vehicle sites; picnic area; swimming; fishing.

Darien

DARIEN LAKES STATE PARK
(716) 547-9242
LOCATION: Harlow Road.
FACILITIES: Open May - Oct.; 150 sites; water and bathroom facilities; sanitary station; trailer village vehicle sites; picnic area; food service; swimming; boating; boat rental; tent camping.

Farnham

EVANGOLA STATE PARK
(716) 549-1760
LOCATION: North of Farnham on Route 5.
FACILITIES: Open May - Oct.; 51 sites; water and bathroom facilities; sanitary station; trailer village vehicle sites; laundry; picnic area; swimming; fishing; tent camping.

Fayetteville

GREEN LAKES STATE PARK
(315) 637-6111
LOCATION: 3 mi. east of Fayetteville.
FACILITIES: Open May - Oct.; 137 sites; water and bathroom facilities; sanitary station; electrical hookup; trailer village vehicle sites; laundry; picnic area; swimming; boating; fishing; tent camping.

Hamlin

HAMLIN BEACH STATE PARK
(716) 964-2121
LOCATION: 3 mi. north of Hamlin.
FACILITIES: Open May - Oct.; 264 sites; sanitary station; electrical hookup; trailer village vehicle sites; laundry; picnic area; food service; swimming; fishing; tent camping.

Hudson

LAKE TAGHKANIC STATE PARK

(518) 851-3631
LOCATION: 11 mi. south of Hudson.
FACILITIES: Open May - Oct.; 64 sites; water and bathroom facilities; trailer village vehicle sites; picnic area; swimming; boating; boat rental; fishing; tent camping.

Ithaca

BUTTERMILK FALLS STATE PARK
(607) 273-5761
LOCATION: 3 mi. south of Ithaca.
FACILITIES: Open May - Oct.; 60 sites; water and bathroom facilities; sanitary station; trailer village vehicle sites; picnic area; swimming; fishing; tent camping.

ROBERT H. TREMAN STATE PARK
(607) 273-3440
LOCATION: 5 mi. south of Ithaca.
FACILITIES: Open May - Oct.; 137 sites; water and bathroom facilities; electrical hookup; trailer village vehicle sites; swimming; fishing; tent camping.

TAUGHANNOCK FALLS STATE PARK
(607) 387-6739
LOCATION: 10 mi. north of Ithaca on Route 89.
FACILITIES: Open May - Oct.; 84 sites; water and bathroom facilities; sanitary station; electrical hookup; trailer village vehicle sites; picnic area; swimming; boating; fishing; tent camping.

Massena

ROBERT MOSES STATE PARK
(315) 388-5636
LOCATION: 2 mi. north of Route 87, east of Massena.
FACILITIES: Open May - Oct.; 401 sites; sanitary station; electrical hookup; trailer village vehicle sites; laundry; picnic area; food service; swimming; boating; boat rental; fishing; tent camping.

Middleburgh

TOE PATH MOUNTAIN STATE PARK
(518) 827-4711
LOCATION: 8 mi. south of Middleburgh.
FACILITIES: Open May - Oct.; 29 sites; water and bathroom facilities; trailer village vehicle sites; picnic area; tent camping.

Montauk Village

HITHER HILLS STATE PARK
(516) 668-2554
LOCATION: 3 mi. west of Montauk Village.
FACILITIES: Open May - Oct.; 165 sites; water and bathroom facilities; trailer village vehicle sites; picnic area; food service; swimming; fishing; tent camping.

Moravia

FILLMORE GLEN STATE PARK
(315) 497-0130
LOCATION: 1 mi. south of Moravia.
FACILITIES: Open May - Oct.; 50 sites; water and bathroom facilities; sanitary station; trailer village vehicle sites; picnic area; swimming; tent camping.

STATE PARKS (continued)

Morristown

JACQUES CARTIER STATE PARK
(315) 375-6371
LOCATION: River Road.
FACILITIES: Open May - Oct.; 98 sites; water and bathroom facilities; sanitary station; trailer village vehicle sites; picnic area; swimming; boating; boat rental; fishing; tent camping.

Niagara Falls

GOLDEN HILL STATE PARK
(716) 795-3885
LOCATION: Lower Lake Road.
FACILITIES: Open May - Oct.; 50 sites; water and bathroom facilities; sanitary station; electrical hookup; trailer village vehicle sites; fishing; tent camping.

Ogdensburg

EEL WEIR STATE PARK
(315) 393-1138
LOCATION: 3 mi. southwest of Ogdensburg.
FACILITIES: Open May - Oct.; 19 sites; water and bathroom facilities; trailer village vehicle sites; picnic area; swimming; fishing; tent camping.

Oneonta

GILBERT LAKE STATE PARK
(607) 432-2114
LOCATION: 12 mi. northwest of Oneonta.
FACILITIES: Open May - Oct.; 221 sites; water and bathroom facilities; sanitary station; electrical hookup; trailer village vehicle sites; laundry; picnic area; food service; swimming; fishing; tent camping.

Ovid

SAMPSON STATE PARK
(315) 585-6392
LOCATION: 5 mi. north of Ovid on Route 96A.
FACILITIES: Open May - Oct.; 245 sites; water and bathroom facilities; sanitary station; trailer village vehicle sites; swimming; boating; fishing; tent camping.

Oxford

BOWMAN LAKE STATE PARK
(607) 334-2718
LOCATION: 8 mi. west of Oxford.
FACILITIES: Open May - Oct.; 202 sites; water and bathroom facilities; sanitary station; electrical hookup; trailer village vehicle sites; swimming; boating; boat rental; fishing; tent camping.

Penn Yan

KEUKA LAKE STATE PARK
(315) 536-3666
LOCATION: 6 mi. southwest of Penn Yan.
FACILITIES: Open May - Oct.; 150 sites; water and bathroom facilities; sanitary station; trailer village vehicle sites; picnic area; swimming; boating; fishing; tent camping.

Perry

LETCHWORTH STATE PARK
(716) 493-2611
LOCATION: 4 mi. east of Perry.
FACILITIES: Open May - Oct.; 270 sites; water and bathroom facilities; sanitary station; electrical hookup; trailer village vehicle sites; laundry; picnic area; food service; swimming; fishing; tent camping.

Poughkeepsie

MARGARET LEWIS NORRIE STATE PARK
(914) 889-4646
LOCATION: 9 mi. north of Poughkeepsie.
FACILITIES: Open May - Oct.; 45 sites; water and bathroom facilities; trailer village vehicle sites; picnic area; boating; boat rental; fishing; tent camping.

Pulaski

SELKIRK SHORES STATE PARK
(315) 298-5737
LOCATION: 5 mi. west of Pulaski.
FACILITIES: Open May - Oct.; 151 sites; water and bathroom facilities; sanitary station; electrical hookup; trailer village vehicle sites; laundry; picnic area; food service; swimming; tent camping.

Redwood

KRING POINT STATE PARK
(315) 482-9822
LOCATION: Off Route 12.
FACILITIES: Open May - Oct.; 142 sites; sanitary station; electrical hookup; trailer village vehicle sites; picnic area; swimming; boating; boat rental; fishing; tent camping.

Rome

DELTA LAKE STATE PARK
(315) 337-4670
LOCATION: 6 mi. northeast of Rome on Route 46.
FACILITIES: Open May - Oct.; 102 sites; water and bathroom facilities; sanitary station; trailer village vehicle sites; laundry; swimming; boating; fishing; tent camping.

Sackets Harbor

WESCOTT BEACH STATE PARK
(315) 646-2239
LOCATION: 4 mi. south of Sackets Harbor on Route 3.
FACILITIES: Open May - Oct.; 207 sites; sanitary station; electrical hookup; trailer village vehicle sites; picnic area; food service; swimming; fishing; tent camping.

Salamanca

ALLEGANY STATE PARK
(716) 354-2182
LOCATION: Off Route 280.
FACILITIES: Open May - Oct.; 423 sites; water and bathroom facilities; sanitary station; electrical hookup; laundry; picnic area; food service; swimming; boating; fishing; tent camping.

STATE PARKS (continued)

Seneca Falls

CAYUGA LAKE STATE PARK
(315) 568-5163
LOCATION: 7 mi. southeast of Seneca Falls.
FACILITIES: Open May - Oct.; 250 sites; water and bathroom facilities; sanitary station; electrical hookup; trailer village vehicle sites; swimming; boating; boat rental; fishing; tent camping.

Stony Point

HARRIMAN STATE PARK
(914) 947-2792
LOCATION: Off Route 210.
FACILITIES: Open May - Oct.; 220 sites; water and bathroom facilities; sanitary station; trailer village vehicle sites; picnic area; swimming; boating; boat rental; fishing; tent camping.

Three Mile Bay

LONG POINT STATE PARK
(315) 649-5258
LOCATION: Off Route 12E.
FACILITIES: Open May - Oct.; 99 sites; water and bathroom facilities; sanitary station; electrical hookup; trailer village vehicle sites; swimming; fishing; tent camping.

Wading River

WILDWOOD STATE PARK
(516) 929-4262
LOCATION: Off Route 25A.
FACILITIES: Open May - Oct.; 322 sites; water and bathroom facilities; sanitary station; electrical hookup; trailer village vehicle sites; picnic area; swimming; fishing; tent camping.

Wantagh

JONES BEACH STATE PARK
(516) 785-1600
LOCATION: 3 mi. north of Wantagh.
FACILITIES: Open May - Oct.; 200 sites; picnic area; food service; swimming; boating; fishing; tent camping.

Watkins Glen

WATKINS GLEN STATE PARK
(607) 535-4511
LOCATION: Off Route 14.
FACILITIES: Open May - Oct.; 300 sites; water and bathroom facilities; sanitary station; electrical hookup; trailer village vehicle sites; picnic area; swimming; fishing; tent camping.

Wellesley Island

DE WOLFE POINT STATE PARK
(315) 482-2012
LOCATION: North of Thousand Islands Bridge.
FACILITIES: Open May - Oct.; 29 sites; water and bathroom facilities; trailer village vehicle sites; picnic area; boating; fishing; tent camping.

WELLESLEY ISLAND STATE PARK

(315) 482-2722
LOCATION: 2 mi. north of Thousand Islands Bridge.
FACILITIES: Open May - Oct.; 490 sites; water and bathroom facilities; sanitary station; electrical hookup; trailer village vehicle sites; food service; swimming; boating; boat rental; fishing; tent camping.

Woodville

SOUTHWICK BEACH STATE PARK
(315) 846-5338
LOCATION: Off Route 193.
FACILITIES: Open May - Oct.; 110 sites; water and bathroom facilities; sanitary station; electrical hookup; trailer village vehicle sites; food service; swimming; fishing; tent camping.

STATE FORESTS

Department of Environmental Conservation
Forestry Division
Albany, NY 12233
(518) 474-2121

New York State Forests are located in or near major State Parks. For information on exact locations and expanded facilities in the State Forests, contact the Regional Forester.

Bath

Regional Forester
Forest Service
115 Liberty Street
Bath, NY 14810
(607) 776-2165

BIRDSEYE HOLLOW STATE FOREST
LOCATION: Steuben County.
FACILITIES: Open year round; water and bathroom facilities; trailer village vehicle sites; picnic area; hiking; tent camping.

CAMERON STATE FOREST
LOCATION: Steuben County.
FACILITIES: Open year round; water and bathroom facilities; trailer village vehicle sites; picnic area; hiking; tent camping.

COON HOLLOW STATE FOREST
LOCATION: Schuyler County.
FACILITIES: Open year round; water and bathroom facilities; trailer village vehicle sites; picnic area; hiking; tent camping.

GOUNDRY HILL STATE FOREST
LOCATION: Schuyler County.
FACILITIES: Open year round; water and bathroom facilities; trailer village vehicle sites; picnic area; hiking; tent camping.

URBANA STATE FOREST
LOCATION: Steuben County.
FACILITIES: Open year round; water and bathroom facilities; trailer village vehicle sites; picnic area; hiking; tent camping.

Canton

Regional Forester

NEW YORK

STATE FORESTS (continued)

Forest Service
30 Court Street
Canton, NY 13617
(315) 386-4546

BRASHER STATE FOREST
LOCATION: St. Lawrence County.
FACILITIES: Open year round; water and bathroom facilities; trailer village vehicle sites; picnic area; hiking; tent camping.

SOUTH HAMMOND STATE FOREST
LOCATION: St. Lawrence County.
FACILITIES: Open year round; water and bathroom facilities; trailer village vehicle sites; picnic area; hiking; tent camping.

WHISKEY FLATS STATE FOREST
LOCATION: St. Lawrence County.
FACILITIES: Open year round; water and bathroom facilities; trailer village vehicle sites; picnic area; hiking; tent camping.

WOLF LAKE STATE FOREST
LOCATION: St. Lawrence County.
FACILITIES: Open year round; water and bathroom facilities; trailer village vehicle sites; picnic area; hiking; tent camping.

Catskill

Regional Forester
Forest Service
National Bank Bldg..
Catskill, NY 12414
(518) 943-4030

RENSSELAERVILLE STATE FOREST
LOCATION: Albany County.
FACILITIES: Open year round; water and bathroom facilities; trailer village vehicle sites; picnic area; hiking; tent camping.

Cortland

Regional Forester
Forest Service
P.O. Box 1169
Cortland, NY 13045
(607) 753-3095

BEAR SWAMP STATE FOREST
LOCATION: Cayuga County.
FACILITIES: Open year round; water and bathroom facilities; trailer village vehicle sites; picnic area; hiking; tent camping.

CUYLER HILL STATE FOREST
LOCATION: Cortland County.
FACILITIES: Open year round; water and bathroom facilities; trailer village vehicle sites; picnic area; hiking; tent camping.

DANBY STATE FOREST
LOCATION: Tompkins County.
FACILITIES: Open year round; water and bathroom facilities; trailer village vehicle sites; picnic area; hiking; tent camping.

GRIGGS GULF STATE FOREST
LOCATION: Cortland County.
FACILITIES; Open year round; water and bathroom facilities; trailer village vehicle sites; picnic area; hiking; tent camping.

HAMMOND HILL STATE FOREST
LOCATION: Tompkins County.
FACILITIES: Open year round; water and bathroom facilities; trailer village vehicle sites; picnic area; hiking; tent camping.

JAMES D. KENNEDY MEM. STATE FOREST
LOCATION: Cortland County.
FACILITIES: Open year round; water and bathroom facilities; trailer village vehicle sites; picnic area; hiking; tent camping.

MORGAN HILL STATE FOREST
LOCATION: Cortland County.
FACILITIES: Open year round; water and bathroom facilities; trailer village vehicle sites; picnic area; hiking; tent camping.

SEACORD HILL STATE FOREST
LOCATION: Cortland County.
FACILITIES: Open year round; water and bathroom facilities; trailer village vehicle sites; picnic area; hiking; tent camping.

SUMMER HILL STATE FOREST
LOCATION: Cayuga County.
FACILITIES: Open year round; water and bathroom facilities; trailer village vehicle sites; picnic area; hiking; tent camping.

WINONA STATE FOREST
LOCATION: Oswego County.
FACILITIES: Open year round; water and bathroom facilities; trailer village vehicle sites; picnic area; hiking; tent camping.

Herkimer

Regional Forester
Forest Service
225 N. Main Street
Herkimer, NY 13350
(315) 866-6330

BIG BROOK STATE FOREST
LOCATION: Oneida County.
FACILITIES: Open year round; water and bathroom facilities; trailer village vehicle sites; picnic area; hiking; tent camping.

FALL BROOK STATE FOREST
LOCATION: Oneida County.
FACILITIES: Open year round; water and bathroom facilities; trailer village vehicle sites; picnic area; hiking; tent camping.

SWANCOTT HILL STATE FOREST
LOCATION: Oneida County.
FACILITIES: Open year round; water and bathroom facilities; trailer village vehicle sites; picnic area; hiking; tent camping.

TASSELL HILL STATE FOREST
LOCATION: Oneida County.
FACILITIES: Open year round; water and bathroom facilities; trailer village vehicle sites; picnic area; hiking; tent camping.

Jamestown

Regional Forester

STATE FORESTS (continued)

Forest Service
R.D. 1, Box 4
Jamestown, NY 14701
(716) 484-7161

ALLEN LAKE STATE FOREST
LOCATION: Allegany County.
FACILITIES: Open year round; water and bathroom facilities; trailer village vehicle sites; picnic area; water skiing; tent camping.

CARLTON HILL STATE FOREST
LOCATION: Wyoming County.
FACILITIES: Open year round; water and bathroom facilities; trailer village vehicle sites; picnic area; hiking; tent camping.

COYLE HILL STATE FOREST
LOCATION: Allegany County.
FACILITIES: Open year round; water and bathroom facilities; trailer village vehicle sites; picnic area; hiking; tent camping.

FRANKLINVILLE STATE FOREST
LOCATION: Cattaraugus County.
FACILITIES: Open year round; water and bathroom facilities; trailer village vehicle sites; picnic area; hiking; tent camping.

GILLIES HILL STATE FOREST
LOCATION: Allegany County.
FACILITIES: Open year round; water and bathroom facilities; trailer village vehicle sites; picnic area; hiking; tent camping.

MCCARTHY HILL STATE FOREST
LOCATION: Cattaraugus County.
FACILITIES: Open year round; water and bathroom facilities; trailer village vehicle sites; picnic area; hiking; tent camping.

NINE MILE CREEK STATE FOREST
LOCATION: Cattaraugus County.
FACILITIES: Open year round; water and bathroom facilities; trailer village vehicle sites; picnic area; hiking; tent camping.

NORTH HARMONY STATE FOREST
LOCATION: Chautauqua County.
FACILITIES: Open year round; water and bathroom facilities; trailer village vehicle sites; picnic area; hiking; tent camping.

PALMER POND STATE FOREST
LOCATION: Allegany County.
FACILITIES: Open year round; water and bathroom facilities; trailer village vehicle sites; picnic area; hiking; tent camping.

ROCK CITY STATE FOREST
LOCATION: Cattaraugus County.
FACILITIES: Open year round; water and bathroom facilities; trailer village vehicle sites; picnic area; hiking; tent camping.

SOUTH VALLEY STATE FOREST
LOCATION: Cattaraugus County.
FACILITIES: Open year round; water and bathroom facilities; trailer village vehicle sites; picnic area; hiking; tent camping.

VANDERMARK STATE FOREST
LOCATION: Allegany County.

FACILITIES: Open year round; water and bathroom facilities; trailer village vehicle sites; picnic area; hiking; tent camping.

ZOAR VALLEY STATE FOREST
LOCATION: Cattaraugus County.
FACILITIES: Open year round; water and bathroom facilities; trailer village vehicle sites; picnic area; hiking; tent camping.

Lowville

Regional Forester
Forest Service
R.F.D. 3
Route 26A
Lowville, NY 13367
(315) 376-3521

FRANK E. JADWIN STATE FOREST
LOCATION: Lewis County.
FACILITIES: Open year round; water and bathroom facilities; trailer village vehicle sites; picnic area; hiking; tent camping.

LOOKOUT STATE FOREST
LOCATION: Lewis County.
FACILITIES: Open year round; water and bathroom facilities; trailer village vehicle sites; picnic area; hiking; tent camping.

MOHAWK SPRINGS STATE FOREST
LOCATION: Lewis County.
FACILITIES: Open year round; water and bathroom facilities; trailer village vehicle sites; picnic area; hiking; tent camping.

TUG HILL STATE FOREST
LOCATION: Jefferson County.
FACILITIES: Open year round; water and bathroom facilities; trailer village vehicle sites; picnic area; hiking; tent camping.

WINONA STATE FOREST
LOCATION: Jefferson County.
FACILITIES: Open year round; water and bathroom facilities; trailer village vehicle sites; picnic area; hiking; tent camping.

Northville

Regional Forester
Forest Service
Northville, NY 12134
(518) 863-4545

LASSELLSVILLE STATE FOREST
LOCATION: Fulton County.
FACILITIES: Open year round; water and bathroom facilities; trailer village vehicle sites; picnic area; hiking; tent camping.

PECK HILL STATE FOREST
LOCATION: Fulton County.
FACILITIES: Open year round; water and bathroom facilities; trailer village vehicle sites; picnic area; hiking; tent camping.

Ray Brook

Regional Forester
Forest Service
Ray Brook, NY 12977
(518) 891-1370

NEW YORK

STATE FORESTS (continued)

DEER RIVER STATE FOREST
LOCATION: Franklin County.
FACILITIES: Open year round; water and bathroom facilities; trailer village vehicle sites; picnic area; hiking; tent camping.

MACOMB RESERVATION STATE FOREST
LOCATION: Clinton County.
FACILITIES: Open year round; water and bathroom facilities; trailer village vehicle sites; picnic area; hiking; tent camping.

TERRY MOUNTAIN STATE FOREST
LOCATION: Clinton County.
FACILITIES: Open year round; water and bathroom facilities; trailer village vehicle sites; picnic area; hiking; tent camping.

TITUSVILLE MOUNTAIN STATE FOREST
LOCATION: Franklin County.
FACILITIES: Open year round; water and bathroom facilities; trailer village vehicle sites; picnic area; hiking; tent camping.

Sherburne

Regional Forester
Forest Service
P.O. Box 145
Sherburne, NY 13460
(607) 674-2611

CHARLES E. BAKER STATE FOREST
LOCATION: Madison County.
FACILITIES: Open year round; water and bathroom facilities; trailer village vehicle sites; picnic area; hiking; tent camping.

BEAVER CREEK STATE FOREST
LOCATION: Madison County.
FACILITIES: Open year round; water and bathroom facilities; trailer village vehicle sites; picnic area; hiking; tent camping.

BEAVER MEADOW STATE FOREST
LOCATION: Chenango County.
FACILITIES: Open year round; water and bathroom facilities; trailer village vehicle sites; picnic area; hiking; tent camping.

BOWMAN CREEK STATE FOREST
LOCATION: Chenango County.
FACILITIES: Open year round; water and bathroom facilities; trailer village vehicle sites; picnic area; hiking; tent camping.

FIVE STREAMS STATE FOREST
LOCATION: Chenango County.
FACILITIES: Open year round; water and bathroom facilities; trailer village vehicle sites; picnic area; hiking; tent camping.

GENEGANSLET STATE FOREST
LOCATION: Chenango County.
FACILITIES: Open year round; water and bathroom facilities; trailer village vehicle sites; picnic area; hiking; tent camping.

LONG POND STATE FOREST
LOCATION: Chenango County.
FACILITIES: Open year round; water and bathroom facilities; trailer village vehicle sites; picnic area; hiking; tent camping.

NEW MICHIGAN STATE FOREST
LOCATION: Chenango County.
FACILITIES: Open year round; water and bathroom facilities; trailer village vehicle sites; picnic area; hiking; tent camping.

Stamford

Regional Forester
Forest Service
Jefferson Road
Stamford, NY 12167
(607) 652-7364

BURNT-ROSSMAN HILLS STATE FOREST
LOCATION: Schoharie County.
FACILITIES: Open year round; water and bathroom facilities; trailer village vehicle sites; picnic area; hiking; tent camping.

FAIRLANDS STATE FOREST
LOCATION: Schoharie County.
FACILITIES: Open year round; water and bathroom facilities; trailer village vehicle sites; picnic area; hiking; tent camping.

PATRIA STATE FOREST
LOCATION: Schoharie County.
FACILITIES: Open year round; water and bathroom facilities; trailer village vehicle sites; picnic area; hiking; tent camping.

HISTORIC SITES

Huntington

WALT WHITMAN HOUSE - Boyhood home of America's "good gray poet." Located in West Hills.

Hyde Park

FRANKLIN D. ROOSEVELT ESTATE - Birthplace of F.D.R., 32nd President, and home where he grew up and eventually lived with Eleanor and their children. Also contains Presidential library and museum. Located off Route 9.

Lake Placid

JOHN BROWN FARM - Owned by the famous abolitionist, who left in mid-1850s to fight in "Bleeding Kansas." Located on John Brown Road.

Montauk

MONTAUK POINT LIGHTHOUSE - In January, 1796, Washington authorized construction of this lighthouse on a site that had been selected four years earlier. Designed by John McComb, Jr., well-known architect of New York City Hall, the light is the oldest beacon established by the U.S. Government. Located on Montauk Point State Blvd.

Mt. McGregor

GRANT COTTAGE - In June, 1885, Joseph W. Drexel offered his cottage to General Ulysses S. Grant, 18th President, who was

NEW YORK

HISTORIC SITES (continued)

financially destitute and dying of tuberculosis. The residence became the scene of one of the nation's most famous death watches. Located on Route 101.

Mumford

GENESEE COUNTRY VILLAGE - Restored settlement of the early 1880s with some 35 village and farm structures, including working blacksmith shop, print shop, tinsmith and small-scale farm. Located on Flint Hill Road.

New York

STATUE OF LIBERTY - Presented to the U.S. in 1884 by France to commemorate this nation's 100th birthday. Measures 151 feet high on a 156 foot pedestal. Reached by boats running from the Battery. Located on Liberty Island.

THEODORE ROOSEVELT BIRTHPLACE - Restored home of only President born in the city. Located at 28 East 20th Street.

Old Bethpage

OLD BETHPAGE VILLAGE RESTORATION - Pre-Civil War farm village with over 30 original buildings, including inn, store, and church. Located on Round Swamp Road.

Old Chatham

SHAKER MUSEUM - A restored 18th-century Shaker community with many original buildings. Galleries contain over 17,000 simple and beautiful Shaker-designed items. Located off County Road 13.

Oyster Bay

SAGAMORE HILL - Estate of Theodore Roosevelt, 26th President, includes his home, furnished as it was during the years he and his family lived here. Located on Cove Neck Road.

Rome

ERIE CANAL - FORT BULL PROJECT - Restoration of canal village. Steam train and boat ride. Located on Route 49W.

Ticonderoga

FORT TICONDEROGA - Restored Colonial fort built in 1755. Also includes military museum, cannon firing, morter drills, and fife and drum corps.

HOSTELS

Glens Falls

LAKE GEORGE YOUTH HOSTEL
YMCA
Upper Glen Street
Glens Falls, NY 12801
(518) 669-2634

FACILITIES: Open Jun. 1 - Aug. 31; 25 beds, men; 25 beds, women; modern bathroom; nearest hostel: Warrensburg, 18 mi. north; overnight charges: $2.50.

Kingston

HIDDEN VALLEY LAKE YOUTH HOSTEL
CPO Box 190
Kingston, NY 12401
(914) 338-4616
FACILITIES: Open year round; 20 beds, men; 20 beds, women; modern bathroom; nearest hostel: Mt. Tremper, 25 mi. northwest; overnight charges: $3 summer; $4.25 winter; houseparents: hostel staff.

Lacona

SMART HOUSE NATURE CENTER
Smartville Road
Lacona, NY 13083
(315) 387-5521
FACILITIES: Open year round; 22 beds, men and women; modern bathroom; nearest hostel: Old Forge, 72 mi.; overnight charges: $3 May 1 - Sept. 30; $4 Oct. 1 - Apr. 30; houseparents: Alice & John Arneson.

Mt. Tremper

CAMP & RETREAT CENTER
P. O. Box 197
Mt. Tremper, NY 12457
(914) 688-2228
FACILITIES: Open year round; 50 beds, men; 50 beds, women; modern bathroom; overnight charges: $3; houseparents: Harold & Ruth Haar.

New York

NORTH AMERICAN ACCOMMODATIONS SYSTEM
Prince George Hotel
14 E. 28th Street
New York, NY 10016
(212) 685-9207
FACILITIES: Open year round; 200 beds, men; 200 beds, women; modern bathroom; overnight charges: single $19; twin $11; quad or triple $9; houseparent: Richard Garcia.

Old Forge

BROOKER FAMILY LODGE
Route 28
Old Forge, NY 13420
(315) 369-6072
FACILITIES: Open year round; 15 beds, men; 15 beds, women; modern bathroom; overnight charges: $3 summer; $4 winter; houseparents: Marlene & William Brooker.

Paul Smith's

ROTARY YOUTH HOSTEL
Keese Mill Schoolhouse
Paul Smith's, NY 12970
No telephone
FACILITIES: Open year round; 12 beds, men; 12 beds, women; modern bathroom; overnight charges: $2.50 (May - Sept.); $3 (Oct. - Apr.); reservations required; houseparents: Bob & Fran Kleinberg.

NEW YORK

HOSTELS (continued)

Staatsburg

CLUB HIGHVIEW YOUTH HOSTEL
Outdoor Inns
Staatsburg, NY 12580
(914) 266-5667
FACILITIES: Open year round; 20 beds,
men; 20 beds, women; modern bathroom;
overnight charges: $3 summer; $4.25 winter; houseparents: Doug & Nettie Young.

Warrensburg

THE GLEN HOUSE
Route 28
Warrensburg, NY 12885
(518) 494-3250
FACILITIES: Open year round; 12 beds,
men; 12 beds, women; modern bathroom;
overnight charges: $2 summer; $3 winter;
houseparent: Richard Nelson.

POINTS OF INTEREST

Bronx

BRONX ZOO - One of the world's largest and
most famous zoological parks. Located near
177th Street.

NEW YORK BOTANICAL GARDEN - A
230-acre park featuring beautifully landscaped grounds, buildings and large botanical
collection. Located in northwest Bronx Park.

Cooperstown

BASEBALL HALL OF FAME AND MU-
SEUM - Mementos of famous players.

Corning

CORNING GLASS CENTER, STEUBEN
GLASS FACTORY AND MUSEUM - See
glass being made and Steuben glass being
hand-blown. Museum holds more than 14000
glass objects, including a duplicate of the 20-
ton, 200-inch mirror disk made for Mount
Palomar telescope. Located on Route 414.

ROCKWELL GALLERY - World's largest collection of Carder Steuben glass. Located in
Rockwell's Department store.

Goshen

HALL OF FAME OF THE TROTTER MU-
SEUM - Dedicated to harness racing; contains
displays on record-setting horses, collection of
Currier and Ives prints, and library. Located
at 240 Main Street.

Hammondsport

GREYTON H. TAYLOR WINE MUSEUM
AND WINERY - Gold Seal and Great Western
wines made here. Tours available May - Nov.
Located on Bully Hill Road.

Highland

HUDSON VALLEY WINE VILLAGE - The
325-acre estate contains winery, vineyards,
wine village and wine cellars. Tours available
Feb. - Nov. Located on Route 9W.

Ilion

REMINGTON ARMS MUSEUM - Every type
of firearm manufactured by the Remington
Arms Company. Located at municipal marina
on Barge Canal.

Milton

ROYAL-KEDEM WINERY - Wine tasting and
film offered in converted Early American railway station. Tours available May - Nov. Located on Dock Road.

New York

AMERICAN MUSEUM OF NATURAL HIS-
TORY - Explores the origins of man and
world of plant and animal life. Located on
Central Park West at 79th Street.

BROADWAY - World-famous theatrical boulevard featuring at least 35 stage shows. Located off Times Square.

BROOKLYN BRIDGE - World-famous bridge.
Pedestrian walkway from Manhattan to
Brooklyn open year round. Located near
Worth Street.

CENTRAL PARK - A touch of natural beauty
in the midst of towering skyscrapers; includes
ball-playing fields, riding trails, tennis courts,
a theater, picnic areas, jogging trails and thousands of park benches. Located at Fifth Avenue and 59th Street.

CHINATOWN - Area includes Chinese shops,
restaurants, tea houses, and Chinese Museum.
Located near Chatham Square, west of the
Bowery.

THE CLOISTERS - Uptown branch of Metropolitan Museum, these five French cloisters
with lovely gardens celebrate medieval art
treasures. Situated in Fort Tyron Park at
190th St. and Fort Washington Ave.

EMPIRE STATE BUILDING - Extends 1472
feet into the sky, with 2 million square feet of
office space. Elevators run to observation
deck. Located at 5th Avenue and 34th Street.

GREENWICH VILLAGE - Area famed for its
curio shops, bookstores, art shows, coffee
houses, restaurants, and nightclubs. Located
near Avenue of the Americas and 8th Street.

GUGGENHEIM MUSEUM - Designed by
Frank Lloyd Wright; paintings are hung along
a spiral walkway which descends from the
domed top of building to terrace floor. Located on 5th Avenue at 89th Street.

HAYDEN PLANETARIUM - A dazzling, one-
hour sky show depicting space exploration,
development of the planets, black holes, patterns in the stars and distant universes. Lo-

POINTS OF INTEREST (continued)

cated at Central Park West and 81st Street.

METROPOLITAN MUSEUM OF ART - One of the world's greatest museums. Large exhibits on Egyptian, Greek and Roman art, as well as European and American art. Located in Central Park at 5th Avenue and 82nd Street.

MUSEUM OF MODERN ART - Extraordinary collection of modern sculpture, paintings, drawings, prints, and films. Located at 11 West 53rd Street.

ROCKEFELLER CENTER - 21 buildings on a 25-acre area; includes NBC, Radio City Music Hall, and RCA Building. Located at 5th Avenue and 48th Street.

ST. PATRICK'S CATHEDRAL - Famous 5th Avenue Catholic church designed in 13th-century Gothic style. Seats 2200. Located at 50th Street.

THE STOCK EXCHANGES - Both the American Stock Exchange and New York Stock Exchange provide guided tours and visitors galleries. American Stock Exchange located at 86 Trinity Place. New York Stock Exchange located at 20 Broad Street.

TIMES SQUARE - In the heart of the Broadway theater district, a four-square-block area jammed with people and glittering lights. Located at 42nd Street and 7th Avenue.

UNITED NATIONS HEADQUARTERS - Includes Secretariat building, domed General Assembly building, a conference center and Hammarskjold Library. Located on 1st Avenue at 42nd Street.

WALL STREET - Financial center of the U.S. Located in Lower Manhattan.

WORLD'S TRADE CENTER - One of the world's tallest buildings; twin towers reach 110 stories above skyline. Located on Church Street.

Niagara Falls

NIAGARA FALLS - One of the nation's natural wonders; awesome spectacle with falls dropping 200 feet in a single plunge. Located off Route 190.

Rochester

GEORGE EASTMAN HOUSE - Museum covers history of photography. A see-and-touch museum with displays on optics and color. Located at 900 East Avenue.

Saratoga Springs

NATIONAL MUSEUM OF THOROUGH-BRED RACING - Depicts history of thoroughbred racing. Also contains trappings and paintings of famous winners.

Seneca Falls

WOMEN'S HALL OF FAME - Honors women in art, athletics, business, education, government, humanities, philanthrophy and science. Located at 76 Fall Street.

Tarrytown

SLEEPY HOLLOW - Region made famous by Washington Irving. Also, British spy Major John Andre was captured here and exposed treason of Benedict Arnold.

Washingtonville

BROTHERHOOD WINERY - America's oldest winery. Wine-tasting hours available. Located on North Street.

Watkins Glen

NATIONAL MOTOR RACING MUSEUM AND HALL OF FAME - Memorabilia of motor racing past and present. Located at 110 N. Franklin.

West Point

WEST POINT - U.S. Military Academy founded in 1802 to train Army officers. Tours and accommodations available.

NORTH CAROLINA

North Carolina, the nation's largest producer of tobacco products, joined the Union in 1789 as the twelfth state. About 15 years before the turn of the 17th century, Sir Walter Raleigh established the first English settlement on Roanoke Island, which lasted only one year. His second attempt to colonize North Carolina lasted as long, and ended in a mystery. All members of the settlement disappeared for no apparent reason, creating speculation as to to what really happened to the "Lost Colony."

Early settlers were engaged in numerous Indian conflicts which eventually ended in the 1760s. This hindered the state's development, as did the density of its forests, which at that time covered nearly 60 percent of the state.

Tobacco farming in North Carolina began early and grew steadily, establishing the present base for the state's economy. North Carolina has a significant textile industry. With the Atlantic Ocean forming the eastern border of the state, tourism is another important revenue source.

State capital: Raleigh. State bird: Cardinal. State tree: Pine. State flower: Dogwood.

NORTH CAROLINA

WEATHER

The total area of North Carolina is 52,712 square miles, of which 49,142 square miles are land and 3,570 square miles are water. The range of altitude is the greatest of any state east of the Mississippi River, ranging from sea level along the Atlantic coast to 6,684 feet at the summit of Mount Mitchell, the highest peak in the eastern United States.

The most important single influence contributing to the variability of North Carolina climate is altitude. In all seasons of the year, the average temperature varies more than 20 degrees F from the lower coast to the highest elevations. The annual temperature at Southport on the lower coast is nearly as high as that of interior northern Florida, while the average on the summit of Mount Mitchell is lower than that of Buffalo, NY.

In winter, the mountain ranges partially protect the greater part of North Carolina from the frequent outbreaks of cold air which move southeastward across the Central States.

Differences in temperatures over the various parts of the state are no less pronounced in summer than in winter. The warmest days are found in the interior rather than near the coast in summer.

Average daily temperature for each month.

	Eastern	Western
Jan.	54.6 to 34.0	46.3 to 24.4
Feb.	56.9 to 35.6	49.1 to 26.1
Mar.	63.0 to 41.6	57.0 to 32.2
Apr.	72.2 to 49.8	67.9 to 41.3
May	78.5 to 57.8	76.0 to 49.7
Jun.	84.0 to 65.7	82.1 to 57.3
Jul.	87.2 to 69.9	84.5 to 61.3
Aug.	86.6 to 69.6	84.0 to 60.2
Sept.	82.0 to 64.6	79.6 to 53.8
Oct.	74.3 to 54.8	69.5 to 42.1
Nov.	65.4 to 44.1	57.7 to 32.4
Dec.	57.7 to 36.2	49.1 to 26.7
Year	71.9 to 52.0	66.9 to 42.3

STATE CHAMBER OF COMMERCE

North Carolina Citizens Association, Inc.
P.O. Box 2508
Raleigh, NC 27602
(919) 828-0758

STATE & CITY TOURISM OFFICES

State

Industrial Development Division
North Carolina Department of Commerce
430 N. Salisbury Street
Raleigh, NC 27611
(919) 733-4151

Travel Department Section
North Carolina Department of Natural &
    Economic Resources

P.O. Box 27687
Raleigh, NC 27611
(919) 733-4171

STATE HIGHWAY DEPARTMENT

Department of Transportation
1 South Wilmington Street
Raleigh, NC 27611
(919) 829-2520

HIGHWAY WELCOMING CENTERS

Kings Mountain

KINGS MOUNTAIN CENTER - Interstate 85, south, south of Gastonia.

Norlina

NORLINA CENTER - Interstate 85, north, near Virginia border.

Roanoke

ROANOKE RAPIDS CENTER - Interstate 95, north, near Virginia border.

Roland

ROLAND CENTER - Interstate 95, south.

Waynesville

WAYNESVILLE CENTER - Interstate 40.

STATE POLICE

Department of Public Safety
Raleigh, NC 27611
(919) 733-3911

HUNTING & FISHING

Hunting

Resident licenses may be obtained only by those who have resided for 6 months or have been permanently domiciled for 60 days within the state; by non-residents under 18 who are visiting their resident parent; and by non-resident members of the armed forces, their spouses, and children under 18 when stationed in this state. County licenses are limited to county residents, non-resident landowners, and non-resident servicemen and their families stationed in this state.

In general, non-resident landowners are required to possess the appropriate non-resident license prior to hunting.

A resident landowner or person leasing land primarily for cultivation, his spouse, and dependent children under 18 may hunt and trap on such land without a license. A person under 16, being a member of a resident family, may hunt under the license of his parent

HUNTING & FISHING (continued)

or guardian when in possession of the license or accompanied by the parent or guardian.

Resident

Sportsman's, $25; combination hunting and fishing, $10; statewide hunting, $7.50; county hunting, $3.50; big game, $3.50; statewide trapping, $10; county trapping, $5.

Lifetime combinations: disabled veterans, $7.50; over age 65, $10; over age 70, no charge.

Non-resident

Sportsman's, $50; annual hunting, $26; 6-day hunting, $21; landowner's county hunting, $10; big game, $15; trapping, $60.

Other licenses & permits

Primitive weapons, $5; controlled shooting preserve, $10; game lands use permit, $8; hunting guides, $5.25.

Fishing

Resident licenses may be obtained only by those who have resided within the state for 6 months; those who have been permanently domiciled within the state for 60 days; or by non-resident members of the armed forces, their spouses and children under 18 when such members of the armed forces are stationed in this state. A county license may be used only in the county of residence.

The following exemptions to the license requirements are noted: (1) persons under 16 years of age are exempted from fishing license requirements, (2) a landowner or person leasing land primarily for cultivation, his spouse and dependent children under 18 may fish on such land without a license, (3) a resident may fish with natural bait in his county of residence without an ordinary hook-and-line fishing license. This exemption does not apply to the special trout license or the game lands use permit. The game lands use permit is not required to fish on the central or eastern game lands or in any waters not designated as trout waters.

Resident

Sportsman's, $25; combination hunting and fishing, $10; statewide fishing, $7.50; state 3-day fishing, $3; county fishing, $3.50; trout waters, $3.25; special device personal use, $3; special device nonpersonal use, $10.

Lifetime licenses: disabled veterans, $7.50; over age 65, $10; over age 70, no charge; blind, no charge; totally disabled persons, no charge.

Non-resident

Sportsman's, $50; annual fishing, $12.50; 3-day fishing, $5.50; trout waters, $6.25; special device personal use, $10; special device nonpersonal use, $25.

Game lands use permit, $8.

For more information contact:

Wildlife Resources Commission
Raleigh, NC 27611
(919) 733-7123

CAMPGROUNDS

Private

Ashville

TANGLEWOOD KOA KAMPGROUND
(704) 686-3121
LOCATION: U.S. 70 east.
FACILITIES: Open Apr. - Nov.; 200 sites; water and bathroom facilities; sanitary station; electrical hookup; trailer village vehicle sites; laundry; food service; swimming; boating; fishing; hiking; tent camping.

Brevard

LITTLE RIVER CAMPING RESORT
(704) 877-4475
LOCATION: 12 mi. east of Brevard off U.S. 64.
FACILITIES: Open May 15 - Sept. 4; 240 sites; water and bathroom facilities; sanitary station; electrical hookup; trailer village vehicle sites; laundry; food service; swimming; boating; fishing; hiking; tent camping.

Burnsville

MOUNTAIN WILDERNESS
(704) 682-3244
LOCATION: Hwy. 197.
FACILITIES: Open year round; 240 sites; water and bathroom facilities; sanitary station; electrical hookup; trailer village vehicle sites; laundry; food service; swimming; boating; fishing; hiking; tent camping.

Charlotte

FROG CREEK
(704) 588-2600
LOCATION: At Carowinds, I-77 south.
FACILITIES: Open year round; 210 sites; water and bathroom facilities; sanitary station; electrical hookup; trailer village vehicle sites; laundry; food service; swimming; hiking; tent camping.

Cherokee

CHEROKEE KOA KAMPGROUND
(704) 497-9151
LOCATION: 7 mi. north of Cherokee on Big Cove Road.
FACILITIES: Open Mar. 1 - Nov. 15; 212 sites; water and bathroom facilities; electrical hookup; trailer village vehicle sites; swimming; fishing; tent camping.

HOLIDAY INN-TRAV-L-PARK
(704) 497-9109
LOCATION: 3 mi. east of Cherokee on Hwy. 19.
FACILITIES: Open Mar. - Nov.; 347 sites; water and bathroom facilities; sanitary station; electrical hookup; trailer village vehicle

NORTH CAROLINA

CAMPGROUNDS (continued)

sites; laundry; food service; swimming; boating; fishing; hiking; tent camping.

RAMADA CAMP INN
(704) 497-9711
LOCATION: 6 mi. north of Cherokee on Big Cove Road.
FACILITIES: Open Apr. 1 - Jan. 15; 320 sites; water and bathroom facilities; sanitary station; electrical hookup; trailer village vehicle sites; laundry; food service; swimming; fishing; hiking; tent camping.

Conover

NEW LAKE HICKORY CAMPGROUND
(704) 256-8615
LOCATION: Route 4, off Route 16.
FACILITIES: Open year round; 250 sites; water and bathroom facilities; sanitary station; electrical hookup; trailer village vehicle sites; laundry; food service; swimming; boating; fishing; hiking; tent camping.

Denver

CROSS COUNTRY CAMPGROUND
(704) 483-5897
LOCATION: Hwy. 150, 1½ mi. off Hwy. 16, 8 mi. off I-77.
FACILITIES: Open year round; 400 sites; water and bathroom facilities; sanitary station; electrical hookup; trailer village vehicle sites; laundry; food service; swimming; fishing; hiking.

HOLIDAYLAND
(704) 483-5746
LOCATION: 18 mi. north of Charlotte on Hwy. 16.
FACILITIES: Open year round; 250 sites; water and bathroom facilities; sanitary station; electrical hookup; trailer village vehicle sites; food service; swimming; boating; fishing; hiking; tent camping.

Elizabethtown

CLEARWATER CAMPGROUND
(919) 862-3365
LOCATION: In Elizabethtown.
FACILITIES: Open Apr. - Oct.; 275 sites; water and bathroom facilities; electrical hookup; trailer village vehicle sites; swimming; fishing; tent camping.

Ellerbe

ELLERBE SPRINGS FAMILY CAMP-
GROUND
(919) 652-5600
LOCATION: 1 mi. north of Ellerbe on U.S. 220.
FACILITIES: Open year round; 200 sites; water and bathroom facilities; sanitary station; electrical hookup; trailer village vehicle sites; laundry; food service; swimming; boating; fishing; hiking; tent camping.

Emerald Isle

HOLIDAY INN TRAV-L-PARK

(919) 326-3010
LOCATION: ½ mi. after Cameron Langston Bridge on Hwy. 58.
FACILITIES: Open year round; 216 sites; water and bathroom facilities; sanitary station; electrical hookup; trailer village vehicle sites; food service; swimming; boating; fishing; hiking; tent camping.

Hatteras

SURF-N-SOUND
(919) 986-2505
LOCATION: 3 mi. north of Hatteras on Hwy. 12.
FACILITIES: Open Apr. - Dec.; 250 sites; water and bathroom facilities; sanitary station; electrical hookup; laundry; food service; swimming; boating; fishing; tent camping.

Littleton

AMERICAN HERITAGE
(919) 586-4121
LOCATION: 17 mi. west of I-95 exit on U.S. 158.
FACILITIES: Open year round; 200 sites; water and bathroom facilities; sanitary station; electrical hookup; trailer village vehicle sites; laundry; food service; swimming; boating; fishing; hiking; tent camping.

Maggie Valley

PRESLEY'S CAMPGROUND
(704) 926-1904
LOCATION: On U.S. 19.
FACILITIES: Open Apr. 15 - Oct. 25; 306 sites; water and bathroom facilities; sanitary station; electrical hookup; trailer village vehicle sites; laundry; food service; swimming; fishing; hiking; tent camping.

Manteo

SANDPIPERS TRACE, LTD.
(919) 473-3471
LOCATION: 3 mi. west on U.S. 64.
FACILITIES: Open year round; 200 sites; water and bathroom facilities; sanitary station; electrical hookup; trailer village vehicle sites; laundry; food service; swimming; boating; fishing; hiking; tent camping.

Mooresville

PIER MARINA
(704) 663-4225
LOCATION: Hwy. 150 west.
FACILITIES: Open year round; 215 sites; water and bathroom facilities; sanitary station; electrical hookup; trailer village vehicle sites; food service; swimming; boating; fishing; hiking; tent camping.

Morehead City

SALTER PRATH FAMILY CAMPGROUND
(919) 726-2710
LOCATION: ½ mi. west of Salter Prath.
FACILITIES: Open Mar. 20 - Nov. 1; 200 sites; water and bathroom facilities; sanitary station; electrical hookup; trailer village vehicle sites; food service; swimming; boating; fishing; hiking; tent camping.

CAMPGROUNDS (continued)

Rodanthe

CAPE HATTERAS KOA KAMPGROUND
(919) 987-2250
LOCATION: 1 mi. south of Rodanthe on
Hwy. 12.
FACILITIES: Open Mar. - Dec.; 196 sites; water and bathroom facilities; sanitary station;
electrical hookup; trailer village vehicle sites;
laundry; food service; swimming; fishing; tent
camping.

HOLIDAY INN TRAV-L-PARK
(919) 987-2307
LOCATION: Hwy. 12, Hatteras Island.
FACILITIES: Open Mar. 15 - Dec. 1; 250
sites; water and bathroom facilities; sanitary
station; electrical hookup; trailer village vehicle sites; laundry; food service; swimming;
boating; fishing; hiking; tent camping.

Salisbury

TOMAHAWK - CRAZY HORSE CAMP-
GROUND
(704) 636-7848
LOCATION: 9½ mi. southeast of Salisbury
on Stokes Ferry Road, to St. Matthews
Church Road, then left.
FACILITIES: Open year round; 189 sites; water and bathroom facilities; sanitary station;
electrical hookup; trailer village vehicle sites;
laundry; food service; swimming; boating;
fishing; tent camping.

Sherrills Ford

WILDLIFE WOODS CAMPGROUND
(704) 486-5611
LOCATION: Hwy. 150, 2 mi. east of Hwy.
16 on Lake Norman.
FACILITIES: Open year round; 300 sites; water and bathroom facilities; sanitary station;
electrical hookup; trailer village vehicle sites;
laundry; food service; swimming; boating;
fishing; hiking; tent camping.

White Lake

CAMP CLEARWATER
(919) 862-3365
LOCATION: On Route 1515, ½ mi. north of
Route 53.
FACILITIES: Open year round; 350 sites; water and bathroom facilities; sanitary station;
electrical hookup; trailer village vehicle sites;
laundry; food service; swimming; boating;
fishing; hiking; tent camping.

RESORTS & BEACHES

Kitty Hawk

OUTER BANKS AREA - On sunny, sandy
beaches that stretch 100 miles or more along
the Atlantic coast, you can surf, sail, swim or
just relax and watch the sea gulls circle overhead. Then, when the spirit moves you, ride
the sand dunes at Jockey's Ridge, highest on
the east coast, or visit the Wright Brothers
Memorial.

Shallotte

SOUTH BRUNSWICK ISLAND AREA - With
the Gulf Stream only 30 miles away, the
beaches are a subtropical delight nearly every
day of the year. You can golf, play tennis,
fish from a pier or sample the fare at all 20
seafood restaurants in the nearby fishing village of Calabash, "the Seafood Capital of the
World."

Wilmington

WRIGHTSVILLE BEACH AREA - Stroll
white sandy beaches, sun-bathe, swim, fish in
the surf or rent a small boat and go sailing.
Then visit nearby historic Wilmington, where
the charm of a bygone era has been recreated.

BOATING AREAS

Asheville

LAKE LURE
LOCATION: 20 mi. east of Asheville.
FACILITIES: Launching.

Davidson

LAKE NORMAN
LOCATION: Near Davidson.
FACILITIES: Launching.

Elizabethtown

WHITE LAKE
LOCATION: Near Elizabethtown.
FACILITIES: Launching.

Fontana Dam

FONTANA LAKE
LOCATION: Near Fontana Dam.
FACILITIES: Launching.

Gaston

LAKE GASTON
LOCATION: Near Gaston.
FACILITIES: Launching.

Henderson

KERR LAKE
LOCATION: Near Henderson.
FACILITIES: Launching.

New Holland

LAKE MATTAMUSKEET
LOCATION: Near New Holland.
FACILITIES: Launching.

Roxboro

HYCO LAKE (Carolina Power Lake)
LOCATION: 10 mi. west of Roxboro.
FACILITIES: Launching.

Salisbury

HIGH ROCK LAKE
LOCATION: Near Salisbury.
FACILITIES: Launching.

NORTH CAROLINA

BICYCLE TRAILS

No information was available on Bicycle Trails in North Carolina.

TRAILS

Canton

BILTMORE CAMPUS TRAIL - 1 mi. foot trail. This trail, located within 30 miles of Asheville, departs from the Cradle of Forestry Visitor Center. It crosses U.S. 276 through a tunnel under the highway, makes a loop through the forest and returns to the tunnel and terminates at the Visitor Center parking lot. Featured along the trail are two historic buildings, circa 1880s and 1896, four reconstructed buildings and an open blacksmith shop. The trail surface is blacktopped. The buildings are furnished in the 1906 style and are open to the public.

Providence

BOB'S CREEK TRAIL - 8 mi. foot trail. This trail consists of an 8-mile loop and a 3.5-mile loop and leads to and through a 500-acre pocket wilderness area adjoining timber lands. Hardwood forests, dense laurel thickets, small waterfalls, rock formations, and numerous species of woodland plants and wild flowers can be viewed along the trail.

SKI AREAS

Banner Elk

BEECH MOUNTAIN
Banner Elk, NC 28604
(704) 387-4231
LOCATION: Near Banner Elk.
FACILITIES: 5 chairlifts; 2 J-bars; 3 tow ropes; ski instruction; ski rental; nursery; 809 ft. vertical drop; restaurants; lodging.

SUGAR MOUNTAIN
Banner Elk, NC 28604
(704) 898-4521
LOCATION: Off Route 184.
FACILITIES: 3 chairlifts; 1 T-bar; 1 tow rope; ski instruction; ski rental; nursery; 1200 ft. vertical drop; restaurants; lodging.

Blowing Rock

APPALACHIAN SKI MOUNTAIN
Blowing Rock, NC 28605
(704) 245-7951
LOCATION: Off U.S. 321.
FACILITIES: 2 double chairlifts; 3 tow ropes; ski instruction; ski rental; 336 ft. vertical drop; restaurants; lodging.

HOUND EARS
Blowing Rock, NC 28605
(704) 963-4321
LOCATION: Near Blowing Rock.
FACILITIES: 1 double chairlift; 200 ft. vertical drop; restaurants; lodging.

Boone

MILL RIDGE
Boone, NC 28607
(704) 963-4500
LOCATION: Near Boone.
FACILITIES: 1 double chairlift; ski instruction; ski rental; 225 ft. vertical drop; restaurants; lodging.

SEVEN DEVILS
Boone, NC 28607
(704) 963-5702
LOCATION: Off Route 105.
FACILITIES: 1 chairlift; 2 tow ropes; ski instruction; ski rental; 607 ft. vertical drop; restaurants; lodging.

Maggie Valley

CATALOOCHEE SKI SLOPES
Maggie Valley, NC 28751
(704) 926-0285
LOCATION: On U.S. 19.
FACILITIES: 1 double chairlift; 1 T-bar; 2 tow ropes; ski instruction; ski rental; 740 ft. vertical drop; restaurants; lodging.

Mars Hill

WOLF LAUREL
Mars Hill, NC 28754
(704) 689-4111
LOCATION: Off U.S. 23.
FACILITIES: 1 chairlift; 1 T-bar; 1 tow rope; ski instruction; ski rental; 700 ft. vertical drop; restaurants; lodging.

Roaring Gap

HIGH MEADOWS
Roaring Gap, NC 28668
(919) 363-2221
LOCATION: Near Roaring Gap.
FACILITIES: 2 tow ropes; ski instruction; ski rental; 80 ft. vertical drop; restaurants; lodging.

Sapphire Valley

SAPPHIRE VALLEY SKI AREA
Sapphire, NC 28774
(704) 743-3441
LOCATION: Off U.S. 64.
FACILITIES: 1 chairlift; 1 tow rope; ski instruction; ski rental; 325 ft. vertical drop; restaurants; lodging.

AMUSEMENT PARKS & ATTRACTIONS

Asheville

ASHEVILLE RECREATION PARK & ZOO
Old Swannanoa Road
Asheville, NC 28805
(704) 298-4311
FACILITIES: 8 major rides; 4 kiddie rides; 5 games; refreshment stand; arcade; shooting gallery; picnic facilities; zoo; free gate; free parking; open May 30 - Labor Day.

NORTH CAROLINA

AMUSEMENT PARKS (continued)

Carolina Beach

BLOCKADE RUNNER MUSEUM
U.S. 421
North Carolina Beach
Carolina Beach, NC 28428
(919) 458-5746
FACILITIES: Museum; exhibits; picnic facilities.

SEA SHORE AMUSEMENT PARK
Boardwalk
Carolina Beach, NC 28428
(919) 458-8781
FACILITIES: 9 major rides; 4 kiddie rides; arcade; open Mar. - Labor Day.

Charlotte

CAROWINDS
P.O. Box 15514
Charlotte, NC 28210
(704) 588-2600
FACILITIES: 20 major rides; 6 kiddie rides; 20 refreshment stands; 7 restaurants; arcade; shooting gallery; exhibits; stage shows; pay gate; pay parking; open Memorial Day - Labor Day; weekends: Apr., May, & Sept.

Cherokee

FRONTIERLAND
U.S. 19
Cherokee, NC 28719
(704) 497-4311
FACILITIES: 11 major rides; 9 kiddie rides; refreshment stand; restaurant; arcade; museum; picnic facilities; stage shows; pay parking; free parking; open May 20 - Sept. 4; weekends: Sept.

Elizabethtown

CRYSTAL BEACH
White Lake
Elizabethtown, NC 28337
(919) 862-4326
FACILITIES: 9 major rides; 5 kiddie rides; fun house; walk thru; 300 games; 4 refreshment stands; 2 restaurants; beach; arcade; sightseeing boat; fishing; picnic facilities; miniature golf; orchestras; free acts; free gate; pay parking; open Easter - Sept. 30.

Maggie Valley

GHOST TOWN IN THE SKY
U.S. 19
Maggie Valley, NC 28751
(704) 926-1140
FACILITIES: 10 major rides; 9 kiddie rides; 3 refreshment stands; restaurant; arcade; shooting gallery; museum; exhibits; picnic facilities; Western Town; theater; Mountaineer Town; Mining Town; gun fights; saloon shows; Country and Western shows; Indian village; pay gate; free parking; open May 6 - Oct. 29.

New Bern

TYRON PALACE RESTORATION COMPLEX (Attraction)

613 Pollock Street
New Bern, NC 28560
(919) 638-5109
FACILITIES: 3 historic restoration houses; guided tours; museum; exhibits; gardens; pay gate; free parking; open all year.

STATE FAIR

North Carolina State Fair
1025 Blue Ridge Blvd.
Raleigh, NC 27607
(919) 733-2145
DATE: October

NATIONAL PARKS

See TENNESSEE, National Parks, Great Smokey Mountain National Park.

NATIONAL FORESTS

National Forests
Southern Region
1720 Peachtree Road, NW
Atlanta, GA 30309
(404) 881-4177

Asheville

CROATAN NATIONAL FOREST
ATTRACTIONS: Historic New Bern, founded 1710; Civil War breastworks; deer, bear, turkey, quail, migratory bird hunting; fishing; boating; swimming.
FACILITIES: 2 camp and picnic sites, 2 picnic only; 2 swimming sites; resorts and motels nearby.
NEARBY TOWNS: Goldsboro, Morehead City, New Bern, Wilmington.

NANTAHALA NATIONAL FOREST
ATTRACTIONS: 60 miles of Appalachian Trail; European wild boar, deer, turkey, bird hunting; bass, trout fishing; hiking; swimming; boating; scenic drives.
FACILITIES: 19 camp and picnic sites, 10 picnic only; swimming site.
NEARBY TOWNS: Bryson City, Franklin, Hayesville, Highlands, Murphy, Robbinsville.

PISGAH NATIONAL FOREST
ATTRACTIONS: Mount Mitchell, 6,684 feet, highest point east of the Mississippi; deer, bear, small-game hunting; purple rhododendron; trout, bass, perch fishing; hiking; horseback riding; swimming; scenic roads and trails.
FACILITIES: 6 camp and picnic sites, 9 picnic only; 4 swimming sites; resorts and cabins available nearby.
NEARBY TOWNS: Brevard, Burnsville, Canton, Hot Springs, Lenoir, Marion, Waynesville.

UWHARRIE NATIONAL FOREST
ATTRACTIONS: Hunting in Uwharrie Wildlife Management Area; fishing in Uwharrie River and Badin Lake.
FACILITIES: Camp and picnic site.
NEARBY TOWNS: Asheboro, Troy, Albemarle.

NORTH CAROLINA
STATE PARKS

Headquarters

Division of Parks and Recreation
P.O. Box 27687
Raleigh, NC 27687
(919) 733-5133

Albemarle

MORROW MOUNTAIN STATE PARK
LOCATION: 7 mi. east of Albemarle.
FACILITIES: Open year round; 106 sites; water and bathroom facilities; sanitary station; trailer village vehicle sites; cabins; picnic area; food service; swimming; boating; fishing; hiking; horseback riding; tent camping.

Carolina Beach

CAROLINA BEACH STATE PARK
LOCATION: 1 mi. northwest of Carolina Beach.
FACILITIES: Open year round; 70 sites; water and bathroom facilities; sanitary station; trailer village vehicle sites; picnic area; food service; boating; fishing; hiking; tent camping.

Creswell

PETTIGREW STATE PARK
LOCATION: 9 mi. south of Creswell.
FACILITIES: Open year round; 13 sites; water and bathroom facilities; trailer village vehicle sites; picnic area; boating; boat rental; fishing; hiking; tent camping.

Elizabethtown

JONES LAKE STATE PARK
LOCATION: 4 mi. north of Elizabethtown.
FACILITIES: Open year round; 18 sites; water and bathroom facilities; trailer village vehicle sites; picnic area; food service; swimming; boating; fishing; hiking; tent camping.

Goldsboro

CLIFFS OF THE NEUSE STATE PARK
LOCATION: 14 mi. southeast of Goldsboro.
FACILITIES: Open year round; 35 sites; water and bathroom facilities; sanitary station; trailer village vehicle sites; picnic area; food service; swimming; boat rental; fishing; tent camping.

Raleigh

WILLIAM B. UMSTEAD STATE PARK
LOCATION: 10 mi. northwest of Raleigh.
FACILITIES: Open year round; 28 sites; water and bathroom facilities; trailer village vehicle sites; picnic area; boat rental; fishing; hiking; tent camping.

Winston-Salem

HANGING ROCK STATE PARK
LOCATION: 32 mi. north of Winston-Salem.
FACILITIES: Open year round; 74 sites; water and bathroom facilities; trailer village vehicle sites; cabins; picnic area; food service; swimming; boat rental; fishing; hiking; tent camping.

STATE FORESTS

Forest Service
1512 Salisbury
Raleigh, NC 27611
(919) 733-2162

Clayton

CLEMMONS STATE FOREST
(919) 553-5651
LOCATION: 1 mi. west of Clayton.
FACILITIES: Open year round; water and bathroom facilities; trailer village vehicle sites; picnic area; hiking; tent camping.

Hendersonville

HOLMES STATE FOREST
(704) 692-0100
LOCATION: 1.7 mi. east of Transylvania County line.
FACILITIES: Open year round; water and bathroom facilities; trailer village vehicle sites; hiking; tent camping.

Lenoir

TUTTLE STATE FOREST
(704) 758-5645
LOCATION: 1 mi. west of Route 18.
FACILITIES: Open year round; water and bathroom facilities; trailer village vehicle sites; hiking; tent camping.

HISTORIC SITES

Bath

BATH - The oldest town in North Carolina was settled in 1696 and was the first meeting place of the state's colonial assembly. St. Thomas Episcopal Church is the oldest church building in the state that has been in continuous use.

Concord

CONCORD - The first gold nugget discovered in America was found near Concord in 1799 by 12-year-old Conrad Reed at what became the Reed Mine. North Carolina was the nation's foremost gold-mining state until 1850.

Flat Rock

CARL SANDBURG'S HOME (CONNEMARA) - Poet and Lincoln biographer chose nearby Flat Rock for his retirement home, a 240-acre farm near the Flat Rock Playhouse.

Henderson

ASHLAND PLANTATION - In this home, Colonel Henderson, in violation of the orders of King George III, commissioned Daniel Boone to explore territory which is now eastern Tennessee and Kentucky. Located 3 mi. northeast of Henderson.

HISTORIC SITES (continued)

Hertford

OLDEST HOUSE - North of Edenton off U.S. 17 is what historians believe to be the oldest house in North Carolina.

Kitty Hawk

KITTY HAWK - In 1900 Orville and Wilbur Wright began glider experiments that led to the first powered flight on December 17, 1903. Dominating the area is Wright Brothers National Memorial, with its monument rising from the crest of Kill Devil Hill. You will also see the launching apparatus, the hanger and the living quarters of the Wrights. A museum deals with the early history of the Wright Brothers and includes a life size replica of the Kitty Hawk.

Manteo

FORT RALEIGH - Site of first English colony in America established by Sir Water Raleigh in 1585; also the "lost colony" because settlers had disappeared by 1590. Restored fort and gravestone of Virginia Dare, first English child born in the New World.

Old Salem

OLD SALEM - A serene reminder of what life was like in a Moravian congregation town some 200 years ago. Historic Salem Tavern once provided food and lodging for George Washington.

Pineville

JAMES K. POLK BIRTHPLACE - Memorial to the 11th President, a reconstructed and furnished log house. Events in Polk's life are depicted at the site in Visitor Center exhibits and a film program.

Southport

FORT FISHER MUSEUM - See items salvaged from Confederate blockade runners. Take the Southport-Fort Fisher Ferry across the Cape Fear River to reach the museum.

Statesville

FORT DOBBS - Named for Royal Governor Arthur Dobbs, it was built in 1756 to protect western settlers from hostile Indians. The outpost was abandoned in 1764 as settlements extended further westward.

HOSTELS

Bryson City

NANTAHALA OUTDOOR CENTER
Star Route Box 68
Bryson City, NC 28713
(704) 488-6407
FACILITIES: Open year round; 6 beds, men;

modern bathroom; overnight charges: $3; motel rooms available for families; houseparents: John Payson & Aurelia Kennedy.

POINTS OF INTEREST

Asheville

BILTMORE HOUSE - Stately mansion built by George Vanderbilt is the world's largest private home and one of the most imposing structures in the world, reflecting the inspiration of the noted French Renaissance chateaux, Chenonceaux, Blois and Chambord.

BLUE RIDGE PARKWAY - Along the eastern edge of the city of Asheville passes the Blue Ridge Parkway, a balcony from which you may enjoy an uninterrupted view of the vastness of the Southern Appalachian Mountains. South from Asheville on the Parkway, turn east at Wagon Road Gap. Down this steep, winding road lies the Cradle of Forestry where the first school of forestry was begun.

THOMAS WOLFE MEMORIAL - As a youth, Wolfe lived in a boarding house operated by his mother, which became "Dixieland" in his classic novel, "Look Homeward, Angel."

Bailey

DOCTORS' MUSEUM - Tribute to country family doctors who fought ignorance, as well as disease and death, with crude instruments and large doses of courage. Medical antiques dating from 1700 to 1900.

Cape Hatteras

CAPE HATTERAS LIGHTHOUSE - Tallest in the country, this 208-foot lighthouse warns ships away from Diamond Shoals, the "graveyard of the Atlantic."

Charlotte

CHARLOTTE NATURE MUSEUM - One of the finest children's nature museums in the country; special attractions include a planetarium, motion-picture showings and classes for adults and children alike, tamed wild animals, and "Century III," an exhibit depicting the history of Charlotte and Mecklenburg County from 1500 A.D. to the present. Located at 1658 Sterling Road.

Cherokee

OCONALUFTEE VILLAGE - A vivid reminder of what life was like among the Cherokee 250 years ago is provided by Oconaluftee Indian Village on the reservation. The village contains structures of woven cane and clay used by the earliest Cherokee. Also here are dirt-floored cabins introduced by white traders.

Linville

GRANDFATHER MOUNTAIN - Highest in the Blue Ridge Range at 5,964 feet, it is be-

NORTH CAROLINA

POINTS OF INTEREST (continued)

lieved to be one of the oldest rock formations in the world. Also famous mile-high swinging bridge nearby. Located near Linville.

Pinehurst

THE WORLD GOLF HALL OF FAME - Among the items of interest is the gallery featuring the clubs and photographs of the golfing heads of state. In this exhibit are President Eisenhower's favorite putter engraved with his signature and five stars, his brown-and-white golf shoes, and the golf cart that he used.

Other features include several collections of golf artifacts and the portraits of the golfing greats who have been inducted into the Golf Hall of Fame. Located adjacent to Pinehurst Number Two course.

Winston-Salem

JOSEPH SCHLITZ BREWING COMPANY - Facility is the largest plant under one roof in North Carolina and produces over 4 million barrels of beer annually.

R.J. REYNOLDS TOBACCO COMPANY - One of the world's largest tobacco manufacturing firms. Offers free guided tours of its facilities.

NORTH DAKOTA

North Dakota, where farming is big business, joined the Union in 1889 as the thirty-ninth state. In the period from 1857 to 1878, a number of forts were built to protect the newly arriving settlers from disgruntled Indians. By the early 1880s, however most of the Indians were resettled on reservations and the hostilities subsided.

The largest influx of settlers in North Dakota was prompted by the Homestead Act, which granted 160 acres free to anyone, who would settle and work the land for five years.

Today, the state's farms, which are highly mechanized and nearly two-and-one-half times larger than the average American farm, produce abundant crops of wheat (second only to the state of Kansas), rye, potatoes, feed corn and barley.

The cattle industry also produces a sizeable income for the state, as does tourism, which features excellent big game hunting and fishing.

State capital: Bismarck. State bird: Western meadowlark. State tree: American elm. State flower: Wild prairie rose.

WEATHER

North Dakota is made up of three main regions: the Red River Valley along the eastern border, the Young Drift Plains just west of this strip and, in the southwest, the Great Plains. The eastern part of the state is flat, with a gradual rise of terrain westward until an elevation of 3,468 feet is reached at Black Butte in the southwestern part of the state.

North Dakota has a continental climate marked by wide temperature variation. The annual mean temperature ranges from about 36 degrees F in the northeast to 43 degrees F in the south. Temperatures can range from 60 degrees below zero in winter to 120 degrees F in summer. Hot winds and periods of prolonged high temperatures can occur, but nights are cool. Winters are long and cold.

Average daily temperature for each month.

	Northern	Southern
Jan.	11.4 to --7.9	17.5 to --3.9
Feb.	19.1 to --1.7	24.1 to 2.4
Mar.	30.7 to 11.0	35.0 to 13.8
Apr.	50.2 to 28.2	53.2 to 29.6
May	65.4 to 39.5	67.4 to 41.1
Jun.	75.4 to 50.3	76.3 to 51.7
Jul.	80.9 to 54.7	83.7 to 56.3
Aug.	79.9 to 53.0	83.6 to 54.7
Sept.	67.4 to 41.9	70.7 to 43.2
Oct.	55.6 to 31.8	59.5 to 33.4
Nov.	33.6 to 16.2	38.9 to 18.0
Dec.	19.3 to 1.3	24.6 to 4.5
Year	49.1 to 26.5	52.9 to 28.7

STATE CHAMBER OF COMMERCE

Greater North Dakota Association - State
   Chamber of Commerce
P.O. Box 2467
Fargo, ND 58102
(701) 237-9461

STATE & CITY TOURISM OFFICES

State

Business and Industrial Development Department
State Office Building
Bismarck, ND 58501
(701) 224-2810

North Dakota Travel Division
State Highway Department
Capitol Grounds

Bismarck, ND 58505
(701) 224-2525

STATE HIGHWAY DEPARTMENT

North Dakota Highway Department
State Highway Building
Capitol Grounds
Bismarck, ND 58505
(701) 224-2500

HIGHWAY WELCOMING CENTERS

Apple Creek

APPLE CREEK CENTER - Interstate 94, at Bismarck.

Beach

BEACH CENTER - Interstate 94.

Painted Canyon

PAINTED CANYON OVERLOOK WELCOME CENTER - Painted Canyon entrance.

Pempina

PEMPINA CENTER - Canadian border.

STATE POLICE

Department of Public Safety
Bismarck, ND 58505
(701) 224-2500

HUNTING & FISHING

Hunting

License to hunt and fish in the state is required for: residents 16 years of age or older; non-residents 12 years of age or older; and resident and non-resident servicemen.

To qualify for a resident's license, a person must reside in the state of North Dakota for 6 months prior to application.

Resident

General game license 1, $1; small-game stamp, $5; deer bow stamp, $10; antelope bow stamp, $10; furbearer (trapping) license, $5.

Non-resident

General game license 1, $1; small-game stamp (additional to license required for waterfowl, $5) 2, $40; deer bow stamp, $30; antelope bow stamp, $30; non-game stamp 3, $15.

Fishing

See hunting regulations above.

Resident

Fishing license, $5; family fishing license (husband and wife), $8; senior citizen fishing license (65 and over), $1; totally or permanently disabled resident fishing, $1.

Non-resident

Fishing license, $10; 7-day fishing license, $2.

For more information contact:

Game and Fish Department
2121 Lavett Avenue
Bismarck, ND 58505
(701) 224-2180

CAMPGROUNDS

Private

Belfield

EXIT 10 CAMPGROUND
(701) 575-4203
LOCATION: Exit 10, I-94 and U.S. 85.
FACILITIES: Open year round; 50 sites; water and bathroom facilities; sanitary station; electrical hookup; trailer village vehicle sites; picnic area; swimming; tent camping.

Bismarck

BISMARCK KOA KAMPGROUND
(701) 255-0873
LOCATION: Exit 37, I-94, 1 mi. north.
FACILITIES: Open year round; 106 sites; water and bathroom facilities; sanitary station; electrical hookup; trailer village vehicle sites; picnic area; fishing; tent camping.

HILLCREST ACRES TRAILER PARK
(701) 223-4505
LOCATION: Exit 37, I-94, 1½ mi. south, then 1½ mi. east.
FACILITIES: Open year round; 60 sites; water and bathroom facilities; sanitary station; electrical hookup; trailer village vehicle sites; picnic area; tent camping.

Dickinson

KIMM KAMPERAMA
(701) 225-5308
LOCATION: Exit 13, I-94.
FACILITIES: Open year round; 60 sites; water and bathroom facilities; sanitary station; electrical hookup; trailer village vehicle sites; picnic area; tent camping.

KOA KAMPGROUND ON THE HEART
(701) 225-9600
LOCATION: Exit 12, I-94, 2 mi. south.
FACILITIES: Open year round; 150 sites; water and bathroom facilities; sanitary station; electrical hookup; trailer village vehicle sites; picnic area; fishing; tent camping.

NORTH DAKOTA

CAMPGROUNDS (continued)

Eckelson

SCOTTY'S KAMPSITE
(701) 646-6510
LOCATION: In Eckelson.
FACILITIES: Open year round; 60 sites; water and bathroom facilities; sanitary station; electrical hookup; trailer village vehicle sites; picnic area; swimming; fishing; tent camping.

Fargo

FARGO-MOORHEAD KOA KAMPGROUND
(218) 233-0671
LOCATION: 3 mi. east of Moorhead.
FACILITIES: Open year round; 140 sites; water and bathroom facilities; sanitary station; electrical hookup; trailer village vehicle sites; picnic area; tent camping.

Grand Forks

WEST SIDE TRAILER PARK & CAMPING
(701) 772-7165
LOCATION: 3 mi. west of Grand Forks on Hwy. 2.
FACILITIES: Open year round; 97 sites; water and bathroom facilities; sanitary station; electrical hookup; trailer village vehicle sites; picnic area; tent camping.

Hillsboro

KAMP DAKOTA
(701) 436-5760
LOCATION: Exit 104, I-29.
FACILITIES: Open year round; 46 sites; water and bathroom facilities; sanitary station; electrical hookup; trailer village vehicle sites; picnic area; tent camping.

Jamestown

BLOOM EXIT CAMPGROUND
(701) 252-5070
LOCATION: 4 mi. east of Jamestown.
FACILITIES: Open year round; 60 sites; water and bathroom facilities; sanitary station; electrical hookup; trailer village vehicle sites; picnic area; tent camping.

FRONTIER FORT CAMPGROUND
(701) 252-7492
LOCATION: Off I-94.
FACILITIES: Open year round; 48 sites; water and bathroom facilities; sanitary station; electrical hookup; trailer village vehicle sites; picnic area; tent camping.

SMOKEY'S CAMPSITE & LANDING
(701) 252-0659
LOCATION: 7 mi. north on Hwy. 281, then 2 mi. east.
FACILITIES: Open year round; 100 sites; water and bathroom facilities; electrical hookup; trailer village vehicle sites; picnic area; swimming; boating; fishing; tent camping.

Minot

FRONTIER GARDENS
(701) 838-7487

LOCATION: Route 4 and U.S. 52 east.
FACILITIES: Open year round; 66 sites; water and bathroom facilities; sanitary station; electrical hookup; trailer village vehicle sites; picnic area; tent camping.

Velva

H BAR B VALLEY RANCH
(701) 338-5931
LOCATION: West of Velva at Hwys. 52 & 41 junction.
FACILITIES: Open year round; 60 sites; sanitary station; electrical hookup; trailer village vehicle sites; swimming; tent camping.

Williston

BUFFALO TRAILS KOA KAMPGROUND
(701) 572-3206
LOCATION: 3 mi. north of Williston.
FACILITIES: Open year round; 50 sites; water and bathroom facilities; electrical hookup; trailer village vehicle sites; tent camping.

DRIFTWOOD CAMPGROUND
(701) 572-6302
LOCATION: 2 mi. west of Williston.
FACILITIES: Open year round; 50 sites; water and bathroom facilities; sanitary station; electrical hookup; trailer village vehicle sites; picnic area; tent camping.

RESORTS & BEACHES

Most of the state's resort activities center around the major lakes and include fishing, swimming, boating, water skiing, and camping. (See Boating Areas and State Parks.)

BOATING AREAS

Bismarck

LAKE OAHE
LOCATION: South of Bismarck.
FACILITIES: Launching.

Bottineau

LONG LAKE
LOCATION: Near Bottineau.
FACILITIES: Launching.

Coleharbor

LAKE AUDUBON
LOCATION: Near Coleharbor.
FACILITIES: Launching.

Devils Lake

DEVILS LAKE
LOCATION: Near Devils Lake.
FACILITIES: Launching.

Foxholm

LAKE DARLING
LOCATION: 6 mi. north of Foxholm.
FACILITIES: Launching.

BOATING AREAS (continued)

Glen Ullin

LAKE TSCHIDA
LOCATION: 15 mi. south of Glen Ullin.
FACILITIES: Launching.

Perkin

STUMP LAKE
LOCATION: Near Perkin.
FACILITIES: Launching.

Pettibone

ROUND LAKE
LOCATION: Near Pettibone.
FACILITIES: Launching.

Riverdale

LAKE SAKAKAWEA
LOCATION: Near Riverdale.
FACILITIES: Launching.

Valley City

LAKE ASHTABULA
LOCATION: 10 mi. north of Valley City.
FACILITIES: Launching.

BICYCLE TRAILS

No information was available on Bicycle Trails in North Dakota.

TRAILS

Bottineau

OLD LAKE TRAIL - 3 mi. foot trail. This nature trail, located 13 miles north of Bottineau, in Lake Metigoshe State Park, is designed for year-round use and is named for the 200-year-old Bur Oak which grows along the trail. Also found along the trail, which passes through a hilly, forest environment, are different types of vegetation, animals, birds, and insects. A half-way exit has been established for those people who do not wish to cover the total length of the trail.

SKI AREAS

Arvilla

VILLA VISTA SKI AREA
Arvilla, ND 58214
(701) 594-4234
LOCATION: Near Arvilla.
FACILITIES: 4 tow ropes; ski instruction; ski rental; 100 ft. vertical drop; longest run, 900 ft.; restaurants; lodging.

Bottineau

WINTER PARK SKI AREA
Bottineau, ND 58318
(701) 263-4556
LOCATION: Near Bottineau.
FACILITIES: 1 T-bar; 3 tow ropes; ski instruction; ski rental; 200 ft. vertical drop; longest run, 1200 ft.; restaurants; lodging.

Devils Lake

SKY-LINE SKY-WAY SKI AREA
Devils Lake, ND 58301
(701) 662-3295
LOCATION: Near Devils Lake.
FACILITIES: 1 tow rope; ski instruction; ski rental; 200 ft. vertical drop; longest run, 1200 ft.; restaurants; lodging.

Fort Ransom

FORT RANSOM SKI AREA
Fort Ransom, ND 58033
(701) 683-4834
LOCATION: Near Fort Ransom.
FACILITIES: 4 tow ropes; ski instruction; ski rental; 300 ft. vertical drop; longest run, 2640 ft.; restaurants; lodging.

Minot

TRESTLE VALLEY SKI AREA
Minot, ND 58701
(701) 839-5321
LOCATION: Near Minot.
FACILITIES: 1 T-bar; 1 platter pole; ski instruction; ski rental; 200 ft. vertical drop; longest run, 2200 ft.; restaurants; lodging.

Rolla View

ROLLA VIEW SKI AREA
Rolla View, ND 58367
LOCATION: Near Rolla View.
FACILITIES: 3 tow ropes; ski instruction; ski rental; 400 ft. vertical drop; longest run, 1200 ft.; restaurants; lodging.

Walhalla

FROST FIRE SKI AREA
Walhalla, ND 58282
(701) 549-3600
LOCATION: Near Walhalla.
FACILITIES: 3 tow ropes; ski instruction; ski rental; 400 ft. vertical drop; longest run, 2600 ft.; restaurants; lodging.

AMUSEMENT PARKS & ATTRACTIONS

Medora

ROUGH RIDE COUNTRY
P.O. Box 198
Medora, ND 58645
(701) 623-4444
FACILITIES: Walk thru; restaurant; museum; exhibits; miniature golf; zoo (native animals); trail rides through Badlands; fishing; stage shows.

NORTH DAKOTA

STATE FAIR

North Dakota State Fair
P.O. Box 1796
Minot, ND 58701
(701) 852-3113
DATE: July

NATIONAL PARKS

There are no National Parks in North Dakota.

NATIONAL FORESTS

There are no National Forests in North Dakota.

STATE PARKS

Headquarters

North Dakota Parks and Recreation
P.O. Box 139
Mandan, ND 58554
(701) 663-9571

Arvilla

TURTLE RIVER STATE PARK
LOCATION: 2 mi. north of Arvilla.
FACILITIES: Open year round; water and bathroom facilities; electrical hookup; trailer village vehicle sites; picnic area; swimming; fishing; tent camping.

Bismarck

FORT LINCOLN STATE PARK
LOCATION: 3 mi. southwest of Bismarck.
FACILITIES: Open year round; water and bathroom facilities; sanitary station; electrical hookup; trailer village vehicle sites; picnic area; fishing; tent camping.

Bottineau

LAKE METIGOSHE STATE PARK
LOCATION: 10 mi. north of Bottineau.
FACILITIES: Open year round; water and bathroom facilities; sanitary station; electrical hookup; trailer village vehicle sites; picnic area; swimming; boating; fishing; tent camping.

Bowman

BUTTE VIEW STATE PARK
LOCATION: 3 mi. north of Bowman.
FACILITIES: Open year round; water and bathroom facilities; sanitary station; electrical hookup; trailer village vehicle sites; picnic area; tent camping.

Burnstad

BEAVER LAKE STATE PARK
LOCATION: 2 mi. north of Burnstad.
FACILITIES: Open year round; water and bathroom facilities; sanitary station; electrical hookup; trailer village vehicle sites; swimming; boating; fishing; tent camping.

Garrison

FORT STEVENSON STATE PARK
LOCATION: Near Garrison.
FACILITIES: Open year round; water and bathroom facilities; trailer village vehicle sites; picnic area; swimming; boating; fishing; tent camping.

Hallson

ICELANDIC STATE PARK
LOCATION: 2 mi. north of Hallson.
FACILITIES: Open year round; water and bathroom facilities; sanitary station; electrical hookup; trailer village vehicle sites; picnic area; swimming; boating; fishing; tent camping.

Killdeer

LITTLE MISSOURI BAY STATE PARK
LOCATION: 10 mi. northeast of Killdeer.
FACILITIES: Open year round; water and bathroom facilities; picnic area; horseback riding; tent camping.

Medora

SULLY CREEK STATE PARK
LOCATION: 3 mi. south of Medora.
FACILITIES: Open year round; water and bathroom facilities; picnic area; horseback riding; tent camping.

Pick City

LAKE SAKAKAWEA STATE PARK
LOCATION: Near Pick City.
FACILITIES: Open year round; water and bathroom facilities; sanitary station; electrical hookup; trailer village vehicle sites; picnic area; swimming; boating; fishing; tent camping.

Streeter

STREETER MEMORIAL STATE PARK
LOCATION: In Streeter.
FACILITIES: Open year round; water and bathroom facilities; picnic area; swimming; boating; tent camping.

Watford City

LEWIS AND CLARK STATE PARK
LOCATION: 10 mi. north of Watford City.
FACILITIES: Open year round; water and bathroom facilities; sanitary station; electrical hookup; trailer village vehicle sites; picnic area; swimming; boating; fishing; tent camping.

Wishek

DOYLE MEMORIAL STATE PARK
LOCATION: 2 mi. southwest of Wishek.
FACILITIES: Open year round; water and bathroom facilities; picnic area; swimming; boating; fishing; tent camping.

STATE FORESTS

Forest Service
North Dakota State University and Institute
    of Forestry
Bottineau, ND 58318
(701) 263-4085

Bottineau

TURTLE MT. STATE FOREST
LOCATION: 10 mi. north of Bottineau.
FACILITIES: Open year round; water and
bathroom facilities; trailer village vehicle sites;
picnic area; swimming; hunting; fishing; hiking; tent camping.

Dunseith

HOMEN STATE FOREST
LOCATION: 10 mi. northwest of Dunseith.
FACILITIES: Open year round; water and
bathroom facilities; trailer village vehicle sites;
picnic area; boating; hunting; fishing; hiking;
tent camping.

Towner

MOUSE RIVER STATE FOREST
LOCATION: Near Towner.
FACILITIES: Open year round; water and
bathroom facilities; sanitary station; picnic
area; hunting; fishing; tent camping.

HISTORIC SITES

Devils Lake

FORT TOTTEN - Best-preserved fort of Indian Wars period; contains 15 original brick
buildings.

Medora

THEODORE ROOSEVELT NATIONAL

MEMORIAL PARK - Named in honor of 26th
President, contains original log cabin from his
ranching days in the Badlands in the 1880s.

Williston

FORT BUFORD - Sioux Indians and Chief
Sitting Bull surrendered here a short while after the Battle of Little Bighorn. Stone powder
magazine and Field Officers' quarters still
stand.

HOSTELS

There are no Hostels in North Dakota.

POINTS OF INTEREST

Bismarck

NORTH DAKOTA STATE HISTORICAL
SOCIETY MUSEUM - Outstanding collection
of Indian artifacts and other examples of
prairie history. Located on Capitol Grounds.

Dunseith

INTERNATIONAL PEACE GARDEN - A
2300-acre natural area on U.S.-Canadian border commemorates 150 years of peace between the two nations.

Jamestown

FRONTIER VILLAGE - Features world's
largest buffalo statue and reconstructed frontier buildings.

Mandan

SLANT INDIAN VILLAGE - Display of Indian homes and villages. Located in Fort Lincoln State Park.

OHIO

Ohio, the epitome of this country's midwestern ideals and ideas, joined the Union in
1803 as the seventeenth state. Indian conflicts
plagued the early settlers in the state until the
late 1700s.

Since 1835, Ohio has had two border disputes with it neighbor, Michigan, over who
owns what land along Lake Erie. The first,
settled by Congress in 1835, was in favor of
Ohio. The most recent disagreement, involving oil and natural gas rights, is still in the
courts.

During the Civil War, Ohio strongly
backed the Union cause and helped many a
runaway slave escape through the "Underground Railroad."

Major industry developed in the state following the War Between the States, and today
Ohio is a leading producer of iron and steel
products and by-products. Livestock production is another major source of the state's
revenues, as is tourism, which relies primarily
on attractive state parks and forests.

State capital: Columbus. State bird: Cardinal. State tree: Buckeye. State flower:
Scarlet carnation.

WEATHER

The topography of Ohio is greatly varied.
Less than one-half of its area is occupied by
plains, while most of eastern, and much of
southern, Ohio is hilly.

OHIO

WEATHER (continued)

Located north and west of the Appalachian Mountains, Ohio has a climate essentially continental in nature, characterized by moderate extremes of heat and cold, wetness and dryness. Summers are moderately warm and humid, although temperatures rarely exceed 100 degrees F. Winters are cold, with an average of about five days of subzero weather. Cool, dry, and invigorating weather prevails throughout most of the autumn. Variations over the state are due mainly to differences in latitude and topography, but the immediate lake shore area experiences a moderating effect due to its proximity to a large body of water.

Average daily temperature for each month.

	Northwestern	Southwestern
Jan.	33.7 to 17.5	41.2 to 21.2
Feb.	36.0 to 18.7	44.4 to 23.2
Mar.	45.0 to 26.4	53.0 to 30.7
Apr.	59.9 to 37.8	66.1 to 40.7
May	70.0 to 47.0	75.6 to 49.9
Jun.	78.5 to 56.0	83.8 to 58.6
Jul.	82.1 to 60.2	87.6 to 62.9
Aug.	80.8 to 58.5	86.8 to 61.1
Sept.	74.7 to 52.9	81.0 to 54.3
Oct.	63.9 to 42.7	70.2 to 42.8
Nov.	49.1 to 32.4	55.3 to 32.7
Dec.	37.3 to 22.4	44.5 to 25.2
Year	59.3 to 39.4	65.8 to 41.9

STATE CHAMBER OF COMMERCE

Ohio Chamber of Commerce
17 South High Street
8th Floor
Columbus, OH 43215
(614) 228-4201

STATE & CITY TOURISM OFFICES

State

Travel Bureau
Ohio Department of Economic & Community Development
30 East Broad Street
Columbus, OH 43215
(614) 466-8844

Local

Greater Cincinnati Chamber of Commerce
120 West Fifth Street
Cincinnati, OH 45202
(513) 721-3300

Cleveland Convention and Visitor's Bureau
511 Terminal Tower
Cleveland, OH 44113
(216) 621-4110

Columbus Convention and Visitor's Bureau
50 West Broad Street
Room 2540
Columbus, OH 43215
(614) 221-6623

Dayton Area Chamber of Commerce
111 West First Street, Room 200
Dayton, OH 45402
(513) 226-1444

STATE HIGHWAY DEPARTMENT

Ohio Department of Transportation
25 S. Front Street
Columbus, OH 43215
(614) 466-2335

HIGHWAY WELCOMING CENTERS

Ashtabula

ASHTABULA CENTER - Interstate 90, south.

Bellmont

BELLMONT CENTER - Interstate 70, west, near Pennsylvania border.

Preble

PREBLE CENTER - Interstate 70, east, near West Alexandria.

STATE POLICE

Department of Public Safety
Columbus, OH 43205
(614) 466-2660

HUNTING & FISHING

Hunting

A hunting and trapping license is required each year as of Sept. 1. A license is required regardless of age. Hunters under 16 years of age must be accompanied by an adult.

A hunting and trapping license is not required of persons who are: (1) members of the U.S. Armed Forces carrying current annual leave papers; (2) landowners or their children while hunting or trapping on their land; (3) tenants or managers or their children while hunting or trapping on the land where they reside.

Resident licenses are for persons who have resided in Ohio for the last 6 months preceding application for a license.

Resident

Hunting license, $4; persons 65 years of age or older, $4; deer permit, $10; turkey permit, $10.

HUNTING & FISHING (continued)

Non-resident

Hunting license, $30.

Fishing

A fishing license is required in Ohio waters, including Lake Erie, to take fish, frogs, turtles, or mussels.

A fishing license is not required of a resident who is 66 years of age or older, or a person who is: (1) less than 16 years of age; or (2) physically handicapped; or (3) fishing only in a private pond; or (4) fishing only on land and water which he or his parents own; (5) fishing only on land and water where he or his parents are tenants and on which he resides; or (6) a member of the U.S. Armed Forces.

A resident is any person who has resided in Ohio for at least 6 months just prior to applying for a license.

Resident

Annual resident license (for resident age 16 through 65), $7.

Non-resident

Annual non-resident fishing license, $14; 7-day non-resident tourist's license, $7.

For more information contact:

Division of Wildlife
Building C
Fountain Square
Columbus, OH 43224
(614) 466-7313

CAMPGROUNDS

Private

Ashtabula

HIDE-A-WAY
(216) 998-1431
LOCATION: 2020 S. Ridge West.
FACILITIES: Open May - Oct.; 300 sites; water and bathroom facilities; sanitary station; electrical hookup; trailer village vehicle sites; laundry; food service; swimming; fishing; tent camping.

Brunswick

BRUNSWICK LAKE
(216) 225-6023
LOCATION: 3466 Center Road.
FACILITIES: Open May 15 - Nov. 1; 300 sites; water and bathroom facilities; sanitary station; electrical hookup; trailer village vehicle sites; swimming; fishing; tent camping.

WILLOW LAKE PARK
(216) 225-6580
LOCATION: 2434 Substation Road.
FACILITIES: Open May - Nov.; 300 sites; water and bathroom facilities; sanitary station; electrical hookup; trailer village vehicle sites; laundry; swimming; fishing; tent camping.

Cadiz

SALLIE BUFFALO PARK
(614) 942-3213
LOCATION: 1 mi. south on Route 9.
FACILITIES: Open year round; 1300 sites; water and bathroom facilities; sanitary station; electrical hookup; trailer village vehicle sites; boating; fishing; tent camping.

Caledonia

RIVER BEND PARK
(614) 389-4179
LOCATION: 7 mi. east of Marion off Route 95 at South Caledonia.
FACILITIES: Open Apr. - Nov.; 467 sites; water and bathroom facilities; sanitary station; electrical hookup; trailer village vehicle sites; laundry; food service; swimming; boating; fishing; tent camping.

Canal Fulton

CLAY'S PARK RESORT
(216) 854-3961
LOCATION: 13185 Patterson Road.
FACILITIES: Open year round; 1200 sites; water and bathroom facilities; sanitary station; electrical hookup; trailer village vehicle sites; food service; swimming; boating; fishing; horseback riding; tent camping.

Champion

WILLOW LAKE PARK CLUB
(216) 847-8614
LOCATION: 6863 Mahoning Ave. northwest.
FACILITIES: Open May - Oct.; 600 sites; water and bathroom facilities; sanitary station; electrical hookup; trailer village vehicle sites; swimming; tent camping.

East Rochester

PARADISE LAKE PARK
(216) 525-7726
LOCATION: 6940 Rochester Road.
FACILITIES: Open Apr. - Nov.; 750 sites; water and bathroom facilities; sanitary station; electrical hookup; trailer village vehicle sites; laundry; food service; swimming; boating; fishing; tent camping.

Galena

BERKSHIRE LAKE
(614) 965-2321
LOCATION: 1848 Alexander Road.
FACILITIES: Open Apr. - Nov.; 400 sites; water and bathroom facilities; sanitary station; electrical hookup; trailer village vehicle sites; food service; swimming; fishing; tent camping.

Geneva-On-The-Lake

INDIAN CREEK CAMPING, INC.
(216) 466-8191
LOCATION: Lake Road East.
FACILITIES: Open year round; 410 sites; water and bathroom facilities; sanitary station;

OHIO

CAMPGROUNDS (continued)

electrical hookup; trailer village vehicle sites; laundry; swimming; boating; fishing; tent camping.

Grover Hill

BLUE WATER CAMP
(419) 587-3433
LOCATION: 3 mi. east of Grover Hill.
FACILITIES: Open year round; 300 sites; water and bathroom facilities; sanitary station; electrical hookup; trailer village vehicle sites; swimming; boating; fishing; tent camping.

Hillsboro

BABINGTON CAMPING AREA
(513) 466-2323
LOCATION: 8 mi. southeast of Hillsboro off Route 124, then 3 mi. northeast of Marshall off Route 506.
FACILITIES: Open Apr. 15 - Nov. 1; 320 sites; water and bathroom facilities; sanitary station; electrical hookup; trailer village vehicle sites; laundry; boating; fishing; tent camping.

Kings Mills

KINGS ISLAND CAMPING
(513) 398-2901
LOCATION: In Kings Mills.
FACILITIES: Open year round; 300 sites; water and bathroom facilities; sanitary station; electrical hookup; trailer village vehicle sites; laundry; food service; swimming; tent camping.

Lakeside

FORT FIRELANDS
(419) 734-1237
LOCATION: 5800 E. Harbor Road.
FACILITIES: Open May 1 - Oct. 31; 300 sites; water and bathroom facilities; sanitary station; electrical hookup; trailer village vehicle sites; food service; swimming; boating; hunting; fishing; horseback riding; tent camping.

Loudonville

OCTOBER HILL
(419) 994-4828
LOCATION: 9 mi. south of Loudonville on Wally Road.
FACILITIES: Open Apr. - Nov.; 1000 sites; water and bathroom facilities; sanitary station; electrical hookup; trailer village vehicle sites; laundry; food service; swimming; boating; fishing; horseback riding; bicycle trail; tent camping.

ROSE-LINN CAMP
(419) 994-3691
LOCATION: 6 mi. south of Loudonville on Route 3.
FACILITIES: Open May - Nov.; 500 sites; water and bathroom facilities; sanitary station; electrical hookup; trailer village vehicle sites; laundry; food service; swimming; boating; fishing; tent camping.

Louisville

SUNSET TRAILER PARK
(216) 935-2733
LOCATION: 8000 Edison Avenue.
FACILITIES: Open year round; 400 sites; water and bathroom facilities; sanitary station; electrical hookup; trailer village vehicle sites; laundry; food service; tent camping.

Mantua

ROUNDUP LAKE PARK
(216) 562-6500
LOCATION: 3392 Route 82.
FACILITIES: Open year round; 500 sites; water and bathroom facilities; sanitary station; electrical hookup; trailer village vehicle sites; laundry; food service; swimming; boating; fishing; tent camping.

Mifflin

CHARLES MILL LAKE PARK
(419) 368-6885
LOCATION: ½ mi. west of Mifflin.
FACILITIES: Open year round; 527 sites; water and bathroom facilities; sanitary station; electrical hookup; trailer village vehicle sites; swimming; boating; hunting; fishing; tent camping.

Mount Sterling

CROWNOVER MILL
(614) 869-3519
LOCATION: ½ mi. east of Deer Dam on Crownover Mill Road.
FACILITIES: Open year round; 300 sites; water and bathroom facilities; sanitary station; electrical hookup; trailer village vehicle sites; food service; swimming; boating; hunting; fishing; tent camping.

New London

CLARE-MAR LAKES
(216) 647-3318
LOCATION: New London Eastern Road.
FACILITIES: Open May - Nov.; 500 sites; water and bathroom facilities; sanitary station; electrical hookup; trailer village vehicle sites; food service; swimming; boating; fishing; horseback riding; tent camping.

Norwalk

LEMAR LAKE
(419) 668-0425
LOCATION: 282 Whittlesey Avenue.
FACILITIES: Open May - Oct.; 300 sites; water and bathroom facilities; sanitary station; electrical hookup; trailer village vehicle sites; food service; swimming; fishing; tent camping.

Orwell

PINE LAKES
(216) 437-6218
LOCATION: On Hague Road.
FACILITIES: Open May 1 - Oct. 31; 600 sites; water and bathroom facilities; sanitary station; electrical hookup; trailer village vehicle sites; food service; swimming; boating; fishing; tent camping.

CAMPGROUNDS (continued)

Pebbles

MINERAL SPRINGS LAKE RESORT
(513) 587-3132
LOCATION: Route 41 & 32, southwest of Bainbridge.
FACILITIES: Open year round; 300 sites; water and bathroom facilities; sanitary station; electrical hookup; trailer village vehicle sites; laundry; swimming; boating; hunting; fishing; horseback riding; tent camping.

Pemberville

TOONERVILLE JUNCTION
(419) 833-5311
LOCATION: 4301 Devil Hole Road.
FACILITIES: Open May 20 - Nov. 1; 300 sites; water and bathroom facilities; sanitary station; electrical hookup; trailer village vehicle sites; swimming; fishing; tent camping.

Peninsula

TAMSIN PARK
(216) 653-6316
LOCATION: 5008 Akron-Cleveland Road.
FACILITIES: Open May - Nov.; 300 sites; water and bathroom facilities; sanitary station; electrical hookup; trailer village vehicle sites; swimming; fishing; tent camping.

Pioneer

FUNNY FARM
(419) 737-2467
LOCATION: Exit 2, Ohio Turnpike, off U.S. 20 on Route 576.
FACILITIES: Open year round; 300 sites; water and bathroom facilities; sanitary station; electrical hookup; trailer village vehicle sites; food service; swimming; boating; fishing; tent camping.

LAZY RIVER
(419) 485-4411
LOCATION: Intersection of U.S. 20 & U.S. 20 A.
FACILITIES: Open Apr. - Nov.; 500 sites; water and bathroom facilities; sanitary station; electrical hookup; trailer village vehicle sites; food service; swimming; boating; hunting; horseback riding; tent camping.

Ravenna

BRADY LAKE PARK
(216) 673-4651
LOCATION: 6381 Lakeview Drive.
FACILITIES: Open May - Oct.; 300 sites; water and bathroom facilities; sanitary station; electrical hookup; trailer village vehicle sites; swimming; boating; fishing; tent camping.

Rootstown

HICKORY HILLS PARK
(216) 325-7425
LOCATION: 4527 Hattrick Road.
FACILITIES: Open Apr. - Nov.; 400 sites; water and bathroom facilities; sanitary station; electrical hookup; trailer village vehicle sites; food service; swimming; boating; fishing; tent camping.

Salem

PONDEROSA PARK
(216) 337-9023
LOCATION: 9362 Salem-Warren Road.
FACILITIES: Open Apr. 15 - Oct. 15; 500 sites; water and bathroom facilities; sanitary station; electrical hookup; trailer village vehicle sites; food service; swimming; fishing; tent camping.

Sandusky

CAMPER VILLAGE
(419) 626-0830
LOCATION: Cedar Point on Lake Erie.
FACILITIES: Open May 14 - Sept. 6; 380 sites; water and bathroom facilities; sanitary station; electrical hookup; trailer village vehicle sites; laundry; food service; tent camping.

Sinking Springs

CAVE LAKE PARK
(513) 588-2752
LOCATION: 5 mi. southeast of Sinking Springs.
FACILITIES: Open year round; 400 sites; water and bathroom facilities; sanitary station; electrical hookup; trailer village vehicle sites; laundry; food service; swimming; boating; fishing; tent camping.

South Vienna

CRAWFORD'S CAMPGROUND & FARM MARKET
(513) 568-4266
LOCATION: U.S. 40 at South Vienna, east of Springfield.
FACILITIES: Open year round; 500 sites; water and bathroom facilities; sanitary station; electrical hookup; trailer village vehicle sites; laundry; food service; swimming; fishing; tent camping.

Streetsboro

MAR-LYNN LAKE PARK
(216) 653-8998
LOCATION: 187 Route 303.
FACILITIES: Open May 1 - Oct. 15; 400 sites; water and bathroom facilities; sanitary station; electrical hookup; trailer village vehicle sites; swimming; fishing; tent camping.

Thornville

MEMORY LANE
(614) 536-7355
LOCATION: 6470 Oakthorpe Road.
FACILITIES: Open Apr. 1 - Nov. 15; 569 sites; water and bathroom facilities; sanitary station; electrical hookup; trailer village vehicle sites; food service; swimming; boating; fishing; tent camping.

Upper Sandusky

INDIAN MILL CAMPING
(419) 294-2715

OHIO

CAMPGROUNDS (continued)

LOCATION: On County Road.
FACILITIES: Open May - Nov.; 300 sites; water and bathroom facilities; sanitary station; electrical hookup; trailer village vehicle sites; swimming; fishing; tent camping.

Wadsworth

OSAGE PARK
(216) 336-2971
LOCATION: 7741 Boneta Road.
FACILITIES: Open May - Nov.; 600 sites; water and bathroom facilities; sanitary station; electrical hookup; trailer village vehicle sites; food service; swimming; boating; fishing; tent camping.

Wausen

SUNNY'S SHADY RECREATION AREA
(419) 337-3101
LOCATION: On County Road.
FACILITIES: Open Apr. 30 - Nov. 1; 425 sites; water and bathroom facilities; sanitary station; electrical hookup; trailer village vehicle sites; swimming; boating; fishing; tent camping.

Wilmington

HILLSIDE HAVEN
(513) 382-8591
LOCATION: 295 Todd's Fork Road.
FACILITIES: Open Apr. - Nov.; 315 sites; water and bathroom facilities; sanitary station; electrical hookup; trailer village vehicle sites; food service; swimming; fishing; tent camping.

Zanesfield

KAMP-A-LOTT
(513) 593-7871
LOCATION: 1 mi. east of Zanesfield.
FACILITIES: Open year round; 300 sites; water and bathroom facilities; sanitary station; electrical hookup; trailer village vehicle sites; food service; swimming; fishing; tent camping.

RESORTS & BEACHES

Most of the state's resort activities center around the major lakes and include fishing, swimming, boating, water skiing, and camping. (See Boating Areas and State Parks.)

BOATING AREAS

See also State Parks.

LAKE ERIE

Ashtabula

ASHTABULA TOWNSHIP PARK
LOCATION: Off Route 11.
FACILITIES: Launching; canoeing; water skiing; fishing; camping; picnic area.

Bono

WARDS CANAL (METZGER MARSH)
LOCATION: 1 mi. east of Bono.
FACILITIES: Launching; fishing.

Cleveland

EDGEWATER MUNICIPAL PARK
LOCATION: Edgewater Drive.
FACILITIES: Launching; sailing; water skiing; fishing; picnic area.

GORDON MUNICIPAL PARK
LOCATION: East 72 Street.
FACILITIES: Launching; sailing; water skiing; fishing; picnic area.

WILDWOOD PARK
LOCATION: Neff Road.
FACILITIES: Launching; sailing; water skiing; fishing.

Fairport

FAIRPORT BOAT LANDING
LOCATION: Water Street.
FACILITIES: Launching; sailing; water skiing; fishing; lodging.

Geneva-On-The-Lake

GENEVA-ON-THE-LAKE
LOCATION: Off Route 534.
FACILITIES: Launching; sailing; canoeing; water skiing; fishing.

Grand River

RUTHERFORD'S LANDING
LOCATION: Off Route 283.
FACILITIES: Launching; sailing; canoeing; water skiing; fishing.

Oregon

COOLEY CREEK COUNTY RAMP
LOCATION: Near Oregon on Maumee Bay.
FACILITIES: Launching; sailing; canoeing; water skiing; fishing; picnic area.

Port Clinton

LITTLE PORTAGE RIVER ACCESS
LOCATION: 5 mi. west of Port Clinton.
FACILITIES: Launching; sailing; canoeing; water skiing; fishing.

PORTAGE RIVER ACCESS
LOCATION: 17 mi. west of Port Clinton.
FACILITIES: Launching; canoeing; water skiing; fishing.

TURTLE CREEK (MAGEE MARSH)
LOCATION: 17 mi. west of Port Clinton.
FACILITIES: Launching; canoeing; fishing.

WEST HARBOR PUBLIC BOAT LAUNCH
LOCATION: In Port Clinton.
FACILITIES: Launching; sailing; canoeing; water skiing; fishing.

Sandusky

EAST BATTERY MUNICIPAL PARK

BOATING AREAS (continued)

LOCATION: Water & Meigs Streets.
FACILITIES: Launching; sailing; canoeing; water skiing; fishing; picnic area; lodging.

GREEN HARBOR
LOCATION: Off Route 53.
FACILITIES: Launching; sailing; water skiing; fishing.

WHITE'S LANDING
LOCATION: Sandusky Bay.
FACILITIES: Launching; sailing; canoeing; water skiing; fishing.

Toledo

CULLEN MUNICIPAL PARK
LOCATION: Summit & 101st Streets.
FACILITIES: Launching; sailing; canoeing; water skiing; fishing; picnic area.

WALBRIDGE MUNICIPAL PARK
LOCATION: East Broadway.
FACILITIES: Launching; sailing; canoeing; water skiing; fishing; picnic area.

MUSKINGUM RIVER PARKWAY

Beverly

MUSKINGUM LOCK 4
LOCATION: Off Route 60.
FACILITIES: Launching; canoeing; water skiing; fishing; picnic area.

Ellis

MUSKINGUM LOCK 11
LOCATION: Off Route 60.
FACILITIES: Launching; canoeing; water skiing; fishing; picnic area.

Luke Chute

MUSKINGUM LOCK 5
LOCATION: Off Route 266.
FACILITIES: Launching; canoeing; water skiing; fishing; picnic area.

Stockport

MUSKINGUM LOCK 6
LOCATION: Off Route 376.
FACILITIES: Launching; canoeing; water skiing; fishing; picnic area.

OHIO RIVER

Chesapeake

INDIAN GUYAN CREEK
LOCATION: 3 mi. east of Chesapeake.
FACILITIES: Launching; water skiing; fishing.

SYMMES CREEK
LOCATION: Off Route 7, east of Chesapeake.
FACILITIES: Launching; water skiing; fishing; picnic area.

Cincinnati

RIVERSIDE PARK
LOCATION: Riverside & South Side Avenue.
FACILITIES: Launching; water skiing; fishing.

SCHMIDT PLAYGROUND
LOCATION: Kellogg Avenue.
FACILITIES: Launching; water skiing; fishing.

Cleves

MIAMI BOAT RAMP
LOCATION: South of Cleves on River Road.
FACILITIES: Launching; canoeing; water skiing; fishing.

Franklin Furnace

GINAT RUN
LOCATION: Braulin Road.
FACILITIES: Launching; water skiing; fishing; picnic area.

Gallipolis

GALLIPOLIS PUBLIC ACCESS
LOCATION: South end of First Avenue.
FACILITIES: Launching; water skiing; fishing; picnic area.

Higginsport

WHITE OAK CREEK
LOCATION: ½ mi. east of Higginsport.
FACILITIES: Launching; water skiing; fishing; camping; picnic area.

Ironton

RIVERVIEW PARK
LOCATION: Foot of Railroad Street.
FACILITIES: Launching; water skiing; fishing.

Manchester

ISLAND CREEK PUBLIC ACCESS
LOCATION: ½ mi. east of Manchester on U.S. 52.
FACILITIES: Launching; water skiing; fishing; picnic area.

Middleport

MIDDLEPORT PUBLIC ACCESS
LOCATION: Off Route 7.
FACILITIES: Launching; fishing; picnic area.

Pomeroy

POMEROY PUBLIC ACCESS
LOCATION: Main Street.
FACILITIES: Launching; water skiing; fishing.

Portsmouth

PORTSMOUTH PUBLIC ACCESS
LOCATION: Foot of Court Street.
FACILITIES: Launching; water skiing; fishing.

Proctorville

OLD LOCK AND DAM 27
LOCATION: 3 mi. west of Proctorville.

OHIO

BOATING AREAS (continued)

FACILITIES: Launching; water skiing; fishing; picnic area.

Ripley

EAGLE CREEK
LOCATION: ½ mi. east of Ripley.
FACILITIES: Launching; water skiing; fishing; camping; picnic area.

Rome

OHIO BRUSH CREEK
LOCATION: ½ mi. west of Rome.
FACILITIES: Launching; water skiing; fishing; picnic area.

Steubenville

ISLAND CREEK RAMP
LOCATION: 5 mi. north of Steubenville.
FACILITIES: Launching; water skiing; fishing; picnic area.

STEUBENVILLE PUBLIC RAMP
LOCATION: Corner Market & Water Street.
FACILITIES: Launching; water skiing; fishing.

Warrington

INDIAN SHORT CREEK PUBLIC RAMP
LOCATION: South of Warrington.
FACILITIES: Launching; water skiing; fishing; picnic area.

Wellsville

WELLSVILLE PUBLIC RAMP
LOCATION: Corner 18th & Nevada Streets.
FACILITIES: Launching; water skiing; fishing.

BICYCLE TRAILS

LITTLE MIAMI RIVER TRAIL - 105 mi.; any bicycle.
Make this ride in either direction along Ohio's longest bikeway. The Little Miami River winds through the scenic countryside of southwestern Ohio.
Trail: Newtown to Milford to Loveland to South Lebanon to Morrow to Oregonia to Waynesville to Spring Valley to Yellow Springs.

OLD MILL TRAIL - 30 mi.; any bicycle.
Along this route you will see a covered bridge, an old cemetery and the Cedarville College Campus.
Trail: Yellow Springs to Clifton.

TRAILS

Cleveland

HARRIET L. KEELER WOODLAND TRAIL, Brecksville Reservation - .5 mi. foot and Braille trail. This is a 6-foot-wide asphalt foot and Braille nature trail which loops through a natural area featuring exotic trees.

Nearly level, the trail can be used independently by the handicapped. A plastic-coated guidewire aids the blind and provides a convenient handhold for other handicapped persons. Braille markers dot the route.

SKI AREAS

Bellbrook

SUGAR CREEK SKI HILLS
P.O. Box 265
Bellbrook, OH 45305
(513) 848-6211
LOCATION: 15 mi. from Daytona via I-75 & Route 725.
FACILITIES: 1 quad chairlift; 2 T-bars; 4 tow ropes; 1 poma; slopes for expert, intermediate and beginning skiers; ski instruction; ski rental; 200 ft. vertical drop; longest run, 1600 ft.; lodging.

Bellefontaine

MAD RIVER MOUNTAIN
P.O. Box 22
Bellefontaine, OH 43311
(513) 599-1015
LOCATION: 6 mi. west of Bellefontaine.
FACILITIES: 2 double chairlifts; 1 T-bar; 4 tow ropes; slopes for expert, intermediate and beginning skiers; ski instruction; 300 ft. vertical drop; longest run, 300 ft.; restaurants; lodging.

Butler

CLEAR FORKS SKI AREA
P.O. Box 308
Butler, OH 44822
(419) 883-2000
LOCATION: 20 mi. south of Mansfield.
FACILITIES: 2 double chairlifts; 3 T-bars; 3 tow ropes; slopes for expert, intermediate and beginning skiers; ski instruction; ski rental; 375 ft. vertical drop; longest run, 1½ mi.; restaurants; lodging.

Chesterland

ALPINE VALLEY
10620 Mayfield Road
Chesterfield, OH 44026
(216) 285-2211
LOCATION: 10 mi. east of I-271.
FACILITIES: 1 chairlift; 2 T-bars; 2 tow ropes; slopes for expert, intermediate and beginning skiers; ski instruction; ski rental; 250 ft. vertical drop; longest run, 1500 ft.; restaurants; lodging.

Mansfield

SNOW TRAILS SKI AREA
Possum Run Road
Mansfield, OH 44901
(419) 522-7393
LOCATION: 5 mi. south of Mansfield.
FACILITIES: 2 triple chairlifts; 2 double chairlifts; 2 T-bars; 5 tow ropes; slopes for expert, intermediate and beginning skiers; ski instruction; ski rental; 300 ft. vertical drop; longest run, 2000 ft.; restaurants; lodging.

SKI AREAS (continued)

Northfield

BRANDYWINE SKI CENTER
P.O. Box 343
Northfield, OH 44607
(216) 467-8197
LOCATION: 1 mi. from Northfield.
FACILITIES: 2 quad chairlifts; 1 triple chairlift; 1 double chairlift; 2 T-bars; 10 tow ropes;
slopes for expert, intermediate and beginning
skiers; ski instruction; ski rental; 241 ft. vertical drop; longest run, 1710 ft.; restaurants;
lodging.

Peninsula

BOSTON MILLS SKI AREA
Riverview and Boston Mills Roads
Peninsula, OH 44264
(216) 657-2334
LOCATION: 10 mi. north of Akron.
FACILITIES: 3 triple chairlifts; 2 double
chairlifts; 5 tow ropes; slopes for expert, intermediate and beginning skiers; ski instruction; ski rental; 240 ft. vertical drop; longest
run, 1700 ft.; restaurant; lodging.

AMUSEMENT PARKS & ATTRACTIONS

Akron

PLAYLAND PARK
2135 Massillon Road
Akron, OH 44312
(216) 644-5768
FACILITIES: 16 major rides; 16 kiddie rides;
walk thru; 6 games; 3 refreshment stands; arcade; roller rink; exhibit (German band organ); picnic facilities; miniature golf; ponies;
orchestras; pay gate; free parking.

Aurora

GEAUGA LAKE
1060 Aurora Road
Aurora, OH 44202
(216) 562-7131
FACILITIES: 32 major rides; 17 kiddie rides;
21 games; 14 refreshment stands; 2 restaurants; arcade; shooting gallery; picnic facilities; miniature golf; stage shows; pay gate;
free parking; open May 1- Sept. 6.

SEA WORLD OF OHIO (Attraction)
1100 Sea World Drive
Aurora, OH 44202
(216) 562-8101
FACILITIES: 5 restaurants; arcade; picnic
facilities; aquatic theater; whale, dolphin, seal
and penguin shows; Japanese pearl diving; seal
and dolphin pools; trout ponds; exhibits; deer
park; pay gate; free parking; open May 29 -
Sept. 12.

Bellevue

SENECA CAVERNS (Attraction)
Bellevue, OH 44811
(419) 483-6711

FACILITIES: Caverns; picnic facilities; pay
gate & parking; open Memorial Day - Labor
Day; weekends: Apr., May, Sept., Oct.

Canton

DINE AMUSEMENTS INC.
4075 Martindale Road, N.E.
Canton, OH 44705
(216) 492-1475
FACILITIES: 20 major rides; 10 kiddie rides;
2 fun houses; 5 walk thrus; 30 games; 10 refreshment stands; restaurant; open Apr. 1 -
Oct. 15.

Chippewa Lake

CHIPPEWA LAKE
County Road 19
Chippewa Lake, OH 44215
(216) 769-2074
FACILITIES: 18 major rides; 10 kiddie rides;
fun house; walk thru; 15 games; 11 refreshment stands; 2 restaurants; arcade; shooting
gallery; beach; picnic facilities; miniature golf;
cruise boat; speed boat; stage shows; pay gate;
free & pay parking; open May 24 - Labor Day.

Cincinnati

CINCINNATI ZOO
3400 Vine Street
Cincinnati, OH 45220
(513) 861-4981
FACILITIES: 6 major rides; 6 kiddie rides; 38
refreshment stands; 3 restaurants; penny arcade; shooting gallery; picnic facilities; name
bands; pay gate.

Delaware

OLENTANGY INDIAN CAVERNS & OHIO
FRONTIER LAND (Attraction)
1779 Home Road
Delaware, OH 43015
(614) 548-7917
FACILITIES: Recreation of Ohio Frontier
Land; caverns; 2 refreshment stands; arcade;
swimming pool; museum; picnic facilities;
miniature golf; gun fights; pay gate; free parking; open Apr. 1 - Nov. 1.

Kings Mills

KINGS ISLAND (Theme)
P.O. Box 400
Kings Mills, OH 45034
(513) 241-5600
FACILITIES: 40 major rides; 8 kiddie rides;
10 games; 25 refreshment stands; 2 restaurants; arcade; shooting gallery; picnic facilities; zoo; theatre; stage shows; free acts; pay
gate; pay parking; open mid-Apr. - mid-Oct.;
weekends: Apr., May, Sept. & Oct.

Middletown

FANTASY FARM PARK
R.R. No. 1
Middletown, OH 45042
(513) 539-8864
FACILITIES: 12 major rides; 20 kiddie rides;
2 walk thrus; 10 games; 4 refreshment stands;
fun house; restaurant; miniature bowling; arcade; swimming pool; exhibits; picnic facili-

OHIO

AMUSEMENT PARKS (continued)

ties; zoo; miniature golf; museum; stage shows; pay gate; open Memorial Day - Labor Day; weekends: May & Sept.

AMERICANA, THE GREAT AMERICAN AMUSEMENT PARK
5757 Hamilton-Middletown Road
Middletown, OH 45042
(513) 539-7339
FACILITIES: 27 major rides; 11 kiddie rides; 15 games; 9 refreshment stands; restaurants; arcade; shooting gallery; picnic facilities; western town; horses; ponies; live animals; pay gate; free parking.

Powell

ZOO AMUSEMENT PARK
10101 Riverside Drive
Powell, OH 43065
(614) 889-8465
FACILITIES: 10 major rides; 10 kiddie rides; 10 games; 4 refreshment stands; 2 restaurants; arcade; shooting gallery; miniature golf; zoo; picnic facilities; pay gate; free parking; open Apr. 26 - Labor Day.

Sandusky

CEDAR POINT, INC.
P.O. Box 759
Sandusky, OH 44870
(419) 626-0830
FACILITIES: 39 major rides; 16 kiddie rides; fun house; 46 games; 50 refreshment stands; 10 restaurants; arcade; shooting gallery; beach; museum; exhibits; picnic facilities; miniature golf; zoo; theatre; crafts; stage shows; pay gate; free parking; open mid-May - Labor Day.

South Zanesville

MOXAHALA PARK
Moxahala Park Road
South Zanesville, OH 43701
(614) 452-3398
FACILITIES: 12 major rides; 8 kiddie rides; 4 games; 3 refreshment stands; arcade; roller rink; picnic facilities; race track; miniature golf; zoo; pool; free acts; free gate; free parking; open May 25 - Labor Day.

Youngstown

THE IDORA AMUSEMENT PARK
Canfield Road
Youngstown, OH 44511
(216) 782-1161
FACILITIES: 17 major rides; 14 kiddie rides; walk thru; 21 games; 9 refreshment stands; restaurant; fun house; exhibits; stage shows; arcade; shooting gallery; picnic facilities; miniature golf; free acts; pay gate; pay parking; open Apr. 24 - Sept. 11; weekends: Apr. 24-Jun. 12.

STATE FAIR

Ohio State Fair
632 East 11th Street

Columbus, OH 43123
(614) 294-5441
DATE: August

NATIONAL PARKS

There are no National Parks in Ohio.

NATIONAL FORESTS

National Forests
Eastern Region
633 West Wisconsin Avenue
Milwaukee, WI 53203
(414) 291-3693

Ironton

WAYNE NATIONAL FOREST
ATTRACTIONS: Old charcoal furnaces; hunting; fishing; horseback riding; auto tours; scenic lookout points.
FACILITIES: 1 camp and picnic site, 3 picnic only; swimming site; motels, tourist homes, hotels.
NEARBY TOWNS: Athens, Jackson, Marietta.

STATE PARKS

Headquarters

Department of Natural Resources
Division of Parks and Recreation
Fountain Square
Columbus, OH 43224
(614) 466-2838

Adelphi

TAR HOLLOW STATE PARK
LOCATION: 10 mi. south of Adelphi.
FACILITIES: Open year round; 96 sites; water and bathroom facilities; trailer village vehicle sites; picnic area; swimming; hunting; fishing; tent camping.

Andover

PYMATUNING STATE PARK
LOCATION: 2 mi. east of Andover.
FACILITIES: Open year round; 434 sites; water and bathroom facilities; sanitary station; electrical hookup; trailer village vehicle sites; cabins; picnic area; food service; swimming; boating; hunting; fishing; tent camping.

Athens

STROUDS RUN STATE PARK
LOCATION: Off U.S. 33 from Athens.
FACILITIES: Open year round; 80 sites; water and bathroom facilities; trailer village vehicle sites; picnic area; swimming; boating; hunting; fishing; tent camping.

Bellefontaine

INDIAN LAKE STATE PARK
LOCATION: 12 mi. northwest of Bellefontaine.

STATE PARKS (continued)

FACILITIES: Open year round; 443 sites; water and bathroom facilities; sanitary station; electrical hookup; trailer village vehicle sites; picnic area; food service; swimming; boating; hunting; fishing; tent camping.

Belle Valley

WOLF RUN STATE PARK
LOCATION: Off Route 821 at Belle Valley.
FACILITIES: Open year round; 140 sites; water and bathroom facilities; sanitary station; trailer village vehicle sites; laundry; picnic area; tent camping.

Belmont

BARKCAMP STATE PARK
LOCATION: 1 mi. east of Belmont.
FACILITIES: Open year round; 150 sites; water and bathroom facilities; trailer village vehicle sites; picnic area; swimming; boating; hunting; fishing; hiking; tent camping.

Blue Rock

BLUE ROCK STATE PARK
LOCATION: 3 mi. north of Blue Rock.
FACILITIES: Open year round; 103 sites; water and bathroom facilities; trailer village vehicle sites; picnic area; swimming; boating; fishing; tent camping.

Cambridge

SALT FORK STATE PARK
LOCATION: 8 mi. northeast of Cambridge.
FACILITIES: Open year round; 212 sites; water and bathroom facilities; sanitary station; electrical hookup; trailer village vehicle sites; cabins; picnic area; swimming; boating; hunting; hiking; handicapped access/restroom; tent camping.

Chillicothe

SCIOTO TRAIL STATE PARK
LOCATION: South of Chillicothe.
FACILITIES: Open year round; 62 sites; water and bathroom facilities; trailer village vehicle sites; picnic area; swimming; boating; hunting; fishing; tent camping.

Circleville

A.W. MARION STATE PARK
LOCATION: 4 mi. northeast of Circleville.
FACILITIES: Open year round; 60 sites; water and bathroom facilities; trailer village vehicle sites; picnic area; boating; hunting; fishing; hiking; tent camping.

Clarksville

COWAN LAKE STATE PARK
LOCATION: 3½ mi. east of Clarksville.
FACILITIES: Open year round; 237 sites; water and bathroom facilities; sanitary station; electrical hookup; trailer village vehicle sites; cabins; picnic area; food service; swimming; boating; hunting; fishing; hiking; bicycle trail; tent camping.

Defiance

INDEPENDENCE DAM STATE PARK
LOCATION: 3 mi. east of Defiance.
FACILITIES: Open year round; 41 sites; water and bathroom facilities; picnic area; boating; hunting; fishing; tent camping.

Delaware

DELAWARE STATE PARK
LOCATION: 8 mi. north of Delaware.
FACILITIES: Open year round; 214 sites; water and bathroom facilities; sanitary station; electrical hookup; trailer village vehicle sites; picnic area; swimming; boating; hunting; fishing; tent camping.

Dovola

MUSKINGUM RIVER STATE PARK
LOCATION: Near Dovola.
FACILITIES: Open year round; 20 sites; water and bathroom facilities; trailer village vehicle sites; picnic area; boating; fishing; tent camping.

Edenton

STONELICK STATE PARK
LOCATION: Near Edenton.
FACILITIES: Open year round; 153 sites; water and bathroom facilities; sanitary station; electrical hookup; trailer village vehicle sites; picnic area; swimming; boating; hunting; fishing; bicycle trail; tent camping.

Fayette

HARRISON LAKE STATE PARK
LOCATION: 5 mi. southwest of Fayette.
FACILITIES: Open year round; 201 sites; water and bathroom facilities; sanitary station; electrical hookup; trailer village vehicle sites; picnic area; swimming; boating; fishing; tent camping.

Glouster

BURR OAK STATE PARK
LOCATION: Northeast of Glouster.
FACILITIES: Open year round; 90 sites; water and bathroom facilities; sanitary station; trailer village vehicle sites; cabins; picnic area; food service; swimming; boating; hunting; fishing; hiking; tent camping.

Hillsboro

PAINT CREEK STATE PARK
LOCATION: 17 mi. east of Hillsboro.
FACILITIES: Open year round; 199 sites; water and bathroom facilities; sanitary station; electrical hookup; trailer village vehicle sites; picnic area; boating; hunting; fishing; tent camping.

ROCKY FORT STATE PARK
LOCATION: 6 mi. southeast of Hillsboro.
FACILITIES: Open year round; 227 sites; water and bathroom facilities; sanitary station; electrical hookup; trailer village vehicle sites; picnic area; food service; swimming; boating; hiking; tent camping.

OHIO

STATE PARKS (continued)

Kelleys Island

KELLEYS ISLAND STATE PARK
LOCATION: On Kelleys Island.
FACILITIES: Open year round; 108 sites; water and bathroom facilities; trailer village vehicle sites; picnic area; swimming; boating; hunting; fishing; tent camping.

Lisbon

GUILFORD LAKE STATE PARK
LOCATION: 4 mi. west of Lisbon.
FACILITIES: Open year round; 82 sites; water and bathroom facilities; trailer village vehicle sites; picnic area; swimming; boating; fishing; tent camping.

Logan

HOCKING HILLS STATE PARK
LOCATION: Southwest of Logan.
FACILITIES: Open year round; 170 sites; water and bathroom facilities; sanitary station; electrical hookup; trailer village vehicle sites; laundry; picnic area; swimming; hunting; hiking; tent camping.

Loudonville

MOHICAN STATE PARK
LOCATION: Southwest of Loudonville.
FACILITIES: Open year round; 225 sites; water and bathroom facilities; sanitary station; electrical hookup; trailer village vehicle sites; cabins; picnic area; food service; swimming; boating; fishing; bicycle trail; tent camping.

Minster

LAKE LORAMIE STATE PARK
LOCATION: 1 mi. south of Minster.
FACILITIES: Open year round; 184 sites; water and bathroom facilities; trailer village vehicle sites; picnic area; swimming; boating; hunting; fishing; tent camping.

Morgantown

PIKE LAKE STATE PARK
LOCATION: 5 mi. northwest of Morgantown.
FACILITIES: Open year round; 150 sites; water and bathroom facilities; sanitary station; electrical hookup; trailer village vehicle sites; cabins; picnic area; food service; swimming; boating; fishing; tent camping.

Mt. Gilead

MT. GILEAD STATE PARK
LOCATION: 1 mi. east of Mt. Gilead.
FACILITIES: Open year round; 60 sites; water and bathroom facilities; sanitary station; trailer village vehicle sites; picnic area; swimming; fish.ng; tent camping.

Mt. Sterling

DEER CREEK STATE PARK
LOCATION: South of Mt. Sterling on Route 207.
FACILITIES: Open year round; 232 sites; water and bathroom facilities; sanitary station; electrical hookup; trailer village vehicle sites; picnic area; swimming; boating; hunting; fishing; tent camping.

Oxford

HUESTON WOODS STATE PARK
LOCATION: 5 mi. northwest of Oxford.
FACILITIES: Open year round; 531 sites; water and bathroom facilities; sanitary station; electrical hookup; trailer village vehicle sites; cabins; picnic area; food service; swimming; boating; fishing; hiking; tent camping.

Port Clinton

EAST HARBOR STATE PARK
LOCATION: East of Port Clinton.
FACILITIES: Open year round; 570 sites; water and bathroom facilities; sanitary station; trailer village vehicle sites; picnic area; swimming; boating; hunting; fishing; hiking; tent camping.

Portsmouth

SHAWNEE STATE PARK
LOCATION: Northwest of Portsmouth.
FACILITIES: Open year round; 107 sites; water and bathroom facilities; sanitary station; electrical hookup; trailer village vehicle sites; cabins; picnic area; food service; swimming; boating; hunting; fishing; tent camping.

Quincy

KISER LAKE STATE PARK
LOCATION: 7 mi. south of Quincy.
FACILITIES: Open year round; 150 sites; water and bathroom facilities; sanitary station; trailer village vehicle sites; picnic area; swimming; hunting; fishing; hiking; tent camping.

Ravenna

WEST BRANCH STATE PARK
LOCATION: 4 mi. east of Ravenna.
FACILITIES: Open year round; 103 sites; water and bathroom facilities; trailer village vehicle sites; picnic area; swimming; boating; hunting; fishing; tent camping.

Reedsville

FORKED RUN STATE PARK
LOCATION: West of Reedsville.
FACILITIES: Open year round; 198 sites; water and bathroom facilities; sanitary station; trailer village vehicle sites; laundry; picnic area; food service; hiking; tent camping.

Richmond

JEFFERSON LAKE STATE PARK
LOCATION: Northwest of Richmond.
FACILITIES: Open year round; 100 sites; water and bathroom facilities; trailer village vehicle sites; picnic area; swimming; boating; hunting; fishing; hiking; tent camping.

Saint Marys

GRAND LAKE SAINT MARYS STATE PARK

STATE PARKS (continued)

LOCATION: 2 mi. west of Saint Marys.
FACILITIES: Open year round; 206 sites; water and bathroom facilities; sanitary station; electrical hookup; trailer village vehicle sites; picnic area; swimming; boating; tent camping.

South Bass Island

SOUTH BASS ISLAND STATE PARK
LOCATION: On South Bass Island.
FACILITIES: Open year round; 125 sites; water and bathroom facilities; trailer village vehicle sites; cabins; boating; fishing; tent camping.

South Newbury

PUNDERSON STATE PARK
LOCATION: Near South Newbury.
FACILITIES: Open year round; 201 sites; water and bathroom facilities; sanitary station; electrical hookup; trailer village vehicle sites; cabins; picnic area; swimming; boating; fishing; tent camping.

Van Buren

VAN BUREN STATE PARK
LOCATION: Southeast of Van Buren.
FACILITIES: Open year round; 50 sites; water and bathroom facilities; trailer village vehicle sites; picnic area; swimming; hunting; fishing; tent camping.

Warren

MOSQUITO STATE PARK
LOCATION: 10 mi. northeast of Warren.
FACILITIES: Open year round; 234 sites; water and bathroom facilities; trailer village vehicle sites; picnic area; swimming; boating; hunting; fishing; tent camping.

Waverly

LAKE WHITE STATE PARK
LOCATION: 4 mi. southwest of Waverly.
FACILITIES: Open year round; 75 sites; water and bathroom facilities; trailer village vehicle sites; picnic area; swimming; hunting; fishing; tent camping.

Wellington

FINDLEY STATE PARK
LOCATION: 2 mi. south of Wellington.
FACILITIES: Open year round; 283 sites; water and bathroom facilities; sanitary station; trailer village vehicle sites; laundry; picnic area; food service; swimming; boating; hunting; fishing; hiking; tent camping.

Wellston

LAKE ALMA STATE PARK
LOCATION: 1 mi. northeast of Wellston.
FACILITIES: Open year round; 60 sites; water and bathroom facilities; trailer village vehicle sites; picnic area; swimming; hunting; fishing; hiking; tent camping.

Yellow Springs

JOHN BRYAN STATE PARK
LOCATION: 2 mi. east of Yellow Springs.
FACILITIES: Open year round; 75 sites; water and bathroom facilities; trailer village vehicle sites; picnic area; swimming; fishing; hiking; tent camping.

Zaleski

LAKE HOPE STATE PARK
LOCATION: 4 mi. north of Zaleski.
FACILITIES: Open year round; 223 sites; water and bathroom facilities; sanitary station; trailer village vehicle sites; cabins; laundry; picnic area; swimming; fishing; hiking; tent camping.

Zanesville

DILLON STATE PARK
LOCATION: 8 mi. northwest of Zanesville.
FACILITIES: Open year round; 195 sites; water and bathroom facilities; sanitary station; electrical hookup; trailer village vehicle sites; cabins; picnic area; swimming; boating; hunting; fishing; hiking; tent camping.

STATE FORESTS

Department of Natural Resources
Division of Forestry
Fountain Square
Columbus, OH 43224
(614) 466-7842

Bloomingdale

FERNWOOD STATE FOREST
LOCATION: Near Bloomingdale.
FACILITIES: Open year round; trailer village vehicle sites; hunting; hiking; horseback riding; tent camping.

Blue Rock

BLUE ROCK STATE FOREST
LOCATION: Near Blue Rock.
FACILITIES: Open year round; hunting; hiking; horseback riding; guided tour.

Byer

RICHLAND FURNACE STATE FOREST
LOCATION: Near Byer.
FACILITIES: Open year round; hunting; hiking.

Chillicothe

SCIOTO TRAIL STATE FOREST
LOCATION: Near Chillicothe.
FACILITIES: Open year round; hunting; hiking; horseback riding.

Friendship

SHAWNEE STATE FOREST
LOCATION: Near Friendship.
FACILITIES: Open year round; hunting; hiking; horseback riding; primitive campsites.

STATE FORESTS (continued)

Latham

PIKE STATE FOREST
LOCATION: Near Latham.
FACILITIES: Open year round; hunting; hiking; horseback riding.

Londonderry

TAR HOLLOW STATE FOREST
LOCATION: Near Londonderry.
FACILITIES: Open year round; hunting; hiking; horseback riding; primitive campsites.

Pedro

DEAN STATE FOREST
LOCATION: Near Pedro.
FACILITIES: Open year round; hunting; horseback riding.

Peebles

BRUSH CREEK STATE FOREST
LOCATION: Near Peebles.
FACILITIES: Open year round; hunting; horseback riding.

Perrysville

MOHICAN-MEMORIAL STATE FOREST
LOCATION: Near Perrysville.
FACILITIES: Open year round; hunting; horseback riding.

Reedsville

SHADE RIVER STATE FOREST
LOCATION: Near Reedsville.
FACILITIES: Open year round; hunting; horseback riding.

Rockbridge

HOCKING STATE FOREST
LOCATION: Near Rockbridge.
FACILITIES: Open year round; hunting; hiking; horseback riding; primitive campsites.

Swanton

MAUMEE STATE FOREST
LOCATION: Near Swanton.
FACILITIES: Open year round; hunting; hiking; horseback riding.

Zaleski

ZALESKI STATE FOREST
LOCATION: Near Zaleski.
FACILITIES: Open year round; trailer village vehicle sites; hunting; hiking; horseback riding; tent camping.

HISTORIC SITES

Columbus

OHIO VILLAGE - Reconstructed community of 19th-century Ohio. Working craftspeople include a printer, blacksmith, weaver, tin-smith, cabinetmaker, gunsmith, saddle-and-harness maker and photographer. The village also offers a museum, lawyer's and physician's offices, glass and china shop, town hall and general store. Meals from a 19th-century menu available in the hotel. Located at 17th Avenue and I-71 junction.

Jackson

BUCKEYE FURNACE - Iron furnace of the Hanging Rock district, charging house, charcoal and casting sheds and company store. Several nature trails wind through the lush forests that surround the site. Located on County Road 58.

Marion

WARREN G. HARDING HOME - From the front porch of this house the 30th President conducted his 1920 campaign. Museum behind the home has Harding momentoes. Located at 380 Mt. Vernon Avenue.

Mentor

LAWNFIELD - Restored home of James A. Garfield, containing personal possessions of the 20th President. Located on U.S. 20.

New Philadelphia

SCHOENBRUNN - Reconstruction of Ohio's first Christian settlement, established in 1772 by Moravian missionaries and their Indian converts. Costumed guides demonstrate a variety of pioneer crafts. Located on U.S. 250 and Route 800.

Newark

MOUND BUILDERS EARTHWORKS - Ceremonial "Great Circle" earthworks built by the Hopewell Indians. The Ohio Prehistoric Indian Art Museum at the site features exhibits on the artistic creations of these early people. Octagon Mound, on North 33rd Street, is another ceremonial complex that was once joined to the Great Circle earthworks. Located on North 21st Street.

Perrysburg

FORT MEIGS - Largest reconstructed walled fort in America, built by General William Henry Harrison in 1813. Uniformed "soldiers" carry on demonstrations of military life. Located on Route 65.

Piqua

THE PIQUA HISTORICAL AREA - Farmstead of Colonel John Johnston, an early 19th-century Ohio Indian agent, offers demonstrations of pioneer cooking, spinning, weaving, candle and soap making. Historic Indian Museum displays rare artifacts, and lifelike mannequins portray the story of Indian culture in Ohio in the 1700s and 1800s. Located on Hardin Road.

HOSTELS

Bowling Green

WINTERGARDEN LODGE YOUTH HOSTEL
Wintergarden Road
Bowling Green, OH 43402
(419) 352-9806
FACILITIES: Open year round; 16 beds, men; 16 beds, women; modern bathroom; overnight charges: $2 summer; $2.50 winter; houseparent: Sue Butler.

Cincinnati

UNIVERSITY OF CINCINNATI
Sander Hall
Mail Location No. 5
Cincinnati, OH 45221
(513) 475-6461 (day)
FACILITIES: Open year round; 800 beds, men and women; modern bathroom; overnight charges: $7; $10, double occupancy.

Lucas

MALABAR FARM YOUTH HOSTEL
Route 1
Lucas, OH 44842
No telephone
FACILITIES: Open year round; 20 beds, men; 10 beds, women; modern bathroom; nearest hostel: Bowling Green, 110 mi.; overnight charges: $2.50 summer; $3.50 winter; houseparents: Mr. & Mrs. Jim Berry.

New Plymouth

COMMUNITY CAMP YOUTH HOSTEL
Route 1
New Plymouth, OH 45654
(614) 385-7207 (summer)
FACILITIES: Open Mar. - May and Sept. - Nov. in large houses; Jun. - Aug.: outdoor camping facilities; 20 beds, men; 20 beds, women; modern bathroom; overnight charges: $1.50 summer; $2 winter; houseparent: Paul Gelsleichter.

POINTS OF INTEREST

Canton

PRO FOOTBALL HALL OF FAME - Football-shaped building has busts of great players and pictures of famous teams. Located at 2121 Harrison Avenue, NW.

Kelleys Island

GLACIAL GROOVES - America's largest set of exposed limestone glacial scratchings. Outdoor exhibits describe history of the grooves. Inscription Rock, nearby, is a large boulder on which prehistoric Indians carved pictographic writings. Located on Kelleys Island; take ferry from Marblehead.

Marietta

THE OHIO RIVER MUSEUM - Exhibits in this "museum on stilts" depict the natural history of rivers, the Golden Age of steamboats and relationship of man and the river. A 16-projector multi-media theater presents "The River." The sternwheeler W.P. Snyder and a river flatboat are docked at the museum and open to visitors. Located on Front Street.

Piqua

GENERAL HARRISON - A mule-drawn canal boat ride over more than a mile of the Miami and Erie Canal.

Wapakoneta

THE NEIL ARMSTRONG AIR & SPACE MUSEUM - Dozens of exhibits on Ohio's flight pioneers, from early balloonists to the state's space explorers. Located on I-75.

Wright-Patterson AFB

UNITED STATES AIR FORCE MUSEUM - Oldest and largest military aviation museum in the world. Exhibits include 130 aircraft and missiles, plus aeronautical items spanning the period from Kitty Hawk to the present. Located 6 mi. northeast of Dayton at Wright-Patterson Air Force Base.

Zanesville

THE LORENA - Sternwheeler was Bicentennial project for Zanesville. Public rides Tue. - Sun. Located at Putnam Landing Park, south of 6th Street Bridge.

THE NATIONAL ROAD — ZANE GREY MUSEUM - Showcase of Ohio land transportation history. Antique vehicles displayed on the roadbeds they traveled. Life-sized mannequins inhabit recreations of blacksmith and wagon shops, a travelers' inn and a pioneer campsite. The life of Zanesville native Zane Grey, "father of the adult western," occupies a special section of the museum. Located at the Norwich exits of U.S. 40 and I-70.

OKLAHOMA

Oklahoma, the land of the American Indian, entered the Union in 1907 as the forty-sixth state. In the early 1800s, the federal government set up a huge land trust called the Indian Territory and forced five major tribes from all parts of the country to relocate there.

For nearly a century prior to the relocation, most of the Indians had been living and working closely with white men, and had become accustomed to the new way of life. So when the Civil War began, Indians from the South readily joined the Southern cause.

OKLAHOMA

INTRODUCTION (continued)

After the war, all Indians on the land trust were reprimanded for the few who had sympathized with the South, and a large part of their land was confiscated.

Today, Oklahoma's primary income is derived from heavy industry and oil, both of which are centered around Tulsa and Oklahoma City. With the recent development of the state park resorts and the dozens of man-made lakes, tourism adds significantly to the state's income, also.

State capital: Oklahoma City. State bird: Scissortailed flycatcher. State tree: Redbud. State flower: Mistletoe.

WEATHER

Oklahoma is located in the southern Great Plains. Of the 50 states, it ranks 18th in size with an area of approximately 70,000 square miles, only 935 of which are covered by lakes and ponds. The terrain is mostly rolling plains, sloping downward from west to east. The plains are broken by scattered hilly areas and by a mountainous area in the southeast.

The climate of Oklahoma is continental in type, as in all of the central Great Plains. Warm, moist air moving northward from the Gulf of Mexico exerts much influence at times, particularly over the southern and more eastern sections of the state. As a result, humidities and cloudiness are generally greater and precipitation considerably heavier than in the western and northern sections.

Summers are long and occasionally very hot. Winters are shorter and less rigorous than those of the more northern Plain States. Periods of extreme cold are infrequent. Low humidities and good southerly breezes usually accompany the high summer temperatures and somewhat lessen their discomforting effect. Nights are generally comfortable because the clear skies and dry air allow for rapid cooling after sunset.

Average daily temperature for each month.

	Northern	Southern
Jan.	47.3 to 23.0	55.1 to 28.7
Feb.	53.2 to 27.5	60.7 to 33.0
Mar.	61.1 to 34.6	68.5 to 40.4
Apr.	72.9 to 46.3	78.3 to 51.2
May	81.9 to 56.1	85.1 to 59.3
Jun.	91.6 to 65.6	93.1 to 67.3
Jul.	96.4 to 70.4	98.2 to 71.0
Aug.	95.1 to 68.6	98.4 to 69.7
Sept.	86.2 to 60.5	90.1 to 62.8
Oct.	75.8 to 49.1	79.6 to 51.8
Nov.	60.0 to 35.7	65.9 to 39.6
Dec.	49.4 to 26.7	57.4 to 31.8
Year	72.6 to 47.0	77.5 to 50.6

STATE CHAMBER OF COMMERCE

Oklahoma State Chamber of Commerce
4020 North Lincoln Boulevard
Oklahoma City, OK 73105
(405) 424-4003

STATE & CITY TOURISM OFFICES

State

Department of Industrial Development
Office of the Governor
Oklahoma City, OK 73105
(405) 521-2401

Tourism Promotion Division
Oklahoma Tourism and Recreation Department
500 Will Rogers Building
Oklahoma City, OK 73105
(405) 521-2406

Local

Oklahoma City Convention and Tourism Center
1 Santa Fe Plaza
Oklahoma City, OK 73102
(405) 232-6381

STATE HIGHWAY DEPARTMENT

Oklahoma Department of Transportation
200 NE 21st Street
Oklahoma City, OK 73105
(405) 521-2631

HIGHWAY WELCOMING CENTERS

Blackwell

BLACKWELL CENTER - Interstate 35.

Colbert

COLBERT CENTER - U.S. 69 & 75.

Erick

ERICK CENTER - Interstate 40.

Lawton

LAWTON CENTER - City limits.

Miami

MIAMI CENTER - Interstate 44.

Sackerville

SACKERVILLE CENTER - Interstate 35.

WELCOMING CENTERS (continued)

Sallisaw

SALLISAW CENTER - Interstate 40.

STATE POLICE

Department of Public Safety
3600 N. Eastern Avenue
Oklahoma City, OK 73111
(405) 424-4011

HUNTING & FISHING

Hunting

An Oklahoma hunting license is required of all persons who hunt except: (1) legal resident owners or tenants who hunt only on land owned or leased by them (not including hunting leases); (2) residents 65 years or older; (3) legal resident veterans with 60 percent or more disability; (4) citizens of Oklahoma in the U.S. Armed Forces serving outside Oklahoma and on authorized leave; (5) residents under 16 years of age; (6) non-residents under 14 years of age. License (or proper proof of exemption) must be carried on hunter's person while hunting and displayed upon request by an Oklahoma citizen or ranger.

Resident

Hunting, $5; combination hunting and fishing, $9; turkey tag, $3; deer-gun tag, $5; deer-archery tag, $5; deer-primitive firearms tag, $5; deer-bonus deer tag, $5; deer-hunting with dog tag, $5; elk tag, $10; amateur trapping, $1.25; professional trapping, $50; federal duck stamp, $5.

Non-resident

Hunting, $30; turkey tag, $3; deer-gun tag, $50; deer-archery tag, $50; deer-primitive firearms tag, $50; deer-bonus deer tag, $50; deer-hunting with dog tag, $50; elk tag, $50; non-resident trapping, $250; federal duck stamp, $5.

Fishing

An Oklahoma resident or non-resident fishing license is required of all persons who take or attempt to take fish or other aquatic dwelling organisms by any method in Oklahoma except: (1) residents under 16; (2) non-residents under 14; (3) resident owner or tenants on land owned or leased by such owner or tenant; (4) residents 65 years or over; (5) resident disabled veterans with 60 percent or more disability; (6) any person who fishes with pole and line, trotline or throwline in streams, natural ponds and mine pits in or forming the boundary of the county in which he is a bona fide resident, when using any bait other than commercial or artificial bait, blood, stink bait, cut fish, and shrimp; (7) any legally blind person or physically impaired person.

Resident

Fishing, $5; combination hunting and fishing, $9; trout license, $3.

Non-resident

10-day fishing, $4.75; annual, $9.25; trout license, $3.

For more information contact:

Department of Wildlife Conservation
1801 North Lincoln Boulevard
Oklahoma City, OK 73105
(405) 521-3855

CAMPGROUNDS

See State Parks.

RESORTS & BEACHES

There are seven resorts in Oklahoma: Arrowhead, Fountainhead, Lake Murray, Lake Texoma, Quartz Mountain, Roman Nose and Western Hills. All but Western Hills (Sequoyah State Park) are located in State Parks of the same name. For information on lodging facilities and activities at these resorts, see State Parks.

BOATING AREAS

Ardmore

LAKE MURRAY
LOCATION: 7 mi. south of Ardmore on I-35, then 2 mi. east on Route 77.
FACILITIES: Launching; fishing; swimming; camping.

Atoka

ATOKA LAKE
LOCATION: 3 mi. northeast of Atoka.
FACILITIES: Launching; fishing; swimming; camping.

Barnsdall

BIRCH LAKE
LOCATION: 1½ mi. south of Barnsdall.
FACILITIES: Launching; fishing; swimming; camping.

Binger

FT. COBB RESERVOIR
LOCATION: Hwy. 152 west from Binger, then Hwy. 146 south.
FACILITIES: Launching; fishing; swimming; camping.

Broken Bow

BROKEN BOW LAKE
LOCATION: Near Broken Bow.
FACILITIES: Launching; fishing; swimming; camping.

OKLAHOMA

BOATING AREAS (continued)

Canton

CANTON LAKE
LOCATION: West from the city of Canton on Hwy. 51.
FACILITIES: Launching; fishing; swimming; camping.

Claremore

OOLOGAH LAKE
LOCATION: 10 mi. north of Claremore on Hwy. 88.
FACILITIES: Launching; fishing; water skiing; camping.

Clinton

FOSS LAKE
LOCATION: Northwest of Clinton.
FACILITIES: Launching; fishing; swimming; camping.

Davis

LAKE OF THE ARBUCKLES
LOCATION: South of Hwy. 7 between Davis and Sulphur.
FACILITIES: Launching; fishing; swimming; camping.

Enid

GREAT SALT PLAINS LAKE
LOCATION: Hwy. 64, north of Enid.
FACILITIES: Launching; fishing; swimming; camping.

Grove

WEBBERS FALLS LAKE
LOCATION: 3 mi. west of Grove.
FACILITIES: Launching; fishing; swimming; camping.

Hardesty

OPTIMA LAKE
LOCATION: 3 mi. northwest of Hardesty off Hwy. 3.
FACILITIES: Launching; fishing; camping.

Henryetta

LAKE EUFAULA
LOCATION: I-40 east from Henryetta.
FACILITIES: Launching; fishing; swimming; camping.

Hugo

HUGO LAKE
LOCATION: U.S. 70 east from Hugo.
FACILITIES: Launching; fishing; swimming; camping.

Kingston

LAKE TEXOMA
LOCATION: 5 mi. east of Kingston on U.S. 70.
FACILITIES: Launching; fishing; swimming; camping.

Langley

GRAND LAKE
LOCATION: Near Langley.
FACILITIES: Launching; fishing; swimming; camping.

Lawton

LAKES ELLSWORTH AND LAWTONKA
LOCATION: Near Lawton.
FACILITIES: Launching; fishing; swimming; camping.

Lone Wolf

ALTUS RESERVOIR
LOCATION: 7 mi. south of Lone Wolf.
FACILITIES: Launching; fishing; swimming; camping.

Mountain Park

TOM STEED RESERVOIR
LOCATION: 10 mi. north of Mountain Park off U.S. 183.
FACILITIES: Launching; fishing.

Muskogee

FT. GIBSON LAKE
LOCATION: Hwy. 80 north from Muskogee to the Ft. Gibson area.
FACILITIES: Launching; fishing; swimming; camping.

Norman

LAKE THUNDERBIRD
LOCATION: Exit south-bound I-35 on Route 9 at Norman.
FACILITIES: Launching; fishing; swimming; camping.

Pawhuska

HULAH LAKE
LOCATION: Near Pawhuska.
FACILITIES: Launching; fishing; swimming; camping.

Ponca City

KAW LAKE
LOCATION: 15 mi. east of Ponca City.
FACILITIES: Launching; fishing; swimming; camping.

Pryor

LAKE HUDSON
LOCATION: East of Pryor on Hwy. 20.
FACILITIES: Launching; fishing; swimming; camping.

Sallisaw

ROBERT S. KERR LAKE
LOCATION: Near Sallisaw on I-40.
FACILITIES: Launching; fishing; swimming; camping.

Spavinaw

LAKES SPAVINAW AND EUCHA

BOATING AREAS (continued)

LOCATION: Near Spavinaw.
FACILITIES: Launching; fishing; swimming; camping.

Tahlequah

LAKE TENKILLER
LOCATION: Hwy. 82 south from Tahlequah.
FACILITIES: Launching; fishing; swimming; camping.

Tulsa

KEYSTONE RESERVOIR
LOCATION: West of Tulsa.
FACILITIES: Launching; fishing; swimming; camping.

Waurika

WAURIKA LAKE
LOCATION: 6 mi. northeast of Waurika off Hwy. 5.
FACILITIES: Launching; fishing; swimming; camping.

Wister

LAKE WISTER
LOCATION: Near Wister.
FACILITIES: Launching; fishing; swimming; camping.

Woodward

FT. SUPPLY LAKE
LOCATION: Near Woodward.
FACILITIES: Launching; fishing; swimming; camping.

Wright City

PINE CREEK LAKE
LOCATION: 5 mi. north of Wright City.
FACILITIES: Launching; fishing; swimming; camping.

BICYCLE TRAILS

No information was available on Bicycle Trails in Oklahoma.

TRAILS

Oklahoma City

RED STICK TRAIL - 1.5 mi. foot trail. This nature trail in the Dr. J.T. Martin Park Nature Center begins at a 5-acre man-made lake which provides habitat for a variety of plant and animal life. The loop trail offers scenic views of the 130-acre protected wildlife area. Some 30 species of trees occur along the trail, and there are several interesting large rock outcroppings. Interpretive facilities are located at points of interest, and a trail guide is available at the Nature Center.

SKI AREAS

There are no organized Ski Areas in Oklahoma.

AMUSEMENT PARKS & ATTRACTIONS

Anadarko

INDIAN CITY, U.S.A. (Attraction)
P.O. Box 695
Anadarko, OK 73005
(405) 247-5661
FACILITIES: Guided tours through 7 Indian villages; pay gate; free parking; open all year.

Cache

EAGLE PARK
Route 1
Cache, OK 73527
(405) 429-3238
FACILITIES: 10 major rides; 8 kiddie rides; fun house; walk thru; 5 refreshment stands; 2 restaurants; arcade; roller rink; museum; rodeo; picnic facilities; miniature golf; free acts; free gate; free parking; open Apr. 1 - Sept. 1.

Oklahoma City

FRONTIER CITY, U.S.A.
11601 N.E. Expressway
Oklahoma City, OK 73111
(405) 478-2412
FACILITIES: 11 major rides; 6 kiddie rides; fun house; 3 refreshment stands; 3 restaurants; 5 games; arcade; shooting gallery; picnic facilities; Indian village; Indian dancers; gunfights; train robbers; wax museums; trail & pony rides; stage shows; pay gate; free parking; open May 23 - Labor Day; weekends, Easter - Memorial Day and Sept.

SPRING LAKE AMUSEMENT PARK
1800 Springlake Drive
Oklahoma City, OK 73111
(405) 424-1405
FACILITIES: 17 major rides; 6 kiddie rides; fun house; mirror maze; 6 walk thrus; 6 games; 5 refreshment stands; restaurant; arcade; picnic facilities; miniature golf; amphitheatre; circus acts; free acts; pay gate; free parking.

Tahlequah

CHEROKEE NATIONAL HISTORICAL SOCIETY (Attraction)
P.O. Box 515
Tahlequah, OK 74474
(918) 456-6007
FACILITIES: Museum; exhibits; theater; Trail of Tears historic drama; ancient Cherokee village; Cherokee National Museum; free parking; open May 1 - Sept. 1.

Tulsa

BELL'S AMUSEMENT PARK
21st Street at S. New Haven
Tulsa, OK 74104

OKLAHOMA

AMUSEMENT PARKS (continued)

(918) 932-1989
FACILITIES: 22 major rides; 10 kiddie rides;
walk thru; 2 games; 2 refreshment stands; arcade; picnic facilities; miniature golf; free
acts; free gate; free parking.

STATE FAIR

State Fair of Oklahoma
500 Land Rush Street
Oklahoma City, OK 73107
(405) 942-5511
DATE: September

NATIONAL PARKS

There are no National Parks in Oklahoma.

NATIONAL FORESTS

National Forests
Southern Region
1720 Peachtree Road, NW
Atlanta, GA 30309
(404) 881-4177

See OUACHITA NATIONAL FOREST -
Arkansas.

STATE PARKS

Headquarters

Tourism and Recreation Department
Division of Parks and Recreation
500 Will Rogers Bldg.
Oklahoma City, OK 73105
(405) 521-2646

Ardmore

LAKE MURRAY STATE PARK (Resort)
Ardmore, OK 73401
(405) 223-6600
LOCATION: 7 mi. south of Ardmore on U.S.
77.
FACILITIES: Open year round; water and
bathroom facilities; sanitary station; electrical
hookup; trailer village vehicle sites; cabins;
picnic area; food service; swimming; boating;
boat rental; fishing; water skiing; horseback
riding; tent camping; lodging.

Broken Bow

BEAVER'S BEND STATE PARK
Broken Bow, OK 74728
(405) 584-3800
LOCATION: 7 mi. north of Broken Bow on
Hwy. 259, east on Hwy. 259A.
FACILITIES: Open year round; water and
bathroom facilities; sanitary station; electrical
hookup; trailer village vehicle sites; cabins;
picnic area; food service; swimming; boating;
boat rental; fishing; water skiing; hiking.

Canadian

ARROWHEAD STATE PARK (Resort)
Canadian, OK 74425
(918) 339-2711
LOCATION: 10 mi. south of Eufaula, off
U.S. 69.
FACILITIES: Open year round; water and
bathroom facilities; sanitary station; electrical
hookup; trailer village vehicle sites; cabins;
picnic area; food service; swimming; boating;
boat rental; fishing; water skiing; horseback
riding; tent camping; lodging.

Checotah

FOUNTAINHEAD STATE PARK (Resort)
Checotah, OK 74426
(918) 689-2501
LOCATION: 9 mi. south of Checotah on U.S.
69 and west on Hwy. 150.
FACILITIES: Open year round; water and
bathroom facilities; sanitary station; electrical
hookup; trailer village vehicle sites; cabins;
picnic area; food service; swimming; boating;
boat rental; fishing; water skiing; horseback
riding; tent camping; lodging.

Fort Cobb

FORT COBB STATE PARK
Fort Cobb, OK 73038
(405) 643-2249
LOCATION: 4 mi. north of Fort Cobb.
FACILITIES: Open year round; water and
bathroom facilities; sanitary station; electrical
hookup; trailer village vehicle sites; picnic
area; food service; swimming; boating; boat
rental; fishing; water skiing; horseback riding;
tent camping.

Foss

FOSS STATE PARK
Route 1, Box 59C
Foss, OK 73647
(405) 592-3171
LOCATION: 14 mi. west of Clinton on Hwy.
73.
FACILITIES: Open year round; water and
bathroom facilities; sanitary station; electrical
hookup; trailer village vehicle sites; picnic
area; food service; swimming; boating; boat
rental; fishing; water skiing; tent camping.

Kingston

LAKE TEXOMA STATE PARK (Resort)
Kingston, OK 73439
(405) 564-2311
LOCATION: 5 mi. east of Kingston on U.S.
70.
FACILITIES: Open year round; water and
bathroom facilities; sanitary station; electrical
hookup; trailer village vehicle sites; cabins;
picnic area; food service; swimming; boating;
boat rental; fishing; water skiing; horseback
riding; tent camping; lodging.

Lone Wolf

QUARTZ MOUNTAIN STATE PARK (Resort)
Lone Wolf, OK 73655
(405) 563-2424

STATE PARKS (continued)

LOCATION: 12 mi. east of Mangum on U.S. 283 and Hwy. 44, north on Hwy. 44A.
FACILITIES: Open year round; water and bathroom facilities; sanitary station; electrical hookup; trailer village vehicle sites; cabins; picnic area; food service; swimming; boating; boat rental; fishing; water skiing; tent camping; lodging.

New Prue

WALNUT CREEK STATE PARK
New Prue, OK 74060
(918) 242-3362
LOCATION: Between Tulsa and Cleveland on North Loop Hwy. off Hwy. 99.
FACILITIES: Open year round; water and bathroom facilities; sanitary station; electrical hookup; trailer village vehicle sites; picnic area; food service; swimming; boating; boat rental; fishing; tent camping; lodging.

Norman

LITTLE RIVER STATE PARK
Route 4
Norman, OK 73069
(405) 321-7038
LOCATION: 12 mi. east of Norman on Hwy. 9.
FACILITIES: Open year round; water and bathroom facilities; sanitary station; electrical hookup; trailer village vehicle sites; picnic area; swimming; boating; boat rental; fishing; water skiing; hiking; horseback riding; tent camping.

Pawhuska

OSAGE HILLS STATE PARK
Pawhuska, OK 74056
(918) 336-4141
LOCATION: 14 mi. northeast of Pawhuska.
FACILITIES: Open year round; water and bathroom facilities; sanitary station; electrical hookup; trailer village vehicle sites; cabins; swimming; boat rental; fishing; tent camping.

Vian

TENKILLER STATE PARK
Star Route
Vian, OK 74962
(918) 489-5641
LOCATION: 14 mi. west of Vian on Hwys. 82 and 100.
FACILITIES: Open year round; water and bathroom facilities; sanitary station; electrical hookup; trailer village vehicle sites; cabins; food service; swimming; boating; boat rental; fishing; water skiing; tent camping.

Wagoner

SEQUOYAH STATE PARK (Resort)
Wagoner, OK 74467
(918) 772-2545
LOCATION: 6 mi. east of Wagoner on Hwy. 51.
FACILITIES: Open year round; water and bathroom facilities; sanitary station; electrical hookup; trailer village vehicle sites; cabins; picnic area; food service; swimming; boating;

boat rental; fishing; water skiing; hiking; horseback riding; tent camping; lodging.

Watonga

ROMAN NOSE STATE PARK (Resort)
Watonga, OK 73772
(405) 623-7281
LOCATION: 7 mi. northwest of Watonga on Hwys. 8 and 8A.
FACILITIES: Open year round; water and bathroom facilities; sanitary station; electrical hookup; trailer village vehicle sites; cabins; picnic area; swimming; boating; boat rental; fishing; horseback riding; tent camping; lodging.

Wilburton

ROBBER'S CAVE STATE PARK
Wilburton, OK 74578
(918) 465-2562
LOCATION: 5 mi. north of Wilburton on Hwy. 2.
FACILITIES: Open year round; water and bathroom facilities; electrical hookup; trailer village vehicle sites; cabins; picnic area; food service; swimming; boating; boat rental; fishing; tent camping.

Wister

WISTER STATE PARK
Wister, OK 74966
(918) 655-7212
LOCATION: 9 mi. southwest of Poteau on U.S. 270.
FACILITIES: Open year round; water and bathroom facilities; sanitary station; electrical hookup; trailer village vehicle sites; cabins; food service; swimming; boating; boat rental; fishing; tent camping.

STATE FORESTS

There are no State Forests in Oklahoma.

HISTORIC SITES

Broken Bow

CHIEF GARDNER MANSION/MUSEUM, CYPRESS TREE - 1880s home of Jefferson Gardner, principal chief of Choctaw Indians. Prehistoric and historic Indian artifacts, pioneer artifacts from eastern Oklahoma. 2000-year-old cypress tree, largest in the state, stands nearby. Located 6 mi. east of Broken Bow on U.S. 70.

Claremore

J.M. DAVIS GUN MUSEUM - Collection of 20,000 guns, 70 saddles, 750 steins, hundreds of animal horns and trophy heads, Indian artifacts, 600 W.W.I posters, extensive "John Rogers Statuary" collection. Located at 333 Lynn Riggs Blvd.

Cookson

FORT CHICKAMAUGA - Only authorized re-

OKLAHOMA

HISTORIC SITES (continued)

creation of an early-day horse cavalry post in the U.S. "Soldiers" maintain customs and styles of the 1870s army. Many of the fort buildings over 100 years. Located ½ mi. north of Cookson on Hwy. 82.

Oologah

WILL ROGERS BIRTHPLACE - Relocated ranch house where Will Rogers, America's great humorist, was born. Located 1 mi. north on Hwy. 169 and 2 mi. east of Oologah.

Tahlequah

CHEROKEE NATIONAL MUSEUM, TSA-LA-GI VILLAGE - Cherokee history from earliest known beginnings to present. Also Tsa-La-Gi Village, recreated Cherokee village of the 17th century, with Cherokee living as their ancestors did 300 years ago. Located 2½ mi. south and 1 mi. east of Tahlequah off Hwy. 82.

HOSTELS

There are no Hostels in Oklahoma.

POINTS OF INTEREST

Ardmore

ELIZA CRUCE HALL DOLL MUSEUM - Three hundred of the world's finest dolls, ranging from famed "Court Dolls" belonging to Marie Antoinette, to Italy's Lenci. Also miniature tea sets of gold, silver, brass, pewter, wood, ivory and glass. Located on Grand at E, northwest.

Bartlesville

FRANK PHILLIPS HOME - Twenty-six room mansion of Frank Phillips, founder of Phillips Petroleum Co. Located at 1107 Cherokee.

Dewey

TOM MIX MUSEUM - Personal collection, clothing, saddles, trophies, pictures and records of the movie star. Located on 8th and Don Tyler.

Enid

MIDGLEY MUSEUM - Home built from rock and petrified wood, filled with displays of rocks and minerals, big game trophy heads, crystal and glassware, antique furniture. Located at 1003 Sequoyah.

Lawton

U.S. ARMY FIELD ARTILLERY AND FORT SILL MUSEUM - Seven exhibit buildings, including Geronimo Guardhouse, Old Stone Corral, graves of Geronimo and other Indian chiefs. History of field artillery from Revolutionary War to present. Located 4 mi. north of Lawton.

Muskogee

FIVE CIVILIZED TRIBES MUSEUM - History and artifacts of Cherokee, Chickasaw, Choctaw, Creek and Seminole tribes. Traditional Indian art gallery. Located on Agency Hill, Honor Heights Drive.

U.S.S. BATFISH - Submarine used in World War II. Continuous tours. Located ¾ mi. from Hyde Park exit, off Muskogee Turnpike northeast of city in War Memorial Park.

Oklahoma City

NATIONAL COWBOY HALL OF FAME AND WESTERN HERITAGE CENTER - Western art by Russell, Remington, Moran, sculptor James Fraser and others. National Rodeo and Great Western Performers Halls of Fame. Re-creation of an old pioneer town and Indian village. Located at 1700 N.E. 63rd St.

NATIONAL SOFTBALL HALL OF FAME AND MUSEUM - History, memorabilia and displays on every aspect of softball. Located at 2801 N.E. 50th.

OKLAHOMA HERITAGE CENTER - Fine mansion containing French, German, Italian, English and American classical paintings and furniture. Oklahoma Hall of Fame gallery, Oklahoma Heritage Galleria, memorial chapel and heritage gardens. Located at 201 N.W. 14th.

Ponca City

PIONEER WOMAN STATUE - Bryant Baker's famous statue of the pioneer woman. Located at 701 Monument Road.

Yale

JIM THORPE HOME - Restored and furnished home of the internationally famous Oklahoma athlete, who lived here from 1917 to 1923. Located at 706 E. Boston.

OREGON

Oregon, a land of forests, lakes and mountains, entered the Union in 1859 as the thirty-third state. Several early explorers passed through or by the state on their way to other destinations. Captain Cook, looking for the Northwest Passage to the Atlantic Ocean, sailed along and charted its coastline in the late 1700s. A few years later Lewis and Clark entered the region, but were just looking.

Oregon's forests, which cover nearly 50

INTRODUCTION (continued)

percent of the state's land area, are its most abundant and profitable natural resource. The leading state in the lumber industry, Oregon produces more than two-thirds of this nation's plywood supply.

The state's other natural resources. 13 national forests and a national park that contains Crater Lake, this country's deepest lake, and picturesque mountain ranges attract thousands of travelers each year, creating a considerable tourism trade for Oregon.

State capital: Salem. State bird: Western meadowlark. State tree: Douglar fir. State flower: Oregon grape.

WEATHER

Oregon enjoys a mild, though varied, climate. The single most important geographic feature of the climate of Oregon is the Pacific Ocean, whose coastline makes up the western border of the state.

Three mountain ranges also exert an important influence on Oregon's climate. The Coast Range, beginning near and following the coast the full length of the state, is the farthest west of the three. Some of the heaviest annual rainfalls occur along the higher western slopes. The Cascade Mountains parallel the Coast Range about 75 miles to the east and to within 50 to 75 miles of the California border, where the two ranges merge. The third range, the Blue Mountains, extends from the northeast corner southwestward to central Oregon.

Winter minimum and summer maximum temperatures in the west, and to a lesser extent in the eastern portion, are greatly moderated by the influence of the Pacific Ocean. The occurrence of extreme low or high temperatures is generally associated with the occasional invasion of the continental air masses.

Average daily temperature for each month.

	Northeastern	Southwestern
Jan.	37.9 to 22.8	47.9 to 34.2
Feb.	43.5 to 26.1	54.0 to 36.0
Mar.	49.0 to 28.1	57.6 to 36.3
Apr.	57.8 to 32.6	63.8 to 38.8
May	66.6 to 38.7	70.3 to 43.6
Jun.	73.8 to 44.8	76.5 to 49.3
Jul.	84.7 to 48.9	84.2 to 52.3
Aug.	83.0 to 47.6	83.2 to 51.9
Sept.	74.8 to 41.0	78.5 to 47.5
Oct.	62.6 to 33.9	66.6 to 42.9
Nov.	47.8 to 28.8	54.3 to 39.3
Dec.	39.3 to 24.0	48.4 to 35.6
Year	60.1 to 34.8	65.4 to 42.3

STATE CHAMBER OF COMMERCE

Associated Oregon Industries, Inc.
1149 Court Street, N.E.
P.O. Box 12519
Salem, OR 97309
(503) 588-0050

STATE & CITY TOURISM OFFICES

State

Oregon Department of Economic Development
317 South Alder Street
Portland, OR 97204
(503) 229-5535

Travel Information Section
101 Highway Building
Salem, OR 97310
(503) 378-3438

Portland Chamber of Commerce
824 S.W. Fifth Avenue
Portland, OR 97204
(503) 228-9411

STATE HIGHWAY DEPARTMENT

Department of Transportation
State Transportation Building
Salem, OR 97310
(503) 378-6388

HIGHWAY WELCOMING CENTERS

Ashford

ASHFORD CENTER - Interstate 5.

Astoria

ASTORIA CENTER - Columbia River Bridge.

Brookings

BROOKINGS CENTER - U.S. 101, south.

Klamath Falls

KLAMATH FALLS CENTER/MIDLAND - U.S. 97.

Ontario

ONTARIO CENTER - Interstate 80, north.

OREGON

Portland

PORTLAND CENTER - Interstate 5 at the Bridge.

Salem

SALEM CENTER - In city, Capitol Building.

STATE POLICE

Department of Public Safety
Salem, OR 97310
(503) 378-3720

HUNTING & FISHING

Hunting

Every person 14 years of age or older must have a hunting license on his person to hunt any wildlife.

No license is required for a resident to hunt wildlife on land he owns and upon which he resides, except for those species for which a tag or permit is required.

No person less than 14 years of age is required to possess a license for hunting wildlife, except for those species for which a tag or permit is required, provided that an adult accompanies the youngster on lands other than those owned or leased by the parents or guardians.

Any person who has not resided in Oregon for a period of at least 6 months immediately prior to application must purchase a non-resident hunter's license, except that members of the Armed Forces assigned to permanent duty status in Oregon and alien students attending school in Oregon under a foreign student exchange program may purchase licenses at resident rates.

Resident

Hunter's license, $7; bow hunting when purchased with hunting license, $2; bow hunting when purchased separately from hunting license, $5; combination angler's and hunter's license, $15; juvenile hunter's license, $2; general deer tag, $4; general elk tag, $15; elk bow tag, $15; bear tag, $4; antelope tag, $5; sheep tag, $10; cougar tag, $10; disabled war veterans (residents only): hunting license, $1; angling license, $1; elk tag, $2.50; pioneers (65 years old-50 years immediately prior residence in state): hunting license, $1; angling license, $1; elk tag, $2.50; senior citizens hunting and fishing license (70 years old-5 years immediately prior residence in state, free; resident trapper's license for furbearers, $6; beaver tag (trapper's license required).

Non-resident

Hunter's license, $75; general deer tag, $35; general elk tag, $75; elk bow tag, $75; bear tag, $35.

Fishing

A valid angling license is required of all persons 14 years or over to angle for game fish, except Oregon residents on their own land or on land owned by a member of their immediate family and upon which they reside.

Oregon residents must comply with Oregon regulations when angling for game fish anywhere in the Snake River (except from Idaho shore).

When angling for salmon 24 inches or over, or steelhead 20 inches or over, all anglers, regardless of age, must have a salmon-steelhead tag in possession, except for daily anglers (1-2-or 3-day) license holders.

The Oregon salmon-steelhead tag and daily angler licenses are not valid in the ocean within the 3-mile limit off the coasts of Washington or California.

A resident is any person who has resided in the state for at least 6 months immediately before applying for a license.

Resident

Annual angling, $9; annual combination angling and hunting, $15; daily angling, $2.50; annual juvenile angling, $2; annual salmon-steelhead tag, $2; annual senior citizen angling (70 years of age and 5 years Oregon resident), free; annual pioneer angling (65 years of age and 50 years Oregon resident), $1; annual disabled war veteran angling, $1.

Non-resident

Annual angling, $25; 10-day angling, $10; daily angling, $2.50; annual salmon-steelhead tag, $2.

For more information contact:

Department of Fish and Wildlife
506 SW Mill Street
Portland, OR 97208
(503) 229-5403

CAMPGROUNDS

See National Parks, National Forests, State Parks and State Forests.

RESORTS & BEACHES

Most of the state's resort activities center around the major lakes and include fishing, swimming, boating, water skiing, and camping. (See Boating Areas, National Parks, National Forests, State Parks, and State Forests.)

BOATING AREAS

Ashland

HOWARD PRAIRIE RESERVOIR
LOCATION: Northeast of Ashland.
FACILITIES: Launching.

BOATING AREAS (continued)

LAKE O' WOODS
LOCATION: Northeast of Ashland.
FACILITIES: Launching.

Baker

PHILLIPS RESERVOIR
LOCATION: Southwest of Baker.
FACILITIES: Launching.

Blue River

COUGAR RESERVOIR
LOCATION: Southeast of Blue River.
FACILITIES: Launching.

Burns

CHICKAHOMINY RESERVOIR
LOCATION: West of Burns.
FACILITIES: Launching.

Cottage Grove

COTTAGE GROVE RESERVOIR
LOCATION: South of Cottage Grove.
FACILITIES: Launching.

DORENA RESERVOIR
LOCATION: East of Cottage Grove.
FACILITIES: Launching.

Crescent

CRESCENT LAKE
LOCATION: In Crescent.
FACILITIES: Launching.

Detroit

ELK LAKE
LOCATION: North of Detroit.
FACILITIES: Launching.

Diamond Lake

DIAMOND LAKE
LOCATION: Near Diamond Lake.
FACILITIES: Launching.

Dilley

HENRY HAGG LAKE
LOCATION: West of Dilley.
FACILITIES: Launching.

Estacada

NORTH FORK RESERVOIR
LOCATION: Southeast of Estacada.
FACILITIES: Launching.

Eugene

FALL CREEK RESERVOIR
LOCATION: East of Eugene.
FACILITIES: Launching.

LOOKOUT POINT RESERVOIR
LOCATION: East of Eugene.
FACILITIES: Launching.

Florence

MERCER LAKE
LOCATION: North of Florence.
FACILITIES: Launching.

MUNSEL LAKE
LOCATION: North of Florence.
FACILITIES: Launching.

SILTCOOS LAKE
LOCATION: South of Florence.
FACILITIES: Launching.

WOAHINK LAKE
LOCATION: South of Florence.
FACILITIES: Launching.

Fort Klamath

CRATER LAKE
LOCATION: North of Fort Klamath.
FACILITIES: Launching.

Juntura

BEULAH RESERVOIR
LOCATION: North of Juntura.
FACILITIES: Launching.

Klamath Agency

AGENCY LAKE
LOCATION: South of Klamath Agency.
FACILITIES: Launching.

Klamath Falls

KLAMATH LAKE
LOCATION: Northwest of Klamath Falls.
FACILITIES: Launching.

Lakeside

SOUTH TENMILE LAKE
LOCATION: In Lakeside.
FACILITIES: Launching.

Lakeview

DREWS RESERVOIR
LOCATION: Southwest of Lakeview.
FACILITIES: Launching.

LaPine

WALDO LAKE
LOCATION: Northwest of LaPine.
FACILITIES: Launching.

WICKIUP RESERVOIR
LOCATION: West of LaPine.
FACILITIES: Launching.

Lincoln City

DEVILS LAKE
LOCATION: In Lincoln City.
FACILITIES: Launching.

New Pine Creek

GOOSE LAKE
LOCATION: West of New Pine Creek.
FACILITIES: Launching.

OREGON

BOATING AREAS (continued)

Oakridge

HILLS CREEK RESERVOIR
LOCATION: South of Oakridge.
FACILITIES: Launching.

ODELL LAKE
LOCATION: East of Oakridge.
FACILITIES: Launching.

Pendleton

MCKAY RESERVOIR
LOCATION: South of Pendleton.
FACILITIES: Launching.

Port Orford

GARRISON LAKE
LOCATION: West of Port Orford.
FACILITIES: Launching.

Prineville

OCHOCO RESERVOIR
LOCATION: East of Prineville.
FACILITIES: Launching.

PRINEVILLE RESERVOIR
LOCATION: Southeast of Prineville.
FACILITIES: Launching.

Reedsport

LOON LAKE
LOCATION: Southeast of Reedsport.
FACILITIES: Launching.

TAHKENITCH LAKE
LOCATION: North of Reedsport.
FACILITIES: Launching.

Riley

MOON RESERVOIR
LOCATION: South of Riley.
FACILITIES: Launching.

Roseburg

COOPER CREEK RESERVOIR
LOCATION: Northeast of Roseburg.
FACILITIES: Launching.

Sisters

LAKE BILLY CHINOOK
LOCATION: North of Sisters.
FACILITIES: Launching.

SUTTLE LAKE
LOCATION: Northwest of Sisters.
FACILITIES: Launching.

Summer Lake

SUMMER LAKE
LOCATION: Near Summer Lake.
FACILITIES: Launching.

Sweet Home

FOSTER RESERVOIR
LOCATION: East of Sweet Home.
FACILITIES: Launching.

PETER GREEN RESERVOIR
LOCATION: Quartzville Road.
FACILITIES: Launching.

Unity

UNITY RESERVOIR
LOCATION: North of Unity.
FACILITIES: Launching.

Wallowa

WALLOWA LAKE
LOCATION: In Wallowa.
FACILITIES: Launching.

BICYCLE TRAILS

CRATER LAKE TRAIL - 35 mi.; rugged terrain, high elevation; 10-speed bicycle recommended.

This is high-altitude cycling at its best. Although the elevation of the lake is around 6100 feet, the rim road goes above 8000 feet in several places and drops to around 6500 feet in others. The scenery is unsurpassed, with the deep blue water contrasting with the coniferous forests and the rocky cliffs. This road is normally free of snow from July to the end of September, but make local inquiries.

Trail: Around Crater Lake in Crater Lake National Park near Union Creek.

CROSS-OREGON TRAIL - 400 mi.; mountainous terrain; hot, dry climate; long distances per day; 10-speed bicycle necessary.

Start in Reedsport on the Pacific Coast with its cool breezes and heavy clouds even in summer. Enjoy the sea breeze while you can as the interior of Oregon can be plenty hot.

After Eugene you will pass through pretty mountain country. You will have stiff climbs at McKenzie, Dixie, and Blue Mountain passes. Once out of the mountains you will find the flat country dry and monotonous. Take it easy on the descent into the Grand Canyon of the Snake River. This is a trip for experienced cyclists to make between May and the middle of October.

Trail: Reedsport to Gunter to Eugene to Sisters to Prineville to Mitchell to John Day to Unity to Baker.

OREGON COAST TRAIL - 41 mi.; fog and wind, some hills; 10-speed bicycle recommended.

The sea stacks (picturesque, offshore rocks) along this trail are numerous and the road has a wide shoulder or an extra lane most of the way. Things that may give you trouble are fog, lumber trucks and chilly ocean winds.

Trail: Gold Beach south to Brookings.

WILLAMETTE RIVER TRAIL - 45 mi.; any bicycle.

This ride is over flat country along the Willamette River, south of Portland, and features two free ferry rides.

434

BICYCLE TRAILS (continued)

Trail: Wilsonville to Wheatland Ferry to Lincoln to Independence to Buena Vista to Buena Vista Ferry to Interstate 5.

TRAILS

Eugene

WILLAMETTE RIVER TRAIL - 1.84 mi. foot trail. This trail follows the southwest bank of Willamette River from Briarcliff Street to the Ferry Street Bridge. Parts of the trail run through developed park land which includes a rose garden and affords splendid views of distant scenery. The main recreational opportunity in the undeveloped areas is wild blackberry picking and passive recreation along the riverfront. There are several picnic sites and a wide variety of activities and natural attributes in the area.

Klamath Falls

LINK RIVER TRAIL - .75 mi. foot trail. This level, dead-end trail is 3 feet wide and located within a hydroelectric development project area consisting of a small division dam and two canals. The trail parallels the impoundment and is alongside a company maintenance road. The road is not open for public use. Abundant vegetation, birds and small animals can be found in the area.

Medford

BEAR CREEK BIKEWAY AND NATURE TRAIL - 3.4 mi. foot trail. Paved trail adjacent to Bear Creek. Running through the downtown Medford area, the trail offers opportunities to enjoy nature and outdoor recreation activities. Eventual extension of the trail is planned.

Portland

WILDWOOD TRAIL - 14 mi. foot trail. The Wildwood Trail lies within the 5,000-acre Forest Park, Portland's largest park. All but the first ½-mile is heavily forested with Douglas Fir, Western Hemlock, Western Red Cedar, Sword Ferns and Salal Bush. Special features include Pittock Mansion, which is associated with Portland's early history, a bird sanctuary and a self-guided nature trail. Connecting trails go through the 200-acre Hoyt Arboretum.

Seaside

TILLAMOOK HEAD TRAIL - Ecola State Park - 6 mi. foot trail. This trail, located between Seaside and Cannon Beach on the northern Oregon coast, provides access to a spruce-hemlock-alder forest environment and to precipitous seaside lands. Wildlife includes deer, elk, and smaller animals, plus numerous birds. Sea-birds may be observed on offshore rocks. The park on Tillamook Head tends to have generally steep terrain and is precipitous on the west side. There is an interesting history involving the Lewis and Clark Expedition and remnants of World War II coast defense works.

SKI AREAS

Ashland

MT. ASHLAND SKI AREA
P.O. Box 220
Ashland, OR 97520
(503) 482-6406
LOCATION: 20 mi. south of Ashland off Route I-5.
FACILITIES: 2 double chairlifts; 1 T-bar; 1 tow rope; 1 poma; ski instruction; ski rental; restaurants; lodging.

Bend

MT. BACHELOR SKI AREA
Bend, OR 97701
(503) 382-2442
LOCATION: 22 mi. west of Bend.
FACILITIES: 1 triple chairlift; 6 double chairlifts; 1 tow rope; ski instruction; ski rental; restaurants; lodging.

Government Camp

MULTORPOR-SKI BOWL
Government Camp, OR 97028
(503) 272-3330
LOCATION: Near Government Camp.
FACILITIES: 4 double chairlifts; 8 tow ropes; ski instruction; ski rental; restaurants; lodging.

SUMMIT SKI AREA
P.O. Box 85
Government Camp, OR 97028
(503) 272-3351
LOCATION: Near Government Camp.
FACILITIES: 1 T-bar; 4 tow ropes; ski rental; restaurants; lodging.

TIMBERLINE SKI AREA
Government Camp, OR 97028
(503) 272-3311
LOCATION: Near Government Camp.
FACILITIES: 4 double chairlifts; 2 tow ropes; ski instruction; ski rental; restaurants; lodging.

Hood River

COOPER SPUR SKI AREA
401 Monticello
Hood River, OR 97031
(503) 386-3381
LOCATION: 24 mi. south of Hood River.
FACILITIES: 1 T-bar; 1 tow rope; ski instruction; ski rental; restaurants; lodging.

John Day

DIXIE MOUNTAIN
121 SE Elm
John Day, OR 97845
(503) 575-1367
LOCATION: 5 mi. northeast of Prairie City.
FACILITIES: 1 tow rope; ski rental; 600 ft. vertical drop; restaurants; lodging.

OREGON

SKI AREAS (continued)

Klamath Falls

TOMAHAWK SKI BOWL
123 N. Spruce Street
Klamath Falls, OR 97601
LOCATION: 24 mi. northwest of Klamath Falls.
FACILITIES: 1 tow rope; 1 poma; ski instruction; ski rental; 630 ft. vertical drop; restaurants; lodging.

Lakeview

WARNER MOUNTAIN
P.O. Box 1204
Lakeview, OR 97630
(503) 947-1212
LOCATION: 10 mi. northeast of Lakeview.
FACILITIES: 1 T-bar; ski instruction; ski rental; 730 ft. vertical drop; restaurants; lodging.

Mt. Hood

MT. HOOD MEADOWS SKI AREA
Mt. Hood, OR 97041
(503) 337-2222
LOCATION: Near Mt. Hood.
FACILITIES: 6 double chairlifts; 3 tow ropes; ski instruction; ski rental; restaurants; lodging.

North Powder

ANTHONY LAKES SKI AREA
North Powder, OR 97867
(503) 898-2261
LOCATION: Near North Powder.
FACILITIES: 1 double chairlift; 1 poma; ski instruction; ski rental; restaurants; lodging.

Sisters

HOODOO SKI BOWL
Sisters, OR 97759
(503) Ask operator for Hoodoo No. 2.
LOCATION: Near Sisters.
FACILITIES: 3 chairlifts; 2 tow ropes; ski instruction; ski rental; restaurants; lodging.

Weston

SPOUT SPRINGS SKI AREA
Weston, OR 97886
(503) 566-2015
LOCATION: 40 mi. from Walla Walla.
FACILITIES: 2 double chairlifts; 2 T-bars; 1 tow rope; ski instruction; ski rental; 550 ft. vertical drop; restaurants; lodging.

AMUSEMENT PARKS & ATTRACTIONS

Newport

OREGON UNDERSEA GARDENS (Attraction)
267 S.W. Bay Blvd.
Newport, OR 97365
(503) 265-7541

FACILITIES: Underwater aquarium; scuba diving shows; free parking.

Portland

OAKS AMUSEMENT PARK
Portland, OR 97202
(503) 233-5777
FACILITIES: 17 major rides; 6 kiddie rides; 4 games; 4 refreshment stands; penny arcade; roller rink; picnic facilities; free acts; free gate; free parking; open Memorial Day - Labor Day; weekends all year.

Seaside

FAMILY FUN CENTER
117 Broadway
Seaside, OR 97138
(503) 325-5348
FACILITIES: 6 major rides; 8 kiddie rides; 8 games; 2 refreshment stands; arcade; shooting gallery; beach; miniature golf; golf driving range; bowling; aquarium; free gate; free parking; open Jun. 5 - Sept. 5; weekends all year.

STATE FAIR

Oregon State Fair
Salem, OR 97310
(503) 378-3247
DATE: August

NATIONAL PARKS

Crater Lake

CRATER LAKE NATIONAL PARK
Crater Lake, OR 97604
(503) 594-2211

LOST CREEK
LOCATION: Pinnaclos Road.
FACILITIES: Open Jul. 15 - Oct. 1; entrance fee; limit of stay: 14 days; 12 sites; NPS campsite fee: $2; water and bathroom facilities; cabins; picnic area; food service; swimming; fishing; hiking; snowmobile route; exhibit; environmental study area; living history program; NPS guided tour; self-guiding tour; lodging.

MAZAMA
LOCATION: 0.3 mi. east of Annie Springs entrance.
FACILITIES: Open Jul. 1 - Oct. 1; entrance fee; limit of stay: 14 days; 200 sites; NPS campsite fee: $3; water and bathroom facilities; sanitary station; cabins; picnic area; food service; swimming; fishing; hiking; snowmobile route; exhibit; environmental study area; living history program; NPS guided tour; self-guiding tour; lodging.

NATIONAL FORESTS

National Forests
Pacific Northwest Region
319 SW Pine Street
Portland, OR 97208
(503) 221-2971

NATIONAL FORESTS (continued)

Baker

WALLOWA-WHITMAN NATIONAL FORESTS (Two National Forests).
ATTRACTIONS: Snowcapped peaks; lakes; glaciers; alpine meadows and rare wild flowers; stream and lake trout fishing; elk, deer, bear hunting; saddle and pack trips; scenic drives.
FACILITIES: 50 camp and picnic sites, 3 picnic only; Anthony Lake Winter Sports Area; resorts; dude ranches; motels.
NEARBY TOWNS: Enterprise, Halfway, La Grande, Union.

Bend

DESCHUTES NATIONAL FOREST
ATTRACTIONS: Snowclad peaks; ice and lava caves; waterfalls; rainbow trout fishing; deer hunting; scenic drives; saddle and pack trips; skiing.
FACILITIES: 119 camp and picnic sites, 21 picnic only; 4 swimming sites; winter sports area; 42 boating sites; dude ranches; motels; resorts.
NEARBY TOWNS: Crescent, Redmond, Sisters.

Corvallis

SIUSLAW NATIONAL FOREST
ATTRACTIONS: Ocean, lake, and stream fishing; deer, bear, cougar, migratory bird hunting; swimming; boating; clam digging; scuba diving; scenic drives.
FACILITIES: 31 camp and picnic sites, 8 picnic only; 6 boating sites; resorts; motels.
NEARBY TOWNS: Eugene, Florence, Mapleton, Reedsport, Tillamook, Waldport.

Eugene

WILLAMETTE NATIONAL FOREST
ATTRACTIONS: Most heavily timbered National Forest in the United States; snowcapped peaks, lakes, waterfalls, and hot springs; lava beds; stream and lake fishing; deer and bear hunting; scenic drives; saddle and pack trips; winter sports area.
FACILITIES: 73 camp and picnic sites, 9 picnic only; 19 boating; 5 swimming sites; 2 winter sports areas; motels; cabins; pack trip outfitters.
NEARBY TOWNS: Albany, Lebanon, Salem.

Grants Pass

SISKIYOU NATIONAL FOREST
ATTRACTIONS: Beautiful Oregon coast; famous salmon fishing; early-day gold camps; home of rare species, including Port Orford cedar, "Oregon myrtle", rock rhododendron; cutthroat and steelhead trout, salmon fishing; deer, bear, cougar hunting; boat trips; saddle and pack trips; scenic drives.
FACILITIES: 26 camp and picnic sites, 2 picnic only; resorts; pack trip outfitters; cabins in and near the National Forest.
NEARBY TOWNS: Brookings, Gold Beach, Port Orford, Powers.

John Day

MALHEUR NATIONAL FOREST
ATTRACTIONS: Fossil beds of prehistoric plants and animals; steelhead, rainbow trout fishing; elk, deer hunting; archers' hunting reserve; scenic drives; saddle and pack trips.
FACILITIES: 36 camp and picnic sites, 2 picnic only; winter sports area; motels; cabins in and near the National Forest.
NEARBY TOWNS: Burns, Dayville and Prairie City.

Klamath Falls

WINEMA NATIONAL FOREST
ATTRACTIONS: Half the forest consists of former tribal lands of Klamath Indians; teeming waterfowl areas in adjacent Upper Klamath Lake, Oregon's largest lake; trout fishing; deer (both black-tailed and mule), migratory bird hunting.
FACILITIES: 26 camp and picnic sites, 9 picnic only; 6 boating and 2 swimming sites; Tomahawk Ski Bowl; resorts; cabins; motels; pack trip outfitters.
NEARBY TOWNS: Chemult, Chiloquin.

Lakeview

FREMONT NATIONAL FOREST
ATTRACTIONS: Indian paintings and writings; protected herds of antelope; deer, bird hunting; winter sports; Abert geologic fault east of Lake Abert, second largest vertical fault in the world.
FACILITIES: 33 camp and picnic sites, 3 picnic only; winter sports area; 3 boating sites; motels.
NEARBY TOWNS: Bly, Chemult, Klamath Falls, Paisley, Silver Lake.

Medford

ROGUE RIVER NATIONAL PARK
ATTRACTIONS: Mammoth sugar pine roadside specimen; Table Rock, site of bloody war with Rogue River Indians; rainbow and steelhead trout fishing; deer hunting; scenic drives; saddle and pack trips; skiing.
FACILITIES: 45 camp and picnic sites, 7 picnic only; swimming site; Union Creek and Mt. Ashland Winter Sports Areas; resorts; motels; cabins.
NEARBY TOWNS: Ashland, Grants Pass, Klamath Falls.

Pendleton

UMATILLA NATIONAL FOREST
ATTRACTIONS: Hot sulfur springs; steelhead, rainbow trout fishing; elk, deer, pheasant, other bird hunting; saddle and pack trips; scenic drives; skiing.
FACILITIES: 54 camp and picnic sites, 16 picnic only; 3 boating sites; tollgate-Spout Springs Winter Sports Area; hotels; resorts; dude ranches.
NEARBY TOWNS: La Grande, OR; Clarkston, Pomeroy, Waitsburg, and Walla Walla, WA.

Portland

MOUNT HOOD NATIONAL FOREST

OREGON

NATIONAL FORESTS (continued)

ATTRACTIONS: Glaciers; lakes; hot springs; flower-filled alpine meadows; stream and lake fishing; swimming; saddle and pack trips; huckleberry picking; winter sports; scenic drives.
FACILITIES: 107 camp and picnic sites, 24 picnic only; 6 winter sports areas; Timberline Lodge; Multnomah Falls Lodge, and other resorts in and near the National Forest.
NEARBY TOWNS: Gresham, Hood River, Maupin, Oregon City.

Prineville

OCHOCO NATIONAL FOREST
ATTRACTIONS: Beaver colonies; frontier-day army posts; scenes of early-day range wars; trout fishing; elk, deer hunting; scenic drives.
FACILITIES: 27 camp and picnic sites, 3 picnic only; 4 boating sites; motels; cabins.
NEARBY TOWNS: Bend, Burns.

Roseburg

UMPQUA NATIONAL FOREST
ATTRACTIONS: Unique stands of incense-cedar; steelhead and rainbow trout fishing; deer, bear, cougar hunting; scenic drives; saddle and pack trips; skiing.
FACILITIES: 53 camp and picnic sites, 19 picnic only; 6 boating sites; Taft Mountain Winter Sports Area; resorts; dude ranches; motels.
NEARBY TOWNS: Canyonville, Cottage Grove.

See KLAMATH NATIONAL FOREST - California.

STATE PARKS

Headquarters

State Parks and Recreation Branch
525 Trade Street, SE
Salem, OR 97310
(503) 378-6305

Astoria

FORT STEVENS STATE PARK
LOCATION: 10 mi. west of Astoria.
FACILITIES: Open year round; 483 sites; water and bathroom facilities; sanitary station; electrical hookup; trailer village vehicle sites; picnic area; swimming; hunting; fishing; tent camping.

Bandon

BULLARDS BEACH STATE PARK
LOCATION: 1 mi. north of Bandon.
FACILITIES: Open year round; 192 sites; water and bathroom facilities; electrical hookup; trailer village vehicle sites; picnic area; swimming; boating; fishing; tent camping.

Brookings

HARRIS BEACH STATE PARK

LOCATION: 2 mi. north of Brookings.
FACILITIES: Open year round; 151 sites; water and bathroom facilities; sanitary station; electrical hookup; trailer village vehicle sites; picnic area; swimming; fishing; tent camping.

LOEB STATE PARK
LOCATION: 10 mi. northeast of Brookings.
FACILITIES: Open year round; 53 sites; water and bathroom facilities; electrical hookup; trailer village vehicle sites; picnic area; swimming; fishing; tent camping.

Coos Bay

SUNSET BAY STATE PARK
LOCATION: 12 mi. southwest of Coos Bay.
FACILITIES: Open year round; 137 sites; water and bathroom facilities; electrical hookup; trailer village vehicle sites; swimming; boating; fishing; tent camping.

Detroit

DETROIT LAKE STATE PARK
LOCATION: 3½ mi. west of Detroit.
FACILITIES: Open year round; 320 sites; water and bathroom facilities; electrical hookup; trailer village vehicle sites; picnic area; swimming; fishing; tent camping.

Estacada

MILO MCIVER STATE PARK
LOCATION: 5 mi. west of Estacada.
FACILITIES: Open year round; 42 sites; water and bathroom facilities; sanitary station; electrical hookup; trailer village vehicle sites; picnic area; swimming; boating; fishing; tent camping.

Eugene

ARMITAGE STATE PARK
LOCATION: 5 mi. north of Eugene.
FACILITIES: Open year round; 32 sites; water and bathroom facilities; picnic area; fishing; tent camping.

Florence

JESSIE M. HONEYMAN STATE PARK
LOCATION: 3 mi. south of Florence.
FACILITIES: Open year round; 423 sites; water and bathroom facilities; sanitary station; electrical hookup; trailer village vehicle sites; picnic area; swimming; boating; fishing; tent camping.

Grants Pass

VALLEY OF THE ROGUE STATE PARK
LOCATION: 12 mi. east of Grants Pass.
FACILITIES: Open year round; 174 sites; water and bathroom facilities; sanitary station; electrical hookup; trailer village vehicle sites; picnic area; swimming; boating; fishing; tent camping.

John Day

CLYDE HOLLIDAY STATE PARK
LOCATION: 7 mi. west of John Day.
FACILITIES: Open year round; 30 sites; wa-

STATE PARKS (continued)

ter and bathroom facilities; sanitary station; electrical hookup; trailer village vehicle sites; picnic area; tent camping.

Joseph

WALLOWA LAKE STATE PARK
LOCATION: 6 mi. south of Joseph.
FACILITIES: Open year round; 310 sites; water and bathroom facilities; sanitary station; electrical hookup; trailer village vehicle sites; picnic area; swimming; boating; fishing; tent camping.

LaGrande

HILGARD JUNCTION STATE PARK
LOCATION: 8 mi. west of LaGrande.
FACILITIES: Open year round; 18 sites; water and bathroom facilities; electrical hookup; trailer village vehicle sites; picnic area; fishing; tent camping.

Lakeview

GOOSE LAKE STATE PARK
LOCATION: 15 mi. south of Lakeview.
FACILITIES: Open year round; 48 sites; water and bathroom facilities; electrical hookup; trailer village vehicle sites; swimming; boating; fishing; tent camping.

Lincoln City

DEVILS LAKE CAMP STATE PARK
LOCATION: Near Lincoln City.
FACILITIES: Open year round; 100 sites; water and bathroom facilities; electrical hookup; trailer village vehicle sites; boating; fishing; tent camping.

Madras

THE COVE PALISADES STATE PARK
LOCATION: 15 mi. southwest of Madras.
FACILITIES: Open year round; 272 sites; water and bathroom facilities; sanitary station; electrical hookup; trailer village vehicle sites; picnic area; swimming; boating; fishing; tent camping.

Manzanita Junction

NEHALEM BAY STATE PARK
LOCATION: 3 mi. south of Manzanita Jct.
FACILITIES: Open year round; 292 sites; water and bathroom facilities; sanitary station; electrical hookup; trailer village vehicle sites; picnic area; swimming; boating; fishing; tent camping.

Newberg

CHAMPOEG STATE PARK
LOCATION: 7 mi. east of Newberg.
FACILITIES: Open year round; 48 sites; water and bathroom facilities; sanitary station; electrical hookup; trailer village vehicle sites; picnic area; fishing; tent camping.

Newport

BEVERLY BEACH STATE PARK
LOCATION: 7 mi. north of Newport.
FACILITIES: Open year round; 278 sites; water and bathroom facilities; electrical hookup; trailer village vehicle sites; picnic area; swimming; fishing; tent camping.

SOUTH BEACH STATE PARK
LOCATION: 2 mi. south of Newport.
FACILITIES: Open year round; 257 sites; water and bathroom facilities; sanitary station; electrical hookup; trailer village vehicle sites; picnic area; swimming; fishing; tent camping.

Nyssa

LAKE OWYHEE STATE PARK
LOCATION: 33 mi. southwest of Nyssa.
FACILITIES: Open year round; 30 sites; water and bathroom facilities; sanitary station; electrical hookup; trailer village vehicle sites; picnic area; swimming; fishing; tent camping.

SUCCOR CREEK STATE PARK
LOCATION: 30 mi. south of Nyssa.
FACILITIES: Open year round; 198 sites; water and bathroom facilities; picnic area; fishing; tent camping.

Ontario

FAREWELL BEND STATE PARK
LOCATION: 25 mi. northwest of Ontario.
FACILITIES: Open year round; 53 sites; water and bathroom facilities; sanitary station; electrical hookup; trailer village vehicle sites; picnic area; swimming; boating; fishing; tent camping.

Pendleton

EMIGRANT SPRINGS STATE PARK
LOCATION: 26 mi. southeast of Pendleton.
FACILITIES: Open year round; 51 sites; water and bathroom facilities; electrical hookup; trailer village vehicle sites; picnic area; tent camping.

Port Orford

CAPE BLANCO STATE PARK
LOCATION: 9 mi. north of Port Orford.
FACILITIES: Open year round; 58 sites; water and bathroom facilities; sanitary station; electrical hookup; trailer village vehicle sites; picnic area; swimming; fishing; tent camping.

HUMBUG MOUNTAIN STATE PARK
LOCATION: 6 mi. south of Port Orford.
FACILITIES: Open year round; 105 sites; water and bathroom facilities; electrical hookup; trailer village vehicle sites; picnic area; swimming; fishing; tent camping.

Portland

AINSWORTH STATE PARK
LOCATION: 37 mi. east of Portland.
FACILITIES: Open year round; 45 sites; water and bathroom facilities; sanitary station; electrical hookup; trailer village vehicle sites; picnic area; tent camping.

Prineville

OCHOCO LAKE STATE PARK

OREGON

STATE PARKS (continued)

LOCATION: 7 mi. east of Prineville.
FACILITIES: Open year round; 22 sites; water and bathroom facilities; picnic area; swimming; fishing; tent camping.

PRINEVILLE RESERVOIR STATE PARK
LOCATION: 17 mi. southeast of Prineville.
FACILITIES: Open year round; 70 sites; water and bathroom facilities; electrical hookup; trailer village vehicle sites; picnic area; swimming; boating; fishing; tent camping.

Reedsport

UMPQUA LIGHTHOUSE STATE PARK
LOCATION: 6 mi. south of Reedsport.
FACILITIES: Open year round; 63 sites; water and bathroom facilities; electrical hookup; trailer village vehicle sites; swimming; boating; fishing; tent camping.

WM. M. TUGMAN STATE PARK
LOCATION: 8 mi. south of Reedsport.
FACILITIES: Open year round; 115 sites; water and bathroom facilities; sanitary station; electrical hookup; trailer village vehicle sites; picnic area; swimming; boating; fishing; tent camping.

Roseburg

SUSAN CREEK STATE PARK
LOCATION: 29 mi. east of Roseburg.
FACILITIES: Open year round; 31 sites; water and bathroom facilities; electrical hookup; trailer village vehicle sites; picnic area; fishing; tent camping.

Salem

SILVER FALLS STATE PARK
LOCATION: 26 mi. east of Salem.
FACILITIES: Open year round; 61 sites; water and bathroom facilities; electrical hookup; trailer village vehicle sites; picnic area; tent camping.

Selma

DEER CREEK STATE PARK
LOCATION: 6 mi. east of Selma.
FACILITIES: Open year round; 16 sites; water and bathroom facilities; electrical hookup; trailer village vehicle sites; picnic area; fishing; tent camping.

Sweet Home

CASCADIA STATE PARK
LOCATION: 14 mi. east of Sweet Home.
FACILITIES: Open year round; 26 sites; water and bathroom facilities; picnic area; swimming; fishing; tent camping.

The Dalles

DESCHUTES RIVER STATE PARK
LOCATION: 17 mi. east of The Dalles.
FACILITIES: Open year round; 34 sites; water and bathroom facilities; sanitary station; electrical hookup; trailer village vehicle sites; picnic area; fishing; tent camping.

MEMALOOSE STATE PARK
LOCATION: 11 mi. west of The Dalles.
FACILITIES: Open year round; 110 sites; water and bathroom facilities; sanitary station; electrical hookup; trailer village vehicle sites; picnic area; tent camping.

Tillamook

CAPE LOOKOUT STATE PARK
LOCATION: 12 mi. southwest of Tillamook.
FACILITIES: Open year round; 246 sites; water and bathroom facilities; electrical hookup; trailer village vehicle sites; picnic area; swimming; fishing; hiking; tent camping.

Ukiah

UKIAH-DALE STATE PARK
LOCATION: 3 mi. southwest of Ukiah.
FACILITIES: Open year round; 25 sites; water and bathroom facilities; electrical hookup; trailer village vehicle sites; fishing; tent camping.

Unity

UNITY LAKE STATE PARK
LOCATION: 5 mi. north of Unity.
FACILITIES: Open year round; 16 sites; water and bathroom facilities; electrical hookup; trailer village vehicle sites; picnic area; swimming; boating; fishing; tent camping.

Waldport

BEACHSIDE STATE PARK
LOCATION: 4 mi. south of Waldport.
FACILITIES: Open year round; 80 sites; water and bathroom facilities; electrical hookup; trailer village vehicle sites; picnic area; swimming; fishing; tent camping.

STATE FORESTS

Forestry Department
2600 State Street
Salem, OR 97310
(503) 378-2560

Forest Grove

ELK CREEK STATE FOREST
LOCATION: 22 mi. west of Forest Grove.
FACILITIES: Open year round; 9 sites; water and bathroom facilities; fishing; tent camping.

GALES CREEK STATE FOREST
LOCATION: 15 mi. west of Forest Grove.
FACILITIES: Open year round; 38 sites; water and bathroom facilities; electrical hookup; trailer village vehicle sites; fishing; hiking; tent camping.

Mohler

NEHALEM FALLS STATE FOREST
LOCATION: 10 mi. east of Mohler.
FACILITIES: Open year round; 15 sites; water and bathroom facilities; electrical hookup; trailer village vehicle sites; fishing; tent camping.

STATE FORESTS (continued)

Tillamook

DIAMOND MILL STATE FOREST
LOCATION: 24 mi. east of Tillamook.
FACILITIES: Open year round; 30 sites; water and bathroom facilities; trailer village vehicle sites; fishing; tent camping.

JONES CREEK STATE FOREST
LOCATION: 23 mi. east of Tillamook.
FACILITIES: Open year round; 50 sites; water and bathroom facilities; sanitary station; electrical hookup; trailer village vehicle sites; picnic area; fishing; tent camping.

KEENIG CREEK STATE FOREST
LOCATION: 18 mi. east of Tillamook.
FACILITIES: Open year round; 30 sites; water and bathroom facilities; electrical hookup; trailer village vehicle sites; fishing; tent camping.

PENINSULA PARK STATE FOREST
LOCATION: 11 mi. east of Tillamook.
FACILITIES: Open year round; 6 sites; water and bathroom facilities; fishing; tent camping.

TRASK RIVER STATE FOREST
LOCATION: 15 mi. east of Tillamook.
FACILITIES: Open year round; 90 sites; water and bathroom facilities; sanitary station; electrical hookup; trailer village vehicle sites; fishing; tent camping.

HISTORIC SITES

Jacksonville

HISTORIC JACKSONVILLE - Abounds with buildings dating from the mid-1800s. Included are the Eagle Brewery Saloon, the butcher shop, and Kahler's Law Office. Many are private residences still in use. A county museum is located in the old Courthouse.

Newberg

MINTHORN HOUSE - Home of Herbert Hoover, the 31st President, from 1884-1889. Contains many of the original furnishings and souvenirs of his boyhood. Hoover was raised by his uncle, Henry John Minthorn. Located at 115 South River Street.

Portland

MCLOUGHLIN HOUSE - One of the few remaining pioneer dwellings in the region once known as the Oregon Country (Oregon, Washington, Idaho, and parts of Montana and Wyoming). The house was built in 1845-46 by Dr. John McLoughlin, chief factor and superintendent of the Columbia department of the Hudson's Bay Company. Located in McLoughlin Park between 7th and 8th Streets.

Salem

DEEPWOOD - Queen Anne Mansion built in 1894 by Dr. Luke A. Port. House features oak paneling, Tiffany style windows, donated period furnishings. Located at 116 Mission Street, SE.

MISSION MILL MUSEUM - Includes home of Reverend Jason Lee, the first to establish an Indian mission in the Pacific Northwest, home of John D. Boon, an early Oregon pioneer, and Methodist Mission with furnishings. Located off Mill Street between 12th and 14th Streets, SE.

Wolf Creek

WOLF CREEK TAVERN - Unique among other surviving Oregon stage stations, it has been in continuous use as a depot from the beginning. A fine example of 19th-century Classical Revival style architecture. Located on I-50, 20 mi. north of Grants Pass.

HOSTELS

Coos Bay

SEAGULL
P.O. Box 847
Coos Bay, OR 97420
(503) 267-6114
FACILITIES: Open Jun. 15 - Labor Day; 15 beds, men; 15 beds, women; modern bathroom; nearest hostel: Mt. Shasta, CA; Portland, OR; overnight charges: $1.75; houseparents: hostel staff.

Mitchell

OREGON HOTEL
Box 12
Mitchell, OR 97750
No telephone
FACILITIES: Open year round; 24 beds, men; 24 beds, women; modern bathroom; nearest hostel: Portland; overnight charges: $2.50; houseparent: Donna Heller.

Portland

N.W. PORTLAND YOUTH HOSTEL
1809 N.W. Johnson Street
Portland, OR 97209
(503) 227-1488
FACILITIES: Open year round; 16 beds, men; 14 beds, women; modern bathroom; nearest hostels: Coos Bay, Mitchell; overnight charges: $3; houseparent: Rev. Donald Slakie.

POINTS OF INTEREST

Florence

INDIAN FOREST - Authentic replicas of Indian villages, including earth lodges, tepees, bark house, and sweat lodge. Live buffalo, and Indian arts and crafts. Located on Hwy. 101.

SEA LION CAVES - Modern elevator takes you to one of the world's largest sea caves. One mainland home of the Stellar Sea Lion. No special clothing needed. Located on Hwy. 101, north of Florence.

OREGON

POINTS OF INTEREST (continued)

Gleneden Beach

ALDER HOUSE II - A glassblowing studio where artisans work in traditional off-hand method, with each piece being completely individualized in design. Located east of Hwy. 101 on Immonen Road.

MOSSY CREEK POTTERY - Small pottery workshop with gallery featuring the work of some of Oregon's finest artists and craftspeople. Located off Hwy. 101 on Immonen Road.

Nehalem

NEHALEM BAY WINERY - Visitors are invited to taste premium wines made from fruits grown in the Pacific Northwest. Tours through winery plus a tasting room.

Portland

INTERNATIONAL ROSE TEST GARDEN - One of 24 gardens nationwide designated as an official test garden by AARS (All-American Rose Selections). You can wander among 8000 roses of 400 different varieties. Located at 400 S.W. Kingston.

The Dalles

SASQUATCH EXHIBIT - An unusual museum depicting the lore of the Northwestern legend of Bigfoot, a huge ape-like animal. Located near Hwy. 80.

Tillamook

TILLAMOOK CHEESE FACTORY - Produces 80 percent of all cheese made in Oregon. Viewing window and slide show explain process. Located on Main Street.

PENNSYLVANIA

Pennsylvania, from the beginning a natural leader in industry, entered the Union in 1787 as the second state. William Penn, a Quaker, founded the original colony and established a liberal form of government which fostered creativity and growth. In 1728, Ben Franklin of Philadelphia published "The Saturday Evening Post," this country's first magazine.

About 66 years later, the Philadelphia-Lancaster Turnpike became the first paved highway in the nation. Then near Titusville, the world's first oil well was drilled in 1859.

The electronic communications industry was inaugurated in Pennsylvania, too, when America's first radio station, Pittsburgh's KDKA, went on the air in 1920.

Today, the state leads in the mining of hard coal and is one of the country's foremost producers of steel. Agriculture, especially dairy products and livestock, and tourism add substantially to Pennsylvania's income.

State capital: Harrisburg.   State bird: Ruffed grouse.   State tree: Hemlock.   State flower: Mountain laurel.

WEATHER

Pennsylvania, comprising 45,126 square miles, is characterized by notable contrasts in topography and climate. The Appalachian Mountain system divides the Commonwealth into three major topographical sections: the Piedmont Plateau in the southeast; the Ridge and Valley Region northwest of the Piedmont; and the Allegheny Plateau, which extends north to the New York border and west to Ohio. In addition, two plains areas of relatively small size exist: the Coastal Plain in the southeast and the Lake Erie Plain in the northwest.

Pennsylvania is generally considered to have a humid continental type climate, but the varied physiographic features have a marked effect on the weather and climate of the various sections within the state. In the Southeastern Coastal Plain and Piedmont Plateau, the summers are long and, at times, uncomfortably hot, in general, the winters are comparatively mild. The Ridge and Valley Province does not have a true mountain type of climate, but it does have many of the characteristics of such a climate. Tempera-

tures are more extreme than in the southeastern part of the state. The Allegheny Plateau has a continental type of climate, with changeable temperatures and more frequent precipitation than other parts of the state. In the more northerly sections, conditions serve to make this the coldest area in the state. The region of the Lake Erie Plain has a unique climate typical of much of the coastal area surrounding the Great Lakes.

Average daily temperature for each month.

	Northwestern	Southeastern
Jan.	34.8 to 16.9	40.4 to 20.1
Feb.	36.7 to 16.9	43.2 to 21.9
Mar.	45.5 to 24.8	52.0 to 29.5
Apr.	59.9 to 35.2	65.1 to 38.9
May	70.5 to 44.0	75.0 to 48.3
Jun.	79.0 to 53.4	83.5 to 57.7
Jul.	82.8 to 57.5	87.5 to 62.3
Aug.	81.3 to 56.3	85.6 to 60.4
Sept.	75.0 to 49.8	79.1 to 53.9
Oct.	64.4 to 39.6	68.1 to 42.1
Nov.	49.8 to 31.6	55.2 to 33.3
Dec.	38.2 to 22.5	43.8 to 24.7

WEATHER (continued)

Year 59.8 to 37.4   64.9 to 41.1

STATE CHAMBER OF COMMERCE

Pennsylvania Chamber of Commerce
222 North 3rd Street
Harrisburg, PA 17101
(717) 232-4121

STATE & CITY TOURISM OFFICES

State

Bureau of Travel Development
Pennsylvania Department of Commerce
431 South Office Building
Harrisburg, PA 17120
(717) 787-5453

Pennsylvania Department of Commerce
South Office Building
Harrisburg, PA 17120
(717) 787-3003

Local

Convention and Tourist Bureau
1525 John F. Kennedy Blvd.
Philadelphia, PA 19102
(215) 864-1976

Convention and Visitors Bureau
3001 Jenkins Arcade
Pittsburgh, PA 15222
(412) 281-5723

STATE HIGHWAY DEPARTMENT

Department of Transportation
1220 Transportation & Safety Building
Commonwealth & Forester Streets
Harrisburg, PA 17120
(717) 787-5574

HIGHWAY WELCOMING CENTERS

Cumberland

CUMBERLAND/NEWVILLE CENTER - Interstate 81, north.

Delaware Water Gap

DELAWARE WATER GAP CENTER - Interstate 80, west of New Jersey line.

Erie

ERIE CENTER - Interstate 90, near North East .

Fulton

FULTON CENTER - Interstate 95, north, north of Maryland border.

Marcus Hook

MARCUS HOOK CENTER - Interstate 95, north, north of Delaware line.

Mercer

MERCER COUNTY CENTER - Interstate 80, east, east of Ohio line.

Sideling Hill

SIDELING HILL CENTER - Pennsylvania Turnpike, east & west bound, near Waterfall.

Trevose

TREVOSE CENTER - Pennsylvania Turnpike.

Yardley

YARDLEY CENTER - Interstate 95, south.

Zelienople

ZELIENOPLE CENTER - Pennsylvania Turnpike, Beaver Valley Interchange Exits 2 & 3.

STATE POLICE

Department of Public Safety
1800 Elmerton Avenue
Harrisburg, PA 17120
(717) 783-5599

HUNTING & FISHING

Hunting

A current license, signed in ink with the owner's signature, is required to hunt, trap, take or kill any wild bird or wild animal in Pennsylvania. License valid from September 1 to the following August 31, inclusive.

It is unlawful for any person under the age of 12 years to receive a hunting license under any circumstances. It is unlawful for any person under 16 years of age to receive a hunting license without presenting a written request to the issuing agent, signed by his or her mother, father or legally constituted guardian. Persons 12 or 13 years of age must be accompanied while hunting by a parent or legal guardian, or some other person who is serving in place of a parent or guardian, or some other member of the family at least 18 years of age. Hunters 14 or 15 years of age must be accompanied by an adult of at least 18 years of age. Persons 16 years of age and older my hunt alone although they only possess a valid junior license. Farm youths, ages 12-16, may hunt alone on property upon which they reside. No hunting license will be issued to any person under the age of 16 years unless he or she presents either (a) evidence that he or she has held a hunting license in Pennsylvania or

PENNSYLVANIA

HUNTING & FISHING (continued)

another state in a prior year, or (b) a certificate of competency showing that he or she has successfully completed a course of instruction in the safe handling of firearms and bows and arrows.

No license (including antlerless deer and archery) is required by any citizen residing upon and regularly and continuously cultivating lands on a commercial basis. Such person may also hunt or trap privately owned lands adjacent to his or her own without a license, if written consent is given by owner or lessee.

Resident

Junior hunting and trapping license, $5.25 (12-16 years of age); adult hunting and trapping license, $8.25; senior hunting and trapping license, $5.25; antlerless deer, $3.35; archery, $2.20; muzzleloader deer, $3.25.

Non-resident

Hunting, $40.35; trapping, $40; 3-day regulated shooting grounds, $3.15.

Fishing

A current license, signed in ink, is required to fish or angle for any species of fish herein legally provided for, and to take fishbait or baitfish, and is required of persons of any age to take frogs, tadpoles and turtles.

License valid from January 1 to December 31, inclusive.

You qualify for a resident fishing license if you have been a bona fide resident of Pennsylvania for at least 60 consecutive days immediately prior to buying your license.

License not required of resident owners or lessee and family residing on a farm and persons regularly employed upon a farm which includes an artificial pond. Pond's water source must be wholly within the farm, or contain no game fish. Visitors must possess a license while fishing and must abide by all Commission rules and regulations.

Resident

Adult fishing, $7.50; senior fishing, $2.

Non-resident

Fishing, $12.50; 7-day tourist, $7.50.

For more information contact:

Pennsylvania Game Commission
Harrisburg, PA 17120
(717) 787-6286

Pennsylvania Fish Commission
Harrisburg, PA 17120
(717) 787-6487

CAMPGROUNDS

Private

Bellefonte

BELLEFONTE KOA KAMPGROUND
(814) 355-7912
LOCATION: North on Hwy. 26.
FACILITIES: Open May - Nov.; water and bathroom facilities; sanitary station; electrical hookup; trailer village vehicle sites; laundry; food service; swimming; hiking; tent camping.

Bentleyville

CAMPGROUND 70
(412) 239-5522
LOCATION: 1 mi. north of Bentleyville.
FACILITIES: Open year round; water and bathroom facilities; sanitary station; electrical hookup; trailer village vehicle sites; laundry; food service; tent camping.

Brookville

CONTENTED VALLEY CAMPGROUND
(814) 328-2651
LOCATION: On Gravel Road.
FACILITIES: Open May - Nov.; water and bathroom facilities; sanitary station; electrical hookup; trailer village vehicle sites; laundry; hunting; hiking; tent camping.

Burnt Cabins

YE OLDE MILL CAMPGROUND
(717) 987-3244
LOCATION: On Cowan Cap Road.
FACILITIES: Open year round; water and bathroom facilities; sanitary station; electrical hookup; trailer village vehicle sites; laundry; food service; hunting; fishing; hiking; tent camping.

Bushkill

KEN'S WOODS CAMPGROUND
(717) 588-6381
LOCATION: 2 mi. north on Hwy. 209, then 7 mi. east.
FACILITIES: Open May - Nov.; water and bathroom facilities; sanitary station; electrical hookup; trailer village vehicle sites; laundry; food service; swimming; fishing; hiking; tent camping.

Catawissa

J & D TRAILER COURT
(717) 672-2097
LOCATION: Between Catawissa and Elysburg on Route 487.
FACILITIES: Open May - Nov.; water and bathroom facilities; sanitary station; electrical hookup; trailer village vehicle sites; food service; swimming; boating; fishing.

Champion

CUTTY'S FAMILY RESORT CAMP-GROUND
(412) 455-3300
LOCATION: Off Pennsylvania Turnpike, Exit

CAMPGROUNDS (continued)

9, 4 mi. south on Route 711.
FACILITIES: Open year round; water and bathroom facilities; sanitary station; electrical hookup; trailer village vehicle sites; laundry; food service; swimming; boating; fishing; hiking; tent camping.

Coudersport

DEER LICK CAMPING AREA
(814) 274-9950
LOCATION: 2 mi. south of U.S. 6 on Hwy. 872.
FACILITIES: Open year round; water and bathroom facilities; sanitary station; electrical hookup; trailer village vehicle sites; food service; hunting; hiking; tent camping.

Danville

PINE-N-OAK CAMPGROUNDS
(717) 437-3291
LOCATION: 3 mi. west of Danville, left at sign, then 1½ mi. to campground.
FACILITIES: Open May - Nov.; water and bathroom facilities; sanitary station; electrical hookup; trailer village vehicle sites; food service; swimming; fishing; hiking; tent camping.

Denver

HICKORY RUN FAMILY CAMPGROUND
(215) 267-5785
LOCATION: 2 mi. west on Greenville Road.
FACILITIES: Open year round; water and bathroom facilities; sanitary station; electrical hookup; trailer village vehicle sites; laundry; food service; swimming; boating; hunting; fishing; hiking; tent camping.

Drums

HAZELTON — WILKES-BARRE KOA KAMPGROUND
(717) 788-3382
LOCATION: I-80 & I-81 Junction.
FACILITIES: Open May - Nov.; water and bathroom facilities; sanitary station; electrical hookup; trailer village vehicle sites; laundry; food service; swimming; hunting; hiking; tent camping.

East Stroudsburg

TIMOTHY LAKE CAMP-RESORT
(717) 583-6631
LOCATION: I-80, Exit 52, U.S. 209, 8 mi. north to Winona Falls Road, then left 5 mi.
FACILITIES: Open year round; water and bathroom facilities; sanitary station; electrical hookup; trailer village vehicle sites; laundry; food service; swimming; boating; hunting; fishing; hiking; tent camping.

Ebensburg

WOODLAND PARK CAMPGROUND
(814) 472-9857
LOCATION: ¼ mi. west of Ebensburg Airport on Route 22.
FACILITIES: Open May - Nov.; water and bathroom facilities; sanitary station; electrical hookup; trailer village vehicle sites; laundry; food service; fishing; hiking; tent camping.

Ellwood City

BENTEL'S CAMPGROUND
(412) 758-5761
LOCATION: South of Ellwood on Route 65.
FACILITIES: Open May - Nov.; water and bathroom facilities; sanitary station; electrical hookup; trailer village vehicle sites; swimming; boating; hunting; tent camping.

Emporium

YESTER-YEN CAMPING AREA
(814) 486-9825
LOCATION: 3 mi. north of Emporium.
FACILITIES: Open May - Nov.; water and bathroom facilities; sanitary station; electrical hookup; trailer village vehicle sites; laundry; food service; hunting; fishing.

Falls

THE BIG "4" CAMPGROUND
(717) 388-6626
LOCATION: 1 mi. south of Falls on U.S. 92.
FACILITIES: Open May - Nov.; water and bathroom facilities; sanitary station; electrical hookup; trailer village vehicle sites; food service; boating; fishing; hiking; tent camping.

Gettysburg

GRANITE HILL FAMILY CAMP RESORT
(717) 642-8749
LOCATION: 6 mi. west of Gettysburg on Route 116.
FACILITIES: Open May - Nov.; water and bathroom facilities; sanitary station; electrical hookup; trailer village vehicle sites; laundry; food service; swimming; boating; fishing; hiking; tent camping.

Hatfield

OAK GROVE PARK
(215) 723-2007
LOCATION: North Main St.
FACILITIES: Open year round; water and bathroom facilities; sanitary station; electrical hookup; trailer village vehicle sites; laundry; swimming; tent camping.

Hershey

HERSHEY HIGHMEADOW CAMP
(717) 566-0902
LOCATION: On Chocolate Ave.
FACILITIES: Open year round; water and bathroom facilities; sanitary station; electrical hookup; trailer village vehicle sites; laundry; food service; swimming; boating; fishing; tent camping.

Honesdale

KEEN LAKE CAMPING-COTTAGE RESORT
(717) 488-6161
LOCATION: 7 mi. west of Honesdale on U.S. 6.
FACILITIES: Open year round; water and

PENNSYLVANIA

CAMPGROUNDS (continued)

bathroom facilities; sanitary station; electrical hookup; trailer village vehicle sites; laundry; food service; swimming; boating; fishing; hiking; tent camping.

Honey Brook

HONEY BROOK FAMILY CAMPGROUND
(215) 273-3152
LOCATION: On Route 10, 9 mi. south of Pennsylvania Turnpike, Exit 22.
FACILITIES: Open year round; water and bathroom facilities; sanitary station; electrical hookup; trailer village vehicle sites; laundry; food service; swimming; hunting; fishing; hiking.

Hop Bottom

SHORE FOREST MANOR CAMPGROUND
(717) 289-4666
LOCATION: 4 mi. west on Loomis Lake Road.
FACILITIES: Open May - Nov.; water and bathroom facilities; sanitary station; electrical hookup; trailer village vehicle sites; laundry; food service; swimming; boating; fishing; tent camping.

Huntingdon

RAYSTOWN COUNTRY CAMPING RESORT
(215) 867-9080
LOCATION: On Water Street.
FACILITIES: Open year round; water and bathroom facilities; sanitary station; electrical hookup; trailer village vehicle sites; swimming; boating; fishing; hiking; tent camping.

Jonestown

MEMORIAL LAKE KOA KAMPGROUND
(717) 865-2526
LOCATION: I-78 exit for Fredericksburg, 4 mi. west on Route 22.
FACILITIES: Open May - Nov.; water and bathroom facilities; sanitary station; electrical hookup; trailer village vehicle sites; laundry; food service; swimming; hiking; tent camping.

Kittanning

SILVER CANOE CAMPGROUND
(412) 783-6367
LOCATION: Between Kittanning and Indiana on Route 210.
FACILITIES: Open May - Nov.; water and bathroom facilities; sanitary station; electrical hookup; trailer village vehicle sites; food service; boating; hunting; fishing; hiking; tent camping.

Knox

WOLF'S KOA KAMPGROUND
(814) 797-1103
LOCATION: In Knox.
FACILITIES: Open May - Nov.; water and bathroom facilities; sanitary station; electrical hookup; trailer village vehicle sites; laundry; food service; swimming; boating; fishing; tent camping.

Kutztown

OLD DUTCH MILL PARK CAMPGROUND
(215) 683-3959
LOCATION: From I-78, 3 mi. south on Route 737.
FACILITIES: Open year round; water and bathroom facilities; sanitary station; electrical hookup; trailer village vehicle sites; food service; boating; hunting; fishing; hiking; tent camping.

Lewisburg

WINFIELD RIVER EDGE CAMP
(717) 524-0453
LOCATION: 4 mi. south of Lewisburg.
FACILITIES: Open May - Nov.; water and bathroom facilities; sanitary station; electrical hookup; trailer village vehicle sites; laundry; food service; swimming; boating; fishing; tent camping.

Lewistown

IDLE ACRES CAMPING AREA
(717) 899-6307
LOCATION: 10 mi. west of Lewistown.
FACILITIES: Open year round; water and bathroom facilities; sanitary station; electrical hookup; trailer village vehicle sites; swimming; fishing; hiking; tent camping.

Liverpool

FERRYBOAT CAMPSITES
(717) 444-3200
LOCATION: In Liverpool.
FACILITIES: Open May - Nov.; water and bathroom facilities; sanitary station; electrical hookup; trailer village vehicle sites; food service; swimming; boating; hunting; fishing; hiking.

Marchburg

KINZUA EAST KOA KAMPGROUND
(814) 368-3662
LOCATION: 1½ mi. west of Marchburg.
FACILITIES: Open May - Nov.; water and bathroom facilities; sanitary station; electrical hookup; trailer village vehicle sites; laundry; food service; swimming; hunting; hiking; tent camping.

Mercer

SKY-VIEW CAMPING RESORT
(412) 662-5317
LOCATION: 2½ mi. northwest of Mercer on Route 258.
FACILITIES: Open May - Nov.; water and bathroom facilities; sanitary station; electrical hookup; trailer village vehicle sites; laundry; swimming; fishing; hiking; tent camping.

Mercersburg

SAUNDEROSA PARK CAMPGROUND
(717) 328-2216
LOCATION: 2 mi. south of Hwys. 456 & 16 junction.
FACILITIES: Open May - Nov.; water and bathroom facilities; sanitary station; electrical

CAMPGROUNDS (continued)

hookup; trailer village vehicle sites; laundry; food service; swimming; hiking; tent camping.

Mexico

WALKER CAMPING AREA
(717) 436-2481
LOCATION: ¼ mi. southwest of Mexico.
FACILITIES: Open year round; water and bathroom facilities; sanitary station; electrical hookup; trailer village vehicle sites; laundry; food service; boating; hunting; fishing; hiking; tent camping.

Mt. Holly Springs

MOYER'S MOUNTAIN RETREAT CAMPGROUND
(717) 486-5281
LOCATION: 2 mi. south on Hwys. 34 & 94, then 1 mi. east on County Road.
FACILITIES: Open year round; water and bathroom facilities; sanitary station; electrical hookup; trailer village vehicle sites; laundry; food service; swimming; hunting; hiking; tent camping.

New Castle

ROSE POINT PARK
(412) 924-2415
LOCATION: On U.S. 422 at Rose Point.
FACILITIES: Open year round; water and bathroom facilities; sanitary station; electrical hookup; trailer village vehicle sites; laundry; food service; swimming; hunting; fishing; hiking; tent camping.

New Ringold

LAUREL LAKE CAMPSITES
(717) 386-5301
LOCATION: ½ mi. west of Hwys. 309 & 895 junction.
FACILITIES: Open year round; water and bathroom facilities; sanitary station; electrical hookup; trailer village vehicle sites; boating; hunting; fishing; tent camping.

New Stanton

FOX DEN ACRES CAMPGROUND
(412) 925-7054
LOCATION: 1¼ mi. north of junction Hwy. 119, I-70 & Exit 8 of Pennsylvania Turnpike.
FACILITIES: Open year round; water and bathroom facilities; sanitary station; electrical hookup; trailer village vehicle sites; food service; boating; hunting; fishing; hiking; tent camping.

New Tripoli

ALLENTOWN - LEHIGH VALLEY KOA KAMPGROUND
(215) 298-2160
LOCATION: I-78, Fogelsville Exit, Route 100 North.
FACILITIES: Open May - Nov.; water and bathroom facilities; sanitary station; electrical hookup; trailer village vehicle sites; laundry; food service; swimming; hunting; fishing; hiking; tent camping.

Penns Creek

GRAY SQUIRREL CAMPSITES
(717) 524-6984
LOCATION: Between Penns Creek & Troxelville.
FACILITIES: Open year round; water and bathroom facilities; sanitary station; electrical hookup; trailer village vehicle sites; laundry; food service; hunting; fishing; hiking; tent camping.

Portersville

BEAR RUN CAMPGROUND
(412) 368-3564
LOCATION: North on Badger Hill Road.
FACILITIES: Open year round; water and bathroom facilities; sanitary station; electrical hookup; trailer village vehicle sites; food service; swimming; boating; hunting; fishing; hiking; tent camping.

Portland

DRIFTSTONE-ON-THE-DELAWARE CAMPGROUND
(717) 897-6859
LOCATION: 4 mi. south of Portland on River Road.
FACILITIES: Open May - Nov.; water and bathroom facilities; sanitary station; electrical hookup; trailer village vehicle sites; laundry; food service; swimming; boating; fishing; hiking; tent camping.

Quakertown

LITTLE RED BARN CAMPGROUNDS
(215) 536-3357
LOCATION: 3 mi. east to Route 536, north to Old Beth Road, then 1 mi. northwest.
FACILITIES: Open year round; water and bathroom facilities; sanitary station; electrical hookup; trailer village vehicle sites; laundry; food service; swimming; hunting; fishing; hiking; tent camping.

Ridgway

BOOT JACK KOA KAMPGROUND
(814) 722-4135
LOCATION: 6 mi. south of Ridgway on U.S. 219.
FACILITIES: Open year round; water and bathroom facilities; sanitary station; electrical hookup; trailer village vehicle sites; laundry; food service; swimming; hunting; tent camping.

Schellsburg

ALLEGHENY VILLAGE CAMPGROUND
(814) 733-4254
LOCATION: 5 mi. east of Schellsburg on Route 30.
FACILITIES: Open year round; water and bathroom facilities; sanitary station; electrical hookup; trailer village vehicle sites; laundry; food service.

Shunk

BUTTERMILK FALLS KOA KAMPGROUND

PENNSYLVANIA

CAMPGROUNDS (continued)

(717) 857-9616
LOCATION: ¼ mi. off Route 154.
FACILITIES: Open May - Nov.; water and bathroom facilities; sanitary station; electrical hookup; trailer village vehicle sites; laundry; food service; swimming; hunting; fishing; hiking; tent camping.

Somerset

PIONEER PARK CAMPGROUND
(814) 445-6348
LOCATION: Route 31 West.
FACILITIES: Open May - Nov.; water and bathroom facilities; sanitary station; electrical hookup; trailer village vehicle sites; laundry; food service; swimming; boating; hunting; fishing; hiking; tent camping.

Spartansburg

HEMLOCK LAKES PARK
(814) 664-2994
LOCATION: Hyde Road.
FACILITIES: Open year round; water and bathroom facilities; sanitary station; electrical hookup; trailer village vehicle sites; laundry; food service; swimming; boating; hunting; hiking; tent camping.

Stony Fork

STONY FORK CREEK CAMPING GROUNDS
(717) 724-3096
LOCATION: 2 mi. south of Stony Fork.
FACILITIES: Open year round; water and bathroom facilities; sanitary station; electrical hookup; trailer village vehicle sites; laundry; swimming; hunting; fishing; hiking; tent camping.

Sunbury

IRISH VALLEY CAMPGROUND
(717) 644-1214
LOCATION: 7 mi. south of Sunbury on Route 890.
FACILITIES: Open year round; water and bathroom facilities; sanitary station; electrical hookup; trailer village vehicle sites; food service; hunting; fishing; tent camping.

Tionesta

KIBBE'S ISLAND PARK CAMPGROUND
(814) 755-3364
LOCATION: 4 mi. on Route 62 at Hunter Station Bridge.
FACILITIES: Open May - Nov.; water and bathroom facilities; sanitary station; electrical hookup; trailer village vehicle sites; swimming; boating; hunting; fishing; hiking.

Tyrone

BALD EAGLE CAMPSITE
(814) 684-3485
LOCATION: 4 mi. north of Tyrone.
FACILITIES: Open May - Nov.; water and bathroom facilities; sanitary station; electrical hookup; trailer village vehicle sites; food service; hunting; fishing; hiking; tent camping.

Union City

CANADOHTA LAKE PARK CAMP-GROUND
(814) 694-2012
LOCATION: 5 mi. south of Union City on Route 8, then 2 mi. west.
FACILITIES: Open May - Nov.; water and bathroom facilities; sanitary station; electrical hookup; trailer village vehicle sites; laundry; food service; swimming; boating; hunting; fishing; hiking.

Waterford

COUNTRY VIEW RESORT CAMP-GROUNDS
(814) 438-3004
LOCATION: Route 97 to Union City Dam.
FACILITIES: Open May - Nov.; water and bathroom facilities; sanitary station; electrical hookup; trailer village vehicle sites; laundry; food service; swimming; hunting; fishing; hiking; tent camping.

Waterville

HAPPY ACRES CAMPGROUND
(717) 847-3221
LOCATION: 3½ mi. on Route 41021 after Waterville Bridge.
FACILITIES: Open year round; water and bathroom facilities; sanitary station; electrical hookup; trailer village vehicle sites; laundry; food service; swimming; boating; hunting; fishing; hiking; tent camping.

West Hickory

INDIAN VALLEY CAMPGROUND & CANOE LIVERY
(814) 755-3578
LOCATION: 5 mi. south of West Hickory.
FACILITIES: Open year round; water and bathroom facilities; sanitary station; electrical hookup; trailer village vehicle sites; food service; swimming; boating; hunting; fishing; hiking; tent camping.

White Haven

WAGON TRAIN CAMPGROUND
(717) 443-9191
LOCATION: 5 mi. north of Exit 41, I-80 West, on Hwy. 940.
FACILITIES: Open year round; water and bathroom facilities; sanitary station; electrical hookup; trailer village vehicle sites; laundry; food service; swimming; hunting; fishing; hiking.

Wind Ridge

LYON CAMPGROUND
(412) 428-3362
LOCATION: 1 mi. west of Ryerson State Park turnoff on Route 21.
FACILITIES: Open May - Nov.; water and bathroom facilities; sanitary station; electrical hookup; trailer village vehicle sites; food service; hunting; fishing; tent camping.

CAMPGROUNDS (continued)

Woodland

WOODLAND - PLEASANT VALLEY KOA KAMPGROUND
(814) 875-7820
LOCATION: ½ mi. off I-80 at Exit 20.
FACILITIES: Open year round; water and bathroom facilities; sanitary station; electrical hookup; trailer village vehicle sites; laundry; food service; swimming; boating; hunting; fishing; hiking; tent camping.

Wyalusing

ENDLESS MOUNTAINS CAMPGROUND
(717) 265-9055
LOCATION: 6 mi. north of Wyalusing on Hwy. 187.
FACILITIES: Open May - Nov.; water and bathroom facilities; sanitary station; electrical hookup; trailer village vehicle sites; laundry; food service; swimming; hunting; fishing; hiking; tent camping.

York

CREEK AYR CAMPGROUND
(717) 292-2535
LOCATION: 12 mi. west of York.
FACILITIES: Open May - Nov.; water and bathroom facilities; sanitary station; electrical hookup; trailer village vehicle sites; food service; boating; hunting; fishing; hiking; tent camping.

RESORTS & BEACHES

Stroudsburg

POCONO MOUNTAINS - A spectacular view, clean, crisp air and every outdoor and indoor activity imaginable make these mountains a four-season playground for families and honeymooners alike. There's swimming, boating, golf, skiing, hunting, riding trails, tennis, snowmobiling, basketball, and, of course, great trout fishing. But perhaps you'd rather sit in the shade of a beach umbrella beside a shimmering swimming pool with a cool drink in your hand. There's that, too.

BOATING AREAS

Beltzville

BELTZVILLE LAKE
LOCATION: Near Beltzville.
FACILITIES: Launching.

Blanchard

BLANCHARD LAKE
LOCATION: 2 mi. west of Blanchard.
FACILITIES: Launching.

Borough of Edinboro

EDINBORO LAKE
LOCATION: Near borough of Edinboro.
FACILITIES: Launching.

Brackney

QUAKER LAKE
LOCATION: Near Brackney.
FACILITIES: Launching.

Butler

LAKE ARTHUR
LOCATION: West of Butler.
FACILITIES: Launching.

Danville

MONTOUR PRESERVE
LOCATION: Near Danville.
FACILITIES: Launching.

Erie

LAKE ERIE
LOCATION: Off Route 5.
FACILITIES: Launching.

Glenhazel

EAST BRANCH CLARION RIVER RESERVOIR
LOCATION: Near Glenhazel.
FACILITIES: Launching.

Hanover

LAKE MARBURG
LOCATION: 2 mi. southeast of Hanover.
FACILITIES: Launching.

Harveys Lake

HARVEYS LAKE
LOCATION: Near borough of Harveys Lake.
FACILITIES: Launching.

Hesston

RAYSTOWN LAKE
LOCATION: Near Hesston.
FACILITIES: Launching.

Honesdale

DUCK HARBOR POND
LOCATION: 15 mi. north of Honesdale.
FACILITIES: Launching.

Jamestown

PYMATUNING LAKE
LOCATION: Near Jamestown.
FACILITIES: Launching.

Jim Thorpe

MAUCH CHUNK LAKE
LOCATION: West of Jim Thorpe.
FACILITIES: Launching.

Leesport

ONTELAUNEE RESERVOIR
LOCATION: Near Leesport.
FACILITIES: Launching.

PENNSYLVANIA

BOATING AREAS (continued)

Lititz

SPEEDWELL FORGE LAKE
LOCATION: 6 mi. north of Lititz.
FACILITIES: Launching.

Meadville

CONNEAUT LAKE
LOCATION: 7 mi. east of Meadville.
FACILITIES: Launching.

TAMARACK LAKE
LOCATION: 3 mi. south of Meadville.
FACILITIES: Launching.

Newtown Square

SPRINGTON RESERVOIR
LOCATION: Near Newtown Square.
FACILITIES: Launching.

Oxford

CHESTER-OCTORARO RESERVOIR
LOCATION: 4 mi. west of Oxford.
FACILITIES: Launching.

Patton

GLENDALE LAKE
LOCATION: Near Patton.
FACILITIES: Launching.

Pleasant Mount

BELMONT LAKE
LOCATION: 2½ mi. north of Pleasant Mount.
FACILITIES: Launching.

Pond Hill

LILY LAKE
LOCATION: Near Pond Hill.
FACILITIES: Launching.

Sandy Lake

LAKE WILHELM
LOCATION: North of Sandy Lake.
FACILITIES: Launching.

Schellsburg

SHAWNEE LAKE
LOCATION: Near Schellsburg.
FACILITIES: Launching.

Sharpsville

SHENANGO LAKE
LOCATION: Near Sharpsville.
FACILITIES: Launching.

Somerset

HIGH POINT LAKE
LOCATION: 30 mi. south of Somerset.
FACILITIES: Launching.

YOUGHIOGHENY DAM
LOCATION: 25 mi. south of Somerset.

FACILITIES: Launching.

Tionesta

TIONESTA LAKE
LOCATION: ¼ mi. south of Tionesta.
FACILITIES: Launching.

Troxelville

CLARENCE WALKER DAM
LOCATION: 1 mi. south of Troxelville.
FACILITIES: Launching.

Warren

ALLEGHENY RESERVOIR
LOCATION: 7 mi. east of Warren.
FACILITIES: Launching.

BICYCLE TRAILS

AMISH TRAIL - 42.5 mi.; any bicycle.
"Pennsylvania Dutch" country makes for what may be the best cycling in the mid-Atlantic area. The roads are small and lightly traveled, and the land abounds with well-kept farms and the culture of the Pennsylvania Dutch people.
Trail: Bowmansville Youth Hostel to Five-pointville to Terre Hill, left on Main Street, right on Lancaster Avenue, left on Grist Mill Road, continue on Linden Grove Road, left on Shirk Road, right on S. Shirk Road, right on Zeltenreich Road, left on Musser School Road, right on Groffdale Road, left on E. Elby Road, left on Stumptown Road to Mascot, left on Newport Road, right on Hess Road, left on Old Philadelphia Road, left on Ridge Road, left on Hollander Road, left on Custer Road, right on Conestoga Street, left on N. Railroad Avenue, right on Lindengrove Road, right on Lancaster Road to Terre Hill, right on Main Street, left on Center Avenue, right on Linden Street, left on Wentzel Road, left at dead end, Hwy. 625 to Bowmansville.

BUCKS COUNTY TRAIL - 26 mi.; any bicycle.
This ride in Bucks County features two covered bridges. Roads indicated with five numbers are county roads, and they are well marked along the routes.
Trail: Weisel to Applebachville to Pleasant Valley to Hwy. 485, left on Hwy. 418, right on 09137 to Durham to 09061 to Applebachville to Weisel.

DELAWARE CANAL TRAIL - 30 mi.; poor surfaces, some hills; 10-speed bicycle recommended.
The canal follows roughly the path of Route 32.
At two places the canal crosses streams on aqueducts with only narrow catwalks on the side. It is advisable to detour onto Route 32 to bypass these points. The towpath surface is rough in spots.
Trail: Start at the town of Upper Black Eddy and continue south to Uhlerstown to Erwinna to Tinicum to Pt. Pleasant to Lumberville to Center Bridge to New Hope to Washington Crossing.

BICYCLE TRAILS (continued)

DELAWARE RIVER TRAIL - 250 mi.; hilly terrain; 10-speed bicycle recommended.

The highlights of this ride include the Pocono Mountains, the Delaware River, and the Delaware Water Gap National Recreation Area. It is 250 miles if you start in Philadelphia and complete the northern loop. Add 80 miles if you plan to pedal back to Philadelphia.

Trail: Philadelphia to Weisel to Riegelsville to Phillipsburg, NJ, to Belvidere to Shoemakers, PA to Bushkill to Dingman's Ferry to Port Jervis, NY to Barryville to Hawley, PA to La Anna to Shoemakers, return to Philadelphia.

GETTYSBURG-CATOCTIN PARK TRAIL - 52 mi.; some hills; 10-speed bicycle recommended.

Here is a ride that connects the historic town of Gettysburg with the new Catoctin National Park. Most of this ride is on rural roads with light traffic.

Trail: Gettysburg to Emmitsburg, MD to St. Anthony to Thurmont to Catoctin Park to Foxville to Lantz to Sabillasville to Greenstone, PA to Fairfield to Gettysburg.

MIDDLE ATLANTIC TRAIL - 625 mi.; long distances per day, hills; 10-speed bicycle necessary.

This is a popular long-distance bicycle trip that includes most of the Delaware Valley.

Trail: Philadelphia to Hwy. 352 west, Hwy. 282 to Geigertown to Hershey to Harrisburg to Gettysburg to Hwy. 116, Hwy. 491 to Raven Rock Campground to Shady Hook Hostel to Seneca Hostel to Washington, DC to Annapolis to Easton to Trap Pond State Park, DE to Nanticoke River Ferry to Assateague State Park to Lewes, DE to ferry to Cape May, NJ to Ocean City to Hammonton to Evesboro to Philadelphia.

MORAINE PARK TRAIL - 95 mi.; poor road surfaces, some hills; 10-speed bicycle recommended.

North of Pittsburgh, in Butler County, some fine cycling is to be found on the secondary roads. There are some bumps and rough bridge surfaces on this trip.

Trail: North Park to Gibsonia to Mars to Evans City to Prospect to Moraine State Park.

PENNSYLVANIA DUTCH TRAIL - 250 mi.; some poor roads, hills; 10-speed bicycle recommended.

This trail works out to an average of less than 40 miles per day with spring, summer and fall being suitable traveling times.

Trail: Philadelphia to Ridley Creek State Park to Downington to Geigertown to Parksburg to Georgetown to Strasburg to Lititz to Brickerville to Ephrata to Bowmansville to Birdsboro to Gilberts to Spinnerstown to Weisel to Pipersville to Washington Crossing to Bryn Athyn to Philadelphia.

See MARYLAND - Seneca-to-Gettysburg Trail.

See NEW YORK - Susquehanna Crescent Trails.

VALLEY FORGE TRAIL - 78 mi.; hilly terrain; 10-speed bicycle recommended.

During part of this trip you will be traveling the route of the historic Horse Shoe Trail.

Trail: Philadelphia to Narberth to Old Gulph Road to New Centerville to Valley Forge Park to Williams Corner to Charleston to Rapps Corner to Chester Springs to Nantmeal Village to Warwick to French Creek State Park. Retrace to Rapps Corner to Malvern to Whitehorse to Oakmont to Narberth to Philadelphia.

TRAILS

Holtwood

KELLY'S RUN - PINACLE TRAIL SYSTEM - 4.75 mi. foot trail. Located at the Holtwood Hydro electric project near Holtwood, the system is comprised of four interconnecting loop trails located in rolling hills that drop sharply into the Susquehanna River Valley. This rugged natural area includes pine plantations, oak forests and old-growth hemlock trees with rosebay rhododendron beneath.

Jeannette

FLOUR SAK BATTLE BICENTENNIAL TRAIL - 1 mi. foot trail. This nature trail is in Bushy Run Battlefield State Park and contains special provisions for use and enjoyment by the blind. A series of learning posts describes in Braille the historical significance of sites along the trail. Tape recorders are also available which give a narrative description of the trail's historic significance. A special feature of the trail is the variety of tree species planted as part of the overall effort to reclaim strip-mined lands for park and recreation purposes.

Philadelphia

FAIRMOUNT PARK BIKE PATH - 8.5 mi. foot trail. Located in one of the oldest and largest urban parks in the nation, this trail follows the banks of the Schuylkill River. Five and one-half miles of connecting trails lead users throughout the park. Fairmount was the site of the national centennial of 1876. Numerous mansions, remaining from original country estates, have been preserved. An internationally famous art museum graces one end of the trail. Hikers will find a great variety of flowers and flowering shrubs, as well as trees, in this well-maintained example of the 19th-century landscape park concept.

WISSAHICKON TRAIL - 5.4 mi. foot trail. This nature trail is within Wissahickon Valley, a National Natural Landmark. Natural and man-made attractions include the only remaining covered bridge in the Philadelphia area, unique rock formations, and waterfalls, one of which is a very popular fishing spot for Philadelphians. There is an outstanding hemlock preserve near the trail, and there are several features of historic significance, such as statues of William Penn and Delaware Indian Chief Tedyuscung.

PENNSYLVANIA

TRAILS (continued)

Reading

UNION CANAL WALKING AND BICYCLE TRAIL - 2.3 mi. foot trail. A portion of the historical Union Canal Towpath in Berks County forms the basis for this trail. Various recreation facilities of Tulpehocken Creek Valley Park are linked through this aggregate surfaced trail. Recreation opportunities along the level towpath include walking, bicycling, jogging, nature study and historical interpretation of the canal, locks, blacksmith shop and covered Red Bridge (the longest in Pennsylvania).

SKI AREAS

Buck Hill Falls

BUCK HILL
Buck Hill Falls, PA 18323
(717) 595-7441
LOCATION: 8 mi. from Mt. Pocono.
FACILITIES: 2 pomas; ski instruction; ski rental; nursery; restaurants; lodging.

Bushkill

FERNWOOD
Bushkill, PA 18324
(717) 588-6661
LOCATION: On Route 209.
FACILITIES: 1 tow rope; ski instruction; ski rental; nursery; restaurants; lodging.

SAW CREEK
Bushkill, PA 18324
(717) 588-6611
LOCATION: Off Route 209.
FACILITIES: 1 chairlift; ski instruction; ski rental; restaurants; lodging.

Cambridge

MT. PLEASANT
Cambridge, PA 16403
(814) 734-1641
LOCATION: 7 mi. southeast of Edinboro on Washington Valley Road.
FACILITIES: 1 T-bar; 1 poma; ski instruction; ski rental; restaurants; lodging.

Canadensis

TIMBER HILL
Canadensis, PA 18325
(717) 595-7571
LOCATION: On Route 447.
FACILITIES: 2 T-bars; 1 poma; ski instruction; ski rental; restaurants; lodging.

Chadds Ford

CHADDS PEAK
Chadds Ford, PA 19317
(215) 388-6476
LOCATION: 4 mi. west of Route 202.
FACILITIES: 3 tow ropes; 1 poma; ski instruction; ski rental; restaurants; lodging.

Champion

HASELTINE HILLS
Champion, PA 15622
(412) 455-3311
LOCATION: 10 mi. southeast of Donegal.
FACILITIES: 1 tow rope; 2 pomas; ski instruction; ski rental; restaurants; lodging.

SEVEN SPRINGS
Champion, PA 15622
(814) 352-7777
LOCATION: 10 mi. off PA Turnpike Exit 9.
FACILITIES: 6 chairlifts; 5 tow ropes; 2 pomas; ski instruction; ski rental; nursery; restaurants; lodging.

Claysburg

BLUE KNOB
Claysburg, PA 16625
(814) 239-5111
LOCATION: At Bedford, Routes 220 to 869, left at Osterburg to area.
FACILITIES: 2 chairlifts; 2 pomas; ski instruction; ski rental; restaurants; lodging.

Coudersport

DENTON HILL
Coudersport, PA 16915
(814) 435-6372
LOCATION: Route 6, east of Coudersport.
FACILITIES: 1 chairlift; 3 pomas; ski instruction; ski rental; restaurants; lodging.

Eagles Mere

HANLEY'S HAPPY HILL
Eagles Mere, PA 17731
(717) 525-3461
LOCATION: On Route 42.
FACILITIES: 2 tow ropes; ski instruction; ski rental; restaurants; lodging.

Fairfield

SKI LIBERTY
Fairfield, PA 17320
(717) 642-8282
LOCATION: 8 mi. southwest of Gettysburg on Route 116.
FACILITIES: 3 chairlifts; 1 J-bar; ski instruction; ski rental; nursery; restaurants; lodging.

Flinton

GLENDALE
Flinton, PA 16640
(814) 687-2575
LOCATION: 20 mi. northwest of Altoona.
FACILITIES: 1 tow rope; ski instruction; restaurants; lodging.

Hazelton

EAGLE ROCK
Hazelton, PA 18201
(717) 384-3231
LOCATION: 5 mi. south on Route 924.
FACILITIES: 2 chairlifts; 1 mitey mite; ski instruction; ski rental; restaurants; lodging.

SKI AREAS (continued)

Honesdale

HICKORY RIDGE
Honesdale, PA 18431
(717) 253-2000
LOCATION: 5 mi. south of Honesdale.
FACILITIES: 1 T-bar; 1 tow rope; ski instruction; ski rental; nursery; restaurants; lodging.

Hughesville

MONT SAINT ONGE
Highesville, PA 17737
(717) 584-2698
LOCATION: 7 mi. off Route 220.
FACILITIES: 1 tow rope; 1 poma; ski instruction; ski rental; restaurants; lodging.

Lackawaxen

MASTHOPE
Lackawaxen, PA 18435
(717) 685-7101
LOCATION: Near Hawley.
FACILITIES: 1 chairlift; 1 J-bar; ski instruction; ski rental; nursery; restaurants; lodging.

Lake Coma

MOUNT TONE
Lake Coma, PA 18437
(717) 798-2707
LOCATION: 2 mi. from Route 247.
FACILITIES: 1 chairlift; 1 T-bar; 2 tow ropes; ski instruction; ski rental; restaurants; lodging.

Lake Harmony

BIG BOULDER
Lake Harmony, PA 18624
(717) 722-0101
LOCATION: 5 mi. from Blakeslee.
FACILITIES: 4 chairlifts; 1 T-bar; 1 J-bar; ski instruction; ski rental; nursery; restaurants; lodging.

SPLIT ROCK
Lake Harmony, PA 18624
(717) 443-9571
LOCATION: Near Lake Harmony.
FACILITIES: 1 T-bar; ski instruction; ski rental; nursery; restaurants; lodging.

Latrobe

SUGARBUSH MOUNTAIN
Latrobe, PA 15650
(412) 238-9655
LOCATION: Ridge Road between Youngstown and Darlington.
FACILITIES: 1 tow rope; ski instruction; ski rental; restaurants; lodging.

Lewisberry

SKI ROUNDTOP
Lewisberry, PA 17339
(717) 432-9631
LOCATION: Between Harrisburg and York.
FACILITIES: 5 chairlifts; 1 J-bar; ski instruction; ski rental; nursery; restaurants; lodging.

Ligonier

LAUREL MOUNTAIN
Ligonier, PA 15658
(412) 238-6622
LOCATION: 7 mi. east of Ligonier.
FACILITIES: 1 chairlift; 3 tow ropes; 2 pomas; ski instruction; ski rental; restaurants; lodging.

Macungie

DOE MOUNTAIN
Macungie, PA 18062
(215) 682-7107
LOCATION: 15 mi. southwest of Allentown.
FACILITIES: 2 chairlifts; 1 J-bar; 1 tow rope; ski instruction; ski rental; restaurants; lodging.

Mt. Pocono

MT. AIRY
Mt. Pocono, PA 18344
(717) 839-8811
LOCATION: 3 mi. south of Mt. Pocono.
FACILITIES: 1 chairlift; ski instruction; ski rental; nursery; restaurants; lodging.

Muncy Valley

NORTH MOUNTAIN
Muncy Valley, PA 17758
(717) 482-2541
LOCATION: 2 mi. north of Muncy Valley.
FACILITIES: 1 J-bar; 1 tow rope; ski instruction; ski rental; restaurants; lodging.

Orefield

APPLE HILL
Orefield, PA 18069
(215) 395-4241
LOCATION: 8 mi. northwest of Allentown, left off Route 309.
FACILITIES: 1 T-bar; 3 tow ropes; ski instruction; ski rental; restaurants; lodging.

Phillipsburg

BLACK MOSHANNON
Phillipsburg, PA 16866
(814) 342-1101
LOCATION: 10 mi. east of Phillipsburg.
FACILITIES: 2 pomas; restaurants; lodging.

Plum Boro

BOYCE PARK
Plum Boro, PA 15239
(412) 325-1516
LOCATION: East of Pittsburgh off Monroeville Parkway in Plum Boro.
FACILITIES: 1 T-bar; 1 tow rope; 3 pomas; ski instruction; ski rental; restaurants; lodging.

Pocono Manor

POCONO MANOR
Pocono Manor, PA 18349
(717) 839-7111
LOCATION: 15 mi. northwest of Stroudsburg off Route 611.
FACILITIES: 1 T-bar; 1 J-bar; ski instruction; ski rental; nursery; restaurants; lodging.

PENNSYLVANIA

SKI AREAS (continued)

Shawnee on Delaware

SHAWNEE MOUNTAIN
Shawnee on Delaware, PA 18356
(717) 421-7231
LOCATION: Near Stroudsburg.
FACILITIES: 2 chairlifts; ski instruction; ski rental; nursery; restaurants; lodging.

Somerset

HIDDEN VALLEY
Somerset, PA 15501
(814) 445-6014
LOCATION: 12 mi. west of Somerset.
FACILITIES: 4 chairlifts; 1 tow rope; 2 pomas; ski instruction; ski rental; nursery; restaurants; lodging.

Spring Mount

SPRING MOUNTAIN
Spring Mount, PA 19478
(215) 287-7900
LOCATION: 30 mi. north of Philadelphia off Routes 29 and 73.
FACILITIES: 2 chairlifts; 3 tow ropes; ski instruction; ski rental; restaurants; lodging.

Tafton

TANGLEWOOD
Tafton, PA 18464
(717) 226-9500
LOCATION: Route 390 off Routes 6 and 507.
FACILITIES: 1 chairlift; 2 T-bars; 1 J-bar; ski instruction; ski rental; nursery; restaurants; lodging.

Tannersville

CAMELBACK
Tannersville, PA 18372
(717) 629-1661
LOCATION: Northwest of Stroudsburg.
FACILITIES: 4 chairlifts; 2 T-bars; 1 J-bar; ski instruction; ski rental; restaurants; lodging.

Union Dale

ELK MOUNTAIN
Union Dale, PA 18470
(717) 679-2611
LOCATION: 9 mi. east of I-81.
FACILITIES: 4 chairlifts; ski instruction; ski rental; nursery; restaurants; lodging.

White Haven

JACK FROST MOUNTAIN
White Haven, PA 18661
(717) 443-8425
LOCATION: 3 mi. west of Blakesdale.
FACILITIES: 5 chairlifts; 1 J-bar; ski instruction; ski rental; nursery; restaurants; lodging.

Youngsville

PEEK'N MOUNTAIN
Youngsville, PA 16371
(814) 563-9210

LOCATION: 7 mi. west of Warren.
FACILITIES: 1 chairlift; 2 T-bars; 1 mitey mite; ski instruction; ski rental; restaurants; lodging.

AMUSEMENT PARKS & ATTRACTIONS

Allentown

DORNEY PARK COASTER
3830 Dorney Park Road
Allentown, PA 18104
(215) 395-3724
FACILITIES: 25 major rides; 5 kiddie rides; 2 walk thrus; 15 refreshment stands; restaurant; 15 games; arcade; shooting gallery; race track; stage shows; picnic facilities; miniature golf; zoo; free acts; free gate; pay parking.

Altoona

LAKEMONT PARK
118 6th St. & Lakemont
Altoona, PA 16602
(814) 943-4341
FACILITIES: 14 major rides; 6 kiddie rides; 8 games; monster den; 3 refreshment stands; penny arcade; shooting gallery; roller rink; miniature golf; zoo; casino; picnic facilities; free gate; free parking.

Barnesville

LAKEWOOD PARK
Barnesville, PA 18214
(717) 773-2284
FACILITIES: 9 major rides; 4 kiddie rides; 2 games; 6 refreshment stands; restaurant; arcade; picnic facilities; free acts; free gate; free parking; open Memorial Day - Labor Day.

Bushkill

MAGIC VALLEY & WINONA FALLS (Attraction)
Route 209
Bushkill, PA 18324
(717) 588-9411
FACILITIES: 10 major rides; 5 kiddie rides; restaurant; refreshment stands; arcade; games; picnic facilities; shooting gallery; stage shows; petting zoo; ice skating rink; ski slopes; horseback riding; free guided tours; pay gate; free parking; open mid-Apr. - Memorial Day, weekends only; Memorial Day - Labor Day full time; weekends to Nov.

Conneaut Lake

CONNEAUT LAKE PARK
Conneaut Lake, PA 16316
(814) 382-5115
FACILITIES: 25 major rides; 11 kiddie rides; 26 games; 13 refreshment stands; 3 restaurants; beach; boats; miniature golf; arcade; zoo; Fairyland Forest; picnic facilities; stage shows; free acts; free gate; pay parking; open Memorial Day - Labor Day.

Easton

BUSHKILL PARK AMUSEMENT CO.

AMUSEMENT PARKS (continued)

2125 Bushkill Park Drive
Easton, PA 18042
(215) 258-6941
FACILITIES: 12 major rides; 9 kiddie rides; 3
games; walk thru; 3 refreshment stands; arcade; pool; roller rink; miniature golf; picnic
facilities; free acts; free gate; pay parking;
open Memorial Day - Labor Day.

Elysburg

KNOEBEL'S GROVES
Route 487
Elysburg, PA 17824
(717) 672-2641
FACILITIES: 20 major rides; 8 kiddie rides;
penny arcade; shooting gallery; pool; roller
rink; picnic facilities; miniature golf; free
acts; free gate; free parking; open Memorial
Day - Labor Day.

Erie

WALDAMEER PARK, INC.
Peninsula Drive
Route 832 N.
Erie, PA 16505
(814) 838-3591
FACILITIES: 13 major rides; 7 kiddie rides;
12 games; fun house; walk thru; shooting gallery; 2 refreshment stands; gift house; arcade;
picnic facilities; free acts; free gate; free parking; open later part of May - Labor Day.

Gettysburg

FANTASYLAND STORYBOOK GARDENS
Route 1
Gettysburg, PA 17325
(717) 334-1415
FACILITIES: 6 major rides; 6 kiddie rides; 2
games; 4 refreshment stands; theatre; arcade;
picnic facilities; free acts; pay gate; free parking.

Hershey

HERSHEYPARK
Hershey, PA 17033
(717) 534-3900
FACILITIES: 26 major rides; 10 kiddie rides;
5 restaurants; 37 refreshment stands; arcade;
picnic facilities; shooting gallery; ice rink; museum; stage shows; petting zoo; pay gate; free
parking; open mid-May - Labor Day; selected
weekends in Sept.

Lancaster

DUTCH WONDERLAND
2249 Lincoln Hwy. E.
Lancaster, PA 17602
(717) 393-3846
FACILITIES: 12 major rides; walk thru; 3
refreshment stands; restaurant; 30 exhibits;
museum; gardens; picnic facilities; stage
shows; pay gate; free parking; open Memorial
Day - Labor Day; weekends: Easter & after
Labor Day.

Ligonier

IDLEWILD PARK

P.O. Box C
Ligonier, PA 15658
(412) 238-9881
FACILITIES: 16 major rides; 14 kiddie rides;
9 games; 7 refreshment stands; 2 restaurants;
arcade; golf; shooting gallery; pool; picnic facilities; miniature golf; zoo; pay gate; pay
parking; open mid-May - Labor Day.

Mechanicsburg

WILLIAMS GROVE PARK, INC.
1 Park Avenue
Mechanicsburg, PA 17055
(717) 697-8266
FACILITIES: 17 major rides; 10 kiddie rides;
fun house; 10 games; 15 refreshment stands;
arcade; shooting gallery; crafts; picnic facilities; race track; exhibits; museum; theater;
free acts; free gate; pay parking; open Easter -
Sept. 30.

Moosic

GHOST TOWN IN THE GLEN
Rocky Glen Road
Moosic, PA 18057
(717) 457-5641
FACILITIES: 21 major rides; 12 kiddie rides;
arcade; beach; picnic facilities; stage shows;
pay gate; free parking; open May 20 - Sept. 4;
weekends: Sept.

New Castle

CASCADE PARK & CASCADE PARK SWIMMING POOL
1928 E. Washington Street Ext.
New Castle, PA 16101
(412) 652-7661
FACILITIES: 8 major rides; 11 kiddie rides;
3 games; 5 refreshment stands; restaurant;
penny arcade; shooting gallery; pool; beach;
skee ball; miniature golf; trampolines; boats;
picnic facilities; free acts; free gate; free parking.

Philadelphia

KIDDIE PLAYLAND
St. Vincent St. & Roosevelt Blvd.
Philadelphia, PA 19149
(215) 624-9211
FACILITIES: 7 major rides; 14 kiddie rides; 3
refreshment stands; miniature golf; free gate;
free parking.

PHILADELPHIA ZOOLOGICAL GARDEN
    (Attraction)
Girard Avenue
Philadelphia, PA 19104
(215) 243-1100
FACILITIES: Zoo; children's zoo; natural
habitat zoo; free acts; pay gate; free parking;
open all year.

Royersford

LAKEVIEW AMUSEMENT PARK
947 Walnut Street
Royersford, PA 19468
(215) 279-7515
FACILITIES: 19 major rides; 12 kiddie rides;
4 games; walk thru; 3 refreshment stands;
restaurant; penny arcade; miniature golf; pic-

PENNSYLVANIA

AMUSEMENT PARKS (continued)

nic facilities; pay gate; free parking.

West Chester

MAIN LINE PARK
Routes 52 & 100
West Chester, PA 19380
(215) 793-2700
FACILITIES: 10 major rides; 12 kiddie rides;
fun house; 2 walk thrus; 12 games; 4 refreshment stands; 2 restaurants; arcade; shooting
gallery; pool; picnic facilities; free acts; pay
parking; open May 1 - Oct. 31.

West Mifflin

KENNYWOOD PARK
4800 Kennywood Blvd.
West Mifflin, PA 15122
(412) 461-0500
FACILITIES: 36 major rides; 14 kiddie rides;
walk thru; 19 games; 14 refreshment stands;
restaurant; 2 shooting galleries; picnic facilities; miniature golf; free acts; free & pay parking.

West Point

WEST POINT PARK
Park Road
West Point, PA 19486
(215) 699-4329
FACILITIES: 17 major rides; 6 kiddie rides;
shooting gallery; 22 games; 5 refreshment
stands; arcade; picnic facilities; pay gate; open
mid-May - Sept. 14.

STATE FAIR

Allentown State Fair
17th and Chew Streets
Allentown, PA 18104
(215) 433-7541
DATE: May

NATIONAL PARKS

There are no National Parks in Pennsylvania.

NATIONAL FOREST

National Forests
Eastern Region
633 West Wisconsin Avenue
Milwaukee, WI 53203
(414) 291-3693

Warren

ALLEGHENY NATIONAL FOREST
ATTRACTIONS: Trout, bass fishing; deer,
turkey, bear hunting; scenic drives.
FACILITIES: 15 camp and picnic sites, 35
picnic only; 27 roadside tables; 4 swimming
sites; hotels nearby; cabins in Cook Forest
and Allegheny State Parks.
NEARBY TOWNS: Bradford, Kane, Ridgway,
Sheffield, Tionesta.

STATE PARKS

Headquarters

Department of Environmental Resources
Bureau of State Parks
State Office Bldg.
Harrisburg, PA 17120
(717) 787-6640

Barnesville

TUSCARORA STATE PARK
(717) 467-2404
LOCATION: Near Barnesville.
FACILITIES: Open year round; water and
bathroom facilities; picnic area; food service;
swimming; boating; boat rental; fishing; skiing; hiking; horseback riding; bicycle trail;
handicapped access/restroom.

Bedford

SHAWNEE STATE PARK
(814) 733-4218
LOCATION: 9 mi. west of Bedford on U.S.
30.
FACILITIES: Open year round; 300 sites; water and bathroom facilities; trailer village vehicle sites; food service; swimming; boating;
hunting; fishing; hiking; handicapped access/
restroom; tent camping.

Birdsboro

FRENCH CREEK STATE PARK
(215) 582-1514
LOCATION: 6 mi. south of Birdsboro.
FACILITIES: Open year round; 160 sites; water and bathroom facilities; trailer village vehicle sites; swimming; boating; hunting; fishing;
hiking; tent camping.

Canadensis

PROMISED LAND STATE PARK
(717) 676-3428
LOCATION: 11 mi. north of Canadensis on
Route 390.
FACILITIES: Open year round; 453 sites; water and bathroom facilities; sanitary station;
trailer village vehicle sites; swimming; boating;
hunting; fishing; hiking; handicapped access/
restroom; tent camping.

Clarington

CLEAR CREEK STATE PARK
(814) 752-2368
LOCATION: 2 mi. east of Clarington.
FACILITIES: Open year round; 53 sites; water and bathroom facilities; sanitary station;
trailer village vehicle sites; swimming; hunting;
fishing; hiking; handicapped access/restroom;
tent camping.

Cooksburg

COOK FOREST STATE PARK
(814) 744-8407
LOCATION: On Route 36.
FACILITIES: Open year round; 226 sites; water and bathroom facilities; sanitary station;
trailer village vehicle sites; swimming; hunting;

STATE PARKS (continued)

fishing; hiking; handicapped access/restroom; tent camping.

Curwensville

CURWENSVILLE STATE PARK
(814) 236-1184
LOCATION: 2 mi. south of Curwensville.
FACILITIES: Open year round; water and bathroom facilities; picnic area; swimming; boating; boat rental; hunting; fishing; hiking; handicapped access/restroom.

Dallas

FRANCES SLOCUM STATE PARK
(717) 696-3525
LOCATION: 3 mi. west of Dallas.
FACILITIES: Open year round; water and bathroom facilities; picnic area; food service; swimming; boating; boat rental; fishing; handicapped access/restroom.

Dalton

PROMPTON STATE PARK
(717) 253-0411
LOCATION: 1 mi. north of Dalton.
FACILITIES: Open year round; picnic area; swimming; boating; boat rental; hunting; fishing.

Derry

KEYSTONE STATE PARK
(412) 668-2939
LOCATION: 1 mi. north of Derry.
FACILITIES: Open year round; 100 sites; water and bathroom facilities; trailer village vehicle sites; swimming; boating; hunting; fishing; hiking; tent camping.

Erie

PRESQUE ISLE STATE PARK
(814) 838-7672
LOCATION: On Presque Isle.
FACILITIES: Open year round; water and bathroom facilities; picnic area; food service; swimming; boating; boat rental; hunting; fishing; handicapped access/restroom.

Flinton

PRINCE GALLITZIN STATE PARK
(814) 674-3691
LOCATION: Route 53 at Flinton.
FACILITIES: Open year round; 437 sites; water and bathroom facilities; sanitary station; trailer village vehicle sites; food service; swimming; boating; hunting; fishing; hiking; handicapped access/restroom; tent camping.

Ford City

CROOKED CREEK STATE PARK
(412) 763-3161
LOCATION: 4 mi. south of Ford City.
FACILITIES: Open year round; 50 sites; water and bathroom facilities; sanitary station; trailer village vehicle sites; swimming; boating; hunting; fishing; hiking; tent camping.

Fort Loudon

COWANS GAP STATE PARK
(717) 485-3948
LOCATION: 8 mi. north of Fort Loudon on U.S. 30.
FACILITIES: Open year round; 300 sites; water and bathroom facilities; sanitary station; trailer village vehicle sites; swimming; boating; hunting; fishing; hiking; handicapped access/restroom; tent camping.

Gettysburg

CALEDONIA STATE PARK
(717) 352-2161
LOCATION: 15 mi. west of Gettysburg on U.S. 30.
FACILITIES: Open year round; 196 sites; water and bathroom facilities; sanitary station; trailer village vehicle sites; swimming; hunting; fishing; hiking; handicapped access/restroom; tent camping.

Gouldsboro

GOULDSBORO STATE PARK
(717) 894-8671
LOCATION: 1 mi. south of Gouldsboro.
FACILITIES: Open year round; water and bathroom facilities; picnic area; food service; swimming; boating; boat rental; hunting; fishing; handicapped access/restroom.

Greentown

BRUCE LAKE STATE PARK
(717) 676-3428
LOCATION: 5 mi. east of Greentown.
FACILITIES: Open year round; hunting; fishing; hiking; tent camping.

Hanover

CODORUS STATE PARK
(717) 637-2816
LOCATION: 3 mi. east of Hanover on Route 116.
FACILITIES: Open year round; 198 sites; water and bathroom facilities; sanitary station; trailer village vehicle sites; swimming; boating; hunting; fishing; hiking; handicapped access/restroom; tent camping.

Howard

BALD EAGLE STATE PARK
(814) 625-2775
LOCATION: On Blanchard Reservoir.
FACILITIES: Open year round; water and bathroom facilities; boating; hunting; fishing; hiking; handicapped access/restroom; tent camping.

Jamestown

PYMATUNING STATE PARK
(412) 932-3141
LOCATION: 1 mi. north of Jamestown on U.S. 322.
FACILITIES: Open year round; 832 sites; water and bathroom facilities; sanitary station; trailer village vehicle sites; food service; swimming; boating; hunting; fishing; hiking; handicapped access/restroom; tent camping.

STATE PARKS (continued)

Johnsonburg

ELK STATE PARK
(814) 965-2646
LOCATION: 9 mi. north of Johnsonburg off
U.S. 219.
FACILITIES: Open year round; 75 sites; water and bathroom facilities; sanitary station;
trailer village vehicle sites; swimming; boating;
hunting; fishing; hiking; handicapped access/
restroom; tent camping.

Lehighton

BELTZVILLE STATE PARK
(215) 377-3170
LOCATION: 3 mi. northeast of Lehighton.
FACILITIES: Open year round; water and
bathroom facilities; picnic area; food service;
swimming; boating; hunting; fishing; hiking;
handicapped access/restroom.

McMichaels

BIG POCONO STATE PARK
(717) 629-0320
LOCATION: 2 mi. north of McMichaels.
FACILITIES: Open year round; water and
bathroom facilities; picnic area; hiking; environmental study area; handicapped access/
restroom.

Media

RIDLEY CREEK STATE PARK
(215) 666-4800
LOCATION: 3 mi. northwest of Media.
FACILITIES: Open year round; water and
bathroom facilities; picnic area; food service; fishing; hiking; horseback riding; bicycle
trail; handicapped access/restroom.

Newtown

TYLER STATE PARK
(215) 646-2942
LOCATION: 2 mi. west of Newtown.
FACILITIES: Open year round; water and
bathroom facilities; picnic area; food service;
boating; boat rental; fishing; water skiing; hiking; horseback riding; bicycle trail; handicapped access/restroom.

Nola

YELLOW CREEK STATE PARK
(412) 463-3850
LOCATION: 2 mi. west of Nola.
FACILITIES: Open year round; water and
bathroom facilities; picnic area; food service;
swimming; boating; boat rental; hunting; fishing; hiking; handicapped access/restroom.

Ohiopyle

OHIOPYLE STATE PARK
(412) 329-4707
LOCATION: On Route 381.
FACILITIES: Open year round; 223 sites; water and bathroom facilities; sanitary station;
trailer village vehicle sites; hunting; fishing;
hiking; handicapped access/restroom; tent
camping.

Pavia

BLUE KNOB STATE PARK
(814) 276-3576
LOCATION: 1 mi. north of Pavia on Blue
King Road.
FACILITIES: Open year round; 75 sites; water and bathroom facilities; trailer village vehicle sites; swimming; hunting; fishing; hiking;
tent camping.

Philipsburg

BLACK MOSHANNON STATE PARK
(814) 342-1101
LOCATION: 10½ mi. east of Philipsburg on
Route 504.
FACILITIES: Open year round; 80 sites; water and bathroom facilities; sanitary station;
trailer village vehicle sites; food service; swimming; boating; hunting; fishing; hiking; handicapped access/restroom; tent camping.

Pittsburgh

RACCOON CREEK STATE PARK
(412) 899-2200
LOCATION: 25 mi. north of Pittsburgh on
Route 18.
FACILITIES: Open year round; 161 sites; water and bathroom facilities; sanitary station;
trailer village vehicle sites; swimming; boating;
hunting; fishing; handicapped access/rest-
room; tent camping.

Portersville

MORAINE STATE PARK
(412) 368-8811
LOCATION: Near Portersville.
FACILITIES: Open year round; water and
bathroom facilities; picnic area; food service;
swimming; boating; boat rental; hunting; fishing; hiking; horseback riding; bicycle trail;
handicapped access/restroom.

Pottsville

LOCUST LAKE STATE PARK
(717) 467-2772
LOCATION: 7 mi. northeast of Pottsville.
FACILITIES: Open year round; 282 sites; water and bathroom facilities; sanitary station;
trailer village vehicle sites; swimming; boating;
hunting; fishing; hiking; handicapped access/
restroom; tent camping.

Quakertown

NOCKAMIXON STATE PARK
(215) 536-7095
LOCATION: 3 mi. east of Quakertown.
FACILITIES: Open year round; water and
bathroom facilities; picnic area; food service;
boating; boat rental; hunting; fishing; hiking;
bicycle trail; handicapped access/restroom.

Red Rock

RICKETTS GLEN STATE PARK
(717) 477-5675
LOCATION: 3 mi. south of Red Rock on
Route 487.
FACILITIES: Open year round; 101 sites; wa-

STATE PARKS (continued)

ter and bathroom facilities; sanitary station; trailer village vehicle sites; swimming; boating; hunting; fishing; hiking; handicapped access/ restroom; tent camping.

Renovo

KETTLE CREEK STATE PARK
(717) 923-9925
LOCATION: 5 mi. west of Renovo on U.S. 120.
FACILITIES: Open year round; 84 sites; water and bathroom facilities; trailer village vehicle sites; swimming; boating; hunting; fishing; hiking; tent camping.

Rockwood

LAUREL RIDGE STATE PARK
(412) 455-3744
LOCATION: Near Rockwood.
FACILITIES: Open year round; water and bathroom facilities; hunting; fishing; hiking; handicapped access/restroom; tent camping.

Rossville

GIFFORD PINCHOT STATE PARK
(717) 432-5011
LOCATION: On Route 177 near Rossville.
FACILITIES: Open year round; 340 sites; water and bathroom facilities; sanitary station; trailer village vehicle sites; swimming; boating; hunting; fishing; hiking; handicapped access/ restroom; tent camping.

Sandy Lake

MAURICE K. GODDARD STATE PARK
(412) 253-4833
LOCATION: Near Sandy Lake.
FACILITIES: Open year round; water and bathroom facilities; picnic area; swimming; boating; hunting; fishing; handicapped access/ restroom.

Sinnemahoning

SINNEMAHONING STATE PARK
(814) 647-8945
LOCATION: 8 mi. north of Sinnemahoning.
FACILITIES: Open year round; 40 sites; water and bathroom facilities; trailer village vehicle sites; swimming; boating; hunting; fishing; hiking; handicapped access/restroom; tent camping.

Somerset

LAUREL HILL STATE PARK
(814) 445-7725
LOCATION: 7 mi. west on Route 31, then 2 mi. south.
FACILITIES: Open year round; 270 sites; water and bathroom facilities; sanitary station; trailer village vehicle sites; swimming; boating; hunting; fishing; hiking; handicapped access/ restroom; tent camping.

Tobyhanna

TOBYHANNA STATE PARK

(717) 894-8671
LOCATION: In Tobyhanna.
FACILITIES: Open year round; 140 sites; water and bathroom facilities; trailer village vehicle sites; swimming; boating; hunting; fishing; hiking; tent camping.

Waterville

LITTLE PINE STATE PARK
(717) 847-3209
LOCATION: 2 mi. north of Waterville.
FACILITIES: Open year round; 100 sites; water and bathroom facilities; sanitary station; trailer village vehicle sites; picnic area; food service; swimming; boating; hunting; fishing; hiking; handicapped access/restroom; tent camping.

Waverly

LACKAWANNA STATE PARK
(717) 945-3239
LOCATION: North of Waverly off Route 407.
FACILITIES: Open year round; 96 sites; water and bathroom facilities; sanitary station; trailer village vehicle sites; swimming; boating; hunting; fishing; hiking; handicapped access/ restroom; tent camping.

White Haven

HICKORY RUN STATE PARK
(717) 443-9991
LOCATION: Off Exit 35 of Pennsylvania Turnpike.
FACILITIES: Open year round; 381 sites; water and bathroom facilities; sanitary station; trailer village vehicle sites; swimming; hunting; fishing; hiking; handicapped access/restroom; tent camping.

Wind Ridge

RYERSON STATION STATE PARK
(412) 428-4254
LOCATION: On Route 31.
FACILITIES: Open year round; 50 sites; water and bathroom facilities; sanitary station; trailer village vehicle sites; swimming; boating; hunting; fishing; hiking; handicapped access/ restroom.

STATE FORESTS

Headquarters

Department of Environmental Resources
Forest Bureau
Harrisburg, PA 17102
(717) 787-2708

Cherry Springs

CHERRY SPRINGS STATE FOREST
LOCATION: 1 mi. south of Cherry Springs.
FACILITIES: Open year round; water and bathroom facilities; trailer village vehicle sites; picnic area; tent camping.

PATTERSON STATE FOREST
LOCATION: 6 mi. northwest of Cherry Springs.

PENNSYLVANIA

STATE FORESTS (continued)

FACILITIES: Open year round; water and bathroom facilities; trailer village vehicle sites; picnic area; tent camping.

PROUTY PLACE STATE FOREST
LOCATION: 8 mi. west of Cherry Springs.
FACILITIES: Open year round; water and bathroom facilities; trailer village vehicle sites; picnic area; fishing; tent camping.

Coburn

POE PADDY STATE FOREST
LOCATION: 5 mi. southeast of Coburn.
FACILITIES: Open year round; water and bathroom facilities; trailer village vehicle sites; picnic area; boating; fishing; tent camping.

Milroy

PENN-ROOSEVELT STATE FOREST
LOCATION: 10 mi. west of Milroy.
FACILITIES: Open year round; water and bathroom facilities; trailer village vehicle sites; picnic area; fishing; tent camping.

New Germantown

FOWLERS HOLLOW STATE FOREST
LOCATION: 4 mi. south of New Germantown.
FACILITIES: Open year round; water and bathroom facilities; trailer village vehicle sites; picnic area; fishing; tent camping.

HISTORIC SITES

Allentown

LIBERTY BELL SHRINE (Zion United Church of Christ) - In Sept., 1777, the Liberty Bell was moved from Philadelphia to Allentown and hidden beneath the floor of the church. Also, a rumor was spread that the Liberty Bell had been lost in the Delaware River. Church now contains full-size replica of the original Liberty Bell, along with paintings and other historic displays. Located in Hamilton Mall at Church Street.

Bethlehem

18TH-CENTURY INDUSTRIAL QUARTER-First municipal water system in America. Also, restored industrial area illustrating Moravian economy. Located on Church Street.

Boalsburg

BOAL MANSION AND MUSEUM - Christopher Columbus Family Chapel brought from Spain to this site by descendents of Columbus. Authentic relics of Columbus family. Located on Route 322.

Gettysburg

GETTYSBURG - Site of one of the bloodiest battles of the Civil War and of President Lincoln's Gettysburg Address.

Goshen

ROBERT FULTON HOME - Birthplace of builder of first commercially successful steamboat. Located north of Goshen on U.S. 222.

Great Bend

MORMON MONUMENT - Commemorates spot where Joseph Smith, founder of Mormon religion, interpreted famous "Golden Tablets." Located on Route 81.

Jim Thorpe

JIM THORPE MAUSOLEUM - Final resting place of one of the world's greatest athletes, who won grueling pentathlon and decathlon events in 1912 Olympics. Located on Route 903.

Johnstown

JOHNSTOWN FLOOD MUSEUM - 250 years of Johnstown history plus the Great Flood Story on panoramic map; narration and authentic slides. Located on Walnut and Washington Streets.

Lackawaxen

GRAVE OF UNKNOWN SOLDIER - One of America's earliest unknown soldiers, a casualty of the Battle of Minisink in 1779. Located off Route 590.

ZANE GREY INN - Manuscripts and other memorabilia of the great Western writer. Located off Route 590.

Philadelphia

BETSY ROSS HOUSE - Charming, 2½-story home where Betsy Ross lived and created first national flag. Located at 239 Arch Street.

CARPENTERS' HALL - First Continental Congress met here in 1774. During the Revolutionary War, the hall was used as an American military hospital. Located at 4th and Chestnut Streets.

CHRIST CHURCH AND CEMETERY - More signers of the Declaration of Independence are buried here than anywhere else. Also, site of Benjamin Franklin's grave. Located at 5th and Arch Streets.

INDEPENDENCE HALL - Originally called State House, the Second Continental Congress met here in May, 1775 and on July 4, 1776, approved and signed the Declaration of Independence. Located in Independence Square.

LIBERTY BELL PAVILION - New glass-enclosed building houses original Liberty Bell, symbol of American liberty. Located across from Independence Hall.

Pittsburgh

FORT PITT MUSEUM - Restored bastion of the original fort, built in 1758. Its site in Point State Park is within the Golden Tri-

HISTORIC SITES (continued)

angle, where the Allegheny, Monongahela and Ohio Rivers meet.

Reading

DANIEL BOONE HOMESTEAD - Birthplace of America's great frontiersman. Located east of Reading on Route 422.

Uniontown

FORT NECESSITY - Site of George Washington's only defeat. He yielded this fort to French on July 4, 1754, during early days of the French and Indian War. Located 11 mi. southwest of Uniontown on Route 40.

Wilkes-Barre

OLD FELL TAVERN - In 1808 Judge Jesse Fell first successfully burned anthracite coal on an open grate. Grate still intact. Located on S. Washington Street.

York

GOLDEN PLOUGH TAVERN AND GATE HOUSE - Revolutionary-era tavern where Lafayette made famous "Toast That Saved a Nation," after an attempt to oust Washington as Commander-in-Chief. Located at West Market and Pershing Aves.

YORK COUNTY COLONIAL COURT - HOUSE - Meeting place of Continental Congress, Sept. 30, 1777, through June 27, 1778, where Articles of Confederation and new nation's first Constitution were adopted, creating the United States of America and designating York as the country's first Capital. Located at Market Street and Pershing Ave.

HOSTELS

Bowmansville

BOWMANSVILLE YOUTH HOSTEL
P.O. Box 117
Bowmansville, PA 17507
(215) 445-4831
FACILITIES: Open year round; 20 beds, men; 20 beds, women; modern bathroom; nearest hostels: Denver, 10 mi. west; Geigertown, 11 mi. east; overnight charges: $2.50 May 1 - Sept. 30; $3.25 Oct. 1 - Apr. 30; houseparent: Roger Lawn.

Bushkill

RISING WATER YOUTH HOSTEL
P.O. Box 223
Bushkill, PA 18324
(717) 588-6394
FACILITIES: Open year round; 32 beds for men; family units available; modern bathroom; nearest hostels: Cresco; Layton, NJ; overnight charges: $2.50 summer; $3 winter; houseparent: Ted Pollis.

Cresco

LA ANNA YOUTH HOSTEL
R.R. 2, Box 1026
Route 191
Cresco, PA 18326
(717) 676-9076
FACILITIES: Open year round; 20 beds, men; 20 beds, women; modern bathroom; nearest hostels: Bushkill, 35 mi. east; Quakertown, 55 mi. south; overnight charges: $2.50 May 1 - Sept. 30; $3.25 Oct. 1 - Apr. 30; houseparent: Mr. & Mrs. Roy L. Walter.

Denver

DENVER YOUTH HOSTEL
Steinmetz Road
Denver, PA 17517
(215) 267-5166
FACILITIES: Open Mar. 1 - Nov. 30; send self-addressed, stamped envelope for reservation; 20 beds, men; 20 beds, women; modern bathroom; nearest hostel: Bowmansville, 13 mi. west; overnight charges: $2.50 summer; $3.25 winter; houseparent: Alvin Enck.

Geigertown

SHIREY'S YOUTH HOSTEL
Geigertown Road
Geigertown, PA 19523
(215) 286-9537
FACILITIES: Open Mar. 1 - Nov. 30; 20 beds, men; 20 beds, women; modern bathroom; nearest hostels: Bowmansville, west; Philadelphia, east; overnight charges: $2.50; houseparent: David O. Shirey.

Media

RIDLEY CREEK PARK YOUTH HOSTEL
841 Sycamore Mills Road
Media, PA 19063
(215) 566-9846
FACILITIES: Open year round; 20 beds, men and women; accommodations for families; modern bathroom; nearest hostel: Philadelphia, 16 mi. east; overnight charges: $2.50 May 1 - Sept. 30; $3.25 Oct. 1 - Apr. 30; houseparent: Jerry Kopelman.

Mt. Pleasant

LAURELVILLE CHURCH CENTER
Route 5, Box 145
Mt. Pleasant, PA 15666
(412) 423-2056
FACILITIES: Open year round; 10-15 beds, men; 10-15 beds, women; modern bathroom; overnight charges: $3 summer; $3.25 winter; houseparent: Susie Bontrager.

Philadelphia

CHAMOUNIX MANSION
Philadelphia International Youth Hostel & Community Meeting Center
West Fairmount Park
Philadelphia, PA 19131
(215) 878-3676
FACILITIES: Open Jan. 1 - Nov. 30; reservations required; 20 beds, men; 20 beds, women; modern bathroom; nearest hostels: Quakertown, 40 mi. north; Geigertown, 40

PENNSYLVANIA

HOSTELS (continued)

mi. northwest; Media, 16 mi. southwest; overnight charges: $3; houseparent: Bruce & Deborah Paige.

Quakertown

WEISEL YOUTH HOSTEL
RD 3
Quakertown, PA 18951
(215) 536-8749
FACILITIES: Open year round; 12 beds, men; 12 beds, women; modern bathroom; nearest hostels: Philadelphia, 40 mi. south; Bushkill, 55 mi. north; overnight charges: $1.50 summer; $2 winter; houseparents: Mr. & Mrs. Steven Schafer.

White Haven

LEHIGH GORGE HOSTEL
Star Route, Box 6A
White Haven, PA 18661
(717) 443-9191
FACILITIES: Open year round; 12 beds, men; 12 beds, women; modern bathroom; nearest hostel: Quakertown, 60 mi. south; overnight charges: $3 summer; $4.25 winter; houseparents: Ray & Pat Stressman.

Williamsport

YMCA WAYSIDE
343 W. 4th Street
Williamsport, PA 17701
(717) 323-7134
FACILITIES: Open Apr. 30 - Sept. 30; 20 beds, men; 10 beds, women; accommodations for families; modern bathroom; overnight charges: $2.50; need sleeping bags; houseparent: Roy Tuomisto.

Zelienople

CAMP CARONDOWANNA
RD 1, Box 810
Fombell, PA 16123
(412) 532-6720
FACILITIES: Open year round; 22 beds, men; 15 beds, women; modern bathroom; nearest hostel: Mt. Pleasant, 80 mi. southeast; overnight charges: $2.50 summer; $3 winter; houseparents: Raymond & Elenor Earlin.

POINTS OF INTEREST

Belleville

AMISH COMMUNITIES - Quaint old towns where all goods are still made by hand. Located on Route 655.

Carlisle

"MOLLY PITCHER" GRAVE AND STATUE- During the Revolution, Mary "Molly" Ludwig followed her cannoneer husband into battle. On hot days she carried water to soldiers, who began calling her "Molly Pitcher." At the Battle of Monmouth she replaced her collapsed husband as a member of the gun crew. Located in the Old Cemetery.

Franklin Center

FRANKLIN MINT AND MUSEUM - World's largest private mint and producer of limited edition collections. Tours daily except major holidays. Located on Route 1.

Hershey

HERSHEY'S CHOCOLATE WORLD - Tour through a delightful chocolate world that shows the making of chocolate from the cacao bean to the Hershey bar. Located on Park Blvd.

Kennett Square

LONGWOOD GARDENS - Ultimate expression of 1920s country estate garden. Includes trees planted in early 1800s, spectacular water displays and large conservatories with year round shows of flowers and tropical plants.

Lenhartsville

PENNSYLVANIA DUTCH FOLK CULTURE CENTER - Restored area includes log cabin, school house, farm equipment shed, Folklife Museum, and House of Fashions.

Philadelphia

AFRO-AMERICAN HISTORICAL AND CULTURAL MUSEUM - Displays of events affecting blacks in America. Also includes works of modern black artists and craftsmen. Located at 7th and Arch Streets.

EDGAR ALLEN POE HOME - House in which Poe wrote "The Raven," "The Tell-Tale Heart," and many others. The famous author lived here with his young bride and her mother. Located at 530 N. 7th Street.

FAIRMOUNT PARK TROLLEY BUS - Ride recreation of a turn-of-the-century Victorian trolley. Trolley passes by Fairmont Park, museums along the Parkway, the zoo and historic mansions.

FRANKLIN INSTITUTE SCIENCE MUSEUM - Home of the Benjamin Franklin National Memorial. A do, see, and touch museum including a Boeing 707, a walk-through heart, outdoor science park, and Fels Planetarium. Located at 20th and the Parkway.

LIVING HISTORY CENTER - 200 years of American history presented through modern electronic wizardry and multimedia technology, including huge indoor movie screen. Located at 6th and Race Streets.

NEW MARKET AND PENN'S LANDING - Area of many old buildings containing boutiques and restaurants, tall sailing ships, and sculpture gardens. Located on Philadelphia's famous Society Hill.

NEW YEAR'S SHOOTERS AND MUMMERS MUSEUM - Highlights history of the Mummers and their instruments and costumes. Lo-

POINTS OF INTEREST (continued)

cated at 2nd Street and Washington Avenue.

NORMAN ROCKWELL MUSEUM - Reproductions of all the Rockwell Saturday Evening Post covers and many of his major works. Located at 601 Walnut Street.

PENNSYLVANIA ACADEMY OF FINE ARTS - Restored Victorian building, oldest art museum and school in America. Collections include works by Eakins, Homer, and Peales. Located at Broad and Cherry Streets.

PHILADELPHIA MUSEUM OF ART - Contains over 500,000 priceless paintings, sculptures, drawings, decorative arts, antiques, and Oriental art, making it the third largest museum in America. Located at 26th and the Parkway.

Pittsburgh

CATHEDRAL OF LEARNING - This 42-story building is only college skyscraper in the country. Located at Bigelow Blvd. and 5th Avenue.

Schaefferstown

MICHTER'S DISTILLERY - America's oldest distillery. Tours available.

RHODE ISLAND

Founded on the principle of religious and political freedom, Rhode Island joined the Union in 1790 as the thirteenth state. Roger Williams, unhappy with the Puritans in Plymouth (they were less than estatic with his attitude), moved to Rhode Island to establish the state's first colony in Providence and the country's first Baptist church.

Rhode Island's economy initially flourished during the slave trading days when it exported rum to Africa. Africa in turn sold slaves to the West Indies for molasses, which was then sold to Rhode Island for the making of rum. In the 1770s, the state ceased its involvement with slave traders and the "Triangle Trade Route" and took a strong stand against slavery.

The state's economy today is based on the manufacturing of textiles and electronic products, and commercial fishing, in addition to tourism. Newport, its most famous resort area, is also the nation's yachting center.

State capital: Providence.   State bird: Rhode Island red.   State tree: Red maple. State flower: Violet.

WEATHER

Rhode Island, the smallest of the states, extends for 50 miles in a north-south direction and has an average width of about 30 miles. The total area, including Block Island some 10 miles offshore, is 1,497 square miles, of which Narragansett Bay occupies about 25 percent.

There are three topographical divisions of the state. A narrow coastal plain lies along the south shore and around Narragansett Bay. A second division lies to the north and east of the Bay, with gently rolling uplands of up to 200 feet elevation. The western two-thirds of Rhode Island consist of predominantly hilly uplands.

The chief characteristics of Rhode Island's climate may be summarized as follows: equable distribution of precipitation among the four seasons; large ranges of temperature, both daily and annual; great differences in the same season of different years; and considerable diversity of the weather over short periods of time. These characteristics are modified by nearness to the Bay or ocean, elevation, and nature of the terrain.

Average daily temperature for each month.

	Central	Block Island
Jan.	36.2 to 20.6	37.4 to 25.4
Feb.	37.6 to 21.2	37.2 to 25.3
Mar.	44.7 to 29.0	42.7 to 31.0
Apr.	56.7 to 37.8	51.7 to 38.8
May	66.8 to 46.9	60.4 to 47.2
Jun.	76.3 to 56.5	69.7 to 56.5
Jul.	81.1 to 63.0	75.6 to 63.3
Aug.	79.8 to 61.0	75.3 to 63.1
Sept.	73.1 to 53.6	69.8 to 57.7
Oct.	63.9 to 43.4	61.4 to 49.2
Nov.	52.0 to 34.6	51.8 to 40.1
Dec.	39.6 to 23.4	41.2 to 29.1
Year	59.0 to 40.9	56.2 to 43.9

STATE CHAMBER OF COMMERCE

Rhode Island Chamber of Commerce
206 Smith Street
Providence, RI 02908
(401) 272-1400

STATE & CITY TOURISM OFFICES

State

Rhode Island Department of Economic Development

RHODE ISLAND

TOURISM OFFICES (continued)

One Weybossett Hill
Providence, RI 02903
(401) 277-2614

Tourist Promotion Divsion
Department of Economic Development
One Weybossett Hill
Providence, RI 02903
(401) 277-2614

Local

Convention and Visitor's Bureau
Newport Chamber of Commerce
Newport, RI 02840
(401) 847-1600

STATE HIGHWAY DEPARTMENT

Department of Transportation
State Office Building
Providence, RI 02903
(401) 277-2481

HIGHWAY WELCOMING CENTERS

Charlestown

CHARLESTOWN CENTER - U.S. Route 1.

Coventry

COVENTRY CENTER - U.S. Route 1 & Sandy Bottom Road.

Hopkinton

HOPKINTON CENTER - Interstate 95, near Connecticut border.

Lincoln

LINCOLN CENTER - Interstate 295.

Newport

NEWPORT CENTER - Thames & W. Marlborough Streets.

South Kingstown

SOUTH KINGSTOWN CENTER - Route 138 & U.S. 1.

Westerly

WESTERLY CENTER - City of Westerly, Main Street.

STATE POLICE

Department of Public Safety
P.O. Box 185
North Scituate, RI 02857
(401) 647-3311

HUNTING & FISHING

Hunting

No person shall hunt, pursue, take or kill any wild bird or animal in the State without first having obtained a license.

Persons not having a prior license or not having been a member of the armed forces must have completed a course in safe hunting practices and have been issued a Certificate of Competency to obtain a license.

Every person while hunting shall wear his license plainly visible at all times and shall present it for inspection to any person demanding same. Failure to present license shall make a person liable to penalty as if he were hunting without a license.

Licenses are not transferable and expire on the last day of February.

No license shall be granted to any person for one year after conviction of violation of game laws.

Any transfer or loan of license forfeits same.

Resident

Resident (must be 15 years old), $3.25; combination (hunting & fishing), $5.25; resident (over 65 years), 25 cents; military personnel, $3.25; resident alien, $10.25; shooting preserve, $10; shooting preserve hunting license, $3; deer (bow & arrow), $5; deer (shotgun), $5; trapping (over 15 years of age), $2; trapping (under 15 years of age), no fee for license.

Non-resident

Hunting license, $10.25; military personnel, $3.25; deer (bow & arrow), $20; deer (shotgun), $20; trapping, reciprocal with state in which person applying is a resident, but not less than $15.

Fishing

Fishing licenses are reciprocal with Connecticut (Beach Pond, Killingly Pond, Hazard Pond and Peck Pond) and Massachusetts (Wallum Lake).

Fishing licenses obtained at any city or town clerk's office and from authorized agent.

Must be worn so that it is visible and must be shown upon request.

Expires last day of February annually.

Will be revoked for violation of fishing laws.

Not required of minors 15 years or under.

Not required of citizens or members of their families when fishing from property on which they are actually domiciled.

Special permit required to seine and sell freshwater minnows.

Resident

Fishing license (required of all males between 16-65), $3.25.

Non-resident

Fishing license, $7.25; tourist (3 consecu-

464

HUNTING & FISHING (continued)

tive days), $3.25.
Note: Any resident reaching the age of 65 may obtain a permanent license for a fee of $3.25.

For more information contact:

Department of Environmental Management
Division of Fish & Wildlife
Veterans Memorial Bldg.
Providence, RI 02903
(401) 277-2784

CAMPGROUNDS

Private

Chepachet

BOWDISH LAKE CAMPING AREA
(401) 568-8890
LOCATION: 5 mi. west of Chepachet.
FACILITIES: Open Apr. 15 - Oct. 15; 200 sites; water and bathroom facilities; sanitary station; electrical hookup; trailer village vehicle sites; boating; boat rental; fishing; tent camping.

Coventry

COLWELL'S CAMPGROUND
(401) 397-3605
LOCATION: On Route 117.
FACILITIES: Open Apr. 15 - Oct. 15; 75 sites; water and bathroom facilities; sanitary station; electrical hookup; trailer village vehicle sites; swimming; boating; fishing; hiking; tent camping.

Foster

DYER WOODS NUDIST CAMPGROUND
(401) 397-3007
LOCATION: South Killingly Road.
FACILITIES: Open May - Oct.; 14 sites; water and bathroom facilities; sanitary station; electrical hookup; trailer village vehicle sites; cabins; picnic area; tent camping.

GINNY B FAMILY CAMPGROUND
(401) 397-9477
LOCATION: South from U.S. 6 via Cucumber Hill Road.
FACILITIES: Open May 1 - Sept. 30; 200 sites; water and bathroom facilities; sanitary station; trailer village vehicle sites; laundry; swimming; bicycle trail; tent camping.

WHIPPOORWILL HILL FAMILY CAMP-
GROUND
(401) 397-7256
LOCATION: Old Plainfield Pike.
FACILITIES: Open Apr. 15 - Oct. 15; 150 sites; water and bathroom facilities; sanitary station; electrical hookup; trailer village vehicle sites; swimming; tent camping.

Greene

HICKORY RIDGE FAMILY CAMPGROUND
(401) 397-5025

LOCATION: In Greene.
FACILITIES: Open Apr. 15 - Oct. 15; 200 sites; water and bathroom facilities; sanitary station; electrical hookup; trailer village vehicle sites; swimming; fishing; hiking; tent camping.

Hope Valley

WHISPERING PINES CAMPGROUND
(401) 539-7011
LOCATION: 3 mi. west of I-95 (Exit 3) on Route 138.
FACILITIES: Open May 1 - Oct. 15; 130 sites; water and bathroom facilities; sanitary station; electrical hookup; trailer village vehicle sites; picnic area; food service; swimming; fishing; tent camping.

Hopkinton

FRONTIER CAMPER PARK
(401) 377-4510
LOCATION: On Frontier Road.
FACILITIES: Open Feb. - Dec.; 100 sites; water and bathroom facilities; sanitary station; electrical hookup; trailer village vehicle sites; tent camping.

Richmond

WAWALOAM RESERVATION CAMP-
GROUND
(401) 294-3039
LOCATION: Gardiner and Hillsdale Roads.
FACILITIES: Open year round; 225 sites; water and bathroom facilities; sanitary station; electrical hookup; trailer village vehicle sites; food service; swimming; tent camping.

South Kingston

WORDEN'S POND FAMILY CAMP-
GROUND
(401) 789-9113
LOCATION: 1173 Worden's Pond Road.
FACILITIES: Open year round; 190 sites; water and bathroom facilities; sanitary station; electrical hookup; trailer village vehicle sites; swimming; fishing; tent camping.

Tiverton

SAKONNET OAKS
(401) 624-3655
LOCATION: On Fish Road.
FACILITIES: Open May - Oct.; 150 sites; water and bathroom facilities; sanitary station; trailer village vehicle sites; laundry; food service; tent camping.

Wakefield

STEADMAN'S CAMPGROUND
(401) 783-1503
LOCATION: On Tuckertown Road.
FACILITIES: Open May - Oct.; 150 sites; water and bathroom facilities; sanitary station; trailer village vehicle sites; picnic area; swimming; boating; fishing; tent camping.

West Greenwich

OAK EMBERS CAMPGROUND
(401) 397-4042

RHODE ISLAND

CAMPGROUNDS (continued)

LOCATION: Escoheag Hill Road.
FACILITIES: Open year round; 60 sites; water and bathroom facilities; sanitary station; electrical hookup; trailer village vehicle sites; laundry; picnic area; food service; swimming; boating; fishing; tent camping.

RESORTS & BEACHES

Newport

NEWPORT AREA - A world away from pollution and congestion where you can swim, surf and sun on the beaches. Then try your hand at fishing and boating in Narragansett Bay. And if you like, cheer on your favorites at the America's Cup Yacht Races and tennis tournaments, or quietly enjoy the music festivals, theater, night clubs, boat shows, art exhibits and museums. There is always something special going on in Newport.

BOATING AREAS

The following is a listing of public saltwater and freshwater launching sites. Boat launching facilities may be found at most private marinas, also. Generally these marinas maintain boat supplies and services, in addition to launching facilities, and are located near or adjacent to the public sites.

Saltwater

Bristol

BRISTOL HARBOR
LOCATION: State Street.

BRISTOL NARROWS
LOCATION: Off Route 136.

THAMES STREET
LOCATION: Foot of Church Street, off Route 114.

Charlestown

CHARLESTOWN BREACHWAY
LOCATION: At the Breachway.

QUONOCHONTAUG BREACHWAY
LOCATION: At the Breachway.

TOWN DOCK ROAD
LOCATION: Town Dock Road.

Cranston

PAWTUXET
LOCATION: Aborn Street.

East Greenwich

CROMPTON AVENUE (Pole No. 6)
LOCATION: Greenwich Cove.

East Providence

BEACH ROAD

LOCATION: Off Bullock's Point Avenue.

BOLD POINT
LOCATION: Off Veteran's Memorial Parkway via Mauran Avenue at the end of Pier Road.

HAINES MEMORIAL PARK
LOCATION: Off Metropolitan Park Drive.

SABIN POINT PARK
LOCATION: Off Bullock's Point Avenue, at the end of Shore Road.

Jamestown

EAST SHORE ROAD
LOCATION: In village.

FORT GETTY RECREATION AREA
LOCATION: Off Beavertail Road.

Little Compton

SAKONNET HARBOR
LOCATION: Sakonnet Point Road.

Middletown

THIRD BEACH ROAD
LOCATION: Third Beach Road.

Narragansett

AT SNUG HARBOR
LOCATION: Jerusalem.

GALILEE
LOCATION: Near corner of Galilee Road and Great Island Road.

KENYON FARMS
LOCATION: Off Route 108.

LONG COVE MARINA
LOCATION: Off Route 108.

Newport

KENNY'S BEACH
LOCATION: Directly off Ocean Drive.

KING PARK
LOCATION: Wellington Avenue.

OFF WASHINGTON STREET
LOCATIONS: Elm Street & Poplar Street.

North Kingstown

BISSEL'S COVE
LOCATION: Waldren Street.

ED'S BOAT STATION
LOCATION: Route 1A.

PLEASANT STREET
LOCATION: Wickford.

WICKFORD
LOCATION: U.S. 1 near fire station.

Portsmouth

GULL COVE

BOATING AREAS (continued)

LOCATION: Route 138.

SANDY POINT ROAD
LOCATION: Off Route 138.

STONE BRIDGE
LOCATION: East of junction of Routes 138 and 24 on Park Avenue.

South Kingstown

MARINA PARK EXIT
LOCATION: Route 1.

NARROW RIVER
LOCATION: Off Pettaquamscutt Road, between Middle Bridge Road & Bridgetown Road.

POND STREET
LOCATION: At the end.

SNUG HARBOR
LOCATION: Foot of Gooseberry Road.

Tiverton

AT THE BEACH
LOCATION: Route 77.

SAKONNET RIVER BRIDGE
LOCATION: Sakonnet River Bridge.

SAPOWET POINT
LOCATION: Route 77 to Sapowet Avenue.

Warwick

ARNOLD'S NECK AREA
LOCATION: End of Harrop Avenue.

CHEPIWANOXET
LOCATION: Off U.S. 1, Alger Avenue.

CONIMICUT
LOCATION: Off Route 117, Rock Road.

CONIMICUT POINT
LOCATION: Directly off Point Avenue.

EDGEWATER BEACH
LOCATION: Off Route 117.

EDGEWATER BEACH AREA
LOCATION: Directly off Oak Tree Avenue.

GASPEE COVE
LOCATION: Narragansett Parkway to General Hawkins Drive.

LONG MEADOW
LOCATION: At Long Meadow.

OAKLAND BEACH
LOCATION: Off Oakland Beach Avenue.

WARWICK DOWNS
LOCATION: Off Narragansett Parkway, dirt roads, ledge just below surface of water at launching site.

WARWICK NECK
LOCATION: On Randall Avenue, off Warwick Neck Avenue.

Fresh Water

Burrillville

CLEAR RIVER
LOCATION: Off Sherman Road.

WILSON RESERVOIR
LOCATION: At the reservoir.

Charlestown

DEEP POND
LOCATION: U.S. 1, Kings Factory Road.

Coventry

TIOGUE LAKE
LOCATION: At Tiogue Lake.

ZEKES BRIDGE
LOCATION: At Zekes Bridge.

Cranston

JOHN L. CURRAN PUBLIC FISHING AREA
LOCATION: Fiskeville Reservoir, Seven Mile Road.

Exeter

BREAKHEART POND
LOCATION: In Arcadia Management area.

Glochester

BOWDISH RESERVOIR
LOCATION: U.S. 44, gravel ramp.

KEECH POND
LOCATION: Off Route 102.

LAKE WASHINGTON
LOCATION: Off U.S. 44.

SMITH & SAYLES RESERVOIR
LOCATION: Off Chestnut Hill Road.

Hopkinton

ALTON LANDING
LOCATION: In Alton Landing.

ASHVILLE POND
LOCATION: Route 3 to Canonchet Road.

GRANTVILLE
LOCATION: Hope Valley Road.

LOCUSTVILLE POND
LOCATION: Route 3 to Fairview Avenue.

WOOD RIVER ACCESS
LOCATION: Wood River access.

North Smithfield

UPPER SLATERSVILLE RESERVOIR
LOCATION: Off Route 102.

BOATING AREAS (continued)

Portsmouth

MELVILLE PUBLIC FISHING AREA
LOCATION: Off Route 114.

Providence

MASHAPAUG POND
LOCATION: On Route 2.

Richmond

BISCUIT CITY LANDING
LOCATION: Biscuit City Road, directly off
Route 2.

RICHMOND LANDING
LOCATION: Pawcatuck River at Routes 3 &
138.

WYOMING POND
LOCATION: Off I-95.

South Kingstown

BARBER'S POND
LOCATION: Route 2.

INDIAN LAKE
LOCATION: Off Tower Hill Road, U.S. 1.

TAYLOR'S LANDING
LOCATION: Off Route 138 in West Kingston.

TUCKER'S POND
LOCATION: Ministerial Road to Tuckertown
Road.

WORDEN'S POND
LOCATION: Ministerial Road to Tuckertown
Road.

Tiverton

STAFFORD POND
LOCATION: Stafford Pond Road, off Routes
177 & 81.

Warwick

POTOWOMUT POND
LOCATION: Off U.S. 1.

West Greenwich

BIG RIVER LANDING
LOCATION: Off Weaver Hill Road.

BIG RIVER LANDING
LOCATION: Off Burnt Sawmill Road.

TARBOX POND
LOCATION: Off Hopkins Hills Road.

Westerly

BRADFORD LANDING
LOCATION: On Pawcatuck River, off U.S. 1
at Dunn's Corner, Bradford Road.

CHAPMAN'S POND
LOCATION: Off Westerly-Bradford Road.

BICYCLE TRAILS

No information was available on Bicycle
Trails in Rhode Island.

TRAILS

Newport

CLIFF WALK - 3.5 mi. foot trail. This trail
offers outstanding scenic, historic, and cultural features. The walk is sometimes 50 feet
above the rocky beaches, offering superb
views of the Atlantic Ocean and the shoreline.
Of special cultural appeal are the late-19th-
century summer "cottages" which are passed
as one walks along the trail. These were built
by some of the nation's most prominent families in the 1880-1914 period. The northern
portion of the trail runs along the edge of a
district on the National Register of Historic
Places.

SKI AREAS

Cumberland

DIAMOND HILL SKI AREA
Cumberland, RI 02864
(401) 333-2116
LOCATION: 4 mi. northeast of Cumberland.
FACILITIES: 1 chairlift; slopes for expert, intermediate and beginning skiers; ski instruction; ski rental; restaurants; lodging.

SKI VALLEY
Cumberland, RI 02864
(401) 333-6406
LOCATION: 1 mi. north of Cumberland.
FACILITIES: 1 chairlift; 2 tow ropes; slopes
for expert, intermediate and beginning skiers;
ski instruction; ski rental; restaurants; lodging.

Escoheag

PINE TOP
Escoheag, RI 02821
(401) 397-5656
LOCATION: 5 mi. south of Escoheag.
FACILITIES: 2 tow ropes; slopes for expert,
intermediate and beginning skiers; ski instruction; ski rental; restaurants; lodging.

Slocum

YAWGOO VALLEY
Exeter, RI 02822
(401) 295-5366
LOCATION: 5 mi. west of Slocum.
FACILITIES: 1 chairlift; 3 tow ropes; slopes
for expert, intermediate and beginning skiers;
ski instruction; ski rental; restaurants; lodging.

AMUSEMENT PARKS & ATTRACTIONS

Hope Valley

THE ENCHANTED FOREST OF RHODE
ISLAND

AMUSEMENT PARKS (continued)

Rt. 3
Hope Valley, RI 02832
(401) 539-7711
FACILITIES: 4 kiddie rides; 13 walk thrus;
2 refreshment stands; arcade; exhibits; picnic
facilities; nature trail; petting zoo; pay gate;
free parking.

Riverside

CRESCENT AMUSEMENT PARK
Bullocks Point Avenue
Riverside, RI 02915
(401) 433-0800
FACILITIES: 15 major rides; 11 kiddie rides;
fun house; walk thru; 14 games; 4 refreshment stands; restaurant; arcade; picnic facilities; miniature golf; free acts; pay gate; free
parking; open Jun. - Sept. 6; weekends: Apr.
& Oct.

Warwick

ROCKY POINT PARK
Rocky Point Road
Warwick, PA 02889
(401) 737-8000
FACILITIES: 29 major rides; 11 kiddie rides;
fun house; 30 games; 9 refreshment stands;
3 restaurants; arcade; 2 shooting galleries;
pool; beach; miniature golf; exhibits; petting
zoo; aquarium; free acts; pay gate; free parking; open May 28 - Sept. 6; weekends: Apr.,
May and late Sept.

STATE FAIR

Rocky Hill State Fair
Division Street
East Greenwich, RI 02818
(401) 884-4114
DATE: August

NATIONAL PARKS

There are no National Parks in Rhode Island.

NATIONAL FORESTS

There are no National Forests in Rhode Island.

STATE PARKS

Headquarters

Department of Natural Resources
Parks Division
83 Park
Providence, RI 02903
(401) 277-2632

Charlestown

BURLINGAME STATE PARK
LOCATION: Near Charlestown.
FACILITIES: Open year round; 775 sites; water and bathroom facilities; trailer village vehicle sites; picnic area; food service; swimming;
boating; fishing; tent camping.

CHARLESTOWN BREACHWAY STATE
PARK
LOCATION: Near Charlestown.
FACILITIES: Open year round; 75 sites; water and bathroom facilities; trailer village vehicle sites; boating; fishing; hiking; tent camping.

NINIGRET CONSERVATION AREA STATE
PARK
LOCATION: Near Charlestown.
FACILITIES: Open year round; 50 sites; wa-
ter and bathroom facilities; trailer village vehi-
cle sites; fishing; hiking; tent camping.

Exeter

BEACH POND STATE PARK
LOCATION: Near Exeter.
FACILITIES: Open year round; 48 sites; water and bathroom facilities; trailer village vehicle sites; cabins; picnic area; food service;
swimming; fishing; hiking; tent camping.

Glocester

GEORGE WASHINGTON STATE PARK
LOCATION: Near Glocester.
FACILITIES: Open year round; 47 sites; water and bathroom facilities; trailer village vehicle sites; picnic area; swimming; boating; fishing; hiking; tent camping.

Narragansett

FISHERMEN'S MEMORIAL STATE PARK
LOCATION: Near Narragansett.
FACILITIES: Open year round; 140 sites; water and bathroom facilities; sanitary station;
electrical hookup; trailer village vehicle sites;
picnic area; swimming; boating; fishing; tent
camping.

Richmond

ARCADIA STATE PARK
LOCATION: Near Richmond.
FACILITIES: Open year round; 25 sites; water and bathroom facilities; trailer village vehicle sites; picnic area; food service; swimming;
boating; hiking; tent camping.

STATE FORESTS

There are no State Forests in Rhode Island.

HISTORIC SITES

Block Island

SETTLERS' ROCK - A monument lists the
names of Block Island's first settlers at their
landing place, April, 1661. Located on the
shore of Cow Cove.

Charlestown

INDIAN CHURCH (1859) - Last of three

RHODE ISLAND

HISTORIC SITES (continued)

Christian Indian churches built in Rhode Island. Visitors welcome at Sunday services, 11 am, Palm Sunday to mid-Nov. Located off Route 2.

Coventry

GENERAL NATHANAEL GREENE HOMESTEAD (1770) - "Mount Vernon of the North." Home of George Washington's second-in-command. Located on Taft Street.

Newport

ARTILLERY COMPANY OF NEWPORT, MILITIA - Chartered in 1741, nation's oldest active military organization. Most complete collection of American and foreign military uniforms on view. Located at 23 Clarke Street.

FRIENDS MEETING HOUSE - Built 1699, additions 1710 and 1807. Oldest congregation of New England Friends (1657). Located on Marlborough and Farewell Streets.

OLD STONE MILL - Much time and effort have been spent to determine the mill's origin. Most popular theory is that it was built by Norsemen before Columbus' voyage. Located in Touro Park.

REDWOOD LIBRARY - Oldest continuously used library building in America; outstanding collection of paintings. Used by British during Revolutionary War as an officers' club. Located on Bellevue Avenue.

Pawtucket

SLATER MILL HISTORIC SITE - Birthplace of American Industrial Revolution. Old Slater Mill (1793). Sylvanus Brown House (1758). Wilkinson Mill (1810). Demonstrations of hand spinning, weaving and early textile machinery. Located on Roosevelt Avenue.

Portsmouth

FOUNDER'S BROOK - Site of the landing of the first settlers from Boston in 1638 under Anne Hutchinson, first woman to establish town in nation. The "Portsmouth Compact," an instrument which organized the first truly democratic form of government in the world, is inscribed on a bronze and stone marker. Located off Boyd's Lane.

Providence

EAST SIDE - Architectural historians regard the building of Providence's "East Side" (as historic residential Providence is locally known) as one of America's best examples of 18th-century America. Homes from the colonial period to the contemporary cover every period of architectural importance in American life. The East Side of Providence is not a re-created showplace; these homes have been lived in continuously since before the Revolutionary War.

FIRST BAPTIST CHURCH - Oldest Baptist Church in AMerica, established in 1638 by Roger Williams. Present church, built in 1775, is an artistic triumph, flawlessly preserved. Located at 75 North Main Street at Waterman Street.

JOHN BROWN HOUSE (1786) - Described by John Quincy Adams as "the most magnificent and elegant mansion that I have ever seen on this continent." Headquarters of Rhode Island Historical Society. Located at 52 Power Street.

West Kingstown

SITE OF GREAT SWAMP FIGHT - An obelisk marks the location of the Great Swamp Fight which took place Dec. 19, 1675, during King Philip's War, and resulted in the near annihilation of the Narragansett Indians. Located off Route 2.

HOSTELS

Newport

ARMED SERVICE YMCA
Multi Center
50 Washington Square
Newport, RI 02840
(401) 846-3120
FACILITIES: Open year round; 20 beds, men; 20 beds, women; modern bathroom; nearest hostel: N. Scituate; overnight charges: $3.50; need sleeping bag; houseparent: Robert Johnson.

North Scituate

CAMP PONAGANSETT
RFD 2, Box 472
North Scituate, RI 02857
(401) 647-7377
FACILITIES: Open Apr. 15 - Oct. 15; 10 beds, men; 10 beds, women; modern bathroom; nearest hostel: East Bridgewater, MA 55 mi. northeast; overnight charges: $2.50; houseparents: Walter R. & Ann T. Hamill.

POINTS OF INTEREST

Adamsville

RHODE ISLAND RED MONUMENT - Commemorates the breed established in 1854 and honors the famous edible commodity which gave the poultry industry to the world. Located on Main Street.

Bristol

HERRESHOFF MARINE MUSEUM - A collection, preservation and display of yachts, engines, fittings, photographs and memorabilia of the unique accomplishments of the Herreshoff Manufacturing Company. Located at 18 Burnside Street.

HERRESHOFF MONUMENT - Commemorates the fame of the Herreshoff brothers, designers and builders of successful America's

POINTS OF INTEREST (continued)

Cup defender yachts and U.S. Navy's prototype torpedo boats. Located at 142 Hope Street.

Cumberland

NEW ENGLAND WIRELESS AND STEAM MUSEUM - Exhibits early radio, telegraph and telephone equipment; stationary steam, hot air, gas and oil engines. Located at Frenchtown and Tillinghast Roads.

Fort Adams

SLOOP-OF-WAR PROVIDENCE - This 12-gun, 65 foot ship is a reproduction of the first authorized ship of the Continental Navy and the first command of John Paul Jones.

Little Compton

MONUMENT TO ELIZABETH PABODIE - Gravesite of daughter of Pilgrims John and Priscilla Alden, first white girl born in New England. Located at Commons Burial Ground.

Newport

BELCOURT CASTLE (1891) - King Louis XIII style castle built for Oliver H.P. Belmont and the former Mrs. W.K. Vanderbilt. Exhibits a world-famous collection of antiques, architectural models of Newport joiner and cabinetmaker Merrall Holt, stained glass windows, armor, rugs, paintings, etc. The only golden Coronation Coach in this country. Tea served. Located on Bellevue Avenue.

THE BREAKERS (1895) - Built for Cornelius Vanderbilt. The symmetry of design, opulence and lavish use of alabaster, marble, mosaics and antique woods rival the magnificent northern Italian Renaissance palaces after which it was modeled. Located on Ochre

Point Avenue.

THE ELMS - Neoclassic mansion built in early 1900s for Edward J. Berwind; has formal sunken gardens and many elaborate statues. Located on Bellevue Avenue.

HAMMERSMITH FARM - 28-room "summer cottage" and formal gardens atop 50 rolling acres overlooking Narragansett Bay. Served as a summer White House during the Kennedy administration. Located on Harrison Avenue.

INTERNATIONAL TENNIS HALL OF FAME AND TENNIS MUSEUM, INC. - Birthplace of national tennis tournaments. Site of the Miller Hall of Fame Championships. Located at 194 Bellevue Avenue.

KINGSCOTE - Built by Richard Upjohn as a summer residence for George Noble Jones of Georgia. Considered the nation's first "summer cottage." Located on Bellevue Avenue.

MARBLE HOUSE (1892) - Mansion built for William K. Vanderbilt. Louis XIV period predominates; building utilizes features of the Grand and Petit Trianon at Versailles. Meetings advancing cause of women's suffrage held here. Located on Bellevue Avenue.

TOURO SYNAGOGUE (1763) - Oldest synagogue in the country. Located at 72 Touro street.

Portsmouth

MEMORIAL TO BLACK SOLDIERS - At the Battle of Rhode Island, August 29, 1778, the first Negro regiment to fight for the American flag made a gallant stand at spot marked by flagpole. Located just to the left of the junctions formed by north-bound Routes 114 and 24.

SOUTH CAROLINA

South Carolina, an ardent states' righter, joined the Union in 1788 as the eighth state. Early settlers were in constant combat with the Spanish, French, Indians and pirates; later, when it came to the question of slavery, war again seemed the natural course of action for a truculent state.

South Carolina's economy, just prior to the War Between the States, was based on agricultural crops and slave labor. As the growing national resentment to slavery threatened the state's already shaky economy, a defensive position was struck. On April 12,

1861, Confederate artillery opened fire on troops at Fort Sumter, signalling the start of this nation's bloodiest war.

Today, industry plays a major role in South Carolina's economy, augumented by livestock farming and commercial fishing.

Tourism is on the rise especially in locales such as historic Charleston, and at Hilton Head and John's Island, the state's most luxurious resort area.

State capital: Columbia. State bird: Carolina wren. State tree: Palmetto. State flower: Yellow jessamine.

WEATHER

South Carolina is located on the southeastern coast of the United States between the

southern slopes of the Appalachian Mountains and the Atlantic Ocean.

Factors affecting temperatures are elevation, latitude, and distance inland from the

SOUTH CAROLINA

WEATHER (continued)

coast. All three of these work together in South Carolina to give a pleasant, mild, and humid climate. Lower temperatures can be expected in the Upper Piedmont and Mountain Regions. Higher temperatures are found along the southern coast. Except for small-scale and local irregularities, there is a gradual decrease in annual average temperature from the coast northwestward to the edge of the mountains.

In general, summers in South Carolina are rather hot, and air-conditioning is desirable at elevations below 500 feet. Fall and spring are mild, but winters are rather cool at elevations above 500 feet.

Average daily temperature for each month.

	Northern	Southern
Jan.	54.4 to 29.5	59.7 to 34.7
Feb.	57.7 to 31.6	62.5 to 37.0
Mar.	65.3 to 37.6	69.4 to 42.9
Apr.	75.4 to 47.0	77.8 to 50.9
May	82.3 to 55.4	84.5 to 58.3
Jun.	88.1 to 62.9	88.9 to 65.1
Jul.	90.8 to 66.9	91.1 to 68.7
Aug.	90.0 to 66.2	90.4 to 68.5
Sept.	84.9 to 60.1	85.6 to 63.4
Oct.	75.3 to 48.4	77.8 to 52.2
Nov.	65.3 to 37.6	69.2 to 41.8
Dec.	56.3 to 31.3	61.9 to 36.3
Year	73.8 to 47.9	76.6 to 51.7

STATE CHAMBER OF COMMERCE

South Carolina Chamber of Commerce
1002 Calhoun Street
Columbia, SC 29201
(803) 779-6270

STATE & CITY TOURISM OFFICES

State

Division of Tourism
South Carolina Department of Parks, Recreation and Tourism
1205 Pendleton Street
Columbia, SC 29202
(803) 758-2536

South Carolina State Development Board
P.O. Box 927
Columbia, SC 29202
(803) 758-3145

Local

Charleston Chamber of Commerce
P.O. Box 975
Charleston, SC 29402
(803) 722-8338

STATE HIGHWAY DEPARTMENT

Department of Highways & Public Transportation
State Highway Building
Columbia, SC 29202
(803) 758-2716

HIGHWAY WELCOMING CENTERS

Allendale

ALLENDALE CENTER - U.S. Hwy. 301, south.

Augusta

AUGUSTA CENTER - Interstate 20, west, north of Augusta.

Blacksburg

BLACKSBURG CENTER - Interstate 85, north.

Columbia

COLUMBIA CENTER - State House, Columbia.

Fair Play

FAIR PLAY CENTER - Interstate 85, south.

Hamer

HAMER CENTER - Interstate 95, north.

Landrum

LANDRUM CENTER - Interstate 28, west.

Little River

LITTLE RIVER CENTER - U.S. Hwy. 17, north.

Santee

SANTEE CENTER - Interstate 95.

STATE POLICE

Department of Public Safety
Columbia, SC 29202
(803) 758-2815

HUNTING & FISHING

Hunting

Hunting and fishing licenses are issued for the period July 1 - June 30 of the following year. Duplicate licenses are available at a cost of $.50 from the SCWMRD, Columbia office only. Application forms may be obtained

HUNTING & FISHING (continued)

from a license agent or Conservation Officer. Exchanging or lending licenses is unlawful.

Children under 14 and 100% permanently and totally disabled veterans are not required to purchase a license or Game Management Area Permit.

Military personnel on active duty presenting their official furlough or leave papers are not required to purchase a hunting or fishing license, but must purchase a Game Management Area Permit to hunt on GMA lands.

Resident

Annual state license, $6.25 (good in all counties); combination hunting and fishing license, $10.25 (all privileges of state hunting and fishing license); county license, $3.25 (good only in county of residence); Game Management Area Permit, $4.25 (all licensed hunters and servicemen must have a permit in addition to a S.C. hunting license or official leave papers to hunt on any and all game management areas in the state).

Non-resident

Annual license, $42.50 (good in all counties); 3-day license, $12.50 (three consecutive days only); 10-day license, $22 (ten consecutive days only); Game Management Area Permit, $20.25 (all non-residents 14 and older must also have a S.C. hunting license).

Fishing

See above hunting regulations.

Resident

Annual statewide license, $5.25 (good in all public waters of the state for all types of natural or manufactured tackle or equipment, fly rod, casting rod or artificial bait); combination hunting and fishing license, $10.25 (all privileges of state hunting and fishing license); 14-day license, $2.25 (all privileges of statewide license, but good for 14 consecutive days only); lakes and reservoirs permit, $1.50; (1 permit only required of all residents using ONLY cane poles in Lakes Marion and Moultrie; Murray; Greenwood; Wylie, Fishing Creek and Wateree; Clark Hill and Steven's Creek; Hartwell, Jocassee and Keowee); no license or permit required for cane poles ONLY in other waters.

Non-resident

Annual license, $11.25 (good in all public waters for all types of tackle and equipment); 10-day license, $4.25 (good for 10 consecutive days only).

For more information contact:

Department of Wildlife and Marine Resources
Dutch Plaza
P.O. Box 167
Columbia, SC 29202
(803) 758-6314

CAMPGROUNDS

Private

Fort Mill

PINE TREE SAFARI CAMPGROUND
Route 4, Box 429
Fort Mill, SC 29715
(803) 548-0216
LOCATION: On Gold Mill Road.
FACILITIES: Open year round; 219 sites; water and bathroom facilities; sanitary station; electrical hookup; trailer village vehicle sites; food service; swimming; tent camping.

Hardeeville

LAKE PINES KOA KAMPGROUND
P.O. Box 134
Hardeeville, SC 29927
(803) 784-2529
LOCATION: 2 mi. north of Hardeeville on U.S. 17 and I-95, Exit 8.
FACILITIES: Open year round; 200 sites; water and bathroom facilities; sanitary station; electrical hookup; trailer village vehicle sites; laundry; food service; swimming; fishing; tent camping.

Lexington

LAKE MURRAY FAMILY CAMPGROUND
R.F.D. 1
Gilbert, SC 29054
(803) 892-2222
LOCATION: 8 mi. west of Lexington off U.S. 378 from I-26.
FACILITIES: Open year round; 300 sites; water and bathroom facilities; sanitary station; electrical hookup; trailer village vehicle sites; laundry; food service; swimming; fishing; tent camping.

Myrtle Beach

HOLIDAY INN TRAV-L-PARK
Star Route 2
Myrtle Beach, SC 29577
(803) 449-3714
LOCATION: 9 mi. north of Myrtle Beach on U.S. 17.
FACILITIES: Open year round; 1013 sites; water and bathroom facilities; sanitary station; electrical hookup; trailer village vehicle sites; laundry; food service; swimming; fishing; tent camping.

LAKE ARROWHEAD FAMILY CAMPGROUNDS
Star Route 2
Myrtle Beach, SC 29577
(803) 449-5626
LOCATION: 8 mi. north of Myrtle Beach on U.S. 17.
FACILITIES: Open year round; 1300 sites; water and bathroom facilities; sanitary station; electrical hookup; trailer village vehicle sites; laundry; food service; swimming; fishing; tent camping.

LAKEWOOD FAMILY CAMPGROUND
Hwy. 17 South
Myrtle Beach, SC 29577

SOUTH CAROLINA

CAMPGROUNDS (continued)

(803) 238-5161
LOCATION: 4 mi. south of Myrtle Beach on U.S. 17.
FACILITIES: Open year round; 1535 sites; water and bathroom facilities; sanitary station; electrical hookup; trailer village vehicle sites; food service; swimming; fishing; tent camping.

MYRTLE BEACH KOA KAMPGROUND
5th Avenue South
Myrtle Beach, SC 29577
(803) 448-3421
LOCATION: U.S. 17 and 5th Avenue South.
FACILITIES: Open year round; 225 sites; water and bathroom facilities; sanitary station; electrical hookup; trailer village vehicle sites; laundry; food service; swimming; fishing; tent camping.

OCEAN LAKES FAMILY CAMPGROUND
Hwy. 17 South
Myrtle Beach, SC 29577
(803) 238-5636
LOCATION: 4 mi. south of Myrtle Beach on U.S. 17 and Route 375.
FACILITIES: Open year round; 2500 sites; water and bathroom facilities; sanitary station; electrical hookup; trailer village vehicle sites; laundry; food service; swimming; fishing; tent camping.

PIRATELAND FAMILY CAMPGROUND
Hwy. 17 South
Myrtle Beach, SC 29577
(803) 238-5155
LOCATION: 3 mi. south of Myrtle Beach on U.S. 17.
FACILITIES: Open year round; 110 sites; water and bathroom facilities; sanitary station; electrical hookup; trailer village vehicle sites; laundry; food service; swimming; fishing; tent camping.

PONDEROSA FAMILY CAMPGROUND
Star Route 2
Myrtle Beach, SC 29577
(803) 272-6172
LOCATION: 10 mi. north of Myrtle Beach on U.S. 17.
FACILITIES: Open year round; 483 sites; water and bathroom facilities; sanitary station; electrical hookup; trailer village vehicle sites; laundry; food service; swimming; fishing; tent camping.

North Myrtle Beach

SHERWOOD FOREST FAMILY CAMPGROUND
P.O. Box 2116
North Myrtle Beach, SC 29582
(803) 272-6420
LOCATION: 6 mi. north of North Myrtle Beach on U.S. 17.
FACILITIES: Open year round; 525 sites; water and bathroom facilities; sanitary station; electrical hookup; trailer village vehicle sites; laundry; food service; swimming; fishing; tent camping.

Santee

HOLIDAY INN TRAV-L-PARK
P.O. Box 124
Santee, SC 29142
(803) 478-4444
LOCATION: Santee-Cooper Lakes, ½ mi. off I-95 and U.S. 301.
FACILITIES: Open year round; 280 sites; water and bathroom facilities; sanitary station; electrical hookup; trailer village vehicle sites; laundry; food service; swimming; fishing; tent camping.

ROCKS POND CAMPGROUND
Route 1, Box 432
Eutawville, SC 29048
(803) 492-7711
LOCATION: 6 mi. east of Santee on Route 6.
FACILITIES: Open year round; 569 sites; water and bathroom facilities; sanitary station; electrical hookup; trailer village vehicle sites; swimming; fishing; tent camping.

SANTEE - LAKE MARION KOA KAMPGROUND
Route 2, Box 84
Summerton, SC 29148
(803) 478-2262
LOCATION: Santee-Cooper Lakes, I-95 and U.S. 301, Exit 102.
FACILITIES: Open year round; 200 sites; water and bathroom facilities; sanitary station; electrical hookup; trailer village vehicle sites; laundry; food service; swimming; fishing; tent camping.

SHAWNEE
P.O. Box 137
Santee, SC 29142
(803) 854-2136
LOCATION: Santee-Cooper Lakes, I-95, 2 mi. east on Route 6.
FACILITIES: Open year round; 200 sites; water and bathroom facilities; sanitary station; electrical hookup; trailer village vehicle sites; food service; fishing; tent camping.

RESORTS & BEACHES

Beaufort

HUNTING ISLAND STATE PARK - Fripp Island - If you like beachcombing and wildlife observation, you'll like this park which is located 16 mi. east of Beaufort on U.S. 21. It's an untamed, sub-tropical island that has become one of the most popular of South Carolina's state parks. There are camping facilities, 11 rental cabins, picnic and swimming areas, boat ramp, nature trail, playground, carpet golf and a 1,000-foot boardwalk for observing wildlife. The 136-foot lighthouse here, one of the few remaining on the Atlantic coast, was built in 1873 and used actively until 1933. Just beyond the park, after crossing the Fripp Island Bridge, you enter a modern sanctuary... for people. There is golf to enjoy along with swimming (surf or pool), hiking, bicycling, boating, or you may simply do nothing at all.

RESORTS (continued)

Charleston

KIAWAH ISLAND - Kiawah, about 20 mi. south of Charleston, is one of the newest island resorts along South Carolina's coast. Still basically in its virgin state, the 10,000-acre island was once the home of the Kiawah Indians. The uncrowded beach is 10 mi. long, and at points, 150 yards wide. Many species of birds and wild animals consider the island their home, and visitors may take the Back Island Safari Jeep Tour along old logging trails, around alligator pools and rookeries and into the island wilderness.

Hilton Head Island

HILTON HEAD ISLAND - A vacation to a tropical island paradise can be a lot closer than most people think. Located in the southeastern corner of the state, Hilton Head Island is one of the largest sea islands on the Atlantic coast, with 12 mi. of unspoiled beaches. Major resorts on the island include Sea Pines Plantation, Palmetto Dunes Resort, Port Royal, Shipyard Plantation, Spanish Wells and the Hilton Head Plantation. The island also has many fine inns, hotels and motels, rental villas, condominiums and rental homes. On the island are the remains of the Civil War's Fort Mitchell and Fort Walker and the Baynard Ruins, where massive tabby walls and scattered foundations show the extent of a typical Low-Country plantation.

John's Island

SEABROOK - You can now enjoy the serenity of Seabrook by the day, week, or month, thanks to Seabrook's elegant High Hammock Villas. High Hammock offers the perfect location for golfing islanders and visitors; you can play Seabrook's challenging oceanside course, or simply relax on a villa deck, patio or observation deck. Bask in the warm Carolina sun. Swim in the pool or the ocean, just beyond. Play tennis and fish the tidal creeks, surf or stroll along the white-sand beach. Then savor the Antebellum elegance of historic Charleston, just 20 mi. up the coast.

Little River

THE GRAND STRAND - This 55-mi. stretch of beach, with Myrtle Beach at its hub, extends from the town of Little River in the north to Georgetown in the south. The area offers over 35,000 rooms for visitors, 10,000 campsites, 27 golf courses and nearly 100 tennis courts. History, recreation, fishing, unique shopping complexes and boutiques, fine restaurants, and, of course, the beach make Myrtle Beach and Grand Strand South Carolina's most popular vacation area.

McCormick

See State Parks, Hickory Knob State Park (Resort).

Santee

SANTEE-COOPER - Santee-Cooper country is the area around Lakes Marion and Moultrie (the Santee-Cooper Lakes), famous for their landlocked striped bass. Over 171,000 acres of fresh water surround fishermen as they pit their skills against striped bass, largemouth bass, white bass, bream, crappie and other fish. Over 50 fishing camps are located in the area, as well as many public boat landings. The area also has excellent hunting, golf, camping and water sports.

BOATING AREAS

See Resorts & Beaches and State Parks.

BICYCLE TRAILS

No information was available on Bicycle Trails in South Carolina.

TRAIL

Pumpkintown

TABLE ROCK TRAIL - 9 mi. foot trail. This continuous-loop trail in Table Rock State Park, with parts of it designated by other names, is open year-round to the general public. Its rugged terrain offers hikers a 2,000-foot ascent at its beginning and a 4-mile descent at its end. The trail requires stamina from hikers as it stretches over mountain ridges and winds through oak and hickory forests interlaced with scattered pines and hemlocks. A shorter portion of the main trail serves as a self-interpretive nature trail.

SKI AREAS

There are no organized Ski Areas in South Carolina.

AMUSEMENT PARKS & ATTRACTIONS

Myrtle Beach

GRAND STRAND AMUSEMENT PARK
408 S. Ocean Blvd.
Myrtle Beach, SC 29577
(803) 448-3516
FACILITIES: 11 major rides; 7 kiddie rides; 3 refreshment stands; 2 penny arcades; beach; museum; free acts; free gate; free parking.

LAKEWOOD MAGIC HARBOR
Hwy. 17
Myrtle Beach, SC 29577
(803) 238-0717
FACILITIES: 12 major rides; 6 kiddie rides; 18 games; 6 refreshment stands; free gate; free parking.

MYRTLE BEACH PAVILION & AMUSEMENT PARK
9th & Ocean Blvd.

SOUTH CAROLINA

AMUSEMENT PARKS (continued)

Myrtle Beach, SC 29577
(803) 448-6456
FACILITIES: 15 major rides; 12 kiddie rides;
fun house; 12 refreshment stands; 2 restaurants; arcade; beach; miniature golf course;
picnic facilities; free acts; free gate; pay parking.

STATE FAIR

South Carolina State Fair
P.O. Box 393
Columbia, SC 29202
(803) 799-3387
DATE: October

NATIONAL PARKS

There are no National Parks in South Carolina.

NATIONAL FORESTS

National Forests
Southern Region
1720 Peachtree Road, NW
Atlanta, GA 30309
(404) 881-4177

Columbia

FRANCIS MARION NATIONAL FOREST
ATTRACTIONS: Ruins and remnants of
early colonial settlements and plantations.
Many "Carolina bays" (small lakes, believed
to be caused by meteors). Bass and other fishing; alligator, deer, turkey, quail hunting;
boating.
FACILITIES: 1 camp and picnic site, 1 picnic
only; swimming site; hotels and motels near
the National Forest.
NEARBY TOWNS: Charleston, Georgetown,
McClellanville, Moncks Corner.

SUMTER NATIONAL FOREST
ATTRACTIONS: Trout, bass fishing; quail
hunting; scenic drives.
FACILITIES: 11 camp and picnic sites, 23
picnic only; 4 swimming sites; hotels and motels near the National Forest.
NEARBY TOWNS: Abbeville, Clinton, Edgefield, Greenwood, Newberry, Union, and Walhalla.

STATE PARKS

Headquarters

South Carolina State Parks
P.O. Box 71
Columbia, SC 29203
(803) 758-7507

Aiken

AIKEN STATE PARK
(803) 649-2857
LOCATION: 16 mi. east of Aiken off U.S.
78.
FACILITIES: Open year round; 25 sites; water and bathroom facilities; sanitary station;
electrical hookup; trailer village vehicle sites;
picnic area; swimming; boating; boat rental;
fishing; tent camping.

Anderson

SADLERS CREEK STATE PARK
(803) 226-8950
LOCATION: 13 mi. southwest of Anderson
off U.S. 29.
FACILITIES: Open year round; 100 sites; water and bathroom facilities; sanitary station;
electrical hookup; trailer village vehicle sites;
picnic area; swimming; boating; boat rental;
fishing; tent camping.

Barnwell

BARNWELL STATE PARK
(803) 284-2212
LOCATION: 7 mi. northeast of Barnwell on
Route 3.
FACILITIES: Open year round; 25 sites; water and bathroom facilities; sanitary station;
electrical hookup; trailer village vehicle sites;
picnic area; swimming; boating; boat rental;
fishing; tent camping.

Beaufort

HUNTING ISLAND STATE PARK
(803) 838-2011
LOCATION: 16 mi. east of Beaufort on U.S.
21.
FACILITIES: Open year round; 200 sites; water and bathroom facilities; sanitary station;
electrical hookup; trailer village vehicle sites;
picnic area; swimming; boating; boat rental;
fishing; tent camping.

Bishopville

LEE STATE PARK
(803) 428-3833
LOCATION: 7 mi. east of Bishopville off
I-20.
FACILITIES: Open year round; 50 sites; water and bathroom facilities; sanitary station;
electrical hookup; trailer village vehicle sites;
picnic area; swimming; boating; boat rental;
fishing; tent camping.

Charleston

EDISTO BEACH STATE PARK
(803) 869-2156
LOCATION: 50 mi. southeast of Charleston
on Route 174.
FACILITIES: Open year round; 75 sites; water and bathroom facilities; sanitary station;
electrical hookup; trailer village vehicle sites;
picnic area; swimming; boating; fishing; tent
camping.

Cheraw

CHERAW STATE PARK
(803) 537-2215
LOCATION: 4 mi. southwest of Cheraw on
U.S. 1.

STATE PARKS (continued)

FACILITIES: Open year round; 25 sites; water and bathroom facilities; sanitary station; electrical hookup; trailer village vehicle sites; picnic area; swimming; boating; boat rental; tent camping.

Chester

CHESTER STATE PARK
(803) 385-2680
LOCATION: 3 mi. southwest of Chester on Route 72.
FACILITIES: Open year round; 45 sites; water and bathroom facilities; sanitary station; electrical hookup; trailer village vehicle sites; picnic area; boating; boat rental; fishing; tent camping.

Columbia

SESQUICENTENNIAL STATE PARK
(803) 788-2706
LOCATION: 13 mi. northeast of Columbia on U.S. 1.
FACILITIES: Open year round; 87 sites; water and bathroom facilities; sanitary station; electrical hookup; trailer village vehicle sites; picnic area; swimming; boating; boat rental; fishing; tent camping.

Dillon

LITTLE PEE DEE STATE PARK
(803) 774-8872
LOCATION: 11 mi. southeast of Dillon off Route 57.
FACILITIES: Open year round; 50 sites; water and bathroom facilities; sanitary station; electrical hookup; trailer village vehicle sites; picnic area; swimming; boating; boat rental; fishing; tent camping.

Ehrhardt

RIVERS BRIDGE STATE PARK
(803) 267-3675
LOCATION: 7 mi. southeast of Ehrhardt on Route 641.
FACILITIES: Open year round; 50 sites; water and bathroom facilities; sanitary station; electrical hookup; trailer village vehicle sites; picnic area; swimming; boating; boat rental; fishing; tent camping.

Greenville

PARIS MOUNTAIN STATE PARK
(803) 244-5565
LOCATION: 9 mi. north of Greenville off U.S. 25.
FACILITIES: Open year round; 50 sites; water and bathroom facilities; sanitary station; electrical hookup; trailer village vehicle sites; picnic area; swimming; boating; boat rental; fishing; tent camping.

PLEASANT RIDGE STATE PARK
(803) 836-6589
LOCATION: 22 mi. northwest of Greenville on Route 11.
FACILITIES: Open year round; 25 sites; water and bathroom facilities; sanitary station;

electrical hookup; trailer village vehicle sites; swimming; boating; boat rental; fishing; tent camping.

Greenwood

GREENWOOD STATE PARK
(803) 543-3535
LOCATION: 17 mi. east of Greenwood on Route 702.
FACILITIES: Open year round; 125 sites; water and bathroom facilities; sanitary station; electrical hookup; trailer village vehicle sites; picnic area; swimming; boating; boat rental; fishing; tent camping.

Lancaster

ANDREW JACKSON STATE PARK
(803) 285-3344
LOCATION: 8 mi. north of Lancaster on U.S. 521.
FACILITIES: Open year round; 25 sites; water and bathroom facilities; sanitary station; electrical hookup; trailer village vehicle sites; picnic area; boating; boat rental; fishing; tent camping.

McCormick

BAKER CREEK STATE PARK
(803) 443-5886
LOCATION: 3 mi. southwest of McCormick on U.S. 378.
FACILITIES: Open year round; 100 sites; water and bathroom facilities; sanitary station; electrical hookup; trailer village vehicle sites; picnic area; swimming; boating; boat rental; fishing; tent camping.

HAMILTON BRANCH STATE PARK
(803) 333-2115
LOCATION: 15 mi. south of McCormick on U.S. 221.
FACILITIES: Open year round; 200 sites; water and bathroom facilities; sanitary station; electrical hookup; trailer village vehicle sites; picnic area; boating; boat rental; fishing; tent camping.

HICKORY KNOB STATE PARK (Resort)
(803) 443-2151
LOCATION: 8 mi. southwest of McCormick on U.S. 378.
FACILITIES: Open year round; 75 sites; water and bathroom facilities; sanitary station; electrical hookup; trailer village vehicle sites; cabins; picnic area; boating; boat rental; fishing; tent camping; lodging.

Murrells Inlet

HUNTINGTON BEACH STATE PARK
(803) 237-4440
LOCATION: 3 mi. south of Murrells Inlet on U.S. 17.
FACILITIES: Open year round; 128 sites; water and bathroom facilities; sanitary station; electrical hookup; trailer village vehicle sites; picnic area; swimming; boating; fishing; tent camping.

Myrtle Beach

MYRTLE BEACH STATE PARK

SOUTH CAROLINA

STATE PARKS (continued)

(803) 238-5325
LOCATION: 3 mi. south of Myrtle Beach on U.S. 17.
FACILITIES: Open year round; 300 sites; water and bathroom facilities; sanitary station; electrical hookup; trailer village vehicle sites; picnic area; swimming; boating; fishing; tent camping.

Pickens

TABLE ROCK STATE PARK
(803) 878-9813
LOCATION: 16 mi. north of Pickens on Route 11.
FACILITIES: Open year round; 109 sites; water and bathroom facilities; sanitary station; electrical hookup; picnic area; food service; swimming; boating; boat rental; fishing; tent camping.

Santee

SANTEE STATE PARK
(803) 854-2167
LOCATION: 3 mi. northwest of Santee off I-95.
FACILITIES: Open year round; 150 sites; water and bathroom facilities; sanitary station; electrical hookup; trailer village vehicle sites; picnic area; swimming; boating; boat rental; fishing; tent camping.

Spartanburg

CROFT STATE PARK
(803) 585-1283
LOCATION: 3 mi. southeast of Spartanburg off Route 56.
FACILITIES: Open year round; 50 sites; water and bathroom facilities; sanitary station; electrical hookup; trailer village vehicle sites; picnic area; boating; boat rental; fishing; tent camping.

Summerville

GIVHANS FERRY STATE PARK
(803) 873-0692
LOCATION: 16 mi. west of Summerville on Route 61.
FACILITIES: Open year round; 25 sites; water and bathroom facilities; sanitary station; electrical hookup; trailer village vehicle sites; picnic area; boating; fishing; tent camping.

Sumter

POINSETT STATE PARK
(803) 494-8177
LOCATION: 18 mi. southwest of Sumter off Route 261.
FACILITIES: Open year round; 50 sites; water and bathroom facilities; sanitary station; electrical hookup; trailer village vehicle sites; picnic area; swimming; boating; boat rental; fishing; tent camping.

Walhalla

OCONEE STATE PARK
(803) 638-5353

LOCATION: 12 mi. northwest of Walhalla on Route 107.
FACILITIES: Open year round; 140 sites; water and bathroom facilities; sanitary station; electrical hookup; trailer village vehicle sites; picnic area; swimming; boating; boat rental; fishing; tent camping.

Walterboro

COLLETON STATE PARK
(803) 538-8206
LOCATION: 11 mi. north of Walterboro on U.S. 15.
FACILITIES: Open year round; 25 sites; water and bathroom facilities; sanitary station; electrical hookup; trailer village vehicle sites; picnic area; boating; fishing; tent camping.

York

KINGS MOUNTAIN STATE PARK
(803) 222-3209
LOCATION: 12 mi. northwest of York on Route 161.
FACILITIES: Open year round; 125 sites; water and bathroom facilities; sanitary station; electrical hookup; trailer village vehicle sites; swimming; boating; boat rental; fishing; tent camping.

STATE FORESTS

State Commission of Forestry
P.O. Box 21707
Columbia, SC 29221
(803) 758-2226

Patrick

SAND HILLS STATE FOREST
LOCATION: Near Patrick.
FACILITIES: Open year round; hunting; fishing; hiking; tent camping.

Wedgefield

MANCHESTER STATE FOREST
LOCATION: South of Wedgefield.
FACILITIES: Open year round; boating; hunting; fishing; hiking; tent camping.

HISTORIC SITES

Charleston

DOCK STREET THEATRE - First theater in America (1736), the remodeled building is still used for theatrical performances. Located on Church Street.

FORT SUMTER - One of the series of coastal fortifications built by the United States after the War of 1812. It was here, on April 12, 1861, that the first shot was fired in the War Between the States. Tour boats (the only way to reach the fort is by boat) leave daily from the Charleston Municipal Marina. Located in Charleston Harbor.

HUGUENOT CHURCH - French Protestant Church is country's last remaining Huguenot

HISTORIC SITES (continued)

place of worship. Located on corner of Chruch and Queen Streets.

NATHANIEL RUSSELL HOUSE - Built before 1809 at an estimated cost of $80,000. Charleston's finest example of Adams architecture, it has a beautiful free-standing stairway, oval drawing rooms, and south rooms built along elliptical lines. Located at 51 Meeting Street.

Spartanburg

WALNUT GROVE PLANTATION - Built in 1765, this was the home of Kate Moore Barry, a scout for General Daniel Morgan at the Revolutionary Battle of Cowpens. Located near U.S. 221 and S-42-196 junction.

Sullivan's Island

FORT MOULTRIE - In 1776, Col. William Moultrie and about 400 South Carolinians beat off a squadron of nine British warships at this site. Located on U.S. 17.

HOSTELS

There are no Hostels in South Carolina.

POINTS OF INTEREST

Charleston

THE FRANCIS BEIDLER FOREST IN FOUR HOLES SWAMP - Contains the largest remaining virgin stand of cypress and tupelo trees in the world. A 6500-foot boardwalk trail enables visitors to walk through the swamp and enjoy its natural beauty. The sanctuary is a habitat for abundant and varied wildlife, including deer, raccoons, bobcats, otters, opossums, gray squirrels, alligators and many species of birds. The interpretive center here is heated with solar energy. Located on Hwy. 78 about 35 mi. northwest of Charleston.

MIDDLETON PLACE - Pre-Revolutionary War house with the country's oldest landscaped gardens (1741); the first camellias were transplanted here from France. Located northwest of Charleston on Route 61.

MAGNOLIA PLANTATION AND GAR-

DENS - Drayton family home with beautiful gardens featuring hundreds of varieties of camellia and azalea, plus a 200 year old redwood tree. Located on Ashley River Road.

Darlington

JOE WEATHERLY STOCK CAR MUSEUM - Youngsters and oldsters alike will enjoy sitting behind the wheel of Richard Petty's Dodge and driving the track like one of the pros in the only racing simulator of its kind in the Southeast. Located on Route 34.

Florence

FLORENCE AIR AND MISSILE MUSEUM - Some 38 planes and missiles are on display at the museum. Among them are the BOMARC, a long-range, high-altitude supersonic missile designed to destroy enemy aircraft; the Titan I, an ICBM missile; the F-89-J "Scorpion" jet; and the RB-57-A, a bomber that reaches a speed of over 600-miles per hour and has a range of 2000 miles. Located on U.S. 301, 5 mi. east of I-95.

Greenwood

THE GARDENS OF PARK SEED COMPANY - One of the country's largest seed supply houses. During the city's Festival of Flowers (third week in July), Saturday is "Open House," and Park's "All-American" selections are announced at this time. The stunning beauty of the tea gardens and other floral displays is exciting anytime. Located on Route 254, 6 mi. north of Greenwood.

Hartsville

NUCLEAR INFORMATION CENTER - The state's first commercial nuclear facility. Inside this $200,000 structure are exhibits that tell the story of energy, graphically showing how the atom has been harnessed to do the work of man. The kids can work off some of their excess energy on a bicycle which, when pedaled, lights a 60-watt bulb. Located at Carolina Power and Light's Generating Plant.

Murrells Inlet

BROOKGREEN GARDENS - Four old rice plantations are the site of this tranquil outdoor museum, full of sculpture, rice fields and centuries-old live oaks. The gardens contain more than 350 works representing the history of American sculpture from the 19th and 20th centuries. Located on U.S. 17.

SOUTH DAKOTA

South Dakota, site of the world's largest gold mine, joined the Union in 1889 as the fortieth state. Prior to the discovery of gold in the state, the Sioux Indians roamed the lands pretty much as they pleased, hunting the wild buffalo. Those white settlers who did venture

into the Indian territory were constantly harassed. Then in the 1870s, gold fever struck South Dakota and the white man came in droves to dig in the hills, overwhelming the Indian.

In the process of settling the state, the

SOUTH DAKOTA

INTRODUCTION (continued)

white man killed off the buffalo herds which did as much to defeat the Indians as the cavalry's new repeater rifles.

Gold is still mined in South Dakota today, but now agriculture accounts for a major share of the state's revenues, especially live-stock and its by-products.

Tourism, too, is important to the state, aided by impressive attractions such as Mount Rushmore, and historic Deadwood and Wounded Knee.

State capital: Pierre. State bird: Ring-necked pheasant. State tree: Black Hills spruce. State flower: Pasqueflower.

WEATHER

Rolling plains are the main feature of South Dakota, varying from nearly level land to hilly ridges, and increasing in elevation from the eastern border to the western edge of the state. The Black Hills, an isolated group of forest-covered mountains, have a climate of their own.

Since South Dakota is situated in the heart of the North American continent, it is near the paths of many cyclones and anticyclones, and has the extremes of summer heat and winter cold that are characteristic of continental climates. Rapid fluctuations in temperature are common. Temperatures of 100 degrees F, or higher, are experienced in some part of the state each summer, and on rare occasions such readings have been noted as early as April and as late as October. These high temperatures are usually attended by low humidity, which greatly reduces the oppressiveness of the heat. Below-zero temperatures occur frequently on midwinter mornings, but it is not often that the temperature stays below zero during the entire day. In the north, subzero temperatures can occur in October and April.

Warm, "chinook" winds and frequent sunny skies make the Black Hills area the warmest part of the state in winter. In summer, the higher elevation of the Black Hills results in that section having cooler temperatures than the rest of the state. During this season, the central and southeastern counties are warmest.

Average daily temperature for each month.

	Northern	Southern
Jan.	19.2 to -1.7	32.0 to 9.8
Feb.	26.1 to 5.1	38.0 to 15.2
Mar.	37.3 to 16.1	45.6 to 22.2
Apr.	55.4 to 30.6	61.4 to 34.9
May	68.3 to 41.8	72.6 to 46.7
Jun.	77.4 to 52.3	81.9 to 57.0
Jul.	84.6 to 57.2	89.7 to 62.7
Aug.	84.6 to 55.7	88.2 to 61.2
Sept.	72.5 to 44.4	77.2 to 50.4
Oct.	61.1 to 34.4	65.9 to 39.9
Nov.	40.7 to 19.3	48.5 to 25.9
Dec.	26.0 to 6.6	36.0 to 15.3
Year	54.4 to 30.2	61.4 to 36.8

STATE CHAMBER OF COMMERCE

Greater South Dakota Association
P.O. Box 190
Pierre, SD 57501
(605) 324-5879

STATE & CITY TOURISM OFFICES

State

Department of Economic and Tourism Development
620 South Cliff
Sioux Falls, SD 57103
(605) 339-6779

Division of Tourism
Joe Foss Building
Pierre, SD 57501
(605) 773-3301

Local

Rapid City Chamber of Commerce
P.O. Box 747
Rapid City, SD 57701
(605) 343-1744

Sioux Falls Chamber of Commerce
P.O. Box 1425
Sioux Falls, SD 57101
(605) 336-1620

STATE HIGHWAY DEPARTMENT

Department of Transportation
Transportation Building
East Broadway
Pierre, SD 57501
(605) 224-3265

HIGHWAY WELCOMING CENTERS

Chamberlain

CHAMBERLAIN CENTER - Interstate 90.

Minnesota

MINNESOTA BORDER - Interstate 90.

Salem

SALEM CENTER - Interstate 90, east.

SALEM CENTER - Interstate 90, west.

WELCOMING CENTERS (continued)

Wasta

WASTA CENTER - Interstate 90 east.

STATE POLICE

Department of Public Safety
118 West Capitol Avenue
Pierre, SD 57501
(605) 773-3105

HUNTING & FISHING

Hunting

A license is required for all persons, ages 12 through 69, who hunt and fish in the state. To qualify as a resident, a person must reside in the state 90 days prior to application.

Resident

General hunting license, $1; big game, $12; small game, $3; turkey, $2; pheasant restoration stamp, $5.

Non-resident

General hunting license, $2; big game, $50; small game, $30; turkey, $5; waterfowl, $30; pheasant restoration stamp, $5.

Fishing

See hunting regulations above.

Resident

Annual fishing, $4.

Non-resident

Annual fishing, $15; 5-day fishing, $5.

For more information contact:

Department of Game, Fish and Parks
Pierre, SD 57501
(605) 773-3482

CAMPGROUNDS

Private

Arlington

SIOUXLAND TRAILER PARK & CAMP-GROUND
(605) 983-5930
LOCATION: 24 mi. south of Watertown on U.S. 81.
FACILITIES: Open Apr. 1 - Oct. 15; water and bathroom facilities; sanitary station; electrical hookup; trailer village vehicle sites; food service; tent camping.

Brookings

SOUTH SIDE RECREATION CAMPING

(605) 693-4477
LOCATION: 4 mi. west of Brookings.
FACILITIES: Open May - Oct.; water and bathroom facilities; sanitary station; electrical hookup; trailer village vehicle sites; laundry; picnic area; food service; swimming; boating; tent camping.

Canistota

BATTLE CREEK CAMPGROUND
(605) 296-3163
LOCATION: 23 mi. west of Sioux Falls.
FACILITIES: Open May - Oct.; water and bathroom facilities; sanitary station; electrical hookup; trailer village vehicle sites; laundry; food service; swimming; boating; boat rental.

Chamberlain

FAMILYLAND USA CAMPGROUND
(605) 734-9920
LOCATION: 3 mi. west of Chamberlain on I-90.
FACILITIES: Open May 15 - Oct. 1; water and bathroom facilities; electrical hookup; trailer village vehicle sites; picnic area; tent camping.

Custer

BEAVER LAKE RANCH & CAMPGROUND
(605) 673-2464
LOCATION: 3 mi. west of Custer on U.S. 16.
FACILITIES: Open May 1 - Sept. 30; water and bathroom facilities; electrical hookup; trailer village vehicle sites; laundry; picnic area; food service; fishing; tent camping.

BIG PINE CAMPGROUND
(605) 673-4054
LOCATION: 2 mi. west of Custer on U.S. 16.
FACILITIES: Open May 15 - Oct. 1; water and bathroom facilities; electrical hookup; trailer village vehicle sites; laundry; food service; tent camping.

FLINTSTONES BEDROCK CITY CAMP-GROUND
(605) 673-4664
LOCATION: West Custer, Hwys. 16 & 385.
FACILITIES: Open May 15 - Sept. 15; water and bathroom facilities; electrical hookup; trailer village vehicle sites; laundry; food service; tent camping.

Gettysburg

RIVER'S EDGE CAMPSITE
(605) 765-2550
LOCATION: 16 mi. west of Gettysburg.
FACILITIES: Open May 15 - Sept. 15; water and bathroom facilities; electrical hookup; trailer village vehicle sites; laundry; picnic area; swimming; boating; fishing; tent camping.

Hermosa

BLACK HILLS CAMPGROUND
(605) 666-4609
LOCATION: 11 mi. south of Keystone on Hwy. 16A.
FACILITIES: Open May 1 - Oct. 1; water and

SOUTH DAKOTA

CAMPGROUNDS (continued)

bathroom facilities; sanitary station; electrical hookup; trailer village vehicle sites; cabins; laundry; picnic area; food service; tent camping.

Hill City

HORSE THIEF RESORT
(605) 574-2668
LOCATION: 4 mi. south of Hill City.
FACILITIES: Open May 15 - Sept. 15; water and bathroom facilities; electrical hookup; trailer village vehicle sites; swimming; tent camping; lodging.

MOUNT RUSHMORE HOLIDAY INN TRAV-L-PARK
(605) 574-2349
LOCATION: In Palmer Gulch, 5 mi. west of Mount Rushmore on Hwy. 224 (Old 87).
FACILITIES: Open May - Oct.; water and bathroom facilities; electrical hookup; trailer village vehicle sites; cabins; laundry; swimming; hiking; tent camping.

RAFTER J BAR RANCH CAMPGROUND
(605) 574-2527
LOCATION: At west entrance to Mount Rushmore at intersection of Hwys.16, 385, 87.
FACILITIES: Open Apr. 15 - Oct. 15; water and bathroom facilities; electrical hookup; trailer village vehicle sites; laundry; food service; swimming; fishing; horseback riding; tent camping.

Hot Springs

LARIVE LAKE RESORT
(605) 745-3993
LOCATION: ¼ mi. west of Hot Springs.
FACILITIES: Open Apr. 5 - Oct. 15; water and bathroom facilities; electrical hookup; trailer village vehicle sites; cabins; laundry; swimming; boating; boat rental; tent camping.

Interior

BADLANDS KOA KAMPGROUND
(605) 433-5337
LOCATION: 4 mi. southeast of Interior on Hwy. 44.
FACILITIES: Open May 1 - Oct. 25; water and bathroom facilities; electrical hookup; trailer village vehicle sites; laundry; food service; swimming; hunting; horseback riding; tent camping.

Kadoka

DIRKS CAMPGROUND
(605) 837-2261
LOCATION: I-90 at Kadoka.
FACILITIES: Open year round; water and bathroom facilities; electrical hookup; trailer village vehicle sites; laundry; picnic area; food service; tent camping.

Keystone

KEMPS KAMP
(605) 666-4654
LOCATION: 1½ mi. west of Keystone off Hwy. 16A.

FACILITIES: Open May 15 - Sept. 15; water and bathroom facilities; electrical hookup; trailer village vehicle sites; swimming; tent camping.

RUSHMORE RESORT & CAMPGROUND
(605) 666-4605
LOCATION: 7 mi. south of Rushmore on Hwy. 16 A.
FACILITIES: Open May 20 - Sept. 24; water and bathroom facilities; electrical hookup; trailer village vehicle sites; food service; swimming; fishing; horseback riding; tent camping.

Mitchell

FAMIL-E-FUN CAMPING
(605) 996-8983
LOCATION: 5 mi. west of Mitchell on I-90, Betts Road Exit 325, south 1/8 mi.
FACILITIES: Open May 20 - Sept. 20; water and bathroom facilities; sanitary station; electrical hookup; trailer village vehicle sites; laundry; food service; swimming; tent camping.

Rapid City

SAFARI CAMPING RANCH
(605) 787-4293
LOCATION: 1 mi. north of Black Hawk.
FACILITIES: Open May 1 - Oct. 30; water and bathroom facilities; electrical hookup; trailer village vehicle sites; laundry; food service; swimming; tent camping.

WOODED ACRES
(605) 342-9625
LOCATION: 9 mi. south of Rapid City on Hwy. 16W.
FACILITIES: Open Apr. 1 - Nov. 15; water and bathroom facilities; electrical hookup; trailer village vehicle sites; picnic area; tent camping.

Sioux Falls

MAPLE LANE CAMPGROUND
(605) 334-8688
LOCATION: 1507 East 63rd Street North.
FACILITIES: Open May - Oct.; water and bathroom facilities; electrical hookup; trailer village vehicle sites; laundry; food service; tent camping.

TOWER TOURIST CAMP
(605) 336-7110
LOCATION: Exit 79, I-29.
FACILITIES: Open year round; water and bathroom facilities; sanitary station; electrical hookup; trailer village vehicle sites; laundry; food service; swimming; tent camping.

Spearfish

MOUNTAIN VIEW CAMPGROUND
(605) 642-2170
LOCATION: 2½ mi. southeast of Spearfish via I-90.
FACILITIES: Open May 15 - Oct. 1; water and bathroom facilities; electrical hookup; trailer village vehicle sites; food service; swimming; tent camping.

RESORTS & BEACHES

Most of the state's resort activities center around the major lakes and include fishing, swimming, boating, water skiing, and camping. (See Boating Areas, National Parks, National Forests, and State Parks.)

BOATING AREAS

Fort Pierre

LAKE OAHE
LOCATION: Near Fort Pierre.
FACILITIES: Launching.

Fort Thompson

LAKE SHARPE
LOCATION: Near Fort Thompson.
FACILITIES: Launching.

Pickstown

LAKE FRANCIS CASE
LOCATION: Near Pickstown.
FACILITIES: Launching.

Yankton

LEWIS AND CLARK LAKE
LOCATION: Near Yankton.
FACILITIES: Launching.

BICYCLE TRAILS

See NEBRASKA - Prairie Trail.

TRAILS

Aberdeen

TRAIL OF SPIRITS, Seiche Hollow State Park - 5 mi. foot trail. This self-guiding trail provides access to a series of unique colored springs, rich in Indian lore, that are a registered National Natural Landmark. Expansion of the existing trail network is expected.

Rapid City

SUNDAY GULCH TRAIL, Custer State Park - 4 mi. foot trail. Located at Sylvan Lake, this loop trail along the lakeshore provides access to nearby overlooks. Scenery is spectacular on this rugged, picturesque trail with unusual rock formations, ample wildlife, a crystal-clear lake and beautiful vistas of a timbered mountain setting. The wildlife preserve of Custer State Park is surrounded by the Black Hills National Forest.

Sioux Falls

WOODLAND TRAIL - 1.33 mi. foot trail. The trail is located approximately 20 miles south of Sioux Falls in Newton Hills State Park. Designed to retain a natural condition, the trail winds through the hardwood forest within the park. Thousands of years ago, receding glaciers altered the terrain, providing observant hikers an opportunity to experience a geographically unique area. Interpretive stations along the trail alert visitors to particular interests.

Sturgis

BEAR BUTTE TRAIL - 3.5 mi. foot trail. The trail, in Bear Butte State Park, starts near Indian ceremonial grounds and leads to the summit of Bear Butte, a registered National Natural Landmark. From there, the hiker has outstanding vistas of Bear Butte Lake and, in the distance, snowcapped peaks and the Black Hills National Forest. Unusual features include a natural prairie environment.

SKI AREAS

Lead

DEER MOUNTAIN
Lead, SD 57754
(605) 584-3230
LOCATION: About 3½ mi. south of Lead.
FACILITIES: 1 triple chairlift; 2 pomas; slopes for expert, intermediate and beginning skiers; ski instruction; ski rental; 700 ft. vertical drop; restaurants; lodging.

TERRY PEAK
Lead, SD 57754
(605) 584-2723
LOCATION: In the Black Hills near Lead-Deadwood.
FACILITIES: 2 chairlifts; 3 pomas; slopes for expert, intermediate and beginning skiers; ski instruction; ski rental; 1200 ft. vertical drop; restaurants; lodging.

Sioux Falls

GREAT BEAR SKI VALLEY
Sioux Falls, SD 57101
(605) 338-3516
LOCATION: 2 mi. east of Sioux Falls on Brandon Road.
FACILITIES: 1 tow rope; slopes for expert, intermediate and beginning skiers; ski instruction; ski rental; 250 ft. vertical drop; restaurants; lodging.

AMUSEMENT PARKS & ATTRACTIONS

Custer

FLINTSTONE-BEDROCK CITY
Box 649
Custer, SD 57730
(605) 673-4079
FACILITIES: Campground; Flintstone movies only; Flintstone train and car rides.

Keystone

RUSHMORE CAVE (Attraction)
Keystone, SD 57751
(605) 255-4467
FACILITIES: Cave tours; refreshment stand; pay gate; free parking; open May 1 - Oct. 31.

SOUTH DAKOTA

AMUSEMENT PARKS (continued)

Rapid City

BEAR COUNTRY, U.S.A. (Attraction)
Route 2
Rapid City, SD 57701
(605) 343-2290
FACILITIES: Wild life preserve.

SITTING BULL CRYSTAL CAVERNS
P.O. Box 1649
Rapid City, SD 57701
(601) 342-0911
FACILITIES: Caverns; free parking.

STORY BOOK ISLAND
Sheridan Lake Drive
Rapid City, SD 57701
(605) 342-6357
FACILITIES: Fairy Tale theme park; picnic
facilities; free (donation); open Memorial
Day - Labor Day.

STATE FAIR

South Dakota State Fair
P.O. Box 1275
Huron, SD 57350
(605) 352-3115
DATE: September

NATIONAL PARKS

Hot Springs

WIND CAVE NATIONAL PARK
Hot Springs, SD 57747
(605) 727-2301

ELK MOUNTAIN
LOCATION: 1 mi. north of headquarters.
FACILITIES: Open May 15 - Sept. 15; limit
of stay: 14 days; 100 sites; group camps; NPS
campsite fee: $3; water and bathroom facili-
ties; picnic area; food service; fishing; exhibit;
handicapped access/restroom.

NATIONAL FORESTS

National Forests
Rocky Mountain Region
11177 West 8th Avenue
Lakewood, CO 80225
(303) 234-3914

Custer

BLACK HILLS NATIONAL FOREST
ATTRACTIONS: Spectacular canyons and
waterfalls; crystal caves; historic gold rush
area where famous early-day characters lived
and were buried, including Calamity Jane,
Wild Bill Hickok, Deadwood Dick, and
Preacher Smith; famous Homestake Mine.
Harney Peak, highest east of Rocky Mountains. Mount Rushmore National Memorial
Lake, stream fishing; deer, elk hunting; boating; saddle trips; scenic drives.

FACILITIES: 31 camp and picnic sites, 31
picnic only; 4 swimming sites; winter sports
area; motels, dude ranches in and near the
National Forest.
NEARBY TOWNS: Belle Fourche, Deadwood, Edgemont, Hot Springs, and Rapid
City, SD; Newcastle and Sundance, WY.

See CUSTER NATIONAL FOREST - Montana.

STATE PARKS

Headquarters

Department of Game, Fish and Parks
Pierre, SD 57501
(605) 773-3482

Beresford

UNION COUNTY STATE PARK
LOCATION: 11 mi. south of Beresford.
FACILITIES: Open year round; 25 sites; water and bathroom facilities; trailer village vehicle sites; picnic area; hiking; tent camping.

Canton

NEWTON HILL STATE PARK
LOCATION: 7 mi. south of Canton.
FACILITIES: Open year round; 100 sites; water and bathroom facilities; trailer village vehicle sites; picnic area; hiking; tent camping.

Custer

CUSTER STATE PARK
LOCATION: 6 mi. east of Custer.
FACILITIES: Open year round; 370 sites; water and bathroom facilities; trailer village vehicle sites; picnic area; swimming; boating; fishing; hiking; tent camping.

Garretson

PALISADES STATE PARK
LOCATION: 14 mi. north off I-90 on Route
11.
FACILITIES: Open year round; 46 sites; water and bathroom facilities; trailer village vehicle sites; picnic area; swimming; fishing; hiking; tent camping.

Lake City

ROY LAKE STATE PARK
LOCATION: 3 mi. west of Lake City
FACILITIES: Open year round; 85 sites; water and bathroom facilities; electrical hookup;
trailer village vehicle sites; picnic area; swimming; boating; fishing; hiking; tent camping.

Madison

LAKE HERMAN STATE PARK
LOCATION: 2 mi. west of Madison.
FACILITIES: Open year round; 82 sites; water and bathroom facilities; electrical hookup;
trailer village vehicle sites; picnic area; boating; fishing; hiking; tent camping.

STATE PARKS (continued)

Milbank

HARTFORD BEACH STATE PARK
LOCATION: 15 mi. north of Milbank.
FACILITIES: Open year round; 43 sites; water and bathroom facilities; trailer village vehicle sites; picnic area; swimming; boating; fishing; hiking; tent camping.

Redfield

FISHER GROVE
LOCATION: 7 mi. east of Redfield.
FACILITIES: Open year round; 26 sites; water and bathroom facilities; electrical hookup; trailer village vehicle sites; picnic area; boating; fishing; hiking; tent camping.

Selby

LAKE HIDDENWOOD STATE PARK
LOCATION: 2 mi. east, then 3 mi. north of Selby.
FACILITIES: Open year round; 14 sites; water and bathroom facilities; electrical hookup; trailer village vehicle sites; picnic area; swimming; boating; fishing; hiking; tent camping.

Sturgis

BEAR BUTTE STATE PARK
LOCATION: 6 mi. northeast of Sturgis.
FACILITIES: Open year round; 15 sites; water and bathroom facilities; trailer village vehicle sites; picnic area; swimming; boating; fishing; hiking; tent camping.

Volga

OAKWOOD LAKES STATE PARK
LOCATION: 10 mi. north of Volga.
FACILITIES: Open year round; 57 sites; water and bathroom facilities; electrical hookup; trailer village vehicle sites; picnic area; swimming; boating; fishing; hiking; tent camping.

STATE FORESTS

There are no State Forests in South Dakota.

HISTORIC SITES

De Smet

LAURA INGALLS WILDER SITES - These are the places made famous in the "Little House on the Prairie" books of Laura Ingalls Wilder. Located east of De Smet.

Deadwood

MOUNT MORIAH - "Boot Hill" graves of "Wild Bill" Hickok, Calamity Jane, Preacher Smith, Potato Creek Johnny and others. Located in Deadwood.

Hill City

BLACK HILLS CENTRAL RAILROAD -

1880 Train at Hill City, site of filming of CBS "Gunsmoke." A nostalgic demonstration ride that brought the early prospectors during the gold rush of the 1880s. Vintage coaches and open cars behind one of America's last operating steam locomotives.

Keystone

MOUNT RUSHMORE NATIONAL MEMORIAL - The massive granite sculpture memorializes through the likenesses of four American Presidents - George Washington, Thomas Jefferson, Theodore Roosevelt and Abraham Lincoln - the vigorous beginnings, growth and development of the United States during its first century and a half as a nation.

Madison

PRAIRIE VILLAGE - South Dakota's living museum, containing 25 original buildings furnished with authentic items of state's pioneer heritage. State's largest collection of gasoline and steam tractors, plus a steam train and carousel. Located 2 mi. west of Madison.

Mobridge

SITTING BULL MONUMENT - Carved by Korczak Ziolkowski, the Sitting Bull monument marks the famed chieftain's grave overlooking Lake Oahe. Located west of Mobridge.

Springfield

FIRST SCHOOL - Built in 1859, the log Bon Homme School was the first in Dakota Territory. Located northeast of Springfield off Hwy. 52.

Webster

FORT SISSETON - Well-preserved frontier army outpost built in 1864 to protect settlers in the Coteau des Prairies and closed in 1889 when its usefulness had ended. More than a dozen buildings remain. Located 23 mi. north of Webster.

HOSTELS

RAPID CITY YMCA
815 Kansas City Street
Rapid City, SD 57701
(605) 342-8538
FACILITIES: Open Jun. 1 - Aug. 30; reservation required; men only; modern bathroom; nearest hostel: YMCA, 9th & Cedar, St. Paul, MN; overnight charges: $2; need sleeping bag; houseparent: George Zeise.

POINTS OF INTEREST

Custer

WESTERN WOODCARVINGS - The "Talking Woodcarvings" will amaze and entertain you. The largest collection of "animated" woodcarvings in the world. Hundreds of characters and animals will "come to life" at the push of

SOUTH DAKOTA

POINTS OF INTEREST (continued)

a button. Located on Hwy. 16, west of Custer.

Gettysburg

MEDICINE ROCK - Large rock deeply incised by foot prints. Indians believed the prints were made by the Great Spirit. Located along Hwy. 212 in Gettysburg.

Hot Springs

EVANS PLUNGE - World's largest natural warm-water indoor swimming pool.

Kadoka

BADLANDS PETRIFIED GARDENS - A rare display of Badlands minerals, prehistoric fossils, dinosaur tracks, fossil tree trunks and the Badlands, largest petrified logs. Located at East Kodoka interchange.

Keystone

PARADE OF PRESIDENTS WAX MUSEUM - Walk through the most exciting scenes of America's history with all the presidents from Washington to Carter. Located between Keystone and the entrance to Mt. Rushmore on Hwy. 16A.

Lead

TERRY PEAK CHAIRLIFT - Two double chairlifts. A beautiful ride to the top of the highest mountain east of the Rockies, with a five-state view. Located 3 mi. west of Lead.

Mitchell

CORN PALACE - "The World's Only Corn Palace." Thousands of bushels of natural colored corn, wheats and Sudan grass are used each year to make picture designs on the exterior of this unique structure. Located at Mitchell.

Rapid City

DINOSAUR PARK - A group of life-sized prehistoric reptiles reproduced in concrete. Located on Skyline Drive.

REPTILE GARDENS - The sparkling new sky dome covers America's most beautiful and modern reptile collection set among tropical foliage and orchids. Unique trained animals operate the Bewitched Village. Located 6 mi. south of Rapid City on Hwy. 16.

Sioux Falls

EROS DATA CENTER - The EROS (Earth Resources Observation Systems) Data Center houses nearly 6 million frames of satellite and aircraft photography of the earth. Located northeast of Sioux Falls off I-90 on County Road 121.

TENNESSEE

Tennessee, the home of country music, joined the Union in 1796 as the sixteenth state. The Spanish were the first to set foot in the state, but because they wanted gold more than land, the British were able to move in and take possession. The native Indians resented the intruding white man and resisted all advances until the late 1700s.

Tennessee employed slave labor, but prior to the Civil War its sympathies lay with the Union. Consequently, the state, although part of the Deep South, was the last to secede and the first to ask for readmission to the Union.

Most of the state's income today is derived from the chemical textile and agricultural industries, with tourism adding significantly to the total. Nearly half the state is, forested, and resort-like state parks prove irrisistable to thousands of travelers each year as do attractions like Nashville's Grand Old Opry and the Country Music Hall of Fame and Museum.

State capital: Nashville. State bird: Mockingbird. State tree: Tulip poplar. State flower: Iris.

WEATHER

The topography of Tennessee is quite varied, stretching from the lowlands of the Mississippi Valley to the mountain peaks in the east. The westernmost part of the state, between the bluffs overlooking the Mississippi River and the western valley of the Tennessee River, is a region of gently rolling plains. The hilly Highland Rim, in a wide circle touching the Tennessee River Valley in the west and the Cumberland Plateau in the east, together with the enclosed Central Basin, makes up the whole of Middle Tennessee.

Most aspects of the state's climate are related to the widely varying topography within its borders. The decrease of temperature with elevation is quite apparent, amounting to, on the average, 3 degrees F per 1,000 feet increase in elevation. Across the state, the average annual temperature varies from over 62 degrees F in the extreme southwest to near 45 degrees F atop the highest peaks of the east. While most of the state can be described as

WEATHER (continued)

having warm, humid summers and mild winters, this must be qualified to include variations with elevation. Thus, with increasing elevation, summers become cooler and more pleasant, while winters become colder and more blustery.

Average daily temperature for each month.

	Eastern	Western
Jan.	48.0 to 26.1	46.5 to 29.3
Feb.	51.6 to 28.4	50.7 to 32.7
Mar.	60.2 to 34.7	58.9 to 39.9
Apr.	72.0 to 44.3	71.1 to 51.0
May	79.6 to 52.6	80.2 to 59.3
Jun.	86.1 to 60.9	88.4 to 67.4
Jul.	88.9 to 64.6	90.5 to 70.4
Aug.	88.3 to 63.5	89.5 to 68.5
Sept.	83.7 to 57.4	83.5 to 61.9
Oct.	72.6 to 44.9	73.6 to 50.0
Nov.	59.7 to 34.3	59.6 to 39.4
Dec.	50.6 to 28.4	49.5 to 32.9
Year	70.1 to 45.0	70.2 to 50.2

STATE CHAMBER OF COMMERCE

State Chamber Division
Tennessee Taxpayers Association
1070 Capitol Hill Building
Nashville, TN 37219
(615) 242-1854

STATE & CITY TOURISM OFFICES

State

Department of Economic and Community
Development
1007 Andrew Jackson State Office Building
500 Deaderick Street
Nashville, TN 37219
(615) 741-1888

Tourist Development Division
1028 Andrew Jackson Building
Nashville, TN 37219
(615) 741-2158

Local

Convention and Visitor's Bureau
Memorial Auditorium
399 McCallie Avenue
Chattanooga, TN 37402
(615) 266-5716

Convention and Visitor's Bureau
Greater Knoxville Chamber of Commerce
P.O. Box 2229
Knoxville, TN 37901
(615) 637-4550

Memphis Area Chamber of Commerce
P.O. Box 224

Memphis, TN 38101
(901) 523-2322

STATE HIGHWAY DEPARTMENT

Tennessee Department of Transportation
Highway Building, Corner 6th Ave. N and
Deaderick Streets
Nashville, TN 37219
(615) 741-3011

HIGHWAY WELCOMING CENTERS

Ardmore

ARDMORE CENTER - Interstate 65, south of Nashville, near Alabama line.

Bristol

BRISTOL CENTER - Interstate 81, at Bristol.

Chattanooga

CHATTANOOGA CENTER - Interstate 75, south of Chattanooga on Georgia line.

Jellico

JELLICO CENTER - Interstate 75, north of Knoxville on Kentucky line.

Memphis

MEMPHIS CENTER - Interstate 55, at Mississippi line.

Mitchellville

MITCHELLVILLE CENTER - Interstate 65, north of Nashville on Kentucky line.

Tiftonia

TIFTONIA CENTER - Interstate 24, at Chattanooga.

STATE POLICE

Department of Public Safety
Nashville, TN 37219
(615) 741-2925

HUNTING & FISHING

Hunting

See Fishing for rules & regulations.

Resident

Hunting-fishing combination, $7.80; sportsman's license, $30.30; junior hunting, $3.30; trapping, $5.30; turkey license, $3.30; big game (deer, bear, hog), $7.80; archery, $2.30; waterfowl (16 years & older), $2.30.

TENNESSEE

HUNTING & FISHING (continued)

Non-resident

Hunting, $20.30; hunting-fishing combination, $30.30; junior hunting, $5.30; 3-day hunting (except big game), $8.30; trapping, $15.30; turkey license, $10.30; big game (deer, bear, hog), $7.80; archery, $5.30; waterfowl, $5.30.

Fishing

No licenses needed for the following:
Under 16 years of age.
Owner and tenant of farm land and dependent children fishing on land where they reside.
Fishing in county of residence, except on TWRA lakes, although minnows or lures may not be used, trout may not be taken, and there may not be more than 50 hooks on trotlines.
Military personnel on leave, carrying copy of leave orders. A pass does not meet this requirement.
Residents 65 years of age or older (proof of age required).

Resident

Annual hunting-sport fishing, $7.80; 2-day sport fishing, $1.80; 10-day sport fishing, $3.30; guide license, $5.30; trout license, $3.30; Tellico daily permit, $1.80; wild trout streams daily permit, $1.80; Cherokee WMA permit, annual $3.30, daily $1.30; agency lake permit, daily $1; non-game wildlife certificate, $5; sportsman, $30.30.

Non-resident

Annual hunting-sport fishing, $30.30; annual fishing, $12.30; 3-day sport fishing, $3.30; 10-day sport fishing, $5.30; trout license, $5.30; Tellico daily permit, $1.80; wild trout streams daily permit, $1.80; Cherokee WMA permit annual, $3.30, daily $1.30; agency lake permit, daily $1; non-game wildlife certificate, $5.

For more information contact:

Tennessee Wildlife Resources Agency
P.O. Box 40747
Nashville, TN 37204
(615) 741-1512

CAMPGROUNDS

Private

Crossville

LAKE TANSI RV PARK
(615) 788-6724
LOCATION: Near Crossville.
FACILITIES: Open year round; 250 sites; water and bathroom facilities; sanitary station; electrical hookup; trailer village vehicle sites; laundry; picnic area; food service; fishing; tent camping.

Dickson

RUSKIN CAVE CAMPGROUND
(615) 763-9141
LOCATION: Near Dickson.
FACILITIES: Open Apr. 1 - Nov. 1; 150 sites; water and bathroom facilities; sanitary station; electrical hookup; trailer village vehicle sites; laundry; picnic area; food service; swimming; fishing; tent camping.

Gatlinburg

DUDLEY CREEK TRAVEL TRAILER PARK
(615) 436-5053
LOCATION: 200 Parkway.
FACILITIES: Open Mar. 1 - Oct. 31; 125 sites; water and bathroom facilities; sanitary station; electrical hookup; trailer village vehicle sites; laundry; food service; swimming; tent camping.

SMOKEY MOUNTAIN CAMPGROUND
(615) 436-4434
LOCATION: Near Gatlinburg.
FACILITIES: Open year round; 225 sites; water and bathroom facilities; sanitary station; electrical hookup; trailer village vehicle sites; laundry; picnic area; food service; swimming; fishing; horseback riding; tent camping.

LaFollette

KOA - NORRIS LAKE
(615) 562-9731
LOCATION: On Route 63.
FACILITIES: Open year round; 84 sites; water and bathroom facilities; sanitary station; laundry; picnic area; food service; swimming; boating; tent camping.

Lebanon

TIMBERLINE CAMPGROUND
(615) 449-2818
LOCATION: Near Lebanon.
FACILITIES: Open year round; 150 sites; water and bathroom facilities; sanitary station; electrical hookup; trailer village vehicle sites; laundry; food service; swimming; tent camping.

Maryville

HOLIDAY PARK
(615) 983-7723
LOCATION: 2 mi. south on Hwys. 411 and 129.
FACILITIES: Open year round; 105 sites; water and bathroom facilities; sanitary station; electrical hookup; trailer village vehicle sites; laundry; food service; swimming; fishing; tent camping.

Memphis

LAKELAND CAMPGROUND
(901) 388-7120
LOCATION: Near Memphis.
FACILITIES: Open year round; 200 sites; water and bathroom facilities; sanitary station; electrical hookup; trailer village vehicle sites; laundry; food service; swimming; boating;

CAMPGROUNDS (continued)

boat rental; fishing; horseback riding; tent camping.

Nashville

NASHVILLE KOA KAMPGROUND
(615) 889-0282
LOCATION: Near Nashville.
FACILITIES: Open year round; 250 sites; water and bathroom facilities; sanitary station; electrical hookup; trailer village vehicle sites; laundry; food service; swimming; tent camping.

Pigeon Forge

CAMP PIGEON FORGE
(615) 453-9632
LOCATION: Near Pigeon Forge.
FACILITIES: Open May 1 - Nov. 1; 150 sites; water and bathroom facilities; sanitary station; electrical hookup; trailer village vehicle sites; laundry; picnic area; food service; swimming; fishing; horseback riding; tent camping.

KOA KAMPGROUND
(615) 453-7903
LOCATION: Off Hwy. 441.
FACILITIES: Open Apr. - Nov.; 132 sites; water and bathroom facilities; sanitary station. electrical hookup; trailer village vehicle sites; laundry; swimming; tent camping.

Sevierville

RIVEREDGE TRAVEL TRAILER PARK
(615) 453-5813
LOCATION: Off Route 2.
FACILITIES: Open year round; 100 sites; water and bathroom facilities; sanitary station; electrical hookup; trailer village vehicle sites; laundry; food service; swimming; fishing; tent camping.

Smyrna

NASHVILLE I-24 KOA KAMPGROUND
(615) 459-5818
LOCATION: Near Smyrna.
FACILITIES: Open year round; 150 sites; water and bathroom facilities; sanitary station; electrical hookup; trailer village vehicle sites; laundry; picnic area; food service; swimming; horseback riding; tent camping.

Townsend

SUNDOWN RESORT CAMPGROUND
(615) 448-6936
LOCATION: On Route 73.
FACILITIES: Open year round; 200 sites; water and bathroom facilities; sanitary station; electrical hookup; trailer village vehicle sites; laundry; picnic area; food service; swimming; tent camping.

TREMONT CAMP SITE
(615) 448-6363
LOCATION: On Route 73.
FACILITIES: Open Apr. - Nov.; 150 sites; water and bathroom facilities; sanitary station; electrical hookup; trailer village vehicle sites; swimming; fishing; tent camping.

RESORTS & BEACHES

See State Parks (Resorts).

BOATING AREAS

Big Sandy

KENTUCKY LAKE
LOCATION: Near Big Sandy.
FACILITIES: Launching; fuel; food service; camping.

Bristol

SOUTH HOLSTON LAKE
LOCATION: Near Bristol.
FACILITIES: Launching; fuel; food service; camping.

Chattanooga

CHICKAMAUGA LAKE
LOCATION: Near Chattanooga.
FACILITIES: Launching; fuel; food service; camping.

Cleveland

PARKSVILLE LAKE
LOCATION: Near Cleveland.
FACILITIES: Launching; fuel; food service; camping.

Hampton

WATAUGA LAKE
LOCATION: Near Hampton.
FACILITIES: Launching; fuel; food service; camping.

Jasper

NICKAJACK LAKE
LOCATION: Near Jasper.
FACILITIES: Launching; fuel; food service; camping.

Jefferson City

CHEROKEE LAKE
LOCATION: Near Jefferson City.
FACILITIES: Launching; fuel; food service; camping.

Jonesboro

BOONE LAKE
LOCATION: Near Jonesboro.
FACILITIES: Launching; fuel; food service; camping.

Lenoir City

FORT LOUDOUN LAKE
LOCATION: Near Lenoir City.
FACILITIES: Launching; fuel; food service; camping.

Norris

NORRIS LAKE
LOCATION: Near Norris.

TENNESSEE

BOATING AREAS (continued)

FACILITIES: Launching; fuel; food service; camping.

Oak Ridge

MELTON HILL LAKE
LOCATION: Near Oak Ridge.
FACILITIES: Launching; fuel; food service; camping.

Pickwick Dam

PICKWICK LAKE
LOCATION: Near Pickwick Dam.
FACILITIES: Launching; fuel; food service; camping.

Sevierville

DOUGLAS LAKE
LOCATION: Near Sevierville.
FACILITIES: Launching; fuel; food service; camping.

Watts Bar Dam

WATTS BAR LAKE
LOCATION: Near Watts Bar Dam.
FACILITIES: Launching; fuel; food service; camping.

Winchester

TIMS FORD LAKE
LOCATION: Near Winchester.
FACILITIES: Launching; fuel; food service; camping.

BICYCLE TRAILS

GREAT SMOKY MOUNTAINS TRAIL - 88 mi.; mountainous terrain; 10-speed bicycle recommended.
This is mountain country with 1,000 foot climbs being rather common. Don't feed or pester the bears and be sure to carry insect repellent.
Trail: Start at Trigonia and pedal to Union Grove to Kegley to Carpenter Campground to Maryville to Hubbard, follow the bank of the Little River to Dry Valley, to Wear's Valley to Pigeon Forge, along the rocky banks of the Little Pigeon River to Greenbrier Cove.

See MISSISSIPPI - Natchez Trail.

TRAILS

Dayton

LAUREL-SNOW TRAIL - 8 mi. foot trail. The Laurel-Snow Trail is in the 710-acre "Laurel-Snow Pocket Wilderness" established specifically to preserve unusual scenic and natural values. There are outstanding waterfalls and overlooks in a wilderness environment. The area is managed for public use and enjoyment, although privately owned.

DeRossett

VIRGIN FALLS TRAIL - 8 mi. foot trail. The trail begins at a point approximately 8 miles south of DeRossett and leads to a 317-acre pocket wilderness. There it forms a loop which leads past several unusual natural and scenic areas. At Virgin Falls, which gives the trail its name, a stream emerges from a cave, runs 50 feet, plunges over a 110-foot cliff, and disappears into another cave. This fairly rugged trail takes between 6 and 8 hours to hike completely.

Morris

RIVER BLUFF TRAIL - 3.1 mi. foot trail. Located within a Tennessee Valley Authority Small Wild Area on the Norris Dam Reservation, the trail meanders through a heavily forested area overlooking the scenic Clinch River. Wild flowers and ferns are abundant. A massive limestone bluff overlooks a portion of the trail. Originally constructed in the mid-1930s, the trail rises and falls over the hilly East Tennessee terrain. The tread surface is level and comfortable.

Nashville

FORT HENRY HIKING TRAIL - 26 mi. foot trail. Located approximately 80 miles northwest of Nashville within the Land Between The Lakes, the hiking trails system generally follows the historical route taken by General Grant's troops from Fort Henry to Fort Donelson during the Civil War. In addition to the historical resources in the trail vicinity, the hiker is exposed to a rich variety of hardwood forests along the ridgetop and bottomland, a variety of wildlife, and old home sites.

OLD HICKORY TRAIL - 1.66 mi. foot trail. This hiking trail is located below the Old Hickory Dam and provides a great variety of plant and animal life, making it a unique experience for the urban visitor. The trail is mostly level and consists of separate woodland, willow swamp, and wildlife loops.

Oak Ridge

NORTH RIDGE TRAIL - 7.5 mi. foot trail. This trail runs along Black Oak Ridge, the northern boundary of the city of Oak Ridge, within a 54-acre hardwood forest greenbelt. The trail is easily accessible from several points and offers a relaxing sense of isolation with glimpses of the Cumberland Mountains.

Oneida

HONEY CREEK TRAIL - 5 mi. foot trail. This loop trail leads the hiker through a 109-acre pocket wilderness along the scenic gorges of two streams. At one point, an overlook is available, giving a view of the Big South Fork from a vantage point of 250 feet above the river. The trail passes a number of small waterfalls, cliff and boulder formations, and several natural "rock houses" formerly used by Indians for temporary shelter on hunting expeditions.

SKI AREAS

Gatlinburg

OBER GATLINBURG
1001 Parkway
Gatlinburg, TN 37738
(615) 436-5423
LOCATION: In Gatlinburg.
FACILITIES: 1 chairlift; 2 tow ropes; 1 tram; slopes for expert, intermediate and beginning skiers; ski instruction; ski rental; restaurants; lodging.

AMUSEMENT PARKS & ATTRACTIONS

Knoxville

CHILHOWEE PARK
Hocus Pocus Recreation Area
Magnolia Avenue
Knoxville, TN 37914
(615) 523-8011
FACILITIES: 14 major rides; 12 kiddie rides; 16 games; fun house; 16 refreshment stands; penny arcade; roller rink; miniature golf; picnic facilities; free acts; free gate; free parking.

Memphis

LAKELAND
3970 Canada Road
Memphis, TN 38128
(901) 386-4881
FACILITIES: 12 major rides; 5 kiddie rides; 5 games; 5 refreshment stands; 2 restaurants; penny arcade; 2 walk thrus; picnic facilities; pay gate; free parking; open May 1 - Labor Day.

LIBERTYLAND
Mid-South Fairgrounds
Memphis, TN 38114
(901) 274-1776
FACILITIES: 12 major rides; 2 kiddie rides; 12 games; 23 refreshment stands; 2 restaurants; arcade; shooting gallery; zoo; dolphin show; pay gate; free parking; open Jun. 12 - Sept. 4; weekends: Mar. 24 - Jun. 11.

Nashville

FAIR PARK
State Fairgrounds
Nashville, TN 37214
(615) 256-6494
FACILITIES: 10 major rides; 8 kiddie rides; fun house; 2 games; 2 refreshment stands; restaurant; penny arcade; shooting gallery; free gate; free parking.

OPRYLAND, U.S.A.
P.O. Box 2138
Nashville, TN 37214
(615) 889-6600
FACILITIES: 13 major rides; 4 kiddie rides; 7 restaurants; 12 fast food bars; 11 live shows; arcade; shooting gallery; zoo; free acts; home of the "Grand Ole Opry"; pay gate; pay parking; open year round.

Pigeon Forge

PORPOISE ISLAND (Attraction)
Island Drive
Hwy. 441
Pigeon Forge, TN 37863
(615) 453-4681
FACILITIES: Dolphin, sea lion shows; bird shows; petting zoo; 3 refreshment stands; picnic facilities; free acts; pay gate; free parking; open May 1 - Sept. 30.

STATE FAIR

Tennessee State Fair
State Fairgrounds
Nashville, TN 37210
(615) 255-6441
DATE: September

NATIONAL PARKS

Gatlinburg

GREAT SMOKEY MOUNTAINS NATIONAL PARK (TN, NC)
Gatlinburg, TN 37738
(615) 436-5615

ABRAHAMS CREEK
LOCATION: 31 mi. south of Maryville, TN.
FACILITIES: Open Apr. 14 - Nov. 1; limit of stay: 14 days (7, May 1 - Oct. 15); 16 sites.

BALSAM MOUNTAIN
LOCATION: Near Park Headquarters.
FACILITIES: Open May 15 - Oct. 15; limit of stay: 14 days; 46 sites; NPS campsite fee: $4; water and bathroom facilities; cabins; picnic area; hiking; exhibit; museum; living history program; NPS guided tour; self-guiding tour; lodging.

CADES COVE
LOCATION: 10 mi. southwest of Townsend, TN.
FACILITIES: Open year round; limit of stay: 14 days (7, May 1 - Oct. 15); 180 sites; group camps: 4 (reservations); NPS campsite fee: $4; water and bathroom facilities; sanitary station; cabins; picnic area; food service; fishing; hiking; horseback riding; exhibit; museum; environmental study area; living history program; handicapped access/restroom; NPS guided tour; self-guiding tour; lodging.

CATALOOCHEE
LOCATION: 20 mi. northwest of Waynesville, NC.
FACILITIES: Open Apr. 15 - Nov. 1; limit of stay: 14 days (7, May 1 - Oct. 15); 28 sites; group camps: 5 (reservations); fishing.

COSBY
LOCATION: 7 mi. south of Cosby.
FACILITIES: Open Apr. 1 - Nov. 1; limit of stay: 14 days (7, May 1 - Oct. 15); 174 sites; group camps: 5 (reservations); NPS campsite fee: $4; water and bathroom facilities; sanitary station; cabins; picnic area; fishing; hiking; horseback riding; exhibit; museum; en-

TENNESSEE

NATIONAL PARKS (continued)

vironmental study area; living history program; handicapped access/restroom; NPS guided tour; self-guiding tour; lodging.

DEEP CREEK
LOCATION: 2 mi. north of Bryson City, NC.
FACILITIES: Open Apr. 14 - Nov. 1; limit of stay: 14 days (7, May 1 - Oct. 15); 119 sites; group camps: 3 (reservations); NPS campsite fee: $4; water and bathroom facilities; sanitary station; cabins; picnic area; fishing; hiking; exhibit; museum; environmental study area; living history program; handicapped access/restroom; NPS guided tour; self-guiding tour; lodging.

ELKMONT
LOCATION: 8 mi. west of Gatlinburg.
FACILITIES: Open year round; limit of stay: 14 days (7, May 1 - Oct. 15); 222 sites; group camps: 5 (reservations); NPS campsite fee: $4; water and bathroom facilities; sanitary station; cabins; picnic area; fishing; hiking; exhibit; museum; environmental study area; living history program; handicapped access/restroom; NPS guided tour; self-guiding tour; medical service.

LOOK ROCK
LOCATION: 11 mi. southwest of Walland.
FACILITIES: Open May 6 - Oct. 15; limit of stay: 7 days; 92 sites; NPS campsite fee: $4; water and bathroom facilities; cabins; picnic area; fishing; hiking; museum; environmental study area; living history program; handicapped access/restroom; NPS guided tour; self-guiding tour; lodging.

SMOKEMONT
LOCATION: 6 mi. north of Cherokee, NC.
FACILITIES: Open year round; limit of stay: 14 days (7, May 1 - Oct. 15); 152 sites; group camps: 8 (reservations); NPS campsite fee: $4; water and bathroom facilities; sanitary station; cabins; picnic area; fishing; hiking; horseback riding; exhibit; museum; environmental study area; living history program; handicapped access/restroom; NPS guided tour; self-guiding tour; lodging.

NATIONAL FORESTS

National Forests

Southern Region
1720 Peachtree Road, NW
Atlanta, GA 30309
(404) 881-4177

Cleveland

CHEROKEE NATIONAL FOREST
ATTRACTIONS: Rainbow, brook trout fishing; small, big game, wild boar hunting; hiking; boating; swimming. Ducktown Copper Basin, one of the Nation's worst examples of deforestation through air pollution, with consequent erosion.
FACILITIES: 29 camp and picnic sites, 25 picnic only; 13 swimming sites; hotels and tourist cabins in nearby towns.

NEARBY TOWNS: Cleveland, Erwin, Etowah, Greeneville, Johnson City, Madisonville, Mountain City, Newport, Parksville, Tellico Plains.

See CHATTAHOOCHEE NATIONAL FOREST - Georgia.

STATE PARKS

Headquarters

Parks and Recreation
2611 West End Avenue
Nashville, TN 37203
(615) 741-3251

Buchanan

PARIS LANDING STATE PARK (Resort)
LOCATION: On U.S. 79.
FACILITIES: Open year round; 80 sites; water and bathroom facilities; trailer village vehicle sites; picnic area; food service; swimming; boating; boat rental; hunting; hiking; tent camping.

Burns

MONTGOMERY BELL STATE PARK (Resort)
LOCATION: Off Route 1.
FACILITIES: Open year round; 110 sites; water and bathroom facilities; trailer village vehicle sites; cabins; picnic area; food service; swimming; boating; boat rental; fishing; hiking; horseback riding; tent camping.

Carryville

COVE LAKE STATE PARK
LOCATION: On U.S. 25W and I-75.
FACILITIES: Open year round; 50 sites; water and bathroom facilities; trailer village vehicle sites; picnic area; food service; swimming; boating; boat rental; fishing; hiking; tent camping.

Chapel Hill

HENRY HORTON STATE PARK (Resort)
LOCATION: On U.S. 31A.
FACILITIES: Open year round; 90 sites; water and bathroom facilities; trailer village vehicle sites; cabins; picnic area; food service; swimming; boating; boat rental; hiking; horseback riding; tent camping.

Chattanooga

BOOKER T. WASHINGTON STATE PARK
LOCATION: On Hwy. 58.
FACILITIES: Open year round; 33 sites; water and bathroom facilities; trailer village vehicle sites; picnic area; food service; swimming; boating; fishing; hiking; tent camping.

Crossville

CUMBERLAND MOUNTAIN STATE PARK
LOCATION: On U.S. 127 off I-40.
FACILITIES: Open year round; 135 sites; water and bathroom facilities; trailer village vehi-

STATE PARKS (continued)

cle sites; cabins; food service; swimming; boating; boat rental; fishing; hiking; tent camping.

Eva

NATHAN BEDFORD FORREST STATE PARK
LOCATION: Off U.S. 70.
FACILITIES: Open year round; 50 sites; water and bathroom facilities; trailer village vehicle sites; picnic area; food service; boating; fishing; hiking; tent camping.

Gallatin

BLEDSOE CREEK STATE PARK
LOCATION: On Hwy. 25.
FACILITIES: Open year round; 133 sites; water and bathroom facilities; sanitary station; electrical hookup; trailer village vehicle sites; boating; fishing; tent camping.

Harrison

HARRISON BAY STATE PARK
LOCATION: On U.S. 58.
FACILITIES: Open year round; 260 sites; water and bathroom facilities; trailer village vehicle sites; picnic area; food service; swimming; boating; boat rental; fishing; hiking; tent camping.

Henderson

CHICKASAW STATE PARK
LOCATION: On Hwy. 100.
FACILITIES: Open year round; 75 sites; water and bathroom facilities; trailer village vehicle sites; cabins; picnic area; food service; swimming; boating; boat rental; fishing; hiking; tent camping.

Jamestown

PICKET STATE PARK
LOCATION: On Hwy. 154.
FACILITIES: Open year round; 50 sites; water and bathroom facilities; trailer village vehicle sites; cabins; picnic area; food service; swimming; boating; boat rental; fishing; hiking; tent camping.

Jellico

INDIAN MOUNTAIN STATE PARK
LOCATION: At Jellico off I-75.
FACILITIES: Open year round; 50 sites; water and bathroom facilities; sanitary station; electrical hookup; trailer village vehicle sites; picnic area; boating; boat rental; fishing; hiking; tent camping.

Kingsport

WARRIOR'S PATH STATE PARK
LOCATION: On U.S. 23.
FACILITIES: Open year round; 160 sites; water and bathroom facilities; trailer village vehicle sites; picnic area; food service; swimming; boating; boat rental; fishing; hiking; horseback riding; tent camping.

Lawrenceburg

DAVID CROCKETT STATE PARK
LOCATION: On U.S. 64.
FACILITIES: Open year round; 100 sites; water and bathroom facilities; trailer village vehicle sites; picnic area; food service; swimming; boating; boat rental; fishing; hiking; bicycle trail; tent camping.

Lebanon

CEDARS OF LEBANON STATE PARK
LOCATION: On U.S. 231 and Hwy. 10.
FACILITIES: Open year round; 166 sites; water and bathroom facilities; trailer village vehicle sites; picnic area; food service; swimming; hiking; horseback riding; tent camping.

Livingston

STANDING STONE STATE PARK
LOCATION: On Hwy. 52.
FACILITIES: Open year round; 50 sites; water and bathroom facilities; trailer village vehicle sites; cabins; picnic area; food service; swimming; boating; boat rental; hiking; tent camping.

Maynardville

BIG RIDGE STATE PARK
LOCATION: Off Hwy. 61.
FACILITIES: Open year round; 50 sites; water and bathroom facilities; trailer village vehicle sites; picnic area; food service; swimming; boating; boat rental; fishing; hiking; horseback riding; tent camping.

Memphis

T.O. FULLER STATE PARK
LOCATION: On U.S. 61.
FACILITIES: Open year round; 30 sites; water and bathroom facilities; trailer village vehicle sites; picnic area; food service; swimming; hiking; tent camping.

Millington

MEEMAN-SHELBY FOREST STATE PARK
LOCATION: On U.S. 51.
FACILITIES: Open year round; 50 sites; water and bathroom facilities; trailer village vehicle sites; cabins; picnic area; food service; swimming; boating; boat rental; fishing; hiking; horseback riding; bicycle trail; tent camping.

Morristown

PANTHER CREEK STATE PARK
LOCATION: On U.S. 11E.
FACILITIES: Open year round; 50 sites; water and bathroom facilities; sanitary station; electrical hookup; trailer village vehicle sites; picnic area; boating; fishing; hiking; tent camping.

Norris

NORRIS DAM STATE PARK (Resort)
LOCATION: On U.S. 441.
FACILITIES: Open year round; 50 sites; wa-

TENNESSEE

STATE PARKS (continued)

ter and bathroom facilities; trailer village vehicle sites; cabins; picnic area; food service; swimming; boating; fishing; hiking; tent camping.

Pickwick Dam

PICKWICK LANDING STATE PARK (Resort)
LOCATION: On Hwy. 57.
FACILITIES: Open year round; 50 sites; water and bathroom facilities; trailer village vehicle sites; cabins; picnic area; food service; swimming; boating; boat rental; fishing; hiking; tent camping.

Pikeville

FALL CREEK FALLS STATE PARK (Resort)
LOCATION: On Hwy. 30.
FACILITIES: Open year round; 60 sites; water and bathroom facilities; trailer village vehicle sites; cabins; picnic area; food service; swimming; boating; boat rental; fishing; hiking; horseback riding; bicycle trail; tent camping.

Roan Mountain

ROAN MOUNTAIN STATE PARK (Resort)
LOCATION: On Hwy. 143.
FACILITIES: Open year round; 50 sites; water and bathroom facilities; trailer village vehicle sites; picnic area; hiking; tent camping.

Rock Island

ROCK ISLAND STATE PARK
LOCATION: On U.S. 705.
FACILITIES: Open year round; 50 sites; water and bathroom facilities; trailer village vehicle sites; picnic area; swimming; boating; fishing; hiking; tent camping.

Silver Point

EDGAR EVINS STATE PARK
LOCATION: At Center Hill Lake.
FACILITIES: Open year round; 60 sites; water and bathroom facilities; trailer village vehicle sites; picnic area; food service; swimming; boating; fishing; tent camping.

Tiptonville

REELFOOT LAKE STATE PARK (Resort)
LOCATION: On Hwy. 21.
FACILITIES: Open year round; 75 sites; water and bathroom facilities; trailer village vehicle sites; cabins; picnic area; food service; boating; boat rental; fishing; hiking; tent camping.

Wildersville

NATCHEZ TRACE STATE PARK (Resort)
LOCATION: Off I-40.
FACILITIES: Open year round; 50 sites; water and bathroom facilities; trailer village vehicle sites; cabins; picnic area; food service; swimming; boating; boat rental; fishing; hiking; horseback riding; tent camping.

Winchester

TIMS FORD STATE PARK
LOCATION: West of Winchester on Hwy. 130.
FACILITIES: Open year round; 50 sites; water and bathroom facilities; electrical hookup; trailer village vehicle sites; cabins; picnic area; swimming; boating; bicycle trails; tent camping.

STATE FORESTS

Division of Forestry
2611 West End Avenue
Nashville, TN 37013
(615) 741-3326

Chattanooga

PRENTICE-COOPER STATE FOREST
LOCATION: Near Chattanooga.
FACILITIES: Open year round; picnic area; hunting; hiking.

Erwin

STEWART STATE FOREST
LOCATION: Near Erwin.
FACILITIES: Open year round; picnic area; hunting; hiking.

Henderson

CHICKASAW STATE FOREST
LOCATION: Near Henderson.
FACILITIES: Open year round; picnic area; hunting; hiking.

Hohenwald

LEWIS STATE FOREST
LOCATION: Near Hohenwald.
FACILITIES: Open year round; picnic area; hunting; hiking.

Jamestown

PICKET STATE FOREST
LOCATION: Near Jamestown.
FACILITIES: Open year round; picnic area; hunting; hiking.

SCOTT STATE FOREST
LOCATION: Near Jamestown.
FACILITIES: Open year round; picnic area; hunting; hiking.

Lebanon

CEDARS OF LEBANON STATE FOREST
LOCATION: Near Lebanon.
FACILITIES: Open year round; picnic area; hunting; hiking.

Livingston

STANDING STONE STATE FOREST
LOCATION: Near Livingston.
FACILITIES: Open year round; picnic area; hunting; hiking.

STATE FORESTS (continued)

Pikeville

BLEDSOE STATE FOREST
LOCATION: Near Pikeville.
FACILITIES: Open year round; picnic area; hunting; hiking.

Sewanee

FRANKLIN STATE FOREST
LOCATION: Near Sewanee.
FACILITIES: Open year round; picnic area; hunting; hiking.

Sharps Chapel

CHUCK SWAN STATE FOREST
LOCATION: Near Sharps Chapel.
FACILITIES: Open year round; picnic area; hunting; hiking.

Wartburg

LONE MOUNTAIN STATE FOREST
LOCATION: Near Wartburg.
FACILITIES: Open year round; picnic area; hunting; hiking.

Wildersville

NATCHEZ TRACE STATE FOREST
(See State Parks, Natchez Trace.)

HISTORIC SITES

Columbia

JAMES K. POLK ANCESTRAL HOME - The only surviving Tennessee structure in which lived James K. Polk, eleventh President of the United States, lived. The two-story Federal style house, was built in 1816 by prospering Samuel Polk, father of the future president, to accommodate his large and growing family.

Greeneville

ANDREW JOHNSON NATIONAL MONUMENT - The Andrew Johnson home has been restored to the period 1869-1875, when the former President returned to Greeneville and made his home there until his death in 1875. The house is furnished with many pieces used by, or connected with, the Johnson family. Located on Main Street.

Jamestown

ALVIN YORK'S FARM AND GRIST MILL - General John J. Pershing described Sgt. York, a World War I Medal of Honor recipient, as "the greatest soldier of the war." Located south of Jamestown on Hwy. 28.

Johnson City

DAVY CROCKETT BIRTHPLACE PARK - Humorist, bear hunter, hero in the Creek Indian War (1813-14), State Legislator, U.S. Congressman for three terms, and martyr in the cause of Texas independence. Crockett was born in 1786 on the banks of the Nolichucky River. Located off U.S. 11E and 411, west of Johnson City.

Memphis

CHUCALISSA PREHISTORIC INDIAN TOWN - A rebuilt village, complete with grass-thatched huts and a great, conical temple on its flat-topped mound; an excavated cemetery group with forty burials on exhibit; and a new modern museum. Located on Mitchell Road.

Morristown

DAVID CROCKETT TAVERN & MUSEUM - In the 1790s John Crockett opened a small, six room tavern on the Abingdon-Knoxville Road, near the present city of Morristown. It was at this tavern that Davy Crockett spent his younger years. On a wall hangs the legendary coonskin cap and a rifle similar to "Old Betsy." Located on U.S. 11E.

Nashville

BELLE MEADE MANSION - The "Queen of Tennessee Plantations," was the focal point of the 5300-acre plantation owned by the Harding family. John Harding founded the plantation in 1807, and gradually added land to what was to become one of the finest farms in the country. Located on Leake Avenue, off U.S. 70.

THE HERMITAGE & TULIP GROVE - The home of Andrew Jackson, stately Hermitage, and its graceful neighbor, Tulip Grove, stand today as monuments to this prominent Tennessean and his family. Located on Rachel's Lane.

Smyrna

SAM DAVIS HOME - Sam Davis, "the Boy Hero of the Confederacy," lived here until he went to military school and subsequently the Civil War. He was captured, convicted as a spy and hanged after refusing a pardon. Located on Route 102, off U.S. 70 S.

Tiftonia

REFLECTION RIDING - A beautiful and historic drive through 300 acres of unspoiled natural beauty. It provides nature trails with 45 varieties of trees and 65 kinds of wildflowers identified for visitors, pioneer dwellings, and the world's only known double profile, which the Indians called "Father Stone." Located off U.S. 41 at Route 11.

HOSTELS

There are no Hostels in Tennessee.

POINTS OF INTEREST

Jackson

CASEY JONES HOME - Last residence of the

TENNESSEE

POINTS OF INTEREST (continued)

valiant engineer who died in the famous train crash of "Old 382" on April 30, 1900. Located at 211 West Chester Street.

Nashville

THE COUNTRY MUSIC HALL OF FAME & MUSEUM - 16,000 square feet of exhibits, including: Elvis' "solid gold" Cadillac, a country star's touring bus, Walkway of the Stars, costumes of the greats, a simulated recording session and a shrine to the leaders of a world-famous music. Located at 4 Music Square East.

THE PARTHENON - An exact reproduction of the Parthenon of Pericles' time, when Athens was the hub of western civilization. Located in Centennial Park.

Norris

MUSEUM OF APPALACHIA - The most authentic and complete replica of pioneer Appalachian life in the world. Over 20,000 pioneer relics are on display in a number of cabins.

Oak Ridge

AMERICAN MUSEUM OF ATOMIC ENERGY - Explores nuclear energy and its uses in agriculture, industry, medicine, and research. Located at Tulane and Illinois Avenue.

Winchester

HUNDRED OAKS CASTLE - The castle was built in 1891 by Arthur Handly Marks, son of Tennessee's 21st governor, Albert S. Marks. The Hundred Oaks Castle was named for the oak trees which surround the area. The castle contains a library which is an exact replica of the one in Sir Walter Scott's castle in Abbotsford, Scotland.

THE JACK DANIELS DISTILLERY - The oldest registered distillery in the United States. Located on Hwy. 55, north of Winchester.

TEXAS

Texas, second only to Alaska in area, entered the Union in 1845 as the twenty-eighth state. Stephen F. Austin, the "Father of Texas," led thousands of homesteaders into the state on the authority of a Spanish land grant given his father, thus establishing the first permanent American settlement there.

Mexico became disturbed by the "invasion" and sent troops to curtail it, but it was too late. Resistance by the Texas-Americans was gallant, the most famous battle being that staged at the Alamo in 1836, where Davey Crockett, Jim Bowie and 300 others lost their lives. Because of the heroism at the Alamo, the soldiers under Sam Houston's authority rallied and soundly defeated the Mexicans, ending their rule in the state.

Today, Texas produces more cattle, cotton, gas and oil than any other state. In addition, heavy industry, associated with the NASA space program in Houston, and tourism play an important part in the state's economy.

State capital: Austin. State bird: Mockingbird. State tree: Pecan. State flower: Bluebonnet.

WEATHER

Texas contains 267,339 square miles, or 7.4 percent of the nation's total area. It may be described as a vast amphitheater, sloping upward from sea level along the coast of the Gulf of Mexico to more than 4,000 feet general elevation along the Texas-New Mexico line. While much of the state is relatively flat, there are 90 mountains a mile or more high, all of them in the Trans-Pecos region.

Wedged between the warm waters of the Gulf of Mexico and the high plateaus and mountain ranges of the North American continent, Texas has diverse meteorological and climatological conditions. Continental, marine, and mountain types of climates are all found in Texas. While the changes in climate across the state are considerable, they are nevertheless gradual; no natural boundary separates the moist east from the dry west or the cool north from the warm south.

The vast land area of Texas experiences a wide range of temperatures. The High Plains have low temperatures in winter; however, extended periods of subfreezing temperatures are rare. In summer, the temperature contrast is much less pronounced from north to south, with daily highs generally in the 90's.

Average daily temperature for each month.

	Northern	Southern
Jan.	53.0 to 25.4	67.4 to 47.4
Feb.	57.3 to 28.8	69.8 to 50.9
Mar.	64.9 to 34.3	74.4 to 55.9
Apr.	74.5 to 44.4	80.4 to 63.0
May	82.1 to 54.3	85.9 to 69.1
Jun.	91.4 to 63.6	90.5 to 74.0
Jul.	92.4 to 66.5	93.5 to 74.6
Aug.	91.7 to 65.8	93.8 to 74.5
Sept.	84.4 to 58.4	90.1 to 71.4
Oct.	74.8 to 47.5	84.5 to 64.5
Nov.	62.4 to 33.3	73.8 to 54.3

WEATHER (continued)

Dec.	54.7 to 27.3	68.8 to 49.5
Year	73.6 to 45.8	81.1 to 62.4

STATE CHAMBER OF COMMERCE

Texas State Chamber of Commerce
1004 International Life Building
Austin, TX 78701
(512) 459-5526

STATE & CITY TOURISM OFFICES

State

Texas Industrial Commission
716 Sam Houston State Office Building
Capitol Station, Box 12728
Austin, TX 78711
(512) 475-5551

Texas Tourist Development Agency
Box 12008, Capitol Station
Austin, TX 78711
(512) 475-4326

State Department of Highways and Public
Transportation
Texas Highway Building
11th and Brazos Streets
Austin, TX 78701
(512) 475-2081

Local

Dallas Convention and Tourist Bureau
Dallas Chamber of Commerce
1507 Pacific Avenue
Dallas, TX 75201
(214) 651-1020

El Paso Chamber of Commerce
10 Civic Center Plaza
El Paso, TX 79944
(915) 544-7880

Tarrant County Convention and Visitor's
Bureau
700 Throckmorton Street
Fort Worth, TX 76102
(817) 336-2491

Greater Houston Convention and Visitor's
Council
1006 Main Street, Suite 1101
Houston, TX 77002
(713) 224-5201

San Antonio Convention and Visitor's Bureau
2200 Tower Life Building
San Antonio, TX 78298
(512) 223-9133

STATE HIGHWAY DEPARTMENT

State Department of Highways and Public
Transportation
Texas Highway Building
11th and Brazos Street
Austin, TX 78701
(512) 475-2081

HIGHWAY WELCOMING CENTERS

Amarillo

AMARILLO CENTER - Interstate 40.

Anthony

ANTHONY CENTER - Interstate 10, north of
El Paso.

Austin

AUSTIN CENTER - State Capitol.

Dennison

DENNISON CENTER - U.S. 75.

Gainesville

GAINESVILLE CENTER - Interstate 35.

Laredo

LAREDO CENTER - Interstate 35.

Orange

ORANGE CENTER - Interstate 10, near
Louisiana border.

Roy Bean

ROY BEAN VISITOR CENTER - U.S. 90, at
Langtry.

Texarkana

TEXARKANA CENTER - Interstate 30.

Waskom

WASKOM CENTER - Interstate 20, between
Dallas & Shreveport, LA.

Wichita Falls

WICHITA FALLS CENTER - Red River Expressway - U.S. 287.

STATE POLICE

Department of Public Safety
Austin, TX 78773
(512) 452-0331

TEXAS

HUNTING & FISHING

Hunting

A license is required for all persons, ages 17 through 65, who hunt in the state. Exempt from the license requirement are those who hunt game (excluding deer or turkey) in the county of their residence.

To qualify as a resident, a person must reside in the state 90 days prior to application.

Resident

Hunting, $5.25.

Non-resident

Hunting, $37.50; resort hunting, $5; 5-day license (migratory game birds), $10.25.

Fishing

A license is required for fishing in Texas waters except for:

Any person with a throw line or fishing pole with no winding device when fishing in the county of his residence.

Any person under 17 or over 65 years of age.

Any person fishing in private waters.

Resident

Fishing, $4.25; 3-day saltwater license, $1.25.

Non-resident

Fishing, $4.25; 3-day salt water license, $1.25.

For more information contact:

Parks and Wildlife Department
4200 Smith School Road
Austin, TX 78744
(512) 475-4907

CAMPGROUNDS

See National Parks, National Forests, State Parks, and State Forests.

RESORTS & BEACHES

Most of the state's resort activities center around the major lakes and include fishing, swimming, boating, water skiing, and camping. (See Boating Areas, National Parks, National Forests, and State Parks.)

BOATING AREAS

Athens

LAKE CEDAR CREEK
LOCATION: 10 mi. west of Athens.
FACILITIES: Launching.

Atlanta

WRIGHT PATMAN LAKE
LOCATION: Near Atlanta.
FACILITIES: Launching.

Austin

LAKE TRAVIS
LOCATION: Near Austin.
FACILITIES: Launching.

Borger

MEREDITH LAKE
LOCATION: 10 mi. west of Borger.
FACILITIES: Launching.

Buchanan Dam

BUCHANAN LAKE
LOCATION: Near Llano and Burnet.
FACILITIES: Launching.

Dallas

LAKE LEWISVILLE
LOCATION: 27 mi. north of Dallas.
FACILITIES: Launching.

RAY HUBBARD LAKE
LOCATION: 10 mi. east of Dallas.
FACILITIES: Launching.

Del Rio

AMISTAD RESERVOIR
LOCATION: Off U.S. 90.
FACILITIES: Launching.

Denison

LAKE TEXOMA
LOCATION: North of Denison.
FACILITIES: Launching.

Greenville

LAKE TAWAKONI
LOCATION: 16 mi. southeast of Greenville.
FACILITIES: Launching.

Houston

LAKE HOUSTON
LOCATION: 18 mi. northeast of Houston.
FACILITIES: Launching.

Jacksonville

LAKE PALESTINE
LOCATION: 13 mi. northwest of Jacksonville.
FACILITIES: Launching.

Jasper

LAKE B.A. STEINHAGEN
LOCATION: Midway between Jasper and Woodville.
FACILITIES: Launching.

LAKE SAM RAYBURN
LOCATION: 20 mi. north of Jasper.
FACILITIES: Launching.

BOATING AREAS (continued)

Jefferson

LAKE O' THE PINES
LOCATION: 10 mi. west of Jefferson.
FACILITIES: Launching.

Lavon

LAKE LAVON
LOCATION: Near Lavon.
FACILITIES: Launching.

Livingston

LAKE LIVINGSTON
LOCATION: 6 mi. west of Livingston.
FACILITIES: Launching.

Mathis

LAKE CORPUS CHRISTI
LOCATION: Near Mathis.
FACILITIES: Launching.

Monaham

IMPERIAL RESERVOIR
LOCATION: 25 mi. south of Monaham.
FACILITIES: Launching.

Orla

RED BLUFF LAKE
LOCATION: 5 mi. north of Orla.
FACILITIES: Launching.

Robert Lee

E.V. SPENCE RESERVOIR
LOCATION: Near Robert Lee.
FACILITIES: Launching.

Roma

FALCON RESERVOIR
LOCATION: 14 mi. northwest of Roma.
FACILITIES: Launching.

San Augustine

TOLEDO BEND RESERVOIR
LOCATION: Near San Augustine.
FACILITIES: Launching.

San Jacinto

LAKE CONROE
LOCATION: Near San Jacinto.
FACILITIES: Launching.

Whitney

LAKE WHITNEY
LOCATION: Near Whitney.
FACILITIES: Launching.

Wichita Falls

LAKE ARROWHEAD
LOCATION: 20 mi. southeast of Wichita
Falls.
FACILITIES: Launching.

LAKE KEMP
LOCATION: 48 mi. southwest of Wichita
Falls.
FACILITIES: Launching.

BICYCLE TRAILS

No information was available on Bicycle
Trails in Texas.

TRAILS

Austin

TOWN LAKE WALK AND BIKEWAY - 9.75
mi. foot trail. The trail linking the Town Lake
Linear Park system follows the bed of the
Colorado River through the center of Austin.
Popular uses of the trail and linear park system include hiking, bicycling, jogging, fishing, picnicking and boating. The 8-foot-wide
trail is constructed of compacted gravel with
flagstone and concrete used on the inclined
areas. The design allows for use by handicapped persons.

Fort Worth

GREER ISLAND NATURE TRAIL - 3 mi.
foot trail. This self-guided nature trail is on a
32-acre island in Lake Worth (within the city
of Fort Worth) connected by causeway to the
main shoreline. The environment is an extension of the eastern deciduous forest in near-
primitive condition, with a disturbed area providing an example of ecological succession.

Longview

CARGILL LONG PARK TRAIL - 2.5 mi.
foot trail. This trail, which extends the length
of a narrow linear park, was built on an abandoned railroad right-of-way through a residential area and connects several neighborhoods.
It is lighted for night use and is to be developed with diverse facilities for recreation
activities. Most of the trail is heavily wooded
and is tended by local garden clubs.

SKI AREAS

There are no organized Ski Areas in Texas.

AMUSEMENT PARKS & ATTRACTIONS

Abilene

ZOO WORLD
Nelson Park
Abilene, TX 79604
(915) 672-0039
FACILITIES: 9 major rides; 9 kiddie rides; 3
refreshment stands; restaurant; swimming
pool; beach; picnic facilities; zoo; free gate;
free parking; open Mar. - Nov.

TEXAS

AMUSEMENT PARKS (continued)

Amarillo

WONDERLAND AMUSEMENT CENTER
Thompson Park
Hwy. 287 North
Amarillo, TX 79106
(806) 383-4712
FACILITIES: 13 major rides; 8 kiddie rides; 6 games; 2 refreshment stands; arcade; shooting gallery; miniature golf; slide; picnic facilities; pay gate; free parking; open mid-Mar. - mid. - Oct.; weekends: Mar., Sept. & Oct.

Arlington

SIX FLAGS OVER TEXAS
2201 Road to Six Flags
Arlington, TX 76010
(817) 461-1200
FACILITIES: 33 major rides; 5 kiddie rides; 25 games; 35 food outlets; arcade; shooting gallery; museum; exhibits; picnic facilities; free acts; pay gate; pay parking; open mid-Mar. - Nov. 30; weekends: Spring & Fall.

Dallas

SANDY LAKE AMUSEMENT PARK
Dallas, TX 75234
(214) 242-7449
FACILITIES: 8 major rides; 6 kiddie rides; 3 refreshment stands; pool; arcade; picnic facilities; miniature golf; par 3 golf; free acts; pay gate; free parking.

STATE FAIR PARK
Fair Park
Dallas, TX 75226
(214) 823-9931
FACILITIES: 19 major rides; 10 kiddie rides; 16 games; 11 refreshment stands; restaurant; penny arcade; shooting gallery; ice rink; Cotton Bowl Stadium; music hall; coliseum; wax museum; picnic facilities; free gate; free parking.

El Paso

WESTERN PLAYLAND, INC.
Ascarate Park
El Paso, TX 79902
(915) 772-3914
FACILITIES: 13 major rides; 11 kiddie rides; fun house; 3 refreshment stands; 8 games; arcade; electronic shooting gallery; golf driving range; free acts; pay gate; free parking; open Mar. 1 - Nov. 30.

Houston

ASTROWORLD
9001 Kirby Drive
Houston, TX 77054
(713) 748-1234
FACILITIES: 26 major rides; 10 kiddie rides; 32 games; 19 food service stands; 4 restaurants; 2 arcades; shooting gallery; exhibits; picnic facilities; petting zoo; free acts; pay gate; pay parking; open mid-Mar. - Thanksgiving.

BUSCH BIRD PARK
9660 I-10 East at Gellhorn

Houston, TX 77029
(713) 675-9131
FACILITIES: Free-flight cage and waterfowl display; exhibits; bird circus; zoo; free gate; free parking.

San Antonio

PLAYLAND AMUSEMENT PARK
2222 N. Alamo
San Antonio, TX 78215
(512) 227-4983
FACILITIES: 12 major rides; 7 kiddie rides; fun house; walk thru; 15 games; 3 refreshment stands; arcade; shooting gallery; miniature golf; picnic facilities; pay gate; free parking; open Mar. - Sept. 1.

Wichita Falls

FUNLAND AMUSEMENT PARK
2006 Southwest Parkway
Wichita Falls, TX 76302
(817) 767-7911
FACILITIES: 8 major rides; 6 kiddie rides; 2 games; refreshment stand; arcade; miniature golf; free acts; free gate; free parking; open Mar. 12 - Oct. 31; weekends: Mar. 12 - Jun. 6.

STATE FAIR

State Fair of Texas
P.O. Box 26010
Dallas, TX 75226
(214) 823-9931
DATE: October

NATIONAL PARKS

Big Bend National Park

BIG BEND NATIONAL PARK
Big Bend National Park, TX 79834
(915) 477-2251

CHISOS MOUNTAINS LOWER BASIN
LOCATION: 10 mi. southwest of headquarters.
FACILITIES: Open year round; limit of stay: 14 days; 58 sites; group camps: 3; NPS campsite fee: $2; water and bathroom facilities; sanitary station; picnic area; food service; hiking; horseback riding; bicycle trail; lodging.

PANTHER JUNCTION TRAILER COURT
LOCATION: Park headquarters.
FACILITIES: Open year round; trailer village vehicle sites: 7 ($3.75); picnic area; food service; hiking; horseback riding; bicycle trail; exhibit; NPS guided tour; self-guiding tour; lodging.

RIO GRANDE TRAILER VILLAGE
LOCATION: Near Park Headquarters.
FACILITIES: Open year round; trailer village vehicle sites; food service; boating; fishing.

RIO GRANDE VILLAGE
LOCATION: 20 mi. southeast of headquarters.
FACILITIES: Open year round; limit of stay: 14 days; 99 sites; group camps: 3; NPS camp-

NATIONAL PARKS (continued)

site fee: $2; water and bathroom facilities; sanitary station; laundry; picnic area; food service; boating; fishing; hiking.

Dell City

GUADALUPE MOUNTAINS NATIONAL PARK
Dell City, TX 79837
(915) 828-3385

PINE SPRINGS CANYON
LOCATION: Near Park Headquarters.
FACILITIES: Open year round; limit of stay: 7 days; 20 sites; picnic area; hiking; bicycle trail; exhibit; NPS guided tour.

NATIONAL FORESTS

National Forests
Southern Region
1720 Peachtree Road, NW
Atlanta, GA 30309
(404) 881-4177

Lufkin

ANGELINA NATIONAL FOREST
ATTRACTIONS: Bass, catfish fishing; quail, dove hunting.
FACILITIES: 7 camp and picnic sites, 5 picnic only; 2 swimming sites.
NEARBY TOWNS: Jasper, San Augustine.

DAVY CROCKETT NATIONAL FOREST
ATTRACTIONS: Bass, catfish fishing; deer hunting.
FACILITIES: 2 camp and picnic sites, 4 picnic only; swimming site.
NEARBY TOWNS: Alto, Crockett, Groveton.

SABINE NATIONAL FOREST
ATTRACTIONS: Bass, catfish fishing; fox hunting.
FACILITIES: 4 camp and picnic sites, 4 picnic only; swimming site.
NEARBY TOWNS: Center, Hemphill, Jasper, and San Augustine.

SAM HOUSTON NATIONAL FOREST
ATTRACTIONS: Bass, catfish fishing.
FACILITIES: 3 camp and picnic sites, 2 picnic only; swimming site.
NEARBY TOWNS: Cleveland, Conroe, Huntsville.

See LINCOLN NATIONAL FOREST - New Mexico.

STATE PARKS

Headquarters

Parks and Wildlife Department
4200 Smith School Road
Austin, TX 78744
(512) 475-4888

Albany

FT. GRIFFIN STATE PARK
LOCATION: Near Albany.
FACILITIES: Open year round; water and bathroom facilities; sanitary station; electrical hookup; trailer village vehicle sites; picnic area; fishing; exhibit; museum; tent camping.

Atlanta

ATLANTA STATE PARK
LOCATION: Near Atlanta.
FACILITIES: Open year round; water and bathroom facilities; sanitary station; trailer village vehicle sites; picnic area; swimming; boating; fishing; water skiing; tent camping.

Austin

MCKINNEY FALLS STATE PARK
LOCATION: Near Austin.
FACILITIES: Open year round; group camps; water and bathroom facilities; sanitary station; electrical hookup; trailer village vehicle sites; picnic area; boating; fishing; exhibit; museum; tent camping.

Balmorhea

BALMORHEA STATE PARK
LOCATION: Near Balmorhea.
FACILITIES: Open year round; water and bathroom facilities; trailer village vehicle sites; swimming; tent camping.

Bastrop

BASTROP STATE PARK
LOCATION: Near Bastrop.
FACILITIES: Open year round; water and bathroom facilities; sanitary station; electrical hookup; trailer village vehicle sites; cabins; picnic area; swimming; fishing; tent camping.

Blanco

BLANCO STATE PARK
LOCATION: Near Blanco.
FACILITIES: Open year round; water and bathroom facilities; sanitary station; electrical hookup; trailer village vehicle sites; picnic area; swimming; fishing; tent camping.

Bonham

BONHAM STATE PARK
LOCATION: Near Bonham.
FACILITIES: Open year round; water and bathroom facilities; electrical hookup; trailer village vehicle sites; picnic area; swimming; fishing; tent camping.

Brownwood

LAKE BROWNWOOD STATE PARK
LOCATION: Near Brownwood.
FACILITIES: Open year round; water and bathroom facilities; sanitary station; electrical hookup; trailer village vehicle sites; cabins; picnic area; food service; swimming; boating; fishing; tent camping.

Buffalo Gap

ABILENE STATE PARK
LOCATION: Near Buffalo Gap.
FACILITIES: Open year round; water and

TEXAS

STATE PARKS (continued)

bathroom facilities; electrical hookup; trailer village vehicle sites; cabins; picnic area; swimming; tent camping.

Burnet

INKS LAKE STATE PARK
LOCATION: Near Burnet.
FACILITIES: Open year round; water and bathroom facilities; sanitary station; electrical hookup; trailer village vehicle sites; picnic area; food service; swimming; boating; boat rental; fishing; water skiing; tent camping.

Caddo

POSSUM KINGDOM STATE PARK
LOCATION: Near Caddo.
FACILITIES: Open year round; water and bathroom facilities; sanitary station; electrical hookup; trailer village vehicle sites; cabins; picnic area; food service; swimming; boating; boat rental; fishing; water skiing; tent camping.

Canyon

PALO DURO CANYON STATE PARK
LOCATION: Near Canyon.
FACILITIES: Open year round; water and bathroom facilities; sanitary station; electrical hookup; trailer village vehicle sites; picnic area; food service; tent camping.

Cleburne

CLEBURNE STATE PARK
LOCATION: Near Cleburne.
FACILITIES: Open year round; water and bathroom facilities; electrical hookup; trailer village vehicle sites; picnic area; food service; swimming; boating; fishing; tent camping.

Colorado City

LAKE COLORADO CITY STATE PARK
LOCATION: Near Colorado City.
FACILITIES: Open year round; water and bathroom facilities; sanitary station; electrical hookup; trailer village vehicle sites; picnic area; swimming; boating; fishing; water skiing; tent camping.

Concan

GARNER STATE PARK
LOCATION: Near Concan.
FACILITIES: Open year round; water and bathroom facilities; sanitary station; trailer village vehicle sites; cabins; picnic area; food service; swimming; fishing; tent camping.

Daingerfield

DAINGERFIELD STATE PARK
LOCATION: Near Daingerfield.
FACILITIES: Open year round; water and bathroom facilities; sanitary station; electrical hookup; trailer village vehicle sites; cabins; picnic area; swimming; boating; fishing; tent camping.

Denison

EISENHOWER STATE PARK
LOCATION: Near Denison.
FACILITIES: Open year round; water and bathroom facilities; sanitary station; electrical hookup; trailer village vehicle sites; picnic area; swimming; boating; fishing; water skiing; tent camping.

El Paso

HUECO TANKS STATE PARK
LOCATION: Near El Paso.
FACILITIES: Open year round; water and bathroom facilities; sanitary station; electrical hookup; trailer village vehicle sites; picnic area; exhibit; tent camping.

Fairfield

FAIRFIELD LAKE STATE PARK
LOCATION: Near Fairfield.
FACILITIES: Open year round; water and bathroom facilities; electrical hookup; trailer village vehicle sites; picnic area; swimming; boating; fishing; water skiing; tent camping.

Ft. Davis

DAVIS MOUNTAINS STATE PARK
LOCATION: Near Ft. Davis.
FACILITIES: Open year round; water and bathroom facilities; sanitary station; electrical hookup; trailer village vehicle sites; picnic area; exhibit; museum; tent camping.

Galveston

GALVESTON ISLAND STATE PARK
LOCATION: Near Galveston.
FACILITIES: Open year round; water and bathroom facilities; sanitary station; electrical hookup; trailer village vehicle sites; picnic area; swimming; fishing; tent camping.

Glen Rose

DINOSAUR VALLEY STATE PARK
LOCATION: Near Glen Rose.
FACILITIES: Open year round; group camps; water and bathroom facilities; electrical hookup; trailer village vehicle sites; picnic area; exhibit; tent camping.

Goliad

GOLIAD STATE PARK
LOCATION: Near Goliad.
FACILITIES: Open year round; water and bathroom facilities; sanitary station; electrical hookup; trailer village vehicle sites; picnic area; fishing; exhibit; museum; tent camping.

Groesbeck

OLD FT. PARKER STATE PARK
LOCATION: Near Groesbeck.
FACILITIES: Open year round; water and bathroom facilities; electrical hookup; trailer village vehicle sites; exhibit; museum; tent camping.

STATE PARKS (continued)

Huntsville

HUNTSVILLE STATE PARK
LOCATION: Near Huntsville.
FACILITIES: Open year round; water and bathroom facilities; sanitary station; electrical hookup; trailer village vehicle sites; picnic area; food service; swimming; boating; boat rental; fishing; self-guided trail; tent camping.

Jacksboro

FT. RICHARDSON STATE PARK
LOCATION: Near Jacksboro.
FACILITIES: Open year round; water and bathroom facilities; sanitary station; electrical hookup; trailer village vehicle sites; picnic area; fishing; exhibit; museum; tent camping.

Jasper

MARTIN DIES, JR. STATE PARK
LOCATION: Near Jasper.
FACILITIES: Open year round; water and bathroom facilities; sanitary station; electrical hookup; trailer village vehicle sites; picnic area; swimming; boating; fishing; water skiing; tent camping.

Johnson City

PEDERNALES FALLS STATE PARK
LOCATION: Near Johnson City.
FACILITIES: Open year round; group camps; water and bathroom facilities; sanitary station; electrical hookup; trailer village vehicle sites; picnic area; swimming; fishing; tent camping.

Karnack

CADDO LAKE STATE PARK
LOCATION: Near Karnack.
FACILITIES: Open year round; water and bathroom facilities; sanitary station; electrical hookup; trailer village vehicle sites; cabins; picnic area; swimming; boating; fishing; water skiing; tent camping.

Kerrville

KERRVILLE STATE PARK
LOCATION: Near Kerrville.
FACILITIES: Open year round; water and bathroom facilities; sanitary station; electrical hookup; trailer village vehicle sites; picnic area; swimming; boating; fishing; tent camping.

Lockhart

LOCKHART STATE PARK
LOCATION: Near Lockhart.
FACILITIES: Open year round; water and bathroom facilities; sanitary station; electrical hookup; trailer village vehicle sites; picnic area; swimming; tent camping.

Lubbock

MACKENZIE STATE PARK
LOCATION: Near Lubbock.

FACILITIES: Open year round; water and bathroom facilities; electrical hookup; trailer village vehicle sites; picnic area; swimming; tent camping.

Luling

PALMETTO STATE PARK
LOCATION: Near Luling.
FACILITIES: Open year round; water and bathroom facilities; sanitary station; electrical hookup; trailer village vehicle sites; picnic area; fishing; tent camping.

Mathis

LAKE CORPUS CHRISTI STATE PARK
LOCATION: Near Mathis.
FACILITIES: Open year round; water and bathroom facilities; sanitary station; electrical hookup; trailer village vehicle sites; picnic area; food service; swimming; boating; fishing; water skiing; tent camping.

Meridian

MERIDIAN STATE PARK
LOCATION: Near Meridian.
FACILITIES: Open year round; group camps; water and bathroom facilities; sanitary station; electrical hookup; trailer village vehicle sites; picnic area; swimming; fishing; water skiing; tent camping.

Mexia

FT. PARKER STATE PARK
LOCATION: Near Mexia.
FACILITIES: Open year round; group camps; water and bathroom facilities; sanitary station; electrical hookup; trailer village vehicle sites; picnic area; swimming; boating; fishing; water skiing; tent camping.

Mission

BENTSEN-RÍO GRANDE VALLEY STATE PARK
LOCATION: Near Mission.
FACILITIES: Open year round; water and bathroom facilities; electrical hookup; picnic area; fishing; tent camping.

Monahans

MONAHANS SANDHILLS STATE PARK
LOCATION: Near Monahans.
FACILITIES: Open year round; water and bathroom facilities; sanitary station; electrical hookup; trailer village vehicle sites; picnic area; boating; tent camping.

Moody

MOTHER NEFF STATE PARK
LOCATION: Near Moody.
FACILITIES: Open year round; water and bathroom facilities; sanitary station; electrical hookup; trailer village vehicle sites; picnic area; fishing; tent camping.

Quanah

COPPER BREAKS STATE PARK
LOCATION: Near Quanah.

TEXAS

STATE PARKS (continued)

FACILITIES: Open year round; water and bathroom facilities; electrical hookup; trailer village vehicle sites; picnic area; swimming; boating; fishing; tent camping.

Rockport

GOOSE ISLAND STATE PARK
LOCATION: Near Rockport.
FACILITIES: Open year round; water and bathroom facilities; sanitary station; electrical hookup; trailer village vehicle sites; picnic area; swimming; boating; fishing; water skiing; tent camping.

Rusk

TEXAS STATE RAILROAD STATE PARK
LOCATION: Near Rusk.
FACILITIES: Open year round; water and bathroom facilities; sanitary station; electrical hookup; trailer village vehicle sites; picnic area; food service; fishing; tent camping.

San Felipe

STEPHEN F. AUSTIN STATE PARK
LOCATION: Near San Felipe.
FACILITIES: Open year round; water and bathroom facilities; sanitary station; electrical hookup; trailer village vehicle sites; picnic area; swimming; fishing; exhibit; museum; tent camping.

Smithville

BUESCHER STATE PARK
LOCATION: Near Smithville.
FACILITIES: Open year round; water and bathroom facilities; electrical hookup; trailer village vehicle sites; picnic area; fishing; tent camping.

Somerville

LAKE SOMERVILLE STATE PARK
LOCATION: Near Somerville.
FACILITIES: Open year round; water and bathroom facilities; sanitary station; electrical hookup; trailer village vehicle sites; picnic area; swimming; boating; fishing; water skiing; tent camping.

Stonewall

LYNDON B. JOHNSON STATE PARK
LOCATION: Near Stonewall.
FACILITIES: Open year round; water and bathroom facilities; trailer village vehicle sites; picnic area; swimming; boating; fishing; tent camping.

Tyler

TYLER STATE PARK
LOCATION: Near Tyler.
FACILITIES: Open year round; water and bathroom facilities; sanitary station; electrical hookup; cabins; food service; swimming; boating; boat rental; fishing; tent camping.

Weches

MISSION TAJAS STATE PARK
LOCATION: Near Weches.
FACILITIES: Open year round; water and bathroom facilities; sanitary station; electrical hookup; trailer village vehicle sites; cabins; fishing; tent camping.

Whitney

LAKE WHITNEY STATE PARK
LOCATION: Near Whitney.
FACILITIES: Open year round; water and bathroom facilities; sanitary station; electrical hookup; trailer village vehicle sites; picnic area; swimming; boating; fishing; water skiing; tent camping.

Wichita Falls

LAKE ARROWHEAD STATE PARK
LOCATION: Near Wichita Falls.
FACILITIES: Open year round; water and bathroom facilities; sanitary station; electrical hookup; trailer village vehicle sites; picnic area; food service; swimming; boating; fishing; water skiing; tent camping.

Zapata

FALCON STATE PARK
LOCATION: Near Zapata.
FACILITIES: Open year round; water and bathroom facilities; sanitary station; electrical hookup; trailer village vehicle sites; picnic area; swimming; boating; fishing; water skiing; tent camping.

STATE FORESTS

Texas Forest Service
College Station, TX 77843
(713) 845-2641

Conroe

JONES STATE FOREST
LOCATION: 5 mi. south of Conroe.
FACILITIES: Open year round; picnic area; swimming; fishing; self-guided trail; tent camping.

Kirbyville

SIECKE STATE FOREST
LOCATION: 5 mi. southeast of Kirbyville.
FACILITIES: Open year round; picnic area; fishing; self-guided trail; tent camping.

Rusk

FAIRCHILD STATE FOREST
LOCATION: 13 mi. west of Rusk.
FACILITIES: Open year round; picnic area; swimming; fishing; self-guided trail; tent camping.

Woodville

KIRBY STATE FOREST
LOCATION: 14 mi. south of Woodville.
FACILITIES: Open year round; picnic area; self-guided trail; tent camping.

HISTORIC SITES

Austin

LYNDON B. JOHNSON LIBRARY - Archives/museum relating to LBJ, 36th President, and Office of Presidency in general; colorful highlights of political campaigns. Exhibits include gifts from foreign heads of state, classical Western art, a moon rock, and replica of Oval Office. Located at 2300 Red River Street.

Bonham

SAM RAYBURN LIBRARY - Elegant structure of white Georgia marble; library contains exact duplicate of Speaker Rayburn's U.S. Capitol office, from pattern on the tile floor to barrel-vaulted ceiling. Over desk is crystal chandelier, more than a century old, which hung in both White House and Capitol. Located on U.S. 82, 4 blocks west of downtown.

Clifton

NORSE SETTLEMENT - "Capital" of Norwegian settlement in Texas. Cleng Peerson, "the father of Norse immigration to America," and Ole Knutson brought groups of Norwegian immigrants to area in 1850s. Peerson's grave, in churchyard of Our Savior's Lutheran Church in Norse community, is honored by Norwegian descendants throughout America. Old World customs celebrated each November. Located on Route 182 north.

Dallas

JOHN F. KENNEDY MEMORIALS - Polished granite marker at Houston and Main Streets designates spot where President Kennedy, 35th President, was assassinated during motorcade, November 22, 1963. Cenotaph and Memorial Park at Main and Market Streets. Landscaped city block with open-style monument dedicated to the slain President. John F. Kennedy Museum. Oversize reproductions of assassination stories from newspapers of 50 states; detailed model of city tracing route of motorcade; films and narrations. Located at Dealey Plaza.

Denison

EISENHOWER BIRTHPLACE - On Oct. 14, 1890, Dwight D. Eisenhower, 34th President, was born in two-story white frame house. Home restored to 1890 appearance. Located at 208 E. Day Street.

Farmersville

BIRTHPLACE OF AUDIE L. MURPHY - Hometown of World War II Medal of Honor recipient and most decorated United States soldier.

Franklin

WALTER WILLIAMS GRAVE - In rural Mount Pleasant church cemetery a few miles southeast of Franklin is grave of last survivor of War Between the States. Walter Williams, Confederate soldier who survived all veterans, both South and North.

Huntsville

SAM HOUSTON MEMORIAL PARK - Many of the buildings and personal effects of Gen. Sam Houston, twice president of Republic of Texas. Buildings include "Steamboat House," the Sam Houston Museum, law office, carriage house and one of the general's homes. His tomb in Oakwood Cemetery bears Andrew Jackson's tribute, "The world will take care of Houston's fame." Located at 1804 Avenue L.

Iraan

DISCOVERY WELL A NO. 1 - Gusher blew in more than 4 decades ago, remains one of largest-producing oil wells in North America. Tremendous jet of oil sprayed tent city 4 miles away.

Johnson City

LYNDON B. JOHNSON NATIONAL HISTORIC SITE - Frame structure nearly 100 years old where Lyndon Johnson, 36th President, lived while attending public school. Furnishings include Johnson family household items and period furniture.

Langtry

JUDGE ROY BEAN VISITOR CENTER - Features rustic saloon, courtroom and billiard hall of Judge Roy Bean, the colorful and controversial "Law West of the Pecos" in 1880s. Center preserves historic site where Judge Bean ruled with high-handed, but appropriate, brand of homespun law, outrageous humor, and six-shooter justice.

San Antonio

THE ALAMO - In 1718 Spanish Viceroy of Mexico authorized Father Antonio de Olivares to establish the mission that was to become internationally famous as "the Alamo." The church structure was begun about 1775. Less than a century later, in 1836, it established undisputed claim as the "Cradle of Texas Liberty." During 13 days to glory (Feb. 23 to Mar. 6) it became the focal point of one of the most heroic struggles in the annals of mankind. Outnumbered Texans at the Alamo gallantly challenged a seasoned Mexican army, but in vain. The defenders died to the last man, among them such storied names as William Travis, Davy Crockett and Jim Bowie. Located in Alamo Plaza.

SPANISH GOVERNOR'S PALACE - In 1772 San Antonio became seat of Spanish government in Texas, headquartered at 10-room Spanish Governor's Palace on Military Plaza. Many commandants of Presidio de Bexar and Spanish governors lived and ruled here. And here, in 1830, the dashing Jim Bowie courted his beautiful aristocratic future wife, daughter of Mexican vice-governor (later governor) of Texas. Located on Camaron Street at Military Plaza.

TEXAS

Waco

HOMER GARRISON MEMORIAL TEXAS RANGER MUSEUM (FORT FISHER) - Replica of original Texas Ranger fort established 1837. Displays commemorate history and heritage of Texas Rangers. Headquarters for present Company F, Texas Rangers. Also houses Texas Rangers Hall of Fame. Located along Route 35 at Riverside Drive.

HOSTELS

Austin

AUSTIN YOUTH HOSTEL
1312 Newning Avenue
Austin, TX 78704
(512) 442-1584
FACILITIES: Open year round; 10 beds, men; 10 beds, women; modern bathroom; overnight charges: $2 summer; $2.50 winter; houseparent: Father Damian Klauber.

POINTS OF INTEREST

Austin

O. HENRY HOME - Residence of William Sydney Porter, eminent short-story writer who signed his works "O. Henry." Porter lived in Austin 1885 - 95. Desk, writing materials and other furnishings of the period. Located at 409 E. 5th Street.

Del Rio

VAL VERDE WINERY - Family enterprise in its fourth generation, founded in 1880s by Italian immigrants. Grapes grown in the area since 1825, but other varieties from Spain, America and Mexico were introduced. Still operated by the family, the winery welcomes visitors during regular business hours and sells their wine only at the winery.

El Paso

SIERRA DE CRISTO REY - The Mountain of Christ the King, looms above El Paso at point where territories of Texas, Mexico and New Mexico meet. Atop the 4,576-foot summit stands a massive monument of Christ on the Cross. Built of Cordova cream limestone quarried near Austin, figure and cross stand 33.5 feet high. A 4-mile foot trail winds to the summit. Access via guided tour only.

Galveston

SEAWOLF PARK - Picturesque location provides close look at ocean-going vessels entering and departing port and yacht basin. Main attraction is naval exhibit featuring tours of WW II submarine USS Cavalla, destroyer escort USS Stewart, Navy jet and military vehicles. Located on Pelican Island.

Georgetown

INNER SPACE - Texas' newest and most accessible cavern; subterranean beauty of stalactites, stalagmites and flowstones plus remains of prehistoric mastodons, wolves and Ice Age animals. Creative lighting and acoustics dramatize the natural beauty. Located on Route 35.

Hereford

NATIONAL COWGIRL HALL OF FAME - Pays tribute to all women who contributed to development of the West and pioneer spirit of women everywhere. Located temporarily in Deaf Smith County Library.

Houston

LYNDON B. JOHNSON SPACE CENTER - Visit the headquarters of America's space program, the famous "Mission Control" that guided pioneering astronauts, and throughout the 1980s will direct the vast Space Shuttle project. At the Visitor Orientation Center see actual lunar rocks, photographs from Mars, movies about space flights and orbital rendezvous. Exhibits include spacecraft that have been to the moon and back, a full-scale Skylab and examples of space-technology spinoff even beyond the imagination of Star Trek fans. Located 3 mi. east of Route 45 on NASA Road 1.

Killeen

FORT HOOD - Nation's greatest concentration of armored power. Headquartered at base named for Confederate General John Bell Hood are the Army's III Corps, 1st Cavalry Division ("Old Ironside"), and 2nd Armored Division ("Hell on Wheels"). Base is open facility which welcomes visitors without requirements for special passes. Museums of 2nd Armored Division and 1st Cavalry Division feature venerable combat hardware from N. African and European campaigns of W.W. II. Main gate on U.S. 190.

Kingsville

KING RANCH - Largest ranch in continental U.S., famous King Ranch established in 1853 when Capt. Richard King purchased 75,000 acres which had been Spanish land grant called Santa Gertrudis. Holdings today comprise some 823,000 acres spreading over Nueces, Kennedy, Kleberg and Willacy Counties. Originally based upon Texas Longhorns, ranch led in introducing purebred cattle such as Hereford, Shorthorn and Brahman. Now-famous Santa Gertrudis breed, first strain of cattle originated in Western Hemisphere, was developed on King Ranch. Because of size and complexity of operations, casual visitors are not accepted, but ranch makes available a 12-mile loop route which leads past headquarters, stables, other points of interest. Located immediately west of Kingsville off Hwy. 141.

Livingston

ALABAMA-COUSHATTA INDIAN RESER-

POINTS OF INTEREST (continued)

VATION - Home of several hundred Alabama and Coushatta Indians, part of southern forest tribe. Reservation is in densely wooded area known as the Big Thicket. Sam Houston, a staunch friend of the Indians, was influential in having reservation created in the 1850s. Visitor program features Living Indian Village where tribal members employ traditional techniques to make jewelry, basketry and feather items.

Marlin

HIGHLANDS MANSION - Although not as imposing on the outside as some mansions of its day, this 19th-century house displays exceptional elegance within. Building reflects graciousness of its era in details including a leaded stained-glass dome, cut-glass china cabinet and tufted leather paneling. Located on Route 147, 1 mi. northeast of Marlin.

Nederland

WINDMILL MUSEUM - Built by Nederland population to preserve Dutch heritage; 3-story building with 25-foot revolving blades houses artifacts dating from city's founding.

Odessa

JACKRABBIT STATUE - Billed as "World's Largest Jackrabbit," 10-foot statue is a popular photo spot. Located in 400 block of N. Lincoln Street.

San Antonio

SPORTSWORLD WAX MUSEUM - "Stop action" of great moments in sports created in lifelike figures in authentic settings. Sound effects use actual recordings. Located at 123 Alamo Plaza.

Sonora

CAVERNS OF SONORA - Discovered and opened to public only a few years ago. Formations called "impossible" grow in delicate crystal beauty and amazing profusion. Every hue of the rainbow shimmers from intricate networks of cave growth. Located 15 mi. southwest of Sonora on U.S. 290.

Waco

OLD SUSPENSION BRIDGE - Still in use crossing Brazos River. The bridge was nation's largest suspension bridge when built in 1870. The famous Brooklyn Bridge was later patterned after it.

UTAH

Utah, home of the Mormon church, joined the Union in 1896 as the forty-fifth state. The first settlers in the state were members of the Church of Jesus Christ of Latter-day Saints who left the East Coast because of religious persecution.

During the 1860s, the Federal Government tried unsuccessfully to regain control of Utah and diminish the power of the Mormons. The outbreak of the Civil War marked the withdrawal of federal troops and the end of the power struggle.

For nearly half a century, Congress saw fit to deny Utah statehood because of the Mormon practice of polygamy, i.e., having more than one wife at a time. Finally in 1896, Utah was admitted after it outlawed polygamy.

Utah's main revenue sources are agriculture, especially livestock and its by-products, industry, and mining of copper and coal. Tourist attractions like the Great Salt Lake and the national parks and monuments also add significantly to Utah's income.

State capital: Salt Lake City. State bird: Seagull. State tree: Blue spruce. State flower: Sego lily.

WEATHER

The topography of Utah is extremely varied, with most of the state being mountainous. A series of mountains (including the Wasatch Range), which runs generally north and south through the middle of Utah, and the Uinta Mountains, which extend east and west through the northeast portion, are the principal ranges. The lowest area is the Virgin River Valley in the southwest. Western Utah is almost entirely within the Great Basin, with no outlet to the sea. It is the largest closed basin in North America.

There are definite variations in temperature with altitude and with latitude. Naturally, the mountains and the elevated valleys have the cooler climates, with the lower areas of the state having the higher temperatures. The southern counties generally have average annual temperatures 6 to 8 degrees higher than northern counties at similar altitudes. Temperatures above 100 degrees F occur occasionally in summer in nearly all parts of the state. However, low humidity makes these high temperatures more bearable than in more humid regions. Temperatures below zero during winter and early spring are uncommon in most areas of the state, and prolonged periods of extremely cold weather are rare.

Utah experiences relatively strong insolation during the day and rapid nocturnal cooling, resulting in wide daily ranges in temperature. Even after the hottest days, nights are

UTAH

WEATHER (continued)

usually cool.

Average daily temperature for each month.

	Northern	Southern
Jan.	33.2 to 10.6	41.9 to 16.3
Feb.	35.5 to 10.3	46.1 to 21.0
Mar.	40.9 to 16.0	52.4 to 25.5
Apr.	52.8 to 26.1	61.0 to 32.3
May	65.3 to 34.3	71.8 to 41.0
Jun.	73.7 to 40.4	82.8 to 49.1
Jul.	83.3 to 46.6	89.7 to 57.7
Aug.	81.3 to 45.2	87.0 to 56.4
Sept.	72.3 to 36.9	79.5 to 46.7
Oct.	60.0 to 28.6	67.2 to 36.0
Nov.	44.2 to 21.1	52.4 to 25.1
Dec.	34.8 to 13.8	42.8 to 17.5
Year	56.4 to 27.5	64.6 to 35.4

STATE CHAMBER OF COMMERCE

Utah Travel Council
Council Hall, Capitol Hill
Salt Lake City, UT 84114
(801) 533-5681

STATE & CITY TOURISM OFFICES

State

Department of Development Service
State Capitol
Salt Lake City, UT 84114
(801) 533-5961

Utah Travel Council
Council Hall, Capitol Hill
Salt Lake City, UT 84114
(801) 533-5681

Local

Salt Lake Valley Convention and Visitor's
Bureau
The Salt Palace
Salt Lake City, UT 84101
(801) 521-2822

STATE HIGHWAY DEPARTMENT

Utah Department of Transportation
603 State Office Building
Salt Lake City, UT 84114
(801) 533-4000

HIGHWAY WELCOMING CENTERS

Echo Junction

ECHO JUNCTION - Interstate 80.

St. George

ST. GEORGE CENTER - Interstate 15.

STATE POLICE

Department of Public Safety
Salt Lake City, UT 84114
(801) 533-5621

HUNTING & FISHING

Hunting

Resident means any person (12 years old or older) who has been domiciled in the state of Utah for 60 consecutive days immediately preceding the purchase of a license, and who does not claim residency for hunting, fishing or trapping in any other state or country.

Non-residents attending an institution of higher learning in Utah as full-time students and who do not claim residency for hunting, fishing or trapping in any other state or country may qualify as Utah residents.

The license year begins January 1 and continues through December 31 of the same year.

Resident

Big game, $7; small game (ages 12-15), $3; small game (ages 16 & over), $6; combination, $18; trapping, $10; commercial area bird, $3.

Non-resident

Big game, $75; small game, $20; commercial area bird, $3.

Fishing

See hunting regulations above.

Resident

Fishing (ages 12-15), $3.50; fishing (ages 16-64), $8; fishing (ages 65 & over), $4.

Non-resident

Fishing, 1 day, $2; fishing, 5 days, $7.50; fishing season, $25.

For more information contact:

Division of Wildlife Resources
1596 West North Temple
Salt Lake City, UT 84116
(801) 533-9333

508

CAMPGROUNDS

Private

Beaver

UNITED CAMPGROUND
(801) 438-2808
LOCATION: South of Beaver.
FACILITIES: Open year round; 188 sites; water and bathroom facilities; electrical hookup; trailer village vehicle sites; boating; fishing; tent camping.

Cedar City

CEDAR CITY
(801) 586-9872
LOCATION: 1121 N. Main Street.
FACILITIES: Open year round; 100 sites; water and bathroom facilities; sanitary station; electrical hookup; trailer village vehicle sites; laundry; boating; fishing; tent camping.

Coalville

COALVILLE
(801) 336-5954
LOCATION: On I-80 Interchange.
FACILITIES: Open year round; 143 sites; water and bathroom facilities; sanitary station; electrical hookup; trailer village vehicle sites; boating; fishing; tent camping.

Green River

UNITED CAMPGROUND
(801) 564-3212
LOCATION: ½ mi. east on Hwys. 6 & 50.
FACILITIES: Open Mar. 1 - Oct. 15; 240 sites; water and bathroom facilities; electrical hookup; trailer village vehicle sites; laundry; swimming; tent camping.

Hatch

RIVERSIDE CAMPGROUND
(801) 735-4224
LOCATION: 1 mi. north on Route 89.
FACILITIES: Open May 15 - Nov. 1; 100 sites; water and bathroom facilities; sanitary station; electrical hookup; trailer village vehicle sites; food service; boating; fishing; tent camping.

Kaysville

CHERRY HILL CAMPING
(801) 867-2104
LOCATION: 1325 S. Main.
FACILITIES: Open Apr. - Oct.; 214 sites; water and bathroom facilities; sanitary station; electrical hookup; laundry; food service; tent camping.

St. George

UNITED CAMPGROUND
(801) 673-2970
LOCATION: 2 mi. north of St. George.
FACILITIES: Open year round; 100 sites; water and bathroom facilities; sanitary station; electrical hookup; trailer village vehicle sites; laundry; tent camping.

Salt Lake City

CAMP V.I.P.
(801) 328-0224
LOCATION: 1350 West North Temple.
FACILITIES: Open year round; 188 sites; water and bathroom facilities; sanitary station; electrical hookup; trailer village vehicle sites; laundry; food service; tent camping.

DENMAN'S
(801) 355-1192
LOCATION: 1400 West North Temple.
FACILITIES: Open year round; 213 sites; water and bathroom facilities; sanitary station; electrical hookup; trailer village vehicle sites; laundry; food service; swimming; boating; fishing; tent camping.

TRUCKERS CAMPGROUND
(801) 262-6437
LOCATION: 2198 S. 300 West.
FACILITIES: Open year round; 144 sites; water and bathroom facilities; sanitary station; electrical hookup; trailer village vehicle sites; laundry; food service; swimming; tent camping.

RESORTS & BEACHES

Most of the state's resort activities center around the major lakes and include fishing, swimming, boating, water skiing, and camping. (See Boating Areas, National Parks, National Forests, and State Parks.)

BOATING AREAS

Antimony

OTTER CREEK RESERVOIR
LOCATION: 5 mi. north of Antimony.
FACILITIES: Launching.

Cedar City

NAVAJO LAKE
LOCATION: Near Cedar City.
FACILITIES: Launching.

Coalville

ECHO RESERVOIR
LOCATION: Coalville.
FACILITIES: Launching.

Garden City

BEAR LAKE
LOCATION: Near Garden City.
FACILITIES: Launching.

Heber City

DEER CREEK RESERVOIR
LOCATION: 5 mi. southwest of Heber City.
FACILITIES: Launching.

STRAWBERRY RESERVOIR
LOCATION: Near Heber City.
FACILITIES: Launching.

UTAH

BOATING AREAS (continued)

Junction

PIUTE RESERVOIR
LOCATION: North of Junction.
FACILITIES: Launching.

Manila

FLAMING GORGE RESERVOIR
LOCATION: Near Manila.
FACILITIES: Launching.

Morgan

EAST CANYON RESERVOIR
LOCATION: 10 mi. south of Morgan.
FACILITIES: Launching.

Ogden

PINEVIEW RESERVOIR
LOCATION: Near Ogden.
FACILITIES: Launching.

Panguitch

PANGUITCH LAKE
LOCATION: Near Panguitch.
FACILITIES: Launching.

Provo

UTAH LAKE
LOCATION: Near Provo.
FACILITIES: Launching.

Richfield

FISH LAKE
LOCATION: Near Richfield.
FACILITIES: Launching.

Salt Lake City

GREAT SALT LAKE
LOCATION: Salt Lake City.
FACILITIES: Launching.

Scofield

SCOFIELD RESERVOIR
LOCATION: Near Scofield.
FACILITIES: Launching.

Vernal

STEINAKER RESERVOIR
LOCATION: Near Vernal.
FACILITIES: Launching.

Virgin

VIRGIN RESERVOIR
LOCATION: Near Virgin.
FACILITIES: Launching.

Wahweap

LAKE POWELL RESERVOIR
LOCATION: Near Wahweap.
FACILITIES: Launching.

Wanship

ROCKPORT RESERVOIR
LOCATION: 1½ mi. south of Wanship.
FACILITIES: Launching.

Willard

WILLARD BAY RESERVOIR
LOCATION: Near Willard.
FACILITIES: Launching.

BICYCLE TRAILS

ST. GEORGE TRAILS - 28, 50 & 60 mi.;
steep hills, dry climate; 10-speed bicycle necessary.
  Tucked away in the southwest corner of
Utah is the town of St. George. This area has
many types of scenery, including beautiful
red and pink sandstone cliffs, pine forest, rolling dry hills, farmland, and miles and miles of
nothing.
  Trails: (1) St. George to Dixie State Park
Central to Pine Canyon - 28 mi.; (2) St.
George to Anderson Junction to Hurricane to
Route 17 to St. George - 50 mi.; (3) St.
George to Hurricane to Virgin to Kolob Res-
ervoir - about 60 mi.

TRAILS

There are no National Trails System Foot
Trails in Utah.

SKI AREAS

Alta

ALTA
Alta, UT 84070
(801) 742-3333
LOCATION: 28 mi. southeast of Salt Lake
City.
FACILITIES: 6 double chairlifts; 4 tow
ropes; slopes for expert, intermediate and beginning skiers; ski instruction; ski rental; 2000
ft. vertical drop; longest run, 3 mi.; restaurants; lodging.

Beaver

MT. HOLLY
Beaver, UT 84713
(801) 438-2488
LOCATION: I-15 to Beaver exit, 17 mi. east
on Hwy. 153.
FACILITIES: 1 double chairlift; 1 T-bar; 1
tow rope; slopes for expert, intermediate and
beginning skiers; ski instruction; ski rental;
1500 ft. vertical drop; restaurants; lodging.

Brighton

BRIGHTON SKI BOWL
Brighton, UT 84121
(801) 359-3283
LOCATION: 25 mi. east of Salt Lake City.
FACILITIES: 4 double chairlifts; 46 runs;
slopes for expert, intermediate and beginning

SKI AREAS (continued)

skiers; ski instruction; ski rental; 1525 ft. vertical drop; restaurants; lodging.

Cedar City

BRIAN HEAD
Cedar City, UT 84720
(801) 586-4636
LOCATION: I-15 to Parowan exit; 12 mi. southeast on Hwy. 143.
FACILITIES: 2 double chairlifts; 1 T-bar; slopes for expert, intermediate and beginning skiers; ski instruction; ski rental; 1280 ft. vertical drop; restaurants; lodging.

Eden

NORDIC VALLEY
Eden, UT 84310
(801) 745-3511
LOCATION: I-15 to Ogden, 12th Street exit, 17 mi. northeast via Ogden Canyon (U-39) to U-162.
FACILITIES: 2 double chairlifts; 10 runs; slopes for expert, intermediate and beginning skiers; ski instruction; ski rental; 1500 ft. vertical drop.

POWDER MOUNTAIN
Eden, UT 84310
(801) 745-3771
LOCATION: I-15 to Ogden, 12th Street exit; 17 mi. northeast via Ogden Canyon (Hwy. 39) to Hwy. 162.
FACILITIES: 1 triple chairlift; 2 double chairlifts; 26 runs; slopes for expert, intermediate and beginning skiers; ski instruction; ski rental; 1960 ft. vertical drop; restaurants; lodging.

Logan

BEAVER MOUNTAIN
Logan, UT 84321
(801) 753-0921
LOCATION: 27 mi. east of Logan via U.S. 89.
FACILITIES: 3 double chairlifts; 16 runs; slopes for expert, intermediate and beginning skiers; ski instruction; ski rental; 1632 ft. vertical drop.

Monticello

BLUE MOUNTAIN
Monticello, UT 84535
(801) 587-2612
LOCATION: 5 mi. west of Monticello.
FACILITIES: 1 poma; 5 runs; slopes for expert, intermediate and beginning skiers; ski instruction; ski rental; 800 ft. vertical drop; restaurants; lodging.

Ogden

SNOW BASIN
Ogden, UT 84403
(801) 392-9196
LOCATION: 19 mi. east via Ogden Canyon (U-39).
FACILITIES: 1 triple chairlift; 4 double

chairlifts; 30 runs; slopes for expert, intermediate and beginning skiers; ski instruction; ski rental; 2600 ft. vertical drop.

Park City

PARK CITY
Park City, UT 84060
(801) 649-8111
LOCATION: 27 mi. east of Salt Lake City.
FACILITIES: 10 chairlifts; 1 tram; slopes for expert, intermediate and beginning skiers; ski instruction; ski rental; nursery; 3100 ft. vertical drop; longest run, 3½ mi.; restaurants; lodging.

PARK WEST
Park City, UT 84060
(801) 649-9663
LOCATION: 24 mi. east of Salt Lake City.
FACILITIES: 5 double chairlifts; 33 runs; slopes for expert, intermediate and beginning skiers; ski instruction; ski rental; 2000 ft. vertical drop; restaurants; lodging.

PARLEY'S SUMMIT RESORT
Park City, UT 84060
(801) 649-9840
LOCATION: 15 mi. east of Salt Lake City via I-80, take ranch exit just east of Parley's Summit.
FACILITIES: 1 double chairlift; 2 surface lifts; slopes for expert, intermediate and beginning skiers; ski instruction; ski rental; 500 ft. vertical drop.

Provo

SUNDANCE
Provo, UT 84601
(801) 225-4100
LOCATION: I-15 to Orem.
FACILITIES: 1 triple chairlift; 2 double chairlifts; 25 runs; slopes for expert, intermediate and beginning skiers; ski instruction; ski rental; 1800 ft. vertical drop.

Snowbird

SNOWBIRD RESORT
Snowbird, UT 84070
(801) 742-2222
LOCATION: 31 mi. southeast of Salt Lake City.
FACILITIES: 5 chairlifts; 1 tram; slopes for expert, intermediate and beginning skiers; ski instruction; ski rental; nursery; 3100 ft. vertical drop; longest run, 2½ mi.; restaurants; lodging.

Solitude

SOLITUDE SKI RESORT
Salt Lake City, UT 84117
(801) 534-1400
LOCATION: 23 mi. east of Salt Lake City.
FACILITIES: 1 triple chairlift; 2 double chairlifts; 20 runs; slopes for expert, intermediate and beginning skiers; ski instruction; ski rental; 1800 ft. vertical drop; restaurants; lodging.

AMUSEMENT PARKS & ATTRACTIONS

Lehi

SARATOGA RESORT & CAMPGROUND
Lehi, UT 84043
(801) 768-8206
FACILITIES: 12 major rides; 8 kiddie rides; 2 refreshment stands; penny arcade; shooting gallery; miniature golf; picnic facilities; free acts; pay parking; open Easter - Labor Day.

Salt Lake City

LAGOON
Salt Lake City, UT 84101
(801) 363-4451
FACILITIES: 24 major rides; 10 kiddie rides; fun house; 25 games; 11 refreshment stands; restaurant; penny arcade; shooting gallery; miniature golf; picnic facilities; free acts; free gate; pay parking.

STATE FAIR

Utah State Fair
State Fairgrounds
Salt Lake City, UT 84116
(801) 533-5858
DATE: September

NATIONAL PARKS

Bryce Canyon

BRYCE CANYON NATIONAL PARK
Bryce Canyon, UT 84717
(801) 834-5322

NORTH
LOCATION: Headquarters.
FACILITIES: Open May 1 - Nov. 1; entrance fee; limit of stay: 14 days; 111 sites; NPS campsite fee: $2; water and bathroom facilities; sanitary station; cabins; laundry; picnic area; food service; hiking; snowmobile route; exhibit; museum; medical service; lodging.

SUNSET
LOCATION: 1 mi. south of headquarters.
FACILITIES: Open Jun. 1 - Labor Day; limit of stay: 14 days; 115 sites; group camps: 3; NPS campsite fee: $2; water and bathroom facilities; cabins; laundry; picnic area; hiking; horseback riding; snowmobile route; exhibit; museum; NPS guided tour; self-guiding tour; medical service; lodging.

Moab

ARCHES NATIONAL PARK
Moab, UT 84532
(801) 259-7166

DEVIL'S GARDEN
LOCATION: 18 mi. north of Visitor Center.
FACILITIES: Open Mar. - Oct.; entrance fee; limit of stay: 14 days; 53 sites; group camps: 2 (reservations); NPS campsite fee: $3; water and bathroom facilities; picnic area; fishing;

guide for hire; hiking; horseback riding; exhibit; museum; living history program; handicapped access/restroom; NPS guided tour; self-guiding tour; free camping; no water Nov. - Feb.

CANYONLANDS NATIONAL PARK
Moab, UT 84532
(801) 259-7166

SQUAW FLAT
LOCATION: 35 mi. west of Hwy. 163.
FACILITIES: Open year round; limit of stay: 14 days; 31 sites; group camps: 1; NPS campsite fee: $2; water and bathroom facilities; sanitary station; picnic area; swimming; boating; boat rental; fishing; guide for hire; hiking; horseback riding; exhibit; museum; living history program; NPS guided tour; self-guiding tour; primitive sites.

Springdale

ZION NATIONAL PARK
Springdale, UT 84767
(801) 772-3256

SOUTH
LOCATION: South entrance.
FACILITIES: Open Apr. 15 - Sept. 15; entrance fee; limit of stay: 14 days; 144 sites; NPS campsite fee: $2; water and bathroom facilities; sanitary station; cabins; picnic area; food service; swimming; hiking; horseback riding; exhibit; museum; handicapped access/restroom; lodging.

WATCHMAN
LOCATION: South entrance.
FACILITIES: Open year round; entrance fee; limit of stay: 14 days; 229 sites; group camps: 1; NPS campsite fee: $2; water and bathroom facilities; sanitary station; cabins; picnic area; food service; swimming; hiking; horseback riding; exhibit; museum; handicapped access/restroom; NPS guided tour; self-guiding tour; lodging.

Torrey

CAPITOL REEF NATIONAL PARK
Torrey, UT 84775
(801) 425-3871

CAPITOL REEF
LOCATION: 1¼ mi. south of Hwy. 24.
FACILITIES: Open year round; limit of stay: 14 days; 53 sites; NPS campsite fee: $2; water and bathroom facilities; picnic area; food service; hiking; exhibit; museum; lodging.

NATIONAL FORESTS

National Forests
Intermountain Region
324 25th Street
Ogden, UT 84401
(801) 399-6484

Cedar City

DIXIE NATIONAL FOREST
ATTRACTIONS: Table Cliff Point with vista

NATIONAL FORESTS (continued)

into 4 states (Colorado, Arizona, Nevada, and Utah); spectacularly colored cliffs; deer, elk, cougar hunting; lake and stream fishing.
FACILITIES: 27 camp sites, 4 picnic only; Cedar Canyon Winter Sports Area; resorts; motels; dude ranches.
NEARBY TOWNS: Enterprise, Escalante, Panguitch, Parowan, St. George, UT; Las Vegas, NV.

Logan

CACHE NATIONAL FOREST
ATTRACTIONS: Fishing; deer, elk hunting; horseback riding and hiking trails.
FACILITIES: 49 camp sites, 8 picnic only; Beaver Mountain and Snow Basin Winter Sports Areas.
NEARBY TOWNS: Brigham, Ogden, UT; Montpelier, Preston, Soda Springs, ID.

Price

MANTI-LA SAL NATIONAL FOREST
ATTRACTIONS: Indian hieroglyphics and cliff dwellings; world's largest aspen tree; fishing; deer, elk hunting; scenic drives; horseback riding and hiking trails; limited skiing.
FACILITIES: 15 camp sites, 7 picnic only; Bluebell Flat Winter Sports Area.
NEARBY TOWNS: Blanding, Ferron, Huntington, Manti, Moab, Monticello, Mount Pleasant.

Provo

UINTA NATIONAL FOREST
ATTRACTIONS: Fishing; deer, elk hunting; hiking trails.
FACILITIES: 36 camp and picnic sites, 12 picnic only; 1 winter sports area; 4 valley-view overlook points; hotels; motels.
NEARBY TOWNS: American Fork, Heber, Nephi, Spanish Fork.

Richfield

FISHLAKE NATIONAL FOREST
ATTRACTIONS: Beaver Mountains, Thousand Lake Mountain Scenic Area, Fish Lake, Petrified Wood; lake and stream fishing; deer, elk hunting; scenic drives.
FACILITIES: 21 camp sites, 9 picnic only; resorts; hotels; motels.
NEARBY TOWNS: Beaver, Delta, Fillmore, Kanosh, Loa, Monroe, Salina.

Salt Lake City

WASATCH NATIONAL FOREST
ATTRACTIONS: Big Mirror Lake; lake and stream fishing; deer, elk hunting; boating; swimming; horseback riding and hiking trails; wilderness trips; outstanding skiing; skating; mountain climbing.
FACILITIES: 45 camp and picnic sites, 29 picnic only; 4 winter sports areas, including the famous developments at Alta and Brighton; numerous resorts; motels; dude ranches.
NEARBY TOWNS: Heber, Kamas, Murray, Ogden, Provo, UT; Evanston, WY.

Vernal

ASHLEY NATIONAL FOREST
ATTRACTIONS: Exposed geological formations a billion years old; numerous scenic gorges, natural erosion formations; lake and stream fishing; deer, elk, antelope hunting; horseback riding trails; wilderness pack trips.
FACILITIES: 50 camp and picnic sites, 12 picnic only; winter sports site; resorts; motels; dude ranches.
NEARBY TOWNS: Green River, Rock Springs, WY; Duchesne, Manila, Roosevelt, UT.

See CORONADO NATIONAL FOREST - Arizona.

See CARIBOU NATIONAL FOREST and SAWTOOTH NATIONAL FOREST - Idaho.

STATE PARKS

Headquarters

State Division of Parks and Recreation
1596 West North Temple
Salt Lake City, UT 84116
(801) 533-6012

Crescent Junction

DEAD HORSE POINT STATE PARK
LOCATION: 45 mi. south of Crescent Junction off Hwy. 163.
FACILITIES: Open year round; 20 sites; water and bathroom facilities; sanitary station; electrical hookup; trailer village vehicle sites; tent camping.

Midway

WASATCH MOUNTAIN STATE PARK
(801) 363-3232
LOCATION: Near Midway.
FACILITIES: Open year round; 285 sites; water and bathroom facilities; sanitary station; trailer village vehicle sites; picnic area; fishing; hiking; tent camping.

Provo

UTAH LAKE STATE PARK
LOCATION: 2 mi. west of Provo.
FACILITIES: Open year round; 60 sites; water and bathroom facilities; trailer village vehicle sites; picnic area; food service; boating; boat rental; tent camping.

St. George

SNOW CANYON STATE PARK
LOCATION: 7 mi. north of St. George.
FACILITIES: Open year round; 32 sites; water and bathroom facilities; electrical hookup; trailer village vehicle sites; boating; tent camping.

Salt Lake City

GREAT SALT LAKE STATE PARK (Saltair Beach)
(801) 533-4080
LOCATION: 16 mi. west of Salt Lake City.

UTAH

STATE PARKS (continued)

FACILITIES: Open year round; 50 sites; water and bathroom facilities; electrical hookup; trailer village vehicle sites; food service; tent camping.

PIONEER TRAIL STATE PARK
LOCATION: 5 mi. east of Salt Lake City.
FACILITIES: Open year round; water and bathroom facilities; exhibit; museum.

Syracuse

GREAT SALT LAKE STATE PARK (Antelope Island)
(801) 533-4080
LOCATION: 6½ mi. from Syracuse.
FACILITIES: Open year round; 17 sites; water and bathroom facilities; trailer village vehicle sites; picnic area; swimming; boating; tent camping.

STATE FORESTS

Division of State Lands, Forestry & Fire Control
444 Empire Bldg.
231 East 400 South
Salt Lake City, UT 84111
(801) 533-5439

All Utah State Forests are essentially wilderness areas with no developed facilities. It is recommended that you travel in these forests in 4-wheel drive vehicles.

Antimony

PARKER MOUNTAIN STATE FOREST
LOCATION: South of Antimony off Hwy. 22.
FACILITIES: Open year round; hunting; hiking; primitive campsites.

Bryce

FLAKE MOUNTAIN STATE FOREST
LOCATION: 2 mi. west of Bryce off Hwy. 12, then 3 mi. dirt trail.
FACILITIES: Open year round; hunting; primitive campsites.

East Carbon City

PATMOS RIDGE STATE FOREST
LOCATION: 5 mi. east of East Carbon City.
FACILITIES: Open year round; hunting; primitive campsites.

Fruitland

TABBY MOUNTAIN STATE FOREST
LOCATION: North of Fruitland off Hwy. 40.
FACILITIES: Open year round; hunting; primitive campsites.

Glendale

ORDERVILLE CANYON STATE FOREST
LOCATION: 1 mi. east of Glendale.
FACILITIES: Open year round; hunting; primitive campsites.

Green River

BOOK CLIFFS STATE FOREST
LOCATION: I-70 east from Green River.
FACILITIES: Open year round; hunting; hiking; primitive campsites.

Logan

FRANKLIN BASIN STATE FOREST
LOCATION: 25 mi. east of Logan, then west on improved gravel road.
FACILITIES: Open year round; hunting; hiking; primitive campsites.

Manila

PHIL PICO STATE FOREST
LOCATION: 2 mi. west of Manila.
FACILITIES: Open year round; hunting; primitive campsites.

Moab

LASAL MOUNTAIN STATE FOREST
LOCATION: 11 mi. south along Pack Creek paved road, then follow jeep trail for 10 mi.
FACILITIES: Open year round; hunting; hiking; primitive campsites.

Ogden

MONTY CRISTO STATE FOREST
LOCATION: 35 mi. northeast of Ogden off Hwy. 39.
FACILITIES: Open year round; hunting; primitive campsites.

HISTORIC SITES

Monticello

NEWSPAPER ROCK STATE HISTORIC MONUMENT - Indian petroglyphs inscribed on the face of a large, flat rock present a fascinating example of Indian rock art form at least three distinct periods of native American culture. This priceless cliff mural is one of Utah's archaeological treasures. Located 24 mi. northwest of Monticello.

Ogden

EPISCOPAL CHURCH OF GOOD SHEPHERD - Designed by Gordon W. Lloyd, reported to be the oldest building in continuous use in Ogden; built in 1874 of stone from the Mendron area. Located at 24th and Grant.
OPEN: Mon. - Fri., 9 a.m. - 12:30 p.m.

MILES GOODYEAR CABIN - Built about 1845, believed to be the oldest "home" in Utah. Located at Temple Square.

CHARLES HARDING HOME - Classic Greek Revival rock house built c. 1870 by Shadrach Jones and Charles Harding. He and his brother, George, brought the first mowing machine and reaper to Utah and freighted for Walker Bros. in Salt Lake City. Located at 142 South Main.

HISTORIC SITES (continued)

St. George

BRIGHAM YOUNG WINTER HOME AND OFFICE - Built in 1872 as a winter retreat for Brigham Young; front wing added in 1874. Located 2nd North and 1st West.
OPEN: Mon. - Sat., 8:30 a.m. - 5 p.m.

ST. GEORGE TEMPLE - Built during 1871-77, it was the first Mormon temple completed in Utah. Architect was Truman O. Angell. Walls are red sandstone stuccoed over and painted white. Located at 2nd and 3rd East, 4th and 5th South.

Salt Lake City

BEEHIVE HOUSE - Designed by Truman O. Angell, this lovely pioneer home was built by Brigham Young in 1854. It served as his official residence. Located at 67 East South Temple.
OPEN: Mon. - Sat., 9:30 a.m. - 4:30 p.m.

BIG MOUNTAIN - When the pioneers reached the top of this mountain, they caught their first glimpse of the distant Salt Lake Valley. At the eastern base of Big Mountain, breastworks can still be seen, the remains of fortifications built in 1857 to intercept the forces of Johnston's Army, which tried to route the Mormons.

BRIGHAM YOUNG FARM HOUSE - Constructed between 1861-63, the farm house served as a family home and place to entertain guests. Agricultural experiments were conducted on the farm. Five of Brigham Young's wives lived there at one time or another. Located at 732 Ashton Avenue.
OPEN: Mon. - Sat., 9:30 a.m. - 4 p.m.

CAPITOL HILL — AVENUES - These were some of the earliest areas to be settled in the city, and many of the early small plastered adobe houses can still be seen. The west side of Capitol Hill has been called the Marmalade District because the streets are named for fruit trees.

HEBER C. KIMBALL GRAVE - Heber C. Kimball, one of the most important leaders of the Mormon Church, was born in 1801 in Vermont, died here in 1868, and was buried in the family burial ground. Located at Gordon Place.

MORROW-TAYLOR HOME - Built by William Morrow c. 1868, purchased in 1884 by John W. Taylor, son of the Latter Day Saints President John Taylor. It is said that the house once contained a hidden room where President Taylor hid during polygamy persecution. Located at 390 Quince Street.

HOSTELS

There are no Hostels in Utah.

POINTS OF INTEREST

Abraham

TOPAZ WAR RELOCATION CENTER - In existence from July, 1942, to October, 1945, the 19,800-acre project included a mile-square city designed to house 9,000 persons. The 623 buildings have been removed, and all that remains of Topaz are some concrete foundations. It was one of ten camps in the U.S. to which more than 110,000 Japanese-Americans were evacuated during the war hysteria of World War II.

Circleville

CIRCLEVILLE - Known chiefly as the birthplace of George LeRoy Parker, alias "Butch Cassidy," Utah's most notorious bandit.

Corinne

CORINNE METHODIST-EPISCOPAL CHURCH - Built in 1870, this is the first Methodist-Episcopal church dedicated in Utah; funds were raised by subscription in Corinne. Previously closed due to decline in population, the church is being restored. Located at corner of Colorado and South 6th Street. Ask for key at house across the street.

Grantsville

ALEX JOHNSON HOME - Built in 1899, this is one of the more handsome houses in Grantsville. The outside walls are burned brick (mailed from California, each brick wrapped in paper, because postal rates were less than freighting rates), the interior walls are adobe brick. Small building to the west is a two-story summer sleeping house. Located at corner of Hale and Main Street.

Huntsville

ABBEY OF OUR LADY OF THE HOLY TRINITY - Established in 1947, the Trappist-Cistercian Abbey is commonly known as "the Monastery." The monks offer a delicious variety of cheese, honey, bread and other items for sale at their store on weekdays only. Located southeast of Huntsville.

Ogden

JOHN MOSES BROWNING HOME - Built in 1899 by renowned gun inventor. Now remodeled as Y.W.C.A. Located at 505 27th Street.

Old Frisco

OLD FRISCO - Discovered accidentally in 1875 by two prospectors, the Horn Silver Mine, on the hill a mile west of Frisco, was the richest silver producer in Utah. By 1879, the town was booming. A sheriff named Peterson, hired to clean up the town, had a simple law enforcement policy:"leave town or shoot it out." A "body wagon" made the rounds every morning to pick up the corpses. In 1885 a mine cave-in started the exodus that made Old Frisco a ghost town today.

UTAH

POINTS OF INTEREST (continued)

Pine Valley

PINE VALLEY - Discovered by Isaac Riddle in 1855 while looking for a stray cow. The first settlers came to operate a sawmill, using the excellent timber in the valley, which furnished lumber to much of the southwest area and supplied logs for organ pipes in the Salt Lake Tabernacle. The brick used for building in Pine Valley has a lovely clear red color unlike bricks in surrounding towns.

Salt Lake City

"CAST-IRON FRONT" OF Z.C.M.I. - Was one of the first department stores in the U.S. Although major modifications have occurred in the building, the center cast-iron front is original. Located at 15 South Main.

MORMON TEMPLE AND TABERNACLE - The granite Temple has six spires 212 feet high; a golden statue of the Angel Moroni tops the east tower. The Tabernacle, with its large domed roof and splendid acoustics, seats more than 7,000 persons. It is also the home of the world-famous Tabernacle Choir. Located on Temple Square, the site of the Seagull Monument and other interesting statues.

Vernal

NATURAL HISTORY STATE MUSEUM - Located in the heart of Utah's Dinosaurland. Exhibits of ancient fossils, skeletal reproductions, archaeology, geology, fluorescent minerals, full-size replicas of dinosaur species and other natural history aspects of Utah's Uintah Basin are featured.

VERMONT

Vermont, renowned for its maple syrup and gem-like marble, entered the Union in 1791 as the fourteenth state. Early Vermont settlers were farmers of a fiercely independent nature who resisted all attempts at domination. There were border conflicts with New Hampshire and New York, which were solved as a condition of statehood.

True to form, while most states were limiting the rights of the individual, Vermont created a constitution that outlawed slavery and allowed any man to vote, property owner or not. At the time, it was customary for only men of means to have a say in the government.

Agriculture, once the state's mainstay, is being replaced today by the electronic, lumber and asbestos industries.

Tourism is also an important business in Vermont. The quaint villages and shops, covered bridges, magnificent mountain scenery, and most recently, winter ski resorts, attract throngs of visitors each year.

State capital: Montpelier. State bird: Hermit thrush. State tree: Sugar maple. State flower: Red clover.

WEATHER

"The Green Mountain State" occupies 9,609 square miles, fully one-seventh of New England's total area. Although Vermont is the only New England state without a coastline on the Atlantic Ocean, most of its boundary is water. The terrain is hilly to mountainous. The Green Mountains extend the length of the state. Two-thirds of Vermont is forest, contained in national, state, municipal, and private reserves and in farm woodlands.

Vermont shares with other New England states the following characteristics: changeableness of the weather; large range of temperature, both daily and annual; great differences between the same seasons in different years, equable distribution of precipitation, and considerable diversity from place to place. The regional climatic influences are modified in Vermont by varying elevations, types of terrain, and distances from the Atlantic Ocean and from Lake Champlain.

Summer temperatures are comfortable as a rule, and they are reasonably uniform over the state. Comparative regional temperatures vary more in winter than in summer.

Average daily temperature for each month.

	Northern	Southern
Jan.	24.4 to 2.9	30.5 to 9.0
Feb.	28.3 to 4.4	33.5 to 10.1
Mar.	37.4 to 15.9	41.9 to 22.0
Apr.	51.2 to 29.0	55.6 to 33.2
May	64.9 to 40.0	68.2 to 42.2
Jun.	75.1 to 50.0	78.0 to 53.0
Jul.	79.2 to 54.5	82.8 to 57.4
Aug.	76.7 to 52.3	80.7 to 55.1
Sept.	69.1 to 45.1	72.9 to 48.1
Oct.	57.4 to 35.9	62.1 to 37.2
Nov.	41.7 to 26.0	46.9 to 28.9
Dec.	28.5 to 10.7	33.9 to 15.9
Year	52.8 to 30.6	57.3 to 34.3

STATE CHAMBER OF COMMERCE

Vermont State Chamber of Commerce
P.O. Box 37
Montpelier, VT 05602
(802) 223-3443

516

STATE & CITY TOURISM OFFICES

State

Office of Information
Agency of Development and Community Affairs
61 Elm Street
Montpelier, VT 05602
(802) 828-3236

Vermont Agency of Development and Community Affairs
Montpelier, VT 05602
(802) 828-3211

STATE HIGHWAY DEPARTMENT

Department of Highways
133 State Street
Montpelier, VT 05602
(802) 828-2657

HIGHWAY WELCOMING CENTERS

Guilford

GUILFORD/BRATTLEBORO CENTER - Interstate 91.

High Gate Springs

HIGH GATE SPRINGS CENTER - Interstate 89.

STATE POLICE

Department of Public Safety
Montpelier, VT 05602
(802) 828-2115

HUNTING & FISHING

Hunting

A person of any age engaged in fishing, hunting or taking any wild animals must be properly licensed, except as listed below:

A resident owner of land in Vermont, his or her spouse and minor children may hunt on this land and take fish within said land without a license. A non-resident has equal privilege, except in archery deer season, if his lands are not posted.

Any person under 15 years of age may take wild animals by legal trapping and may take fish according to regulations without a license.

In order to obtain resident licenses, a person must have lived in Vermont for the 6 months immediately prior to applying for a license and not have claimed residence elsewhere for any reason.

Resident

Hunting, $5; combination, $8; bow and arrow (hunting license also needed), $4; trapping, $4.

Non-resident

Hunting, $40.75; combination, $45.75; bow and arrow (hunting license also needed), $7.50; trapping, $300; alien hunting, $100.75; alien combination, $105.75; alien trapping, $500.

Fishing

See regulations above.

Resident

Fishing license, $4.

Non-resident

Fishing license, $12.25; 14-day fishing, $8.75; 3-day fishing, $4.75.

For more information contact:

Vermont Fish & Game Department
Montpelier, VT 05602
(802) 828-3371

CAMPGROUNDS

Private

Andover

HORSESHOE ACRES
(802) 875-2960
LOCATION: 4½ mi. east of Weston.
FACILITIES: Open year round; entrance fee: $4 - $5; 90 sites; group camps: 60; water and bathroom facilities; sanitary station; electrical hookup; trailer village vehicle sites; picnic area; swimming; hiking; tent camping.

Arlington

CAMPING ON THE BATTENKILL
(802) 375-6663
LOCATION: ¾ mi. north of Arlington.
FACILITIES: Open Apr. 1 - Dec. 1; 80 sites; water and bathroom facilities; trailer village vehicle sites; picnic area; swimming; fishing; tent camping.

Ascutney

RUNNING BEAR CAMPGROUND
(802) 674-6417
LOCATION: 1 mi. north on Route 5.
FACILITIES: Open year round; 106 sites; water and bathroom facilities; sanitary station; electrical hookup; trailer village vehicle sites; picnic area; swimming; tent camping.

Bomoseen

LAKE BOMOSEEN CAMPGROUND
(802) 273-2061
LOCATION: On Route 30.

VERMONT

CAMPGROUNDS (continued)

FACILITIES: Open May 1 - Oct. 15; entrance fee: $4.50; 85 sites; water and bathroom facilities; sanitary station; electrical hookup; trailer village vehicle sites; picnic area; swimming; boat rental; tent camping.

Braintree

MOBILE ACRES TRAILER PARK
(802) 728-5548
LOCATION: 2 mi. north of Randolph on Route 12A.
FACILITIES: Open May 15 - Oct. 1; 89 sites; water and bathroom facilities; sanitary station; electrical hookup; trailer village vehicle sites; laundry; picnic area; swimming; tent camping.

Charlotte

OLD LANTERN CAMPGROUND
(802) 425-2120
LOCATION: On Greenbush Road.
FACILITIES: Open May 1 - Oct. 15; 83 sites; water and bathroom facilities; electrical hookup; trailer village vehicle sites; picnic area; tent camping.

Colchester

LONE PINE CAMPSITES, INC.
(802) 878-5447
LOCATION: On Route 127.
FACILITIES: Open May 1 - Nov. 1; 250 sites; water and bathroom facilities; sanitary station; electrical hookup; trailer village vehicle sites; laundry; picnic area; swimming; tent camping.

Gaysville

WHITE RIVER VALLEY CAMPING AREA
(802) 234-9115
LOCATION: On Route 107.
FACILITIES: Open Apr. 15 - Dec. 1; 80 sites; water and bathroom facilities; sanitary station; electrical hookup; trailer village vehicle sites; laundry; picnic area; food service; swimming; hunting; fishing; hiking; tent camping.

Georgia

HOMESTEAD MOTOR COURT
(802) 524-2356
LOCATION: On I-89.
FACILITIES: Open May 1 - Oct. 15; 135 sites; water and bathroom facilities; sanitary station; electrical hookup; trailer village vehicle sites; cabins; picnic area; playground; tent camping.

Hero

APPLE ISLAND CAMPGROUND & MARINA
(802) 372-4666
LOCATION: Exit 17 (Champlain Islands) off I-89, west Route 2, 6 mi. to Sand Bar.
FACILITIES: Open May 1 - Oct. 15; 200 sites; water and bathroom facilities; sanitary station; electrical hookup; trailer village vehicle sites; laundry; picnic area; swimming; boating; boat rental; fishing; tent camping.

Island Pond

LAKESIDE CAMPING AREA
(802) 723-6649
LOCATION: Near Island Pond.
FACILITIES: Open mid-May - mid-Sept.; 100 sites; water and bathroom facilities; sanitary station; electrical hookup; trailer village vehicle sites; laundry; picnic area; swimming; boating; fishing; tent camping.

Newport

TOP DECK CAMPGROUND
(802) 334-2008
LOCATION: On Lake Road.
FACILITIES: Open May 15 - Oct. 15; 150 sites; water and bathroom facilities; sanitary station; electrical hookup; trailer village vehicle sites; laundry; picnic area; boat rental; fishing; tent camping.

Randolph Center

LAKE CHAMPAGNE CAMPGROUND
(802) 728-5293
LOCATION: On Route 66.
FACILITIES: Open May 30 - Oct. 15; 120 sites; water and bathroom facilities; sanitary station; electrical hookup; trailer village vehicle sites; laundry; picnic area; swimming; tent camping.

Salisbury

LAKE DUNMORE KAMPERSVILLE
(802) 352-4501
LOCATION: On Route 53.
FACILITIES: Open May - Oct.; 150 sites; water and bathroom facilities; sanitary station; electrical hookup; trailer village vehicle sites; laundry; picnic area; swimming; boating; tent camping.

Stowe

GOLD BROOK CAMPGROUND
(802) 253-7683
LOCATION: On Route 100.
FACILITIES: Open year round; 100 sites; water and bathroom facilities; sanitary station; electrical hookup; trailer village vehicle sites; picnic area; swimming; hunting; fishing; hiking; tent camping.

Townshend

BALD MOUNTAIN CAMPGROUND
(802) 365-7510
LOCATION: On State Forest Road.
FACILITIES: Open year round; 140 sites; water and bathroom facilities; sanitary station; electrical hookup; trailer village vehicle sites; laundry; swimming; hiking; tent camping.

CAMPERAMA RESORT CAMPGROUND
(802) 365-4451
LOCATION: On Route 30.
FACILITIES: Open May - Oct.; 250 sites; water and bathroom facilities; sanitary station; electrical hookup; trailer village vehicle sites; picnic area; swimming; tent camping.

RESORTS & BEACHES

Burlington

LAKE CHAMPLAIN ISLANDS - Warm summer days and cool nights are ideal for swimming, boating, camping, golfing or whatever your favorite sport is. Or maybe you just want to rent one of the many cottages available on the islands and relax in the unhurried atmosphere of the country. As the leaves turn bright red and gold, pick your own apples from the island's famous apple orchards. And when the snows come, bundle up for skiing, snowmobiling and sledding in a winter playground of fun and adventure.

BOATING AREAS

See State Parks and State Forests.

BICYCLE TRAILS

ALL-STATE TRAIL - 665 mi.; hilly terrain, long distances; 10-speed bicycle is necessary.

A long tour of Vermont that starts and ends in Massachusetts and includes small portions of New York and Quebec and requires a lot of planning. It is a fine trip for a group of fairly experienced riders who want to bicycle in a scenic area for two to four weeks. You will need to check a good state map closely.

Trail: Stockbridge, MA, to Williamstown, MA - Routes 102, 41, 20, 22, 43. Williamstown, MA, to Manchester, VT - proceed with caution on Route 7. Avoid Sun. and holidays. Manchester to West Castleton - West Road, Routes 30, 4A. West Castleton to Middlebury - Route 30. Middlebury to Shelburne - Route 116 and Falls Road. (Don't take Route 7 as an alternate.) Shelburne to Jeffersonville - follow un-numbered road to Mechanicsville, Richmond, Jericho Center, Underhill Flats, Underhill Center, Pleasant Valley, Cambridge, and Jeffersonville. Jeffersonville to Richford - Routes 109, 118, and 105. Richford to Lowell - Routes 105, 105A into Canada, 101 and 100. Lowell to Craftsbury Common. Craftsbury Common to Montpelier - Route 14, Vincent Flats Road, Cherry Hill Road. Montpelier to South Royalton - Routes 12, 107, 14. South Royalton to Ludlow - Routes 107, 12, 106, 131, and 103. Ludlow to Putney - Routes 103, 35, 121 and through Westminister West. Putney to Northfield, MA - Routes 5, 123, 12, and 63. Northfield, MA to Sunderland, MA - Take Route 63 south ½ mi. to Route 10 west. Turn left off Route 10 toward Mt. Hermon, Gill and Mantague City. This road joins Route 5 north of Deerfield. Proceed on Route 5 south to Route 116. Head east on 116 to Sunderland. Sunderland to Windsor State Forest - take Route 116 to Savoy. Windsor State Forest to Stockbridge - Routes 116, 8A, 9, 8, 20, 41 and 102.

GREEN MOUNTAIN TRAIL - 150 mi.; low mountains, gravel trails; 10-speed bicycle necessary.

On this ride you will travel through much of the Green Mountain chain of Vermont.

Summer is good for this trip, but for autumn color select late Sept. or Oct.

Trail: Ludlow on Route 100 to Rochester to Warren to Waterbury Center to Eden, turn on Route 118 to Montgomery, Richford to East Franklin.

TRAILS

There are no National Trails System Foot Trails in Vermont.

SKI AREAS

Barnard

SONNENBERG (SUNNY MOUNTAIN)
(802) 234-9874
LOCATION: East of Barnard on East Barnard Road.
FACILITIES: 2 pomas; ski instruction; ski rental; restaurants; lodging.

Bolton

BOLTON VALLEY
(802) 434-2131
LOCATION: 4 mi. off Route 2 between exits 10 & 11 on I-89.
FACILITIES: 4 double chairlifts; ski instruction; ski rental; nursery; restaurants; lodging.

Brattleboro

LIVING MEMORIAL PARK
(802) 454-5808
LOCATION: On Route 9, west of Brattleboro.
FACILITIES: 1 T-bar; ski instruction; ski rental; restaurants; lodging.

Brownsville

MT. ASCUTNEY
(802) 484-7711
LOCATION: On Route 44 in Brownsville.
FACILITIES: 2 double chairlifts; 3 T-bars; ski instruction; ski rental; nursery; restaurants; lodging.

Chittenden

APPLE HILL
(802) 483-2311
LOCATION: 10 mi. northeast of Rutland off Route 4.
FACILITIES: 1 T-bar; ski instruction; ski rental; restaurants; lodging.

East Burke

BURKE MOUNTAIN
(802) 626-3305
LOCATION: Just off Route 114, 8 mi. north of Lyndonville, I-91 exit 24.
FACILITIES: 2 double chairlifts; 1 T-bar; 2 pomas; ski instruction; ski rental; nursery; restaurants; lodging.

Jay

JAY PEAK INCORPORATED
(802) 988-2611

VERMONT

SKI AREAS (continued)

LOCATION: 8 mi. west of North Troy off Route 101 on Route 242.
FACILITIES: 2 double chairlifts; 3 T-bars; 1 tram; ski instruction; ski rental; restaurants; lodging.

Jeffersonville

SMUGGLERS' NOTCH
(802) 644-8851
LOCATION: On Route 108, 5 mi. south of Jeffersonville.
FACILITIES: 3 double chairlifts; 1 tow rope; ski instruction; ski rental; nursery; restaurants; lodging.

Killington

KILLINGTON
(802) 422-3333
LOCATION: 11 mi. east of Rutland off junction U.S. 4 and Route 100 N.
FACILITIES: 3 triple chairlifts; 7 double chairlifts; 1 poma lift; 1 gondola; ski instruction; ski rental; restaurants; lodging.

Londonderry

MAGIC MOUNTAIN
(802) 824-5566
LOCATION: 2½ mi. east of Londonderry on Route 11.
FACILITIES: 3 double chairlifts; 1 T-bar; 1 mini ski school lift; ski instruction; ski rental; nursery; restaurants; lodging.

Ludlow

OKEMO MOUNTAIN
(802) 228-4041
LOCATION: 1 mi. north of Ludlow.
FACILITIES: 3 double chairlifts; 6 poma lifts; ski instruction; ski rental; nursery; restaurants; lodging.

Lyndonville

LYNDON OUTING CLUB
(802) 626-9876
LOCATION: 1 mi. east of Lyndonville.
FACILITIES: 1 T-bar; 1 tow rope; ski instruction; ski rental; nursery; restaurants; lodging.

Manchester

SNOW VALLEY
(802) 297-1000
LOCATION: On Route 30, 1 mi. south of Routes 11 and 30 intersection.
FACILITIES: 1 double chairlift; 1 T-bar; 1 poma lift; 1 mitey mite; ski instruction; ski rental; nursery; restaurants; lodging.

Manchester Center

BROMLEY MOUNTAIN
(802) 824-5522
LOCATION: On Route 11 in Peru.
FACILITIES: 5 double chairlifts; 1 J-bar; ski instruction; ski rental; nursery; restaurants; lodging.

Marlboro

HOGBACK
(802) 464-5494
LOCATION: On Route 9, 15 mi. west of Brattleboro.
FACILITIES: 4 T-bars; ski instruction; ski rental; restaurants; lodging.

Middlebury

MIDDLEBURY COLLEGE SNOW BOWL
(802) 388-4356
LOCATION: On Route 125, 9 mi. off Route 7 at East Middlebury.
FACILITIES: 1 chairlift; 3 poma lifts; ski instruction; ski rental; restaurants; lodging.

Mount Snow

MOUNT SNOW SKI RESORT
(802) 464-3333
LOCATION: On Route 100, 9 mi. north of Wilmington.
FACILITIES: 1 triple chairlift; 10 double chairlifts; 2 gondolas; ski instruction; ski rental; nursery; restaurants; lodging.

Newport

CHAMBERLIN BIRCH
(802) 334-6345
LOCATION: 2 mi. south of Newport on Lower Glen Road.
FACILITIES: 1 tow rope; ski instruction; ski rental; restaurants; lodging.

Northfield

NORWICH UNIVERSITY SKI AREA
(802) 485-9311
LOCATION: 5 mi. north of Northfield.
FACILITIES: 1 double chairlift; 1 poma; 1 mitey mite; ski instruction; ski rental; nursery; restaurants; lodging.

Plymouth Union

ROUND TOP MOUNTAIN
(802) 672-5152
LOCATION: On Route 100.
FACILITIES: 2 double chairlifts; 1 T-bar; 1 handlebar tow; ski instruction; ski rental; nursery; restaurants; lodging.

Randolph

PINNACLE MT.
(802) 728-3300
LOCATION: 2 mi. south of exit 4, I-89.
FACILITIES: 2 poma lifts; ski instruction; ski rental; nursery; restaurants; lodging.

Readsboro

DUTCH MT.
(802) 423-5312
LOCATION: 12 mi. north of North Adams, MA., on Routes 8 and 100.
FACILITIES: 1 T-bar; 1 J-Bar; 1 tow rope; ski instruction; ski rental; nursery; restaurants; lodging.

SKI AREAS (continued)

Richmond

COCHRAN
(802) 434-2479
LOCATION: 1 mi. south of Old Round Church on Cochran Road.
FACILITIES: 1 T-bar; 2 tow ropes; 1 mitey mite; ski instruction; ski rental; restaurants; lodging.

Rutland

PICO
(802) 775-4345
LOCATION: On Route 4, 9 mi. east of Rutland.
FACILITIES: 1 triple chairlift; 5 double chairlifts; 2 T-bars; 1 poma lift; ski instruction; ski rental; nursery; restaurants; lodging.

Springfield

SPRINGFIELD SKI AREA
(802) 885-2727
LOCATION: 139 Main Street.
FACILITIES: 1 tow rope; ski instruction; ski rental; restaurants; lodging.

Stowe

STOWE (MT. MANSFIELD)
(802) 253-7311
LOCATION: On Route 108, 6 mi. northwest of Stowe Village.
FACILITIES: 3 double chairlifts; 1 single chairlift; 3 T-bars; 1 gondola; ski instruction; ski rental; nursery; restaurants; lodging.

Stratton Mountain

STRATTON MOUNTAIN
(802) 297-2200
LOCATION: 4 mi. off Route 30.
FACILITIES: 1 triple chairlift; 7 double chairlifts; ski instruction; ski rental; nursery; restaurants; lodging.

Underhill Center

UNDERHILL SKI BOWL
(802) 899-4677
LOCATION: 1½ mi. east of Underhill Center on Stevensville Road.
FACILITIES: 1 tow rope; 1 poma lift; ski instruction; ski rental; restaurants; lodging.

Waitsfield

GLEN ELLEN
(802) 496-3301
LOCATION: 3 mi. west of Waitsfield on Route 100.
FACILITIES: 4 double chairlifts; 1 T-bar; ski instruction; ski rental; nursery; restaurants; lodging.

MAD RIVER GLEN
(802) 496-3551
LOCATION: On Route 17, 5 mi. off Route 100 at Waitsfield.
FACILITIES: 3 double chairlifts; 1 single chairlift; ski instruction; ski rental; nursery; restaurants; lodging.

Warren

SUGARBUSH VALLEY
(802) 583-2381
LOCATION: Between Warren and Waitsfield.
FACILITIES: 1 triple chairlift; 4 double chairlifts; 2 poma lifts; 1 gondola; ski instruction; ski rental; nursery; restaurants; lodging.

West Dover

CARINTHIA
(802) 464-5461
LOCATION: On Route 100, adjacent to Mount Snow.
FACILITIES: 1 T-bar; 1 tow rope; ski instruction; ski rental; nursery; restaurants; lodging.

West Dummerston

MAPLE VALLEY
(802) 254-6083
LOCATION: On Route 30 near Brattleboro.
FACILITIES: 2 double chairlifts; 1 T-bar; 1 tow rope; ski instruction; ski rental; nursery; restaurants; lodging.

Wilmington

HAYSTACK
(802) 464-5321
LOCATION: 2½ mi. north of Wilmington on Route 100 to Coldbrook Road.
FACILITIES: 2 double chairlifts; 1 shuttle chairlift; 3 T-bars; ski instruction; ski rental; nursery; restaurants; lodging.

Windham

TIMBER RIDGE
(802) 824-6806
LOCATION: 7 mi. east of Londonderry on Route 121.
FACILITIES: 1 chairlift; 1 T-bar; ski instruction; ski rental; restaurants; lodging.

Woodstock

SUICIDE SIX
(802) 457-1666
LOCATION: Near Woodstock.
FACILITIES: 2 double chairlifts; 1 J-bar; ski instruction; ski rental; restaurants; lodging.

AMUSEMENT PARKS & ATTRACTIONS

Bellows Falls

STEAMTOWN U.S.A. (Attraction)
P.O. Box 71
Bellows Falls, VT 05101
(802) 463-3937
FACILITIES: Museum of Steam Railroadiana; steam train excursions; exhibits; refreshment stands; picnic facilities; free parking.

Putney

SANTA'S LAND U.S.A.
U.S. 5 & Interstate 91

VERMONT

AMUSEMENT PARKS (continued)

Putney, VT 05346
(802) 387-5550
FACILITIES: Major ride; refreshment stand;
restaurant; post office; candlemaking; glass
blowing; antique German carousel; picnic
facilities; zoo; animal forest; Santa's workshop; free movies; Santa Claus in person; free
parking.

STATE FAIR

Vermont State Fair
Rutland Fairgrounds
Rutland, VT 05701
(802) 775-5200
DATE: September

NATIONAL PARKS

There are no National Parks in Vermont.

NATIONAL FORESTS

National Forests
Eastern Region
633 West Wisconsin Avenue
Milwaukee, WI 53203
(414) 291-3693

Rutland

GREEN MOUNTAIN NATIONAL FOREST
ATTRACTIONS: Battlegrounds of Revolutionary and French and Indian Wars; winter
sports; hiking and bridle trails; deer, ruffed
grouse, rabbit, black bear hunting; fishing;
scenic drives.
FACILITIES: 29 camp and picnic sites, 10
picnic only; swimming site; Mount Snow and
Sugarbush Winter Sports Areas; summer resorts and famous New England inns; hotels;
cabins.
NEARBY TOWNS: Brandon, Burlington,
Manchester, Middlebury, Rochester.

STATE PARKS

Headquarters

Department of Forests, Parks and Recreation
Montpelier, VT 05602
(802) 828-3471

Bennington

WOODFORD STATE PARK
(802) 447-7169
LOCATION: 11 mi. east of Bennington on
Route 9.
FACILITIES: Open Jun. - Oct.; 104 sites; water and bathroom facilities; sanitary station;
trailer village vehicle sites; picnic area; swimming; boating; boat rental; hiking; tent camping.

Brattleboro

FORT DUMMER STATE PARK
(802) 254-2610
LOCATION: 2 mi. south of Brattleboro.
FACILITIES: Open Jun. - Oct.; 61 sites; water and bathroom facilities; sanitary station;
trailer village vehicle sites; hiking; tent camping.

Brookfield

ALLIS STATE PARK
(802) 276-2975
LOCATION: At Brookfield, 7 mi. south of
Northfield.
FACILITIES: Open Jun. - Oct.; 21 sites; water and bathroom facilities; sanitary station;
trailer village vehicle sites; picnic area; tent
camping.

East Dorset

EMERALD LAKE STATE PARK
(802) 362-1655
LOCATION: 22 mi. south on U.S. 7 at North
Dorset.
FACILITIES: Open Jun. - Oct.; 105 sites; water and bathroom facilities; sanitary station;
trailer village vehicle sites; picnic area; swimming; boating; boat rental; hiking; tent camping.

Enosburg Falls

LAKE CARMI STATE PARK
(802) 933-8383
LOCATION: 17 mi. northeast of St. Albans
on Lake Carmi.
FACILITIES: Open Jun. - Oct.; 177 sites; water and bathroom facilities; sanitary station;
trailer village vehicle sites; picnic area; food
service; swimming; boating; boat rental; tent
camping.

Fair Haven

BOMOSEEN STATE PARK
(802) 265-4242
LOCATION: 21 mi. northwest of Rutland.
FACILITIES: Open Jun. - Oct.; 134 sites; water and bathroom facilities; sanitary station;
trailer village vehicle sites; picnic area; food
service; swimming; boating; boat rental; hiking; tent camping.

Grand Isle

GRAND ISLE STATE PARK
(802) 372-4300
LOCATION: 20 mi. northwest of Burlington
on Lake Champlain.
FACILITIES: Open Jun. - Oct.; 154 sites; water and bathroom facilities; sanitary station;
trailer village vehicle sites; food service; swimming; boating; boat rental; tent camping.

Lake Elmore

ELMORE STATE PARK
(802) 888-2982
LOCATION: 5 mi. southeast of Morrisville
on Route 12.
FACILITIES: Open Jun. - Oct.; 64 sites; wa-

STATE PARKS (continued)

ter and bathroom facilities; sanitary station; trailer village vehicle sites; picnic area; food service; swimming; boating; boat rental; hiking; tent camping.

North Hero

NORTH HERO STATE PARK
(802) 372-8727
LOCATION: 8 mi. north of North Hero village on Lake Champlain.
FACILITIES: Open Jun. - Oct.; 77 sites; water and bathroom facilities; sanitary station; trailer village vehicle sites; swimming; boating; hiking; tent camping.

North Stratford

MAIDSTONE STATE PARK
(802) 676-3930
LOCATION: 27 mi. southeast of Island Pond on Maidstone Lake.
FACILITIES: Open Jun. - Oct.; 83 sites; water and bathroom facilities; sanitary station; trailer village vehicle sites; picnic area; swimming; boating; boat rental; hiking; tent camping.

St. Albans Bay

BURTON ISLAND STATE PARK
(802) 524-6353
LOCATION: ½ mi. southwest of St. Albans Point (accessible only by boat).
FACILITIES: Open Jun. - Oct.; 52 sites; water and bathroom facilities; electrical hookup; trailer village vehicle sites; picnic area; swimming; boating; boat rental; hiking; tent camping.

Vergennes

BUTTON BAY STATE PARK
(802) 475-2377
LOCATION: 7 mi. west of Vergennes.
FACILITIES: Open Jun. - Oct.; 70 sites; water and bathroom facilities; sanitary station; trailer village vehicle sites; picnic area; swimming; boating; boat rental; fishing; tent camping.

Windsor

ASCUTNEY STATE PARK
(802) 674-2060
LOCATION: 3 mi. northeast of Ascutney Village.
FACILITIES: Open Jun. - Oct.; 49 sites; water and bathroom facilities; sanitary station; trailer village vehicle sites; picnic area; tent camping.

STATE FORESTS

Department of Forests, Parks and Recreation
Montpelier, VT 05602
(802) 828-3471

Marshfield

GROTON STATE FOREST

(802) 584-3820
LOCATION: Midway between Montpelier and St. Johnsbury.
FACILITIES: Open Jun. - Oct.; 223 sites; water and bathroom facilities; sanitary station; trailer village vehicle sites; picnic area; food service; swimming; boating; boat rental; hunting; fishing; hiking; tent camping.

Plymouth

CALVIN COOLIDGE STATE FOREST
(802) 672-3612
LOCATION: 2 mi. north on Route 100A.
FACILITIES: Open Jun. - Oct.; 60 sites; sanitary station; trailer village vehicle sites; picnic area; hiking; tent camping.

Waterbury

MOUNT MANSFIELD STATE FOREST
(802) 244-7103
LOCATION: 6 mi. northwest of Waterbury.
FACILITIES: Open Jun. - Oct.; 109 sites; water and bathroom facilities; sanitary station; trailer village vehicle sites; picnic area; swimming; hiking; tent camping.

HISTORIC SITES

Fairfield

BIRTHPLACE OF CHESTER A. ARTHUR - A modest one-story clapboard house on a remote ledge hillside northeast of Fairfield Station. The original house of the 21st President disappeared long ago, but a replica was reconstructed from a photograph. Located off Route 36.

Middlebury

U.V.M. MORGAN HORSE FARM - World-famous home of the Morgan, 60 registered stallions, mares, foals. Statue of Justin Morgan. Guided tours, slide-tape show. Located 2 mi. from Middlebury.

Plymouth Notch

BIRTHPLACE OF CALVIN COOLIDGE - Boyhood home of the 30th President from the time he was 4 years old through years in local grade school and later at Black River Academy in neighboring Ludlow. Located on Route 100A.

Shelburne

SHELBURNE MUSEUM - Over 3 centuries of Americana. 35 buildings on 45 acres. Electra Havemeyer Webb Memorial Building with founders' European paintings and furniture. American art galleries. Early furnished homes. Sidewheeler S.S. Ticonderoga and lighthouse. R.R. station and private car. Located on U.S. 7.

Townshend

SCOTT COVERED BRIDGE - The longest single span (over the West River) of any bridge in the state. The total length of its

VERMONT

three spans is 276 feet. Located on Route 30.

Windsor

THE OLD CONSTITUTION HOUSE - On July 8, 1777, meeting in a tavern at Windsor, representatives of the New Hampshire Grants adopted the first Constitution of the "free and independent State of Vermont." Since the January convention at Westminister earlier the same year when the Grants had declared their independence, the area had been known as the "separate state of New Connecticut." Located on Route 5.

HOSTELS

Burlington

TRINITY COLLEGE
Colchester Avenue
Burlington, VT 05401
(802) 864-7784
FACILITIES: Open Jul. 1 - Aug. 14; 50 beds, men; 100 beds, women; modern bathroom; nearest hostel: Waterbury Center; overnight charges: $2.50; no blankets or pillows; houseparent: Linda Chiasson.

Johnson

JOHNSON STATE COLLEGE
Sterling House
c/o Summer Session
Johnson, VT 05656
(802) 635-2356 Ext. 234
FACILITIES: Open Jun. 15 - Aug. 20; 30 beds, men; 30 beds, women; modern bathroom; overnight charges: $2; houseparent: J. MacDowell.

Ludlow

LUDLOW YOUTH HOSTEL
44 Pleasant Street
Ludlow, VT 05149
(802) 228-8475
FACILITIES: Open year round; 20 beds, men; 20 beds, women; modern bathroom; nearest hostel: Grantham, NH; overnight charges: $3 summer; $4 - $5 winter; houseparent: Richard Russo.

Rochester

SCHOOL HOUSE YOUTH HOSTEL
Rochester, VT 05767
(802) 767-9384
FACILITIES: Open May 15 - Oct. 15, Nov. 15 - Apr. 15; 35 beds men; 35 beds, women; modern bathroom; nearest hostels: Ludlow, 44 mi. south; Warren, 25 mi. north; overnight charges: $2 summer; $4 winter; houseparent: David Marmor.

Warren

OLD HOMESTEAD YOUTH HOSTEL
2½ Miles E. Warren Road
Warren, VT 05674
(802) 496-3744

FACILITIES: Open year round; 45 beds, men; 45 beds, women; modern bathroom; nearest hostel: Waterbury Center, 22 mi. north; overnight charges: $2.50; houseparent: Mrs. Thelma Ricketts.

Waterbury Center

SKI HOSTEL LODGE YOUTH HOSTEL
Waterbury, VT 05677
(802) 244-8859
FACILITIES: Open May 1 - Nov. 15; 80 beds, men; 80 beds, women; modern bathroom; nearest hostel: Warren, 22 mi.; overnight charges: $2.50; houseparent: Mrs. Martha Guthridge.

POINTS OF INTEREST

Barre

ROCK OF AGES GRANITE QUARRIES - World's largest monumental granite quarry and craftsman center. Quarry train ride Jun. 1 - Aug. 31. Quarry and plant operations open to visitors year round except Jul. 4 - 18.

Bellows Falls

STEAMTOWN FOUNDATIONS - World's largest collection of steam locomotives and railroad equipment. Located on Route 5.

Cabot

CABOT FARMERS' CO-OPERATIVE - New England's largest and most modern manufacturer of cheddar cheese and butter. Large picture windows allow you to view the manufacture of famous "Cabot Vermont Cheddar Cheese." Located in the village of Cabot.

Cavendish

CAVENDISH MILLS - Grist mill and saw mill location since 1784, on the beautiful Black River. Contains original equipment, tools, and record books on display. Located just off Route 131 on Carlton Road.

Healdville

CROWLEY CHEESE FACTORY - Vermont's oldest and only old-time cheese factory. Cheese made by hand just as it was in the last century. Located 2 mi. off Route 103 between Ludlow and Rutland.

Old Bennington

BENNINGTON MUSEUM - One of America's outstanding regional museums. Exhibits include Bennington pottery, American glass, fine art, military history, the famous Bennington flag, Grandma Moses paintings, Grandma Moses schoolhouse Museum. Located 1 mi. west of junction of Route 9 and U.S. 7.

Proctor

OTTER VALLEY RAILROAD - 8 mi. long scenic tourist railroad ride up mountain, past

POINTS OF INTEREST (continued)

abandoned quarries to panoramic views of Otter Valley and Green Mountains. Located on Route 3, northwest of Rutland.

WILSON CASTLE - Architectural masterpiece built in the middle of the 19th century. The furnishings are European and Far Eastern. Located on West Proctor Road.

Quechee

DEWEY'S AT QUECHEE GORGE ("Vermont's Little Grand Canyon") - A mile-long chasm through which the Ottauquechee River flows at a depth of 162 feet below the new highway bridge on U.S. 4. Vermont's unique natural wonder.

St. Johnsbury

MAPLE GROVE MAPLE MUSEUM - World's largest maple candy factory. Also Old Sugar House Museum with old and new sugaring equipment. Located on Route 2.

Vergennes

KENNEDY BROS., INC. - Watch as raw Vermont pine wood is transformed into fine wooden furniture and gift accessories, through large picture windows. Located on Route 22A, just off U.S. 7.

Weston

WESTON BOWL MILL - Watch bowls and many other wood products being made. A magnificent collection of Vermont-made woodenware is on display in the Annex. Located on Route 100 in Weston.

VIRGINIA

Virginia, the site of this country's first settlement, entered the Union in 1788 as the tenth state. One hundred and sixty-nine years after the Pilgrims established a colony in Jamestown, Richard Lee introduced a motion before the Continental Congress to sever all ties with England. Shortly thereafter, George Washington, another Virginian, took to the field as Commander-in-Chief of the Continental Army, finally defeating the enemy in Yorktown where General Cornwallis surrendered. Thomas Jefferson, also from Virginia, penned the Declaration of Independence and became this country's third President.

Virginia's leading agricultural commodity, tobacco, has been a significant contributor to its economy since the time of John Rolfe, the husband of Pocahontas, who produced the state's first crop.

In a state so rich in history and historic sites, tourism accounts for a sizeable portion of the overall income.

State capital: Richmond. State bird: Cardinal. State tree: American dogwood. State flower: American dogwood.

WEATHER

Virginia, located on the east coast of the North American continent, is triangular in shape, with the longest north-south distance about 200 miles and the longest east-west distance more than 400 miles. There are 40,815 square miles, of which 1,200 square miles are inland waters. The state is composed of three natural topographic regions; namely, the Tidewater or coastal plains area, the Piedmont plateau or middle Virginia, and the western mountain region.

The climate of Virginia is determined by its proximity to the Atlantic Ocean, latitude, and topography. The mountains provide the usual elevation effects on temperatures, which are distinctly lower in this section, and there are wide variations over short distances as elevations change. Summers in the mountains are comparatively cool, and winters are more severe. In addition, these mountains produce various steering, blocking, and modifying effects on storms and general air movements in their vicinity. Temperature variations within the state due to latitude alone are very small; yearly averages are only 2 to 3 degrees F higher in the south than in the north. The longitudinal variations, however, show a sharper contrast, from the mountain extremes in the west toward an ocean influence in the east.

Average daily temperature for each month.

	Eastern	Western
Jan.	48.4 to 25.8	41.8 to 21.7
Feb.	51.0 to 27.6	44.1 to 23.0
Mar.	59.1 to 34.0	52.2 to 29.1
Apr.	70.7 to 43.8	64.2 to 38.6
May	78.3 to 53.1	73.4 to 47.2
Jun.	85.2 to 61.5	79.8 to 54.6
Jul.	88.6 to 65.9	82.7 to 58.6
Aug.	87.0 to 64.9	81.4 to 58.0
Sept.	81.1 to 57.6	75.3 to 51.6
Oct.	71.3 to 45.8	65.4 to 41.2
Nov.	61.1 to 35.8	53.2 to 31.7
Dec.	50.5 to 28.2	43.4 to 24.5
Year	69.4 to 45.3	63.1 to 40.0

VIRGINIA

STATE CHAMBER OF COMMERCE

Virginia State Chamber of Commerce
611 East Franklin Street
Richmond, VA 23219
(804) 643-7491

STATE & CITY TOURISM OFFICES

State

Virginia Division of Industrial Development
1010 State Office Building
Richmond, VA 23219
(804) 786-3791

Virginia State Travel Service
6 North Sixth Street
Richmond, VA 23219
(804) 786-4484

Local

Norfolk Convention and Visitor's Bureau
P.O. Box 238
Norfolk, VA 23501
(804) 441-5266

STATE HIGHWAY DEPARTMENT

Department of Highways and Transportation
1221 E. Broad Street
Richmond, VA 23219
(804) 786-2801

HIGHWAY WELCOMING CENTERS

Bracey

BRACEY CENTER - Interstate 85.

Bristol

BRISTOL CENTER - City of Bristol.

Clear Brook

CLEAR BROOK CENTER - Interstate 81.

Covington

COVINGTON CENTER - Interstate 64.

Fredericksburg

FREDERICKSBURG CENTER - Interstate 95.

Manassas

MANASSAS CENTER - Interstate 66.

STATE POLICE

Department of Public Safety
Richmond, VA 23261
(804) 272-1431

HUNTING & FISHING

Hunting

Landowners, their husbands or wives, children and minor grandchildren do not need a license to hunt, trap or fish within the boundaries of their own lands and inland waters. Tenants, on the land they rent and occupy, are not required to have a license, but must have the written permission of the landowners. Residents 65 years of age and over do not need a license to hunt or trap on private property in their county of residence. A lifetime license is available to residents over 65.

Those entitled to buy a resident license are: (1) persons who have physically resided in the city, county or state for six consecutive months immediately preceding the date of application for license; (2) persons who have been domiciliary residents of the state for at least two months upon approval of a completed affidavit to be furnished by the Game Commission. Legal voters, members of the Armed Forces on active duty stationed in Virginia, and students residing in Virginia who are enrolled in bona fide Virginia schools also qualify. Unnaturalized owners of real property in Virginia who have resided in a county for five years immediately prior to making application for a license may apply for resident licenses only in the county where they qualify.

Resident

County or city residents, to hunt & fish in county or city of residence, $5; state resident to hunt statewide, $5; state resident big-game license to hunt bear, deer and turkey statewide required in addition to county or state hunting license, $5; special stamp to hunt deer, bear in Alleghany, Bath, Bland, Botetourt, Craig, Floyd, Giles, Grayson, Highland, Patrick, Rockbridge, Russell, Scott, Smyth, Tazewell, Washington, Wise and Wythe counties, in addition to other licenses, and sold only by the clerks of those counties, $1; lifetime hunting, trapping & fishing licenses for residents 65 years of age and over, available from the commissioner's Richmond office only, $5; national forest permit (stamp) to hunt, fish or trap on national forests, required in addition to hunting license, $1; permit to hunt or trap on Appomattox-Buckingham-Cumberland-Prince Edward and Pocahontas state forests (sold by the Division of Forestry) may be obtained from forest headquarters or clerk of court in local counties, $1; federal migratory bird hunting stamp to take migratory waterfowl, required of persons 16 years of age and over, in addition to hunting license and sold at U.S. Post Offices, $5; county resident to trap in county of residence, $5; state resident to trap statewide, $15.

HUNTING & FISHING (continued)

Non-resident

Hunting statewide, $20; big-game license to hunt bear, deer and turkey statewide, required in addition to hunting license, $20; hunting on shooting preserves, only obtainable in counties in which preserves are located, $5; trap statewide, $50.

Fishing

Non-resident licenses are required for all visitors to Virginia who fish in waters where freshwater fish are found, except for children under 12 accompanied by licensed adult, and guests fishing in individually owned ponds.

Resident

Annual license, $10; trout license, $7.50; 5-day license, daily fee; net permit, $2; national forest stamp, $1.

Non-resident

Annual, $10; 5-day license, $3.

For more information contact:

Commission of Game and Inland Fisheries
P.O. Box 11104
Richmond, VA 23230
(804) 257-1000

CAMPGROUNDS

Private

Berryville

WATERMELON PARK CAMPGROUND
(703) 955-1121
LOCATION: 5½ mi. southeast of Berryville.
FACILITIES: Open Apr. - Nov.; 500 sites; water and bathroom facilities; sanitary station; electrical hookup; trailer village vehicle sites; food service; swimming; fishing; tent camping.

Cheriton

CHERRYSTONE BAYSHORE CAMP-GROUND
(804) 331-3063
LOCATION: On Chesapeake Bay, on Route 680, 2 mi. west of U.S. 13.
FACILITIES: Open Apr. 1 - Nov. 30; 500 sites; water and bathroom facilities; sanitary station; electrical hookup; trailer village vehicle sites; laundry; swimming; fishing; tent camping.

Chincoteague

CAMPERS RANCH CAMPGROUND
(804) 336-6371
LOCATION: On Chincoteague Island, 13 mi. east of U.S. 13 via Route 175.
FACILITIES: Open Apr. - Nov.; 325 sites; water and bathroom facilities; sanitary station; electrical hookup; trailer village vehicle

sites; laundry; food service; tent camping.

INLET VIEW WATERFRONT CAMP-GROUND
(804) 336-5126
LOCATION: At southern end of Chincoteague Island, 11 mi. east of U.S. 13 via Route 175.
FACILITIES: Open Mar. - Jan.; 200 sites; water and bathroom facilities; sanitary station; electrical hookup; trailer village vehicle sites; laundry; food service; swimming; fishing; tent camping.

MADDOX SAFARI CAMPGROUND
(804) 336-6648
LOCATION: On Maddox Boulevard, Chincoteague Island, 11 mi. east of U.S. 13 via Route 175.
FACILITIES: Open year round; 310 sites; water and bathroom facilities; sanitary station; electrical hookup; trailer village vehicle sites; food service; swimming; tent camping.

TOM'S COVE CAMPGROUND
(804) 336-6498
LOCATION: On Tom's Cove Waterfront, southeast of Chincoteague Island via Route 175 from U.S. 13.
FACILITIES: Open year round; 600 sites; water and bathroom facilities; sanitary station; electrical hookup; trailer village vehicle sites; laundry; food service; swimming; fishing; tent camping.

Colonial Beach

MONROE BAY CAMPGROUND
(804) 224-6411
LOCATION: On Potomac River on Route 628, 2 mi. east of Route 205.
FACILITIES: Open Apr. 1 - Nov. 15; 370 sites; water and bathroom facilities; sanitary station; electrical hookup; trailer village vehicle sites; food service; swimming; fishing; tent camping.

Deltaville

BUSH PARK CAMPGROUND
(804) 776-3135
LOCATION: At mouth of Rappahannock River near Deltaville.
FACILITIES: Open Apr. - Nov.; 400 sites; water and bathroom facilities; sanitary station; electrical hookup; trailer village vehicle sites; food service; swimming; fishing; tent camping.

Lenexa

CHICKAHOMINY OUTPOST CAMP-GROUND
(804) 966-2318
LOCATION: 1 mi. south of U.S. 60 on Chickahominy River.
FACILITIES: Open year round; 200 sites; water and bathroom facilities; sanitary station; electrical hookup; trailer village vehicle sites; laundry; food service; fishing; tent camping.

ED ALLEN'S CAMPGROUND
(804) 966-2582

VIRGINIA

CAMPGROUNDS (continued)

LOCATION: 16 mi. east of Williamsburg on Chickahominy River.
FACILITIES: Open year round; 200 sites; water and bathroom facilities; sanitary station; electrical hookup; trailer village vehicle sites; laundry; swimming; fishing; tent camping.

Saluda

CAMP NIMCOCK
(804) 758-2744
LOCATION: 2¼ mi. north of Saluda.
FACILITIES: Open year round; 200 sites; water and bathroom facilities; sanitary station; electrical hookup; trailer village vehicle sites; food service; swimming; fishing; tent camping.

CYPRESS SHORES KOA KAMPGROUND
(804) 693-3792
LOCATION: 8 mi. southeast of Saluda.
FACILITIES: Open Apr. - Nov.; 300 sites; water and bathroom facilities; sanitary station; electrical hookup; trailer village vehicle sites; laundry; food service; swimming; fishing; tent camping.

South Hill

LAKE GASTON AMERICAMP
(804) 636-2668
LOCATION: On Lake Gaston, 12 mi. south of South Hill via I-85 and Route 637.
FACILITIES: Open Mar. 11 - Nov. 30; 240 sites; water and bathroom facilities; sanitary station; electrical hookup; trailer village vehicle sites; laundry; food service; swimming; fishing; tent camping.

Topping

GREY'S POINT CAMP
(804) 758-2485
LOCATION: On Grey's Point near southern end of Route 3 bridge across the Rappahannock River near Chesapeake Bay.
FACILITIES: Open Apr. - Jan.; 400 sites; water and bathroom facilities; electrical hookup; trailer village vehicle sites; food service; swimming; fishing; tent camping.

Virginia Beach

NORTH BAY SHORE FAMILY CAMPGROUND
(804) 426-7911
LOCATION: 12 mi. south of Virginia Beach via Route 615.
FACILITIES: Open Apr. 1 - Oct. 15; 200 sites; water and bathroom facilities; sanitary station; electrical hookup; trailer village vehicle sites; food service; fishing; tent camping.

SURFSIDE AT SANDBRIDGE CAMPGROUND
(804) 426-2911
LOCATION: 15 mi. south of Virginia Beach via Route 149 and Sandbridge Road.
FACILITIES: Open year round; 225 sites; water and bathroom facilities; sanitary station; electrical hookup; trailer village vehicle sites; swimming; fishing; tent camping.

VIRGINIA BEACH KOA KAMPGROUND
(804) 428-1444
LOCATION: At Prosperity Road, 3 mi. south of Rudee Inlet Bridge.
FACILITIES: Open Apr. - Nov.; 700 sites; water and bathroom facilities; sanitary station; electrical hookup; trailer village vehicle sites; laundry; food service; swimming; fishing; tent camping.

Williamsburg

HOLIDAY INN TRAV-L PARK
(804) 229-1453
LOCATION: 9 mi. west of Williamsburg at Chickahominy River.
FACILITIES: Open year round; 332 sites; water and bathroom facilities; sanitary station; electrical hookup; trailer village vehicle sites; laundry; swimming; fishing; tent camping.

JAMESTOWN BEACH CAMPSITES
(804) 229-8366
LOCATION: 3½ mi. south of Williamsburg.
FACILITIES: Open year round; 500 sites; water and bathroom facilities; sanitary station; electrical hookup; trailer village vehicle sites; laundry; food service; swimming; fishing; tent camping.

NEWPORT NEWS PARK CAMPGROUND
(804) 887-5381
LOCATION: 8 mi. east of Williamsburg.
FACILITIES: Open year round; 200 sites; water and bathroom facilities; sanitary station; electrical hookup; trailer village vehicle sites; laundry; fishing; tent camping.

WILLIAMSBURG CAMPSITES
(804) 564-3101
LOCATION: 5 mi. west of Williamsburg on U.S. 60.
FACILITIES: Open year round; 250 sites; water and bathroom facilities; sanitary station; electrical hookup; trailer village vehicle sites; laundry; swimming; tent camping.

RESORTS & BEACHES

Virginia Beach

VIRGINIA BEACH AREA - With the Gulf Stream practically next door, swimmers and surfers frolic in the warm ocean waters from early spring to late fall. And there's plenty of sunshine, too, which makes for great golfing, tennis, fishing or strolling along the 28 miles of soft, sandy beaches.

BOATING AREAS

Abingdon

SOUTH HOLSTON RESERVOIR
LOCATION: Southeast of Abingdon off Route 75.
FACILITIES: Launching.

Boydton

BUGGS ISLAND LAKE
LOCATION: Near Boydton.

BOATING AREAS (continued)

FACILITIES: Launching.

Gasburg

LAKE GASTON
LOCATION: Near Gaston off Route 626.
FACILITIES: Launching.

Gretna

LEESVILLE LAKE
LOCATION: North of Gretna off Route 29.
FACILITIES: Launching.

Halifax

KERR RESERVOIR
LOCATION: East of Halifax on Route 58.
FACILITIES: Launching.

Haysi

J.W. FLANNAGAN RESERVOIR
LOCATION: West of Haysi off Route 63.
FACILITIES: Launching.

Henry

PHILPOTT RESERVOIR
LOCATION: West of Henry on Route 605.
FACILITIES: Launching.

Huddleston

LEESVILLE RESERVOIR
LOCATION: South of Huddleston.
FACILITIES: Launching.

Leesville

LEESVILLE RESERVOIR
LOCATION: West of Leesville.
FACILITIES: Launching.

Mannboro

LAKE CHESDIN
LOCATION: Off Route 612.
FACILITIES: Launching.

Newport News

CHICKAHOMINY LAKE
LOCATION: Off Route 60, east of Providence Forge.
FACILITIES: Launching.

DIASCUND RESERVOIR
LOCATION: On Route 60, east of Providence Forge.
FACILITIES: Launching.

Penhook

SMITH MOUNTAIN LAKE
LOCATION: North of Penhook off Route 40.
FACILITIES: Launching.

SMITH MOUNTAIN RESERVOIR
LOCATION: Near Penhook off Route 40.
FACILITIES: Launching.

Radford

CLAYTOR LAKE
LOCATION: West of Radford.
FACILITIES: Launching.

Rocky Mount

SMITH MOUNTAIN RESERVOIR
LOCATION: North of Rocky Mountain.
FACILITIES: Launching.

Thornburg

LAKE ANNA
LOCATION: 20 mi. west of Thornburg.
FACILITIES: Launching.

Woodbridge

OCCOQUAN RESERVOIR
LOCATION: North of Woodbridge off Route 123.
FACILITIES: Launching.

BICYCLE TRAILS

See WEST VIRGINIA - Bartow Trail.

BURKE LAKE TRAIL - 36.3 mi.; hilly terrain; 10-speed bicycle recommended.
A loop tour through southern Fairfax County.
Trail: Springfield, west on Rolling Road, left on Burke Road, left on Burke Lake Road, left on Ox Road to Burke Lake Park, right on Henderson Road, left on Hampton Road, right on Ox Road, left on Furnace Road, left on Lorton Road, right back on Furnace Road, left on Old Colchester Road, right on Gunston Hall Road to Pohick Bay Regional Park, right back on Gunston Hall Road, right on Old Colchester Road, left on U.S. 1, right on Pohick Road, right on Rolling Road to Springfield.

CHARLOTTESVILLE TRAIL - 117.3 mi.; hilly terrain, sections of dirt trail; 10-speed bicycle recommended.
Originating at Mt. Vernon, this route explores rural Virginia on predominantly lightly-traveled back roads. Sections of the route are improved dirt and will be difficult with tubular tires or in the rain.
Trail: Mount Vernon to Pohick to Route 638, left on Route 641, left on Route 645, left on Route 610, right on Route 643, left on Route 612, right on Route 663, left on Route 667, left on Route 688, right on Route 234 at Lake Jackson, left on Route 649 to Brentsville to Aden, left on Route 612, right on Route 609, left on Route 806 to Morrisville to Kelley's Ford to Lignum, left on Route 647 to Rapidan to Orange, Route 20 south to Charlottesville to University of Virginia.

GREAT FALLS TRAIL - 18.6 mi.; rolling hills; 10-speed bicycle recommended.
A lightly-traveled route from Chain Bridge above the Chesapeake and Ohio Canal to Great Falls Park on Virginia bank of

VIRGINIA

BICYCLE TRAILS (continued)

the Potomac.

Trail: Chain Bridge, left on Glebe Road, right on Chesterbrook Road, left on Kirby Road, right on Great Falls Road, left on Idylwood Road, right ·on Williams Avenue, left on Electric Avenue, right on Woodford Road, left on Old Courthouse Road, right on Trap Road through Wolf Trap Farm Park, left on Towlson Road, left on Old Dominion Drive to Great Falls Park.

LEXINGTON TRAIL - 32 mi.; some hills; 10-speed bicycle recommended.

All roads are hard surfaced for this loop trip.

Trail: Lexington to Rockbridge Baths to George Washington National Forest to Goshen Pass and return.

MANASSAS TRAIL - 46 mi.; hilly terrain; 10-speed bicycle recommended.

A good one-day loop through rural Virginia countryside to the Manassas National Battlefield Park.

Trail: Start at Cardinal Forest Plaza Shopping Center, Springfield, right on Rolling Road, left on Burke Road, left on Burke Lake Road, right on Pohick Road, left on Ox Road (Route 123), right on Wolf Run Shoals Road to Clifton, left on Clifton Road, left on Compton Road, right on Bull Run P.O. Road, left on Lee Highway, left on Sudley Road (Route 234) to Manassas Battlefield Park, south on Sudley Road, becomes Grant Avenue, left on Center Street (Route 28) in Manassas, right on Fairview Street, becomes Davis Ford Road (663), left on Yates Ford Road, right on Henderson Road, left on Wolf Run Shoals Road, right on Clifton Road, right on Burke Road, right on Rolling Road back to Springfield.

RICHMOND TRAIL - 141 mi.; rolling hills, long distances; 10-speed bicycle recommended.

The Richmond Trail originates at Mt. Vernon and continues to Coatesville and Capitol Square.

Trail: Mount Vernon to Pohick to Lake Jackson to Brentsville to Aden to Kelly's Ford to Route 682 to Chancellorsville to Payne Store to Spotsylvania to Shell to Blades Corner to Marye to Blanton to Chilesburg to Hewlitt to Coatesville to Negro Foot to Lanes Corner to Hunton, right on Woodman Road onto Hermitage Road to Richmond to Capitol Square.

ROANOKE BLUE RIDGE TRAIL - 102 mi.; hilly terrain; 10-speed bicycle necessary.

A challenging but beautiful century ride in southwest Virginia. The route is marked by white painted arrows on the road (except along the Blue Ridge Parkway), with all turns indicated by the direction of the arrow before the intersection and confirmed by an arrow after the intersection.

Trail: Vinton Recreation Center to Route 634 east, cross Hardy Ford Bridge, north on Route 122, right on Route 616, right on Route 670, right on Route 674, right on Route 674 to Rocky Mount, right on U.S. 220, left on Route 40, right on Route 640, to Route 602

to Adney's Gap to Blue Ridge Parkway north toward Roanoke, right on Route 24 west, left to continue on Route 24 to Vinton Recreation Center.

See MARYLAND - Seneca-Leesburg Trail.

SKYLINE DRIVE TRAIL - 31 mi.; some steep hills; 10-speed bicycle recommended.

Originating at the Rotunda of the University of Virginia, the trail winds through rural Albemarle County along much of the Trans-America Trail to Rockfish Gap and the Skyline Drive.

Trail: Rotunda of University of Virginia, west on University Avenue, left on McCormick Road, right on Alderman Road, left on Ivy, right on Route 754, right on Route 601, straight on Route 676, Route 614 to Whitehall to Crozet, right on Route 691, right on Route 690, right on Route 796 to Rockfish Gap and Skyline Drive.

WILLIAMSBURG TRAIL - 226 mi.; easy hills, long distances; 10-speed bicycle necessary.

This trail originates at Mt. Vernon and continues to the state's colonial capital and ultimately Yorktown, along much of the Trans-America Trail.

Trail: Mount Vernon to Pohick to Lake Jackson to Brentsville to Aden to Kelly's Ford to Route 682 to Chancellorsville to Payne's Store to Spotsylvania to Shell to Blades Corner to Marye to Blanton to Chilesburg to Hewlitt to Coatsville, left on Route 738, right on Route 667 to Ashland City limits; left on Route 657, right on Route 656, left on Route 637 to Mechanicsville through Richmond Battlefield to Old Cold Harbor, south on Grapevine Road to Memorial Drive, left on Charles City Road to Glendale, south on Route 156 and Route 5 to Charles City to Rustic to Jamestown, left on Colonial Parkway to Williamsburg to Yorktown.

TRAILS

Pearisburg

CASCADES TRAIL, Jefferson National Forest - 4 mi. foot trail. This hiking trail is located within the Jefferson National Forest. The first half of the trail generally follows the banks of Little Stony Creek. The return trail follows an old logging road, passing an old rock slide and Barney's Wall, a 50-foot rock cliff that angles up the slope to the top of the ridge.

SKI AREAS

Bryce

BRYCE RESORT
P.O. Box 3
Bryce, VA 22810
(703) 856-2121
LOCATION: 11 mi. west of Mt. Jackson on Route 263.
FACILITIES: 2 double chairlifts; 2 tow ropes; 1 mighty mite; slopes for expert, intermediate and beginning skiers; ski instruction;

SKI AREAS (continued)

ski rental; 500 ft. vertical drop; restaurants; lodging.

Fancy Gap

CASCADE MOUNTAIN
Route 2
Fancy Gap, VA 24328
LOCATION: On Route 608, 1½ mi. north of Route 52.
FACILITIES: 1 mighty mite; slopes for expert, intermediate and beginning skiers; ski instruction; ski rental; longest run, 3000 ft.; restaurants; lodging.

Hot Springs

HOMESTEAD
Hot Springs, VA 24445
(703) 839-5500
LOCATION: On U.S. 220.
FACILITIES: 1 T-bar; 1 tram; 2 tow ropes; slopes for expert, intermediate and beginning skiers; ski instruction; ski rental; 550 ft. vertical drop; restaurants; lodging.

McGaheysville

MASSANUTTEN VILLAGE SKI RESORT
McGaheysville, VA 22840
(703) 289-2711
LOCATION: Near Harrisonburg.
FACILITIES: 4 chairlifts; 1 J-bar; slopes for expert, intermediate and beginning skiers; ski instruction; ski rental; 795 ft. vertical drop; longest run, 5600 ft.; restaurants; lodging.

New Market

MOUNTAIN RUN
P.O. Box 217
New Market, VA 22844
(703) 477-3149
LOCATION: Near New Market.
FACILITIES: 1 double chairlift; 2 tow ropes; slopes for expert, intermediate and beginning skiers; ski instruction; ski rental; restaurants; lodging.

Wintergreen

WINTERGREEN RESORT
Wintergreen, VA 22938
(804) 361-2200
LOCATION: On Route 664.
FACILITIES: 1 double chairlift; 2 triple chairlifts; slopes for expert, intermediate and beginning skiers; ski instruction; ski rental; restaurants; lodging.

AMUSEMENT PARKS & ATTRACTIONS

Buckroe Beach

BUCKROE BEACH AMUSEMENT PARK
Box 4067
Buckroe Beach, VA 23364
(804) 851-8981
FACILITIES: 10 major rides; 10 kiddie rides; 16 games; 6 refreshment stands; 2 restaurants; arcade; shooting gallery; beach; miniature golf; monkey display; picnic facilities; free gate; pay parking; open Memorial Day - Labor Day.

Doswell

KINGS DOMINION
Box 166
Doswell, VA 23047
(804) 876-3371
FACILITIES: 26 major rides; 7 kiddie rides; walk thru; 8 refreshment stands; 10 restaurants; arcade; zoo preserve; free acts; pay gate; pay parking; open Memorial Day - Labor Day; weekends: Apr. 3 - May 23, and Sept. 11 - Oct. 31.

Norfolk

OCEAN VIEW AMUSEMENT PARK
End of Granby Street
Norfolk, VA 23503
(704) 587-1011
FACILITIES: 15 major rides; 10 kiddie rides; fun house; slide; 6 refreshment stands; arcade; shooting gallery; beach; miniature golf; picnic facilities; free acts; pay parking; open Mar. 22 - Labor Day.

Salem

LAKESIDE AMUSEMENT PARK
1526 E. Main Street
Salem, VA 24153
(703) 366-8871
FACILITIES: 25 major rides; 9 kiddie rides; 4 refreshment stands; arcade; restaurant; shooting gallery; miniature golf; picnic facilities; free acts; pay gate; free parking.

Virginia Beach

SEASIDE PARK
31st.St. & Atlantic Avenue
Virginia Beach, VA 23451
(804) 428-1199
FACILITIES: 6 major rides; 6 kiddie rides; 4 refreshment stands; 2 restaurants; arcade; shooting gallery; beach; picnic facilities; free gate; open May 13 - Labor Day.

Williamsburg

BUSCH GARDENS - "THE OLD COUNTRY"
Hwy. 60, East
Williamsburg, VA 23185
(804) 220-2000
FACILITIES: 15 major rides; 4 kiddie rides; fun house; 3 walk thrus; 30 refreshment stands; 17 restaurants; arcade; shooting gallery; exhibits; picnic facilities; zoo; stage shows; pay gate; pay parking; open Apr. - Oct.; weekends: spring and fall.

COLONIAL WILLIAMSBURG (Attraction)
P.O. Box C
Williamsburg, VA 23185
(804) 229-1000
FACILITIES: Restoration of Virginia's eighteenth-century capital; colonial homes; shops; public buildings; museum; exhibits; picnic facilities; 9 restaurants; open all year.

VIRGINIA

STATE FAIR

State Fair
P.O. Box 26805
Richmond, VA 23261
(804) 329-4437
DATE: September

NATIONAL PARKS

Luray

SHENANDOAH NATIONAL PARK
Luray, VA 22835
(703) 999-2266

MILEPOST 22.1
LOCATION: Mathews Arm.
FACILITIES: Open mid-Apr. - Oct.; limit of stay: 14 days; 186 sites; group camps; NPS campsite fee: $3; water and bathroom facilities; sanitary station; cabins; picnic area; food service; fishing; hiking; exhibit; museum; environmental study area; living history program; self-guiding tour; lodging.

MILEPOST 51.2
LOCATION: Big Meadows.
FACILITIES: Open year round; limit of stay: 14 days; 253 sites; group camps; NPS campsite fee: $3; water and bathroom facilities; sanitary station; cabins; laundry; picnic area; food service; fishing; hiking; horseback riding; exhibit; museum; environmental study area; living history program; self-guiding tour; lodging.

MILEPOST 57.5
LOCATION: Lewis Mountain.
FACILITIES: Open mid-May - Oct.; limit of stay: 14 days; 32 sites; group camps; NPS campsite fee: $3; water and bathroom facilities; cabins; picnic area; fishing; hiking; exhibit; museum; environmental study area; living history program; self-guiding tour; lodging.

MILEPOST 79.5
LOCATION: Loft Mountain.
FACILITIES: Open mid-Apr. - Oct.; limit of stay: 14 days; 231 sites; group camps; NPS campsite fee: $3; water and bathroom facilities; sanitary station; cabins; laundry; picnic area; food service; fishing; hiking; exhibit; museum; environmental study area; living history program; self-guiding tour; lodging.

NATIONAL FORESTS

National Forests
Southern Region
1720 Peachtree Road, NW
Atlanta, GA 30309
(404) 881-4177

Harrisonburg

GEORGE WASHINGTON NATIONAL FOREST
ATTRACTIONS: Sinks and other unusual geological sites; Civil War iron furnaces; Trout, bass fishing; black bear, deer, turkey, grouse, squirrel hunting; scenic drives.
FACILITIES: 23 camp and picnic sites, 24 picnic only; swimming site; hotels; resorts, and numerous small cabins available nearby.
NEARBY TOWNS: Front Royal, Luray, Staunton, Lexington, Lynchburg, Waynesboro, Charlottesville, Winchester, VA; Franklin, Moorefield, WV.

Roanoke

JEFFERSON NATIONAL FOREST
ATTRACTIONS: Mount Rogers, 5719 feet, highest in Virginia; transitional zone between northern and southern flora; Civil War iron furnaces. Fishing; white-tailed deer, grouse, squirrel, bear, raccoon, elk hunting.
FACILITIES: 42 camp and picnic sites, 19 picnic only; 2 swimming sites; resorts; hotels; cabins.
NEARBY TOWNS: Bristol, Bluefield, Lexington, Lynchburg, Marion, Radford, Wytheville.

STATE PARKS

Headquarters

Virginia State Parks
Division of Parks
1201 State Office Bldg.
Capitol Square
Richmond, VA 23219
(804) 786-2134

Appomattox

HOLIDAY LAKE STATE PARK
(804) 248-6308
LOCATION: 6 mi. northeast of Appomattox.
FACILITIES: Open Apr. - Dec.; water and bathroom facilities; sanitary station; trailer village vehicle sites; picnic area; food service; swimming; boating; boat rental; fishing; tent camping.

Bassett

FAIRY STONE STATE PARK
(703) 930-2424
LOCATION: 8 mi. west of Bassett.
FACILITIES: Open Apr. - Dec.; water and bathroom facilities; sanitary station; trailer village vehicle sites; cabins; picnic area; food service; swimming; boating; boat rental; fishing; horseback riding; tent camping.

Burkeville

GOODWIN LAKE - PRINCE EDWARD STATE PARK
(804) 392-3435
LOCATION: 3 mi. west of Burkeville.
FACILITIES: Open Apr. - Dec.; water and bathroom facilities; sanitary station; trailer village vehicle sites; cabins; picnic area; food service; swimming; boating; boat rental; fishing; tent camping.

Clarkesville

OCCONEECHEE STATE PARK
(804) 374-2210

VIRGINIA

STATE PARKS (continued)

LOCATION: 2 mi. east of Clarkesville.
FACILITIES: Open Apr. - Dec.; water and bathroom facilities; sanitary station; trailer village vehicle sites; picnic area; food service; swimming; boating; fishing; tent camping.

Clifton Forge

DOUTHAT STATE PARK
(703) 862-0612
LOCATION: 6 mi. north of Clifton Forge.
FACILITIES: Open Apr. - Dec.; water and bathroom facilities; sanitary station; trailer village vehicle sites; cabins; picnic area; food service; swimming; boating; boat rental; tent camping.

Clinchport

NATURAL TUNNEL STATE PARK
(703) 940-2674
LOCATION: 1 mi. north of Clinchport.
FACILITIES: Open Apr. - Dec.; water and bathroom facilities; sanitary station; trailer village vehicle sites; picnic area; hiking; tent camping.

Dillwyn

BEAR CREEK LAKE STATE PARK
(804) 492-4410
LOCATION: 7 mi. east of Dillwyn.
FACILITIES: Open Apr. - Dec.; water and bathroom facilities; sanitary station; trailer village vehicle sites; picnic area; food service; swimming; boating; boat rental; fishing; tent camping.

Marion

HUNGRY MOTHER STATE PARK
(703) 783-3422
LOCATION: 4 mi. north of Marion.
FACILITIES: Open Apr. - Dec.; water and bathroom facilities; sanitary station; trailer village vehicle sites; cabins; picnic area; food service; swimming; boating; boat rental; fishing; horseback riding; tent camping.

Oak Grove

WESTMORELAND STATE PARK
(804) 493-6167
LOCATION: 3 mi. east of Oak Grove.
FACILITIES: Open Apr. - Dec.; water and bathroom facilities; sanitary station; trailer village vehicle sites; cabins; picnic area; food service; swimming; boating; boat rental; fishing; tent camping.

Pulaski

CLAYTOR LAKE STATE PARK
(703) 674-5492
LOCATION: 8 mi. east of Pulaski.
FACILITIES: Open Apr. - Dec.; water and bathroom facilities; sanitary station; trailer village vehicle sites; cabins; picnic area; swimming; boating; boat rental; fishing; horseback riding; tent camping.

Richmond

POCAHONTAS STATE PARK
(804) 748-5929
LOCATION: 14 mi. southwest of Richmond.
FACILITIES: Open Apr. - Dec.; water and bathroom facilities; sanitary station; trailer village vehicle sites; picnic area; food service; swimming; boating; boat rental; fishing; horseback riding; tent camping.

South Boston

STAUNTON RIVER STATE PARK
(804) 572-4623
LOCATION: 9 mi. east of South Boston.
FACILITIES: Open Apr. - Dec.; water and bathroom facilities; sanitary station; trailer village vehicle sites; cabins; picnic area; food service; swimming; boating; boat rental; fishing; hiking; tent camping.

Virginia Beach

SEASHORE STATE PARK
(804) 481-2131
LOCATION: 6 mi. north of Virginia Beach.
FACILITIES: Open Apr. - Dec.; water and bathroom facilities; sanitary station; trailer village vehicle sites; cabins; picnic area; food service; swimming; boating; fishing; tent camping.

Volney

GRAYSON HIGHLANDS STATE PARK
(703) 579-7092
LOCATION: 4 mi. east of Volney.
FACILITIES: Open Apr. - Dec.; water and bathroom facilities; sanitary station; trailer village vehicle sites; picnic area; hiking; tent camping.

STATE FORESTS

Virginia Division of Forestry
P.O. Box 3758
Charlottesville, VA 22903
(804) 977-6555

There are four State Forests in Virginia and each comprises a State Park with developed facilities and a Wildlife Management Area. The latter is reserved for hunting, fishing and primitive camping only.

Appomattox

APPOMATTOX - BUCKINGHAM STATE FOREST

See State Parks, Holliday Lake State Park.

Burkeville

PRINCE EDWARD - GALLION STATE FOREST

See State Parks, Goodwin Lake - Prince Edward State Park.

Dillwyn

CUMBERLAND STATE FOREST

VIRGINIA

STATE FORESTS (continued)

See State Parks, Bear Lake State Park.

Richmond

POCAHONTAS STATE PARK & FOREST

See State Parks, Pocahontas State Park.

HISTORIC SITES

See also District of Columbia.

Alexandria

CHRIST CHURCH - George Washington's pew is preserved in this lovely English country style church built of native brick and stone between 1767 and 1773. Robert E. Lee was confirmed in the church and later attended while living at Arlington House. Located at Cameron and N. Washington Streets.

ROBERT E. LEE'S BOYHOOD HOME - Light Horse Harry Lee, Revolutionary War hero and father of the more famous Robert E. Lee, brought his family to this house in 1812. Robert E. Lee lived and studied here in his formative years. Beautifully furnished with rare antiques and Lee memorabilia. Located at 607 Oronoco Street.

Appomattox

APPOMATTOX COURT HOUSE - Site of the Confederate surrender ending the Civil War on April 9, 1865. The restored village of 27 houses and stores includes the McLean House, where Generals Lee and Grant negotiated the peace. The Court House itself is a Civil War museum. Located on Route 24.

Fredericksburg

FREDERICKSBURG AND SPOTSYVANIA NATIONAL MILITARY PARK - Included in the 5,000-acre park are four famous Civil War battlefields: Fredericksburg, Spotsylvania Court House, Chancellorsville, and the Wilderness campaigns. All are within 17 miles of Fredericksburg.

RISING SUN TAVERN - Built about 1760 by Charles, brother of George Washington. It was the favorite meeting place of early patriots. House is considered to be an architectural gem. Located at 1306 Caroline Street.

Hampton

FORT MONROE - Never attacked by the Confederacy because Lee knew its strength; he helped build it. Fort Monroe denied to the Confederacy access from the ocean to Norfolk and Richmond. Jefferson Davis was imprisoned here after being accused falsely of plotting Lincoln's assassination. Located 8 mi. southeast of Richmond.

Jamestown

JAMESTOWN - First permanent English set-tlement in America, established May, 1607. Setting where Pocahontas, John Rolfe, Captain John Smith, Governor Sir George Yeardley, Nathaniel Bacon and a host of others left their imprint on the pages of history.

Leesburg

MORVEN PARK - A Greek-Revival-style mansion on a 1200-acre estate with unmatched boxwoods. Estate has the distinction of having been the home of the governors of two states, Thomas Swann, Maryland, and Westmoreland Davis, Virginia. Located 2 mi. north of Leesburg on Route 698.

OATLANDS - Meticulously preserved Federal mansion built in 1800 by George Carter, great-grandson of Robert "King" Carter. Also, one of Virginia's finest hunt race courses has been installed and equestrian activities scheduled throughout the season. Located 6 mi. south of Leesburg on Route 15.

WATERFORD - Restored Quaker village dating back to 1733 was named by Thomas Moore, a shoemaker, for his birthplace in Ireland. Located on Route 698.

WHITE'S FERRY - Last ferry boat still in operation on the Potomac was named for Gen. Jubal Early, a famous Confederate general. Generals Jeb Stuart and Robert E. Lee crossed the river here with their armies during the Civil War. Once known as Conrad's Ferry. Located 4 mi. north of Leesburg off Route 15 on Route 655.

Lexington

STONEWALL JACKSON HOUSE - Largest collection of Jackson relics anywhere. Exhibits show him as churchman, family man, teacher, citizen and soldier.

Lorton

GUNSTON HALL - Home of George Mason. Sometimes called the "Pen of the Revolution," Mason wrote the Virginia Declaration of Rights on which the Federal Bill of Rights was based. Palladian room in the mansion has been described as one of the "100 most beautiful rooms in America."

Monticello

MONTICELLO - Unique and vital spirit of Thomas Jefferson, 3rd President, is seen in the design of this classic mansion, its furnishings, and its grounds.

Richmond

THE WHITE HOUSE OF THE CONFEDERACY - Jefferson Davis, the first and only President of the Confederacy, lived here four years, 1861-1865. Located at 12th and Clay Streets.

Williamsburg

BERKELEY - Most-visited and historic of the

HISTORIC SITES (continued)

great James River plantations. Site of the first official Thanksgiving in 1619. Located on Route 5.

SHERWOOD FOREST - Home of John Tyler, 10th President, built in 1780. One of the longest private dwellings in America, 300 feet in length. Now occupied by President Tyler's great-grandson. Located 20 mi. from Williamsburg on Route 5.

Yorktown

THE BATTLEFIELD - Site of British surrender to General Washington in 1781, ending the Revolutionary War. Markers show positions of British and American armies at the Siege of Yorktown, including site of Washington's Headquarters. Battlefield Tour Road runs through Colonial National Historical Park, in and around Yorktown.

HOSTELS

There are no Hostels in Virginia.

POINTS OF INTEREST

Chincoteague

CHINCOTEAGUE - Island made famous by miniature horse Misty and her ponies. Round-up of ponies on Assateague Island and annual swim to Chincoteague on Pony Day.

Front Royal

SKYLINE DRIVE AND BLUE RIDGE PARKWAY - From the northern end of the Shennandoah National Park at Front Royal, this mountain-top highway follows the ridges for 320 miles of panoramic beauty southward through Virginia.

Jamestown Island

JAMESTOWN FESTIVAL PARK - Tours of full-scale models of the Susan Constant, the Godspeed, and the Discovery, three tiny ships in which 104 men and boys reached Virginia. Also, glassblowers reproduce early wares nearby at the replica of the glasshouse of 1608. At Jamestown the tower of the church of 1639 stands sentinel near the foundations of the early village. An auto train cuts through the swamp and forest landscape at Jamestown Island.

MOUNTAIN GAP SCHOOL - Little school sits alone on a spur of the old road between Leesburg and Oatlands and serves as a reminder to future generations of a way of education before the turn of the century. Located 4 mi. south of Leesburg on Route 15.

Natural Bridge

NATURAL BRIDGE - One of the seven natural wonders of the world, this towering arch was surveyed by Washington and once was owned by Jefferson. Nightly during the season, there is a drama on the story of creation. Located on U.S. 11.

Norfolk

GARDENS-BY-THE-SEA - Beautiful camellia, azalea, and rhododendron blooms from spring through late summer. Adjoins Norfolk Airport.

Petersburg

BROWN & WILLIAMSON TOBACCO CORPORATION - Company produces 50 billion cigarettes per year. Tour of the facility available. Located at Brown and Perry Streets.

Richmond

THE AMERICAN TOBACCO COMPANY - One of the nation's major cigarette firms, has continuously manufactured tobacco products in the Richmond area since 1890. Tour of the facility available. Located at 26th and Cary Streets.

MUSEUM OF THE CONFEDERACY - World's largest collection of Confederate memorabilia is housed in this modern building dedicated in 1976, adjacent to the White House of the Confederacy. Located at 12th and Clay Streets.

Williamsburg

CARTER'S GROVE PLANTATION - Host to patriots and presidents for more than two centuries, has been called "the most beautiful house in America." Named by the fabulously wealthy planter, Robert (King) Carter, it was built in 1750-1753. The mansion with its 200-foot facade, is a masterpiece of Virginia architecture. Located 6 mi. east of Williamsburg on U.S. 60.

THE WILLIAMSBURG NATIONAL WAX MUSEUM - Depicts the first 200 years of colonial America. Starting with Queen Elizabeth I granting the charter of the New World to Sir Walter Raleigh, and ending with Declaration of Independence. Located 3 mi. west of Williamsburg on Route 60.

WASHINGTON

Washington, a key element in a boundary dispute with the British, entered the Union in 1889 as the forty-second state. In 1844, the

federal government had set the country's northern boundary well into Canadian territory (50 degrees and 40 minutes latitude),

WASHINGTON

INTRODUCTION (continued)

which irritated the British. The slogan, "Fifty-four forty or fight," won the Presidency for James K. Polk, who eventually agreed to territorial limits at the 49th parallel.

Early settlers in the state experienced little if any trouble with the native Americans; however, when gold was discovered in the 1850s, and thousands of settlers followed, the Indians went on the warpath.

Today, Washington's main source of revenue is its manufacturing industry. Agriculture, too, is important, especially its world-famous apple crop.

And with the increasing popularity of outdoor activities, Washington is experiencing a rapidly expanding tourist trade.

State capital: Olympia. State bird: Willow goldfinch. State tree: Western hemlock. State flower: Western rhododendron.

WEATHER

The location of the state of Washington on the windward coast in mid-latitudes is such that the climatic elements combine to produce a predominantly marine-type climate west of the Cascade Mountains, while east of the Cascades the climate possesses both continental and marine characteristics. Considering its northerly latitude, Washington's climate is mild.

Washington's western boundary is formed by the Pacific Ocean. Two ranges of mountains parallel the coast: the Coastal Range and the Cascade Range. The Cascade Mountains, 90 to 125 miles inland and 4,000 to 10,000 feet in elevation, are a topographic and climatic barrier separating the state into eastern and western Washington.

West of the Cascade Mountains, summers are cool and comparatively dry, and winters are mild, wet and cloudy. East of the Cascades, summers are warmer, with low relative humidity and high temperatures; winters are colder and precipitation is less than in western Washington.

Average daily temperature for each month.

	Eastern	Western
Jan.	31.4 to 19.2	43.6 to 33.0
Feb.	37.4 to 22.5	47.0 to 34.5
Mar.	47.0 to 29.1	51.3 to 36.2
Apr.	58.6 to 35.9	58.2 to 40.1
May	69.3 to 43.1	65.6 to 45.3
Jun.	74.5 to 49.3	69.9 to 49.7
Jul.	85.6 to 55.4	75.6 to 54.1
Aug.	83.0 to 52.9	74.6 to 53.6
Sept.	74.7 to 47.0	69.3 to 50.5
Oct.	60.1 to 38.0	60.3 to 44.4
Nov.	42.9 to 28.5	49.6 to 38.1
Dec.	35.9 to 24.2	45.9 to 35.7
Year	58.4 to 57.1	59.2 to 42.9

STATE CHAMBER OF COMMERCE

Association of Washington Business
P.O. Box 658
Olympia, WA 98507
(206) 946-1600

STATE & CITY TOURISM OFFICES

State

Department of Commerce and Economic Development
General Administration Building
Olympia, WA 98504
(206) 753-5630

Travel Development Division
Department of Commerce and Economic Development
General Administration Building
Olympia, WA 98504
(206) 753-5610

Local

Seattle-King County Convention and Visitor's Bureau
1815 Seventh Avenue
Seattle, WA 98101
(206) 622-5022

Visitor's and Convention Bureau
Spokane Chamber of Commerce
P.O. Box 2147
Spokane, WA 99210
(509) 624-1393

STATE HIGHWAY DEPARTMENT

Washington State Highway Commission
Department of Transportation
P.O. Box 29
Olympia, WA 98507
(206) 753-6170

HIGHWAY WELCOMING CENTERS

Anacortes

ANACORTES CENTER - City Chamber of Commerce.

Blaine

BLAINE CENTER - Interstate 5.

WELCOMING CENTERS (continued)

Clarkston

CLARKSTON CENTER - City of Clarkston, 749 6th Street.

Oroville

OROVILLE CENTER - Route 1.

Port Angeles

PORT ANGELES CENTER - U.S. Hwy. 101.

Seaview

SEAVIEW VISITOR CENTER - City Chamber of Commerce.

Spokane

SPOKANE CENTER - Route 1.

Vancouver

VANCOUVER CENTER - City, 905 Pacific Freeway.

STATE POLICE

Department of Public Safety
Olympia, WA 98504
(206) 753-6540

HUNTING & FISHING

Hunting

A license is required for all persons who hunt (ages 10 through 69) and fish (ages 16 through 69) in the state. To qualify as a resident, a person must reside in the state 90 days prior to application.

Resident

State hunting license, $7.50; county hunting and fishing license, $9; state deer tag, $5; state elk tag, $11; state goat and sheep tags, $11; state trapping license, $11; state turkey tag, $3; state bear tag, $3; archery and/or muzzle-loading rifle permit, $6; upland bird permit, $3.

Non-resident

State hunting license, $60; state elk tag, $42; state goat and sheep tags, $42.

Fishing

See hunting regulations above.

Resident

State fishing license, $8.50; county fishing license, $7.

Non-resident

State 7-day fishing license, $7.25; state fishing license, $24.

For more information contact:

Department of Game
600 N. Capitol Way
Olympia, WA 98504
(206) 753-5700

CAMPGROUNDS

See National Parks, National Forests, State Parks and State Forests.

RESORTS & BEACHES

Most of the state's resort activities center around the major lakes and include fishing, swimming, boating, water skiing, and camping. (See National Parks, National Forests and State Parks.)

BOATING AREAS

See National Parks, National Forests and State Parks.

BICYCLE TRAILS

CENTRAL WASHINGTON TRAILS - 200 mi.; hilly terrain; 10-speed bicycle recommended.

This is a bicycle camping trip in the beautiful farm and forest country of central Washington.

Trails: Ellensburg to Wish Poosh to Baker to Ellensburg to French Cabin Creek to Fish Lake to Wish Poosh to Beverly to Swauk to Bonanza to Baker to Ellensburg.

DARRINGTON HOSTEL TRAILS - 85 & 110 mi.; some gravel surfaces, hilly terrain; 10-speed bicycle recommended.

Most of the trip is on secondary paved roads, but the south loop has about 20 miles of gravel.

Trails: (1) Darrington to Monte Cristo to Silverton to Granite Falls to Arlington to Route 530 to Darrington - 85 mi.; (2) Darrington to Bennett to Rockport to Concrete to Sedro Woolley to Big Lake to McMurray to Arlington to Route 530 to Darrington - 110 mi.

LONGVIEW TRAIL - 6.5 mi.; some hills; any bicycle.

The bicycle trail is asphalt and varies from four to six feet in width.

Trail: Sacajawea Lake to Columbia River to Mount Solo to Roy Morse Park.

SLIGO CREEK BICYCLE TRAIL - 3.7 mi.; narrow trails; any bicycle.

A bicycle trail in Montgomery County from Wayne Avenue to Wheaton Regional Park.

Trail: Wayne Avenue, go north on trail, cross Colesville Road, cross Forest Glen Road, cross Route 193, left on Franwell Avenue, right on Nairn Road to Wheaton Regional Park.

WASHINGTON

BICYCLE TRAILS (continued)

STRAITS AND SOUNDS TRAIL - 120 mi.; 10-speed bicycle recommended.

July and August are good months for this easy ride.

Trail: Begin in Seattle. Take Washington State Ferry to Winslow located on Bainbridge Island to Agate Pass Bridge to Poulsbo to Hood Canal Floating Toll Bridge. You will pass by the Kitsap Memorial State Park, available for camping, to Port Townsend; take ferry to Fort Casey, facilities available on Whidbey Island, to Coupeville to Deception Pass State Park to Anacortes; take ferry through the San Juan Islands to Sidney on Vancouver Island to Victoria to Port Townsend and retrace your route to Seattle.

VASHON ISLAND TRAIL - 26 mi.; some hills; 10-speed bicycle recommended.

Vashon Island is just a ferry ride from both Seattle and Tacoma, and it offers some fine biking.

Trail: Ferry from Seattle to Vashon Heights to 99th Street southwest to Marina to Tahlequah to 131st Street southwest to 135th to 123rd to Vashon Heights.

TRAILS

Seattle

DISCOVERY PARK LOOP TRAIL - 2.8 mi. foot trail. This trail is located in Discovery Park, the largest component of the city's park system. The park is a 400-acre natural retreat. The trail winds along the perimeter of the park and meanders through a shrub-lined corridor, forest groves and open meadows. Trail users enjoy superb views of Puget Sound and the Olympic Mountains as they pass along the top of 300-foot bluffs overlooking the beach.

LAKE WASHINGTON BICYCLE PATH - 3.2 mi. foot trail. This is a segment of a longer trail along the west shore of Lake Washington. The trail lies in a landscaped linear park parallel to Lake Washington Boulevard and provides additional access to Seward Park. The environment consists of grass and trees along the lakeshore. Users are afforded views of the distant Cascade Mountains, as well as recreational boating and sailboat races on the lake.

LAKE WASHINGTON SHIP WATERSIDE TRAIL - .25 mi. foot trail. Located in the city of Seattle, the trail lies beside the Montlake Cut, a canal connecting Lake Washington to Puget Sound (via the Hiram M. Chittenden locks). The area is heavily developed urban-industrial, but the immediate trail environment has been landscaped with flowering ornamentals, evergreens and a wide variety of shrubs and ground plantings. The major attraction on the trail is a steady parade of vessels using the canal.

Tacoma

FRED CLEATOR INTERPRETIVE TRAIL - Federation Forest State Park - 1.3 mi. foot trail. Located 35 miles from Tacoma and 45 miles from Seattle on Old Naches Trail, which crosses the Cascade Range, the trail is constructed so that wheelchairs may be used during the summer. Emphasis is given to interpreting major northwest tree and shrub communities. The site is also of historic interest in that it once was considered a possible link between the Puget Sound area and eastern Washington.

SKI AREAS

Bandera

SKI ACRES
Seattle, WA 98199
(206) 282-6893
LOCATION: Near Bandera.
FACILITIES: 6 double chairlifts; 14 tow ropes; ski instruction; ski rental; restaurants; lodging.

Bellingham

MOUNT BAKER
Bellingham, WA 98225
(206) 734-8083
LOCATION: Off Route 542.
FACILITIES: 7 double chairlifts; 5 tow ropes; ski instruction; ski rental; restaurants; lodging.

Berne

SNO COUNTRY STEVENS PASS
Leavenworth, WA 98826
(206) 973-2500
LOCATION: 2 mi. northwest of Berne off Route 2.
FACILITIES: 1 triple chairlift; 6 double chairlifts; 2 tow ropes; ski instruction; ski rental; nursery; restaurants; lodging.

Chewelah

49 DEGREES NORTH
Chewelah, WA 99109
(509) 935-6649
LOCATION: Near Chewelah.
FACILITIES: 3 chairlifts; ski instruction; ski rental; restaurants; lodging.

Crystal Mountain

CRYSTAL MOUNTAIN
Crystal Mountain, WA 98022
(206) 663-2265
LOCATION: Near Northeast corner of Mount Rainier National Park.
FACILITIES: 1 triple chairlift; 5 double chairlifts; 1 T-bar; 10 tow ropes; ski instruction; ski rental; restaurants; lodging.

Granite Falls

MOUNT PILCHUK
Granite Falls, WA 98252
(206) 355-8109
LOCATION: 8 mi. east of Granite Falls.
FACILITIES: 2 double chairlifts; 3 tow ropes; ski instruction; ski rental; restaurants; lodging.

SKI AREAS (continued)

Hyak

HYAK
Seattle, WA 98101
(206) 623-0330
LOCATION: 50 mi. southeast of Seattle off
U.S. 90.
FACILITIES: 4 double chairlifts; 7 tow
ropes; ski instruction; ski rental; restaurants;
lodging.

SNOQUALMIE SUMMIT
Seattle, WA 98112
(206) 322-5450
LOCATION: 47 mi. southeast of Seattle off
U.S. 90.
FACILITIES: 2 triple chairlifts; 6 double
chairlifts; 9 tow ropes; 2 pomas; ski instruction; ski rental; nursery; restaurants; lodging.

Leavenworth

LEAVENWORTH
Leavenworth, WA 98826
(509) 548-5596
LOCATION: Near Leavenworth.
FACILITIES: 2 tow ropes; restaurants; lodging.

Mead

MOUNT SPOKANE
Mead, WA 99021
(509) 238-6281
LOCATION: 5 mi. north of Mead.
FACILITIES: 5 double chairlifts; 3 tow
ropes; ski instruction; ski rental; restaurants;
lodging.

Pateros

LOUP LOUP
Pateros, WA 98846
(509) 826-0537
LOCATION: 1 mi. north of Twisp off Route
20.
FACILITIES: 2 tow ropes; 2 pomas; ski instruction; ski rental; restaurants; lodging.

Port Angeles

HURRICANE RIDGE
Port Angeles, WA 98362
(206) 452-9235
LOCATION: In Olympia National Park.
FACILITIES: 2 tow ropes; 1 poma; ski instruction; ski rental; restaurants; lodging.

Pullman

NORTH SOUTH BOWL
ASWSU Rec.
Washington State University
Pullman, WA 99163
(509) 335-2651
LOCATION: 45 mi. north of Moscow on U.S.
95A in Emida.
FACILITIES: 1 double chairlift; 2 tow ropes;
ski instruction; ski rental; 450 ft. vertical
drop; restaurants; lodging.

Snoqualmie Pass

ALPENTAL
Snoqualmie Pass, WA 98068
(206) 434-6112
LOCATION: 47 mi. from Seattle via I-90.
FACILITIES: 4 double chairlifts; 4 tow
ropes; 1 poma; ski instruction; ski rental; restaurants; lodging.

Tonasket

SITZMARK
Tonasket, WA 98855
(509) 486-4238
LOCATION: 10 mi. northeast of Tonasket.
FACILITIES: 1 tow rope; 2 pomas; ski instruction; ski rental; restaurants; lodging.

Waterville

BADGER MOUNTAIN
Waterville, WA 98858
(509) 745-4261
LOCATION: Near Waterville.
FACILITIES: 5 tow ropes; ski instruction; ski
rental; restaurants; lodging.

Wenatchee

MISSION RIDGE
Wenatchee, WA 98801
(509) 663-6543
LOCATION: Near Wenatchee.
FACILITIES: 4 double chairlifts; 3 tow
ropes; ski instruction; ski rental; restaurants;
lodging.

Yakima

WHITE PASS VILLAGE
Yakima, WA 98907
(509) 453-8731
LOCATION: 14 mi. southeast of Mount Rainier National Park on U.S. 12.
FACILITIES: 3 double chairlifts; 1 tow rope;
1 poma; ski instruction; ski rental; restaurants; lodging.

AMUSEMENT PARKS & ATTRACTIONS

Seattle

FUN FOREST AMUSEMENT PARK
370 Thomas Street
Seattle, WA 98109
(206) 624-1585
FACILITIES: 16 major rides; 6 kiddie rides; 5
refreshment stands; arcade; miniature golf;
free gate; pay parking; open Mar. - Nov.;
weekends: Mar., Apr., Sept. & Nov.

KIDDY AMUSEMENTS
700 N. 50th Street
Seattle, WA 98103
(206) 633-5540
FACILITIES: 10 major rides; 4 kiddie rides.

WASHINGTON

STATE FAIR

Washington State Fair
Interstate Fairgrounds
Spokane, WA 99210
(509) 535-1766
DATE: August

NATIONAL PARKS

Ashford

MOUNT RAINIER NATIONAL PARK
Tahoma Woods
Longmire, WA 98397
(206) 569-2211

COUGAR ROCK
LOCATION: 8 mi. northeast of Wisqually entrance.
FACILITIES: Open Jun. - Oct.; entrance fee; limit of stay: 14 days; 200 sites; group camps: 5; NPS campsite fee: $3; water and bathroom facilities; sanitary station; picnic area; food service; guide for hire; hiking; snowmobile route; exhibit; museum; handicapped access/restroom; NPS guided tour; self-guiding tour; lodging.

ISPUT CREEK
LOCATION: 5 mi. east of Carbon River entrance.
FACILITIES: Open May - Oct.; limit of stay: 14 days; 32 sites; NPS campsite fee: $1; water and bathroom facilities.

LONGMIRE
LOCATION: 6 mi. northeast of Wisqually entrance.
FACILITIES: Open Jul. - Labor Day; limit of stay: 14 days; 110 sites; group camps: 1; NPS campsite fee: $3; water and bathroom facilities; picnic area; food service; guide for hire; hiking; snowmobile route; exhibit; museum; handicapped access/restroom; NPS guided tour; self-guiding tour; lodging.

OHANAPECOSH
LOCATION: 1½ mi. south of Stevens Canyon entrance.
FACILITIES: Open May - Oct.; entrance fee; limit of stay: 14 days; 232 sites; NPS campsite fee: $3; water and bathroom facilities; sanitary station; picnic area; food service; fishing; hiking; snowmobile route; exhibit; museum; handicapped access/restroom; NPS guided tour; self-guiding tour; lodging.

SUNSHINE POINT
LOCATION: 1/5 mi. east of Wisqually entrance.
FACILITIES: Open year round; limit of stay: 14 days; 30 sites; NPS campsite fee: $1; water and bathroom facilities.

WHITE RIVER
LOCATION: 5 mi. west of White River entrance.
FACILITIES: Open Jul. - Oct.; entrance fee; limit of stay: 14 days; 125 sites; NPS campsite fee: $3; water and bathroom facilities; picnic area; food service; guide for hire; hiking; snowmobile route; exhibit; museum;

handicapped access/restroom; self-guiding tour; lodging.

Port Angeles

OLYMPIC NATIONAL PARK
Port Angeles, WA 98362
(206) 452-9235

ALTAIRE
LOCATION: 13 mi. west of Port Angeles.
FACILITIES: Open May - Oct.; limit of stay: 14 days; 29 sites; NPS campsite fee: $3; water and bathroom facilities; fishing; hiking; horseback riding.

BOULDER
LOCATION: 20 mi. west of Port Angeles.
FACILITIES: Open Jun. - Sept.; limit of stay: 14 days; 50 sites; water and bathroom facilities; fishing; hiking; horseback riding; walk in.

DEER PARK
LOCATION: 22 mi. southeast of Port Angeles.
FACILITIES: Open Jun. - Sept.; limit of stay: 14 days; 10 sites; no trailers.

DOSEWALLIPS
LOCATION: 15 mi. west of Brinnon.
FACILITIES: Open May - Sept.; limit of stay: 14 days; 33 sites; water and bathroom facilities; fishing; hiking; horseback riding; no trailers.

ELWHA
LOCATION: 10 mi. west of Port Angeles.
FACILITIES: Open year round; limit of stay: 14 days; 23 sites; NPS campsite fee: $3; water and bathroom facilities; fishing; hiking; horseback riding.

ERICKSON BAY
LOCATION: West shore of Ozette Lake.
FACILITIES: Open year round; limit of stay: 14 days; 15 sites; swimming; boating; fishing; access by boat or trail.

FAIRHOLM
LOCATION: 26 mi. west of Port Angeles.
FACILITIES: Open May - Oct.; limit of stay: 14 days; 90 sites; NPS campsite fee: $3; water and bathroom facilities; sanitary station; food service; swimming; boating; fishing; hiking; horseback riding.

GRAVES CREEK
LOCATION: 20 mi. east of Amanda Park.
FACILITIES: Open year round; limit of stay: 14 days; 45 sites; water and bathroom facilities; fishing; hiking; horseback riding.

HEART O' THE HILLS
LOCATION: 5¼ mi. south of Port Angeles.
FACILITIES: Open May - Oct.; limit of stay: 14 days; 100 sites; NPS campsite fee: $3; water and bathroom facilities; hiking; horseback riding.

HOH
LOCATION: 22 mi. southeast of Forks.
FACILITIES: Open year round; limit of stay: 14 days; 95 sites; NPS campsite fee: $3; water and bathroom facilities; sanitary station; fishing; hiking; horseback riding.

NATIONAL PARKS (continued)

JULY CREEK
LOCATION: 6 mi. northeast of Amanda Park.
FACILITIES: Open year round; limit of stay: 14 days; 31 sites; water and bathroom facilities; fishing; hiking; horseback riding; walk in.

KALALOCH
LOCATION: 35 mi. south of Forks, on coast.
FACILITIES: Open year round; limit of stay: 14 days; 195 sites; NPS campsite fee: $3; water and bathroom facilities; sanitary station; food service; swimming; fishing; hiking; horseback riding.

MORA
LOCATION: 15 mi. west of Forks.
FACILITIES: Open year round; limit of stay: 14 days; 91 sites; NPS campsite fee: $3; water and bathroom facilities; sanitary station; swimming; fishing; hiking; horseback riding.

NORTH FORK QUINAULT
LOCATION: 20 mi. northeast of Amanda Park.
FACILITIES: Open May - Sept.; limit of stay: 14 days; 10 sites; fishing; no trailers.

QUEETS
LOCATION: 25 mi. southeast of Queets.
FACILITIES: Open year round; limit of stay: 14 days; 26 sites; fishing.

SOLEDUCH
LOCATION: 40 mi. southwest of Port Angeles.
FACILITIES: Open May - Oct.; limit of stay: 14 days; 84 sites; NPS campsite fee: $3; water and bathroom facilities; sanitary station; food service; swimming; fishing; hiking; horseback riding.

STAIRCASE
LOCATION: 19 mi. northwest of Hoodsport.
FACILITIES: Open May - Sept.; limit of stay: 14 days; 50 sites; NPS campsite fee: $3; water and bathroom facilities; fishing; hiking; horseback riding.

Sedro Wooley

NORTH CASCADES NATIONAL PARK
Sedro Woolley, WA 98284
(206) 855-1331

STEHEKIN VALLEY CAMPGROUND
LOCATION: Near Park headquarters.
FACILITIES: Open May - Oct.; limit of stay: 14 days; 18 sites; bathroom facilities; fishing; hiking; horseback riding; primitive site; access by shuttle bus or trail.

NATIONAL FORESTS

Pacific Northwest Region
319 SW Pine Street
Portland, OR 97208
(503) 221-2971

Bellingham

MOUNT BAKER NATIONAL FOREST
ATTRACTIONS: Numerous glaciers; alpine lakes; heavy stands of Douglas fir up to 200 feet in height; steelhead, rainbow trout fishing; deer, bear hunting; skiing; saddle and pack trips; mountain climbing.
FACILITIES: 87 camp and picnic sites, 6 picnic only; Mount Baker and Mount Pilchuck Winter Sports Areas; hotels; resorts; experienced guides.
NEARBY TOWNS: Darrington, Everett, Granite Falls.

Colville

COLVILLE NATIONAL FOREST
ATTRACTIONS: Hunting in area noted for large mule deer, record weight of 440 pounds; lake and stream fishing.
FACILITIES: 25 camp and picnic sites, 7 picnic only; 6 swimming sites; Chewelah Peak Winter Sports Area; resorts and cabins.
NEARBY TOWNS: Chewelah, Republic.

Okanogan

OKANOGAN NATIONAL FOREST
ATTRACTIONS: Lake and stream fishing; boating; saddle and pack trips; mountain climbing; winter sports.
FACILITIES: 61 camp and picnic sites, 2 picnic only; 9 boating and 2 swimming sites; Loup Winter Sports Area; dude ranches; motels.
NEARBY TOWNS: Brewster, Tonasket, Twisp.

Olympia

OLYMPIC NATIONAL FOREST
ATTRACTIONS: Dense rain forests; big trees; spectacular snow peaks; salmon, steelhead trout fishing; deer, bear, cougar, elk hunting; scenic drives; saddle and pack trips.
FACILITIES: 20 camp and picnic sites; 2 boating sites; swimming site; resorts; motels; dude ranches.
NEARBY TOWNS: Aberdeen, Port Angeles, Quileene, Shelton.

Seattle

SNOQUALMIE NATIONAL FOREST
ATTRACTIONS: Snoqualmie Falls, 250 feet high; scenic giant Douglas firs; snow peaks; salmon, steelhead trout fishing; black-tailed mule deer, bear, elk hunting; scenic drives; saddle and pack trips; skiing.
FACILITIES: 103 camp and picnic sites; 9 boating sites; 5 winter sports areas; motels and outfitters locally available.
NEARBY TOWNS: Cle Elum, Everett, Tacoma, Yakima.

Vancouver

GIFFORD PINCHOT NATIONAL FOREST
ATTRACTIONS: Historic Indian huckleberry fields; lake and stream trout fishing; deer, bear hunting; spectacular auto tours; saddle and pack trips; mountain climbing; winter sports.

WASHINGTON

NATIONAL FORESTS (continued)

FACILITIES: 65 camp and picnic sites, 15
picnic only; 5 boating sites; resorts; motels;
cabins.
NEARBY TOWNS: Castle Rock, Morton,
Stevenson, White Salmon.

Wenatchee

WENATCHEE NATIONAL FOREST
ATTRACTIONS: Lake Chelan, bottom 389
feet below sea level; trout fishing; deer, bear
hunting; scenic drives; boat trip; saddle and
pack trips; winter sports.
FACILITIES: 120 camp and picnic sites, 5
picnic only; 4 winter sports areas; motels and
dude ranches.
NEARBY TOWNS: Cashmere, Chelan, Cle
Elum, Ellensburg, Leavenworth.

See COEUR D'ALENE NATIONAL FOREST
and KANIKSU NATIONAL FOREST - Idaho.

See UMATILLA NATIONAL FOREST - Oregon.

STATE PARKS

Headquarters

State Parks and Recreation Commission
7150 Cleanwater Lane
Olympia, WA 98504
(206) 753-5755

Bellingham

LARRABEE STATE PARK
LOCATION: 7 mi. south of Bellingham.
FACILITIES: Open year round; 100 sites; water and bathroom facilities; sanitary station;
electrical hookup; trailer village vehicle sites;
picnic area; swimming; boating; fishing; hiking; tent camping.

Coulee City

SUN LAKES STATE PARK
LOCATION: 6 mi. south of Coulee City.
FACILITIES: Open year round; 209 sites; water and bathroom facilities; sanitary station;
electrical hookup; trailer village vehicle sites;
food service; swimming; boating; boat rental;
fishing; hiking; handicapped access/restroom;
tent camping.

Ellensburg

GINKGO STATE PARK
LOCATION: 29 mi. east of Ellensburg.
FACILITIES: Open year round; water and
bathroom facilities; picnic area; hiking; living
history program.

Grand Coulee

STEAMBOAT ROCK STATE PARK
LOCATION: 11 mi. south of Grand Coulee.
FACILITIES: Open year round; 100 sites; water and bathroom facilities; electrical hookup;
trailer village vehicle sites; food service; swimming; boating; boat rental; fishing; hiking;

handicapped access/restroom; tent camping.

Granite Falls

MOUNT PILCHUCK STATE PARK
LOCATION: 20 mi. east of Granite Falls.
FACILITIES: Open year round; 3 sites; water
and bathroom facilities; trailer village vehicle
sites; picnic area; food service; hiking; tent
camping; lodging.

Hadlock

FORT FLAGLER STATE PARK
LOCATION: 8 mi. northeast of Hadlock, on
Marrowstone Island.
FACILITIES: Open year round; 114 sites; water and bathroom facilities; sanitary station;
trailer village vehicle sites; food service; swimming; boating; boat rental; fishing; hiking;
tent camping.

Hoodsport

LAKE CUSHMAN STATE PARK
LOCATION: 7 mi. west of Hoodsport on
Staircase Road.
FACILITIES: Open year round; 80 sites; water and bathroom facilities; sanitary station;
electrical hookup; trailer village vehicle sites;
swimming; boating; fishing; hiking; handicapped access/restroom; tent camping.

Iiwaco

FORT CANBY STATE PARK
LOCATION: 2 mi. west of Iiwaco.
FACILITIES: Open year round; 250 sites; water and bathroom facilities; sanitary station;
electrical hookup; trailer village vehicle sites;
picnic area; food service; swimming; boating;
fishing; handicapped access/restroom; tent
camping.

Leavenworth

LAKE WENATCHEE STATE PARK
LOCATION: 22 mi. north of Leavenworth.
FACILITIES: Open year round; 197 sites; water and bathroom facilities; sanitary station;
trailer village vehicle sites; food service; swimming; boating; fishing; hiking; horseback riding; handicapped access/restroom; tent camping.

Oak Harbor

DECEPTION PASS STATE PARK
LOCATION: 8 mi. north of Oak Harbor.
FACILITIES: Open year round; 254 sites; water and bathroom facilities; trailer village vehicle sites; picnic area; food service; swimming;
boating; fishing; hiking; handicapped access/
restroom; tent camping.

Olympia

MILLERSYLVANIA STATE PARK
LOCATION: 10 mi. south of Olympia on
Tilly Road.
FACILITIES: Open year round; 216 sites; water and bathroom facilities; sanitary station;
electrical hookup; trailer village vehicle sites;
swimming; boating; fishing; hiking; tent camping.

STATE PARKS (continued)

Pateros

ALTA LAKE STATE PARK
LOCATION: 2 mi. southwest of Pateros.
FACILITIES: Open year round; 200 sites; water and bathroom facilities; sanitary station; electrical hookup; trailer village vehicle sites; picnic area; swimming; boating; fishing; hiking; tent camping.

Rosario

MORAN STATE PARK
LOCATION: Near Rosario, on Orcas Island.
FACILITIES: Open year round; 160 sites; water and bathroom facilities; sanitary station; trailer village vehicle sites; picnic area; swimming; boating; boat rental; fishing; hiking; handicapped access/restroom; tent camping.

Spokane

MT. SPOKANE STATE PARK
LOCATION: 30 mi. east of Spokane.
FACILITIES: Open year round; 12 sites; water and bathroom facilities; trailer village vehicle sites; picnic area; food service; hiking; horseback riding; tent camping; lodging.

RIVERSIDE STATE PARK
LOCATION: 3 mi. northwest of Spokane.
FACILITIES: Open year round; 110 sites; water and bathroom facilities; trailer village vehicle sites; boating; fishing; hiking; tent camping.

Vancouver

BEACON ROCK STATE PARK
LOCATION: 35 mi. east of Vancouver via Hwy. 14.
FACILITIES: Open year round; 34 sites; water and bathroom facilities; sanitary station; trailer village vehicle sites; picnic area; swimming; boating; fishing; hiking; horseback riding; handicapped access/restroom; tent camping.

Washtucna

LYON'S FERRY STATE PARK
LOCATION: 20 mi. southeast of Washtucna.
FACILITIES: Open year round; 50 sites; water and bathroom facilities; sanitary station; trailer village vehicle sites; picnic area; food service; swimming; boating; fishing; hiking; handicapped access/restroom; tent camping.

Westport

TWIN HARBORS STATE PARK
LOCATION: 3 mi. south of Westport.
FACILITIES: Open year round; 295 sites; water and bathroom facilities; electrical hookup; trailer village vehicle sites; swimming; hiking; tent camping.

STATE FORESTS

There are no State Forests in Washington.

HISTORIC SITES

Brewster

FORT OKANOGAN - First structure in the state to fly the U.S. flag. Artifacts from fur trade era.

Lake Whatcom

RAILROAD MUSEUM AND EXCURSION TRAINS - Three steam railroad excursions: Lake Whatcom Railway Excursion from Lake Whatcom to Wickersham; Puget Sound Railway Museum at Snoqualmie; and the Steam Train at the Camp Six Logging Museum in Point Defiance Park.

Olympia

OLYMPIA - Monument marking the end of the Oregon Trail is in Sylvester Park in downtown Olympia.

STATE CAPITOL MUSEUM - Features exhibits from territorial days and early days of statehood. Legislative Building (1928) is one of the last of the traditional domed capitol buildings built in the U.S.

Port Townsend

PORT TOWNSEND - Thriving port city of the 1870s and 1880s with many restored mansions and many handsome old buildings in the downtown section.

San Juan Island

SAN JUAN ISLAND NATIONAL HISTORICAL PARK - Commemorates the Pig War 1859-1872, which led to final boundary settlement with England. English campsite includes original blockhouse, commissary and one of the barracks. English cemetery nearby. American camp has earthworks used by U.S. troops.

Spokane

SPOKANE HOUSE - Site of first fur trade post (1811). Footings of original fur trading post, some artifacts from site on display. Located on Little Spokane River near Spokane.

Vancouver

FORT VANCOUVER - The hub of the Hudson's Bay Company's Pacific Northwest empire from 1825 to 1846. Slide presentation, dioramas. Stockade of Fort Vancouver and six buildings have been reconstructed.

Whidbey Island

FORT CASEY - Coast artillery fort of Spanish American War period. Two 10-inch guns on display.

WASHINGTON

HOSTELS

Chinook

FT. COLUMBIA YOUTH HOSTEL
Route 101
Chinook, WA 98614
No telephone
FACILITIES: Open Jun. 1 - Labor Day; 30 beds, men; 16 beds, women; modern bathroom; nearest hostel: Portland, 110 mi. southeast; Lilliwaup, 145 mi. northeast; overnight charges: $2.50; houseparent: hostel staff.

Davenport

COTTONWOOD SPRINGS YOUTH HOSTEL
P.O. Box 716
Davenport, WA 99122
(509) 725-7901
FACILITIES: Open Jun. 1 - Aug. 31; 15-20 beds, men; 10-12 beds, women; modern bathroom; overnight charges: $2; houseparents: David & Nancy Edwards.

Lilliwaup

MIKE'S BEACH
R. 1, Box 95 N.
Lilliwaup, WA 98555
(206) 877-5324
FACILITIES: Open Apr. 15 - Oct. 15; 36 beds, men; 10 beds, women; modern bathroom; nearest hostel: Port Townsend, 50 mi. north; overnight charges: $3.25 summer; $4.25 winter; houseparents: Robert & Trudy Schultz.

Nordland

FORT FLAGER HOSTEL
Nordland, WA 98358
(206) 385-1288
FACILITIES: Open May 1 - Sept. 30; 10 beds, men; 10 beds, women; modern bathroom; nearest hostels: Port Townsend, 19 mi.; Seattle, southeast 50 mi. plus ferry; overnight charges: $2.50; houseparents: Val & Cathy Benavidez.

Port Townsend

FORT WORDEN YOUTH HOSTEL
Route 113
Ft. Worden State Park
Port Townsend, WA 98368
(206) 385-0655
FACILITIES: Open year round; 13 beds, men; 16 beds, women; modern bathroom; nearest hostels: Nordland, 19 mi.; Seattle 50 mi. southeast plus ferry; overnight charges: $2.50; houseparents: Lockwood & Hiroko Dennis.

Seattle

SEA HAVEN YOUTH HOSTEL
1431 Minor Avenue
Seattle, WA 98101
(206) 624-8012
FACILITIES: Open year round; 150 beds men and women; modern bathroom; nearest hostel: Port Townsend, 94 mi.; overnight charges: $3; houseparents: Brother Joseph Curl & Sister Gail Falkenhagen.

POINTS OF INTEREST

Hoquiam

HOQUIAM'S CASTLE - A restored lumber baron's mansion with an excellent collection of late 19th-century Americana.

LaConner

LACONNER - Old fishing village on Swinomish channel.

Seattle

LONGHOUSE AT SEATTLE CENTER - A reconstructed longhouse using original totem and house poles.

TILLICUM VILLAGE ON BLAKE ISLAND - Authentic Indian-style baked salmon and Indian dances. Boat tour from Seattle.

Tacoma

LOGGING MUSEUM - Camp Six in Point Defiance Park.

Walla Walla

FORT WALLA WALLA - Pioneer village and a very extensive museum filled with artifacts of early days.

Wenatchee

ROCKY REACH DAM - Complete story of development of electricity.

WASHINGTON, D.C.

See District of Columbia

WEST VIRGINIA

West Virginia, not one to shy away from fueding and fighting, joined the Union in 1863 as the thirty-fifth state. Much of its early history is entwined with neighboring Virginia, since before the Civil War, Virginia and West Virginia were one and the same state. However, at the war's onset, Virginia seceded from the Union against the wishes of its northern counties which established their own rule and remained loyal to the Union.

Perhaps just as famous a feud erupted between two neighboring families, the Hatfields of West Virginia and Kentucky's McCoys. (See Introduction under Kentucky.)

In the 1930s, the United Mineworkers' Union won its long and often bloody struggle to organize the state's coal fields. Today, the working conditions in the mines are much improved, due in part to the efforts of the union.

West Virginia is also a ruggedly beautiful state that appeals to the outdoorsman, making tourism another important source of state income.

State capital: Charleston. State bird: Cardinal. State tree: Sugar maple. State flower: Rhododendron.

WEATHER

West Virginia has an area of over 24,000 square miles, and its main portion is roughly oblong in shape. It has the highest average elevation (1654 feet) of any state east of the Mississippi River. The rugged topography of the "Mountain State" features some elevation differences greater than 3000 feet within individual counties.

West Virginia's climate is much more of the continental than of the maritime type. The most important aspect of this type of climate is the marked temperature contrast between summer and winter, with four distinct seasons. The state has a moderately severe winter climate, accentuated and prolonged in the mountains, with frequent alternations of fair and stormy weather. Summer is marked by hot and showery weather. The heat is less pronounced in the mountains, but this area is more subject to thunderstorms and has fewer clear days the year round. Little more can be said in the way of general climatic characteristics, because there are marked variations in the weather elements due to rugged topography. Large differences occur not only between the mountains and plateau areas, but even between different parts of the same county.

Average daily temperature for each month.

	Northeastern	Southwestern
Jan.	41.7 to 18.1	44.2 to 24.1
Feb.	43.3 to 20.3	47.9 to 25.6
Mar.	51.6 to 28.0	56.8 to 32.5
Apr.	64.0 to 37.9	69.3 to 41.9
May	73.4 to 46.4	78.5 to 51.0
Jun.	81.5 to 54.9	85.5 to 59.8
Jul.	85.6 to 59.1	88.5 to 64.5
Aug.	84.3 to 57.4	87.5 to 63.6
Sept.	78.5 to 50.2	82.6 to 56.7
Oct.	67.9 to 38.8	71.5 to 44.4
Nov.	55.3 to 30.2	57.4 to 33.7
Dec.	44.4 to 22.0	47.2 to 27.7
Year	64.3 to 38.6	68.1 to 43.8

STATE CHAMBER OF COMMERCE

West Virginia Chamber of Commerce

P.O. Box 2789
Charleston, WV 25330
(304) 345-0770

STATE & CITY TOURISM OFFICES

State

Department of Economic and Community Development
Governor's Office
Charleston, WV 25305
(304) 348-2000

Travel Development Division
West Virginia Department of Commerce
1900 Washington Street, East
Charleston, WV 25305
(304) 348-2286

STATE HIGHWAY DEPARTMENT

West Virginia Department of Highways
1900 Washington Street, East
Charleston, WV 25305
(304) 348-3456

HIGHWAY WELCOMING CENTERS

Bunker Hill

BUNKER HILL CENTER - Interstate 81, north.

Falling Waters

FALLING WATERS CENTER - Interstate 81, south.

Huntington

HUNTINGTON CENTER - Interstate 64.

Mineralwells

MINERALWELLS CENTER - City limits.

WEST VIRGINIA

WELCOMING CENTERS (continued)

Shepherdstown

SHEPHERDSTOWN CENTER - Near Harpers Ferry.

White Sulphur Spring

WHITE SULPHUR SPRING CENTER - In City.

STATE POLICE

Department of Public Safety
So. Charleston, WV 25309
(304) 348-6370

HUNTING & FISHING

Hunting

See fishing regulations below.

Resident

Statewide bow or gun hunting and trapping license (Class A), $6; bear stamp, bear damage stamp (required in order to hunt or pursue bear; bear damage stamp is to be affixed to Class A, AB, C, E, L or M license), $4; antlerless deer license (Class N) must be applied for (not valid without eligibility card), $8; statewide combination bow or gun hunting, trapping and fishing license (Class AB), $10; small arms hunting license (Class A-1), $5; national forest fishing and hunting license (Class 1) required on the Monongahela, George Washington and Jefferson National Forests in addition to regular license, $1.

Non-resident

Bow only hunting and fishing license (Class L), license entitles licensee to employ a long or compound bow and arrow in taking game, fish and frogs, $15; bow or gun hunting license (Class E), $40; commercial shooting preserve license (Class MO), $3; small game hunting license (6 days) (Class H), $8.

Fishing

License not required for:
Any bona fide resident of this state who is totally blind.
Any resident 65 years of age or older. In lieu of such license any such person shall at all times while hunting, trapping or fishing, carry on his person a card issued by the Director stating name, address and date of birth.
Any non-resident or resident under 15 years of age.
Any resident of West Virginia on active duty in the Armed Forces of the United States of America, while on leave or furlough. Leave or furlough papers shall serve in lieu of any such license and shall be carried on the person at all times while fishing.
Bona fide resident landowners or their resident children, or bona fide resident tenants of such land, may hunt, trap or fish on their own land during open seasons in accordance with the laws and regulations applying to such hunting, trapping and fishing, unless such lands have been designated as a wildlife refuge preserve.
Resident parents to fish, hunt or trap on their resident children's land in West Virginia during regular open season.

Resident

Combined statewide hunting and fishing license (Class AB), $10; statewide fishing license (Class B), $6; trout fishing license, required by holders of Class B or Class AB license who fish or trout (Class O), $3; National forest hunting and fishing license (required on the Monongahela, George Washington, and Jefferson National Forests in addition to regular license) (Class 1), $1.

Non-resident

Statewide fishing license (Class F), $20; statewide bow and arrow hunting and fishing license (Class L), $15; statewide tourist fishing license (6 consecutive days) (Class K), $5; plus trout stamp, when trout fishing, $5; state park and family license (available at parks and forests). head of family (1 week only) (Class G), $3; each additional member of the family (Class G-1), 50 cents.

For more information contact:

Department of Natural Resources
Division of Wildlife Resources
1800 Washington St., E
Charleston, WV 25305
(304) 348-2771

CAMPGROUNDS

Private

Belington

TWIN LAKES CAMPGROUND
(304) 823-2021
LOCATION: 1¾ mi. from Audra State Park.
FACILITIES: Open year round; 200 sites; water and bathroom facilities; sanitary station; electrical hookup; laundry; food service; swimming; hunting; fishing; self-guided trail; tent camping.

Berkeley Springs

COOLFRONT RECREATION CAMP-GROUND
(304) 258-1793
LOCATION: 3 mi. from Berkeley Springs.
FACILITIES: Open year round; 140 sites; water and bathroom facilities; sanitary station; electrical hookup; trailer village vehicle sites; laundry; food service; swimming; boating; boat rental; fishing; self-guided trail; tent camping.

Bowder

ALPINE SHORES CAMPGROUND
(304) 636-4311

CAMPGROUNDS (continued)

LOCATION: 10 mi. east of Elkins.
FACILITIES: Open year round; 150 sites; water and bathroom facilities; sanitary station; electrical hookup; trailer village vehicle sites; food service; hunting; fishing; hiking; tent camping.

Buckhannon

MIDDLE FORK RIVER FOREST CAMP-GROUND
(304) 472-3400
LOCATION: 1¾ mi. south of Audra State Park.
FACILITIES: Open year round; 230 sites; water and bathroom facilities; sanitary station; electrical hookup; trailer village vehicle sites; laundry; food service; swimming; boating; hunting; fishing; hiking; tent camping.

Charleston

GREENBERRY FARM KOA KAMP-GROUND
(304) 984-9933
LOCATION: 4 mi. off I-77 on Grapevine Creek.
FACILITIES: Open year round; 100 sites; water and bathroom facilities; sanitary station; electrical hookup; trailer village vehicle sites; laundry; food service; swimming; fishing; self-guided trail; tent camping.

Harpers Ferry

HARPERS FERRY KOA KAMPGROUND
(304) 535-6895
LOCATION: 1 mi. west of Harpers Ferry.
FACILITIES: Open Mar. 1 - Dec. 15; 300 sites; water and bathroom facilities; sanitary station; electrical hookup; trailer village vehicle sites; food service; swimming; hiking; tent camping.

YOGI BEAR'S JELLYSTONE CAMP
(304) 535-2221
LOCATION: 1 mi. south of Harpers Ferry on U.S. 340, then ½ mi. north on Bakerton Road.
FACILITIES: Open Mar. 1 - Dec. 25; 225 sites; water and bathroom facilities; sanitary station; electrical hookup; trailer village vehicle sites; food service; swimming; tent camping.

Hinton

BASS LAKE PARK CAMPGROUND
(304) 466-1057
LOCATION: Route 20, north of Hinton.
FACILITIES: Open year round; 200 sites; water and bathroom facilities; sanitary station; trailer village vehicle sites; food service; swimming; boating; hunting; fishing; hiking; tent camping.

Milton

FOX FIRE CAMPING
(304) 743-5622
LOCATION: Mile post 25 on I-64.
FACILITIES: Open year round; 250 sites; water and bathroom facilities; sanitary station; electrical hookup; trailer village vehicle sites; laundry; food service; swimming; fishing; hiking; tent camping.

Pence Springs

PENCE SPRINGS CAMPGROUND
(304) 466-1757
LOCATION: Route 3, Pence Springs.
FACILITIES: Open year round; 150 sites; water and bathroom facilities; sanitary station; trailer village vehicle sites; swimming; boating; fishing; hiking; self-guided trail; tent camping.

Romance

RIPPLING WATERS CAMPGROUND
(304) 984-0701
LOCATION: Romance.
FACILITIES: Open year round; 230 sites; water and bathroom facilities; sanitary station; electrical hookup; trailer village vehicle sites; laundry; food service; swimming; fishing; hiking; tent camping.

Sugar Grove

SUGAR GROVE CAMPGROUND
(304) 249-5421
LOCATION: In Sugar Grove.
FACILITIES: Open year round; 100 sites; water and bathroom facilities; sanitary station; electrical hookup; trailer village vehicle sites; laundry; food service; swimming; boating; hunting; fishing; tent camping.

Summersville

SUMMERSVILLE MOUNTAIN MANOR CAMPGROUND
(304) 872-4220
LOCATION: 1 mi. south of Summersville.
FACILITIES: Open year round; 230 sites; water and bathroom facilities; sanitary station; electrical hookup; trailer village vehicle sites; laundry; food service; hiking; tent camping.

Wheeling

DALLAS PIKE CAMPGROUND
(304) 547-0940
LOCATION: 9 mi. east of Wheeling.
FACILITIES: Open Apr. - Nov.; 100 sites; water and bathroom facilities; sanitary station; electrical hookup; trailer village vehicle sites; laundry; food service; swimming; hiking; tent camping.

White Sulphur Springs

YOUNG'S CAMPGROUND
(304) 536-2200
LOCATION: North of White Sulphur Springs.
FACILITIES: Open year round; 125 sites; water and bathroom facilities; sanitary station; electrical hookup; trailer village vehicle sites; laundry; food service; boating; boat rental; hunting; fishing; hiking; tent camping.

RESORTS & BEACHES

Most of the state's resort activities center

WEST VIRGINIA

RESORTS (continued)

around the major lakes and include fishing, swimming, boating, water skiing, and camping. (See Boating Areas, National Forests, State Parks and State Forests.)

BOATING AREAS

Hinton

BLUESTONE LAKE
LOCATION: Near Hinton.
FACILITIES: Launching; fishing; swimming; camping.

Mardsville

CHEAT LAKE
LOCATION: 5 mi. east of Mardsville.
FACILITIES: Launching; fishing; swimming; camping.

Newville

SUTTON LAKE
LOCATION: Near Newville.
FACILITIES: Launching; fishing; swimming; camping.

Summersville

SUMMERSVILLE LAKE
LOCATION: Near Summersville.
FACILITIES: Launching; fishing; swimming; camping.

Wayne

EAST LYNN LAKE
LOCATION: 10 mi. north of Wayne.
FACILITIES: Launching; fishing; swimming; camping.

Weston

STONEWALL JACKSON LAKE
LOCATION: 3 mi. south of Weston.
FACILITIES: Launching; fishing; swimming; camping.

Whitewater Rafting

For complete information on whitewater rafting in West Virginia, write or call the organizations listed below:

Maryland

Cheat River Outfitters, Inc.
Box 134
Ellicott City, MD 21043
(301) 329-9816

Ohio

North American River Runners
7817 Shaftesbury Drive
Sylvania, OH 43560
(419) 882-8654

Pennsylvania

Cheat Canyon Expeditions
Box 106
Ohiopyle, PA 15470
(412) 329-5942

Mountain Streams and Trails Outfitters
Box 106
Ohiopyle, PA 15470
(412) 329-8810

West Virginia

Appalachian Wildwaters, Inc.
Box 126
Albright, WV 26519
(304) 329-1665

West Virginia River Adventures, Inc.
Box 10185
Charleston, WV 25312
(304) 744-9005

TransMontane Outfitters, Ltd.
Box 325
Davis, WV 26260
(304) 259-5117

Blue Ridge Outfitters
Harpers Ferry, WV 25425
(304) 725-3444

Mountain Rivers Tours, Inc.
Box 88
Hico, WV 25854
(304) 658-5817

Jerry E. Starcher
Kingwood, WV 26537
(304) 789-6171

Songer Enterprises, Inc.
Box 677
Morgantown, WV 26505
(304) 296-5772

Five Rivers Canoe Company
420 Second Street
Parsons, WV 25936
(304) 478-2811

New River Adventures
Star Route, Box 25
Thurmond, WV 25936
(304) 469-9627

Wildwater Expeditions Unlimited, Inc.
Box 55
Thurmond, WV 25936
(304) 469-2551

BICYCLE TRAILS

BARTOW COUNTY TRAIL - 63 mi.; mountainous terrain; 10-speed bicycle necessary.
A trip through the Virginias with some spectacular mountain scenery.
Trail: From Bartow, intersection Route 28 and U.S. 250 south on Route 28 over nearly flat to moderately rolling terrain to Arbovale and Green Bank. Continue on Route 28 to

BICYCLE TRAILS (continued)

Frost, then left on Route 84 and make easy ascent to Virginia line at Mill Gap. Descend and after about 14 miles from VA- W. VA line left on 640 and ascend to Hightown. Here, left on US 250 and begin hard ascent over Lantz Mountain, elevation 3,600 feet, descend then ascend and cross over Red Oak Knob, again descend then start final effort over Allegheny Ridge, elevation 4,271 feet. At summit, cross West Virginia line and start long descent to Thornwood at intersection of Route 28. Left on Route 28 and go to Bartow.

TRAILS

Huntington

THE GENTLE TRAIL - .4 mi. foot and Braille trail. The trail is oriented toward nature education and recreation, with special emphasis on providing services to the blind and handicapped. The trail is a loop traversing through an immature maple complex and a more mature oak-hickory complex. There is a fragrance garden at the end of the trail. There are many interpretive signs in both regular print and Braille.

SKI AREAS

Davis

CANAAN VALLEY
LOCATION: Near Davis.
FACILITIES: 2 double chairlifts; 1 poma; 1 mitey mite; slopes for expert, intermediate and beginning skiers; ski instruction; ski rental; nursery; 850 ft. vertical drop; longest run, 1 mi.; restaurants; lodging.

Morgantown

CHESTNUT RIDGE
LOCATION: 15 mi. northeast of Morgantown on U.S. 48.
FACILITIES: 1 tow rope; ski rental; 170 ft. vertical drop; longest run, 1200 ft.

Slatyfork

SNOWSHOE
LOCATION: On U.S. 219 north of Slatyfork.
FACILITIES: 3 chairlifts; slopes for expert, intermediate and beginning skiers; ski instruction; ski rental; nursery; 700 ft. vertical drop; longest run, 7500 ft.; restaurants; lodging.

Terra Alta

ALPINE LAKE
LOCATION: Near Terra Alta.
FACILITIES: 2 pomas; 1 pony lift; slopes for expert, intermediate and beginning skiers; ski instruction; ski rental; 400 ft. vertical drop; longest run, 2200 ft.; restaurants; lodging.

Wheeling

OGLEBAY PARK

LOCATION: At Wheeling.
FACILITIES: 2 pomas; 1 tow rope; slopes for expert, intermediate and beginning skiers; ski instruction; ski rental; restaurants; lodging.

AMUSEMENT PARKS & ATTRACTIONS

Beckley

HATFIELDS & MCCOYS/HONEY IN THE ROCK (Attraction)
Grandview State Park
Beckley, WV 25801
(304) 253-8313
FACILITIES: Camping; exhibits; picnic facilities; theatre; crafts; free gate ; free parking; open Jun. 21 - Labor Day.

Huntington

CAMDEN PARK RECREATION CENTER
U.S. Route 60 West
P.O. Box 1794
Huntington, WV 25718
(304) 429-4231
FACILITIES: 12 major rides; 6 kiddie rides; 8 games; 10 refreshment stands; restaurant; penny arcade; shooting gallery; roller rink; miniature golf; zoo; horseshow grounds; picnic facilities; books vaudeville; fireworks; free acts; pay gate; free parking.

STATE FAIR

State Fair of West Virginia
P.O. Box 829
Lewisburg, WV 24901
(304) 645-1090
DATE: August

NATIONAL PARKS

There are no National Parks in West Virginia.

NATIONAL FORESTS

National Forests
Eastern Region
633 West Wisconsin Avenue
Milwaukee, WI 53203
(414) 291-3693

Elkins

MONONGAHELA NATIONAL FOREST
ATTRACTIONS: Spruce Knob, 4860 feet, highest peak in West Virginia; Seneca Rocks on historic Seneca Indian Trail; botanically curious Cranberry Glades; unexplored limestone caves; bear colonies; trout, bass fishing; deer, turkey, squirrel, bear, grouse, and other game hunting; swimming; horseback riding; scenic drives.
FACILITIES: 43 camp and picnic sites, 17 picnic only; 5 swimming sites; tourist homes and motels.
NEARBY TOWNS: Charleston, Lewisburg, Petersburg.

WEST VIRGINIA

NATIONAL FORESTS (continued)

See GEORGE WASHINGTON NATIONAL FOREST - Virginia.

STATE PARKS

Headquarters

Department of Natural Resources
Division of Parks and Recreation
State Capitol
Charleston, WV 25305
(304) 348-2764

Ansted

HAWKS NEST STATE PARK (Resort)
Ansted, WV 25812
(304) 658-5212
LOCATION: Near Ansted.
FACILITIES: Open year round; cabins; picnic area; food service; swimming; boating; fishing; lodging.

Berkeley Springs

CACAPON STATE PARK (Resort)
Berkeley Springs, WV 25411
(304) 258-1022
LOCATION: Near Berkeley Springs.
FACILITIES: Open year round; cabins; picnic area; food service; swimming; boating; boat rental; fishing; hiking; horseback riding; lodging.

Buckhannon

AUDRA STATE PARK
Buckhannon, WV 26201
(304) 457-1162
LOCATION: Near Buckhannon.
FACILITIES: Open year round; 65 sites; water and bathroom facilities; sanitary station; trailer village vehicle sites; picnic area; food service; swimming; fishing; hiking; tent camping.

Cairo

NORTH BEND STATE PARK (Resort)
Cairo, WV 26337
(304) 643-2931
LOCATION: Near Cairo.
FACILITIES: Open year round; 55 sites; water and bathroom facilities; sanitary station; electrical hookup; trailer village vehicle sites; picnic area; food service; swimming; fishing; hiking; tent camping; lodging.

Clifftop

BABCOCK STATE PARK (Resort)
Clifftop, WV 25822
(304) 438-6205
LOCATION: Near Clifftop.
FACILITIES: Open year round; 40 sites; water and bathroom facilities; sanitary station; electrical hookup; trailer village vehicle sites; cabins; picnic area; food service; swimming; boating; boat rental; fishing; hiking; tent camping.

Davis

BLACKWATER FALLS STATE PARK (Resort)
Davis, WV 26260
(304) 259-5216
LOCATION: Near Davis.
FACILITIES: Open year round; 65 sites; water and bathroom facilities; electrical hookup; trailer village vehicle sites; cabins; food service; swimming; boating; boat rental; fishing; hiking; horseback riding; tent camping; lodging.

CANAAN VALLEY STATE PARK (Resort)
Davis, WV 26260
(304) 866-4121
LOCATION: Near Davis.
FACILITIES: Open year round; 34 sites; water and bathroom facilities; sanitary station; electrical hookup; trailer village vehicle sites; cabins; food service; swimming; boating; fishing; hiking; horseback riding; tent camping; lodging.

Glenville

CEDAR CREEK STATE PARK
Glenville, WV 26351
(304) 462-7158
LOCATION: Near Glenville.
FACILITIES: Open year round; 22 sites; water and bathroom facilities; sanitary station; trailer village vehicle sites; picnic area; swimming; fishing; hiking; tent camping.

Grafton

TYGART LAKE STATE PARK (Resort)
Grafton, WV 26354
(304) 265-2320
LOCATION: Near Grafton.
FACILITIES: Open year round; 40 sites; water and bathroom facilities; trailer village vehicle sites; cabins; picnic area; food service; swimming; boating; boat rental; fishing; tent camping; lodging.

Hacker Valley

HOLLY RIVER STATE PARK (Resort)
Hacker Valley, WV 26222
(304) 493-6353
LOCATION: Near Hacker Valley.
FACILITIES: Open year round; 88 sites; water and bathroom facilities; sanitary station; electrical hookup; trailer village vehicle sites; cabins; picnic area; food service; swimming; fishing; hiking; tent camping.

Hinton

BLUESTONE STATE PARK (Resort)
Hinton, WV 25951
(304) 466-1922
LOCATION: Near Hinton.
FACILITIES: Open year round; 81 sites; water and bathroom facilities; sanitary station; electrical hookup; trailer village vehicle sites; cabins; picnic area; food service; swimming; boating; boat rental; hunting; fishing; hiking; tent camping.

STATE PARKS (continued)

Logan

CHIEF LOGAN STATE PARK
Logan, WV 25601
(304) 752-8558
LOCATION: Near Logan.
FACILITIES: Open Apr. 15 - Nov. 1; picnic area; food service; swimming; hiking; tent camping.

Marlinton

WATOGA STATE PARK (Resort)
Marlinton, WV 24954
(304) 799-4087
LOCATION: Near Marlinton.
FACILITIES: Open year round; 38 sites; water and bathroom facilities; sanitary station; trailer village vehicle sites; cabins; picnic area; food service; swimming; boating; boat rental; fishing; hiking; horseback riding; tent camping; lodging.

Mathias

LOST RIVER STATE PARK (Resort)
Mathias, WV 26812
(304) 897-5372
LOCATION: Near Mathias.
FACILITIES: Open year round; cabins; picnic area; food service; swimming; hiking; horseback riding; lodging.

Mullens

TWIN FALLS STATE PARK (Resort)
Mullens, WV 25882
(304) 294-4000
LOCATION: Near Mullens.
FACILITIES: Open year round; 47 sites; water and bathroom facilities; electrical hookup; trailer village vehicle sites; cabins; picnic area; food service; swimming; hiking; tent camping; lodging.

New Manchester

TOMLINSON RUN STATE PARK
New Manchester, WV 26056
(304) 564-3651
LOCATION: Near New Manchester.
FACILITIES: Open May 15 - Nov. 1; picnic area; swimming; boating; fishing.

Pipestem

PIPESTEM STATE PARK (Resort)
Pipestem, WV 25979
(304) 466-1800
LOCATION: Near Pipestem.
FACILITIES: Open year round; 50 sites; water and bathroom facilities; sanitary station; electrical hookup; trailer village vehicle sites; cabins; picnic area; food service; swimming; boating; fishing; hiking; horseback riding; tent camping; lodging.

STATE FORESTS

Department of Natural Resources
Division of Parks and Recreation

State Capitol
Charleston, WV 25305
(304) 348-2764

Bruceton Mills

COOPERS ROCK STATE FOREST
(304) 296-6065
LOCATION: Near Bruceton Mills.
FACILITIES: Open Apr. 15 - Nov. 1; 24 sites; water and bathroom facilities; trailer village vehicle sites; picnic area; hunting; fishing; hiking; tent camping.

Caldwell

GREENBRIER STATE FOREST
(304) 536-1944
LOCATION: Near Caldwell.
FACILITIES: Open Apr. 15 - Nov. 1; 16 sites; water and bathroom facilities; trailer village vehicle sites; cabins; picnic area; food service; swimming; boating; boat rental; hunting; hiking; tent camping.

Camp Creek

CAMP CREEK STATE FOREST
(304) 425-9481
LOCATION: Near Camp Creek.
FACILITIES: Open Apr. 15 - Nov. 1; 12 sites; water and bathroom facilities; trailer village vehicle sites; picnic area; hunting; fishing; hiking; tent camping.

Charleston

KANAWHA STATE FOREST
(304) 346-5654
LOCATION: Near Charleston.
FACILITIES: Open Apr. 15 - Nov. 1; 43 sites; water and bathroom facilities; sanitary station; electrical hookup; trailer village vehicle sites; picnic area; hunting; hiking; tent camping.

Dunlow

CABWAYLINGO STATE FOREST
(304) 385-4255
LOCATION: Near Dunlow.
FACILITIES: Open Apr. 15 - Nov. 1; 44 sites; water and bathroom facilities; trailer village vehicle sites; cabins; picnic area; food service; swimming; hunting; fishing; hiking; tent camping.

Dunmore

SENECA STATE FOREST
(304) 799-6213
LOCATION: Near Dunmore.
FACILITIES: Open Apr. 15 - Nov. 1; 10 sites; water and bathroom facilities; trailer village vehicle sites; cabins; picnic area; food service; boating; hunting; fishing; hiking; tent camping.

Huttonsville

KUMBRABOW STATE FOREST
(304) 335-2219
LOCATION: Near Huttonsville.
FACILITIES: Open Apr. 15 - Nov. 1; 12 sites;

WEST VIRGINIA

STATE FORESTS (continued)

water and bathroom facilities; trailer village vehicle sites; cabins; picnic area; hunting; fishing; hiking; tent camping.

Panther

PANTHER STATE FOREST
(304) 938-2252
LOCATION: Near Panther.
FACILITIES: Open Apr. 15 - Nov. 1; 6 sites; water and bathroom facilities; trailer village vehicle sites; picnic area; swimming; hunting; fishing; hiking; tent camping.

HISTORIC SITES

Fairmont

PRICKETTS FORT - Life on the Virginia frontier during the Revolutionary War is accurately portrayed in authentic reconstruction of a typical stockade fort of the period. Original log buildings were dismantled and used as building materials to recreate a refuge fort.

Moundsville

LITTLE GRAVE CREEK INDIAN MOUND - World's largest Indian mound and complete museum of Indian artifacts.

Oglebay Park

OGLEBAY MANSION - Once the summer home of Cleveland industrialist Earl W. Oglebay, this historic mansion features period rooms, art gallery and an exceptional glass collection including the famous Sweeney Punch Bowl and the largest known cut-blown moulded piece in the world.

Philippi

PHILIPPI BRIDGE - On June 3, 1861, a small garrison of Confederate soldiers, some of them billeted in the bridge itself, were surprised by Union cannon fire. The Confederates were driven from the town in the skirmish known as the first land battle of the Civil War.

Wheeling

WEST VIRGINIA INDEPENDENCE HALL - One of the country's best examples of Civil War architecture, Independence Hall was the site of the famous meeting which declared Virginia's secession from the Union unlawful and gave birth to the new state of West Virginia.

HOSTELS

Morgantown

CHESTNUT RIDGE CAMP
P.O. Box 590
Morgantown, WV 26505
(304) 292-4773

FACILITIES: Open year round; dormitory accommodations with beds & bunks for men and women; modern bathroom; overnight charges: $1.25; houseparent: Mary M. Adkins.

POINTS OF INTEREST

Bluefield

SKYLAND'S RIDGE RUNNER - Shortest interstate railroad in the nation, where you can cross the West Virginia/Virginia state line four times on top of the East River Mountain.

Caldwell

ORGAN CAVE - Once called Lee's Underground Powder Works, and one of the largest caves in the United States, contains 37 well-preserved saltpeter hoppers in one room, and features the Rock Organ, a large flowstone. Located on U.S. 60.

Charleston

SUNRISE - Two magnificent mansions and a beautiful 16-acre estate, the Sunrise complex provides facilities for the Children's Museum and Planetarium, the Charleston Art Gallery of Sunrise, and the Sunrise Garden Center. Located at 746 Myrtle Road.

Hillsboro

STULTING HOUSE - Home of Pearl S. Buck has been renovated, but still contains many of the furnishings that were there when the famous author was born.

Lewisburg

LOST WORLD CAVERNS - Walk on a prehistoric ocean floor and along a scenic trail which travels over a subterranean mountain of rock to rooms larger than a football field. Also, visit an ancient beach over 300,000 years old.

Moundsville

FOSTORIA GLASS COMPANY - Highly skilled workmen engage in making nationally famous hand-crafted glassware and Fostoria lead crystal.

New Martinsville

VIKING GLASS COMPANY - Since the turn of the century, Viking Glass has been fashioning treasured glassware. Tours of the facility are offered daily.

Oglebay Park

GOOD ZOO - Like no other zoo in the world, a unique presentation of animals indigenous to North America in their natural surroundings.

Talcott

BIG BEND TUNNELS - The legend of big

POINTS OF INTEREST (continued)

John Henry began here when he beat the steam drill in a race in 1873. The famous twin railroad tunnels are 6,500 feet long; the older one nearer the highway is the legendary entry. A statue of John Henry is erected overlooking the tunnel. Located off Route 3.

WISCONSIN

Wisconsin, famous for its dairies and breweries, joined the Union in 1848 as the thirtieth state. Back in 1636, the French, too busy fighting the native Indians to establish a permanent settlement, lost out to the British, whose rapport with the Indians was somewhat better. When Indian hostilities finally subsided in the late 1730s, Wisconsin was solidly in the hands of the British and remained so until after the War of 1812.

Preceding the Civil War, Wisconsin saw a great influx of Europeans, mostly Germans and Scandinavians who became dairy farmers, miners, and lumberjacks. Brewmasters also immigrated to the state and set up distilleries. Today, Wisconsin is the nation's leading beer supplier, in addition to being the foremost producer of dairy products.

A picturesque state, being partially surrounded by two of the Great Lakes, Wisconsin draws thousands of visitors each year, making tourism another substantial state industry.

State capital: Madison. State bird: Robin. State tree: Sugar maple. State flower: Wood violet.

WEATHER

Wisconsin lies in the upper Midwest between Lake Superior, Upper Michigan, Lake Michigan, and the Mississippi and Saint Croix Rivers. Its greatest length is 320 miles, greatest width, 295 miles, and total area, 56,066 square miles. The Northern Highlands, a plateau extending across northern Wisconsin, is an area of about 15,000 square miles with elevations from 1,000 to 1,800 feet. This area has many lakes. A comparatively flat, crescent-shaped lowland lies immediately south of the Northern Highlands and embodies nearly one-fourth of Wisconsin. The eastern ridges and lowlands are located to the southeast of the Central Plains and are the most densely populated. The uplands of southwestern Wisconsin, west of the ridges and lowlands and south of the Central Plains, make up about one-fourth of the state.

The Wisconsin climate is typically continental with some modification by Lakes Michigan and Superior. The cold, snowy winters favor a variety of winter sports, and the warm summers appeal to thousands of vacationers each year. The average annual temperature varies from 39 degrees F in the north to about 50 degrees F in the south.

Average daily temperature for each month.

	Northern	Southern
Jan.	19.1 to 1.0	27.4 to 9.6
Feb.	25.0 to 3.8	32.4 to 13.9
Mar.	35.5 to 15.4	42.2 to 23.5
Apr.	51.5 to 30.7	58.9 to 36.8
May	64.1 to 41.3	70.8 to 46.7
Jun.	73.3 to 51.3	80.2 to 56.4
Jul.	77.3 to 55.9	84.2 to 60.7
Aug.	75.1 to 54.0	82.5 to 59.2
Sept.	65.4 to 45.3	75.0 to 51.5
Oct.	55.9 to 36.9	64.0 to 42.1
Nov.	37.2 to 23.0	46.2 to 29.2
Dec.	24.3 to 9.0	32.6 to 17.0
Year	50.3 to 30.6	58.0 to 37.2

STATE CHAMBER OF COMMERCE

Wisconsin Association of Manufacturers & Commerce
111 E. Wisconsin Avenue
Room 1600
Milwaukee, WI 53202
(414) 778-0640

STATE & CITY TOURISM OFFICES

State

Division of Business Development Services
123 W. Washington Avenue
Madison, WI 53702
(608) 266-3222

Division of Tourism
Department of Business Development
123 W. Washington Avenue
Madison, WI 53702
(608) 266-2161

Local

Green Bay Visitor's and Convention Bureau, Inc.
Brown County Arena
P.O. Box 3278
Green Bay, WI 54303
(414) 494-9507

Milwaukee Convention and Visitor's Bureau
828 N. Broadway
Milwaukee, WI 53202
(414) 273-3950

WISCONSIN

STATE HIGHWAY DEPARTMENT

Department of Transportation
4802 Sheboygan Avenue
Madison, WI 53702
(608) 266-1113

HIGHWAY WELCOMING CENTERS

Beloit

BELOIT CENTER - Interstate 90, Wisconsin and Illinois border.

Genoa City

GENOA CITY CENTER - U.S. 12.

Hudson

HUDSON CENTER - Interstate 94, east.

Kenosha

KENOSHA CENTER - Interstate 94, Wisconsin and Illinois border.

Prairie du Chien

PRAIRIE DU CHIEN CENTER - U.S. 18, Iowa and Wisconsin border.

Rockland

ROCKLAND CENTER - Interstate 90, east.

Superior

SUPERIOR CENTER - U.S. 53, Minnesota border.

STATE POLICE

Department of Public Safety
P.O. Box 7912
Madison, WI 53702
(608) 266-3212

HUNTING & FISHING

Hunting

No hunting licenses shall be issued to any person under the age of 12 years.

Members of the Armed Forces stationed in Wisconsin, and registered full-time undergraduate students in residence at a college or university located in this state and offering a bachelor degree, may purchase a resident small-game and deer license.

A fishing and small-game hunting license shall be issued without charge to any Wisconsin member of the Armed Forces of the United States who exhibits proof that he/she is in active service with such Armed Forces and that he/she is a Wisconsin resident on furlough or leave.

A citizen of a foreign country temporarily residing in this state while attending a Wisconsin high school or an agricultural short course at the University of Wisconsin may purchase a resident small-game and deer license.

All licenses expire on August 31, except the Armed Forces license, which expires on December 31.

A resident is defined as any person who has maintained his/her place of permanent abode in this state for a period of 30 days immediately preceding the application for license.

Resident

Deer license, $7.25; bear license, $7.25; small-game license, $5.25; sportsman's license, $16.50; archer's license, $6.25 (under 19, $3.25); trapping license, $4.25.

Non-resident

General license, $100.50; deer-bear license, $70.50; small-game license, $50.50; archer's license, $25.50; trapping license not available to non-residents.

Fishing

Resident fishing license is required of all resident fishers 16 to 65 years of age for fishing in inland, boundary and outlying waters. Members of the Armed Forces stationed in Wisconsin, and registered full-time undergraduate students in residence at college or university located in this state and offering a bachelor degree may purchase a resident license.

A fishing and small-game hunting license shall be issued without charge to any Wisconsin member of the Armed Forces of the United States who exhibits proof of active service with such Armed Forces and is a Wisconsin resident on furlough or leave.

Any person who has not been a permanent resident of Wisconsin continuously for 30 days prior to the date of application for a license is considered a non-resident. A non-resident is required to have a fishing license when taking smelt.

A trout stamp is required for all persons who must obtain a fishing license who intend to fish trout in inland waters of the state. The stamp must be signed across its face and attached to the fishing license.

Resident

Fishing license, $4.25; permanent resident if blind or over 65, free; combination fishing license, $7.50; voluntary sportsman's license, minimum fee, $16.50; trout stamp, $2.50.

Non-resident

Annual fishing license, $12.50; annual family fishing license, $18; 15-day fishing license, $7.50; 4-day fishing license, $5.50; trout stamp, $2.50.

For more information contact:

Department of Natural Resources
P.O. Box 7921

HUNTING & FISHING (continued)

Madison, WI 53702
(608) 266-3696

CAMPGROUNDS

Private

Atkinson

YOGI BEAR'S JELLYSTONE CAMP
(414) 563-5714
LOCATION: 6 mi. south of Ft. Atkinson on Route 26, 1 mi. west on Koshkonong Lake Road.
FACILITIES: Open May - Nov.; 300 sites; water and bathroom facilities; sanitary station; electrical hookup; trailer village vehicle sites; laundry; food service; swimming; fishing; tent camping.

Campbellsport

BENSON'S CAMPING RESORT
(414) 533-8597
LOCATION: 2 mi. north of Dundee on Route 67, on Long Lake.
FACILITIES: Open Apr. - Nov.; 250 sites; water and bathroom facilities; sanitary station; electrical hookup; trailer village vehicle sites; food service; swimming; boating; boat rental; fishing; tent camping.

Edgerton

HICKORY HILLS CAMPGROUND
(608) 884-6327
LOCATION: 856 Hillside Road.
FACILITIES: Open May 1 - Oct. 15; 250 sites; water and bathroom facilities; sanitary station; electrical hookup; trailer village vehicle sites; food service; boating; boat rental; fishing; tent camping.

Elkhart Lake

PLYMOUTH ROCK CAMPING RESORT
(414) 892-4252
LOCATION: 4 mi. north of Plymouth.
FACILITIES: Open year round; 200 sites; water and bathroom facilities; sanitary station; electrical hookup; trailer village vehicle sites; laundry; food service; swimming; boating; boat rental; fishing; tent camping.

Elkhorn

TROUT VALLEY CAMPGROUND
(414) 723-3210
LOCATION: 5 mi. east of Elkhorn on Route 11.
FACILITIES: Open Apr. - Nov.; 325 sites; water and bathroom facilities; sanitary station; electrical hookup; trailer village vehicle sites; food service; swimming; boating; boat rental; fishing; tent camping.

Kingston

SPORTSMAN'S HAVEN CAMPGROUND
(414) 394-3643
LOCATION: 2½ mi. west of Kingston.

FACILITIES: Open May - Dec.; 300 sites; water and bathroom facilities; sanitary station; electrical hookup; trailer village vehicle sites; laundry; food service; hunting; fishing; tent camping.

Lodi

GANNON'S BIRCHWOOD RESORT & CAMPGROUND
(608) 592-3757
LOCATION: 11 mi. west of I-90 and I-94 on Hwy. 60.
FACILITIES: Open year round; 400 sites; water and bathroom facilities; sanitary station; electrical hookup; trailer village vehicle sites; laundry; food service; fishing; tent camping.

Lyndon Station

CLIFF HOUSE RESORT & CAMPGROUND
(608) 666-3121
LOCATION: 4 mi. east of Lyndon Station on Hwy. HH.
FACILITIES: Open year round; 250 sites; water and bathroom facilities; sanitary station; electrical hookup; trailer village vehicle sites; laundry; food service; swimming; hunting; fishing; tent camping.

Milton

LAKELAND CAMP & TRAILER PARK
(608) 868-4255
LOCATION: 2 mi. east of I-90 on Route 59.
FACILITIES: Open May 15 - Oct. 1; 350 sites; water and bathroom facilities; sanitary station; electrical hookup; trailer village vehicle sites; food service; swimming; boating; boat rental; fishing; tent camping.

Montello

WILDERNESS CAMPGROUND
(414) 297-2002
LOCATION: 7 mi. south of Montello on Route 22.
FACILITIES: Open Apr. 15 - Oct. 15; 350 sites; water and bathroom facilities; sanitary station; electrical hookup; trailer village vehicle sites; laundry; food service; swimming; fishing; tent camping.

Pardeeville

INDIAN TRAILS CAMPGROUND
(608) 429-3244
LOCATION: 1 mi. north of Pardeeville on Route 22, then 1 mi. west on Haynes Road.
FACILITIES: Open year round; 275 sites; water and bathroom facilities; sanitary station; electrical hookup; trailer village vehicle sites; laundry; food service; swimming; boating; boat rental; tent camping.

Redgranite

FLANAGANS PEARL LAKE CAMPSITE
(414) 566-2758
LOCATION: 3 mi. north of Redgranite on Route EE.
FACILITIES: Open year round; 300 sites; water and bathroom facilities; sanitary station; electrical hookup; trailer village vehicle sites;

WISCONSIN

CAMPGROUNDS (continued)

laundry; food service; swimming; hunting; fishing; tent camping.

Sturgeon Bay

YOGI BEAR'S JELLYSTONE CAMP
(414) 743-9001
LOCATION: 7 mi. southwest of Sturgeon Bay.
FACILITIES: Open May - Nov.; 308 sites; water and bathroom facilities; sanitary station; electrical hookup; trailer village vehicle sites; laundry; food service; swimming; hunting; fishing; tent camping.

Tomahawk

THE OUTPOST
(715) 453-3468
LOCATION: 6 mi. north of Tomahawk on Route 51, then 1 mi. east on Hwy. N.
FACILITIES: Open May 1 - Oct. 15; 250 sites; water and bathroom facilities; sanitary station; electrical hookup; trailer village vehicle sites; laundry; food service; swimming; boating; boat rental; fishing; tent camping.

Watertown

RUBIDELL RECREATION
(414) 261-5112
LOCATION: 8 mi. west of Watertown.
FACILITIES: Open Apr. 15 - Oct. 20; 450 sites; water and bathroom facilities; sanitary station; electrical hookup; trailer village vehicle sites; laundry; food service; swimming; boating; boat rental; tent camping.

Wautoma

LAKE OF THE WOODS
(414) 787-3601
LOCATION: 8 mi. south of Wautoma on Route 22, 1 mi. west on Hwy. JJ, then ½ mi. south on 14th St.
FACILITIES: Open year round; 250 sites; water and bathroom facilities; sanitary station; electrical hookup; trailer village vehicle sites; laundry; food service; swimming; boating; boat rental; hunting; fishing; tent camping.

West Bend

LAZY DAYS CAMPGROUND
(414) 675-6511
LOCATION: 7½ mi. northeast of West Bend.
FACILITIES: Open Apr. - Dec.; 300 sites; water and bathroom facilities; sanitary station; electrical hookup; trailer village vehicle sites; laundry; food service; swimming; boating; boat rental; fishing; tent camping.

Whitewater

LAURSEN'S T.C. CAMPGROUND
(608) 883-2920
LOCATION: 8 mi. south of Whitewater.
FACILITIES: Open May 1 - Oct. 15; 250 sites; water and bathroom facilities; sanitary station; electrical hookup; trailer village vehicle sites; laundry; food service; swimming; tent camping.

Wild Rose

EVERGREEN CAMPSITES
(414) 622-3498
LOCATION: 4½ mi. east of Wild Rose.
FACILITIES: Open year round; 300 sites; water and bathroom facilities; sanitary station; electrical hookup; trailer village vehicle sites; laundry; food service; swimming; boating; boat rental; hunting; fishing; tent camping.

RESORTS & BEACHES

Most of the state's resort activities center around the major lakes and include fishing, swimming, boating, water skiing, and camping. (See National Forests, State Parks and State Forests.)

BOATING AREAS

Wisconsin has more than 30,000 lakes, the largest of which are Lake Michigan, the state's eastern boundary, and Lake Superior, the boundary to the north. For Boating Areas in major recreational areas throughout the state, see National Forests, State Parks and State Forests.

BICYCLE TRAILS

KINNICKINNIC TRAIL - 100 mi.; any bicycle.

The ride may be taken in either direction in the spring, summer, or fall. Wisconsin County roads are designated by single or double letters rather than by numerals.

Trail: River Falls to SS north, left on N to Hudson to MM south to QQ south to Q to Diamond Bluff to E, left on O to Trimbelle to O north to Beldenville to J to Martell to Y north, left on M to River Falls.

LAKE SUPERIOR TRAIL - 350 mi.; long distances; 10-speed bicycle recommended.

This north-south tour of Wisconsin starts on the shores of Lake Superior, one of the largest lakes in the world, and ends on the banks of the mighty Mississippi River. Between these two points it skirts many lakes and streams.

Trail: Red Cliff to Port Wing to Parkland to Gordon to Hayward to Edgewater to Mikana to Chetek to Bloomer to Chippewa Falls to Eau Claire to Eleva to Arcadia to New Amsterdam to La Crosse.

TOMAHAWK TRAIL - 225 mi.; hilly terrain, long distances; 10-speed bicycle recommended.

This is a long jaunt that starts at Deepwood Ski Lodge Hostel between Colfax and Wheeler.

Trail: Colfax to Wheeler to Bloomer to Route 178 to Longwood to Golby to Wisconsin River to Merrill to Tomahawk to Spirit Falls to Phillips.

TRAILS

Elroy

ELROY-SPARTA TRAIL - 30 mi. foot trail. This portion of the Wisconsin Bikeway is constructed on an abandoned railroad right-of-way. The trail passes through three tunnels to provide easy riding in a hilly, scenic area of Wisconsin. An unusual feature of the trail is that it is designated as a snowmobile trail during winter, and all motorized travel is prohibited in summer. It is strongly supported by local communities along the trail.

Madison

SUGAR RIVER STATE TRAIL - 23 mi. foot trail. Approximately one-half hour's drive from Madison, this trail is located on an abandoned railroad right-of-way. The trail environment is of a rural character in gently rolling farmland in the most scenic part of Green County. The Sugar River Valley abounds with wildlife. The railroad bed has been modified by adding a hard pack of limestone screenings, providing a smooth and solid base for the trail activities.

Milwaukee

ICE AGE TRAIL - 25 mi. foot trail. Located 40 miles north of Milwaukee, the Ice Age Trail in Kettle Moraine State Forest passes through several types of forested areas, both highland and swamp, and past kames, eskers, kettle holes, and moraine lakes. The State Forest is noted for its special geological feature of continental glaciers during the Ice Age. There are five trailside shelters along the trail.

Sturgeon Bay

AHNAPEE STATE PARK TRAIL - 15 mi. foot trail. An abandoned railroad right-of-way has been used in Wisconsin's scenic Door Peninsula. Major features of the trail environment include the Ahnapee Wildlife Area, a peat swamp, the Ahnapee River, and extensive farm lands. Sturgeon Bay and Algoma, near the northern and southern ends of the trail respectively, provide water-oriented recreation opportunities.

Torrington

GRASSROOTS TRAIL - .94 mi. foot trail. The trail runs through the center of Torrington along a greenbelt of mini-parks. The mini-parks are unique, having been constructed on land reclaimed by tiling and covering an open irrigation canal. The canal dates to 1883 and is part of the New North Platte Irrigation Canal that now flows under the trail.

SKI AREAS

Antigo

KETTLEBOWL
Antigo, WI 54409
(715) 623-3560
LOCATION: 15 mi. northeast on South 52.
FACILITIES: 5 tow ropes; 200 ft. vertical drop; longest run, 2000 ft.; restaurants; lodging.

Arena

TIMBERLANE
Arena, WI 53503
(608) 753-2315
LOCATION: 30 mi. west of Madison on South 14.
FACILITIES: 1 chairlift; 1 T-bar; 1 tow rope; ski instruction; ski rental; longest run, 2200 ft.; restaurants; lodging.

Bayfield

PORT MOUNTAIN
Bayfield, WI 54814
(715) 779-3227
LOCATION: 3 mi. south of Bayfield on South 13.
FACILITIES: 4 chairlifts; 1 T-bar; ski instruction; ski rental; 817 ft. vertical drop; longest run, 5000 ft.; restaurants; lodging.

Boscobel

BULL RUN LTD
Boscobel, WI 53805
(608) 375-4789
LOCATION: 1.5 mi. west of Boscobel on South 133.
FACILITIES: 2 tow ropes; ski instruction; ski rental; 320 ft. vertical drop; longest run, 3500 ft.; restaurants; lodging.

Bruce

CHRISTIE MOUNTAIN
Bruce, WI 54819
(715) 868-7800
LOCATION: 7 mi. northwest of Bruce.
FACILITIES: 1 chairlift; 1 T-bar; 1 tow rope; ski instruction; ski rental; longest run, 4000 ft.; restaurants; lodging.

Cable

MT. TELEMARK
Cable, WI 54821
(715) 798-3811
LOCATION: 3 mi. east of Cable.
FACILITIES: 3 chairlifts; 3 T-bars; 10 tow ropes; ski instruction; ski rental; 370 ft. vertical drop; longest run, 2600 ft.; restaurants; lodging.

Coleman

MT. LEBETT
Coleman, WI 54112
(414) 897-2290
LOCATION: 5 mi. west of Coleman.
FACILITIES: 1 chairlift; 3 tow ropes; ski instruction; ski rental; 310 ft. vertical drop; longest run, 1500 ft.; restaurants; lodging.

Crivitz

WINTERSET
Crivitz, WI 54114
(715) 854-7935
LOCATION: 5 mi. west of Crivitz.
FACILITIES: 3 tow ropes; ski instruction; ski

WISCONSIN

SKI AREAS (continued)

rental; 180 ft. vertical drop; longest run, 1800 ft.; restaurants; lodging.

Delafield

VELKOMMEN
Delafield, WI 53018
(414) 367-6967
LOCATION: Southwest of I-94 and South 83, Delafield exit.
FACILITIES: 1 chairlift; 6 tow ropes; ski instruction; ski rental; longest run, 1300 ft.; restaurants; lodging.

DePere

HILLY HAVEN
DePere, WI 54115
(414) 336-6204
LOCATION: 6.5 mi. south of DePere.
FACILITIES: 5 tow ropes; ski instruction; ski rental; 100 ft. vertical drop; longest run, 800 ft.; restaurants; lodging.

PINK PANTHER
DePere, WI 54115
(414) 336-1122
LOCATION: 3½ mi. south of DePere on South 32.
FACILITIES: 1 T-bar; 3 tow ropes; ski instruction; ski rental; longest run, 1000 ft.

Dresser

TROLLHAUGEN
Dresser, WI 54009
(715) 755-2955
LOCATION: .75 mi. east of Dresser.
FACILITIES: 2 quad chairlifts; 1 chairlift; 1 T-bar; 7 tow ropes; ski instruction; ski rental; 250 ft. vertical drop; longest run, 2500 ft.; restaurants; lodging.

Duluth

MONT DULAC
Duluth, WI 55808
(715) 636-9991
LOCATION: 17 mi. south of Duluth.
FACILITIES: 1 chairlift; 1 T-bar; 3 tow ropes; ski instruction; ski rental; 300 ft. vertical drop; longest run, 2400 ft.; restaurants; lodging.

East Troy

ALPINE VALLEY
East Troy, WI 53120
(414) 642-7374
LOCATION: 3 mi. south of East Troy.
FACILITIES: 1 triple chairlift; 11 chairlifts; 1 tow rope; beginners slope; ski instruction; ski rental; 288 ft. vertical drop; longest run, 3300 ft.; restaurants; lodging.

Florence

KEYES PEAK
Florence, WI 54121
(715) 528-3228
LOCATION: 4 mi. south of Florence on South 101.

FACILITIES: 3 tow ropes; 200 ft. vertical drop; longest run, 1760 ft.; restaurants; lodging.

Friendship

SKYLINE
Friendship., WI 53934
(608) 339-3421
LOCATION: ¼ mi. northwest of Friendship off South 13.
FACILITIES: 1 triple chairlift; 1 chairlift; 2 tow ropes; ski instruction; ski rental; 335 ft. vertical drop; longest run, 2880 ft.; restaurants; lodging.

Gays Mills

SNOWBOWL
Gays Mills, WI 54631
(608) 735-9479
LOCATION: ½ mi. south of Gays Mills via South 131 then east 1 mi. on Town Road.
FACILITIES: 1 tow rope; ski instruction; ski rental; longest run, 1500 ft.

Gilman

PERKINSTOWN WINTER SPORTS AREA
Gilman, WI 54433
(715) 447-8211
LOCATION: 4 mi. north of South 64.
FACILITIES: 5 tow ropes; ski rental; 150 ft. vertical drop; longest run, 1500 ft.; restaurants; lodging.

Gleason

HARRISON HILLS
Gleason, WI 54435
(715) 873-2235
LOCATION: 20 mi. northeast of Merrill on South 17.
FACILITIES: 3 tow ropes; 200 ft. vertical drop; longest run, 2000 ft.; restaurants; lodging.

Hancock

NORDIC MOUNTAIN
Hancock, WI 54943
(414) 787-3324
LOCATION: 8 mi. north of Wautoma.
FACILITIES: 1 triple chairlift; 1 chairlift; 1 tow rope; 1 poma; ski instruction; ski rental; 240 ft. vertical drop; longest run, 2500 ft.; restaurants; lodging.

Hilbert

CALUMET COUNTY PARK
Hilbert, WI 54129
(414) 439-1008
LOCATION: 3 mi. north of Stockbridge on south 55.
FACILITIES: 5 tow ropes; ski instruction; ski rental; 155 ft. vertical drop; longest run, 5000 ft.; restaurants; lodging.

Houlton

BIRCH PARK
Houlton, WI 54016
(715) 549-6777

SKI AREAS (continued)

LOCATION: Houlton WI, 3 mi. east of Stillwater, MN.
FACILITIES: 3 chairlifts; 1 T-bar; 7 tow ropes; ski instruction; ski rental; 230 ft. vertical drop; longest run, 2000 ft.; restaurant; lodging.

Kewaskum

SUNBURST
Kewaskum, WI 53040
(414) 626-4605
LOCATION: Near Kewaskum.
FACILITIES: 1 chairlift; 1 T-bar; 4 tow ropes; 1 cable grip ski instruction; ski rental; 214 ft. vertical drop; restaurants; lodging.

LaCrosse

MT. LACROSSE
LaCrosse, WI 54601
(608) 788-0044
LOCATION: 2 mi. south of LaCrosse on South 35.
FACILITIES: 2 chairlifts; 3 tow ropes; ski instruction; ski rental; 516 ft. vertical drop; longest run, 5300 ft.; restaurants; lodging.

Lake Geneva

INTERLAKEN
Lake Geneva, WI 53147
(414) 248-9121
LOCATION: 3 mi. west of Lake Geneva on South 50.
FACILITIES: 2 tow ropes; ski instruction; ski rental; longest run, 950 ft.; restaurants; lodging.

MAJESTIC
Lake Geneva, WI 53147
(414) 248-6128
LOCATION: 8 mi. south of Lake Geneva.
FACILITIES: 3 chairlifts; 5 tow ropes; ski instruction; ski rental; 230 ft. vertical drop; longest run, 1400 ft.; restaurants; lodging.

MT. FUJI
Lake Geneva, WI 53147
(414) 248-6553
LOCATION: 2 mi. northeast of Lake Geneva at Junction South 36 and Krueger Road.
FACILITIES: 4 chairlifts; 1 T-bar; 2 tow ropes; 235 ft. vertical drop; longest run, 2700 ft.; restaurants; lodging.

PLAYBOY
Lake Geneva, WI 53147
(414) 248-8811
LOCATION: 3 mi. from Lake Geneva adjacent to South 50.
FACILITIES: 3 chairlifts; 2 tow ropes; ski instruction; ski rental; 211 ft. vertical drop; longest run, 1320 ft.; restaurants; lodging.

Lakewood

PAUL BUNYAN
Lakewood, WI 54138
(715) 276-7610
LOCATION: 2 mi. north of Lakewood on North Road.
FACILITIES: 1 T-bar; 4 tow ropes; ski in-

struction; ski rental; 110 ft. vertical drop; longest run, 1050 ft.; restaurants; lodging.

Land O'Lakes

GATEWAY LODGE
Land O'Lakes, WI 54540
(715) 547-3321
LOCATION: 2 blocks east of Land O'Lakes off South 45.
FACILITIES: 3 tow ropes; ski instruction; ski rental; longest run, 2000 ft.; restaurants; lodging.

Manitowoc

HIDDEN VALLEY
Manitowoc, WI 54220
(414) 863-2713
LOCATION: 13 mi. north of Manitowoc on U.S. 141.
FACILITIES: 1 chairlift; 4 tow ropes; ski instruction; ski rental; 200 ft. vertical drop; longest run, 3600 ft.

Mauston

WOODSIDE DUDE RANCH
Mauston, WI 53948
(608) 847-4275
LOCATION: 7 mi. east of Mauston on South 82.
FACILITIES: 1 tow rope; ski instruction; ski rental; 75 ft. vertical drop; longest run, 800 ft.; restaurants; lodging.

Merrimac

DEVIL'S HEAD
Merrimac, WI 53561
(608) 493-2251
LOCATION: South of Baraboo.
FACILITIES: 1 triple chairlift; 6 chairlifts; 3 tow ropes; ski instruction; ski rental; 495 ft. vertical drop; longest run, 4500 ft.; restaurants; lodging.

Montreal

WHITECAP
Montreal, WI 54550
(715) 561-2227
LOCATION: 7 mi. west of Hurley on Hwy. 77.
FACILITIES: 4 chairlifts; 4 tow ropes; ski instruction; ski rental; 400 ft. vertical drop; longest run, 5000 ft.; restaurants; lodging.

Mt. Horeb

TYROL BASIN
Mt. Horeb, WI 53572
(608) 437-5440
LOCATION: 3.5 mi. west of Mt. Horeb off South 18.
FACILITIES: 1 chairlift; 1 T-bar; 3 tow ropes; ski instruction; ski rental; 380 ft. vertical drop; longest run, 3600 ft.; restaurants; lodging.

Neillsville

BRUCE MOUND
Neillsville, WI 54456

WISCONSIN

SKI AREAS (continued)

(715) 743-2490
LOCATION: 11 mi. north of Black River Falls.
FACILITIES: 2 T-bars; 2 tow ropes; ski instruction; ski rental; 300 ft. vertical drop; longest run, 2500 ft.; restaurants; lodging.

New London

VIEWRIDGE
New London, WI 54961
(414) 982-9982
LOCATION: 1 mi. east of New London.
FACILITIES: 3 tow ropes; ski instruction; longest run, 2400 ft.

Oconomowoc

OLYMPIA
Oconomowoc, WI 53066
(414) 567-0311
LOCATION: North of I-94 on Route 67 south, exit 282, 26 mi. west of Milwaukee.
FACILITIES: 2 chairlifts; 2 tow ropes; ski instruction; ski rental; 196 ft. vertical drop; longest run, 2800 ft.; restaurants; lodging.

Portage

CASCADE MOUNTAIN
Portage, WI 53901
(608) 742-2550
LOCATION: 4.5 mi. southwest of Portage on I-90-94, then south on Route 33 east or Route 78 to Cascade Mountain Road.
FACILITIES: 1 chairlift; 1 T-bar; 2 tow ropes; 1 pony lift; beginners area; ski instruction; ski rental; 460 ft. vertical drop; longest run, 5300 ft.; restaurants; lodging.

Reedsburg

HOGSBACK HILL
Reedsburg, WI 53959
(608) 524-2649
LOCATION: 4 mi. south of Reedsburg.
FACILITIES: 1 tow rope; longest run, 600 ft.; open when weather permits.

Rhinelander

CAMP 10
Rhinelander, WI 54501
(715) 362-6900
LOCATION: 10 mi. southwest of Rhinelander.
FACILITIES: 2 T-bars; 3 tow ropes; ski instruction; ski rental; 255 ft. vertical drop; longest run, 2000 ft.; restaurants; lodging.

Rice Lake

HARDSCRABBLE
Rice Lake, WI 54868
(715) 234-3412
LOCATION: 5 mi. east of Rice Lake.
FACILITIES: 2 T-bars; 5 tow ropes; ski instruction; ski rental; 400 ft. vertical drop; longest run, 400 ft.; restaurants; lodging.

Shiocton

NAVARINO HILLS

Shiocton, WI 54170
(715) 758-2211
LOCATION: 10 mi. east of Clintonville.
FACILITIES: 1 chairlift; 4 tow ropes; ski instruction; ski rental; 106 ft. vertical drop; longest run, 1200 ft.; restaurants; lodging.

Slinger

LITTLE SWITZERLAND
Slinger, WI 53086
(414) 644-5020
LOCATION: 25 mi north of Milwaukee on Route 41 south.
FACILITIES: 1 quad chairlift; 4 chairlifts; ski instruction; ski rental; longest run, 1800 ft.; restaurants; lodging.

Somerset

SNOWCREST
Somerset, WI 54025
(715) 247-3852
LOCATION: 10 mi. north of I-94, take Hudson exit north on South 35.
FACILITIES: 2 chairlifts; 1 T-bar; 7 tow ropes; ski instruction; ski rental; 280 ft. vertical drop; longest run, 3500 ft.; restaurants; lodging.

Spring Green

WINTERGREEN
Spring Green, WI 53588
(608) 583-2124
LOCATION: 3 mi. south of Spring Green on Route 23 south.
FACILITIES: 2 chairlifts; 1 J-bar; ski instruction; ski rental; 400 ft. vertical drop; longest run, 4100 ft.; restaurants; lodging.

Spring Valley

SPRING VALLEY
Spring Valley, WI 54767
(715) 778-5513
LOCATION: 1.5 mi. northwest of Spring Valley on Route 29 south.
FACILITIES: 1 tow rope; longest run, 1200 ft.; restaurants; lodging.

Stevens Point

STANDING ROCKS
Stevens Point, WI 54481
(715) 346-3510
LOCATION: 1.25 mi. south on Town Road, then ¼ mi. east on Town Road.
FACILITIES: 2 tow ropes; ski instruction; ski rental; 100 ft. vertical drop; longest run, 1000 ft.; restaurants; lodging.

Strum

VIKING SKYLINE
Strum, WI 54770
(715) 696-3525
LOCATION: .5 mi. east of Strum on South 10.
FACILITIES: 3 tow ropes; ski instruction; ski rental; longest run, 1100 ft.

Three Lakes

SHELTERED VALLEY

SKI AREAS (continued)

Three Lakes, WI 54562
(715) 546-3535
LOCATION: 8 mi. east of Three Lakes on
South 32 to Military Road, 2 mi. to Sheltered
Valley Road then 2 mi.
FACILITIES: 3 tow ropes; 1 poma; ski in-
struction; ski rental; 200 ft. vertical drop;
longest run, 2000 ft.; restaurants; lodging.

Wausau

RIB MOUNTAIN
Wausau, WI 54401
(715) 845-2846
LOCATION: 3 mi. southwest of Wausau on
Route 51 Bypass south.
FACILITIES: 2 chairlifts; 2 T-bars; 3 tow
ropes; ski instruction; ski rental; 600 ft. vertical drop; longest run, 3800 ft.; restaurants;
lodging.

SYLVAN HILL PARK
Wausau, WI 54401
(715) 842-2141
LOCATION: In Wausau.
FACILITIES: 4 tow ropes; ski instruction; ski
rental; 90 ft. vertical drop; longest run, 1800
ft.; restaurants; lodging.

Wheeler

DEEPWOOD
Wheeler, WI 54772
(715) 658-1394
LOCATION: 9 mi. northwest of Colfax.
FACILITIES: 2 T-bars; 8 tow ropes; ski instruction; ski rental; 293 ft. vertical drop;
longest run, 3200 ft.; restaurants; lodging.

Wilmot

WILMOT MOUNTAIN
Wilmot, WI 53192
(414) 862-2301
LOCATION: 15 mi. west of I-94.
FACILITIES: 3 triple chairlifts; 4 chairlifts;
1 T-bar; 8 tow ropes; ski instruction; ski rental; 230 ft. vertical drop; longest run, 2500 ft.;
restaurants; lodging.

Wisconsin Dells

CHRISTMAS MOUNTAIN
Wisconsin Dells, WI 53965
(608) 254-2531
LOCATION: 4.5 mi. west of Wisconsin Dells.
FACILITIES: 2 chairlifts; 3 tow ropes; ski instruction; ski rental; 205 ft. vertical drop;
longest run, 2800 ft.; restaurants; lodging.

Wisconsin Rapids

POWERS BLUFF
Wisconsin Rapids, WI 54494
(715) 423-3000
LOCATION: 17 mi. northwest of Wisconsin
Rapids.
FACILITIES: 1 tow rope; ski rental; 250 ft.
vertical drop; longest run, 1750 ft.; restau-
rants; lodging.

AMUSEMENT PARKS & ATTRACTIONS

Baraboo

CIRCUS WORLD MUSEUM (Attraction)
426 Water Street
Baraboo, WI 53913
(608) 356-8341
FACILITIES: 3 refreshment stands; restaurant; museum; exhibits; picnic facilities; circus shows; free acts; pay gate; free parking;
open mid-May - mid-Sept.

Fish Creek

THUMB FUN
P.O. Box 128
Highway 42
Fish Creek, WI 54212
(414) 868-3418
FACILITIES: 9 major rides; 5 kiddie rides;
walk thru; 5 games; picnic facilities; restaurant; 2 refreshment stands; arcade; miniature
golf; golf driving range; free gate; free parking;
open May - Oct. 15; weekends: May, Sept. &
Oct.

Green Bay

BAY BEACH AMUSEMENT PARK
E. Shore Drive
Green Bay, WI 54301
(414) 437-0641
FACILITIES: 7 major rides; 4 kiddie rides; 4
refreshment stands; restaurant; wildlife sanctuary; picnic facilities; free gate; free parking;
open Apr. 22 - Sept. 5.

GREEN BAY PACKER HALL OF FAME
MUSEUM (Attraction)
1901 S. Onieda
Green Bay, WI 54303
(414) 499-4281
FACILITIES: Museum; exhibits; theater; pay
gate; free parking; open all year.

Muskego

DANDILION PARK
P.O. Box 66
Muskego, WI 53150
(414) 679-2400
FACILITIES: 19 major rides; 9 kiddie rides; 8
refreshment stands; restaurant; arcade; beach;
picnic facilities; pay gate; free parking; open
Memorial Day - Labor Day.

Wisconsin Dells

FAMILYLAND
Hwy. 12
Wisconsin Dells, WI 53965
(608) 254-7766
FACILITIES: 9 major rides; 10 kiddie rides;
fun house; walk thru; 2 refreshment stands;
shooting gallery; arcade; miniature golf; picnic facilities; pay gate; free parking; open
May 15 - Sept. 30.

FORT DELLS
P.O. Box 27
Wisconsin Dells, WI 53965
(608) 254-2535

WISCONSIN

AMUSEMENT PARKS (continued)

FACILITIES: 6 major rides; 2 kiddie rides; 3 refreshment stands; restaurant; 2 walk thrus; museum; exhibits; arcade; zoo (farm animals); picnic facilities; 335-foot totem tower; free acts; pay gate; free parking; open May 13 - Oct. 1.

RIVERVIEW AMUSEMENT PARK
Hwys. 12 and 23
Wisconsin Dells, WI 53965
(608) 254-8336
FACILITIES: 12 major rides; 15 kiddie rides; walk thru; 4 refreshment stands; arcade; shooting gallery; picnic facilities; trampolines; batting cage; miniature golf; books country & bluegrass stage shows; free gate; open mid-May - Sept. 5; weekends: Oct. 17.

RON & JUDY'S AMUSEMENT PARK
Hwy. 12
Wisconsin Dells, WI 53965
(608) 254-2450
FACILITIES: 15 major rides; 8 kiddie rides; fun house; 50 games; 4 refreshment stands; arcade; shooting gallery; picnic facilities; miniature golf; crafts; stage shows; free gate; free parking; open May 15 - Labor Day.

STATE FAIR

Wisconsin State Fair
2822 S. 19th Street
West Allis, WI 53227
(414) 257-8800
DATE: August

NATIONAL PARKS

There are no National Parks in Wisconsin.

NATIONAL FORESTS

National Forests
Eastern Region
633 West Wisconsin Avenue
Milwaukee, WI 53203
(414) 291-3693

Park Falls

CHEQUAMEGON NATIONAL FOREST
ATTRACTIONS: Muskellunge fishing; deer and small game hunting; canoe travel on Flambeau and Chippewa Rivers; skiing.
FACILITIES: 21 camp and picnic sites, 6 picnic only; 11 swimming sites; winter sports area; resorts and cabins.
NEARBY TOWNS: Ashland, Eau Claire, Hayward, Medford, Superior, Washburn.

Rhinelander

NICOLET NATIONAL FOREST
ATTRACTIONS: Muskellunge, pike, bass, trout fishing; deer, bear, grouse, duck hunting; swimming; boating; canoe trips; snowshoeing and skiing.
FACILITIES: 24 camp and picnic sites, 17 picnic only; 16 swimming sites; Sheltered Valley Ski Area; numerous resorts and private cabins on private lands within and near the National Forest.
NEARBY TOWNS: Eagle River, Green Bay, Marinette.

STATE PARKS

Headquarters

Department of Natural Resources
P.O. Box 7921
Madison, WI 53702
(608) 266-2621

Baraboo

DEVIL'S LAKE STATE PARK
(608) 356-8301
LOCATION: Near Baraboo.
FACILITIES: Open year round; 471 sites; water and bathroom facilities; sanitary station; electrical hookup; trailer village vehicle sites; picnic area; food service; swimming; boating; fishing; hiking; handicapped access/restroom; tent camping.

Blanchardville

YELLOWSTONE STATE PARK
(608) 523-4427
LOCATION: Near Blanchardville.
FACILITIES: Open year round; 129 sites; water and bathroom facilities; sanitary station; electrical hookup; trailer village vehicle sites; picnic area; food service; swimming; boating; fishing; hiking; handicapped access/restroom; tent camping. '

Blue Mounds

BLUE MOUNDS STATE PARK
(608) 437-5711
LOCATION: Near Blue Mounds.
FACILITIES: Open year round; 78 sites; water and bathroom facilities; sanitary station; trailer village vehicle sites; picnic area; hiking; tent camping.

Burkhardt

WILLOW RIVER STATE PARK
(715) 386-5931
LOCATION: Near Burkhardt.
FACILITIES: Open year round; 72 sites; water and bathroom facilities; sanitary station; electrical hookup; trailer village vehicle sites; picnic area; food service; swimming; boating; fishing; hiking; handicapped access/restroom; tent camping.

Chippewa Falls

LAKE WISSOTA STATE PARK
(715) 382-4574
LOCATION: Near Chippewa Falls.
FACILITIES: Open year round; 76 sites; water and bathroom facilities; sanitary station; electrical hookup; trailer village vehicle sites; picnic area; food service; swimming; boating; fishing; hiking; bicycle trail; handicapped access/restroom; tent camping.

STATE PARKS (continued)

Cornwell

BRUNET ISLAND STATE PARK
(715) 239-6888
LOCATION: Near Cornwell.
FACILITIES: Open year round; 69 sites; water and bathroom facilities; sanitary station; electrical hookup; trailer village vehicle sites; picnic area; swimming; boating; fishing; hiking; bicycle trail; tent camping.

Dodgeville

GOVERNOR DODGE STATE PARK
(608) 935-2315
LOCATION: Near Dodgeville.
FACILITIES: Open year round; 266 sites; water and bathroom facilities; sanitary station; electrical hookup; trailer village vehicle sites; picnic area; food service; swimming; boating; fishing; hiking; horseback riding; handicapped access/restroom; tent camping.

Fish Creek

PENINSULA STATE PARK
(414) 868-3258
LOCATION: Near Fish Creek.
FACILITIES: Open year round; 457 sites; water and bathroom facilities; sanitary station; electrical hookup; trailer village vehicle sites; picnic area; food service; swimming; fishing; hiking; bicycle trail; handicapped access/restroom; tent camping.

Fountain City

MERRICK STATE PARK
(608) 687-4936
LOCATION: Near Fountain City.
FACILITIES: Open year round; 76 sites; water and bathroom facilities; sanitary station; electrical hookup; trailer village vehicle sites; swimming; boating; fishing; handicapped access/restroom; tent camping.

Friendship

ROCHE A CRI STATE PARK
(608) 339-3385
LOCATION: Near Friendship.
FACILITIES: Open year round; 45 sites; water and bathroom facilities; trailer village vehicle sites; picnic area; hiking; handicapped access/restroom; tent camping.

Lake Delton

MIRROR LAKE STATE PARK
(608) 254-2333
LOCATION: Near Lake Delton.
FACILITIES: Open year round; 83 sites; water and bathroom facilities; sanitary station; electrical hookup; trailer village vehicle sites; picnic area; swimming; boating; fishing; handicapped access/restroom; tent camping.

Lake Geneva

BIG FOOT BEACH STATE PARK
(414) 248-2528
LOCATION: Near Lake Geneva.

FACILITIES: Open year round; 100 sites; water and bathroom facilities; trailer village vehicle sites; picnic area; food service; swimming; fishing; hiking; handicapped access/restroom; tent camping.

Merrill

COUNCIL GROUNDS STATE PARK
(715) 536-2711
LOCATION: Near Merrill.
FACILITIES: Open year round; 55 sites; water and bathroom facilities; sanitary station; electrical hookup; trailer village vehicle sites; picnic area; swimming; fishing; hiking; handicapped access/restroom; tent camping.

Prairie du Chien

WYALUSING STATE PARK
(608) 996-2261
LOCATION: Near Prairie du Chien.
FACILITIES: Open year round; 131 sites; water and bathroom facilities; sanitary station; electrical hookup; trailer village vehicle sites; picnic area; food service; boating; fishing; hiking; handicapped access/restroom; tent camping.

St. Croix Falls

INTERSTATE STATE PARK
(715) 483-3747
LOCATION: Near St. Croix Falls.
FACILITIES: Open year round; 96 sites; water and bathroom facilities; trailer village vehicle sites; picnic area; swimming; boating; fishing; hiking; handicapped access/restroom; tent camping.

Sheboygan

KOHLER-ANDRAE STATE PARK
(414) 452-3457
LOCATION: Near Sheboygan.
FACILITIES: Open year round; 105 sites; water and bathroom facilities; sanitary station; electrical hookup; trailer village vehicle sites; picnic area; food service; swimming; fishing; hiking; handicapped access/restroom; tent camping.

Sherwood

HIGH CLIFF STATE PARK
(414) 989-1106
LOCATION: Near Sherwood.
FACILITIES: Open year round; 54 sites; water and bathroom facilities; trailer village vehicle sites; picnic area; food service; swimming; boating; fishing; hiking; handicapped access/restroom; tent camping.

Stoughton

LAKE KEGONSA STATE PARK
(608) 873-9695
LOCATION: Near Stoughton.
FACILITIES: Open year round; 68 sites; water and bathroom facilities; sanitary station; trailer village vehicle sites; picnic area; swimming; boating; fishing; hiking; handicapped access/restroom; tent camping.

WISCONSIN

STATE PARKS (continued)

Sturgeon Bay

POTAWATOMI STATE PARK
(414) 743-5123
LOCATION: Near Sturgeon Bay.
FACILITIES: Open year round; 125 sites; water and bathroom facilities; electrical hookup; trailer village vehicle sites; picnic area; boating; fishing; hiking; bicycle trail; handicapped access/restroom; tent camping.

Superior

PATTISON STATE PARK
(715) 399-2115
LOCATION: Near Superior.
FACILITIES: Open year round; 59 sites; water and bathroom facilities; sanitary station; electrical hookup; trailer village vehicle sites; picnic area; food service; swimming; boating; fishing; hiking; bicycle trail; tent camping.

Trempealeau

PERROT STATE PARK
(608) 534-6409
LOCATION: Near Trempealeau.
FACILITIES: Open year round; 104 sites; water and bathroom facilities; sanitary station; electrical hookup; trailer village vehicle sites; picnic area; food service; boating; fishing; hiking; handicapped access/restroom; tent camping.

Washington Island

ROCK ISLAND STATE PARK
(414) 847-2235
LOCATION: Near Washington Island.
FACILITIES: Open year round; 40 sites; water and bathroom facilities; trailer village vehicle sites; picnic area; swimming; boating; fishing; hiking; tent camping.

Waupaca

HARTMAN CREEK STATE PARK
(715) 258-2372
LOCATION: Near Waupaca.
FACILITIES: Open year round; 100 sites; water and bathroom facilities; sanitary station; trailer village vehicle sites; picnic area; swimming; boating; fishing; hiking; handicapped access/restroom; tent camping.

Wisconsin Dells

ROCKY ARBOR STATE PARK
(608) 254-2333
LOCATION: Near Wisconsin Dells.
FACILITIES: Open year round; 69 sites; water and bathroom facilities; sanitary station; electrical hookup; trailer village vehicle sites; picnic area; handicapped access/restroom; tent camping.

STATE FORESTS

Department of Natural Resources
P.O. Box 7921

Madison, WI 53702
(608) 266-2621

Black River Falls

BLACK RIVER STATE FOREST
(715) 284-5301
LOCATION: Near Black River Falls.
FACILITIES: Open year round; 90 sites; water and bathroom facilities; trailer village vehicle sites; picnic area; swimming; boating; fishing; hiking; handicapped access/restroom; tent camping.

Boulder Junction

NORTH HIGHLAND - AMERICAN LEGION STATE FOREST
(715) 385-2727
LOCATION: Near Boulder Junction.
FACILITIES: Open year round; 926 sites; water and bathroom facilities; sanitary station; trailer village vehicle sites; picnic area; swimming; boating; fishing; hiking; handicapped access/restroom; tent camping.

Brule

BRULE RIVER STATE FOREST
(715) 736-2811
LOCATION: Near Brule.
FACILITIES: Open year round; 37 sites; water and bathroom facilities; trailer village vehicle sites; picnic area; boating; fishing; hiking; tent camping.

Campbellsport

KETTLE MORAINE (N.) STATE FOREST
(414) 626-2116
LOCATION: Near Campbellsport.
FACILITIES: Open year round; 391 sites; water and bathroom facilities; sanitary station; electrical hookup; trailer village vehicle sites; cabins; picnic area; food service; swimming; boating; fishing; hiking; horseback riding; handicapped access/restroom; tent camping.

Eagle

KETTLE MORAINE (S.) STATE FOREST
(414) 594-2135
LOCATION: Near Eagle.
FACILITIES: Open year round; 225 sites; water and bathroom facilities; sanitary station; electrical hookup; trailer village vehicle sites; picnic area; swimming; boating; fishing; hiking; horseback riding; handicapped access/restroom; tent camping.

Phillips

FLAMBEAU RIVER STATE FOREST
(715) 332-5271
LOCATION: Near Phillips.
FACILITIES: Open year round; 60 sites; water and bathroom facilities; sanitary station; trailer village vehicle sites; picnic area; swimming; boating; fishing; hiking; tent camping.

Two Rivers

POINT BEACH STATE FOREST
(414) 794-7480
LOCATION: Near Two Rivers.

STATE FORESTS (continued)

FACILITIES: Open year round; 149 sites; water and bathroom facilities; electrical hookup; trailer village vehicle sites; cabins; picnic area; food service; swimming; fishing; hiking; bicycle trail; handicapped access/restroom; tent camping.

HISTORIC SITES

Appleton

WORLD'S FIRST HYDROELECTRIC CENTRAL STATION - In 1882, a water wheel supplied the energy to generate enough current for 250 50-watt lamps. Located at 807 S. Oneida Street.

Coon Valley

NATION'S FIRST WATERSHED PROJECT - First large-scale soil and water conservation project was organized here beginning in 1933. Many of the farm practices used today were first demonstrated in the 90,000-acre Coon Creek Watershed. Located ½ mi. west of Coon Valley, on Hwy. 14.

Fond du Lac

BROWN-HANSEN OCTAGON HOUSE - Architecturally unique, grout octagon house built in 1856 and used as part of the "underground railroad," during the Civil War. Secret room and tunnel. Located at 276 Linden Street.

Greenbay

NATIONAL RAILROAD MUSEUM - Over 50 steam locomotives and passenger and freight cars. Guided tours and train rides during regular season. Located at 2285 S. Broadway.

ROI-PORLIER-TANK COTTAGE - The oldest standing house in Wisconsin. Built in 1776 by fur trader Joseph Roi. Niels Otto Tank, a wealthy Norwegian missionary bought the home in 1850. Much of the furniture was handed down from his wife's Dutch ancestors. Located in Union Park.

Greenbush

OLD WADE HOUSE, BUTTERNUT HOUSE, AND THE WESLEY W. JUNG CARRIAGE MUSEUM - Wade House, an 1850s stagecoach inn, was a popular stopping place between Fond du Lac and Sheboygan, and contains much of its original furnishings. Butternut House is a typical mid-19th-century home. Carriage museum features more than 100 vehicles in one of America's finest carriage collections. Located on Hwy. 23.

Janesville

THE TALLMAN RESTORATIONS - Complex includes Tallman House, where Abraham Lincoln was a guest in 1859; 1842 Stone House; Carriage House, a local history museum. Located at 44 N. Jackson Street.

Milwaukee

INVENTION OF THE TYPEWRITER - In 1869, C. Latham Sholes perfected the first practical typewriter, at the C.F. Kleinsteuber machine shop. His daughter, Lillian, became known as the first woman stenographer. Located at 4th and State Streets.

New Glarus

CHALET OF THE GOLDEN FLEECE - Authentic Swiss-style chalet containing Swiss antiques and jewelry. Located at 618 2nd Street.

SWISS HISTORICAL VILLAGE - Replica of pioneer village includes 12 buildings. Located at 6th Avenue and 7th Street.

Ripon

BIRTHPLACE OF REPUBLICAN PARTY - Dissatisfaction with the Whig party and opposition to slavery brought together 53 citizens on March 3, 1854, in this schoolhouse. The result was a new party, although not formally named until two years later. Located at intersection of Hwys. 24, 44 and 49 in downtown Ripon.

Watertown

FIRST KINDERGARTEN - America's first kindergarten, established by Margarethe Meyer Schurz, in 1856. It was moved to this site in 1956. Located at 919 Charles Street.

HIGHWAY MARKING - In 1917, the Wisconsin Highway Commission began naming and numbering highways, the first such system in the United States. Located 7 mi. east of Watertown on Hwy. 16.

HOSTELS

Cable

Ches Perry Youth Hostel (Ski hostel)
Cable, WI 54821
(715) 798-3367
FACILITIES: Open year round; reservations after Apr.; 30 beds, men; 30 beds, women; modern bathroom; overnight charges: $1.75 summer; $2.50 winter; houseparent: Marryn Olson.

Dodgeville

SPRING VALLEY TRAILS
Route 2
Dodgeville, WI 53533
(608) 935-5725
FACILITIES: Open year round; 20 beds, men; 20 beds, women; sleeping bags recommended; modern bathroom; overnight charges: $3; houseparents: Rev. & Mrs. Philip Yeager.

Greendale

THE RED BARN YOUTH HOSTEL
Greendale, WI 53219

WISCONSIN

HOSTELS (continued)

(414) 327-5952 or 461-3429
FACILITIES: Open May 1 - Oct. 31; 20 beds, men; 20 beds, women; modern bathroom; overnight charges: $2.

Turtle Lake

TIMBERLAKE LODGE
Route 2
Turtle Lake, WI 54889
No telephone
FACILITIES: Open year round; 15 beds, men; 15 beds, women; modern bathroom; nearest hostel: Cable, 80 mi. north; overnight charges: $3.25 summer; $4 houseparent: Ron Brohmer.

POINTS OF INTEREST

Baraboo

CIRCUS WORLD MUSEUM - Preserves sights and sounds of the great American circuses. World's largest collection of circus wagons and art. Daily shows include loading of circus train, circus parade, acrobatic and animal acts. Located in original winter quarters of Ringling Brothers Circus.

MID-CONTINENTAL RAILWAY MUSEUM - Operating railroad museum. Also, 9-mile steam train ride. Located 7 mi. west of Baraboo on Hwy. 136.

Hudson

OCTAGON HOUSE, CARRIAGE HOUSE AND MUSEUM AND GARDEN HOUSE - Authentically furnished mid-19th-century house; doll collection, Carriage and garden house exhibits include blacksmith shop, country store, early farm machinery, lumbering. Located at 1004 3rd Street.

Keshena

MENOMINEE LOGGING CAMP MUSEUM - Complete logging camp complex including camp office, bunkhouse, cook shanty, wood butcher's shop, blacksmith, saw filer's shack and horse barn. Thousands of logging artifacts. Located ¼ mi. north of Keshena.

Spring Green

FRANK LLOYD WRIGHT HOME - Wisconsin-born and world-renowned architect lived and worked at Taliesin, his home, studio and school of architecture. Located east of Spring Green on Hwy. 14.

WYOMING

Wyoming, the least populated of the contiguous states, joined the Union in 1890 as the forty-fourth state. Herds of wild animals roamed much of the state prior to the arrival of white settlers, when Wyoming was the bountiful hunting ground of the Plains Indians. They violently resented the encroachment until the mid-1860s. By then most of the herds were destroyed, and the Indian warriors were sorely outnumbered and outgunned.

Following the Indian wars, classic western-style range wars broke out between the cattlemen and sheepherders in the 1890s.

Herds of cattle and sheep still graze much of Wyoming today, making livestock the state's leading agricultural product. But, spurred by the energy crunch, Wyoming's oil industry has grown by leaps and bounds and is the state's number one source of revenue.

Tourism also does a brisk business in the state, aided by big game hunting, splendid fishing opportunities, and attractions such as Yellowstone National Park.

State capital: Cheyenne. State bird: Meadowlark. State tree: Cottonwood. State flower: Indian paintbrush.

WEATHER

Wyoming's outstanding features are its majestic mountains and high plains. Its mean elevation is about 6,700 feet above sea level, and even when the mountains are excluded, the average elevation over the southern part of the state is well over 6,000 feet, while much of the northern portion is some 2,500 feet lower. The topography and variations in elevation make it difficult to divide the state into homogeneous climatological areas.

Because of its elevation, Wyoming has a relatively cool climate. Above the 6000-foot level the temperature rarely exceeds 100 degrees F. The warmest parts of the state are the lower portion of sections of the Big Horn

Basin, the lower elevations of the central and northeast portions, and along the eastern border.

Summer nights are almost invariably cool, even though daytime readings may be quite high at times. In the wintertime it is characteristic to have rapid and frequent changes between mild and cold spells. During warm spells in the winter, nighttime temperatures frequently remain above freezing. "Chinooks," warm downslope winds, are common along the eastern slopes.

Average daily temperature for each month.

	Northern	Southern
Jan.	30.2 to 5.2	32.5 to 9.3

WYOMING

WEATHER (continued)

Feb.	38.8 to 13.2	35.1 to 10.9
Mar.	47.2 to 19.9	39.3 to 15.0
Apr.	57.9 to 30.1	50.0 to 24.0
May	69.7 to 41.6	62.2 to 33.7
Jun.	79.4 to 49.7	72.6 to 41.9
Jul.	89.0 to 54.5	80.3 to 47.9
Aug.	87.0 to 51.9	78.3 to 46.2
Sept.	73.8 to 40.6	69.1 to 37.2
Oct.	62.3 to 30.2	57.8 to 27.9
Nov.	44.8 to 19.1	42.3 to 17.1
Dec.	34.0 to 9.5	34.4 to 10.7
Year	59.5 to 30.5	54.5 to 26.8

STATE CHAMBER OF COMMERCE

Wyoming Travel Commission
1-25 at Etchepare Circle
Cheyenne, WY 82002
(307) 777-7777

STATE & CITY TOURISM OFFICES

State

Department of Economic Planning and Development
Barrett Building
Cheyenne, WY 82002
(307) 777-7234

Wyoming Travel Commission
2320 Capitol Avenue
Cheyenne, WY 82002
(307) 777-7777

Local

Jackson Hole Chamber of Commerce
P.O. Box E
Jackson Hole, WY 83001
(307) 733-3316

STATE HIGHWAY DEPARTMENT

Wyoming Highway Department
State Highway Office Building
Cheyenne, WY 82001
(307) 777-7471

HIGHWAY WELCOMING CENTERS

Cheyenne

CHEYENNE CENTER - Interstate 25.

Jackson

JACKSON CENTER - U.S. 187, 26 and 89.

St. George

ST. GEORGE CENTER - Interstate 15.

Sheridan

SHERIDAN CENTER - Interstate 90.

STATE POLICE

Department of Public Safety
Cheyenne, WY 82001
(307) 777-7301

HUNTING & FISHING

Hunting

No one under 14 may hunt big or trophy game. Non-residents under 14 may fish or hunt small game without a license, if they're with an adult who has a license and their bag is counted as part of the adult's bag limit. These persons may also buy a regular non-resident license and take their own limit. All game-bird and waterfowl hunters must hold a license. If they're under 12, they must be with an adult.

Resident

Antelope, $10; deer, $10; elk (elk & fish), $15; moose, $25; bighorn sheep, $30; black bear, $5; mountain goat, $30; mountain lion, $20; turkey, $5; bird, $5; small game, $3; archery, $3; falconry, $5; interstate game tag, $1.

Non-resident

Antelope, $50; deer, $50; elk (elk & fish), $125; moose, $125; bighorn sheep, $150; black bear, $30; mountain goat, $150; mountain lion, $100; turkey, $20; bird, $25; small game, $10; archery, $5; falconry, $5; interstate game tag, $1.

Fishing

Residents and non-residents: No person 14 years or older, nor any non-resident person less than 14 years, shall fish in or on any Wyoming waters, except a catchout pond located on a licensed fish hatchery or a fishing preserve, without first obtaining a proper license. A non-resident person less than 14 years need not obtain a proper fishing license if accompanied by an adult possessing a valid Wyoming fishing license.

Resident

Fishing license, $5; youth fishing license (between 14th and 19th birthdays), $2; military fishing license, $5; underwater fishing license (game fish), $3; 5-day fishing license, $3; special 30-day fishing license, $12.50.

Non-resident

Fishing license, $25; tourist 5-day license,

WYOMING

HUNTING & FISHING (continued)

$5; tourist youth 5-day fishing license (children under 14), $2; national girl scout west, 15-day fishing license, $2.

For more information contact:

Wyoming Game and Fish Department
Communications Branch
Cheyenne, WY 82002
(307) 777-7735

CAMPGROUNDS

Private

Buffalo

INDIAN CAMPGROUND
(307) 684-9601
LOCATION: Near Buffalo.
FACILITIES: Open Apr. 15 - Nov. 1; 122 sites; water and bathroom facilities; electrical hookup; trailer village vehicle sites; picnic area; tent camping.

Casper

FORT CASPER CAMPGROUND
(307) 234-3260
LOCATION: Near Casper.
FACILITIES: Open year round; 117 sites; water and bathroom facilities; electrical hookup; trailer village vehicle sites; picnic area; tent camping.

Cheyenne

KARL'S KOA KAMPGROUND
(307) 638-6371
LOCATION: Near Cheyenne.
FACILITIES: Open year round; 128 sites; water and bathroom facilities; sanitary station; electrical hookup; trailer village vehicle sites; laundry; picnic area; food service; tent camping.

Cody

BUFFALO BILL VILLAGE
(307) 587-5544
LOCATION: Downtown Cody.
FACILITIES: Open May - Sept.; 110 sites; water and bathroom facilities; sanitary station; electrical hookup; trailer village vehicle sites; picnic area; food service; swimming; tent camping.

CODY KOA KAMPGROUND
(307) 645-2468
LOCATION: Near Cody.
FACILITIES: Open May 1 - Oct. 1; 149 sites; water and bathroom facilities; electrical hookup; trailer village vehicle sites; horseback riding; tent camping.

WAPITI VALLEY INN CAMPER VILLAGE
(307) 587-3961
LOCATION: 18 mi. west of Cody.
FACILITIES: Open May 1 - Nov. 15; 226 sites; water and bathroom facilities; electrical hookup; trailer village vehicle sites; picnic area; food service; hunting; fishing; hiking; tent camping.

Douglas

JACKALOPE KOA KAMPGROUND
(307) 358-2164
LOCATION: Near Douglas.
FACILITIES: Open year round; 128 sites; water and bathroom facilities; electrical hookup; trailer village vehicle sites; swimming; tent camping.

Gillette

TUMBLEWEED CAMPGROUND
(307) 682-3665
LOCATION: Near Gillette.
FACILITIES: Open May 1 - Oct. 15; 107 sites; water and bathroom facilities; electrical hookup; trailer village vehicle sites; picnic area; swimming; tent camping.

Jackson

A-1 CAMPGROUND
(307) 733-2697
LOCATION: Near Jackson.
FACILITIES: Open year round; 100 sites; water and bathroom facilities; electrical hookup; trailer village vehicle sites; picnic area; tent camping.

JACKSON HOLE CAMPGROUND
(307) 733-2927
LOCATION: Near Jackson.
FACILITIES: Open May 15 - Sept. 15; 121 sites; water and bathroom facilities; electrical hookup; trailer village vehicle sites; laundry; food service; swimming; fishing; tent camping.

Laramie

LARAMIE KOA KAMPGROUND
(307) 742-6553
LOCATION: Near Laramie.
FACILITIES: Open year round; 125 sites; water and bathroom facilities; sanitary station; electrical hookup; trailer village vehicle sites; laundry; food service; swimming; boating; fishing; hiking; horseback riding; tent camping.

OVERLAND TRAIL INN KOA KAMPGROUND
(307) 742-6830
LOCATION: 38 mi. west of Laramie.
FACILITIES: Open May 15 - Oct. 15; 125 sites; water and bathroom facilities; electrical hookup; trailer village vehicle sites; picnic area; hiking; tent camping.

Moran

FLAGG RANCH VILLAGE
(307) 543-2861
LOCATION: Near Moran.
FACILITIES: Open Jun. 1 - Aug. 31; 175 sites; water and bathroom facilities; electrical hookup; trailer village vehicle sites; picnic area; tent camping.

S.R. KOA KAMPGROUND
(307) 543-2483

CAMPGROUNDS (continued)

LOCATION: Near Moran.
FACILITIES: Open May 1 - Nov. 15; 113 sites; water and bathroom facilities; sanitary station; electrical hookup; trailer village vehicle sites; picnic area; food service; tent camping.

Pine Bluffs

SCENIC BLUFFS PARK
(307) 245-3665
LOCATION: Near Pine Bluffs.
FACILITIES: Open year round; 102 sites; water and bathroom facilities; electrical hookup; trailer village vehicle sites; picnic area; tent camping.

Rawlins

RAWLINS KOA KAMPGROUND
(307) 324-9987
LOCATION: Near Rawlins.
FACILITIES: Open year round; 130 sites; water and bathroom facilities; electrical hookup; trailer village vehicle sites; picnic area; swimming; tent camping.

WESTERN HILLS CAMPGROUND
(307) 324-2592
LOCATION: Near Rawlins.
FACILITIES: Open year round; 152 sites; water and bathroom facilities; electrical hookup; trailer village vehicle sites; laundry; tent camping.

Rock Springs

ROCK SPRINGS KOA KAMPGROUND
(307) 362-3063
LOCATION: Near Rock Springs.
FACILITIES: Open May 30 - Oct. 1; 106 sites; water and bathroom facilities; electrical hookup; trailer village vehicle sites; picnic area; swimming; boating; fishing; tent camping.

Sundance

SUNDANCE/DEVILS TOWER KOA KAMP-GROUND
(307) 283-1557
LOCATION: Near Sundance.
FACILITIES: Open May 15 - Nov. 15; 170 sites; water and bathroom facilities; electrical hookup; trailer village vehicle sites; tent camping.

Teton Village

TETON VILLAGE KOA KAMPGROUND
(307) 733-5354
LOCATION: Near Teton Village.
FACILITIES: Open May 1 - Oct. 1; 110 sites; water and bathroom facilities; electrical hookup; trailer village vehicle sites; horseback riding; tent camping.

RESORTS & BEACHES

Guest Ranches

Bondurant

TRIANGLE F RANCH
Bondurant, WY 82922
(307) 773-3237
LOCATION: U.S. 187, halfway between Jackson and Pinedale.
FACILITIES: Horseback riding; fishing.

Buffalo

FRENCH CREEK RANCH
P.O. Box 143
Buffalo, WY 82834
(307) 684-5124
LOCATION: 6 mi. northwest of Buffalo.
FACILITIES: Horseback riding; fishing; hunting.

PARADISE GUEST RANCH
P.O. Box 790
Buffalo, WY 82834
(307) 674-4496
LOCATION: 15 mi. west of Buffalo on U.S. 16.
FACILITIES: Horseback riding; fishing; pack trips; snowmobiling.

Cody

ELK CREEK RANCH
802 Lane Drive
Cody, WY 82414
(307) 587-3902
LOCATION: 40 mi. northwest of Cody.
FACILITIES: Horseback riding; clay pigeon shooting; gymkhanas; swimming; fishing.

FEW ACRES RANCH
P.O. Box 1567
Cody, WY 82414
(307) 587-5037
LOCATION: 23 mi. from northeast entrance to Yellowstone National Park.
FACILITIES: Horseback riding; fishing; hunting; pack trips.

GRIZZLY RANCH
Cody, WY 82414
(307) 587-3966
LOCATION: Between Cody and Yellowstone National Park.
FACILITIES: Horseback riding; fishing; hiking; tennis; pack trips; hunting.

HIDDEN VALLEY RANCH
Route 2, Box 3650
Cody, WY 82414
(307) 587-5090
LOCATION: 6 mi. southwest of Cody.
FACILITIES: Horseback riding; pack trips; hunting; fishing.

HUNTER PEAK RANCH
Cody, WY 82414
(307) 587-3711
LOCATION: 67 mi. northwest of Cody.
FACILITIES: Horseback riding; fishing; pack trips; hunting.

RESORTS (continued)

SEVEN D RANCH
P.O. Box 109
Cody, WY 82414
(307) 587-3997
LOCATION: 50 mi. northwest of Cody.
FACILITIES: Horseback riding; fishing; hunting; back pack trips; pack trips.

SIGGINS TRIANGLE X RANCH
Cody, WY 82414
(307) 587-2031
LOCATION: 38 mi. southwest of Cody.
FACILITIES: Horseback riding; pack trips; fishing; hayrides; working ranch activities; hunting.

VALLEY RANCH
South Fork Star Route W
Cody, WY 82414
(307) 587-4661
LOCATION: East entrance to Yellowstone National Park.
FACILITIES: Horseback riding; hiking; fishing.

Douglas

DEER FORKS RANCH
Route 6
Douglas, WY 82633
(307) 358-2033
LOCATION: In Douglas.
FACILITIES: Horseback riding; hiking; fishing.

Dubois

BITTERROOT RANCH
Dubois, WY 82513
(307) 347-3257
LOCATION: 26 mi. northeast of Dubois.
FACILITIES: Horseback riding; fishing; hunting; pack trips.

BROOKS LAKE LODGE
P.O. Box 333
Dubois, WY 82513
(307) 455-2559
LOCATION: 29 mi. northwest of Dubois.
FACILITIES: Horseback riding; hiking; boating; pack trips; hunting.

CM RANCH
Dubois, WY 82513
(307) 455-2331
LOCATION: 6 mi. from Dubois.
FACILITIES: Horseback riding; hiking; gymkhanas; pack trips; fishing; hunting; swimming.

CROSS MILL IRON RANCH
Crowheart, WY 82512
(307) 486-2279
LOCATION: 20 mi. south of Dubois.
FACILITIES: Horseback riding; fishing; hunting; pack trips.

HIGHLAND MEADOW GUEST RANCH
Dubois, WY 82513
(307) 455-2401
LOCATION: 16 mi. northwest of Dubois.
FACILITIES: Horseback riding; fishing; hunting; pack trips.

LAVA CREEK RANCH
P.O. Box 25
Dubois, WY 82513
(307) 455-2351
LOCATION: 19 mi. west of Dubois.
FACILITIES: Horseback riding; fishing; hunting; pack trips; snowmobiling.

LAZY L AND B RANCH
Dubois, WY 82513
(312) 945-0107
LOCATION: On East Fork.
FACILITIES: Horseback riding; pack trips; fishing.

TIMBER LINE RANCH
Dubois, WY 82513
(307) 455-2215
LOCATION: 16 mi. west of Dubois.
FACILITIES: Horseback riding; fishing; hunting; pack trips.

TRIANGLE C RANCH
Dubois, WY 82513
(307) 455-2225
LOCATION: 18 mi. northwest of Dubois.
FACILITIES: Horseback riding; fishing; hunting; river float trips; pack trips.

Encampment

A BAR A RANCH
P.O. Box 36
Encampment, WY 82325
(307) 327-5454
LOCATION: 85 mi. west of Laramie.
FACILITIES: Horseback riding; fishing; tennis; swimming; golf; target ranges.

Jackson

BONANZA BUTTE RANCH
P.O. Box 982
Jackson, WY 83001
(307) 733-3779
LOCATION: 4 mi. north of Jackson.
FACILITIES: Horseback riding; swimming.

GOOSEWING RANCH
P.O. Box 496
Jackson, WY 83001
(307) 733-2768
LOCATION: Gros Ventre Road, 30 mi. from U.S. 26, 89, and 187.
FACILITIES: Horseback riding; pack trips; hiking; fishing; hunting; snowmobiling; cross-country skiing.

MAD DOG RANCH
P.O. Box 1645
Jackson, WY 83001
(307) 733-3729
LOCATION: Halfway between Jackson and Teton Village.
FACILITIES: Horseback riding; fishing; hunting.

RIMROCK RANCH
P.O. Box 485
Jackson, WY 83001
(307) 733-3093
LOCATION: 26 mi. southeast of Jackson.

RESORTS (continued)

FACILITIES: Horseback riding; hiking; swimming; fishing; hunting; pack trips; cross-country skiing.

SPOTTED HORSE RANCH
Jackson, WY 83001
(307) 733-2097
LOCATION: 17 mi. south of Jackson.
FACILITIES: Horseback riding; river float trips; swimming; fishing.

TWIN CREEK RANCH
P.O. Box 958
Jackson, WY 83001
(307) 733-2929
LOCATION: 6 mi. east of Jackson.
FACILITIES: Horseback riding.

Jackson Hole

DIAMOND D RANCH OUTFITTERS
P.O. Box 11
Moran, WY 83013
(307) 543-2479
LOCATION: 4 mi. east of Moran Junction.
FACILITIES: Horseback riding; pack trips; fishing; hunting; snowmobiling; skiing.

FLYING V RANCH
P.O. Box 205, Kelly
Jackson Hole, WY 83011
(307) 733-2799
LOCATION: 17 mi. from Jackson Hole.
FACILITIES: Horseback riding; fishing; pack trips.

Laramie

T BAR K GUEST AND CATTLE RANCH
Rex Route
Laramie, WY 82070
(307) 745-5926
LOCATION: 30 mi. west of Laramie.
FACILITIES: Horseback riding; hiking; fishing; hunting.

VEE BAR RANCH
Rex Route, Box 198
Laramie, WY 82070
(307) 742-5741
LOCATION: 21 mi. west of Laramie on Hwy. 130.
FACILITIES: Horseback riding; wild game study; hiking; backpacking trips; fishing; hunting; skiing; snowmobiling.

Moose

LOST CREEK RANCH
Moose, WY 83012
(307) 733-3435
LOCATION: In Jackson Hole.
FACILITIES: Horseback riding; shooting ranges; swimming; tennis; pack trips; fishing.

MOOSE HEAD RANCH
P.O. Box 214
Moose, WY 83012
(307) 733-3141
LOCATION: 26 mi. north of Jackson.
FACILITIES: Horseback riding; fishing; river float trips; golf; tennis; swimming.

TRIANGLE X RANCH
Moose, WY 83012
(307) 733-2183
LOCATION: 26 mi. northeast of Jackson.
FACILITIES: Horseback riding; fishing; hunting; river float trips; pack trips.

WHITE GRASS RANCH
Moose, WY 83012
(307) 733-3329
LOCATION: 20 mi. north of Jackson.
FACILITIES: Horseback riding; fishing; swimming; hiking.

Moran

BOX K RANCH
Moran, WY 83013
(307) 543-2407
LOCATION: In Moran.
FACILITIES: Horseback riding; snowmobiling; fishing; hunting.

FIR CREEK RANCH
Moran, WY 83013
(307) 543-2416
LOCATION: In Moran.
FACILITIES: Horseback riding; fishing; hunting; pack trips; cross-country skiing.

HEART SIX GUEST RANCH
Moran, WY 83013
(307) 543-2477
LOCATION: 4 mi. east of Moran Junction.
FACILITIES: Horseback riding; fishing; hunting; river float trips; snowmobiling; pack trips.

TURPIN MEADOW RANCH
P.O. Box 48
Moran, WY 83013
(307) 543-2496
LOCATION: 14 mi. east of Moran Junction.
FACILITIES: Horseback riding; fishing; hunting; pack trips; snowmobiling; cross-country skiing.

Pinedale

BOULDER LAKE RANCH
P.O. Box 725
Pinedale, WY 82941
(307) 367-4627
LOCATION: 12 mi. from U.S. 187 and Boulder.
FACILITIES: Horseback riding; hunting; fishing.

FALL CREEK RANCH
P.O. Box 181
Pinedale, WY 82941
(307) 367-4649
LOCATION: 8 mi. east of Pinedale.
FACILITIES: Horseback riding; fishing; hunting; pack trips; river float trips; snowmobiling.

Rock Springs

SWEETWATER GAP RANCH
P.O. Box 26
Rock Springs, WY 82901
(307) 362-2798
LOCATION: 24 mi. north of Hwy. 28.
FACILITIES: Horseback riding; pack trips; mountain climbing; fishing; hunting.

WYOMING

RESORTS (continued)

Savery

THE BOYER YL RANCH
Savery Post Office, WY 82332
LOCATION: 9 mi. north of Savery.
FACILITIES: Horseback riding; camping;
cookouts; swimming; tennis; fishing.

Sheridan

SPEAR-O-WIGWAM RANCH INC.
P.O. Box 1081
Sheridan, WY 82801
(307) 674-4496
LOCATION: 30 mi. southwest of Sheridan.
FACILITIES: Horseback riding; fishing; hunt-
ing; pack trips; snowmobiling; cross-country
skiing.

Smoot

FOREST DELL GUEST RANCH
P.O. Box 33
Smoot, WY 83126
(307) 886-5665
LOCATION: 13 mi. south of Afton on U.S.
89.
FACILITIES: Horseback riding; hunting; fish-
ing; pack trips.

Tie Siding

TWO BAR SEVEN RANCH
P.O. Box 67-W
Tie Siding, WY 82084
(307) 742-6072
LOCATION: 24 mi. south of Laramie on U.S.
287.
FACILITIES: Horseback riding; hunting; fish-
ing; pack trips; nature study.

Wapiti

BROKEN H RANCH
Wapiti, WY 82450
(307) 587-5053
LOCATION: 6 mi. west of Cody on U.S. 14,
16, and 20.
FACILITIES: Horseback riding; pack trips;
swimming; river float trips; fishing; hunting.

CIRCLE H RANCH
Wapiti, WY 82450
No telephone listed.
LOCATION: 25 mi. east of the Yellowstone
National Park entrance.
FACILITIES: Horseback riding; riding for
cattle; wrangling horses; fishing; hunting.

CROSSED SABRES RANCH
P.O. Box WTC
Wapiti, WY 82450
(307) 587-3750
LOCATION: 9 mi. east of Yellowstone Na-
tional Park.
FACILITIES: Horseback riding; pack trips;
fishing; river float trips.

SWEETWATER LODGE
Wapiti, WY 82450

(307) 587-5788
LOCATION: 20 mi. from east entrance of
Yellowstone National Park.
FACILITIES: Horseback riding; hunting; fish-
ing; pack trips.

Wolf

EATON'S RANCH
Wolf, WY 82844
(307) 655-9285
LOCATION: In Wolf.
FACILITIES: Horseback riding; swimming;
fishing; pack trips.

BOATING AREAS

Big Piney

FONTENELLE RESERVOIR
LOCATION: Near Big Piney.
FACILITIES: Launching; lodging; camping.

Buffalo

LAKE DESMET
LOCATION: Near Buffalo.
FACILITIES: Launching; camping.

Casper

ALCOVA RESERVOIR
LOCATION: Near Casper.
FACILITIES: Launching; lodging; camping.

PATHFINDER LAKE
LOCATION: Near Casper.
FACILITIES: Launching; camping.

Cody

BUFFALO BILL RESERVOIR
LOCATION: Near Cody.
FACILITIES: Launching; lodging; camping.

Farson

BIG SANDY LAKE
LOCATION: Near Farson.
FACILITIES: Launching; camping.

Glendo

GLENDO LAKE
LOCATION: Near Glendo.
FACILITIES: Launching; lodging; camping.

Green River

FLAMING GORGE LAKE
LOCATION: Near Green River.
FACILITIES: Launching; lodging; camping.

Jackson

JACKSON LAKE
LOCATION: Near Jackson.
FACILITIES: Launching; lodging; camping.

Kemmerer

VIVA NAUGHTON RESERVOIR
LOCATION: Near Kemmerer.
FACILITIES: Launching; lodging; camping.

BOATING AREAS (continued)

Laramie

LAKE HATTIE
LOCATION: Near Laramie.
FACILITIES: Launching; camping.

Lovell

BIG HORN LAKE
LOCATION: Near Lovell.
FACILITIES: Launching; camping.

Pinedale

FREMONT LAKE
LOCATION: Near Pinedale.
FACILITIES: Launching; lodging; camping.

WILLOW LAKE
LOCATION: Near Pinedale.
FACILITIES: Launching; lodging; camping.

Rawlins

SEMINOE RESERVOIR
LOCATION: Near Rawlins.
FACILITIES: Launching; lodging; camping.

Riverton

OCEAN LAKE
LOCATION: Near Riverton.
FACILITIES: Launching; lodging; camping.

Shoshoni

BOYSEN RESERVOIR
LOCATION: Near Shoshoni.
FACILITIES: Launching; lodging; camping.

BICYCLE TRAILS

No information was available on Bicycle Trails in Wyoming.

TRAILS

Casper

LEE MCCUNE BRAILLE TRAIL - Approximately .3 mi. foot and Braille trail. Located in Casper Mountain Park, this trail is designed to acquaint the blind, as well as the sighted, with flora, fauna, and geology. A recreation-education self-guiding facility, the loop trail has signs in both Braille and English at 36 interpretive way stations. The trail has safety ropes for guidance.

SKI AREAS

Alta

GRAND TARGHEE SKI AREA
(307) 353-2308
LOCATION: 42 mi. northwest of Jackson.
FACILITIES: 3 double chairlifts; 1 tow rope; ski instruction; ski rental; restaurants; lodging.

Casper

HOGADON SKI AREA
(307) 266-1600
LOCATION: 11 mi. south of Casper on Route 251.
FACILITIES: 1 T-bar; 1 poma; slopes for expert, intermediate and beginning skiers; ski instruction; ski rental; 650 ft. vertical drop; restaurants; lodging.

Centennial

MEDICINE BOW SKI AREA
(307) 745-5750
LOCATION: 32 mi. west of Laramie on Route 130, in Medicine Bow National Forest.
FACILITIES: 1 double chairlift; 2 T-bars; slopes for expert, intermediate and beginning skiers; ski instruction; ski rental; 600 ft. vertical drop; restaurants; lodging.

Cody

SLEEPING GIANT SKI RESORT
(307) 587-4044
LOCATION: 48 mi. west of Cody on U.S. 14, 16, and 20.
FACILITIES: 1 T-bar; 1 tow rope; slopes for expert, intermediate and beginning skiers; ski instruction; ski rental; 450 ft. vertical drop; restaurants; lodging.

Evanston

EAGLE ROCK SKI AREA
(307) 789-2871
LOCATION: 11 mi. east of Evanston on old U.S. 30.
FACILITIES: 1 chairlift; 2 tow ropes; slopes for expert, intermediate and beginning skiers; ski instruction; ski rental; 680 ft. vertical drop; restaurants; lodging.

Greybull

ANTELOPE BUTTE SKI AREA
(307) 347-3257
LOCATION: 38 mi. east of Greybull.
FACILITIES: 1 T-bar; 1 poma; slopes for expert, intermediate and beginning skiers; ski instruction; ski rental; restaurants; lodging.

Jackson

SNOW KING SKI AREA
(307) 733-2851
LOCATION: In Jackson.
FACILITIES: 1 double chairlift; 1 tow rope; slopes for expert, intermediate and beginning skiers; ski instruction; ski rental; restaurants; lodging.

Lander

SINKS CANYON SKI AREA
(307) 332-2135
LOCATION: 14 mi. southwest of Lander.
FACILITIES: 1 tow rope; beginners area; ski instruction; ski rental; 100 ft. vertical drop; restaurants; lodging.

Laramie

HAPPY JACK SKI AREA

WYOMING

SKI AREAS (continued)

(307) 745-9583
LOCATION: 10 mi. east of Laramie.
FACILITIES: 2 T-bars; ski instruction; ski
rental; restaurants; lodging.

Pinedale

WHITE PINE SKI AREA
(307) 367-4531
LOCATION: 10 mi. northeast of Pinedale.
FACILITIES: 1 T-bar; 1 tow rope; slopes for
expert, intermediate and beginning skiers; ski
instruction; ski rental; restaurants; lodging.

Teton Village

JACKSON HOLE SKI AREA
(307) 733-2291
LOCATION: 12 mi. northwest of Jackson on
Route 390.
FACILITIES: 4 double chairlifts; 1 tram;
slopes for expert, intermediate and beginning
skiers; ski instruction; ski rental; restaurants;
lodging.

Worland

MEADOWLARK SKI AREA
(307) 366-2409
LOCATION: Halfway between Buffalo and
Worland on U.S. 16.
FACILITIES: 2 pomas; slopes for expert, intermediate and beginning skiers; ski instructions; ski rental; restaurants; lodging.

AMUSEMENT PARKS & ATTRACTIONS

Cheyenne

PLAYLAND AMUSEMENT PARK
Lions Park
Cheyenne, WY 82001
(307) 638-9428
FACILITIES: 5 major rides; 6 kiddie rides; 6
games; refreshment stand; cafe; picnic facilities; miniature golf; show boat on the lake;
free gate; free parking.

Cody

BUFFALO BILL VILLAGE (Attraction)
Cody, WY 82414
(307) 587-3654
FACILITIES: 8 games; 3 refreshment stands;
2 restaurants; pool; museum; exhibits; picnic
facilities; stage shows; orchestras; free & pay
parking; open Jun. - Sept.

STATE FAIR

Wyoming State Fair
Drawer 10
Douglas, WY 82633
(307) 358-3473
DATE: August

NATIONAL PARKS

Moose

GRAND TETON NATIONAL PARK
Moose, WY 83012
(307) 733-2752

COLTER BAY
LOCATION: 9 mi. northwest of Moran.
FACILITIES: Open May 15 - Oct.15; entrance fee; limit of stay: 14 days; 350 sites;
group camps: 9; NPS campsite fee: $3; water
and bathroom facilities; sanitary station;
cabins; laundry; picnic area; food service;
swimming; boating; boat rental; fishing;
guide for hire; hiking; horseback riding; bicycle trail; snowmobile route; exhibit; museum; environmental study area; living history
program; NPS guided tour; self-guiding tour;
lodging.

COLTER BAY TRAILER VILLAGE
LOCATION: 9 mi. northwest of Moran.
FACILITIES: Open May 15 - Oct. 15; entrance fee; trailer village vehicle sites: 122
($7.25); cabins; laundry; food service; swim-
ming; boating; boat rental; fishing; hiking;
horseback riding; bicycle trail; snowmobile
route; environmental study area; living history
program; NPS guided tour; self-guiding tour;
medical services; lodging.

GROS VENTRE
LOCATION: 10 mi. southeast of Moose.
FACILITIES: Open May 15 - Oct. 15; entrance fee; limit of stay: 14 days; 360 sites;
group camps: 5; NPS campsite fee: $3; water
and bathroom facilities; sanitary station; cabins; picnic area; hunting; fishing; guide for
hire; hiking; bicycle trail; snowmobile route;
exhibit; museum; environmental study area;
living history program; NPS guided tour; self-
guiding tour; lodging.

JENNY LAKE
LOCATION: 7 mi. north of Moose.
FACILITIES: Open May 25 - Oct. 15; entrance fee; limit of stay: 10 days; 49 sites;
NPS campsite fee: $3; water and bathroom
facilities; cabins; picnic area; boating; boat
rental; hunting; fishing; guide for hire; hiking; horseback riding; bicycle trail; snowmobile route; exhibit; museum; environmental study area; living history program; NPS
guided tour; self-guiding tour; tents only;
lodging.

LIZARD CREEK
LOCATION: 17 mi. northwest of Moran.
FACILITIES: Open Jun. 10 - Sept. 10; entrance fee; limit of stay: 14 days; 60 sites;
NPS campsite fee: $3; water and bathroom
facilities; cabins; picnic area; swimming; boating; boat rental; hunting; fishing; guide for
hire; hiking; bicycle trail; snowmobile route;
exhibit; museum; environmental study area;
living history program; NPS guided tour; self-
guiding tour; lodging.

SIGNAL MOUNTAIN
LOCATION: 7 mi. southwest of Moran.
FACILITIES: Open Jun. 1 - Sept. 15; en-
trance fee; limit of stay: 14 days; 84 sites;

NATIONAL PARKS (continued)

NPS campsite fee: $3; water and bathroom facilities; sanitary station; cabins; picnic area; food service; swimming; boating; boat rental; hunting; fishing; guide for hire; hiking; bicycle trail; snowmobile route; exhibit; museum; environmental study area; living history program; NPS guided tour; self-guiding tour; lodging.

Yellowstone National Park

YELLOWSTONE NATIONAL PARK (WY, ID, MT)

Yellowstone National Park, WY 82190
(307) 344-7381

BRIDGE BAY
LOCATION: 3 mi. southwest of Lake Junction.
FACILITIES: Open Jun. - Sept.; entrance fee; limit of stay: 30 days (14, Jul. 1 - Labor Day); 438 sites; group camps; NPS campsite fee: $3; water and bathroom facilities; sanitary station; cabins; laundry; picnic area; food service; boating; boat rental; fishing; guide for hire; hiking; bicycle trail; snowmobile route; exhibit; museum; living history program; NPS guided tour; self-guiding tour; medical service; lodging.

CANYON
LOCATION: ¼ mi. east of Canyon Junction.
FACILITIES: Open Jun. - Aug.; entrance fee; limit of stay: 30 days (14, Jul. 1 - Labor Day); 280 sites; group camps; NPS campsite fee: $3; water and bathroom facilities; sanitary station; cabins; laundry; picnic area; food service; fishing; guide for hire; hiking; horseback riding; bicycle trail; snowmobile route; exhibit; museum; living history program; NPS guided tour; self-guiding tour; medical service; lodging.

FISHING BRIDGE
LOCATION: 1 mi. east of Lake Junction.
FACILITIES: Open Jun. - Aug.; entrance fee; limit of stay: 30 days (14, Jul. 1 - Labor Day); 308 sites; group camps; NPS campsite fee: $3; water and bathroom facilities; sanitary station; cabins; laundry; picnic area; food service; boating; boat rental; fishing; guide for hire; hiking; bicycle trail; snowmobile route; exhibit; museum; living history program; NPS guided tour; self-guiding tour; medical service; lodging.

FISHING BRIDGE TRAILER COURT
LOCATION: 1½ mi. east of Lake Junction.
FACILITIES: Open Jun. - Sept. 14; entrance fee; limit of stay: 30 days (14, Jul. 1 - Labor Day); water and bathroom facilities; trailer village vehicle sites: 358 ($4.50); cabins; laundry; picnic area; food service; boating; boat rental; fishing; guide for hire; hiking; bicycle trail; snowmobile route; exhibit; museum; living history program; NPS guided tour; self-guiding tour; medical service; lodging.

GRANT VILLAGE
LOCATION: 2 mi. south of West Thumb Junction.
FACILITIES: Open Jun. - Sept.; limit of stay: 30 days (14, Jul. 1 - Labor Day); 433 sites; group camps; NPS campsite fee: $3; water and bathroom facilities; sanitary station; cabins; laundry; picnic area; boating; boat rental; fishing; guide for hire; hiking; bicycle trail; snowmobile route; exhibit; museum; living history program; NPS guided tour; self-guiding tour; medical service; lodging.

INDIAN CREEK
LOCATION: 7 mi. south of Mammoth.
FACILITIES: Open Jun. - Sept.; limit of stay: 30 days (14, Jul. 1 - Labor Day); 78 sites; NPS campsite fee: $2; fishing.

LEWIS LAKE
LOCATION: 10 mi. south of West Thumb.
FACILITIES: Open Jun. - Oct.; limit of stay: 30 days (14, Jul. 1 - Labor Day); 100 sites; NPS campsite fee: $2; boating; fishing.

MADISON
LOCATION: ¼ mi. west of Madison Junction.
FACILITIES: Open Jun. - Sept.; entrance fee; limit of stay: 30 days (14, Jul. 1 - Labor Day); 292 sites; group camps; NPS campsite fee: $3; water and bathroom facilities; sanitary station; cabins; picnic area; fishing; guide for hire; hiking; bicycle trail; snowmobile route; exhibit; museum; living history program; NPS guided tour; self-guiding tour; medical service; lodging.

MAMMOTH
LOCATION: ½ mi. north of Mammoth.
FACILITIES: Open year round; entrance fee; limit of stay: 30 days (14, Jul. 1 - Labor Day); 87 sites; group camps; NPS campsite fee: $3; water and bathroom facilities; cabins; picnic area; food service; fishing; guide for hire; hiking; horseback riding; bicycle trail; snowmobile route; exhibit; museum; living history program; NPS guided tour; self-guiding tour; medical service; lodging.

NORRIS
LOCATION: 1 mi. north of Norris Junction.
FACILITIES: Open Jun. - Aug.; entrance fee; limit of stay: 30 days (14, Jul. 1 - Labor Day); 116 sites; group camps; NPS campsite fee: $3; water and bathroom facilities; cabins; picnic area; fishing; guide for hire; hiking; bicycle trail; snowmobile route; exhibit; museum; living history program; NPS guided tour; self-guiding tour; medical service; lodging.

PEBBLE CREEK
LOCATION: 7 mi. southwest of northeast entrance.
FACILITIES: Open Jun. - Aug.; limit of stay: 30 days (14, Jul. 1 - Labor Day); 36 sites; NPS campsite fee: $2; fishing.

SLOUGH CREEK
LOCATION: 10 mi. east of Tower Fall Junction.
FACILITIES: Open Jun. - Aug.; limit of stay: 30 days (14, Jul. 1 - Labor Day); 26 sites; NPS campsite fee: $2; fishing.

TOWER FALL
LOCATION: 3 mi. east of Tower Fall Junction.
FACILITIES: Open Jun. - Aug.; limit of stay: 30 days (14, Jul. 1 - Labor Day); 38 sites; NPS campsite fee: $2; food service; fishing; horseback riding.

WYOMING

NATIONAL FORESTS

National Forests
Intermountain Region
324 25th Street
Odgen, UT 84401
(801) 399-6484

Cody

SHOSHONE NATIONAL FOREST
ATTRACTIONS: Gannett Peak, 13,785 feet, highest in Wyoming; largest glaciers in Rocky Mountains; fishing; mountain sheep, elk, moose, deer, antelope, black grizzly bear, game bird hunting; saddle and pack trips; scenic drives.
FACILITIES: 30 camp and picnic sites, 9 picnic only; 2 winter sports areas; motels and dude ranches in and near the National Forest.
NEARBY TOWNS: Dubois, Lander, WY; Cooke City, Red Lodge, MT.

Jackson

TETON NATIONAL FOREST
ATTRACTIONS: Unspoiled scenic back-country famous for big-game herds; famous Jackson Hole country; outstanding skiing; stream, lake fishing; moose, elk, deer, mountain sheep, grizzly bear hunting; scenic drives.
FACILITIES: 10 camp sites, 2 picnic only; 2 swimming sites; 3 winter sports areas, including Jackson and Teton Pass Ski Runs; resorts; dude ranches; cabins.
NEARBY TOWNS: Dubois, WY; Rexburg, ID.

Kemmerer

BRIDGER NATIONAL FOREST
ATTRACTIONS: Live glaciers; Gannett Peak, highest in Wyoming at 13,785 feet; lake and stream fishing; bear, moose, elk, mountain sheep, deer hunting; scenic drives.
FACILITIES: 23 camp sites, 2 picnic only; swimming site; Divide and Surveyor Park Winter Sports Areas; resorts; hotels; cabins; dude ranches.
NEARBY TOWNS: Afton and Pinedale.

Laramie

MEDICINE BOW NATIONAL FOREST
ATTRACTIONS: Numerous beaver colonies; fishing; deer hunting; saddle and pack trips; scenic drives.
FACILITIES: 36 camp and picnic sites, 10 picnic only; 3 winter sports areas; motels and dude ranches in and near the National Forest.
NEARBY TOWNS: Cheyenne, Encampment.

Sheridan

BIGHORN NATIONAL FOREST
ATTRACTIONS: Curious prehistoric Indian medicine wheel on Medicine Mountain; Indian battlefields; fishing; elk, deer, bear, duck hunting; saddle and pack trips; scenic drives.
FACILITIES: 40 camp and picnic sites, 14 picnic only; 2 winter sports areas; motels and dude ranches in and near the National Forest.
NEARBY TOWNS: Buffalo, Greybull, Lovell, Worland.

See CARIBOU NATIONAL FOREST and TARGHEE NATIONAL FOREST - Idaho.

See BLACK HILLS NATIONAL FOREST - South Dakota.

See ASHLEY NATIONAL FOREST and WASATCH NATIONAL FOREST - Utah.

STATE PARKS

Headquarters

Wyoming Recreation Commission
Cheyenne, WY 82002
(307) 777-7695

Cheyenne

CURT GOWDY STATE PARK
LOCATION: Between Cheyenne and Laramie on I-80.
FACILITIES: Open year round; water and bathroom facilities; trailer village vehicle sites; picnic area; hiking; tent camping.

Cody

BUFFALO BILL STATE PARK
LOCATION: East of Cody.
FACILITIES: Open year round; water and bathroom facilities; trailer village vehicle sites; picnic area; fishing; tent camping.

Glendo

GLENDO STATE PARK
LOCATION: 4 mi. east of Glendo.
FACILITIES: Open year round; water and bathroom facilities; electrical hookup; trailer village vehicle sites; cabins; picnic area; food service; boating; fishing; tent camping.

Guernsey

GUERNSEY STATE PARK
LOCATION: 3 mi. from Guernsey on U.S. 26.
FACILITIES: Open year round; water and bathroom facilities; trailer village vehicle sites; picnic area; swimming; boating; fishing; tent camping.

Lander

SINKS CANYON STATE PARK
LOCATION: 10 mi. southwest of Lander.
FACILITIES: Open year round; trailer village vehicle sites; swimming; boating; fishing; hiking; tent camping.

Shoshoni

BOYSEN STATE PARK
LOCATION: Off U.S. 20.
FACILITIES: Open year round; water and bathroom facilities; trailer village vehicle sites; picnic area; food service; swimming; boating; fishing; tent camping.

Sinclair

SEMINOLE STATE PARK
LOCATION: 28 mi. south of Sinclair.

STATE PARKS (continued)

FACILITIES: Open year round; water and bathroom facilities; trailer village vehicle sites; picnic area; fishing; hiking; tent camping.

Sundance

KEYHOLE STATE PARK
LOCATION: On I-90.
FACILITIES: Open year round; water and bathroom facilities; trailer village vehicle sites; picnic area; swimming; boating; hunting; fishing; tent camping.

Thermopolis

HOT SPRINGS STATE PARK
LOCATION: Near Thermopolis.
FACILITIES: Open year round; water and bathroom facilities; trailer village vehicle sites; swimming; hiking; tent camping.

STATE FORESTS

There are no State Forests in Wyoming.

HISTORIC SITES

Bridger

FORT BRIDGER - Established in 1843 on the Black's Fork of the Green River by frontiersman Jim Bridger, trapper, trader and scout. At first a trading post, the Fort later played key roles in the history of western overland transportation, communication, military affairs and agriculture.

Buffalo

FORT PHIL KEARNY - Sioux and Cheyenne Indians fought successfully to prevent invasion of their hunting grounds by men headed for the Montana gold fields. Fort Phil Kearny was the focus of siege after siege in Red Cloud's War before being abandoned and burned in 1868. Located west of I-90 between Buffalo and Sheridan.

Fort Washakie

FORT WASHAKIE; ST. MICHAEL'S MISSION - Chief Washakie, the Shoshone leader for whom the post was named, was one of the most respected Indian chiefs in the history of western America. St. Michael's Mission, east of Fort Washakie, was established as an Episcopal mission in 1887 by the Reverend John Roberts. The mission is the home of valuable collections of Arapahoe artifacts and cultural materials.

Kaycee

HOLE-IN-THE-WALL - A famous hideout of cattle rustlers and other thieves. Nature provided a huge lush valley surrounded by a steep wall of red rocks that had limited access. Allegedly the home of Butch Cassidy and "The Wild Bunch." The "hole" lies on private property, and with permission of the landowners, plus a four-wheel drive vehicle and some shoe leather, the outlaws' haven can be explored. Located west of Kaycee.

Medicine Bow

COMO BLUFF: MEDICINE BOW AND "THE VIRGINIAN" - Was the site of world-famous 19th-century geologic quarries. The still-productive bluff has yielded countless tons of near-perfect dinosaur and other fossil remains to supply natural history museums throughout the world. To the west is Medicine Bow, a favorite country of author Owen Wister and location for his famous novel about the west and the cowboy, "The Virginian." Located between Medicine Bow and Rock River and just north of U.S. 30.

South Pass City

SOUTH PASS CITY, SWEETWATER MINING DISTRICT - A number of original buildings remain in this former gold camp which became the center of the Sweetwater Gold Rush of 1867. South Pass City gained lasting fame when its representatives led the Wyoming Territorial Legislature (established 1868) in action to become the first government unit in the world to grant suffrage to women. Located off Hwy. 28 about 35 mi. southwest of Lander, and then south on a dirt road for 2½ mi.

HOSTELS

Jackson Hole

THE HOSTEL
P.O. Box 16
Teton Village, WY 83025
(307) 733-3415
FACILITIES: Open year round; 260 beds for men and women; reservations required; modern bathroom; overnight charges: $15 one or two; $18, three or four; houseparents: Colby & Joey Wilson.

POINTS OF INTEREST

Afton

BUFFALO HERD - One of Wyoming's largest buffalo herds. Located 12 mi. north of Afton.

INTERMITTENT SPRING - Spring gushes a huge volume of water from its orifice in solid rock for an 18-minute period, then completely ceases to flow for a like period. It is believed to be a siphon spring. Located in Swift Creek Canyon, 5 mi. east of Afton.

Cody

BUFFALO BILL MONUMENT - World's largest bronze equestrian statue; designed and built by Gertrude Vanderbilt Whitney. Located northwest of Buffalo Bill Historical Center.

WHITNEY GALLERY OF WESTERN ART -

WYOMING

POINTS OF INTEREST (continued)

Finest collection of Western art, artifacts and displays found in America. Large collections of works by Frederick Remington, Charles Russell and many other famous western artists. Located at western edge of Cody.

Douglas

AYRES NATURAL BRIDGE - Nature created one of the world's most perfect stone bridges. During eons of beating violently against sandstone rock, the cascading waters of LaPrele Creek formed an arch 150 feet long and 50 feet high. The turnoff for the bridge is halfway between Douglas and Glenrock on I-25.

THE JACKALOPE - One glance at the statue is all that is needed to see the strange fellow defies classification. Were it not for the mule deer-like antlers, it might be confused with a jackrabbit. If not for the body markings, it might be mistaken for a North American pronghorn antelope. It is not usually vicious, but oddly enough, coyotes have a keen respect for its sharp antlers, and they maintain a healthy distance from this creature. If anyone has still "mythed" the point, it's a put-on! Located in downtown Douglas.

Lovell

PRYOR MOUNTAIN WILD HORSE RANGE - First ever established by the Bureau of Land Management in the United States (1968). Home for more than 200 free-roaming wild horses on 31,000 acres of BLM land in northern Wyoming and southern Montana.

Sundance

DEVILS TOWER - This colossal stone tower has nearly perpendicualr sides and fluted columns, resembling a huge tree trunk. It rises 865 feet above the wooded base. Permission to climb the tower requires a special permit; mountain climbing demonstrations are held daily at the Visitors' Center. Located off Route 24 or U.S. 14.

INYAN KARA MOUNTAIN - A symbol of the early exploration and history of the Black Hills, this prominent landmark juts upward 6600 feet above sea level. In 1874 General George A. Custer, leading an exploratory expedition into the Black Hills, climbed Inyan Kara and inscribed his name in granite on top of the peak. Located west of Route 585, 10 mi. south of Sundance.

Acknowledgments

We would like to thank the following organizations and their staff members for helping us put this book together. Without their invaluable assistance, we could not have compiled so comprehensive a volume.

Alabama Bureau of Publicity and Information
Alaska Division of Tourism
American Youth Hostels, Inc., Delaplane, VA
Arizona Office of Tourism
Arkansas Department of Parks and Tourism
California Department of Navigation and Ocean Development
California Office of Visitor Services, Department of Economic
    and Business Development
Chamber of Commerce of the United States, Washington, DC
Colorado Campground Association, Boulder, CO
Colorado Ski Country USA, Denver, CO
Colorado Travel Market Section, Colorado Division of Commerce and
    Development
Connecticut Tourism Promotion Service, Connecticut Department of
    Commerce
Delaware State Visitors Service, Division of Economic Development
District of Columbia - Washington Area Convention and Visitors Bureau
Far West Ski Association, Los Angeles, CA
Florida Division of Tourism, Florida Department of Commerce
Georgia Tourist Division, Bureau of Industry and Trade
Hawaii Visitors Bureau
Idaho Division of Tourism and Industrial Development
Illinois Office of Tourism, Department of Business and Economic
    Development
Indiana Tourism Development Division, Indiana Department of Commerce
International Association of Amusement Parks and Attractions, North
    Riverside, IL
Iowa Department of Public Instruction
Iowa Travel Development Division, Iowa Development Commission
Kansas Tourist Division, Kansas Department of Economic Development
Kentucky Division of Advertising and Travel Promotion
Louisiana Tourist Development Commission
Maine Department of Conservation, State of Maine Publicity Bureau
Maryland Division of Tourist Development, Department of Economic and
    Community Development
Massachusetts Division of Tourism, Massachusetts Department of Com-
    merce and Development
Michigan Department of State, Michigan History Division
Michigan Travel Commission
Minnesota Association of Campground Operations, Inc., Minneapolis, MN
Minnesota Tourism Division, Minnesota Department of Economic
    Development
Mississippi Travel and Tourism Department, Mississippi Agricultural and
    Industrial Board
Missouri Division of Tourism
Montana Travel Promotion Unit, Montana Department of Highways

National Association of State Development Agencies, Falls Church, VA
National Oceanic and Atmospheric Administration
National Police Chiefs and Sheriffs Information Bureau, Milwaukee, WI
Nebraska Division of Travel and Tourism, Nebraska Department of Economic Development
Nevada Tourism Division, Department of Economic Development
New Hampshire Office of Vacation Travel, Division of Economic Development
New Jersey Office of Tourism and Promotion
New Mexico Tourist Division, Department of Tourism
New York Division of Tourism, New York State Department of Commerce
North Carolina Travel Development Section, North Carolina Department of Natural and Economic Resources

North Dakota Travel Division, State Highway Department
Ohio Travel Bureau, Ohio Department of Economic and Community Development
Oklahoma Tourism Promotion Division, Oklahoma Tourism and Recreation Department
Oregon Travel Information Section
Pennsylvania Bureau of Travel Development, Pennsylvania Department of Commerce
Redwood Empire Association
Rhode Island Tourist Promotion Division, Department of Economic Development
South Carolina Division of Tourism, South Carolina Department of Parks, Recreation, and Tourism
South Dakota Division of Tourism
Tennessee Tourist Development Division
Texas Tourist Development Agency
U.S. Department of Agriculture
U.S. Department of Commerce, U.S. Travel Service
U.S. Department of the Interior
U.S. Department of Transportation
Utah Travel Council
Vermont Agency of Environmental Conservation
Vermont Office of Information, Agency of Development and Community Affairs
Virginia State Travel Service
Washington Travel Development Division, Department of Commerce and Economic Development
West Virginia Travel Development Division, West Virginia Department of Commerce
Wisconsin Association of Campground Owners, Madison, WI
Wisconsin Division of Tourism, Department of Business Development
Wyoming Travel Commission

We would also like to thank Jean Dolan, Sue Geraci, Diane Urbanek and Marti Worthen for their editorial assistance.

Finally, a very special thanks to Keyo Ross and Beverley Winterburn whose skill and dedication over the past year made the compilation of this massive amount of information appear easy and, at times, fun.

NOTES

NOTES

NOTES

NOTES

NOTES

NOTES

NOTES